HOSPITAL MANAGEMENT

S.M. JHA
Ph.D., D.Litt.
Professor
Department of Commerce and Business Administration
L.N. Mithila University, Darbhanga-846 008.

ISO 9001:2015 CERTIFIED

First Edition : 2001
Reprint : 2005, 2007, 2008
Second Revised Edition : 2011
Reprint : 2019
Reprint : 2021

Published by : Mrs. Meena Pandey for **Himalaya Publishing House Pvt. Ltd.**,
Ramdoot, Dr. Bhalerao Marg, Girgaon, Mumbai - 400 004
Phone: 022-23860170/23863863; **Fax:** 022-23877178
E-mail: himpub@bharatmail.co.in; **Website:** www.himpub.com

Branch Offices :

New Delhi : Pooja Apartments, 4-B, Murari Lal Street, Ansari Road, Darya Ganj, New Delhi - 110 002. Phone: 011-23270392, 23278631; Fax: 011-23256286

Nagpur : Kundanlal Chandak Industrial Estate, Ghat Road, Nagpur - 440 018. Phone: 0712-2738731, Telefax: 0712-2721216

Bengaluru : Plot No. 91-33, 2nd Main Road, Seshadripuram, Behind Nataraja Theatre, Bengaluru - 560 020. Phone: 080-41138821; Mobile: 09379847017, 09379847005

Hyderabad : No. 3-4-184, Lingampally, Besides Raghavendra Swamy Matham, Kachiguda, Hyderabad - 500 027. Phone: 040-27560041, 27550139

Chennai : New No. 48/2, Old No. 28/2, Ground Floor, Sarangapani Street, T. Nagar, Chennai-600 017. Mobile: 09380460419

Pune : First Floor, Laksha Apartment, No. 527, Mehunpura, Shaniwarpeth (Near Prabhat Theatre), Pune - 411 030. Phone: 020-24496323, 24496333; Mobile: 09370579333

Lucknow : House No. 731, Shekhupura Colony, Near B.D. Convent School, Aliganj, Lucknow - 226 022. Phone: 0522-4012353; Mobile: 09307501549

Ahmedabad : 114, SHAIL, 1st Floor, Opp. Madhu Sudan House, C.G. Road, Navrang Pura, Ahmedabad - 380 009. Phone: 079-26560126; Mobile: 09377088847

Ernakulam : 39/176 (New No. 60/251), 1st Floor, Karikkamuri Road, Ernakulam, Kochi - 682011. Phone: 0484-2378012, 2378016; Mobile: 09387122121

Cuttack : New LIC Colony, Behind Kamala Mandap, Badambadi, Cuttack - 753 012, Odisha. Mobile: 9338746007

Kolkata : 108/4, Beliaghata Main Road, Near ID Hospital, Opp. SBI Bank, Kolkata - 700 010, Phone: 033-32449649; Mobile: 07439040301

DTP by : Times Printographics

Printed at : M/s. Aditya Offset Process (I) Pvt. Ltd., Hyderabad. On behalf of HPH.

Preface

Of course, the inventions and innovations in the field of medical sciences have considerably transformed the perception of service quality. The developments in the field of information and communication technology have been playing a positive role in defining and redefining healthcare services. We find India, of late, emerging as a global healthcare brand and credibility for the same goes to the world class medical and paramedical personnel playing an incremental role in the development process. We have a number of world class hospitals both in the public and private sectors serving and subserving the interests of domestic as well as the global users. However, we need to accelerate the pace of qualitative-cum-quantitative transformation so that the benefits of development do not remain confined to the affluent sections of the society rather are also affordable to the weaker sections. This in a natural fashion focusses our attention on developing a team of thematically sound, professionally excellent, value based personnel and in addition, a mix of sophisticated and low cost indigenous technologies.

The management of biological system of human beings becomes vitally significant to make their bodies insensitive and resistive to the disease-prone environmental conditions. A majority of the Indian population fails in managing health which makes its bodies very sensitive and receptive to the multi-dimensional health hazards. Our wrong decisions, sins and misdeeds, violation of the law of nature, temptation to the animal culture and even more than that, irrational industrial development plans substantially influence the nature and character of disease profile. We cannot negate that during yester decades, the high intensity of frequency in almost all the areas has gained a rapid momentum which has necessitated worldclass professional excellence in the management of organisations in general and healthcare organisations in particular. It is against this background that we need to manage hospitals and healthcare organisations in a bit different way with a new vision, new strategy and new vigour.

With the rising demographic pressure, we find a big jump in our healthcare requirements. The demand side is expanding fast but the supply side is not showing an analogous change. Undoubtedly enough, the shrinking public health spending has been found expanding the gap between demand and supply. The private hospitals have been found very much instrumental in bridging the gap but unless we find the government hospitals increasing their contributions, the general masses are to suffer. In a true sense, the government hospitals need to improve the quality of their services but this is not to be possible unless they are professionally, technologically and financially sound. Countering the problem of financial crunch seems to be an urgent need of the hour.

The government hospitals in particular have been facing numerous problems on that account. The public healthcare spending is found shrinking. The hospitals do not have freedom of mobilizing finance from the internal sources because they have to prove their excellence as a non-profit organisation. And the charities and donations from the individuals or organisations have not been getting the required support. On the other hand, the inputs used for improving the quality of services are also becoming much more expensive. This makes a strong advocacy in favour of a sound financial management.

Quality in totality is required to be our avowed mission which would help us in making our services nationally and globally competitive. Service uniqueness makes it essential that a hospital manager synchronises curative, supportive and peripheral services in such a fashion that patients and attendants witness an additional attraction. The first priority, of course, is to be given to the quality of services delivered to the patients but in addition, we find service ambience or services capes, surroundings and premises and behavioural profile of medical and paramedical staff playing an incremental role in processing and generating worldclass service. The increasing cases of indecent behaviour, misbehaviour, cheating, absence of sympathy and empathy make it essential that hospital managers and almost all the staff are well aware of the behavioural dimensions.

In the modern business world where we find corporatisation becoming an integral part of socio-economic transformation, it is pertinent that the healthcare sector also momentises the process of developing corporate culture. The holistic concept of management needs due attention of healthcare policymakers so that health professionals find it easier to practise the same in the larger interests of society. It is not only significant that you make yourself strong. It is much more impact generating that your strengths are protecting and promoting the interests of almost all the sections. Development of small affluent islands around the vast sea of backwardness cannot serve our purpose. It is equally pertinent that like the affluent sections albeit the weaker sections have been harnessing the benefits of qualitative improvements. The holistic management if conceptualised in a right way would make it possible.

The healthcare sector has been found emerging with a high pace. According to the Price Water House Coopers, the health sector would have an investment of about 40 billion US $ by 2010. It is also expected that medical tourism or health tourism would have an attractive market both at national and international levels and by 2012, the medical tourism would have a market of around 2 billion US $. Capitalising on the opportunities makes it essential that we are in a position to predict with the support of a well developed techno-driven information system. This helps us in making our strategical and tactical decisions of world class enabling us to excel competition. Enriching our strengths thus requires priority attention without which we cannot even survive then what to talk of thriving. "Compete or Perish" is the slogan that requires transcendental priority in the development agenda of corporate sector without which we cannot nurture corporate culture.

Excelling competition makes it essential that hospitals activate the process of multi-dimensional transformation. The hospital architects, consultants, planners, medical and paramedical personnel and health professionals need to develop hospitals and healthcare organisations in such a fashion that evolving technologies and changing requirements are given due weightage. An ideal and a pragmatic plan is to be formulated so that our investments prove to be productive. The changing needs and requirements of different segments are to be studied, the emerging trends in the disease profile are to be identified and development and expansion plans are to be finalized. The behavioural management is to be given due place, the techno-driven information system is to be promoted, low cost indigenous technologies are to be given due weightage and sincere and honest efforts are to be made to fulfill the mounting levels of expectations of patients and attendants. Additionally, the surroundings and premises are to be made environment-friendly. We cannot deny that changing levels of expectations of patients and attendants cannot be fulfilled unless we develop and motivate medical, para-medical, technical and managerial staff. Enriching the knowledge bank of different categories and echelons of staff and retaining them with the help of lucrative incentives need priority attention.

The service environment of a hospital is found different to others. We find hospitals a place for the generation of tension which may depress patients and attendants and the working people. The vulnerable units like emergency ward, operation theatres, mortuary houses, mismanaged wastes considerably and adversely influence the quality of service environment where tension is but natural. This makes it essential that possible measures are initiated to improve the quality of service environment. In addition, it is also pertinent that health professionals make it sure that whatsoever the incentives are given to them also prove to be a source for gaining satisfaction and new experiences while delivering and using. The psychosomatic complaints received from the medical staff need to be redressed. Job stress is found of high magnitude in hospitals and healthcare services. The emergency staff in particular witnesses high magnitudes of job stress which can be diffused by offering lucrative incentives and efficiency-friendly service environment. A majority of the hospitals have been found undermining this component in the Indian hospitals.

The management of waste is an important problem in the hospitals which have not received due attention of health professionals. Of course, the corporate hospitals are found taking care of different types of wastage but the small private hospitals and government hospitals in general have not been found sincere to this problem. Aesthetic sense becomes an integral part of hospital management. It also helps in minimising the recovery period. The hospital waste proves to be a carrier for the vulnerable diseases. The biomedical degradable and non-degradable wastage need priority attention of health professionals. They need scientific devices to manage the waste. In a true sense, we need rigid regulations to remove the problem of waste.

The government policy makers, the boardrooms of the corporate hospitals need an attitudinal change. They have also to focus on locating speciality hospitals preferably in the rural areas so that weaker sections of the society also harness the benefits of sophisticated developments in the healthcare services. If we find hospitals having proper accessibility, the urban segment would not have any problem. The multiplier effects would be active and the process of rural economic development by transforming rural areas into urban areas would also be found easier. The corporate hospitals also need to promote the use of new generation of technology so that telediagnosis and telemedicine significantly serve the interests of rural population. While undertaking research activities, they should devise low cost indigenous technologies in addition to the diversified use of information technology.

Since we find a majority of the hospitals in the government sector facing the problem of financial crunch, the PPP mode may be motivated. The state governments in particular need to promote PPP mode by offering a number of incentives. The Central Government may play an incremental role making provisions for tax holiday and other incentives. In this context, it is to be made sure that the incentives offered to them are repaid in the shape of subsidised or even free of charge services to the weaker section of the society.

In the years to come, the multidimensional hazards would make the disease profile much more vulnerable. This would aggravate the intensity of problem. This makes it essential that a hospital manager in addition to the blending of core and peripheral services also promotes preventive services so that the rural masses are sensitised and the food-prone, water-prone, pollution-prone and communicable diseases are minimised. The creative promotional measures of health professionals would also be instrumental in the sensitisation process. A healthcare or hospital manager hears the responsibility of improving the level of efficiency because this is the most effective prescription to make the medicare services cost effective. Improving the quality of inputs used in the process; improving the quality of people engaged in the process; improving the strengths of hospitals; understanding the expectations of patients and attendants and healthcare personnel; synchronising the marketing resources in tune with the changing needs and requirements of patients, improving the quality of knowledge technology to activate the innovation process are some of the vital responsibilities before the healthcare professionals for which they need world class excellence. We need to develop health professionals having he potentials to discharge the multi-dimensional functional responsibilities failing which either government hospitals or private hospitals would find it difficult to improve the quality of their services. Managing the services environment and the concerned people and technology in such a way that patients are found satisfied with the services delivered and working people are satisfied with the service environment and incentives made available to them remain the key areas where the health professionals need to show their world class excellence.

In today's context, the hospitals are required to be developed as a healthcare brand. We cannot deny that Indian healthcare sector is potentially sound to establish a global brand name. With the development of corporate culture, the contours of development have undergone radical changes which have made ways for the development and growth of corporate hospitals. World class medicare services at a competitive price structure and in addition providing opportunities for enjoying at tourist destinations are the key areas for the development of healthcare sector as an industry. Even if we talk about subsidized or free of charge services, this is not possible unless hospitals get an opportunity to earn something more from the affluent sections of the society both at domestic and global levels. It is right to mention that globalisation of economy has engineered a sound foundation for the development of healthcare services where professionals may be successful in marketing India as a healthcare destination. We have been selling healthcare services as a hot cake and have also been successful in luring multitudes of Europeans, Asians and NRIs to undertake international travel for health purposes. Our services are of worldclass and the users get First World Services at Third World Costs where we find enough scope for capitalising on the opportunities both in national and global markets. McKinsey, a consulting firm estimates that India's medical tourism industry could yield as much as 2.2 billion of annual revenue by 2012. We have been growing at 30 per cent annually and expect to march forward with a high pace provided we keep on moving the process of defining and redefining quality.

Shifting from an administrative structure to a managerial structure and adding much more flavour to our services in the shape of professional excellence needs due attention of government policy makers. Attitudinal transformation proves to be a focal point for qualitative transformation. Corporatisation, technological sophistication and humanisation are some of the properties in the modern healthcare services where we need priority attention.

2010 **S.M. JHA**

Contents

The Foundation of Hospital Management

Our wrong decisions, sins and misdeeds, violation of the law of nature, irrational economic transformation policy and emergence of live-in in culture have considerably influenced the disease profile. We need to develop hospitals efficacious of sensitising the society and instrumental in improving the service quality. This focusses on world-class professional excellence.

CHAPTER OBJECTIVES

Introduction—Management of Non—profit Organisations—Hospital: the Concept—Types of Hospital—Hospital Management: the Concept—Significance of Hospital Management—Hospital Management: Shift from Professional to the Manager—Functional Areas in Hospital Management—Managing Sensitive Issues in Hospitals—Management By Objectives in Hospitals—Hospital: A Non-profit Organisation—Hospital: A Social Institution—Hospital: An Institution for Human Capital Formation—National Health Policy—Ethical Dimensions in Hospitals—Consumer Protection Act, 1987—AYUSH: An Overview—E—Health in Indian Perspective—Thrust Areas in Managing Hospitals—An Ideal Hospital Manager—Summary—Key Terms—Review Questions—Application Exercises—End Notes.

LEARNING OBJECTIVES

This chapter of the book aims at studying the different dimensions of the basics of hospital management. Engineering of a foundation plays a decisive role in the development process. The task of managing a non-profit organisation is found difficult, specially in a country like India where the government managed hospitals even till date are traditionally managed. With the emergence of corporate culture and the incremental role of e-Health, it is pertinent that hospital professionals develop their awareness of the changing levels of expectations of users vis-a-vis the multi-dimensional developments in the field of information and communication technology which would help in improving the service quality and satisfying the users.

Introduction

In a country like India where high rate of demographic pressure, illiteracy, environmental pollution and insensitivity amongst the masses have considerably been responsible for generating and aggravating the multi-pronged diseases, we need concerted efforts to make an assault on the food-prone, water-prone, pollution-prone and communicable diseases on a priority basis. Often we talk about speeding up the process of socio-economic transformation but less we do for human capital formation. Even in an age of high-tech, the proverb, "Health is above Wealth", is found relevant. The national policy makers bear the responsibility of making available to the masses at least the basic medical facilities. The voluntary social organisations, non-government organisations and albeit the corporate sector need to evince interests in the process of social transformation. Of course, the state exchequer has been allocating huge funds for healthcare services but the results in a true sense are found very much disappointing. The medical and paramedical personnel serving hospitals and healthcare centres in different capacities, specially in the government sector have not been found serving and subserving the interests of those segments who need it on a priority basis. It is against this backdrop that we need to assign due weightage to the hospital management so that professional excellence and professional ethics help in protecting and promoting the interests of almost all the sections and segments.

In the group of service-generating organisations, we find two broad categories, viz. profit-making and non-profit-making organisations. The profit making organisations have a legitimate right of making profits whereas the non-profit making organisations do not have the same right. However, they can generate surpluses to make possible qualitative and quantitative transformation in their potentials. We find hospitals in the second category.

The hospitals bear multi-faceted responsibilities of curative and preventive nature. On the one hand, they are supposed to make available to the patients quality medical aid while on the other hand, they are also supposed to sensitise the masses. We cannot deny that the track record of hospitals working under the government sector has not been found satisfactory. The prime reason for the same is faulty national health policy which has been responsible for contracting the potentials of hospitals. It is high time that government administration, hospital planners and hospital managers make a microscopic audit of the unproductive results and formulate a strategy which will improve the quality of services in both the rural and urban areas of the country.

The organisation and management of hospitals need due care of the hospitals planners. A sound organisational structure making provisions for the quality medical and paramedical personnel of different echelons need priority attention. The vulnerable catchment areas need expertise in the face of prevailing diseases. The recruitment possesses, training facilities, motivational plans and performance appraisal are some of the areas where professional excellence of hospital administrators would play a meaningful role. In a true sense, they need managerial proficiency of worldclass. Of late, the leading private and government hospitals have been found providing quality services specially with the help of new generation of technology. They need to define and redefine service quality by promoting research and development activities in which the techno-driven information system would play an incremental role.

We cannot deny that in the hospital and healthcare services, the medical and paramedical personnel and the nursing staff significantly contribute to the process of service quality upgradation but even the quality inputs fail in delivering quality outputs if we find an organisation facing the problem of managerial deficiency. The OT is ready for a surgeon to perform but we cannot expect anything concrete unless he/she is made available a team of dedicated personnel and the supporting infrastructural facilities. On the other hand, we also find cases where the supporting infrastructural facilities are available but in absence of a professionally sound hospital manager, the investments are found to be unproductive. This makes it clear that the service quality requires a fair synchronization of quality medical and paramedical personnel, quality supporting infrastructural facilities, quality technology and a quality manager performing in a quality ambience.

In an age of hybrid technology, the hospitals and healthcare centres are required to make huge financial investments for quality inputs and therefore, they need mobilisation of adequate financial resources from the diverse sources. On the one hand, they need to pave avenues for charities, donations and grants while on the other hand, they have also to make use of the internal sources. The formulation of a sound budget, the scientific documentation and filing, computer-based accounting, techno-based investigation, worldclass services ambience are some of key dimensions necessitating priority attention of a hospital manager.

The different functional areas of the medicare organisations need a professional touch, personalised services, professional ethics, sense of commitment and dedication with the mission of serving and subserving the interests of not only the affluents who can afford but even of those who have less affordability. A professional managing hospital needs an attitudinal change where service considerations establish an edge over other considerations. Managing a non-profit organisation is, of course, a challenging task where we find an acid test of a professional. Enriching the inputs, adding new feathers in their services, maintaining cost-effectiveness, promoting humanised leadership, managing accounts, inventories, identifying irregularities, removing the sore spots make it essential that professionals managing hospitals have worldclass excellence. The most arduous task before a hospital manager is to conceptualise marketing. The motive is to enable hospitals to enrich inputs so that the process of value-addition and quality up-gradation in the larger interests of society gains a rapid momentum. While managing hospitals, the administrative expenses are to be made optimal to minimise the costs. The accounting processes need due care to identify the financial irregularities. The materials and stores are found to be vulnerable areas for promoting the unfair practices. The management of finance in a hospital is considerably influenced by the pricing strategy and of late, when we talk about hospital marketing, a close link between both the administrators, managing two different functional responsibilities, viz. finance and marketing need due attention. The avenues for the mobilisation of internal sources are to be paved and in the process, the fee structure cannot be undermined.

The management of human resources in hospitals draws priority attention of hospital managers on the availability of worldclass medical and paramedical personnel and the other categories of staff. In a majority of the government hospitals, we find unproductive human resources not only increasing the costs of services generation but also degenerating the quality of services. Right from the recruitment to performance-evaluation, the hospital administrators need to be sincere and honest. The process of recruitment must be fair to make available to the hospitals quality people within the shortest possible duration specially with the support of new generation of information and communication technology. The processes of educating, training and developing their potentials must be consistent. The compensation and incentives for motivating them must be linked to their performance levels. The behavioural profile of para-medical or other staff must be based on human considerations. The thematical competence, professional excellence, personal commitment and value-orientation are the properties to be developed on a regular basis.

Another important dimension of management is the marketing of services generated by the hospitals. This constituent of functional management occupies a place of outstanding significance because offering services of worldclass involve huge costs and make the services expensive. The modern hospitals considerably depend on a new generation of technology and quality supporting infrastructural facilities. The managers thus need to adopt a fee structure which is not only meant for the affluent sections of society but also to serve and subserve the interests of weaker sections. Making the services cost-effective would pave avenues for rationalsing the price structure. The fee structure resolving the problem of financial crunch, ensuring cost-effective services to the masses and paving avenues for qualitative improvements need due attention of hospital marketers. Affordability remains to be the most judicious criterion to protect and promote the interests of almost all the sections. The mobilisation of financial resources through charities and donations need priority attention of hospital marketers.

A discriminatory pricing strategy may be preferred to protect and promote the interests of weaker sections of the society. The product uniqueness generates attractions which requires an optimal blending of core and peripheral services. But to be more specific, in hospital services, we find core services establishing an edge over the peripheral services.

The leading private hospitals have been found assigning due weightage to aesthetic management. This focuses out attention of management of surroundings and premises. We cannot negate the contribution of environmentfriendly hygienic surroundings to the quick recovery of patients. The hehavioural studies help in studying and understanding the levels of expectations of patients and attendants. The study of segmentation helps in knowing the needs and requirements of particular segment.

Of course, we find hospital professionals playing a big role in improving the quality of services but we cannot underestimate the instrumentality of National Policy makers in the entire process. It is right to advocate in favour of National Health Policy ensuring at least the basic medical facilities to the poorest of the poor. Though, since Independence, India has built up a vast health infrastructure and health personnel at primary, secondary and tertiary levels in public, voluntary and private sectors and a number of medical and paramedical institutions including Ayurveda, Yoga and Naturopathy, Unani, Siddha and Homeopathy (AYUSH) institutions have also been set up but a majority of the population even till date lacks the basic healthcare services. We are aware of the fact that even the users of hospital services get protection from the Consumer Protection Act and therefore, the policy makers and hospital professionals need to motivate the personnel for an attitudinal change. Though the ethical dimensions leave no scope for negligence, still we find a number of cases where patients suffer mainly on account of inefficiency and mismanagement.

We expect positive results from the e-Health initiatives focussing on training, education and capacity building for e-health; monitoring by e-enabled HMIS to ensure timely flow of data, Geographical information System, Resources Mapping of various health facilities, disease surveillance, tele-consultations, health helpline, district hospital referral net and e-enabled mobile medical units. Achieving a New Vision based on faster, broad-based and inclusive growth needs priority attention on structural transformation in the national policies.

The management of a social institution is no doubt a challenging task which is found much more complicated in the Indian society where we find high intensity of insensitivity. Contrary to other organisations, the hospitals not only bear the responsibility of speeding up the recovery process but also bring down the number of potential users by developing mass awareness. The print media, broadcast and telecast media need to inform and sense the masses regarding the waterprone, food-prone, communicable and viral diseases.

The management of hospitals requires professional excellence of world class. It is not only significant that we raise the budgetary provisions and make financial allocation. It is not only pertinent that we employ quality medical and paramedical personnel. It is much more impact generating that we make the environment conducive to the healthy living conditions which on the one hand develop the resistance power of masses while on the other hand also make possible quick recovery of patients.

A healthier society is our target. Promoting healthcare services is our mission. Making possible affordability is our objective. The poor and underprivileged segments need priority attention. A comprehensive approach encompassing individual healthcare, public health, sanitation, clean drinking water, access to food, nutritional awareness, sensitivity to vaccination culture, knowledge of hygience and feeding practices etc. are some of the key issues for minimizing the health problems.

During the yesteryears, the Centre as well as the State Governments have initiated a wide variety of PPP arrangements to meet people's growing healthcare needs. The services like cleaning and maintenance of buildings, security, waste management, scavenging, laundary and diet have been contracted out to the private sector by many states. In the Indian perspective, we find contracting as a predominant model for PPP. The Most important functional responsibility before a government is to create an environment found unfriendly to diseases.

In an age of information, it is imperative that we assign due weightage to the development of information-driven healthcare organisation. It is in this context that we find Clinical Data Warehouses (CDWs) to improve clinical performance and decrease costs. A CDW is a milestone along the path towards a fully electronic, living medical record system integrating data entry with archival and retrieval into one seamless system. It is much more judicious that benefits of technological sophistication are made available albeit to the hospitals or healthcare organisations. Monitoring by e-enabled HMIS to ensure timely flow of data and collation to be used at various levels, Geographical Information System, Resource Mapping of various health facilities, tele-consultations and health helpline are some of the benefits of tech-driven information system considerably helping hospitals and healthcare organisations in maintaining cost economy. The government policy makers need to deal with rising costs of healthcare and growing expectations of people. The challenge of quality health services in remote rural regions has to be urgently met. In a true sense, we need to transform public healthcare into an accountable, accessible and affordable system efficacious of offering quality services.

Let the policy makers realise the instrumentality of management in hospitals and healthcare organisations. Let the professionals make use of their worldclass excellence for translating the inefficients into star performers. Let them make the services affordable. Let them minimise the possibilities of water-prone, food-prone, viral and communicable diseases.

Management of Non-profit Organisations

Profitwise, we classify organisations into two categories, viz. profit making and non-profit making. Managerial proficiency constitutes a place of outstanding significance for both categories of organisations. It is in this context that we find educational institutions, hospitals and healthcare organisations, political organisations and religious organisations conceptualizing the principles of holistic concept of management to accomplish the organisational objectives. Qualitative and quantitative transformation are found meaningful even for the non-profit organisations because if they start stagnating or moving in the reverse gear, the interests of society in general and the weaker sections in particular would considerably be affected. We cannot deny that either for an individual or for an organisation or institution, strengths carry important meaning. If we are strong enough to counter the challenges and threats, we also find ourselves efficacious of serving and subserving social interests. This makes a strong advocacy in favour of enriching our strength and for that we need managerial proficiency vis-a-vis the financial solvency. An organisation found to be managerially proficient is found to be financially solvent. Of course, the non-profit organisations do not have a legitimate right of making profits but if we realise their significance to the process of protecting and promoting the social interests, we cannot be allowed to regulate their rights of generating surpluses which would open new vistas for their development.

In the Indian perspective, we find the boardrooms very much indifferent to the development and well-being of non-profit organisations which has been obstructing the process of their qualitative or quantitative improvements. A contraction in their potentials of bearing the social costs makes them insignificant to the social transformation process. It is against this background that we find important government managed social institutions like educational institutions, and hospitals and healthcare organisations are glaring examples of deficient management. They are found virtually trapped in the vicious circle and a majority of them are found struggling just for protecting their existences. The intensity of the problem is found at its peak which would hardly be reversed unless we take up the problem on a priority basis.

The holistic concept of management[1] draws out prime attention on the conceptualisation process. This focusses on social or public interests. The most important thing in the social transformation process is increasing the social costs bearing capacity of an organisation which cannot be possible if they depend solely on the state exchequer. The process of mobilisation of internal resources and charities and donations need top priority to bring things back on the rail. The government managed universities, colleges, institutes, hospitals and healthcare centres are found crumbling. It is high time that the policy makers make possible an attitudinal change and are positive to these institutions. In addition, the professional managing hospitals and healthcare centres explore avenues for generating finance and increasing surpluses to make them more sound. A basic change in the character and structure of these organisations appears to be the need of hour. It is against this backdrop that we find professional excellence a subject of priority consideration for managing hospitals and healthcare organisations.

The process of social engineering makes it essential that we conceptualise the principles of social management for managing the social-welfare oriented institutions. There are a number of factors found responsible for influencing the human quality index but the level of education and healthcare facilities assume a place of outstanding significance. Both the services are found under the purview of non-profit organisations where managerial proficiency can play an incremental role in their development process. If the educational institutions are not delivering goods to the society; if quality medicare services are not made available to the society; if the political organisations are found witnessing serious comments; if the religious organisations have been facing the image problem, it is due mainly to their professional deficiency. It is hoped that the holistic concept of management would help them in many ways.

The management principles make it essential that the hospitals or other non-profit making organisations formulate a rational plan in tune with the changing social requirements. They take help of techno-driven information system, study and understand the levels of expectations of customers or users, improve the quality of their services, make possible cost-effectiveness, set a fee which is found affordable, enrich their potentials of bearing the social costs and pave avenues for their qualitative and quantitative improvements. All the functional areas need due care of a professional. The management of human resources, finance, stores and inventories, supporting infrastructural facilities, surroundings and premises, service ambience, sensitive points like OTs, etc, need priority attention. The marketing dimension looks significant even in the non-profit organisations. In addition to other aspects, the marketing professional would also help hospitals and healthcare organisations in increasing charities and donations, sensitising and influencing the donors and activating the preventive measures.

In view of the above mentioned facts, it is right to mention that the management of non-profit organisations requires due attention of policy makers, boardrooms and hotel professionals because they are found pledged to subserve the social interests. It is right to mention that in the modern hospitals, we find huge expenses on new generation of information and communication technology, hybrid technology and equipments and instruments in addition to the supporting infrastructural facilities. So far as the private hospitals are concerned, they make it possible but the government managed hospitals find it difficult mainly on account of the problem of financial crunch. Conceptualisation of holistic concept of management would make their tasks easier and proactive.

HOSPITAL: THE CONCEPT

At the outset, we go through the concept of a hospital. With a change in the time cycle, it is natural that we find a change in the concept and perception. Yesterday, the hospitals were considered to be "alms houses" which were endowed for the support and lodging of the poor. These houses were set up as a charity institution to take care of sick and poor. Today, we consider hospital a place for the diagnosis and treatment of human ills, for the education and training and research, for the promotion of healthcare activities and to some extent, a centre also helping big-social research. The document of World Health Organisation (WHO) focusses on the concept of a hospital. In the document of WHO, it is stated that hospital is an integral part of a social and medical organisation, the function of which is to provide for the population complete healthcare, both curative and preventive and whose out-patient services reach out to the family in its home environment; the hospital is also a centre for training of health workers for big-social research.[2]

In the face of the viewpoints expressed in the documents of WHO, of late, we find modern hospitals responsible for offering a number of preventive and curative services. When we talk about an environment for hospitals, the WHO document makes it clear that the environment of hospitals should be similar to the home environment.

The WHO documents further consider hospital a complex organisation.[3] It is complex in the sense that multi-faceted developments in the society have made the masses more conscious of their rights. Today, we find masses expecting more from the hospitals. They want everything, not within the four walls of the hospitals but at their doorstep or in the vicinity of living places. On the other hand, we find different types of diseases spreading due to environmental problems that increase the functional responsibilities of hospitals. This also makes it a complex organisation.

Of late, we consider hospital a major social institution for offering healthcare services and for offering a considerable advantage to both the patients and society. It is considered to be a place for the diagnosis and treatment of human ills and restoration of health and well-beings of those temporarily deprived of.[4]

The aforesaid facts make it clear that hospital is a complex social institution to subserve the interests of society by offering preventive and curative medicare services in addition to the educational and training facilities for the medicos and paramedical personnel. The significant developments in the society have made possible a basic change in the concept and perception of hospitals. It is in this context that of late we find the organisation and management of hospitals in a bit different way. When we consider it a managerial process, our focus is on managing hospitals with the help of professionally sound personnel so that the masses get the required medicare services on time. Of late, we talk about hospital management and in the same context, we also deliberate upon the instrumentality of hospital managers to improve the quality of medical services offered by hospitals. With the growing significance of the holistic concept of management, we find management of hospital as a social institution and more so as a no-profit making organisation.

TYPES OF HOSPITALS

There are different types of hospitals[5] established with the motto of offering the medicare services and educational and training facilities. In a natural way, we find distinction in their structure, function and performance. The classification is found based on different criteria as mentioned below:

Objectives: The first criterion for the classification is the objective. The main objective of establishing a hospital is to offer the medical services but we also find education, training and research as the secondary objectives. In Fig. 1.1, we find classification on the basis of objective.

- The Teaching-cum-Research hospitals, the first in the category, are established to make available to the medicos and paramedical personnel the teaching aid. These hospitals are found instrumental in offering the educational and research facilities in addition to the medical services. As for example, we find All India Institute for Medical Sciences, Postgraduate Education and Research Institute, Chandigarh and others established as teaching-cum-research hospitals.
- General Hospitals, the second category, also offer teaching and research facilities but here, we find these objectives of secondary nature. The main objective is to offer the medical services.

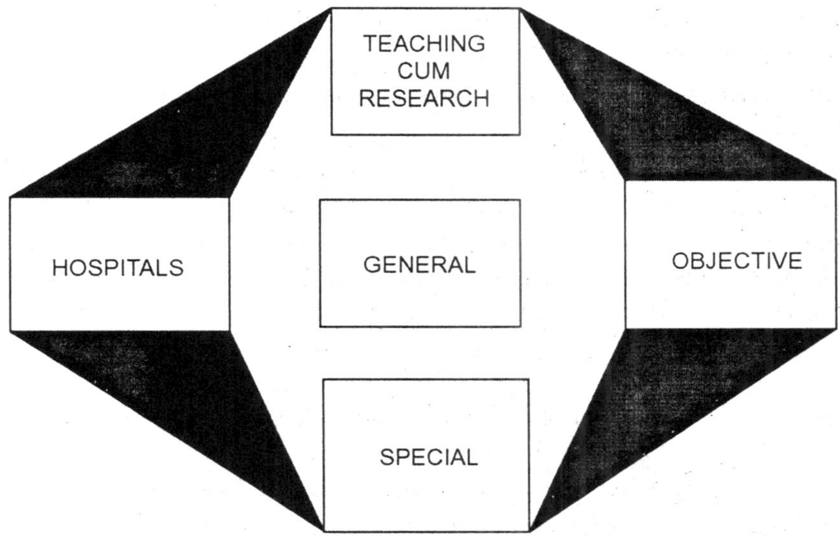

Fig. 1.1. Classification on the Basis of Objective

- Special Hospitals, the third category, are meant for specific purposes. These hospitals offer specialised services in the selected areas. They concentrate on a particular organ of the body or a particular disease.

Ownership: We also find classification on the basis of ownership. The different categories in the very context are mentioned in Fig, 1.2.

Government Hospitals: It is the first type in the ownership category. The government hospitals are owned, managed and controlled by the government whereas the semi-government hospitals are found acting as an autonomous body.

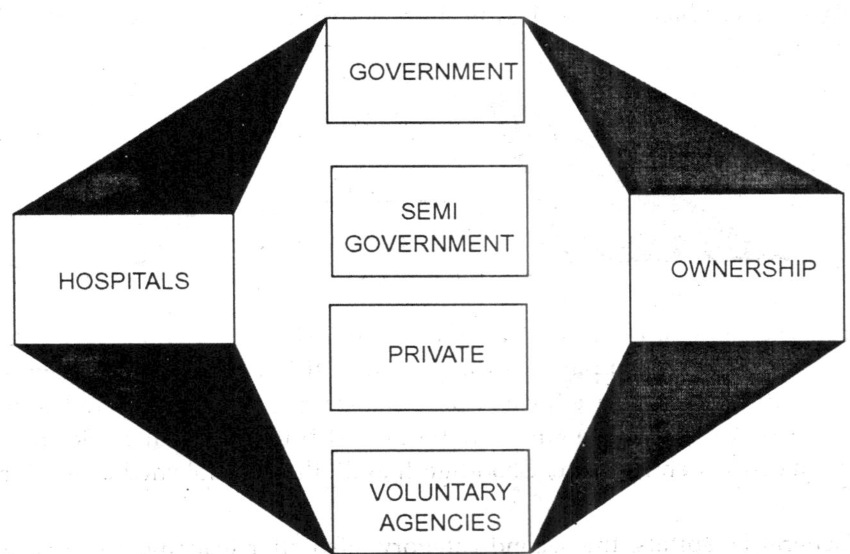

Fig. 1.2. Classification on the Basis of Ownership

Semi-government Hospitals: Such type of hospitals act as an autonomous body. The governmental regulations control the functioning of hospitals.

Voluntary Agencies Hospitals: The voluntary organisations manage and control hospitals coming under this category.

Private Charitable Hospitals: Some of the hospitals are managed by charitable trusts.

Path of Treatment: This is also a base for the classification of hospitals. In this category, we find Allopathic, Ayurvedic, Homeopathic and Unani hospitals. In Figure 1.3, we find classification on the basis of path of treatment. In different types of hospitals classified on the basis of medicine or path of treatment, we find a difference in the nature and character of treatment.

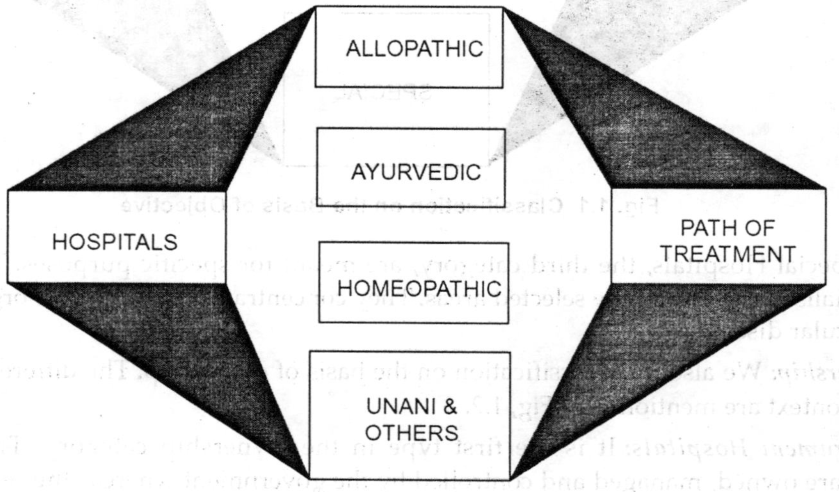

Fig. 1.3. Classification on the Basis of Path of Treatment

Size: This is also a base for the classification of hospitals. In Fig. 1.4, we find classification on the basis of size.

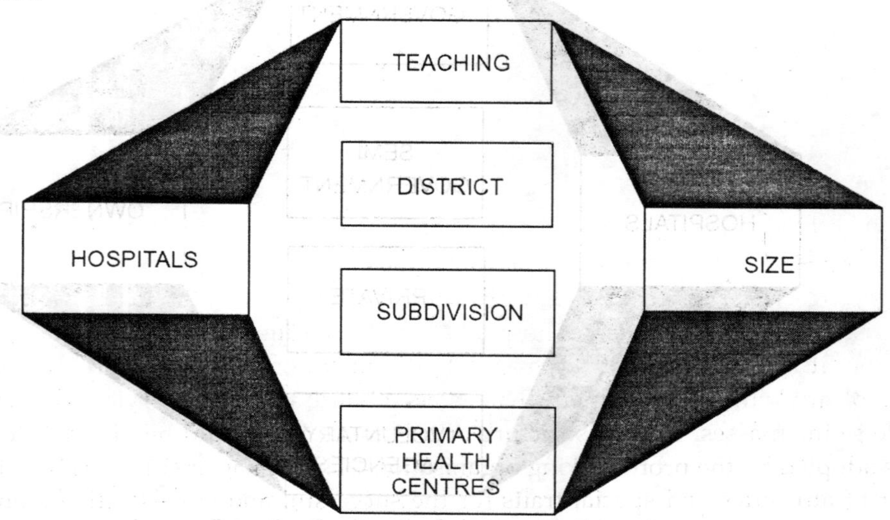

Fig. 1.4. Classification on the Basis of Size

Teaching Hospital: The teaching hospitals generally have five hundred beds which can be increased according to the number of students.

District Hospital: The district hospitals generally have two hundred beds which can be raised to three hundred depending upon the population in a catchment area.

Tehsil, Taluk, Subdivisional Hospital: Such type of hospitals generally have fifty beds that can be raised to one hundred beds depending upon the population in the catchment area.

Primary Health Centres: In this category, we find six beds which can be raised to ten.

HOSPITAL MANAGEMENT—THE CONCEPT

At the outset, let's go through the conceptual aspects of hospital management. Since we find here a combination of two worlds, it is natural that by hospital management, our focus would be on the management principles pertaining to the management of no-profit making organisations. Management of hospitals thus draws our attention on planning, organising, staffing, directing, communicating and controlling a social institution professionally which makes available to the patients quality medicare services at an affordable price. It also gravitates our attention on managing the functional areas of hospitals with the motto of serving the society, such as management of material, management of human resources, management of finance and management of marketing. We find hospital management a science because the services generated by hospitals are found based on researches and experiments taking place in the medical sciences. The machines and equipment used in the process of diagnosis and treatment, the medicines produced by the pharmaceutical industry and the inventions and innovations in the modes of treatment are considerably governed by the scientific developments. Most of us find it a profession because the personnel managing hospitals need professional excellence which requires proper education and training facilities specifically in the face of evolving technologies. We can't expect from ordinary or common persons to be an efficient hospital manager. The professionals managing hospitals are supposed to be aware of the principles of management and to be more specific, familiar with the principles of holistic concept of management, specially for the no-profit making organisations. We can't negate a basic difference in the nature and character of profit and no-profit making organisations. The professionals acting as hospital managers are required to understand the salient features of services generated by hospitals vis-a-vis the requirements and expectations of patients and attendants. This makes it essential that the hospital managers undertake an in-depth study of the behavioural profile so that the medical and paramedical personnel and the nursing staff realise the significance of behavioural sciences in minimising the duration of recovery. Thus, we find hospital management a fair synchronisation of science and profession. The hospital managers bear the responsibility of making available to the patients the quality services at an affordable fee structure. This necessitates cost-effectiveness. He/she is required to manage finance efficiently of course with a different vision. Because we consider hospital a social institution and more so a no-profit making organisation, it is pertinent that the hospital administrators/managers are familiar with the principles of marketing management. This is essential to make the services remunerative but affordable to the masses. The fee structure or treatment cost would be different to the pricing strategies adopted by the profit making organisations. The management/personnel thus require a number of attributes and special traits for the successful and cost-effective management of hospitals.

In view of the aforesaid facts, we perceive the following facts for a right perception of hospital management:

- Hospital management is an aggregation of two words—"Hospital" and "Management."
- It is a managerial process of practising the principles of management.
- It is a social process because we also consider hospital a social institution.
- It is based on the holistic concept of management that necessitates subserving of social interests.
- It is a science and more so a profession because the hospital managers/administrators need proper education and training for achieving perfection.
- It is the management of an organisation which is not supposed to make profits.
- It is based on professional excellence where an administrator is required to blend optimally the core and peripheral services.

Significance of Hospital Management

There are a number of persons till now not considering the relevance of managing hospitals professionally. They advocate that the doctors bear the responsibility of managing and controlling the hospitals. It is against this background that we focus on some of the issues testifying the instrumentality of hospital administrators/managers in managing almost all the categories of hospitals. The expertise can't be generalised. We find medical and paramedical personnel acquiring expertise in the related areas which can't be efficiently done by the management experts. Like this, we find different functional areas of management which can't be carried forward effectively by the medical and paramedical personnel. The patients and attendants come to a hospital with the motto of quality medicare services to be made available to them on time. The hospitals may have different amenities and facilities but it is not essential that all the required amenities and facilities are made available to them. We are well aware of the fact that time honoured and decent and efficient offering or processing of services is the result of a well-formulated team. Since a number of machines, equipment and infrastructural facilities help the process of diagnosis and treatment, the professional excellence occupies a place of outstanding significance. Thus, we can't devalue hospital management for generating efficiency and making the process of treatment cost effective. The following facts testify the importance of hospital management:

1. Formulation of a pragmatic plan: The most important thing for the proper functioning and an optimal development of an organisation is the formulation of a rational plan found of pragmatic nature which is implemented within the stipulated time and budget. A professionally sound administrator/manager finds it convenient to estimate the changing requirements within the available potentials. The schemes for development, modernisation and expansion are found in the face of available financial strength which is not to result into the delayed implementation or reallocation or additional allocation of funds. The hospital planners formulate short and long-term plans keeping in view the expected number of the potential users in the catchment area. Unplanned development or the formulation of an overambitious plan would not serve our purpose. Since the hospital administrators/managers take the support of a well-developed and a technology-driven Management Information System, it is easier to estimate the requirements vis-a-vis to assess the strength. The time honoured implementation is possible because the administrators design the monitoring mechanism consisting of personally-committed employees. Since the management of time is given an overriding priority, we find cost effectiveness at the different stages of implementation.

2. Formulation of an efficient and personally committed team: We are well aware of the fact that hospital administrators/managers bear the responsibility of constituting a team of personally-committed and efficient medical and paramedical personnel in consultation with the specialists of the respective areas. The quality and number of assisting personnel, the supporting equipment and the infrastructural facilities required by a particular team can only be finalised by experts. The hospital administrators/managers are required to be vigilant that personnel included in the team perform satisfactorily. Of course, the doctors know better about the quality and size of a team to be formulated but once the team has been constituted, the administrators/ managers bear the responsibility of making it sure that all of them are available and performing as per the set norms, defined ways and fixed time.

3. Availability of supporting infrastructural facilities: For performing efficiently, effectively and timely, it is pertinent that the hospital administrators/ managers come to know about the supporting infrastructual facilities such as light, water, oxygen, emergency drugs, dresses and instruments in right order, equipment helping doctors are in proper condition, sophisticated communication facilities are available in a working condition or so. We can't expect even from an efficient team to perform efficiently if the supporting infrastructural facilities are not available. It is right to mention that in a majority of the government hospitals, the supporting infrastructural facilities of course are available but the working teams fail to get them on time which questions the performance of medical and paramedical personnel vis-a-vis tarnishes the image of hospitals. This is due mainly to the fact that efficient hospital administrators/managers are not working there. If the hospitals have professionally sound administrators, the supporting infrastructural facilities would be made available to the doctors attending on the patients.

4. Optimising the cost: The hospital administrators/managers are supposed to be well aware of the fact that how and in what way, the administrative and other unproductive expenses are to be made optimal to the changing requirements. There are a number of expenses found unproductive in nature and very much instrumental in raising the cost of treatment. The medical personnel find it difficult to regulate. The wastes of water, light, poor maintenance and operation of machines and equipment, the mismanagement and unfair practices in the purchase of materials and stores, etc. increase the operational costs. Of course, the required infrastructural facilities and other, administration expenses are essential but we talk about mismanagement or misuse of funds at the different stages. The hospital administrators/managers identify the points of wastes and make sincere or concerted efforts to control which make the diagnosis-cum-treatment processes cost effective. In an age of sophisticated technologies, we find hospitals taking the support of infrastructural facilities considerably. The proper operation and maintenance of technologies used in the process of diagnosis and treatment need an intensive care. Thus, the task of making the process cost effective rests on the shoulders of hospital administrators/managers having the worldclass managerial excellence.

5. Acceleration of overall productivity: We can't negate that even hospitals need to increase the rate of overall productivity. This requires proper use of technologies and the human resources. If we use machines and equipments in tune with their potentials, if the medical and paramedical personnel work efficiently and maintain punctuality the rate of overall productivity would go up. Earlier we have talked about cost-effectiveness which makes it essential that all the components involved in the process are managed in a right fashion. If we fail in raising the rate of productivity, the cost of diagnosis and treatment would go up which can't be welcome specially in countries like ours where masses need pocket-friendly services. The efficient management of hospitals thus only not makes the process cost effective but as a result, also increases the rate of productivity which increases the strength or potentials of hospitals to subserve the social interests in tune with the principle of holistic concept of management.

6. Creativity in the promotional efforts: When we talk about the services of hospitals, the preventive services assume a place of outstanding significance. We can't negate that hospital administrators/managers know well the skill of making possible creativity in the promotional measures. Of late, it is essential that masses, specially living in the rural areas and particularly related to the illiterate segment of the society are informed and sensed in a right fashion so that the water-prone, food-prone, environment-prone, communicable, viral diseases and their harmful effects are minimised considerably. This necessitates creativity in the promotional measures and campaigns and the hospital administrators/managers having professional and managerial excellence can make it possible. In addition, we also realise the relevance of promotional measures in generating work culture that almost all is found vanishing. By creative promotional measures, we focus on advertising and publicity measures having the potentials to influence the masses. The preventive services depend sizeably upon the creative promotional measures. We can't negate that only a professional can make it possible which would help hospitals in many ways.

7. Management of Behaviour: We can't negate that efficiency of medical and paramedical personnel, availability of supporting infrastructural facilities, sophistication of machines and equipments are essential to enrich the quality of medicare services but in this context, the behavioural management also assumes a significant place. The behavioural profile of personnel working in the hospitals plays an incremental role in minimising the recovery period. The doctors and paramedical personnel serving hospitals need an indepth study of behavioural management so that the possibilities of indecent behaviour and confrontation with the patients and attendants are minimised considerably. The hospital administrators/managers being aware of the behavioural management, can be successful in improving the behavioural profile of different echelons of employees working in the hospitals which would make the departmental relationship cohesive and friendly.

The aforesaid facts make it clear that management of hospitals by the professionally sound administrators/managers provide a number of benefits. The efficiency index, the behavioural profile, the satisfaction to users are some of the problems which can't be overcome satisfactorily failing the sound management of hospitals by the world class professionally sound managers. It is in this context that we find rationale behind practising management principles in the health care organisations. Not only do the private hospitals but even the government hospitals need to conceptualise the holistic concept of management for subserving the social interests. Quality medicare services to the patients and proper development of hospitals are the key objectives which can't be fulfilled satisfactorily unless the hospitals are managed professionally. Besides, the efficient personnel serving the hospitals efficiently would also be rewarded suitably if we find hospital managers managing things properly. Professionals having worldclass excellence are required to be recruited in all the hospitals to improve the quality of services.

HOSPITAL MANAGEMENT—THE TRANSITION FACTORS

Shift from Professional to Manager

The transition factors in the process of shift from a professional to a manager[6] need your due case to meet the expectations of users/patients. Your instrumentality as a professional, no doubt is significant to improve the quality of services but keeping in view the multidimensional developments in the business and social environmental conditions, you need to establish your success as a manager. We can't deny the fact that your professionalism as a manager would open new vistas for qualitative-cum-quantitative improvements in the healthcare services which would cater to the ever increasing expectations of customers/ users. This makes it clear that personnel engaged in administering the hospitals, of late, need to prove that their excellence as a manager would make possible an attitudinal change in their orientation. You work as an administrator and in this context, your responsibility is confined to the tasks assigned to you. But when you start acting as a manager, your functional responsibilities and areas are enlarged because you are found responsible for the performance of all. You are accountable even for the mistakes committed by others. Thus, a shift from self-direction to selfless service makes the ways for a circumstantial control or supervision. Of late, the leading hospitals in the world make strong advocacy in favour of developing the hospital administrator as a manager. In this context, we find four types of shifts as mentioned in Fig. 1.5.

Shift-1 is from self-direction to selfless service.

Shift-2 is from autonomous control to circumstantial control.

Shift-3 is from quantitative outcomes to the qualitative outcomes.

Shift-4 is from definite criteria to gray area.

In Figure 1.5, we find focus on multifaceted shifts. The moment you switch on the process of circumstantial control, the copious avenues are paved for qualitative improvements. The stellar performance helps you in establishing your image as a personally committed manager. In a very

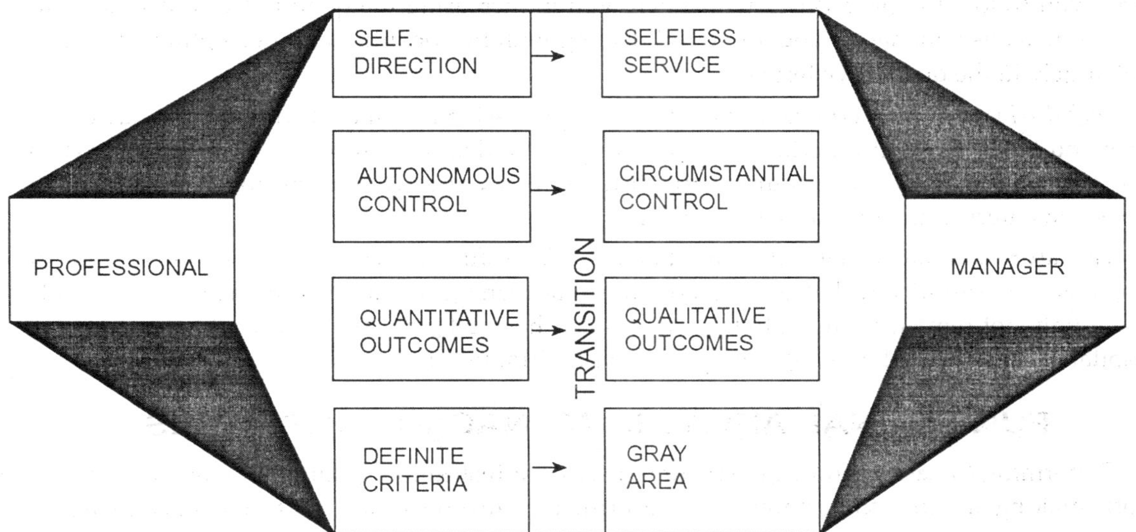

Fig. 1.5. Transition Factors in Shift from Professional to Manager

natural way, you then enter the gray area where all healthcare executives and managers consent to the way you adopt.

The aforesaid facts make it clear that to make possible an improvement in the quality of services offered by hospitals to the masses, specially in the overpopulated countries like ours, such a shift is essential. We go through the multidimensional shifts being influenced by your instrumentality as a manager.

Shift-1—From self-direction to selfless services: In this context, when you act as a professional, it is quite natural that you are self-directed. You are supposed to be responsible for your own performance. You have defined ways and your footsteps follow the same. It is self that guides the formation of attitude. It is self that proves your instrumentality positive to all or just to a few selected areas. When you act as a manager, you are responsible not only for your own performance but for the performance of all directly or indirectly linked to the services offered by the hospitals. We can't negate that in both the processes, the qualitative difference in the result is apparent. When you act as an administrator, your area is self-directed but when you act as a manager, your area is selfless service since you are also supposed to supervise the activities of others. This results into qualitative improvements in the services offered by hospitals.

Shift-2—From autonomous control to circumstantial control: Your instrumentality as a professional makes possible autonomous control but if you act as a manager, the situational or circumstantial control is possible. In the first case, you are influenced by a job description in which proven practices guide your decisions but when you act as a manager, the emerging trends or the changing conditions or circumstances govern the flow of your action. In this context, we find flexibility playing an incremental role but it necessitates a change in your approach and attitude. Since you are supposed to be reactive, adaptable, flexible and versatile, the success in mobilising the entire department specially in an emergency like condition can't be doubtful.

Shift-3—From quantitative to qualitative outcomes: When you act as a professional, you succeed in having the quantitative outcomes. As a job technician, staff pharmacist, plant engineer, staff nurse, you follow the procedures which help you in increasing the quantitative outcomes. But when you act as a manager, you are found dealing with personalities and perceptions then you deal largely in the qualitative terms.

Shift-4—From Definite criteria to gray areas: As a professional, you deal with definite outcomes. Since you have clear-cut criteria, it is easier for you to identify your own contributions. When you work as a manager, it is found difficult to get black and white performance criteria. You succeed in entering an area known as gray area.

The aforesaid facts make it clear that for successful and cost effective functioning of hospitals, it is significant that we promote hospital managers since as a manager the benefits would only not remain confined to the patients and hospital personnel but would also go to the hospital organisations that would open doors for multidimensional developments.

FUNCTIONAL AREAS IN MANAGING HOSPITALS

Performing the assigned responsibilities as a social institution, testifying excellence as a no-profit making organisation, practising the principles of holistic concept of management for subserving social interests and paving avenues for the development and expansion make it essential that the healthcare organisations assign due weightage to the management of functional areas. On the one hand, the hospitals need to make possible quantitative improvements to cater to the medicare services to be offered to the increasing population while on the other hand, they also require qualitative improvements to enrich the quality of services. This in addition to other improvements requires innovative strategies to manage the functional areas, specially with the support of professionally sound managers. The key functional areas are management of human resources, management of finance and the management of marketing the hospital services. This in a natural way requires an indepth study of behavioural profile, segmentation, information management or so.

Managing the Human Resources: We are well aware of the fact that in the medicare organisations, different categories of medical and paramedical personnel work. The management needs due attention on establishing a proportionate relationship in between the different categories of personnel. Since we find the medicare service a result of optimally blended team of different categories of personnel, the administrators need to estimate the requirements and to process for their recruitments with the support of concerned specialists. While recruiting, it is essential that the specialists take into consideration a number of essentials and attributes. The first and foremost thing is efficiency which makes it essential that the personnel to be recruited have knowledge of fundamentals related to the discipline or area for which the recruitments are to be made. But this is not the only thing to be considered since of late we find a number of cases where even efficients have failed in delivering goods. It is in this context that we need quality people even for the medicare organisations. This in a natural way makes it essential that we need to go through the problem in a bit different way. We need quality people who focus our attention on a number of attributes. We need to perceive the essentials required for quality people in a right fashion. We expect doctors to be punctual but in a majority of the cases, they are not. We except doctors to be decent but generally they are found aggressive in character and indecent in behaviour. We expect doctors to be personally committed but they in most of the cases are found not even professionally committed. Not only this, a step ahead, they are found instrumental even in degenerating values and promoting private practice. Of course, the private hospitals are found establishing an edge over the government hospitals, specially in the context of behavioural profile. The medicare organisations need personally committed personnel who at all the time think for the welfare of patients, for the development of hospitals and for improving the quality of services. We can't negate the fact that an organisation can't think about personal commitment unless the personnel serving there get due financial and non-financial incentives. Thus, the hospital managers need to make possible a fair synchronisation of performance orientation and employee orientation. A fair blending of the two would make available to the hospitals value based, personally committed, efficient personnel. The managers are supposed to be vigilant that personnel serving the hospitals get due incentives. We find a close relation between personal-commitment and employee-orientation. With the evolving technologies, the training programmes need to be restructured, the syllabi need to be changed and the refresher courses need to be made regular. The efficients are to be given due incentives whereas the inefficients are to be demotivated.

An appraisal of the performance of employees would help in identifying the efficient personnel. There is no doubt in it that the hospital managers need to assign due weightage to the behavioural profile of different categories of personnel serving the hospitals. In addition, the medical and paramedical personnel need to have humanity which require due emphasis on human values. This makes it essential that attributes like humane, humanity and human values are given due weightage while educating and training the personnel. To be more specific in the medicare services, we can't expect quality results unless the personnel have human values.

Managing Finance: We can't negate the fact that this aspect of hospital is found critical as well as challenging, specially in the Indian context, where masses find it difficult to afford the expensive services. Of late, we find hospitals using expensive inputs which requires generation of adequate finance from different sources. While mobilising the internal sources, they need to adjust the losses on account of cost-based or subsidised services with the high structure of fee charged from the effluents. Besides, it is also pertinent that avenues are explored for charity, grants and donations. The national and international social organisations are to be approached for financial support. The corporate sector in particular has to be liberal to the donations to be given to the healthcare organisations. The holistic concept of management makes it essential that the corporate sector should only not take part in the development process but also come forward to subserve the public interests. They should promote cause-related marketing to help the poorest of the poor who find it difficult to afford even the cost-based services. Of late, we find the government hospitals experiencing the problem of financial crunch. The state exchequer finds it difficult to cater to the increasing financial requirements of hospitals. The regulations deprive them of generating finance from the internal sources and the poorest segment of the society prove to be the worst sufferers. Thus, the hospitals need to tap both the internal and external sources and to minimise their dependence on the state exchequer. In addition, the hospital managers/administrators also need to regulate or minimise the unproductive expenses. Proper accounting, filing, documentation need due attention to control the misuse of funds. The most sensitive or vulnerable points are required to be monitored with the help of sophisticated information technologies. The problem of overstaffing is to be removed. The cases of unfair practices are to be checked. The wastes of supporting infrastructural facilities are to be regulated. Thus, the hospital managers are supposed to be careful only not to the generation of funds but also to be vigilant that the unfair practices are arrested. We agree with the view that in the government hospitals, the cases of misuse of funds and financial irregularities aggravate the financial burden. This makes it essential that hospitals, public or private, small or big, manage finance in a right fashion so that quality inputs are made available to the hospitals to deliver quality services. The hospital managers need two-pronged strategies—first exploring avenues for the mobilisation of financial resources and second checking the misuse of funds. The hospital managers are supposed to manage finance in such a way that even the internal sources of finance generate adequate fund to meet the multifaceted requirements. Besides, they also need to tap the external sources.

Managing Marketing: This component of the functional area occupies a place of outstanding significance because in this context, we talk about formulation of a sound marketing mix for the hospitals. The hospital managers/ administrators bear the responsibility of blending the different constituents in such a way that quality services, at an affordable fee structure/price, are made available to the users besides copious avenues are paved for the development, expansion and modernisation of hospitals in tune with the latest developments in the medical sciences. We find it the most significant functional area of management because in this context, we take a decision regarding the generation of funds from the internal sources by adopting a rational fee structure. At the outset, we talk about the formulation of a sound marketing mix for hospitals.

The service/product mix focusses our attention on the curative and preventive services made available by the hospitals. While formulating the services mix, the hospital managers are supposed to synchronise the peripheral services, specially to make the services unique. The hospital managers need professional excellence since the water-prone diseases, foodprone diseases, communicable diseases and viral diseases are found spreading like a wild fire. In vulnerable areas found sensitive to the multi-faceted diseases, the hospital mangers are required to assign due weightage to the preventive services so that masses are informed and sensed in a right fashion. To be more specific, in the Indian context where masses are illiterate, the promotional measures are required to be made creative since creativity in the promotional measures would inculcate awareness and the increasing pressure on hospitals would considerably be minimised. There are different components of promotion, such as advertising, publicity, sales promotion, word-of-mouth promotion, personal selling and telemarketing which, if blended optimally, would minimise the pressure on hospitals. If they succeed in publicising with a sense of creativity and if they succeed in informing and sensing the masses, a number of problems would be arrested at an early stage of their development. The advertising professionals bear the responsibility of making the advertisement slogans, campaigns and messages creative so that the illiterate rural masses come to know about the significance of healthcare management. The main thing in the process of advertising is to sensitise the masses regarding the types of services available. Further, the sales promotion measures also need an intensive care, specially to motivate the personnel and the users. The professionals also need to think about personal selling so that they succeed in developing a team of personnel efficacious enough in understanding the attitudes and expectations of attendants as well as the patients. The personnel acting as motivators would be paid suitable incentives. If we find hospitals sincere to the offering or processing of services, there would be a substantial increase in the number of word-of-mouth promoters since the satisfied group of users and attendants would promote the services of hospitals. If they start acting as a hidden salesforce, the potential users would be benefited in many ways. In an age of sophisticated information and communication technologies, we find telemarketing emerging as an important constituent of the marketing mix which focusses our attention on developing hospital personnel specially managing the windows or acting as a front line employee, receptionist or so. This would promote the services of hospitals in an effective way. We are aware of the fact that telemarketing helps in promoting and selling the services/goods with the help of sophisticated information and communications technologies and sensitive communications. The efficient telemarketers would help hospitals in transmitting and receiving different types of messages.

The aforesaid facts make it clear that the different constituents of promotion are required to be blended optimally. It is quite natural that in the medicare organisations, we find publicity, word-of-mouth promotion and telemarketing more effective in sensitising the promotional messages. While blending the different constituents, the hospital managers/administrators need to perceive the features of a particular region or the catchment area which would let them know about the nature and character of problems found instrumental in generating and aggravating the diseases.

We find pricing an important mix of marketing which focusses our attention on the pricing or fee strategy adopted by the hospitals. The government hospitals working in the Indian society need more precautions while formulating the pricing strategy since the masses find it difficult to afford even the cost based services then what to talk of the expensive services. Hence, the hospital managers need to go through the problem with a new vision. The state exchequer finds it difficult to offer adequate financial support to the hospitals and the crux of the problem is that they are even not allowed to generate finance from the internal sources. The most significant responsibility before the hospital managers is to pave the avenues for pocket-friendly pricing strategy.

Of course, we find quality of services important to the hospitals or medicare organisations but they can't undermine the way of processing the services. Efficient services are to be offered in a decent way and at the right time. This gravitates our attention on the behavioural profile of medical and paramedical personnel serving the hospitals. We can't negate the fact that in the government hospitals, this dimension of marketing mix is found very much neglected. In this context, we also need to go through the location points for establishing hospitals. The hospitals are to be accessible in addition to the availability of the required infrastructural facilities. The professionals need to be careful that places selected for establishing hospitals are not hazardous.

In addition to the aforesaid mixes, we also need to focus on people mix assuming a place of outstanding significance, specially in the Indian perspective. The quality medical and para-medical personnel and nursing staff would make an assault on the multi-dimensional problems. The hospital managers need a fair synchronisation of performance-orientation and employee-orientation in order to develop personally-committed personnel. Besides, the personnel serving the hospitals also need to have humanity and human values.

Of late, we find physical attractions emerging as an important component of the marketing mix. This draws our attention on the dresses, uniform, make-up and physique. The medical and paramedical personnel need to distinct themselves by adding physical attractions. The hospital managers can't undermine this mix of the marketing mix.

In view of the aforesaid facts, it is right to mention that the hospital administrators/ managers need to blend the different constituents of marketing mix in such a way that quality services are made available to the users, on time and even at an affordable price. It is in this context that we need to go through the problem of managing the hospital services. Of course, we need a new vision to manage the no-profit making organisations since the social and economic conditions in the Indian perspective are found a bit different than the developed countries.

MANAGING SENSITIVE ISSUES IN HOSPITALS

Managing Time: An individual or an institution can't think of meeting the desired goals or achieving the targeted success unless the management of time is given due weightage. It is the right management of time that makes your task easier. It is proper management of time that helps you in different ways. This makes it essential that the healthcare organisations manage time in a right fashion because the mismanagement of time, specially in hospitals, may result into the irrepairable losses. Of course, it was against this background that in USA, the corporate giants advocated much in favour of time management approximately three decades earlier.[7] They seized on the management of time not only as a training theme but as an essential ingredient of success and prosperity. To be more specific, when we talk about time management in the hospitals or medicare organisations, our focus is on eliminating the misappropriation of time due to unscientific or inadequate preparations. Thus, a healthcare organisation and specially the hospital managers/administrators need to gravitate due attention on four proven strategies such as sequencing of time, prioritising assessing needs and wants and assessing the relative importance.

In Fig. 1.6 we find focus on the same.

The Stoplight System: In this system, we find three categories—first no time limit, second within time limit and third, immediate attention. We call it stoplight system where time parameter is used. Green represents for no time limit, yellow represents for within time limit and red represents for immediate attention.

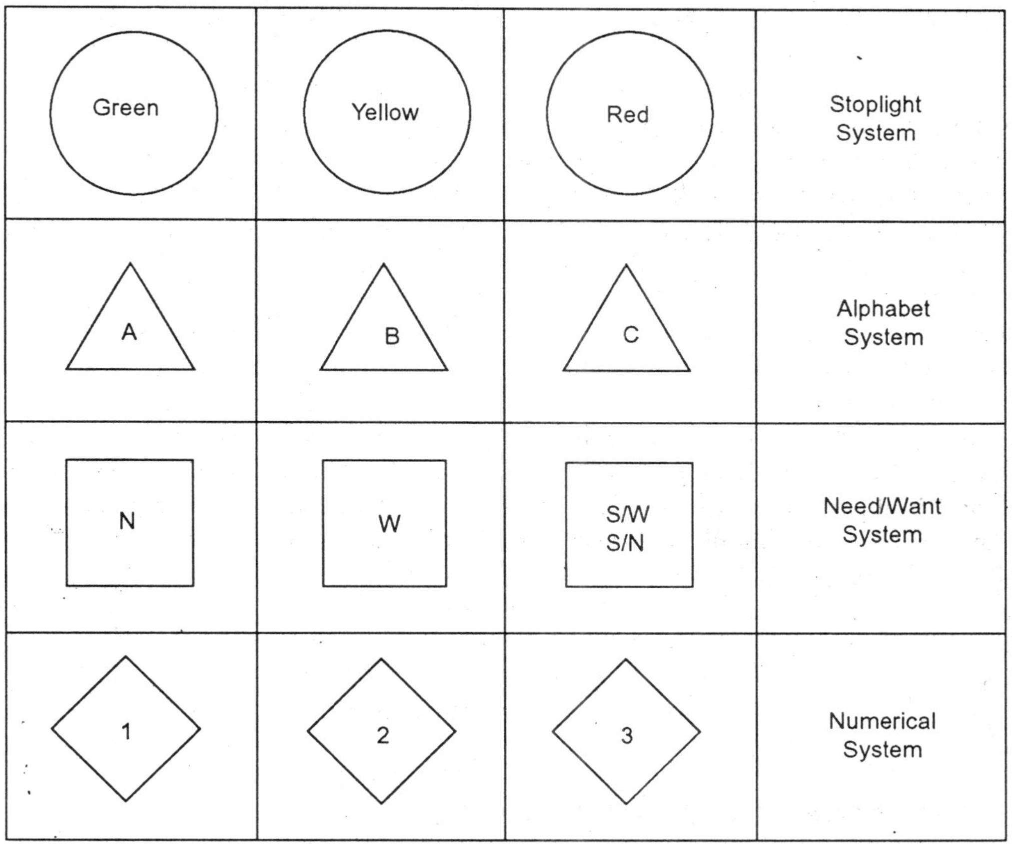

Fig. 1.6. Managing Time —Power Proven Strategies

Adapted from: Donald L. Lombardi; Healthcare'; p. . 151.

The Alphabet System: We call it the alphabet system in which the priority parameter is used. A represents for top priority, B represents for important priority and C represents for low/no priority. It is the alphabet system since different alphabets are used as indicators.

The Need/Want System: In this system, we use action parameter. It is need/want system which is found based on demand. Here, N refers to a particular task you need to do immediately in which we don't find element selectiveness or electiveness attached to the job. Need items are mostly on a par with red-light or yellow-light items or priority A or priority B items. W refers to want items. Want items are job tasks you might like to do. Here, we find an immediate sense of election or selection. The S/W or S/N relates to someone else who wants or needs a particular task to be completed.

Numerical System: This is the fourth system of time management. Here, we find the scale 1-3. The number 1 identifies a task as critically important whereas number 2 identifies it as significantly important. Here, the number 3 refers to least important or immaterial. This technique can also be used in combination with any of the other three techniques, such as spot-light, alphabet, need/want.

In managing time, you need to select that which of the system would suit your level of comfort vis-a-vis provides the most potential worth. You can also create your own unique system of time management which would be incorporated as a routine practice. The routine would allow you to sort mail, manage communications and set priorities found fruitful and efficient throughout your management career. This would afford you a certain peace of mind in addition to the freedom to pursue the assigned tasks.

The aforesaid facts make it clear that for managing time, you can use any number of techniques. The fourproven strategies discussed earlier focus on time sequencing, prioritising, assessing needs and wants and assessing the relative importance. You are supposed to review each strategy and to take a decision that which one is appropriate for you. You can use an independent strategy or even can make a combination of different strategies which would of course be dictated by your responsibilities. We can't deny the fact that the time management is critical in the healthcare environment where in the capacity of a manager, you are charged with top-level performance though you may face the resource constraint. We are well aware of the fact that the mismanagement of time, specially in the hospitals or healthcare organisations may result into irreparable losses. This makes it essential that you are sincere to the preparations to be made for a particular treatment plan to be implemented. Of course, the specialists bear the responsibility of making your schedule result-oriented but being a manager, you are supposed to make it sure that the requirements of specialists are fulfilled. It is not possible unless you make necessary preparations and go through all the items to be used by the specialists. You are supposed to make it sure that OT is ready. You are supposed to make it sure that the related instruments to be used in the process are sterilised and disinfected properly. You are also supposed to make it sure that the infrastructural facilities are available. In addition, you also bear the responsibility of making it sure that medical and paramedical personnel included in the team are available.

Thus, we come to this conclusion that in the medicare organisations, the management of time occupies a place of outstanding significance and the hospital managers/administrators bear the responsibility of managing everything in the face of changing conditions or situations.

AESTHETIC MANAGEMENT IN HOSPITALS

Of late, the management experts have often been found talking about the instrumentality of aesthetic management in the business world. They advocate that human beings in general are found fascinated to the points generating attractions. They argue that attractions make the way for uniqueness which create a positive sense vis-a-vis influence the impulse. Attractive things and good looking things gravitate our attention. It is against this background that the decision makers attempt to generate attractions in the goods or services produced or generated by them. We can't negate that even the medicare organisations find this dimension of management impact generating. To be more specific in the hospitals, we find aesthetic management significant also with the viewpoint of generating healthy conditions. We can't negate that hygiene plays an incremental role in minimising the duration of recovery period of the patients. Besides, a number of diseases can be prevented if the surroundings and premises of hospitals are found healthy.[8] The management of hospital waste, drains, sanitation, general waste, plantation, gardening become important in the very context. It is right to mention that private hospitals have been found assigning due weightage to aesthetic management whereas in a majority of the Government hospitals, this dimension of management has not even been incorporated on the development agenda. The mismanagement of hospital waste, drains and sanitation and water services become instrumental in engineering a sound foundation for the development of a number of diseases. Thus, it is pertinent that hospitals and the healthcare centres think over the problem on a priority basis.

Civic sense makes the ways for aesthetic sense which in addition to hygiene also includes in its purview attractions. Neat and clean, good looking buildings, planned plantation and gardening, interiors generating attraction become instrumental in inducing the patients and attendants. We can't negate that a majority of the hospitals are found not assigning any weightage to aesthetic management which has been making the surroundings and premises of hospitals sensitive to epidemics. In almost all the hospitals we find mismanagement of mortuary houses which makes the surroundings and premises unhygienic. This makes it essential that the hospitals and the healthcare centres consider aesthetic management an integral part of hospital management and make concerted efforts to generate an aesthetic sense.

There is no doubt in it that in a country like India where even a majority of the population lack civic sense, it is very difficult to expect from them the aesthetic sense. However, we have no option but to make ways for the same otherwise, the pressure on hospitals would be found at its peak. The marketing managers of the hospital services need to assign a transcendental priority to the process of inculcating awareness by making possible creativity in the advertisement messages and publicity measures. At the very outset, they need to generate civic sense. Cultivating the habits of spitting at the place meant for that, throwing hospital wastes at the point meant for that look easier but very much difficult specially in the Indian society. The voluntary social organisations also need to accept the responsibility of sensitising the process of keeping the surroundings and premises of hospitals and healthcare centres neat and clean. The NSS is required to promote afforestation and gardening with the support of students. The students' associations need to accept it as a challenging task. Thus, we need multi-cornered efforts to bring things on the rail.

Aesthetic management includes in its purview a number of components. The hospital managers/administrators, planners and even the policymakers need priority attention. There are different constituents influencing the process, such as plantation and gardening, mortuary and management of hospital waste. We go through the management of waste in detail since this has been found very much instrumental in making the environment of hospitals prone to different types of diseases. We need multi-cornered efforts in the very context as explained below.

Disinfection Process: The process of disinfection is found significant to the use of services specially related to the management of sanitation and beds of the patients. The vulnerable areas need an intensive care because a majority of the patients lack awareness regarding the benefits of clean and healthy living conditions. The floors, toilets, urinals, drains and operation theatres are some of the vulnerable spots influencing and aggravating the process of infection. The hospital administrators/managers need to assign due weightage to the regular administration of the disinfecting devices. In addition, it is also right to mention that a large number of patients and attendants lack civic sense and the promotional measures of the hospitals require to inculcate mass awareness regarding where to spit, where to urinate, where to throw the waste or so. All these contribute substantially to the disinfection process which in the long run would help hospitals in making the environment healthy. In addition, the instruments used for operation of the patients, linen are required to be sterilised and disinfected properly. The hospital managers are required to make it sure that the materials, instruments, dresses are disinfected regularly Disinfection makes the ways for a healthy environment. It is in this context that we find it an essential component of the aesthetic management.

Mortuary Management: In a majority of the hospitals, we don't find proper management of mortuary houses which again aggravates the intensity of problem. The vagabond dogs around the mortuary houses, the improper and in human discharge of dead bodies and the stinking surroundings testify the mismanagement of mortuary houses. This makes it clear that the hospital managers/administrators need to be careful regarding the mismanagement of mortuary houses in hospitals and the hospital planners are required to select a suitable point for the construction of mortuary houses.

Plantation and Gardening: In the context of aesthetic management, it is pertinent that the hospital planners and managers assign due weightage to plantation and gardening. Often we find hospitals neglecting this aspect of aesthetic management. The government hospitals in general are found a grazing or even a breeding ground for vagabond animals. This makes it essential that from the very beginning of the establishment of hospitals, the planners make provisions for fencing, plantation and gardening and the hospital administrators/managers are particular to the protection and maintenance of plants and trees. We can't negate that proper plantation and gardening would make hospitals a place for proper care and the recovery period would also be minimised. Not only this, the availability of fresh air to the patients would make the task of treatment easier. It is against this background that we find plantation and gardening assuming a place of outstanding significance while activating the process of aesthetic management.

The aforesaid fats make it clear that the hospital managers/administrators also need to care for the aesthetic sense helping the medical and paramedical personnel in many ways. The most important aspect in the very context is the management of waste in the hospitals which require proper care of hospital planners and managers.

Management of Hospital Waste

In a majority of the hospitals, we don't find proper management of waste which opens doors for infection of high magnitude. To be more specific in the government hospitals, the scattered garbages, hospital wastes known as biomedical waste need due care of the hospital planners and managers. At the outset, they need due care of wastes and thereafter, they also require to throw them at the safe points not creating problems to the population. It is found that mismanagement of waste is resulting into a multifaceted disease. We also find cases of throwing the hospital waste into the rivers and ponds contaminating the water and generating a number of problems. This necessitates a sound management of hospital waste.

Biomedical waste is mostly of two kinds—biodegradable in the form of used bandages, human body parts and blood and non-biodegradable like syringes, plastic bottles and glass items. A Non-government Organisation, Shrishti released its fourth survey of hospital waste management. Shrishti found that hospitals were still going ahead with some distributing actions making ways for the generation of irrepairable losses.[9] The following facts are found very alarming since we do not find any step for their treatment or healthy and eco-friendly management.

- Many hospitals are burning plastics. The entire plastic waste is being incinerated.
- Hospitals are using red bags for incineration while the rules specify yellow bags since red bags have cadmium dyes which are harmful when burnt.
- Incinerator ash is being collected by workers without any protective gear and is being dumped with general waste. The rules specify that incinerator ash is a separate category and should be collected in black bags to be disposed of in landfills.
- Incinerators in other Indian cities are banned within city limits but Delhi had incinerators very close to the residential areas.
- Many private hospitals want a common waste facility as they could not set up individual disposable facilities.
- There are a number of nursing houses and private clinics dumping their biomedical waste without either disinfecting it or even segregating it into municipal corporation dustbins all over the city.

The aforesaid facts make it clear that the management of hospital waste requires due attention of hospital planners and managers. We need different arrangements for both types of wastes. So far as the general wastes are concerned, the hospital managers need to make suitable arrangements so that the municipal corporations or the civic bodies discharge them at the proper places not generating short or long-run problems. The main thing in the management of waste is to think and plan for the management of biomedical waste. The government hospitals, private clinics and hospitals need to think over the problem on a priority basis. They need to promote two-pronged measures, first related to the uses of biomedical items. Both the items bio-degradable and non-bio-degradable need to be used in a rational fashion. We focus here on the quality or types of materials used in the process.

It is high time that the hospitals regulate the use of plastic materials, specially used in the forms of bottles and packing materials. The glass items also require a sound management. Thus, non-biodegradable waste can sizeably be minimised if the hospital management, of course, with the support of specialists explore and think about the alternatives. So far as the bio-degradable waste is concerned, the hospital managers need to think about their proper discharge. The bandages, human body parts and blood are to be stored and preserved scientifically till their final discharge. The time gap is also to be minimised considerably because these wastes are found very much sensitive to the health hazards. It is, of course, a crime to mix the general waste with the biomedical waste. The municipal corporations or the civic bodies or even the social organisations need to come forward to throw the non-biomedical waste at the points far off from the residential areas. On the other hand, the hospital managers need to take suitable steps for the management of biomedical waste. It is significant that they make it possible on a priority basis since these wastes are found dangerous to the living beings in general and the human beings in particular. It is proper that they think in favour of a scientific management of waste in consultation with experts. In the Indian perspective, we don't find governmental regulations very much effective to control the mismanagement of hospital biomedical waste. Hence, the government policymakers and the boardrooms of hospitals need to plan about the proper management of hospital biomedical waste. We can't deny the fact that private clinics and the small private hospitals throw different types of wastes here and there or even into ponds or rivers. This becomes instrumental in generating the problem of water contamination resulting into the spread of water borne diseases to the human beings and animals.

In view of the above, it is right that the management of waste in hospitals is assigned due weightage. The medical and paramedical personnel need proper training facilities for the same so that the biomedical waste are discharged within the limited possible time. The hospital managers/ administrators need to make an assault on the problem so that waste is not dumped without disinfecting or even segregating the same. The hospitals in general and the government hospitals in particular have been undermining the importance of management of waste. In this context, they need to formulate a strategy for disinfecting and segregating. All of the medicare organisations though are aware of the rules and the harmful effects are still going ahead with disturbing actions.

The following strategic decisions would help the hospital managers in managing the waste in a right fashion:

- They need to have two different strategies for managing waste.
- The general waste in the form of garbage, dust and other particles need a strategy for dumping at a proper place and removing the same with the cooperation of municipal corporations and civic bodies or even the non-governmental social organisations.
- The biomedical waste, both of biodegradable and non-biodegradable types need a different strategy. The staff specially of low echelon responsible for collecting the same and the medical and paramedical personnel using and throwing the same need to understand the harmful effects of mismanagement.
- The most vulnerable point in this connection is the OT generating a number of bio-medical waste which requires proper care of hospital administrators and managers so that collection, dumping and disposing off processes are completed before the disinfection process starts.

Management of Tension in Hospitals

It is pertinent that the patients visiting the hospitals are treated as human beings with the holistic approach and his/her attendants are granted full rights of knowing about his/ her patient's illness, outcome, prognosis, investigation and treatment plan. We often talk about the instrumentality of high behavioural profile of medical and paramedical personnel in speeding up the process of treatment and recovery vis-a-vis the diffusion of tension. We accept the fact that the stress and tension need to be managed by the hospital personnel in a right fashion so that the psycho-bio equilibrium of attendants is not disturbed. It is quite natural that attendants knock at the door of hospitals with high expectations. The patients and the intensity of problem generated by the same make the ways for the generation of anxiety, stress and tension. The hospital personnel treat both categories of patients —acute and non-acute. In case of acute patients, the intensity of tension to the attendants is found of high magnitude. A number of apprehensions disturb the attendants. Contrary to it, in the case of non-acute patients, we find patients more disturbed because the attendants are aware of the outcome, prognosis and the results. Hence, the hospital personnel need to perceive the magnitude of problem of anxiety, stress and tension of the patients and attendants and should make sincere, honest and concerted efforts to diffuse the same.

Anxiety refers to a fear reaction in which the cause of the fear is not a specific object.[10]

Stress refers to a condition resulting from disturbances to physical or psychological well-being. "

Tension refers to the readiness for action generally with no action possible and often refers to the strain resulting from stress.[12]

The team of the medical profession should have professional excellence in the art of influencing other people to lessen the agony of attendants and patients. It is against this background that we go through the problem of diffusion of tension with the help and cooperation of almost all categories of the hospital personnel. The management scientists often make strong advocacy for understanding the behavioural profile of providers and users so that the treatment paves avenues for the diffusion of tension. We can't negate the fact that the hospital personnel need to have empathy and to incorporate the same in the treatment plan to maintain the psycho-bio-equilibrium of patients and attendants besides improving the quality of medical treatment. It is right to say that medical treatment has a close link with the psycho treatment and if the hospital personnel succeed in blending the two optimally, the treatment plan is found productive.

The existing environment, specially in the government hospitals makes it clear that the medical personnel in a majority of the cases are found aggressive in nature, inhuman in approach and indecent in behaviour. Such an attitude found in a large number of the government hospitals makes it essential that we educate and train them in the field of behavioural management. The hospital administrators/managers bear the responsibility of making it clear to the medical and paramedical personnel that the medical treatment needs hospital personnel with a sound behavioural profile.

They need to perceive the following facts in a right fashion so that the process of diffusion of tension moves in the right directions.

- Appeals to action establish an edge over the appeals to inhibit.
- Perceive the needs, apprehensions, expectations of attendants and patients in a right fashion.
- Take support of effective communications and prefer to use the language in the face of the cultural and social background of the patients and attendants.
- Select appropriate words for communication.
- Take support of body language and use less words.
- "Talk less—communicate more", is found effective in the process.
- Promise less and offer more. This would simplify the task of influencing them effectively.
- Use voice, body language effectively.

- Your approach should be personalised.
- Try to perceive things and conditions from the viewpoints of others.
- Don't make hasty decisions.
- Take the support of empathy which focusses our attention on sharing the stress and anxiety of patients and attendants by using soft words.
- Be careful while saying 'no.'
- Clear communications should be preferred to transmit the messages related to outcome, prognosis, investigation and treatment plan.

The aforesaid facts would help the medical and paramedical personnel in diffusing the tension of patients and attendants in an effective way. It is not only essential that the hospitals think about the medical treatment plan. It is much more impact generating to blend the same with the behavioural plan. If they succeed in synchronising the two optimally, the process of diffusion of tension is found activated. It is against this background that the behavioural scientists make a strong advocacy in favour of studying the behavioural profile and making available to the hospital personnel the knowledge of behavioural management. Aggressive nature, indecent behaviour and inhuman approach complicate the task of hospital personnel While soft nature, decent behaviour and humanism pave the avenues for the diffusion of tension. If we feel that tension plays a significant role in generating and aggravating the magnitude of the problem, we need honest efforts to diffuse the same.

In view of the above, it is right to say that the management of tension is an important part of the treatment plan and the hospital personnel assigning due weightage to the same succeed in satisfying the users and attendants in a right perspective. In the Indian society, we find the problem more complicated that makes the task of hospital personnel much more difficult. It is difficult to communicate something to the illiterate patients and attendants. This makes it essential that the medical and paramedical personnel develop communication excellence keeping in view the reception capacity of the patients and attendants. The problem of diffusing tension is much more related to the behavioural studies.

MANAGEMENT BY OBJECTIVES (MBO) IN HOSPITALS

The students of management are well aware of the MBO playing a significant role in the management process. Destination, if fixed, minimises the possibilities of deviation. The professionals well aware of the destination find it easier to formulate a strategy which helps them considerably in making the efforts cost effective vis-a-vis productive. It is in this context that we talk about Management By Objectives, in short known as MBO.

Of course, Management By Objectives is practised all over the world but a very few of us are well aware of the conceptual aspect of MBO. Some of us think it as an appraisal tool and some others find it a motivational tool. We also find a few of us considering MBO a planning and control device. This makes it clear that we need to perceive the concept in a right fashion because definitions and applications of MBO differ widely. The definition given by Koontz and Weihirich is given below.

"Management By Objectives is a comprehensive managerial system that integrates many key managerial activities in a systematic manner and that is consciously directed toward the effective and efficient achievement of organisational and individual objectives." This view of MBO as a system of managing is not shared by all because most of us find it something different and therefore, define MBO in a very limited way. In view of the multidimensional changes and opinions of a number of experts regarding the concept of MBO, it is right to perceive it as a system approach.

We consider MBO an instrument for motivating individuals, a technique for performance appraisal and very recently we have identified it as a part of strategic planning. However, we don't find the perception complete since a number of managerial subsystems are found missing, such as formulation of organisational structure, portfolio management, management development, career development, compensation programmes and budgeting. George Odiorne, an authority of MBO considers it a system of managerial leadership. And this concept in a true sense is found most appropriate in the present management world. Thus, we find MBO as a system of managerial leadership.

With the passage of time, we find a number of changes in the management world. Against this background, we find MBO fast becoming an important yardstick of contemporary management. The hospital managers/administrators bear the responsibility of making available to the users quality services. This makes it essential that they turn their eyes on other areas, get themselves apprised of the contributions of other no-profit making organisations so that they are familiar with the objectives in the face of changing social systems, nature and character of spreading diseases, the capacity of users to pay tee and so on. This, of course, would make it easier to integrate the efforts for accomplishing the organisational goals.

Justifications for MBO in Hospitals: We can't negate the instrumentality of setting objectives even in the hospitals. In addition to hospitals, even other no-profit making organisations also find MBO relevant. We find the rationale behind its application since in the Indian environment, we find a number of hospital personnel even not aware of their functional responsibilities which influences the level of efficiency adversely. If we find it essential that hospitals are to be managed in a right fashion, it is pertinent that they have a system for setting the time-honoured objectives, fixing of accountability, a thorough follow-up and a visible feedback. We agree with this view that in the Indian condition, the hospitals are mismanaged that complicates the task of accomplishing the organisational objectives. If we practise MBO, the rate of productivity would go up since the level of efficiency would sizeably be increased. The following facts make it clear that MBO would benefit hospitals in many ways:[13]

- Working out economic alternatives.
- Using zero-based budgeting.
- Applying MBO for measuring individual performance.
- Preparing short and long-range objectives and plans.
- Installing effective control system.
- Engendering atmosphere of trust and confidence.
- Devising a sound organisational structure.

The aforesaid measures would substantially help hospital managers in improving the level of efficiency of hospital personnel which at present is found abysmally low. The main thing in the process is setting the time honoured objectives.

Setting of Time-honoured Objectives: We agree with this view that setting of objectives is a difficult task. To be more specific when we talk about the MBO, it is pertinent that whatever the objectives we set are in tune with the changing conditions of the catchment area and the potential users. Since we find hospitals working in the Indian society facing the image problem, it is significant that a number of considerations are given due weightage while setting the objectives. The following facts need due weightage while setting objectives:

- Personal commitment is the most significant aspect to be given due weightage.
- There should be top-level goal setting since effective planning usually begins with the top people setting the preliminary goals in conference and in consultation with other members with the organisation. Goals stated should be specific and quantifiable.
- The objective setting should also be at all levels, such as corporate, departmental and individual. Everyone should have a clear perception of objectives.
- The significant areas should be prioritised. This helps identifying the sensitive problems.
- There must be participation of subordinates in setting the objectives.
- While implementing plans, there must be autonomy. Once the objective is set, an individual should have discretion while implementing the same.
- There should be a careful review of the performance. The review would be periodic to identify the weaknesses in the implementation process and to correct them at the early stage.
- The procedures should be appropriate. In case of conflicts between the objectives and procedures, the objectives need to be considered supreme.
- The role should be clarified.
- There should be multi-pronged constituencies of accountability. The multiple centres of accountability is essential because everyone is found responsible for the positive or negative results.

Hospital—A Non-profit Organisation

An organisation not having a legitimate right of making profits is known as a no-profit making organisation. We consider hospital a no-profit making organisation because it doesn't have a legitimate right of making profits. There is no doubt in it that a number of hospitals knowing well the organisational limitations have been making profits sizeably which has been found violating the norms set for the management of no-profit making organisations. To be more specific, the private hospitals practice the same in the name of investment of huge capital for establishment, maintenance and modernisation. The government hospitals are not allowed to mobilise internal resources which has been seen obstructing the normal flow of their developments. It is in this context that we need to go through the problem of profit generation by the hospitals.

We can't negate the fact that the modern hospitals need a number of machines, equipments, medical and paramedical personnel, buildings in addition to the supporting infrastructural facilities known as inputs. Besides, they are also supposed to make huge investments for promoting research and development facilities. Thus, to offer quality medicare services, the hospitals of today need to make huge investment, of capital for quality and expensive inputs. The state exchequer finds it difficult to finance and the governmental regulations strict them while mobilising finance from the internal sources. This results into a degeneration in the quality of services offered by the government hospitals. It is against this background that the private hospitals have been charging exhorbitantly. It is right to mention that the management scientists treat no-profit organisations in a bit different way. They feel that the hospitals—government or private, rural or urban need to work in tune with the defined principles of the holistic concept of management. They advocate that for subserving the interests of poorest of the poor, the hospitals have no option but to practise pocket-friendly pricing strategy based on the principle of what the traffic will bear.

A no-profit making organisation restricts generation of profits but requires proper maintenance and time-honoured developments which can't be possible unless hospitals generate surpluses. This makes it essential that hospitals, public or private look at the problems with a new vision. The private hospitals charge more because we find a difference between the two specially in respect of financial support from the government. It is also argued that hospitals and healthcare centres need to mobilise donations from private sources. The national and international social organisations, red cross societies and charitable trusts need to accept the responsibility of mobilising finance. The affluent sections of society also need to be positive to the financial problem of hospitals.

In view of the aforesaid facts, it is right to say that hospitals and healthcare centres need to be treated as a no-profit making organisation. This is found essential, specially in a country like India where masses find it difficult to avail the expensive services of private hospitals. At the same time, it is also judicious that a legitimate right of making profits would allow hospitals to promote unfair practices and exploitation and the ultimate sufferers would be the poorest of the poor which can't be socially, constitutionally or even morally fair.

Hospital—A Social Institution

We consider hospitals a social institution[15] since the services generated by them are directly related to the public interests. About the society, an expert opines :

"Society is a system of usages and procedures and mutual aid of many groupings and divisions of control of human behaviour and liberties. This ever changing complex system we call a society. It is the web of social relationships. And it is always changing. The perception of society is thus related to a system that provides a healthy environment to all the living beings to survive and thrive. Wherever there is life, there is society. It is in this context that we find the hospital emerging as a social institution.

In society, we find emphasis on the survival, development and well-being of the living beings in general and the human beings in particular. If we talk about the medicare organisations or hospitals and the health centres, they are found throwing a big impact on the healthy living conditions without which the living beings would find it difficult to survive and thrive. The curative and preventive services of hospitals influence the Quality Life Index (QLI) vis-a-vis the quality of human index. By informing and sensing the masses, we find hospitals exploring new devices of treatment besides the creation of healthy living conditions. It is against this background that we find them acting as a social institution.

The hospitals take responsibility of an institution since number of machines, equipments, medical and paramedical personnel in addition to the supporting infrastructural facilities are required to activate the process of diagnosis and treatment which is found institutionalised. An individual based on his/her expertise finds it difficult to offer all the services which is found easier with the institutional efforts. We find social development an everchanging complex system in which positive and negative developments take place pari-passu. Since the scientific inventions and innovations make the ways for the negative developments, it is quite natural that positive developments engineer a foundation for countering the negative developments. The services of hospitals make an assault on the harmful effects of economic development.

Since we find hospitals a social institution, it is imperative that whatever the principles, policies and strategies we formulate for their working are to benefit the masses. This necessitates conceptualisation of the holistic concept of management in a right fashion so that even poorest of the poor avail the services. The mounting demographic pressure, haphazard development of industries, specially within the cities precincts, illiteracy and insensitivity in the masses are some of the basic reasons complicating the functional responsibilities of hospital managers/administrators. If we consider the hospital a social institution, the quality life index of human beings would start moving upward. This would substantially contribute to the process of human capital formation.

The aforesaid facts testify that hospitals need to work as a social institution. We can't imagine the existence of society without human beings and we can't think about the survival of the human beings if the hospitals become non-existent.

Hospital—An Institution for Human Capital Formation

The quality of human index contributes substantially to the process of human capital formation. There are a number of constituents influencing the Quality Life Index of human beings, such as the living conditions, level of income, standard of education, environmental conditions or so. The living conditions include the life styles, food habits, nutritional awareness, physical soundness, quality of water, sanitation, noise and pollution free environment, aesthetic sense, civic sense or so. More sound the living conditions, less chances we find for fatigue, diseases and illness. The healthcare services thus become a part and parcel of our living conditions. We can't confine the boundary of healthcare services only to the offering of medicare services. In addition to the medical services, the healthcare services include a number of services helping the masses in improving the health and increasing the resistance power. The services creating awareness prove to be significant to enrich the healthcare services. It is against this background that we find different dimensions of healthcare services. Contributing sizeably to the process of improving the quality life index activates the process of human capital formation.

The hospitals, healthcare centres, social organisations, educational institutions, red cross societies and the communication organisations bear the responsibility of improving the quality of healthcare services. If the allied or supporting organisations evince their interests in improving the healthcare services, the hospitals and healthcare centres would find it easier to enrich the quality of human life index. Contrary to it, if they start taking rest, the hospitals would find it difficult to cater to the increasing pressure. Thus, the healthcare services gravitate our attention on a priority basis since the task of human capital formation can't be processed in a right direction unless all the related organisations keep themselves engaged in raising their contributions.

By human capital, our focus is on the fact that human resources enrich their potentials, prove to be productive in the defined areas of their workings and help an organisation in accelerating the rate of overall productivity. It is in this context that we find healthcare services throwing a telling impact on the transformation of human resource into human capital. If we find human beings realising their responsibilities, perceiving the instrumentality of healthy living conditions in a right fashion, making themselves fully aware of the nutritional values, assigning due weightage to the physical fitness, regulating the food habits and respecting the norms and following the guidelines suggested by the specialists; a sound foundation is engineered for the formation of human capital.

The aforesaid facts make it clear that the healthcare services have an important bearing on the formation of human capital. The healthcare services depend considerably on the national health policy. If we find a sound national health policy, the supporting organisations find no option but to discharge their responsibilities in the defined way. When we start drinking safe water, when we regulate our food habits, when we evince our interests in improving our physique, when we have safe sanitation and ventilation facilities, when we are aware of the nutritional values; the avenues for ailments and diseases start shrinking considerably.

National Health Policy

Policy determines the effectiveness of strategy. If we formulate polices in the face of changing socio-economic and technological conditions, the strategies prove to be effective. Contrary to it, if we find something wrong with the making of policies, the strategies prove to be insensitive. It is against this background that the policymakers or the boardrooms play a significant role in the process of increasing the sensitivity of strategies. If we have failed in providing healthcare services to the masses, it is due mainly to our faulty policies. This makes it essential that we turn our eyes on the National Health Policy with a new vision that caters to the changing needs and requirements of the increasing population and spreading multi-dimensional diseases. We can't negate the fact that after the attainment of independence in 1947 and to be more specific, after the beginning of Five Year Plans in 1951, the contours of developments underwent radical changes. There is no doubt in it that during the yester plans, we witnessed multifaceted developments in the process of socio-economic emancipation but the process of social transformation could not be activated in the right directions because even the essential constituents of social transformation like health and education remained neglected. This deprived the masses of albeit the basic education and medical aid then what to talk of the world class services. It is in this context that we go through the National Health Policy.

The National Health Policy (1983) reiterated India's commitment to attain Health for All (HFA) by 2000 AD. The deadline is over but even till now we are lagging far behind the target. Of course, the policymakers assigned due weightage to the eradication of small pox and plague but at the same time, it is also right to say that the morbidity rate and mortality on account of malaria, cholera and various other diseases have considerably declined. However, HFA is long way off.[16] Malaria has again come back in a dangerous form because the existing medicines are found not so effective and complicate the problems of treatment. The new viral diseases have been found spreading. We have, of course, been successful in reducing the prevalence and incidence of communicable diseases but AIDS has been found spreading like a wild fire. The government hospitals and healthcare centres find it difficult to cope up with the increasing pressure. The private hospitals have been proved to be expensive and therefore, not subserving the interests of masses. The rural masses are the worst sufferers.

Present century breeds the next century. We have a long-run target of having a healthier 21st century and a short-run target of improving the quality of existing medical services in different hospitals and the healthcare centres. We bear the constitutional responsibility of providing the basic medical aid to the masses. We are morally and socially pledged of offering quality medicare services. But we don't find good auguries since the increasing pressure of population and disappointing rate of literacy have been found standing as an important barrier. This makes it essential that the policy planners, scientists, social scientists, professionals and more so, the medical experts review the National Health Policy. The multidimensional developments in the field of medical sciences are yet to be conceptualised in a right fashion. The masses are found unaware of the ways for managing the healthy living conditions. Inadequacy of quality medical and paramedical personnel, lack of personal commitment and work culture, negative attitudes towards performance-orientation and employee-orientation, contracting potentials of the state exchequer and restrictions in the process of mobilising finance from the internal sources are some of the obstacles complicating the task of HFA in many ways. This necessitates a rational policy—a policy that ensures essential medicare services to all, a policy that makes the services pocket-friendly and a policy that achieves world class excellence.

We can't negate that during the yester decades, there have been major changes in the disease profile and healthcare infrastructure and healthcare seeking behaviour of the population. Several new techniques and technologies for diagnosis and management of health problems have been devised. These, in turn have widened the gap between what is possible and what is feasible and affordable at the level of an individual and the country. Increasing expectations of population, rising cost of diagnosis and treatment and diminishing resources have brought into the issue of optimising the rising medical bill. The essential interlinkages between healthcare services delivery and health and manpower development are still not fully understood and operationalised.

In view of the above, it is essential that National Health Policy undergoes a reappraisal and reformation so that it provides a reliable and relevant policy framework not only for improving healthcare but also for measuring and monitoring the delivery systems and healthy states of the population during the coming decades. Amidst multi-dimensional health hazards, we need a new national policy for health which ensures healthcare services to the masses. We need to improve the efficiency of existing healthcare infrastructure at primary, secondary and tertiary levels, care setting through appropriate institutional strengthening, improvement of referral linkages and operationalisation of Hospital Management Information System (HMIS). A new vision is needed to promote the development of human resources for health. We also need to improve the safety of the work environment and workers' health in organised and unorganised industrial and agricultural sectors, specially among vulnerable groups of the population. The research potentials need due weightage. A mismatch between personnel and equipment is required to be bridged. This requires development of human resources in tune with the evolving technologies. Further, we need to create and strengthen primary healthcare infrastructure through reorganising and restructuring the existing institutions.

Since the Consumer Protection Act includes in its purview even the services offered by the healthcare organisations and agencies, it is essential that the human resources working there either as medical or as paramedical personnel or acting as managers/administrators are made accountable to the mistakes and errors committed deliberately. Such a step would make the ways for sincerity and punctuality which would improve the quality of services offered vis-a-vis would minimise the possibilities of negligence. The public or private hospitals are required to realise the significance of time management. We need personally-committed and value-based personnel which would be possible when the policymakers make possible a structural change in the syllabi. Ethical dimensions and behavioural management seem to be effective in sensitising the process of offering the time-honoured services.

In view of the aforesaid facts, the policy makers need to review the National Health Policy. The following facts need due attention while reviewing the policy:

- **The Demographic Transition:** It is well-known that the National Health Policy was formulated way back in 1983. In view of the emerging problems, we need a National Population Policy activating the process of population control. The pressure on account of increasing population is required to be minimised by innovating and promoting the motivational and demotivations schemes. On the one hand, the persons controlling population are to be motivated suitably whereas on the other hand, the persons responsible for increasing population are to be demotivated sizeably. If we are really interested in streamlining the health policy, we have no option but to make the National Health Policy effective, failing which the healthcare measures would remain non-optimal to the increasing rate of population.

- **The Epidemiological Transition:** During the 1980s and 1990s, we found a major change in the disease profile, healthcare infrastructure and healthcare seeking behaviour of the population. A number of new generation of sophisticated technologies have been devised to make the process of diagnosis and treatment more scientific. This has been found instrumental in increasing the cost of treatment and diagnosis. In the Indian perspective, we find a majority of our population not in a position to afford the expensive medicare services. This makes it essential that we review the National Health Policy and make the services pocket-friendly so that the masses are in a position to avail the services. The healthcare delivery systems also need an appraisal. The changing disease profile in which we find communicable diseases, viral diseases, water-prone, food-prone, pollution-borne diseases spreading like a wild fire; the preventive measures need to be innovated so that the masses are found aware of the same.

- **Expansion of Healthcare Infrastructure:** Of late, we find that the government hospitals and healthcare centres lack the supporting infrastructural facilities which have been found degenerating the quality of services. This makes it essential that while reviewing the National Health Policy' the policy makers think about the infrastructural facilities on a priority basis. Unless we enrich the inputs, it is meaningless to think about the quality of outputs. To be more specific in the rural areas, we find almost all the health centres facing the problem of infrastuctural constraints. The policy makers need to go through the problem of rural health with a new vision.

- **Changes in Health Seeking Behaviour:** With a change in the process of treatment and diagnosis vis-a-vis the sophistication in knowledge technologies, we find a major change in the health seeking behaviour of the population which has been found increasing the level of their expectations. The hospitals and healthcare centres need to conceptualise the principles of modern management where the professionals are made available to fulfil the increasing level of expectations of the users by motivating the medical and paramedical personnel.

- **Promoting the Private Hospitals:** Because we find the government hospitals and healthcare centres not in a position to cater to the increasing demand, it is pertinent that the private hospitals are promoted. We need to promote the corporate sector. In addition, we also need to make possible a structural change in the working of the government hospitals. This is essential to improve the quality of services.

We cannot deny that over the last six decades, a number of efforts have been made in some of the key areas to improve health standards such as life expectancy, child mortality, infant mortality and maternal mortality. Small pox and guineaworm have been eradicated and there is hope that poliomyelitis will be contained in the near future. The Eleventh Five year plan has been found focussing on restructuring policies to achieve a New Vision based on faster, broad based and inclusive growth. The poor and the underprivileged are to get top priority. We expect special attention on adolescent girls, women of all ages, children below the age of three, older persons, disabled and primitive tribal groups.

The goals of Eleventh Five Year Plan if fulfilled would improve the quality of health. The key areas are reducing Maternal Mortality to 1 per 1000 live births; reducing Infant Mortality Rate to 28 per 1000 live births; reducing Total Fertility Rate to 2.1; providing drinking water for all; reducing malnutrition among children of age group 0-3 to have its present level; reducing anaemia among women and girls by 50% and raising the sex ratio for age group 0-6 to 935 by 2011-12 and 950 by 2016-17.[17]

The most important task before the national policy makers is to channelise the healthcare and medicare services to the rural areas where the masses have failed in availing the benefits of new generation of low cost technology considerably influenced by e-Health. It is high time that the policy makers focus priority attention on developing AYUSH and mainstreaming it under NRHM. Making Health Care Affordable to the common people is the mission which requires emphasis on low-cost technology but it is hardly to be possible unless we find Jan Swasthya Sahyog (JSS) gaining popularity specially in the rural areas of the country where masses have poor affordability.

Ethical Dimensions in Hospital

When the process of value-engineering starts moving backward, more so in a social institution, it becomes prime responsibility of each of us to energise the process of value-orientation so that it starts moving forward. We agree with this view that during the yesterdecades, there has been a considerable degeneration in the process of value orientation in almost all the areas. Since we find hospitals a place for offering healthcare services to the human beings, such a degeneration is found influencing the ethical dimensions. We can't deny the fact that value-orientation and ethics are found closely related. If doctors start making a goodbye to ethics, the process of social engineering would adversely be influenced. In the Indian perspective, we find almost all the government hospitals facing a problem like this which has been found endangering the social interests. It is against this background that we find justifications for promoting ethical dimensions in hospitals.

Of course, knowledge is power but character is superpower. The most precious human possessions are health, harmony, happiness, wisdom and above all is our character which is found instrumental in reflecting ethical and human values. Manifestation of these values in our thoughts, speech, action and decisions help us in becoming high performers. Human and ethical values constitute the wealth of character. The metal contents of the good person are called moral and ethical values. Fearlessness, courage, purity of mind and heart, action and behaviour, generosity, spirit of sacrifice for the sake of social interests, inspired ideals and vision, creativity, empathy, love and affection, patience, faith, fairness, steadfastness, uprightness, harmlessness, charity, gentleness, truthfulness, loyalty, integrity, fortitude, vigour, cheerfulness, simplicity and optimism are the different facets of values which help a manager to be a personally committed and dedicated force not only helping him in accomplishing the organisational goals but even in accomplishing wonders. Human values consist of moral and ethical values. The established business values such as service, communication, excellence, credibility, innovation, creativity and coordination are closely related to the human values. The managerial functions, such as direction, control, supervision and communication, integration and coordination are found easier if we find human values in the managers.

We find ethical management a case of normative ethics. We can't negate its instrumentality for the welfare, development and prosperity of an organisation. Values are the means of perfection, values bring about excellence. With the passage of time, we find a change in the skills but the values remain existent. Ethics and values must be an integral part of management and work culture. In the process of economic transformation, we have made a direct attack on both—physical environment and ethical-moral fabric of our society. Effectiveness in the performance of managers and workers is a function of values and skills together. An ideal manager has strength in both values and skills. The boardrooms of any organisation bear the responsibility of inculcating values. Values need to be an integral part of corporate mission. A manager or a worker is basically a human being who can manage himself with the ethical and spiritual human values and the human resources centred round with human values can bring about the desirable managerial transformation. It is in this context that we go through ethical dimensions in hospitals where a majority of the medical and paramedical personnel have made a final good-bye to values.

The oaths taken by doctors while getting the degrees focus on the values they need to promote in discharging the functional responsibilities assigned to them. The professional commitment of doctors is thus found linked to the ethical dimensions. Of late, we find cases that doctors treating or attending on the patients leave them in the same condition, if they feel that fees promised by the patients would not be paid. In this context, we find a complete departure from ethical values. Such a degenerating condition makes it essential that hospital managers assign due weightage to the ethical dimensions and make it an essential criterion for rating their performance. We can't negate the fact that a majority of the doctors now prefer to be money minters. Of course, in this materialistic world they need money to lead a comfortable life but it is not meant that they do everything found undesirable. It is also right to say that values and ethics move together. It is a process that takes much more time for coming to a final shape. There is no doubt in it that it is inherited but we can also inculcate the same by changing the environmental conditions, innovating the education and training facilities and imposing the regulatory barriers.

The increasing cases of value-degeneration have resulted into the development of unfair practices, carelessness, negligence or so. If we find degeneration in other areas, we have time to set things in the right directions. But if degeneration is found in the hospital or healthcare services, we get less time or even don't get any time for setting things in the right directions. Since delay of a few seconds or minutes is to result into a big loss found of irreparable nature, the continuing degeneration in the process of value-engineering is required to be checked. It is important to mention that self-regulation is found much more impact generating and the doctors need to promote the same. Since they have developed expertise and excellence for protecting the precious human beings, it is essential that they regulate their behaviour, actions and decisions found instrumental in degenerating the quality of healthcare services. If we find self-regulation not getting a suitable place, the boardrooms and the policy makers have no option but to take the support of rigid regulations.

Since we find value-orientation a process, it is pertinent that an institution like a hospital is regulated by the social regulations where the social organisations, social reformists, social activists, social leaders and opinion leaders need to play a dominating role. The media need to promote values specially in the hospitals. The social regulations need to control the unfair and inhuman practices promoted by the doctors. The syllabi and the training facilities designed for educating and training the doctors and paramedical staff need to assign due weightage to the ethical dimensions. In a true sense, we need to turn our eyes on the system of education right from the basic education to the higher education and at all the levels and stages, we need to make ethics an integral part of the course structure. The important sources for value degeneration are our acts, decisions, misdeeds, signs, and unfair practices promoted in a family. If we start witnessing everything wrong in our families right from the stage of learning, the task of value-engineering becomes much more difficult. We can't negate the fact that in most of the Indian families, the parents don't find it essential to promote values. Contrary to it, they provide an opportunity to witness wrong, unfair, unethical practices getting a respectable position. This engineers a sound foundation for value-degeneration and by that time, we become matured and the roots are found deeper. They find their counterparts minting money by adopting unethical, unfair practices because their children believe in lifestyles based on luxury and status symbol. The vicious circle for value-degeneration has been continuing and would continue till we start its reversal from our own homes. When all the other sectors are influenced, why not the health and education?

We find doctors adopting a number of unethical practices and the latest one is found in the business related to the different organs of the body. The poorest of the poor and orphans are the worst sufferers. The cases of kidnapping of children for the purpose of using their organs have been found increasing with the connivance of doctors. The persons enriching excellence for the welfare and protection of human beings are found engaged in endangering their interests just for money. Not only this, we also find cases of promoting even the spurious drugs by the doctors only for earning money. A number of pharmaceutical industries with their help and cooperation have been found flourishing. Once again the poorest of the poor and illiterate suffer. We find height of degeneration when the doctors found inefficient, knowing well the fact that they are not in a position to diagnose and treat a patient start diagnosing and administering the wrong medicines resulting into the death of the patients. These facts make it clear that a degeneration in values promoted by a few has been tarnishing the image of even those doctors who are dedicated, value-based and personally committed.

In view of the above, it is essential that we think over the problem on a priority basis and make sincere and honest efforts to bring things on the track. Since we find the process of value-degeneration at its peak, it is pertinent that governmental and social regulations make joint efforts. The voluntary social organisations, social reformists and opinion leaders need to accept the responsibility of motivating the doctors for value-based and fair practices. They even need to raise their voice against those doctors who have been promoting it. In addition, the governmental regulations need due attention on the prevailing conditions. We need special laws and regulations because the existing legal processes and formalities are so long that everything is found complicated. Of course, we find the Consumer Protection Act helping patients in many ways but again, the government hospitals, where we find unethical and unfair practices on a large scale are not found under the purview of the Act since in a majority of the cases we find them offering free of charge services. This makes it essential that hospitals in general think over the problem on a priority basis. The policy makers, the boardrooms and the hospital managers need to identify those doctors promoting unethical practices and punish them in the face of their sins and misdeeds.

But the only permanent solution to the problem is activating the process of value engineering. This gravitates our attention on inculcating values. The process is to be started right from the primary stage and is to continue forever. The syllabi at all the stages and the levels are to be restructured. The audio/visual exposure would make the process more creative. The producers of TV serials and movies need to present stories, events and sequences promoting ethics. The educational institutions need to educate and train them. The parents bear the responsibility of presenting an adducible example and to set new paradigms to their children based on values and ethics. The multi-cornered attempts would make the environmental conditions conducive where values and ethics would get a suitable milieu to grow and prosper. We need to define ethical behaviour and a small number of core values because the regulation-based approach to ethics does not work well.[18]

Consumer Protection Act

Way back in 1987 when the Consumer Protection Act came into existence, nobody even could imagine that this Act would be a lesson to the medical and paramedical personnel not aware of their functional responsibilities. The Supreme Court on 13th November 1995, upheld the National Consumer Commission's judgement of April 1992 whereby patients who received deficient services by medical profession and hospitals are entitled to claim damages under the Consumer Protection Act. In a true sense, the acts, laws and regulations depend on right interpretation of cases. We produce goods, we generate services. We produce goods for making profits and we generate public utility services for serving the society; or even for making profits. Since we talk here everything related to the no-profit making organisations, the application of the different provisions of the Consumer Protection Act are required to be clarified in a right way. The hospitals bear the responsibility of protecting or subserving the social interests. You charge or may not charge. You charge more or charge less. The prime focus on the provisions of the Consumer Protection Act is on the fee you charge from the patients for the services you make available to them. By charging fee, you turn the patients to be a consumer and therefore, if your actions and decisions influenced by carelessness or negligence damage the interests of patients, you are supposed to compensate the losses on that account. You have adopted a double pronged fee strategy. For the same services, you charge more from the affluents and less or even nothing from the weaker sections. Such a discrimination is based on the holistic concept of management that is not to deprive the patients of their rights of getting the same quality or standard of treatment that you offer to those who pay more. When the patients, specially belonging to the poor section use your subsidised or free of charge services, they don't feel that such a discrimination in the fee structure is to influence the quality of treatment. And you practise it. If the patients suffer, you are supposed to compensate the losses. If you don't charge anything from any of the patients, you are not under the purview of the Act.

The aforesaid facts make it clear that different provisions of the Consumer Protection Act focus on the circumstances or conditions when you transform patients as a consumer. The private hospitals, clinics, and even the government hospitals charging for the services offered more or less are under the purview of the Act. Before we make an anatomy of the different provisions of the Act making you liable to make up the losses, it is pertinent that we focus on the job responsibility or professional commitment of doctors. We can't deny the fact that to be more specific in the Indian perspective, a majority of the doctors are not aware of the professional commitments, ethical dimensions and personal commitments. If they come to know the real meaning of these words directly related to the promises and oaths they had taken before accreditation, they would themselves find it judicious that whatever the applications we find of the Consumer Protection Act are judicious and lawful. If we turn our eyes on the attitudes of doctors, specially serving the government hospitals, it is right to comment that they have forgotten about professional commitments. The doctors in general are found commercialising their expertise. They work seriously in the private clinics. They are found well aware of their commitments when they work in their own clinics but when they come to the hospitals where they are employed, they forget their commitments and start working with a different attitude. Except a very few, we find a majority of the doctors working with a negative attitude. This, of course, engineers a sound foundation for the application of Consumer Protection Act which is now found even troubling the doctors conceptualising professional commitments in a right fashion.

Cases

We go through two important decisions of the Supreme Court made in this regard.

The First Case: IMC Vs. V. P. Institute (1995)

The decision made in 1995 made it clear that the health services offered by public as well as the private hospitals would come under the purview of Consumer Protection Act. It was clarified that the hospitals offering cost-based or even free of charge services are under the purview but in this context, it is essential that the hospitals are following the double-pronged strategy or say, they have been charging more from one segment, charging less or even free of charge services from another segment. In this case, the patients paying more fee, or paying less fee or paying nothing would be under the purview of the Act. This is due to the fact that the hospitals promise uniformity in the quality of services to the different categories of patients and therefore, a discrimination in the quality of services offered is not desirable and the losses on that account to the patients would be payable.

The Second Case: IMC Vs. Prashant (1999)

In the case of *Prashant Vs. IMC*, it was clarified by the Supreme Court that hospitals offering free of charge services to the patients are not under the purview of the Consumer Protection Act.

The two aforesaid cases form a base for the hospitals and doctors.

In this context, it is pertinent that we go through the justifications and the legal provisions which include hospitals under the purview of the Consumer Protection Act 1987.

Consumer[19]

In this Act, unless the context otherwise requires (d) ii, "Consumer means any person who hires or avails of any services for a consideration which has been paid or promised or partly paid and partly promised, or under any system of deferred payment and includes any beneficiary of such services other than the person who hires or avails of the services for consideration paid or promised or partly paid and partly promised under any system of deferred payment when such services are availed of with the approval of the first mentioned person;

Explanation: For the purpose of sub-clause (1), "Commercial purpose" does not include use by a consumer of goods bought and used by him exclusively for the purpose of earning his livelihood, by means of self-employment.

Service[20]

In this Act, unless the context otherwise requires—

"Service means service which is made available to potential users and includes the provision of facilities in connection with banking, financing, insurance, chit fund, real estate, transport process, supply of electrical or other energy, board or lodging both, entertainment, amusement, or the purveying of news or other information but does not include the rendering of any service free of charge or under a contract of personal service."

The aforesaid definitions of Consumer and Service make it clear that hospitals offering free of charge services are not under the purview of the Consumer Protection Act, 1987 since the explanation of the term makes it clear that it is not to include the rendering of any service free of charge or under a contract of personal service. It is based on this provision that in the case of IMC Vs. *Prashant,* the Supreme Court made it clear that legal provisions under the Consumer Protection Act are not applicable to those hospitals where free of change services are offered. In the first case, it was clarified that hospitals offering both categories of services free of cost and cost-based would be under the purview of the Act.

The aforesaid facts make it clear that the Consumer Protection Act and its different provisions make doctors liable of the losses to the patients on account of their negligence and carelessness. This makes it essential that hospitals and the doctors attending on the patients don't neglect them and make available the promised diagnosis and treatment facilities. We can't negate the fact that the focus is found on the attitudes of doctors and hospitals. If the patients feel that whatever the losses they have incurred would have been avoided if proper care would have been taken by the hospitals and doctors, they have a legitimate right of claiming for the compensation.

The provisions of the Consumer Protection Act, 1987 don't include hospitals where the patients get free of charge services. Here, it is important to mention that in almost all the government hospitals, we find a provision for free-of-charge services and therefore, they are not under the purview of the Act. This is due mainly to the fact that patients getting treatment facilities there are not considered to be a consumer.

The hospitals and doctors in a majority of the cases (both of them) are found critical to the application of Consumer Protection Act, 1987 but they need to confess that some of the doctors and hospitals don't follow the required norms for the diagnosis and treatment of patients. We also find cases where they are found deliberate in neglecting the patients paying less fee. We can't negate that there have also been a gross misuse of the Act and it has been making the task difficult to the hospitals and doctors while admitting the patients covering more risk in course of treatment. On the one hand, we consent to the provisions of the Act while on the other hand, we also find it judicious that cases of misuse are checked.

In view of the aforesaid facts, it is right to mention that the Consumer Protection Act may regulate the attitudes of carelessness and negligence but there are avenues for making some amendments in the Act keeping in view the emerging trends. The private hospitals and clinics managed and controlled by the private doctors and the government hospitals need a code that makes the way for regulating the attitudes or the behavioural profile of hospital personnel irrespective of the types and nature of hospitals. If we go to the government hospitals and the patients are admitted there, the promises of offering the required services are made by the hospitals. The hospital managers may have a number of excuses but the hospitals never make it clear that they are financially bankrupt, professionally deficient and technologically obsolete and therefore, the quality of services promised to them are not to be made available. In this case, we find enough scope even for the inclusion of government hospitals under the purview of Consumer Protection Act.

Medical Regulations

We agree with this view that the legal aspect of hospital management and private practice assume a place of outstanding significance so that the doctors and hospitals are found successful in avoiding the complications and projecting a positive image. A number of books on medicine and surgery deal with various matters, prescribe certain norms for prevention and infection and medical complications which may also result in death. This is to aggravate the problems of doctors, paramedical staff, nursing staff and the managerial staff specially while testifying it that the death was not due to their negligence. It is in this context that we talk about regulations related to private practice and hospital. There are a number of conditions where negligence of doctors and paramedical staff may result into infections. Superficial or deep wounds may become infected by organisms from the patient, that is, self-infection or even by cross-infection from other patients or from members of hospital staff but in this context, the most sensitive component is found in the mismanagement of OTs where hospital "Staph aureus" (bacterium found in clustered masses) and "Gram Negative bacilli" (antibiotic obtained from certain bacteria and used against gram-positive bacteria) are found dangerous sources and should not enter the OTs. It is the prime responsibility of medical and paramedical staff that they are careful and adopt the preventive measures. But we find several cases where they have not been serious to the problem and due to their negligence, the patients have suffered irreparable losses. It is in this context that we talk about medical regulations.[21]

As and when we find a mishap, the basic question is to judge whether a medical man personally or the Hospital Management in general are guilty of culpable negligence. The relevant legal provisions are contained in Sections 81, 87, 88, 89 and 92 of the Indian Penal Code.

Section 81 lays down that nothing is an offence merely by reason of it being done with the knowledge that it is likely to cause harm, and in good faith for the purpose of preventing or avoiding other harm to persons or property. The explanation to this section states that it is a question of fact in each case whether the harm is to be prevented or avoided was of such nature and so imminent as to justify or excuse the risk of doing the act with the knowledge that was likely to cause harm.

Section 87 of the Indian Penal Code is also an important provision which deals with the matter of consent by persons suffering the harm, who in a medical case would be the patient himself. The Section says that nothing which is not intended to cause death, or grievous hurt is an offence by a person by reason of any harm which it may cause to any person, above 18 years of age who has given his consent, whether express or implied, to suffer that harm, or by reason of any harm which it may be known by the doer to be likely to cause to any such person who has consented to take the risk of the harm.

Section 88 of the Indian Penal Code says that nothing which is not intended to cause death is an offence by reason of any harm which it may cause to any person for whose benefit it is done in good faith and who has given a consent, whether express or implied, to suffer that harm or to take the risk of that harm. As for example, Mr. X, a surgeon, knowing well that a particular operation is likely to cause the death of Mr. A who is suffering from pain, but not intending to cause Mr. A's death and intending, in good faith Mr. X's benefit performs that operation on Mr. A with Mr. A's consent. Mr. X has committed no offence.

Section 89 of the Indian Penal Code covers Acts done in good faith for the benefit of a child or insane person or by consent of the guardian. The Section says that nothing, which is done in good faith for the benefit of a person under 2 years of age or unsound mind or by consent, either express or implied of the guardian or other person having lawful charge of that person is an offence by reason of a harm which it may cause, or to be intended by the doer to cause or be known by the doer to be likely to cause that person. The proviso to this section says that this immunity shall not extend to the intentional causing of death or attempting to cause death. Another proviso states that the immunity will not be available for voluntary causing of grievous hurt unless it be for the purpose of preventing death or curing of a grievous disease or infirmity. As is obvious, the section relates to harm caused to persons below 12 years of age or of unsound mind, by the guardian himself or by another person with the guardian's consent, in good faith for the benefit of the said child or the person of unsound mind.

Section 92 of the Indian Penal Code says, "92 Act done in good faith for benefit of a person without consent. Nothing is an offence by reason of any harm which it may cause to a person for whose benefit it is done in good faith, even without that person's consent, if the circumstances are such that it is impossible for that person to signify consent, or if that person is incapable of giving consent and has not a guardian or other person in lawful charge of him from whom it is possible to obtain consent in time for the thing to be done with benefit.

Provided

First—that the exception shall not extend to the intentional causing of death, or attempting to cause death;

Second —that this exception shall not extend to the doing of anything which the person doing it knows to be likely to cause death, for any purpose other than the preventing of death or grievous hurt, or the curing of any grievous disease or infirmity;

Third—that this exception shall not extend to the voluntary causing of hurt, or attempting to cause hurt, for any purpose other than the preventing of death or hurt;

Fourth—that this exception shall not extend to the abetment of any offence, to the committing of which offence it would not extend.

Meaning of Negligence

The meaning of the word 'Negligence' as derived from observations made in decided cases is, the omission to which a reasonable man, guided upon the instructions, which ordinarily regulate the conduct of human affairs, would do or doing something which a prudent and reasonable man would not do. Negligence is not a question of evidence. It is an inference to be drawn from proved facts. Negligence is not an absolute term but is a relative one, rather it is a comparative term. Where there is a duty to exercise care must be taken to avoid acts or omissions which could be reasonably foreseen to be likely to cause physical injury to persons. The degree of care required, of course, depends upon determination of various facts.

There are three basic elements of this tort, viz.:

(*i*) An act or omission on the part of defendant;

(*ii*) Intention or negligence or the breach of a strict duty on the part of the defendant.

(*iii*) Damage resulting to plaintiff from the wrongful act of the defendant which is not too remote.

Proof of Negligence

The honourable Supreme Court has held that proof of negligence is necessary before any compensation can be claimed. The normal rule is that it is for the plaintiff to prove negligence but in some of the cases, considerable hardship is caused to the plaintiff as the true cause is not known to him but is solely within the knowledge of the defendant who caused it. In such cases, the plaintiff can prove the basic facts of the accident but is unable to prove how it happened to establish negligence on the part of the defendant. This hardship is sought to be avoided by applying the principle of *Res Ipsa Luquitur,* which means that the accident "speaks for itself" or "tells its own story." However, this principle applies essentially to the law of tort and is not applicable to a criminal prosecution. As regards the quantum of proof regarding negligence on the part of the respondent, the burden is not as heavy in the case of tort as is required to prove a criminal charge, basically for the reason that under criminal jurisprudence, a person is presumed to be innocent till he is found to be guilty.

Medical Negligence

In the case of medicalmen, negligence means failure to act in accordance with the standard of reasonably competent medicalman at that time. In order that a medical man may be held liable for negligence, it is not necessary to prove that he expressly professed or promised to use proper skill or care. The fact that he styles himself as a medical man warrants an assumption that he professes to use such skill. However, it has been held that a medical man was not answerable merely because some other more experienced and able practitioner might possibly have shown greater skill and knowledge.

Some instances of medical negligence may be noticed. A reasonably competent doctor would not prescribe an overdose of any medicine. Therefore, if a Doctor prescribes an overdose of medicine and the patient, following the advice, takes the excess dose and suffers from the ill-effects of the medicine, the doctor would be liable for negligence. Similarly, if a surgeon carelessly fails to remove any of the swabs put into a patient at the time of operation, he would be guilty of negligence. Even a nurse who by inadvertence administers a poisonous medicine which causes injury to the patient, would be guilty of professional negligence.

Negligence or Misadventure

In a true sense, we find difference between negligence and misadventure or errors of judgement. It has been held that it is not every slip or mistake which imports negligence and in the case of a surgeon, it is necessary to have regard to different kinds of circumstances that may present themselves for urgent attention. Lord Justice Denning succinctly observed it in an English case as follows:

"It is easy to be wise after the event and to condemn as negligence that which was only a misadventure. We ought always to be on guard against it, especially in cases against hospitals and doctors. Medical science has conferred great benefits on mankind, but these benefits are attuned by risk. We cannot take the benefit without taking the risk. Every advance in technique is also attuned by risk. Doctors, like the rest of us, have to learn by experience and experience often teaches in a hard way. Something goes wrong and shows up a weakness, and then it is put right. That is just what happened here."

In another case, the same learned Judge made the following observations:

"Counsel had stopped to compare the case against the hospital to motor car accident or accident in a factory. There ought not to be accident if everyone used proper care. But in a hospital, when a person who was ill and came in for treatment, no matter what care was used, there was always a risk and it would be wrong and bad law to say that simply because a mishap had occurred, the hospital and the doctor were liable. Indeed, it would be disastrous to the community. It would mean that the doctor examining a patient or a surgeon operating at the table, instead of getting on with his work, would be even for looking over his shoulder to see if someone was coming up with a dagger; for an action for negligence against the doctor was like a dagger. His professional reputation was as dear to him as his body and perhaps more so, and an action for negligence would wound his reputation as severely as a dagger could his body. The Jury must, therefore, not find him negligent simply because one of the risks inherent in an operation actually took place or because in a matter of opinion, he made an error of judgement. They should only find him guilty when he had fallen of the standard of reasonable medical care when he was deserving of censure."

Precautions

In view of the above, it is pertinent that the precautionary measures are adopted by the Hospital Management in general and also by the surgeons and medical practitioners, during the course of treatment rendered by them. For prevention of hospital infection, those responsible for the administration and functioning of the institute should make all efforts for reducing the sources of pathogens (an organism or substance that causes disease) and restricting their spread. For this purpose, all hygienic measures have to be adopted. Indeed, infection may creep in despite these measures but as long as proper precautions and safeguards have been adopted, no negligence, whether under the tort or criminal law can be attributed to the administration. The question as to whether the required measures for disinfecting various articles and instruments, etc. used for performing surgical operations had been carried out or not would be a question of fact requiring proof in a particular case, if the matter goes to court.

In the case of patients who are attended by the Casuality/Emergency Ward of the hospital, the doctors attending the patients need much more precaution to avoid infection of wounds by Tetanus organism. They need to record everything on the "Treatment Card" whether the patient according to him or his attendant, in case a patient is not in a position to speak, was immunised for Tetanus within one year of the date of examination or not. If such immunisation has not been done, the same must be done expeditiously with the latest technology and medicine.

AYUSH: AN OVERVIEW

Ayurveda, Yoga and Naturopathy, Unani, Siddha and Homoeopathy known as AYUSH focus on holistic systems of health care especially in the prevention and management of chronic lifestyle related non-communicable diseases and systemic diseases. We cannot deny that no single system of health care has the capacity to solve all the needs of society and therefore, a mix of all may not only benefit the users but even the providers because we have tremendous potentials and opportunities for becoming a world leader specially·in the era of integrative medicine. We cannot negate that India is the only country in the world having a sound mix of Western biomedical sciences and immensely rich and mature indigenous medical heritage of its own found effective in improving the quality of services and making them affordable to the masses. We can develop them both at national and global levels where the focus must be on the thrust areas such as strengthening professional education, strategic research programmes, promotion of best clinical practices, technology upgradation in industry, setting internationally acceptable pharmacopoeic standards, conserving medicinal flora, fauna, metals and minerals, utilizing human resources for AYUSH in the national health programmes with the ultimate aim of enhancing the outreach of AYUSH health care in an accessible, acceptable, affordable and qualitative manner.

Of course, we have found upgradtion programmes related to educational standards, quality control and standardization of drugs, improving the availability of medicinal plant material, R&D and awareness development programme about the national and international potentials of the systems. We need to make possible optimum utilization of AYUSH for meeting the unmet needs of the population. The primary health care has considerably been benefited but the secondary and tertiary health care system have marginally been benefited and therefore, the AYUSH clinics are required to be expanded specially for Panchkarma considered as specialized therapies. It is a need of the hour that national policymakers consider integration of mainstream health care system with the AYUSH which would sizably benefit the population integrating AYUSH into NRHM especially with the availability of a large number of practitioners in this field.

Interventions of AYUSH under NRHM have been found gaining a rapid momentum. The co-location of AYUSH dispensaries in a good number of PHCs in different states, appointment of a large number of AYUSH doctors, inclusion of AYUSH modules in graining of ASHA, inclusion of Punarnavdi Mandoor in the ASHA kit for management of anemia during pregnancy, inclusion of Ayurvedic and Unani medicines in the RCH programme, establishment of speciality clinics, specialized therapy centres and AYUSH wings in district hospitals supported through CSS are the measures to channelise the benefits of AYUSH to the Indian population in general and the rural population in particular. The development of AYUSH as in industry makes it essential that we assign due weightage to the development of quality human resource.

The AYUSH educational institutions providing both Undergraduate and Post-Graduate educational aid and training facilities need to be sincere and honest to the quality. It is need of the hour that AYUSH education is made contemporary and provide generous support to centres of excellence in government and non-government sectors. The CCIM (Central Council of India Medicine) needs to make it sure that the educational institutions related to AYUSH maintain the prescribed standards. The development of professional education is also required to be promoted by AYUSH. It is also essential that formal accredited programmes for the training of AYUSH paramedics viz. nurses, pharmacists and panchkarma therapists are launched for qualitative improvements.

The AYUSH can be developed as an industry but in this context, we need professional orientation. Currently, we find a major portion of AYUSH exports consisting of raw materials and the process of value addition has been found neglected. The major challenge for the AYUSH industry is to transform its global image from that of a raw material supplier to a knowledge products industry. This would require investments in upgrading the processing technology, research and development activities including collaborative research with reputed international institutions and quality control. The intersectoral cooperation among AYUSH, CSIR, ICMR, private sector R&D, NGOs and Ministry of Commerce for meeting global requirements of quality and safe natural medicinal products. The technical and financial support to the industry in this direction may boost up our exports.

The CCRAS (Central Council for Research in Ayurveda and Siddha), CCRUM Central Council for Research in Unani Medicine), HCCRH (Homeopathy Central Council for Research in Homeopathy), CCYN (Central Council of Yoga and Naturopathy) need to promote the research activities to improve the quality of AYUSH products which would create a big market for exports. The research base of AYUSH is largely plants. Around 6000 species of medicinal plants are documented in published medical and ethno-botanical literatures. Wild populations of a large number of these species are under threat in their natural habitats. The government and the PPP mode may be used for the conservation of gene pools and cultivation of medicinal plants.

The AYUSH dispensaries are found neglected. The mainstreaming of AYUSH under NRHM, strengthening of AYUSH dispensaries, hospitals and for supply of AYUSH medicinal kits in rural areas and development of AYUSH specialised treatment centres under PPP mode may pave avenues for the development of AYUSH industry which at present suffers from small scale of operation and low technology that requires to be upgraded. "Drug Quality Control" requires to be promoted and for that, sophisticated technology, packing and packaging machines, medicinal plants storage, testing facilities and marketing need due attention. India can be a brand leader provided we find professionalised efforts for marketing the AYUSH products. The central government investments, the state governments financial provision and motivation to PPP mode need due weightage.

Role of e-Health in Indian Perspective

The sky-rocketing sophistication in the field of information technology has helped defining and redefining the quality of services in almost all the areas. We cannot deny the multi-dimensional uses of IT for an enhanced role in healthcare and governance. The healthcare providers, trainers, beneficiaries and civil society may share the benefits of National Grid. A strong fibre backbone and indigenous satellite communication technology with trained human resources have been benefiting the healthcare sector in many ways. During the yester years, we have found private concerns, NGOs, medical colleges and research institutions setting up a number of pilot projects on e-Health which have benefited both the providers and users. We are well aware of the increasing role of HMIS in improving the quality of healthcare services. Not only the urban areas of the country but even the rural areas need to make use of the benefits of e-

Health. Telemedicine may be helpful in bringing specialized healthcare services albeit to the remotest areas of the country. The telediagnosis, especially in the areas of cardiology, pathology, dermatology and radiology besides Continuing Medical Education (CME) need priority attention of hospitals and health care organisations because the services even till date are confined to selected areas of the country. The rural and remote hospitals need priority attention while developing e-health services. Geostationary Satellites services of ISRO need to be extended to all the district hospitals and government medical colleges.

The central as well as the state governments bear the responsibility of activating the e-health initiatives. The important dimensions necessitating their priority attention are the following:

- Training, education and capacity building for e-health.
- Monitoring by e-enabled HMIS to ensure timely flow of data and collation at various levels.
- Geographical Information system (GIS), Resource Mapping of various health facilities (Allopathic and AYUSH, Laboratories, Training Centres, Health Manpower and other inputs to optimize utilization).
- Providing service delivery and other e-enabled activities like disease surveillance, tele-consultations, health helpline, district hospital referral net and e-enabled mobile medical units.

In a country like India where we find remotest parts of the country completely unaware of the sophisticated development taking place in some of the selected areas of the country, the telemedicine programmes need to be channelised. The ISRO, DIT, NEC Telemedicine programme for NE States, State Governments and NGOs are to evince special interests in making the telemedicine programme proactive. The projects already commissioned like NE Project, J & K Project, Southern India Project, Armed Forces Medical Services Project, Asia Heart Foundation, South India Project, Sankara Nethralaya Palemedicine Project, Workhardt Hospital and Heart Institute Project and Apollo Hospitals Project need to benefit the rural segment on a priority basis.

The motives entailed behind using new generation of technology are to improve the service quality and to minimise the cost so that even poor segments of society find the services affordable. The service quality in respect of hospital and healthcare depends on the utilisation of appropriate technologies for diagnosis and treatment. Over the last few years, the health related technology has developed at a rapid pace but its impact on public health services has been minimal. This has deprived the weaker sections of the society of the benefits of new technology. This makes a strong advocacy in favour of low cost or cheaper technologies found cost effective and proactive. The critical equipments like anaesthesia machine, surgical equipment, lighting, sterilization equipment, defibrillator, ventilator, electrocardiogram, blood pressure monitoring equipment, pulse oxymeter, etc. must be affordable to the masses. In addition, the public health related technologies need to be used at all levels of health care.

Making health care affordable is a crying need of the hour specially in the Indian context to serve the interests of weaker sections of society who find the expensive services unfriendly to their pockets. It is in this context, we focus on the experience of Jan Swasthya Sahyog (JSS) with the motto of making health in the hinterlands available, accessible, and affordable. It is an effort of a group of dedicated team of young doctors from institutes like CMC, Vellore, and AIIMS.

They have been working since a decade back even at the cost of their lucrative jobs, sparkling city lights and hefty pay packets to develop cheap, accurate and easy-to-use technology used for prevention, diagnosis and treatment of diseases in remote tribal areas of Bilaspur and Chattisgrah. An early detection of UTI infection costs less than Rs. 2 per test; Rs. 2, diabetes test; Rs. 1 anemia test; Rs. 3 pregnancy test. They have also developed low cost mosquito repellent creams, breath counters for detection of pneumonia among children, low-cost delivery kits just for Rs. 40, electrophoresis just Rs. 20, etc. For malaria detection, they have innovative strategy. In a true sense, the rural India requires JSS technology which can be useful for peripheral, remote areas and can be used by all health workers to make diagnosis.

Health Management Information System is now found making use of new generation of technology. Telemedicine has been found helping population found in the remotest corners of the country. Telediagnosis specially in the areas of cardiology, pathology, dermatology and radiology have been found benefiting a number of population but we need to expand the services particularly to the rural areas of the country. The e-health if intelligently and professionally used and strategically channelised may be cost-effective. But in this context, the ISRO, DIT and NEC need to play a catalytic role. The NGOs and state governments also need to make the health care technology much more appropriate so that the services are affordable, accessible and affordable to the general masses.

Thrust Areas in Hospital Management

We can't deny the fact that managing a social institution is a difficult task. To be more specific, when we find hospitals working as a no-profit making organisation, the task of a manager is much more complicated. All of us are well aware of the quality of health and medicare services made available to the masses, specially by the government hospitals and the healthcare centres. In a true sense, we find the government hospitals in a depleted condition. The masses find it difficult to afford the expensive services of private hospitals. This makes it essential that the government policy makers make sincere and honest efforts to improve the working conditions of hospitals. It is against this background that we focus on the thrust areas to be effective in the process of improving the quality of services.

Strategic Planning is Essential: At the very outset, we find it significant that the hospitals, government or private, think about the formulation of a strategic plan which is related to the designing of an action plan in the face of emerging changes and the increasing requirements. There have been a number of developments in medical sciences which have changed the way, pattern and cost of diagnosis and treatment. We can't deny that in a majority of the government hospitals, even the minimum supporting infrastructural facilities are not available. On the one hand we find that the pressure on government hospitals is increasing fast while on the other hand, the potentials of hospitals are found shrinking sizeably. A mismatch between the demand generated by the masses and existing potentials of hospitals is due mainly to the fact that we don't think about the formulation of a strategic plan. Our focus is here on the formulation of an action plan based on the findings of the Management Information System for hospitals. A change in disease profile becomes natural when we lack awareness and are not serious to the contamination of water and pollution of environment. The strategic plan is required to be prepared at least for a period of five years so that the hospitals find it possible to mobilise the financial resources for enriching the inputs. Since the rural health centres are found virtually non-existent, it is pertinent that we think about an integrated plan in which the health centres and the hospitals would have a direct link. In almost all the government hospitals, we find inadequacy of quality, value-based and personally committed personnel. The strategic plan needs to consider the number and potentials of medical and paramedical personnel to meet the requirements. Thus, the first and foremost thing in the process is the formulation of a strategic plan in which we can't devalue the instrumentality of professionals to manage hospitals in a right fashion.

Holistic Concept of Management to be Conceptualised: We focus here on the holistic concept of management which expands the functional boundaries for the government and private hospitals. Of course, we find expensive inputs used in the process of offering quality service which defends or makes a claim for a high fee structure for hospitals but the holistic concept of management makes it essential that the organisations, specially the no-profit making organisations, assign an overriding priority to the subserving of social interests. If we turn our eyes on the Indian society, it is apparent that a majority of the population are not in a position to afford the expensive services. It is against this background that the concept makes a strong advocacy in favour of pocket-friendly or user-friendly fee strategy.

Not only the government hospitals but even the private hospitals need to realise the instrumentality of fee strategy in managing hospitals effectively. This also draws our attention on the preventive services of hospitals with the motto of increasing mass awareness. Since the society is illiterate and unconscious, it is pertinent that hospitals inform and sense them in a right fashion.

Well-managed and a technology-driven MIS: In an age of information explosion, it is essential that like other organisations even the hospitals or the healthcare organisations and agencies assign due weightage to information management. Of late, we find knowledge technologies playing an incremental role in managing an organisation. To be more specific in hospitals, the MIS is found essential to help the medical personnel in improving the quality of services besides enriching their knowledge bank in the field of medical sciences. The task of educating and training the medical and paramedical students would be simplified considerably, if we find a well developed and technology driven information system. Besides, the documentation, filing and accounting processes would be made more scientific, if we take the support of the information system. The nature and character of diagnosis and treatment would fantastically be changed with the help of knowledge technology. It is significant to mention that the conditions of health centres located in the rural areas would also be improved with the help of a sound information system. It is against this background that we make a strong advocacy in favour of a technology-driven information system for hospitals. The policy makers need to realise the instrumentality of MIS in improving the quality of services offered by hospitals. Of late, we talk about integrated healthcare and the MIS can simplify the integration process. Thus, the curative as well as the preventive services of hospitals can be given a new direction if an MIS is developed. The government hospitals need to assign due weightage to the same because the private hospitals have been found assigning an overriding priority to the same. Whatever the qualitative improvements we find in their functional areas are due to the use of advanced information technology. We are well aware of the fact that in managing hospitals, the quality of diagnosis plays a contributory role in improving the quality of treatment. An MIS helps substantially in improving the quality of diagnosis which simplifies the treatment process. The case history of patients can be maintained in a scientific way if we have a developed knowledge technology. The increasing cases of financial irregularities can also be minimised considerably if we have a technology-driven information system. These facts are a mute testimony to this proposition that for managing hospitals efficiently as MIS requires an intensive care.

Behavioural Management: Behavioural scientists are of the view that behavioural influences play an incremental role in improving the quality of services offered by hospitals. The doctors as well as paramedical personnel need to understand the importance of behavioural management. The medical and paramedical personnel need to behave properly so that the patients as well as the attendants feel that whatever the services have been offered by the hospitals are the best they can. We can't underestimate the role of behaviour in minimising the recovery period. We talk about the management of tension in hospitals and the behavioural influences play a significant role in diffusing the tension. This makes it essential that the healthcare organisations assign due weightage to the behavioural management and the syllabi for educating and training the students include the same on a priority basis.

The refresher and capsule courses for medical and paramedical personnel need to include behavioural management. We can't negate that particularly in the government hospitals, a large number of personnel are found aggressive in nature and indecent in behaviour which mounts to the generation of tension among the patients and attendants. It is in this context that we make much more advocacy in favour of behavioural management.

Professional Touch in the Functional Areas: In this context, we talk about different functional areas of hospitals. The most important functional area is related to the management of hospital personnel. We are well aware of the fact that different echelons of personnel serve hospitals and it is joint efforts that results are found positive. The management scientists now talk about quality people in hospitals. By quality people, our focus is on personnel having personal commitment in addition to a strong base of fundamentals of the subject. In other words, the medical and paramedical personnel serving the hospitals should have an in depth knowledge of the subject besides the supportive knowledge consisting of value-addition, personal-commitment, decent behavioural profile or so. This makes it essential that hospital managers assign due weightage to the management of hospital personnel where a fair blending of employee orientation and performance orientation is made possible. The personnel are motivated, the efficients are rewarded suitably and at the same time, the dishonest and inefffficient people are demotivated and penalised. Of course, we find infrastructural support, equipment, technologies playing a significant role improving the level of efficiency of hospitals but ultimately, it is the quality of hospital personnel who play a dominating role. This makes it essential that the hospital managers/administrators assign an overriding priority to the management of hospital personnel. Right from the process of recruitment to the process of control, they are required to make it sure that value-based, ethically sound, personally-committed and intelligent personnel are made available to the hospitals. This is essential because in a majority of the government hospitals, we find efficient personnel but since they are not value-based and personally-committed, the level of efficiency is found almost zero.

Another component of the functional area is the management of finance. To be more specific, the government hospitals have been found facing the problem of financial crunch and this makes it essential that the managers also think about the management of finance so that the hospitals are found successful in mobilising the internal sources of generating finance. It is essential that the government hospitals are allowed freedom in the very context because the state exchequer finds it difficult to extend financial support as per the increasing requirements. The hospital managers need to act professionally[22] so that avenues for the generation of finance are paved. The governmental regulations need to promote charity, donation and the participation of corporate sector to improve the financial health of hospitals. While managing finance, it is to be made sure that the cases of financial irregularities and unfair practices are checked. This in a natural way gravitates our attention on the workings of store and purchase department because in a majority of the cases, we find irregularities inviting a stage of financial disaster. Besides, the management of finance would also improve the system of accounting. The hospital managers/administrators need to be vigilant so that the mismanagement of finance is checked.

An important and of course, the most important component is the marketing of hospital services which substantially influences the process of generation of finance from the internal sources. The hospital managers bear the responsibility of formulating a sound mix for the hospital services. They are supposed to blend the core and peripheral services optimally so that the services offered by them prove to be distinct to others. This would inject life to the principles of Product Uniqueness Proposition. In addition, the different constituents of promotion mix are to be blended optimally so that the customers/users are informed and sensed in a right fashion. Besides, they bear the responsibility of formulating a rational fee strategy so that the financial health of hospitals is sound enough to enrich the supporting infrastructural facilities. In view of the paying capacity of Indian society, the hospitals need a pocket-friendly fee strategy so that even poorest of the poor gets an opportunity to avail the services. The hospital managers/administrators are supposed to process the services in an effective way so that the promised services are made available to the users without making any distortion. The front-line staff, the medical and paramedical personnel and the nursing staff need to go through the problem of behavioural management. The People mix of marketing thus is found occupying a place of outstanding significance because by improving the quality of different echelons of hospital personnel, the level of efficiency would sizeably be increased.

Thus the different functional areas of management are to be managed professionally[23] and the hospital managers/administrators are supposed to discharge the assigned functional responsibilities in an effective way resulting into the emergence of a satisfied group of users.

Management of Ambience: Since we talk about the management of hospitals, it is judicious that we also talk about the management of surroundings and premises. This focuses our attention on keeping hospitals neat and clean, promoting plantation and gardening, assigning due weightage to the management of hospital waste and general waste, proper sanitation, lighting and ventilation facilities around the compound and inside the hospitals or so. The management scientists feel that hospitals, specially the government hospitals don't consider it significant to manage the surroundings and premises which makes the environment polluted, prone to multi-faceted diseases influencing the level of efficiency of hospitals. It is against this background that we need to assign due weightage to the management of surroundings and premises. It is right to mention that hospitals may seek the cooperation of Social Organisations, NSS, Scouts, Municipal Corporations, Civic Bodies and even the Forest Department. The plantation of ornamental plants generating flowers and oxygen would keep the environmental conditions healthy which would help hospitals in increasing the level of efficiency. Here, we need a plan so that plantation is not to generate problems while expanding the transportation, communications and power facilities.

The aforesaid thrust areas need an intensive care of hospital managers/administrators. In a true sense, we need an attitudinal change. The policy makers, the medical and paramedical personnel and the hospital managers are required to make it sure that the hospitals and healthcare centres keep themselves engaged in subserving the public interests. Managing professionally a social institution would, of course, be an effective device to bring the derailed healthcare systems on the rail.

An Ideal Hospital Manager

The operational efficiency of an organisation is considerably influenced by the positive or negative contributions of managers. If managers work with a positive attitude; if they are value-driven; if they are emotional; if they are candid; if they are ethical; if they are careful then the accomplishment of organisational goals is found easier. Because we talk about the qualities for a manager serving a no-profit-making organisation, it is essential that they are well aware of the principles of holistic concept of management. To be more specific, in the government hospitals we find the problem of low level of efficiency very alarming. Except a very few, we find almost all the government hospitals establishing a record in the respect of degeneration of efficiency. Of course, the deficient management has sizeably been responsible for the present disappointing results. The policy panels like Mudaliar Committee and Siddhu Committee have made it clear that hospitals need to be managed by personnel having managerial excellence but the government policy makers are yet to think over the problem. Sooner or later, we have no option but to make provisions for world class professionals for managing the hospitals. The private hospitals, no doubt, have been found evincing their interests in managing hospitals professionally but even they have been found making half-hearted efforts. The healthcare organisations and hospitals while selecting and developing managers need to assign due weightage to the following properties or attributes:

1. **A hospital manager needs to be professionally sound:** At the outset, we talk about the professional excellence of managers because they are supposed to manage an organisation almost in a depleted condition. On the basis of world class professional excellence, they can be successful in bringing the derailed healthcare system on the rail. By the professional excellence our focus is on the qualifications and experiences related to the management of a hospital. They are supposed to be an MBA (Hospital Administration) or they should at least have a Post-graduate Diploma in Hospital Administration. A degree in Hospital Management is to be preferred. Here, we concentrate on the subjective knowledge of personnel to be recruited as a hospital manager. If we find an MBBS having a degree in Hospital Management/a diploma in Hospital Administration, he/she would be most suitable for the post of a hospital manager.

2. **A hospital manager should be ethical and value-driven:** Of late, we find almost all the organisations assigning due weightage to ethics and values. It is against this background that we find corporate ethics getting a priority position on the development agenda of boardrooms or the policy makers. Because we talk about hospitals, it is pertinent that we assign an overriding priority to this property of a hospital manager. A hospital manager should have respect for values and ethics. A number of internationally acclaimed management experts feel that regulation-based approach to ethics is not to serve the purpose of organisations in general and the hospitals in particular. It is in this context that the executives feel that the hospitals need to promote self-regulation. You define a small number of core values that every employee and manager must use to guide their decisions and behaviour. Policing and punishing your

employees for not following the rules and regulations defining human behaviour would not serve our purpose. This makes it essential that we promote value based approach. The essential qualities that you need to go through are honesty, promise-keeping, fairness, respect for others, compassion and integrity.

In the face of growing unethical and unfair practices in the hospitals, we need an overriding priority to value orientation and ethics.

3. A manager needs to be candid: Candour and honesty are of late getting due significance in the policy decision making. We find business magnets often advocating for a liberal environment or a regulation-free environment. In a true sense, the managers are required to ensure their credibility by defining specific operating standards and developing ways of self-policing, showing hospitality to critics, recognising the legitimacy of different opinions, avoiding litigation as a way to work out or resolve conflicts. This makes it clear that credibility of a manager occupies a place of outstanding significance. Lack of credibility among the managers is required to be removed.

4. A manager requires to be emotional: A manager should have the efficacy to communicate his/her feelings, views in strong but decent words. May be that your efforts are innovative and more proactive but your subordinates or even superiors and peers don't welcome it because they feel that by making it possible they would face a number of problems. It is not meant that you keep mum and don't respond to the persons found critical to your innovative efforts. It is in this context that we focus on the emotional quality of a manager because you may emotionally urge them to battle the challenges on account of innovative efforts. We agree with this view that one of the essential qualities of a successful manager is the ability to convey his/her strong feelings about a subject. The best managers are not only emotional, they know just the right time to inject emotion into a business situation. The sign of an ideal manager is the ability to make ordinary people to do extraordinary things when the odds are against them.

5. A manager should be personally committed: By personal commitment, our focus is on involving an individual into the work situations. If you are personally committed, your responsibility is found enlarged substantially. Even if you are at home, you think about your organisation. May be that you are in a supermarket or a departmental store for shopping but albeit there, you think about your organisation. It is in this context that we find personal commitment something different from the professional commitment. To be more specific in the Indian condition, we assign due weightage to this property of a manager because our bitter experiences testify the perception that specially in hospitals, we can't think of a good patient care unless we have personally committed managers and other hospital personnel. It is personal commitment that motivates you to work even if the working conditions are not conducive.

6. A manager should have human values: It is humanity, human, humane, human values requiring due attention of a HRD manager. The doctors may be professionally sound but if they lack humanity, the patients would fail in getting the quality services. The managers may be professionally sound but if they lack humanity, the real constraints and handicaps obstructing the process of quality medicare would not be taken due care. It is against this background that we find experts advocating much more in favour of human values, specially in hospitals.

7. A manager should be professionally committed: We consider professional commitment an essential quality for a successful manager. This is due to the fact that professionally committed managers would keep themselves all the time engaged in enriching their professional excellence. Since we find sky the only limit to perfection, the hospital managers need to be professionally-committed.

Professional excellence is found essential to make them potentially sound and the professional commitment is pertinent to motivate them to use their potentials in a productive fashion. A hospital manager is required to be professionally-committed because the services of hospitals are found of sensitive nature.

8. A manager should have aesthetic sense: In addition, it is also significant that a manager is aesthetic because this expands scope for maintaining and developing the surroundings and premises containing aesthetic sense. It is essential that plantation, gardening and neatness are given due weightage while managing a hospital. In hospital management, we find aesthetic management occupying a place of outstanding significance because it is found helpful in making the environment friendly and attractive. The patients in addition to the treatment also need a pollution-free environment. This makes it essential that a hospital manager manages the surroundings and premises and develops a landscape making hospitals eco-friendly. This in a natural way makes a strong advocacy in favour of managing the premises for managing the hospital waste because in a majority of the hospitals we find the medical and biomedical waste very much instrumental in making the premises dirty and prone to different types of diseases.

9. A manager should have leadership quality: A hospital manager is supposed to play the role of a successful leader. He/she needs all the qualities found essential for a leader. This makes it essential that the managers are competent enough to face the multidimensional challenges. He/she has patience, an indepth knowledge of the behavioural management, capacity to understand the problem, ethical and moral values, carefulness, high communications ability, art of influencing the persons and diffusing the tension, empathy or so. Because we find hospital managers facing a number of problems, it is essential that he is never perturbed by his/her decisions. The universal characteristics of leadership focus on some of the traits, such as visibility or vision, a steady hand in all the departmental circumstances and situation, they are hands-on in their approach to leadership or so. In the healthcare organisations where illness and death are ever present, it is essential that a hospital manager maintains a lighter side through sharing a witty anecdote, relating a tasteful joke or laughing at your own foibles. Besides, it is also essential that he/she has the capacity to accept the errors to increase his/her credibility.

The aforesaid qualities of a hospital manager make it clear that development of an ideal or a sound hospital manager is a difficult task that requires proper education and training. May be that some of the qualities are inherent or by educating and training, the qualities or potentials can be developed. There is no doubt in it that an indepth knowledge of hospital management is essential for a manager but in addition, he/she requires a number of qualities as narrated above. We can't negate the fact that a large number of problems in hospitals are due to deficient management and an efficient manager bears the responsibility of improving the quality of management so that the wrongs are corrected and the concept of good patient care is practised in the right perspective. We have been spending a lot of money on other personnel but our investment on management cadre is very inadequate. This necessitates development of an ideal manager who is professionally as well as personally committed.

We agree with this view that the spirit behind management-in-action is leadership. Of course, there are a number of aspects to be given due weightage while developing an ideal hospital manager but he/she should have all the qualities required for a successful leader because this would help him/her in communicating the mission, vision, values, ethics and objectives of hospitals to the public at large.

Thus, an ideal hospital manager should have futuristic vision, dynamism, respect to others, spirit of sacrifice, high behavioural profile, ethical and human values, carefulness, aesthetic sense, candour, emotion, empathy because an optimal mix of different properties would help a hospital manager in proving his/her excellence as a super performer. We can not negate that by and large, almost all the government hospitals and even a good number of private hospitals have not been assigning due weightage to managerial proficiency which has considerably been affecting the service quality. Of course, we find governments spending huge money on the development of hospitals and healthcare centres but in a majority of them, we find problems of managerial deficiency. This makes a strong advocacy in favour of a managerially sound and professionally profound hospital to be efficacious of delivering goods to the society. Though we find hospitals realizing the significance of a professional for managing hospitals but they have not been placing the same on their development agenda. It is high time that the policy makers realise the outstanding contributions of a potentially sound hospital manager which would help hospitals in different ways. The quality of services would be improved, the services would be affordable, accessible and available not only to a few selected segments but to all who need.

The hospital professionals in the very context would be required to strengthen training programmes for different categories of paramedical and medical personnel which would be helpful in sensitising them to the emerging trends and the evolving developments in the field of medical sciences. The thematical competence, no doubt, assume a place of outstanding significance but in any case, they cannot undermine the role of professional excellence. For the hospital services, it is pertinent that paramedical or medical personnel have been achieving world class excellence. Today, it is not only a national issue but even international concern because we find a number of people from the overseas countries coming to India for getting medical aid. Professional ethics, commitments, personalized services or personal-touch-in-service, sincerity, honesty and empathy would be helpful in projecting the image of a hospital in a positive way. Almost all the staff working in any capacity need human touch in behaviour.

Particularly the government managed hospitals need priority attention where we find service quality not to the desired level of patients. In addition to other aspects, the hospitals need to assign due weightage to the management of surroundings, premises and service ambience because the hospital services considerably rest on the aesthetic sense. Cleanliness is considered to be an essential consideration for a hospital and therefore, a hospital manager while managing surroundings and premises need due attention on aesthetic management. The plantation if planned would help hospitals in minimising the recovery period. In a majority of the hospitals we find mismanagement of biodegradable and non-biodegradable medical waste becoming a centre for infection and development of health hazards. A manager needs to manage them in a scientific way.

SUMMARY

In this chapter, you have gone through the fundamentals of hospital management. After going through the chapter, be sure that the following facts are well versed:

Management of No-profit-making Organisations: The organisations not having a legitimate right of making profit are the no-profit-making organisations, such as the educational institutions, hospitals or healthcare centres, social organisations and political organisations.

Hospital—the Concept: We consider hospital a place for diagnosis and treatment. It is also considered to be a social institution because it bears the responsibility of subserving the social interests.

Types of Hospitals

The different types of hospitals are teaching-cum-research, general, special, government, private, semi-government, allopathic, homeopathic, unani, ayurvedic, district, sub-division and health centres.

Hospital Management—the Concept: By the management of hospital, we mean professional management of hospitals in line with the principles of holistic concept.

Significance of Hospital Management: Managing hospitals professionally is found significant with the viewpoints of formulating a pragmatic plan, constitution of an efficient team of hospital personnel, availability of the supporting infrastructural facilities, optimising the overall costs, accelerating the rate of overall productivity, making possible creativity in the promotional measures, managing the behavioural profile and satisfying the patients and attendants.

Hospital Management—Shift from Professional to Manager: With the passage of time, we find a significant change in the nature and character of managing hospitals which has necessitated a shift from administration to a manager because such a shift makes possible selfless service, circumstantial control, qualitative outcomes or so.

Functional Areas in Hospital Management: The hospital managers bear the responsibility of managing the different functional areas such as managing the services, finance, human resources and marketing.

Managing Sensitive issue in Hospitals: In the management of sensitive issues, we go through the problem of management of time, management of hospital and general waste, management of tension and aesthetic management.

Management By Objectives in Hospitals: The hospitals need to realise the instrumentality of MBO in managing the hospitals. This helps hospital managers in setting the time honoured objectives and making an appraisal of the performance of hospital personnel.

Hospital—A No-profit-making Oreganisation: We consider hospitals a no-profit making organisation since they don't have a legitimate right of making profits.

Hospital—A Social Institution: We consider hospitals a social institution since the mission of a hospital is to justify its existence in the society by protecting the public interests.

Hospital—An Institution of HCF: The process of Human Capital Formation is activated by hospitals.

National Health Policy: We go through the salient features of National Health Policy, 1983 and its review in 2000.

Ethical Dimensions in Hospitals: It is pertinent that we make possible integration of ethics the healthcare services that requires fuelling of the process of value-engineering by education and training.

Consumer Protection Act 1987: We go through the application of Consumer Protection Act in the hospitals. The hospitals charging more or charging less are under the purview of the Act.

AYUSH: An Overview: Ayurveda, Yoga and Naturopathy, Unani, Siddha and Homeopathy are known as AYUSH which we consider as a holistic system of healthcare.

e-Health in Indian Perspective: A number of new generation of technology are used for improving the service quality and minimising the costs.

Thrust Areas in Managing Hospitals: Strategic planning, holistic concept, MIS, Behavioural Management, Functional Areas, Surroundings and Premises need priority attention.

An Ideal Hospital Manager: Professional excellence value-driven, candid, emotion, personal touch, human touch are essentials for an ideal hospital manager.

KEY TERMS

Paramedical	Mortuary
AYUSH	Hospital Waste
e-health	Biodegradable
HMIS	Non-biodegradable
Tele-consultation	Syringe
PPP	Incinerator
Clinical Data Warehouses	Cadmium
Non-profit Organisation	Psycho-bio-equilibrium
Hybrid Technology	MBO
WHO	Empathy
Tehsil	Zero-based Budgeting
Taluk	Social Institution
Creativity	Human Capital
Gray Area	Quality Life Index
Aesthetic	Quality Human Index
Hygiene	HFA
Disinfection	AIDS
Consumer Protection Act	Epidemiological
Demographic	Mortality
IMC	IPC
Antibiotic	Misadventure
CCIM	CCRUM
CCRAS	CCYN

REVIEW QUESTIONS

1. Focus on the management of Non-profit Organisations.
2. What do you mean by Hospital? Discuss its different types.
3. What do you mean by Hospital Management? Throw light on the significance of hospital management to the development of healthcare services.
4. Explain the advantages of a shift from administration to management.
5. Discuss the different functional areas of hospital management.
6. Explain the significance of time management in hospitals.
7. Focus on the management of hospital waste.
8. Throw light on the different sensitive issues in the management of hospitals.
9. Explain the management of tension in hospitals.
10. What do you mean by MBO? Explain Management By Objectives in the context of hospital.
11. Explain the importance of aesthetic management in hospital management.

12. Discuss the following:
    (*a*) Hospital: A Social Institution
    (*b*) Hospital: A Non-profit Organisation
    (*c*) Hospital: A Place for Human Capital Formation.
13. Critically examine the National Health Policy.
14. Write a short note on the ethical dimensions in hospitals.
15. Explain Consumer Protection Act in the context of hospital services.
16. Focus on the essential qualities for an ideal Hospital Manager.
17. Discuss the different Sections of IPC related to the private practice by a doctor.

APPLICATION EXERCISES

1. As a marketing professional, focus on the considerations influencing the management of a non-profit organisation.
2. "The hospital managers are required to act as a professional". Comment on this statement as a hospital manager.
3. The hospital staff is required to have an indepth knowledge of time management. Comment in the capacity of a hospital manager.
4. You have been acting as a hospital manager. Focus on the key functional areas you need to manage.
5. The management of hospital waste has been found creating numerous health problems. In the light of this statement, throw light on the measures you will adopt for managing biomedical waste.
6. Throws light on the key areas to be managed on a priority basis by a hospital manager.
7. In the capacity of a hospital professional, focus on the role of aesthetic management in improving the quality of service environment.
8. Comment on the ethical dimensions in the context of hospital management.
9. "The Consumer Protection Act has been found complicating the task of private hospitals and clinics. "Do you find it judicious to bring the hospital services under the purview of Consumer Protection Act? Defend your arguments.
10. Identify thrust areas in the health care services on which a hospital manager needs priority attention to improve the level of efficiency of hospitals.
11. Throw light on the different Sections of Indian Pena Code on which doctors need due care.

END NOTES

1. Gurner Spur, *Management in the Industrial Society of Future*, Siemens Review, 1/90, pp. 4-9.
2. *WHO Technical Report Series 1968*, 395, p. 6.
3. *WHO Technical Report Series 1957*, 122, p. 4.
4. Goel S.L. and Kumar R., *Challenges of the Administration of Hospital Services*, Hospital Administration, Vol. 1, pp. 9-10.
5. Jha S.M., *Services Marketing*, Himalaya Publishing House, Mumbai, 1994, pp. 304-6.
6. Donald N. Lombardi, *Handbook for the New Healthcare Manager*, p. 7-9.
7. *Bid.*, pp. 1490-50.
8. Jha, S.M., *Social Marketing*, Himalaya Publishing House, Mumbai, Chap. 8, pp. 169-200.

9. *Times of India,* Delhi, February 8, 2000.
10. Goel S.L. and Kumar R., *Hospital Administration,* Vol. 2, p. 209.
11. *Ibid.*
12. *Bid.*
13. Mangla K.K.: *Applying MBO in Hospitals*: Hospital Administration, Vol. I pp. 285-313
14. Jha, S.M. : *Services Marketing;* Himalaya Publishing House, Mumbai, 2009
15. *WHO Technical Report Series, 1957,* 122 P.4
16. *Ninth Five Year Plan;* Vol. I Nabhi's Chap. 3
17. *Eleventh Five Year Plan;* Vol. II pp. 57-127
18. *Business Today,* March 22, 1999 pp. 138-39
19. *Consumer Laws,* Malhotra Brothers P.6
20. *Ibid.*
21. Singh Surinder, *Medical Practice and Law* pp. 165-78
22. Nalini V.Dave; *Hospital Management* p.31
23. *Ibid.*

Total Quality Management in Hospitals

We live in an age where we do not find any boundary for quality. An organisation defining and redefining quality succeeds whereas others compromising with quality perish. TQM makes ways for quality in totality.

CHAPTER OBJECTIVES

Introduction—Quality: the Perception—Misperception of Quality—Total Quality Management: the Concept—TQM in Hospitals—Quality Assurance—Dimensions of TQM in Hospitals—Technical Quality—Functional Quality—Infrastructural Quality—TQM in Hospital Personnel—Team and TQM in Hospitals—Principles of Building a Team in Hospital—Justifications for TQM in Hospitals—Quality Circle—Practising QCs in Hospitals—Quality in Totality in Indian Hospitals—Summary—Key Terms—Review Questions—Application Exercises—End Notes.

LEARNING OBJECTIVES

This chapter aims at studying the different dimensions of Total Quality Management which is also known as TQM. The hospitals and healthcare organisations need to improve the service quality which requires conceptualisation of TQM. In the Indian perspective, it is essential that low-cost technologies are used to make the services cost-effective and affordable. The hinterlands of India have not been getting the benefits of e-Health and new generation of information and communication technology. The readers after going through this chapter develop their awareness of practising quality in totality.

Introduction

Innovations make the ways for perfection. Our dedication, commitments and optimism play an incremental role in generating excellence which is the result of perfection. But our eyes and minds need to be receptive. Innovators prove to be a market leader because they develop the potentials of defining and redefining quality. Sooner or later, today or tomorrow, an individual or an institution succeeds in thriving, if they do not fix any boundary for quality and nurture the perception that sky is the limit for quality because sky is the limit for perfection. We are suitably rewarded for defining quality and considerably demotivated and punished for denying or delaying the process of innovation. Like other organisations, the hospitals also need to focus on the concept of quality in totality for which they will be required to practise Total Quality Management.

In an age of new generation of information and communication technology, modern instruments and equipments and techno-driven Health Information System, the hospitals are in a position to make their services nationally and globally competitive. We find leading private and government hospitals completely depending on technology of new generation and this has been found increasing the costs vis-a-vis fee which can not be affordable to a majority of the Indian population. This makes a strong advocacy in favour of low cost technology specially in the interest of weaker sections of society.

The concept of Total quality Management (TQM) is based on the principle that for achieving perfection, we need to synchronise the different constituents in such a fashion that services are cost and qualitywise competitive. Our excellence, no doubt, is coiled in the essence of understanding the instrumentality of a particular constituent at a particular time and occasion. In the generation of service quality, we find blending of a number of constituents such as new generation of technology, supporting infrastructural facilities, a techno-driven health information system and the important of all world class medical and paramedical personnel working and serving hospitals and healthcare organisations with a sense of conviction and commitment.

Service quality is more a function of attitude than that of technology as most of us believe. But here, we are influenced by this perception that there must be an optimal combination of attitude and technology. On the one hand, we need new generation of technology while on the other hand also realise the significance of positive attitudes of people administering, managing and controlling the development processes. Of late, we find a string base of hybrid technology which has resulted into the mergence of techniculture and hospitals and healthcare centres promoting the same succeed in establishing an edge over the competitors and ultimately, become a quality leader.

A number of organisations both in profit and non-profit segments have been found practising TQM which has considerably helped them in redefining quality. Particularly in the hospital and healthcare services where we find a majority of the organisations facing the problem of quality, the conceptualisation of TQM would open new vistas for qualitative and quantitative transformation.

Tomorrow would be an age for quality leaders and those hospitals and healthcare organisations who practise TQM would have an edge over others. This draws our attention on promoting research and development activities so that inventions and innovations in the field of medical sciences help Indian society and Indian economy in different ways. The researchers and scientists need to assign due weightage to the development of low-cost technology which protects and promotes the interests of weaker sections of society. The teaching-cum-research hospitals, healthcare institutes bear an outstanding responsibility of devising new devices of immunisation, vaccination, diagnosis, investigations and treatment so that the expanding disease profile is regulated, the cost-effectiveness is made possible, the risk elements and side effects are minimised and healthcare services of world class do not remain confined to a few selected segments of the society. In almost all the areas, we need innovations such as equipment, instrument, information and communication, medicines and so on.

We cannot deny that supporting infrastructural facilities play an important role in improving the quality of healthcare services. This focusses our attention on the availability of power, water, transportation, communication, information, sanitation and other facilities making the task of hospital personnel easier and the stay of patients and attendants economic and comfortable. We make a strong advocacy in favour of new generation of technology but in absence of supporting infrastructural facilities, we can not expect the desired level of services from them. This makes it essential that hospital professionals also ensure availability of uninterrupted infrastructural facilities.

The TQM makes it essential that we assign an overriding priority to the quality of personnel. We are well aware of the fact that different echelons of medical and paramedical personnel are required for smooth running of hospitals. The hospital professionals have to make it sure that required attributes and properties are available for the working people and therefore, they can organise training and development programmes with the support of experts. The TQM makes it essential that in addition to the thematical competence, the working people are value-based, personally committed and human oriented. The patients expect not only quality treatment but in addition, they also expect decent behaviour, sympathy and empathy, personal touch and friendly service environment where service culture may be nurtured. This necessitates a structural change in the syllabi at almost all the stages and levels of service delivery. We expect from medical and paramedical personnel a sense of social service and personal touch in addition to the world class excellence. The hospital personnel biding a good-bye to human values and ethics are hardly to serve our interests.

The hospital professionals need to develop a leadership quality where ethics, emotions, carefulness and candidness need priority attention. It is well experimented that regulation based approaches provide only a lukewarm response because there we find possibilities for deviation. We need to define ethical behaviour and a small number of core values based on the principles of honesty, promise-keeping, fairness, respect for others, compassion and integrity. Unless you lead well, you manage well and if you manage well, you not only succeed in accomplishing he organisational goals but also make yourself potentially sound to show many wonders.

The TQM thus draws out attention on the different constituents required to make available to the general masses the quality healthcare services. The first and foremost thing is quality of medical and paramedical personnel and for which the education and training facilities need priority attention. The quality of equipment, instrument, machines, information and communication technology, internet services, provision for telemedicine programmes, etc. also influence TQM. It is significant that we develop cheaper technologies found effective as the expensive technologies. The technological solutions for making crucial equipment affordable, for example, anesthesia machine, surgical equipment and lighting, sterilization equipment, defibrillator, ventilator, electrocardiogram, blood pressure monitoring equipment, pulse oxymeter and the like need due attention. In this context, the supporting infrastructural facilities such as transportation, sanitation, water, communication, gas, etc. need an uninterrupted supply. The construction of hospital building is a matter of prime concern and for which we need to make use of the services of world class hospital planners, designers, architects, consultants, professionals and other experts for development of service ambience. Scientific management of hospital waste is an integral part of hospital management.

In view of the above, it is right to mention that managing a particular constituent is not to serve out purpose. We need qualitative and quantitative transformation which requires a fair synchronisation of all the constituents making medicare services proactive and cost effective to serve more and earn more so that the medical tourism plays a catalytic role in the development of quality healthcare services. The TQM would serve our purpose.

QUALITY-THE PERCEPTION

At the outset, we go through the perception of "Quality" based on the multidimensional developments. Here, our focus is on service quality which focuses out attention on the productivity of the resources used for service generation and delivery. The service quality can be classified into two parts viz. technical quality and the functional quality.[1] We find quality as a result of the sincere efforts of people and technology in addition to the different types of inputs used in the process. The techniquality of goods or services can be improved with the help of new generation of sophisticated technology whereas the functional quality of human resources can be improved by strong emphasis on attitudes, service mindedness, accessibility, interpersonal relations, appearance and commitment.[2]

This makes it essential that organisations generating services and to be more specific, when they are supposed to act as a no-profit-making organisation, assign due weightage to the functional quality of human resources or people serving the organisation. We can't negate the fact that of late, we find technologies playing an important role in improving the quality of healthcare services. In this context, it is pertinent that the professionals while developing quality make sincere and honest efforts to blend the two optimally so that a new perception of quality is developed.

The perception of quality is found ever changing because the processes of inventions and innovations make the way for technological sophistication and the organisations using sophisticated technologies establish an edge over the organisations managing everything manually. It is against this background that a number of organisations have developed a new perception of service quality. The banks, insurance companies, the airways and airlines, the hotels, the tourist organisations, the tour operators and the leading hospitals of the globe have been successful in developing a new perception of quality. The hospitals using sophisticated instruments, equipment and machines are found improving the quality of diagnosis and treatment and this has very much been instrumental in increasing the level of expectations of patients as well as the attendants. In this context, if hospitals keep on moving with traditional technologies, the quality would of course be inferior resulting into dissatisfaction since the prospects have perceived a new perception of diagnosis and treatment. Thus, the quality perception in the healthcare services is fantastically influenced by technical quality. On the other hand, we also find new devices and new course structure for educating and training the medical and paramedical professionals in addition to the development of worldclass hospital managers. The functional quality helps in increasing the outcomes of technical quality.

Scientific inventions and innovations thus change the perception of quality and the hospitals believing in making things happen develop a new perception of quality. This shapes the level of expectations of patients and attendants and for satisfying them, it becomes essential that other hospitals also follow the same.

MISPERCEPTION OF QUALITY

Quality does not happen by chance because each and every stage of the life cycle of your product requires due care at a number of stages, sources and failing due care, it is distorted. In a true sense, we find quality the totality of characteristics of an entity that bear on its ability or efficacy to satisfy stated and implied needs. Quality, specially in the Indian perspective is regarded as a socially desirable objective and we find nothing wrong in this observation but it is not to be forgotten that quality is also to make the ways smooth to increase the market share, establish leadership and make considerable amount of profits. There are some wrong observations regarding the concept of quality; to be more specific, in the developing and less developed countries which have been found obstructing the process of development. Unless they remove the misconceptions and perceive the concept of quality in a right fashion, the qualitative transformation would continue to remain for them simply a socially desirable objective. It is against this background that we need to remove the misconceptions regarding quality.

Quality is not the result of only high costs: A majority of us believe that higher quality costs more and therefore, we fail in activating the process of qualitative transformation. In a true sense, the most widely perceived misconceptions regarding quality is required to be removed on a priority basis. The new insights into the mechanism of quality building and manufacturing processes have not only been visible rather have testified it in almost all the cases that quality does not always cost more. Quality is first defined on paper and then the design is translated into an actual product by the right manufacturing and generating processes. There is no doubt in it that the process of quality transformations requires use of expensive inputs and sophisticated technologies but in addition, there are a number of factors to influence the process. The main thing in the process is the increasing craze among the prospects for the new perception of quality which makes the process cost-effective and in due course, we find the costs coming down because the intensity of competition is found moving upward.

Process of quality transformation decelerates the rate of productivity: We also perceive the fact that quality leads to low rate of productivity but this is not true in all the cases. We can't negate that quality and productivity are found interrelated. It is not essential that for accelerating the rate of productivity and for improving the quality of goods or services manufactured and generated by us, we have to minimise the quantity because late physical inspection of end-product is not the only thing for quality transformation. Since we talk about quality in totality, there are a number of stages and sources where we need to be careful and vigilant. If we are sincere and honest at all the concerned stages, the process of quality transformation would not affect the increase of quantity. Thus, both the processes of improvements, viz., qualitative and quantitative transformation can be activated simultaneously, if we practise the concept of Total Quality Management.

Human Resources or people are not only responsible for quality upgradation or quality degeneration: We also need to remove the misconception among the masses that as and when we find something wrong with the quality of goods or services, it is only due to the insincerity or inefficiency of employees working there. A microscopic analysis of the problem makes it clear that workers/employees are found responsible for a degeneration in quality only when the management has thoroughly trained the operators of process of equipment with the evolving technologies, detailed instructions have been given to them as and when the circumstances necessitated so, the contributions of employees have been evaluated at a reasonable gap. But in a very few cases we find completion of these formalities by a manager. Often we find a gap between the evolving technologies and the human resources or people available to handle, operate and maintain the existent technologies. The organisations, no doubt, assign, due weightage to the process of technological transformation but delay the process of developing and training the people.

Quality upgradation requires large investments: We also need to remove the misperception that quality improvement requires huge investments in all the cases. Of course, we find cases when the process of quality upgradation proves to be expensive due to capital intensive technologies and expensive raw materials or inputs but this is not the only thing. In this content, it is essential to make it clear that plants and equipment constitute only one component of a total quality system. The process of technological transformation is not the only thing that we need to improve. It is also not essential that in all the cases only capital-intensive plants and equipment play a positive role because we also find cases where low-cost, indigenous technologies have been successful in establishing an edge over the expensive technologies.

Quality can be ensured by strict inspection and control: In addition to the aforesaid misperceptions, we also find masses believing that quality can be assured just by strict inspection and control. Of course, we find inspection and control essential to improve the quality of goods and services but it is also not to be forgotten that the prescription of the beginning of the 20th century has now lost its sensitivity because there are a number of stages and areas where we find possibilities of quality degeneration. It is right to mention that inspection can only lead to the segregation of good from bad places. It can't by itself improve the quality of a manufactured product. The researches, illustrations and cases reveal that in a majority of the cases, a degeneration in the quality of product is considerably influenced by the faults or lapses in areas such as design, process engineering and purchasing. We have found particular to the degeneration process at a particular stage and we find avenues in a very good number where the process of quality degeneration is activated and we fail to identify.

The aforesaid facts regarding the perception and misperception of quality make it clear that the less developed countries like ours need to remove the misconceptions and only then the process of total quality management can successfully be switched on. Quality generation and quality control are influenced by a number of factors and it is your professional excellence that you are well aware of at all the stages or points where the process of degeneration is switched on. If we delay the process of making possible a microscopic identification or detection, our efforts for quality upgradation can't get a positive response. The hospitals and healthcare organisations need to improve the quality of healthcare services and for improving the quality, it is not the only thing that you have a quality hospital or healthcare personnel. In addition, you need quality technology,, materials, drugs and medicines and favourable conditions. The process of distortion can be switched on at any stage and therefore, being a professionally sound manager, it is expected from you that you know about the sources and identify them at the very initial stage of their developments. Since we talk about quality in totality, you need care at a number of stages.

TOTAL QUALITY MANAGEMENT

When we talk about Total Quality Management (TQM), our prime focus is on tailoring of the management resources in tune with the changing level of expectations of users of the services so that an organisation succeeds in satisfying them in addition to the accomplishment of organisational goals and showing some wonders by developing a new perception of quality. This also diverts our attention on the level of satisfaction of human resources serving the organisation. The management of total quality is a managerial process that requires the excellence of world-class professionals.[3] We can't negate the fact that the world class excellence makes the ways for worldclass services. The personnel engaged in the process of making inventions and innovations shape a new perception of quality. The TQM is considered to be a way to develop a new perception. The TQM focusses our attention on managing everything directly or indirectly instrumental in improving the quality of services. Thus, we find TQM an effort based on inventions and innovations. The TQM thus draws our attention on the following facts:

- Quality is an aim having a top position.
- Sky is the limit for quality generation.
- Best in the world applies to the effective management of functional quality that focusses our attention on improving the quality of people.
- The personnel serving an organisation prove to be a problem solver rather than a problem generator.
- The technical quality is given due weightage and the uses of sophisticated technologies are promoted.
- Development of people is found in the face of evolving technologies and therefore, new course structure and training facilities are offered.
- The employee-orientation is given due weightage on the development agenda of HRD manager. This requires due weightage on the motivational plans for employees or the human resources working in different positions.
- The performance-orientation also requires an intensive care and this gravitates our attention on the education and training facilities in addition to dedication, personal and professional commitments.
- The professionals need to synchronise employee-orientation and performance orientation which would make it easier to develop personally-committed human resources, efficacious in showing some wonders.
- The professionals would continue to undertake an indepth study of the strategies adopted by the competitive organisations.
- The professionals would make possible a microscopic study of the changing behavioural profile of customers and would develop the management resources accordingly.
- The policy makers/boardrooms would require to have an attitudinal change.

- The gap between the services promised and services offered would be bridged over.
- Innovations would be an ongoing process to develop a new perception of quality much earlier than your competitors even plan to do such.
- Your offerings would continue to establish an edge over the promises.
- The organisation would then have total quality management which would help them in different ways.

TQM IN HOSPITALS

The conceptualisation of total quality management in hospitals draws our attention on the generation of quality of curative, preventive and supportive services helping patients in getting quality medical aid, attendants in diffusing tension and masses in informing, educating and sensing regarding the healthy living conditions. Since we find TQM a corporate management strategy, it is quite natural that the boardrooms or the top management is fully committed to provide visible leadership to TQM. The professional excellence in the management process makes it easier to offer total satisfaction to customers/patients or attendants. The concept of Total Quality Management focuses on the culture of an organisation to satisfy the customers in totality and in the hospitals, it is related to the satisfaction of patients. An integrated system of tools, techniques, education and training facilities makes possible a complete change in the system of generating and offering the services. An organisation practising TQM must implement changes in all the areas of management. The strategies are reviewed, plans are reformulated and the processes and procedures are changed in the face of changing needs and requirements of customers or users. In the hospitals, we find a complete change in the processes of diagnosis of treatment in the face of changing disease profile and latest developments in the medical sciences. We can't negate the fact that TQM is a way of life, it is not a magic formula. The management/hospital managers bear the responsibility of making possible qualitative improvements in almost all the areas so that the healthcare services to be offered are found of world class. The problems of leadership, product profile, offering and processing of services, physical attractions, quality of people, quality of instruments and equipment, quality of supporting infrastructural facilities, and quality of environment at working and living places are found completely changed which result into the availability of quality healthcare services.

The concept of total quality is based on totality which demands honest and sincere total efforts of managers as well as the medical and paramedical personnel. In the hospital services, the active participation of nursing staff, medical and paramedical personnel, the professional commitments of doctors and hospital managers become essential to achieve total quality. This draws our attention on the holistic total efforts. We agree with this view that the concept of TQM is substantially influenced by the management's right perception of quality. It is well-known to all of us that the perception of quality is found everchanging which makes it essential that the hospital managers are well aware of the latest developments in the medical sciences and quality efforts practised by the leading hospitals of the world are given due weightage while developing the perception. It is significant that the hospital managers keep their minds all the time active and eyes open so that the technology-driven information system makes available to them the information feedback for changing the perception of quality. The new devices of diagnosis and treatment, the new equipment and instruments used in the process of diagnosis and treatment and the new medicines with less or zero side-effects are to be conceptualised in a right fashion.

In view of the above, it is right to mention that the TQM is a management process that helps an organisation in formulating a development strategy for improving the quality of goods or services.[4] The concept of TQM makes it essential that the healthcare organisations and hospitals start believing in making things happen since this makes the ways for frequent inventions and innovations without which the TQM is just a dream.

Quality Assurance

In an age of fierce competition, we find quality generation the only way to get the desired success. We agree with this view that the promotional efforts help you in informing and sensing the customers but ultimately, it is quality that simplifies your task of excelling competition. The promises regarding quality need due attention of hospital managers. Not only the promises but they are also required to make it sure that the gap between the services-promised and the services-offered is bridged over. It is against this background that we talk about quality assurance. The first stage is making the promises and the second stage is making it sure that whatever the promises are made are processed in a decent way. Our assurances, our promises are to be based on our potentials. Unless we find ourselves competent enough to fulfil the promises, whatever the managerial efforts we make regarding promotion are only to aggravate the magnitude of problem. This makes it essential that at the outset, the hospital managers develop an innovative perception of quality and then make it sure that they have potentials to generate services of that quality and only thereafter make promises and promote with more creativity.

Quality Assurance is thus found helping hospital managers in making the ways for qualitative transformation in the product profile. If the features of your services click with the changing needs of patients and attendants, it is quite natural that you succeed in fulfilling their expectations. Unless we find an organisation innovating for quality, the conceptualisation of total quality management would remain a dream. A sweeping renewal of organisational culture, a complete change in the management philosophy and an unswerving commitment towards increasing excellence if practised in right fashion engineer a sound foundation for the TQM. Total Quality Management and value-oriented Management are found complementary to each other. Thus, an organisation interested in achieving quality in totality has no option but to explore avenues for developing a new perception of quality that makes possible innovative services throwing a positive imprint on the attitudes of customers.

In the healthcare services, we find a number of changes influenced by the recent developments in the medical sciences. The sophisticated technologies are used, the world class doctors and paramedical professionals are engaged, the professionally sound managers work and therefore, we find the development of a new concept of diagnosis and treatment showing multi-dimensional positive effects. The hospitals efficacious enough in achieving excellence offer quality assurance or promise world class healthcare services to the patients and attendants. Such an assurance to the patients and attendants shapes the levels of expectations. The professionally sound hospital managers find themselves in a position to offer the promised quality of services and therefore, the services are found in tune with the changing levels of expectations.

Assurances become dangerous and project a negative image when the users find that assurances are simply the lip-promises to delude them. This makes it essential that at the outset, an organisation develops its potentials and only then the assurances and promises take a shape.

"Promise-less and serve-more" is found to be an effective strategy to win the heart of patients and attendants.

Dimensions of TQM in Hospitals

The perception of TQM makes it clear that in the hospital services for total quality management, it is essential that a fair blending of technical quality, functional quality and infrastructural quality is made possible. While blending, the hospital managers bear the responsibility of identifying the changing needs and requirements of patients, increasing levels of expectations of patients and attendants and making it sure that the services offered by hospitals would fulfil in totality the same. This requires an indepth study of the different dimensions of TQM with the viewpoint of hospital services. In Fig. 2.1, we find different dimensions of TQM.

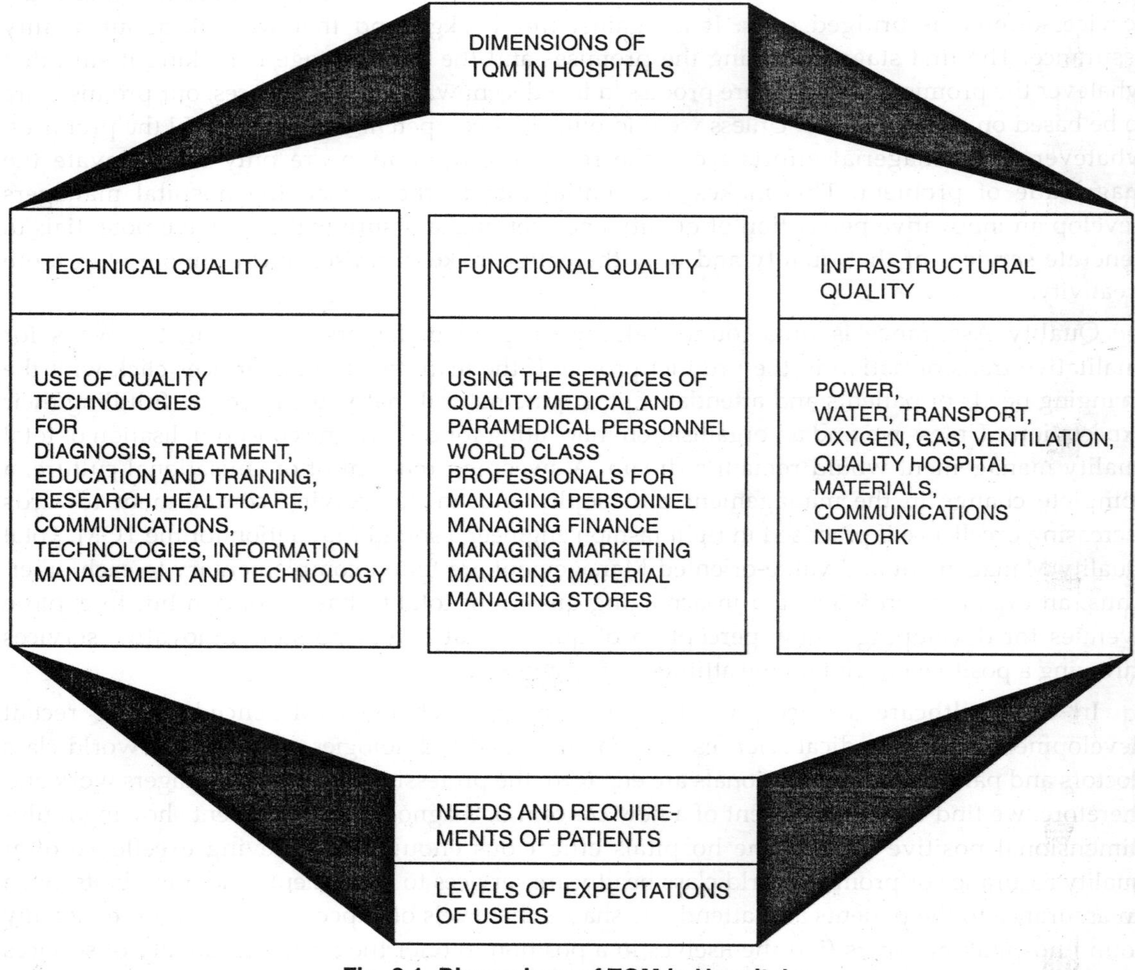

Fig. 2.1. Dimensions of TQM in Hospitals

Technical Quality: In an age of technology, it is quite natural that we assign an overriding priority to the process of technological sophistication because even in the hospitals, we find almost all the services directly or indirectly influenced by technologies. The modern devices of diagnosis, treatment and education and training facilities are substantially influenced by different types of instruments, equipment, plants and information and communication technologies. The technological sophistication has been successful in minimising the time gap, maximising the accuracy and bringing down the side effects besides countering the risk factors. With the help of sophisticated equipment and plants, the results of diagnosis are found authentic. The processes of operating different organs of body, grafting and laser devices have made possible qualitative improvements in the medicare services.

It is due mainly to the technological advances that a number of vital diseases are now diagnosed at the initial stage which simplifies the task of doctors. There have been a large number of qualitative improvements in the area of surgery. The risk factors are now considerably minimised. Almost all organs of our body are now found successfully operated and a large number of organs are also grafted. We can't negate the fact that the task of hospitals and doctors has sizeably been simplified and the credibility of the same goes to the processes of technological advances. We agree with this view that in the process of qualitative improvements in the healthcare services, the pharmaceutical industry has played an incremental role. The inventions and innovations, researches, dedication and commitments of a few of the medical scientists have resulted into the supply of a number of life saving medicines. Whatever the developments we find in the field of immunisation, which in the long-run is to minimise the pressure on hospitals, is the result of research and development programmes. There are a number of instances to testify the positive contributions of the pharmaceutical industry in activating the process of qualitative transformation in the field of medical sciences. Of late, we find a number of sophisticated plants, equipment, instruments and machines for different purposes. The modern hospitals are found establishing an edge over the traditional hospitals and this is mainly on account of the techniculture which of late is given due weightage. They assign a transcendental priority to the improvement of technical quality as and when new developments take place. It is against his background that we find them successful in minimising the duration of recovery period vis-a-vis the intensity of risk factors.

In view of the above, it is right to say that in the healthcare services, we find techniculture gaining popularity the world over. If we think about quality in totality, we have no option but to make the ways for improving the quality of technologies required for that very purpose. The scientists and the doctors (senior) may provide sufficient feedback to the hospital managers in the very context. The hospital managers, in consultation with the specialists, need to improve the quality of technologies. Besides, they are also supposed to make it sure that sophisticated technologies used by the hospitals are maintained in a right fashion. A number of government hospitals in the Indian perspective of course have installed sophisticated technologies to improve the quality of diagnosis and treatment but they have not been found delivering goods due mainly to poor maintenance. We can't negate the fact that sophisticated technologies need sophisticated environmental conditions for delivering goods and if we fail in doing such, the results would be very disappointing.

In view of the changing disease profile, the hospital managers in consultation with the specialists are required to make available to the different departments and sections of the hospitals, the new generation of technologies found instrumental in improving the quality of healthcare services. In this context, it is also important to mention that information technology has considerably been successful in educating and training the medical and paramedical personnel, improving the quality of documentation and filing, accounting, identification of errors, preparation of case histories or so. This makes it essential that hospital managers/administrators recognise the increasing instrumentality of information and communication technologies in the healthcare services.

Functional Quality: The second important constituent of total quality is the functional quality which draws our attention on improving the functional areas of managing hospitals. The first and foremost area of operation is the performance of medical and paramedical personnel and this makes it essential that world class doctors, nursing and paramedical personnel are made available to the hospitals. To be more specific, when we talk about the. hospitals promoting research and offering educational and training facilities, it is pertinent that the research scientists and the faculty are of world-class. It is not only important that hospitals are made available sophisticated technologies. It is much more impact generating that quality medical and paramedical personnel are available to operate and maintain the same. It is against this background that while improving the functional quality, we assign due weightage to the quality of hospital personnel. In this context, the hospital managers/administrators are required to make it sure that world class specialists are available in the special wards and departments. They, of course, are efficient because their credentials are very rich but in addition, they also need to be value-based, personally-committed and professionally sound in addition to the decent behavioural profile. We advocate much in favour of the supportive traits to be found in the medical and paramedical personnel since we find a number of cases where the doctors are efficient but they lack values, ethics, humanity, decency, personal and professional commitments and therefore, the quality is degenerated and the patients and attendants remain dissatisfied with them. If we talk about quality in totality, it is pertinent that we also think about these traits and make it sure that the hospital personnel are well aware of the same. If we expect from the specialists not only to serve the patients but also to show some wonders, that would hardly be possible unless they have personal and professional commitments. It is against this background that the functional quality specially related to the offering of healthcare services assumes a place of outstanding significance.

In this context, we also realise the instrumentality of other functional areas, such as the instrumentality of managers in managing finance, human resources and marketing. In a majority of the government hospitals, we find that due to financial crunch, they are not in a position to offer even the basic medical aid, then what to talk of the world class services. The stage of financial bankruptcy is to be removed and this requires world-class financial managers to improve the financial health of hospitals. We can't negate the fact that whatever the improvements we expect in the context of technological sophistication need adequate finance. The state exchequer is not in a position to cater to the increasing financial requirements of hospitals. At this juncture, we can't leave hospitals in a depleted condition because the masses have no option but to avail the services of government hospitals since they can't afford the expensive services of leading private hospitals. This makes it essential that hospitals pave avenues for the generation of financial resources from internal as well as the external sources. They need to follow a fee strategy that makes the ways for resource generation and at the same time, they also need to explore avenues for mobilising the external sources, such as charity, donations, organisation of cultural and entertainment programmes, seeking the cooperation of corporate sector or so. This requires efficient hospital managers capable of improving the financial health of hospitals.

Despite of the technological advances, we find human resources playing a commanding role in almost all the areas. If we expect the best from the new generation of technologies, we need quality medical and paramedical personnel. The hospital managers need to make it sure that their development plans related to the installation of new generation of technologies have a correlation with the education and training facilities. We, for quality in totality, need quality medical and paramedical personnel in addition to the other administrative and supervisory or even low echelon of personnel. For TQM, it is pertinent that the hospital managers perceive a new perception of quality people. This makes it essential that in addition to the knowledge related to the discipline for which they have been recruited, they are value-based, personally and professionally-committed and are well aware of the significance of human values. The managers responsible for organising the training programme and the refresher courses need to make it sure that value-inculcation process is given due weightage.

While going through the functional areas, the hospital managers also need to gravitate their attention on the marketing of healthcare services. They are required to act as a marketer and this makes it essential that they are well aware of the art of blending the different mixes of marketing optimally so that the increasing level of expectations of patients and attendants are fulfilled and the hospitals are found successful in making available the promised quality of services to the patients on time. It is against this background that we need due emphasis on marketing. When we talk about TQM, our prime focus is on availability of the healthcare services in totality so that the patients are cured, their expectations are fulfilled and the expanding disease profile is made smaller. The formulation of a sound service mix makes it essential that the hospitals are in a position to make available the improved quality of curative, preventive and supportive services. The promotion mix makes it essential that the hospital managers promote their services with the help of a sensitive tool of promotion. They advertise and publicise with the motto of informing and sensing the patients and attendants the quality of services and other required information for improving the living conditions. They need to offer innovative tools of sales promotion for promoting the hospital personnel as well as the patients and attendants. In addition, they need to pave avenues for the word-of-mouth promoters and activate personal selling. The telemarketers are also supposed to play an incremental role in the process of informing and sensing the patients. In addition to the promotional measures, the pricing strategy also occupies a place of outstanding significance, specially in the Indian perspective because the masses find it difficult to afford the expensive services. The location points for the hospital should be accessible, safer and peaceful and possibly far off from the vulnerable areas. The processing should be time honoured and decent specially with the cooperation of front line staff, such as the receptionists, enquiries, nurses, sisters or so. The hospital personnel also need to think about physical attractions where the uniform dresses used by them and their physique and make-up are found important.

Since we find multi-faceted functional responsibilities of technical and managerial importance, the hospital managers/administrators need world class excellence to make possible quality in totality. We go through the problem of total quality management and in view of the same, we have focussed on functional quality bearing an outstanding significance in the management of quality

Infrastructural Quality: Quality medicare services are well supported by a number of infrastructural facilities failing which even the sophisticated technologies, quality medical and paramedical personnel find it difficult to practise quality in totality. Availability of power, water, communications services, gas, oxygen and transportation play an incremental role without which the hospitals even of world-class would find it difficult to work in totality. It is against this background that we find availability of time honoured and adequate infrastructural facilities essential for improving the quality of healthcare services. Uninterrupted supply of power is the most significant aspect because almost all the sophisticated technologies used for diagnosis, treatment or education and training are found operated by electricity. The organisations supplying the power facilities need to realise the adverse effects of interruption in the process of distribution, the level of voltage fluctuation, the cases of leakage in distribution or transmission, the safe positioning of wire or so. The hospital managers bear the responsibility of making stand-by provisions for the emergency cases.

Water also assumes a place of outstanding significance for improving the quality of healthcare services. Almost all the wards, departments and operation theaters need supply' of water for drinking and other purposes. The municipal corporations or civic bodies responsible for the supply of water need to understand the importance and to make possible adequate supply of safe water. It is right to mention that in most of the cases, we find hospitals developing their own water supply systems and this draws our attention on a number of points. The hospital managers need to make it sure that authorities responsible for managing the water assign due weightage to an uninterrupted supply besides the quality of water. On the other hand, it is also pertinent that in some of the sensitive areas, we take an intensive care, such as the lavatories and the operation theatres. Of late, we talk about the management of aesthetics and this makes it essential that water is also made available in the surroundings or on the promises of hospitals to nurture and protect the plants and trees.

In an age of superhighway for communications, it is quite natural that information technology serve multi-faceted purposes of hospitals. For time honoured transmission of information and instructions, for avoiding the cases of delay, for countering the crisis like situations, for safety provisions, for arranging the transportation facilities, for consultation, discussions and immediate actions, it is pertinent that almost all the hospitals irrespective of nature and size are made available sophisticated communication facilities. We can't negate the fact that information technology in general is found linked to the communications network and therefore, the Telecommunications Corporation of India need to consider the requirements of hospitals on a priority basis. The hospital managers are required to make it sure that Internet services, e-mail services, fax services and the telephonic services are working round-the-clock. It is right to mention that in a majority of the government hospitals, we don't find even telephonic services in right order then what to talk of other services. To be more specific, the doctors are to be made available the Internet services so that they are in a position to know about the recent developments in the field of medical sciences. This would help enriching the contributions of hospitals in subserving the social interests. Interruption in the supply of communication services may result into big losses found of irreparable nature which the hospital managers need to remember.

In the infrastructural quality, the transportation facilities play an important role. The prime focus is found here on the provisions for ambulance by the hospitals or other agencies. The hospital managers need to make it sure that the round-the-clock ambulance facilities are available and the emergency cases reach to the hospitals on time. In a number of government hospitals, we find inadequacy of ambulance which in addition to inconveniences to the patients and attendants also result into causalities, specially in the emergency cases. The enquiry or the reception centres or the emergency services where the ambulances are available should be managed by efficient front-line-personnel. The parking places for the ambulances should be barrier-free. To increase the supply position, the hospital managers need to seek the cooperation of agencies and organisations offering the services of ambulance even free of charge. The main thing is to increase the number because the government hospitals in particular find it difficult to cater to the increasing requirements.

Oxygen is found playing a significant role in a number of cases to save the life of patients. To be more specific, in the emergency case and more particularly in the operation theatres and ICUs, the availability of oxygen is found essential. The hospital managers need to make it sure that at all the emergency points, the supply of oxygen is optimal to the requirements. It is amazing that in a majority of the government hospitals, we find inadequacy of oxygen creating difficulties to the doctors and irreparable losses to the patients and attendants.

Of late, we find use of gas in place of anaesthesia. The availability of gas in the operation theatres is essential. In a majority of the government hospitals we find inadequacy of gas and the hospital managers need to make it sure that whatever the devices are preferred by the specialists are made available at the required points.

The aforesaid facts make it clear that TQM is related to almost all the aspects of hospitals without which the quality in totality is not possible. There are a number of considerations to help hospital managers in estimating the infrastructural requirements of a particular hospital. In the face of the character of a particular catchment area, nature and types of hospital, size of hospital, the hospital managers find it easier to take a decision regarding technical quality, functional quality and the infrastructural quality. The level of expectations of patients and attendants and the changing needs and requirements of patients in the face of changing disease profile would help hospital managers in practising TQM in a right fashion.

The perception of TQM focusses our attention on the level of satisfaction and the hospital managers are required to be sure that the patients and attendants using the services of hospitals are satisfied. It is against this background that they also need to have an indepth study of the needs and requirements of patients and the level of expectation because we find both of them everchanging. With the expansion of Internet services, we find the expectations of patients and attendants very high since they go through the recent developments in the field of medical sciences taking place the world over and expect that hospitals and their doctors are competent enough to make available to them the same quality of services. The information superhighway has thus played an important role in increasing the level of expectations of users and the hospitals may also be efficacious in improving their potentials, if they like so.

TQM and Hospital Personnel

There is no doubt in it that new generation of sophisticated technologies has been found playing a significant role in improving the quality of health care services but at the same time, it is also right to say that ultimately, it is the instrumentality of hospital personnel that occupies a place of outstanding significance. The hospital managers/administrators need to realise that failing the cooperation and participation of hospital personnel, all of their efforts are to be turned into a fiasco. This makes it essential that they assign due weightage to their interests. It is ascertained that they are working at a safe place where the working conditions are friendly and conducive. This draws their attention on the quality of working conditions. In addition, they also bear the responsibility of making it sure that the hospital personnel have been leading a quality life. This gravitates their attention on the quality of personal life of the hospital personnel. We can't negate the fact that both of the conditions influence the potentials of hospital personnel. If they face the problem of infrastructural constraints and even if they are efficient, the quality of healthcare services can't be improved. If they face the problem of unsafe and unhygienic working conditions, their life would be in danger. This makes it essential that the hospital managers/administrators make available to them a safe and conducive environment at the work place. In addition to the professional requirements, they are also made available amenities and facilities to counter monotony and fatigue. This would substantially be helpful in increasing the level of their efficiency. Contrary to it, if they find everything disturbing at the work place, the task of evincing their personal interests would be much more difficult. It is right to mention that in a majority of the government hospitals, we find inadequacy of the supporting infrastructural facilities to fulfil the professional commitments then what to talk of the personal requirements at the workplace. The doctors and paramedical personnel need a sound physical environment inside the four walls of hospitals.

Another important aspect in the very context is related to the psychological environment. This makes it essential that the hospital managers/administrators make it sure that the hospital personnel find themselves comfortable and safe even at the places where they live. This draws our attention on the living conditions of the hospital personnel. The housing or accommodation facilities for them, the water, power, communications facilities in their houses, the nature of population living close to their houses, the recreation and entertainment facilities adjacent to their quarters and the education and medicare facilities for their children are some of the important aspects involving hospital personnel and their family members personally. The hospital managers need to realise the instrumentality of personal involvement of a family in increasing the level of efficiency of the hospital personnel. We talk much about professional commitments but do nothing for personnel orientation. In a true sense, we find performance orientation and personnel orientation correlated. Professional commitments and personal commitments are the result of a fair blending of the two. The hospital managers not realising the significance of both the environmental conditions would hardly be successful in increasing the level of efficiency of the hospital personnel. For TQM, it is essential that we find personal involvement of the hospital personnel. This requires due emphasis on both the environmental conditions—physical as well as the psychological. The hospital managers/healthcare managers bear the responsibility of making available at the work place conducive working conditions helpful in the generation of level of efficiency, providing to them safety and security, peace and comforts which would require a sound management of the different constituents of physical environment. The quality of life at the workplace where the medical and paramedical personnel and other employees work would influence the quality of services generated by them. In Fig. 2.2, we find focus on physical and psychological environmental conditions influencing the quality of services of hospitals.

While improving the quality of physical environment, the hospital managers need to make it sure that adequate light, temperature and ventilation facilities are available. The arrangements for sitting and relaxing for the doctors, the peace around the hospitals, the hygienic conditions and the cohesive departmental relationship are found friendly to the professional requirements. This would provide them an opportunity to work efficiently.

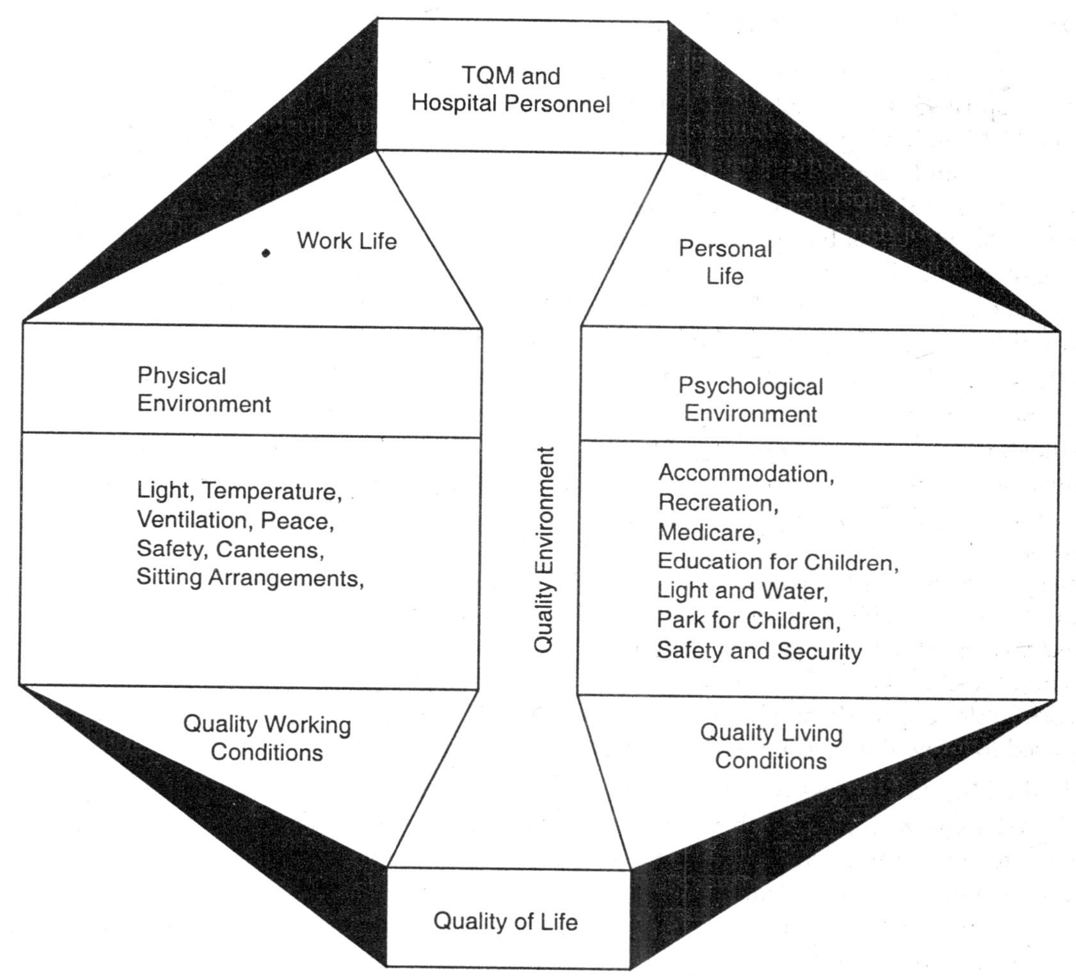

Fig. 2.2. Quality of Life of Hospital Personnel

In addition, the hospital managers also need to focus their attention on the quality of the living conditions of the medical and paramedical personnel. This draws our attention on the psychological environment. The accommodation facilities inside the compound, educational facilities for the children of hospital personnel, medicare facilities, safety and security arrangements and parks for hospital personnel are some of the important constituents of the psychological environment playing a very significant role in improving the quality of life of the hospital personnel.

The hospital managers are supposed to synchronise both the environmental conditions optimally so that we find hospital personnel completely involved in the process of offering the world class healthcare services. The formation of a positive attitude makes it essential that people serving the organisation find attraction in their job which makes the way for performance-orientation and in the due course, they prove to be super performers. In a true sense, the hospitals of today need high performers because they have been found experiencing the intensity of work load at its peak.

Team and TQM in Hospitals

We can't negate the fact that the healthcare services are of quality when we find team work and team spirit. Quality in totality can't be possible with the involvement and participation of an individual albeit having world class excellence. The physicians for writing a prescription require the assistance and cooperation of a big team helping him in diagnosing the disease. The surgeons can't be successful in operating on a patient if he/she fails in getting the cooperation of a full team. It is against this background that the excellence of a hospital manager is coiled in the essence of getting the full support of a team constituted in consultation with the specialists. If we talk about quality in totality in the healthcare services, we have to think regarding the constitution of an efficient, dedicated team. The team spirit and team culture simplify the task of doctors attending on the patients. Like this, an efficient team simplifies the task of hospital managers.

In the hospitals, we find the concept of total quality to be practised as a mission. As and when we talk about a mission, the enormous cooperation of a team becomes essential. It is togetherness or unity of our efforts that transforms impossible into possible, difficult into easy. Mutual trust, mutual respect, mutual cooperation become essential constituents of team spirit. The spirit of cooperation helps a team in fulfilling the mission. Of course, the specialists better know about the efficient persons, dedicated persons, value-based persons, professionally and personally-committed persons, working at different levels of a hospital. It is also right that all persons can't be suitable for all the teams. This is due to the psychological conditions or temperament of an individual feeling pleasure in working under the leadership of one person but getting it difficult to work under the leadership of another. The hospital managers while constituting a team are supposed to know the personal feelings of different categories of personnel.

In the hospital services, we find instrumentality of cross-functional teams from the different functional areas working together. For diagnosing, we find involvement of different teams, of course, the areas may be different but the ultimate motto is to find out the reason of a particular disease. A number of small teams are found involved in the process with the motto of helping a physician or a surgeon to diagnose. It is quite natural that here, self-interest is subdued. Self-activated towards the total satisfaction of patients and attendants draws our attention on the involvement of all in a particular team, well-integrated, intelligently knitted and gently performing the functional responsibilities assigned to them. We agree with this view that to be more specific in the healthcare services, working together really brings the positive results.

There is no doubt in it that value-engineering is found significant to almost all the organisations but to be more specific in hospitals we find it assuming a place of outstanding significance. The hospital managers need to perceive different terminologies in a right fashion such as Mission, Vision, Values and Total Quality.

The Mission of a hospital is to make available to the patients quality healthcare services with a dismal scope for side effects of diagnostic or other devices.

The Vision makes it clear that in the eyes of patients and attendants, the hospital in which they are getting the medical services are the best. This necessitates offering of the world class services.

The Value orientation makes it clear that the doctors and the different members of the team are dedicated, personally and professionally-committed, sincere and honest. All of them do their best to treat the patients with the motto of curing—not with the motto of exploiting and earning.

The Total Quality makes it clear that the available potentials in a hospital would optimally be used to make available to the users the required services. Since it is quality in totality, the services offered would of course, be of world class bearing the instrumentality of satisfying the patients and attendants.

The hospital personnel in general and the hospital managers in particular need to perceive the aforesaid terminologies. In the healthcare organisations, we find managers playing a commanding role and therefore, it is pertinent that he/she is supported by a number of small teams bearing some of the essential properties or attributes as shown in Fig. 2.3.

In Fig. 2.3, we find the total quality system that makes it clear that the hospital managers get the cooperation of a number of teams known as supporting team of managers bearing the traits like high communication ability, global vision, humility, commitment, ability to earn trust, mental capacity to perceive values, efficient in collaboration or extending cooperation or seeking or soliciting cooperation, assigning an overriding priority to the interest of a team, compassion for others, willingness to perform the role of superiors, maturity, emotional stability, self-control, self-discipline, integrity, ethical and human values and more so, humanity while acting in the capacity of a manager. It is right to mention that in the hospital services, we find more scope for human, humane and humanity. The doctors without human values can't be successful in fulfilling the mission of hospitals. The attributes thus makes it essential that the team constituted for a particular job includes quality people. The term "quality" focusses our attention on all the properties.

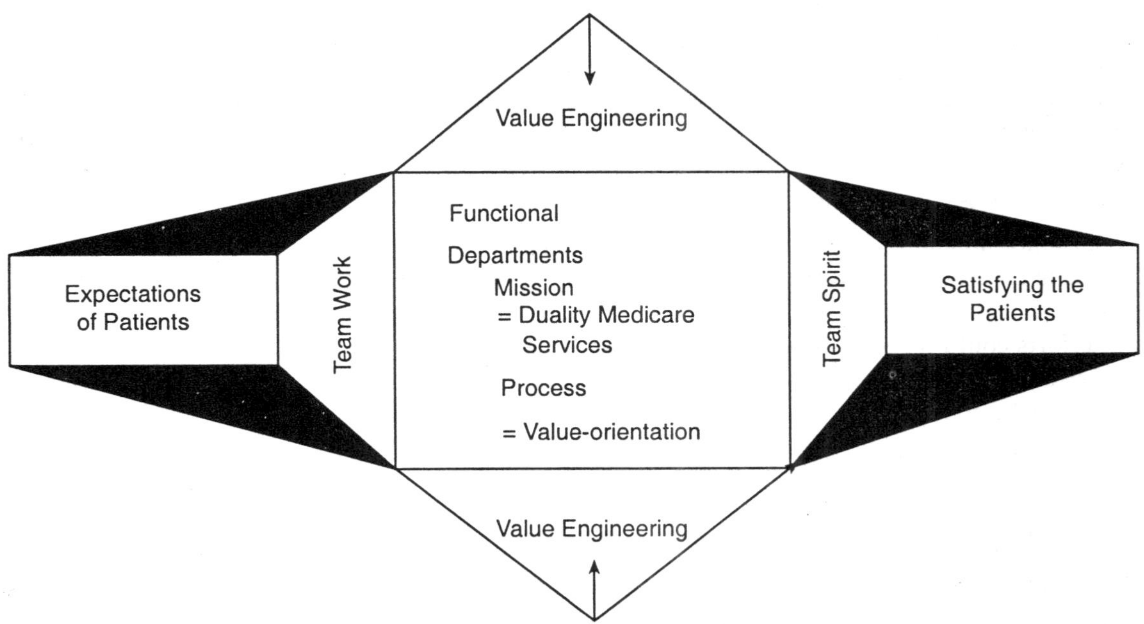

Fig 2.3. Total Quality System

Principles of Building a Team in Hospitals

We are well aware of the fact that the services offered by a hospital are based on team work. This makes it essential that the hospital managers know the art of formulating a team that succeeds in achieving the goals. There are some of the essentials to be given due care in the process.

1. *Defining the Roles:* The first task before you is to define a policy which may be implicit or explicit. The defining of roles would be your important task in the very context. It is essential that each member of a team knows about his/her role which requires to define the role in a receptible fashion. This simplifies the task of a member. At the outset, you need to review with each staff member his/her primary role; then compile, refine or update a job description for each individual. It is to be ascertained that you have established an objective for your group work.

2. *Strong Interest in Objectives and Goals::* The second aspect while building a team is to make it sure that your team is committed to profession. If you feel that personnel acting as members of your team are not committed, you need to discuss with them the reason for that. May be that a member is not in a position to perceive the goal in a right fashion; may be that he/she is deviated; may be that he/she is apathetic. Make it sure that you try your best to motivate them to the defined goals. If you find a case like this that despite your efforts they have not improved their performance, please go through the comments helping you in knowing about their contributions in past and the process of making disproportionate contributions if continues for a long time, you need to place him elsewhere in the organisation or you may even terminate him.

3. *Open Communications System:* Being a manager, you need to realise the instrumentality of open communications. The process of open communications with all members of your staff would help you in many ways. It is in this context that you need to hold a regular staff-meeting in which you should discuss the objectives of department, recent developments and the organisational information. A round table discussion having the participation of all members and open communications with each member would let you know the day-to-day developments. You need to discuss with them work dynamics. One-to-one "Coffee Conference," once in a week would let you know not only the developments but also the constraints and the difficulties they feel in the process of achieving the goals.

4. *Ability to Bounce Back:* This quality is related to your ability to "Bounce Back" where we find focus on assessing the situations and finding out the reasons for a negative result. It is not essential that all the time you get success. We also find cases where you could not be successful or your efforts could receive a lukewarm response. This makes it essential that specially during the adverse situations, you call a staff meeting in which some of the important questions would be required to be answered.

- What went wrong with you?
- How could it have been avoided?
- What have you learned from this?
- What would be your efforts in the same situations coming again?

By doing this, you provide to each and every one an opportunity to improve. If they realise, the corrective measure can be taken. If not you would have to think in a bit different way.

5. *A Diversity of Talent and Variety of Perspectives:* While building a team, it is essential that you try your best to use the potentials of your staff. May be that some of your staff has a long experience and you may encourage him to share their ideas and perspectives. We find a number of managers making the mistake of trying to force "group think" which often turns into "group

stink." Ask people for their opinion and encourage them to share their opinions and to interact in a positive way with an optimistic approach.

Of course, the aforesaid five principles of team orientation are found important but in addition, we also find other considerations requiring your due attention. "Common values", "clarity of purpose" and growth and development are found important considerations while building a team. In Fig. 2.4, we find a complete picture of the essential considerations. An ideal team should have common values which would be based on a "sense of allegiance." A clear vision is found essential. Above all, you are supposed to act a mentor.[5] You are also required to make possible the growth and development of your staff.

You are not supposed to forget that each staff person is an expert at his/her particular job and a confident leader is not afraid of or threatened by strong individual contribution. The members of your team should develop a positive attitude that you really trust them and you will find trust in a two-way street. If you succeed in exhibiting your professional excellence, they would place their trust in you as a leader. Thus, the team spirit and a team culture would be existent. Unless you trust on your staff, it is difficult for them to be sure that you are professionally sound to achieve the organisational goals. If we find a team managed in a right fashion; if we find a team managed professionally; if we find a team not promoting breach of trust; a manager is to get success. Since you need to show some wonders, you have to be

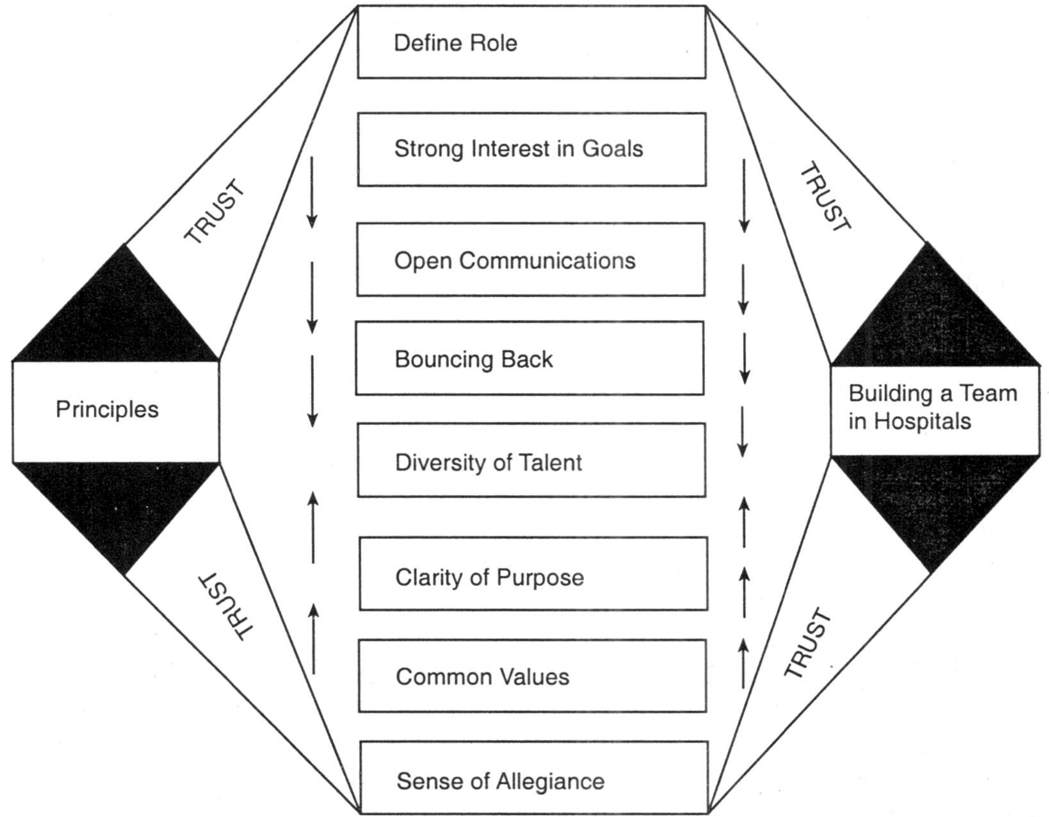

Fig. 2.4. Principles of Building a Team

optimistic. You commit mistakes, it is but natural. You repeat, it is blunder. With this notion, you need to prove yourself professionally sound and the TQM thereafter, would not remain a dream.

Justifications for TQM in Hospitals

Each and everyday we find new developments in the field of medical sciences and expect the process to continue uninterrupted even in future. In an age of globalization where process of technological sophistication has gained a rapid momentum, it is quite natural that we find its impact even on the hospital and healthcare services. The emergence of techniculture has paved avenues for defining and redefining quality and the hospitals enriching their potentials are in demand not only in the domestic markets but even in the global markets. What to talk of the developing countries when we find people coming to India for their treatment even from the developed countries because our medical services are of world class and affordable albeit to the common people. The conceptualisation of TQM is found judicious in the Indian perspective. The following facts justify application.

1. For promoting techno-driven services: The emergence of techniculture has immensely affected the service quality in the Indian hospitals and healthcare centres. In a true sense, we find technology dominating the process of service delivery. Since we find a majority of the hospitals and healthcare centres facing the problem of poor quality, it is imperative that new generations of technology is incorporated to get the desired results. The application of TQM would require the use of appropriate technologies for diagnosis and treatment of diseases. To make the healthcare and medicare services much more competitive, we need to develop cheaper technologies found as effective as the expensive ones. Apart from the secondary and tertiary care, there is need and scope to introduce the use of public health related technologies and public health related practices at all levels of healthcare. Besides, we also need to promote the appropriate use of IT for an enhanced role in healthcare governance. Since we have a strong fibre backbone and indigenous satellite communication technology with trained human resources in this regard, the avenue for generalising the benefits of new generation of technology to primary, secondary and tertiary healthcare services would be tapped with the help of TQM.

2. For making cost-effective services: In the Indian perspective, the hospitals bear the social responsibility of making the services cost-effective because a large number of population face the problem of affordability. Besides, we also need to make the services costwise competitive which would be possible with the help of TQM. While promoting technology, it is not only essential that we concentrate on expensive technologies bur explore avenues for developing new generation of low-cost technologies such as anesthesia machine, surgical equipment and lighting, sterilization equipment, defibrillator, ventilator, electrocardiogram, blood pleasure monitoring equipment, pulse oxymeter, etc. and make use of the same even in the small hospitals and health care centres. This would minimise the cost of services vis-à-vis the fees structure to be charged at domestic or global levels. The modern hospitals need sophisticated technologies so that correct and quick diagnosis improve the service quality and minimise the service cost.

3. For making available to the hospitals quality people: For practising TQM, it is also significant that we have quality manpower potentially sound for diversifying the use of technologies. A number of medical and paramedical personnel belonging to different levels of management play an incremental role in improving the quality of services. The hospital professionals need to ensure training and development of human resources related different areas. While imparting training facilities, we need to make use of techno-driven devices. The conceptualisation of TQM would make it possible. For becoming a quality leader, if we need new generation of technology, we also realise the outstanding significance of world class medical and paramedical personnel. With the conceptualisation of TQM, the development of human resources is found in the face of emerging trends which make the resources productive both in the domestic and global perspectives.

4. For the constitution of a right team: The hospital and healthcare services are the results of involvement of a complete team and the processes of TQM are found based on team work and team spirit. It would be difficult for physicians or surgeons to perform if they do not get the cooperation of channels providing to them the investigation reports. The medical personnel cannot perform, if they do not get cooperation of paramedical personnel. There are a number of investigating centres administered and managed with the help and cooperation of a number of specialists and experts. While constituting a team, the hospital professionals need to take into account the thematical competence as well as the attitudinal similarities so that the possibilities of confrontation or non-cooperation are minimised. They need to remember that team spirit and team culture cannot be possible if we find something wrong in the constitution of a team. The hospital professionals need to consider the needs and requirements and preferences of doctors while constituting a team.

5. For promoting healthcare education: We find development an ongoing process. The emergence of techniculture, changes in the disease profile and levels of expectations of users make it essential that the hospitals and healthcare organisations are made available quality medical and paramedical personnel. The hospitals bear the responsibility of making available to the society curative as well as the preventive services. This draws our attention on creating mass awareness related to the lifestyles, food and drinking culture, harmful effects of malnutrition, food-borne, water-borne, viral and communicable diseases. Particularly in the Indian perspective, where we find masses insensitive to the health problems, the hospital professionals bear the responsibility of making the society much more conscious to the healthy living conditions. The vaccination and immunization culture need due attention of hospital professionals. The doctors also need to play an important role in the sensitisation process for which the media would be required to extend the best possible cooperation for strengthening the publicity measures. The messages and themes for the rural people and women need a distinct approach. The preventive measures would minimise the number of patients and would also minimise the pressure on hospitals. The hospital managers with the help of information system may also be successful in identifying the star performers, performers and non-performers. The TQM makes it essential that the motivational plans must be based on their performance. The hotel professionals are supposed to play a decisive role in sensitising the rural masses found insensitive to the health problems. The TQM makes a strong advocacy in favour of effective communication which in the long run would be successful in minimising the pressure on hospitals. Creativity in promotional measures would simplify the task of professionals.

6. For identifying hospital personnel to motivate them: It is judicious that hospital professionals identify star performers for providing to them special incentives. If we find medical and paramedical personnel or other staff significantly contributing to the process of improving service quality, they should be rewarded suitably. Contrary to it, the personnel with the minimum level of efficiency should be made available proper training facilities. The hospital managers by practising TQM find it convenient to differentiate the efficients and inefficients. This paves avenues for transforming the inefficients into efficients.

7. ***For creating service uniqueness:*** The conceptualisation of TQM is found judicious with the view point of adding additional attractions to the services so that the services are found unique. With the help of a sound techno-driven Health Information System, the professionals get information regarding the diagnosis and treatment processes adopted by the leading hospitals of the globe. This helps them in improving the level of efficiency.

The aforesaid facts make it clear that conceptualisation of TQM may bring multi-dimensional qualitative and quantitative improvements in the hospital and healthcare services.

QUALITY CIRCLE

Quality Circle is found to be a unique tool for making available to the customers users the goods or services of world class. It is considered to be a key to quality products. We cannot deny that quality is never an accident but a result of consistent and intelligent efforts. After the World War II, the Japanese integrated the American Behavioural Sciences and Statistical Theories and techniques in the development of Quality Circles (QCs). Right from 1945 till the present, they have conceptualized quality circles for improving the quality of achieving quality in totality in almost all the sectors or areas which has considerably helped them in defining and redefining quality. Ishikawa (1963) recommended that foremen should establish book reading articles within their group works to promote quality concept. Gradually, the suggestions of Ishikawa has been conceptualised the world over. The work-based groups moved from theoretical study to problem-solving which emerged into Quality Circles. This move focussed on group decentralization and participative decision making. Education and training, the quality concepts and techniques were extended to include every level of the organisation from the top management to shop floor.

A Quality Control Audit (QCA) was introduced and computers were used for quality control activities.[6] Thus, we find the emergence of the concept of quality circle which is found based on group culture. The Japanese feel about the quality circles that the real problem in an organisation remains often unknown and therefore, the process of involving all categories of employees in the process of working and decision-making would make it easier to identify the real problems and to adopt the suitable corrective measures.

The QCs are found aimed at :

- Making possible self and mutual development.
- Increasing quality and cost awareness.
- Utilising the creativity of the workforce.
- Improving the morale of the workers.
- Developing managerial ability and leadership.
- Building team spirit through participative decision making.
- Implementing and managing the accepted ideas.
- Improving task resulting into a better product and process at work.
- Improving productivity.

We can't negate the fact that the success of QCs depend upon effective communications. The mutual trust between the management and workers is a must without which an organisation can't survive then what to talk of its development and prosperity. The workers/ employees/human resources/people must be convinced that management is not only interested in getting their valuable suggestions, indeed they are anxiously waiting for the same. Such an attitude of management would develop a feeling of elevated position and due weightage. It is right to mention that the Japanese see their people as the most valuable resources. This is evident in the saying, "Making Every Man Manager." The development of potentials of employees is found possible by imparting to them the training facilities. Dr. Ishikawa believed that training should be a part of an overall development programme of an organisation. Since the development processes keep on moving, it is pertinent that an organisation continues the process of enriching the potentials of their employees. We find communications and human relations essential constituents of the training programme.

The training of participative management and knowledge regarding its techniques are made available to the employees with the help of Pareto Charts, Ishikawa diagram, histogram, scatter diagram, check-sheet and control charts. An adequate time is given for training to ensure widespread acceptance and systematic exposure.

QCs are found process-oriented and the different processes deal with the system of production indirectly due to their predominantly preoccupation with production analysis and the collective department of production improvement plans. To implement QCs, an organisation is required to make the necessary preparations. The following steps are found important in the very context:

- A dialogue between the management and people closest to the means of production is found useful. The neutrally knowledgeable third party consultant may perform this responsibility.
- The current organisational climate requires an intensive audit.
- The QC leaders and members need proper education and training and for this, the collection of resources is essential.
- The objectives-setting process requires involving supervisors and middle managers.
- In all the phases of implementation, the involvement of unions is found impact generating. The unions need to feel that the QCs don't infringe upon the collective bargaining process.
- After the formation of QCs, the education and training programmes need to be intensified at all the levels of an organisation. All the employees are to be given an opportunity to assume leadership.
- After processing, the impact is to be measured and the objectives are to be reviewed and analysed, if necessary also revised.
- The QCs are found effective when we allow to implement suggestions.
- The problem regarding incentives need to be resolved by measuring the value of contributions.
- High degree of trust and cooperation, open communications between workers and managers is found essential.

We can't negate the fact that the formation of QCs would be effective even in the healthcare organisations. Of course, the approaches would be a bit different while practising the implementation programme since we find hospitals a no-profit-making organisation, and more so, a service generating organisation based on the holistic concept of management. We are well aware of the fact that hospitals need the cooperation of a number of employees of different cadres and positions for the successful offering of the diagnostic, curative, preventive and supportive services. In a true sense, we find it a team work and this is the main reason for recognising the instrumentality of QCs in the hospitals. The sensitivity rate of management of people for hospitals is found of high degree because right from the development of knowledge, by promoting the education and training programmes to the stage of making them a successful practitioners, we find importance of people participation, group participation and team participation which result into the offering of world class medicare services.

Practising QCs in Hospitals

Quality in totality is our aim. Offering the world services is our motto. Justifying our existence in the society is our mission. Frequent innovation in the process of development is our work culture. The hospitals need to conceptualise the same as and when they think of practicing QCs. We are well aware of the fact that the concept of QCs is based on the concept of

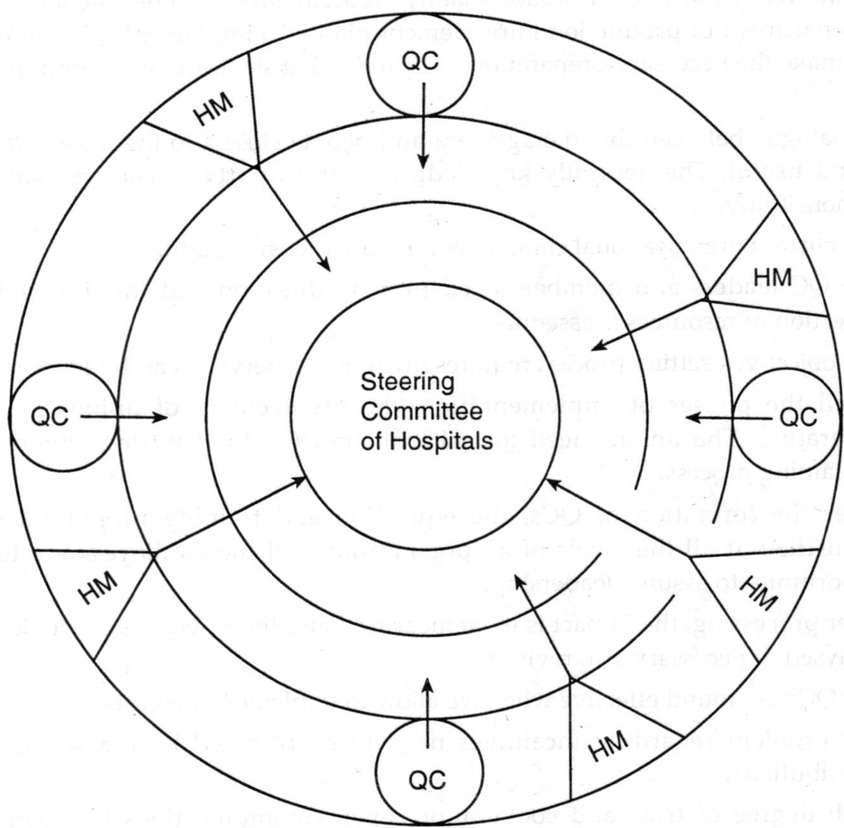

Fig. 2.5. Quality Circles

performance orientation with the help of people orientation. It is in this context that we find development of knowledge assuming a place of outstanding significance in the formation of QCs. Effective communications, participation of all in the management, offering of incentives in the face of contributions, assigning due weightage to the suggestions of even low cadre of employees and promoting research as an ongoing process are some of the important facets of QCs which improve the quality of services offered by hospitals. The QCs would benefit hospitals in many ways. The Fig. 2.5 shows Quality Circles and on the basis of this figure, we can realise the instrumentality of QCs in the healthcare organisations.

In Fig. 2.5, we find Quality Circles considering steering committee in an important or a central position. When we say about the steering committee, our focus is on the formation of a leading committee, assigning to the team and groups certain responsibilities, making the ways for interactions or communications, pointing out the suggestions and exploring avenues for qualitative improvements in the entire process. When we talk about the concept of quality in totality, specially in hospitals, it becomes important that we solicit the cooperation of different teams and groups. A doctor, even of world class, a surgeon albeit acquiring world class excellence can't do anything unless a full team of diagnostic and supporting groups extend to him constructive cooperation. They are considered to be sound enough to reach to a conclusion and making the ways for a physician to write a prescription and surgeon to proceed on operation. It is against this background that we find formation of a Quality Circle essential to make possible quality in totality. Education and training programmes are required to be innovated with the evolving technologies and developing concepts or principles.

The different groups and committees and the leading and supporting teams would play an incremental role in policymaking decisions by the hospitals. Since the members of the different committees and teams are supposed to be expert in their areas of specialisation, they are supposed to know the best about the diagnosis and treatment facilities and the feedback received from them would help hospital managers in many ways. In a true sense, the hospital managers are to coordinate everything and therefore, whatever the feedback they get from different teams would make the ways for quality in totality. It is presumed that the hospitals have a well-developed and a technology-driven information system and therefore, they would be in a position to make possible frequency in the use of sophisticated technologies for the diagnosis and treatment. The quality circles would help hospital managers in devising new or innovative peripheral services and thus would be successful in adding attractions to the mix of services offered by the hospitals. The information related to recent developments in the field of medical sciences would be made available to the hospital managers and the supporting source would be the teams of different specialists meant for that purpose who are supposed to be aware of the latest developments, specially with the support of the management information system preferably through Internet operations, or information superhighway.

In view of the above, it is right to say that the formation of quality circles would make possible quality in totality. The hospitals would find the services in tune with the changing requirements of patients. The potentials of hospitals would be enriched and the qualitative transformation would be an ongoing process. The increasing level of expectations of the patients and attendants would be fulfilled and the hospitals would justify their existence in the society. Thus, it is right to opine that development of quality circles is essential to achieve quality in totality.

Quality in Totality in Indian Hospitals

We cannot deny that that healthcare sector in India is marching forward by leaps and bounds. Corporatisation has also influenced the hospital sector and it is against this background that we find big corporate players investing in the hospital sector. Of late, we find five-star hospitals like Escorts and Max Healthcare[8] making available to the users world class healthcare services found very expensive and not affordable to the common people. While on the other hand, we also find state hospitals like AIIMS, Ram Manohar Lohia, of course, providing quality services with affordability as an important consideration. The most important thing that we find with the state hospitals is positive attitude of masses because they witness that world class doctors are working there. Another important thing that we find with the state hospitals is their network even in the rural areas of the country. The private sector has not entered the rural areas as yet and this happens to be an important feature which keeps the state managed hospitals at the top level.

In a country like India where we find a majority of our population insensitive to the health problem, it is imperative that both the public and private hospitals play a meaningful role by sensitising the masses. Quality remains an important consideration in the healthcare services and therefore we make a strong advocacy in favour of conceptualisation of Total Quality Management. Poverty and insensitivity are the two important barriers depriving the Indian masses of getting the quality healthcare services. The mounting demographic pressure makes it essential that the Hospital Services Consultancy Corporation (HSCC) assigns due weightage to the qualitative-cum-quantitative transformation so that a large number of our population get the quality healthcare services.

The strategic decisions focus our attention on some of the key measures such as encouraging the private sector to go to the rural areas, increasing government grants to the state managed hospitals, exploring avenues for charities and donations and the most important of all is taking support of PPP mode. The corporate sector may go to the rural areas if they are offered a number of incentives such as tax holiday, free land, supporting infrastructural facilities, etc. The HSCC has two important functional responsibilities, first expanding healthcare services to the rural areas so that rural population are benefited and second, improving the quality of services by intensifying the uses of low cost technologies of new generation. An important device to reach the far-off population is telemedicine.

Of late, we find a number of low-cost technologies of course, indigenous but found very effective. The development and utilization of appropriate technologies for diagnosis and treatment of diseases is essential. During the yesteryears, we have witnessed rapid developments in the health related technology.

The sophisticated technology of the new generation has considerably served the affluent sections of the society. But its impact on the public health has been found minimal. This makes it essential that we develop cheaper technologies that are as effective as the expensive technologies. The national policy makers need to find technological solutions for making crucial equipments affordable. The public health related technologies are required to be used at all levels of healthcare. The experience of Jan Swasthya Sahyog (JSS)[9] may be useful for the rural population who fail in getting even the basic healthcare facilities. This would help to prevent outbreaks of water-borne, food-borne diseases, maternal mortality related to unsafe deliveries and postpartum infections, anemia, prevent acquisition of malaria and deaths due to childhood pneumonias, etc.

For practising quality in totality in the hospital and healthcare services, we also need to think over the appropriate use of IT. In this context, it is pertinent that we set up a National Grid to be shared by healthcare providers, trainers, beneficiaries and the civil society. Since we have already have the advantage of a strong fibre backbone and indigenous satellite communication technology with trained human resources, it is easier for us to diversify the uses of technology in the larger interests of society.

The most important consideration for initiating and activating the process of qualitative and quantitative transformation is to enrich the Health Management Information System. A computerised web-enabled data capturing and analytical systems are to be established to provide valid and reliable data and reports for use at all levels. This would not only facilitate proper ME of different programmes under implementation but would also help in various aspects of service delivery. The HMIS would also integrate the various vertical systems having their own reporting machinery into an integrated umbrella of holistic ME to cater to the needs of Sarva Swasthya Abhiyan.

The telemedicine could help to bring specialized healthcare to the remotest parts of the country through which the advantages of tele-diagnosis especially in the areas of cardiology, pathology, dermatology and radiology besides continuing medical education (ME) are to be diversified. We find the process of immense use for diagnostic and consultive purposes for patients getting treatment from the secondary level healthcare facilities. The network established by the Indian Space Research Organisation has been found benefiting the rural segments but in a very limited areas of the country. It is significant that superspeciality hospitals and mobile telemedicine vans and rural and remote hospitals across the country through its geostationary satellite benefit not only the district hospitals and government medical colleges but also move to the remotest parts of the country where even basic healthcare services are not available.

For initiating and activating the process of qualitative transformation, we need to speed up e-Health initiatives. It is in this contest that we talk about e-enabled HMIS to ensure timely flow of data and collation at various levels.

It is pertinent that we focus on training, education and capacity building for e-Health. An optimal utilization of e-Health needs due attention on Geographical Information System (GIS), Resources Mapping of various health facilities (Allopathic and AYUSH), Laboratories, Training Centres, Health Manpower and other inputs.[10] The activities like disease surveillance, tele-consultations, health helpline, district hospital referral net and e-enabled mobile medical units would inject new life and strength to the process of qualitative transformation. The ISRO, DIT, NEC, NGOs and State Governments need to extend their best support and cooperation to telemedicine programmes.

Development of a small affluent island around the vast sea of backwardness cannot serve our purpose. In a true sense, we need to develop a healthcare system that serves and subserves the interests of all the sections and regions of all the income groups. The curative as well as the preventive measures need due attention. The benefits of new generation of information technology need to be diversified and channelised to the poor people who, even today are deprived of the primary education and healthcare services. If we find general masses insensitive to the health problems, it is due mainly to the fact that they are illiterate and lack sensitivity. They are unaware of water-prone, food-prone and communicable diseases. They lack nutritional awareness and are insensitive to the immunization culture. One the one hand, they are illiterate and on the other hand, they are poor. This throws them in the reverse gear and traps them in the disease circle. The teleconferencing would considerably benefit rural India.

In the face of emerging trends, it is essential that we throw light on all the three levels such as governmental measures through state hospitals and healthcare centres, private measures with the help and cooperation of leading private hospitals as a part of their corporate social responsibility and PPP mode in which public and private players would make joint efforts to improve the quality of healthcare services. We are well aware of the significant developments in the field of medical sciences. We are also aware of the latest development in the field of information and communication technology. The world class excellence of out medical and paramedical personnel are well known to the globe. The large players in the private sector have a profitable opportunity to capitalise on. They may promote their world class services in a different way in which the promotional measures would focus on "India-A Global Healthcare Brand" vis-a-vis "India-A Tourist Destination. They have an edge over the global players both in terms of quality and cost. The only thing they need is creative promotional measures for sensitising the potential customers in different parts of the world. By tapping this segment, the private players would be in a position to generate surpluses which may be used for the welfare of the rural segment. In addition, the government also needs an attitudinal change. The state hospitals need not to continue with the problem of financial crunch. Not only the allocation but in addition, managerial proficiency of hospitals and healthcare centres also need priority attention to regulate misuse and promote productive use.

An important dimension necessitating priority attention of national policy makers is a structural transformation in the system of ME. It is not only significant that our medical and paramedical personnel have thematical competence. It is equally pertinent that they have behavioural decency, sense of personal and professional commitments, knowledge of ethical dimensions, fascination of temptation to value system and humanity which would inject new life and strength to the recovery measures adopted by them. This focuses out attention on a fair synchronisation of formal and non-formal or informal systems while educating and training the medical and paramedical professionals.

The surrounding and premises of hospitals and healthcare centres also add to the quality of healthcare services. In a number of cases, we find diseases influenced by environmental considerations or the quality ambience bears the efficacy of minimising the duration of recovery. The hospital professionals need to ensure development of hospital surroundings and premises like a think park where plantation based on scientific and aesthetic considerations would make the environment disease free. The cleanliness is an important consideration for hospitals and healthcare centres. The hospital professionals are supposed to make it sure that all the avenues for infection have been sealed. The disinfection of all the sources need due attention of hospital professionals. The service ambience governs the magnitude of positive or negative influences. Hence, quality in totality also makes it essential that they are honest and sincere to the aesthetic management.

We live in an age where we do not find any boundary for quality. An organisation showing sincerity and continuity to the process of research and development activities succeeds in defining and redefining quality which opens new vistas for its developments because it find profitable niche markets to capitalise on. The large domestic players both in public and private sectors have world class potentials to establish an edge over the global players. They need to nurture the second line of defence. The district hospitals or talukas or rural healthcare centres need due support from the large players. The benefits of new generation of information and communication technology are required to be channelised to the neglected areas of the country.

Making health in the hinterlands available, accessible and affordable is our target. Easy-to-use technology and low-cost technology need priority attention of policy planners. The hospital professionals need innovative strategy to make Health for All by the end of 12th Five Year Plan. In addition to other strategic decisions, we may also think in favour of urbanisation which focusses out attention on locating world class health care centres and hospitals preferably in the hinterlands or rural areas of the country specially with the support of PPP mode which would initiate and activate multiplier effects and a number of hotels, educational institutions, trade centres established in the adjoining areas would help in transforming the rural areas into the urban areas. Since we find well connected roads, even the people living in towns and cities may use the services.

We need quality in totality. We need huge financial resources and world class human resources for accelerating the pace of qualitative or quantitative transformation. We need managerial proficiency and professional excellence which focusses on quality medical education. Conceptualising TQM provides everything that we need.

SUMMARY

In this chapter, you have gone through Total Quality Management in Hospitals. After reading this chapter, be sure that the following facts are well versed.

Quality-the Perception: Quality focusses our attention on the outcome of the resources and activities expanded to offer the goods/services against the increasing level of expectations of customers/ users.

Total Quality Management: By TQM, our focus is found on managing all the activities professionally helping quality in totality. It is a managerial process.

TQM in Hospitals: The concept of total quality management is practised in hospitals with the motto of making available to the users the services of world class. The technologies, personnel and the infrastructural facilities are managed to improve the quality of healthcare services.

Quality Assurance: By quality assurance, we mean the services assured to the patients and attendants for the fee/charges paid by them or even free of charge.

Dimensions of TQM in Hospitals: The total quality management is a fair synchronisation of technical quality, functional quality and the infrastructural quality. The technical quality focuses our attention on the different types of managerial functions in the hospitals and the infrastructural quality gravitates our attention on the supporting infrastructural facilities used in the process.

TQM and Hospital Personnel: There is no doubt in it that a fair combination of different constituents results into quality in totality but we can't negate the fact that of all the constituents, we find different categories of hospital personnel playing a commanding role in improving the quality of healthcare services.

Team and TQM in Hospitals: As and when we talk about the total quality management, our prime focus is found on team work or team spirit. The formation of an efficient team thus becomes significant to make possible TQM. The hospital managers in consultation with experts bear the responsibility of co-ordinating the different teams and groups. In a true sense, they play the role of a coordinator.

Justifications for TQM in Hospitals: For technological sophistication, managerial excellence, cost-effectiveness, efficient people, right team, healthcare education, efficiency-based motivation and service uniqueness, the hospitals find it judicious to practise TQM.

Quality Circle: The concept of Total Quality Management and more so, the quality circles have often been practised by the Japanese. It is considered to be a unique tool for making available to the customers/users goods or services of world class. Since we talk about the concept of quality circle in the context of hospitals, it is pertinent that the team of different specialists are well coordinated by the hospital managers who are supposed to follow the guidelines of the steering committee.

Practising QCs in Hospitals: The concept of QCs can ever be practised in hospitals where the hospital managers in consultation with a specialist conceptualise quality circles in which the steering committee plays an effective role.

Quality in Totality in Indian Hospitals: In a majority of the Indian hospitals both, in the public and private sectors, we find problems of quality. This makes it essential that the HSCC make possible conceptualisation of TQM where focus must be on quality of medical and paramedical personnel, quality of equipmental instrument and information technology; quality of surroundings and premises where the hospitals are located and the quality of hospital professionals bearing the responsibility of ensuring the service quality delivery. The behavioural profile, personal and professional commitments, and professional ethics also become significant for improving quality.

KEY TERMS

Total Quality Management	Technical Quality
Quality Circle	Functional Quality
Telemedicine	Infrastructural Quality
Teleconferencing	Information Superhighway
Low-cost Technology	Team Spirit
Anaesthesia Machine	Team Culture
Sterilization Equipment	Value Engineering
Defibrillator	PPP Mode
Ventilator	Satellite Communication
Electrocardiogram	Strong Fibre Backbone
Pulse Oxymeter	Telediagnosis
Quality Assurance	e-Health
Laser Devices	Disease Circle

REVIEW QUESTIONS

1. Define the Concept "Quality". Do you find Total Quality Management a unique tool to achieve quality in totality? Defend your arguments.
2. Focus on the misperception of Quality.
3. What do you mean by Total Quality Management? Throw light on its conceptualisation in hospitals.
4. Discuss in brief the different constituents of TQM.
5. What do you mean by Technical Quality? Explain its role for improving the quality of diagnostic and curative services.
6. What do you mean by Functional Quality? Explain its role in hospital management.
7. Focus on the instrumentality of a team in improving the quality of hospital and healthcare services.

8. Justify application of TQM in the Indian perspective.
9. What do you mean by Quality Circle?
10. Discuss the principles to be considered while building an efficient team in a hospital for improving the operational efficiency.
11. Conceptualise quality in totality in the Indian hospitals.
12. Discuss the principles to be considered while building an efficient team in a hospital.
13. Do you find low-cost technologies essential for making the hospital and healthcare services available, accessible and affordable? Justify you opinion.

APPLICATION EXERCISES

1. A majority of the hospitals in the Indian perspective have been facing quality problem. As a hospital professional focus on the instrumentality of TQM is improving the medicare and healthcare services.
2. In the capacity of a hospital professional focus on the different constituents you would like to manage for practising TQM.
3. As a hospital manager, your professional excellence is coiled in the essence of blending the different constituents of quality in such a way that world class healthcare services are made available.
4. Out of all the dimensions of quality transformation, we find quality of medical and paramedical personnel occupying a place of outstanding significance. Do you agree with this view? Justify your arguments as a hospital manager.
5. The quality of services offered by a hospital considerably depends on the constitution of a right team. In the light of this statement focus on the instrumentality of a team in improving the quality of healthcare services.

ENDNOTES

1. Singh J.D., *Indian Journal of Management*, 3/2 1985, pp.48-63.
2. *Ibid.*
3. Benentt R.C., *The Services Sector in India: Some Heretical Thoughts*, Indian Management, pp. 12-16.
4. Jha S.M., *Services Marketing*, New Edition, Chap. 3 Total Quality Management, pp. 81-101.
5. Donald N. Lombard, *Healthcare Manager*, pp. 92-95.
6. Pause M.L., *Quality Circles: A Key for Quality Product Management*, Vol. II/1, 1985, pp. 8-14.
7. Sherlekar S.A., *Management – Value-oriented Holistic Approach*, Chap. 6 Total Quality Management, pp. 98-108.
8. Kumar Ashok, *Indian Hospitals Need Good Managers and IT*; Journal of Marketing & Communication, Jan-April, 2006 Vol. I/3 pp. 77-81.
9. Eleventh FiveYear Plan, *Planning Commission, Government of India*, New Delhi, Vol. II, Chapter 3 pp. 57-127.
10. *Ibid.*

Hospital Management Information System

MIS, of late, is found techno-driven. With a rich potential and the multi-dimensional features, we find HMIS helping in defining and redefining quality. The hospitals and healthcare organisations need to practise MIS to improve the quality of their decisions.

CHAPTER OBJECTIVES

LEARNING OBJECTIVES

This chapter aims at studying the different dimensions of information management in the context of healthcare services. In an age of information superhighway, it is imperative that hospitals and healthcare organisations take help of a techno-driven information system which would considerably help them in improving the quality of healthcare services. The telemedicine, telediagnosis and teleconferencing have been found instrumental in protecting and promoting the interests of even the rural population. The readers develop their awareness of the MIS helping them in many ways.

Introduction

Environmental pollution, noise pollution, water contamination, malnutrition, unawareness of food-prone and water-prone diseases, insensitivity to vaccination culture, increasing temptation to live in relationship and sexual behaviour are some of the important reasons for the development of a volatile disease profile. On the one hand, we look sincere to the new developments in the field of medical sciences while on the other hand, we are very much unregulated in ordering socio-cultural norms and the economic transformation processes. The hospitals bear the responsibility of making available to the society different types of healthcare services helping them in leading a normal lifestyle. Objectives can not remain static because we find multidimensional changes in the environmental conditions taking place everyday. With a change in the objectives and priorities, the policy makers or the boardrooms need to bring a change in their policy decisions failing which he strategic decisions would show only lukewarm response. The scientific inventions and innovations keep on moving which pave avenues for a number of developments in the medical sciences. By breaking law of nature, we complicate he tasks of medical scientists but their sincere, dedicated, professionally and personally committed efforts continue to devise ways for making an invasion on the frequently changing disease profile.

Like other areas, we also find the healthcare services considerably influenced by the evolving process of technological sophistication. A number of new instruments, equipments, machines, information and communication technologies are the outcome of scientific advances. An organisation or an institution found conscious and sensitive perceives the recent developments in different areas and conceptualizes them for enriching their potentials, credentials, properties and strengths. It is quite natural that based on their credentials and world class professional excellence, they succeed in capitalizing on the opportunities. Because we find their efforts innovative and the practices creative and sensitive, they thrive even without a gap. Contrary to it, an individual or an institution keeping their eyes closed and minds inactive fail in doing such. It is against this background that we need to remain conscious to know about the emerging trends in the different areas. This necessitates a sound knowledge bank.

Management Information System, of late, is found techno-driven because new generation of computers are found influencing the operational mechanism. With a rich potential and the multi-dimensional faculties, we find info-tech now helping an individual or an institution in activating the process of qualitative transformation. It is in this context that we talk about the relevance of an MIS in improving the quality of hospital and healthcare services. The hospitals taking the support of sophisticated information technology succeed in establishing an edge over the hospitals managed manually. The multifaced improvements in the diagnosis, treatment, communication and information services enrich the potential of hospitals to deliver quality services and project a positive image.

The policy decisions play a significant role in the development of an organisation. It is felt that hospitals lack a sound policy that obstructs the flow of development. The Health Management Information System simplifies the task of formulating a sound policy not only for a few selected segments of society living in the urban areas but even for those living in the backward rural areas. The boardrooms or the top management of hospitals with the help of a techno-driven information system come to know about the emerging trends in the health scenario, the latest developments in the field of medical sciences, the potentials of hospitals to serve the users, the recent developments in the field of low-cost technologies for diagnosis, investigations and treatment.

The setting of objectives and scheduling a rescheduling of the order of priorities also occupy an important place in the smooth functioning of a hospital. The hospital planners with the support of an MIS make an appraisal of the weaknesses and lapses of a plan. The objectives are evaluated and the priorities are reviewed in the face of changing requirements of the catchments area. In addition, the hospital managers with the support of an MIS find it convenient to formulate a sound strategy. In a true sense, we find a close relation between policy, objectives and strategies. If we find policy makers formulating policy without knowing the healthcare requirements if we find hospital planners setting objectives without knowing the policy decisions and if we find that the hospital managers formulating a strategy processes are delayed, cost-effectiveness becomes difficult and the hospitals find it difficult to accomplish the organizational objectives. It is in this context tat we realize the significance of a techno-driven information system for managing hospitals. The boardrooms or policy planners or hospital planners, hospital designers and architects, hospital consultants and more so, the hospital managers move in the right directions if they take the support of MIS.

To be more specific, in the Indian society where the masses are found insensitive and lack nutritional awareness, face the problem of nutritional deficiency or malnutrition, do not realize the significance of healthy lifestyles, are not aware of food-borne, water-borne, viral and communicable diseases, the healthcare education needs an intensive care. We cannot negate that with the support of sophisticated information and communication technology, we find ample scope for sensitizing the insensitive and illiterate segments for the society. The system of healthcare education can be made result oriented by the Internet services and audio-visual exposure. The illiterate rural masses would considerably be benefited with the help of telemedicine and teleconferencing. The mission of hospitals and healthcare organisation thus, would easily be achieved. We need to make use of the latest devices for which the hospitals are to be well equipped.

It is significant to mention that in the context of healthcare management, we find HSCC playing an important role, In addition to the upgrading of the management system in hospitals, the agency is also looking at the issue of healthcare insurance. It is thought that with the development of healthcare insurance, the quality of services would drastically be improved. Accreditation of hospitals is an important consideration and we find the agency pushing the matter very sincerely and aggressively. The accreditation certification would be a base for the users for making a decision. Waste management and Information Technology are the two important areas that the agency is currently following up with different hospitals. The HSCC has been found initiating and activating the process of making IT much more relevant and popular in the field of hospital or healthcare sector. The agency has been found working towards taking modern healthcare facilities to the weaker sections of the society.

The Eleventh Five Year Plan has been looking sincere and honest to the large scale uses of Information Technology in the healthcare sector. It is thought that the establishment of a National Grid would be much more impact generating. The healthcare providers, trainees, beneficiaries and civil society would immensely be benefited. We find ourselves in a position to make use of indigenous satellite communication and against this background, we find a good number of pilot projects of e-Health during the yesteryears undertaken by private concerns, NGOs, Medical

Colleges and Research Institutions. Health Management Information System would considerably be benefited with the innovative developments in the filed of IT. The availability of data supported by web would help strengthening the research activities. The qualitative improvements in the field of medical education and the service delivery processes would benefit users of services. The Integrated Disease Surveillance Project (IDSP) a by-product of HMIS would the benefit health care services in different ways. The penetration of computers even at the block level would benefit the rural segments. The demand-driven management and redistribution of medicines nearing date of expiry would minimise the wastage of medicines. The telemedicine would bring specialized healthcare to the remotest parts of the country.

Thus, the techno-driven management of information would make ways for a number of qualitative improvements in the field of healthcare sector. The research and activities would gain a rapid momentum which would pave avenues for the development of low-cost technologies in the larger interest of weaker sections of the community. The large players both, in the public and private sectors would have an opportunity to benefit the hospitals and patients residing in the remotest parts of the country. Besides, the multidimensional developments in the field of healthcare sector may be transmitted for promoting the Medical Health Tourism which would benefit hospitals as well as the tourism industry.

MIS-THE CONCEPT

MIS is not new, only its computerization is new. Before computers, the MIS techniques existed to supply managers the information permitting them to plan and control operations. The computer has added one or more dimensions such as speed, accuracy and increased volumes of data for alternatives in a decision. The MIS is a combination of three words, Management, Information and System. We are aware of management. In brief, we find management comprising planning, organising, staffing, directing, communicating and controlling the operations. The managers plan by setting strategies and goals and select the best course of action to achieve the plan. They organise, staff, direct, communicate and control with the motto of accomplishing the organisational goals. We find decision making a fundamental prerequisite to all the processes, thus the job of an MIS becomes that of facilitating decisions necessary for the different functions of management.

By Information, our focus is on the result of transformation of data. Data are facts and figures not currently being used in a decision making process and usually take the form of historical records, not recorded and filed without immediate intent to retrieve for decisionmaking. Information consists of data that have been retrieved, processed or otherwise used for informative or inference purposes, argument or as a basis for forecasting or decision-making.

By System, we mean a set of elements joined together for a common objective. A subsystem is a part of a larger system with which we are concerned. All systems are found to be the parts of larger systems. For our purposes, the organisation is the system and the parts (divisions, departments, functions, units) are the subsystems.

The system concept of MIS is therefore, one of optimizing the output of the organisation by connecting the operating subsystems through the medium of information exchange.)

In brief, we are concerned with three subsystems, such as the social system called the organisation; a system of management that is used in practice to improve the operations and accelerate the productivity of the organisation and its subsystems and the management information system which provides the information for making decisions regarding the integration of the organisation through the process of management.

An MIS is thus a process of transforming the data into information in which the personnel and technologies work together. Of late, we talk about a technology-driven management information system and therefore, our prime focus is found on the quality of information technology used in the process of transformation. With the evolving technologies, we also think about the quality of computer professionals serving the system and the quality of researchers and the research scientists supplying to the system the data known as inputs.

The term management information system has been used differently by various authors. It is defined here as a formal system of gathering, integrating, comparing, analyzing and dispersing information internal and external to the enterprise in a timely, effective and efficient manner.[2] It is quite natural that the system is tailored to specific needs and also include routine information, such as monthly reports, information that points out expectations, especially at critical points and information necessary to predict the future.

Of course, we find the system even managed manually but the frequent use of computers for managing the information made possible a number of improvements in the system. The electronic equipment permits fast and economical processing of huge amounts of data. The computers can with proper programming, process data towards logical conclusions, classify them and make them readily available for a manager's use. In fact, data do not become information until they are processed into a usable form. That task is done by the MIS.

In view of the above, it is right to mention that an MIS is a systematic effort to transform the data into information. The process of transformation can be managed manually or can be done with the support of information technology

HOSPITAL INFORMATION SYSTEM

Of late, we find almost all the organisations making use of MIS for improving the quality of policy decisions or even for the time-honoured and cost-effective implementation of policies and projects. At almost all the levels of managing an organisation, we find use of information because a number of developments take place everyday in the environmental conditions where an organisation is supposed to work, exist and thrive. If you have to survive and thrive, the only option in your hand is to believe in making things happen. This requires innovative efforts and we find an MIS proving its instrumentality in the very context. Right from the formulation of policies to their time-honoured and cost-effective implementation, we need different types of information to improve the quality of our decisions. We are aware of the fact that hospital is a no-profit-making organisation which bears the responsibility of subserving the social interests by making available quality healthcare services to almost all the segments of the society. The latest developments in the medical sciences, the emerging trends in the disease profile, the increasing unawareness and the growing malnutrition make the task of modern hospitals much more difficult. If they fail in making available to the society the quality medicare services in tune with the changing level of their expectations, the dissatisfaction would grow and the image problem would aggravate. Thus, the hospitals are supposed to be aware of the latest developments in almost all the areas and to improve the quality of their services in tune with the available potentials. It is against this background that we talk about the instrumentality of managing information in the process of improving the quality of healthcare services.

The Hospital Information System is thus to manage the information related to the developments and workings of hospitals either manually or with the support of sophisticated information technology. It is a device to help hospitals in the formation of policies, setting of objectives, scheduling of the order of priorities, formulation of strategic decisions for planning implementation and evaluation.

It is quite natural that information needs of all the organisations can't be uniform. The hospitals need different types of information for different purposes, different personnel and different departments. The doctors performing the role of a clinician need information related to the diagnostic services and other patient data generally made available by the nurses and sisters. The senior and junior doctors are found using the data. The management of shift of doctors and paramedical personnel can be made scientific with the help of hospital information system. The hospital managers need information about patient data on the basis of clinical investigation and about the pressure of work on the different categories of hospital personnel. Besides, the financial information would help the managers in managing finance. Information of all concerned problems are required for planning, budgeting and controlling. They need information related to the pay-roll, work distribution, promotion and transfer. The inventory of drugs, linen, other supplies of important materials, blood, etc. are significant to the management and information related to them are to be collected. The information related to the generation of finance from the internal and external sources would help managers in maintaining the cash flow. The cases of financial irregularities and fraudulent practices can easily be identified. The hospital managers also need information related to the marketing of services. We can't negate the fact that the formulation of a sound marketing mix is possible with the help of latest information related to the different mixes. The latest developments in the field of medical sciences are to be made available to the doctors and the students. For improving the quality of core services, it is pertinent that modern diagnostic and treatment facilities are available. The surgical equipment of new generation, sophisticated machines and instruments, internet operations and the time honoured transmission of information play an incremental role in improving the quality of health care services. In the process of developing knowledge, the doctors and students need to be aware of the multi-dimensional developments. The hospitals of today have also been found offering a number of peripheral services to the patients with the motto of making their services unique. The communication and information technologies play a dominating role in educating the patients and masses regarding the instrumentality of healthcare. The task of creating mass awareness is fantastically simplified with the help of audio-visual exposure. It is significant that information related to the different areas are made available to the concerned personnel. The hospital managers need to inform and sense the masses and for that, the sensitivity rate of the different constituents of promotion need to be increased by making possible creativity. The advertising, publicity, sales promotion, personal selling, word-of-mouth promotion and telemarketing are to be blended optimally so that the masses are sensitised and the cost effectiveness is made possible. The sales promotion measures need due attention because the hospital personnel and the patients and attendants are required to be motivated. The fee structure is to be made pocket-friendly and the processes of offering the services are to be made decent. The different categories of hospital personnel need physical attractions, dedication professional and personal commitments.

The aforesaid facts make it clear that hospitals need different types of information. It is against this background that we make a strong advocacy in favour of a well-developed and a technology driven information system for hospitals. An MIS proves to be a process and with the use of computers, we find a dramatic change in the capacity, memory and accuracy of the system.

It is a system to help all the policy makers, the hospital planners, the hospital architects, the hospital consultants and more so, the hospital managers. In innovating different types of services, the hospital managers use the information system since based on information. They find it easier to go through strategic decisions followed by other leading hospitals. The task of informing, sensing and motivating the patients is done successfully by making the slogans and messages creative. The strategic decisions related to fee are made optimal and the processing of services is done in a right fashion.

The process of gathering, integrating, comparing, analysing and dispersing internal and external information help different levels of employees in increasing the level of efficiency. Thus, we find the system acting as a guide. The gathering of data is done by the researchers or even with the help of sisters and nurses found personally involved in the process of interactions with the patients and attendants. Of course, we can manage the system manually but of late, we find focus on technology-driven information system that makes it a joint endeavour of highly skilled personnel and the most sophisticated information technology.

Information Technology

Of late, in an age of information revolution, we find a number of organisations making sincere efforts to build a superhighway for communications and the credibility for the same goes to the increasing sophistication in the process of developing information technology. Electronic equipment permits fast processing of huge amounts of data. The computer can process data toward logical consideration with the help of proper programming and in addition can also classify them and make them readily available for a manager's use. We are well aware of the fact that the data can't take the shape of information unless they are processed into a usable form that informs. The computers can store, retrieve and process information. Often a discussion is found regarding the different types of computers. The main frame is a full scale very expensive computer. We find them capable of handling huge amounts of data. The supercomputers are used for engineering, simulation and the manipulation of larger data bases. The minicomputer has less memory and is found smaller than the mainframe narrated earlier. This kind of computer is often connected with peripheral equipment. The microcomputer is even smaller and may be a desk computer, home computer, personal computer, portable computer or small computer for a business system. The requirements for materials, planning, servicing or manufacturing, project costing, inventory control and purchasing are some of the important operations done with the help of the computers. The computer also aids in designing and engineering besides processing financial information such as accounts receivable and accounts payable, payroll, capital budgeting and financial planning.

We can't negate the fact that we live in an age of information revolution where information technology dominates the scene. The increasing knowledge gap, the embracing information, education and widening access to technology are some of the factors fuelling the information revolution. Today, we find a new divide emerging which is found dividing the world into two parts—"high-tech countries" and the "low-tech countries."[3] You can tell the rich from the poor by their Internet operations and there can be little argument against the fact that information and freedom move together.

The information revolution is inconceivable without democracy and true democracy is unthinkable without freedom of information. Global interdependence means that those who receive and disseminate information have an edge over those who curtail it. And its consequences are apparent in the field of human endeavour. At the simplest level, the students need information to compete in the society, farmers need information about the weather conditions and market prices, businessmen need to exchange information with potential partners, the profit making organisations need information to increase the level of profits and the no-profit making organisations to make the quality of services of world class. The challenges facing the world today are how to widen the reach of information, how to make it available to people everywhere, whether they live in the industrialised world or in the developing world. We must increase access to information. Individuals or institutions, of late, can't exist failing the accessibility to information. The ability to receive, download and send information through electronic networks and the capacity to share information including publishing newspapers and journals without censorship or restrictions have already become the hallmarks of development. Communications and information technology have enormous potentials in furthering sustainable development specially in the less developed countries like ours. The challenges are to promote greater, freer and fairer access to information for developing countries which means improving infrastructure and sharing technological advances.

In the Indian context, we need to enrich the information potentials of different categories of no-profit-making organisations, specially the educational institutions and hospitals where high flow of information would make possible multifaceted qualitative improvements. We can't negate that with the help of advanced information technology, the healthcare education would be made more sensitive and proactive which would minimise the pressure on hospitals. The rural society of India would considerably be benefited since we find there the problem of insensitivity. The creation of mass awareness is found essential to improve the quality of human life index. It is right to mention that a majority of our population is not aware of the healthy living conditions due to which they don't assign due weightage to their food habits. They often consume contaminated water. They create a hazardous living condition found dangerous to them and sensitive to multi-pronged food-borne, water-borne, viral and communicable diseases. The hospital information system would only not help doctors in improving the quality of diagnosis and treatment but would also be efficacious in making the masses more conscious. In almost all the hospitals, specially under the government control, we find the problem of unfair, unethical, illegal practices making the task difficult to a few of the right thinking persons. The hospital information system would play a significant role in improving the system of financial management. The budgeting, accounting and auditing processes would be found easier. The task of identifying the unfair practices would not be so much difficult. The hospital managers would find it convenient to identify the inefficient personnel and the compensation and motivational plans can be made efficiency-oriented, scientific and rational. The efficients would suitably be rewarded whereas the inefficients would considerably be demotivated or penalised. Thus, the level of efficiency of the hospital personnel can be increased significantly.

It is high time that the government policy decisions are liberal to the development of information technology. The private hospitals assign due weightage to the development of hospital information system. And the small hospitals procure information from the big hospitals.

Computer-driven MIS

From a manual MIS to a technology-driven MIS, the contours of development have undergone radical changes. Speed, accuracy and memory have been significantly increasing in the technology-driven system which paved copious avenues for its multidimensional uses. Qualitative transformation in computers made infotech an integral part of the MIS and it was against this background that almost all the organisations evinced their interests in using information technology. It is right to mention that with the use of computers for managing information, the managers have, of late, been successful in improving the quality of their decisions. Like other organisations, we also find hospitals of today using computers for managing information. What to talk of the organisational uses of computers when of late, we find microprocessors even in the toys of children. The pocket calculators, industrial robots, home appliances and many others have been using microprocessors. In a true sense, we don't find even a single machine, instrument, equipment or information system without a microprocessor.

The computers of new generation have virtually changed everything in our modern personal, social and institutional or organisational systems. The first four generation of computers were based on the technology of the age to which they belonged. They were found based on the vacuum tube technology, the transmission and printed circuit technology, the integrated circuit technology and the Very Large Scale Integrated (VLST) technology, respectively.

Today, we classify computers as mainframe computers, mini-computers and micro-computers.

Mainframe Computers: The mainframe computers are expensive, large, centralised computer facilities where a super computer like the (RAY or CYBER or a large computer like the IBM 3033, CDC 7600, DEC 10, IBM 370 models are found important. We find mainframe computers connected to several terminals. A multi-user mainframe computer has a large memory and is found capable of the speed of several millions of floating point operations per second (Mflops).

Micro-computers: The microcomputers are found based on standard micro-processors marketed by Zilog, Intel, Motorola etc. A micro-processor is a single silicon electronic chip which contains the ALU and the control unit. Some of the most commonly used micro-processors are Intel's 8086,8088,80286,80386 and Motorola's 6800,68000,68010, 68020, 68030. Micro-computers are often called Personal Computers or PCs because they are originally to be single user devices either at the office or at the home.

Miniframe Computers: The miniframe computers are also multiuser computers having lesser memory and operating at slower speeds. In the miniframe computers, the extremely popular PDP' 11 and VAX 11 computers of the Digital Equipment Corporation are found important.

The aforesaid computers are found used for multidimensional purposes and the MIS has also been using computers for managing information and against this background, we call the system technology-driven.

Programming Language

We classify computerware into two parts—hardware and software. The five functional units of a computer built with electronic circuits and electromechanical devices constitute the hardware. Software refers to the range of programmes or routines used on the hardware to perform various functions. Programming is the art of writing a programme. It is an internal hardware structure of a machine that makes provision for a unique level language called the machine language. To make free the programmer from the tedium of writing a program, we find development of a number of high-level and low-level languages. The high-level languages are comprehensible representation of machines code using memories in the assembly language. Of these, FORTRAN (Formula Translation), ALGOL (Algorithmic Language) and BASIC (Beginners All-purpose Symbolic Instructions Code) are found to be the most widely accepted general-purpose programming Languages while COBOL (Common Business Oriented Language) is the programming language for business applications. C language is the recent and most powerful one. It is available for DOS, Windows, OS/2 and Unix platforms. There are new versions of C like C+ +, Visual C, Quick C & Turbo C.

The World of Micro: The microcomputer/industry was found revolutionised by the entry of IBM which started marketing PCs in 1980. Essentially, we find microcomputers consisting of a System Unit, the keyboard and Visual Display Unit (VDU). The printer is an auxiliary unit found essential to get the output from the micro-computer as a hard copy. The standard typewriter keys A to Z, 0 to 9 and certain special characters together constituting the alpha-numeric characters are an essential part of all the micro-computer key boards.

Floppy Disks: The most widely used form of auxiliary storage in microprocessor is the floppy disk storage. A floppy diskette is a round vinyl disk enclosed within a plastic cover. The 3 1/2" diskettes are becoming universal and are fast replacing 5 1/4" diskettes.

The Printer: The printer usually used along with a microcomputer is a dot matrix printer wherein a 9 pin (vertical) head creates matrix pattern to form the characters. The character size may range from 5 to 16.5 characters per inch.

Networking: All networks cater to common requirements and consist of interconnected service locations. A network is the means by which computers share and exchange information and resources across either short distances (Local Area Network) or globally (Wide Area Networks). Making the best use of networking technology means making better use of business resources, accelerating productivity and increasing efficiency. The networking helps an organisation to communicate with and share resources with everyone else giving them access to data held in individual PCs by remote office sites or external suppliers and giving users an opportunity to share printer, fax CD-ROM and modern technology, etc.

The aforesaid facts are fundamentals which the hospital managers need to know because the MIS would require a large scale use of these terminologies while making use of the information to be received from the system.

Information Superhighway

It is right to mention that the Internet is a network of networks, an internationally linking of tens of thousands of business, universities and research organisations with millions of individual users. The Internet originated in 1969 in the hands of the US military as a doomsday communication system impervious to nuclear war. By the end of 1980s, we found Internet an important computer network for people for a number of academic researchers. Today, the internet has users in more than 50 countries.[4] In 1993, when the commercial providers were first permitted to sell internet connections to individuals, we found the beginning of network explosion because a large number of new users came on within months. Thus, a new area of computer communication gained the momentum.

The internet is a global electronic community of over 50,000 interconnected computer networks or say more than 50 million people are linked together which we of late know as information superhighway. The salient feature of the Internet is that there is no administrator, no coordinating authority and yet, starting from a small network set by the US Defence Department, we find internet today growing as a global supermarket. We can't negate the fact that the internet has changed our life styles and has been adding a new dimension to our existence. It gives each of us the option to be the publisher of our information and views. The Internet offers a number of business opportunities. Of late, we find a number of business organisations making use of internet for promoting their business. It is a source of up-to-date information and assistance related to business, share market, education, medical advances, etc. Communication is another critical use of the internet making it invaluable as a resource. We also find organisations setting up intranet. This is a network used on the Internet to communicate and share information across the organisation.

The demand for internet technology implementation and applications is found gaining popularity in the corporate world. Intranets are already evolving towards offering of new services. A full Service Intranet is a corporate TCP/IP network with reliable features and rich applications, sharing five core, standard-based services, viz., directory, e-mail, file, print and network management.

It is right to mention that with the development of a superhighway for information, we call this age an age of information revolution in which an individual or an organisation can't exist unless we find them making sincere efforts to enrich the knowledge bank. Information technology is found making its place as a knowledge technology. The hospitals need different types of information, specially related to the medical sciences failing which qualitative improvements would hardly be possible. It is against this background that we make a strong advocacy in favour of making available to the different categories of hospitals the benefits of information technology so that the small and big hospitals, rural or urban hospitals keep on moving the process of offering the world class healthcare services to the society. Unless we have latest information, we can't think about qualitative improvements because we fail to know about others.

Application of Information Technology in Hospitals

In an age of information revolution, it is quite natural that like other organisations, the hospitals also take the benefits of information technology for the qualitative improvements of their services. Of late, we find almost all the important hospitals using information technology for the making of policies, formulation of plans and management of functional areas. In Fig. 3.1, we find the different areas where the hospitals use or may use information technology. At almost all the levels of management, we find information technology significant because an MIS simplifies the task of improving the quality of decisions.

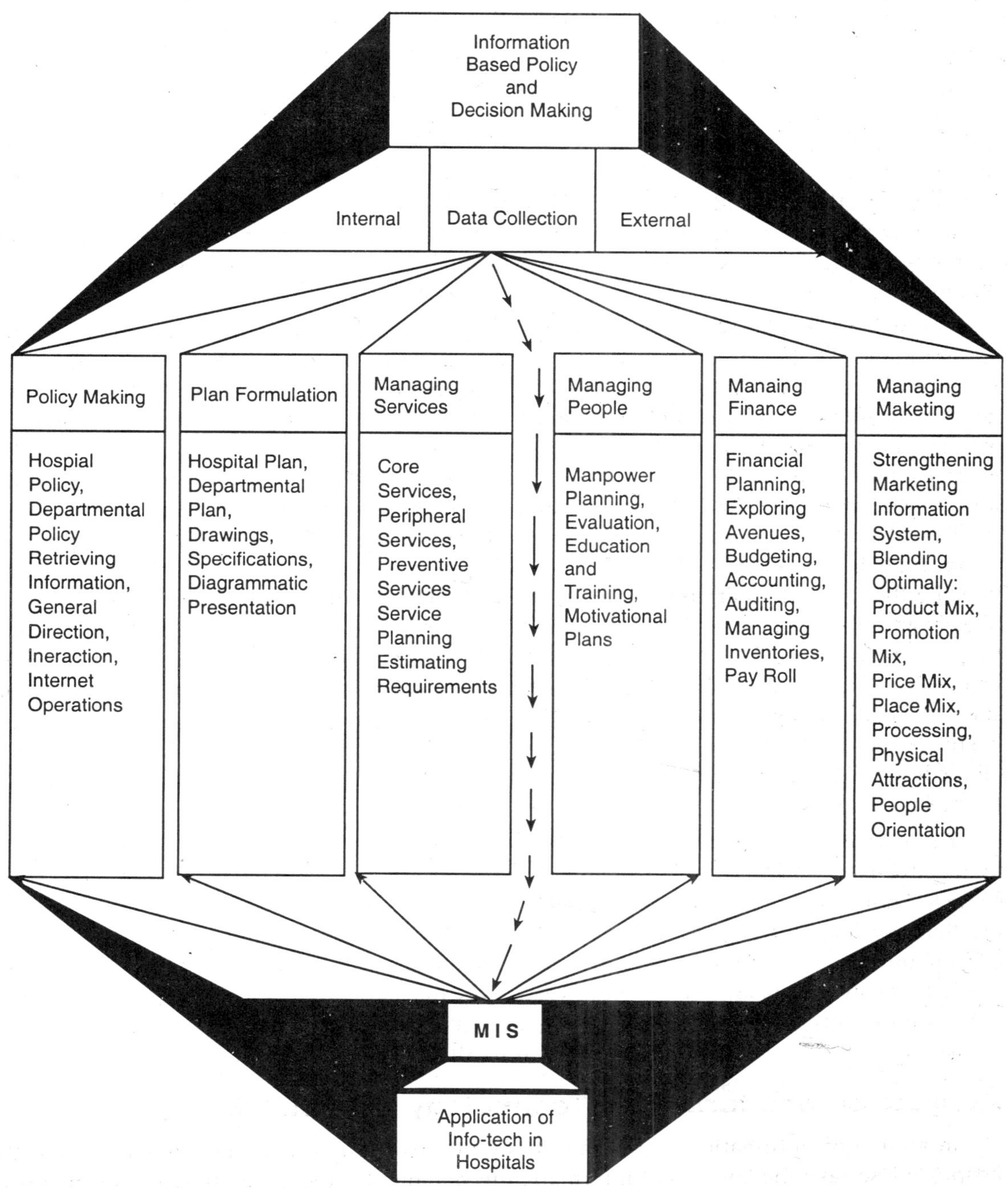

Fig. 3.1. Application of Information Technology

Information Related to Policy Making

The top level managers, the boardrooms or the policy makers bear the responsibility of formulating a sound policy for hospitals, specially when we talk about the management of private hospitals.

In addition to the general direction of the hospitals, they are also responsible for the appropriate interaction as and when the circumstances necessitate so. They can use the computers to retrieve information from a database that facilitates the application of decision models. It is quite natural that a number of changes take place in the environmental conditions, medical sciences, disease profile and the application of computers makes possible timely responses to the changes taking place in the medical world. We agree with this view that in the Indian perspective, we find hospitals not assigning due weightage to the time-to-time evaluation of policy in the face of changing conditions and therefore, a mismatch between the potentials of hospitals making the way for changes and the hospitals continuing with traditional devices is but natural.

The making of policies requires different types of information specially related to the external environment. At the same time, the top level manager and the boardrooms also bear the responsibility of studying the recent developments in the medical sciences so that the hospitals get the benefits of modern equipment, machines, instruments and information technology to activate the process of qualitative improvements. The policy makers can't be spared from the responsibility of promoting hospitals in a right fashion. The middle-level managers and the lower-level managers find it convenient to formulate sound strategic decisions for the implementation of policies if they get the support of boardrooms. The policy for the development of hospitals is related to the National Health Policy. Since we find the government hospitals freezing their potentials for initiating qualitative improvements, it is high time that the policy makers pave the avenues for the development of private hospitals. Even if they prefer to promote the government hospitals, it becomes essential that the policy decisions make the way for the generation of financial resources from the internal sources. We are well aware of the fact that the state exchequer finds it difficult to meet the increasing financial requirements of government hospitals and resulting from which we find a degeneration in the quality and capacity of almost all the hospitals managed and controlled by the government. This necessitates a basic change in the making of policies.

The computers simplify the task of top-level managers specially while enriching their knowledge bank related to the developments taking place in the medical sciences. They also come to know about the quality of services made available to the masses vis-a-vis the changing health care requirements of society. If they find it judicious to activate the process of qualitative-cum-quantitative improvements, they can take the support of information technology. An interaction between the different levels of managers would simplify the task of making a sound policy for the development of hospitals. Besides, the government policy makers would also be in a position to review the outcome of National Health Policy and the necessary changes can be incorporated. It is against this background that we make a strong advocacy in favour of promoting the use of information technology for the making of policies. With the development of internet operations, it is easier for the policy makers to know about the developments taking place in other countries and their efforts for the formulation of a sound policy. An MIS thus proves its instrumentality in the making of policies.

Information Related to Plan Formulation

The hospital planners bear the responsibility of formulating an ideal plan for hospitals. The hospital architects, consultants are also to be involved in the process. The plan may be for short-term and even for the long-run. The planners and the full team related to planning need the services of information technology. The designing of a hospital building requires excellence and the hospital architects and hospital consultants with the support of information technology design a building found comfortable, purpose-oriented and cost-effective. The hospital architects need a number of information and also require to keep in their minds the future development plans of hospitals so that modernisation and expansion processes are not to face any problem. If they feel necessary, the hospital consultants may also be consulted for that very purpose. It is the responsibility of hospital managers to make available to the architects and consultants their requirements at present and of future so that they make provisions for expansion, alternation or so. When the hospitals are to be constructed in the cities' precincts, the space constraint is found to be a major problem and therefore, in this context, the hospital architects need excellence to accommodate everything within the available space and means. While locating hospitals, the planners need to go through a number of facts and figures. They are supposed to select a site where there is enough scope for a planned development and expansion. The modern hospitals are not just a place for diagnosis and treatment but something more than that. The development of surroundings and premises staff quarters, gardening and plantation, entertainment facilities for the children of the hospital personnel, amusement park and think park are some of the additional attractions of modern hospitals where patients and hospital personnel feel themselves comfortable. This in a very natural way requires adequate space where all these amenities and facilities are to be made available. It is in this context that the hospital planners need to think about the availability of space and landscape on a priority basis.

Budgeting is an important part of planning. The hospital managers need to go through the requirements of hospitals in the very context. The information technology helps them in making plan allocation, testing the allocation for a particular head, gauging the impact of inflationary pressure during the estimated period of construction or a provision for inflationary accounting, a fair match between the plan allocation and resource generation or so. We can't negate that there is a great deal to be done before drawings are undertaken. Of course, there are some of the problems for which we don't need graphics but there are a large number of problems for which the graphics are needed and the information technology is found useful in the very context. Cost of land, cost of movable furnishing and equipment, cost of engineering, such as the fees of architects, consultants, engineers, etc., cost of roads, yard work and landscaping, diagnostic and therapeutic facilities, higher level of technical equipment for the research-oriented hospitals are some of the important points to be given due weightage while budgeting.[5] In a true sense, we find planning, designing, construction substantially based on graphics and therefore, the information technology helps hospital planners considerably.

In addition to other aspects, they are also required to be aware of the size and type of hospital since the requirements would vary in respect of primary, secondary and tertiary hospitals. We are aware of the fact the local or community clinics, often called dispensaries are primary hospitals.

Community hospitals are known as secondary hospitals and teaching hospitals are known as tertiary hospitals. The requirements in all the three cases would vary. There are different units, such as nursing unit, therapeutics, admission, out-patient department (OPD), general configuration and requirements in all the cases can't be uniform. The hospital planners, architects, consultants need not forget that the designing of the hospital building should be made anatomically so that it can function properly. This in a natural way requires formulation of a programme. We consider programme a basis for architect work. While making available different types of information to the hospital architects, the hospital managers need to make it sure that a programme listing only the number of rooms and their approximate size is most inadequate. The practical information on organisation, personnel, etc. may be useful to the architects. The planning for departments and premises are found significant in the very context. The hospital architects and consultants are considered to be the technical personnel specially in respect of hospital planning and therefore, the hospital managers and doctors need not to interfere.

The drawings and specifications are the most important aspects where we find use of information technology.[6] Small-scale diagrammatic plans and the large-scale diagrammatic plans are formulated with the support of computers. The flow-diagrams for goods, equipment and personnel are also found important in the very context. The results of thinking and planning are set down on drawings and written in specification in full detail. The architect, structural, mechanical and electrical engineers are found engaged in the process. These are the documents from which the contractors prepare the tenders and on which the construction contracts are finally based. The construction works start thereafter.

The aforesaid facts make it clear that hospital planning is an important dimension of hospital management which is found of technical nature and therefore, the hospital architects, consultants, designers and engineers are required to be engaged for that purpose. The main focus is here on the instrumentality of information technology and we can't negate that almost in all the processes of planning and designing, we find use of information technology. We can't say that without the use of information technology it is impossible but at the same time, it is also right to mention that with the support of information technology, we find perfection in almost all the areas. Since we think of constructing modern hospital, it is pertinent that in addition to other areas, we also practice information technology for planning and designing. The cost effectiveness, comforts and conveniences with the view point of patients, smooth accessibility, beautiful landscape, and peaceful atmosphere are some of the essential features drawing due attention of hospital managers and for which they are free to take the support of experts. The planning is considered to be an important aspect because mistakes committed at this stage are not to be corrected.

While planning, the hospital managers need to be innovative in approach because of late, we find a basic change in the concept of hospital. Of course, we find hospital a centre for diagnosis and treatment but today, we also consider it a place where the patients feel comfortable, a place where the medical and paramedical personnel feel pleasure while working and a place where the attendants are found tension free.

Information Related to the Management of Services

In the management of services, the computers have been playing a significant role. In the health care services, the curative services occupy a place of outstanding significance in which the diagnostic and treatment facilities are found important. All of us are well aware of the different diagnostic services with the help of computers. The use of computers in this context has been successful in making available authentic investigation reports to the doctors which help them in writing prescriptions. In the hospitals, the computers are also used for the maintenance of hospital records, medical research and analysis.

We can't deny the fact that in the management of hospitals, the management of records is found significant and we find computers helping hospital managers in the very context. In a majority of the hospitals, we don't find proper arrangement for the maintenance of records. The computerisation of registration of patients may help hospital management in many ways. If we manage records manually, the task of locating them becomes much more difficult. Valuable data about the patients and diseases stored in patients' file can't be traced easily, if it is managed manually. The emergency departments present a very gloomy picture, in respect of management of records. Besides, the problem of storage, missing page or records due to mismanagement make the task much more difficult. It is in this context that we talk about the instrumentality of information technology in managing the records. The researchers, doctors find them useful in solving complicated problems and undertaking the valuable researches. We agree with this view that the problem of record department would be simplified considerably if the whole registration and record system is computerised. Of course, the task is a bit difficult since at the initial stage, a number of things are to be managed properly but in due course, the doctors, the researchers, and the medical scientists would find them very much useful in activating inventions and innovations. There is no doubt in it that the experts would think over the mechanics and application of the system.

In the context of registration, we go through a model of compterised registration.[7] A model for a large hospital consists of a mainframe computer. Each patient coming for consultation is given a unique registration number. Even if we find patients related to the different departmental clinics, the same number may be used. The details of age, address, sex, marital status and other administrative data are recorded. In each of the clinic dealing with the patients, we find a complete computerised patient registration records. Thus, a single database suffices the needs of all. The multiplicity of records can be minimised considerably with the help of a single database. The users get the unique "passwords" and therefore, it is easier for the computer to identify and record. The hospitals need worldclass computer professionals to manage the system.

In the Central Registration Department, we find a master index of all patients and as and when we find patients reporting for a routine check-up with the help of master index, it is found easier to follow up consultation. It is pertinent that new facts and figures related to the patients are recorded specially related to his/her revisits, admissions, discharges, transfers or so.[8] We find a continuous monitoring essential for updating everything.

In view of the above, it is right to say that we find a large scale use of computers in managing the different types of services related to the health care of patients.

In the medical research, we find computers playing a commanding role with the help of computerised testing of equipment and data collection, storage, retrieval, statistical analysis and research planning. Almost all categories of modern equipment now has built-in computer systems, such as computerised spirometers, blood chemistry and gas analysers, ultrasound scanners and CT scanners.[9] In addition, of late, even small equipments go through computerised testing. The second aspect is related to research where we find computers playing a big role. The research planning is an important aspect where we find computers instrumental in addition to the analysis of data and statistics. It is quite natural that different categories of researchers need computer for different purposes, such as the physiologists require computers for creating mathematical models or for the analysis of biological signals, records, graphs and images. By using computers, they find it convenient to activate the process. The analysis is found fast, simple and reliable and even mandatory because they can use it when the manual calculations are found impractical. In Fig. 3.2, we find a list of some of the important uses of computer in the medical services.

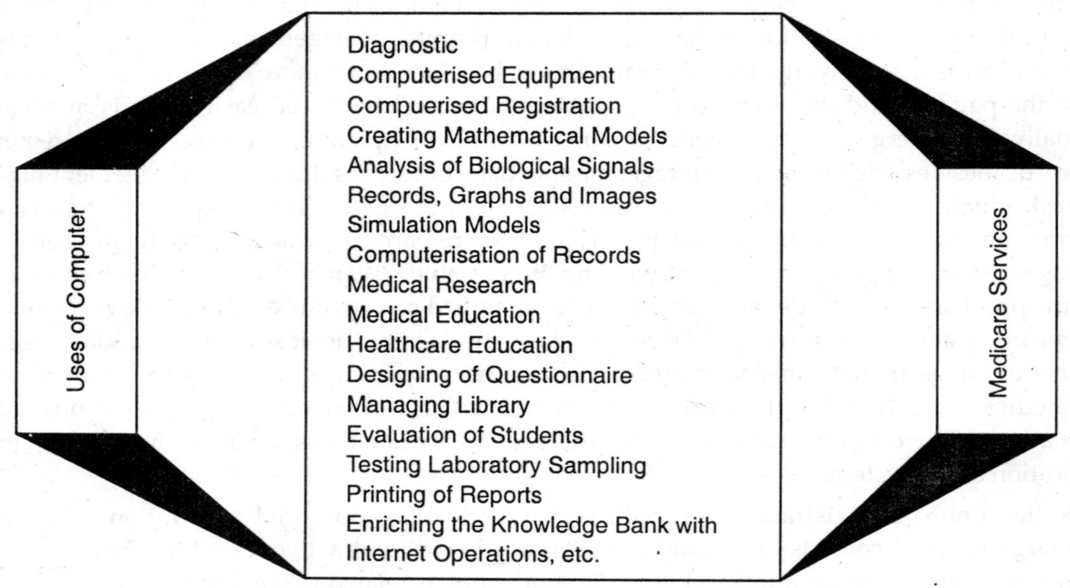

Fig. 3.2. Uses of Computer in the Medical Services

In respect of medicine, we find it of common use for the clinicians and epidemiologists. So far as the manual recording is concerned, we find it useful for the small data. The computer is found useful for large data and a number of variables are used in the process. We find "Programming" used here as a technical terminology which depends upon the understanding of the problem of the methodology of analysis. We can't negate the importance of knowledge of statistics in planning a research project and therefore, the services of statistics knowing computers would be of much use. It is also clear that a small data can be analysed with a microcomputer whereas we need medium or a mainframe computer for large data. The creation of software is found as per the changing needs in the big hospitals where we find use of a central facility of a mainframe computer.

The designing of questionnaires is also an important use of computer which is required for a particular software package. The questionnaires are required to be simple and clear to avoid the irrelevant things. The coding of responses to questions should be easily understandable. Closed ended questions and open ended questions can be used for the collection of information. We find hybrid questions, a mixture of the two where the respondents are supposed to answer in brief. For the precoded questions, we find a different code. Storage of a large number of data and the analysis involve statistics.

The use of computers in the field of library management is well-known to all. For searching literature or for keeping a track on the movement of books, we find computers useful. It is right to mention that the manual search of references is found difficult as well as time taking but we find computers helping researchers in the very context. Of late, the Internet operations have added a new dimension in the information technology and the researchers find it convenient to know about the references in detail. The most commonly used database Medline contains all the material cited in the printed index Medicus plus. The name of BLAISE (British Library Automated Information System) is found significant in the very context. The use of computer is also found for controlling the circulation of books and journals. We find book-cataloguing an on-line process where you can know about the availability of a book.

In addition to the above, we also find other uses of computers for imparting educational and training facilities to the medical and paramedical students. Computer models simulating diseased states can be created and the students can play with the model as we find in a computer video game. The parameters can be changed and the effects can be studied. We find simulation models for abdominal pain, coma, arterial blood gases, GI, bleeding, hypertensive emergencies and many others. In the evaluation of students, we find use of computers for assessment. We find creation of Question Data Bank and the evaluation system is selected. In the context of testing laboratory, we find computers playing a significant role. Sampling, recording and analysis, calculation of results, printing of report, future references, transmission of results are some of the important uses.

In the context of health education, we find information technology playing a contributory role. The knowledge bank of individuals or institutions can be enriched with the help of information technology. With the beginning of Internet operations, we find a number of qualitative improvements in the uses of information technology. The hospitals bear an outstanding responsibility of using the same for students, faculty or even for masses for informing and sensing. In an age of information revolution, it is quite natural that like other disciplines, the medical discipline also makes use of computers and we find the beginning since a number of diagnostic and treatment devices are now governed by computers. It is pertinent that like big hospitals, we also find small hospitals making use of computers for improving the quality of health care services. Of course, the policymakers, specially the government policy makers, are required to develop a positive attitude.

Information Related to the Management of People

We can't negate the fact that of all the resources instrumental in activating the healthcare services and the human resources occupy a place of outstanding significance. There is no doubt in it that a number of developments have taken place in the medical sciences and resulting from which we find modern devices for diagnosis and treatment but failing the cooperation of people, our efforts are not to be proactive. We talk about information technology, we also talk about the information superhighway and tomorrow, we may talk something more but ultimately, the human resources command everything. The computerised instruments and equipment may be made available to the hospitals, even the robot culture is promoted but who would care for the innovative developments in the process of technological sophistication. This makes it clear that the hospitals need to use the information technology for the development of human resources so that information technology proves to be a knowledge technology.

In the development of human resources, we find more emphasis on the development of professional excellence. We can't negate that professional excellence happens to be an integral part of HRD but at the same time, we find development of value-engineering process the most significant aspect for the development of personally-committed hospital personnel. Since of late, we talk about information superhighway and also find a number of sophisticated communication technologies playing an incremental role in the inculcation process, it is high time that the hospitals of different categories make use of the available knowledge technology and succeed in developing professionally sound, professionally and personally-committed medical and para-medical personnel. We assign as overriding priority to this dimension of the people management because we find a number of cases where doctors, nurses, sisters and hospital administrators are professionally sound but very insentive while perceiving the significance of Human, Humane and Humanity. This stands as a barrier specially while making available quality and personalised services to the patients who in a majority of the cases need the same on a priority basis.

The recent developments in the field of information technology and more so, our efforts for developing information superhighway have rich potentials of inculcating personal values as an essential attribute for the development of successful hospital personnel. Of course, we can use and we have also started using information superhighway for educating and training the hospital personnel but whatever the efforts we find at present are nothing but a drop in the ocean. So far as the instrumentality of information superhighway in inculcating human values is concerned, we don't find even the beginning, rather it has been found instrumental in activating the degeneration process because most of us are well aware of the misuse of BroadBand and DSL connections even by kids, teens and practically by a majority of us. If the negative developments in the process of building a superhighway for information start establishing an edge over the positive developments, the masses become the ultimate suffers. It is against this background that we make a strong advocacy in favour of a code for transmission. The tertiary hospitals and even primary and secondary hospitals need to promote knowledge technology but essentially with a sense, otherwise the generation of nuisance is quite natural.

We are well aware of the fact that three different categories of employees are found involved in the process of improving the quality of healthcare services, viz., the doctors, the paramedical personnel and the managerial staff. The information technology would be useful in improving the credentials of almost all the categories of employees. The students and researchers would be benefited by getting advanced and latest information related to the medical sciences. The reference made available to them would enrich their knowledge bank and the qualitative improvements in the field of developing professionalism can't be negated. The medical scientists and the research-oriented doctors would make intensive efforts to show wonders with the help of information superhighway. The library would be made rich and scientific. Thus, the information made available by the MIS would benefit the hospital personnel in many ways. Not only this, the task of evaluating or rating the performance of hospital personnel would also be found easier which would make the motivational plans more rational vis-a-vis efficiency oriented. It is well-known to us that the most of the services offered by hospitals are the result of a team work and the teams showing wonders and performing efficiently would suitably be motivated. The task of evaluating is found difficult as well as time taking when we find its processing with a manual information system. The use of computers would make the task of evaluating and rating process more logical.

The task of manpower planning[10] is found significant to the efficient management of hospitals and the information technology would help hospital managers in knowing the requirements and potentials of the medical and paramedical personnel to be recruited. Based on the same, the education and research and training facilities or the refresher courses can be made up-to-date. The problem of over or understaffing would considerably be minimised. The information technology would make available to the hospital managers the information related to the quality environment at the workplace or at the living places of the hospital personnel. Thus, the task of improving the quality of environment at both the levels would be made easier for the hospital managers.

The most significant aspect in the very context is related to value engineering process and the information technology would make it easier to identify or detect the cases of unethical, unfair, illegal and inhuman practices promoted by the hospital personnel. This would provide to the hospital management two-pronged benefits—first the process would be made cost-effective since fixing of accountability would be easier and second, the human values would also be promoted. The vanishing work culture found almost in all the government hospitals makes it essential that the hospital managers make use of the information technology for regulating the unfair and inhuman practices. But this requires due support of the government policy makers because in a majority of the cases due to regulatory barriers, the government hospitals offering free of charge services get free hands in promoting the quality degeneration process. We appreciate the recent developments in the field of information superhighway but nothing would inject strength to appreciation unless the government hospitals, where masses avail the services harness the benefits.

Information Related to the Management of Finance

In the management of hospital, we find management of finance playing an important role. The hospital managers or account officers responsible for managing finance need different types of information for the formulation of budget, accounting and auditing purposes. The increasing cases of irregularities and unproductive expenses make it essential that the accounting and auditing processes are given due weightage. In the context of purchase for stores, we find unfair practices and the uses of information technology make it easier for the hospital managers to detect the cases and regulate the same. They bear the responsibility of securing utmost values for the limited financial resources of hospitals. Improvements in methods and increase in the efficiency are therefore, a must. Installation and maintenance of modern methods of accounting and financial and cost control are required to be adopted. Estimates of income and expenditure, methodical recording of income and expenditure and receipts and payments, maintenance of double entry system of accounting, stores records and accounts, inventories, cost accounting, unit cost, periodical returns are related to effective financial management. Budgetary control, salary and wage payments, organisation of financial procedures, creditors and debtors accounts, financial and other statistics and graphic charts are the essential components for the management of finance. They need to design an integral system of departmental and cost accounting with appropriate units cost for the effective financial control. Standard costs along with budgetary control may be incorporated while designing the system.

The application of information technology for managing finance draws our attention on the accounting processes because this is considered to be the focal point helping a manager in many ways. The books of accounts and registers, preparation of cash book, journal and ledger, accounts receivable, accounts payable, pay roll, salary allocation are now found easier because computers have been found helping the process. In a number of hospitals, we now find preparation of payroll by the computers.

The material management is an important dimension of financial management." In hospitals, we find about 30 per cent of the expenses or even more than that related to materials. It is therefore, necessary that the material management is given due weightage. The availability of right quality of materials at the right time and at the right place and prices are found important in the very context. The materials like drugs, instruments/equipment, linen are found important materials in hospitals generally marketed by the manufacturers. Thus, the selection of right materials is an important aspect where the specialists of the related areas should be made accountable for the quality as per the specifications. In a hospital, we find inventory in a true sense a direct money and that is found limited. This makes it essential that supply of inventory is as per the requirements so that the cases of over or undersupply are checked. In addition, the supply of excess inventory would also create a number of problems like more space for storage, damages or so. Here, the managers need excellence to estimate the requirements and to make available the inventory as per the requirements. The computers on the basis of information would help in estimating the requirements.

It is the prime responsibility of a manager to regulate the unproductive expenses mainly related to establishment. With the use of computers, we find enough scope for minimising the bill on employees for accounting, filing and other operations.

The formulation of a sound financial plan is found essential to manage finance efficiently and the instrumentality of information technology in the very context can't be underestimated. The proposed plans for modernisation, expansion and development of hospitals make it essential that the required financial resources are made available on time. There are a number of heads related to the day-to-day workings of the hospitals but in addition, they also need to make provisions for expansion and development. The new equipment, instruments and sophisticated diagnostic devices need huge money but are found essential to improve the quality of services. Since the government hospitals have been facing the problem of financial crunch on account of inadequate governmental support, it is pertinent that the financial planners pave avenues for the generation of finance from the external sources, such as charity, donation, organisation of sponsored events, borrowings or so. So tar as the internal sources are concerned, we find regulatory barrier and on account of that, they find it difficult to generate finance from fees. Of course, the private hospitals are found using the internal sources which simplify their task of modernisation, expansion and development and it is against this background that in some of the cases, they are found offering the worldclass services. The mismanagement of finance in the government hospitals is found at an alarming stage and this makes the responsibility of financial managers a bit complicated and challenging. We can't deny the fact that information technology helps to have an effective control on the unproductive expenses, simplifies the process of detecting irregularities and unfair practices and makes the accounting practices much more easier and transparent.

The aforesaid facts make it clear that the application of information technology for managing finance would check mismanagement and make the administration bill optimal. The financial requirements for the sensitive heads would be secured while the unnecessary expenses would be regulated. It is in this context that we find use of computers helping the management of finance in hospitals. So far as the private hospitals are concerned, they have been found making sincere efforts in the very context but in a majority of the government hospitals, the application and uses are delayed deliberately. This makes it essential that almost in all the government hospitals, the computers play a dominating role in the management of finance. There are a number of heads in which we expect significant improvements with the computerised management. The inventory management is an important area where the use of computers would regulate a number of expenses on account of the lapses found in the manual operations of registers and accounts. Like this, the payroll if computerised would also control excess payments. Budgetary control is considered to be an important dimension of financial management and the computers help streamlining the wrong processes. Thus, there are a number of areas where we expect qualitative improvements in the management of finance.

Information Related to the Management of Marketing

The hospitals, being a no-profit-making organisation need to market the healthcare/medicare services with a different motive. So far as the profit making organisations are concerned, the task of marketing is found influenced by the generation of profits and therefore, we find attitudes influencing their marketing decisions. The hospital managers bearing the responsibility of marketing the services need different types of information related to the different areas so that the quality services are made available to the patients. The holistic concept of management makes it clear that no-profit-making organisations like hospitals and the educational institutions need more care while managing the different mixes of marketing, specially the price mix. The formulation of a sound marketing mix for hospital would be much more difficult if the managers are not aware of the latest developments in the medical sciences. In addition to the core services, they need information even for managing the peripheral services so that additional attractions are added to the services mix.[12] The task is to satisfy the patients and attendants and unless they know about the level of their expectations, we can't think of satisfying them. The task is to inform and sense the masses in a creative way and unless we make possible creativity in our promotional efforts, it is not possible. Thus, the hospital managers are supposed to blend the different constituents of marketing in such a way that two-pronged motives are fulfilled—first, the hospitals succeed in serving the masses and second, the hospitals keep on moving the process of initiating qualitative-cum-quantitative improvements in tune with the latest developments in medical sciences and the changing requirements of patients. Thus, they need information related to curative services, preventive services and the peripheral services so that quality healthcare services are offered by the hospitals.

The hospitals in addition to the offering of quality services also bear the responsibility of informing and sensing the patients and attendants regarding the services to be made available, amenities and facilities to be provided and the fees to be charged. In a majority of the cases, we find patients and attendants even not aware of the nature and type of services made available by the hospitals. In addition, the task of sensing the patients related to the precautions to be followed, nutritional awareness and healthy living conditions help in minimising a number of food-borne, water-borne viral and communicable diseases. This requires information related to the various areas of promotion so that the hospital managers find it possible to blend them optimally. The different components of promotion are advertising, publicity, sales promotion, personal selling, word-of-mouth promotion and telemarketing. The information related to the advertising agencies, advertising budget, behavioural profile of patients and attendants, level of education of the patients and attendants become important to make possible creativity in the advertisement messages and slogans. They need information related to the magazines and dailies preferred by the users or prospects and to promote with the support of print media. The information related to the media personnel and opinion leaders become important to publicise the services. The motive is to influence them to write about the positive and constructive contributions of the hospital.

The sales promotion schemes are to be made innovative and this requires a knowledge of the tools offered by the competitive hospitals. The hospital personnel as well as the patients and users are to be influenced with the motto of increasing the quality of services. In the context of personal selling, the sisters, nurses, the receptionists and the doctors are required to promote hospitals. If we find hospitals offering services to cater to the changing level of expectations of the patients and attendants, it is quite natural that the satisfied group of users acts as a hidden sales force and the potential users come to know about the services even without advertisement and publicity. Of late, we find telemarketing helping hospitals substantially in promoting and selling the services. The telemarketers bear the responsibility of making available to the users or the potential users necessary information. Besides, they are also required to answer to the queries of visitors and attendants. We can't negate the fact that the functional responsibilities of hospital are considerably simplified if a person with innovative physical attractions and creative communication ability is appointed as a telemarketer. The hospital managers may procure a number of important information from the telemarketers because they are supposed to have a dialogue or conversation with patients, attendants, visitors or others. The marketing information system may get a number of important information from the telemarketers. The hospital managers may use telemarketers as an authentic source for the feedback and may come to know about the complaints and behavioural profile of different categories of hospital personnel. The marketing information system thus simplifies the task of blending the different constituents of promotion in such a way that patients are informed and sensed in a creative way but the promotional expenses are not to be disproportionate or non-optimal to the general budget of hospitals.

The most important decision making area in the hospital management is pricing/fee that requires more excellence because the hospitals are not supposed to make profits. We are well aware of the fact that masses in the Indian perspective need subsidised and cost-based services. The government hospitals, of course, offer free of charge services but except a few, we find all the government hospitals in the same boat. It against this background that the level of efficiency in the government hospitals draws an intensive care. The problem of financial crunch is to be avoided and the quality of services is to be improved. But the state exchequer finds it difficult to extend the required financial support to the hospitals. This makes it essential that we have a different fee strategy so that the internal resources of finance are mobilised in a right way. The hospital mangers need enormous cooperation of the information system because an indepth study of catchment area becomes impact generating in the very context. The level of paying capacity of the different segments, the cost incurred on offering the services are found important for formulating a few structure subserving the interests of all. It is in this context that we talk about a pocket-friendly fee strategy. To be more specific, the government hospitals have to make the ways for the poorest of the poor because they can't afford the services of private hospitals. Since we talk about the uses of quality inputs for improving the quality of services, the general fee structure would be high.

The pocket-friendly or income-based fee strategy would only not help the weaker sections but would also mobilise adequate financial resources for the development of hospitals. The hospital managers need information to manage fee.

The placement needs due care of hospital managers and in this context, they need to collect information for the fulfilment of two different purposes, first the location points for hospitals are easily accessible, free of health hazards, pollution free and second, the services assured by the hospitals are processed in a decent way. This makes it essential that front-staff, sisters, nurses and doctors in addition to the processing of time honoured services also assign due weightage to their behavioural profile. The information related to the locational points and the behavioural profile would help hospital managers in formulating a sound place mix.

The processing of services occupies a place of significance to bridge over the gap between services assured and services offered. It is often found that the medical and paramedical personnel degenerate the quality deliberately and thus, the image of hospital is found tarnished making a place for fear psychosis among the patients and attendants. It is in this context that we need to make available to the patients the assured quality of services. The marketing information system with the help of a marketing intelligence system would inform the hospital managers the details about personnel doing extraordinarily well, personnel doing well and personnel degenerating efficiency. The hospital managers on the basis of report available from the system would be efficacious in identifying, demotivating and penalising the inefficients and rewarding and motivating the efficients. The recruitment processes, specially for the hospital personnel would study the behavioural profile which would make available to the patients the assured services.

Of late, we find physical attraction playing a significant role in almost all the areas. To be more specific, in the hospitals we find provision for uniforms for different categories of personnel. It is essential that the physical attraction of hospital personnel project a positive image of hospitals. The doctors, sisters, nurses, receptionists, telemarketers and others need to look smart and attractive. The moment we find them wearing uniform, a sense of responsibility is found existent.

The management of marketing people is found significant with the view point of increasing the quality of services. It is against this background that we often talk about people-orientation because professional commitments make it essential that hospital personnel are well aware of human and ethical values. The education and training programmes, the syllabi and the refresher courses need to assign due weightage to the process of value engineering.

The aforesaid facts make it clear that the hospital managers need different types of information for managing the marketing of medicare services. The marketing information system, the marketing intelligence system, the marketing research, analytical marketing and the different subsystems of the system would enrich the knowledge bank of medical and paramedical personnel. The day-to-day developments based on frequent inventions and innovations make it essential that the hospital personnel are well aware of the recent developments in medical sciences.

Knowledge Technology in the Armoury of Hospital Management

In a large number of organisations, we find people and machines complemented by a third production factor which is often found to be a bottleneck in the process of development since we find systems allowing access to information already documented. The conventional systems of storing, processing and disseminating information developed during the yester decades, have now brought us to the threshold of a new age in which the dissemination of knowledge demands engineering solutions.[13] It is against this background that we find a need for the computerised knowledge distribution system. Since we find information technology playing a contributory role in the process of enriching the knowledge bank, it is widely known as knowledge technology.

Knowing is becoming increasingly complex in this age of information revolution. It is likely to invite a situation in which the individual may feel overwhelmed and paralysed. The implementation of systems providing raid access to knowledge bases is found much more important. With the passage of time, the knowledge-based systems are going to play an increasingly significant role in modern organisations and in this context, it is pertinent to mention that ongoing developments which would make the ways for the development of the new science of knowledge engineering following the development of systems and machines to support and facilitate the processing of knowledge of people. Systems for storing and processing knowledge are likely to play a role in growing number of human spheres of activity. Of course, the results are to be of quantitative and qualitative values in the overall potentials of knowledge-born intelligence. It is quite natural that the knowledge-based work systems would have a much greater impact when experts from other disciplines enter and use the system without any special training. Assuming that the pace of inventions and innovations keep on moving at the same pace as in other technologies, it would take not less than fifty years to reach technology to this level of sophistication. The work already done on the development of expert systems can be considered to be the first step towards the evolution of genuine industrial knowledge technology.

After all, we can't negate the fact that the knowledge technology is to play an important role in the management of hospitals. The continuing developments in the field of computers, the building of superhighway for information and the consistent efforts of the scientists make it clear that the hospitals and the hospital personnel would be required to take the benefits of incoming developments in the field of knowledge technology failing which the world class quality in the healthcare services would not be possible. All of us are well aware of the fact that Internet operations related to the medical sciences are found helping the researchers, doctors and managers in many ways. Of course, till now, a very few of the hospitals have been found enriching their knowledge technology but we find good auguries and the continuing pace of adoption make it clear that in the decades to come, the hospitals would have no option but to depend upon the knowledge technology. The researchers and medical scientists can't think of activating the process of quality research, if they don't promote e-mailing, Internet and intranet operations.

The information technology is found witnessing a number of qualitative improvements but we don't find development of computer professionals parallel to that pace which is likely to create a gap in the development of knowledge since the potentials of computers would hardly be used optimally. We are well aware of the fact that a number of developments have been taking place in the medical sciences and even till now, a number of doctors and hospital managers are found not aware of the same which has been contracting the returns for our investments. This makes it essential that while developing management information systems, the hospital managers make it sure that quality information technology has been making available to the concerned segments quality knowledge. Again it is to be ascertained that medical and paramedical personnel have been making available to the hospitals the benefits of their rich knowledge bank. The development of a sound management information system, supported by sophisticated information technology would hardly be meaningful unless the medicare services made available to the poor patients are found tasting the fragrance of the same. It is in this context that we need certain precautions while developing the information technology in hospitals.

We agree with this view that in the Indian perspective, there are a number of small hospitals and health centres which lack the potentials of using the sophisticated information technology partially on account of the knowledge constraint and substantially on account of the financial crunch. In addition, the constraints related to the availability of supporting infrastructural facilities have also been aggravating the magnitude of problem. This makes it essential that the government policy makers and the hospital policy formulators assign an overrising priority to the development of knowledge technology in a right fashion.

In the health scenario of India, we find village India presenting a very gloomy picture. Even the primary health centres though effectively operational on papers are found nonexistent in practice. The masses fail in getting even the basic medicare facilities then what to talk of the medicare services of world class. We can't negate that it is also on account of a faulty National Health Policy of the Union and State Governments. A number of secondary and tertiary hospitals are found in a depleted condition because most of them have been found facing the problem of financial crunch. The state exchequer is not to amend the regulations to pave avenues for the development of private hospitals. At this critical juncture, it is judicious that the policy makers bring an attitudinal change so that copious avenues are paved and new vistas are opened for the participation of corporate sector in the health care services. The opening of private hospitals would be efficacious in increasing the level of efficiency of the government hospitals.

In view of the above, it is right to say that an optimal use of knowledge technology in the health care services would activate the process of qualitative transformation. The masses wait for the same anxiously, let the policy makers think about the same seriously. It is high time that the health sector is given an overriding priority.

Emerging Trends in Healthcare Management Information system

Managerial decisions considerably rest on information technology. Since the beginning of 21st century, we have witnessed a number of developments in the IT which have helped the healthcare sector in defining and redefining quality. Around the globe, we find processes of diagnosis, investigation and treatment changing very fast. The advent of Internet services have virtually revolutionised the process of managing hospitals and healthcare services. Almost for all the purposes, we find new generation of information and communication technology commanding the HMIS. The public as well as the private hospitals have been successful in initiating and penetrating qualitative transformation with the help of IT. However, a good number of hospitals need to channelise the multidimensional uses of information and communication technology for protecting and promoting the interests of users. The healthcare providers and trainers have been found initiating a structural transformation with the help of IT. Since India has the advantage of a strong fibre backbone and indigenous satellite communication technology; the hospitals and healthcare centres may enrich their potentials.

The IT has been successful in managing data in a right way. We find direct flow of data from the periphery. The HMIS is found in a position to integrate the various vertical systems with the help of own reporting machinery into an integrated umbrella of holistic management education to cater to the needs of Sarva Swasthya Abhiyan[14]. We find penetration of computerization even at a block level which has been instrumental in channelising the benefits of IT to the remotest areas. We find scope for minimising the wastage of drugs due to expiry of date. The credibility of demand-driven management goes to the new generation of IT.

Today, we find telemedicine helping the remotest corners of the country in bringing specialised health care to them. The advantage of telediagnosis specially in the areas of cardiology, pathology, dermatology and radiology are well known to us. The development of secondary level healthcare facilities has been possible due to new developments in the field of information and communication technology. The diagnostic and consultative uses have been found benefiting the masses. The Indian Space Research Organisation (ISRO) has played an important role in connecting superspeciality hospitals with mobile telemedicine vans and rural and remote hospitals. It is high time that they expand the services to a larger number of rural hospitals and health care centres. The organisations like DIT, NEC, NGOs and State Governments need to extend active support to the telemedicine and telediagnosis programme. The e-enabled mobile medical units are found due to new generation of IT but we find limited uses of the same which need priority attention of central as well as the state governments.

The hospitals and healthcare centres not only succeed in improving the quality of their services but in addition, they also find themselves successful in promoting the services.

In the changing perspective, it is pertinent that the hospitals and healthcare organisations make use of Internet for advertising their services. When we find a number of hospitals of global standard both in the public and private sectors, advertising online would help them in having an access to a global market where the cost-effectiveness is found of high intensity. Advertising on the web pertains to build the eye-catching banner. In the Indian perspective, we find a significant increase in the Internet connections and by large, around the world, we find the same trend and therefore, the hospital and healthcare organisations may use banner advertisement. We find hyper banner the largest global banner exchange on the Web. Of late, when we find India efficacious of marketing medical or healthcare tourism, it is significant that we make use of banner advertisement.

The significant developments in the field of information and communication technology have also made it easier to promote medical education[15]. The leading hospitals of the country who are considered to be potentially sound may promote medical education with the help of teleconferencing. We find medical colleges or institutes gearing themselves to invest their resources in terms of time, manpower and money to mould themselves to groom students. The teleconferencing may be helpful in promoting educational aid and training facilities to the students. Besides, this device may also be used for developing mass awareness related to the food prone and water-prone or communicable diseases. The information related to nutritional awareness of vaccination and immunisation may also be transmitted to the masses as preventive measures.

The sophisticated IT has also simplified the process of making payments. The hospitals or the users of services find it convenient to get payment solutions. The e-payment has been found gaining popularity. In the modern society, we find Internet as the gold mine. The hospitals and healthcare organisations are required to make payment to the different agencies or parties where e-payment makes their task convenient. In addition, the users of services also get their payment solutions. The accounting and filing are found much more authentic. The evaluation and control processes have become easier.

For activating the process of development, it is essential that we undertake research and development activities. In this connection management of inputs (data) and management of outputs (information) are found significant. Electronic Date Interchange (EDI) minimises scope for paperwork.[16] The loads of paperwork can be minimised with the help of EDI. The conventional paper documents have virtually been replaced by EDI. The office system is found completely automated. The information flow is found faster and we also find possibilities of accuracy. The hospitals are also found in a position to get the logistic benefits. The forecasting and planning for the healthcare services have gained a rapid momentum due to EDY. Accessibility to a particular command area is found possible. The hospitals are in a position to get the competitive advantage.

Proper governance is an essential consideration for the smooth functioning of hospitals and healthcare organisations. The hospital managers with the help of e-governance can monitor the operational mechanism. All the functional responsibilities need time honoured monitoring and reporting. With the development of HMIS, we find integration of various vertical systems with the help of own reporting machinery into an umbrella of holistic medical education to cater to the needs of the weaker sections of the society. The integrated Disease Surveillance Project would help in the right diagnosis.

It is in the larger interest of the society that we develop information driven healthcare organisations. We are well aware of the fact that healthcare is basically a labour-intensive service industry considerably depending on knowledge and information as a product. Right diagnosis, time-honoured diagnosis, proper treatment and care, decent behaviour and administering accurate dose of drugs are some of the important dimensions necessitating due attention for the delivery of promised quality of services by the healthcare organisations. Since in the Indian perspective, we find demographic pressure of high magnitude standing as a barrier for providing proper medicare services to a majority of our population, it is imperative that with the help of research and development activities, we evolve low-cost and indigenous technologies. We cannot deny that during the yesteryears, the research and development activities have resulted into the development of sophisticated technologies for diagnosis and treatment of diseases but we find them expensive and therefore, on account of affordability, the poor sections of the Indian society fail in harnessing the benefits. It is in this context that researchers and scientists need intensive efforts to making crucial equipments affordable such as anesthesia machine, surgical equipment and lighting, sterilization equipment, pulse oxymeter, defibrillator, ventilator, electrocardiogram and blood pressure monitoring equipment. The public health related technologies and public health related practices at all levels of healthcare need priority attention.

The above mentioned facts make it clear that in the Indian perspective we need to view the situation with a different vision. On the one hand, we have been developing healthcare devices of world class helping us in generating foreign currency or promoting the interests of affluent sections of the society and on the other hand, we also need to make available health care services to the weaker sections of the society living in the backward rural areas. Low-cost or cheaper technologies and telemedicine and teleconferencing are the devices which would help us in meeting Health for All which has not been given due weightage by the national policy planners. We have high level of expectations from the techno-driven management information systems and we are hopeful that they would not disappoint us. E-Health and E-Governance need priority attention. Not only the state hospitals but even corporate private hospitals have to accept social responsibility which would protect and promote the interests of humanity.

SUMMARY

In this chapter of the book, you have gone through the different dimensions of Management Information System. After going through all the components, be sure that the following facts are well versed.

MIS-the Concept: The Management Information System is a device to transform the data into information. The data are the raw facts and figures collected from the different sources whereas the information focuses our attention on the disseminated information for the use of managers.

Hospital Information System: The management information system for hospitals draws our attention on managing the facts and figures helping the policy and decision makers in different ways. The system may be managed manually or with the help of computers. The hospital information system helps hospital managers in making right decisions efficacious in satisfying the patients and attendants.

Information Technology: In the context of information technology, we find prime focus on the instrumentality of computers in managing the information system. The miniframe, microframe and mainframe computers are used for this purpose.

Computer-driven MIS: Of late, we talk about a computer-driven system because almost all the organisations prefer to use different types of computers for managing the information. We also call it a technology-driven information system.

Programming Language: Programming is an art of writing a programme. To make free the programmer from the tidum of writing a programme, we find high level and low level languages. The high level languages are comprehensible representation of machine code using mnemonics in the assembly language.

Information Superhighway: Internet operations increasing accessibility to multidimensional information.

Application of MIS in Hospitals: Like other organisations, the hospitals may also use the information system for different purposes, such as formulation of hospital and departmental policies, formulation of hospital and departmental plans and managing the functional areas, such as services, hospital personnel, finance and marketing.

The policy makers find it significant to formulate a sound policy for the development of hospitals. The hospital managers find it important to the management of services for the tailoring of hospital potentials to the changing requirements of patients. In addition, the management of hospital people is found result-oriented. The management of finance is also given a new direction and the marketing practices are made innovative. Thus, the application of a technology-driven MIS may serve hospitals in different ways.

Knowledge Technology in the Armoury of Hospital Management: Since we find information technology helping us in enriching our knowledge, we also call it the knowledge technology. With the development of information superhighway or the internet services, the hospitals find the system useful even in enriching the knowledge of hospital personnel.

Emerging Trends in Healthcare Management Information System: During yester decades, we have witnessed a number of changes in the information technology which has considerably influenced the Health Care Management information System. The telemedicine, teledignosis, teleconferencing, computerised filing, accounting, reporting, online payments and banner advertising are some of the important developments helping hospital professionals in defining and redefining service quality. Of late, we find ourselves potentially sound for developing Medical or Health Tourism. It is high time that national policy makers and corporate boardrooms concentrate priority attention on practising IT for the development of healthcare organisations vis-a-vis multidimensional improvements in the quality of healthcare services with due focus on rural areas.

KEY TERMS

Management Information System	Software
Techno-driven Information	Hardware
Information Technology	Programming
Internet Services	Floppy Disks
Linen	Networking
Inventory Management	Information Superhighway
CARY	OPD
CYDER	Therapeutics
Mainframe Computers	Primary Hospital
Micro-Computers	Secondary Hospital
Miniframe Computers	Tertiary Hospital
ALGOL	Immunisation
COBOL	Vaccination
DOS	Knowledge Technology
BASIC	Satellite

REVIEW QUESTIONS

1. What do you mean by MIS? Focus on the instrumentality of a computer driven MIS in managing the hospitals.
2. What do you mean by Hospital Information System? Explain the instrumentality of information system in formulating a sound development policy for healthcare organisations.
3. Explain the role of information technology in managing the information for hospitals and healthcare organisations.
4. Discuss in brief the uses of computers in managing the hospitals and healthcare organisations.
5. Explain the role of information technology in enriching the knowledge bank of medical and paramedical personnel.
6. Focus on the role of information system in managing finance in hospitals and health care organisations.
7. Explain the contributions of a tech-driven information system in the formulation of a sound policy for the development of healthcare services in the Indian perspective.
8. Explain the contributions of a tech-driven information system in evaluating and motivating hospital personnel.
9. Focus on the instrumentality of MIS in marketing the healthcare services.
10. Throw light on the role of MIS in the development of healthcare services in the rural areas of the country.
11. Explain the relevance of HMIS for promoting Medical Tourism.
12. Focus on the role of Jan Swasthya Sahyog (JSS) in the development of affordable healthcare services for rural India.

APPLICATION EXERCISES

1. The hospital planners, hospital architects and consultants get a number of support from the HMIS which helps them in formulating a sound development plan for hospitals. Comment on this statement as a hospital professional.
2. With the development of information superhighway, we find HMIS considerably helping the medical and paramedical personnel in enriching their knowledge bank. Focus on this statement in the capacity of a hospital manager.
3. A tech-driven MIS helps the policy makers in many ways. Comment on this statement as a hospital professional.
4. In the capacity of a hospital professional, focus on the relevance of Jan Swasthya Sahyog (JSS) for making the healthcare services affordable to the poor rural people who fail in availing the expensive healthcare services.
5. The use of computers would help hospital managers identifying and controlling the financial irregularities found in government hospitals.
6. Being a hospital manager, you bear the responsibility of satisfying the patients and attendants by offering to them the quality healthcare services. In the light of this statement, focus on the practices of MIS in satisfying the users.
7. You are working as a hospital manger. Throw light on the role of new generation of information and communication technology in developing user-friendly healthcare services in the Indian perspective.

END NOTES

1. Murdick, Ross Claggett, *INformation System for Modern Management,* p. 6.
2. Koontz & Weihrich, *Essentials of Management,* pp. 428-29.
3. *Manorama Year Book 2000,* pp. 224-25.
4. *Manorama Year Book 2000,* pp. 229-30.
5. Bhatti S.S., *Hospital Planning,* pp. 87-88.
6. *Ibid.*
7. Surinder K. Jindal, and Umesh N. Jindal, *Computers in Hospital Administration,* pp. 213-32.
8. *Ibid.*
9. *Ibid.*
10. Goel S.L., *Manpower Planning,* p. 253.
11. Goel S.L., *Materials Management with Special Reference to Equipment and Drugs,* pp. 233-53.
12. Jha S.M., *Hospital Marketing,* Chap. 12, *Services Marketing,* pp. 494-525.
13. *Simens Review,* 1/90, p. 5.
14. Eleventh Five Year Plan; Planning Commission, Vol. II
15. Kumar Ashok, Government of India, New Delhi, 2008 *Indian Hospitals Need Good Managers and IT;* Journal of Marketing & Communication Vol. 1/3, 2006
16. Kristie J. Loescher, *The Information-Driven Healthcare Organisation SCMS Journal of Indian Management* Vol. III/1 2006

Management of Behaviour in Hospitals

India has been emerging as a leading global Healthcare Brand and this makes it essential that we keep on moving the process of defining and redefining quality. Behavioural and ethical dimensions add to the quality of healthcare services.

CHAPTER OBJECTIVES

Introduction—Behaviour: the Perception—Theory of Human Nature—Maslow's Theory—Behavioural Influences—Behavioural Management in Hospitals—Relationships—Ethics in Hospitals—Behavioural conflict in Hospitals—Indian Hospitals need Behaviorally and Ethically Sound People—Summary—Key Terms—Review Questions—Application Exercises—End Notes.

LEARNING OBJECTIVES

This chapter of the book aims at studying the different dimensions of behavioral profile in relation to hospital services. The hospital professionals need to make it sure that relationships between superiors, peers and subordinates and doctor-patients and others are friendly. The concept of humanised leadership needs due attention of professionals. In a true sense, the doctor-patients relationships, if friendly and humanised, help in minimising the recovery period. The readers come to know the different facets of behavioural management in hospitals.

Introduction

Scientific inventions and innovations shape the levels of out expectations. If we get more, we expect more. Our expectations thus motivate the inventors to keep themselves all the time engaged in offering something innovative which their counterparts can't. The process of new inventions and innovations thus keep on moving. The behavioural scientists feel that a change in the behavioural profile of users is a natural phenomenon because the development processes cannot remain static. It is against this background that almost all the organisations are found serious to an indepth study of the changing behavioral profile of users. This in a true sense helps them in making things happen.

During yesteryears, we have witnessed a number of inventions and innovations in the field of medical sciences. The research organisations, pharmaceutical industries, tertiary hospitals and albeit individuals have been making sincere efforts to invent something new which help in improving the quality of services. The dedicated and personally committed efforts of scientists have helped the human beings in many ways. The new devices for diagnosis, investigations and treatment, the sophisticated technologies for improving the quality of healthcare services; the new drugs for improving the recovery rate and new generation of information and communication technology for defining and redefining service quality are the results of sincere, honest and consistent efforts of medical scientists. Increasing access of masses to information and knowledge plays an incremental role in increasing the levels of expectations. The information superhighway has activated the process of knowledge transformation. It is due to these innovative developments that our expectations, preferences, needs and requirements, attitudes and behavioural profile have witnessed multidimensional transformation.

Organisations producing goods or generating services assigning due weightage to the changing levels of expectations of users succeed in making a place whereas others keeping their eyes closed and minds inactive perish. This makes it essential that hospitals and healthcare organisations assign number one priority to the behavioural dimensions. In addition, they also need to consider ethical dimensions, human values, personal commitments which are virtually found to be the offshoots of our behavioural profile. You are thematically of world class but morally unsound. You are efficient but dishonest. You are a star performer but lack humanity. Thus, development of a few properties cannot serve our purpose unless we find transformation in totality. In plain words, we need quality medical and paramedical personnel, professional sound hospital managers and thus, a mix of quality people of different echelons makes the ways for worldclass healthcare services. Of course, we find new generation of sophisticated technology helping them in getting the desired results but failing the availability of quality doctors, we find everything turning into a fiasco. This focuses on the development of quality people and in the process of development, required properties and attributes are to be inculcated.

The tertiary hospitals and medical institutes have been found assigning due weightage to the professional requirements but they are yet to make behavioural dimension an essential criterion for the development of quality people. It is against this background that in a majority of the hospitals and healthcare organisations, the relationships amongst the different categories of personnel and the relationships of doctors, nurses or other hospital personnel with the patients and attendants are not decent. This makes it essential that the hospitals and institutes performing the responsibility of developing different categories of medical and paramedical personnel assign due weightage to the development of behavioral dimensions so that inter-departmental and intradepartmental relationships and doctor-patients relationships are found congenial.

Thus, we find two important dimensions of behavioural profile in hospitals-the first is departmental relationships or relationships of superiors with the superiors and the relationships of superiors with the subordinates and vice versa and the second is relationships of hospital personnel with the patients and attendants. The behavioural scientists feel that it is possible to inculcate the faculty by educating and training the personnel in a right fashion. We agree with their viewpoints because we find a sea difference in the behavioural profile of hospital personnel working in some of the leading hospitals and institutes where their schooling is found with a new approach and a distinct vision. Particularly, the leading private hospitals and institutions have been found assigning priority attention to the behavioural traits. In the state hospitals, we find behavioural dimension not getting due attention and therefore, in a majority of the state hospitals, the doctor-patients relationships and the doctor-doctor relationships obstruct the process of increasing the operational efficiency vis-a-vis the productivity.

The quality of relationships plays an incremental role in satisfying the health of the customers. It is in this context that interactions of doctors with the patients considerably influence the quality of services and further, the physicians' relationships with healthcare organisations also influence healthcare services and quality. This makes a strong advocacy in favour of improving the relationships at all levels because it is found directly related with the operational efficiency. Involving patients in the decision making process is found significant with the viewpoint of improving the relationships. There are a number of ways and avenues in which the community and users may participate in the development of health care policy. These can range from passive consultations to structural participation where control of community is preferred.

The healthcare service industry is complex where we find a different scenario. Earlier, the users were not involved in the process of designing the product and service delivery processes. But today, we find a shift to an organisation model in which the users have been found to be the focal point and therefore, we find an attitudinal change and a structural transformation. This has been making the ways for new quality focus where healthcare organisations assign due weightage to preferences, feelings and realisations of patients and attendants.

An indepth study of the management of behaviour in hospitals and healthcare organisations is found essential to improve the quality of healthcare services. The cohesive interdepartmental relationships and intradepartmental relationships make it essential that while educating and training the hospital personnel of different categories, the syllabi, the training programme and the motivational dimensions get priority attention. The hospital managers in the very context bear the responsibility of making it sure that the relationships make the working or service environment friendly. The cases of confrontation, ego-conflict, indecent behaviour of superiors with the subordinates and vice versa, the behaviour of hospital personnel with the patients and attendants are given due weightage while making an appraisal of the different categories of hospital personnel. It is right to mention that degenerating relationships make an invasion on the efficiency of an individual or a group. Since we find working of a hospital based on a team, it is pertinent that cases of confrontation are checked and a sense of coordination is promoted. There are a number of variables influencing the behavioural profile of personnel and the hospital managers need to make it sure that while motivating the personnel in addition to their operational efficiency and performance level, they assign weightage even to the behavioural profile. We cannot deny that service quality in the healthcare organisations sizably rests on the behavioural profile of different categories of hospital personnel.

BEHAVIOUR-THE PERCEPTION

Before we go through the management of behaviour in hospitals, it is essential that we understand the perception of behaviour in a right fashion. There are certain principles which represent universal truths. Because we go through the perception of behavioural in the context of healthcare organisations, it is right to consider behaviour a systematic effort to understand the behaviour of people serving an organisation and further understanding the behaviour of customers or users related to the organisations. This understanding the behaviour of customers or users, nurturing an organisation and understanding the behaviour of personnel serving an organisation become the key areas while studying behaviour. Because we find behaviour a combination of a large number of factors, it is pertinent to go through the psychological, sociological, political and economic factors considerably influencing the behavioural profile. The biological fallacy makes it clear that behaviour is partially influenced by inner needs or motives which we bring with us as members of a biological species. Of course, we find money or the financial incentives influencing and motivating a large number of people but we also find a case where the instrumentality of money in influencing and motivating the people is found at the zero level. This is due mainly to the fact that our perception regarding the way of life, needs and requirements, status and condition determine our requirements for money. The family tradition and family background also develop the perception of behaviour. Suppose you come from a very humble origin and have finally achieved a reasonable subsistence level and perceive yourself as "having made it" by whatever standards you assimilated in the subculture in which you grew up, you will react very differently to a monetary incentive than an MBA from an ordinary institute starting out at the bottom of career, aspiring to get a high level position in the organisation and to a position of wealth which will prove to the world that you have really made it "to the top."' This makes it clear that behaviour in different cases is found different since expectations in all the cases can't be uniform.

We can't deny the fact that the study of behaviour thus becomes a difficult task because we find a number of considerations proving one theory right but rejecting another. It is right to mention that the theory of behavioural psychology was first developed by Prof. J.B. Waston (1919). He was of the view that behaviour could be explained in mechanistic terms. He felt that stimulation has necessary responses. A well-known experiment made by Pavlov on his dogs proved that when dogs were conditioned to the sounding of the bell with the offering of the food, the Saliva dropped from their jaws whenever the bell was sounded even if the food was not served. This speaks of the fact that our actions or decisions have a close relation with our habits and behaviour.[2]

The perception of behaviour is thus found focusing our attention on our family background, the changes in the social systems, the growing influence of materialism in the society, our perception regarding the materialistic achievements, the constitution and support of a family, the family background of spouse or a number of factors not only directly but even indirectly making possible an attitudinal change. It is against this background that we find behaviour a more complicated study in the management science. The organisations, irrespective of their nature and character are required to study the behavioural problems, because this is to help them in surviving and thriving.

Theory of Human Nature

In the annals of behavioural sciences, a number of steps have been taken to know about the nature of human beings and the factors motivating them. Till now whatever the answers we have received only elude us. Efforts are on, discussions are taking place, issues are deliberated upon but still we find enough scope for a debate. In a true sense, there is no one answer to perceive the real facts regarding the motivational factors. The management of people is thus becoming a challenging task for the managers of an organisation. A powerful influence we find of McGregor's Theory X and Theory Y.[3]

In Exhibit 4.1, we find the two theories.

Theory X	*Theory Y*
The typical person dislikes work.	Work is as natural as play and rest, if the conditions are favourable.
The typical person lacks ambition and responsibility and prefers to be directed.	People are not inherently lazy. They have become that way as a result of experience.
The typical person must be closely controlled and often coerced to achieve organisational objectives.	People have potential. Under proper conditions, they learn to accept and seek responsibility. They have imagination, ingenuity and creativity that can be applied to work.

Exhibit 4.1. McGregor's Theory X and Theory Y

In Theory X, the managers are found controlling the employees by adopting even the coercive measures. But in Theory Y, we find managers developing the potentials in the employees and helping them to release the potential towards the accomplishment of common objectives. We also find another theory in the very context. Our focus is here on Maslow's theory.[4]

In the Maslow's theory, it is found that the behaviour of an individual at a particular moment is determined by his strongest need and it may be physiological, social, esteem and self actualisation as presented in Fig. 4.1.

We can't negate the fact that human behaviour and their relationships have been existent since the very beginning of the civilisation, but here it is also right to mention that the art and science of trying to deal with them, specially in the complex organisations has been found different. Harvard University also studied on the nature of human behaviour and the Hawthorne experiment in the very context is known to all of us that an organisation is a social system and an individual employed therein is a very important element and human beings in an organisation are complex personalities interacting in a group situation that often is difficult to understand. The different theories and observations make it clear that the task of understanding the human nature and behaviour is complex. We can't negate that such a situation is due mainly to the different conditions guiding and influencing all of us in a different way. It is the prime responsibility of a manager to understand the obscure human personalities, reacting and behaving against our presumptions. However, we find needs and requirements influencing human behaviour considerably and it is in this context that we find focus on Maslow's theory.

Maslow's Theory

In the world of behavioural sciences, the theory of Maslow occupies an outstanding place. Maslow, an important authority, focuses on the hierarchy of needs. He was of the view that motives related to human behaviour are innate which move in an ascending order. In his opinion, for moving to the next level, it is essential that one need is fully or at least partially fulfilled. Thus, the psychological studies indicate that human activity including the behaviour is directed toward satisfying certain needs. Of course, the clinical psychologists don't agree but a number of authorities on the problem agree with the Maslow's theory. According to Maslow, an individual normally tries to satisfy the most basic needs first and after satisfying the basic needs, he/she feels free to devote his/her efforts to the next as shown in Fig. 4.1. The hierarchy of needs enumerated by Maslow makes it clear that our efforts to get more continue till we completely exhaust or reach to the peak of using our potentials. Thus, the efforts of masses to get more transform expectations and the task of the concerned organisation is found complicated. The more we offer, the more they expect. We can't negate that the instrumentality of the competitive organisations plays an important role in the process of shaping of our expectations.

Basic Needs: In the very beginning, it is quite natural that all of us make efforts to fulfil the basic needs, such as food to satisfy our hunger, water to meet out thirst, clothes to look civilised, shelter to sleep and essential medicare facilities to survive. If we succeed in getting the aforesaid essentials, we march forward and our expectations keep on moving.

Safety and Security: After satisfying the basic needs, we expect safety and security so that we get a place in the society where we live. Here, the physical safety is not so much significant because we also find persons taking risk to fulfil their expectations.

Belonging: After getting safety and security, we expect affectionate relations with individuals and a place in the society. This is found important since its absence proves to be a common cause of maladjustment. This makes the ways for existence.

Esteem Needs: The fulfilment of esteem needs provides a feeling of self confidence and usefulness whereas the non-fulfilment provides feelings of insecurity.

Achievement: This is related to self-actualisation. Here, we expect the maximum of our capabilities or potentials.

The aforesaid classification of needs enumerated by Maslow has been found meaningful to the managers for making decisions. Almost all categories of organisations take the support of people and the managers are supposed to satisfy them. The goods manufacturing or service generating, the profit-making or not-for-profit making, the private sector or the public sector need to motivate the people so that the level of efficiency is sizeably increased. It is against this background that we find rationale behind studying the problem of behavioural management even to the hospital managers because unless they keep the hospital personnel fully satisfied, the expectations of patients and attendants would remain unfulfilled. Of course, a number of factors influence behaviour but the needs have a special position.

Implications of Maslow's Theory

We agree with this view that the theory of Maslow is found relevant to all categories of organisations. The hospitals, being a not-for-profit making organisation are also supposed to make possible an indepth study of the behavioural profile so that the hospital managers are found successful in making the work environment conducive to make available to the patients quality services.

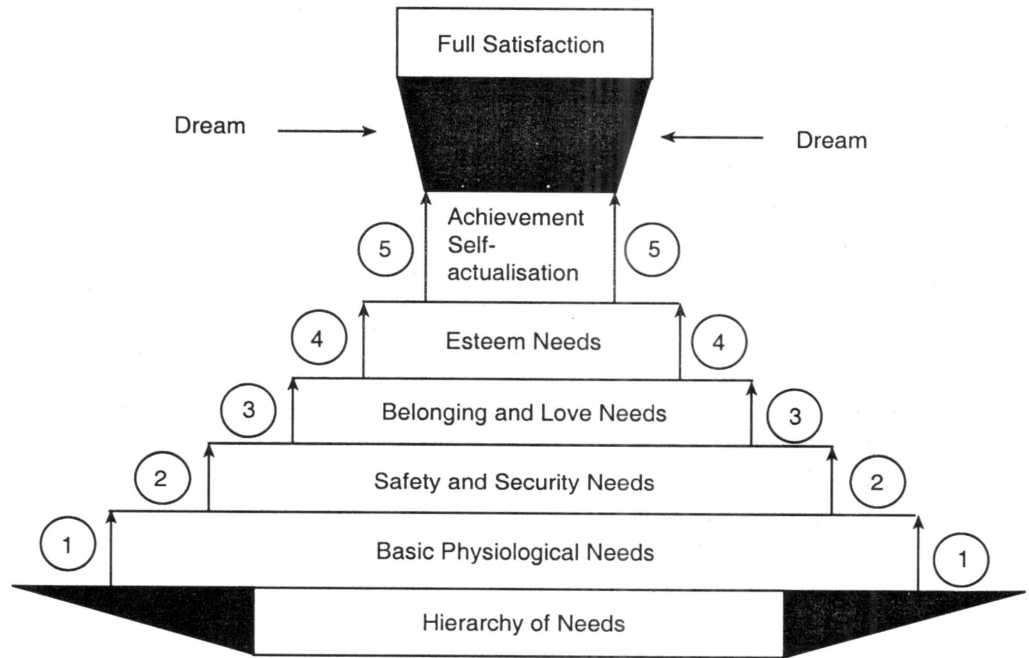

Fig. 4.1. Maslow's Hierarchy of Needs
Adopted from *Motivation and Personality*, Harper Brothers,, New York, pp. 80-85.

Since we talk about the essential services occupying an important place in the family budget of an individual, the problems are analysed with a different vision. We are well aware of the fact that we provide an overriding priority to our medicare or healthcare requirements. The increasing health consciousness in the society is now found assigning due weightage to the healthcare and therefore, we find an attitudinal change in the prospects requiring the services of hospitals. On the other hand, the hospital personnel working in different capacities are supposed to play a dominating role in fulfilling the expectations of patients and attendants. It is pertinent that hospital managers keep themselves informed with the behavioural profile of all categories of personnel.

The emerging positive developments in the medical sciences have substantially influenced the level of expectations of patients and attendants because they find their counterparts getting quality medicare services in some of the hospitals. In addition, the hospital personnel have also developed a high level of expectations being influenced by consumerism/materialism. The theory of Maslow is thus found relevant albeit to the healthcare organisations. It is in this context that we make a strong advocacy in favour of undertaking an indepth study of the behavioural profile.

Behavioural Influences

There are a number of factors found instrumental in influencing the human behaviour. The managers bear the responsibility of making smooth ways for the satisfaction of hospital personnel, patients and attendants. If they are aware of the different variables, the task of improving the quality of hospital services would considerably be simplified. It is against this background that we go through the different variables, viz., social, cultural, economic. The Fig. 4.2 focuses on social factors.

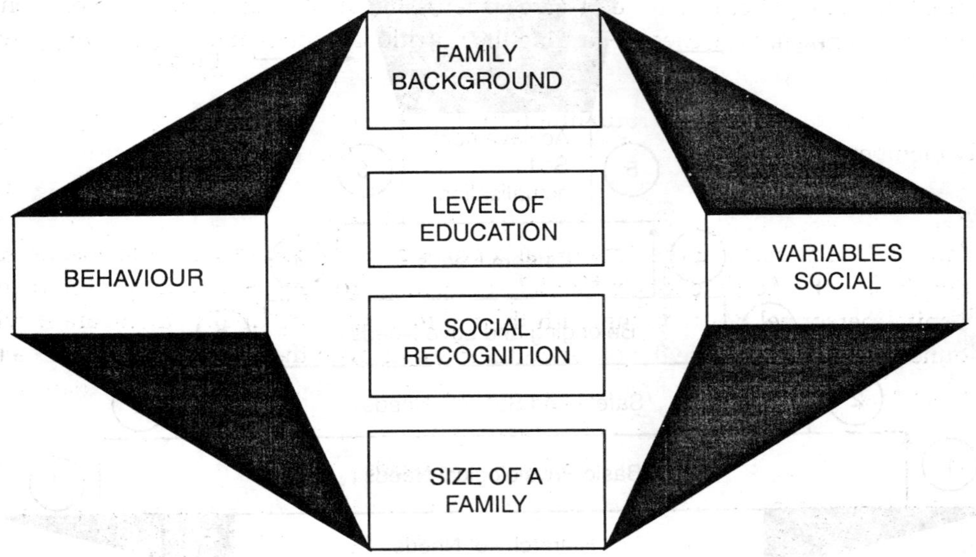

Fig. 4.2. Social Factors Influencing Human Behaviour

The different constituents in the social profile are the family background, level of education, social recognition and size of a family.

Family Background: Among the social variables, we find family background sizeably influencing the human behaviour. By the family background, our focus is on the socio-cultural background of a family from which the hospital personnel and the patients come from. The sociologists, cultural activists believe that the background of a family is engineered as a process, taking years and years and generation-to-generation for having a shape. It is quite natural that expectations of an individual coming from a high family background in which the level of thinking is found culturally sound would commonly be high unless we find the process of degeneration taking a place. If in a family, we find the tradition of maintaining values and intellects having an edge over others, the level of expectations would be high. Such a tradition found developing without a break prepares a sound family background. If the personnel serving the hospitals or the patients and attendants coming to hospitals belong to a family having a rich cultural background, it is quite natural that both of them would have high expectations. The hospital managers are supposed to understand the behavioural profile of personnel and the personnel are supposed to understand the behavioural profile of patients and attendants. This simplifies the task of satisfying both the segments which makes the process of improving the quality of services easier.

Level of Education: It is an important social variable influencing the human behaviour. Since we find education playing an incremental role in increasing awareness, generating values, improving the level of thinking, the educational background of a family needs to be given due weightage while understanding the behaviour. The expectations of educated patients and attendants to the hospitals would be different from the expectations of uneducated or illiterate patients. Since in the Indian perspective we find mass illiteracy, it is pertinent that the hospitals come to know about the educational background of the concerned catchment area in which the hospitals are functioning. Because the educated patients and attendants are found more conscious and are supposed to have awareness regarding the nutritional values and hygienic or unhygienic conditions, the hospital personnel would find it easier to convince and satisfy them.

Social Recognition: The social recognition focuses our attention on the weightage given by the family members on the healthcare devices. It is linked to the education and tradition. If in the society, we find healthcare devices getting an important place in the family budget, the pressure on hospitals is found considerably minimised. In addition, this variable also influences the behavioural influences because the patients and attendants are found well informed regarding the new developments and practices in the field of health care devices and medical sciences. The task of hospital personnel not working with the motto of offering quality medicare services to them is found complicated. Since they keep in their minds even the small things not directly but even indirectly influencing the treatment results, the hospital personnel need not to perceive even small things lightly.

Size of a Family: Among the social variables, we find size of a family occupying a place of significance. The patients and attendants having a big family or say, having more children have less expectations because they can't keep themselves a detailed information of even small things playing an important role in the healthcare. This influences the levels of their expectations and increases the functional responsibilities of hospital personnel. Unmanageable family is thus found a place for the developments of diseases and the Indian masses are substantially influenced by this variable. We don't find nutritional awareness and health consciousness. The dirty living conditions play an incremental role in aggravating the problem of making available the medicare services. The village health centres are found a glaring example of the same where even the maternity services become unmanageable. What to talk of the primary hospitals, when we find even the secondary and tertiary hospitals sizeably influenced by this variable.

The aforesaid social variables make it clear that for improving the quality of healthcare services, minimising the diagnostic and treatment complications, meeting the expectations of patients and attendants, simplifying the task of hospital personnel and more so for increasing the level of efficiency of hospital managers, it is essential that the social variables are given due weightage by the hospital personnel. This would make it easier to get the positive results and to satisfy the patients and attendants in the face of their changing levels of expectations. Ultimately, the hospital managers are found responsible for the level of efficiency of hospitals and therefore, it is essential that besides enriching their own knowledge, they inform and interact with the hospital personnel. To be more specific, the government hospitals, where we find everything in mess, it is pertinent that the hospital personnel in general and the hospital managers in particular come to know about the influences of social variables. This would only not increase the level of efficiency but would also minimise the work pressure on hospitals.

Economic Influences: The human behaviour is substantially influenced by the economic variables. In the context of economic variables, we find the level of income of the society playing an important role. The hospital managers are supposed to be aware of the emerging trends in the level of income of the masses living in the catchment or command area. We can't deny the fact that ultimately, it is the level of income of patients or attendants playing an incremental role in generating demand and influencing supply. Of late, we find medicare services expensive since the process of diagnosis and treatment need the support of sophisticated technologies and expertise. In addition, a number of supporting infrastructural facilities become essential to improve the quality of services. It is in this context that we find economic variables requiring due attention of the hospital managers. Because the health care requirements and medicare demand get a position of top priority in our family, it is significant that the hospital managers know about the emerging trends in the disposable income. There are a number of requirements influencing the scale of disposable income, such as the pressure of inflation and the changing life styles. We can't negate the instrumentality of changing economic conditions. We are supposed to spend for food, accommodation and clothes and in addition on our medicare. If the pressure of inflation is found moving upward, the share of medicare is sizeably minimised. This makes it essential that the hospital managers understand the emerging trends in inflation. If the inflationary pressure is found low, the masses get more disposable incomes for availing the medicare facilities. In this context, even the expensive services may be used by the masses. But contrary to it, if we find the pressure of inflation high, the masses even knowing well the significance of medicare services find it difficult to spend for the same.

The policy makers also need to be aware of the same because the government hospitals, where masses are found availing the facilities can't make the services, cost disproportionate to the levels of income. This draws our attention on the instrumentality of medical experts in promoting the medicare services found of low cost and affordable to the masses. The research and development activities by the medical scientists are required to be intensified to devise low-cost services based on Indian traditional medical science. Unless the policy makers evince their interests in promoting research, the task would remain much more difficult to the hospital managers and the research and the medical scientists. To be more specific, the tertiary government hospitals draw our attention in the very context because they bear the responsibility of educating, training and undertaking and conducting research. Besides, the global health organisations also need to promote the research-oriented hospitals and institutes even in the private sector. The masses in the Indian perspective find it difficult to afford the expensive medicare services. We don't find the steps taken by any of the governmental and non-governmental organisations positive to make the medicare services economic.

The aforesaid factors make it clear that the human behaviour is influenced by a number of factors and the hospital managers, hospital personnel specially of high echelon need to think over the problem on a priority basis. We can postpone our other requirements but not the medicare requirements. The expectations of prospects can't be minimised because the sophisticated communication technologies are found sensitising the same.

Psychological Influences

We can't underestimate the instrumentality of psychological factors on the behavioural profile of patients, attendants and hospital personnel. Since we go through the behavioural influences, it is essential to make it clear that hospital personnel need to go through the psychological problems because they are supposed to satisfy the patients and attendants. On the other hand, the hospital personnel can counter the problem related to the departmental conflicts if they are well aware of the psychological factors influencing the behaviour and shaping the expectations. This focuses our attention on attitudes and motivation.

Attitudes: In the hospital services, the attitudes of patients and attendants are influenced by a number of factors. The educated segment of the patients and attendants is guided with a different attitude. The level of income and family background also influence attitudes. The regional considerations become significant due to communications facilities. The expectations are influenced by all these factors. To be more specific, the latest developments in the field of communications technologies and information superhighway play a significant role in influencing the level of expectations. If the patients and attendants are found aware of the recent developments in the medical sciences and the sophisticated services offered by some of the hospitals, they expect the same quality of services from other hospitals. The hospital managers bear the responsibility of satisfying the patients and attendants and therefore, they are supposed to know about the influences of psychological factors.

The different categories of hospital personnel engaged in offering the different types of services expect lucrative incentives from the employers. There is no doubt in it that the hospital personnel expect handsome salaries and other incentives. It is the responsibility of hospital managers to study the levels of their expectations from the organisation and to make suitable arrangements to fulfil them. In addition, it is also pertinent that the managers keep in their minds the comforts and conveniences of hospital personnel so that they find it convenient to discharge their functional responsibilities up to the expectations of patients and attendants. It is in this context that we find the instrumentality of hospital managers in fulfilling the expectations of personnel to deliver world class services.

Motivation: Unless you motivate the employees in a right fashion, the level of efficiency can't be increased. There are different components of motivation and the hospital managers are supposed to be aware of all of them to motivate the hospital personnel. The financial incentives, the non-financial incentives, the quality of environment at the workplace and the quality of environment at the places of livings are the different aspects to be given due weightage by the hospital managers. Handsome salaries, welfare facilities, promotional avenues, decent behaviour, availability of supporting infrastructual facilities at the work place, the availability of essential infrastructural facilities and the civic amenities at the living places, involvement of family members in the development of hospitals are some of the components of motivation playing a dominating role in increasing the level of efficiency of the hospital personnel. The hospital managers by increasing the level of efficiency would also be successful in making the services cost-effective. Motivational schemes of world class would make the ways for the development of quality hospital personnel not only professionally sound but personally-committed too, where we may also expect some wonders.

Behavioural Management in Hospitals

We are well aware of the fact that being a no-profit-making organisation, the hospitals need to go through a number of problems. On the one hand we find an increase in the cost of diagnosis and treatment and on the other hand, the hospitals are also supposed to subserve the interests of masses. They are also supposed to charge optimally and to be careful so that the expectations of patients and attendants are fulfilled. We can't negate that such a critical situation makes it essential that hospital managers formulate a strategy that improves the relationships in the different concerned areas.[5]

This draws our attention on the behavioural management in hospitals where different categories of staff are found participating in the different types of services. By the management of behaviour, we find our emphasis on studying the level of expectations of patients and attendants, identifying the expectations of hospital personnel and watching the attitudes of trade unions or staff associations. The hospital managers bear the responsibility of making their decisions innovative so that all the related segments are found satisfied vis-a-vis the organisational interests are protected. In the face of changing environmental conditions, the hospital managers need to formulate a strategy that opens new vistas for quantitative-cum-qualitative improvements in the healthcare services. It is against this background that we go through the problem of behavioural management.

We can't negate that all the variables influencing the human behaviour need due attention of hospital managers. They are required to go through the motivational factors in detail because unless the hospital personnel are motivated suitably, the task of accomplishing the organisational goals would remain unfulfilled. The motivational factors draw our attention on the devices found instrumental in improving the service conditions in addition to the improvement of quality at the work and living places. At the outset, we go through different dimensions of behavioural management. Attitudes and expectations are the two important facets playing a contributing role in the very process.

Attitudes play an important role in influencing the levels of expectations. Like other personnel, the hospital personnel also develop a positive or negative attitude. Of course, we find a big variation in the nature and character of services. Unlike other services, the services offered by hospitals are found essential/emergent in nature and character. In addition, we also find the services playing an informative role. This make it essential that motivational schemes for the hospital personnel are made so much lucrative that we don't find even a minor scope for the formation of a negative attitude. Of late, we find financial incentives playing a dominating role in the formation of attitude. We can't deny that such developments have taken place due to the growing influences of consumerism in almost all the areas. The inflationary pressure is found moving upward and the tax burden is also found increasing. The hospital personnel are also supposed to fulfil the 'increasing levels of expectations of the members of their family members. If they fail in doing such, the attitudes are likely to be negative which would not motivate hospital personnel to work efficiently. Besides, the amenities and facilities at the work and living places also influence their attitudes. The hospital managers need to make the environmental condition conducive. In Fig. 4.3, we find the different constituents of environment instrumental in establishing the work culture and effective in increasing the level of efficiency.

The first dimension is financial incentive found very much instrumental in improving the level of efficiency. This makes it essential that the hospital managers make it sure that different categories of hospital personnel get lucrative financial incentives. The second dimension is related to the quality of environment at the work place. This makes it essential that the hospital personnel find the work environment friendly or conducive. The availability of suitable infrastructural facilities and the behaviour of superiors to the subordinates and vice versa become significant in the very context. Even if you are suitably paid, the indecent and aggressive behaviour of superiors to the subordinates makes the work environment prone to tension. The

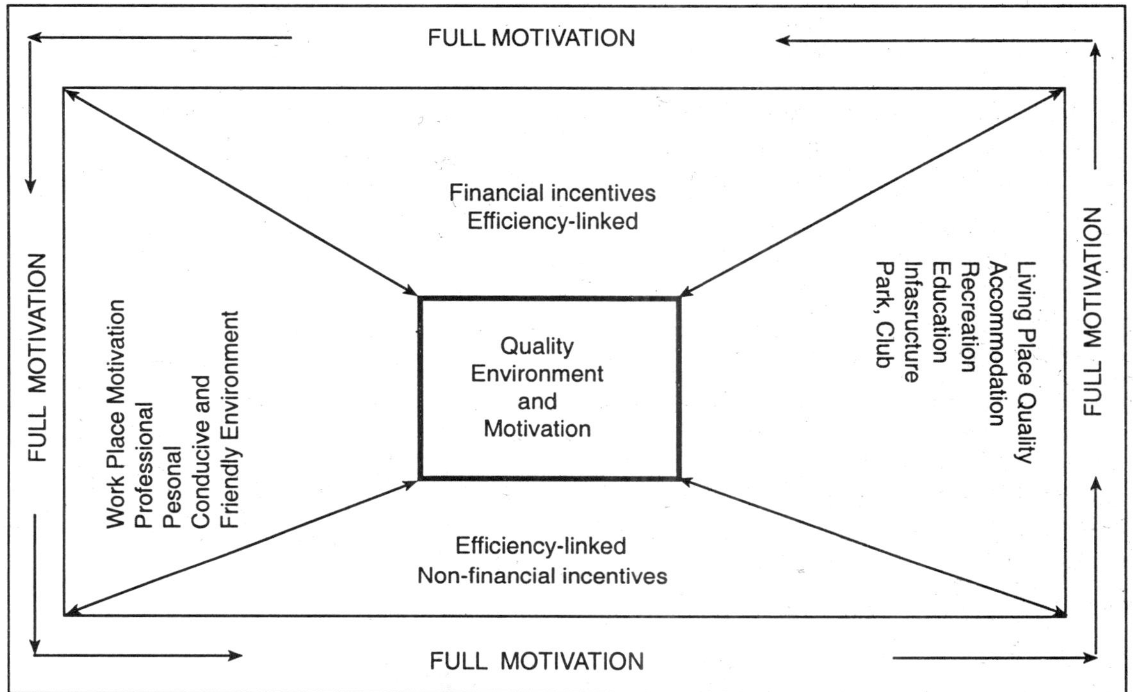

Fig. 4.3. Quality Environment and Motivation

formation of negative attitude among the hospital personnel of low-level can't be denied if doctors start misbehaving with the nurses, sisters and other paramedical personnel. Besides, it is also pertinent that the hospital managers assign due weightage to quality of environment at the living places. This makes it essential that the hospital personnel get suitable accommodation, welfare facilities, infrastructural facilities, the educational facilities for children, the entertainment facilities for children and so on.

A fair combination of the incentives mentioned above improve the quality of environment. This makes the way for the personal commitments because all the members of a family are found directly or indirectly involved in the process. Because in the process of fulfilling the interests of their family members, they are found developing a positive attitude for the development of hospitals, we found personal commitment possible. The harmonious relationships between superiors and superiors, subordinates and subordinates, superiors and subordinates are found essential to improve the work culture resulting from the availability of different types of motivational schemes. The expectations of patients/ attendants can't be underestimated in the very context.

Relationship

Sound management of behaviour makes the way for friendly and harmonious relations, a prerequisite for efficiency generation. The hospitals where we find a team work, it is pertinent that the hospital managers make sincere efforts to improve relationships. Since the hospital personnel bear the responsibility of serving the patients, it is essential that hospital personnel in general are found liberal to the sweet relationships with the patients. This draws our attention on the first dimension of relationships where we go through the problem of improving relationships between hospital personnel and the patients.

The second aspect in the very context is related to the relationships among the different categories of hospital personnel. The interdepartmental and intradepartmental relationship is found important in the very context. The superiors bear the responsibility of behaving decently with the superiors as well as with the subordinates. At the same time, it is also important that subordinates have a sense of respect for the superiors. This is related to the departmental relationships. The last dimension of relationship is related to the relationships of different categories of hospital personnel with the management. This draws our attention on the trade unions and other relationships with the management.

In the sphere of managing behaviour, it is significant that the hospital managers, on the basis of their professional excellence, make possible a sound relationship in all the areas as mentioned in Fig. 4.4. The hospitals may have efficient personnel, they may also have sophisticated amenities and facilities to improve the quality of services but if they don't find a friendly or conducive environment, the patients and attendants can't remain satisfied. It is against this background that we go through different dimensions of relationship and the instrumentality of hospital managers in the very context.

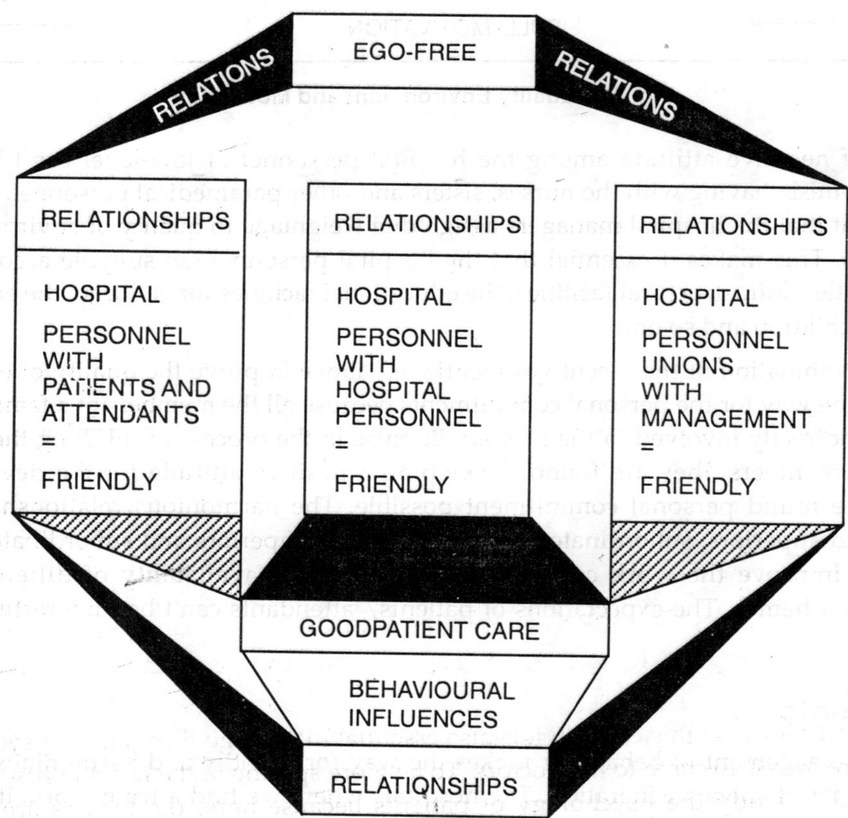

Fig. 4.4. Relationships in Hospitals

Hospital Personnel-Patients Relationship

We classify the relationship of hospital personnel with the patients in two parts, viz., Doctor-patient Relationship and Nurse-patient relationship.

Doctor-Patient Relationship: We assign due weightage to the doctor-patient relationship in the management of hospitals because the concept of goodpatient care is based on the same. On account of conflicting perception in the minds of both, the problem is found a bit complicated. The doctors have expertise or specialisation in a particular discipline. They have professional excellence and are also supposed to have ethical and human values. The patients on the other hand are found in stress with high level of expectations because they consider doctors thoughtful and warm persons and committed to do everything for the welfare of patients. Such a situation increases the responsibility of doctors. It is his/her professional excellence, personal-touch-in-service, humanitarian approach and ethical values that play a big role in the satisfaction of patients. It is also right to mention that unlike western countries, the patients in India feel that doctors bear the responsibility of serving them in all the conditions. We can't deny the fact that such a perception is on account of the constitutional barrier because in the Indian context, the medical attention is claimed as a fundamental right. Since the concept of commercialisation of medicare services is yet to be practised in the Indian hospitals, the doctors need to discharge their functional responsibilities very carefully. There are a number of factors to be taken into consideration while studying the problem of doctor-patient relationship.

Social Environment: We agree with this view that social environment is considered to be an important factor determining his/her exposure and susceptibility to unhygienic conditions prone to multidimensional diseases. The living conditions, health awareness, facilities for entertainment and recreation, management of civic amenities and facilities, nutritional awareness and food habits are the important factors and if not taken due care, generate and aggravate a number of diseases. In addition, we find poverty itself a big disease. In the society, when we find all the systems collapsing, the intensity of problem is found at its peak. The gender, age and profession also determine the nature and character of diseases.

The people and medical care are the two important facets found inter-related. The conflicting interests and priorities make the task much more difficult. Generally, we find patients concerned with the immediate solution of the problem. In a very few cases, we find them thinking about the roots of the problem. But the doctors are supposed to identify the root cause. Thus, we find a stage of conflict in the priorities of both of them. The patients facing the problem of poverty are found believing in making the process economic whereas the doctors have no option but to go through the devices helping the right diagnosis and quick recovery which make the process of treatment expensive. Besides, the doctors in a few of the cases are also influenced by the commercial considerations. Thus, we find a conflict in interest. It is against this background that we find a basic difference in the expectations of educated and uneducated, rural and urban patients and attendants.

Patient Psychology: In this context, it is also essential that we go through the psychology of patients who are forced to come to the doctors. To be more specific in the Indian perspective, we find it essential to study the psychology of patients because here, the masses are illiterate. Understanding the patient's symptoms requires a peep into his/her work environment, his/her relations with the employer and the associates at work, his/her sexual life, his/her social inter-relations and friends. In majority of the cases, we find them not disclosing the real problem. Thus, the basic problem may be physical or emotional and the doctors have no option but to listen relevants or irrelevants. Objectivity and over-identification with the patients result into personal and emotional involvement. The actions of doctors are defined by the law, ethics, time, space and interpersonal relationship. Any contract between a patient and his/her doctor is usually a result of conscious choice on the part of the patient. The doctor-patient relationship is that of expert-layman relationship and it is the physician's expertise which is the ultimate resource in his/her interaction with others. This relationship varies from complete passivity on the part of the patient. The interaction is to help, guide and diffuse the tension so that patients are found in a position to narrate the realities. It may extend to mutual participation where patients are required to take care of themselves specially in the case of diabetes and cardiological diseases. This makes it essential that clinical interaction is promoted so that a good patient-relation is based on the principle of cooperation. Active patients and passive doctors or passive patients and active doctors, both the cases are found problematic. In a true sense, both of them are required to be active resulting into the maximum possible effective communications within the minimum possible duration.

Access to the Organisation: In the context of doctor-patient relationship, we also find this dimension important because in a number of cases, we find that patients don't permit even the essential checking or we also find cases where doctors cross the limits. We can't negate that such a situation would be immoral, scandalous and ridiculous. For examination, it is essential that the doctors expose and touch the required organs but due to a negative attitude of doctors, we find scope for a conflict, tension and a bitter relationship. To see a person naked when this is not required and to touch even sensitive organs in course of examinations may result into a bitter relation but we find it a privileged access vis-a-vis the professional compulsion. The profession of doctors is based on ethical and human values and therefore, the patients are supposed to cooperate with the doctors. At the same time, it is also pertinent that the doctors don't cross the limits which may invite an ugly scene resulting into acrimony.

The Prescription: We find it the most sensitive state and the doctors while writing the prescription are supposed to make it sure that they are not promoting the trial-and-error principle rather than are acting in tune with their potentials. If they find that the results of investigations are confusing, they need to consult the specialists instead of writing a prescription aggravating the problem or delaying the process. If we find doctors adopting such a practice, the doctor-patient relationship may be bitter and more so, even fatal to the patients resulting into a number of problems. At the same time, it is also essential that in a few cases, the doctors are supposed to write a prescription, if they feel that the delay in treatment is to result into irreparable losses. Of course, the side-effects are to be given due weightage but the reparable side-effects may be preferred in place of irreparable losses. It is really amazing that in the Indian context, we also find cases where doctors write a prescription even without diagnosis just to earn. This makes the ways for unfriendly relationships. We can't negate that the doctor-patient relationship would be bitter if the doctors work with a negative attitude.

The Ethical Dimension: The patients and attendants believe that since the doctors have taken the oath to maintain ethical values, they will do everything right for the protection of their interests. We are well aware of the fact that the oath which represents the ethical considerations has its early reference in the first century AD. During that time, the doctors took oath as an ideal to be attained rather than a formality to be completed. This continued till 14th century that it was an obligatory requirement to take the oath before starting the practice of medicine. Of course, we find a number of declarations thereafter but it is well-known to all of us that today it is just a formality to take the oath. In a true sense, we find beginning of degeneration when some of the knotty problems like euthanasia, abortion, forensic medicine iatrogenic diseases are taken up and further, we find application of the same in other areas. The Indian Medical Association has drawn a code of medical ethics which is found comprehensive and now, we find oath even before accreditation of medical degrees but in practice, a majority of the doctors hardly think about the ethical dimension. Since the doctors fail in maintaining ethics, we find enough scope for an acrimonious relation between the patients and attendants.

Indifference to Job: Good patient care makes it essential that the doctors are personally and professionally committed but of late, we find money playing a decisive role in the process of diagnosis and treatment. The government doctors refuse to develop any relationship with the OPD/Ward patients and some of them attend to only VIPs or even they just mark his/her time. This makes the ways for discrimination which paves the avenues for a bitter relation. By and large, in almost all the government hospitals, we find attitude of indifference to job. They may be professionally committed but lack personal commitments. They of course, are available on duty but they don't consider it proper to perform the duty and responsibility assigned to them which invites a number of complications to the patients and attendants. We agree with this viewpoint that it is also an important reason for unfriendly doctor-patient relations.

Impersonal Attitude: In addition to other aspects, the doctors are also found apathetic which makes it essential that they know about empathy and practice it in their profession as a part of their duty. On the other hand, we also find patients having a feeling of nonattendance, neglect and indifference even if the treatment is timely, correct and as per the requirements. Such an attitudinal conflict makes the ways for a bitter relation between the two. We can't deny the fact that an attitudinal change in the doctors is found due to the domination of money in the process and among the patients and attendants, it is due mainly to the negative image of doctors projected by some of them who in a true sense are not the doctors, indeed blood suckers.

The Point of Confrontation: The deteriorating doctor-patient relations makes it essential that we search the conflicting points. We can't call it just an ego-conflict because the existing system of educating and training the doctors, the changing perception of parents of the doctors regarding their sons, the increasing importance of money in the society and the growing significance of consumerism are some of the factors found very much instrumental in the process of degeneration. The aforesaid facts makes it clear that there are a number of reasons for the existing deterioration in the doctor-patient relations and specially, the Indian Medical Association needs to think over the issue on a priority basis.

Nurse-Patient Relations

Another important facet of hospital personnel-relationship is the nurse-patient relationship. Of course, we find a degeneration in the perception of relationship in the field of medicare services but we can't negate the fact that till now this dimension of relationship is found well protected. Except a very few, we find all of them working with a sense of dedication and devotion. They are professionally sound and personally committed and it is due to the fact that the government hospitals in particular are found existent despite of a number of odds. If the nurses and sisters start working with a negative attitude the government hospitals would of course become non-existent. Despite of a number of degeneration in the processes, if there is something left in the government hospitals, it is due to their commitment to profession. It is in this context that we find it an important point for the development of the relationship.

All of us are aware of the fact that nurses play an incremental role in the treatment process and therefore, even a minor degeneration in their attitudes would result into a major loss to the patients. To be more specific, in the government hospitals where we find by and large almost all the employees promoting insincerity, the nurses and sisters find it difficult to work. It is against this background that we find cases of increasing insincerity even among the nurses. This makes it essential that the hospital managers take care of the same so that a vital wing of the medicare services is not to face further degeneration. The cases of exploitation, misbehaviour and multi-dimensional constraints are required to be checked. It is right to mention that in a number of hospitals, we find doctors engaged in exploiting the nurses and sisters. They find themselves handicapped when superiors or their immediate boss start misbehaving with them. The hospital managers bear the responsibility of making it sure that no cases of exploitation stand as a barrier to the discharge of her defined functional responsibilities.

The nurses and sisters need to work with the service motto. Of course, they also need financial incentives to fulfil their essential requirements but it is not to be forgotten that patients have a high level of expectations from them and their actions and behaviour should not frustrate them. They have skill, they are also found personally-committed but the existing scenario and the increasing degeneration in the environment at the work place may disturb them and to counter the same, they need to be strong enough to face the multidimensional challenges.

We agree with this view that nurses and sisters can't discharge the functional responsibilities supposed to be discharged by the doctors and therefore, a number of constraints, infrastructural or professional, are required to be removed. It is in this context that we find the instrumentality of hospital managers in removing the barriers found before the nurses. We talk about relationship and its significance to the process of diagnosis and treatment. The hospital personnel in general need to develop friendly relationships with the patients and attendants so that the tarnished image of hospitals and doctors is reprojected in a positive fashion.

Willingly or unwillingly, we have to accept the fact that hospitals are for the patients and attendants, the educational institutions are for the students and teachers. Whatever the constraints the personnel working in these organisations' experience are not to endanger the interests of ultimate users of the services. By doing such they would project a positive image which would help them in many ways.

Interdepartmental and Intradepartmental Relationships

For the efficient management of an organisation, it is pertinent that personnel working in different capacities in the different departments make possible friendly relations. Superiors would remain superiors even if they are not influenced by ego. The moment we find superiors acting like a superior and behaving like an officer/administrator, the possibilities of a degeneration in the relationships can't be overruled. Because we find the services of hospitals based on a team-work, it is essential that all the personnel irrespective of the rank and position they hold make sincere and honest efforts to accomplish the organisational goals. The superiors successful in developing a sense of affection in the subordinates succeed in generating a sense of respect among the subordinates. The transformation of team-work into a team-spirit and team-culture makes it essential that different echelons of hospital personnel working in the different capacities work with a sense of cooperation and coordination. If we turn our eyes on the workings of government hospitals in particular, this dimension of relationship presents a very gloomy picture. The superiors feel themselves superpowers, they hardly assign any weightage to the instrumentality of low echelon of employees in discharging their responsibilities efficiently. It is against this background that we find a degeneration in the departmental relationship. Even intradepartmental cooperation is found non-existent then what to talk of the interdepartmental relationship. This makes it essential that the hospital managers assign an overriding priority to this dimension and make best of their efforts to make the relationships friendly, cohesive, sweet in which albeit the difficult tasks are performed successfully.

We are well aware of the fact that in hospitals, there are a number of departments, such as finance department, personnel management or human resources department, material and store department, public relations department, medical record department in addition to the technical and medical departments responsible for managing the different types of services and technologies. The different types of services offered are medical services, nursing services, food services, radiology services, outpatient services, engineering services, ward services, fire, lighting security and safety services and a number of other services. All the departments and all the services are based on cooperation and coordination. This makes it essential that we go through the problem of relationships in different ways, such as the relationship of superiors with the superiors, relationship of superiors with the subordinates and the relationship of subordinates with the subordinates.

The hospital managers bear the responsibility of making it sure that a degeneration in relationships between the different categories of employees is not to deteriorate the quality of services offered by the hospitals. Of course, we find efficiency an important indicator to evaluate the excellence of an individual but in no case, we are supposed to underrate behavioural profile of an individual while making an appraisal of their contributions. We can't deny the fact that by and large, in almost all the government hospitals we are yet to assign due weightage to this variable for rating and compensating the quality people.

Your Relationship with your Superiors

The hospital managers bear the responsibility of implementing the policies for the development and smooth functioning of the hospitals. This increases his/her functional responsibilities. The top level management fixes accountability of good patient care to the hospital managers. This in a very natural way makes it essential that on the basis of coordinated efforts he/she is in a position to make available to the top management the necessary feedback. Since we find the senior doctors as a leverspring of a hospital, the hospital managers by their action and behaviour need to be careful that they don't feel themselves neglected. Whatever the strategic decisions are to be taken up, the hospital managers need to consult them to assign due weightage to their valuable solutions. Whatever the constraints they feel, the hospital managers are pledged to remove them so that the time honoured and quality services are made available to the users. Your behaviour profile makes the ways or makes it difficult to accomplish or not to accomplish the organisational goals.

We are well aware of the fact that the policy makers or the top level management bear the responsibility of formulating a sound policy for the development of hospitals and the hospital managers need to support them in this endeavour. When we talk about the relationship of hospital managers with the top-level management, it is quite natural that it is very formal and considerably based on an organised system. Right from planning to its time honoured and cost effective implementation, it is pertinent that hospital managers keep their eyes open and minds active and keep their superiors well informed regarding the developments taking place. There are a number of problems to be discussed in the meetings such as the outstanding contributions of the selected doctors, latest developments in the diagnostic and treatment devices, special incentives to the superperformers, personnel showing some wonders or so. On the other hand, they are also required to deliberate upon the constraints in the process of transacting the sensitive professional responsibilities, such as the neglected attitudes of the municipal corporations or the civic bodies in the due treatment of hospital waste, the misuse of some of the hospital waste by the antisocial elements making the task of doctors and hospital managers difficult, the mass-scale retrenchment problems in case of the use of sophisticated information and communications technologies, the modernisation and expansion plans facing the difficulties or so.

Since we find it a part of your professional obligation, it is pertinent that you convince them. If you consider anything right and even the boardrooms or other senior personnel are critical to it, you are supposed to be strong enough to convince them by making your deliberations logical and factual. It is in this context that we assign due weightage to the hospital managers found candid; showing hospitality to critics, recognising the legitimacy of different opinions and avoiding litigation as a way to work out conflict. Your image in the eyes of public at large is to be positive and you are not supposed to generate a condition losing the confidence of the public. Importance of candour is to be recognised and the clamouring about freedom from government control to improve the working of hospitals may be important. Being a hospital manager, you need to be clear, strong, factual and innovative to convince the top-level management. Your behavioural profile helps you in transforming the negative attitudes of boardroom into a positive one which simplifies your task of accomplishing the organisational goals.

Your Relationship with Your Peers

The hospital managers in this context are required to improve their relations with peers or colleagues. You solicit cooperation or you need to extend cooperation and the relationship with peers[7] assumes a place of outstanding significance. In your day-to-day dealings, the exchange of cooperation plays an incremental role which is found instrumental in increasing the level of your efficiency. This makes it essential that you keep in your minds some of the important points as mentioned below:

Communicating through Daily Interaction

Here, our focus is on open communication with the fellow managers and colleagues. Direct dialogue on the key issues, candid assumption of problems and openness in deliberations help you in many ways. To the extent it is possible and your communications with colleagues should be on an interpersonal basis. You need to stop the practices of sending memos on everything. Given the hyperactivity associated with health care management, it is more expedient to discuss things directly with your colleagues and more so in an open, honest fashion. In all your dealings, you are required to be receptive and to listen carefully to their innovative ideas. You are supposed to know the reasons for a change. You need to capture the rationale behind their thinking. Don't be too quick to dismiss or reject a new idea. Try to be supportive in all management team activities. Encourage colleagues to go ahead with the new ideas when they convince you with their strong arguments and presentation.

Being a hospital manager, you need not forget that creativity is the most important asset a manager can have in countering or solving the problems. Try to lend your creativity in group situations and also try to provide to your colleagues with the benefit of a different slant specially on key issues. You should try to contribute freely to the brainstorming process as and when new ideas are presented by your colleagues. In addition, you need not hesitate to be inquisitive while discussing the work related problems. We agree with this view that an efficient team member acts as an inspiration and also motivates other members of the team. There is no doubt in it that in many occasions, your colleagues would become frustrated or demotivated by the rigors of healthcare management. You would hardly find a day when you don't need the cooperation of your colleagues or peers. Try to make yourself available to give a needed part on the back, a pep talk or a show of empathy.

You also need to render assistance to members of the management team on a regular basis. Besides, you are supposed to learn as much as it is possible from your colleagues. Even if you are new to the hospital, you will have a certain amount of expertise from which your colleagues are to be benefited. Feel free to offer instructions in situations in which your technical expertise and insight might be fruitful. With the thought in mind that "nobody wins unless we will win" recognises that your human, physical and fiscal resources do not belong to you but to the organisation. You are supposed to use your potentials optimally. A true team player uses all of his/her efficacy for the good of the team and not to the good of the individual. Your behavioural profile needs an intensive care on this property.

Basic Communication Ideas: You are required to consider five basic communication ideas while interacting with your colleagues. First, ask questions at all times, valuable information, clear ideas and get the possible information. Second, make appropriate suggestions. We agree with this view that your suggestions and inputs are valuable resources you provide to the team. Third, provide new ideas regularly and bring your suggestions directly to the individual who is apt to use it more efficiently. Fourth, give colleagues second opinions without becoming a second guesser. In providing a second opinion, you are virtually providing an opportunity to your colleagues to give another look at the problem, a view from another angle but a second guesser subversively questions the actions of others with the intent of exposing the individual as incompetent or foolish. And finally, remember that all of your efforts are rated toward cooperating the entire management team.

Networking: As a hospital manager, you are supposed to build a network of individuals on whom you can rely for input and the creative thought. The business cards are required to be exchanged as and when you meet a management counterpart. The counterparts include persons whom you may meet in the course of your personal or professional activities, colleagues at other hospitals, healthcare agencies and organisations. We can't negate that with the development of contact, you will be in a position to enrich your information bank. You need to join a professional organisation because the membership in a strong national or global professional organisation can help you in developing your area of specialisation or expertise. It is quite natural that the organisations would be related to your professional area that would benefit you in many ways.

You are also supposed to involve yourself in the community activities because one of the unique qualities of healthcare is its standing within a community, its image among the masses and its people orientation. It is in this context that you need to make sincere and honest efforts to participate in the community activities. You are required to use your calendar. Try to make at least one contact daily and record the contact's name, organisation, address and phone number in the calendar box. As and when you develop a new contact, please ask as many questions as you can even without becoming impolite or intrusive. Ask about the background, areas of interest and knowledge. You need to consider your internal resources. You need to remember that your organisation represents your biggest bank of internal contacts. Go through critically the problems and in this context, read journals, newsletters, abstracts and other professional literature. You are also required to use mentors and prefer to use your mentors within your organisation, including your supervisor or other senior members of the staff. And finally, join local healthcare groups. You need to remember that your contact network is a two-way street, such that the networking courtesies should be reciprocal. You are not supposed to call someone when you need information only to answer mail from someone who may need your assistance.

The aforesaid facts make it clear that your relationship with the peers is found significant and is substantially influenced by your behavioural profile. The peers/colleagues help you in many ways and therefore, in no case, you are supposed to develop a relation that deprives you of getting their support and cooperation. We find here main focus on communications and networking. The hospital managers with a high communicative ability may be successful in developing good relations with colleagues/peers. At each and every stage, you need cooperation of different departments for discharging your responsibilities efficiently and successfully. If you don't have a sound relation, the task of developing a good relationship is found much more difficult. You can't work successfully unless you get the cooperation of your colleagues/peers and the cooperation is solicited and not claimed which is considerably influenced by your behavioural profile.

Your Relationship with Your Supervisor/Boss

Being a manager, you can't underrate the contributions of your supervisor in helping you considerably in different areas. This makes it essential that you develop good relations with your supervisor. In a true sense, your relationship with your supervisor is an important parameter to rate your performance. They can fulfil several positive roles such as acting as a mentor, educator, conscience keeper and primary supporter. At the same time, they can also play a very negative role, specially when you are facing the rough times. They can be your enemy, destroyer, inhibitor or so.[8] This makes it essential that you develop good relations with your boss or supervisor. There are several steps helping you in improving the relationship.

Setting Goals: While setting goals, establish several initial goals with your supervisor. If you are a new manager, establish five goals at the initial stage of your working. The goals should of course be educational and meaningful. After a few months, add two more goals and finally after a year, add three more goals and the total goals are thus ten in number. The list of ten goals would become your set of objectives for the second year. Unless you have received results of seven goals, you should not include the final three goals.

Maintaining Open Communications: An ongoing communication with your supervisor is essential to develop a good relationship and this focusses on the organisation of regular meetings of at least 20 to 30 minutes. The regular meetings allow you to transmit new developments to you supervisor. To be more specific on the critical issues, they may give you sufficient inputs. The meetings should be organised once in a week and further should be supplemented with monthly meetings, at least for an hour in length. Try to strike a comfortable balance between distance and closeness in your relationship. Other things that you and your supervisor or boss can share are attending meetings, seminars and workshops. This would help you in adding some new dimensions to your relationship. The selection and perception evaluation processes undertaken by you may also be shared by your supervisor. All the efforts for performance evaluation should be reviewed by your supervisor. This allows him an opportunity to help you to define your performance. In addition, while planning work activities for your department, the inputs supplied by your supervisor would be found important.

Ensuring Your Management Development: The final aspect in the very context is to discuss your career needs and desires whenever appropriate. This includes a training or an education programme to be undertaken. It is quite natural that your supervisor is interested in your successful development because it reflects on him/her for having selected you as a manager.

The aforesaid facts make it clear that being a manager, you need to improve your relationship with the supervisor so that you get his/her cooperation as and when you are in trouble. In no case, you are supposed to confront with your supervisor because after top management, we find him/her a competent person to help you or even to harm you. Your behavioural profile is found here important because based on your relations you may satisfy him. Your aggressive nature and indecent behaviour would damage you and therefore, be careful while interacting with your supervisor.

Your Relationship with Your Subordinates

We have gone through your relationships with management, with peers or colleagues and now, we go through your relationship with your subordinates. Since you are supposed to improve the level of efficiency of different departments in which different echelons of employees are found working, it is essential that you try your best to improve your relationship with lower levels of executives and officers. If you fail in getting their cooperation, your task of accomplishing the organisational goals would hardly be fulfilled. It is in this context that we focus on your relationship with the subordinates working with you.

The responsibility of a hospital manager is found of much more significance based on a team and interdepartmental and intradepartmental cooperation. Your behavioural profile with your subordinates becomes a decisive factor in the very context. Your instructions and orders pass through different desks and tables and a delay in the process is to damage your interests. This makes it essential that you assign due weightage to your subordinates and develop even an informal relation with them to seek their cooperation. The superiors are superiors and the subordinates are subordinates. We don't find a place for any confusion or a conflict. The main thing is attitudes of your subordinates regarding you and your behavioural profile. If they find you a hard man, they would act and react in a different way. If they find you a liberal man, they would act and react in a bit different way. And if they find you a good man, they would act and react like a good man. It is your image in the eyes of your subordinates that determines the magnitude of success. Never try to project your image like a very liberal man and at the same time never try to project yourself even like a very tough man. Behave like a friend, act like an administrator and react like a manager. If you behave like a friend, you get the maximum possible cooperation of your subordinates even beyond your expectations. If you act like an administrator; they receive your command seriously and if you react like a manager, you find it easier to understand their positive or negative attitudes and constraint and based on that you can take a decision. Your ultimate responsibility is to help the fulfilment of departmental targets so that the organisational goals are accomplished without making the additional efforts. We find a number of hospital managers not understanding the instrumentality of subordinates in increasing the level of efficiency and resulting from which they often fail in accomplishing the organisational goals. In a true sense, such a negative result is to endanger the interests of a hospital manager.

The hospital managers need not to forget that with the high level of communications, they can seek the cooperation of their subordinates. It is your words, language, tone, volume, body language, informal relations making the task of seeking cooperation much easier or even much more difficult. In a majority of the cases, we find subordinates elevated if the superiors behave with them decently. Just for a few sweet words and empathy, the subordinates have been found extending enormous cooperation to the superiors which can't be possible even with hard words or albeit with lucrative financial incentives. This makes it clear that the hospital managers need to be careful while dealing with the subordinates. The quality environment at the work place makes it essential that superiors solicit the cooperation of their subordinates in place of claiming and not getting.

Your Relationship with Your Associations/Unions

To be more specific in the Indian context where associations and trade unions have been found acting in a negative way, the hospital managers need to behave properly with the leaders of the associations and trade unions. It is really amazing that in the Indian perspective, we find associations and trade unions not realising their responsibilities to the organisations. Of course, they bear the responsibility of protecting the interests of workers and employees but it is not meant that they are insensitive to the negative attitudes of employees making an assault on work culture and just to establish their leadership promoting wrong practices. It is against this background that a study of your relationship with the trade unions and associations is found pertinent.

It is not possible for a hospital manager to bring the derailed systems on the rail. It is not possible for a hospital manager even to declare associations and unions illegal. The only thing that he/she can do is to work tactfully and patiently so that the possibilities of demonstrations, agitations and strikes are considerably minimised. Of course, the trade unions and associations need an attitudinal change because only with the development of organisations they would survive and thrive. They have every right of making it sure that the employees have been getting salaries and benefits as per the service conditions but in this context, they also bear the responsibility of making it sure that the employees are working with sincerity and honesty and in no case their actions are to damage the interest or tarnish the image of the organisations. We can't deny that such an attitudinal change would improve their relationships with the management. On the other hand, the hospital managers also need to make it sure that while interacting with the supervisor, peers and management, they promote their right demand. Thus, improving your relationship with the associations and trade unions is, of course, a challenging task but a hospital manager is required to make it easier.

While developing relationship with the leaders of the associations and trade unions, a hospital manager is required to identify the vocal leaders. They need to convince the leaders regarding the attitudes of management and other superiors regarding their demands. We find a time-to-time interaction with the leaders essential to promote good relations. Since in the Indian context, we find strong trade unionism, specially in the public sector, the hospital managers working in the government hospitals need more care and precautions. While on the one hand, we need to assign due weightage to the leaders of the associations and unions, on the other hand, we also need to be tough when situations warrant so. The hospital managers need to be very informative and to make available to the leaders of the associations and trade unions the performance results of different employees which would be found helpful in transforming their attitudes.

The aforesaid facts make it clear that your relationship with the associations and trade unions assumes a place of outstanding significance and being a manager, you are supposed to remove the feelings of a bias. If the leaders find you a party to the management, the task of convincing and satisfying the union leaders is found difficult. Try to understand the weaknesses and shortcomings of the leaders so that you get an opportunity to sense and influence them in a right fashion. Never try to demoralise them because this will make your task much more difficult.

Departmental Relationship and Good patient Care

We have gone through different areas of relationship and based on the same, we feel that all the facets of relationships influence the process of diagnosis and treatment. Good patient care is the target of a hospital manager and if we find something wrong in the relationships, it is to influence the quality of medicare services. The services offered by a hospital are found based on a team work which is related to the different types of services offered by the different departments. The interdepartmental or intradepartmental relationships, if friendly, make possible coordination and the results are good patient care. Contrary to it, if we find conflicts of different types among the different categories of hospital personnel, even if the hospitals have high potentials of offering the world class services, a gap between the services-assured and services-offered can't be denied. It is against this background that we find it an important area of study requiring due attention of hospital managers. In Fig. 4.4, it is clear that good patient care is the outcome of a friendly relationship which is obstructed by different types of conflicts.

This makes it essential that we make possible ego-free relations in which we don't find any scope for conflicts. The superiors while behaving with the top-level management, with the peers or colleagues, with the subordinates and with the unions and associations are required to be careful so that working environment remains conducive and friendly. The hospital managers bear the responsibility of making the working environment conductive and cohesive. This increases his/her functional responsibilities. While behaving with the doctors, it is to be made sure that his/her communications are not to touch their ego. While behaving with the management, he/she is supposed to be candid so that right facts come in the knowledge of supervisor and the top level management. While deliberating, if he/she considers himself/herself right, even the strong comments are to be answered decently and boldly. While behaving with the subordinates, the hospital managers are required to be very friendly so that they succeed in soliciting their co-operation even if the working conditions are not conducive. While behaving with the unions and associations, the hospital managers are required to be soft and tactful so that the diffusion of tension is made possible and the working conditions are made conducive.

The aforesaid facts make it clear that a study of relationship is essential to improve the quality of environment at the work place which is to influence the level of efficiency. In the medicare services, even the services offered by the low level of employees are found so much significant that failing their cooperation, the doctors would find it difficult to diagnose and treat. Availability of world class doctors, rich infrastructural facilities, attractive and comfortable buildings and sophisticated technologies can't deliver good patient care unless we find the working environment friendly. It is quite natural that different employees even in the same cadre behave in a different way. The hospital managers are supposed to understand the behaviour of an individual or a group/team and to make the working conditions friendly by managing things decently. They bear the responsibility of managing things in such a fashion that possibilities of ego-conflict are considerably minimised. We can't deny the fact that work place relationship is an important dimension of motivation because a number of employees prefer to work in a peaceful condition.

Ethics in Hospital Management

Of late, we find corporate ethics getting an important place in the boardrooms. If we turn our eyes on the globe, it is found that corporate ethics gained prominence during the scandal of "international bribery" involving two giant US corporations—Boeing and Lockheed. The issue of bribery was discussed at great length and the parties involved were penalised.[9] It is essential to mention that today, we find some of the confusing terminologies used in the business world. In the gentlemen's dictionary, we find them appearing as "gifts", "tips", which is nothing but a device to bribe. Societal norms that reflect the culture and traditions of a country may help in differentiating whether a payment made in cash/ kind is gift, bribe or a tip. In a true sense, what is ethical in one society may be unethical in another, what is uncultured in one society may be cultured in another. The issue of corporate ethics is certainly a broad one, ranging from problems of internal policy and treatment of individual employees to environmental and social concerns which may have a global impact.

The pragmatist says, "If it works, it is good." Defining situational ethics for those in the field of business management, Joseph Fletcher says,

"Circumstances alter cases, i.e., in actual problems of conscience, the situational variants are to be weighed as heavily as the theoretical constants, so that circumstances alter not only cases but rules."[10]

Fletcher goes on to note that a business ethic has to be "practical." Any system of ethical absolutes, no matter how clearly stated in our religious books will not serve as a guide for business ethics, if it lacks practical relevance. In this context, we need our attention on four factors: first, the end—the outcome sought; second, the means—the methods employed; third, the motive, the urge which makes the decision necessary in the first place; and fourth, the foreseeable consequences. In classical terms, if any one of those four factors is wrong, the section is immoral.

The situationist, instead of isolating each factor of moral decision making and judging it along looks at all of them together within the framework of the specific situation at hand. " Fletcher quotes a French priest who noted that fanatic love of virtue has done more damage to men and society than all the vices put together. Thus, pragmatist or situanist ethics demand always that very close attention is paid to the changing circumstances. The Japanese officials who accepted millions of dollars in payoffs from Lockheed may believe that they have used their influence to aid their nation in acquiring superior planes, the better to defend the homeland in case of war.

The aforesaid facts make it clear that business ethics are used in a bit different way so whatever we find unfair, immoral in other areas are found fair and moral in the business world. However, we can't negate the fact that fair is always fair and unfair is always unfair. If we promote unethical or unfair practices in the business world, it is to influence the society, the value of social capital, the trust and confidence of society and therefore, we don't find business world acquiring a special position and declaring everything fair, just to get the business.

We go through the problems of a no-profit-making organisation like hospital and to be more specific, in the Indian society, where the masses fail in getting even the basic medicare facilities, the ethical dimension needs an intensive care.

The increasing cases of financial irregularities in the government hospitals, the growing substandard private clinics exploiting the passes, the doctors becoming a party to all the unfair and unethical practices found in government as well as the private hospitals make it essential that we assign due weightage to this dimension which has been aggravating the problem of value degeneration. It is against this background that we talk about ethical dimension in hospitals. It is really amazing that the doctors who have taken the oath to protect the interests of human beings become a part to the value degeneration process. We can't negate the fact that governmental regulations to regulate the unfair, unethical and immoral practices in the hospitals can't be of any use unless the social regulations make possible an attitudinal change in doctors.

To counter the dangers on account of improper sterilising, the concept of disposable syringe came into existence and of late, we are aware of the fact that how with the connivance of doctors and other hospital personnel, the recycling of biomedical nondegradable is practised which generates a number of problems. The concept of legal abortion was to counter the dangers on account of a disabled child and promote family planning but all of us are aware of the misuses of the provisions where the doctors become a party. The concept of issuing medical certificate was to minimise the cases of fraud but in a true sense, we find it promoting fraud. The pharmaceutical industry engaged in producing spurious drugs flourishes with the support of doctors. The purchase of substandard equipment and instruments is promoted by the doctors. We quote here these cases to make it clear that a large number of doctors are found engaged in unethical and immoral practices which has been tarnishing the image of hospitals. The patients and attendants find it difficult to trust the segment who has accepted the responsibility of safeguarding them.

It is not just a matter of earning illegal money. It is really a matter of prime importance because the human beings have no option but to depend on doctors and hospitals and the incidents taking place in the society each and everyday make the ways for a breach of trust. This makes it essential that in addition to the government, the social organisations also think about the increasing incidents of value degeneration in the hospitals. It is in this context that we find ethics in hospital management occupying a place of outstanding significance. The hospital managers bear the responsibility of making available to the patients the assured services and they have to make it sure that a gap in the process is to be bridged over.

There are a number of vulnerable areas where we find enough scope for value degeneration and the hospital managers need to keep their eyes open so that they detect the cases and punish the persons responsible for the same. It is right to mention that inventory is an important area where we find scope for unethical and unfair practices. This draws our attention on the workings of the Material and Store Department. The purchase of expensive instruments and equipment, the engineering services, the food services and housekeeping are some of the selected areas where we find the unethical and unfair practices flourishing like anything. It is the responsibility of the hospital managers that they make possible utmost care to check the same. It is really very amazing to mention that in a few cases, we find the unethical practices even promoted by the government policy makers. This necessitates social regulations because where governmental regulations become insensitive, the social regulations prove to be instrumental. It is high time that we think over the issue on a priority oasis.

Behavioural Conflict in Hospitals

The services of hospitals are based on a team work. This requires enormous cooperation of almost all the departments. The medical services, nursing services, food services, pharmacy services, radiology services, ward services, engineering services, outpatient services and many other services can't be managed by a single department. This makes provisions for departmentation with the motto that all the departments would have a common goal of serving the patients. Thus, cooperation and coordination become essential for managing hospitals efficiently. There are different types of services and therefore, we find different heads of different departments but they are supposed to work with a common goal. The increasing inefficiency in the government hospitals draws our attention on conflicts found in different departments in different forms. The ego-conflict, interest-conflict and priority-conflict are found making the quality of environment at the workplace unfriendly which has been degenerating the quality of hospital services. It is against this background that we need to go through the problem of behavioural conflict. Since the hospital managers bear the responsibility of establishing a creative work environment, it is pertinent that they are serious to the problems obstructing the process.

Being a hospital manager, it is quite natural that you have made best of your efforts to establish trust throughout the work group and to avoid potential conflict but it is human nature that creates an occasion for multidimensional conflicts in the behavioural pattern. The interdepartmental conflict takes place on an interpersonal basis. It is against this background that a number of conflicts like personality conflict and interest conflict crop up. Interpersonal conflict, particularly within a work group is potentially the most damaging type of problem.[12] A hospital manager is supposed to deal with the resolving of multidimensional conflicts. An automatic bomb explodes because the nucleus explodes. If the problems explode from within, the effects are found very dangerous. The problem is of impulsive nature and a hospital manager needs excellence to resolve the same. The interpersonal conflict exists within a department. The drastic negative consequences to the entire department can't be overruled if the wrongs are not abated and healed.

The hospital managers are required to use their own intuition and instinct and to promote examination in a cause-and-effect fashion. The potential symptoms and their potential cause and their effect on your department are mentioned in Fig. 4.5.

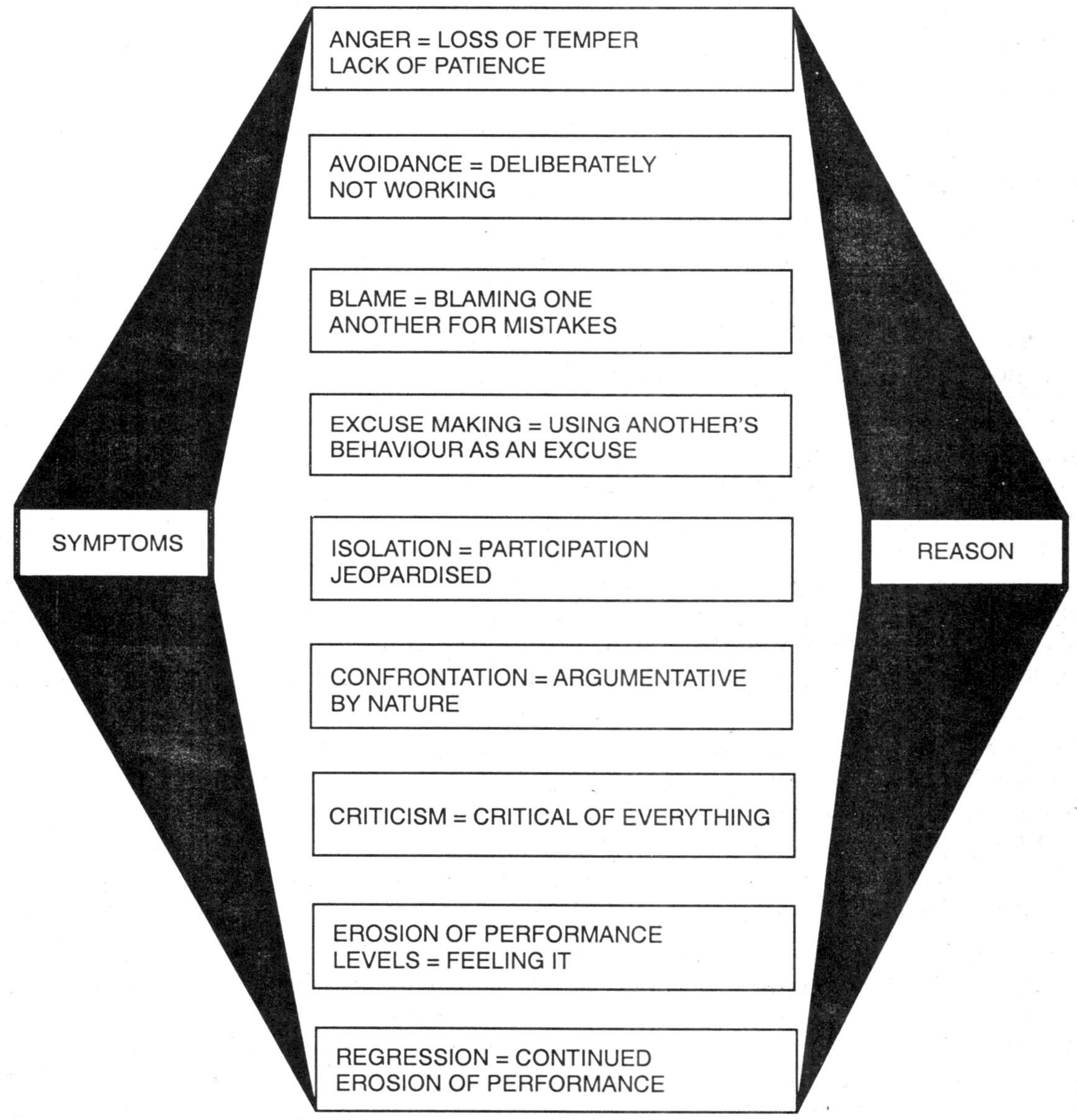

Pig. 4.5. Potential Symptoms and Reasons

In Fig. 4.5, we find potential symptoms and reason. The first interpersonal adversity, anger is found due to loss of temper and lack of confidence or due to the confrontational behaviour. We find it in the interpersonal conflict. The second is avoidance which occurs when an individual declines to work with someone. Due to such a situation, the work can't be done. Avoidance is found more subtle than danger. The third is blame and we find individuals blaming one another for mistakes which creates hostility among team members. The fourth is excuse making when we find an individual using another's behaviour as an excuse for not performing a personal task. The fifth is isolation or fragmentation which jeopardises the participation in the group process. The sixth is confrontation which is the result of certain personality types where we find employees of argumentative nature. The seventh is criticism which is found when an individual is found critical of everything and everyone in the department. The eight is erosion of performance levels which is due to ill feeling and the last one is regression which is due to continued erosion of performance.

Resolving Conflict

We can't deny the fact that conflict is to be resolved to make the working environment friendly or conducive. It is the responsibility of a hospital manager to resolve intradepartmental conflict. This makes it essential that the symptoms are identified and the sources of conflicts are detected. After this, the effects of conflict are to be recognised. In this context, you have to try to define whether the conflict is an individual versus group or faction. This would help you to be more specific even in potential solution. After that, you should try to quantify the person's behaviour by recording in your logbook as many specific incidents as you can. Then you are required to use your notes to analyse whether the problem is related to poor attitude or lack of interpersonal skills, team orientation or technical. Thereafter, determine the full extent of an interpersonal problem and try to ascertain whether a faction is being created by the problem or if one individual seems to be deliberately gathering support from others to form a faction. After collecting and analysing the information, approach the responsible person. In this context, you are required to take five steps. The first, you are required to separate the issues into two categories—first, identify the business related attributes of the problem and second, list personal issues. The second, review the information with the involved party and reach consensus on the facts of the issues and move the discussion to performance focusing specifically on the business effects from the conflict. The third, ask why this behaviour has taken place and how it might be corrected. Try to get the bottom of what they believe in contributing to the problem. The fourth, state clearly, concisely and resolutely your expectations, standards and policies for future action. The fifth, express your confidence that the situation will be corrected and ask if particular assistance is required to do so. Try to strike a delicate balance between expressing optimism that the situation can be corrected.

Because you are going to resolve the most difficult task of resolving intradepartmental conflict, you should incorporate two strategies into your effects. The first strategy is to do a good job of fact-finding every step of the way. It is right to mention that the fact-finding is a process of collecting information from all the involved parties. In this context, you are required to move as quickly as possible. The second strategy related to it is the policy compliance.

You are required to utilise your potential to seek resolution with the conflicting parties. The benefit of your personnel policies would be much more sound if you make use of your documents notebook to record the deliberations of the session and the performance evaluation. We can't deny the fact that the interpersonal conflict particularly within a department is found to be dangerous and therefore, it must be dealt within a timely fashion.

The aforesaid facts make it clear that by exercising your professional excellence, you can resolve conflict which would make the working environment conducive. If we find different departments involved in different types of conflicts, it is ultimately to influence the level of efficiency and the quality of services. This makes it essential that the hospital managers make a microscopic analysis of the changing situations and try to resolve the conflict at the earliest possible. You have also to be careful that some of the conflicts may be generated deliberately, specially by your enemies and therefore, it is upon you to identify the opportune moment, find out the reasons and make efforts for the resolution of conflict.

To be more specific in the government hospitals, we find behavioural conflict very much instrumental in making the departmental relations and working environment unfriendly. Interdepartmental and intradepartmental conflicts are found common. This is also an important reason for the decreasing level of efficiency and the deteriorating quality of services. The hospital managers bear the responsibility of improving the quality of services and they can't think about the same unless we find departmental coordination, cooperation and cohesion. It is in this context that they need to assign top priority to the environmental conditions at the work place. We find behavioural dimension playing a significant role in the very context and even a minor mistake on the part of a hospital manager is to invite a major problem.

This is not to be forgotten that the behavioural profile of personnel plays a big role in determining the success rate of your hospitals. Since we don't find hospital assigning due importance to the behavioural profile in a majority of the cases, they fail to protect the interest of patients. Not only this, we find the problem explosive and even the emergency services of hospitals are paralysed. It is against this background that the conflicts are required to be resolved at the very early stage.

The behavioural scientists feel that different categories of employees working in the hospitals are often found dissatisfied with the motivational schemes offered by the management. The hospital managers fail in resolving the crisis because even they don't assign due weightage to the increasing expectations of employees from the hospitals. Thus, some of the conflicts are due to quality of environment at the work place, some of the conflicts are on account of quality of environment at their living places and some of the conflicts are due to ego. This makes it essential that the hospital managers understand the behavioural profile of employees in a right fashion and perceive the right cause of the existing crisis due to conflict. Directly or indirectly, partially or substantially, we find a majority of the problems associated with the motivation which in a large number of cases are found neglected. This necessitates a right perception of motivation instrumental in resolving the multidimensional conflicts.

Indian Hospitals Need Behaviourally and Ethically Sound People

The hospital and healthcare organisations in the Indian perspective face numerous problems. The education and training programmes initiated and activated by the medical colleges or institutes need to consider some of the key issues which help them in developing potentially sound people. They in a true sense need a mix of different properties which make them thematically sound, professionally excellent, behaviourally decent, ethically sound and considerably humanised. We are aware of the fact that India has been emerging as a leading global Healthcare Brand[13] and this makes it essential that we keep on moving the process of defining and redefining quality. It is in this context that we need concerted efforts to develop medical and paramedical personnel on a priority basis. Not only the private hospitals but even the state hospitals have to work in this direction so that hospitals and healthcare organisations based on product uniqueness establish an edge over the rivals.

The patients and attendants believe that since doctors have taken the oath to maintain ethical values, they will do everything right for the protection and promotion of their interests. It is significant to mention that the oath which represents the ethical considerations has its early reference in the first century AD. During this time, the doctors took oath as an ideal to be maintained rather than a formality to be completed. This continued till 14th century that it was an obligatory requirement to take oath before starting the practice of medicine. Of course, we find a number of declarations thereafter but it is well known to all of us that today it is just a formality to take the oath. In a true sense, we find beginning of degeneration when some of the knotty problems like euthanasia, abortion, forensic medicine and iatrogenic diseases are taken up and further, we find application of the same in other areas. The Indian Medical Association has drawn a code of medical ethics which is found comprehensive and now we find oath even before accreditation of medical degrees but in practice, a majority of the doctors hardly think about the ethical dimensions. Since the doctors fail in maintaining ethics, we find enough scope for an acrimonious relation in between the doctors, patients and attendants. Actually, immoral practices and unethical practices come from the soul of an individual. We cannot find regulations much more effective in controlling unethical practices. Such an attitudinal transformation can be possible when doctors strengthen their realisation that they have adopted the medical profession because they are different from others. Almighty God has sent to them on this planet Earth to protect and promote the interests of human beings and humanity and therefore, they, by promoting immoral and unethical practices commit sins and would be punished. Of course, in a materialistic age they need money to meet their requirements and they earn enough to lead a respectful life. But when we find them activating the process of exploiting the patients, they want to earn more and even earn what they want because patients and attendants have no option and it is not earning but legalized snatching for which God is not to pardon.

Professional ethics, considered an essential dimension of medical services need due attention of medical and paramedical personnel without which the interests of humanity would remain unprotected. Both the public and private hospitals need to make it sure that ethical dimensions get a place in the hearts of all who are concerned with the medical and healthcare services.

The behavioural dimension focuses our attention on the attitudes of medical staff in general with the patients which comes and crops up in the shape of personalized services where the medical and paramedical personnel show not only sympathy but even empathy which help in minimising the recovery period. We cannot deny that rough and aggressive behaviour generate stress and tension which obstruct the process and stand as a barrier while administering the treatment process. The medical and paramedical staff bear the responsibility of satisfying the patients and attendants and for that they need to know about the needs and requirements vis-a-vis the levels of expectations of patients so that they strengthen their realisation that whatsoever the medicare services they are getting are the best to cure them. Attitudes play an incremental role in influencing the levels of expectations. Like other personnel, the hospital personnel also develop positive or negative attitudes. The motivational schemes play an important role in transforming the attitudes of hospital personnel. The policy makers as well as the hospital professionals need to make the motivational schemes much more lucrative so that we do not find any place for the formation of negative attitudes. We cannot deny that keeping in view the services and contributions of hospital personnel whatsoever the incentives that we offer to them are found disproportionate. They witness that other segments of society earn huge money by adopting unfair and unlawful practices. This injects life and strength to their negative feelings and they also start earning more by hook or by crook. We cannot negate that by offering lucrative incentives to them, even something more than other segments, we would make ways for the creation of positive feelings.

Behaviourally sound hospital personnel make the ways for friendly and harmonious relationships. The hospitals where we find a team work, it is pertinent that the hospital professionals make sincere efforts to improve relationships amongst the different echelons. Both, the dimensions of relationships such as doctor-patient relationships and doctor-hospital staff relationships need to be improved. The superiors if found humane to their subordinates make it easier to develop sound relationships because the subordinates find themselves satisfied even with the humanised behavior. Hence, the doctors must be humane to their subordinates which would transform the attitudes of subordinates. The development of team spirit and team culture would be possible which would pave avenues for work culture.

In the Indian perspective, we find it much more essential because the general masses are found dissatisfied[13] with the treatment they get specially in the state hospitals. In a true sense, we find proficient managers to be very much instrumental in the entire process. The hospital professionals are supposed to work as a link between doctors and patients. The hospital personnel serving the state hospitals need to realise the sufferings of general masses who come to the government hospitals because they find it difficult to afford the services of private hospitals. Of course, we find a number of constraints in fulfilling their requirements because the state hospitals are infrastructurally poor. They also face the problem of inadequacy of hospital staff both in medical and paramedical categories. They are financially bankrupt and managerially deficient. And when we find them potentially unsound, how we expect from them even basic medical aids to the poorest of the poor. Hence, the most important task before the state policy makers is to make hospitals and healthcare organisations potentially sound.

The most effective prescription to make Indian hospitals behaviourally and ethically sound is to improve the quality of hospitals personnel. The concept and percept of quality people specially in respect of healthcare services convey something different to others. We often talk about the role of hospital personnel to the society but never talk about the role of society to them. Unless we find an attitudinal change in the society, we cannot expect a change in the attitudes of hospital personnel. We live in a materialistic age where social status rests on money. The corporate culture has injected new life and strength to it where consumerism has trapped all of us. To lead a comfortable and luxurious lifestyle considerably influenced by western culture, we need to earn more which promotes unethical and immoral practices in the society. Since we find other segments of society flourishing with the support of unethical and illegitimate practices, the hospital personnel too adopt the same.

We find investment of huge money on the development of quality medical and paramedical personnel. Both in terms of time and money, the medical personnel have a different graph. They offer the services of distinct nature which cannot be offered by others. Hence, it is judicious that we keep into consideration the relevance of their services and offer to them the financial incentives found adequate to lead a comfortable life. Contrary to it, we find doctors and other paramedical staff getting less than their counterparts. It is amazing that on the one hand we face the problems of poor doctor-patient ratio while on the other hand, we find a number of doctors unemployed. To reverse the vicious circle which has been found making ways for immoral practices, the national policy makers would have to make provisions for a rational motivational plan. Incentives bear the efficacy of transforming our attitudes.

The quality doctors are our assets. We need to offer to them the respect they deserve. We need to provide to them the incentives they need to lead a respectful life. Conversely, we have been found demoralising them, defaming them and depriving them of even the basics. The state hospitals in particular need to promote and motivate quality doctors even if superannuated. The doctors never retire. If we keep on continuing the doctors till they are in a position to serve, the quality gap that we find today would naturally be bridged.

SUMMARY

In this chapter, you have gone through different dimensions of management of behaviour in hospitals. After going through this chapter, be sure that the following facts are well versed:

Behaviour the Perception: The perception of behaviour focuses on our attitudes, family background, changes in the social system, expectations guiding our decisions, reactions and so on.

Theory of Human Nature: In a true sense, we don't find even a single answer that clarifies the nature of human beings. The theory developed by McGregor—Theory X and Theory Y throw light on the human nature.

Maslow's Theory: The theory of Maslow explains the process of shaping of our expectations. Basic needs, safety and security, belonging, esteem needs and achievements are found important in the very context which we know as hierarchy of needs.

Behavioural Influences: The social, economic and psychological factors influence human behaviour considerably. Among the social variables, we find family background, level of education, social recognition and size of a family important. The economic variables include the level of income and the psychological variables include our attitudes and the motivational factors.

Behavioural Management in Hospitals: In the management of hospitals, we find behavioural management playing an important role because the behavioural profile of patients and attendants becomes important in shaping the level of their expectations. The behavioural profile of different categories of employees serving the hospitals becomes significant with the viewpoint of increasing the level of efficiency. If the hospital personnel are well aware of the behavioural profile of patients and attendants, they can gauge the level of their expectations. If the hospital managers are found well aware of the behavioural profile of hospital personnel as well as the patients, they can improve the quality of services.

Relationship: Here, we go through different types of relationships, viz., Hospital personnel and patient relationship, Nurse-patients Relations, Interdepartmental and intradepartmental relationships, Relationship of hospital managers with the supervisor, relationship with peers, relationship with superiors and relationship with the subordinates. An indepth study of relationship with the different categories of employees working in the hospitals helps the resolution of multidimensional conflicts found instrumental in the degeneration of the level of efficiency. The hospital managers are supposed to develop good relations, friendly relations even with the subordinates so that they succeed in getting their cooperation. The departmental coordination, cooperation and cohesion depend on a good relationship. In a true sense, we find a close relation between good-patient care and departmental relationship.

Ethics in Hospitals: The ethical dimension occupies a place of outstanding significance in the management of hospitals because the services of hospitals are found based on human values, humanity and ethics. Unlike profit making organisations, the hospitals and the personnel engaged therein need to work only with the service motto that requires due weightage to ethical values.

Behavioural Conflict in Hospitals: Ego-conflict, interest-conflict, priority-conflict stand as a barrier and therefore, the hospital managers need to resolve it.

Indian hospitals need behaviourally and ethically sound people: It is high time that hospital professionals assign due weightage to the behavioural and ethical dimensions while inculcating faculties in the medical and paramedical personnel. Behaviourally sound hospital personnel help in minimising the recovery period and ethically sound people help in projecting a positive image of hospitals.

KEY TERMS

Behavioural Profile	Hyperactivity
Attitudes	Pep Talk
Typical Person	Empathy
Innate	Boss
Esteem Needs	Unions
Physiological Needs	Associations
Hierarchy of Needs	Bribery
Self-actualisation	Payoffs
Ego	Behavioural Conflict
OPD	Fragmentation
Peers	Euthansia
Superiors	Forensic Medicine
Subordinates	Acrimonious
Accreditation	Percept

REVIEW QUESTIONS

1. What do you mean by Behaviour? Explain the relevance of behavioural management to hospitals.
2. Focus on the Theory X and Theory Y developed by McGregor. Do you find these theories helpful in studying the human behaviour?
3. Explain the Maslow's theory of needs. Discuss the instrumentality of Maslow's theory in studying the levels of expectations of users of hospital services.
4. Discuss the different social variables influencing he behavioural profile.
5. Explain the psychological variables influencing the behaviour.
6. Explain the social, economic and psychological variables influencing the behaviour.
7. Throw light on the behavioural management in hospitals. Do you find an indepth study of behavioural management essential for a hospital manager? Defend your answer.
8. What do you mean by relationship? Explain the relationship of a hospital manager with superiors, peers and subordinates.
9. Focus on the impact of departmental relationship on good patient care.
10. Explain the relationship of hospital personnel with the patients.
11. Throw light on the instrumentality of ethical dimension on improving the working of hospitals.

12. Explain the problem of behavioural conflict in hospitals. Throw light on the resolving of conflicts.
13. Write a short note on the behavioural and ethical dimensions in relation to the Indian hospitals.

APPLICATION EXERCISES

1. You are working as a manager in a private hospital. Focus on you role in improving the quality of healthcare services.
2. In the capacity of a hospital manager focus on the relevance of social variables influencing the behaviour.
3. The psychological variables considerably influence the behavioural profile. Comment on this statement as a hospital professional.
4. You are working as a manager in a government hospital. Focus on the steps you would initiate to improve the interdepartment and intradepartmental relationships.
5. In addition to the quality medicare services, the patients and attendants also expect decent behaviour from the hospital personnel. Comment on this statement as a hospital manager.
6. The services of hospitals considerably rest on nurse-patient relationships. Comment on this statement as a hospital manager.
7. Indian hospitals need behaviourally and ethically sound hospital personnel. Do you agree with this vie? Justify your opinion as a hospital professional.

END NOTES

1. Schein Edge H., *Organisational Psychology*, Prentice Hall of India, pp. 40-41.
2. Jha S.M., *Marketing Management*, Himalaya Publishing House, Mumbai, 1988.
3. Douglas McGregor, *The Human Side Enterprise*, New York, 1960.
4. Maslow A.H., *Motivation and Personality*, Harper and Row, New York, 1954, pp. 80-85.
5. Donald N. Lombardi, *Health Care*, p. 290.
6. Kuma R., *Doctor-Patients Relations: Hospital Administration and Management*, Vol. 3, pp. 179-207.
7. Donald N. Lombardi, *op. cit.*, p. 293.
8. *Ibid.*, p. 290.
9. Berkman H.W., *Corporate Ethics: Who Cares ?* p;. 447.
10. Joseph Fletcher, *Moral Responsibility, Situation Ethics at Work*, Philadelphia, p. 168.
11. Gerald J. Dalcourt, *The Pragmatist and Situationist to Ethics*, Thought, 51, June, 1976, No. 201.
12. Donald N,. Lombardi, *op. cit.*, p. 145.
13. Swati Soni and Makarand Upadhyaya, *India—A Global Healthcare Brand*; Journal of Marketing & Communication; vol. 1/3, January-April, 2006 pp. 69-76
14. Mohd. Masood Ahmed, *Indian Healthcare Delivery System and Customer Satisfaction*; Journal of IPM Meerut; Vol. 6/1 January-March, 2006 pp. 6-13

Hospital Planning

It is planning that helps us in enriching our potentials. It is planning that helps us in tailoring our resources in tune with the changing requirements. Like other organisations, the hospitals and healthcare organisations also need a realistic plan.

CHAPTER OBJECTIVES

Introduction—Hospital Planning: the Concept—Principles of Hospital Planning Components of Hospital Planning Factors Influencing the formulation of Hospital Plan—Instrumentality of MIS in Hospital Planning—Planning the Functional Areas in Hospital—Material Planning—Product Planning—Manpower Planning—Financial Planning—Marketing Planning—Planning the Peripheral Services—Planning for Health Education—Planning for Managing Waste—Summary—Key Terms—Review Questions—Application Exercises—End Notes.

LEARNING OBJECTIVES

This chapter aims at studying the different dimensions of hospital planning. Keeping in view the changing medicare requirements, it is imperative that hospital professionals, with the help of a techno-driven MIS, formulate a realistic plan which serves and subserves the healthcare requirements of society. The readers develop their awareness of the formulation of an ideal plan for hospitals which fulfill the domestic as well as the global requirements. We need hospitals which serve the society and at the same time, generate wealth to enrich their potentials to bear the mounting social costs.

Introduction

An organisation believing in making things happen has no option but to keep on moving the process of innovation so that new products are made available in the markets much earlier than the competitors. If we believe in thriving, the developments to take place and the trends to emerge are to be identified. If we increase our awareness of developments which took place in past, the trends to emerge in future are diagnosed. It is in this context that we talk about planning. It is planning that helps us in enriching our potentials. It is planning that helps us in tailoring our resources in tune with the changing requirements. Like other organisations, the hospitals and healthcare organisations also need to formulate an ideal plan; a plan that is pragmatic, a plan that is meticulous and a plan that is optimistic. We cannot negate that optimism paves the ways for development whereas pessimism becomes instrumental in the contraction of even the potentials available. The hospital planners need to formulate a plan in tune with the multidimensional changes in the disease profile. The increasing levels of expectations of patients and attendants, the growing insensitivity to healthcare and nutritional requirements, the increasing contamination of water, the mounting sound pollution and environmental pollution are some of the key reasons responsible for a significant increase in the disease graph. In addition, our insensitivity to vaccination and immunization, increasing cases of malnutrition and nutritional deficiency have also played a big role in aggravating the intensity of problem.

Of late, we find an age of techniculture. The new generation of sophisticated technology has influenced almost all the sectors. Innovations and inventions in the field of medical sciences make it essential that hospital planners are well aware of the recent developments which would make it easier to formulate an ideal plan. The hospital planners bear the responsibility of formulating short and long-term plans. Since we find hospitals as a capital intensive project, it is essential that whatsoever the developments we propose are in the face of changing needs and requirements. They also need to consider the changing lifestyles and the increasing disposable income of the society. Since we find medical tourism gaining popularity in the Indian perspective, it is also significant that hospital planners and architects also plan for potential users coming from abroad for availing medicare services.

We are well aware of the emerging problems with the rural population. Insensitivity and poor affordability are the two important reasons for multifaceted health problems found aggravating in rural India. The hospital planners also need to consider innovative plans for the development of hospitals in the rural areas. If we find world class hospitals located in villages well equipped with the infrastructural facilities and well connected with roads, the multiplier effects would be found operational. The rural people would avail the healthcare facilities, the development of hotels, educational institutions, communication, transportation and financial services, profitable markets for agricultural produces of the concerned regions would help in transforming the economy of that region. The transformation of rural areas into the urban areas thus would gain a rapid momentum. If the hotel planners are found sensitive to the emerging problems, the rural tourism and medical tourism would also flourish. The most important thing the hospital planners need to consider in the very context is world class services to the users at an affordable price.

The planning for hospitals also need to consider the planning for building, planning for technological advancements, planning for buildings, planning for the availability of quality hospital personnel, planning for the mobilisation and channelisation of financial resources, planning for hospital surroundings and premises, planning for safety, etc. The planners need to make scope for expansion and development, research and modernization intune with the long-term requirements. Since it is considered to be capital intensive, they should also leave scope for all round development of hospitals.

The most neglected aspect in the hospitals and healthcare organisations is concerned with waste management. The different categories of waste need due attention of hospital planners so that from the very beginning, they find it convenient to go for scientific disposal. In a majority of the hospitals, in both the public and private hospitals, the hospital planners keep this item at the bottom of their agenda which proves to be a centre for infection. The used beds, cots, bedsheets, specially in the government hospitals become a point for health hazards. A safe place where these items can be disposed off without any adverse impact is to be identified by the hospital planners.

In the Indian perspective, the hospital planners hardly think about the formulation of an ideal plan of pragmatic nature. Of course, we find some of the leading private hospitals assigning due weightage to a realistic plan and therefore, they are in a position to bring qualitative or quantitative improvements in the face of changing requirements but a number of public or private hospitals do not consider hospital planning an important dimension of hospital management and therefore, the task of development and expansion becomes complicated for them. Particularly the government hospitals need to assign due weightage to an integrated health policy so that primary, secondary and tertiary healthcare centres are found in a position to help each other to touch the target of quality medicare services to the society. We are aware of the fact that state governments bear the responsibility of providing healthcare or medicare services to the population of the concerned but a majority of the healthcare centres are found mismanaged. They lack a positive attitude, professional excellence and supporting infrastructural facilities which make their task of providing quality medicare services much more difficult.

The hospital planners for formulating a realistic plan need to take the support of a techno-driven management information system which would provide to them an indepth knowledge of the changing healthcare requirements of potential users. They can solicite the cooperation of different functional managers for the concerned information. It is right to mention that during the yesteryears, we have witnessed multidimensional changes and with the help of information system, the planners may have an idea of the same for their proper incorporation in the concerned plan. Making provision for the new generation of information and communication technology, sophisticated equipments and instruments, supporting infrastructural facilities, quality materials and world class medical and paramedical personnel are some of the basic requirements without which the healthcare services cannot be optimal to our requirements. The information system would help hospital planners in different ways.

Planning for health education is considered to be significant but we find a majority of the medical colleges and institutes getting it difficult to improve the quality of education. We need a good number of world class medical and paramedical personnel but we find a big gap between demand and supply. The medical colleges and institutes need qualitative-cum-quantitative development to meet the domestic and global requirements. Since we find disease profile becoming much more complicated, the hospital personnel would be required to show their excellence while diagnosing and treating the patients.

In view of the above, it is right to mention that we need a realistic plan for the development of hospital and healthcare services in the Indian perspective. The formulation of an ideal plan must be in the face of development of hospital and healthcare services in all three streams such as public sector, private sector and public–private partnership mode. The primary, secondary and tertiary hospitals need a new vision which will focus on setting a priority order. The services of architects may also be used specially for the development of ambience.

HOSPITAL PLANNING-THE CONCEPT

At the outset, we go through the conceptual aspect of hospital planning which draws our attention on two important components. The first component is hospital and the second component is planning. Here, we find a combination of two words. We have already gone through the conceptual aspect of hospital and now therefore, we focus on the concept of planning. The concept of planning for a hospital is deliberated in a different way. This is due to the fact that we find the multi-pronged developments affecting hospitals in a different way.

Planning throws light on managing the future in a systematic way so that an organisation or an institution is found in a position to work smoothly. The changing requirements of society become a guiding force. The planners need to notice the multidimensional changes.

We find change a natural phenomenon. If we don't plan, our task of managing the future would be much more difficult. It is an ongoing process that continues till the organisations or institutions are found existent. It is a continuous process because today, we complete the implementation of a plan and right from today itself, we start thinking about a new plan.

The term "Hospital Planning" focuses our attention on planning for the development and smooth functioning of hospitals. With the passage of time, we find a number of developments in the society. The increasing population, the degenerating environmental conditions vis-a-vis the changing disease profile, the continuing sophistication in the process of technological advancements, the increasing expectations of hospital personnel, customers/patients and attendants, the changes in the education and training facilities are some of the significant developments making it essential that we make possible an analogous change in the hospitals. It is in this context that we talk about hospital planning. It is a systematic effort to develop hospitals in the changing conditions. If hospitals fail in managing the multi-dimensional changes, the potentials of serving the patients would start shrinking. The hospitals bear the responsibility of making the end-product more benign, wholesome and human.[1] This makes it essential that hospital planners are well aware of the multidimensional changes and plan to develop hospitals accordingly so that a mis-match between the changing conditions and available potentials is ruled out.

Hospital planning in the Indian perspective is required to be viewed in the face of intensity of problem vis-a-vis the resource constraints. In addition, it also requires to consider the process of technological advancements. During the yesterdecades, we have witnessed a number of changes in the technologies in general and the information technology in particular. This has considerably been responsible for a change in the perception of hospital planning. Of late, we find hospital planning a technical problem which is sizeably governed by the management of information. In the Indian context, the hospital planning requires to be viewed in a bit different way because the lack of mass awareness is found making a sound milieu for the development of a different disease profile. The masses lack the potentials to use the expensive services of private hospitals. It is against this background that the hospital planners need an attitudinal change while planning the development of Indian hospitals. The holistic concept of management requires due attention of hospital planners. While planning, they need to make it sure that whatever the services they are going to offer to the end-users would be cost-effective. Thus, we find hospital planning a systematic effort to establish hospitals in the changing environmental and social conditions with due emphasis on technological advancements.

Principles of Hospital Planning

While planning for hospitals, it is essential that the planners are well aware of the principles governing the formulation of an ideal plan that simplifies the task of accomplishing the organisational goals. They bear the responsibility of formulating an ideal plan and in this context, the governing principles[2] as mentioned below need due care:

1. ***Protection:*** The most important thing the planners need to consider on a priority basis is protection to the patients. This requires due attention on multifaceted problems such as the noise generated by the traffic or other sources. If we find too much traffic in the nursing unit corridor, the patients would be disturbed. Besides, the possibilities of noise pollution would also be increased. This requires to make it sure that any unwanted traffic in the surgical suite is regulated. The planners need to consider the importance of good patient care while formulating a plan since this is found to be an important aspect of protection. Besides, the planners also need to make it sure that the drains and hospital waste are not close to the wards or OTs.

2. ***Separation:*** The planners bear the responsibility of separating the quiet and noisy, pleasant and unpleasant functions. The separation of a dissimilar activities is found impact generating because this is also to influence the management of treatment. The different types of personnel, patients, clean and dirty operations must be separated. Like this, the traffic outside and inside the building also requires to be separated. This would improve the level of efficiency of hospitals.

3. ***Circulation:*** We also find circulation an important principle for the formulation of an ideal plan for hospitals. The planners are supposed to make the process cost effective and this makes it residential that they assign due weightage to separation. We need to make the routes efficiency-oriented and this is possible when we find a provision for the short routes. If we find short routes for the nurses, doctors, patients and other personnel, not only would the efficiency be increased but even the intensity of fatigue would also be minimised. In hospitals, all the personnel need to work for the welfare of patients. The time management requires an intensive care in the functioning of hospitals and the principles of circulation would minimise the time gap in the availability of required supporting infrastructural facilities.

4. ***Control:*** For the smooth functioning of hospital, it is pertinent that the related medical and paramedical personnel are in a position to control the diagnosis and treatment processes. The nurses find it significant to have a corridor making their task of control easier. The doctors find it convenient to control and activate the process of supervision, if we find interlinked corridors. Since the visitors and others may carry germs, it is pertinent that the hospital planners make arrangements, specially for the protection of surgical suites. This also draws our attention on separating everything and closing everything as per the required norms so that on the one hand, the efficiency is increased while on the other hand, the possibilities of infection, noise, escape and inconveniences are also minimised.

5. ***The Traffic Streams:*** The principles of hospital planning also need to think about the traffic streams of both categories—exterior and interior. At the outset, we go through the exterior traffic streams.

Exterior Traffic Streams: The exterior traffic streams include in-patients and visitors, out-patients, emergency patients and supplies and fuel.

In-patients and Visitors: We go through the problem of the main entrance meant for the patients using ambulance for admission or leaving the hospitals after discharge. They are supposed to reach to the desk or place meant for admission and would go through the main lobby. In addition, the visitors also use the main gate or even personnel controlling the traffic also use it. Besides, the doctors are also found using the main entrance but they should prefer to use separate entrance so that they are not button-holed or disturbed by the attendants or visitors. They also need a separate parking area. We go through the problem that the hospital planners, in the light of conveniences and inconveniences and time management, plan for the designing of a main gate that is not to generate problems to the users. Of late, we also find automatic gates used in some of the hospitals. The main thing in the process is to make possible a convenient and a safe entrance and exist.

Emergency Entrance: To make possible additional safety and conveniences, it is much more impact generating that the hospital planners keep in their minds entrance provisions specially for emergency patients using the services of ambulance. If we find a separate entrance for ambulance or emergency patients, the problems on account of traffic jam would considerably be minimised. The emergency patients also use private transport facilities for coming to the hospitals. The hospital planners need to gravitate their attention on a number of considerations while designing entrance. It is essential that they are careful to the points that the patients of dirty nature, supported by attendants with a criminal background, or a drunk or cases of major accidents draw due attention of hospital planners.

Out-patients' Entrance: While planning for the hospitals, it is pertinent that planners also think about entrance for the out-patients. It is desirable that a separate gate is provided for the out-patients' entry. They should not get entry to the principal corridors and therefore, we find it significant to make provision for a separate place where they find themselves comfortable but are not disturbing others.

Entrance for Hospital Personnel: While planning, there must be a separate gate or entrance for the hospital personnel. If they make a separate gate for the entry of hospital personnel, a number of problems would be arrested. The hospital planners need to assign due weightage to the gate for the maternity ward because there we find possibilities of generating noise.

Parking: The hospital planners need to think about the parking of vehicles. The main thing while making a provision for parking is related to a separate parking for the doctors. Thus, the space exclusively for doctors would not be used by the visitors and the inconveniences or wastage of time on that account would also be minimised. The parking space for the general visitors should be close to the main gate so that the traffic is not to pollute the environment and to create noise. The planners also need to consider about the parking places for ambulances or vehicles of attendants carrying the emergency cases.

Interior Traffic Streams: The interior traffic streams also become important and therefore, the hospital planners need to go through the problem of different favourites, such as Cruciform, T form. The motive is to control the traffic so gently that the services of hospitals are not to be affected. This is primarily related to the designing process.

The architects have developed a number of designs and the hospital planners are required to go through the same. The size of hospitals, the nature and character of catchment area, the flow of traffic, the location point of hospitals and the influx of patients and attendants are some of the points to be given due weightage while managing the interior traffic streams.

The "Cruciform" is an important plan in the very context. It focuses our attention on a central traffic and cul-de-sac (a street closed at one end). Such an arrangement is found important to provide conveniences to the control of traffic generally found neglected in a majority of the hospitals. The central traffic control is found essential in the hospitals to minimise the problem of interior traffic disturbances.

Another form that we find in the very context is the "T form." Even in the T form, we find a central traffic control. This is to integrate the various medical departments in bases of the letter T floor-by-floor, and nursing units facing south in the top of the letter T.

The aforesaid facts make it clear that interior traffic streams become significant with the viewpoint of a sound traffic control which is not to generate inconveniences and further make possible a sound traffic control. In a majority of the hospitals, we don't find condition-oriented management of traffic control that makes the entire process of diagnosis and treatment inconvenient vis-a-vis time-consuming.

Thus, the hospital planners need to go through the different principles of hospital planning. This is found significant to improve the quality of services. It is in this context that we consider it important to the hospital planning. The motive is to make available to the users quality and time-honoured services. We have gone through a number of problems related to protection, separation, circulation, control and the traffic streams. In the different principles, the main thing that we find is related to the construction of buildings for the hospitals, development and designing of the surroundings and premises, construction of roads and drains, plantation and gardening, exterior and interiors or so. We talk about protection but it is difficult to think about the same unless we find proper construction. The separation element is found important but we can't think about separation unless we design the construction in the face of our requirements and assign due weightage to interiors. We talk about circulation but it is meaningless to think about the same unless we find proper designing. Even if we talk about control, it is not possible unless we plan hospitals intelligently. Thus, the different principles of hospital planning concentrate on comforts and conveniences to the patients, attendants, hospital personnel and in addition, time honoured and cost effective services to the patients since this is the most important thing in the management of hospitals. While planning, the planners can't devalue the cost element because we need to think everything in the Indian perspective where the policy makers find it difficult to extend financial support to the hospitals because they of course, don't consider it a matter of top priority.

It is not only important that we open hospitals. It is much more impact generating that we establish them and think about their planned development which makes the process of diagnosis and treatment time honoured vis-a-vis cost-effective besides keep on moving our efforts for quality upgradation so that users at large are made available the world class healthcare services.

Components of Hospitals Planning

We find hospital a centre for diagnosis and treatment. We find hospitals a place for improving the quality life index. We find hospitals a social institution active in generating mass awareness regarding a healthy living condition. These contributions of a hospital need due weightage when we start planning for hospitals. This makes it essential that the different components of hospital planning are studied in depth.

1. Perceiving the Ideas: The first component in the very context is related to the perception regarding hospital. We find focus on the instrumentality of an architect in translating the ideas into action. An indepth study of catchment area, disease profile and supporting infrastructural facilities is found essential. In this context, we need enormous cooperation of a hospital architect who is supposed to be a specialist in the area. The instrumentality of a consultant of world-class plays an incremental role. May be that an individual possesses both the qualities and if not, an architect should not be hesitant of taking the support of a consultant. In the hospital planning, we find three aspects important. First administrative planning, second physical planning and the third building planning and designing.[3] In a true sense, we need an optimal mix of all the three qualities in an individual. Generally, we feel that an architect specialist in hospital planning would do everything we need.. But all the areas need expertise of world class. It is in this context that we talk about the instrumentality of hospital planners, administrators and managers in perceiving a right idea for designing the hospitals. This makes it essential that even in the syllabi of hospital administration, we make provisions for developing expertise in hospital planning. Like this, the schools of architect need to develop specialisation in the area of hospital planning. This would simplify the problem of perceiving the right perception of hospitals that an organisation, institution and an individual proposes of develop. The hospital managers and architects need to understand the requirements of the catchment area, potentials available for the development of hospitals and the contributions of hospitals when they start serving the society.

2. Selecting the Place for Location: When we find emphasis of the first component of hospital planning on the construction of a suitable building for hospitals the second constituent focuses on the suitability of a place where the hospitals are to be located. An indepth study of the location point is found significant with the viewpoint of understanding the command area and the plus or minus points of the place where the hospital is to be located. The availability of land, supporting infrastructural facilities, cheap labour power for making the construction processes cost-effective are some of the considerations to be given due weightage while formulating an ideal plan for hospitals. In the Indian perspective, the hospital managers and hospital architects need a new vision for approving the location points. We don't find any sense in developing hospitals in the cities' precincts since multifaceted constraints stand as a barrier. This makes it essential that the hospital planners think about the development of big hospitals in the rural areas found close to the big town and cities. Such an approach would show multi-pronged positive results, e.g., the rural areas or villages would be benefited, the urban population would also be benefited because we find well developed roads, the multiplier effects would help villages to activate the process of economic development, the commercialisation of place would change the nature and character of village society, the scope for expansion and development would be available and the process of social transformation would gain momentum. It is in this context that we find urbanisation with the help of hospitals.

3. Finalising the Site: The third component of hospital planning is related to the finalisation of site. The hospital managers and architects need to make it sure that all the required infrastructural facilities are made available to the hospitals before the construction works start. The construction of all-weather proof roads, the power and communications, the water and gas, sewers or so. An indepth study of soil condition is found essential before finalising the site for locating hospitals. This is found essential because we find several cases where due to a negative soil condition, the location was changed resulting into huge financial losses. This makes it essential that we keep in our minds the topographic configuration of the site because the uneven ground conditions create a number of difficulties. The problem of rock excavation would only not be cost-ineffective but even instrumental in delaying the implementation of plan. Hence, the hospital architects need to think over all these problems before finalising the site.

4. Budgeting: This is also found to be an important component of hospital planning because we find finance playing a contributory role in the translation of plans into action. Before drawings are undertaken, it is pertinent that we think about budgeting which would simplify the process of implementation. While budgeting, a number of aspects are to be given due care. There are different methods of budgeting no doubt, but the most widely used in the very context is the assumed gross sum to be spent by an individual, institution and organisation on the project. In this case, we find the first thing is to subtract from it the cost and thereafter, the cost of the movable furnishing and equipment is subtracted, then the cost of engineering which includes fees of architects, engineers, supervisors of construction and finally the cost of roads, yard work and landscaping should be deducted. We find residue the sum available for building purposes. In no case, we should confuse the cost of constructing the building with the gross cost. The balance divided by an assumed cost per square or cft of construction is the area/volume of building in square cubic feet that can be built from the money available. This makes it possible to complete the construction within the area, cubic content and cost. It is essential that the diagnostic and therapeutic facilities of any hospital are optimal to the treatment of the patients. The hospitals meant for imparting educational training and research facilities may require higher level of technical equipment. The budgeting thus is found to be an important component of hospital planning and the hospital planners and architects can't overlook this component if they want cost effective and time honoured completion of the project.

5. Size and Type of Hospital: The hospital planners need to know about the size and nature of hospital because this is to change everything in the process of designing or construction. If we talk about the primary hospitals, or local or community clinics or health centres, the size is small. The community hospitals are of medium-sized to large with 200600 inpatient beds with major diagnostic and treatment specialities. They also offer educational and training facilities to the paramedical personnel. The tertiary or teaching hospitals usually have 600-1000 beds. They house not only the basic services but also offer the sophisticated facilities, adding specialities in tune with the disease profile or a particular organ of the body.

We also find hospitals of a special category which provide for long stay for the elderly, children, psychiatric patients, chronically sick patients, physically handicapped and mentally retarded patients or so.

The large sized hospitals are of two categories, general and referral. In the referral hospitals, the specialised diagnostics and therapeutics are found available.

6. Elements of Hospitals: In hospitals, we find different elements, such as nursing unit, therapeutics, admission, out-patient department and the general configuration. The nursing unit is considered to be an important part of hospital where the patients are nursed. It is right to mention that the nursing unit is the core of the hospital and therefore, this unit requires an intensive care in the formulation of a hospital plan. The therapeutics are related to alleviation and cure of diseases. There are different types of therapy playing a significant role in the treatment process, such as radiation therapy, radio-isotopes and X-ray treatment, operating or surgery, occupational therapy and psychotherapy. The admission process is done by the admitting department. It is also a place where emergency treatment facilities are found available. The OPD is found to be the miniature of the hospital. It is pertinent that they share the diagnostic and therapeutic facilities. In a true sense, we find OPD doing educational, preventive, diagnostic and therapeutic work. The hospital planners are required to go through the different physical elements as mentioned above. In addition, we find general configuration of hospital building, such as window exposure, view, orientation, aesthetics, shape of terrain, engineering considerations and so on. The hospital planners and to be more specific, the hospital architects need to design the hospital building anatomically so that it functions efficiently.

7. Programme Making: We find programme an important base for undertaking the architectural works because the architects get the detailed information not only related to the space but also related to the activity and the organisation and life within the walls. We can't say that a programme just includes the number of rooms and the sizes. In a true sense, it should start with practical information on organisation, personnel or so which would make it easier to plan in tune with the requirements. The hospital consultants and architects bear the responsibility of getting a detailed programme so that they are found successful in completing the designing work efficiently. The hospital administrators/managers bear the responsibility of making available to the hospital architects the detailed programme. The doctors may help him in the preparation work or he/she may seek the cooperation of specialists. But the hospital architects may question the programme made available to them without adequate information. We agree with this view that programme making is an important functional responsibility and the hospital planners are supposed to know about the processes and contents of an ideal programme helping architects in working efficiently.

8. Drawings and Specifications: The drawings and specifications include small-scale diagrammatic plans displaying the corridors, elevators and stairs. In addition, the size, location and relationship are mentioned and the future potentials for expansion are also indicated. Plans are tested by the drawing flow-diagram. The exterior perspectives and elevations are also included to study the architectural form. The architects, structural, mechanical and electrical engineers complete the drawing works and specifications.

Factors Influencing the Formulation of a Hospital Plan

The hospital planners, architects, consultants, managers/administrators need to go through the following facts while formulating an ideal plan for hospitals. The multidimensional developments in the environmental conditions, the changing disease profile, the growing mass unawareness, high rate of illiteracy, the multifaceted developments in the medical sciences, the contracting paying capacity of the masses are some of the key factors to be considered while formulating a plan for hospitals,[4] specially in the Indian perspective.

1. Changing Disease Profile: With increasing non-optimal industrialisation, we find a basic change in the disease profile. We can't negate the fact that the process of industrial transformation has activated the process of economic transformation sizeably but at the same time, has also shown some major negative effects engineering a sound base for the development of a number of diseases. It is against this background that a number of diseases already eradicated in past have been spreading, specially in the rural areas. This makes it essential that hospital planners keep in their minds the changing disease profile of a particular catchment area for which the hospital is to be started. It is quite natural that disease profile substantially influences the designing in and construction of hospitals because special diseases require special diagnostic and treatment facilities which influence the designing process.

2. Increasing Pollution of Environment: Of late, we find the society facing multi-pronged challenges mainly on account of environmental pollution. The air pollution, noise pollution, water contamination use of pesticides and on a large-scale in the process of cultivation, of course has reached to a critical point resulting into multi-dimensional diseases of new character. This has been found affecting the processes and requirements for diagnosis and treatment. The harmful effects of noise pollution has been found inviting a number of diseases. This makes it essential that the hospital planners and architects perceive the multi-dimensional effects of pollution of environment in a particular command area and while designing and planning hospitals for that area assign due weightage to the same.

3. Mass Awareness: We can't negate the fact that increasing mass unawareness is an important reason for the development of diseases because the masses fail in understanding the grave consequences of food-prone and water-borne diseases. They don't know about the nutritional values in maintaining a healthy living condition and thus, generate and aggravate the magnitude of problem. The increasing insensitivity in the Indian society makes the task much more difficult for the hospital planners. The viral diseases and communicable diseases are also found increasing the intensity of problem. Unless and until we find mass awareness in the society, the pressure on hospitals would continue to increase. This complicates the task of hospital planners because they fail to understand the actual requirements of a particular catchement area. It is in this context that we find it important that the hospital planners come to know about the increasing awareness and its impact on the magnitude of problem.

4. High Rate of Illiteracy: It is right to mention that in an illiterate society, the pressure on hospitals is found ever increasing. We find a correlation between the rate of illiteracy and awareness. If we find a high rate of literacy, the society is found fully aware of the healthy or unhealthy living conditions. Not only this, the treatment processes are also found easier when the patients are found literate. Since we find hospital planning directly linked to the nature and character of services made available by the hospitals to the patients, we can't underestimate the rate of literacy influencing the process of planning.

5. Multi-faceted Development in the Medical Sciences: During the yester decades, we have witnessed a number of changes in the process of diagnosis and treatment. This is due mainly to the process of technological sophistication in the field of medical sciences. Frequent inventions and innovations in the instruments, equipment and information technology are found influencing the nature and character of treatment. The hospital planners and architects need to understand the impact of sophisticated technologies because it is sophistication that influences the interior designing on account of space and condition required for increasing the level of efficiency of technologies. The old generation of diagnostic and treatment devices required more space whereas the new generation of technologies need less space for installation and functioning. It is in this context that we focus on the recent developments in the field of medical sciences necessitating due attention of hospital planners and managers.

6. Paying Capacity of the Masses: We are aware of the fact that masses in the Indian society are not in a position to afford even the cheap medical services then what to talk of the expensive services. The latest developments in the medical sciences have also been instrumental in raising the costs of diagnosis and treatment. The hospital planners and managers need to make the process cost-effective so that even poorest of the poor are in a position to avail the medical services required essential. Since we don't find a sign of increase in the disposable income of the masses, it is pertinent that planning for the hospital services make possible economy.

7. Increasing Importance of Specialisation: Of late, we find specialised hospitals gaining popularity because the users feel that the quality of services in the specialised hospitals are of world class. To some extent, it is also right to mention that specialised hospitals establish an edge over the general hospitals. We find a structural change in the nature and character of designing in both the categories of hospitals. This makes it essential that the hospital planners and architects keep in their minds the nature and types of hospitals before they start formulating an ideal plan for the hospitals.

In view of the aforesaid facts, it is right to opine that designing of a plan for the different categories of hospitals and the different types of diseases is a challenging task where world class excellence is needed. We can't devalue the above mentioned facts in the process of formulating an ideal plan for the hospitals. Since planning plays a contributory role in the entire process of diagnosis and treatment, the hospital managers/administrators, architects and consultants need to be careful. They are supposed to formulate a pragmatic and ambitious plan so that avenues are broadened for modernisation, expansion and development. Of late, we find hospital a capital intensive project and therefore, we don't find any sense in investing huge money in a plan that is never to be implemented. On the other hand, we also argue in favour of qualitative-cum-quantitative improvements and this makes it essential that planning processes are followed in a right fashion. It is against this background that we consider the above mentioned factors important to the formulation of a plan for the modern hospitals.

Instrumentality of MIS in Hospitals Planning

We agree with this view that the formulation of a hospital plan is found based on the forecasting results. It is the sound management of information that helps an organisation in formulating a plan having pragmatic approach, time honoured objectives and right setting of the order of priorities. If we find everything managed blindly without turning our eyes on the past and present, the forecasting results confuse us. This makes it essential that whatever the objectives we set and the priorities we change are based on the emerging trends. It is in this context that we talk about the instrumentality of MIS in the formulation of an ideal plan for hospitals.[5] Of late, we talk about a technology driven management information system since significant developments in the field of information and communication technologies have been found making our efforts proactive and result-oriented. The following facts make it clear that formulation of a plan with the support of a well developed information system would minimise the possibilities of a big gap between the planned target and the actuals. When we talk about hospital planning, our prime focus is found on activating the efforts found helpful in offering to the masses quality healthcare services which help them in many ways.

1. MIS makes possible identification of the emerging trends: We are well aware of the fact that formulation and implementation of a plan is an ongoing process that continues till the existence of an organisation. The social conditions change, the disease profile changes, the level of awareness fluctuates and these developments need a change in the plan objectives and priorities.

While formulating a plan, if we find hospital planners doing everything without identifying the emerging trends, the implementation of that plan would only not be a time taking process but even cost-ineffective. In the Indian perspective, we find hospital planners, architects, consultants, managers and administrators not assigning due weightage to the increasing gap between the target and actuals. This forms a vicious circle.

2. MIS helps planners in identifying the errors and shortcomings: It is quite natural that we commit mistakes. It is nothing surprising that our efforts become fruitless. But it is painful that we tail in identifying and confessing and repeat the same mistakes again and again committed earlier. Evaluation thus plays a significant role in identifying the errors and the shortcomings of human resources or technologies. While implementing plan, a mid-term evaluation thus minimises the possibilities of committing mistakes. With the increasing use of information and communications technologies, we find it easier to evaluate the positive or negative contributions. By making a mid-term evaluation, we succeed in minimising the errors. With the completion of a plan, we study the gap between the target and actuals and once again activate the process of identifying the reasons for delayed or cost-ineffective implementation. This engineers a sound foundation for the formulation of an ideal plan in which the least possible errors are to be committed.

3. MIS helps in formulating an ideal compensation plan for the hospital personnel: For achieving the organisational goals, it is pertinent that we increase the level of efficiency of hospital personnel which makes it essential that personnel engaged in the process prove to be high performers. We find a close relation between employee-orientation and performance-orientation. If we continue the process of adopting an attractive compensation plan for personnel, if we reward them suitably, if we pay additional incentives to the high performers, the avenues are paved even for transforming the inefficients into efficients. Contrary to it, if we keep on moving the process of compensating on a uniform basis, even the efficients are demotivated. We can't negate the instrumentality of an MIS in evaluating the performance of an individual or a team. We talk about personally committed hospital personnel and this makes it essential that our compensation and motivational plans are in the face of level of efficiency.

4. Managing finance fairly is possible with a technology-driven MIS: In a majority of the hospitals, we find unfair practices at different levels in the different areas which stand as a major obstacle to the cost effective implementation. With the help of a technology driven management information system, we find filing, accounting, purchase systems and documentation in a right fashion. The unfair practices, the cases of irregularities, the errors and omissions can be identified at the very early stage. Thus, the unfair practices are regulated and the process of maintaining cost economy is also activated in the right directions. We find possibilities of errors and omissions if the accounting practices are managed manually. It is against this background that we make much more advocacy in favour of a technology-driven management information system. Further, the hospital planners, architects, managers and other personnel find it convenient to design the project and to formulate a sound budget. Thus, an MIS helps hospitals in making possible cost-effective implementation of projects.

5. Managing the product of hospitals: For the smooth functioning and high level of efficiency, it is pertinent that an organisation thinks about innovations in the goods or services product. We find product planning an important dimension of hospital management. For meeting the increasing level of expectations of users, it is important that the hospitals offer to them quality services. The hospital managers bear the responsibility of blending the core and supportive services optimally so that the level of satisfaction of users is maximised. This necessitates an indepth study of the multi-dimensional developments in the field of medical sciences, such as the changes in diagnosis and treatment, the side-effects of medicines or so. In addition to the curative services, the hospitals also need to activate the quality of preventive services. Besides, the supportive services also occupy a place of outstanding significance. An MIS simplifies the task of studying the strategies of leading hospitals the world over. The quality of core service vis-a-vis the supportive services can be improved with the help of an MIS. In addition, the increasing pressure on the hospitals mainly on account of malnutrition and a change in the disease profile can also be studied with the help of management information system. Thus, the hospitals are found in a position to formulate a sound short or long-term plan in the face of multi-dimensional developments.

6. Managing the marketing of services: With the increasing cost of inputs used in the hospitals to improve the quality of services, we find a strong emphasis on the fee structure adopted for generating finance from the internal sources. The hospital managers/administrators bear the responsibility of identifying the level of expectations of users and attendants. In addition, the system makes it easier to formulate a sound service mix in the face of changing disease profile and increasing expectations. The task of informing and sensing the society would also be made creative with the help of innovative promotional measures. The gap between the services-promised and services-offered would be bridged over suitably by making possible time honoured and decent processing of services. Thus, the hospital managers are found in a position to blend the product, promotion, price, place and other mixes optimally.

In the face of recent developments, it is pertinent that the hospital managers also think about the blending of three more mixes when they start marketing the healthcare services. The "Processing" is a new mix focusing on the offering of services to the end users. Like other organisations, the hospitals also promise certain quality or standard of services to the patients. In a majority of the cases, we find a gap between the two because the technologies or personnel involved in the process of generating and processing the services deliberately or carelessly make distortions in the quality and the promised services hardly reach to the end users. It is against this background that we find management experts assigning due importance to this mix of marketing. This is related to the management of hospital personnel. Another mix is related to "Physical Attractions." It is right to mention that physical attractions occupy a place of outstanding significance, specially in hospitals where hospital personnel in general need to wear the dresses as per the provisions. This is essential to have a separate identity in addition to the generation of a sense of responsibility linked to the uniform you wear to honour the professional commitments. It is also to mention that because we find hospital a place for offering the healthcare services where the hospital personnel by their physical attractions may present a lesson to the patients, attendants and visitors. They need to look smart, active, energetic and their dresses should generate attraction. Besides, we find "People" assuming a place of significance in almost all the organisation. To be more specific in the hospital services, the hospital personnel in general are found in the group of people mix. We can't negate the fact that it is not the attractive buildings of hospital, it is not the sophisticated technologies used in the process, it is not even the peripheral service mix but it is actually the dedication, personal commitment, value-orientation, humanity, professional excellence of medical and paramedical personnel and managers/administrators without which all the positive developments fail in contributing something substantial to the end users. This generates much more arguments in favour of developing quality hospital personnel.

7. ***Managing the behavioural profile:*** The management scientists are of the view that like other organisations, even hospitals need to make possible an indepth study of the behavioural profile of end users and the attendants. Besides, they also argue in favour of the behavioural profile of hospital personnel because we find several instances to quote that a few of the doctors even achieving world class excellence are so much aggressive in nature and indecent in behaviour that patients and attendants find it difficult albeit to communicate to them their problems/cases. If doctors start misbehaving and if nurses start becoming indecent, the easy recovery of patients would be found in danger. It is against this background that we find it essential to impart detailed knowledge of behavioural management to the hospital personnel in general so that they study the changing level of expectations of the users in a right fashion and make sincere and honest efforts to satisfy them. The hospital planners need to perceive it.

The aforesaid facts make it clear that a technology-driven information management system helps hospitals in formulating a condition oriented plan for hospitals since the information related to almost all the aspects can be collected, processed and disseminated to help managers/administrators, consultants, architects and planners to formulate an ideal plan for hospitals found helpful in subserving the social interests by marching ahead in tune with the changing disease profile and increasing healthcare requirements.

Planning the Functional Areas in Hospitals

The management scientists believe in this proposition that no-profit making organisations like hospitals have suffered a lot mainly on account of an unplanned and a non-optimal development. There are several instances to testify the cases of unplanned development which has been very much instrumental in making the services cost-ineffective and degenerating the level of efficiency. This draws our attention on some of the important constituents as shown in Fig. 5.1.

There are five important constituents gravitating the attention of hospital managers/ administrators, architects, consultants and the specialists to make possible a planned development of hospitals that caters to the increasing healthcare requirements of the Indian society.

- ***Material Planning:*** A material manager in consultation with hospital manager and doctors requires to formulate a material plan.
- ***Product Planning:*** In this context, the core and peripheral or supportive services of hospitals need due care of hospital planners.
- ***Manpower Planning:*** This requires planning the hospital personnel serving in different capacities. The qualitative-cum-quantitative aspects are to be given due weightage.
- ***Financial Planning:*** This gravitates our attention on the management of financial resources so that a stage like the financial crunch is removed and the dependence on the state exchequer is considerably minimised.
- ***Market Planning:*** This draws our attention on the tailoring of marketing resources in the face of changing requirements so that the hospitals are found successful in satisfying the

patients and attendants by conceptualising the holistic concept of management in a right fashion.

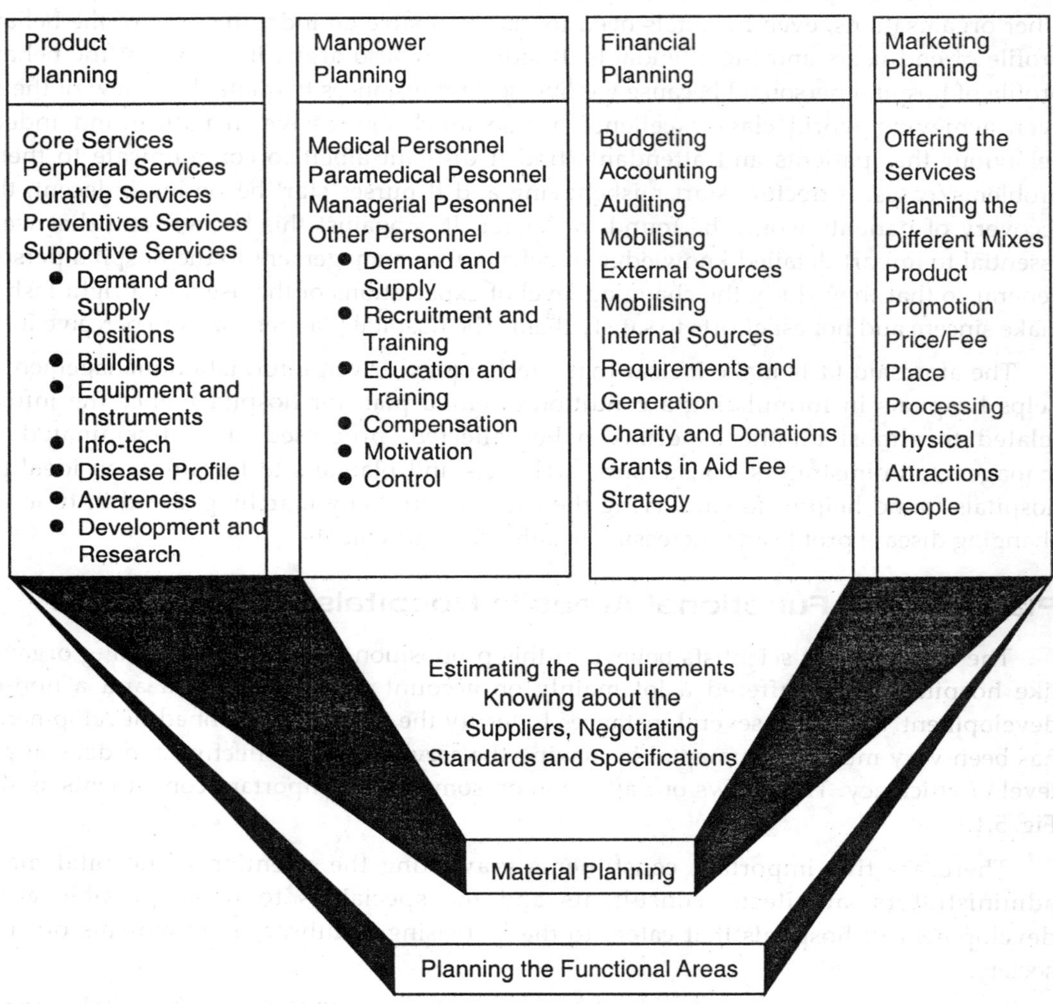

Fig. 5.1. Constituents of Functional Areas

Material Planning

All of us believe in this principle that quality inputs contribute fantastically to the process of qualitative transformation. If we have quality materials, the task of hospital managers is made easier. The doctors find it convenient to perceive a new concept of quality. We can't negate the outstanding contributions of hospital materials in improving the quality of healthcare services. The equipment, instruments, machines, drugs and medicines, food and beverages, linen, housekeeping materials and many other items influence the potentials of hospitals. We find a number of items very expensive and therefore, requiring huge money. Besides, a number of developments take place and the hospitals are supposed to adopt the same. It is against this background that we find material planning occupying a place of outstanding significance.

There are a large number of areas requiring due care in the process of formulating an ideal material plan for the hospitals so that the hospitals or the healthcare organisations find it convenient to plan for the services. At the very outset, it is pertinent that a material manager comes to know about the requirements of development oriented products related to the different types of services offered by the different departments of a hospital. The doctors, managers, paramedical staff and nurses become the key sources for studying the changing requirements. Besides, the policy makers prove to be an important source for the proposed plans and projects. The requirements in terms of quality and quantity would help a material manager in knowing the requirements. It is also significant that they think about the suppliers and prepare a list of different suppliers in the different areas and come to know about their terms and conditions. Before or while preparing the list, a manager is also supposed to know about the past records of the suppliers or manufacturers, specially related to time, cost and quality. They can negotiate and make a deal with the motto of maintaining cost-effectiveness but not at the cost of quality. A list with full descriptions would simplify the process of decision making. A material manager with the support of a hospital manager is supposed to explore the possibilities of making a deal with the suppliers. The time and quality are to be specified to avoid complications.

Of course, we find hospital a complex organisation using a large number of materials. The Advisory Committee for the development of surgical instruments, equipment and appliances (1963) identified 3,200 items of instruments and equipment being used in a hospital. This shows the diversity and variance in the nature and types of materials used in a hospital. It is also right to mention that a hospital has no option but to formulate a scientific plan for materials because we find investment of huge amount of money, i.e., nearly 40 per cent of the total budget of a hospital. Failing the formulation of an intelligent plan, the task of almost all the personnel and departments would be found much more complicated. It is this context that we make a strong advocacy in favour of a pragmatic at the same time an ambitious plan for material but in no case, the material plan is to be overambitious. The technological sophistication, requirements of hospitals and financial health of hospitals are some of the important considerations to be given due importance while designing a plan.

The aforesaid facts make it clear that in the management of hospital, the formulation of a material plan occupies a place of outstanding significance and a material manager has to make It possible.

We agree with this view that in an age of information technology, the task of estimating the requirements, listing the suppliers, budgeting and allocation have become easier. A material manager with the help of computers would be successful in formulating an ideal plan for hospital materials which would be in tune with the changing requirements and potentials of hospitals. It is right to mention that the most sensitive dimension of material management is related to the quality of materials which often create numerous problems before the personnel and departments. The hospital personnel are found involved in the process of supplying substandard materials which degenerate the quality of health care services. It is against this background that a material manager and to be more specific, a hospital manager requires to make it sure that quality of hospital materials is in tune with the standards and specifications defined by the experts. While formulating a plan, it is also pertinent that the hospital manager makes it sure that a material manager is not only efficient but also value-based and honest. He/she knows about information technology and would be efficacious in solving the managerial or financial problems with the support of computers. It is also significant that the concerned departments make available to the material manager their requirements in advance so that the material manager makes available to the concerned personnel and departments the required quantity and quality of materials on time.

Another area related to the planning of material is storage facility for the materials to be bought. This is essential to avoid complications related to safety and damage. If the quality materials are not stored in a right fashion, we find possibilities of their damage. To be more specific, the expensive items related to information and communication technologies or even the diagnostic devices or food and beverages if not stored or preserved as per the required norms, would generate huge financial losses on that account. In addition, the degeneration in quality is also expected. It is against this background that a hospital manager requires to make scientific and spacious storage facilities keeping in view the nature and character of hospital materials to be stored. Your planning is directly related to the management of the store because whatever the materials you buy are to be stored till the items are demanded or required by the concerned department. It is right to mention that in a majority of the hospitals, we find the problem of storage because the administration finds it convenient to promote the unfair practices. The cases of theft and pilferages, specially in small items and particularly in food and beverages make it essential that a hospital manager formulates a suitable plan for storage so that the irregularities are checked. The use of computers would also simplify the process of issue of hospital materials.

The aforesaid facts make it clear that material planning is an important dimension of hospital planning which influences the workings of almost all the departments and personnel. Since we talk about quality in totality, it is pertinent that we assign due weightage to material planning because failing the availability of quality materials, even the superperformers (doctors and management) would find it difficult to accomplish the organisational goals. We, once again, strongly feel that only quality inputs may generate quality outputs. A pragmatic rational, a time-honoured and an ambitious plan for materials would make the ways for qualitative-cum-quantitative transformation.

Product Planning

Regarding Product, Kotler says, 'Anything that can be offered to a market for attention, acquisition, use or consumption; it includes physical objects, services, personalities, places, organisation and ideas.' We find hospital product a service product offering a number of healthcare services both of curative and preventive types. There are different types of hospitals and this brings changes in the nature of services to be offered by them.

Here, we go through product planning which draws our attention on planning both types of services in addition to the peripheral services offered by hospitals. We agree with this view that during the yester decades, a considerable amount of work has been done on the problem of services related to the product planning, however, the different types of services have not been blended optimally. Not only this, we also find problems like a big gap between the demand and supply positions since a number of hospitals fail in identifying the emerging trends in demand and thus, inadequate supply is quite natural. To be more specific, in the Indian perspective where we find the society illiterate and unconscious, it is pertinent that the hospital planners, architects, consultants think over the problem with a new vision. This requires quantitative planning so that the hospitals are in a position to cater to the increasing demand. On the other hand, the hospitals in general have also not been successful in making possible qualitative improvements in the face of recent developments in the field of medical sciences. The inventions and innovations in medical sciences have resulted into a number of qualitative improvements and it is on this account that we find a big gap between the quality of healthcare services made available by the government hospitals and the leading private hospitals. We agree with this view that such a gap in the quality is also due to the faulty hospital planning. In addition, we find a large number of hospitals not conscious of the preventive and supportive services. This mounts to poor quality of supportive and preventive services offered by them.

We, for quality offering of services, find product planning essential for which it is significant to identify the emerging trends in the demand and supply positions, qualitative-cum-quantitative changes and the innovative efforts made by the leading hospitals. In the Indian context, the hospital planning is found very much neglected. It is quite natural that what do we serve today becomes outdated or traditional tomorrow and therefore, the hospitals not sincere to the planning processes, would hardly be successful in offering quality services to the patients. Except a few, we find almost all the hospitals not aware of the recent developments in the field of medical sciences. They don't know about the instrumentality of MIS on hospital planning and therefore, often fail in delivering goods. It is against this background that we need sincere and concerted efforts, to be specially made by the hospital planners, architects, consultants and managers.

We need to plan products in the face of the disparity that we find in the healthcare services between rural and urban areas. We can't negate the fact that the rural masses are found worst sufferers because even the small healthcentres existent on paper in the villages are found on surface non-existent. Since the rural masses are found unaware of the healthy living conditions, it is pertinent that the hospital planners think about creating mass awareness. If the rural masses become sensitive, the increasing pressure on hospitals would considerably be minimised.

While planning for the services, it is essential that they know about specialities of the catchment area. This would help them in knowing details about the existing healthcare requirements at present and to be required in future. A study of the educational background and the level of income would let them know about the strategic decisions for hospital planning. The environmental conditions of the catchment area would help them in knowing the disease profile to emerge in the coming years. In addition, the efforts for creating social awareness specially related to the healthy living conditions would minimise the possibilities of spreading the viral and communicable diseases. The awareness related to the nutritional values would minimise the possibilities of food-borne diseases. And the awareness related to the consumption of safe drinking water would control the water-borne diseases. The programme for expansion of hospitals can be planned based on the aforesaid studies.

The qualitative developments are found essential to make available to the society improved quality of healthcare services. This requires quality inputs and for that, the hospitals need huge money. Since we find the state exchequer not in a position to extend adequate financial support to the hospitals, it is essential that the hospital managers, planners and consultants promote economy. In this context, we need to assign due weightage to the Indian system of medicine and treatment found effective but considerably economic. The research and development activities are required to be promoted to identify the plants and trees having medicinal value and to promote the organised cultivation/farming of the same in the rural areas. This would benefit the rural society in two ways—first, the medical services would be made economic and second, the sources of income of the villagers would also increase.

The hospitals while formulating a plan for the different types of services made available by them need different types of information and this makes a strong advocacy in favour of a well-developed and technology-driven information system. Of late, we find sophistication in the process of developing the knowledge technology which helps hospital planners, architects and managers in different ways. This is found essential not only to improve the quality of curative services but also to make the preventive services more sensitive. The designing of hospital buildings, the knowledge related to the latest developments in the field of medical sciences, the development and research activities would have a new look if the sophisticated information and communications technologies are used for managing the information and guilding the hospital planners.

Of late, we find hospitals assigning due weightage to the development of innovative peripheral services. This includes the services related to the accommodation facilities for the attendants, waiting halls, drinking water facilities, sanitation services, shopping facilities exclusively related to the healthcare services, development of aesthetic sense by making possible creativity in the messages displayed at the signposts, development of surroundings and premises, gardening and plantation, pay-phone services, recreation facilities or the amusement centres and so on. These peripheral services would create uniqueness in the services offered by the hospitals and would motivate patients and attendants besides diffusing their tension. The hospital planners need to keep in their minds the innovative peripheral services offered by leading hospitals of the globe and to plan for the same accordingly so as to improve the quality of product.

The harmful effects of environmental pollution in the urban areas of the country make it essential that the hospital planners view things with a new vision. They are required to promote hospitals preferably in the rural areas of the country well-connected with the all weatherproof roads with the cities and towns which would cater to the healthcare requirements of urban as well as the rural population. The space constraints for expansion and development of hospitals also make it essential that the healthcare planners and the policy makers review the location of hospitals and prefer to locate hospitals either in the suburbs or in the villages. The concept of multistoried culture has been found complicating the task of offering medicare services with the desired effects. In addition, we find certain types of patients and attendants experiencing it difficult to feel comfortable. This also engineers a sound foundation for the development of hospitals far off the big cities and towns where the expansion and development would be much more easier. The development of big surroundings and planned plantation with a traditional touch in the building construction style would only not be comfortable to the patients and attendants but would also be efficacious in minimising the recovery period. It's against this background that the hospital planners need to think about the designing of hospital buildings and management of surroundings and premises on a priority basis.

The leading hospitals of the globe have been found using new generation of instruments, equipment and technologies for microscopic diagnosis and treatment. It is pertinent that the hospital planners, specially in the government hospitals think about the same. We can't negate the tact that due to financial crunch, the government hospitals find it difficult to offer to the patients modern amenities and facilities for diagnosis and treatment. This makes it essential that the planners make double-faceted attempts. They, on the one hand explore avenues for making available to the hospitals the modern amenities and facilities for diagnosis and treatment while on the other hand, also think about the traditional medicare systems based on naturopathy and herbs. By doing so, they would serve the masses since the cost of medicare services would considerably be minimised which would benefit specially the poorest of the poor not in a position to afford the expensive services.

It is high time that we think about the research and development facilities on a priority basis and offer medical experts an opportunity to invent and innovate the medicare devices, medicines having less side-effects and cost-economy. We can't negate the fact that the research and development facilities have not been given due weightage in the Indian perspective, specially in the medical sciences which have been aggravating the intensity for problem. In addition, the preventive services of hospitals need due care of planners so that the sophisticated knowledge and communications technologies play an effective role in sensitising the insensitive segment of the society. Today, we have devices for creating mass awareness, generating nutritional awareness and developing civic and aesthetic sense. The spreading food-borne, water-borne, environment-borne, viral and communicable diseases make it essential that the hospital planners make concerted efforts to use information and communications technologies not only for enriching the diagnosis and treatment modes but also for generating a healthy living condition in which we find less place for the generation of diseases.

The aforesaid facts make it clear that the hospital planners, architects, consultants, managers and doctors bear an outstanding task of formulating an ideal plan for hospitals efficacious in offering quality but economic medicare services to the masses.

Manpower Planning

We agree with this view that of all the resources used in the process of generating and offering the healthcare services and the human resources play an outstanding role. There is no doubt in it that technologies, equipments, instruments, comfortable buildings and supporting infrastructural facilities are found instrumental in improving the quality of medicare services but all our efforts may turn into a fiasco, if we find medical personnel and hospital managers inefficient, inhuman and indecent. The different echelons of personnel serving hospitals play a contributory role in the generation or degeneration processes. It is against this background that we find manpower planning an important constituent of hospital planning.[6]

By the manpower planning, our focus is on making available to the hospitals the required number and quality of personnel on time so that inadequacy of quality human resources is not to keep in danger the product of hospitals. The hospital planners thus bear the responsibility of making suitable provisions for the development of professionally sound, value-based, personally-committed and efficient medical and paramedical personnel. They need to estimate the requirements of a particular hospital because keeping in view the different types of hospitals, the requirements for personnel can't be uniform both in qualitative and quantitative terms. The requirements of research oriented hospitals, special category of hospitals, general hospitals, health centres, referral hospitals vary due mainly to the nature and character of services made available by them. It is quite natural that evolving technologies throw a major impact on the nature and types of our requirements. The hospital planners, if well aware of the process of technological transformation would be successful in bridging over the mismatch. With the evolving technologies, the personnel need training facilities and therefore, the hospital planners are also supposed to keep in their minds the recent developments in the field of medical sciences.

It is right to mention that in the Indian perspective, we find inadequacy of medical and paramedical personnel in almost all categories of hospitals. Thus, we find quantitative transformation an urgent problem so that adequate number of personnel are made available to the hospitals and health centres. In addition, we also find problem of efficiency and work culture. This makes much more advocacy in favour of qualitative transformation. A structural change in syllabi, training facilities becomes pertinent to activate the process of qualitative transformation. It is quite natural that to make the education, research and training facilities in tune with the latest developments in the field of medical sciences, the planners need concerted efforts. It is in this context that we find instrumentality of manpower planning.

The three important categories of personnel draw attention of hospital planners, e.g., medical personnel, paramedical personnel and the managerial personnel. It is right to mention that almost all the government hospitals have been found facing the problem of inadequacy of quality personnel which has been found degenerating the level of efficiency. The planners bear the responsibility of estimating the requirements and making preparation for fulfilling the same on time. Thus, we find prime focus on the demand and supply position. A gap between the two, both, in respects of quality and quantity is to be bridged over.

Planning for the recruitment process is to be made sound so that quality personnel are made available to the hospitals. By the term Quality, our focus is on the personnel having a fair combination of different properties like efficiency, value-orientation, personal-commitment, humanity and decency. We agree with this view that in addition to efficiency, the personnel serving the hospitals also need other properties which would help them to be high performers. This makes it significant that the planners explore avenues for synchronising employee-orientation and performance-orientation. So far as the performance-orientation is concerned, they need to enrich the education and training facilities and to be more particular while recruiting the different categories of personnel having potential or faculties to perceive the required qualities smoothly. The performance-orientation makes it essential that efficiency based handsome and lucrative compensation and motivational plans are adopted without which the employee-orientation would be found much more difficult. A fair combination of the two results into personal commitment. In the Indian perspective, we don't provide suitable incentives to the different categories of personnel serving the hospitals and this stands as a major barrier while generating efficiency. It is against this background that we make much more advocacy in favour of integrating the two.

In view of the prevailing conditions in the Indian healthcare sector, it is pertinent that the medical and paramedical personnel taking part in the processes of generating efficiency are offered suitable incentives in addition to the salaries and welfare facilities they get. If the research-oriented and value-based hospital personnel of even the internationally acclaimed institutions like the All India Institute of Medical Science (AIIMS) and PG Institute of Medical Sciences, Chandigarh are found demoralised, forced to agitate and demonstrate less for their own benefits and much more for the welfare and benefits of the patients, we find a gloomy picture in the healthcare scenario. The hospital planners thus bear the responsibility of formulating a motivational plan which rewards suitably to the efficient and value-based doctors and on the other hand, also demotivate the inefficients and money minters. This makes it essential that we have a plan for making an appraisal of the efficiency of an individual or a team. Today, when we have sophisticated information technology, the task of performance evaluation is easier. It focuses our attention on the control processes found neglected in almost all the sectors.

The changing scenario would pose newer opportunities and challenges for medical and healthcare education. The country has to educate and train an adequate number of health professionals with appropriate knowledge, skill and attitude to meet the future healthcare needs of the people and mounting disease burden. Additionally, we have opportunity to become an important destination for health care services. In view of the increasing demand and growing need for expanding health services, we need systematic studies for estimating the requirements so that the demand and supply positions are found at an optimal point. It is in this context that in the Eleventh Five Year Plan, we find focus on HMIS where we find involvement of concerned Ministries, Professional Councils, Technical Councils, UGC, Central and State Universities, Public Health Institutions and knowledgeable individuals from civil society. NCMH has been found making a strong advocacy in favour of new medical and other institutions, training of village level functionaries and in-service training for health personnel.

The strategic areas where we need priority attention are ensuring availability of medical professionals in rural areas on a permanent basis, posting of doctors with adequate incentives, increasing age of superannuation at least to 65, some of the certificate courses of one year duration for MBBS graduates, expanding the pool of medical practitioners including a cadre of Licentiate Medical Practitioners and Practitioners of Indian System of Medicine and Homeopathy (AYUSH), creating a scientific data bank of health professionals, new medical, nursing and dental colleges in the underserved areas, promoting PPP mode, equipping medical graduates with the skills essential for providing broad-based community healthcare, stemming the high rate of attrition of academics teaching in professional colleges to be made attractive, etc, are some of the measures which would make ways for qualitative and quantitative improvements in the healthcare services.

The hospital and healthcare planners bear the responsibility of suggesting plans commensurate with the changing requirements of the Indian society. They need to keep into consideration national as well as the global requirements so that we find ourselves in a position to project as a Global Healthcare Destinations. The national policy makers need to make it sure that plans are translated into meaningful actions so that the healthcare services not only succeed in improving the service quality but also help in generating wealth. Planning for qualitative and quantitative improvements needs due attention of hospital planners.

Financial Planning

An important constituent of hospital planning is related to financial planning without which all the constituents prove to be unproductive. We plan for services but fail in fulfilling the financial requirements. We plan for manpower development but if financial resources are not available, the task remains unfulfilled. We also plan for marketing but the non-availability of finance considerably affects the development of marketing resources. We are well aware of the problem of financial crunch adversely affecting the functioning of almost all the government hospitals. This makes it essential that our development and expansion plans would simply remain on paper if we do not generate and mobilize financial resources from all the possible internal and external sources. In the very context, the hospital planners, managers, administrators need to assign due weightage to financial planning so that we do not find a mismatch between the existent requirements and the available resources.[7] What to talk of the government hospitals when we find a large number of private hospitals facing the problem of financial insolvency. Of course, the problem of financial planning becomes crucial because like other organisations, the hospitals are not free to charge on the basis of commercial principles. So for as the private hospitals are concerned, they succeed in mobilising finance from the internal sources but the government hospitals face the problem of financial crunch. On the one hand, they face the problem of financial inadequacy while on the other hand, we find a large scale misuse of finance. The financial irregularities, misuse of funds, fraudulent preferences and unfair practices have been found aggravating the magnitude of problem. It is against this background that we need to think over the problem with a new vision so that the hospitals succeed in enriching the quality of inputs to deliver goods to the users.

At the outset, the planners need to estimate the financial requirements for the short and long term projects. There are two important sources for generating finance such as the internal and external. The internal sources consist of the fee charged from the patients for diagnosis and treatment whereas the external sources consist of the grants from governments, charity, donations, borrowings or so. With the limited internal resources, the hospitals are supposed to meet the ever increasing needs and requirements of society. The disease profile is found expanding, insensitivity and unawareness are found increasing and the healthcare services are found contracting. This in a natural way increases the dependence of hospitals on the external sources. It is in this context that the government hospitals need to adopt a strategy allowing them maximum possible generation from the external sources. To the extent it is possible, they should explore venues for charities and donations from individuals or companies. The sources for grants may also be tapped. The government hospitals need to adopt a strategy that allows them generation of finance from the internal sources. Of course, we find a few of the government hospitals generating finance from the shopping complexes, paying wards or so but the problem of subsidy has been found complicating their task. So far as the private hospitals are concerned, they adopt a strategy in tune with the changing conditions and therefore, they are found in a bit improved condition.

In view of the aforesaid problems, it is pertinent that hospitals explore avenues for the generation of finance from the internal sources on a priority basis. The policy makers need to support government hospitals by allowing to them the freedom of generating finance from fee for which the strategic decisions are required to be changed. We make a strong advocacy in favour of using the internal sources since the state exchequer finds it difficult to increase the financial support, specially for modernisation, expansion and development of hospitals. We don't find anything wrong with the pocket-friendly or user-friendly fee strategy that would inject strength to the financial health of hospitals. In addition, they need to use the vacant land of the hospitals for shopping arcades that would also pave avenues for generating finance from the internal sources. Besides, the hospitals need to provide accommodation facilities for attendants and to charge suitably. In addition to the internal sources, they also need to mobilise the external sources. The corporate sector, welfare societies, social organisations, global welfare organisations and financial institutions need an attitudinal change. They are required to extend financial support to the hospitals. The avenues are also to be explored for getting more donations and charity from individuals or organisations for which they need to get rebate while discharging their liabilities related to income tax.

Besides, the mismanagement, cases of irregularities and unfair practices are also to be regulated. In a majority of the government hospitals, we find misuse of funds. This draws our attention on proper budgeting, accounting and auditing. While formulating budget, the hospitals need to control the administrative expenses found of unproductive nature. The bills on account of power and water need due attention of the hospital planners. We can't negate the fact that in almost all the hospitals, the patients, attendants, visitors and even the hospital personnel are found engaged in misusing the infrastructural facilities made available to the hospitals. This results into an increase in the non-optimal administration and establishment expenses. The cases of overstaffing are also to be checked. The purchase system, filing and accounting practices related to the purchase and the stores are some of the sensitive points found very much instrumental in aggravating the financial problem. The delayed implementation of projects also result into an imbalance in the financial management. Of late, we find technologies very much effective in helping the formulation of an ideal budget besides making the accounting and auditing processes transparent.

The aforesaid facts make it clear that hospitals need multicornered efforts to improve the financial health of hospitals. Of course, it requires due cooperation of almost all the segments because in a majority of the government hospitals, the cases of mismanagement have primarily been responsible for a stage like financial crunch. The hospital planners, managers/ administrators bear the responsibility of making available to the hospitals a sound budget formulated in the face of available potentials. While modernising, expanding and developing hospitals, the planners need to make it sure that an ideal strategy has been formulated to counter the increasing problems. The policy makers need an attitudinal change by allowing hospitals to generate finance from the internal sources.

The formulation of a ideal financial plan thus makes it essential that the requirements are estimated in advance and the resources are made available to the different heads optimally. The completion of a project is on time and the individuals and institutions responsible for a delay in implementation are punished. The internal as well as the external sources are used optimally. The budgeting processes are made scientific. The accounting practices are well supported by the sophisticated knowledge technology. The auditing processes identify the errors and fix accountability. The professionally sound financial managers keep their eyes open and regulate the cases of mismanagement and irregularities. The new avenues are explored for the generation of finance, such as organisation of entertainment generating programmes and the support of corporate sector under the head cause-related marketing. The most important thing in the very context is to move forward in tune with the available strength. The hospitals need an intelligent, pragmatic, a meticulous and of course an optimistic plan but in no case an overambitious plan.

Marketing Planning

Marketing the services of no-profit making organisations in general and the hospitals in particular is a difficult task which makes it essential that hospital managers/administrators have world class professional excellence. The planning for the marketing resources is found significant to satisfy the patients and attendants. The marketing professionals serving the hospitals bear the responsibility of formulating an ideal plan so that the availability of marketing resources is in tune with the increasing social requirements and the recent developments in the medical sciences.[8] The marketing professionals are supposed to estimate the requirements for the marketing inputs and further to make available the same in the form of quality healthcare services so that hospitals are found successful in subserving the social interests. It is against this background that we go through the problem of planning for the marketing resources.

We are well aware of the fact that the hospital managers play a significant role in the development of hospitals since the pricing fee strategy formulated by them help the organisation in generating finance from the internal sources. They are supposed to plan for the different mixes of marketing, such as the product, promotion, pricing, place, process, physical attractions and people. We go through the fact that the hospital managers need to forecast the changing healthcare requirements of the society and make available to the patients the facilities found commensurate to the latest developments in the medical sciences. They need to know about the day-to-day developments in the core as well as the peripheral services. The curative and preventive services need due attention of hospital managers. In the group of curative services, the latest developments in the areas of diagnosis and treatment and in the group of peripheral services, we talk about the supportive services adding additional attractions to the service mix and creating uniqueness in the service mix. This requires an indepth study of the specialities of the catchment area and the changing disease profile of that area. In addition, it is also pertinent that the professionals are well aware of the different segments and their profile related to education, population, level of income, rate of sensitivity or so. Since they bear the responsibility of tailoring the service mix to the changing requirements of society, it is significant that they have a detailed knowledge of curative, preventive and supportive services made available by the other leading hospitals vis-a-vis the potentials of hospitals to make available the same. They are supposed to make the services innovative vis-a-vis cost-effective.

After planning for the service mix, the professionals are also required to think about the promotional measures bearing high rate of sensitivity to inform and sense the patients and attendants. There are a number of constituents of promotion, such as the advertisement, publicity, sales promotion, word-of-mouth promotion, personal selling and telemarketing. The hospital managers need to blend them optimally so that the patients and attendants come to know about the quality of services to be made available, the fee structure to be charged for the services offered, besides the preventive measures helping them substantially in maintaining a healthy living condition. While advertising, it is pertinent that the planners formulate a sound budget and make themselves sure that advertisement messages, slogans and appeals carry high rate of sensitivity. They can seek the cooperation of advertising professionals to make possible creativity in advertisement. They are also supposed to make the advertisement budget optimal to the resource potentials of hospitals. Another component of promotion is publicity that makes it essential that the hospital managers plan for developing rapport with the media people and motivate them to write about the positive developments taking place in the hospitals. This would help convincing the patients as well as the attendants. Besides, the sales promotion activities are also to be made proactive. The medical and paramedical personnel and other staff need due incentives to promote the services of hospitals in addition to the incentives to be offered to the patients and attendants. The motive is to attract the users. In the hospital services, we find personal selling playing a significant role since the personnel acting as receptionists, front-line-staff and even the nurses and sisters, by their actions and behavioural profile help hospitals favourably. Further, the word-of-mouth promotion is also found active which is found based on the quality of services made available to the patients. If the attendants feel that hospitals have taken due care of their patients and even the patients are found satisfied, the messages would naturally be transmitted to their close relatives, friends which would promote the business of hospitals. In a true sense, the satisfied group of patients and attendants act as a hidden sales force and promote the business of hospitals without charging anything. Of late, we find telemarketing helping hospitals substantially in promoting the business. In this respect, we find instrumentality of telemarketers and the technologies used for that purpose. The hospital professionals/ managers/administrators and planners need to realise the instrumentality of promotional measures in increasing the business of hospitals. Another aspect of promotion is to create mass awareness so that the patients and even the masses come to know about the healthy living conditions and are careful to the food-borne, water-borne, viral and communicable diseases. This would help hospitals in a bit different way because unlike other profit making organisations, the hospitals bear the responsibility of minimising the number of prospects. If the healthcare organisations start creating mass awareness and the society is found aware of the nutritional values, civic sense, aesthetic sense, importance of food, water, environment and noise in generating and aggravating different types of diseases, there would be a substantial fall in the different types of diseases. Thus, the hospital managers by using world class professional excellence are supposed to promote the preventive measures.

We find pricing an important constituent of marketing that focuses our attention on the fee-strategy adopted by the hospitals. Today, we find it significant that the hospitals explore avenues for generating and mobilising finance from the internal sources. The government hospitals find it difficult due mainly to the governmental regulations because they are not supposed to charge even the cost-based fee structure. The governmental support is found contracting and thus, we find a stage of financial disaster in almost all the government hospitals. This makes it essential that the hospital managers are given freedom of generating finance from the internal sources. The policy makers need an attitudinal change to bring the derailed healthcare systems on the rail. The private hospitals need to formulate a sound fee strategy that on the one hand removes the problem of financial inadequacy while on the other hand also plans for weaker sections of the society not in a position to afford the expensive services. We find pocket-friendly or user-friendly fee strategy a suitable device to help all the sections/segments. It is in this context that the hospital managers need professional excellence to assess the financial requirements of the hospitals and to take suitable steps to tap external as well as the internal sources optimally.

We consider "Place" an important constituent of the marketing mix that focuses our attention on two important facets, first the location point of hospitals and second the instrumentality of hospital personnel in making available, time-honoured services to the users. The hospitals are to be located at a point which is conveniently accessible to the hospital personnel and patients and attendants. This makes a strong advocacy in favour of all-weather proof roads and the transportation facilities. In addition, it is also essential that other infrastructural facilities are available at the hospitals. The hospital planners and managers need to make it sure that the infrastructural constraints are not to affect the comforts and conveniences vis-a-vis the quality of services. This makes it essential that we locate hospitals at a point found convenient to all and in addition, are far off the vulnerable areas. Another consideration is related to the instrumentality of different categories of personnel in making available the promised quality of services to the end users. This draws our attention on the processing of services directly related to the efficiency and behavioural profile of medical and paramedical personnel. It is in this context that we talk about the knowledge of behavioural management to the different categories of personnel servicing the hospitals.

We find physical attractions occupying a place of significance in the hospital services. This gravitates our attention on the uniform and makeup for all categories of personnel. They are supposed to use the dresses as per the professional norms. In addition, they need to be neat and clean, well-dressed so that the patients and attendants perceive a positive opinion about the hospitals. Here, we also talk about the people found to be an important mix of marketing.

There are different categories of personnel found serving the hospitals, such as medical personnel, paramedical personnel, nursing staff and the administrative or managerial personnel. We can't deny the instrumentality of sophisticated instruments and equipment in improving the quality of services made available by the hospitals but at the same, time find strong advocacy in favour of quality of hospital personnel. The different categories of personnel are required to be efficient, value-based, dedicated and personally committed. The planners need to think about the development of personnel in the face of aforesaid properties. Of late to be more specific in the Indian perspective, we find hospital personnel efficient but lacking values, personal commitment and dedication that makes the task of making available quality and time-honoured services to the patients. The hospital planners, managers/administrators are required to make it sure that the syllabi, training programmes, refresher courses and capsule courses assign due weightage to the behavioural profile and ethical dimensions in addition to the generation of efficiency. The government hospitals need an intensive care since in almost all the government hospitals, we find hospital personnel not even aware of the instrumentality of behavioural and ethical dimensions in improving the quality of healthcare services. The hospitals need quality people and the hospital managers need to perceive the perception of "quality people" in a right fashion.

The aforesaid dimensions play a significant role while developing the marketing resources. The hospital managers need to conceptualise the holistic concept of management since no profit making organisations like hospitals are supposed to work with the mission of subserving the social interests.

Planning the Peripheral Services

Of late, services generating organisations in particular need to add additional attractions to the service mix by including innovative peripheral services which their competitors don't offer. The healthcare organisations also need to enrich the peripheral services because in addition to generating attractions, the innovative peripheral services would also help in raising the sensitivity of curative and preventive services offered by hospitals. It is against this background that we need a strong emphasis on innovative peripheral services.

By the peripheral services, our focus is on the allied services creating midusers and making the task of patients and attendants convenient, comfortable and tension free. There are a number of services, of course, not helping the medical and paramedical personnel in course of diagnosis and treatment but we find them playing a significant role in making the task of hospitals easier. The sanitation services, the water facilities, the light and ventilation facilities, the drains and sewage, the accommodation facilities for the attendants, the restaurant and cafeteria services for attendants and visitors, the management of surroundings and premises with the motto of positive environmental effects, the recreation facilities, the development of parks, the placement and positioning of signposts, the seating arrangements for patients and attendants, etc. play an incremental role in improving the quality of healthcare services offered by the hospitals. It is against this background that we find professionals making a strong advocacy in favour of planning for the development of peripheral services as mentioned in Fig. 5.2.

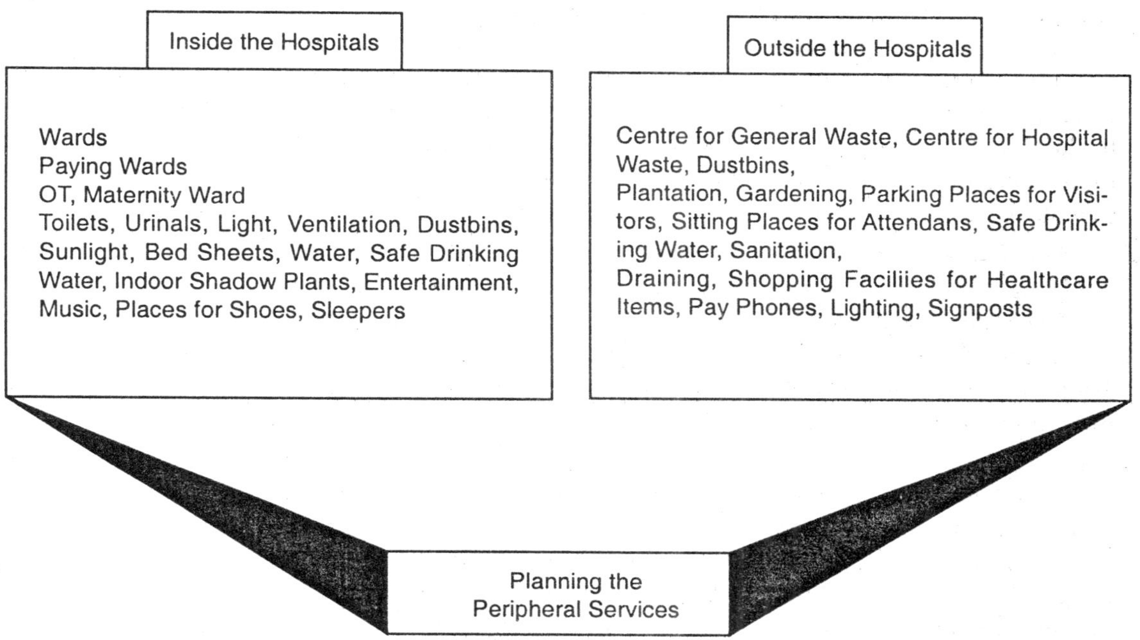

Fig. 5.2. Planning the Peripheral Services for Hospitals

The aforesaid figure makes it clear that modern hospitals need to think over the style and mode of treatment in a bit different way because we find a number of problems generated in course of diagnosis and treatment. If we turn our eyes on the government hospitals, in a majority of the cases, we find nothing in the name of peripheral services. Of course, the core services play a dominating role but we can't underestimate the incremental role of peripheral services.

The environmentalists, the medical scientists, the doctors and the hospital managers can't negate the instrumentality of healthy living conditions in making the process of treatment of patients more effective. For the patients living in wards, the attendants visiting the hospitals and even the medical and paramedical personnel living in a condition found unhealthy or unhygienic the treatment processes become less effective and invite a number of diseases that would complicate the task of hospitals. We don't find any sense in transforming the sensitive healthcare services into an insensitive process. It is against this background that while managing hospitals, the peripheral services need due attention of hospital planners and managers/ administrators.

The most vulnerable areas in the hospitals are toilets, urinals, drains, operation theatres, mortuary houses from where the germs, viruses start the breeding process and make hospitals a sensitive centre for infection. We are well aware of the prevailing conditions, specially in the government hospitals where the peripheral services carry no meaning. Of course, the private hospitals have been found doing something in the name of peripheral services but even they fail in making available to the patients and attendants world class peripheral services. We agree with this view that a majority of the patients, attendants and visitors lack civic sense but such an excuse is not to make an assault on the increasing problems. The hospital planners and managers need to think over the issue on a priority basis and to inform and sense the patients and attendants regarding the harmful effects of their minor mistakes. On other hand, it is also right to mention that the hospital planners/ designers fail in making the sanitation services sophisticated and in addition, the inadequacy of water also complicates the task of users. This makes it essential that the toilets, urinals, dustbins, drains related to operation theatres, the waste related to the maternity wards and biomedical waste or so are given due care. The sweepers need to understand their job responsibilities and the municipal corporations and civic bodies are required to make special arrangements for the treatment of hospital waste.

The management of signposts, their positioning, the messages and instructions displayed on the signposts may play a significant role in sensing and guiding the patients and attendants in a right fashion. The hospital planners and managers/administrators need to make the necessary provisions for sensing the users by making possible creativity in their messages. Since the masses are found illiterate and not aware of the nutritional values, civic sense or so, the task is much more difficult but we have no option than to explore avenues that how and in what way, we get a success.

The development of surroundings and premises need due care of hospital planners and managers. The hospital architects, consultants and managers are required to promote plantation and gardening with a sense. The selection and positioning of plants and trees become significant to get the best and to eliminate the worst creating a number of problems while extending the power and communications or even water facilities. This focuses our attention on a planned development of surroundings and premises. Since we find hospital a centre for offering the healthcare services, they need to understand the importance of fresh air. The ornamental, flower-oriented trees, shadow and oxygen-generating trees need due care of hospital planners. In this context, they need to seek the cooperation of environmentalists.

Planning for Health Education

To be more specific in the Indian context where the rate of illiteracy is high and the masses are not aware of even the civic sense, the insensitivity in its natural way is found at it peak. The hospitals in the very sphere bear an outstanding responsibility of creating mass awareness by educating and sensing the society. This focuses our attention on the outpatient waiting hall where displays with the help of sophisticated audio/visual devices would bring positive results. In addition, the hospitals can also display different paintings, photographs and slogans bearing creativity and found instrumental in sensitising the patients and attendants or even the visitors. Aphorisms displayed artistically on the walls can be much more educative. Lorenz, a pioneer in accident surgery had aphorisms put up in the gymnasium for the benefit of the staff, such as "Keine ubung darf schemerzen verusachen" (No exercise if there is pain) in his Unfall Kranken Haus and its peripheral units at Vienna. National Programmes such as family planning and preventive aspects cannot be compartmentalised but the staff need being reminded; aphorisms put up strategically can help.[9] This makes it clear that waiting halls for outpatients can be an important point for educating and sensing the patients and attendants in different areas. In the Indian society, we find unawareness related to food-borne, water-borne, tobacco-borne, communicable and viral diseases. The displays bearing creativity may create awareness and the future task of hospitals would considerably be simplified.

We find masses not aware of even the civic sense and it is on this account that lavatories, urinals, drains or even the hospital premises often turn to be vulnerable specially with the viewpoint of infection. This makes it essential that with the help of audio-visual exposure, we sense them in a right direction. It is really amazing that in the Indian society, even the educated persons lack civic sense. This makes it essential that in addition to the promotion of healthy education, we also think about punishments. There are different types of hospitals and keeping in view the types of hospitals, the messages and slogans are to be composed with the help of advertising professionals. In the maternity centre, the displays covering the harmful effects of more children on mother or abnormal size of a family complicating the task of managing the family would be found effective. In the cancer centre, the displays covering messages conveying the harmful effects of tobacco would be found useful. We focus on tobacco because in the Indian context, a large number of cancer patients are affected by the use of tobacco. In the cardiological centre, the messages related to food habits, exercise, walking, yoga would be found effective. In the eye centre, the messages related to the care of eyes would be found useful. Like this, the hospitals need to design and compose the slogan in the face of their specialities.

In view of the aforesaid facts, it is right to mention that hospital planners and managers also bear the responsibility of educating and sensing the masses. The preventive services of hospitals focus on health education. We can't deny the fact that a number of diseases can be regulated or at least can be minimised, if we succeed in educating and sensing the society. Almost all categories of hospitals need to promote health education that would, of course be productive; if not in the short-run, without fail in the long-run.

In the India perspective, it is pertinent that Public Health Education draws priority attention for the planners. Presently, we find several institutions engaged in imparting public health and related education. The Public Health Courses are also to be started at the Masters level by some of the medical organisations. The important organisations engaged in the process are Indian Council of Medical Research (ICMR), AIIMS, PGIMER, etc. However, we find a gap between demand and supply and it is hoped that during the Eleventh Five Year Plan,[10] the benefits of knowledge and skills of modern public health will be made available at all levels. It is significant that some of these centres are located in the Universities of Health Sciences and some of the multidisciplinary universities also initiate and activate the process. New Public Health Schools are also to be started within the existing medical colleges, MBA Programme specially tailored for the healthcare and MD (Hospital Administration).

While promoting health education, the rural areas of the country need priority attention because we find a majority of the rural masses insensitive to the healthcare problem. Running social awareness programmes in schools to cover topics like ill effects of tobacco and alcohol, advantages of good sanitation, hygiene, nutrition and safe drinking water would immensely benefit the rural segment. Like this, running free camps for vision tests, health check-ups and immunisation would also benefit the rural masses. Protection against unsafe sex, awareness about locally prevalent communicable and non-communicable diseases, providing non-clinical contraceptives and referring of clinical cases, supervising spray activities, water treatment, sanitary landfill and sanitary latrines, providing emergency primary health services and referrals are some of the steps which would serve the larger interests of rural community.

Thus, we find two-fold measures to be much more effective in the Indian context such as promoting medicare services and sensitising the general masses to make them aware of the preventive measures which would minimise scope for diseases. The hospital planners need to go through both the issues while designing a plan. We cannot deny that in the Indian perspective, we find a big gap in both the areas. The masses in general and the rural masses in particular are the worst sufferers. If we want to regulate the possible avenues for diseases, the planners would have to make the ways for educating the masses. Insensitivity if not removed would expand the gap between demand and supply. The demand position can be regulated with the support of curative and preventive measures. The supply position can be improved with the help of primary, secondary and tertiary level services. The hospital planners need to consider the dangers found at an alarming state mainly due to insensitivity. Unlike other organisations, the success of hospitals and healthcare organisations are coiled in the essence of minimising the demand position.

Planning for Managing Hospital waste

With the development of healthcare organisations, we find problems of managing hospital waste at an alarming stage[11]. It is quite natural that with the increasing number of private clinics in a haphazard way, the intensity of problem aggravates further and we find none doing something positive and concrete to resolve the problem. In addition to other aspects, the mounting popularity of use-and-throw culture has also been found an important reason for the same. The used syringes, plastic bottles and cotton known as hospital non-biodegradable, lack proper management. What to talk of the non-biodegradable when we find even biodegradable in the form of used bandages, human body parts and blood instrumental in aggravating the magnitude of problem. In a majority of the hospitals, public or private, we find mortuary houses injecting new life and strength to the waste problem. The inhuman discharge of dead bodies and the stinking surroundings testify the mismanagement of mortuary house. The hospital planners while planning for the management of waste need due attention on the planning for the management of bio-medical waste in general and bio-degradable in particular. It is amazing that even the government hospitals have not been planning for the management of hospital waste which requires different stages and phases for their final disposal without any side effect on the environment.

The hospital planners need to plan for the management of waste particularly while designing the hospital buildings or even while identifying the points for space for collection. The agencies or people responsible for collection and the safety measures to be adopted by them while collecting the bio-degradable and non-degradable need due attention of hospital planners and architects at the very initial stage. They need maximum care to ensure control on the health hazards which may emerge at any stage. Designing and constructing stores for the safe collection of waste materials cannot be undermined. The second stage in the very context focuses our attention on the disposal centre. There are a number of bio non-degradable products found very dangerous and creating serious problems to the concerned areas or persons engaged in the process. The disposable syringes are found very vulnerable and they are found neglected almost in all the hospitals and clinics. The hospital planners need to make it sure that hospitals have a defined place for different categories of waste and the persons and technologies are available for their proper disposal. The duration between collection and final disposal should not cross the limits.

The hospital waste of private clinics and hospitals need due attention of hospital planners. They are found insincere to the problem of managing waste and playing a big role in aggravating the magnitude of the problem. Making acts, regulations and rules much more rigid cannot be an effective prescription.

SUMMARY

In this chapter, you have gone through different components of hospital planning. After going through the chapter, be sure that the following facts are well versed:

Hospitals Planning—the Concept: Hospital planning is a managerial process to make possible the formulation of an ideal plan that caters to the changing requirements of society. It focusses our attention on planning for the developments in the face of changing healthcare requirements.

Principles of Hospital Planning: The governing principles for the formulation of an ideal plan for hospitals are protection, separation, circulation, control and traffic streams.

Components of Hospital Planning: The different components of hospital planning are perceiving the idea, selecting an ideal place for location, finalising the site for hospitals, budgeting, size and type of hospitals, elements of hospitals, making of programmes, drawings and specifications.

Factors Influencing the Formulation of a Hospital Plan: The different factors influencing the formulation of a pragmatic plan for hospitals are changing disease profile, increasing pollution of environment, mass awareness, high rate of illiteracy, multifaceted developments in the field of medical sciences, paying capacity of the masses and the increasing importance of specialisation of the healthcare services.

Instrumentality of MIS in the Hospital Planning: Since we find the formulation of a plan based on information and as MIS bears the responsibility of making available to the hospital planners different types of information, the MIS plays a big role in the formulation of a plan. The emerging trends can he identified, the errors and shortcomings can be detected, an ideal compensation and motivation plan can be formulated, the irregularities in the management of finance can be identified, the product profile can be managed in a right way, the marketing of services would be helpful to fulfil the increasing level of expectations of patients and attendants.

Planning the Functional Areas: With the formulation of a plan, the different functional areas of planning such as product planning, manpower planning, financial planning and the marketing planning would get due emphasis and the hospitals would be successful in accomplishing the organisational objectives.

Product Planning: It is planning for the product profile of the hospitals which includes different types of services generated by the hospitals, such as curative service, supportive service and preventive service.

Manpower Planning: It is planning for the development of human resources or people serving hospitals. The demand and supply position, recruitment and training programmes, motivation and control are found to be the important constituents of manpower planning.

Financial Planning: It is planning for the management of finance which focuses on generation allocation, accounting and control.

Marketing Planning: It is planning for the development of different mixes of marketing, such as the product mix, promotion mix, price mix, place mix processing, physical attractions and people.

Planning for Peripheral Services: To add additional attraction to the service mix, the hospitals need to plan for the peripheral services.

Planning for Health Education: In the Indian perspective, an important task before the hospital professionals is to educate the insensitive segment of the society by developing mass awareness. Particularly, the rural segment of the society needs due care.

Planning for Managing Waste: The hospital professionals need to plan for the management of bio-degradablė and non-degradable hospitable waste so that environmental problems on that account are minimised. In the process of offering services, the waste in different forms is a natural phenomenon. The hospital professionals need to manage them in a scientific way.

KEY TERMS

Bio-degradable Waste	Cardiological
Bio-non-degradable Waste	Immunisation
Mortuary House	Vaccination
Cruciform	Contraceptives
OPD	Use-and-Throw Product
X-ray	Psychiatric
Radio-isotypes	Therapeutic
Radio Therapy	Viral Diseases
Linen	Disease Profile
Beverages	Pilferages
Peripheral Services	E-governance
Maternity Ward	Rapport

REVIEW QUESTIONS

1. What do you mean by Hospital Planning? Discuss the different principles of hospital planning.
2. Focus on three different components of hospital planning to be covered while formulating a plan for hospitals.
3. Explain the different factors helping the formulation of an ideal plan for hospitals.
4. State and explain the factors making MIS instrumental in the formulation of an ideal hospital plan.
5. Discuss in brief the different functional areas of hospital planning.
6. What do you mean by Product Planning? Discuss the different types of products requiring due attention of hospital planners.
7. Discuss manpower planning with a special reference hospital working in the Indian setting.
8. Explain the importance of financial planning for the purpose of generating financial resources from the internal sources.
9. Discuss in brief the different components of marketing planning for hospitals.
10. Explain the significance of healthcare education for enriching the preventive services of hospitals.
11. Focus on material planning and its importance to hospital planning.
12. Throw light on planning for the peripheral services for hospitals.

APPLICATION EXERCISES

1. You are working as a hospital manager and you need to formulate a plan for the development and expansion of your hospital. Focus on the components you need to consider in the formulation process.
2. As a hospital professional, you need to formulate a plan that is realistic. Throw light on the essentials which would help you in designing an ideal plan.

3. As a hospital manager, how and in what way would you make use of Management Information System for the formulation of a pragmatic plan ?
4. In the changing scenario, focus on the considerations guiding you in the context of manpower planning.
5. Out of all the constituents of manpower planning, we find motivation the most important one. Comment on this statement as a hospital professional.
6. As a hospital professional, what measures you would like to initiate for mobilising the financial resources which may help you in improving the quality of services ?
7. The modern hospitals need an ideal marketing plan. Comment on this statement as a hospital professional.
8. Of late, we find the peripheral services very much effective in adding additional attractions to the healthcare services. Throw light on this statement in the capacity of a hospital manager.
9. How would you plan for materials in your hospital so that supply is optimal to the demand ?
10. As a hospital manager, formulate a pan for the management of waste in you hospital.

ENDNOTES

1. Satya Prakash, *Hospital Planning and Administration*, p.59.
2. Bhatti S.S., *Hospital Planning*, p.79.
3. Goel and Kumar, *Hospital Planning* pp. 85-86.
4. Jha S.M., *Services Marketing*, HPM, Mumbai, 2009.
5. *Ibid.*
6. Goel S.L., *Manpower Planning*, pp. 253-85.
7. Krishna H.R. and Swamy Rao, *Financial Management and Cost Constraint*, pp. 115-95.
8. Jha S.M., *Medicine Marketing, Social* Marketing, HPM, Mumbai, 2009.
9. Satya Prakash, *Hospital Planning and Administration*, op.cit., p.62.
10. *Eleventh FiveYear Plan:* Planning Commission, Government of India, New Delhi, Vol. II, pp. 58-115.
11. Jha, S.M.: *Hazardous Bio-Medical Waste*; The Hindustan Times.

Hospital Organisation and Departmentation

Service quality rests on service culture which requires organisational culture. The organisation and departmentation if professionally managed, simplify cooperation and coordination where we can expect team spirit and team culture. Healthcare and medicare services depend on the involvement of a full team.

CHAPTER OBJECTIVES

Introduction—Organising: the Concept—Departmentation: the Perception—Organising Hospitals—Organisational Structure for Hospitals—Organisation Structure with narrow Span—An Ideal Organisational Structure—Departmentaiton in Hospitals—Functions of management based Departments in Hospitals—Functions of Key Departments on the Medical Side—Promoting a Sound Organisational Structure in Hospitals—Summary—Key Terms—Review Questions—Application Exercises—End Notes.

LEARNING OBJECTIVES

This chapter aims at studying the different dimensions of organisation and departmentaion in relation to the hospitals and healthcare organisations. The motive of this chapter is to sensitise the readers to the instrumentality of organisation and departmentation in establishing organisational culture in which we find tremendous opportunities for establishing service culture. The hospital professionals are supposed to make possible cooperation and coordination so that services are processed and delivered in a right way.

Introduction

Accelerating the rate of productivity is an important functional responsibility before the hospital managers for which they need to ensure an optimal utilisation of different assets with the prime motive of bringing cost-effectiveness and improving service quality. The hospitals and healthcare organisations bearing the responsibility of serving and subserving social interests need a priority attention on maintaining, defining and redefining quality and additionally, minimising the cost so that the services are affordable and competitive. It is not only significant that we have quality people; it is not only essential that we have quality supporting infrastructural facilities. In a true sense, it highly impact generating that we make possible a productive utilisation of the required assets. Particularly in an organisation like a hospital where we find team spirit, team culture becoming essential considerations for work culture, the hospitals, basic responsibility before the society is offering the best and charging the lowest. This draws our attention on managerial proficiency. Almost all management experts believe that failing the cooperation and coordination among the different levels of management, the level of efficiency cannot increased. It is against this background that studying the problem of organisation and departmentation needs due attention of hospital professionals.

The hospital professionals bear the responsibility of organising hospitals and making possible departmentation which would pave avenues for cooperation and coordination. Of course, the boardrooms or the top management has to take a policy decision but ultimately defined functional responsibilities are discharged by the hospital managers. It is quite natural that the nature and character of a hospital prove to be a dominating factor while designing the organisational structure because the services to be offered by hospitals determine the actual size, scale, quality and number of people required for different purposes. This makes it essential that the hospital professionals are well aware of the existing and emerging policies and strategies for development and expansion. The development of a hospital in tune with modern requirements is found to be a capital intensive project. It is not wisdom that we make possible frequent changes. The emerging trends in social awareness, the mounting intensity of environmental pollution, growing insensitivity of masses towards hygienic living conditions are some of important factors influencing the organisation and departmentation of hospitals. Since we find technologies playing an incremental role in the processing of diagnosis and treatment, the hospital managers cannot overlook the infusion of new generation of technology. The main thing in the process is to make possible integration so that organisation and departmenation prove to be fruitful and productive.

The hospitals, of late, are found offering a number of services and for that, they need positive cooperation amongst different departments. It is not possible for a single department to take care of medical services, nursing services, catering, housekeeping, pharmacy, pathological, radiology outpatient, ward and engineering services. Some of the services are provided by the medical personnel whereas some of them are provided by the paramedical and managerial staff. The concept of departmentation, if practised in a right way, helps in improving the quality of services. Materials and Stores Department, Human Resource Department, Finance Department, Marketing Department and Medical Record Department are found helping an increase in the level of operational efficiency.

While organising hospitals and healthcare organisations, the professionals are supposed to formulate an organisational structure that is to bring momentum in the processing of services. In the organisational structure, we find different categories of people related to the different echelons. The prime motive is "Care of Sick" Or "Good-patient Care" for which a big team of medical and paramedical staff with the help of sophisticated technology process and delivery of the services to the patients is required. On the medical side, the clinical activities, general surgical and specialised surgical activities, anaesthsiological activities, pharmaceutical activities, dental, dietary, etc. are found important. On management side, it requires professionalised efforts for managing financial, human resources, material, marketing and other concerned activities to make available to the patients quality medical services. This makes it clear that unless we find cooperation amongst the different departments, the processing and delivery of services cannot be possible.

The main purpose of departmentation is to improve the level of efficiency but here, it is pertinent that coordination, cooperation and cohesion are made possible so that the common goal of a hospital to provide good patient care is accomplished. It is in this context that we find an incremental role of hospital managers in improving the quality of medicare services. It is not only sufficient that hospitals have made provisions for all the services. It is much more significant that the hospital professionals ensure availability of the supporting devices and facilities while offering the services. The availability of a surgeon or a physician cannot serve our purpose unless we find all the supporting devices and equipments and instruments readily made available to the working team of doctors. It is in this context we find hospital managers helping the surgeons and physicians for concentrating their attention on performing excellently. The concept of organisation and departmentation is thus found based on the management principles which makes it essential that an optimal structure is designed to make possible coordination and integration.

In the context of hospital services, we find good time management playing a catalytic role in the entire process. A minor delay or even a small gap may result into irreparable losses. The hospital professionals are supposed to make it sure than on the basis of time honoured cooperation and coordination, all possibilities for delay are minutely sealed. The supporting infrastructural facilities, support of concerned equipments and instruments, cooperation of specialists and experts result into quality service delivery. The professional excellence of a hospital manager is coiled in the essence of integrating all and satisfying all.

It is possible for hospital professionals to open new vistas for the development of team sprit and team culture which would pave avenue for the development of organisational culture without which the services delivered by hospitals and healthcare organisations cannot be personalized and humanised. The quality of environment determines the magnitude of success. The service ambience or environment, surroundings and premises need due attention of hospital professionals which motivate people to perform and technologies to process in order that quality services are delivered to the patients and the hospitals succeed in developing and establishing an internationally acclaimed brand name. Culture nurtures your excellence and provides an opportunity to you to make ways for creativity. It is in this contest that the hospital managers are required to assign due weightage to organisation and departmentation.

A number of departments are found involved in the processing and delivery of healthcare services with the help of world class medical and paramedical personnel and new generation of sophisticated information and communication technology and the hospital managers in the very context may inject new life and strength to the entire process which may result into the generation of service flavour essential for the development of services culture. In the Indian perspective, we find lack of service culture specially in the government hospitals which requires priority attention of hospital professionals because even world class technology cannot replace the quality people.

ORGANISING: THE CONCEPT

At the outset, we go through the conceptual aspect of organising found to be an important function of management. We find organising a process to unify the subsystems and there is a central authority in brain and the nervous system which plans all the related activities. Each and every organ of our body does some specialised work such as the ears hear, the eyes see, the stomach and intestines digest the food consumed by us. We find an excellent coordination amongst the different organs and failing the same, the normal functioning of the body and existence of life system is not possible. In a true sense, we find the process of organising based on the same concept. It is the form of every human association to achieve a common goal. Organisation is not simply a structure or a chart. Virtually, it is the mechanism through which management directs, coordinates and controls the business. It is quite natural that structure makes clarification regarding the quality and number of personnel to be involved in the process. We are well aware of the fact that it is to be maimed by the people and therefore, their quality and credentials, professionalism and personal commitments become significant.

The conceptual exposition made by some leading authorities make it clear that designing and maintaining the roles of different subsystems is the basic managerial function of organising. We find organising a process which makes it clear that those who want to cooperate would work together most effectively if they know the role they have to play in any team operation and the way their roles relate to one another and the process of organising makes it clear. It is in this context that we think of reorganising as—

- The identification and classification of required activities.
- The grouping of activities necessary to attain objectives.
- The assignment of each grouping to a manager with the authority (delegation) necessary to supervise it and the provision for coordination horizontally and vertically; horizontally focusses our attention on the same or similar organisational level and vertical focusses our attention on corporate headquarters, division and department.[1]

The aforesaid facts regarding organising makes it clear that it is a managerial process to make possible coordination and control of the activities of different levels of employees engaged in an organisation. We can't hesitate to mention that it is a process of grouping the activities so that a microscopic analysis of the functional responsibilities of the different levels are made possible and the people having the best of quality are assigned the responsibilities to be discharged efficiently and effectively.

Since we talk about the concept of organising in the context of hospital management, it is to be clarified that in the hospital management, the process is related to the classification of various functional responsibilities, pointing out the qualifications and credentials and the number of personnel of different levels required to make possible smooth discharge of responsibilities by the quality people which would be instrumental in increasing the level of efficiency of hospitals. Thus, by organising hospitals, we mean formulating a sound organisational structure for hospitals keeping in view the nature and character of services they propose to offer.

DEPARTMENTATION—THE PERCEPTION

The concept of departmentation is found based on the formation of different groups. It is a grouping activity and people into the departments make it possible to expand the organisations. It is grouping activities in accordance with the function of an organisation. Departmentation, however, is found a bit different from grouping. We don't find the single best way of departmentalising which is applicable to all the organisations to all the situations. The pattern used would depend on the given situations and what managers believe would make possible the best results. Departmentation by simple numbers, departmentation by time, departmentation by function, departmentation by territory or geography and consumer departmentation are the different types which are practised by the managers in tune with the requirements of an organisation.

An organisation makes provision for departmentation to improve the level of efficiency. It is based on the principle of cooperation and coordination. It is not an end in itself but simply a method of arranging activities to facilitate the accomplishment of objectives.[2] Each method of departmentation has its advantages and disadvantages. In a true sense, the creation of a sound organisational structure is found essential to make possible effective departmentation. There are a number of functional responsibilities to be discharged by an organisation which are found based on specialisation and expertise. It is not possible for all the employees to perform all the responsibilities efficiently and effectively. This makes it essential that only the efficient personnel are made responsible to discharge the defined functional responsibilities for which they have the essential credentials or qualifications and experiences. The concept of departmentation is found based on the grouping of activities or functions of an organisation and making a particular department responsible for that. Since all the departments have a common goal, it is pertinent that to accomplish the organisational goal, they also think about the departmental goals which would be in the face of the organisational goal. This necessitates a correlation between the departmental and organisational goals.

We are well aware of the fact that hospitals are non-profit making organisations. The services or functions of a hospital are based on the team work. A particular department would not be in a position to perform all the functions and therefore, we classify the different services and make responsible different departments to perform the defined responsibilities assigned to them in such a way that coordination and cooperation are made possible. The perception of departmentation in hospitals is due to the variation that we find in the nature of services. The medical and administrative services of hospitals require specialisation of different types. Some of the responsibilities are to be discharged by the medical and paramedical personnel whereas some responsibilities are discharged by the managerial personnel. Both of them need cooperation and coordination. The medical services, nursing services, pharmacy services, pathological and clinical services, food services, housekeeping, radiology services, ward services, outpatient services, fire-lighting security and safety services need different types of specialisation and expertise. The management staff bears the responsibility of making possible professionalism in hospitals and by managing information, behaviour, finance, personnel, services and marketing, they make possible good patient care for which they need the cooperation of different departments.

Organising Hospitals

A sound organisational structure makes possible departmental cooperation and coordination found essential to increase the level of efficiency of an organisation. A manager finds it convenient to work and accomplish the organisational goals if there is management orientation. It is against this background that we make a strong advocacy for formulating a sound organisational structure for hospitals because specially in the government hospitals, we find the level of efficiency very disappointing. It is quite natural that the formulation process for the organisational structure keeps into consideration a number of factors. Availability of quality hospital personnel in the required number is possible if the organisational structure is sound. We are well aware of the fact that the hospital services are team work, necessitating the cooperation of a number of departments having personnel with diverse specialities and expertise. If the departments lack coordination, the offering of quality medicare services on time would not be possible. The motive of organising is to make possible smooth operation. Good patient care is the goal and the hospital managers bear the responsibility of making it possible. We agree with this view that the hierarchical barrier makes the task difficult and by the sound organisational structure, our focus is on a structure having smooth and decent processing.

In the Indian context, we find the governmental hospitals facing the problem of low level of efficiency and an important reason for the same is managerially deficient organisational structure. The hierarchical barrier makes it difficult for the medical and paramedical personnel to improve the quality of services. Even if all the amenities and facilities, machines and equipments, instruments and personnel are available, the patients in a majority of the cases fail in getting quality medicare services. The barrier proves to be an excuse for the degeneration in the quality of medicare services. The health policy makers though don't know even the abc of healthcare services, however, they are found formulating the health policies. Availability of quality services just to a few selected segments is not our target. We bear the responsibility of making it of mass use and in addition to other constraints, the organisational constraint also stands as a barrier. This makes it essential that the government hospitals and the concerned policy makers think over the problem on a priority basis.

The three levels of management are to be given due weightage while formulating the organisational structure. The departmentation is to be in the face of the nature of organisational structure. The requirements of different departments in relations to the quality and personnel or other supporting infrastructural facilities are to be given due weightage. Management orientation is to be made possible and the hospital managers should be given the responsibility of managing the hospitals. It is not only sufficient that we recruit quality medical and paramedical personnel, make available sophisticated technologies and equipment and construct suitable and comfortable buildings. It is much more impact generating that our patients get the benefits of the developmental efforts taken by us. It is believed that management orientation would make the ways for smoothness in the processing of services found essential for a good patient care. It is in this context that we talk about the formulation of a sound organisational structure, specially for the government hospitals because in a majority of the cases, we find private hospitals establishing an edge over the government hospitals specially in the context of processing of services. There are different categories of hospitals and the organisational structure for all of them can't be uniform or identical.

Organisational Structure for Hospitals

In Fig. 6.1, we find a structure commonly found in the government hospitals. The structure in itself speaks of the fact that we need management orientation in the formulation process.

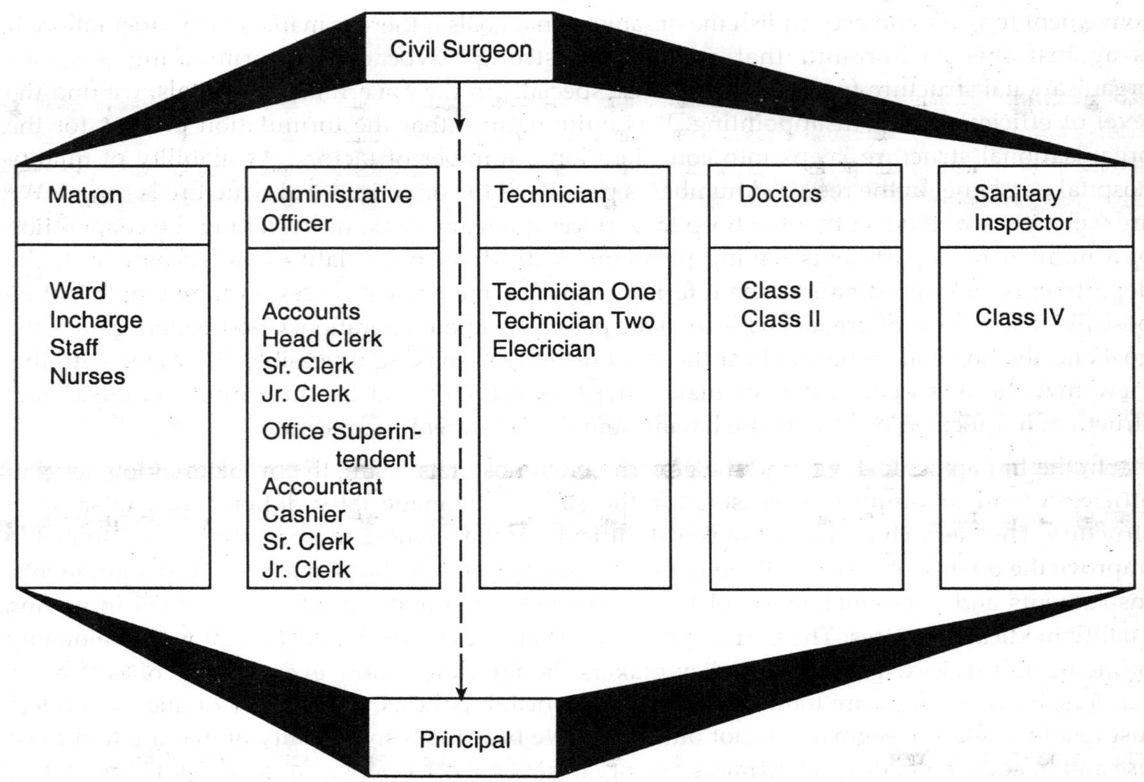

Fig. 6.1. Organisational Structure in Government General Hospitals

If we turn our eyes on the organisational structure presented in Fig. 6.1, it is almost clear that there is no important place for the management personnel in the hierarchical arrangement. We find Civil Surgeon at the top and thereafter, the principal. In the administrative structure, we find a small place for the office superintendent who in a majority of the cases lacks knowledge of management. If we talk about the formulation of a sound organisational structure for the hospitals, our focus is on the fact that management experts or hospital managers need a place of prime importance. The doctors, of course, are expert but just for the skill they have. They are on the operation table but the supporting infrastructural facilities are not available, the personnel of the team constituted for this purpose are not present, the instruments and other requirements are not properly sterilised. The result is that doctors go back and patients suffer. It is against this background that we make a strong advocacy in favour of management orientation so that the doctors are carefree and everything required in the process is available at his/her operation table. This provides to the doctors an opportunity to show his/her professional excellence because they need to concentrate their attention only on their expertise. Of course, there are a number of factors responsible for the degeneration but structural disequilibrium is found occupying a dominating position.

Organisational Structure with a Narrow Span

We can't negate that hospitals for smooth functioning and a close supervision, need a structure with narrow span. Since in a majority of the hospitals we find multidimensional problems while supervising and controlling, the hospital managers find it difficult to manage and control if we find the span wider.

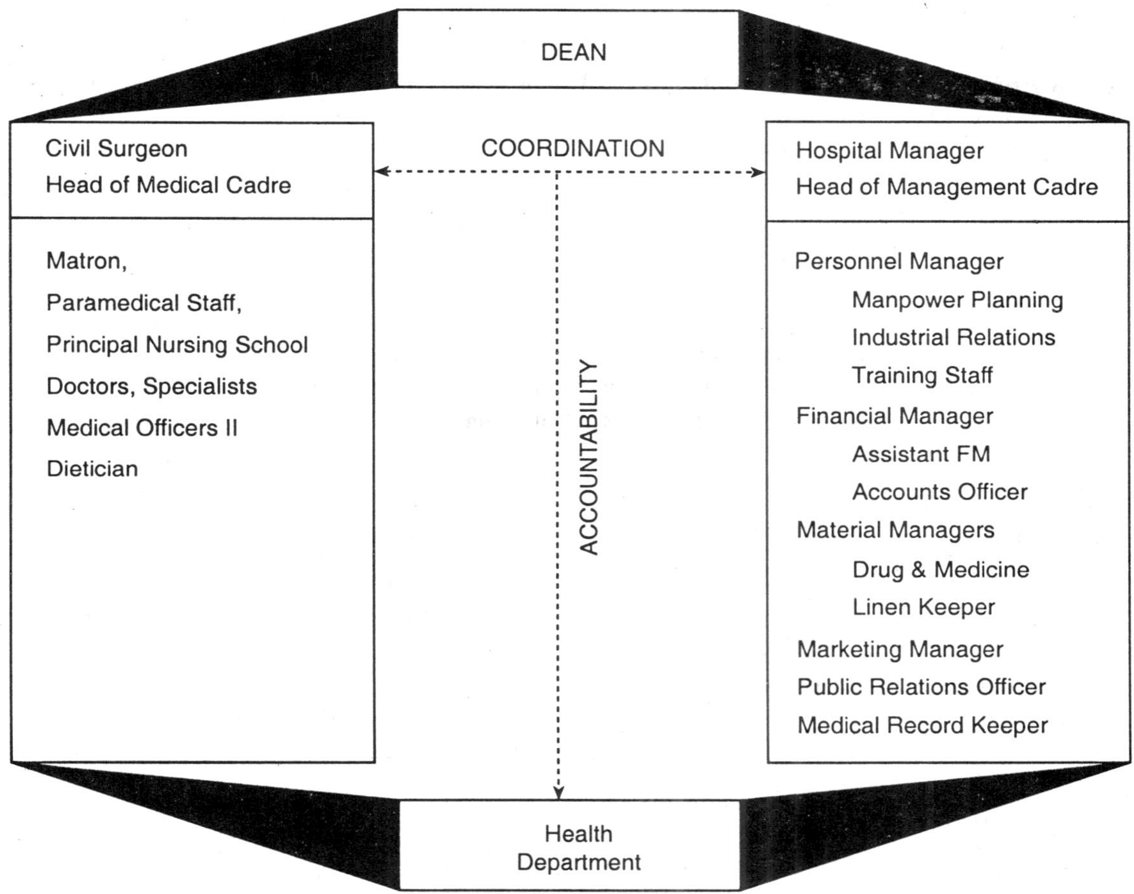

Fig. 6.2. Organisational Structure with Narrow Span

The formation of an organisational structure with a narrow span simplifies the task of close supervision and control. The communication gap between the different echelons of management can successfully be bridged over if we find a narrow span. The fast communications between subordinates and superiors make possible smooth operation and the constraints or difficulties experienced at one level are removed within the shortest possible time. So far as the demerits of narrow span, specially related to the many levels of management and high costs are concerned just with minor modifications and alterations, it is possible to counter the same. It is high time that the top level management recognises the constraints and handicaps on account of a faulty organisational structure and makes posivision for the formulation of an ideal organisational structure that helps hospital managers in making things happen. The traditional structure has outlived its utility in the present set up. Of course, the organisational structure adopted at the different institutes even managed by government is relatively superior, however we find scope for minor modifications and alterations to increase the level of efficiency. Of late, we find pressure on almost all categories of hospitals at its peak and this makes it essential that in addition to other improvements, we also think about management orientation and formulate a structure that keeps hospital managers in a dominating position.

We agree with this view that the government is fully unaware of degeneration in almost all the government hospitals. The two important committees, viz., Health Survey and Planning Committee (Mudaliar Committee) was appointed by the Government of India in 1958 and the second committee—Hospital Review Committee (Siddhu Committee) was appointed in 1978. The observations made by the Mudaliar Committee, "Hospitals were mismanaged because of being run by unqualified administrators"[3] speaks of the fact that knowing well the reason for degeneration, the government looks disinterested in improving the conditions. Another committee, known as Siddhu Committee constituted for reviewing the services of hospitals in Delhi observed, "Hospital Administration be recognised by the government as a distinct medical speciality on par with other specialities of medicine....No person not having formally trained in this specialised discipline be posted to a management position in the hospital."[4] Siddhu Committee makes it clear that the Medical Superintendent should be a person adequately trained in hospital management.

In this context, the report jointly prepared by British Council Team and AIIMS needs an intensive care. The report has recommended three types of administrators.

Type A Hospital Administrator: A highly qualified and experienced administrator competent to take full responsibilities for the largest hospital. He/she should normally be a specialised Masters degree holder including some personal experience of health administration.

Type B Hospital Administrator: A less highly qualified but experienced administrator competent to assist in the administration of a large hospital or to take a full responsibility for a hospital of medium size. He/she should normally be specialised and should have a post-graduate diploma in hospital administration.

Type C Hospital Administrator: A person with sufficient training and experience to take responsibilities for a small hospital or a group of primary health centres or assist the administrator of a large hospital. He/she should have normally a specialised certificate of competence based on a short term training not less than for six months.

While formulating the organisational structure for hospitals, we need to keep in our minds the recommendations of different committees and based on the same, an important position for hospital manager is to be created. Yesterday, we talked about hospital administrator and today, we talk about the hospital manager because we find management principles requiring due weightage for effective hospital management. The structural transformation would make the ways for qualitative transformation without which good patient care is not to be possible. What to talk of the government hospitals when we find even a large number of private hospitals not assigning any significance to hospital management. If you think about management-orientation in hospitals, it is quite natural that a structural change in the process of organising the hospitals would be felt essential. It is important to mention that not only a position but a position having domination in managing, supervising and controlling the hospital operation is a crying need of the hour, if we really feel the urgency of evincing interests in revamping the traditionally managed hospitals. The organisational structure with management orientation would benefit hospitals and doctors or other hospital personnel in many ways.

An Ideal Organisational Structure

The policy makers bear the responsibility of formulating a policy for the sound organisational structure for hospitals which assigns due weightage to the management. In a true sense, both the wings, medical and management need to be coordinated in such a way that quality medicare services are processed in a decent fashion. It is in this context that we present an organisational structure considered to be a model for hospitals. In Fig. 6.3, we find a structure in which we find a position of the hospital manager just after the Vice President making possible a sense of coordination between the medical and managerial cadres. Such type of coordination is essential because different types of services are to be made available to the patients which are made available by the different departments.

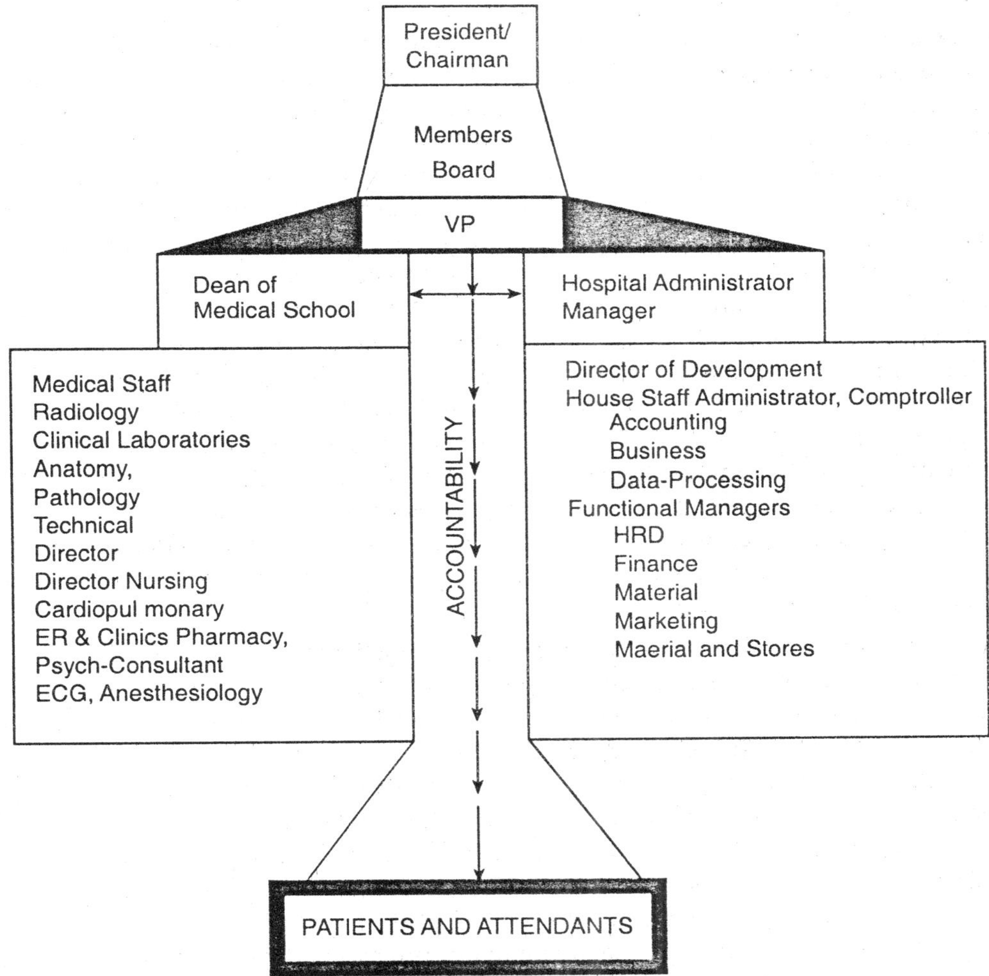

Fig. 6.3. An Ideal Organisational Structure

Ultimate, accountability of hospital is found to the patients and attendants or to the public at large or to the society. In a true sense, the control of government is making the task of the hospital personnel much more difficult in almost all the areas. This necessitates full autonomy to the hospitals so that they get a free hand in controlling and supervising the workings of hospitals. We can't negate that when managerial and medical staff make sincere, honest and joint efforts, the concept of good patient care is to be practised. The expanding gap in the processing of medicare services makes it essential that the expert of the concerned area controls the affairs or workings of hospitals for which they should be made accountable to the Vice President who is accountable to the President or the Chairman. The organisational structure simplifies the process of departmentation.

The role of hospital organisation in health and medicare has, of late, acquired much more significance due to diversification in the nature of services offered and cooperation of a number of allied services essential. The processes of diagnosis and treatment are now more sophisticated and technology-driven. Even a casual observation makes it clear that today, hospitals with their various departments, need the services of various professional groups and multiple relationships among its heterogeneous group present the picture of a complex organisation. The doctors are found competent in their areas of specialisation and we can't expect from them managerial excellence which is found essential to manage hospitals efficiently and effectively. It is right to mention, "Never before in the history of civilization has there been greater need for efficient administration of hospitals."[5] The hospital organisation bears the responsibility of offering to the ailing patients quality medical aid and in addition, they are also supposed to play the role of informing and sensing the masses so that they come to know about essentials for healthy living conditions. To get success in both the areas, it is pertinent that the organisation of hospital is given an overriding priority. Of late, we find the management of a number of hospitals based on the traditional principles in which the seniormost physician/surgeon in the organisation even without having any knowledge of administration and management accepting the responsibility of managing hospitals. The senior most officer is made responsible to look after the day-to-day management of hospitals in addition to his/her clinical obligations. "It is natural that these administrators are not discharging the responsibilities of administration seriously due to dual responsibilities and divided loyalties."[6] We agree with this view that good doctors can't be good managers because even the managerial excellence requires perfection and it is not possible that an individual acts like a super power.

The aforesaid facts make it clear that for efficient functioning, the hospitals of almost all the categories need to be managed by the hospital managers having the knowledge of hospital management. Keeping in view the size of hospital, we have to take a decision regarding the quality and number of hospital managers. Experiences of leading hospitals make it clear that professionally managed hospitals have been successful in establishing an edge over the traditionally managed hospitals. While formulating the organisational structure, it is also to be made sure that span is not so big that the processing of services requires long time or delays diagnosis and treatment. Besides, the experts also need to make it sure that the organisational structure is not to increase the administration bill of the hospitals, otherwise the purpose of making the process cost-effective by managing things professionally would not be fulfilled. It is a sound organisational structure that minimises the scope for over or understaffing. It is a sound organisational structure that makes possible time honoured processing of services. It is a sound organisational structure that makes the ways for fixing accountability. It is against this background that we make a strong advocacy in favour of the formulation of a sound organisational structure.

Organising hospitals successfully is based on professional excellence. In the face of degenerating quality of services, specially in the government hospitals, we have no option but to promote professionalism and to create new positions for hospital managers in the organisational structure.

Departmentation in Hospitals

For the efficient management of hospitals, it is pertinent that the concept of departmentation is practiced in a right fashion. On both the fronts, medical as well as managerial, we find multi-dimensional uses of departmentation. It is right to mention that departmentation from the word "department" designates a distinct area, division or branch of an enterprise over which a manager has authority for the performance of special activities. Thus, departmentation is the process of forming departments, i.e. grouping the activities of an organisation into a number of separate units for the purpose of day-to-day operations and placing each unit under a more or less autonomous administrative head.[7] We consider it a vital step in the process of organising. The increasing pressure and changing nature and character of diagnosis and treatment require multi-faceted operations in hospitals. It is of course, not possible that all the functional responsibilities are discharged by a particular department. It is against this background that the different types of functions and services are now performed and processed by different departments.

On the medical side, we find medical services department, surgical services department, nursing services department, pathological and clinical laboratory services department, radiology services department, dental services department, pharmacy services department, anesthesiology services department and many others depending upon the nature and type of hospitals. For managing each of these departments, we also find formulation of subdepartments and sections, such as the surgical services department are divided into orthopaedic, ophthalmology, gynaecology, general surgery, ENT surgery, etc.[8] On the medical side, we find house keeping and dietary services department, out-patient services department, emergency services department and a few others. Besides, we find library services, medical record services and safety services. A minor variation in the formation of different departments in both the areas can't be overruled.

We find provision for an expert or a specialist for guiding and controlling the working of the department. The specialists or experts bear the responsibility of offering and processing the concerned services with the help of a large number of nursing, paramedical staff and others. Of course, the services related to the surgical and medical sides are the responsibility of the concerned heads of the departments. However, we find hospital managers playing a big role in the very context. In a true sense, the services of hospitals are based on a team-work which require a number of supporting infrastructural facilities in addition to the skilled and unskilled personnel. The hospital managers bear the responsibility of making it sure that all the required amenities and facilities, supporting infrastructure and assisting team of personnel are made available to the doctors attending on the patients so that the time-schedule is maintained and the doctors are made free from the additional responsibilities of controlling and supervising the allied activities resulting into the misuse of their expertise which can be used in a very productive way for treating the patients. It is in this context that we find hospital managers instrumental even in managing the medical and surgical activities, of course, not directly but indirectly with the prime motto of increasing the level of efficiency of hospitals. It is not expected from the doctors to manage and control the supporting devices, of course, they can monitor and supervise that everything is as per their professional needs.

While practicing departmentation, it is pertinent that the personnel heading sections and sub-sections are qualified and the hospital managers monitor everything. We also find departmentation on the management side such as material department, finance department, human resources department, record department and marketing department. In addition, we also find planning departments to process time honoured developments. It is quite natural that all the departments are under the direct control of a senior hospital manager and the departmental managers accept the responsibility of heading and managing the department. In the face of size and character of hospitals, we find minor changes in the process of departmentation.

In Fig. 6.4, we find different departments in hospitals though we find scope for some modifications and alternations.

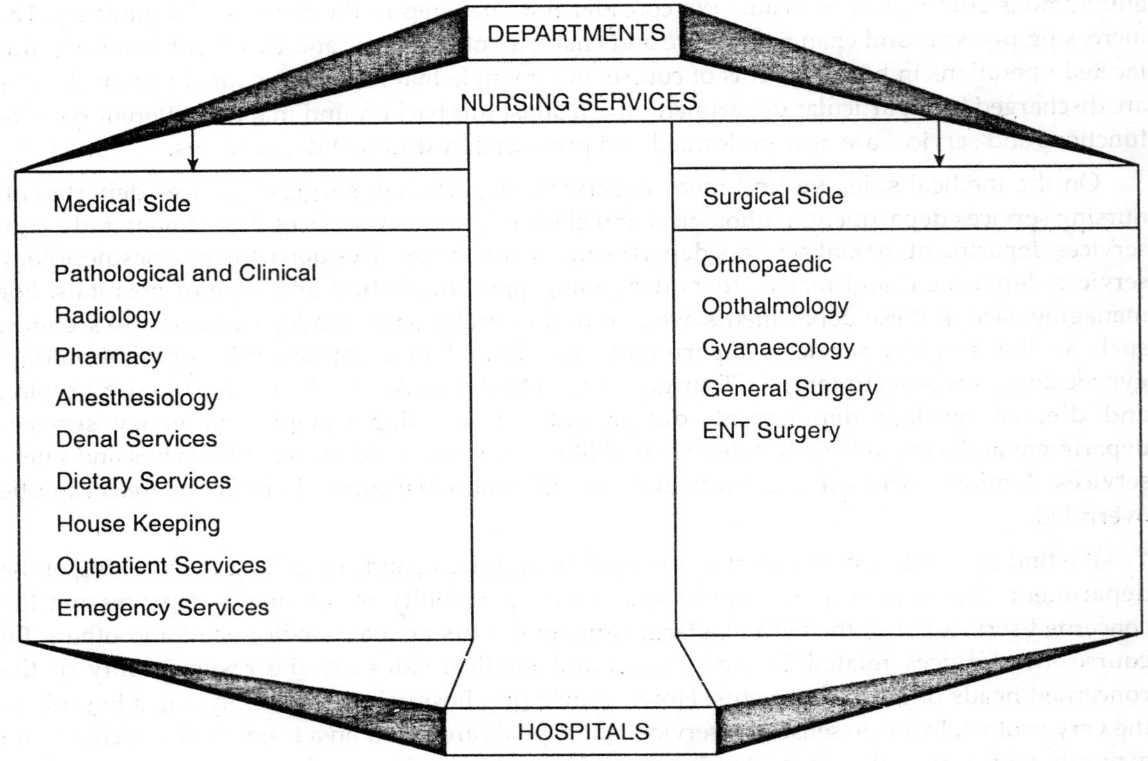

Fig. 6.4. Various Departments on the Medical Side

On the basis of Fig. 6.4, it is right to mention that medical services department, surgical services department and nursing services department are the three main departments and other departments are to assist the working of these departments, such as pathological and clinical laboratory services department, radiology services department, pharmacy services department, anesthesiology services department and specialised services have a separate department which may even be integrated. The surgical services department need some more separate departments such as orthopaedic, ophthalmology, gynaecology, general surgery, ENT surgery and so on.

In Fig. 6.5, we find various departments on the management side. Even on the management side, we find scope for minor modifications and alternations in the formation of departments. The important departments on the management side are the human resources department, finance department, material and stores department and marketing department. We talk about the marketing department in the modern hospitals because of late, the concept of modern marketing is being practised even in the healthcare sector.

In the present context, when a majority of the government hospitals have been found facing the problem of financial crunch, the hospitals have no option but to practise the concept of modern marketing.

Fig. 6.5. Various Departments on the Management Side

In Fig. 6.5, we find various departments on the management side. It is right to say that finance department occupies a place of outstanding significance not only with the viewpoint of regulating the financial irregularities but also with the motto of creating opportunities for the generation and mobilisation of financial resources. It is essential that a financial manager responsible for managing finance makes the ways so that a hospital is found in a position to implement the schemes related to modernisation and expansion. It is against this background that we need a person having specialisation in the discipline of financial management.

The human resources department is supposed to make available to the hospitals quality personnel and this makes it essential that personnel heading the HR has specialisation in managing human resources and he/she is well aware of the changing perception of quality people specially in the context of hospitals. The services of doctors, in addition to other aspects, are based on human and ethical values. The problem of over and understaffing is to be removed and the cost-effectiveness in the process of managing the human resources is to be made possible.

The material and stores department is found to be a very sensitive department specially with the viewpoint of quality of medical services. We also find this department projecting a negative image among the masses because in a number of cases, we find irregularities in the management of inventories which affects the quality of hospital services vis-a-vis the projection of a negative image of the hospitals as well as of the concerned doctors. This makes it essential that a hospital manager is very sincere while selecting a value-based person heading the department sincerely, honestly and with a personal touch.

The marketing department is found to be a new department. Of course, a number of hospitals, specially in the Indian context are yet to realise the instrumentality of marketing department for hospitals. In this context, it is important to mention that with the development of the concept of hospital marketing, we find efforts for opening marketing departments in private hospitals. So far as the government hospitals are concerned due mainly to the regulatory barrier, they currently find it difficult but even they have to move in this direction otherwise, the existing problem of financial crunch in the hospitals would aggravate to such an extent that patients would hesitate to use even their free of charge services. Like other departments, the marketing department is to be headed by a management expert having the specialisation of hospital management in general and marketing the services of hospitals in particular. Because we find hospitals a no-profit-making organisation, it is the responsibility of a manager to make it sure that services processed by the hospitals are in the face of the changing expectations of patients and attendants.

In Fig. 6.6, we find an integration between the two sides of hospital, such as the medical side and the management side.

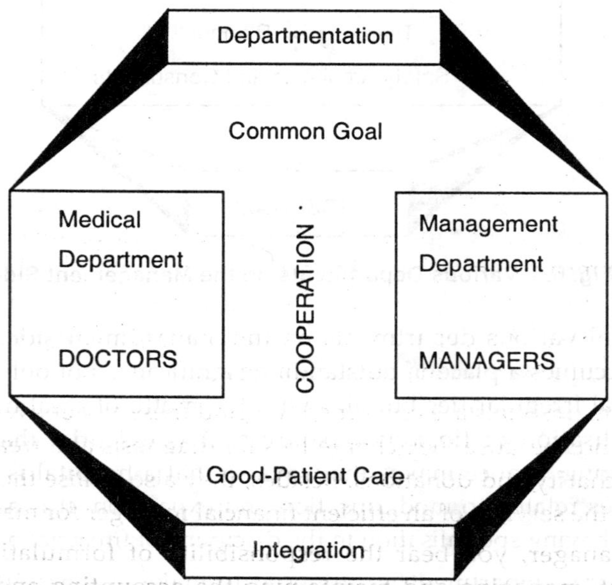

Fig. 6.6. Integration between Medical and Management Departments

We can't negate the fact that medical and paramedical staff, nursing staff and even the staff related to the fourth grade play a dominating role in processing the medicare services but at the same time, it is also to be mentioned that management orientation in hospitals would increase the level of efficiency of all the personnel engaged in offering the medical services. Willingly or unwillingly, even the doctors now feel that it is due mainly to the deficient management that hospitals have been facing the problem of quality degeneration. Almost all the policy panels related to good-patient care have come to this conclusion that management orientation in hospitals is to be the most effective prescription to bring the detailed healthcare system on the rail.

In a true sense, both wings of hospitals need constructive and positive coordination and cooperation because both of them need to work with the motto of improving the quality of services. In no case should the hospital managers develop the feeling that ultimately they have to play a dominating role because they are supposed to play an incremental role.

Functions of Management based Departments in Hospitals

We are well aware of the different departments on the management side in hospitals. These departments help hospitals in different ways. We now go through the functions of different departments in brief.

Finance Department: We can't negate that to be more specific in a no-profit-making organisation, the management of finance is a difficult task. A financial manager working in hospitals is supposed to realise the fact that within the limited means and avenues, they maintain the financial health of hospitals. So far as the government hospitals are concerned, we find there a different systems and therefore, we don't find there enough scope for showing the professional excellence. The limited budget with no avenues for the mobilisation of financial resources complicates the task of a professional. He/she is just supposed to regulate the mismanagement of finance. Of course, there are a number of financial irregularities in the government hospitals, specially related to the material, stores and purchase and a financial manager can check the irregularities and misuse of funds. There are very limited sources from which finance is generated, such as paying wards and in some of the hospitals from subsidised fees and rent received from the shopping complex. And therefore, the most important thing is to regulate the expenditure side. The grants received from the government and in a very few cases, from donors are not so much significant. "In many of the hospitals, more than 60 per cent of the allocated finance is required to be spent on salaries and wages or as establishment expenses and another 25 per cent to 30 per cent on stores and consumables. These expenses are continually rising."[9] This makes it clear that the mismanagement of finance is found at its peak because in almost all the government hospitals, we find stores and consumables presenting a very disappointing picture. In addition, the delayed sanction by government results into the lapse of funds. On the other hand, for most of the heads, we find inadequacy of finance.

So far as the private hospitals are concerned, we find these wider avenues for the generation and mobilisation of funds because they charge fees for diagnosis and treatment and in addition, they also get enough charity and donations. Besides, they also realise the significance of finance and often make use of the services of an efficient financial manager for managing finance.

As a financial manager, you bear the responsibility of formulating the financial plan, preparation of budget, managing and maintaining the accounting and auditing procedures, making efforts to allocate optimal funds to the different heads and maintaining the cash flow.

Human Resources Department: As a human resource manager, you head the human resources department and a number of important responsibilities are discharged by you. Like other organisations, even in hospitals, we find instrumentality of quality people in managing the health care services. Since you bear the responsibility of making available to the hospitals quality people, it is pertinent for you to perceive the real meaning of quality people. Of course, we kind efficiency an important indicator to measure quality but in addition, there are a number of variables or parameters to be given due weightage while recruiting and selecting the personnel for different purposes. You are supposed to make it sure that the doctors to be recruited are not only efficient but value based, professionally and personally committed.

They need personal touch in service, decency in behaviour and positive attitude towards promoting human values and humanity. It is the prime responsibility of a HR manager to impart training facilities to develop awareness of the medical and paramedical staff regarding the behavioural management. It is quite natural that with the latest developments in the medical sciences and increasing sophistication in communication technologies, we find expectations of patients and attendants increasing fast. This makes it essential that the doctors are aware of the increasing level of expectations and process the services accordingly. We can't negate that the boardrooms or the policy makers don't assign due weightage to the compensation and motivational plans related to the medical and paramedical staff. This makes it essential that a HR manager creates a favourable condition for linking the compensation plans to the contributions of hospital personnel. This would motivate the staff to work efficiently. A manager bears the responsibility of improving the quality of environment at the work place as well as at the living places so that the employees are found personally attached to the hospitals. Availability of supporting infrastructural facilities, professional and personal amenities and facilities, accommodation facilities, welfare facilities, rewards and promotional opportunities are some of the motivational schemes sensitising the staff for showing personal commitment. In addition, a HR manager is also responsible for making an appraisal of the performance of employees so that the wrongs, shortcomings, lapses, sore spots are identified and corrected. By formulating an ideal manpower plan, a HR manager keeps on moving the process of enriching the credentials of employees by organising workshops, seminars and refresher courses.

Material and Stores Department: A number of materials are used in the process of diagnosis and treatment. The important functional responsibilities in the very context are planning for material requirement, estimating the demand, procurement, stocking and use. We are aware of the fact that in a majority of the hospitals, almost 40 per cent of the budget is found for materials and therefore, we find enough scope for financial irregularities and frauds. It is essential that the medical and paramedical staff are made available the required materials in tune with the standards and specifications fixed in consultation with the experts. This focuses our attention on quality, time and demand. It is right to mention that by and large, almost all the hospitals fail in managing the materials in a right fashion. Keeping in view the importance of materials in improving the quality of medicare services, it becomes pertinent that a separate department manages materials. Purchasing process is required to be decentralised from the hospitals because in a majority of the cases, we find irregularities in the process of purchase. Of late, we find civil surgeons, pharmacists and line-keepers involved in the process. There is no doubt in it that they know about the quality of materials but it is also right that they know less about the purchasing process. This makes it essential that the concerned experts make available their requirements in terms of quality and quantity to the hospital managers who make available to them the same on right time. It is pertinent that a hospital manager follows systematic and organised efforts for purchasing materials which would not only improve the quality of materials used in the process but would also make the process cost effective.

We are well aware of the fact that in the hospitals, different types of materials are used, for example medical items such as perfusion materials, surgical disposables, instruments, etc. electrical, mechanical and civil engineering items for maintenance, house-keeping materials, linen, big-medical equipment, spares, medicines and drugs, stationery items, food and beverage materials, etc. The advisory Committee for development of surgical instruments, equipments and appliances (1963) identified 3200 items of instruments and equipments being used in a hospital. This makes it clear that a hospital manager needs to minimise the number of materials to be used so that the problem of planning and control is not to be found difficult.

We find quality of materials an important aspect drawing the attention of a hospital manager because in a number of cases, we find complaints regarding poor quality. We expect a lot from the hospital managers in the very context because they can interact with the doctors and suppliers for improving the quality of materials to be supplied. We are well aware of the fact that responsibility of material management is found on the shoulders of a material manager and this makes it essential that utilises cost control and cost reduction techniques. Besides, inventory control, standardisation, waste-reduction, value analysis and alternate source development can also be helpful. Of course, we find use of ABC system but operation research techniques like PERT/CPM considered to be scientific tools, are not adequately used in hospitals.[10] In view of the increasing cases of use of poor quality of materials used by the hospitals, it is essential that hospitals make provision for a separate department headed by a material manager.

Marketing Department: We find marketing department an important department which is yet to gravitate the attention of even a number of private hospitals. Of late, the management experts talk about hospital marketing and it is in this context that we also need to think about the marketing department. The department headed by a hospital manager or even by a marketing manager is found responsible for formulating a sound marketing mix for hospitals. In the product mix, they are supposed to blend the core and peripheral services in such a way that the services offered by hospitals benefit and attract the patients and attendants. It is quite natural that the service mix is to take into consideration the latest developments in the field of medical sciences. So far as the core services are concerned, the doctors would let them know about the package of amenities and facilities related to the same. In the context of a peripheral services, the marketing manager has to keep into consideration the new facilities to be made available to the patients and attendants. Since in the formulation of service mix, we find focus on innovation, the doctors as well as the hospital managers need to think over the latest developments in the field of medical sciences and to make available to the patients sophisticated devices for diagnosis and treatment. Productive and attractive core and peripheral services would be instrumental in attracting the patients.

Another important constituent is promotion that makes it essential that a marketing manager blends the different constituents of promotion with the motto of informing and sensing the patients and attendants. To make available to the prospects, the information related to diagnosis, treatment and more so healthy living conditions, the hospital managers need to advertise with the help of reputed advertising professionals so that creative messages and slogans are used. They also need to make possible cost-effectiveness and to take support of print media for that very purpose. Besides, the public relations activities are also to be promoted with the support of media people and the public relations officer.

By motivating the media people, a marketing manager may be successful in getting an important coverage. Another constituent of promotion, i.e., sales promotion is also to be used for influencing the patients and attendants as well as the front-line personnel, such as the receptionists, nurses and sisters, tele-marketers or even the small ranking doctors and paramedical staff. The offerings may be in the form of small gifts, coupon or so. The personal selling is required to be used and in this context, the important doctors of the hospitals and the hospital managers need to develop rapport with important institutions and organisations who reimburse the medical bills of their employees. The efforts taken for improving the quality of medicare services would increase the number of satisfied group of users and thus, in a very natural way they would act as a word-of-mouth promoter. Of late, we find telemarketing also used by important private hospitals with the motto of informing, influencing and removing the confusions.

The fee structure of hospital is an important decision-making area for the marketing professionals. We agree with this view that modern hospitals of late use expensive inputs and therefore, the cost of diagnosis and treatment is to be high. In a majority of the government hospitals, we find free of charge services and therefore, the problem is specially related to the private hospitals. We are well aware of the fact that hospitals are to be managed as a no-profit making organisation in which the holistic concept of management is to be given due weightage. This makes it essential that even the private hospitals think about the fee structure in a different way. They need to make the structure pocket-friendly so that even the low income group of the society gets an opportunity to avail their services. Here, our focus is on the income based fee structure to be promoted by both categories of hospitals —government as well as the private. To be more specific in the Indian perspective, if we are really interested in improving the quality of services of government hospitals, we have no option but to promote hospital marketing.

The processing of medicare services is also an important functional responsibility of the marketing department which makes it essential that the personnel engaged in offering the services make it sure that the assured quality of services are made available to the users without making any distortion. The nurses, sisters, paramedical staff and Jr. Doctors if work sincerely and honestly, the existing gap in the quality of services made available to the users would considerably be bridged over. A marketing manager/ hospital manager needs to make it sure that personnel are not to distort the quality of services.

The physical attractions become significant because the hospital personnel are also required to project a positive image and in the process their looks carry some meaning, we can't negate. The medical as well as the paramedical staff, nurses and sisters and even the fourth grade staff need to use the uniform made available to them by the hospitals. They are supposed to look smart, neat and clean. Besides, it is also to be made sure that people serving the hospitals have a sense of dedication, involvement and commitment. They have human, morale and ethical values.

The aforesaid facts make it clear that the marketing department is required to play an important role in improving the financial health of hospitals not by exploiting the users but by fulfilling their increasing expectations and a marketing manager can sizeably help hospitals in this endeavour.

Department of Records: To promote research and to benefit the patients, it is pertinent the we assign due weightage to the management of records generally found neglected in almost all the hospitals. For getting correct data related to recovery of the patients, complaints and their redressal, positive or negative remarks of the patients and attendants require much more attention to improve the working of hospitals. It is in this context that we talk about the management of records and recommend a separate department for records so that the management information system gets the required information, specially from the internal sources. The management of records simplifies the task of making an appraisal of the functions or workings of the hospitals and their personnel. It is significant that records present a comprehensive picture of patients' illness with the physical findings and special reports such as X-ray and laboratory reports. All the records are required to be properly filed and today we can use information technology even for putting in memory the records. If on account of cost constraint or budgetary limits, the hospitals don't find it possible to start a separate department for records, it is essential that the library department of a hospital is assigned the responsibility of managing and indexing the records.

Department of Stores: Because a number of expensive materials are used by the hospitals and more so we find a majority of them requiring proper attention for preservation, it is essential that we think about the management of stores. The Department of Stores would be linked to the department of material where a material manager is supposed to discharge the responsibility of managing the materials. If we find in hospitals a separate department for stores, it is quite natural that much more emphasis would be given to the proper conditioning of some of the sensitive items. In a majority of the hospitals, we find the stores department attached to the material department and therefore, in this context we need to establish the Department of Material and Stores bearing the responsibility of managing and preserving or protecting the materials. We can't negate the fact that to be more specific in the government hospitals, we find this department an important source for unfair practices. It is responsibility of a hospital manager to make it sure that the medical, biomedical and general items are stored in the face of the essential conditions they need.

Department of Library: Since we talk about promoting research and increasing the knowledge of medical and paramedical staff, it is essential that a hospital manager also thinks about the library department with computerised cataloguing and indexing. If we find the department of library rich, the management of records would not remain a problem before the hospital managers because an efficient librarian would make necessary provisions for the safety and protection of important books, medical journals, periodicals, important records of hospitals and so on. We find it significant specially with the viewpoint of promoting research.

In view of the above, it is right to say that various departments on the management side play a significant role in improving the working of hospitals. It is against this background that we find leading hospitals of the globe assigning an overriding priority to the management of hospitals because they feel that technical staff getting more time for performing may offer the quality services to the patients. Moreover, they don't know about management and therefore, it is even judicious that the responsibility of managing hospitals is the responsibility of hospital managers.

Functions of Key Departments on the Medical Side

There are a number of departments in the hospitals to offer medicare services. It is really the joint efforts and a sense of coordination and cooperation that various departments in hospitals offer different types of services related to diagnosis and treatment of patients. Besides, we also find hospitals instrumental in promoting the health care education as a preventive measure. The following departments play a key role in the hospitals.

Department of Medicine: In the context of medical services, we find the department of medicine playing an important role. On the medical side, this department is found related to the diagnosis and treatment of different types of diseases. The physicians manage the department under the headship of a senior doctor. We agree with this view that doctors are the backbone of a hospital. A number of junior doctors and the nursing staff help doctors in processing the medicare activities. Clinical investigations and pathological investigations help doctors in diagnosing the disease and writing a prescription. To be more specific in the government hospitals, the patients get free of charge services. Since we don't find any specialisation here, the general type of diseases are diagnosed and treated. A number of subdepartments exist, specially in the tertiary hospitals.

Department of Surgery: Like the medicine department, we find the department of surgery headed by a senior surgeon. A number of junior surgeons are to assist him while performing. Of course, the surgeons bear the responsibility of heading the department but they need a number of infrastructural facilities to conduct operations. In addition to the investigation report, the surgeons also need well sterilised instruments and infection free operation theatre. The management of linen is also an important aspect. This makes it essential that hospital managers take care of the professional requirements of surgeons and make available to them everything they need for conducting operations efficiently. Besides, a number of nursing staff is also required to assist the doctors and help the patients. While managing OT, it is quite natural that a surgeon makes it sure that before conducting operations everything is ready—either the assisting team or the supporting infrastructure. There are some of the important subdepartments related to surgery such as Orthopaedic,. Opthalmology, Gynaecology, General surgery and ENT.

Nursing Department: The primary purpose of the nursing department is to give comprehensive, safe, effective and well-organised nursing care to patients as to accomplish these ends. The nursing department constitutes the largest single group of hospital employees averaging almost 50 per cent of the total staff. We can't negate that if properly administered, it is the mainstay of hospital from the standpoint of supporting administrative requirements, giving effective patient care and promoting good public relations. This department serves as a focal point for much of the administrative coordination.[12] There are three major types of functional responsibilities discharged by them:

1. *Bed-side nursing:* This includes receiving patients, investigating patients, sending them to the respective clinics, rounds with the Medical Officer and assisting the doctors.

2. *Other than bed-side nursing:* This includes IP registration, instructions to servant and other personnel related to proper sterilisation, routine drug, supervision and so on.

Time Spent on Visitors: This includes answering to the questions and queries of visitors and directing the visitors so that they don't face any problem. Of late, we find nurses very much instrumental in guiding the patients.

We agree with this view that the management of nursing staff is found facing a number of problems. The nursing job is found strenuous. We find stress a set of circumstances under which an individual can't respond to the environmental stimuli. Nursing job creates fatigue. A ward nurse often walks and covers a long distance during the duty hours.

Department of Dietary Services and Housekeeping: We find the dietary department playing an important role in the recovery of patients. To be more specific in the government hospitals, we find provision for the supply of free of charge food to the admitted patients. We agree with this view that dietary department needs due care of doctors as well as the hospital managers. Food service is one of the most important activities in almost all the hospitals. It contributes substantially to the process of therapeutic measures because scientifically prepared diet-chart contributes substantially to the quick recovery of patients. It is also essential that we focus on the problem of housekeeping. Here, almost all the formalities are needed as we find in the hotels. Good housekeepers also need technical knowledge of housekeeping as we find in the hotels. It is essential that the housekeepers are schooled in the fundamentals of home economics and the physical sciences considered essential to their defined duties. The important functions of the housekeepers are routine cleaning, dusting, mopping, waxing, window and wall-washing and thus, helping in keeping the place health friendly neat and clean. They are also supposed to perform the task of bed making. We agree with this view that the dietitians and housekeepers play an important role in improving the quality of healthcare services. The dietitians should also have the knowledge of nutrition. A dietitian should be a person with degree either in B.Sc. Home Science with the Postgraduate Diploma in Dietetics and Nutrition or M.Sc. (Food and Nutrition).

It is essential that hospital mangers bear the responsibility of managing the food services and housekeeping. Though a number of people feel that this department should work under the direction of the plant operating superintendent or engineer but we don't find any logic behind the same because it is a responsibility related to management of food and housekeeping.

Department of Pharmacy: Generally, the pharmacy department of a hospital is found clubbed with the central sterilisation and stores. We find hospital pharmacy an important dimension of hospital management, specially on the medical side. The staff is required to be well trained so that they perform efficiently the responsibility of labelling, storage and distribution of drugs and sterilised material. We find pharmacy playing an incremental role in improving the quality of medicare services. Employment of a full time pharmacist is found essential. The doctors on the panel need to make it sure that pharmacists with proper qualifications, training and experiences are recruited for this department. In hospitals, specially of large size, it is essential that a separate department under the direction and control of a professionally competent and legally qualified pharmacist is created. The pharmacists bear the responsibility of making it sure that quality and right medicines are supplied to the hospitals. They are found responsible to regulate the supply of spurious drugs. This makes it essential that personnel with suitable qualifications and experiences are recruited so that the image of hospitals and doctors is not tarnished. Since, it is a department of medical art which consists of collecting, preparing, preserving and dispensing of medicines, the doctors need to watch the working very carefully.

Department of Pathology and Clinical Laboratory Services: We find the services of modern hospitals based on laboratory services because this helps the right diagnosis. The laboratory services include providing information to assist the physicians in diagnosing, treating and preventing the multidimensional diseases. The services also include enriching of the training programme and helping the researchers to invent something new. To be more specific in the surgical services, the laboratory services help surgeons in coming to a right conclusion. And so far as the services related to the department of medicine are concerned, we find laboratory services helping the physicians in different ways. It is quite natural that the department of

Pathology and Laboratory Services are under the direct control of experienced physicians. We can't negate that in a majority of the hospitals, this department is found neglected and the laboratory personnel are not given due weightage but they do play a dominating role in improving the quality of medicare services. This makes it essential that both types of hospitals— the government as well as the private— assign due weightage to the laboratory services. In a true sense, we find them an integral part of the medical services since failing their cooperation, even the most efficient doctors would hardly be successful in making the diagnosis.

Department of Radiology: The radiology department of a hospital bears the responsibility of making the diagnosis more authentic by using radiography, fluroscopy and radioisotopes and high voltage acceleration. A competent radiologist is to head the department who should have specific training and experience in the area of expertise. Developing as diagnostic and therapeutic arms of the hospitals, we find radiology department contributing substantially to the process of using the potentials of doctors.

Department of OPD: Of late, the increasing pressure on hospitals has made the task of admission/registration much more difficult. Besides, it is insignificant that in all the cases, the patients are admitted because a large number of patients can be treated even without admitting them as indoor patients. The growing importance of outpatient services in almost all the hospitals makes it clear that specially in the Indian perspective where masses find it difficult to afford expensive medicare services, the hospitals need to expand out-patient services. We find emergency clinic as a major unit of the out-patient department. Since we find in-patient services based on the observations of out-patient services, the hospital management needs to concentrate its attention even on the out-patient services.

Department of Emergency Services: For serious type of patients, it is pertinent that the medical aid is made available to them on time. This draws our attention on the emergency services of the hospitals playing a special role in projecting the positive image or even tarnishing the positively projected image. The doctors while managing the department need to place the staff found personally committed and professionally dedicated so that the treatment processes start immediately. The medical and paramedical personnel in addition to the other staff should have an indepth knowledge of behavioural management in addition to empathy. We find time management playing a contributory role in managing the department because even a delay of few seconds may result into irreparable losses. For improving the quality of emergency services, it is essential that we enrich the emergency infrastructural facilities like power, oxygen, life saving drugs in addition to a team found available round-the-clock.

Promoting A Sound Organisational Culture in Hospitals

Even without an exception, almost all the management experts believe that the effectiveness of an organisation is considerably influenced by the organisational culture. The quality of environment at the workplace plays an incremental role in governing the organisational culture. It is quite natural that efficient personnel are influenced by the weightage to efficiency while compensating. Because we talk about an organisation in which we find a different condition, the organisational culture would play an incremental role in improving the level of efficiency. The government hospitals need a culture in which the policy makers need to think about the quality of environment at the workplace. We are well aware of the fact that organisational culture is the general pattern of behaviour, shared beliefs and values that members have in common.[13]

Culture can be inferred from what people say, do and think within an organisational setting. It involves the learning and transmission of knowledge, beliefs and patterns of behaviour over a period of time which means that an organisational culture is fairly stable and does not change fast.[14] It often sets the tone for an organisation and establishes implied rules for the way people should behave.

Since in a majority of the government hospitals we find poor level of efficiency, it is pertinent that we think about the organisational culture on a priority basis. What ails the degeneration process?

We can't negate the fact that hospitals working in the Indian environment face a number of problems. The relationships among the different categories of employees if not sound, influence the culture of an organisation. It is also to influence the behavioural patterns and the superiors and subordinates are found confronting albeit on small issues. This in a very natural way makes the quality of environment at the workplace very unfriendly in which all the personnel having values and a sense of respect find it difficult to work. Because efficiency is not to remain an important base for compensating and motivating the people, even the efficients in due course are transformed into inefficients. The process that results into a domination of inefficient people at the work place and the process of degeneration of efficiency starts gaining the momentum. We don't find work culture and all the echelons of employees are found involved in the process of degeneration. We agree with this view that in the government hospitals in particular, whatever the degeneration we find at present has considerably been influenced by the same process.

The aforesaid facts make it clear that organisational culture is the off-shoots of organisational efforts. The most important thing influencing the process is quality of environment at the work-place. If medical and the paramedical staff don't get the supporting infrastructural facilities, if they are constrained by the negative attitudes of the boardrooms or the policy makers or the top-level management, the task of middle-level management is found much more complicated. It is against this background that we find doctors not successful in establishing a work culture and necessitating the presence of an efficient, value-based, professionally and personally committed hospital manager. It is high time that the government policy makers realise the gravity of the situation and assign due weightage to the organisational culture failing which albeit the most sophisticated technological support made available to the hospitals would fail in delivering goods to the publics at large.

The quality of environment at the work place or hospitals need an intensive care if we are really interested in improving the work culture. We can't deny the fact that organisation and departmentation play an effective role in making possible an appropriate organisational culture. If the hospitals make possible departmentation in which cooperation and coordination is possible, goals are set with a great deal of participation, authority is widely defined and decentralised, people are elected on the basis of performance criteria, training is imparted in many functional areas, concerted efforts are made to develop world class people, participative leadership is practised, communication flow is top-down, bottom-up, horizontal and diagonal, a great deal of self control is exercised, the employees working at different levels and round satisfied and evince keen interests in accelerating the operational efficiency. In a true sense, the doctors serving the hospitals and administrating and controlling the working are found nowhere in the policy decision processes. They face a number of constraints but are not in a position to resolve them. They have a number of excuses and grounds for inefficiency and the authorities find themselves helpless. The ambience at the work place is found unfriendly to the work culture.

Creating and developing an ambient condition at the work place fall on the shoulders of hospital managers but in the government hospitals, they face a number of constraints. The police makers are found responsible for creating a sound nexus at the work place. We find their values influencing the direction of an organisation. Although, the term "Value" is used differently. A value can be defined as a fairly permanent belief about what is appropriate and what is not proper which guides the actions and behavioural profile of employees responsible for fulfilling the organisational goals. Values can be thought of as forming an ideology that permeates everyday decisions. In a number of healthcare organisations, the value-driven corporate leaders serve as role models, set the performance standard, motivate employees and make the organisations unique or distinct. It is quite natural that when people participate in the decision-making processes and exercise self-direction and self-control, they feel committed to their own plans. The exposed values need to be reinforced through rewards and incentives, ceremonies, stores and symbolic actions. A clear vision of common purpose elicits commitment.

If we talk about hospital as an organisation, the role model is here set by a doctor or his/her team. He/her sets the performance standard, motivates the people in his/her team and on the basis of his/her world class excellence makes hospital distinct to others. There are a number of examples, when particularly in the government hospitals we find even world class doctors feeling themselves helpless when political interferences make their decisions ineffective.

If we turn our eyes on the private hospitals, of courses, we find a majority of them getting an appropriate work culture because the policy makers realise the significance of organisational culture for work culture. They assign due weightage to the senior doctors, managers and even paramedical staff in the policy decision making processes. They define and set goals knowing well their potentials and therefore, are found successful in facilitating the same. If the senior doctors and professionals create a favourable climate, if they are found value-driven, find enough scope for the development of work culture. The service quality is improved because we find there involvement of a full team. The value-driven doctors and professionals motivate employees to extend their cooperation and this makes the ways for personal commitment. The organisational culture thus makes the ways for team culture *vis-a-vis* the work culture.

SUMMARY

In this chapter, you have gone through the organisation and departmentation of hospitals. After going through the chapter, be sure that the following facts are well versed.

Organising—the Concept: Organising is a managerial process which makes it clear that those who want to cooperate would work together most effectively if they know the role they have to play in any team operation.

Departmentation—the Perception: Departmentation is the formation of different small groups in the face of the defined function of an organisation. It is found based on the principle of coordination and cooperation.

Organising Hospitals: Like other organisations, the hospital, a no-profit making organisation is also organised so that different levels of management cooperate each other to achieve the organisational goals. This is a process of formulating a sound organisational structure for the hospitals.

Organisational Structure for Hospitals: There are different types and categories of hospitals and the process of formulation of a structure is considerably influenced by the same. The general and special hospitals need a different structure. We also find a change in the structure of government hospitals. In this context, it is pertinent that the organisational structure has a narrow span.

An Ideal Organisational Structure: There are a number of considerations making a structure sound or unsound, proportionate or disproportionate, effective or ineffective and optimal and non-optimal. An ideal organisational structure of hospitals contains more autonomy and a hospital manager is found there getting a dominating position.

Departmentation in Hospitals: It is a managerial process of establishing the different departments in hospitals with the motto of increasing the level of efficiency. Medical Services Department, Surgical Services Department, Nursing Services Department, Pathological and Clinical Laboratory Services Department, Radiology Services Department, Dental Services Department, Pharmacy Services Department, Anaesthesiology Services Department and many other small departments and subdepartments are found in the hospitals. Like this, on the management side we also find a number of departments, such as Finance Department, Human Resources Department, Material and Stores Department, Marketing Department, Department of Records, Department of Stores, Department of Library, The Catering Department, Development of Food Services and Housekeeping, Engineering Department, Information and Communications Department also work as important departments.

Promoting a Sound Organisational Culture in Hospitals: The effectiveness of an organisation is sizeably influenced by the organisational culture. The quality of environment at the workplace plays a significant role in governing the organisational culture which we find off-shoots of the positive efforts of management to establish work culture. In a majority of the hospitals, we find lack of work culture. This makes it essential that the organisational structure is made sound.

The culture where we find medical and paramedical personnel getting a service ambience commensurate with the professional requirements. The service environment where we find employees getting pleasure in performing and the users gaining new experiences while using,. Additionally, the equipments, instruments and information technology get the best results while processing. Such an organisational culture paves avenues for work culture. In the Indian perspective, we need to promote such an organisational culture which would make the services of healthcare sector much more productive.

KEY TERMS

Departmentation	Gynaecology
Coordination	Opthalmology
Dietary	Orthopaedic
Anaesthesiological	ENT
Maternity	PERT
Pathological	CPM
Housekeeping	Dietetics
Radiology	Clinical Laboratory
Paramedical	Topdown
Hierarchical	Bottom-up
Cardiopul monary	Organisational Culture
Anatomy	Team Culture
ECG	Horizontal
Catering	Diagonal

REVIEW QUESTIONS

1. Focus on the concept of organisation and explain the rationale for managing hospital professionally.
2. What do you mean by organising hospitals? Discuss the organisational structure found effective for organising hospitals.
3. Focus on the effective organisational structure for hospitals.
4. What do you mean by departmentation? Discuss in brief the managementbased departments in hospitals.
5. Explain the services provided by the different medical-based departments in hospitals.
6. As a hospital manager, throw light on the essentials you find necessary while formulating an ideal organisational structure for hospitals.
7. Focus on the instrumentality of organisational structure in improving the work culture in hospitals.
8. Explain the organisational structure for the general and special hospitals.
9. Discuss the functions of Materials and Stores department in a hospital.
10. Explain the functions of Human Resource Department in a hospital.
11. Focus on the functions of Finance Department in a hospital.
12. Throw light on the role of organisational culture in hospitals for the development of team spirit and work culture.

APPLICATION EXERCISES

1. A hospital manager bears the responsibility of managing the management based departments and his/her professional excellence also simplifies the task of doctors while monitoring and supervising the medical based departments. Comment on this statement as a hospital professional.
2. Being an ideal hospital manager you need to promote an organisational structure which helps in improving the operational efficiency of different departments. Explain how and in what way you will perform and discharge your functional responsibilities.
3. "An organisational structure with a narrow span increases the level of efficiency. In the light of this statement, focus on the organisational structure for hospitals."
4. As a hospital manager, focus on the essentials you find necessary while formulating an ideal organisational structure for the organisation where you serve.
5. Focus on your role as a hospital manager in developing organisational culture which helps in developing service culture.

END NOTES

1. Koontz & Weirich, *Essential of Management*, McGraw-Hill, New York
2. *Ibid*.
3. Lt. Col. M. Srivaastava, *Professional Management of Hospitals, Health Administraton*, Vol. 4/2, December 1986, Official Publication of Indian Society of Health Administration (ISHA).
4. *Ibid*
5. Malcolm, TNC Enchern, *Hospital Organisation and Management, Physician's Record Library*, USE, 3rd Edition.
6. Lt. Col. M. Srivaastava, *op.cit*.

7. Dava, Nalini V., *Hospitals Management*, p. 70.
8. Ibid
9. Sahani A., *Hospitals and Health Administration*, ISHA PDS 1, 1988, p.143.
10. S. L. Goel, *Programmes Evaluation and Review Technique and Critical Path Method*, Modern Management Techniques, New Delhi, 1987, pp/278-93
11. John R. McGibony, *Principles of Hospital Administration*, New York, 1969, p. 426
12. *Ibid*, p. 427.
13. Vijay Sathe, *Some Action Implications of Corporate Culture*, Organisational Dynamics Autumn, 1983, pp. 4-23.
14. B. Littal, *The corporate Culture Vultures, Fortune*, Oct. 17 1983, pp. 66-72.

Management of Hospital Materials and Stores

Quality curative, preventive, supportive and diagnostic services depend on quality materials. Professionally and ethically sound hospital professionals with the help of a sound management of materials and stores may inject new life to the value addition process.

CHAPTER OBJECTIVES

Introduction—Materials Management: the Perception—Materials Used in Hospitals—Essential Principles for Managing Hospital Materials—Objectives of Materials Management—Process of Materials Management—Management of Equipment—Management of Biomedical Equipment—Biomedical Engineering–Management of Drugs—Sensing Patients about Drugs—Management of Inventory—Import Formalities for Medical Equipment—Production and Quality Control of Drugs—Standardisation and Quality Control of ASHU Drugs—Professional and Ethical Dimensions in the Management of Stores—Summary—Key Terms—Review Questions—Application Exercises—End Notes.

LEARNING OBJECTIVES

This chapter aims at studying the different dimensions of managing materials and stores. The readers develop their awareness of the significance of management of materials and stores for improving the quality and regulating the price. The professionals are supposed to sense and sensitise the users not aware of the dangers of mismanagement of drugs and medicines. A techno-driven, e-based devices are found effective in the management of stores and materials. Quality outputs cannot be expected unless we provide to the hospitals quality inputs.

Introduction

To get the quality output, we need quality input. We are well aware of the fact that in the hospital services, a large number of materials of diversified nature and character are used to provide the quality curative, preventive, supportive and diagnostic services. The physician, surgeons and paramedical staff make use of a number of instruments and equipments and if we find something wrong with their quality and uses, the desired results cannot be achieved. Of course, we cannot deny the instrumentality of quality hospital personnel in improving the quality of healthcare services; the equipments, instruments, machines, plants, drugs, linen, disinfecting items and surgical equipments are just to mention a few considerably influencing the quality of medicare services. Being a hospital manager, it is your prime responsibility to ensure supply of quality materials on time so that the medical and paramedical personnel succeed in performing excellently. Since you belong to a managerial cardre, it is essential that your managerial proficiency and professional excellence help hospitals in getting quality material on time and at a moderate price. It is quite natural that personally committed and professionally sound medical and paramedical staff getting quality supporting materials on time succeed in processing and delivering quality services. It is against this background that we find management of hospital materials assuming a place of outstanding significance in improving the healthcare service quality.

It is really amazing that in a majority of the hospitals, we find management of materials and stores very much neglected which not only degenerates the quality of services but also proves to be a fertile ground for the germination and growth of unfair and unethical practices. The deteriorating services and the tarnished image of hospitals make it difficult for the hospitals to win and retain the confidence of users. On the one hand, the users are badly affected while on the other hand, the hospitals gradually become financially bankrupt. It is in this context that we realise the importance of management of materials and stores.

The government hospitals need priority attention on the management of materials and stores where we find unethical practices becoming chronic. In an age of information technology, the hospitals need due attention on e-governance, e-accounting and e-filing to regulate the unfair practices. We find private hospitals managing materials and stores with the help of e-devices and they have also have started the process but they have to go a long way to get the desired results.

In the hospitals, on an average, 30 to 40 per cent of the total budget is spent on materials and this necessitates techno-driven management of stores.

It is right to mention that scientific and information-based management of stores would help in regulating the financial losses due to unfair practices. The increasing cases of theft and pilferages and misuse of drug and other materials can be checked with the help of techno-driven management. Since in the government hospitals we find the problem at an alarming stage, it is imperative that they assign priority attention on e-based devices.

While managing materials and stores, the hospital managers are required to focus on different facets such as planning for materials and stores, collecting materials of quality from the different sources, making scientific arrangements for the safe storage, supplying the required materials to the different departments and making it sure that the concerned departments have been using the materials in a right way. The hospital professionals in the very context need to make use of their excellence so that they succeed in getting quality materials at a moderate price on time.

The first aspect in this context draws our attention on planning which makes it essential that the hospital managers are well aware of the changing quality and quantity of different types of materials. The instruments and equipments to be used for diagnosis and treatment and the requirements of drugs of different types occupy an outstanding place because we find these materials directly influencing the quality of diagnosis and treatment. The hospital managers or in a big hospital, a material manager needs to understand the quality of instruments and equipments needed and the concerned potentially sound suppliers both at national, and international levels. Of course, they need to consult the experts to ensure quality. Since in a majority of the hospitals, supply of materials is found to be a sensitive place for corrupt practices, the hospital managers need to explore avenues for regulating the same. We cannot negate that drugs, linen, surgical equipments and the concerned items are required in a very large quantity. The supply of poor quality materials may affect the service quality and therefore, the policy decision makers need to regulate the process.

The management of stores is also an important problem because we find some of the items of perishable nature requiring special care for preservation and some of the items are found of expensive nature. It is the responsibility of hospital managers dealing with stores to make provisions for proper storage so that we do not find cases of damage and loss due to unscientific and improper storage facilities. The cases of theft and pilferages are required to be regulated by promoting e-governance or other possible devices. The process of issue of materials is required to be made scientific and e-based devices or computer-based inventory, filing, recording and accounting have been found helpful in minimising the unfair and unethical practices.

The above mentioned facts make it clear that management of materials and stores focus our attention on material accounting. The material accounting would help maintenance of continuous records of materials on hand, record of purchases of goods received at cost, correlating procurement of raw materials and the requirements of different departments of hospitals, improving purchases by indicating appropriateness of past purchases for the required uses, etc. Since we find a number of items particularly drugs having much more perishability, it is pertinent that hospital managers or material or stores incharge have an indepth knowledge of the materials and stores.

Today, we have devices to regulate unfair and unethical practices. We cannot deny that in the entire process, information and communication technology play an incremental role. However, we can not undermine the role of working people in managing the same because if we find dishonest people at the workplace, the avenues for unfair practices are paved. Hence, we need two-pronged measures, e.g. first, related to technology helping in managing materials and stores and second, people responsible for managing them. Since the department of materials and stores is to influence the quality of performance of almost all the departments, it is pertinent that different methods and techniques are used and devised so that the quality and costs of service are found regulated. Maintaining cost economy and improving service quality are the two important dimensions where poor management of materials and stores may degenerate the quality and increase the costs.

We are aware of the fact that healthcare services in India have been emerging as a Global Healthcare Brand and therefore, we need to seal all possible avenues which may stand as a barrier while promoting quality and affordability. This makes a strong advocacy in favour of organisational culture which is not to be possible unless we find all the echelons of management cooperating each other in the service generation and delivery processes. We need quality people and at the same time we also need quality materials.

MATERIALS MANAGEMENT-THE PERCEPTION

In the hospitals and healthcare services, a large number of materials are used and therefore, a major portion of the hospital budget is spent on materials. The management of material draws our attention on different components so that the hospitals or healthcare organisation are made available right materials, in right quantity, at right price and on right time. The different components to be given due weightage in the process are determining the nature and types of materials required by particular department, procuring the material of quality from the right sources, ensuring time-honoured supply, ensuring scientific storage and effective delivery, developing an effective control mechanism through good record-keeping, effective distribution at the point of use, ensuring plugging the leakages and making available quality people to manage materials. Do it manually or take the help of technology; the most important thing is your motive which if wrong, manages to search avenues even if most sophisticated technology has been used.

The aforesaid facts make it clear that management of materials is an important dimension of hospital management because a number of components are to be managed for making possible a sound management of materials. Since we talk about the management of materials, it is pertinent that right from the materials planning to effective control, we go through a number of methods and techniques helping qualitative and cost-effective control of materials and stores. We find the material manager directly responsible for the management and control of materials, of course in consultation with a hospital manager. This makes it essential that he/she is well aware of the different types of materials used in the hospitals and knows about their sources of supply at regional, national and even at international levels.

The management of materials makes it essential that a material manager knows about the requirements of different doctors, departments and formulates a plan known as material plan. It is quite natural that the planning processes are based on the influences of technologies on the quality of materials because technological sophistication changes the nature and character of materials to be used in the process. We find improved quality of instrument, equipment, drug, machine, surgical item and the quality of medicare or healthcare substantially influencing the quality of material used in the process. A material manager knows about requirements, formulates a plan, procures the required material, stores them in the required condition, makes available to the persons or departments who requires the same, records them properly and makes it sure that materials collected by different persons and departments are used in a right fashion. Thus, right from planning to supervision and control, we find a number of formalities and steps to be taken to improve the quality of materials.

The motive of material management is to make possible an optimal supply so that mismanagement of materials is checked. It also draws our attention on the quality of materials because unless the quality materials are used in the process, we can't expect the services to be of quality. Thus, it is a managerial process to maintain economy and improve quality. The hospitals may use new generation of information technology even for managing the materials.

Materials used in Hospitals

Healthcare services or Medicare services are the result of a number of materials used in the process. Before we go through the problem of management of materials, it is pertinent that we know about the materials. Medical items, such as perfusion materials, surgical disposables, instruments, electrical, mechanical and civil engineering items for maintenance, house-keeping materials, linen, biomedical equipments, spares, medicine and drugs, food and beverage materials, play an effective role in improving the quality of healthcare services. In Fig. 7.1, we find the list of important materials used by hospitals.

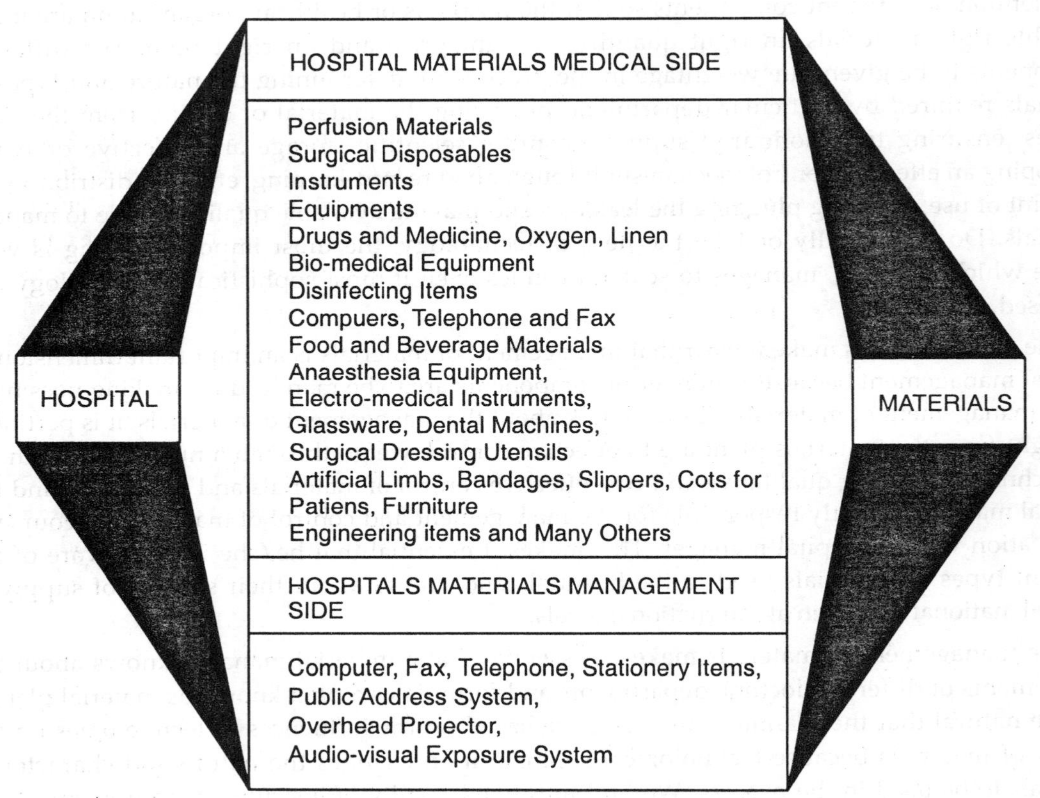

Fig. 7.1. Materials used in Hospitals

The selected items presented in Fig. 7.1 make it clear that diverse nature and character of materials are used in the hospitals. Some of the materials are found very expensive, some of the items are found covering more space, some of the items are found perishable and some of the items are found sensitive to the climatic condition. It is the responsibility of a material manager to make it sure that the storage facilities for the materials are in the face of their requirements. Since we talk about the use of computers, fax, telephones and Internet for different purposes, it is essential that a material manager keeps in his/her mind the essentials for sound storage. Drugs and medicines are found very sensitive to the atmosphere and the sophisticated instruments are found prone to dampness. A number of surgical items need proper care. It is supposed that a material manager is well aware of the requirements and acts in consultation with the hospital manager and the departmental heads. Since we go through the problem of management of materials to be used as inputs for getting the outputs, the professional excellence of a material manager can help doctors as well as a hospital manager in different ways.

Essential Principles for Managing Hospital Materials

The Report of Bureau of Public Enterprises (1984-85) makes it clear that the management of materials is one of the key factors for improving the performance of any unit. Higher inventories saddle an organisation with avoidable costs besides blocking the scarce funds which might be required by the enterprise for its own operations for some other essential development programmes. Proper management of materials, therefore, assumes considerable importance in corporate functioning as well as in the national economy. We are well aware of the fact that in the hospitals, a large number of items of diverse nature and character are used. Since almost all the departments fully or partially are influenced by the supply of materials by the Department of Materials and Stores, it is quite natural that a major portion of the total budget of hospitals is for the purchase of different types of materials. It is said that about 40 per cent of total budget of a hospital is found spent on materials. This makes it essential that a material manager and more so, a hospital manager assigns due weightage to the management of materials. It is against this background that we go through the different principles of managing materials because this would simplify the task of a material manager besides making the management process scientific. Of late, we find a majority of the government hospitals facing the problem of financial crunch and a sound management of materials would make the ways for minimising the financial irregularities, saving the unnecessary expenses, regulating the wastage of materials and more so, improving the quality of materials found essential for improving the quality of hospital services.

In Figure 7.2, we focus on the principles to be practised for the sound management of materials. The seven underlying principles are Quantity, Price, Source, Delivery, Methods, People and the most important one is Quality.[2]

Quantity: This gravitates our attention on the quantity of materials to be demanded by a hospital/material manager. This makes it essential that the estimation process is based on the changing requirements of hospitals in a particular command or catchment area. It is quite natural that quantitative requirements in all the area can't be uniform because we find a change in the disease profile of different areas. However, we find some of the materials of common use are used in almost all hospitals. The main thing in the management process is to make it sure that quantitative requirements of different hospitals are fulfilled. To be more specific in the healthcare services, we find more fluctuation in requirements because in case of viral/epidemic diseases, we find use of a few selected items in a very large quantity. This makes it essential that a material manager and more so a hospital manager makes a time-to-time evaluation of the changing requirements of the command areas.

Price: Another consideration is price which draws our attention on making possible cost-effectiveness. When we find hospitals spending almost 40 per cent of the total budget on materials, even a minor care would maintain economy and at the same time albeit a small mistake would promote cost ineffectiveness. We are well aware of the fact that to be more specific in the Indian context, the material manager/hospital manager bears the responsibility of minimising the cost of services. This necessitates a control on the misuse of materials. Besides, a material manager is also supposed to explore avenues for the supply of materials at a reasonable price which requires professional excellence while negotiating with the suppliers and making a deal. In this context, it is to be remembered that maintaining cost economy is not to result into a degeneration in the quality of materials.

Source: We find a number of suppliers, manufacturers, agents and dealers supplying the hospital materials. Of course, you have a contact with suppliers who have been supplying to you the materials but your wisdom is coiled in the essence of developing rapport with a large number of suppliers and manufacturers so that in case of crisis failure, you don't face any problem. You need to minimise your dependence on a particular supplier even if you find with him everything right. With the help of computers, you can list the different suppliers at national and international levels. Your motive is to get quality materials at a moderate price. If you have alternatives, the task is much more easier. Always promote direct contact and never trust on others.

Delivery: It is also essential that whatever the deals you have finalised are materialised in the defined ways. The supply of materials should be in the face of specifications and standards. The assured or promised quality of materials is to be supplied and therefore, you are supposed to be careful that the gap between the quality promised and the quality delivered is bridged over. Time honoured delivery of materials is found significant to improve the quality of hospital services. While placing orders, you need to mention the time and to make it sure that the suppliers follow the schedule. After getting delivery, you need to make verification before putting the materials in the stores. The quality, quantity and price are to be as per the agreements. However, you are supposed to keep yourself ready for the emergency like situations and therefore, don't invite the stage when the materials are out of stock.

Methods: In the context of managing hospital materials, it is pertinent that you adopt the best method. There are a number of techniques to help you in managing the materials, such as ABC (Always Better Control), HML (High, Medium, Low unit price), VED (Vital, Essential, Desirable component), FSN (Fast-moving, Slow-moving, Non-moving component), SDE Scare, Difficult, (Easy to obtain), GOLF (Government, Ordinary, Local, Foreign Sources), SOS (Seasonal off-seasonal items). You are supposed to take the decision regarding a particular method depending upon the nature and character of materials bought by you. All the methods are found useful no doubt but a majority of the hospitals prefer ABC technique found very simple but substantially effective.

Quality: We find quality an important principle governing the supply of materials management. Coiling more sensitivity in its nature and character, we find medical or healthcare services sizeably influencing the quality of our product. Since we find the risk element at its peak, it is significant that in no case, you compromise with quality. Even a small item used in the medical services contains a big importance. Both categories of hospitals, government or private, are required to make it sure that world class materials are used in the process so that we expect quality services from the hospitals. To be more specific in the Indian perspective, where we find organisations even engaged in manufacturing spurious drugs, recycling and reusing the bio-non-degradable medical waste, a material manager and more so, a hospital manager is required to be more vigilant. A minor mistake can result into a major loss which may even be irreparable. Since it is the prime responsibility of a material manager to make it sure that materials made available to the different departments are of world class, he/she needs attributes helpful in making possible the same. Almost all the hospitals have been found experiencing the problem of quality degeneration mainly on account of the mismanagement of materials and stores department specially related to the quality of materials. To be more specific in the government hospitals, we find the problem at an alarming point. This makes it essential that a material manager uses his/her excellence in identifying the problems and correcting them with the support and cooperation of a hospital manager.

In Fig. 7.2, we find essential principles governing the management of hospital materials.

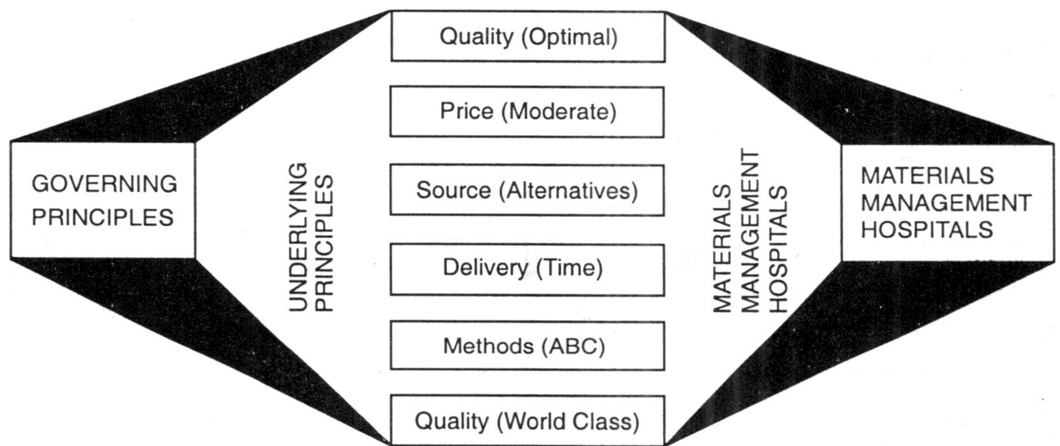

Fig. 7.2. Material Management Governing Principles

Of course, it is the prime responsibility of a material manager to ensure quality of the materials supplied but we can't free the hospital manager and even the doctors from the responsibility of qualitative transformation which is not possible unless all the related personnel make a joint effort.

In addition to the aforesaid facts, it is also essential that a material manager is well aware of the latest developments in the field of medical sciences and have an in depth knowledge about the sophisticated machines, instruments, equipment, information and communication technologies and drugs and medicines so that he/she is not misguided by the suppliers. How to make a deal or how to negotiate so that quality materials are made available to the hospitals at a reasonable price requires professional excellence. The commission culture needs a final departure, if we are really interested in improving the situations very much instrumental in jeopardising the norms specially in the government hospitals. The motive of material management is to make possible cost-effectiveness so that even the private hospitals find it easier to minimise the fee structure. It is really amazing that government hospitals spending a lot of money for the purchase of different types of materials have generally been facing the problem of inadequacy of almost all types of materials to be used by the different departments. This necessitates a sound management of materials based on professionalism. A hospital manager bearing the ultimate responsibility of improving the quality of medicare services is supposed to make it sure that wrongs, lapses, irregularities, unfair and unethical practices to be more specific in the materials and stores department are checked.

Objectives of Materials Management

Like other organisations, the hospitals also need a scientific management of materials with diverse objectives. There is no doubt in it that effective and intelligent management of materials would make the ways for cost-effectiveness which is the most burning problem before hospitals specially in the Indian perspective. A number of researches reveal that by and large in almost all the hospitals, we find mismanagement of materials which has been raising the cost of diagnosis and treatment. We go through primary and secondary objectives of materials management. In Fig. 7.3, we find a list of multidimensional objectives of hospitals.

Primary Objectives: In the group of primary objectives, we find focus on the following objectives:

- Right Price
- Low Procurement and Storage Cost
- Continuity of Supply
- Consistency in Quality
- High Turnover
- Development of Personnel
- Good relationship with the Suppliers
- Good Information System

Right Price: The hospital managers bear the responsibility of making the process of generating the services found to be cost-effective. This is possible when we find hospitals optimising the budget for materials. An organisation where a large number of materials are used, it is pertinent that even a minor scope for mismanagement is checked. We are well aware of the fact that in the hospitals, different types of materials are used related to the core, peripheral and supportive services. In this context, it is the prime responsibility of a material manager to explore possibilities of getting the materials of right quality at a moderate price. Thus, the management of hospital material is also with the motto of making available materials to the hospitals at the right price.

Low Procurement and Storage Cost: We agree with this view that management of procurement and storage cost is also to influence the cost of materials. There are several instances to testify the misuse of materials while storing the same. Besides, we also find cases of unscientific collection of materials instrumental in raising the cost. It is the prime responsibility of a material manager that he/she with the help and cooperation of a hospital manager makes sincere efforts to develop contact with the suppliers available at the closest point. While taking a decision, the total costs on collection of materials would be computed and on the basis of a comparative analysis of the costs, a decision would be taken, of course, in favour of a supplier supplying quality materials at a reasonable price. A material manager needs professional excellence for negotiating and making a deal. The management of stores is also an important area for increasing the costs on materials because mismanagement in storage is found instrumental in increasing the costs. This draws our attention on stores management.

Continuity of Supply: While managing materials, a material manager is supposed to remove the chances of a gap in supply. Even if we find something wrong with the supplies, the doctors and paramedical staff can't wait because an emergency like situation can't be deferred. This necessitates consistency in the supply of materials and to make it possible, a hospital manager/a material manager requires to make an appraisal of the changing qualitative-cum-quantitative requirements of different departments so that they come to know about the emerging trends. The main thing in the process of management is to fulfil the requirements. It is in this context that we talk about the continuity in supply. A material manager bears the responsibility of making it sure that in no case any department of a hospital is likely to face a gap between the demand and supply. Even in an abnormal condition, when in a particular catchment area we find an abnormal increase in the demand of a few selected items due to epidemics or natural calamities, the gap is to be avoided.

Consistency in Quality: Of course, it is an important consideration because the quality of heathcare services is substantially influenced by the quality of materials. A material manager is supposed to be more careful, specially in the Indian perspective where unfortunately, we find business ethics not getting a place even in the healthcare sector. The objective of material management is to ensure quality in the supply of hospital materials. In any case, a material manager is not expected to make a compromise with quality because this may cause irreparable losses to the patients. Since we talk about quality in totality, the quality of hospital materials appears to be a focal point as failing the supply of superior quality of hospital materials, even the world class doctors and professionals would find it difficult to improve the quality `of health care services.

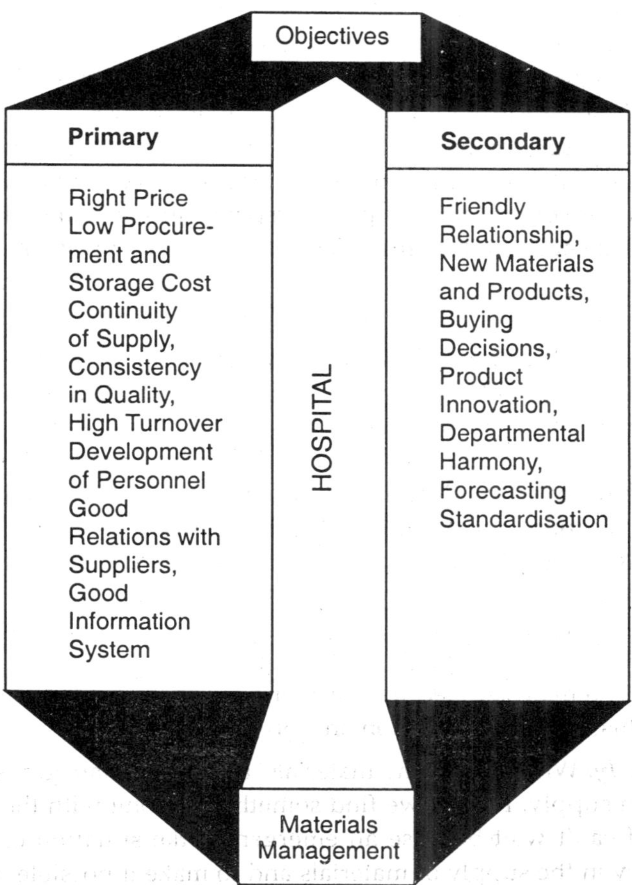

Fig. 7.3. Objectives of Materials Management in Hospitals

High Turnover: The management of hospital materials is also aimed at increasing the rate of turnover. This draws our attention on high turnover. We don't find any sense in' collecting the materials in stores, even we don't find it practical to promote unnecessary supply. The main thing in the process is to make possible a high degree of mobility in the demand and supply of hospital materials. A material manager bears the responsibility of increasing the turnover so that all the departments in a hospital get the required quantity and quality of materials on time.

Development of Personnel: Even the world class doctors and paramedical staff would fail in delivering goods to the patients, if they are not supplied the quality materials on time. The excellence of hospital personnel is thus substantially influenced by the availability of superior quality of materials. It is the responsibility of a hospital manager that he/she makes sincere efforts to understand the changing requirements of time and keeps on moving the process of bridging over the gap between demand and supply. The availability of superior quality of hospital materials simplifies the task of hospital personnel while proving their excellence. Thus, the management of materials is also aimed at developing personnel by providing to them an opportunity to show wonders.

Good Relationship with the Suppliers: We can't negate that the success of a material manager/ hospital manager is fantastically influenced by the supply position. This makes it essential that both of them make sincere efforts to develop rapport with the suppliers so that they succeed in getting the materials even if situations are not favourable. To be more specific in the healthcare organisations, we find possibility of a non-optimal supply because abnormal conditions, natural calamities, epidemics and viral diseases generate a gap. If you develop and maintain good relationship with the suppliers, they may help you even in an abnormal condition. It is also possible that due to official formalities, you fail in making payments to the suppliers on time and if you have friendly relations with your suppliers, they would cooperate with you.

Sound Information System: In an age of information technology where we find information superhighway simplifying the task of hospital managers, it is pertinent that you have a sound information system. This is essential to know about the supply position and the past records of suppliers. This is also found helpful in estimating the fluctuating demand and supply positions. We are well aware of the fact that a technology-driven information system serves multifaceted objectives. Even while ascertaining the quality of materials supplied by the suppliers you would find the instrumentality of computers simplifying your task. It is against this background that we have gone through the problem of a sound management information system for hospitals.

Consistency in Quality: Of course, the most important thing in the management of hospital materials is consistency in the quality of materials made available to you by the suppliers. If you don't make available to the doctors and paramedical staff, the materials of superior quality, it is quite natural that the services would start degenerating which would endanger the interests of all the related parties, such as patients, attendants, doctors, paramedical staff, nursing staff and management personnel. This necessitates a close look at the quality of materials supplied to a material manager. We agree with this view that material management aims at ensuring the quality of materials. It is the prime responsibility of a material manager/ hospital manager to make it sure that consistency in the supply of hospital materials of superior quality is made possible.

The aforesaid primary objectives make it clear that management of materials serves multi-faceted objectives and hospitals can't think of serving well if the management of materials is not effective. In addition to the primary objectives, we also go through the secondary objectives.

Secondary Objectives: The secondary objectives of materials management are:

- Maintaining friendly relationship with the suppliers
- New Materials and Product
- Buying Decision
- Product Innovation
- Departmental Harmony
- Forecasting and Standardisation

Friendly Relationship: In the management discipline, we find relationship occupying a place of outstanding significance. The management of materials aims at maintaining friendly relationship or harmonious relationship with the suppliers so that a material manager finds it convenient to procure the required materials on time. Your suppliers fix the destiny of your development. Your image, quality of your services, convenience or inconveniences are substantially influenced by the harmonious relationship you have made possible while working as a material manager. If you fail, your task is found much more difficult. This necessitates professional excellence so that you develop rapport with the suppliers and are found successful in maintaining a harmonious relationship with them.

New Material and Product: If you serve the Department of Materials and Stores as a material manager, it is quite natural that you pave avenues for innovation for which it is essential that as and when new materials are launched, you activate the process of making available the same to the hospitals. We are well aware of the fact that scientific advances have made possible more frequency in the innovation process. It is against this background that we find new materials related to the healthcare services coming to the markets everyday. The changes in the process of diagnosis and treatment make it essential that whatever the materials you make available are in the face of latest developments. The management of materials thus is found aimed at the availability of new generation of materials.

Buying Decision: It is important to mention that being a manager, you are well aware of the buying processes or transforming the dialogues into a deal. Since you work as a material manager, it is essential that by negotiating, you succeed in getting quality materials at a moderate price. You are supposed to know about the quality of materials and if you have any doubt or confusion, you need to get it confirmed by the doctors and the hospital managers. The management of materials makes it essential that you activate the buying process and never commit a mistake by allowing the producers/suppliers making available to you the poor quality of hospital materials.

Product Innovation: Because we find change a natural phenomenon, it is quite natural that our services sooner or later prove to be traditional and become less effective. This makes it essential that you keep on moving the process of product innovation. It is in this context that we talk about the instrumentality of materials in innovating the services of hospitals. It is also well-known that hospitals working with the support of quality materials succeed in introducing modern services found establishing an edge over the traditional services.

Departmental Harmony: Earlier we have talked about relationship and a hospital manager not making possible departmental harmony fails in improving the quality of materials.

Process of Materials Management

To make the management of materials more effective, it is essential that a manager moves through the following processes:

1. *Determining the categories:* At the very outset, it is significant that a material manager determines the categories of stock required both in terms of quality as well as the quantity. This simplifies the subsequent processes.

2. *Procuring the items:* The second stage in the very process is to procure the items from negotiated sources of suppliers, agencies, dealers or so. The main thing in the process is to make sure that the suppliers would supply the required items on time and as per the specifications. It is not essential that a material manager concentrates or depends on a particular supplier, rather it is of much more significance that he/she explores avenues both at national and international levels.

3. *Ensuring timely supply:* After taking a decision regarding the procurement of items from a particular supplier or different suppliers, a material manager is required to make it sure that they supply the items on time because a gap in demand and supply is to be avoided.

4. *Ensuring good storage:* After the collection of different types of materials from the different sources, it is pertinent that a material manager makes suitable arrangements regarding storage. In this context, the nature and character of items would determine the storage facilities required for the same. If the items are perishable, the storage facilities are required to be made more scientific so that preservation process is up to the mark. To be more specific in the context of expensive drugs and medicines, he/she is supposed to be more careful.

5. *Developing an effective control mechanism:* After making the appropriate storage facility, it is essential that he/she makes provision for effective control. This necessitates good record keeping. Of late, we find use of computers even for record keeping. Such a provision minimises the possibilities of errors all omissions in the process. An effective control mechanism makes it essential that items are delivered to the right persons on right time and proper entries are made thereafter.

6. *Effective distribution at the points of usage:* To make the process of distribution more sound, it is essential that a material manager makes provision for the distribution of items at the points of usage so that he/she ascertains that materials have actually been delivered to the concerned person or department on time.

7. *Ensuring plugging of loopholes:* It is a well-known fact that the materials and stores prove to be a sensitive point for different types of irregularities, theft and leakages. The cases of pilferages are also found influencing the process. This makes it essential that a material manager makes suitable arrangements for plugging the leakages at the different points.

8. *Employing suitable personnel:* A hospital manager is to make it sure that an efficient and value-based person acts as a material manager. In addition, even the low cadre staff of materials and stores department is required to be honest.

9. *Performance-orientation:* In addition to the aforesaid process, it is also essential that a

hospital manager makes frequent audits or supervision so that cases of irregularities and mismanagement are detected.

Management of Equipment

Of late, we find equipments playing an important role in the healthcare services. A hospital manager and to be more specific, a material manager bears the responsibility of managing equipments in such a way that quality of diagnosis and treatment is found improved. We are well aware of the fact that scientific advances have made possible a basic change in the nature and character of equipments to be used in the hospitals. This makes it essential that we assign due weightage to the management of equipments so that the patients get the benefits of technological sophistication. It is against this background that we go through the problem of equipment management. The following procedures draw attention of a hospital manager:

1. *Ordering equipment:* In this context, we find our past experiences and future requirements playing an important role. The process of ordering of equipment requires more care and precaution failing which we find an increase in the unproductive expenses. Unnecessary purchases are to be avoided and this necessitates ordering. It is quite natural that all the equipments to be used can't have a uniform or identical character. Some of them are found essential whereas we can defer or postpone our requirements for some other equipments. The ordering helps us in setting the order of priorities. You are not supposed to cross the budgetary or financial limits and the ordering of equipment would help you in maintaining the financial discipline. In this context, you are supposed to take the help of a catalogue which would help you in knowing or understanding the instrumentality of equipment. Besides, you also have the past experiences and based on the same you can come to a particular conclusion. After going through the catalogue, you are supposed to prepare a requisition form mentioning details and specifications. You are required to understand the importance of modern equipment. Place an order in the face of your requirements.

2. *Storing equipment:* After getting equipments, you bear the responsibility of storing the same. We agree with this view that storing of equipment is found necessary because the cases of theft and pilferages or breakage may result into huge financial losses. Proper arrangement for storage is found essential and keeping in view the nature and character of equipment, you are supposed to make suitable arrangements. A manager is required to make it sure that inventory of the store is well maintained and proper accounting practices have been adopted through stock ledgers. A separate page is to be spared for a particular item to be entered. Whenever you procure new equipments, an additional page is needed for making entries. You are supposed to make the process scientific so that as and when you need to know the stock position, the task is easier.

3. *Issuing equipment:* We are well aware of the fact that in each hospital, we find a number of wards and laboratories where equipment are used. You are supposed to make it clear that as and when you issue equipments to a particular department, after receiving the same, the concerned department bears the responsibility of managing and controlling them properly. However, we can't negate that the departmental heads are required to have a direct liaison with the store to replenish the consumed articles. A material and stores manager is required to take care of the issue voucher since the person receiving or signing the voucher bears the accountability. Taking proper care of apparatus and equipment is the responsibility of the departmental head or the person who has received it.

You are supposed to keep a copy of the issue voucher. There is no doubt in it that you bear the responsibility of making it sure or getting it confirmed that the concerned department requires the particular equipment or apparatus and the issued items are actually used by them. Increasing cases of misuse of equipment and apparatus necessitates time-to-time supervision.

4. *Controlling and maintaining equipment:* After issue, the responsibility is now found shifted to the receiving person or the departmental head. However, you are required to ascertain that the equipment issued to the various departments are used in a right fashion, maintained properly and keeping-up process is found regular. In a majority of the hospitals, we find that equipments remain unused or are even misused. The cases of mechanical defects are to be identified at the very early stage so that necessary steps are taken to repair the same. We are well aware of that almost in all the hospitals, the increasing number of non-working equipments has been generating numerous problems. We also find cases where the departments find it difficult to keep them at the proper places. It is really amazing that hospitals in a few cases have also been found making the equipment unworkable deliberately so that they don't have any pressure of operating and maintaining the equipment. Besides, they also oblige the private practitioners for which they are paid commission. In a majority of the government hospitals, we find cases like collecting money from the private practitioners and directing the patients to go there for examination or investigation.

5. *Coding and standarisation:* In almost all the hospitals, we find use of a large number of equipments and apparatus for different purposes. You have stored a good number of items in the stores. The coding processes would help you in identifying a particular equipment. There are two systems, viz., Birch System and the Kodak System commonly used for this purpose. While coding, you bear the responsibility of classifying the different items on functional basis which would help you in identifying the same. It is not possible that you provide a separate code for all the items and therefore, you are supposed to know the similar or identical items and to provide a code. You also bear the responsibility of cataloguing the same mentioning details for making use of reference.

In Fig. 7.4, we find different processes of managing equipment.

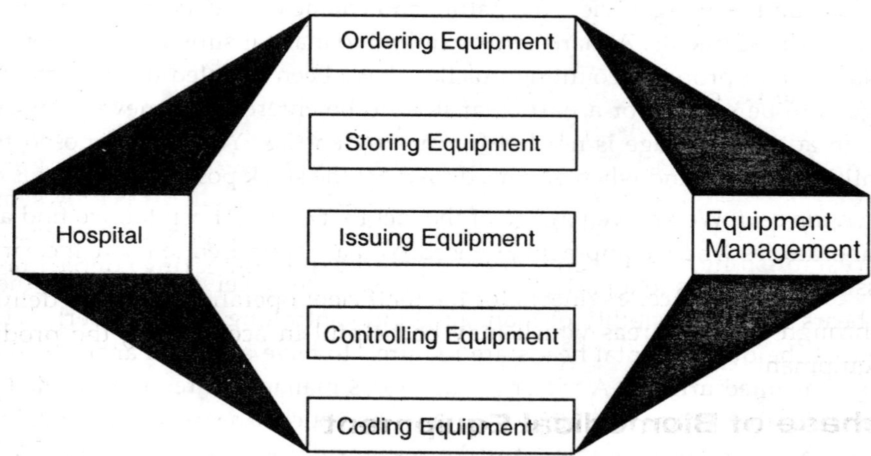

Fig. 7.4. Process of Equipment Management

As a material manager, you bear the responsibility of managing the equipment and apparatus in such a way that the cases of misuse, non-optimal use and improper keeping-up are detected and the responsible persons/departments are penalised.

Managing Biomedical Equipment

For quality in totality, we find it essential to manage the biomedical equipment in a right fashion because the doctors even of world class fail in diagnosing and treating the patients if they don't get the support of sophisticated equipments and apparatus. We are well aware of the fact that medical developments have been creating a demand for complex medical equipments for diagnosis, therapy, monitoring, visualisation, prosthesis, life support system, etc. Of course, we find a number of hospitals evincing keen interests in having sophisticated biomedical equipment but only a few of them have been found interested in managing, maintaining and operating them as per the defined norms. It is really amazing that a number of biomedical equipments used in the hospitals are found lying unserviceable, ill-maintained and roughly operated which decelerate their productivity. It is against this background that we find it an important problem requiring due care of a hospital manager to deliver goods to the patients. The personnel managing, maintaining and operating the sophisticated biomedical equipment are found inefficient and not well aware of the techniculture resulting into a big capital loss to a majority of the hospitals. This makes it essential that we think over the problem on a priority basis.

Sophistication invites complications. We can't deny the fact that the sophisticated biomedical equipment have sizeably been helping the doctors specially while diagnosing. But we fail in managing them properly. It is quite natural that improper management or mismanagement degrades the quality of medical services and in the long-run, results into a major capital loss. We are well aware of the fact that with the use of more sophisticated biomedical equipment, we need specialised services for maintenance and repair which requires biomedical engineering support. The BME makes it sure that whatsoever the equipment you use works in a proper condition, help you in increasing the efficiency and never provides you the confusing results. Maintenance and Repair Policy thus occupies a place of outstanding significance specially while managing the biomedical equipment. If we make possible a well-planned preventive maintenance programme, the life expectancy of equipment would be high and the repair and maintenance costs would also come down. It is in this context that management of biomedical equipment draws our attention on a priority basis. To be more specific, the government hospitals need an intensive care because in a majority of the government hospitals, we find the situation very alarming. Even in the private hospitals, we don't find management of biomedical equipment satisfactory. It is estimated that if all the unserviceable biomedical equipment in the Indian hospitals are serviced and taken due care, the avenues would be paved for equipping 10 new hospitals.[3] This draws our attention on a number of issues such as the purchase of biomedical equipment, the electrical safety procedures, establishing an independent biomedical engineering department, fixing accountability to the biomedical engineers for the inefficient operation and poor delivery and so on. We go through the key areas which may be helpful in accelerating the productivity of biomedical equipment.

The Purchase of Biomedical Equipment

At the outset, we go through the problem of purchase of biomedical equipment. It is pertinent that the purchase of BME is based on a collaborative study by the medical user as well as the BME staff. Presently, we find the knowledge of medical user and the marketing of manufacturing organisations the influencing factors. Such a change in the purchase process would increase the contributions of biomedical equipment because the BME staff are supposed to be well aware of the nature and character of the same. Besides, the hospitals also need a policy for the replacement of biomedical equipment because after some time, we find it unprofitable to repair and operate the same.

Replacing the Biomedical Equipment

We need a plan for the replacement of biomedical equipment and to make necessary financial provision so that we are in a position to replace the same as and when we find repairing process likely to be uneconomic. Of course, BME staff needs to use the replaced equipment as a stand-by or to make available the same to the teaching and research department of the hospitals or even they can use spares of old equipment for the repair of new equipment. By and large, almost all the hospitals, specially in the Indian perspective find it difficult to replace the new generation of biomedical equipment due mainly to the problem of financial inadequacy. However, we find a very few of them making it sure that they have adequate funds to move with the evolving technological sophistication. A manager managing finance needs to appropriate annually to the replacement Fund so that the equipments are replaced as and when the circumstances necessitate so.

A System Approach for Safe and Economic Operation

We can't deny the fact that in almost all the hospitals, the cases of uneconomic operations are found rampant. The safety to a patient undergoing diagnosis and treatment is found significant because we find use of several instruments simultaneously. This necessitates a system approach to keep safe the patients from the electrical hazards. Proper earthing shielding and facilities for fault identification would ensure safety to the patients. Of course, an efficient technical personnel may help us in this context. A hospital manager requires more precaution and excellence while selecting new generating of equipment as for example, installation by technically sound personnel, operation and maintenance by the efficient biomedical engineering staff and so on. A system approach would make the ways for the right purchase, efficient operation, economic maintenance and the minimum operational costs found instrumental in making the medicare services economic.

A Model Biomedical Engineering

Keeping in view the intensity of problem, we find it essential to develop a model for the different categories of hospitals so that all categories of hospitals make use of the new generation of biomedical equipment.

For Big Hospitals: To be more specific in the big or large-sized hospitals, we feel the urgency of having an in-house department of Biomedical Engineering. The three important components to be taken care are personnel, laboratory and space. Since we talk about the new generation of equipment, it is quite natural that our requirements of personnel would not be so taxing. In view of the nature and character of equipment, we need Biomedical Engineer-Incharge, Maintenance Supervisor, Bio-medical Engineering Technicians and the recurring expenditure. The laboratory equipments needed in the very context are Oscilloscope, Valve Tester, Transistor Tester, Megger,

Avometer, RLC bridge, VTVM, Soldering irons and general engineering tools and non-recurring expenditure. The BME servicing laboratory requires near about 4000 sq. ft. space.

For Small Hospitals: In the small hospitals, the requirements in a very natural way would relatively be less than the big hospitals related to personnel, laboratory and the space. In the small hospitals, we don't need a biomedical engineer-incharge because even a maintenance supervisor is found sufficient to perform efficiently. The requirements even for the biomedical engineering technicians would be half the requirements of big hospitals. So far as the laboratory equipments are concerned, they need Megger, Avometer, RLC bridge, Transistor Testor, soldering irons and general engineering tools. The requirements for space would not be more than 2000 sq. ft.

Biomedical Engineering Department

It is right that hospitals assign due weightage to the establishment of a biomedical engineering department. In the face of increasing mismanagement of biomedical equipments found in the hospitals in general and the government hospitals in particular, we need to think over the problem on a priority basis. If we find a separate department for biomedical equipments, a biomedical engineer-incharge in case of big or large-sized hospitals and a maintenance supervisor in case of small hospitals would be required to accept the responsibility of managing the department.

He/she bears multidimensional responsibilities.

- Regular preventive maintenance of biomedical equipments is found essential. It is also pertinent that calibrations of all ranges of biomedical equipment are checked regularly.
- Major servicing is required half yearly or at least annually.
- The developing faults are required to be identified and corrected.
- It is also essential that in tune with the changing requirements of hospitals, the steps related to modifications are taken up.
- The list of all the spares required for smooth functioning of the equipment is prepared and it is made sure that the spares are available in the stock.
- We can't negate the fabrication of small biomedical devices not to be available in the market.
- We also need to fabricate spares not locally available.
- With the evolving technologies, it is significant that new generation of bio-medical equipments are made available to the hospitals and therefore, it is essential that a sound information system develops the awareness regarding the evolving technologies.
- The old generation of personnel needs to accept the responsibility of developing efficient personnel who are competent enough to maintain, repair and operate the evolving technologies efficiently.
- The old generation of biomedical equipments should not be thrown into the waste box, rather the technical and engineering department of the hospitals should use the same to promote research and enrich know-how of the personnel to be developed.
- To make it sure that equipments used for the diagnosis and treatment of patients would not create electric hazards.
- It is also essential that a biomedical engineer-incharge works as a team member specially with the doctors in the OTs or other areas.

- As and when you install sophisticated biomedical equipments make it sure that you have technical personnel who know and understand the same.

The aforesaid steps no doubt would increase the operational productivity of the biomedical equipment. Besides, the patients would also be benefited. If we gravitate our attention on the poor maintenance of sophisticated equipment and apparatus particularly in the government hospitals, the realities force us to comment that we are playing not only with the hospital finance and state exchequer but even with the patients who despite of the fact that equipments are available fail in the getting the benefits of the same. It is against this background that we need the following measures to bring the mismanaged techniculture of hospitals on the right track.

We need to activate the following measures:

- Assigning due weightage to the BME in the management of technology in hospitals.
- An overriding priorly to the BME profession.
- Establishing a separate department of BME in all the hospitals.
- In big hospitals, establishing a training centre for BME professionals to enrich their knowledge bank.
- Fixing accountability for the poor management and faulty operation of biomedical equipment.
- Before installation of equipment, making it sure that efficient personnel is present to operate, repair and maintain the equipment you are going to install.
- A liaison with doctors and hospital managers so that the doctors get the benefits of new generation of equipments and apparatus for diagnosing and treating the patients.
- Promoting innovation in the development of biomedical equipments and motivating BME professionals in this endeavour.
- Keeping in view the depleted condition of government hospitals and the rural health centres, specially in the Indian perspective and developing a centre for biomedical equipment research and training.

The aforesaid measures would help hospitals in many ways. They would be in a position to take the benefits of technologies they have. In addition, they would also be encouraged to develop a craze for techniculture for the right diagnosis and treatment. To be more specific, the government hospitals need to think over the problem on a priorly basis because there we find mismanagement at a very large scale. It is really amazing that biomedical technicians working in the hospitals have been found playing a game in the very context. They deliberately develop faults so that the private diagnostic centres and hospitals get the business. For personal benefit, we find them playing with the interests of poorest segment of the society who find it difficult to afford the high fee structure adopted by the private centres, hospitals and so on. It is against this background that we feel the urgency of fixing accountability for the mismanagement and poor maintenance of biomedical equipment.

Management of Drugs

Proper management of drugs is found essential because the mismanagement in addition to the financial losses would also be dangerous if not rightly administered. The WHO documents focus on the problem of drug management in hospitals. Making productive use of drugs and regulating the waste of drugs are the important objectives of drug management and therefore, a material manager/ hospital manager needs to be careful that necessary steps are taken for the management of drugs. There are a number of factors[4] found instrumental in increasing the waste of drugs and some of them are the following:

Causes of Hospital Waste

A non-optimal use of drugs results into waste. We find cases where a number of drugs are administered on one patient when he/she requires an optimal dose. This results into waste and in addition to the side-effects, we also find non-availability of drugs for the needed patients.

Some of the doctors develop a craze for using expensive drugs when we find low cost drugs equally effective. This draws our attention on brand loyalty resulting into a waste, and an increase in the medicare costs.

"Just to try it" or "Trial and Error" method has been found common. A large number of drugs though not necessary for the patients are used by the doctors. This in addition to an increase in the cost of treatment is also to generate side-effects. It is really amazing that some of the doctors just to get commission from the dispensaries adopt such a practice which is to result into the waste of drugs, vis-a-vis over medication.

Disproportionate dose also results into a waste. We also find cases where the doctors administer a larger dose of drugs when even smaller dose would have been equally effective.

Providing drugs to those patients who don't use and throw them. Or, the patients not serious to the management of treatment avoid to use the drugs regularly resulting into the waste of drugs.

Over supply is also to result into a waste. We also find cases that just to get commission, the over supply of drugs is practised and we have no option but to throw them because of the expiry date.

Inadequate provisions for preserving the expensive and sensitive drugs also result into a waste. This is due to the fact that proper refrigeration or preservation facilities are not made available. Vaccines in a majority of the cases are no longer effective and we throw them.

Mismanagement of drugs is also found due to improper steps such as exposing drugs to sunlight or heat.

A non-optimal supply by the stores also results into a waste.

The aforesaid reasons generate huge financial losses and in addition also increase the costs on treatment. It is against this background that we make a strong advocacy in favour of a scientific management of drugs so that cases of waste are checked and financial losses to the hospitals are regulated. It is the prime responsibility of a material/stores/hospital manager to take due care of drugs so that the increasing cases of waste are checked.

Sensing Patients about Drugs

To be more specific in the Indian society where we find the rate of literacy low, it is the prime responsibility of a hospital manager to educate and sense the patients in a right fashion so that the increasing cases of overmedication are checked. It is really amazing that in the Indian society, a majority of us believe that taking more drugs and expensive drugs would solve their problems but in lieu of getting relief from the medicines, they face the problem of side effects and invite a number of serious health problems. This makes it essential that we educate and sense the masses and patients with creative slogans and messages so that they come to know about the side effects of wrong drugs or overmedication. It is against this background that we talk about innovating the promotional measures or revolutionising the process of healthcare communications. The following steps are to be effective in sensing the patients.

Narrating the Facts: At the very outset, it is the responsibility of doctors attending on the patients to explain to their attendants. Write on the prescription the required dose of medicines to be used by them. Let them know about the side effects of excess dose and overmedication. It is essential because in a number of cases we find patients and attendants believing in the principle of taking excess dose of medicines.

Explaining Facts in Catalogue: In the library of hospitals, we find catalogue detailing the list of medicines. It is considerably important that a hospital manager with the consultation of doctors explain the dose and duration to be followed by the patients. The facts should be mentioned in the catalogue and all the doctors should be made available the literature regarding the same so that they keep in their minds the details and explain the same to the patients while writing the prescriptions.

Displaying Signposts: For sensing the patients and attendants, it is also pertinent that some of the selected medicines often prescribed by the doctors should be mentioned in the signposts detailing the dose and duration besides the side effects. At different important places of the hospitals where patients and attendants assemble in a large number, the display of signposts would be instrumental in informing and sensing them. Since the hospital managers are supposed to know about creativity in messages and slogans, the task of sensitising the patients and attendants in a right fashion would be found easier.

Informative Packaging: In addition, the pharmaceutical industry also bears the responsibility of informing and sensing the patients and attendants with the help of detailed information regarding the dose, duration and the side effects. If the patients and attendants come to know about the details, there would be less scope for taking the excess dose.

Social Advertising to be Promoted: Besides the media, pharmaceutical industry, health department, social organisations and leading hospitals bear the responsibility of promoting social advertising. This would let the patients and attendants know about the side-effects and over-medication due to the excess dose of medicines. To be more specific in the Indian society, we find it essential because the masses are illiterate and they don't know about the harmful effects of taking excess dose and overmedication.

Explaining the Use of Drugs: It is pertinent that we explain to the patients the right way of using the medicines. Each drug has a particular effect in a particular condition and therefore, a drug taken by an individual will not help another. They should be made clear that the optimal dose of medicines plays an important role. If it is too little, the effects are very slow and if it is too high, the reactions and side effects can't be avoided. The dose for children is found different. They should be made it clear that regularity or continuity in treatment plays an effective role because it helps in maintaining the required dose of medicines in the body. We find treatment as a course and the patients need to complete the full course. If the course remains incomplete, the possibilities of relapse resulting into an even more dangerous condition can't be ruled out. The place for drugs should be out of the reach of the small children who may use it and the effects may be very dangerous.

Explaining the Importance of Life saving Drugs: While sensing the patients, it is also significant that we explain to them the importance of life saving drugs. In a few cases, we find the condition of patients so acute that immediate use of drugs is found essential since a delay in the use of drugs may result in irreparable losses. The materials and stores manager should be advised to keep the stock of life saving drugs. It is essential that they are made available a list of vital or the life saving drugs and should place them in a shelf. The shelf is required to be checked frequently.

The aforesaid facts make it clear that patients and attendants are required to be sensed in a right way so that effects of medicines help them in quick recovery, besides the side-effects are also checked. To be more specific in the Indian condition, we find it essential because the masses are illiterate and they don't know about the right or proper use of medicines. They believe that medicines are to be taken and a minor change in dose and duration carries no meaning for them whereas the realities are found something different. We find medicines essential but at the same time we can't negate the side effects to be more dangerous because the side effects are found resulting into even irreparable losses. We find frequent cases of overmedication specially at places where the patients are not conscious. Of course, this also requires proper education to the doctors who prescribe the medicines. The practices of trial and errors have been found resulting into hazardous side effects. The doctors in a few cases don't know about the importance of dose and duration. While educating and training, they should be made clear that side-effects and over-medication are more dangerous.

In the management of hospital, we find marketing of hospital services significant and while explaining the promotional measures, we have gone through the problem in detail. It is in this context that we talk about healthcare communications. Educating, informing and sensing the patients or even the masses are found important, specially in the Indian condition where the doctors take it very lightly. Proper instructions or guidelines to patients are found essential to counter the possibilities of the hazardous side effects. In a true sense, it is a major problem requiring due attention of almost all the segments. The doctors, the media, the social organisations and the red cross societies need to understand the importance of use of drugs or medicines to get the positive effects and remove the side effects.

Management of Inventory

The actual meaning of the word "inventory" focuses our attention on cataloguing the materials related to stores. It is a list or schedule of articles. Inventory is considered to be an ideal resource that possesses economic values. It is nothing but a stock of goods that we maintain to facilitate the continuous production of goods or services.[5] Like other organisations, the hospitals also need to manage inventory because a large number of materials are used by hospitals for which we find an independent Materials and Stores Department. It is the prime responsibility of a material manager that he/she in consultation with the hospital manager manages inventory in such a way that possibilities of misuse of materials are checked. In a majority of the government hospitals, we find mismanagement of inventory which has been very much instrumental in the waste, misuse, theft and pilferages resulting into the huge financial losses. The mismanagement of inventory increases the cost of healthcare services. In an age of information technology, it is easier to manage the inventory in a right fashion. A material manager with the support of computers would be successful in cataloguing the materials and proper documentation would be made regarding the issue of inventory to the persons and departments. The management of inventory thus paves the avenues for optimising the costs of medicare services besides making available materials to the patients which increase the quality of healthcare services. It is in this context that we need to go through the problem of management of inventory.

Inventory Control

It is in a true sense the objective of controlling the inventory that determines the suitability of a particular method as mentioned in Fig. 7.5. ABC, HML, VED, FSN, SDE, GOLF and SOS6 are the different methods of control. In a majority of the hospitals, we find ABC, i.e., Always Better Control, method generally preferred because we find it the simplest of all.

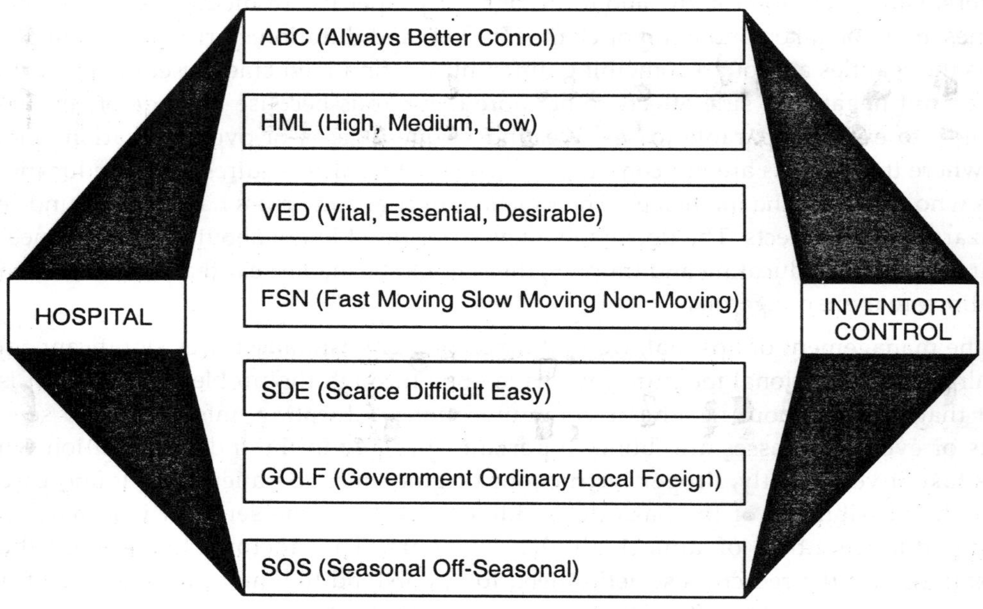

Fig. 7.5. Inventory Control Methods

ABC Method: This method of inventory control separates inventories into three letters A, B and C. To make possible ABC analysis, the list of all the items and their annual consumption in value is computed.

The ABC analysis makes it essential that a list of all the store items and their annual consumption in value is tabulated on the basis of records. We list separately each individual item and its annual consumption value and then the list is rearranged in a descending order beginning with the item of lowest value. After making such an analysis, it is found that the first 10 per cent of the items (A) approximately accounts for 70-80 per cent of the value, next 20 per cent of items (B) accounts for 20-25 per cent and the last (C) accounts for just 5-10 per cent. We agree with this view that the ABC analysis helps hospitals in maintaining economy because our focus is found on A & B items. The following processes are followed in this regard:

- At the outset, a list is prepared of the different items and their annual usage in terms of money (rupees) is calculated. For this, we multiply the quantity (number of units) of the items consumed in one year by its unit price.

• Thereafter, we arrange all these items in the descending order. This is meant that the first item in the list will show the maximum annual usage in rupees, the second item, the second maximum and like this, the last would be the third item. After this, we put the total of annual usage in rupees at the bottom of the list.

• The items covering 70 per cent of the total annual usage may be categorised as A items. Similarly would be items contributing 20-25 per cent would be as B items and the rest would be C items.

• Based on this classification, we place the orders.

The aforesaid classification makes it clear that A class inventories are very few and they involve high cost and therefore, we need scientific techniques to control quantity and re-order time. It is essential that a detailed record of receipts, issues, availability and usage are maintained for these inventories. The B class items need relatively less close control. The order quantity and the reordering points for B items would be determined on the basis of past trends in their usage. We need to maintain detailed records as found in A. It is also essential that a periodic review is made. The C class items are the "trivial many" as they constitute 70 per cent of the total inventory and they don't need close control.

The facts mentioned above make it clear that ABC analysis requires selective control. It is estimated that in the Indian context, we spend around Rs. 1,000 crores annually on the medical supplies. The latest figure is found even more than that. Since the control makes possible economy, even we find hospitals saving 5 per cent and the total savings in monetary terms would amount to several crores of rupees. The material economy thus makes it possible for the hospitals to determine the optimal level of inventory. This makes it essential that almost all the hospitals assign due weightage to the control of inventory because this would enable them to make possible a productive use of inventory. In Fig. 7.6, we find graphic approach to ABC analysis.

- Category A : Maximum or the highest velocity or speed of usage (Expensive)
- Category B : Average velocity or speed of usage (less Expensive)
- Category C : Low velocity or speed of usage (Economic)

It is upon a material manager that he/she in consultation with the departmental heads and the hospital manager comes to know about the instrumentality of different items.

In the graph presented in Fig. 7.6, the A items account for 10 per cent but on the basis of value, the percentage of A items is 60. This makes it clear that a material manager needs to assign due weightage to A category of items. The B category of items account for 30 per cent and therefore, relatively we find less attention on the items in this group. Even on the basis of value, we find its percentage 30. The C category of items account for 60 per cent but on the basis of value, it is only 10 per cent and therefore, we find a material manager not assigning so much significance accordingly so that even if we find something wrong with the management of material, it is not to result into a huge financial loss. It is quite natural that a material manager assigns much more significance to the A category of items because the items in the category are found very expensive and therefore, even a minor mistake is to result into a big financial loss.

Like other organisations, even in hospitals, we don't find all the materials used in the process very expensive or less expensive. Of course, we also find items of economic nature and therefore, it is essential that a material manager on the basis of ABC analysis comes to know about the velocity or speed of usage. On the basis of ABC analysis, he/she would be in a position to understand the weekly or fortnightly requirements of different items and orders can be placed

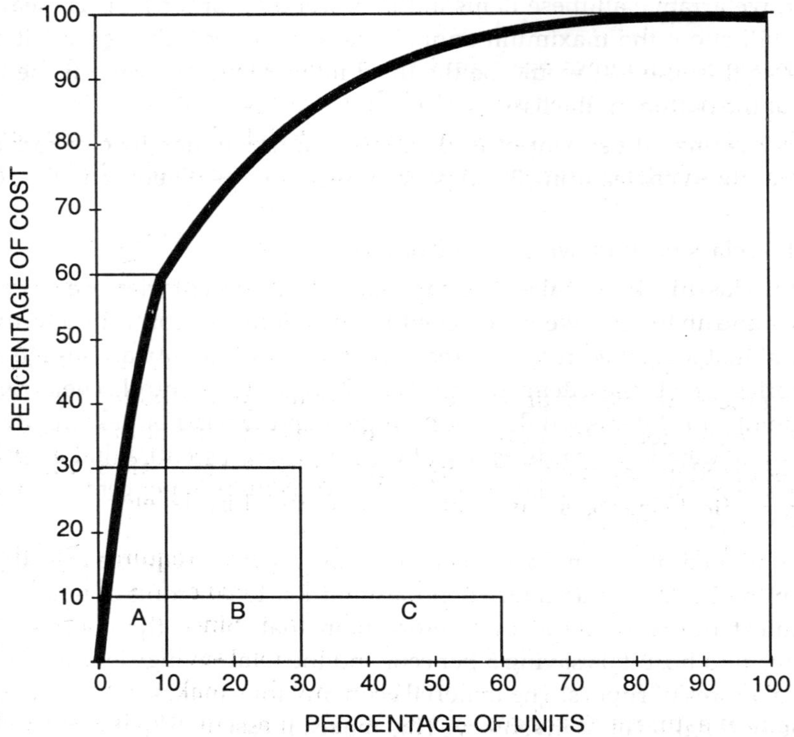

Fig. 7.6. Graphic Approach to ABC Analysis

accordingly. Without ABC analysis, the ordering policy of a hospital would be to order all items once a quarter and position would be a bit different.

The aforesaid facts make it clear that ABC analysis[7] can be used as a guide for economising the purchase processes and controlling the stores by concentrating attention on A & B items having high velocity and relatevely less attention on C category of items having less velocity. The ABC concept tries to isolate the vital few so that the bulk of resources be devoted to control this. Separating inventories is found instrumental in having a better control. Thus, we find ABC analysis an important method of controlling the inventories. At the same time, it is also right to mention that to be more specific in the healthcare sector, we also find some of the items though very cheap but assuming high significance with the viewpoint of the urgency and quality of treatment.

Import Formalities for Medical Equipment

Medical practice in the 21st century would be fantastically different from what we witnessed in the 20th century. One indication of the shape of things to come is the fruitful marriage of medicine and information technology. Romantics in the 1950s thought that very soon a day would come when computers would solve all diagnostic problems and the physicians would outlive their instrumentality in the process. And of late, we find things moving in the same direction. The union of the two frontline areas in modern technology, viz., computational power and molecular genetics are found showing a number of wonders. Use of robots in surgery is another area which is still the realm of experiment but very soon we expect its application. Artificial intelligence programmes are found instrumentalising the diagnostic measures and treatment devices. Lasers have come into use to help the surgeon cut and shape defective tissues with the perfection of laser surgery. Newer synthetic materials are being discovered which may he helpful in creating artificial organs and part of organs. Intraocular lenses, cardiac valves, vessel graft and joint parts made of artificial material are found subserving the interests of human beings. New drug delivery systems where a drug molecule can be delivered with precision to the exact anatomical spot are to come true. And a number of developments right now in pipe line are likely to transform the myths of 20th century into the realities.

The aforesaid facts make it clear that the face and shape of healthcare services are fast changing and the process would continue even in the coming years. In the Indian perspective, the masses need due cooperation of the health sector because they are not in a position to afford the expensive services based on sophisticated biomedical equipment and information technology. Till now, the Indian medical scientists have not been successful in developing advanced medical technologies of their own and the government exchequer finds it difficult to import advanced or new generation of equipment, apparatus, instruments or so to deliver goods to the society. Of course, we find a few of the private hospitals and healthcare organisations interested in getting the new generation of technologies but so far as the government hospitals are concerned, we find a very gloomy picture. It is really amazing and painful that even if they manage to get the expensive biomedical equipment, the management and maintenance are found so poor that the masses fail in getting the benefits. This makes it essential that the government policy makers promote private sector for improving the quality of healthcare services even if by importing and borrowing the technologies they need. Of course, the second stage would be to motivate the medical scientists to develop technologies of their own by developing expertise and excellence with the support of information superhighway and other qualitative developments. It is against this background that a hospital manager is supposed to be aware of the import formalities so that they equip their healthcare centres in the face of latest developments in the medical sciences.

The Imports (Control) Order 1955, issued by the Central Government in exercise of the power conferred on it by the Imports and Exports (Control) Act, 1947 prohibits the import of any goods, except under and in accordance with a licence of a customs permit granted by the Central Government or by any officer specified. However, with the liberalisation of foreign trade regulations, the process is now made easier and motivational if the healthcare organisations appear interested.

The most important thing in this context focuses on the non-availability of the same quality of equipment in the domestic market. Despite of a number of concessions and reliefs, it is pertinent that the hospitals and healthcare organisations are given more incentives while importing medical technologies from abroad. It is in this context that we find it essential that a hospital manager is well aware of the formalities to be completed. The following facts would help a healthcare manager in importing the technologies from abroad to improve the quality of health care services.

Licensing: Of course, we find the foreign trade regulations more liberal. However, a hospital manager is required to be aware of the fact that an application for a licence is to be submitted in the prescribed form.

Completing the Application From: It is to be made sure that all the columns have been filled neatly and accurately as per the instructions. Your statements are to be substantiated by the supporting papers.

Application Fee: The original bank receipt and bank draft showing the payment of the application fee of the value applied for should be attached to the application form.

Supporting Documents: All the supporting documents are to be attached and all the enclosures are to be detailed in the covering letter of the application, furnishing particulars of each document found essential.

Signature: The application form is required to be signed by an authorised person mentioning his/her address and position held by him/her.

Mailing Address: The mailing address of the applicant should be given in complete form mentioning the address, telephone number, fax number, e-mail and so on.

Posting: The application form complete in all respects should be sent by post to the appropriate licensing authority or as per the provision or delivered at the counter of the office of the licensing authority or sponsoring authority.

Code Number: If any code number is allotted, it is to be quoted. If no code number has been allotted, the word "not allotted" should be mentioned.

A Consolidated Application: The actual users need to submit a consolidated application covering the requirements of the unit in respect of raw materials and components for each end-product.

Furnishing the List: While furnishing the list of materials/items to be imported, the applicants require to ensure that the lists are prepared on a good and durable paper to avoid inconveniences at the time of custom clearance of the goods.

Be Sure: While getting the licence, it is essential that the licensee checks everything and makes it confirmed that each page of the list has been duly signed by the licensing authority, the seal is properly affixed, the changes have been duly attested, the conditions mentioned are duly signed by the licensing authority and every signature of the licensing authority appearing on the licence or on the list attached to the licence or on the conditions attached to the licence has been duly authenticated by a security seal affixed above the signature.

The aforesaid formalities are found essential but the policy makers need to simplify the process so that the healthcare organisations and hospitals are motivated and the hospitals are found well-equipped to offer the world class services to the patients.

Production and Quality Control of Drugs

Provisions of appropriate drugs of good quality at affordable cost is essential for the success of disease control programme. Equally important is to restrict, eliminate the use of irrational drug formulation, and detect and eliminate spurious drugs. The Central Government is found responsible for the control over the quality of imported drugs, control over the manufacture of and import of new drugs into the country, amendments to the Drugs and Cosmetics (D&A) Act and Rules. The need of the country for essential drugs are still not fully met. Patent laws do not cover 95 per cent of the essential drugs. It is high time that we explore the possibilities of providing a dual pricing system for generic and brand drugs with the motto of making available the essential drugs to the masses at an affordable price. The supply of essential drugs, vaccine/devices hold the key to any disease control programme. The funds for drugs used for different categories of healthcare centres come partly from the State Funds and partly from the Central Fund. This is found aggravating the problem since we find variation in procurement and distribution. The inefficient indenting procedures adversely affect the process of drug procurement.

Poor inventory management results into unsatisfactory drug procurement and distribution. This gravitates our attention on a priority basis. It is high time that the policy makers assign due weightage to the procurement and inventory control and distribution of drugs at state and central levels. Based on the pattern of Tamil Nadu, it is essential that other states of the country also think in favour of establishing a Medical Services Corporation. A list of essential drugs is to be prepared and the purchase process and storage of drugs need to be made scientific. We need effective inventory control specially in the government hospitals.

In addition to other aspects, it is also pertinent that provisions of the Drugs and Cosmetic Acts assign due weightage to the regulations controlling the spurious drugs. We can't deny the fact that a number of fake pharmaceutical industries have been found manufacturing the spurious drugs—the large sized customers such as hospitals and healthcare organisations become the customers of such spurious drug manufacturing industries. This very often draws our attention on the provisions of D&C Act.

In order to take up drug pricing, quality, clinical trials, etc., as recommended by the Mashelkar Committee (2003) and NCMH (2005), a National Drug Authority (NDA) with an autonomous status was required to be set up and accordingly, we find Central Drugs Authority if India functioning with the motto of improving quality and regulating price. The NDA has been emerging as an important regulatory authority accepting all the responsibilities of National Pharmaceutical Pricing Authority created under the aegis of Ministry of Chemicals and Fertilizers. The National Policy Makers are supposed to perform and serve in the larger interests of weaker sections of the society who find themselves not in a position to afford the expensive drugs. The Central Government is required to provide assistance to States for strengthening the drug regulatory system. They need to prepare essential drug lists for all levels of institutions and to ensure availability of essential drugs of food quality in adequate quantities in all government health facilities. They are supposed to increase efficiency, economy and transparency in drug procurement, warehousing and distribution. Ensuring safe drugs and rational use of drugs are considered essential. It is also significant that information on essential drugs to the medical professionals, pharmacists and to the people are disseminated. The concept of Standard Treatment Guidelines in the service and preservice training programmes of the doctors and health workers is required to be implemented.

In the context of essential drug supply, we may quote Tamil Nadu experience. All the state governments are required to encourage the model practised by Tamil Nadu Medical Services Corporation which would make possible availability of drugs to hospitals at cheaper rates. In Exhibit 7.1, we find the Model.[8]

Exhibit 7.1

Essential Drug Supply-Tamil Nadu Experience

Activities

Finalising list of Essential Drugs selected from the model list by the WHO.

Ensuring adequate funds and human resources for supply of drugs from its warehouse to various points of healthcare delivery.

Testing drugs for quality.

Supplying drugs only in strips and blister packing.

Selecting drugs on the basis of disease pattern, safety, effectiveness and cost.

Including only generic drugs.

Making proper arrangements for storage of drugs in modern warehouses.

Training the pharmacists regarding storage and distribution of drugs.

Revising store keeping procedures and storing drugs according to the first come first out basis and generic name.

Achievements

Preparation of the Essential Drugs list catering to various needs of different levels of healthcare. Provision of good quality, generic drugs. Provision of drugs specific to the need and level of healthcare. Rational use of drugs. Availability of accurate up to date stock in information on the computer linkage of all warehouse telephonically with the TNMSC headquarters in Chennai.

Source: Eleventh Five Year Plan Vol. II Page 77

In view of the increasing intensity of problem, it is essential that we concentrate on creating mass awareness. The illiterate masses find it difficult to protect themselves from the harmful effects of spurious drugs. We make much more advocacy in favour of controlling the quality of drugs because failing the same, the doctors would find it difficult to cure the patients. Of course, diagnostic measures and the professional excellence of doctors are found impact generating but failing the availability of standard quality of drugs, they would find it difficult to prove their excellence. It is against this background that we need to assign an overriding priority to quality control and inventory management. We can't negate the fact that sophisticated information technology would be helpful in making the inventory management more scientific. For the preservation of drugs in a right fashion, we also realise the significance of making the storage system more scientific. Despite of a number of constraints in the process, it is to be made sure that the patients and hospitals are supplied standard quality of drugs.

Ensuring quality and bringing in accountability in healthcare provided is of utmost importance. Development and utilisation of appropriate technologies for diagnosis and management of patients at primary, secondary and tertiary care centres is an essential prerequisite for quality in totality. Realising the significance of quality supportive and diagnostic services, a separate working group was constituted. The Committee made several recommendations to improve the quality of inputs or materials used in the process of generating the healthcare services. A national mechanism for total quality appraisal of new technologies would serve the desired purpose of making the technologies result oriented. This requires concerted efforts in different areas for the development and testing of appropriate technologies found inexpensive. This draws our attention on the following:

- Measuring weight and height to facilitate early detection of undernutrition in adults and children.
- Colourimeters for biochemical tests to improve diagnostic facilities at the Public Health Centres.
- Accurate self-recording instruments for measuring arterial blood pressure for use by ANMs/male multipurpose workers.
- Hand-held electronic data entry machines for ANM/MMPW to enable record maintenance and updating the Health and Family Welfare Programmes.

The aforesaid facts make it clear that in the medical sciences, the modern technologies, or equipment, instruments, apparatus and machines are going to play a commanding role for improving the quality of healthcare services. The diagnostic and treatment devices are to be changed and to be made result-oriented. Of course, the small hospitals would find it difficult to have the support of expensive biomedical equipments but if the big hospitals develop a network, the task of even small hospitals would considerably be simplified. This necessitates a close link between the primary, secondary and tertiary hospitals. This requires a sense of cooperation and coordination among the private and government hospitals.

Since we talk about quality in totality, it is pertinent that hospitals and health care organisations assign due weightage to the management of quality hospital materials and inventory. Unless we have quality inputs, we can't think about quality outputs. We talk about quality drugs, we talk about quality biomedical equipment, we talk about quality management of materials and these things simplify the process of generating and maintaining quality in totality. It is in this context that we find quality drugs and quality equipment playing an important role in the process of total quality management. Of late, the government hospitals in particular need to assign due weightage to the management of drugs and equipments because we find a large number of cases of mismanagement in the process of managing the quality. It is not only sufficient that government hospitals are made available quality drugs and quality equipment and apparatus because we also find cases of mismanagement in the process of maintaining them. This makes it essential that they are made available quality technicians and engineers and more so develop techniculture to ensure the best use of biomedical equipments.

Of course, a number of steps have been taken to regulate the spurious drugs. However, we find frequent cases of manufacturing and marketing the spurious drugs which aggravate the magnitude of problem. Drugs and medicines form a substantial portion of the out-of-pocket spending on health by households. The weaker sections of the society are found to be the worst sufferers. More so, due to illiteracy and awareness, we find them frequently affected by diseases and are least able to purchase and utilise the health services such as drugs. Timely supply of drugs of good quality that involves procurement as well as logistics management is of critical importance in any health system. Increasing accessibility to essential drugs and medicines is a crying need of the hour.

The National Drug Authority is supposed to play a dominating role. In the Indian perspective, we find Central Drug Authority of India having an autonomous status. Keeping in view the increasing cases of spurious drugs and rising prices of drugs and medicines, the NDA would also have to play a commanding role in regulating the price. The state governments with the support of central government are required to strengthen the drug regulatory system. On the one hand, the NDA requires to make the drugs and medicines accessible to the masses while on the other hand, they are also required to promote AYUSH. Standardisation and quality control are the two important dimensions to make the AYUSH medicines accessible and affordable albeit to the weaker sections of the society. Standardisation and Quality Control of Ayurveda, Siddha, Unani and Homoeopathy Drugs:

Standardisation and Quality Control of Ayurveda, Siddha, Unani and Homeopathy Drugs

Evolving uniform standards in preparation of drugs of ASU&H and prescribing working standards for single drug as well as compound formulations are the objectives of four different Pharmacopoeia Committees. These committees have published standards for around 40% of the raw materials and around 15% of formulations, Drug Control Cell (AYUSH) is working in the Department of AYUSH to deal with the matters pertaining to licensing and regulation of Ayurvedic, Unani and Siddha drugs. We expect a lot from the Central Drug Authority for centralized licensing and enforcement of provisions of Drugs and Cosmetics Act and Rules in ensuring quality and safety of ASU&H drugs. The department of AYUSH intends to convert Pharmacopoeial Committees of various systems into modern pharmacopoeial commission with adequate representation of stakeholders and to develop standards in line with internationally acceptable pharamcopoeial standards and quality parameters of ASU&H drugs.

The Central Government has established research councils for Ayurveda and Siddha known as CCRAS for Unani CCRUM, for Homoeopathy, HCCRH and for Yoga and Naturopathy, CCYN. These councils have been carrying out a wide range of research activities. Department of AYUSH has also been administering an Extramural Research Scheme supporting project-based research studies form accredited scientific and medical institutions. The resource base of AYUSH is largely plants. Around 6000 species of medicinal plants are documented in published medical and ethno-botanical literature. The infrastructure and capacities of AYUSH research councils require upgradation to enable them to carry out state-of-the art scientific work related to drug standardization and quality control, botanical standardisation, laying down of pharmacopoeial standards and clinical trials.

In the Eleventh Five Year Plan,[9] the regulatory mechanism is strengthened for ensuring safety, control and efficacy of AYUSH medicines as a priority area. Strengthening the enforcement of Drugs and Cosmetics Act in the country with regard to Ayurveda, Siddha, Unani and Homoeopathy manufacturing units to create public confidence in India and abroad need priority attention.

Golden Triangle Research partnership initiated by the Department of AYUSH with the collaboration of CCRAS, ICMR and CSIR aimed at scientific validation and development of R&D based drugs as well as development of herbal drugs based on traditional medicinal knowledge for prioritised disease conditions may bring qualitative improvements.

Strengthening of AYUSH dispensaries, hospitals and supply of AYUSH medicinal kits in the rural areas and development of AYUSH treatment centres under PPP mode are required to benefit the rural segments of society. Drug Quality Control is an important issue so that we find masses developing a sense of confidence.

Professional and Ethical Dimensions in the Management of Stores :

There have been significant developments in the field of technology which has virtually changed the way of managing materials and stores. In a true sense, e-filing, accounting and controlling measures are found defining and redefining quality where computer professionals pay a dominating role. The concept of e-governance has simplified the task of a material manager. Estimating the requirements, establishing contacts with number one suppliers, getting the materials and storing them properly, issuing materials and managing inventories are some of the key issues requiring due focus on professional as well as ethical dimensions. Since we find increasing cases of unfair practices, it is pertinent that hospital managers also consider honesty as an essential property for the people working as manger for stores.

Being a material and stores manager, you bear the responsibility of making available to the different departments and sections, the materials/items they need to discharge their functional responsibilities. You are supposed to bridge the gap between demand and supply. You are required to be punctual. You need to work with the motto of making the process of the management of stores cost-effective. You need to minimise the cases of waste. This makes it essential that you are professionally sound and are well aware of the demand-side of different departments. Professional excellence makes you sound enough to realise and perceive the functional responsibilities in a right fashion. In a majority of the government hospitals, we find stores presenting a very gloomy picture and showing the disappointing results. In a number of cases, we find them a source for value-degeneration. The irregularities, frauds and wastes are found common in almost all the stores of hospitals. This makes it essential that we gravitate our attention on some of the sensitive issues helping materials and stores manager to make positive contributions to activate the process of qualitative transformation. If doctors, paramedical and nursing staff fail in getting the required materials on time, the quality of medicare services can't be improved. It is against this background that we go through some of the key issues making possible a positive change in the management of stores.

We are well aware of the fact that different types of materials are used in hospitals and keeping in view the nature and character of items, you need to store them properly so that within the minimum possible time you make available the required items to the concerned hospital personnel and the departments. Some of the items are found very expensive, some of the items are less expensive, some of the items are perishable, some of the items are very sensitive to the atmosphere, some of the items need more space and some of the items are very sophisticated requiring minimum space but maximum care. It is the responsibility of hospital planners, hospital architects, hospital consultants and hospital managers that they while designing and constructing hospital stores keep in their minds all the requirements so that the task of a material and stores manager is made easier. Of course, we find cataloguing, indexing, management of inventory occupying a place of outstanding significance but it is not the only thing that we need to improve the quality of services. In addition, the material managers are required to be value-based, honest, sincere and professionally sound so that they realise gravity of the situation and never fail in making available to the hospital personnel the materials they need, specially in an emergency case. Of late with the development of information technology, your task is simplified considerably but the most important thing that we find in the process of managing stores is value-orientation. Knowing well the facts that the drugs and medicines supplied to you, the vaccines made available to you, the instruments and equipment stored are not of quality; you are not sensitised. The increasing insensitivity is a big problem and this necessitates an attitudinal change.

We talk about he professional commitments because this would let you know not only the skill and expertise for managing stores efficiently but would also make you aware of the ethical dimensions, professional and personal commitments, value-orientation or so. Even if you are professionally sound and you lack personal commitments, you need to confess it. Unless you confess, the mistakes can't be corrected. And unless the mistakes are not corrected, the blunders are but natural.

In a majority of the stores, specially in the government hospitals, we find the cases very alarming. The materials are available but only for a few selected segments, the waste of material is very common, expensive instruments and equipment are found thrown like waste materials, the drugs and medicines are of poor quality, the food and beverages are not stored properly or so. We can't negate that they don't understand the significance of scientific storage and fail in making suitable arrangements for storage. On the one hand, we find the hospitals facing the problem of financial crunch and on the other hand, we find waste of even the expensive items. It is against this background that we make a strong advocacy in favour of a professionally sound and personally committed material and stores manager. Of course, we find the situation a bit improved, specially in the private hospitals because they are serious to the mismanagement of finance and the losses of materials result into a capital loss.

The aforesaid facts make it clear that the hospital managers and to be more specific a material and stores manager needs to realise the gravity of the situation and to make sincere efforts to bring the derailed systems on the rail. The personnel managing materials and stores are required to be professionally sound. This makes it essential that they know about the specific requirements to store and preserve different types of materials in a scientific way so that the cases of waste are regulated. They are required to be punctual because this would make possible time management and the concerned departments and the personnel would get the required materials on time. They are required to be value-based so that the cases of irregularities are checked. Besides, they are also supposed to be human so that the cases of indiscrimination are checked. They need an indepth knowledge of information and communications technologies so that the task of proper cataloguing and indexing, information related to the suppliers and quality of materials are found procured and the decisions are taken accordingly. They need to keep their eyes all the time open so that even the low echelons of staff inside the management of stores are not to promote the unfair practices.

The quality of services offered by hospitals cannot be improved unless the materials and stores department is managed in a right fashion. The availability of improved quality of materials makes possible an improvement in the quality of medicare services. Because we talk about quality in totality, it is pertinent that in addition to other aspects, we also consider the management of materials and stores by a proffessionally-sound, value-based and personally-committed manager. The quality and punctuality are the essential dimensions and for that the materials and stores manager requires to be sincere while making use of technology for this purpose.

The government hospitals in particular need due care because we find there unfair practices in the management of materials and stores. The boardrooms, top-level executives, manager materials and stores bear the joint responsibility of regulating the unfair practices. The doctors also need to involve themselves in the process because their excellence and expertise become unproductive if they do not get the quality materials on time. It is not only related with the quality of medicare services but we find its impact even on the image of hospitals and doctors. Hence, it is significant that management of materials and stores gets priority attention of hospital managers.

In the management process, we expect positive contributions of Health Management Information System. Wastage of drugs due to expiry of date also needs to be curtailed by demand-driven management and redistribution of medicines nearing date of expiry. HMIS will be successful in tracking demand and supply and monitoring the drug situation. The penetration of computerization appears to be essential to get the best results from the management of materials an stores. It is also significant to mention that some of the medicines are found very expensive and therefore, we need proper care so that there is nothing wrong with the quality. Scientific storage and warehousing, specially for the expensive and perishable items need due care. The HMIS will be successful in improving the reporting system which will clarify the demand and supply position,

In view of the above mentioned facts, it is right to say that management of materials and stores requires to be well supported by new generation of information and communication technology. All the categories of hospitals viz. primary, secondary and tertiary need due attention on the techno-driven management of materials and stores. The scenario that we find in the government hospitals or also in a majority of the private hospitals cannot be considered to be up to the mark.

SUMMARY

In this chapter, you have gone through different dimensions of materials and stores. After going through the chapter, be sure that the following facts are well versed.

Materials Management—the Perception: By materials management, our focus is on planning, estimating the requirements, placing order, developing rapport with the suppliers and manufacturers, procuring the materials and making it sure that the materials supplied to them are as per the standards and specifications.

Materials Management in Hospitals: In hospitals, a large number of materials are used. Some of the items are expensive whereas some other items though not expensive but very sensitive to the atmospheric conditions. This necessitates sound materials management promoted by an efficient material manager. It is a managerial device to make the demand and supply position optimal.

Essential Principles for Managing Hospitals: While managing materials, a material manager requires to go through a number of factors. He/she requires to make it sure that required quantity of materials are supplied, the price structure is moderate, a number of alternatives are listed, delivery is made on time and more so, the quality is as per the specification.

Objectives of Materials Management: With diverse objectives and motives, we manage hospital materials. The different underlying principles are right price, low procurement and storage cost, continuity of supply, consistency in quality, high turnover, development of personnel, good relationship with the suppliers and good information system. The secondary objectives are maintaining friendly relationship with the suppliers, getting new quality of materials, product innovation, departmental harmony, forecasting and standardisation.

Process of Materials Management: The different processes for material management are determining the categories, ensuring timely supply, procuring the materials as per the specifications, ensuring sound storage, developing an effective control mechanism, effective distribution at the point of usage, ensuring plugging of loopholes, employing suitable personnel and performance-orientation.

Management of Equipment: The management of equipment happens to be an important component of materials management. This draws our attention on ordering equipment, storing equipment, issuing equipment, controlling and maintaining equipment, coding and standardisation.

Management of Drugs: The management of drugs occupies a place of outstanding significance because we find drugs very sensitive to the changing atmosphere. The hospitals suffer a lot on account of poor management of drugs and medicines and this makes it essential that causes responsible for the waste are taken care.

Sensing Patients about Drugs: This is related to creative healthcare education. To be more specific in the Indian society, we find this dimension of management significant because the masses are illiterate and therefore, not aware of the care and precautions while taking medicines. The creative promotional measures need due attention of materials and hospital managers.

Management of Inventory: This problem draws our attention on cataloguing and indexing of materials to make the process of managing materials and stores effective. ABC, HML, VED, FSN, SDE, GOLF and SOS are the different methods but we find ABC the simplest one.

Production and Quality Control of Drugs: The Central Drug Authority of India is found responsible for regulating the Drugs & Cosmetics. Improving quality and regulating price are the two important motives. For evolving uniform standards in ASU & H, we find Drug Control Cell.

Professional and Ethical Dimensions in the Management of Stores: In hospitals, we find stores a vulnerable place for the development of unfair practices and therefore, a manager materials and stores must be honest. Since it is to affect the quality of services in hospitals, it is pertinent that a manager is professionally sound. It is important to mention that a techno-driven information system may be helpful in regulating the management of materials and stores.

KEY TERMS

INPUT	ABC
Output	HML
Drugs	VED
Linen	GOLF
Surgical Equipments	SOS
Computer-based Inventory	SDE
Bio-medical Equipment	Standardisation
Perfusion Materials	Therapy
Oxygen	Oscilloscope
Artificial Limbs	Valve Tester
Anaesthesia Equipment	Megger
Glassware	Avometer
Beverages	FSN
Medicines	Intraocular Lenses
Lasers	Vessel Graft

REVIEW QUESTIONS

1. What do you mean by Management of Materials? Focus on the management of materials in hospitals.
2. Explain the underlying principles for managing hospital materials.
3. Discuss the different objectives of materials management in hospitals.
4. Throw light on the different processes for managing materials in hospitals.
5. Explain the management of equipment and drugs in hospitals.
6. Explain the precautions you need to adopt while managing drugs and medicines.
7. Explain creative measures to sensitise the illiterate and unaware segments of society to make them aware of the uses of drugs and medicines.
8. What do you mean by Management of Inventory? Explain the instrumentality of ABC analysis as an important method for the management of inventory in hospitals.
9. Explain the Standardisation and Control of Drugs in the Indian perspective.
10. Throw light on the professional and ethical dimensions for the management of stores and materials in hospitals.
11. Explain the standardisation and control of ASUH drugs in the Indian Perspective.

APPLICATION EXERCISES

1. The rural masses in India lack drug awareness. As a hospital professional, focus on the creative measures you will initiate to sense and sensitise them.
2. Do you find management of equipments and drugs requiring due attention of a material manager? Defend your arguments.
3. "Drugs and medicines found sensitive to the atmospheric condition need suitable storage facility." In the light of this statement, explain the precautions you need to adopt while managing drugs and medicines.
4. As a hospital professional, focus on the instrumentality of ABC analysis for the management of inventory in hospitals.
5. "The management of materials and stores requires professionally and ethically sound managers." Comment on this statement in the Indian perspective.
6. In the capacity of a hospital manager, throw light on the standardization and control of drugs and medicines in the Indian Perspective.
7. Do you find standardisation and control of ASUH drugs essential to benefit the rural masses? Justify your opinion in the Indian perspective.

END NOTES

1. Ashok Sahani, *Hospital and Health Administration*, ISHA Professional Development Series I, ICHA Bangalore, 1988, p.46.
2. Goel, S. L., *Material Management with Special Reference to Equipment and Drugs*, pp. 233-63.
3. N. M. Murali, *Bio-Medical Equipment: Maintenance Management Programme*, pp. 195-201.
4. Goel, S. L., *op. cit.*
5. Joseph G. Monks, *Operations Management: Theory and Practice*, p. 325.
6. Goel, S. L., *op. cit.*
7. Dave, N. V., *Hospital Management*, pp. 78-80.
8. *Eleventh Five Year Plan*: Planning Commission, Government of India, New Delhi, Vol. II p. 7-11.
9. *Ibid* p. 114.

Management of Hospital Services

Quality if superior, rewards you and quality if inferior, punishes you. This focuses on defining and redefining healthcare and medicare services so that services delivered are affordable and accessible albeit to the weaker sections of the society.

CHAPTER OBJECTIVES

Introduction—Hospital Product: the Perception—Types of Hospital Product—Line Services—Supportive Services—Auxiliary Services—Peripheral Services—Medical Education—Medical Training—Medical Research—Planning for Hospital Services—Life Cycle of Hospital Product—Innovation Diffusion and Adoption—New Product Development Dilemma—Managerial Proficiency for the Key Medical Services—Innovative Product Profile—Promoting e—Health—Policies Influencing Hospital Product—Summary—Key Terms—Review Questions—Application Exercises—End Notes.

LEARNING OBJECTIVES

This chapter aims at studying the different types of hospital services considered as hospital products. The readers develop their awareness of the role of hospital managers in improving the quality of services. With the changing disease profile and increasing sophistication in information and communication technology, we find opportunities for defining and redefining hospital services. The motive of this chapter is to sensitise the readers to the instrumentality of healthcare services in improving the quality and minimising the costs so that quality services are affordable and accessible even to the weaker sections of the society.

Introduction

Quality if superior, rewards you and quality if inferior, punishes you. The goods manufactured by you or services generated by you get a positive response, if you keep on moving the process of defining and redefining quality. We are aware that during yester decades, there have been multi-dimensional developments in the medical sciences which have opened new vistas for qualitative transformation. Today, we find the healthcare services in an advanced form. Credit goes to the medical scientists who have innovated the medicare services. The process of technological sophistication has been efficacious in making the process of diagnosis and treatment much more innovative and result-oriented. New generation of equipments, instruments, information and communication technology have enriched the potentials of hospitals of modern age. The medical and paramedical staff today find themselves potentially sound and make available to the users quality medicare services. This has made possible a significant increase in the levels of expectations of users. It is in this context that service quality assumes a place of outstanding significance in the hospitals and healthcare organisations.

The modern hospitals provide a number of core, peripheral and supportive services. A number of services are found technology-based and therefore, the hospitals not well equipped find it difficult to maintain quality. In a true sense, quality inputs make the ways for quality outputs. If hospitals make use of quality inputs, the cost on providing medicate services are found high and resulting from which the services become unaffordable to general masses. This makes a strong advocacy in favour of devising low-cost technology which helps in minimising the costs. Low cost and indigenous technologies for diagnosis and treatment would serve and subserve the larger interests of weaker sections of the society. It is of prime importance to find technological solutions for making crucial equipments, defibrillator, ventilator, electrocardiogram, blood pressure monitoring equipment, pulse oxymeter, etc.

For improving the quality of healthcare services, it is also pertinent that our scientists explore avenues for low-cost drugs and medicines. On the one hand, they have to take the benefits of allopathic medicines while on the other hand, they have also to promote the use of AYUSH which would be economic and specially for the segments found poor, illiterate and insensitive residing in the rural areas. Standardisation and control need due attention of Central Drug Authority of India to regulate the spurious and substandard drugs and medicines.

The most important thing for value addition and quality upgradation focuses our attention on the quality of medical, paramedical and managerial staff. The staff working in different categories need personal-touch-in service. They need not only professional excellence but in addition, they also require professional ethics. They need not only sympathy but even empathy. They are required to be behaviourally sound. This makes it essential that medical colleges and institutes while educating and training people make it sure that all the properties required for medical and paramedical staff have been inculcated and cultivated. We find human-touch-in-service also essential for the medical profession.

The medicare and healthcare services are the result of a team operation where not an individual but (a term is involved with) the team spirit and team culture can be possible if we find humanised and professionalised leadership. Right treatment depends on right diagnosis which makes it essential that medical and paramedical staff and additionally the managerial staff have been cooperating each other at each and every stage. The quality of core services requires top priority because in the medical services, the users do not mind the peripheral services if they realise that they have been getting the best quality of medical aid.

Additionally, our focus may be on the peripheral services which make their stay in the hospitals comfortable, convenient and safe. The civic amenities and facilities, the availability of safe drinking water, lodging arrangements for the attendants, transportation facilities, entertainment facilities, banking services, communication services, shopping facilities, catering services, etc. are some of the peripheral services which bring in the mix of services additional attractions and uniqueness. Hence, the hospital professionals need to improve the quality of peripheral services so that they are in a position to project their positive image.

Since we have potentials to compete, it is pertinent that the health care sector also assigns due weightage to the development of surroundings and premises. Developing India as a healthcare brand makes it essential that our hospitals have a sound ambience found instrumental in offering an opportunity to the users to have new experiences. The hospital planners, designers, architects need to make provision for the same at the initial stage so that hospitals prove to be a centre for quick recovery. Conversely, we find a majority of the government hospitals in a bad shape. Actually, we find them stinking and becoming a centre for infections. Service fragrance makes it essential that medical and paramedical people engaged in the process of offering the medicare services find something new and special in the ambience where they work. Like this, the patients and attendants availing the services also gain new experiences in the sound environment. Indian hospitals need to make it possible where we find lack of aesthetic sense. We cannot deny the role of civic sense, aesthetic sense and quality service environment in making the medicare and healthcare services much more productive.

In the hospital services, we find primary, secondary and tertiary hospitals offering multi-dimensional services. Of course, we find a few of the hospitals of world class but a majority of them require qualitative transformation to cater to the changing healthcare requirements of different segments of society. The line services, supportive services, auxiliary services and peripheral services need to be made condition oriented. The central as well as the state governments need an attitudinal change so that the benefits of technological sophistication are made available to the healthcare sector. Though we cannot deny that since independence, India has built up a vast health infrastructure and health personnel in all the three streams but it is also right to mention that a big gap between demand and supply continuing since long is yet to be bridged. The challenges of quality health services in remote rural regions has to be urgently met. In view of the high intensity of problem, we need to transform public healthcare into an accountable, accessible and affordable system of quality services. A new vision based on faster, broad-based and inclusive growth makes a call in favour of an opportunity to restructure policies. Structural transformation would make the ways for qualitative-cum-quantitative transformation.

The hospital professionals need world class excellence to improve the quality of medicare services. The curative as well as preventive services need due attention. On the one hand, the hospitals and healthcare organisations need to improve the quality of services while on the other hand, they also need to sensitise the masses. On the one hand, they need to promote the use of new generation of sophisticated technology while on the other hand, they also need to develop low cost indigenous technology. On the one hand, they need to promote modern allopathic treatment while on the other hand they also need to inject new life and strength to AYUSH. In a true sense, a mix of all would serve the multifaceted requirements of diverse segments.

HOSPITAL PRODUCT-THE PERCEPTION

At the outset, it is essential that we clarify the perception of hospital product. Generally, we feel that products in all the conditions are tangible and therefore, the services are not the product. But the management experts feel that even banking, insurance, transport, tourism, hotel, consultancy, electricity, communications, education, medicare of healthcare services etc., though intangible in nature, considered as product. It is against this background that we treat hospital services as product. To put it another way, product or outputs are the results of the should be aggregation or combination of different types of inputs. Even to generate services, we make use of a number of inputs and therefore, the services that we get as consideration are the outputs. The perception of product makes it clear that tangibility or intangibility is not the real theme to define the product. Indeed, it is synchronisation of different types of inputs which shapes the perception.

Internationally acclaimed authorities have also gone through the problem. Kotler says, Nothing that can be offered to a market for attention, acquisition, use or consumption; it includes physical objects, services, personalities, places, organisation and idea which are the product.' This also makes it clear that even the services rendered by the hospitals or healthcare organisations are products and this in a very natural way requires managerial excellence to manage the services generated by them. It is in this context that we find hospital services as the product and we go through all the precautions and promote professionalism that we need for manufacturing goods. The hospitals or health care organisations use different types of materials known as inputs. Unless they use equipments, instruments, infrastructural facilities, it is not possible for the hospital personnel to generate the healthcare services. It is difficult for doctors even having world class professional excellence to offer quality services without getting the support of materials/inputs because only the quality inputs processed by quality professionals results into quality goods/services (outputs).

Transformation of inputs into outputs requires due support of doctors, nurses and the para-medical staff. Besides, a large number of materials are used in the process of transformation, such as equipments, instruments, plants, machines, power, gas, drugs and medicines and so on. We find generation of services a managerial process because failing the professional commitments, even the quality inputs fail in generating the quality services.

The management of hospital product is found a bit different to the product of other service generating organisations. This is due mainly to the fact that we find hospitals, educational institutions, social organisations and the political organisations in the category of no-profit-making organisations. Technically and ethically, they don't have a legitimate right of generating profits. Managing the services/product of a no-profit-making organisation is found difficult and therefore, the professionals having world class excellence and personal commitments are found successful in this endeavour. The hospitals or health care organisations are found generating different types of services. The key services offered by them are medical services containing line services, supportive services and auxiliary services. Besides, they also offer educational and training facilities and intensify medical research. Thus, we find a big list of services/product, specially of the leading healthcare institutes and the secondary and tertiary hospitals.

Types of Hospital Product

Of course, we find general hospitals only generating medicare or healthcare services but secondary and tertiary hospitals and the leading healthcare institutes in addition to the generation of medical services also offer other services like medical education, research and training. It is against this background that we go through almost all the services generated by hospitals and the health care organisations. In Fig. 8.1, we find different types of hospital product.

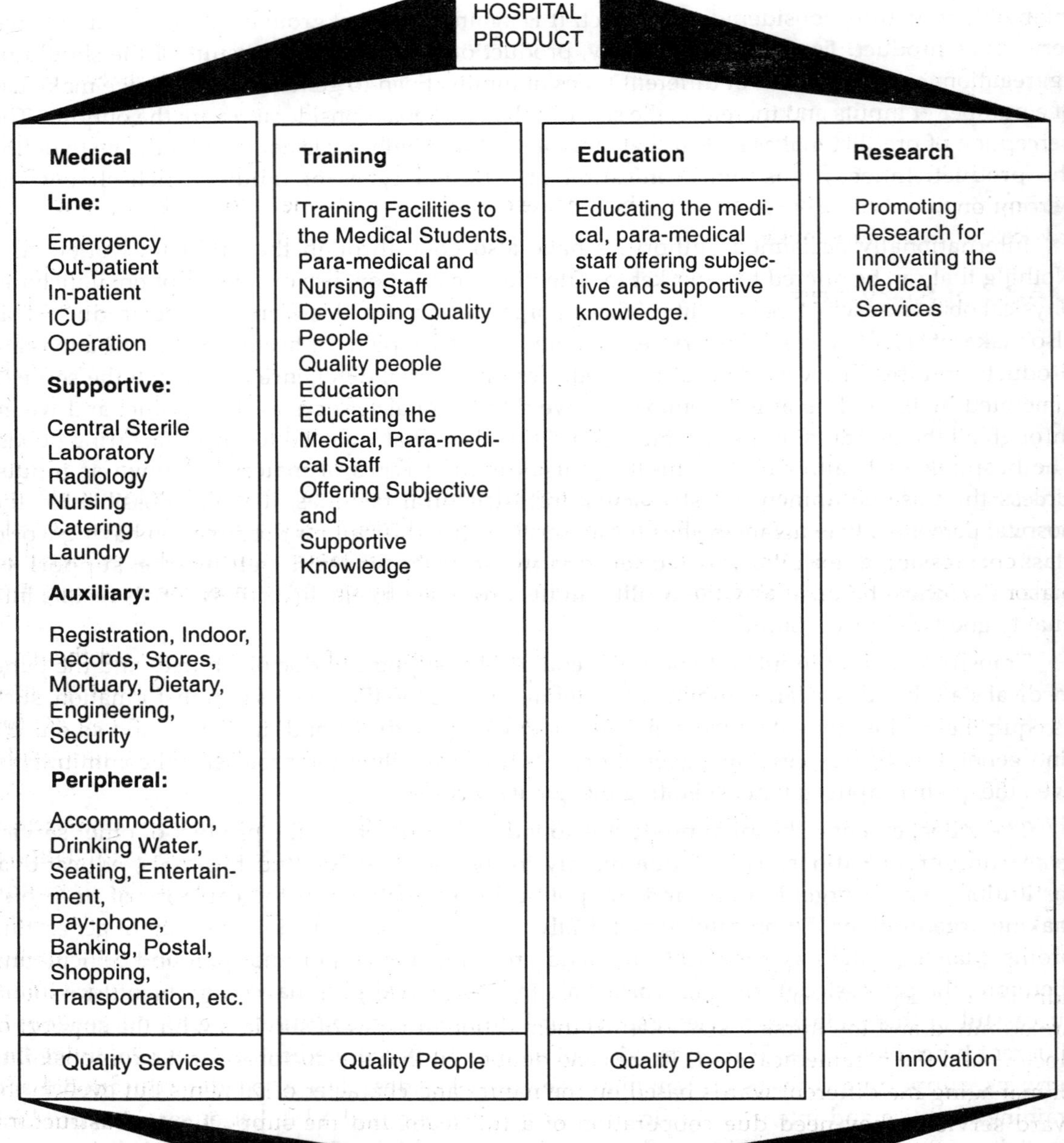

Fig. 8.1. Types of Hospital Product

In Fig. 8.1, we find four main types of products, such as medical services, medical training, medical education and medical research. In the group of medical services, we find line services considered to be the core services of hospitals. In addition, we find supportive services helping core services such as central sterile supply, laboratory, radiology, nursing, catering and laundry. Besides, we also find auxiliary services, such as registration, indoor case, records, stores and issues, transport, mortuary, dietary, engineering and security. Modern hospitals also offer or generate a number of peripheral services to add additional attractions to the product, such as accommodation facilities for the attendants, pay-phone, banking, restaurants, shopping complex, entertainment and health care education. The core services and the supportive services no doubt are found of essential nature and therefore, the patients and attendants claim to have the same but the peripheral services, if of innovative nature, bear the efficacy of generating attractions and motivating the patients and attendants. Because we find the concept of hospital marketing gaining popularity, the hospitals or the healthcare organisations also need to make the peripheral services attractive and innovative.

Medical Services

Line Services: In the group of line services, we find emergency services, out-patient services, in-patient services, intensive care and operation. All these services are considered to be the important or key products of hospitals. It is the prime responsibility of a hospital manager to make it sure that these services reach to the ultimate users or patients in a right fashion. He/she bears the responsibility of making available to the doctors all the supporting infrastructural facilities in addition to the team of assisting personnel so that the doctors perform without any constraint. We are well aware of the fact that emergency services are considered to be the most vital component of hospital care product because this necessitates a different approach and personal commitments in addition to the professional excellence. Of course, the doctors better know about the situational requirements but it is the responsibility of a hospital manager to interact and to make available to them everything in offering the time honoured emergency services. Since the services necessitate due emphasis on time management, it is pertinent that a hospital manager is very careful while managing for the emergency services.

It is right to mention that almost in all the hospitals, we find out-patient services an important wing of hospital which proves to be an important source for the in-patient services. In addition to the emergency services, we also need to take care of the out-patient services because a number of patients need primary care and diagnosis of the out-patient department and this makes it essential that a hospital manager keeps in his/her minds the requirements of OPD and helps patients in getting the time honoured services.

In-patient services are related to the services made available to the patients after getting admission or registration.[2] The services focus due care on ward management where the patients are admitted and the nursing staff offer to them different types of services with the support of doctors and the paramedical staff. There is no doubt in it that the doctors bear the responsibility of managing the different wards based on the nature and character of ailments but even in the ward services, they need due cooperation of a full team and the supporting infrastructural facilities. This makes it essential that a hospital manager in consultation with the doctors acting as incharge knows about their requirements and makes available to them the support they need to offer quality services. Right from admission to discharge, a number of formalities are required to be completed and the task of doctors attending on the patients is simplified considerably if an efficient hospital manager is to help them.

We find Intensive Care Unit (ICU), the most sensitive wing of the line services requiring immediate attention of doctors, nurses, and paramedical personnel. The management of ICU is based on professional excellence. Right from the organisation of ICU to its final processing and day-to-day maintenance, a number of infrastructural facilities are found essential on a priority basis. Since we find the services of emergency nature, it is pertinent that a hospital manager assigns due weightage and an overriding priority to the ICU. He/ she in consultation with the specialists needs to manage everything with professional excellence of world class.

In addition to other services, we also find operation services as an important wing of the lines services. This also requires fulfilment of a number of formalities besides the integration and coordination in the availability of different types of services. We find it a team work and therefore, it is the responsibility of a hospital manager that the requirements of a surgeon are fulfilled on a priority basis. The supporting infrastructural facilities, nursing staff, junior doctors, anesthetist, availability of investigation reports and oxygen are some the essential requirements without which a surgeon can't operate. It is the responsibility of a hospital manager to make it sure that a surgeon gets everything ready on his/her table before starting the operation. Since we find it the most sensitive wing of hospital, a hospital manager requires to fulfil the requirements of OT on a priority basis. In addition to other aspects, a hospital manager requires to take care of the degradable and non-degradable biomedical waste since we find them hazardous.

Supportive Services: For the generation of effective core services or line services, it is pertinent that we also take care of the supportive services. It is right to mention that sterilisation is an important wing of hospital requiring due care of doctors as well as a hospital manager. To be more specific in the surgical services, we find it playing a contributory role. To avoid infection and further complications, we find it playing an important role requiring due care of all.

A laboratory plays an important role in diagnosing and therefore, all the wings of hospitals need their services. It is difficult for the doctors to treat the patients unless they have an authentic investigation report. We find sophistication in the process, specially with the introduction of new generation of equipments. It is the responsibility of doctors as well as of the hospital managers to fulfil the requirements of the laboratory so that the personnel working there find it convenient to support the doctors.

Radiology happens to be the specialised supportive services. As a diagnostic and therapeutic arm of the hospital, we find radiology services playing an important role. The medical staff can show their excellence only when radiology services are available. The radiology department is found responsible for assisting the process of diagnosis through the use of radiography, fluoroscopy and radioisotopes and high voltage acceleration. Radiography and fluoroscopy constitute to be a major part of the workload in the hospitals. We find radiologists responsible for managing the department.

Nursing is a vital part of the hospital services without which it is difficult to offer the medicare or healthcare services. To be more specific, the ward services rest on the instrumentality of nursing staff. It is the responsibility of a hospital manager to make it sure that the nursing staff required by the wards are present on duty.

Food and beverages play a significant role in the quick recovery of patients. It is against this background that we talk about the catering services. The dieticians bear the responsibility of making available a diet-chart and the nursing staff are supposed to make it sure that the patients get food and beverages on the basis of the chart prepared by doctors or the dietitians. It is the responsibility of a hospital manager to make it sure that the food and beverages department is managed in a right fashion so that the patients get nutritional support in addition to the required medical aid.

We find laundry for washing clothes. In this context, we find special emphasis on linen keeping in view the disinfection provision. The hospital clothes are required to be washed very carefully.

Auxiliary Services

Registration: This is an important service related to the registration or admission of patients. While registering or admitting patients, we of late, find even the use of computers. The details of candidates are found mentioned while registering them so that while documenting the same, the record department is not to find it difficult to locate the case history as and when the circumstances necessitate so. It is an important function of hospitals for making available to them the different types of services they need while diagnosing or treating.

Indoor Services: We find the indoor service related to the patients already admitted in different wards of the hospitals as per their requirements. The diagnostic or treatment facilities are made available to the admitted patients. The food and beverages and drug administration are found as per the chart made available by the doctors to the nursing staff. We find different wards in the hospitals which is made clear while admitting the patients. The nursing staff plays an incremental role in improving the quality of indoor services.

Records Management: We find a separate department for documenting the records. It is the responsibility of the department to record the details and case histories of patients. The treatment plan, the effects and side-effects and the results are mentioned and recorded by the department. While undertaking medical research, we find the old records playing an important role. The computers are now also used for documenting the case histories of patients.

Stores: In almost all the hospitals, we find the stores department to store the different types of hospital materials. It is the responsibility of a material and stores manager to store different items in such a way that proper indexing or cataloguing is made possible. The issue and inventories play an important role in managing the stores. A manager is supposed to know the requirements for storing and preserving sophisticated equipment, instruments, food and beverages so that we don't find a degeneration in their quality.

Mortuary: It is a department found responsible to preserve the dead bodies. In case of post-mortem, we find this department playing an important role. The management of mortuary house requires special care and precaution so that inhuman treatment is not found with the dead bodies. Right from the construction of the mortuary house *to* it *its* proper working, a hospital manager bears the responsibility of making it sure that there is no adverse impact on the atmosphere and environment.

Dietary: The management of food and beverages is found significant with the viewpoint of making available to the patients food and drinks in tune with the diet-chart prepared by the doctors or the dieticians. The food and drinks having nutritional values are to be served to the patients. The dietary department is found managed by a person having the required qualification to be a dietician.

Engineering: This department is related to the construction of buildings or making available the power, communications, water and other technical services. The technocrats are found responsible for managing the department in consultation with hospital architects, consultants and managers. Repairing services and development works are also managed by this department.

Security: To protect the property and assets of hospitals, we find the security department. It is also responsible for maintaining peace within the four walls of the hospitals.

Peripheral Services

Modern hospitals in addition to the aforesaid services also offer peripheral services specially with the motto of adding additional attractions to their product. Since we find the concept of modern marketing even practiced in the hospitals or health care organisations, a majority of the private hospitals make efforts to make their services distinct to others by introducing innovative peripheral services.[3] The following services are found important in the group of peripheral services.

Accommodation for the Attendants: We find hospitals and healthcare organisations making available accommodation facilities even to the attendants of course on payment basis. In the accommodation facilities, all the amenities are made available.

Safe Drinking Water: To be more specific in the Indian condition where we often find the problem of water contamination, the patients and attendants feel that safe drinking water facilities are made available to them. Our focus is here not only on the bottles of mineral water but on the supply of safe drinking water.

Comfortable Seating Arrangements: We also find hospitals making available comfortable seating arrangements both for the patients and attendants so that they don't face any problem. To be more specific, we find attendants very much neglected in the government hospitals and this makes it essential that the stay of attendants in the hospitals is made comfortable.

Entertainment: To avoid monotony to the patients and attendants, we also find hospitals making available entertainment facilities. This helps them in spending time and diffusing tension. With the development of telecast media, it is now easier to offer the entertainment facilities.

Pay-phone Services: To bridge over the communication gap, the modern hospitals also make available pay-phone service to the patients and attendants so that they can transmit and receive messages, of course on a payment basis.

Courier Services: The Department of Posts or even the private courier services are found in the hospitals to provide maximum comforts to the patients and attendants for communications.

Shopping Complex In addition, we also find hospitals making available the facilities for shopping by developing a shopping arcade or complex. This is also to help hospitals in generating and mobilising internal finance.

Banking: The banking services are also made available in the modern hospitals so that in addition to the hospital personnel, the patients and attendants get an opportunity to transact.

The aforesaid peripheral services add additional attractions to the product of hospital. The professionals feel that like other organisations, even hospitals need to improve the quality of their peripheral services so that the patients and attendants get an additional attraction. It is against this background that we find hospitals making efforts to innovate their peripheral services so that they make their services unique. Of course, the core and other services are important but we don't find anything wrong if the peripheral services are also enriched and made attractive to offer comforts and conveniences to the patients and attendants.

Medical Education

Hospital personnel play a contributory role in improving the quality of healthcare services. Of course, we find sophisticated equipments and apparatus playing an incremental role but sophistication of technologies carries no meaning failing the inadequacy or non-availability of quality personnel. The secondary hospitals, the tertiary hospitals, the healthcare institutes, the paramedical institutes and the nursing institutes are found engaged in developing hospital personnel of different categories. We consider it an important product of hospital which draws attention of institutions and institutes bearing the responsibility of developing hospital personnel. The health policy makers also need an attitudinal change to help institutions in developing quality hospital personnel. The holistic concept of management makes it clear that practising education marketing is essential to improve the quality of hospital product because in a majority of the hospitals, we find the problem of financial crunch standing as a major obstacle while promoting medical education. There is no doubt that the government hospitals charge very nominal fees for educating the hospital personnel but at the same time, it is also right to mention that they in a majority of the cases have not been found serious to quality. This is partially due to financial problem but substantially due to the negative attitudes of the policy makers. To produce quality hospital personnel, we need a basic change in our attitudes.

For the development of quality hospital personnel, there are two important areas, viz., professional excellence, and personal commitment. The heads of the medical institutions need to perceive the concept of Quality Hospital Personnel in the right perspective. Unless we optimally blend the two attributes—professional excellence and personal commitments—the desired results can't be achieved. It is in this context that we gravitate our attention on both the traits.

Professional Excellence

During the yester decades, the contours of development in the medical sciences have undergone radical changes. Scientific advances have made possible a number of developments in the medical sciences. The information and communication technologies have been found helping the students and faculty substantially. The information superhighway is found opening knowledge gateway for enriching the excellence of faculty and students. Even if you don't have a rich library, the Internet services make-up the losses. The sophisticated equipments and apparatus are available to simplify your task. If you have quality inputs, we don't find anything wrong in expecting the outputs to be of superior quality. The buildings are there, the supporting infrastrutural facilities are there, the audio-visual exposure devices are there but the products that you make available to the society are not of a good quality. The hospital personnel in general fail in developing their excellence in the face of latest developments in the medical sciences. This draws our attention on the management of medical institutions engaged in educating and training the hospital personnel of tomorrow.

In a majority of the government institutions or hospitals, we find senior doctors as faculty and not very much sincere to their functional responsibilities. Of course, they are free to promote private business but not at cost of the parent institutions in which they work. Unless we find the faculty personally the committed, the professionally committed people can't be developed. Hence, it is pertinent that quality faculty, personally and professionally-committed faculty accept the responsibility of educating the students. They are required to update their knowledge and in this context, the information superhighway would help them significantly. The hospital managers, the policy makers need to think over the problem on a priority basis. The faculty is to be motivated and at the same time its contributions to the discipline are also to be evaluated. The syllabi need a structural change. The ethical dimension, value-engineering process are to be given due weightage while educating the students because we also find cases where the doctors are professionally sound, they are even extraordinarily efficient but lack values and humanity which stand as a major barrier while developing quality students. We need to make possible professional excellence and for that the students are required to be given quality education aid. The universities, autonomous institutes and deemed universities should not devalue their certificates, degrees and diplomas, or they need to make them costlier.

Personal Commitments

In addition to improving the professional excellence, we also need to make the students personally committed. This draws our attention on the ethical values, humanity, human values or so. If in the society, we find inefficient people rewarded suitably, the avenues are paved even for the transformation of efficients into inefficients. A vicious circle is thus formed in the development process that makes the task of value-engineering much more difficult. The hospital personnel are professionally sound but they lack personal-touch-in-service. They are efficient but lack humanity. They are present on duty but absent. Since we need to develop quality hospital personnel, it is essential that in addition to the subjective knowledge that we make available to them on a priority basis, they also need something more. It is the pace of value-orientation which is abnormally slowed down. It is not enough that you take an oath and forget. It is much more impact generating that even if you don't commit, you remember your functional responsibilities. It is against this background that we need to incorporate necessary changes in our syllabi, specially related to the medical education. Right from the very beginning to the final day when they are accreditated, we need to activate the process of brainwashing.

Personal commitment thus makes it essential that the medical students of today and the hospital personal of tomorrow bring an attitudinal change. They have to realise that humanity is an essential part of medical profession. They need to conceptualise that quality doctors in addition to professional excellence also need personal-touch-in-service. Since we talk here about the medical students who are going to accept the vital responsibility of serving the society just tomorrow, it is pertinent that we assign due weightage to personal commitments. We can't force faculty to teach honestly; we can't force doctors to treat patients sincerely and unless we make the ways for value-orientation, the task remains unfulfilled. The excellence of faculty is substantially influenced by their intuition and if they lack values, the task is much more difficult. It is against this background that for developing personally committed personnel, the teachers or the faculty are required to be motivated. Actually, we find a large-scale degeneration on the campus and within the four walls of hospitals, the policy makers need to realise it. The dedicated, personally-committed faculty may simplify our task and therefore, we have no option but to motivate them suitably.

Medical Training

Sky is the limit for perfection. Gone are the days when we believed in this principle that chromosomes, family background, racial and genetic considerations determine the development of personality. Of late, we find inculcation process instrumental in sensitising the process of developing people. It is in this context that we talk about development of training facilities to the students as well as to the medical and paramedical personnel. Today, you find yourself competent but just tomorrow you feel that you need to be more sound. This is due mainly to the fact that the development processes keep on moving. If your eyes are open and minds are active, you can realise your shortcomings. The training programme may be short or long-term, for senior doctors or for junior doctors, for paramedical staff or for the nursing staff, for regular students or for trainees. The main thing is to make available to the personnel or the students the excellence they need to perform extraordinarily.

In a majority of the government hospitals, we find doctors educated and trained in the old schools not well aware of the behavioural management. They lack decency and proficiency. They are not only inefficient but also dishonest. They are not only inhuman but even play a role of blood sucker. They don't know anything about sympathy then what to talk of empathy. It is in this context that we make a strong advocacy in favour of result-oriented training programme. Believe it or not, we find a sea change in the behavioural profile of doctors educated and trained in the modern management oriented institutes where behavioural and ethical dimensions are given due weightage, and contrary to it, in the traditional schools, this aspect is found absolutely neglected.

The medical training programme should be instrumental in updating the knowledge of trainees in the medical sciences no doubt but in addition, it also requires to promote ethics and values. For enriching knowledge, it is essential that we take the support of quality faculty and the sophisticated information and communications technologies. Of late, the information superhighway is found simplifying the task of faculty, if they are really interested in developing their knowledge. The hospital managers need to make it sure that faculty or experts acting as a resource person are given suitable incentives to develop knowledge to the trainees. In addition to the medical scientists, the behavioural scientists are also expected to educate and train the medicos or medical and paramedical personnel because we are supposed to develop quality students who prove themselves to be high or super performers. Of course, we find professional excellence a prerequisite for the development of quality medicos but we can't negate that if they lack empathy, our efforts for promoting medicare services are likely to be turned into a fiasco.

We need to make our training programme informative, educative and interesting. This necessitates creativity in our efforts. We promote technologies but fail in developing personnel in line with the evolving technologies that deprives the masses of getting the benefits of scientific and technological advances. This makes it essential that we establish a correlation between the two and even in this context, we find creative training programme very much effective. Since we find quality upgradation an ongoing process, it is quite natural that our training programme is also found to be a continuous process. The training facilities thus need a new vision, a new strategy, a new approach and a fresh look.

Medical Research

Development processes can't remain static. Scientific advancements make the way for new developments. Whatever the developments that we find in the medical sciences today are due to intensive research promoted by the medical scientists. The tertiary hospitals, healthcare institutes and the Indian Council for Medical Research (ICMR) Universities are the different sources for promoting research. The Council for Scientific and Industrial Research (CSIR) is also found engaged in undertaking research. In addition, we also find non-governmental organisations evincing interests in promoting medical research.

The major thrust areas of research include existing problems of communicable diseases, emerging problems of non-communicable diseases, improvement of health and nutritional status of women and children and increasing contraceptive acceptance and continuation. Indigenous development of immuno-diagnostic, research studies on improved drug regimens to combat emerging resistance among several bacteria, alternative strategies for vector control in view of the increasing insecticide resistance among vectors and testing innovative disease control strategies through increased community participation have been the major areas of research in the medical sciences.

The Indian Council for Medical Research include existing problems of non-communicable diseases and researches in the field are anti-tobacco community and oral cancers in both sexes, lifestyle modification to reduce the rising morbidity due to hypertension and cardiovascular diseases, documenting the health problems associated with lifestyle changes and increasing longevity of life. Keeping in view the magnitude of the problem of providing effective comprehensive healthcare to the population, the major research and development activities in the country are required to be promoted to improve quality, coverage, efficiency and cost-effectiveness of healthcare services. Research studies to test the operational feasibility and economic viability of comprehensive health services schemes similar to the National Health Services (NHS) of UK is required to be taken up in the Indian perspective.[4]

The key or thrust areas for research are:

- Immuno-diagnostic tests for common infections.
- Development of new drugs for treatment of common infections in view of the increasing resistance to antibiotics.
- Development of resistance modulating agents to combat the increasing bacterial resistance to antibiotics.
- Development, testing, and quality control of new drugs in the modern system of medicine.
- Newer drug delivery systems for better targeting of drugs and reduction in the side effects.
- Development of therapeutic and prophylactic vaccines for infections, utilising newer big-technological tools so that they are thermostable, have long shelf life, free from side-effects and are affordable.
- Development of newer vector control measures including testing of bio-pesticides like "neem."

The hospitals and the healthcare institutes need to promote research because they have quality personnel to undertake and conduct.

While promoting research, they need to consider the interests of poor section of the society on a priority basis. The most important task before the medical scientists is to make the process of medicare or healthcare services cost effective. The increasing costs on modern diagnostic and treatment processes and the expensive medicines are found making the task of getting medicare services difficult to the masses. This makes it essential that intensive efforts are made to devise affordable medicare services.

The increasing resistance to antibiotics is to be countered. The vector control measures are to be innovated. The Indian Council for Medical Research bears the responsibility of controlling the non-communicable diseases. Keeping in view the quality, coverage and cost-effectiveness, the researches are to be promoted. Because we find development of Hospital Information System based on sophisticated information technology, the task of researchers would considerably be simplified. The universities, healthcare institutes and non-government organisations are required to intensify research so that the rural masses are benefited. The Indianised system of medicines based of herbal products draws attention of researchers. It is not judicious that we make the medicare services so expensive that the poorest of the poor find it difficult to afford. The health department bears the responsibility of ensuring the basic medical services to the masses but the efforts taken by them don't appear encouraging. Thus, we need multi-cornered efforts to promote research.

The leading medical institutes of the country have been facing the problem of financial crunch. To be more specific, the government managed institutes find it difficult to intensify research because they lack funds. The medical scientists are interested in promoting research but they face the financial, infrastructural and other constraints. Even the universities have been experiencing multidimensional problems. To promote research, it is essential that Internet operations are channelised, the hospital information system is innovated and motivational factors are given due weightage.

The aforesaid facts make it clear that in the Indian perspective, the policy makers have not been sincere and serious to the health problems which have been found inviting even those diseases which were considered to be eradicated. Malaria, kalazar and Japanese Encephalitis have been found spreading specially in the rural areas. The tribal area is found most vulnerable since more than 60 per cent of the more dangerous P. Falciparum malaria is found in those areas. The hospitals and particularly, the research institutes need to promote research to get an affordable solution. Immunisation, of course, is considered to be important problem and we need to promote universal immunisation. We are well aware of the fact that vaccines are considered to be the most cost-effective agents for the control of communicable diseases. We need a revolution, specially on the vaccinology front. Tuberculosis is another problem. Of course, we have vaccine like BCG in the immunisation programme but it is not found to be more effective and this focuses our attention on promoting research activities. Typhoid is also a major problem and an oral vaccine found affordable to the masses is required to be introduced. We cannot negate that medical research if intensified in the right directions would make the healthcare services cost-effective innovative and competitive.

The most burning problem that we find obstructing the innovation process is inadequacy of finance. It is often observed that Government Medical Colleges and Hospitals are on the verge of derecognisation mainly because they fail to adhere to the infrastructure, equipment and staff norms as laid down by the Medical Council of India. This makes it essential that central as well as the state governments provide adequate financial support to those institutions concentrating on undertaking research for developing low cost indigenous technologies. Like this, the low cost drugs and medicines are also to be given due weightage in order that the quality healthcare services reach even to the poorest of the poor. The National Drug Authority requires to evince keen interests in promoting research activities so that quality drugs at an affordable price are made available to the weaker sections of the society. We need to take into consideration the recommendations of Mashelkar Committee (2003) and NCMH (2005) so that NDA emerges as a leader to promote quality and minimise price.

The policy makers need multidimensional efforts to initiate qualitative and quantitative transformation. The establishment of Hospital Development Committee in all government hospitals, improvement of supporting infrastructural facilities in the district hospitals, provision of high quality secondary healthcare services for every block in the country, creation of state-of-the-art medical education, research and care institutions in all disciplines of medicine, creation of new institutions and upgradation of existing tertiary care hospitals and mainstreaming of AYUSH systems to actively supplement the efforts of the allopathic systems are some of the steps to improve the quality of healthcare services.

On the one hand, we need to strengthen the medicare services made available by the government hospitals and healthcare sectors while on the other hand, we also realise the instrumentality of promoting PPP mode. During yesteryears, the Centre as well as the State Governments have initiated a wide variety of PPP arrangements to meet the increasing healthcare needs of masses. However, we need innovative efforts to promote PPP mode. We need to develop a generic framework for different categories of PPPs at primary, secondary and tertiary levels of healthcare to improve cost-effectiveness, enhance quality and expand access through extensive stakeholders' consultations.

Expanding avenues for qualitative and quantitative transformation makes it essential that research and development activities are to be promoted at each and every stage by each and every healthcare systems with the prime motive of making the healthcare services accessible and affordable to the masses.

During yesteryears, we have witnessed significant developments in the field of Ayurveda, Yoga, Siddha and Unani drugs but we need to develop this industry in line with internationally acceptable pharmacopoeial standards and quality parameters so that the existent potentials in the AYUSG are tapped to protect and promote the interests of weaker sections of the society who on account of low affordability fail in harnessing the benefits of modern development in the field of medical sciences. The Central Government has established research councils for Ayurveda and Siddha known as Central Council for Research in Ayurveda and Siddha (CCRAS); for Unani, Central Council for Research in Unani Medicine (CCRUM); for homoeopathy, Central Council for Research in Homoeopathy (CCRH) ; and for Yoga, Central Council for Research in Yoga and Naturopathy (CCRYN). We find these councils engaged in promoting research activities. Additionally, other government departments have also carried out a wide range of research activities, e.g. ICMR, CSIR, DST, DBT and ICAR. Despite participation of a number of agencies, organisations and individuals, we do not find concrete results for some of common health problems like malaria, filariasis, hepatitis, anaemia. We lack professionalism and financial support obstructing the process of intensifying research activities. We expect a lot from the Golden Triangle Research Programme for the development of AYUSH drugs.

The Research initiatives have been shown in Exhibit 8.1

Exhibit 8.1

Research Initiatives for AYUSH

Literary Research:

Medico-historical Studies, transcription/translation of rare words

Fundamental Research

Pharamacopoeial work and standardisation of formulations/therapies.

Drug Research:

Medico-Botanical survey, pharmacognostical/phsytochemical studies.

Clinical Research:

Therapeutic trials of drugs for specified diseases, Drug providing or Homoeopathic Pathogenestic Trials.

Tribal Healthcare Research Programme,

Family Welfare and RCH Programme:

Old contraceptive (Pippalyadi Yoga)

Spermicidal Agent (Neem Oil)

Bal Rasayan and Ayush Ghutti for children's health Scientific Validation of Ayurvedic and Siddha Medicines for RCH programme

Development of Cosmaceutical/neutraceutical products based on traditional medicines knowledge.

Source: Eleventh Five Year Plan, Vol. II P.112

In addition, we find mainstreaming of AYUSH in public health, technology upgradation of AYUSH industry, assistance to Centres of Excellence and revitalization and validation of community based local health traditions of Ayush. It is significant that AYUSH industry is made available a team of quality people. National Institutes of various AYUSH systems have been set up by the central government to set benchmarks for teaching, research and clinical practices. It is need of the hour that we transform these institutes into a centre of excellence which would require enormous cooperation of the central government. The AYUSH dispensaries are to be strengthened and the supply of kits of AYUSH for the development of specialised AYUSH treatment centres under PPP mode need priority attention.

The most important task for promoting AYUSH industry is to gain the confidence of masses and for that, we need multidimensional efforts. Development of common drug testing and other infrastructural facilities for AYUSH industry clusters need due attention. We find a majority of the AYUSH units facing the problem of financial crunch and therefore, financial assistance to the concerned units for capacity building and improving quality control and research and development activities would make ways for an improvement in the quality of services. In addition, they need support in different forms such as support to centres for excellence in AYUSH education, drug development, clinical research and tertiary care cannot be underestimated. Additionally, development of backward and forward linkages for in-situ conversations and ex-situ cultivation of medicinal plants can make this industry much more sustainable. Provision of marking and value-added services to medicinal plant farmers and expansion of international cooperation and exchange programme with focus on global positioning of AYUSH systems cannot be delayed.

The hospital planners and government policy makers cannot undermine the qualitative or quantitative improvements in the field of AYUSH because it is to benefit the users or customers in different ways. Particularly, we find the rural segment as an important beneficiary because they are poor and the services provided are found either free of charge or at the lowest possible cost.

The hospital professionals in the very context need to make it sure that world class services are made available to the users. It is service quality that would help AYUSH industry in gaining popularity and serving the users. The research and development activities bear the efficacy of momentising the innovations process. Quality control of drugs is also an important consideration because the spurious drugs or ineffective drugs and medicines would tarnish the image of AYUSH. The National Accreditation Board for Testing and Calibration Laboratories bears the responsibility of accreditating the laboratories. The Drugs and Cosmetics Act has not been found properly enforced and therefore, to get the desired results, we need to strengthen the Act which would help in gaining popularity.

Planning for the Hospital Product

We agree that during the yesterdecades, a considerable amount of work has been done on the problem of services in the context of product planning in the hospitals. The increasing sophistication in medical sciences has complicated the task of hospital planners. Besides, the changing disease profile has also been making the problem more complicated. The modern equipment and instruments have been found increasing the budget of hospitals. The traditional diagnostic and treatment processes are now found outdated. The increasing problem of environmental pollution, water-contamination, noise-pollution, communicable diseases, vector-borne diseases have made it essential that hospitals of today formulate a strategic plan so that they are in a position to make available medicare services to the needy patients. A majority of the government hospitals have been facing the problem of financial crunch which has been obstructing them while increasing the healthcare services. The demand side is increasing but the supply side is not to cater the same. This gravitates our attention on the formulation of a plan so that we find both categories of hospitals— government as well as the private—to fulfil the medicare requirements of society. It is in this context that we go through the problem of product planning in hospitals. While formulating a plan, the hospital managers need to consider a number of factors. The hospital planners bear the responsibility of formulating a plan but they require due cooperation of a hospital manager who has a detailed knowledge of the demand side. The following facts are to be considered while formulating a product plan for the hospitals.[5]

1. *Studying the disease profile:* At the outset, it is essential that a hospital manager studies in depth the changing disease profile in a particular command area so that the hospitals or the healthcare centres serving the area can make available the required services. Currently, we find water-borne, food-borne, pollution-borne and communicable diseases spreading like a wild fire and this makes it essential that the hospitals while formulating a plan make provision for curative as well as the preventive measures. The vector-borne diseases make it essential that hospitals make budgetary provisions for immunisation and promote healthcare communications.

2. *Increasing sophistication in the medical sciences:* We can't negate that during the yester decades, there have been multifaceted developments in the medical sciences which have made possible a basic change in the diagnostic and treatment processes. A majority of the hospitals in

the Indian conditions lack sophisticated biomedical equipments to innovate the process of diagnosis. Even if they make provision, the inadequacy of efficient Bio-medical Equipment, engineers and technicians make it difficult to take the benefits of latest technologies. The diagnostic and treatment processes, traditional in nature, are not to serve the interests of society. This makes it essential that hospital planners in cooperation with the hospital managers make sincere efforts to make available to the hospitals equipments and instruments of new generation.

3. *Use of expensive inputs:* We are well aware of the fact that of late, expensive inputs are needed to improve the quality of healthcare services but to be more specific, the government hospitals find it difficult to raise the budgetary provisions mainly on account of financial constraints. The state exchequer is not in a position to increase grants and the hospitals are not free to generate finance from the international sources.

We can't deprive the society of getting the basic medicare facilities and this makes it essential that a hospital manager explores avenues for the generation of finance by promoting charity and donations. In addition, it is also pertinent that the concept of modern marketing is practiced even in the healthcare sector. Unless the hospitals are allowed to generate finance from the internal sources, the expensive inputs can't be made available to the hospitals.

4. *Seeking the cooperation of hospital architects, consultants and planners:* In the face of the emerging trends, the products of hospitals are to be innovated and for that we need the support of hospital architects, consultants and planners. Keeping in view the nature and character of a hospital, they can formulate an ideal plan that would cater to the increasing demand. We can't deny the fact that the process of product development, modifications and innovation would require due cooperation of experts. Since we talk about modernising the hospitals, it is pertinent that we take care of space, finance, expertise and formulate an action plan.

5. *The medical services are to be innovated:* The hospital planners while formulating a product plan also need to innovate all the medical services, such as core services, supportive services, auxiliary services or even the peripheral services. We agree with this view that like the goods manufacturing organisations even the healthcare organisation would also be required to declare their services outdated. The diagnostic measures, the treatment processes, the equipment and instruments need due care. In addition, the hospital planners also need to think about the peripheral services which in a majority of the government hospitals have been found neglected. The goods manufacturing organisations have been found promoting the slogan "Differentiate or Die" and we find the slogan relevant even to the healthcare organisations. The leading private hospitals have been found innovating all types of services and therefore, they have been successful in adding additional attractions to their product profile. Here, our focus is on Product Uniqueness that would be possible by differentiating the services or making the services distinct.

6. *Specialised centres need due attention:* While formulating a plan for the hospital products, we need to take care of the specialised centres meant for a particular organ of the body. The specialisation may also be linked to a particular type of disease. The plan arrangements for general and specialised hospitals can't be identical.

7. *Location point for hospitals:* Till now, we have concentrated on the urban areas and it is against this background that we find big hospitals located only in the big cities and towns. The rural masses find it difficult to avail the services and to simplify their task, it is essential that we promote hospitals in the rural areas where the villagers and the poor sections would get the benefits of development. Besides, the development of big hospitals in the rural areas would

change the economy of that place because the goods and services produced and generated in that area would get an attractive price besides the multiplier effects would open new vistas for development. It is in this context that we need to promote the concept of world class hospitals preferably in the rural areas. Of course, we need all weather-proof roads so that even the population of cities and towns are benefited.

Life Cycle of Hospital Product

With scientific advancements, a number of developments have taken place in the medical sciences. In a true sense, we find a basic change in the nature and character of diagnostic and treatment devices. The services innovative for yesterday have proved to be outdated for today. And the services innovative for today are of course to be outdated tomorrow. It is in this context that we talk about the life cycle of hospital product. A hospital manager bears the responsibility of making available to the patients innovative services. This makes it essential that he/she is aware of the stage of the life cycle of the services so that the diffusion and adoption processes are given due weightage.

We find different stages in the life cycle, such as introduction stage or beginning stage when you introduce new services. The patients, of course, are found tempted to the new services and therefore, they start using the same which keep the services to the growing stage. If the innovative services are well tested, the process of demand generation keeps on moving and you find your services at the maturity stage. It is a stage where a manager requires to be careful to modify or alter so that the stage of stagnation is not to decrease the demand. After this, we find the declining stage. Since the inventions and innovations keep on moving, you can't fulfil the expectations of users with the old services and this necessitates introduction of new services.

The aforesaid facts make it clear that a hospital manager bears the responsibility of studying the emerging new trends in the medical sciences and to innovate the services accordingly. To be more specific in the hospital services, the patients and attendants prefer to use the sophisticated services even if we find them expensive. It is due mainly to the fact that patients and attendants want to use the best possible services even if they can't afford. It is against this background that a basic change in the diagnostic and treatment devices in the traditional small and big hospitals is felt urgent. It is also important to mention that in the life cycle of the services, we find a different trend specially when the services are found very expensive or are likely to show major side-effects. With the development of information technology and frequent use of computers for diagnosing and other medical purposes, we find patients developing a craze for these services and it is in this respect that the traditional diagnostic and curative services are found virtually at the declining stage.

The leading hospitals and healthcare institutes have been found making sincere efforts to innovate new services and therefore, they succeed in motivating the patients. In a majority of the government hospitals, we find traditional devices existent and therefore, the patients and attendants have been found hesitant to use the services of government hospitals. Of course, we find a few of the government and autonomous hospitals and institutes having world class excellence and they have also been found adopting the latest sophisticated devices for diagnosis and treatment.

In view of the above, it is right to mention that the hospitals and healthcare institutes need to make possible frequent innovation so that new services are made available to the patients. When to introduce or offer the new services is an important problem and an indepth study of product life cycle simplifies the task of a hospital manager.

Product Innovation, Diffusion and Adoption

Since we go through the hospital product, it is right to mention that diagnostic and treatment devices of yesterday are now found outliving their significance in the modern medical sciences. A hospital manager bears the responsibility of formulating a sound product strategy for hospitals so that the services offered by the hospitals are found innovative vis-a-vis affordable. Here, we go through three problems, viz., innovation, diffusion and adoption.

Product Innovation

At the outset, we clarify the concept of innovation.

"An innovation refers to any goods or services or ideas perceived by someone as new. The idea may have a long history but it is an innovation to the person who sees it as new."[6]

In the context of hospital or healthcare services, we use the term innovation for new diagnostic and treatment devices introduced by the hospitals to make available to the patients distinct quality of services. The realisation of patients and attendants in a very natural way would be found impact generating since they are supposed to treat it as new services. The process of innovation takes enough time because innovation is found based on research.

Product Diffusion

Another term "Product Diffusion" according to Rogers is the "spread of a new idea from its source of invention or creation to its ultimate users or adopters."[7]

We find diffusion a process of transmission of idea of innovated goods or services. Unless the idea of innovation is perceived by the prospects in a right fashion, the process of adoption is found taking a rest. This makes it clear that managers bear the responsibility of activating the process of diffusion. The hospital personnel belonging to the group of doctors and researchers are supposed to undertake research. The moment we find new diagnostic and treatment devices innovated, it is quite natural that masses develop a craze for using the same. We find sophisticated information and communications technologies instrumental in transmitting the information related to the new diagnostic and curative services, resulting for which the patients in general develop a temptation. Thus, the process of diffusion, if activated in the right direction, makes the ways for adoption. Innovation becomes ineffective if we don't find transmission of information to the prospects.

Product Adoption

The adoption process focuses on the mental process through which an individual passes from first hearing about an innovation to its final adoption.[8]

The decisions regarding the adoption of new or modern diagnostic and treatment processes are found personalised. Of course, we find modern diagnostic measures. However we find patients and attendants in a number of cases preferring the traditional approaches. Thus, for quick adoption of the innovative diagnostic and treatment processes, it is pertinent that diffusion process are found creative. The more creative and sensitive the diffusion process, the more responsive and proactive are to be the adoption processes.

New Product Development Dilemma

In almost all the organisations, the development of a new product is found to be a risky proposition because the users develop confidence gradually. As and when we find something new to be launched, the process of adoption requires the professional excellence of a manager. Since we find inventions and innovations frequently taking place in the medical sciences, the hospitals and healthcare organisations need to adopt the same to make available to the patients the maximum possible benefits of latest developments. The leading healthcare institutions keep on moving the process of innovation and make it necessary that even others follow the same. We can't deny the fact that the organisations believing in making things happen in addition to other factors also need world class managers. This is found essential to minimise the risk factors that we find in the new services. To be more specific, when we talk about the new services to be incorporated in the product profile of hospitals or the healthcare institutes, it is pertinent that before introducing the same, we go through a number of trials and experiments. This is due to the fact that in the healthcare services, we find involvement of a number of risk factors. The medical scientists innovate something new and the managers bear the responsibility of finding out an opportune moment to introduce the same. The gap between the service-delivery or processing and external communications needs to be bridged and this requires professional excellence. The potential users are to be informed and at the same time, they are also required to be sensitised in the right directions. Your innovative diagnostic measures and treatment processes need to win the heart and the confidence of the prospects. We agree with this view that the development of a new product, specially in the health care services is something like a dilemma. It is the prime responsibility of a hospital manager to insensitise the dilemma. The moment product innovation is talked about, the boardrooms or the policy makers need to make it sure that all the formalities related to the operation and maintenance of technologies, education and training of personnel, generation and retainment of a sense of confidence are completed.

We agree with this view that pioneers always face the difficulties but it is also right that pioneers only succeed in capitalising on the opportunities. It is quite natural that the prospects are not aware of the new services, their outstanding merits, the risk factors, the side-effects and therefore, your responsibility is to generate a sense of confidence by informing and sensing them specially with the help of creative slogans and messages. Of late, we have sophisticated information and communications technologies and therefore it is easier to inform and sense and generate confidence. It is quite natural that new services being expensive in nature may not be acceptable to all. But if we find outstanding merits of services in the product profile, it is quite natural that the potential users if motivated and stimulated or sensitised properly evince interests in the new services. The moment we talk about introducing new services, the collection of different types of information becomes essential because this helps you in knowing the reactions, positive results, feedback, the cost-effectiveness or so. You need to remove the dilemma and this requires managerial excellence and the professional commitments. When to innovate? Where to innovate? What to innovate? How to incorporate? Are some of the basic problems which need to be suitably answered by a professional hospital manager.

As and when new services are incorporated in the product profile, it is the responsibility of a hospital manager to gravitate his/her attention on the following facts:

- *Taking support of sophisticated information and communication technologies:* With the introduction of new services, it becomes the prime responsibility of a hospital manager to inform and sense the prospects and this requires due cooperation of sophisticated information and communication technologies where the creative messages and slogans are to be more effective. Since you bear the responsibility of sensitising the prospects by generating a sense of confidence, it is significant that you leave no scope for any doubt or confusion. You need the support of an efficient telemarketer who removes the confusion and misunderstanding. You need to advertise and publicise in a creative fashion so that the prospects develop a craze for the services to be used. In addition, you are also to be careful regarding the results and the side-effects. The information and communication technologies would let you know the feedback which would help you in making the advertisement plans more proactive.
- *Making it sure that innovative services are risk-free:* Since in the medicare or healthcare services, we find a different condition, the prospects in general avoid to take the risk. It is against this background that we find delayed adoption of the new services but the moment the process of adoption is switched on, the speed is found increasing very fast. If we find one hospital or healthcare institute completing the process successfully, the prospects in general evince their interests in using the same. With the support of print media and publicity measures, you can be successful in winning the heart of potential users of the services.
- *Be sure that innovative services establish, an edge over the traditional services: You* are also required to make it sure that the new services offered by you are of superior quality. The risk factor is minimum, the side-effects are minimal and the patients are to be benefited substantially. As and when you introduce new diagnostic and curative measures, be sure that the new services are superior to the traditional services in all respect. It is quite natural that you take a decision in the face of the paying capacity of prospects. Here, a correlation between the fee charged and the service offered is essential. If the potential users feel that whatever the fee structure they pay to the hospitals or the healthcare institutes for the services they get is not disproportionate, the process of getting a positive response keeps on moving.
- *Beneficial to the vulnerable segment:* Of course, there have been significant developments in the diagnostic and curative measures but it is also right to mention that the poorest of the poor always suffer. In the healthcare services, it is the prime responsibility of a healthcare manager to get it confirmed that not only the affluent sections but even the deprived of sections of the society also get the benefits of product innovation.
- *Declare traditional services obsolete:* To keep on moving the process of product innovation, it is also pertinent that you declare your traditional services outdated much earlier than other hospitals or healthcare institutes even think of it. This would help you in getting the benefits of becoming a leader. Always try to be a leader. This would help you in projecting a positive image, specially among the public at large.

Managerial Proficiency for Key Medical Services

In the management of hospitals, we find some of the important services necessitating world class managerial excellence. Of course, the doctors bear the responsibility of generating emergency services, out-patient and in-patient services, ophthalmic services, rehabilitation services or so but it is the professional-cum-managerial excellence of a hospital manager that simplifies their task. A senior surgeon would find it difficult to operate a patient on his/her table if he/she does not get enormous cooperation of a full team and the supporting infrastructural facilities. This makes it clear that medical and paramedical personnel and the nursing staff, no doubt, contribute substantially to the medicinal and surgical services, but the task of generation is found much more difficult if a professionally sound hospital manager is not to help him/her in this process. We are well aware of the fact that it is the prime responsibility of a hospital manager to know about the requirements of medical and paramedical staff end to make them sure that the required materials, items, personnel and infrastructural facilities would be made available to them on time. It is against this background that we go through the instrumentality of a hospital manager in some of the services of hospital found of sensitive nature.

Out-patient and In-patient Services

In a majority of the hospitals, we find the out-patient and in-patient services very much neglected. This questions the image of hospitals and that of the hospital personnel working there. Here, we go through the out-patient and in-patient services.

Out-patient Services: Since we talk about the instrumentality of a hospital manager in improving the level of efficiency of OPD, it is very natural that we concentrate on managerial excellence in the offering process. We are well aware of the fact that almost in all the hospitals, the OPD is supposed to play an outstanding role because a large number of patients use the services of OPD. In the ordinary hospital, we find the same doctor examining all categories of patients but in the secondary and tertiary hospitals and even in the leading medical institutes, we find specialists examining the patients. It is right to mention that successful management of OPD would minimise the pressure on wards. We can't deny the fact that it is due mainly to the poor quality of services generated by the OPD that masses are forced to go to the private clinics. If we gravitate our attention on the working of OPDs in different government hospitals, it is almost all clear that by and large all of them have been facing the problem of low level of efficiency. May be that doctors are deliberate because this is to question the existence of their private clinics. Delayed services, inadequate laboratory facilities, lack of coordination among different specialists, non-availability of medicine and indecent behaviour of hospital personnel are some of the reasons for the poor performance of the OPDs. In this context, we expect something positive from the hospital managers because they can bring the derailed systems on the rail. To be more specific in the Indian context, we need to improve the working of OPD on a priority basis. This would subserve the interests of the poorest of the poor who can't afford the expensive medical services of private hospitals. It is really amazing that in a majority of the government hospitals, the most neglected aspect is the OPD which requires due attention of hospital manager.

The patients and attendants often complain that doctors neglect and don't like to spare time. In addition, the supporting infrastructural facilities are not available. This results into a delay in diagnosis and treatment. It is in this context that we talk about the managerial excellence of a hospital manager while managing the OPD. If we find a hospital manager serious to the conspicuous absence of doctors or other paramedical staff from the duty and penalises them suitably, the hospital personnel would have no option but to take care of the patients coming to the OPD. While making an appraisal of the performance of hospital personnel, a hospital manager needs to consider his/her performance in serving and satisfying the outpatients.

In-patient Services: We also find hospitals offering in-patient services. The in-patient services are found expensive in nature and therefore, can't be availed by all the patients. The in-patient services are generally offered by a Nursing Unit found in each ward.[9] Since we find patients paying sizeably for the services used, it is judicious that a hospital manager takes care of the comforts and conveniences made available to the in-patients. The diagnostic and curative measures are required to be made available to the patients on time. It is right to mention that the quality of services made available to the in-patients depends upon the quality of nursing units. The American Hospital Association and National League of Nursing Education and Hospital Nursing Service Manual, New York make it clear that the nursing unit should be managed in a right fashion and therefore, assisting the patients with those physical services is found necessary for the well-being and comforts which he/she can't do. The management of record and time-honoured reporting to the doctors is found essential. If we turn our eyes on the performance of the in-patient services, the findings make it clear that a hospital manager is required to make it sure that the in-patient services are administered properly. This makes it essential that right from the construction of nursing units to the admission or registration of patients and offering to them different types of services, we need maximum care. A majority of the hospital personnel complain that due to abnormal size of ward, the offering of services is found complicated. This draws our attention on an optimal size so that control and supervision becomes easier. The inter-personnel relationships also need to be improved because almost in all the hospitals, we find the cases of unfriendly relationships resulting into a degeneration in the level of efficiency. The patients and attendants also complain about the delay in diagnosis and lack of supporting equipment. A hospital manager requires to make it sure that hospital personnel are in the required number and are actually present on duty. Unsatisfactory or non-optimal nurse-patient ratio is also an important reason instrumental in degenerating the level of efficiency. This makes it essential that a hospital manager takes care of nurse-patient ratio and makes it optimal. The most important thing a hospital manager needs is to motivate the nursing staff so that they feel that their services also contribute substantially to the upgradation of quality of hospital services.

Thus, a hospital manager needs to identify the managerial problems instrumental in degenerating the level of efficiency. He/she is supposed to have leadership quality and therefore, very much effective in making possible quality environment at the workplace so that different categories of staff working at both the places are motivated to work efficiently.

Managing the Emergency Services

In almost all the hospitals, the emergency services occupy a place of outstanding significance because here, it is time management and the instrumentality and personal commitment of a hospital manager that play a contributory role. In hospitals, the emergency services have a front-office in the casualty through which the patients enter the portals of the specialised departments.[10] The cases of cardiac attacks, strokes, accidents, natural calamities or so gravitate our attention on a priority basis. In this case, we find the patients and attendants in tension and therefore, they in addition to proper medical aid also need sympathy and empathy. In a majority of the government hospitals, we find even emergency services neglected then what to talk of other services. In a true sense, we find emergency services based on a team work where right decisions are to be taken at the right moment because even a minor delay may result into the irreparable losses. It is against this background that we need a managerial solution to improve the working conditions where a full team is found personally involved in the process.

Of course, we find doctors playing a contributory role in serving the emergency patients and therefore, while formulating or constituting a team, a hospital manager requires to go through the records of the hospital personnel to be placed. All essential formalities such as initial diagnosis, necessary investigations, programming the emergency care and treatment and monitoring processes are to be completed within the available time. This in a very natural way requires a team of professionally sound and personally committed hospital personnel of almost all the categories. Because we find nursing staff also playing an important role in the process, it is pertinent that a hospital manager makes it sure that right from the low echelon of staff to the senior doctors participating in the process are personally and professionally committed.

Availability of hospital personnel on duty, and supporting infrastructural facilities at the work place are to be made sure round-the-clock. It is really amazing that we also find emergency services getting the same treatment as the general services. The managerial, professional, personal excellence of a hospital manager may improve things. While making an appraisal of the performance of hospital personnel, a hospital manager is required to assign due weightage to their performance in offering the emergency services. It is really painful to mention that a majority of the hospital personnel don't prefer emergency services. This necessitates maximum weightage to the emergency services.

It is the prime responsibility of a hospital manager to make it sure that the hospital personnel get or are made available quality environment where they are supposed to work. The working conditions are different and therefore, everything required for the emergency services are to be managed on a priority basis. The ambulance services, the power and communications and the investigation or diagnostic facilities are to be given due weightage so that time-honoured services are made available to the patients. In a true sense, we find emergency services requiring utmost care of a hospital manager because here it is management of time that plays an important role. Any case of negligence of personnel on the emergency duty should be taken up very seriously so that other hospital personnel take a lesson. We need to motivate and we also need to penalise.

'Your motive is to generate efficiency. Your motive is to fulfil the expectations of users and attendants. Your motive is to project a positive image of hospitals. It is your responsibility to make it sure that how and in what way you are going to achieve them.

Willingly or unwillingly, we need to confess that in a majority of the government hospitals, the hospital personnel in general are found disinterested in promoting the work culture because they feel that directly or indirectly, partially or substantially, this is considerably and adversely to affect the workings of their private clinics. Of course, it is an acid test of your professional and managerial excellence. You need to activate the following measures to improve the working of the EMERGENCY DEPARTMENT.

Perceive the Meaning of the word EMERGENCY in a Right Fashion: While going through the management of emergency services, at the outset, try to understand the meaning of emergency. The word "Emergency" is coined from the Latin word "URGENS" and therefore, we find focus on urgency and what is urgent is required to be done without delay. Casualty as defined by the Ministry of Health, London means—a patient who comes to the hospital unannounced with accidental injury and is seen and treated otherwise than at a consultative session. It is against this background that we find emergency department responsible for providing round-the-clock services related to diagnosis and urgent treatment for illness of emergent nature and injuries from accidents. It is in this context that we find emergency department of a hospital a focal point even more than the out-patient department. The surgeons have classified the degree of emergency, such as First Emergency, Second Emergency and Third Emergency. By First Emergency, we find focus on what must be done within a few minutes or hours. By Second Emergency, we mean what must be done within six hours and by Third Emergency, we mean what must be done within 24 hours. It is quite natural that we find a difference in opinion while going through the perception of emergency but one thing can't be denied that it is substantially different to the services that we offer as a part of our routine or time table. If medical and paramedical staff understand the right meaning of the word emergency, it is possible that they would be serious to the emergency duty.

Constitution of a Team of Committed Personnel for the Emergency Department: Though we agree with this view that the senior doctors know better than their peers and subordinates but the task of forming a team is an important functional responsibility of a hospital manager which is to be done in consultation with the senior doctors. The time honoured availability of a team is found significant because we find frequent cases of absence even from the emergency duty. A hospital manager is supposed to have a list of the positive or negative contributions of different categories of personnel. It is a department where you are not supposed to experiment. It is a department where you are not expected to take a chance. It is a department that approves or disapproves your managerial excellence. And therefore, based on past records you need to know about the most efficient personnel of your hospital and to place them on the emergency duty.

Motivate them Sufficiently: We can't negate the fact that motivation bears the efficacy of generating the faculty. If you motivate the personnel serving the emergency department to the level of increasing expectations of patients and attendants, the right or claim of the personnel for getting more incentives can't be denied.

Quality services require quality personnel and quality personnel expect lucrative incentives. It is your prime responsibility to make it sure that the personnel working efficiently are given lucrative incentives. In addition, you also need to link their contributions to incentives. More you work, more you get. Thus, financial and non-financial incentives to the working personnel draw your attention. Besides, you are also supposed to make it sure that quality of environment at the work place is in tune with the requirements. To be more specific, the hospital personnel working in the emergency department are required to work in a different condition. This necessitates availability of infrastructural support so that they don't develop monotony and fatigue. Offering a friendly working environment and efficiency generating environment would provide to them an opportunity to work efficiently. Further, you are also supposed to take care of the environmental conditions at the place where they live. Thus, motivation makes it essential that you provide to them lucrative financial and non-financial incentives; you make available to them quality environment at the work place and ensure quality environment even at their living places.

Availability of Diagnostic and Curative Measures: Since in the emergency department of a hospital, the hospital personnel are supposed to make available quick services, it is your responsibility to see that all the required biomedical equipments are in order. The biomedical equipment incharge, engineers and technicians made available to perform. This makes possible time-honoured availability of investigation or examination reports and the physicians or surgeons are found in a position to take a right decision. Unless the diagnostic reports are made available, the treatment process can't be started. It is really amazing that in a majority of the government hospitals we don't find biomedical equipments in right order. Even if the biomedical equipments are in order, the technicians or engineers are not available. It is against this background that being a hospital manager you have to make available an uninterrupted support of biomedical equipments and to place the efficient personnel at the required place.

Registration Facility: In the emergency department, you need to make a provision for round-the-clock registration facility. All patients coming to the emergency department must be registered. The registration is to be done by the pharmacist on duty. The emergency OPD cases should be registered separately. The registration should be prompt because further line of action would be started only after registration. Every emergency department must have a well organised system of receiving emergency cases. It is right to establish an independent cabin for enquiry close to the emergency department.

Availability of Medicines: It is your responsibility of making it sure that all the medicines and injections for emergency treatment are available. The availability of intravenous fluids and emergency injections would help emergency patients in getting immediate treatment. The central store of the hospital requires to fulfil the demand of the emergency department on a priority basis.

An Efficient Casualty Medical Officer is to be placed: In the emergency department, we find a Casualty Medical Officer playing an outstanding role. This makes it essential that you are placing an efficient medical officer. A Casualty Medical Officer is supposed to admit patient and he/she is also required to refer the patients to the ICU, if they need intensive therapy. A detailed address of patient is recorded by him. Besides, a comprehensive record of patients is to be kept under observation. He bears the responsibility of providing preliminary medical aid to the patients. While treating cases related to the completion of the legal formalities, he/she is supposed to be careful. It is right to mention that in the Indian context, we need an attitudinal change specially related to the treatment of medicolegal cases. We don't find a sense in completing the legal formalities even at the cost of emergency medical aid. Of course, the legal formalities are to be completed but only after making it sure that the legal process is not to harm the patients.

Information and Communication Technologies: In view of the recent changes in the process of diagnosis and treatment, it is pertinent that the emergency department of a hospital is made available sophisticated information and communication facilities to enable them to provide quality medical aid to the emergency patients. The cases of registration, preparation of file, entry of the case diary and the investigation process are of late, considerably influenced by the information technology. It is in this context that we talk about the availability of information and communication technologies. The communication facilitie help a casualty medical officer to speed up the process.

A Frequent Visit: Nothing is secured unless it is done. Nothing is done unless it is monitored frequently and supervised minutely. To be more specific in the Indian perspective where we find absence of a work culture albeit in the hospitals and health care organisations, it is the prime responsibility of a hospital manager to make it sure that everything is going on as per his/her plan and schedule. This necessitates frequent visits of a hospital manager, specially to the emergency department which in a majority of the hospitals is found tarnishing the image of hospitals besides depriving the patients of the quality of treatment they need. Since we find the performance of emergency departments considerably influenced by the services of almost all the departments, even a minor mistake, a small break and interruption even for a few minutes may result into irreparable losses to the patients. If the personnel forget their responsibilities, a manager has no option but to be vigilant and to remind.

The aforesaid measures would bring improvement in the quality of services of the emergency department. The government hospitals draw our attention on a priority basis because except a very few, we find almost all the hospitals not sincere to the working of the emergency department. The hospital personnel just complete their formalities by attending the department. The non-availability of medicines albeit life saving drugs in the emergency department is not found to be a matter of grave concern. The absence of biomedical technicians and poor maintenance and operation of biomedical equipments are not to shock us. The frequent interruption in the supply of power even to the emergency department is not taken up seriously. The non-operational ambulances don't gravitate our attention. The indecent behaviour of personnel with the patients and attendants is not to disturb us. It is against this background that we need a professionally sound and personally committed hospital manager who knows about the significance of the emergency department because he/ she has perceived the meaning of the word "emergency" in a right fashion. It is only the excellence of a hospital manager that can bring the derailed systems of healthcare on the rail. Time management is considered to be the main thing in the emergency department where delay of even a few seconds matters.

Managing Radiotherapy and Oncology

Radiation Oncology is considered to be a highly sophisticated technology-driven area and therefore, availability of power facilities and skilled personnel for that very purpose are found important. The super-voltage cancer radiotherapy has virtually revolutionised the process of cancer treatment. Cancer of uterus and oral cavity are now found curable with radiotherapy. The curative management of cancer is found considerably influenced by radiotherapy. It is in this context that we find radiotherapy and oncology centre[11] gaining prominence in hospitals and healthcare organisations. We agree with this view that the initial management decision is the most critical component in the treatment of cancer, specially in the application of radiation sources. The expertise of radiation oncologists is needed in the very context. Of late, we find the system of surgery well-developed and it requires augmentation to include the modern technological developments. Radiotherapy including chemotherapy is the one discipline which needs to be established in the free cancer standing centres for quality treatment and better cure. A doctor, specialist in the area needs to accept the responsibility of using the centres to benefit the patients and a hospital manager bears the responsibility of making it sure that the radiotherapy and oncology centre is working satisfactorily.

We are well aware of the fact that the management of the centre is found expensive because sophisticated technological support along with skilled team of personnel become pertinent to get the desired benefits from the centre. In this context, we talk about the professional excellence of a hospital manager so that he/she succeeds in removing the financial and the managerial constraints. An effective financial planning is an important consideration to translate the plan into a meaningful action. The cost of service would, of course, be expensive and not affordable to the masses. On the one hand, we find hospitals requiring huge finance to develop radiotherapy and oncology centre while on the other hand, the patients find it difficult to afford the expensive services. This is found making the investment unproductive. It is against this background that we need to promote the centres by making provision for the reimbursement for patient treatment programme. The services of domestic and foreign insurance corporations and companies may be of significant use. In addition, the provincial and union governments also need to promote the centre by reimbursing the medical bills of their personnel. There should be a provision for a special grant from the government and charitable trusts and organisations. We also need to solicit the cooperation of community philanthropists in the development of the centre.

It is right to mention that the two forms of treatment that is, radiation and medical oncology are also known as non-surgical treatment. We consider it to be a part of sophisticated technology development programme benefiting the patients considerably. Since they provide precision treatment and accurate dose delivery to the target volume, a hospital manager requires to think for the development of the centre. It is also significant to mention that the medical oncology is not found so expensive but requires indoor bed facilities and a day-care ward for treatment. Since we talk about the instrumentality of a hospital manager in managing the centre efficiently, it is essential that he/she knows about the essential requirements for the establishment of the centre. Right from the installation and beginning of centre to the stage of delivery, a hospital manager is required to work in a close coordination with the radiotherapist and medical physicist.

Managing Ophthalmic Services

We can't negate that blindness is a curse for a person who is affected vis-a-vis a burden to the family and society. This necessitates concerted efforts to prevent blindness. There are a number of reasons for blindness and in less developed countries like ours, we find unawareness resulting into a sharp increase in the cases of blindness. Blindness due to infections, trauma, poor nutrition, uncorrected refractive errors, glaucoma are found to be preventable if right decisions are taken at the right time.[12] A hospital manager is supposed to create awareness so that the cases of blindness are minimised. The following steps are to show positive results:

Promoting Eye Health Education: Avoidable blindness requires creativity in educating the masses found not aware of the causes. In an age of sophisticated communication technologies, the task is found easier if a hospital manager evinces his/her interests in the process of sensitising the masses. Nutrition, personal hygiene and sanitation, early detection of visual problems, occupational hazards to eye-sight and other injuries, glaucoma, appeals for voluntary eye donation are some of the measures if given due weightage and taken due care, would minimise the cases of blindness. It is high time that a hospital manager realises the gravity of the situation and promotes eye-care communications to create mass awareness.

Mobilising Fund for the Free Operation: It is the responsibility of a hospital manager working in government or private hospitals to generate and mobilise funds for free operation of the poorest sections of the society not in a position to afford the costs. He/she requires to motivate the charitable trusts and organisations to donate substantially to this holy job of curing blindness.

Involving all Doctors: Since we find it a pious work, it is significant that a hospital manager makes efforts to solicit the cooperation of all the doctors for this purpose. Involving all ophthalmic surgeons, introducing a short-term course in ophthalmology, motivating the personnel participating in this endeavour, promoting camps in the rural and neglected areas are some of the measures expected to be helpful in the very context. Even the cooperation of voluntary social organisations and NSS units would be of significant use.

Infrastructural Support: Since we talk about the expansion of services even to the villages, it is pertinent that in the camps, all the supporting infrastructural facilities are made available. Even in the hospitals, we don't find the existing infrastructural facilities helpful to cater to the increasing demand and therefore, it is the prime responsibility of a hospital manager to make it sure that the infrastructural facilities are enriched. All the existing Public Health Centres are to be equipped with basic ophthalmic equipments. In-services training programme is required to be promoted.

Programme Evaluation and Monitoring: A hospital manager is supposed to evaluate and monitor the programme so that the results are evaluated, shortcomings are identified and the corrective measures are taken. A target is to be fixed and the same is to be achieved within the stipulated time and budget.

The aforesaid steps would help minimising the cases of blindness. A hospital manager requires personal-touch-in-services, so that the problem of blindness is minimised.

Managing Nursing Services

All of us accept the positive contributions of the nursing staff in the generation of healthcare and medicare services. In a true sense, we find them standing as an important pillar on which the hospitals are surviving. Of course, we find hierarchy in management and the Director of Nursing manages and controls, to monitor and manage the process but ultimately, a hospital manager bears the responsibility of making it sure that they have been serving the hospitals in a right fashion. It is against this background that we go through the management of nursing services.

At the outset, we go through the concept of nursing. According to Lambertson "Nursing is a dynamic, therapeutic and educative process in meeting the health needs of the society." The International Court of Nurses (1965) makes it clear that the nurse is a person who has completed a programme of basic nursing education and is qualified and authorised in her country to supply the most responsible services of nursing for the promotion of health, prevention of illness and care of the sick. The American Nurse Association defines a professional nurse and says, "One who has met all legal requirements for registration in a state and one who practices and holds position by virtue of her professional knowledge and legal status."

The aforesaid facts make it clear that nurses are persons who have completed the basic nursing education course and are authorised to offer the services of nursing related to the promotion of healthcare services. They are supposed to be professionally sound to nurse the patients as per the requirements. They bear the responsibility of serving the patients with the motto of making available to them the prescribed medical aid.

If we talk about the management of nursing services in a hospital, it is right to mention that in different hospitals, we find different provisions for the management of nursing services. However, we find line and functional organisation as the process of managing and controlling the nursing services. In the line organisation, the Director of Nursing Administration determines the number and types of nurses in the hospitals, makes provisions for their recruitments, trains them, directs them, controls them and makes efforts to motivate them. In the functional organisation, the physicians or doctors prescribe a course of treatment which is carried out on the respective clinical service. The members of the nursing staff are to assist the physicians.[13]

In almost all the hospitals, we find nursing services aimed at the following:

- Offering to the patients the best possible medical care with the minimum inputs.

- Identifying the problems related to patient care and suggesting the best possible solutions to overcome them.
- Strengthening staff development programme to improve the quality of patient care.
- Facilitating inter and intradepartmental coordination for improving the level of efficiency of hospitals.
- Developing quality nurses who are not only professionally sound but even personally committed to show personal-touch-in service.

Here we go through the problem of management and therefore, focus on the instrumentality of a hospital manager in controlling and supervising the nursing staff so that they offer the best possible services to the patients. We are well aware of the fact that it is a service devised to improve patient care by promoting, stimulating and fostering of personal growth and welfare. It is primarily concerned with personnel. It is concerned with physical facilities and equipments only in so far as they affect the quality and care. Because we find nurses playing a contributory role in improving the quality of healthcare services in almost all the hospitals, it is the prime responsibility of a healthcare manager or a hospital manager to make it sure that the process of degeneration is not to take place. A hospital manager by making possible frequent visit of wards may be in a position to identify the lapses in the process. Though we find doctors, matron and director of nursing administration there but keeping in view the significance of nursing services in the good-patient care, a hospital manager is also supposed to make it sure that they are really contributing substantially to the process of offering the best possible services to the patients.

In the nursing services, in addition to professional commitments, we also find the instrumentality of personal commitments. The nurses are supposed to show empathy and it is the personal-touch-in-service that determines the level of their efficiency. May be that doctors don't assign due weightage to empathy; may be that even the matron does not take it up seriously but a hospital manager is supposed to make it sure that they are not only present on duty and offering the services prescribed by doctors and matron but in addition, also keep themselves professionally and personally involved in the process of satisfying the level of expectation of patients so that they are found satisfied and prefer to come to the hospitals if circumstances warrant so.

Since we find nurses placed at the sensitive points, if they are not personally-committed, a degeneration in the quality of services can't be ruled out. There are different types of patients, e.g., some of them are not in a position to move; some of them are not in a position to speak; some of them are decent; some of them are indecent. It is the prime responsibility of a nurse to help them with professional excellence and personal care. A hospital manager requires to make it sure that they are blending the two attributes while performing. He/she bears the responsibility of going through the cases of complaints against the nursing staff personally so that the problems are perceived and appropriate solutions are practiced. A hospital manager is supposed to motivate them so that they serve the patients like a friend. They show not only sympathy to the patients but also promote empathy to diffuse their tension.

In view of the above, it is right to say that a hospital manager also bears the responsibility of improving the quality of nursing services because in almost all the hospitals, this dimension of patient care has been found neglected. Currently, we find degeneration in the quality of nursing services and the process of degeneration is required to be checked without a further delay. A hospital manager with the support of medical and paramedical staff is required to go through the problems in a right fashion so that the nursing staff keeps on moving the process of offering a good-patient care.

Managing the Rehabilitation Services

We find rehabilitation a service to the suffering patients to make them mentally prepared to live in the community. It is a device to bring the patients back to the normal state. Rehabilitation is a specialisation in medicine. It is considered to be an integral part of medicare. The increasing cases of accident, metabolic diseases, neoplastic diseases, cardiovascular diseases and neuro-muscular diseases have made the rehabilitation services essential. According to WHO Technical Series No. 419 (1969) on Medical Rehabilitation, the expert committee recommended to create rehabilitation centres should be established in coordination with social and educational services. In order to promote education in rehabilitation, the faculty of medicine requires to create a provision of rehabilitation personnel. Rehabilitation has a number of connotations. Occupational therapy and physiotherapy are also used in the process.[14]

The WHO makes it clear that the rehabilitation is the combined and coordinated use of medical, social, educational and vocational measures for training or retraining the individual to the highest possible level of functional ability. The physiotherapy deals with physical treatment by means of a course of exercises, cold or hot massage, steam-bath, water-bath, light treatment and electrical massages. The occupational therapy is a medically directed treatment of the physically or mentally disabled by means of constructive activities designed and adopted by a professionally qualified occupational therapist to promote the restoration of useful functions.

Of course, we find the Director of Physical Medicine working as the incharge of the Department of Rehabilitation, but a hospital manager is also required to make a time-to-time supervision of the working of the department to make it sure that patients are not only given the occupational therapy but even the physiotherapy in a right fashion. The Director of Physical Medicine is authorised for admission and discharge of patients. He/she makes an assessment of the plan, coordinates and implements all the programmes related to rehabilitation. He/she proposes budget for the department.

It is important to mention that rehabilitation is a team work and therefore, personal involvement of a number of hospital personnel in the process of offering the services becomes a must. The physicians, physical therapist, occupational therapist, social worker, speech and hearing therapist, nurses, vocational counsellor, psychologists and prosthetic specialist need to participate in the process of offering the rehabilitation services and therefore, the administrative and managerial responsibilities focus on the best possible coordination so that the required services of different specialists are made available to the patients. It is also essential that we focus on the establishment of follow-up clinics in the town or city to be more specific when the patients are discharged from the rehabilitation centre specially to activate the follow up action.

Since we find it a multidimensional functional responsibility promoted by a number of specialists related to a number of disciplines and areas, it is the prime responsibility of a hospital manager to ensure quality services to the patients. Coordination is an important managerial responsibility and a manager requires to ascertain that the prescribed or defined services are processed in a right fashion. It is in this context that we talk about the instrumentality of a hospital manager in making the rehabilitation services result-oriented.

It is significant to mention that with the ongoing health, demographic and socio-economic transitions, the disability profile is changing with an alarming rise in the number of people suffering from chronic disorders and associated morbidity and strength to the problem of mental disabilities mainly due to stress. This makes it essential that government policy makers assign due weightage to train adequate human resources required for medical rehabilitation programme at all the three levels of Healthcare Delivery System. The Physical Medicine and Rehabilitation (PMR) departments in the country need to act as Model Centres. In the Medical Colleges and Teaching Institutions, the PMR Departments are to be set up. The medical rehabilitation services are to be developed by them in Districts, CHCs and PHCs. Additionally, the medical and rehabilitation professionals are to be developed in adequate number for providing secondary and tertiary level rehabilitation services. The training programme is required to be introduced at Diploma, Undergraduate and Post-Graduate levels with due focus on disability prevention, detection and early intervention. The rehabilitation services are to be provided in Medical Hospital and strategies are to be formulated for caring domiciliary and community set up.

We cannot deny that the intensity of problem would aggravate in the coming years because the mounting global financial crisis would increase the number of people facing the problem of stress and tension which would make it essential that almost all the Medical Colleges are potentially sound to counter the emerging challenges and threats. The most dangerous facet which focuses our attention on mental disability requires multicornered support. On the one hand we need to enrich the medicare services while on the other hand, we also find it significant to prevent disability by ordering the social systems where family members would play a commanding role.

Managing Food and Beverage Services

It is right to mention that in a modern hospital, the management of food and beverage services occupy a place of significance. It is not only sufficient that your patients are made available quality diagnostic and treatment facilities. The basic thing in the process is to make possible quick recovery of patients which in addition to the administration of appropriate medicines are also influenced by other factors, such as offering of time honoured quality food and beverages to the patients. It is against this background that a hospital manager is required to make it sure that Dietetics and Food and Beverage Department perform their defined responsibilities in a right fashion. Whatever the diet charts are made available by the doctors or the dieticians, if the Food and Beverage Department follows the same, there is no possibility of qualitative or quantitative degeneration. The establishment of Dietary Department in a hospital is one of the important facilities provided for the due healthcare of the patients. Of course, a hospital or a healthcare organisation is required to manage a number of services but it is not meant that they place the food and beverage services at the bottom of their functional agenda. We agree with this view that the food services is one of the most important functional responsibilities in a hospital which requires expertise vis-a-vis careful monitoring so that the patients get the prescribed dose and quality on the time mentioned in the treatment chart. In this context, it is essential to make it clear that a treatment chart covers everything that a patient requires for quick recovery, such as medicines, food and beverages, therapy prescribed or so. It is due to the fact that in a leading hospital, we find a manager assigning due weightage to the treatment chart.

Food service is one of the most important activities in any hospital. As a therapeutic measure, we find the services contributing substantially to the recovery process. This makes it essential that in hospitals, we find due importance to dieticians, supposed to be an expert in the area. The doctors also help the process of preparing a diet-chart for the patients. It is quite natural that the diet chart is prepared in the face of nature and character of diseases and therefore, this department is required to follow an individualistic approach. The dietetic unit spends a large portion of the hospital budget. It has three important responsibilities, viz., administrative, therapeutic and educational. This makes it essential that in a hospital, we find qualified dieticians discharging their functional responsibilities efficiently. A dietician should be a person with a degree, either B. Sc. (Home Science) with the Postgraduate Diploma in Dietetics and Nutrition or M. Sc. (Food and Nutrition). He/she is found directly responsible to a hospital manager. In the modern hospitals, we find a fullfledged independent department where well-qualified dieticians are placed. To be more specific, in the small hospitals, even doctors can discharge this responsibility or the services of a part-time dietician can be made available.

The Dietary Department is found directly responsible for formulating a diet-chart or menu for the different categories of patients. There are a number of functional responsibilities, such as selection and purchase of food in a close working relationship with the purchase department for receipt and storage of food items, preparation and distribution of food, maintenance of cleanliness and properties, dishwashing in a proper way, coordinating with the medical and nursing staff, sensing and influencing patients regarding the instrumentality of food and beverage in the treatment process and so on. It is in this context that the dieticians need an indepth knowledge of nutrition in addition to the managerial ability to enable him/her to organise his/her staff and their work so as to produce the best possible results at the least possible costs. Thus, to provide food and beverages properly and in time and at prescribed dose and interval, the dieticians are supposed to be careful because this department is often found to be a centre for the unfair practices mainly with the connivance of the purchase department. Since we find the dietetic unit spending a major portion of the hospital budget, the cases of financial irregularities are also found. It is the responsibility of a hospital manager to make it sure that the patients are made available quality foods, in right time and in a decent way.

The beverages also draw our close attention because in addition to food, we find beverages playing an incremental role in the process of formulating an optimal diet chart. By beverage, our focus is on any liquid for drinking, such as tea, coffee, milk, juice, a mixture of cider and water or even a drink. In the hospital management, we find beverages playing an important role because a majority of the hospitals don't consider it an important dimension which in a true sense occupies a place of outstanding significance. The supply of contaminated water, infected or not properly boiled or skimmed milk, not properly preserved juice may invite a number of health hazards to the patients. It is in this context that the dieticians are also required to assign due weightage to beverages in the diet-chart or menu prepared by them.

The aforesaid facts make it clear that we find a close relation between the Department of Dietetics and the Purchase and Stores Department because failing coordination, the chart of dieticians would not be followed. We can't negate that in a majority of the government hospitals, we find both the departments conniving and generating unfair practices. It is against this background that patients in a majority of the government hospitals are not supplied the food and drinks as per the diet-chart. Of course, we find the budgetary provision and the food and drink items are also purchased but not properly preserved. The items are also supplied to the medical superintendent or dietician for their personal consumption, the schedule and timing is not followed, the quality is not maintained and so on. It is the responsibility of a hospital manager to make it sure that the irregularities or unfair practices in the process are checked and the patients are made available the required quality and quantity of food and beverages on time and in a decent and refined way.

On the other hand, it is also right to mention that we find a mismatch between the rising prices and the budgetary provisions. Inadequate financial provision for the food and beverages is found to be common problem in almost all the government hospitals. It is really amazing that even doctors don't assign due weightage to the management of diet in the process of recovery of patients. This necessitates an attitudinal change. The medical, paramedical staff, the nursing staff and the dieticians need to make it sure that quality food and beverages are served to the patients. They are also required to assign due weightage to the time schedule and to the cleanliness and decency while offering the items to the patients. Since we find it an essential part of the prescription of a doctor, a hospital manager bears the ultimate responsibility of ensuring quality and maintaining quantity.

Housekeeping

The housekeeping focusses our attention on the management of wards where patients stay for a long time. We agree with this view that patients in addition to other aspects also need proper care of bedsheets, rooms, essential facilities to the patients or so. We agree with this view that good housekeeping is an asset to a hospital not only because it has physiological effects upon patients and visitors but also with the motto of projecting a positive image. Like hotels, the hospitals also need to consider it an important aspect of good patient care. The housekeepers are found responsible for managing wards in such a fashion that patients, attendants, visiting doctors and other staff feel pleasure in staying or performing. He/she is found directly responsible to a hospital manager or incharge of a particular ward or wards. It is essential that the housekeepers are schooled in the fundamentals of home economics and physical sciences. The primary functions of housekeeping department include routine cleaning, dusting, mopping, waxing, window and wall-washing and similar domestic duties involved in maintaining a high standard of cleanliness in a hospital. They should also have the knowledge of bed-making and other functions necessary in preparing a vacated room for a new patient.

Of course, we find patients and attendants considerably influenced by the healthcare services made available to them but at the same time, it is also right to mention that they are also impressed by the housekeeping facilities made available in the hospitals. If we find wards becoming a place for infection, if we find dust on windows, if we find linen not well maintained, if we find blood-sucking insects on the bed of the patients, the patients are found in trouble. Besides, the medical and paramedical staff and the nursing staff find it difficult to discharge their functional responsibilities efficiently. Criticism of the linen services is one of the most frequent complaints in almost all the government hospitals. We need to take care of it and to use the services of housekeepers as found in the hospitality industry. We agree with this view that we find a number of similarities in the management of housekeeping in both the sectors. Properly planned linen and laundry services, supply of clean and well disinfected linen at a regular interval, frequent change of linen and its effective washing need your due care because in a majority of the hospitals, we don't find even doctors considering the importance of good housekeeping in the easy/quick recovery of patients. In addition to other aspects, the projection of a fair image is also an important functional responsibility of a hospital manager and this requires a culture to be maintained as we find in a well maintained hotel.

The aforesaid facts make it clear that supply of quality food, maintaining cleanliness in the rooms and toilets, maintaining linen, drapery and other furnishing, ensuring supply of safe water for drinking, adequate water in toilets, etc. are some of the important areas not getting due attention of a housekeeper and therefore, a hospital manager requires to make it sure that patients living in wards, attendants or other visiting hospitals, medical, paramedical staff and the nurses serving the patients are motivated and impressed with the management of wards which all are the functional responsibilities of housekeepers. Of course, the professional expertise of doctors and other staff play an important role in improving the quality of healthcare services but we can't negate the fact that food and beverage services and housekeeping till now found at the bottom of almost in all the government hospitals need a priority attention. Quality in totality makes it essential that you assign due weightage even to the small heads.

Laundry Services

As and when we talk about the management of linen, our focus in a very natural way is on the management of laundry services. We can't negate the fact that the hospital personnel in general bear the responsibility of removing the possibilities of infection generated at different sources. Since we find linen an important source of infection and the laundry bears the responsibility of making them clean and infection-free, we need to assign due weightage also to this dimension of hospital services.

The washing operation in general has three objectives, viz., washing, drying and packing. The responsibilities are removing of visible soil or dirt, removal or destruction of invisible living soil-pathogens and/or objectionable micro-organisms and completing removal of "pyrogenic" substances from the surfaces. Here, we go through the problem of cleaning linen and therefore concentrate our attention on the laundry services.

The laundry should have facilities for physically separate places for soiled linen from clean linen. Soiled linen be loaded into one side and clean linens be removed on the other side. In a modern laundry, soiled linens are sorted out and put on to the sling bag for lifting on to water-extractors. The water-extractor unloads on the clean side into a sling and the clean linen is conveyed and dumped into a gas-fired dryer. Linens for ironing are processed across a Braun 3-roll ironer and automatic folder on the discharge end for sheets. Folded sheets are dropped on to a stracker where they are counted automatically and transferred into the clean linen belt conveyer. If clean linens are dropped accidentally on the floor, they are considered to be soiled and are not used. During bed changes, soiled linen is placed in a roll-round soiled linen hampers. Soiled linen from ISOLATION rooms are double bagged frost in a clear plastic water soluble bag and then placed into a red impervious plastic bag marked ISOLATION LINEN. The outer red bag is removed at the washer. The interior bag is not opened but pushed physically into the washer with its contents. This inner bag, being water soluble, disintegrates the washing process and its use protects those handling isolation linens. The laundry is kept spotless including the floor, equipments and overhead pipes.

Of late, we have automatic devices to clean and therefore, the task of the laundry department is considerably simplified. However, it is important that the process of collecting and cleaning the linens get due weightage to minimise the possibilities of infection. The wards and operation theatres need due cooperation of laundry for this purpose. The main thing in the process is to make available clean and well disinfected linen to the different wards and centres where these are used and in the process become dirty. Despite of mechanised drying, we find sunlight playing a significant role in the process of drying because we find it a natural source of disinfection. It is in this context that we find an open space essential for laundry. The personnel engaged in the department are required to make it sure that the time-gap between the linen received for cleaning and linen handed over should be minimised to the extent it is possible.

Safety and Security Services and Fire-Fighting

The protection to hospital assets and personnel in addition to the patients and attendants is found significant and this draws our attention on the safety and security services in a hospital. In addition, the possibilities of fire are also to be minimised and this gravitates our attention on the fire-fighting services.

We can't negate the fact that hospitals can become the victims of fires, thefts and accidents. The dreadful situation is to be avoided and this necessitates proper arrangements of fire-fighting staff, well-trained in preventive measures in addition to their routine task. The fire-alarm system is found essential to signal the personnel. A qualified officer is found responsible to counter the problem with the support and cooperation of a team. The security personnel must be trained and experienced and they should be an asset to the hospital. Since the functional responsibilities of fire services personnel are found of emergent nature, it is pertinent that proper care is taken for their education, training and motivation.

The safety security arrangements are required to be tightened so that the assets of hospitals are found safe. To be more specific, the stores and purchase department where we find possibilities of theft and pilferages need due care of the security officer who is supposed to protect the property of hospitals. At the outset, we have gone through the problem of hospital planning and the hospital architects and consultants need to make suitable arrangements so that security personnel find it convenient to grill the assets and to protect them. It is very painful to mention that in some of the hospitals, we find cases of theft and pilferages with the connivance of hospital personnel and therefore, it is pertinent that a hospital manager keeps his/her eyes open round the clock. While recruiting personnel for the safety and security or even for fire-fighting, we need to prefer the services of retired army personnel who in a majority of the cases are found not only efficient but also honest and dedicated. If we recruit personnel from other sources, it is significant that we assign due weightage to their past records.

Thus, the two important problems influencing the hospital assets and dreadful situation for the sick and their relatives and the hospital personnel working there draw our attention on a priority basis. The cases of safety and security also become important to maintain the problem of law and order. The financial losses due to fire, theft and pilferages are to be removed and this is the responsibility of the safety and security department to take care of the same. To be more specific, the government hospitals need due attention because in a majority of the government hospitals, we find frequent cases of theft and pilferages. Im a true sense, a hospital manager requires to fix accountability because we find involvement of even the senior staff in the operation. Proper fencing of the premises of hospitals, automatic gate and tight security arrangements are some of the measures likely to be effective in minimising the intensity of problem. The main thing in the process is to ensure safety to the patients, attendants, hospital personnel, hospital assets and for this proper safety, security and fire-fighting measures are to be made scientific and result-oriented.

Engineering Services

Right from the first stage of designing hospitals to the stage of construction, repairing and dismantling, we find the engineering department playing an important role in the smooth functioning of hospitals. This makes it essential that different areas for the engineering services, viz., construction of houses, repairing, electricity, power, communications where the engineering section is required play an important role. Being a ship of high seas, a hospital is likely to face a number of emergencies. Sudden failure in some of the installations in OTs ICUs, Kidney unit, etc. can jeopardise the life of patients. This requires proper know-how to counter the multi-dimensional problems. The responsibility of engineering department is required to be assigned to a well-qualified and value-based engineer. It is essential that he/she is familiar with maintenance in diverse areas like water supply, drainage, boilers, laundry, air-conditioning, electronic equipment, electricity, communications and so on. It is essential that he/she is assisted by a small-trained group. A hospital engineer is also responsible to organise some alternative arrangements to ensure that casual absence of some staff is not to create problem to the hospital services.

Management by crisis is an important thing in the proper working of the engineering department of a hospital. It is in this context that we find instrumentality of a dedicated engineer in the hospitals. In addition to the construction and maintenance of buildings in the hospitals, we find engineers also responsible even for the proper functioning of the medical equipments, apparatus, machines and so on. This once again increases the significance of engineering department because we find maintenance technicians and personnel responsible for managing and maintaining the biomedical equipment and apparatus. What is the most important thing that we find in the process is to strengthen the preventive measures. It is hoped that engineers and their team would be helpful to the medical and paramedical staff of the hospitals. The calculation of the expected period during which each and every place of equipment would function satisfactorily and proper arrangements would be made as soon as the troubles start or faults develop or even before that, the equipment would receive service attention or be replaced without the intervention of any one but the engineering staff. This requires much time and efficient personnel. It is the responsibility of engineers working there to constitute an efficient team found successful in discharging the assigned responsibilities.

The aforesaid facts make it clear that engineering department is found to be an important department of hospitals influencing almost all the dimensions, directly or indirectly, partially or substantially. The uninterrupted supply of power and water, the availability of safe drinking water and general water, the communication services, etc. influence the quality of services to be made available by the hospitals. This makes it essential that a hospital manager assigns due weightage to the construction cell of a hospital because the construction and maintenance of buildings if not done properly, the power facilities if not available round-the-clock, the water facilities if not adequate, the communications services if not working satisfactorily influence the quality of services in a hospital. In the Indian perspective, we need due attention of engineers because we not only need professionally sound engineers but also realise the instrumentality of personally committed engineers. The increasing unfair practices in a majority of the hospitals make it essential that engineers or even other staff of the department are efficient and dedicated.

Innovative Product Profile

We have gone through different dimensions of hospital product/services. The scientific advancements have made possible a number of qualitative improvements in the healthcare or medicare services. The process of diagnosis and treatment is now found technology driven. Thus, scientific inventions and innovations have opened copious avenues for the development of healthcare services. The hospitals or healthcare institutions promoting advanced and sophisticated technologies have, of late been found establishing an edge over the traditional hospitals not only in respect of medicare services of core and supportive nature but we also find them very much instrumental in promoting the innovative peripheral services. This in a very natural way has been successful in increasing the levels of expectations of patients and attendants. On the other hand, the traditionally managed hospitals, specially under the government control are found offering traditional medical services. Besides, we also find there the problem of deficient management generating a big gap between the services ensured and the services offered. The patients in general are found dissatisfied. This makes it essential that almost all categories of hospitals keep on moving the process of innovation so that quality medicare services are offered to the patients. It is against this background that we talk about the instrumentality of innovative product profile for the hospitals.

It is quite natural that functional boundaries of hospitals are considerably determined by the nature and character even if we find scope for innovation in almost all the areas. At the very outset, it is the prime responsibility of a hospital manager to make it sure that the medicinal and surgical services are innovated and sophisticated technologies are used for this purpose. In consultation with the senior doctors, a hospital manager is supposed to know about their requirements and to make available to them the required amenities and facilities on time so that they are in a position to perform excellently. We are well aware of the fact that almost all types of diagnostic and treatment processes are now technology-driven. To make possible qualitative improvements, a hospital manager needs to think in this direction. The boardrooms or the policy makers are to be approached and convinced so that we find among them an attitudinal change.

The biomedical equipment have been found playing an important role in improving the quality of medicare or healthcare services. There are a number of sophisticated equipment used for diagnosis and treatment. The biomedical equipment incharge, technicians and supervisors contribute substantially to the process of a productive use of biomedical equipment. It is really amazing that specially in the government hospitals, we find even expensive big-medical equipment, not maintained, operated and repaired properly thus, resulting into a huge financial loss in addition to the degeneration in the quality of service. Inadequacy of efficient professionals in managing the biomedical equipment is found a general problem, particularly in the government hospitals. Thus, to improve the quality of medicare services, it is pertinent that not only should we make available to the hospitals quality and sophisticated biomedical equipment but also ensure proper maintenance and management of the same. It is in this context that we need constructive and positive cooperation of a hospital manager.

The curative services are to be innovated and the task would remain unfulfilled unless we get support of quality personnel and sophisticated equipment. You need to make it sure that mismanagement of technologies used in the process is checked and the accountability is fixed.

In addition to the curative services, you also bear the responsibility of innovating the preventive services. This makes it essential that you promote the use of sophisticated information and communication technologies to educate the masses. Your promotional measures need to sensitise the masses in a creative fashion so that the task of attracting the potential customers /patients is made easier. We agree with this view that a change in the disease profile is well supported by our wrong decisions related to food habits, quality of water, quality of environment, wrong habits and so on. You have the latest sophisticated devices to create mass awareness and you need to make it possible. Audio-visual exposure would help you fantastically in minimising the cases of food-borne, water-borne, environment-prone and noise-borne diseases. Since you bear the responsibility of formulating a sound product profile for your hospitals, it is your prime responsibility to open new vistas for promoting healthcare communications.

"Differentiate or Die" is a slogan required to be practiced by almost all the organisations either producing goods or generating services. The hospitals and healthcare organisations would be successful in differentiating their services/products, if the process of innovation keeps on moving.[15] An organisation needs to believe in making things happen. It is right to mention that a majority of the government or private hospitals have not assigned due weightage to the innovation process. Not only the curative and preventive services but you also need to innovate the peripheral services. The peripheral services add attractions to your product profile because you offer to the patients and attendants a number of services related to their comforts and conveniences. You make suitable provisions for the accommodation of attendants, safe drinking water, modern sanitation, quality seating arrangements, entertainment facilities, pay-phone services, uninterrupted power, sophisticated communication facilities, shopping facilities, restaurant and cafeteria, courier services, personal care services and a number of other facilities helping them in countering the unfavourable conditions, mental tension, monotony and so on. We find modern private hospitals offering innovative peripheral services to the patients and attendants and by doing so, they succeed in making their product profile distinct to others and attracting the patients and attendants.

Because of late, we talk about hospital marketing, you need to show your professional and managerial excellence in many ways. If you continue with the traditional services and other hospitals offer the modern sophisticated services, it is quite natural that potential customers/patients and attendants would prefer to go or use the services of hospitals where they get the refined services of world class. It is against this background that we find innovations essential even in the hospitals. It is quite natural that nature and character of services made available by your organisation would determine the services to be included or eliminated. The main thing that we find in the very context is related to the offering of an innovative product profile which focuses our attention on offering of world class medicare or healthcare services to the patients so that the risk factors are minimised, results are found positive, patients feel satisfied and their expectations are fulfilled. It is not only important that a number of services are included in the product profile, indeed but it is much more impact generating that whatever the services you include in the product profile are of world class.

Promoting e-Health

In an age of information and communication technology, the healthcare sector has also been found making use of new generation of information and communication technology for improving the quality of medicare services. Since we have an advantage of a strong fibre backbone and indigenous satellite communication technology, it is possible for us to define and redefine quality. During the yesteryears, a number of pilot projects on e-health[16] have been set up by private concerns, corporations, NGOs, medical colleges and research institutions and we find their positive impact on service quality. However, we lag far behind because the benefits of technology are yet to be shared by the rural healthcare centres. It is in this context that we find Health Management Information System to be given due weightage. A computerized web-enabled data capturing and the system of analysis are to provide valid and reliable data and reports for use at all levels. The system is also to integrate the various vertical systems having their own reporting machinery into an integrated umbrella of holistic medical education to cater to the needs of Sarva Swasthya Abhigyan. The moment we succeed in momentising the penetration of computerization at the block level, the HMIS would be modular enough to expand the scope to the remotest areas. The increasing cases of wastage of drugs due to expiry of date would also be curtailed by speeding up demand driven management and redistribution of medicines nearing date of expiry. Tracking of demand and supply would be found easier with the help of HMIS.

Additionally, the telemedicine would be helpful in promoting specialised healthcare to the remotest areas of the country. The telemedicine would also provide the advantages of telediagnosis especially in the areas of cardiology, pathology, dermatology and radiology. This will add new feathers in the area of innovative medical education and the users availing the secondary level healthcare facilities would find it easier to meet their diagnostic and consultative requirements. The services of ISRO would be helpful in connecting superspeciality hospitals and mobile telemedicine vans and rural and remote hospitals. The geostationary satellites would channelise the services across the country.

The e-health initiatives thus would redefine service quality. The time honoured flow of date and collation with the help of HMIS, Geographical Information System (GIS), Resources Mapping of various health facilities such as allopathic and AYUSH, need-based training and development of paramedical and medical staff, e-enabled activities like disease surveillance, tele-consultations, health helpline and district hospital referral net mobile medical units would be helpful in innovating the healthcare services not only to a few of affluent segments but albeit to the poor rural masses.

Hence, it is pertinent that the central as well as the state governments evince keen interests in promoting e-health. All the three tiers such as primary, secondary and tertiary systems would immensely be benefited with the innovative devices of e-health.

Policies Influencing Hospital Product

Since we talk about quality in totality, it is imperative that we focus on some of the policies directly or indirectly, partially or substantially influencing the quality of hospital product and making it difficult for the hospital professionals to project a positive image. It is in this context that we go through the problem of drug education, medical education, healthcare education and population. We can't deny the fact that these policies considerably influence the quality of healthcare services.

Drug Policy

Of course the qualitative transformation in the diagnostic and treatment measures have played an incremental role in improving the quality of healthcare services but the task of a doctor is made much more complicated if the pharmaceutical industry is not to make a significant contribution to the process. The quality of drugs supplied by the industry influences the expertise and excellence of doctors vis-a-vis the image of a hospital. Provision of appropriate drugs of good quality and at an affordable price is found essential for the success of disease control programme. Equally important is to restrict the use of irrational drug formulation and detect and eliminate spurious drugs. We are well aware of the fact that the Central Government is found responsible for the control over the quality of imported drugs, control over the manufacturing and import of new drugs into the country, amendment to the Drugs and Cosmetics Act and Rules, coordinating the activities with the State Drug Control authorities for uniform implementation of Drug and Cosmetics Act and Rules, laying down standards for drugs and updating Indian Pharmacopoeia, training of drug analysts and drug inspectors and licensing of whole human blood and blood products, large volume parenterals, sera and vaccines and making provision for strengthening Drug Control Organisations in the states. There is no doubt in it that we find a regulatory control over the process but at the same time, it is also right to mention that substandard and spurious drugs are found floating in the Indian markets and the ultimate sufferers are the patients. For no fault on their part, the hospitals and healthcare organisations find it difficult to project a positive image also on account of the poor quality of drugs. It is in this context that we need to make an anatomy of the existing drug policy and to detect the lapses and shortcomings in the regulations.

All of us agree with this viewpoint that the increasing needs of the country for essential drugs are still not fully met. The Patent laws do not cover over 95 per cent of the essential drugs. Bulk manufacturers of the generic drugs are found dispensing them in inexpensive package to the large-sized or organisational customers like the hospitals and healthcare organisations which would substantially aggravate the intensity of problem. Supply of essential drugs, vaccines/devices holds the key to success to any disease control programme. Funds for drugs used for primary, secondary and tertiary healthcare centres come partly from the State Funds and partly from Central Plan Funds. The procedures for procurement and distribution vary and bottlenecks in these at the national and state levels have been a recurrent problem. We can't deny the fact that the inefficient indenting procedures adversely affect drug procurement. The poor inventory management results in unsatisfactory drug procurement and distribution.

Of course, we find some of the states making due efforts in this context. It is worthwhile to mention that Tamil Nadu has attempted strengthening drug procurement and distribution through formation of a Medical Services Corporation. This Corporation has drawn up an essential drug list, improved purchase and storage of drugs and organised efficient drug distribution within the states and brought about effective inventory control. Thus, we agree with this view that to bring things on the right track, it is pertinent that other states in the country also activate the process of inventory control, specially for managing drugs. Of course, we find The Prevention of Food and Drug Adulteration Act 1954 till now existent, however, a large number of cases have been reported specially related to the manufacturing of spurious drugs by some of the drug manufacturing organisations. The acts and regulations carry no meaning unless we find the doctors, paramedical staff, hospitals and healthcare organisations not evincing interests in identifying the cases of circulation of spurious drugs. It is really amazing that we also find cases of involvement of doctors and hospitals in the use of spurious drugs, specially to promote self interest. This makes it essential that the hospitals and healthcare centres assign due weightage to the management of drugs and at the same time, the policy makers activate the process of making the regulations more rigid.

In view of the above, it is right to mention that the central government as well as the state governments need to assign due weightage to the cases of violation of regulations related to drugs and speed up the process of trial by establishing a special court. Of course, the hospitals and healthcare organisations need to educate and train the staff in the use of drugs but they can't be much more effective, if the regulatory support is not to fuel the process. At several places, we have talked about ethics in the healthcare sector. This is due mainly to the fact that we also find cases of involvement of even the hospital personnel in the supply of substandard and spurious drugs. There is no doubt in it that the pharmaceutical industry is also required to go through the problem because this is also to tarnish their image. The degenerating conditions necessitate multi-corned attack. The State Governments, the Central Government, the Hospitals and Healthcare Centres, the Pharmaceutical Industry, the Medical Association, the Consumer Association and the Non-governmental Social Organisations need to take up the problem on a priority basis.

A majority of the Indian population finds it difficult to buy the expensive imported drugs. This makes it essential that the regulations explore avenues for economic or inexpensive drugs found affordable to the masses. Besides, we also need to promote herbals which would not only be economic but would also have almost dismal side effects. It is right to mention that the expertise of almost all categories of the hospital personnel don't carry any meaning unless the hospitals and healthcare centres assign due weightage to the quality of drugs. It is really painful to mention that we also find cases of involvement of a hospital material manager in the process of buying substandard drugs. The mismanagement of stores and inadequate preservation facilities aggravate the magnitude of problem.

It is a crying need for the hour that accessibility to essential drugs and medicines is increased. The weaker sections of the society are found to be worst affected by diseases and are least able to purchase and utilise the health services such as drugs. We find Central Drugs Authority of India bearing the responsibility of ensuring quality and regulating price. The National Drug Authority came into existence on the recommendations of Mashelkar Committee (2003) and NCMH (2005). With the merger of NDA and National Pharmaceutical Pricing Authority, we find emergence of CDAI and are hopeful that it will be successful in controlling the price and improving the quality.[17]

In addition to the Allopathic drugs and medicines, the regulatory mechanism for AYUSH medicines is also required to be strengthened. The National Accreditation Board for Testing and Calibration Laboratories bar the responsibility of ensuring safety, control and efficacy of AYUSH medicines. This is a high priority area to strengthen the enforcement of Drugs and Cosmetics Act in the country with regard to Ayurveda, Siddha, Unani and Homeopathy manufacturing units to create public confidence in India and abroad.

In the Indian perspective, it is imperative that we promote both so that developments in the field of medicare and healthcare services are made available to all. Affordability is an important consideration in the Indian context which requires priority attention on AYUSH medicines.

Medical Education Policy

New generation of sophisticated biomedical equipments and apparatus has significantly contributed to the process of innovating healthcare services but the Medical Education Policy is not to cater to the changing needs and requirements of society. Both in qualitative and quantitative terms, we need a change in the Medical Education Policy so that a gap between the demand and supply is bridged.

We need to review the medical education policy related to all the three categories of hospitals and healthcare organisations, viz., primary, secondary and tertiary. In the context of primary healthcare, we need strengthening of educational institutes of ISM&H to ensure improvement in the standard of research and teaching in all the systems of ISM&H. In addition, preservation and promotion of cultivation of medicinal herbs and plants need due attention of planners. The completion of pharmacopoeia for all systems of medicines is felt significant. Besides, the drawing up a list of essential drugs and initiating steps to improve their availability at affordable cost is also needed. Ensuing quality control of drugs used and research and development of drugs testing and patenting them appear significant. We are well aware of the fact that beneficiaries of primary healthcare centres are the vulnerable population, specially those residing in urban slums and remote rural and tribal areas and unfortunately, almost all the primary healthcare centres are found in a depleted condition. This necessitates concerted efforts so that the concerned hospital personnel prefer to live in the areas where they are placed in lieu of promoting private practice in the urban areas.

The secondary healthcare facilities don't have linkages with either primary healthcare institutions in ISM & H or with secondary healthcare institutions' modern system of medicine. Very often, we find these institutions lacking support of infrastructure and manpower, Like this, we find all the ISM & H Colleges and institutions in private/government sectors attracting tertiary healthcare hospitals. A majority of the tertiary care institutions lack essential staff, infrastructure and diagnostic facilities.

During the yester decades, there has been a progressive increase in the number of physicians who are qualifying through educational institutions in ISM & H. At present, there are about 350 ISM & H colleges in the country. Available information indicates that the quality of training provided in a majority of ISM & H colleges is suboptimal. The training institutes often lack well qualified teachers; the quality of education provided, especially the practical training in patent management is often not of requisite standard because of the lack of adequately staffed hospitals providing care to patients according to the guiding principles of different systems of ISM & H.

This makes it essential that efforts are activated to improve the quality of human resources development for ISM & H through creation of an appropriate mechanism for quality assurance in educational process in ISM & H educational institutions, strengthening the infrastructure in ISM & H colleges and National Institutes of ISM & H to improve the standard of teaching, creation of appropriate mechanism for funding the government educational institutions and ensuring quality and relevance of training in colleges promoting Continuing Medical Education for all practitioners of ISM & H. We need sincere and honest efforts to ensure that ISM & H colleges are strengthened and monitored in the right directions so that the manpower produced and developed by them has essential skills to tackle health problems in urban and rural areas. It is essential to have appropriate regulations and agencies for implementing the regulations in order to ensure that quality of education is of world class. The Central Council of Indian Medicine

(CCIM), a statutory body constituted in 1970 and the Central Council of Homeopathy (CCH) constituted in 1973 are responsible for laying down and maintaining uniform standard education for courses in Ayurveda, Siddha and Unani and Homeopathy, regulating the practice in Indian Medicine and prescribing standard of professional conduct, etiquette and code of ethics for practitioners and advising the central government in matters relating to recognition of appropriate qualifications of Indian Medicines and Homeopathy. The recommendations of CCIM and CCH are often not acted upon. A system of periodic monitoring by an accreditation committee is to be worked out and implemented to initiate the process of qualitative improvements in the process.

Currently, there are no arrangements in the Department of ISM & H for a degree or diploma in pharmacy nor is ISM & H pharmacy included as one of the options in general pharmacy course. There are no nursing trainees in ISM & H. We need sincere efforts to improve the quality of paramedical and the nursing staff failing which the qualitative improvements in the process would not be possible.

The aforesaid facts make it clear that a number of steps are to be taken to improve the quality of medical education. On the one hand, we need to make the hospital personnel professionally sound and on the other hand, also require to make them personally committed. We also find cases that doctors are of world class but they lack personal-touch-in-service. They lack ethics, values and are found engaged in promoting unfair and unethical practices. This gravitates our attention on including behavioural studies and strengthening ethical dimensions in the syllabi for medical students. We need to make it an integral part of medical education. The medical as well as the paramedical students need to be educated and trained in such a fashion that they prove their excellence by offering quality healthcare services in a decent way. Besides, it is also pertinent that we educate them regarding behavioural management and human and ethical values.

The professional bodies, the universities, the tertiary and private medical institutions need to promote medical education in the face of changing environmental and social conditions. To be more specific in the Indian perspective, we find that due mainly to communication gap, the masses are found unaware of the fundamentals for maintaining a healthy living condition. By promoting medical education, we also assign due weightage to the strengthening of preventive services focussing on the necessity of educating and brainwashing the illiterate society.

In view of the above, it is right to mention that to improve the quality of healthcare services, it is pertinent that we review the health policy of government and make efforts to incorporate necessary amendments so that the medical and paramedical and even the nursing staff are made available world class educational and training facilities.

Healthcare Education Policy

The hospitals and healthcare organisations, specially in the Indian perspective need to promote healthcare education. We agree with this view that the success rate of hospitals and healthcare institutions is substantially influenced by their instrumentality in minimising the number of patients and potential customers/patients. This engineers a strong foundation in favour of healthcare education bearing more creativity. On account of high rate of illiteracy, the masses in India lack nutritional awareness and are found not aware of even the essentials of a healthy living condition. It is against this background that we find increasing cases of food-borne, water borne and pollution-borne diseases. The communicable and vector-born diseases are also found increasing like a wild fire. This makes it essential that hospitals also accept the responsibility of promoting healthcare education.

The curative services no doubt play an important role in the context of hospital product but at the same time, we can't devalue the significance of preventive services. When we talk about the healthcare education, our prime focus is on the preventive services of hospitals. If we educate the society in the desired fashion, it is quite natural that the pressure on hospitals would considerably be minimised. Of late, we have effective devices to sensitise the masses who lack health awareness. Though the educated segment of the society has been found evincing keen interest in the very context, the rural society is yet to be sensitised. Of course, the media and social organisations also need to promote health education but we feel that the effectiveness of the programme would sizeably be increased if the doctors start taking interests in the process. This is due mainly to the fact that a majority of us, specially in health matters trust on doctors. It is in this context that we feel it essential to promote healthcare education specially with the support of the medical staff.

Both categories of hospitals, private as well as government, need to assign due weightage to healthcare education. They can take the support of advertising professionals or even the hospital manager having expertise in the discipline of marketing. The creativity in advertisement and publicity measures would be instrumental in creating mass awareness specially regarding the food habits. The problem of malnutrition is to be checked. The masses are required to be aware of the significance of drinking safe or potable water because number of diseases are found water-borne. The government is required to channelise the distribution of safe drinking water, specially in the rural areas and to be more specific in the tribal areas. The inadequate civic amenities and facilities have also been found very much active in aggravating the health problem. This makes it essential that government as well as the voluntary social organisations and global welfare organisations expand civic amenities and facilities both in urban slums as well as in the villages. The communicable diseases are also found aggravating the magnitude of health problem. The workers living in the big town and cities are not aware of the communicable diseases and their irresponsible sexual behaviour aggravates the problem of AIDS vis-a-vis increases the pressure on hospitals.

The aforesaid facts make it clear that the hospitals and healthcare institutions need to promote healthcare education which would minimise the pressure on hospitals of course in the long-run. If they are found successful in promoting healthcare education, the masses would come to know about the healthy living conditions which would make the task of hospitals and healthcare organisations easier.

Population Policy

Since we go through the policy imperatives for improving the quality of healthcare services, it is essential that we also go through the population policy. Increasing demographic pressure is found increasing the work pressure on the hospitals and healthcare organisations. If we face the problem of overpopulation, the policy makers would find it difficult to improve the facilities found effective in developing human and human value. Ultimately, we find high intensity of problems particularly before hospitals because they are required to make available to a large number of population the improved quality of healthcare services. It is against this background that the population policy gravitates our attention.

India is currently in the midst of demographic transition. Population and sustainable development are key issues requiring due attention of national policy makers. To be more specific, when we find the intensity of population problem at its peak, it is pertinent that the demotivational measures are adopted to regulate or control population. It is the responsibility of hospitals and healthcare organisations that they meet the increasing demand of contraceptives and healthcare of a large number of population. The intensity of problem is likely to be more alarming if it fails in regulating the population. The number of births may remain unaltered but there is an urgent need to bring down maternal and infant mortality. There has been a paradigm shift in the Family Welfare Programme. The ongoing education, info-tech and socio-economic transition have raised awareness and expectations of the population. However, the results of population control measures make it clear that we activate the process with more pace and mass participation.

All of us have witnessed the lukewarm responses of motivational measures for regulating population. And this makes it essential that the policy makers think about the demotivational measures on a priority basis. The hospitals and healthcare organisations bear the responsibility of increasing the popularity of Family Welfare Programme. This necessitates involvement of medical and paramedical personnel because they need to organise a camp in the rural areas where the birth rate is found very high. In a true sense, we are guided by a number of factors. The segment getting governmental support believes that by increasing the number of family members, they would play an important role in the election process. The segment is also influenced by other factors, such as increase in the income of a family because we find all the family members working and earning to live comfortably. Virtually, we find the problem politicalised.

It is difficult for an organisation to cater to the ever increasing healthcare demand of a large number of population. This makes it essential that the hospitals make sincere efforts to promote healthcare education. It is actually our personal commitments to the profession that would show multi-faceted positive results. If we find China successful in controlling population, there is no doubt in the fact that even in the Indian perspective, we expect some wonders, specially from the family planning doctors. It is high time that we consider the significance of sophisticated communication technologies and assign due weightage to the problem of healthcare education. The sophisticated audio-visual exposure facilities would increase the rate of acceptability of the programme because the masses would be sensitised in the right directions.

In view of the above, it is right to mention that critical policy decisions considerably influence the disease profile in a country. If we are conscious of our health and develop our awareness of food-borne, water-borne and communicable diseases, a number of diseases may be controlled. If we are honest to the norms set for healthy lifestyles and sincerely follow the vaccination and immunisation culture, our problems are considerably minimised. If we have a sound national policy for population, the intensity of almost all the problems would naturally be minimised. Like this, our drug policy and medical education policy also influence the quality of medicare services.

The national policy makers need to realise the gravity of the situation that high healthcare costs can lead to entry into or exacerbation of poverty. We need to realise the significance of public provisioning of quality health services. The challenges of quality health services in remote rural regions are to be urgently met. This focuses on transformation of public healthcare into an accountable, accessible and affordable system of quality services. The policies are to be restricted for a new vision based on faster, broad-based and inclusive growth. A comprehensive approach is needed which encompasses individual healthcare, public health, sanitation, clean drinking water, access to food and knowledge of hygiene and feeding practices. Facilitating convergence and development of public health systems and services found responsive to health needs and aspirations of people need priority attention of policy makers.

SUMMARY

In this chapter, you have gone through the hospital product. The motive of this chapter is to sensitise the readers to the different types of services offered by hospitals. After going through the chapter, be sure that the following facts are well versed.

Hospital Product—the Perception: The hospitals or the healthcare organisations offer different types of services for which they make use of the different types of materials vis-a-vis the excellence of personnel. The services though of intangible nature are called the product.

Types of Hospital Products: The hospitals offer different types of services, such as the medical services containing line services, supportive services, auxiliary services and the peripheral services; medical education and training and research facilities. The education, training and research facilities help hospitals in developing professionally sound hospital personnel.

Line Services: The line services include emergency services, out-patient and in-patient services, Intensive Care unit and operation.

Supportive Services: The supportive services include central sterile, radiology, nursing, catering, laundry.

Auxiliary Services: The auxiliary services include registration, indoor, records, stores, mortuary, dietary, engineering and safety.

Peripheral Services: The peripheral services include accommodation for attendants, safe drinking water, entertainment, pay phone, postal or courier, shopping, transportation, sanitation, personal care, banking.

Medical Education: The secondary, tertiary and healthcare institutes offer educational services. They educate medical students and award degrees, diplomas to the successful students.

Medical Training: To develop quality medical personnel, they also offer training facilities so that the personnel are well aware of the recent developments in the medical sciences.

Medical Research: *To* be more specific, the tertiary hospitals, healthcare institutes and even governmental social organisations promote research related to the medical sciences.

Planning for the Hospital Services: Keeping in view the increasing demand and the changing disease profile, the hospitals formulate a plan for product so that they are able to cater to the increasing demand side.

Life Cycle of Hospital Product: It is found that almost all the traditional medical services are not at the declining stage which necessitates innovation.

Innovation, Diffusion and Adoption: Innovation focuses our attention on new medical services. Diffusion means convincing potential users about the outstanding merits of new services and adoption focuses on use of services.

New Product Development Dilemma: The development of a new product is a dilemma because a number of risk factors are there.

Managerial Proficiency for the Key Medical Services: The hospital managers need professional excellence to manage some of the sensitive services, Radiotherapy and Oncology services, Opthalmic services, Nursing services, Rehabilitation services.

Innovative Product Profile: Offering new services found in tune with the latest development in the medical sciences.

Promoting e-Health: With the development of new generation of information and communication technology, we find telemedicine, telediagnosis, management of data, filing, accounting, e-governance defining and redefining the service quality.

Policies influencing Hospital Product: The important policies influencing hospital service are drug policy, medical education policy, healthcare education policy and population policy.

KEY TERMS

Hospital Product	Pippalyadi
ICU	Product Innovation
Out-patient	Product Diffusion
In-patient	Product Adoption
Auxiliary	Oncology
Peripheral	Radiotherapy
Mortuary	Physiotherapy
Line Services	Rehabilitation
Radiology	Linen Services
Fluoroscopy	Bio-medical Equipment
Dietary	Dermatology
Empathy	Geostationary Satellite
CSIR	ISRO
ICMR	Sarva Swasthya Abhigyan
CCRAS	National Drug Authority
CCRUM	AIDS
CCRH	Malnutrition
CCRYN	Dietician

REVIEW QUESTIONS

1. What do you mean by Hospital Product? Explain in brief the different types of services made available by the hospitals.
2. Focus on the line services and their instrumentality in improving the quality of hospital services.
3. What do you mean by the Peripheral Services? Discuss the role of peripheral services in making the hospital product unique.
4. Explain in brief the different types of auxiliary services.
5. Explain the education, training and research services offered by hospitals and healthcare institutes.
6. What do you mean by Product Planning? Explain the process to be followed for formulating a sound plan for hospital product.
7. Explain Innovation, Diffusion and Adoption in the context of hotel product.
8. Do you find development of new services for hospitals a dilemma ?" Defend your answer.
9. Focus on in-patient, out-patient and emergency services.

10. Throw light on the professional excellence of a hospital manager while managing the ophthalmic services.
11. Explain the following in brief:
    (*a*) Drug Policy
    (*b*) Medical Education Policy
    (*c*) Healthcare Education Policy
    (*d*) Population Policy
    (*e*) e-Health

APPLICATION EXERCISES

1. You are working as a hospital manger. How and in what way you would enrich the peripheral services to make your product unique.
2. Focus on your role as a hospital professional while managing the line services in your hospital.
3. "A Hospital manager is required to be more careful while managing the nursing rehabilitation and radiotherapy services." Comment on this statement in the capacity of a hospital manager.
4. There are some important services and vulnerable areas where a hospital manager is supposed to show world class excellence. In the light of this statement, focus on in-patient and out-patient services and emergency services.
5. We find blindness a curse which requires the e excellence of a hospital manager so that the increasing cases of blindness doe to poor nutrition, uncorrected refractive errors, glaucoma, trauma and infections are considerably minimised. In the light of this statement, throw light on the professional excellence of a hospital manger while managing the ophthalmic services.
6. Allopathic as well as the AYUSH streams need standardisation, quality control and cost-effectiveness. Comment on this statement as a hospital manger.

END NOTES

1. Kotler p., *Marketing Management*, Prentice Hall of India, 1995, p. 342.
2. Goel, S. L., *Administration of OPD and In-patients Services*, pp. 9-21.
3. Jha S. M., *Services Marketing*; HPH, Mumbai, 2009.
4. Nabbi's *Ninth Fiver Year Plan*.
5. Jha S. M., *Services Marketing*; (Old Edition), pp. 298-343.
6. Rogers E. M., *Diffusion of Innovating*, Free Press, New York, 1962.
7. *Ibid*.
8. *Ibid*.
9. Goel, S. L., *op. cit*.
10. Balaraman C. S., *Emergency Services in Hospital*, pp. 21-27.
11. Gupta B. D., *Radiotherapy and Oncology Centre- Planning and Management*, pp. 181-93.
12. Saini J.S., *Planning and Management of Ophthalmic Services*, pp. 151-81.
13. Anjana Malhotra, *Nursing Services in Hospitals*, pp. 105-51.
14. Raman, A. V., *Rehabilitation Services*, pp. 197-207.
15. Jha S. M., *Services Marketing*; HPH, Mumbai, 2009.
16. *Eleventh Five Year Plan*: Planning Commission; Government of India, New Delhi Vol. II, pp. 57-115.
17. *Ibid* p. 76.

Management of Human Resources in Hospitals

For conceptualisation of quality in totality, it is pertinent that all the required inputs are of world class and significantly, the human resources serving hospitals prove to be a star performer. Thematically-sound, personally-committed, value-based and human-oriented healthcare and medicare personnel may activate the process of qualitative-cum-quantitative transformation which would make the ways for quality in totality.

CHAPTER OBJECTIVES

LEARNING OBJECTIVES

This chapter aims at studying the different dimensions of human resources management in the context of hospital and healthcare services. The motive is to sensitise the readers to the outstanding features and specialities that we find in the healthcare personnel. The hospital professionals bear the responsibility of making available to the hospitals quality people efficacious of serving the patients and creating a brand name successful in developing India as healthcare destination. The most important task before the hospital personnel is to make the healthcare services cost-effective so that the services are found affordable to the general masses.

Introduction

Sophisticated biomedical equipments and availability of world class infrastructural facilities, of course, sizably influence the quality of healthcare services but ultimately, it is quality of human resources that considerably govern the development processes. Undoubtedly enough, the technicultue carries no meaning in absence of quality people. Since we talk about quality in totality, it is pertinent that all the required inputs are of world class and significantly, the human resources prove to be a star performer. It is in this context that we need to assign due weightage to the development of quality people which is often perceived in a wrong way. A majority of us feel that perception of quality people remains confined simply to the operational efficiency of people engaged in the process but the concept and percept of quality people focus our attention on a number of properties. Professionally sound medical and paramedical staff, technocrats, academically sound teachers and researchers, managers would hardly be successful in delivering goods to the society, if they lack personal-touch-in-service, humanised leadership and commitment to the value system. In a true sense, we find professional excellence helping an organisation in increasing the rate of operational efficiency, accelerating the rate of productivity but failing personal commitment, value-orientation and human touch, the task of achieving perfection in the personality of an individual is found difficult. It is against this backdrop that we need human resources having world class professional excellence; we need human resources having personal commitment; we need human resources having ethical and human touch and only then we find ourselves successful in developing star performers efficacious of making organisations potentially sound and excelling competition by providing innovative services to the users.

Being a non-profit organisation, the hospitals or healthcare organisations are supposed to serve and subserve social interests. The significant developments in the field of medical sciences and latest developments in the field of information superhighway have been found changing the definition of service quality. Today, we live in an age of sophisticated technology where an individual or an organisation is supposed to conceptualise the slogan "Differentiate or Die" or "Compete or Perish." If we keep on moving the process of defining and redefining quality, making goods or services distinct to others, our task of getting success is found easier. The experiences of yester decades testify that we have assigned due weightage to the development of technology but have underrated development of perfect people. This makes it essential that hospitals and healthcare organisations perceive the concept of quality people in a right fashion and inculcate and cultivate the required properties while developing human resources.

In modern hospitals, a number of medical, paramedical and managerial personnel are found working in different capacities. They are supposed to have the expertise and excellence in tune with their defined responsibilities. In a true sense, we find healthcare services a result of team work where team spirit and team culture help in getting the desired results. It is pertinent that hospital professionals are well aware of the changing qualitative and quantitative requirements of different departments and make available to them quality people. It is significant to mention that in the Indian perspective, the expanding gap between demand and supply of people has been creating an imbalance. It is high time that we bridge the gap.

The healthcare services are made available by the primary, secondary and tertiary streams in tune with the changing requirements of the concerned segment. National Rural Health Mission (NRHM) was launched on 12th April, 2005. This focuses on healthcare services as a part of generic public health delivery system from the village to block levels. The multilevel healthcare services cover block level hospital, cluster of Gram Panchayats (GPS), Gram Panchayat Subhealth centre level and village level. At the block-level, we need Health Manager, Accountant and Store Keeper, at the cluster level, we need 3 staff nurses, 1 LHV for 4-5 SHCs, at the Gram Panchayat subhealth centre level, we need RMPs, ANMs, MPW and at village level, we need ASHA, AWWs, in every village. It is significant that we make available to all the levels the required number of people.

The administration of secondary and tertiary care hospitals would be by the professionalised and trained professionals posted as Medical Superintendents. The hospitals are allowed to recruit various staff including junior doctors on ad hoc and contract basis. The district hospitals which play a key role in providing health services to the poor need substantial improvement in infrastructure. It is often observed that Government Medical Colleges and Hospitals fail to adhere to the infrastructure, equipment and staff norms as laid down by the Medical Council of India.

The management of human resources is an important dimension of hospital management. The hospitals need quality people and therefore, the professionals need to recruit quality people with rich credentials. It is also essential that the process of recruitment is made cost effective. They need to make use of new generation of information and communication technology so that the required people are made available on time. In this context, it is also pertinent that hospital professionals organise training and development programmes to enrich the knowledge bank of people. The training programmes may be for short and long duration. On the one hand, the working people need the thematical competence while on the other hand, they also require an indepth knowledge of behavioural profile. The innovative techno-driven devices may be used for training the people of different categories. We may promote teleconferencing for updating the hospital people.

Compensation and motivation play an incremental role in managing the human resources. It is not only significant that we enrich the potentials of people. It is not only significant that we enrich the potentials of people. It is equally important that we make use of their potentials. The financial and non-financial incentives are paid for motivating the people. Since we expect a lot from the hospital people, it is judicious that we pay to them lucrative packages of benefits. The professionals need to blend both the financial and non-financial incentives in such a way that people are motivated to deliver the best. If we want to satisfy the users, it is important that we satisfy the working people. For motivating the hospital people, it is also essential that we make available to them quality service ambience in which they feel pleasure in performing. The hospital professionals need to make it sure that service environment is in tune with the services they have to deliver.

Performance evaluation is an important dimension of human resources management and in this context, the professionals need an in depth study of services delivered to the users by the different echelons of people. Of late, the evaluation process is found easier where the professionals take the support of techno-driven devices. Setting target and getting the desired results are the two dimensions and in both the areas, we expect a lot from the hospital professionals. A hospital manager is required to make a time-to-time evaluation of the personnel working in different capacities. The lapses and shortcomings are to be identified and the redressal measures are to be initiated.

The motive of managing the human resources is to make available to the hospitals world class people. The professionals also need to increase the level of satisfaction of providers and users. Additionally, the service generation and delivery processes are to be made cost-effective. The hospital professionals need not to forget that the service environment for healthcare is considerably influenced by the motivational factors. The services are found to be much more sensitive where the intensity of success sizably rests on the attitudes and behaviour of medical and paramedical staff.

PERCEPTION OF HUMAN AND HUMANE

Before we go through the management of human resources, it is pertinent that our focus is on the concept and percept of human and humane.

Human: The term Human[1] focuses on the genus man. The development of human refers to the development of essential qualities for the genus man. It pertains to man or mankind. In this context, we find emphasis on the qualities or attributes which are developed at the learning stage of human beings mainly from the parents, family members, school teachers or so. There are a number of sources and the outputs made available by the different sources influence the development of human. The media and the healthcare centres also play a significant role in the very context. The properties to be developed at this stage are ethical values, nutritional sense, civic sense, aesthetic sense and in addition, the fundamentals essential to manage a sound physique and helpful in showing better qualities of human beings. This is the first stage which engineers a sound foundation for the development of second stage.

Humane: The term "Humane"[2] refers to the process of humanising or developing humanism. The emphasis in the development process is found on injecting the feelings considered proper to man. This is the second stage of development to be helpful in showing concern and kindness towards others. If we succeed in developing human at the first stage, the task of developing humane is considerably simplified because the receiver becomes more sensitive after successful conceptualisation of the perception of human at the first stage. The educational institutions and the training facilities developed by them make possible a successful transmission of the faculties required to contribute significantly to the process of developing national excellence. Here, our focus is on the feeling proper to a man, hence, the task is to make the human beings more sensitive to receive and perceive in a right fashion and to communicate in a right way as expected in the perspective or working conditions in which he/she is working. In a true sense, the development of "human" is essential for the development of humane and the development of "humane" is essential for the development of "human resources." The technocrats, teachers, bureaucrats, professionals, intellects, scientists, statesmen and doctors well aware of their responsibilities may or may not discharge their defined functional responsibilities in the face of the educational aid and training facilities made available to them at the different stages of developing human by the different sources. It is right to mention that discharging of professional responsibilities is not the only thing that is expected from the human beings. Since you discharge your functional responsibilities in the face of professional requirements but fail in showing humanism, human values and ethical values at the work or living places, the society and the national economy would sizeably suffer. This is a critical stage that we find specially in India. We, of course, have been successful in generating efficiency but have miserably failed in developing human and humane. We find doctors professionally sound but lacking human, humane and human values. This deprives them of being personally committed and they fail becoming super performers as they fail in showing personal-touch-in service and human touch in behaviour.

Human Resources: Since we talk about the development of productive human resources in almost all the areas of managing hospitals, it is pertinent that the professionals in addition to the subjective and supportive knowledge and faculty also possess humanity. This would help an organisation not only in developing professional excellence but would fantastically contribute to the process of developing personal commitments.

Since they have perceived ethical and human values in course of learning at the different stages, they would prove to be the super performers and may show even wonders. This would help the human resources not only in discharging their functional responsibilities efficiently but would also develop their behavioural profile. They would learn not only about sympathy but would also show empathy. Thus, the development of productive human resources would be possible where in addition to the professional excellence, the development of personal commitments would also be ensured. We can't think of developing human resources unless the process of developing human and humanes is found in the right directions. Since almost all the organisations bear the responsibility of developing human resources, it is pertinent that they are well aware of the aforesaid facts.

Developing Human Resources in Hospitals

Our focus here is on the development of human resources for hospitals. To be more specific in the hospitals or healthcare organisations, we find the development of human and humane much more significant because we find several cases where the hospital personnel are efficient but lack human values which stands as a barrier while developing ethical values. Excellence in profession is considered to be the most vital aspect for the sound management of the healthcare services generated by hospitals. Professional excellence draws our attention on perfection which is not possible unless the hospitals get human resources having a fair synchronisation of professional excellence and personal commitments. Of course, the hospitals are yet to recognise the seriousness of some of the attributes essential for hospital personnel which jeopardise all of their productive efforts for the development of quality hospital personnel. There is no doubt in it that leading private hospitals and even a few of the government hospitals have realised the seriousness and therefore, we find a sea change in the behavioural profile of the personnel developed by them or employed and recruited by them. It is not only sufficient that we make available to the hospitals sophisticated biomedical equipments and apparatus; it is even not sufficient that we construct attractive buildings and generate and make available the supporting infrastructural facilities. The most important thing that we don't care is the development of "Quality People!"

Quality Hospital Personnel

In this context, at the outset, we need to make it clear that by saying "Quality Hospital Personnel", our focus is not only on the professional excellence of the hospital personnel. In addition to the world class professional excellence, we also throw light on the personal attributes essential for the hospital personnel. The perception of quality hospital personnel gravitates our attention on producing personnel having a fair blending of the two, viz., Professional excellence and Personal commitments. If they are professionally sound, the patients would get efficient services. And if they are personally committed, the patients would get sympathy, empathy and satisfaction. Thus, the patients would be benefited by getting quality healthcare facilities, decent behaviour and the hospitals would be benefited by having a positive image which would help them in attracting the patients, offering to them the world class healthcare services and thus, a sound base would be engineered for the growth and development of hospitals of world class. It is against this background that we talk about the development of hospital personnel and being an ideal hospital manager, you bear the responsibility of projecting a positive image of an organisation in which you work.

Leadership

Leadership is a nebulous characteristic[3] defined differently by different authorities in different conditions. In the field of healthcare, the leadership takes on a particular level of importance because we find crisis an ever present factor. In the healthcare management, leadership is found essential for accomplishing even the critical objectives. Working with limited resources in a critical condition mandates that leadership must be effective as well as a source of inspiration. In discharging your responsibilities as a healthcare or hospital manager, you not only set direction and participate in the formulation of policy but are also supposed to exemplify a style and to formulate a strategy that motivates personnel to attain their high level of accomplishment. Unless you prove to be a successful leader, your task of developing personally committed human resources would remain unfulfilled. In a true sense, we don't find a magical formula to develop the quality of leadership because the style of leadership is substantially influenced by the type of "followership." This speaks of the fact that the changing working conditions determine the quality that you need and the style that you are supposed to follow to be optimally effective in your decisions. At the same time, it is also right to mention that your own preferences, personality and predilections are equally important. Since you bear the responsibility of winning the heart of your followers, and you accept the task of accomplishing the organisational goals and countering the multidimensional challenges, it is pertinent that you come to know about the influencing factors.

Leadership Influences

Today, you are supposed to play the role of a successful leader and you can't negate the fact that your potentials, credentials, faculties and personality have been influenced by a number of leaders who have played a contributory role in your development. In Fig. 9.1, we find leadership influences.

The first source of your leadership style includes your family—parents and others who have educated and trained you. They were the first leaders you observed firsthand. Whatever you could learn from them are till now existent in your personality and would continue till you exist. The second source that we find in influencing you are your primary and high school teachers who demonstrated a style of leadership in classroom discussions, management of group activities and efforts to inspire you in one of the most intricate processes of human endeavour at the most sensitive stage of your learning. In addition, your scout leaders, dance group leaders, team coaches have also influenced you. Of course and in the process of learning, you were also influenced by the bad leaders and you still have stored them in your memory. Industrial psychologists maintain that we learn more from others' mistakes than we do from their positive attributes.

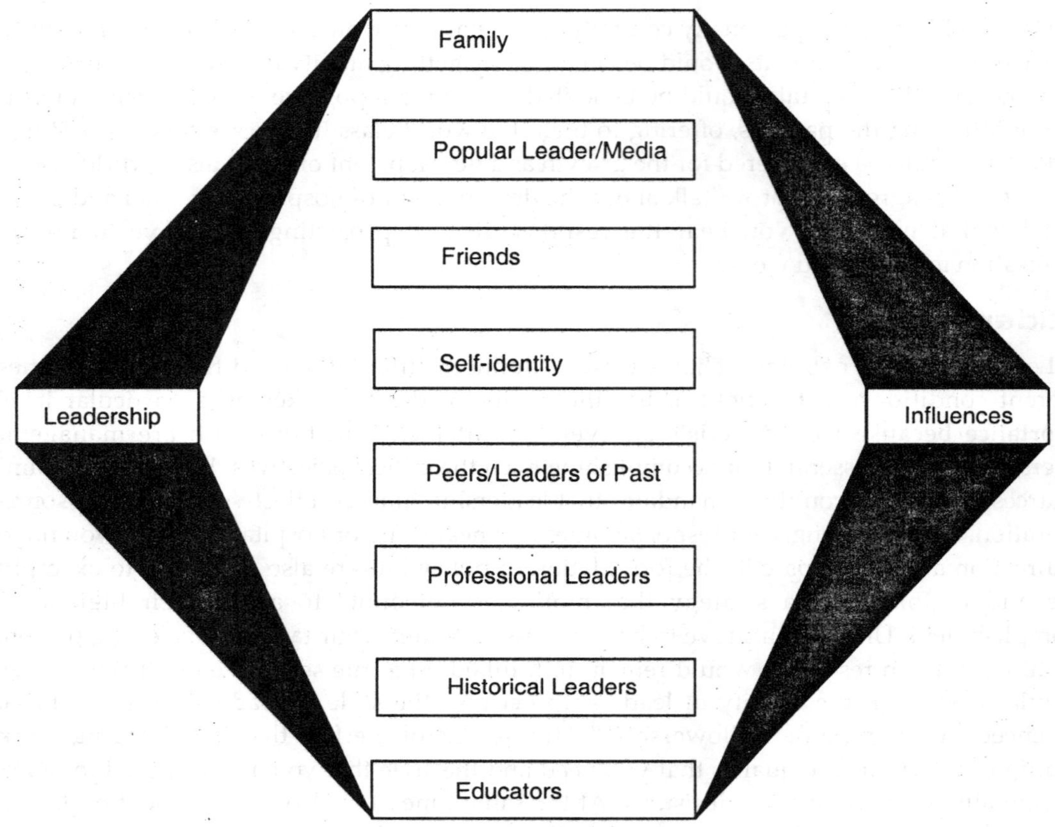

Fig. 9.1. Leadership Influences

Adapted from Lombardi Dobals N., *Healthcare Manager*, p. 73.

Perhaps the leaders outside your healthcare environment—religious, community or civic provide you with action lessons. The manner in which they discharge their responsibilities and perform and educate you as to how you might lead and what options you might select in the leadership process also influence you. The leadership styles among your professional educators, college professors and training instructors have also influenced you considerably. You admire those teachers or educators who convinced you, inspired you, educated and trained you excellently. The great political leaders, social leaders, cultural activists, business leaders and industrial leaders have also influenced you sizeably.

Friends and peers provide a frame of reference for your leadership style in different ways, first by providing feedback in a way that forces you to hone your people skills. If friends and peers are becoming successful, you observe. Similarly, you also observe your own performance and results and make a comparative study of your successes and failures. Thus, you learn from your friends and peers and are motivated by them.

The aforesaid facts make it clear that the development of leadership quality is a process and in a true sense it is a learning process. You start learning from the childhood and keep on moving the process of learning till you find yourself sensitive. We can't negate the fact that the learning process is stopped, if we find demotivational forces becoming stronger and stronger. We find efficiency-generation a process really and an on-going process that gets new life and strength if the sources of learning remain positive.

Being a hospital manager, you are supposed to learn from an organisation which has accepted the responsibility of subserving the social interests. You didn't prefer to be a business leader; you opted to be a leader of an organisation supposed to assign due weightage to social considerations. Of course, you are well aware of the fact that you are leading an organisation not bearing a legitimate right of making profits. Not only this, you are also leading an organisation in which everything is not under your control. The doctors may be of world class, the examination reports may be authentic, the line of treatment may also be right but the results may or may not be positive since you lead an organisation where in addition to your professional excellence, we find almighty "God" playing a contributory role. This makes it essential that you are supposed to be sincere to your efforts and never to be disheartened from the results, rather to learn lessons from your mistakes.

To be more specific in the Indian perspective, you also bear the responsibility of serving the segment who are poorest of the poor, downtrodden in addition to the segments who belong to the affluent sections. You are not supposed to discriminate. You are indeed required to convince the deprived sections that they are getting equal treatment. You bear the responsibility of improving the quality of environment at the work place, making the departmental relationship friendly and cohesive and the environmental conditions favourable. Of course, it is an acid test of your professional excellence and personal commitments.

Universal Characteristics of Leadership

You are supposed to construct your own matrix. We go through some of the characteristics of leaders found universally accepted.[4]

1. *Smartness:* A leader should be both short-term smart and long-term smart. To put it another way, you must make good decisions for the short-term but remember it that your decisions coincide with the long-term mission of your organisation. This would help you in getting an overall positive net effect on your own activities and the activities of your staff.

2. *Visible:* We agree with this view that good leaders must be visible. It is visibility that would help you in making your presence known in any given situation. Such leaders are also found ubiquitous and we feel their importance when they are not physically in the scene. To be more specific in a crisis like situation, we find such type of leaders very effective ill diffusing the problems.

3. *A Steady Hand:* We can't negate while going through the universal characteristics of leadership that good leaders have a steady hand in all departmental conditions and situations. They never back away from making judgements. This is due mainly to the fact that they consider all the necessary criteria in executing actions, transmitting the course of action clearly and getting the positive results.

4. *Emotion:* In the healthcare leadership, we find instrumentality of emotion. A nursing director once remarked that she tries to avoid using "profanity" except on rare occasions. When she does use profanity, she says it is to inspire the performances of a negative staff member and to really get someone's attention. Profanity aside, you need to use emotional outbursts when appropriate and when you seek to make a point. Don't be "even keel" all the time but don't forget that you need to stay true to your own style and personality during emotional moments.

5. *A Sense of Humour:* While going through the universal characteristics, we also talk about a sense of humour. We can't negate that even leaders are human beings subject to human emotions. A sense of humour warmth in executing leadership responsibilities and the strength to be fallible are also universal traits. In the hospitals or healthcare organisations where we find an adverse condition and where illness and death are ever present, you can't and should not make a good-bye to the "Survival Characteristics." You need to share a witty anecdote, relating to a tasteful joke or laughing at your own foibles.

6. *Ability to Confess:* It is not unnatural that you commit mistakes. It is of course blunder that you commit mistakes but never confess the same. This makes it essential that you develop the courage of confession. Ability to admit to errors demonstrates human fallibility and not weakness. Confession also clarifies your positive attitude to reality which would help you in establishing your credibility.

7. *Ability to Listen:* To be more specific in the hospitals and healthcare organisations, you need to develop the strength of listening to your patients, customer or users, to your staff and to your administrators. Don't only listen but also hear because listening shows compassion and involvement in the group process and hearing and understanding show perception.

The aforesaid traits help you substantially in proving your excellence. Since you accept the responsibility of making available to the patients quality healthcare services, you are supposed to be a super performer.

La Guardia Model of Leadership

La Guardia Fiorella was the son of Italian immigrants. His father enlisted in the army and the family travelled across the US. Over time, La Guardia entered civil services, worked in several foreign embassies and enrolled in the law school. He later served six terms in Congress, running under the banner of four different political parties at one time or another. Thus, his adaptability, people skills and experience were sharply honed by the time he assumed "management" of New York City in 1934. A healthcare manager experienced two different situations—the situation during 1930s and 1940s and the situations he/she experiences of late. La Guardia believed that leaders needed six basic leadership necessities[5] as mentioned in Fig. 9.2.

1. *Energy:* According to La Guardia, a leader needs to demonstrate vibrancy and enthusiasm-energy in all activities. His energy was boundless in scope, carrying him through 16 hours days over three terms of six years each. He was of the opinion that energy connotes efforts which needs to be expanded if you have to obtain positive healthcare results. The customers/patients expect energy and effort on the part of the providers. The staff has the same expectations their leaders. Here, you are not required to confuse energy with hyperactivity has rather energy is compatible with your natural style. You complete one work and find yourself competent enough to do another. With the completion of one work, you get energy for another. Thus, from according to La Guardia, a leader is required to be energetic.

2. *Strength:* La Guardia was found strong in making decisions and resolute in defending and maintaining a certain course of action. Managing change is found frequently conceptualised in the healthcare management and this requires strength. He advocates that try to demonstrate strength to your subordinates by handling change in a positive fashion albeit without apparent frustration. It is right to say that showing strength in a leadership position means making the

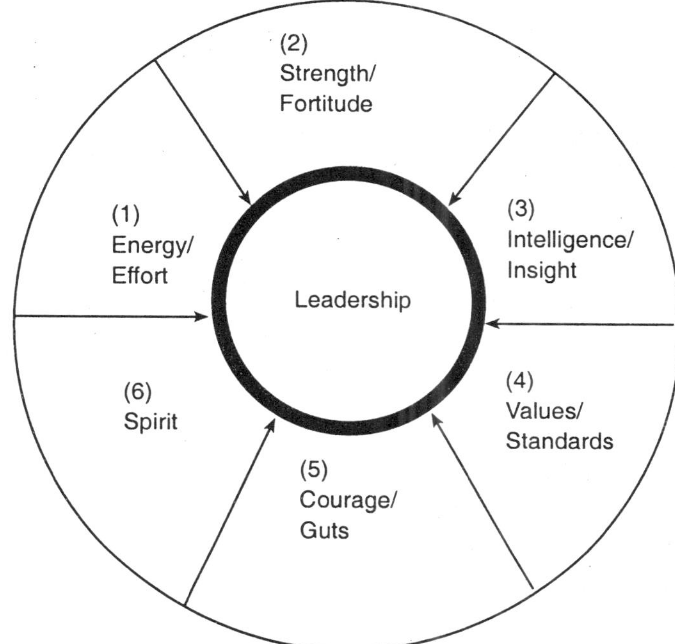

Fig. 9.2. La Guardia's Leadership Necessities
Adapted from Lombardi D.N., *Healthcare Management*, p. 81.

touch call. It is also opined that making tough decisions may be painful today but very much instrumental in making you a strong leader just tomorrow. You need to remember that strong leaders are never ambivalent and never try to "play both sides of the fence", specially in making decisions. Besides, they are not tentative and they prefer to make decisions as soon as they have collected the required facts without being influenced by dubious contrary arguments. In addition, we find a strong leader never retractile.

3. *Intelligence:* Your leadership knowledge starts immediately you resume your job responsibility. As a newly appointed manager, you already have professional excellence. Additionally, you have a wealth of insight into the healthcare business and various dimensions of offering high quality patient care. However, you need to keep on moving the process of learning because sky is the only limit to perfection and you are supposed to be a high performer. Of course, you know about the art of motivating the personnel. You are required to construct a leadership matrix because by doing so, you succeed in enriching your leadership knowledge. This helps you in creating a reflective tool to add to your arsenal of management and leadership frame.

4. *Values:* The underlying principles such a visibility, fully optimisation of resources and dependability are among the ethical standards for leadership strategies and conduct that are essential for value-driven management. We focus here on values and this makes it essential that in addition to the professional excellence that you have of world class, you also need to have ethical values, human values, humanity or so. It is light to mention that a value-driven management is a system of administration and daily management practices that embody

personal values, humanistic standards, business norms and executive principles. To be more specific in the Indian perspective, we find hospital personnel professionally sound but not considering generation of values an essential consideration for a successful healthcare manager.

5. *Courage:* Courage implies that a leader would take an aggressive stand. It is right to mention that during prohibition, La Guardia discovered that several drug stores throughout New York were selling a solution that could easily be converted into alcoholic beer. With a camera crew and radio crew in town, he went to a drug store in a residential area, bought the materials necessary to make beer and concocted the mixture on a table set up right outside the pharmacy. As a healthcare manager, you must take a stand to defend your position in many complex areas and that requires courage. You can't empower others unless you prove to be courageous yourself. Taking the safe position for yourself would not make the ways for the progression of your management career in a forward looking and world class hospital where you work.

6. *Spirit:* Being a healthcare manager, you also need to establish a positive attitude to overcome adverse circumstances. For this, you need to cite team accomplishments to date. You are supposed to be choosy or selective and to prefer office parties or visits to individual workstations to celebrate positive events or outcomes. The importance of establishing a sense of spirit throughout the work group can be minimised, specially in hospitals where crisis and frustration are found breeding freely.

The aforesaid facts make it clear that La Guardia in his model narrated all the essential traits for an effective leader to perform efficiently and satisfactorily as a health care or hospital manager. Since you bear the responsibility of managing the human resources efficiently, it is essential that you do possess the leadership quality.

Categories of Personnel Needed for Hospitals

In modern hospitals, we find different categories of staff working in different capacities. The doctors, nursing staff, paramedical staff, different types of technicians and management personnel contribute substantially to the smooth functioning of the healthcare organisations. Of course, all of them are supposed to work with the single motto of making available to the patients the services up to their expectations but they work in different conditions and make use of the different types of technologies. Before we go through the management of human resources in hospitals, it is essential that we know about the human resources engaged in hospitals. In Fig. 9.3, we find focus on the same.

Doctors: They are considered to be the leverspring of hospitals. Even in this category, we find different subcategories based on credentials, experiences and expertise. They are required to be motivated properly so that they work not only with professional commitments but also show personal commitments, ethics and humanity. They are required to be educated and trained properly so that in addition to the professional excellence, they also come to know about the behavioural management. Since we find degeneration in work culture gaining momentum it is pertinent that we also go through the supervision and control.

Paramedical Staff: In the hospitals, we find a number of paramedical staff working according to their qualifications and expertise. They play an incremental role in improving the quality of hospital services. The diagnostic and treatment processes considerably depend on the expertise of the paramedical staff. It is essential that they are in adequate number and are paid suitably.

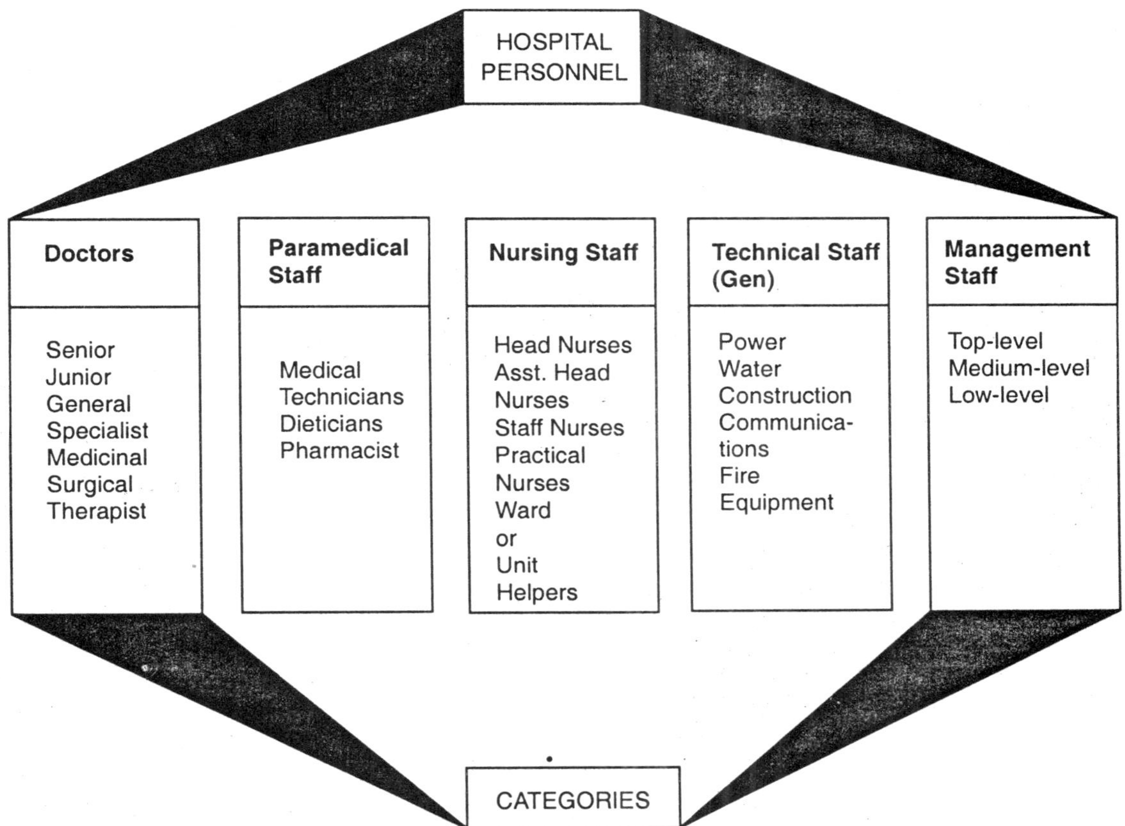

Fig. 9.3. Categories of Hospital Personnel

With the evolving technologies, they also need training facilities. A careful supervision or control is found essential to increase the level of efficiency of the paramedical staff.

Nursing Staff: They are considered to be the backbone of hospitals because in almost all the hospitals and at almost all the points, they are found working with a sense. They need to be given due weightage because despite of their significant contributions to the healthcare services, we don't find suitable incentives for them. Proper education and training facilities required for the nursing staff, sympathy and empathy are found essential for them.

In addition, we also need to motivate them and in this context, we need to make available to them quality environment not only at the places where they work but also at the places where they live so that they are found personally committed. Of late, we find degeneration even in the nursing services and this makes it essential that a rigid supervision and control for increasing the level of efficiency is given due weightage.

Technicians: In addition to the paramedical staff, we also find some general technologies for proper functioning of the hospitals. This draws our attention on the personnel needed for managing, power, water, transportation, communications, construction, repairing or so. Since we find the services of hospitals sizeably influenced by the uninterrupted availability of supporting infrastructural facilities, we need their cooperation at almost all the stages. We need to motivate them so that an increase in the level of their efficiency is made possible. On account of a change in the nature of general technologies, it is pertinent that we make provisions for their training. Besides, we also need to control them.

Management Staff: In almost all hospitals, we find aforesaid categories of personnel working and we are also aware of the poor quality of healthcare services made available by a majority of the hospitals. This speaks of the fact that nothing is managed properly, if we don't have an efficient manager. It is in this context that we talk about hospital management and feel the urgency of different echelons of management to increase the operational or overall productivity of hospitals. We can't deny the fact that professionally sound and personally committed managers help healthcare organisations or hospitals to subserve the organisational as well as the social interests. It is high time that the policy-makers or the boardrooms realise the instrumentality of management staff in making possible a radical change in the quality and costs of healthcare services. To be more specific in the Indian context, it is pertinent that the healthcare managers show their excellence by making possible cost-effectiveness so that the services are made affordable. The increasing cases of mismanagement found at almost all the stages would considerably be minimised if we have world class management staff.

The aforesaid facts make it clear in the hospital services, we find a number of employees working in a different environment. They need time honoured support of the infrastructure as well as the personnel. Since we find it a team work based on the technological and infrastructural support, it is essential that a hospital manager bears the responsibility of managing the different dimensions of the management of human resources. We go through all the dimensions, such as recruitment and selection, education and training, compensation and motivation and supervision and control. As a hospital manager, you bear the prime responsibility of managing hospitals or health care institutions, government or private hospitals, big or small hospitals, rural or urban hospitals. We can't deny the fact that the management of hospital plays an important role and a hospital manager bearing the responsibility of managing the hospitals requires to assign due weightage to the management of hospital personnel. The sophisticated technologies and equipment, no doubt play a significant role in the upgradation of quality but ultimately, it is the quality of personnel assuming a dominance in the entire process of hospital management. It is against this background that we find management of hospital assuming a place of outstanding significance. Now, we go through different constituents of management of human resources specially with the viewpoint of hospitals.

Dimensions of Human Resources Management

Being a hospital manager, you bear the responsibility of managing the hospital personnel in a right fashion so that the hospitals and healthcare organisations succeed in getting quality people. Since we talk about quality in totality, it is pertinent that the hospitals are made available quality personnel. We can't deny the fact that in a majority of the hospitals, the quality of personnel is not found to be superior which has rapidly been decreasing their levels of efficiency. Not only the patients but even we find hospitals facing the consequences of degeneration in the quality of hospital personnel. We agree with this view that a number of hospitals have been made available sophisticated biomedical equipments in addition to the attractive buildings but ultimately, the personnel prove to be a focal point. It is against this background that we go through different dimensions of human resources management, specially with the viewpoint of hospitals or the healthcare organisations. In Fig. 9.4, we find focus on the different constituents of the management of hospital personnel.

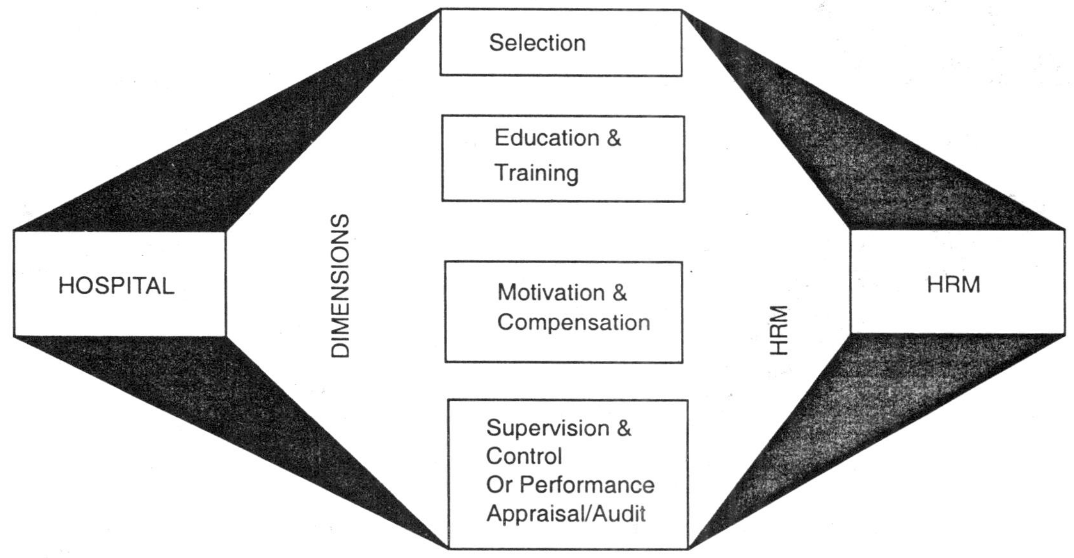

Fig. 9.4. Dimensions of Human Resources Management in Hospitals

On the basis of Fig. 9.4, it is right to mention that while going through the problem, we need to concentrate our attention on the four important constituents, viz., Managing the Selection Process, Managing the Education and Training Programme, Managing Motivation and Compensation and Managing Performance Appraisal or Supervision and Control. A hospital manager while acting or making decisions related to the management of human resources needs to perceive the right meaning of quality hospital personnel so that the task of managing the human resources is found proactive. Your motto is to make the process cost effective so that the hospitals succeed in minimising the administration and establishment bills. Your mission is to generate quality hospital personnel so that the hospitals succeed in defending their existence in the society. Your motive is to make available to the patients good patient care. If you manage the different constituents in a right fashion, the task of fulfilling motto, avowed mission and motives would be made easier. You would prove yourself to be a super performer.

Managing the Preselection Process

You are not supposed to jump into the process of selection but to gravitate your attention on the preselection process. This is essential to make the selection process result oriented. There are five necessary preselection processes as shown in Fig. 9.5.

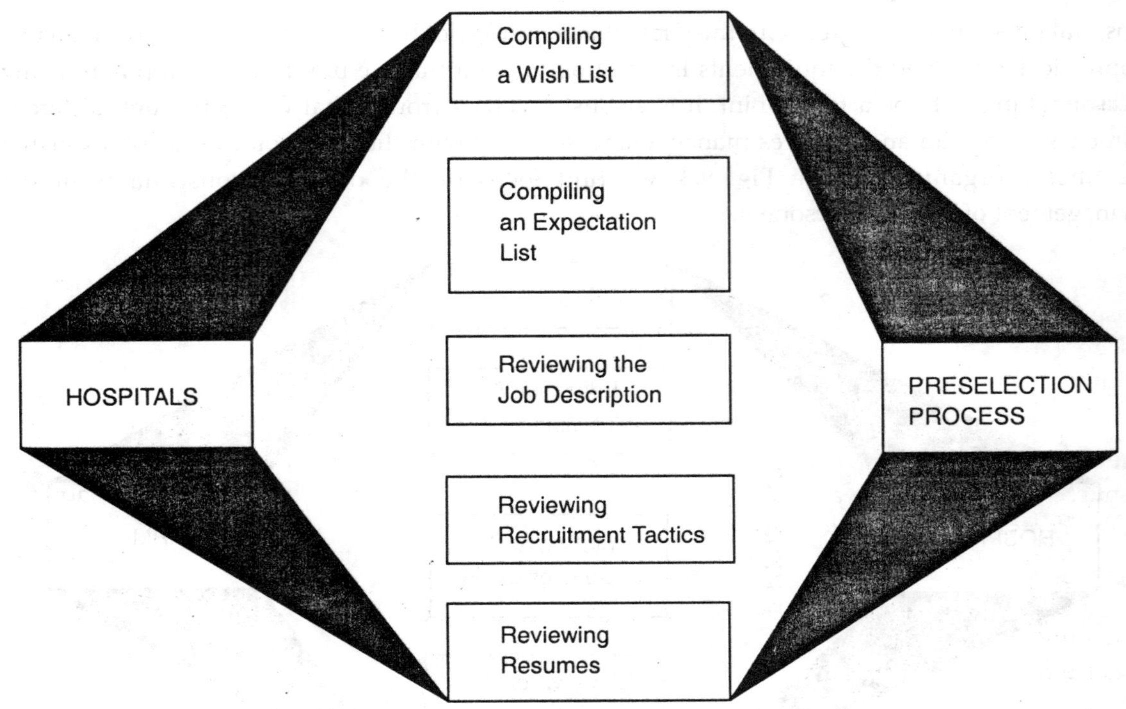

Fig. 9.5. Preselection Process

Adapted from Lombardi D.N., Healthcare Management, p. 233.

1. *A Wish List is to be Compiled:* At the very outset, you need to compile a wish list. It is a type of brainstorming exercise where you are required to review everything you know about the position you need to fill. This requires quantitative as well as the qualitative requisites :

- Job requirements (past, present and future)
- Past success and failures
- Potential expansion of the position
- Collective insight from self, staff and peers

The quantitative requisites are things that can be measured in numbers such as number of years in the field, total years in the field, total years of education, number of technical degrees and accreditation licenses and number of years employed in your specific technical areas and the qualitative requisites, viz., work personality, attitude and work ethics.

2. *Compiling the Expectation List:* After preparing the wish list, you need to compile an expectation list which draws your attention on the things a prospective candidate is expected to do. A good rule of thumb in the every context is to make a "top 10" list which can provide you with a sound frame of reference in monitoring and measuring the performance. Besides, this would also help the candidates in knowing the expectations of employers from them.

3. *Reviewing the Job Description:* Reviewing the job description can be helpful in the pre-selection process. This might not reflect all the activities required in the job. You are supposed to

compare your wish list and expectations list to the job description to ascertain how accurate the job description content is. You need to remember that the job description should have maximum clarity of language. It should be free of jargon. Besides, anything unique or critical to the job position should also be listed as a part of the job description.

4. *Reviewing Recruitment Tactics:* In this context, it is also pertinent that you make efforts to work with your human resources department, develop professional contacts with your supervisor and anyone else who can help you in the recruitment of someone who would match the criteria you established earlier. We find a number of recruitment resources available for your use. There are ten recruitment resources such as human resources department contacts, job fairs, school liaisons, employee referral system, professional contacts, agencies, media coverage, informal staff referrals, internal candidates and community based recruitment.

5. *Reviewing Resumes:* The fifth and final phase of the preselection process is related to the review of resume. Since you have established criteria for the position and know about the ten sources as mentioned earlier, you can now review the resumes to determine who among the applicants are to be selected for an in-person interview.

The aforesaid preselection processes would help you in getting the personnel of your choice. You are supposed to sort out the resumes and organise the candidates into three basic categories—the first category would be individuals who are not qualified, the second category would be of possible candidates who definitely have the quantitative skills and might have additional factors and the third category would consist of probable candidates.

In view of the above, it is right to mention that the preselection process also gives you suitable candidates for the hospitals. The main thing is to be vigilant while going through the formalities. Since you are substantially influenced by time and budget constraints, this helps you in making the process cost effective. So far as the quality of personnel is concerned, if you are careful, a chance of getting inefficient people is almost dismal.

Getting quality people is your motto. Making the process of selection cost effective is your aim. It is your professional excellence that helps you in fulfilling your motto and aim. We have frequently talked about the perception of quality people for hospitals and therefore, you are not supposed to be confused. While selecting personnel, you need professionally sound and personally committed people. Since VC find the working environment in hospitals quite different to the other organisations, it is pertinent that you assign clue weightage to human and humane considerations because failing the same, even professionally-sound personnel would not be helpful in accomplishing the organisational goals. It is against this background that we make much more advocacy in favour of quality people.

Quality people often prove to be top performers or super performers or high performers. When you select a top performer, he/sue may be an example for others. (Conversely, when you select an individual who is inefficient, the negative results can be staggering and to avoid all the possibilities of hiring a poor performer you, need to assign due weightage to the selection process). It is the prowess of selection that minimises the possibilities of getting poor performers. When top performers prove to be an asset to an organisation, the poor performers prove to be a liability. And you are not supposed to increase the liability because you have already a number of social liabilities found very much instrumental in making social costs non-optimal to your potentials.

Managing the Selection Process

The first constituent of the management of human resources is selection or recruitment. The motive is to make available to the hospitals quality personnel of different categories so that they are found playing a positive role in accomplishing the organisational goals. We are well aware of the fact that the hospitals need different categories of personnel in the face of nature, character and expertise needed to deliver goods to the patient care. Being a hospital manager, you are supposed to process the recruitment or selection procedures. You work here with two motives—first to make available to the hospitals quality people, and second, to make the selection process cost-effective. In an age of sophisticated information and communication technologies, you are in a position to minimise the time-gap because the use of these technologies help you in minimising the delay on account of postal transit. Besides, the task of screening or sorting is also made easier. Thus, we find impact of technology even on the selection process and being a hospital manager, you are required to consider them on a priority basis. It is in this context that we go through the selection process.

The first task in the very context is to collect the requirements of different departments in your hospital. It is quite natural that the departmental heads would let you know the number and quality of personnel required. They would also make available to you the specialities required for a particular candidate and the time limit.

Based on the requirements received from the different departments regarding the different categories of personnel, you need to make decisions regarding the newspapers or media through which the advertisements are to be published. In this context, you need to concentrate your attention on the quality of personnel needed and the quality and types of newspapers used by that segment. If you advertise for the class IV position, you keep in your mind the newspapers preferred by that segment. In addition, you also need to take a decision regarding the place and page to be selected for advertisement because we find advertisement tariff depending upon the place of coverage. Of late, we also find use of Internet for selecting the personnel but till now we are not in a position to make it of common use. Thus, in addition to other aspects, a hospital manager while advertising for selection is also required to make the process cost-effective.

After crossing the time limit, you are supposed to go through the applications you have received from the interested candidates. At the outset, you need to sort out by making a comparative analysis of the eligibility that you mentioned in the advertisements and the applicants they mention in their curriculum vitae on the prescribed application form, if it is so. After screening, you need to make it sure that all the formalities and requirements have been fulfilled and a list of candidates is ready for despatching the call letters. While despatching the call letters, make it sure that you are in a position to authenticate that letters were despatched to them on time. Meanwhile, you also need to prepare a list of or panel of experts in consultation with the departmental heads to interview the candidates.

With the tarnishing image of educational institutions, universities and deemed universities or institutes, we find even written examinations organised by the hospitals or other organisations, specially for the elimination process.

This increases the functional responsibilities of board or institutions to process the selection of hospital personnel. To be more specific, for the high positions, even an interview or oral presentation would suffice their needs and therefore, we don't find a sense in delaying the process and increasing the budget. If the recruiting board is fair, the task of getting efficient personnel is not so much difficult and if the board is unfair, even the written examinations can be managed. It is against this background that being a manager, you are supposed to work with the motto of getting quality people within the limited time and budget.

The board to interview the candidates bears the responsibility of selecting the best. Any bias or prejudice would stand as a barrier in the process of elimination and you would fail in making available to the different departments quality hospital personnel. We can't negate that while recruiting or activating the elimination process, the members of the board in addition to the subjective knowledge are also required to assign due weightage to the behavioural profile of personnel to be selected. Of course, we often devalue this dimension of personality which complicates our task in future. Thus, the board without any bias and prejudice needs to be influenced by the traits of the personnel.

After the completion of the elimination process, the letters are sent to the selected candidates after completing the formalities required for the same. The terms and conditions, the motivational and incentive plans and the job responsibilities are to be mentioned in the appointment letters to avoid further complications.

In the contractual job system, you are supposed to mention everything in the contract. You need not forget that of late, negotiation is found essential in the job market. We can't negate that hospitals need to promote the contractual job system so that the personnel in general, evince keen interest in discharging their functional responsibilities. The increasing trade unionism, the growing degeneration in the working or decision making behaviour of the leaders of trade unions and associations of doctors make it essential that we think and deliberate upon reviewing the service conditions. The contractual job system in addition to other benefits would also provide to you a favourable environment for the establishment of work culture because in the Indian perspective, we find personnel in general serving in any organisation considerably regulated by the punishment and coercive measures. If they feel that the performance is to influence their job prospects and existence, they have no option but to work suitably. It is against this background that we find private hospitals establishing an edge over the government hospitals, specially in terms of discipline and work culture.

After the personnel resume their duties, you need to provide to them a short-term refresher course regarding their professional, personal, social and organisational responsibilities. Irrespective of the position, you need to organise a training programme that helps the personnel in knowing about the organisation and its priorities. To be more specific, in a sensitive organisation like hospital, a manager is required to be more careful because the services or product of this organisation are directly and very closely related to the behavioural profile of personnel. If we find psychologists advocating much in favour of behavioural therapy, it is nothing to wonder.

You need to remember that at the initial stage, the appointments are on probation and after one year when you find their performance vis-a-vis the behavioural profile satisfactory, their services are to be confirmed. In the contractual job system, you renew the contracts when they complete their contractual obligations satisfactorily.

Of late, we find use of information technology even for appointing the personnel. The devices like fax and e-mailing are used at different stages to receive and transmit the necessary information and instructions. We agree with this view that sophisticated information and communication technologies have made the process of selection easier. In addition, you also minimise the time limit and are in a position to make the process of selection cost-effective. Since we talk about developing a full-fledged technology-driven management information system in the leading hospitals, the process of selection can be made much more easier. It is against this background that we talk about the use of information technology even for recruiting or selecting the personnel.

After making available to the new employees the initial training facilities to make them aware of the work culture and departmental relationships, you place them, but at this stage, you need to make yourself sure that they are performing satisfactorily.

The aforesaid processes are followed for the selection of personnel in the hospitals and healthcare organisations. To be more specific in hospitals, you find a different environment at the workplaces. Almost all the employees working in different capacities in different departments are required to be used to the environmental conditions found sizeably different from other organisations. It is in this context that we have talked about the behavioural profile of personnel to be selected. It is not supposed from the hospital personnel that they don't show empathy. It is not supposed from them that they are indecent and aggressive rather than it is expected from them that they do their best to diffuse the tension of patients and attendants in addition to the professional excellence they show in the wards, OTs, outdoors, ICUs and so on. While selecting, you also need to make sure that they have all the qualities or traits required for a successful leader.

In the management of hospital personnel, this is the first but the most important component or constituent of the management of human resources. It is so because your task of developing and enriching the knowledge bank of personnel is made much more difficult when you fail in getting the right personnel. We talk about development of faculties but when you get employees without the receiver, the transmission process becomes insensitive. The most important thing to be ascertained is the availability of faculty, you need to remember it. Of course, they need professional excellence on a priority basis but it is not meant that they are not aware of humanity and human values. Since you are supposed to transform even the ordinary personnel into super performers, it is pertinent that you make sure that they have the faculties of development, in tune with your requirements.

In view of the above, it is right to say that the selection process assumes a place of outstanding significance in the management of human resources. There are some underlying principles for recruitment of personnel and being a hospital manager, you need to be aware of the same.

Managing Post-selection Process

A majority of the post-selection processes stars with the employer's orientation process and continues throughout your tenure. It is essential that the orientation process includes the elements as mentioned in Fig. 9.6. Once the candidate has accepted the position for which he/she has selected and agreed on the starting date, the orientation process starts on a personal basis.

Clear Job Expectations	Wage/benefit Information
Exposure to other Team Members	Insurance Forms and Information
Organisation Mandates Standards	Major Project Overviews
Performance Evaluation System	Short-term Performance Goals
Personal Departmental Liaison	Insight into Department Work Goals
Departmental Work Conduct	Department History
Patient Profile	Assistance in Personal Relocation
Future Plans	Assistance in Need (Personal) Acquisition

Fig. 9.6. Potential Orientation Activities

After he/she resumes, you need to introduce your new team member to the rest of our employees and also to make sure that all the members of your team realise that there is no second opportunity to make a first impression because we find the first impression as the last impression. In the orientation process, you are required to involve your human resources department and encourage your old employees to extend to the new employees the maximum possible support. Besides, you need to impart to the new employees the basic knowledge about the organisation. Introduce your new member to your supervisor and finally, make sure that the employee is aware of the type of performance evaluation indices to be used.

Thus, right from the preselection process to the post-selection process, a hospital manager is required to be careful so that the motive of getting quality people for the hospitals or healthcare organisation is fulfilled. It is also explained earlier that while selecting personnel, a hospital manager is also to make the selection cost optimal. We don't find any sense in increasing the costs on selection and delaying the process.

Of course, you need to recruit quality hospital personnel but it is not meant that the personnel selected found best for today retain the top position for ever. This is due mainly to the fact that sky is the only limit for quality. The multidimensional developments take place in the medical sciences everyday and unless you keep on moving your efforts for identifying the evolving changes and developing the training or development programme accordingly, you can't be sure of getting the quality people. Because we find development an ongoing process and a hospital manager keeping his/her eyes closed and mind insensitive can't be successful in accomplishing the organisational goals. It is in this context that the training programme occupies an important place in the personnel or human resources development programme.

Basic Principles Governing Recruitment

We are well aware of the fact that selection is the process through which suitable candidates are selected. It is considered to be a managerial process. If the selection procedure is fair and sound, the hospitals would be in a position to make available to the patients quality health care services. There are some principles and being a hospital they would be in a position to make available to the patients quality healthcare services. There are some basic principles and being a hospital manager, you are supposed to know the same.

1. *Centralised Section:* We can't negate the fact that recruitment should be done from a central pool. Like other organisations, even we find hospitals realising the significance of human resources department for this purpose. Of course, the personnel are selected for different purposes for the different departments but the hospital managers responsible for managing the human resources would make it possible with the cooperation of the departmental heads supposed to be specialists.

2. *Work Analysis:* It is essential that work analysis is made before recruitment. This helps you knowing about the exact requirements for a particular department. You are also supposed to turn your eyes on the future requirements in tune with your development and expansion plan. May be that you have not installed technologies of new generation at present but are likely to install the same in the near future. While selecting, you need to make it sure that employees to be recruited are well aware of the technologies that you are likely to have to promote techniculture.

3. *Use both Internal as well as the External Sources:* While selecting, it is significant that you select employees not only from the external sources but also from the internal sources. If you need an expert and you find that he/she right now serving the hospitals is competent enough to perform efficiently and suitably, you need to select them. But if you get superior quality of personnel from the external sources, you are not supposed to confine yourself to the internal sources.

4. *Required Qualifications and Expertise:* While selecting, you are supposed to make it sure that employees to be selected possess the qualifications and experience you have mentioned in the advertisements. If you fail in getting the personnel in tune with the qualifications and experiences mentioned, it is better to postpone.

5. *Let them know the Future Prospects:* While selecting, it is essential that you communicate to the candidates the future prospects, such as promotional avenues, special incentives to the high performers, norms, culture, discipline and so on. To be more specific, employees or candidates having outstanding credentials have been found interested in knowing their future prospects.

6. *Recruitment Policy should be Made Clear:* It is also pertinent that you communicate to the candidates the recruitment policy. The service conditions, the nature of appointment, the job responsibilities, the superannuation schemes, the post-retirement benefits, etc., are required to be made clear.

7. *Without a Bias:* It is significant that recruitment processes are fair. You are not influenced by personal considerations. You assign due weightage to the quality of personnel to be recruited. You don't consider friendship, brotherhood and at the same time, don't perceive anything negative about a particular candidate.

Developing Hospital Personnel: Education and Training

Since we find multidimensional changes in the medical sciences in addition to the changes in the behaviour profile of patients and attendants, it is essential that the second constituent of the management of personnel or human resources is given due weightage. The increasing cases of food-borne, water-borne, environment-borne, communicable and vector-borne diseases are found changing the disease profile. The available medicines are found to be ineffective and the patients suffer a lot. The plan for the use of the new generation of technologies for innovative diagnostic and treatment measures can't be deferred. This makes it essential that you keep on moving the process of developing the credentials of your personnel. Because we find perfection without a boundary and if you don't make efforts to develop the credentials, it is quite natural that you suffer on that account. It is against this background that we find this component of the management of human resources occupying a place of outstanding significance.

Shrinking operational revenues is also found to be an important factor necessitating innovative efforts. On the one hand, you are required to spend more for the expensive inputs while on the other hand, you don't get avenues for an optimal generation of revenues. This makes ways for a challenging conundrum for any hospital manager found responsible for managing the human resources. With less money to spend on education and training and increased emphasis on improving the quality of the human resources, a hospital manager must install an efficient method of instruction and a training practical to ensure that all the personnel serving the hospitals are to be made available quality environment to work and prosper.

Without a geographical boundary, we find a cut in educational costs which is found complicating the task of a hospital manager not only in India but the world over. In a very natural way, this requires professional excellence to manage everything within the limited time and budget.

In the development process, we talk about the development of knowledge which makes it essential that a hospital manager in addition to other portfolio also proves his/her excellence as a successful educator. Of course, a majority of the technical problems would be dealt by the experts or specialists but the latest basic developments in the discipline are to be made available to the personnel on a priority basis and for that, a hospital manager is supposed to be aware of the multidimensional developments in the medical sciences.

In an age of sophisticated information and communication technologies, the process of sensitising the patients is found easier, specially with the help of audio-visual devices. A hospital manager while developing infrastructural facilities for the training and development programme for the different categories of personnel requires to take the support of sophisticated communications technologies.

Because of the changing role of a hospital manager, specially as an educator, the training and development needs analysis also gravitate our attention. We often talk about the Individual Development Plans (IDPs) which would help you in monitoring and educating your staff. Group training dynamics also prove to be significant and you are supposed to make the group sessions more valuable and beneficial for all the trainees involved. The most overlooked aspect that we find in the development process is delegation and you are required to know the pitfalls and "fail-safes" of delegation so as to make it an educational strategy. Thus, we go through different dimensions of training and development of hospital personnel.

Benefits of Training

Quality personnel benefit an organisation in many ways. If we find hospitals or the healthcare organisations working with the support of world class personnel found professionally-sound as well as personally committed, the patients are found satisfied because they are made available quality health care services. In addition, the hospitals are also benefited. We go through the benefits of training programme.

1. *Benefits to an Organisation/Hospital:* We can't deny the fact that strong training and educational efforts benefit hospitals in different ways. The hospitals for a good patient care need sophisticated technologies no doubt but failing the availability of professionally sound and personally committed personnel, they find it difficult to offer quality healthcare services to the patients. The projection of a positive image becomes too much difficult, if they don't have personnel having up-to-date knowledge. It is due to a well organised training programme that the personnel belonging to different areas get an opportunity to enrich their knowledge bank. We agree with this view that each healthcare employee has his/her own individual performance potential level. Maximising the potential level is the point that separates the strong organisations from the weak ones, specially in an organisation where we find technology-based and people-intensive work environment. It is in this context that we find strong organisations a result of potentially-sound personnel which can't be possible if the training programme is not well organised. We are well aware of the fact that Continuous Quality Improvement (CQI) is an objective held by all the hospital or the healthcare organisations. The CQI starts with each individual employee and therefore, it is much more difficult for an organisation to achieve quality in totality unless it provides due weightage to the education and training to its employees. It is also right to mention that a sense of affiliation is a strong motivation and almost all of us want close affiliation with a "winner" and only the strongest person or organisation proves to be a winner. A well organised training programme makes the ways for increasing the strength.

2. *Individual Employee Development:* We agree with this view that a well-managed training programme is found beneficial to the employees. This is due mainly to the fact that training and development programmes have two-tier effects, viz., an educational effect as well as a motivational impact on the individual employee. Of late, we talk about professional excellence and an ongoing training programme bears the efficacy of making the person professionally-sound. We also assign due weightage to personnel commitments and a well-organised training programme supported and managed by the behavioural scientists generates personal traits in an individual. In addition, we find training and development programmes contributing to the positive motivation of an employee in many ways. We can't deny the fact that with the help of a well managed training programme, an individual gets an opportunity to develop his/her potentials because latest developments in the medical sciences are made available to them. Thus, we agree with the view that training and development programmes in hospitals or healthcare organisations provide profitable opportunities to be capitalised on, specially to the personnel who are found to be professionally-sound and personally-committed.

3. *Management Team Performance:* We agree with this view that strong healthcare organisations have a strong management team. It is right to mention that of late, even in the healthcare sector, we find intensity of competition moving upward. Besides, we also find multi-dimensional developments in the field of medical sciences taking place each and everyday.

This makes it essential that you have a strong team to counter the multidimensional challenges and changes. Strong training and development programmes bear the efficacy to prepare potentially sound managers on the current staff to assume future management roles. The employees get an opportunity to develop whatever the potentials that we find among them are effectively cultivated. Besides, we find the training and development programmes directly assisting the management team in providing the organisation with the high level of operational efficiency found essential to accomplish the organisational goals.

4. *Patient Satisfaction:* The ultimate goals of a hospital or healthcare organisation is to offer to the patients quality healthcare services so that their levels of expectations are fulfilled and they are found satisfied. Of late, we find healthcare organisations or hospitals of course charging exhorbitantly the healthcare bills but we also find a few of them offering the world class healthcare services. This has been successful in increasing the levels of expectations of patients or users of the services. We can't negate that management-orientation in the generation and processing of services improves the quality of services and the patients are offered the services in the face of their expectations. This helps in satisfying the patients. It is against this background that we find an apparent difference in between the quality of services offered by hospitals conceptualising modern management principles and the hospitals offering services having traditional orientation. To win and keep the patients, it is pertinent that we assign due weightage to some of the essentials, such as the hospital personnel should have the widest range of education in their particular areas of technical expertise and business acumen. The personnel need to know the healthcare field at large, such as the emerging trends in business, industry dynamics and all the factors that make the healthcare setting unique and the most important of all that the personnel are skilled in interpersonal communications and other areas contributing substantially to the personal-touch-in services offered. The progressive and positive uses of the training programme relate to development and accomplishment of the organisational goals. Contrary to it, if we find hospitals taking a back seat, the reverse would be true, such as the patients would become disenchanted, the personnel would become disenfranchised and the organisation as a whole would become disruptive and regressive. This speaks of the fact that a well-organised, time-honoured, technology-driven, management-oriented training and education programmes for the hospital personnel pave copious avenues for the satisfaction of patients or users.

5. *Human Capital Formation:* We can't negate the fact that health is above wealth and only physically sound people can be transformed into the productive human resources. The improved quality of healthcare services if made available to the masses help the process of developing physically sound people. It is right to mention that the education and training programmes in addition to the curative services also promote preventive services helping doctors in educating and sensing the patients and attendants in a right fashion. We make efforts to enrich their behavioural profile, communication skills and these things play a big role in sensing the masses in the right directions. If they are aware of the preventive measures, it is quite natural that the increasing cases of diseases prone to food, drinking water, environment and living conditions would considerably be minimised. Contrary to other organisations, the success rate of healthcare organisations depends upon their contributions to the process of bringing down the numbers of potential patients by controlling the multidimensional health hazards.

Education and Development Programme

All of us agree with this view that education is an ongoing process. Because we find education a primary source of achieving perfection and since we don't find any boundary for perfection, the development of education remains to be a continuous process. The moment an organisation feels that the quality of personnel they have are to remain super performers for all the time, we find a full stop to the process of qualitative improvements. It is in this context that we need to assign due weightage to the education development programme so that the process of developing knowledge gains rapid momentum and the employees or personnel get an opportunity to prove to be the top performers. We need to organise the education development programme to enrich the knowledge bank of our employees. It is pertinent that they are well aware of the multidimensional developments in the medical sciences and in addition also succeed in having a high behavioural profile. The process of developing education would make them professionally sound and the process of developing knowledge would make them not only professionally excellent but even personally committed. We go through the problem of development of hospital personnel in two different perspectives. Firstly, we go through the problem of management development and thereafter, turn our eyes on the development of employees.

Management Development

We can't negate the positive contributions of management-orientation to the development of healthcare services. If we keep on moving the process of developing management excellence with the help of education and development programmes, it is quite natural that tomorrow we would have a large number of top performers. Training and development when specifically applied to managers as a management development effort help hospital managers in attaining competence in several basic areas. World class managerial excellence is found essential for the managers serving the healthcare organisations. This draws our attention on the learning curve. Achieving a certain degree of proficiency is essential and this is not possible in a day or two. In Fig. 9.7, we find the learning curve focusing our attention on the level of competence of the healthcare managers.

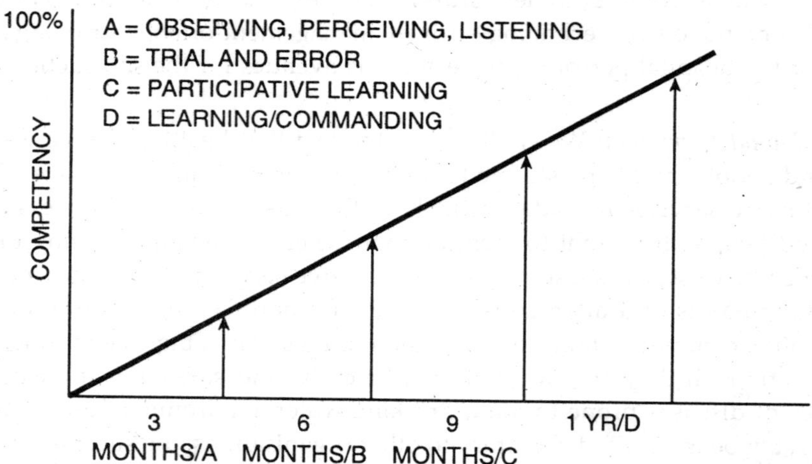

Fig. 9.7. Healthcare Manager's Learning Curve
Adapted from -Lombardi D.N; Healthcare, p. 307

There are different phases of learning, such as first phase—observing, perceiving and listening; second phase—trial and error; third phase—participating, learning and the fourth phase—leading or assuming command. This makes it clear that assuming or leading a command requires consistency in our efforts to educate and develop the managers serving hospitals or healthcare organisations. An analysis of different phases of learning would make it clear that achieving satisfactory level of managerial excellence requires consistent and sincere efforts.

The first phase focuses our attention on observing, perceiving and listening. You are supposed to monitor the progress closely. The performance of your staff, peers and style of managers with whom you work are required to be observed minutely. You are supposed to listen to all of their experiences in the areas of expertise and try to perceive each episode virtually as a lesson. This would provide to you a basic frame of reference in management. Besides, the process of observation would also help you in molding your relationships with peers and superiors.

The second phase draws our attention on trial and error. In the trial and error phase of learning, you are supposed to establish some policy making decisions and operating as an agent of change. We learn from our own mistakes. Unless we commit mistakes, we can't improve or get a lesson. The process of trial and error helps you in identifying the mistakes and even correcting the same.

The third phase is related to participative learning. It takes into account the entire range of activities you learn and practice to your business situation. At this stage, you act as an instructor in delivering information and providing instructions to your staff. In addition, you are also found enriching the expertise of your peers.

The fourth and last phase in the learning process is assuming command. It is expected that you have acquired a certain level of competence. Of course, you are till now at the learning stage. A leadership role is now required to be performed by you. Learning is an ongoing process because perfection is the result of learning that is found an endless process. It is pertinent that while achieving perfection, you keep yourself apprised of the new management techniques, keep yourself well aware of the innovative ways of dealing with the people and are sincere to instrumentalise or sharpen your technical acumen.

In view of the aforesaid facts, it is right to mention that a new manager when he/she resumes his/her functional responsibilities is supposed to go through a learning process. We talk about the top performers but the transformation of new managers into top performers is a process which is found time taking. Achieving excellence or perfection can't be possible within a couple of days or even years because we find multifaceted developments in the medical sciences. For today, you are perfect but just for tomorrow you find yourself imperfect. It is against this background that we focus on the management development programme as an essential part of the personnel development programme. We agree with this view that a successful manager in addition to the professional excellence also requires high communicative ability vis-a-vis a sound behavioural profile. Since you are supposed to manage an organisation in which the working conditions are found sizeably different to other organisations, it is much more impact generating that you have the potentials to counter the adverse situations. If you work and perceive with the motto of enriching your knowledge bank, the task of achieving high level of efficiency would considerably be simplified.

Because you are a new manager and have just started your career, it is essential that you keep your eyes all the time open and make sincere efforts to improve your excellence. This makes it essential that you know about the sources of learning. It would not be out of place to mention that even old and experienced managers also need to learn because we don't find any boundary for perfection.

Sources of Learning

Enriching knowledge is an endless process that requires information sources. The following sources help a new healthcare manager in improving his/her excellence.

1. *Personal Experience:* We learn by our own mistakes. This makes it essential that you take the support of trial and error, try to identify your mistakes and think about the corrective measures to improve. Experience is found to be a source of information. Because you have acquired a certain level of excellence, it is essential that now you rely on your instincts. We can't deny the fact that intuition is the result of experiences and a manager also requires to use his/her intuition.

2. *Look at your Peers:* Whatever you fail to do, your peers succeed in doing the same. May be that your peers fail and you succeed. This speaks of the fact that a new healthcare manager is supposed to gravitate his/her attention on the working styles of peers working with him-her as counterparts. It is quite natural that all the conditions and situations can't be identical. However, it is significant that you not only turn your eyes on the functional behaviour of your peers but also watch the same minutely.

3. *Organisation-supported Education:* It is also essential that in the learning process, you prefer to visit seminars, conferences, workshops, refresher courses and capsule courses organised by your organisation. This provides you an opportunity to learn something. You need to capitalise on the opportunities provided by your organisation specially related to the education development programme.

4. *National and International Conventions:* In the process of improving excellence, it is also essential that you prefer to attend conferences and conventions organised by national and international health associations or medical organisations. This provides you an opportunity to learn something. In addition, you also find yourself in a position to develop rapport with the leading personalities of your discipline. It is important that hospitals or healthcare organisations where you work promote and motivate you for the same.

5. *Journals and other Creative Reading Materials:* You need to develop a habit of reading latest journals and magazines, specially related to the healthcare. This would provide you an opportunity to enrich your knowledge bank. You would come to know about the latest developments in the discipline. In a true sense, you would be in a position to rate your performance. In addition, you are also required to contribute to the journals and magazines, creative literature based on your experiences.

6. *Formal Education:* We are well aware of the fact that being a healthcare manager, you are supposed *to* have a knowledge of different subjects, such as management, its functional areas, viz., management of human resources, management of finance, management of marketing and so on. You are supposed to know even about the other allied subjects such as behavioural science, home science, life science, information technology and so on. Here, our focus is on the fact that you are supposed to be a master of different allied subjects essential for managing the healthcare organisations.

7. *Supervisor Helps You:* You need to remember that the learning material is found at almost all the sources. You learn from your peers, you learn from your boss or supervisor and you learn even from your subordinates. Don't forget that your supervisor can be a valuable source of information. He/she can be a terrific educator.

8. *Information from Staff:* In addition to the aforesaid sources, you also get information from your staff. We can't negate the fact that a healthcare manager who neglects the feedback received from staff would not be successful in his/her efforts for increasing the level of efficiency. You are supposed to watch their day-to-day activities and to store the experiences in your memory bank.

In addition to other aspects, such an attempt would help you in knowing or understanding the fact that what are their weaknesses, how are they motivated and so on.

9. *Outside Sources:* In addition to the internal sources, you get information even from the external sources. You are supposed to establish a network of contacts by developing rapport with the allied businesses. The pharmaceutical manager, the supplier of hospital materials, personnel coordinator, architects, consultants and planners are the different outside sources for getting information.

The aforesaid sources of learning would help a new hospital or healthcare manager in enriching his/her knowledge bank. We agree with this view that even if you have experience, the information is found helpful to learn something. Of late, we find information technology playing an incremental role in enriching the information bank of a hospital or a healthcare manager. The information superhighway, in particular has revolutionised the process of collecting healthcare information. The main thing is the interest you have in improving your excellence. Since we find the intensity of problem of managing government hospitals at its peak, it is pertinent that managers/administrators managing the government hospitals make sincere efforts to develop their expertise. Your world class professional excellence would help government hospitals and the patients admitted in wards in different ways. Because of shrinking revenue and the aggravating problem of financial crunch mainly on account of a drastic cut in the grants related to healthcare, the government hospitals in general are found in a depleted condition. The deficient management has been found aggravating the magnitude of problem. This makes it essential that hospitals in general and the government hospitals in particular take benefits of the services of professionally sound and personally committed healthcare managers.

The aforesaid analysis makes it clear that the healthcare manager requires to enrich his/her knowledge. You are supposed to keep your eyes open all the time so that positive or negative developments in the healthcare sector provide to you an opportunity to learn something new. We can't negate the fact that top level management of the healthcare organisations or hospitals requires to promote the process of learning or management development programme. It is also found that administrators, specially serving the government hospitals are found disinterested in enriching their knowledge bank. The increasing intensity of mismanagement makes it clear that they need to develop the knowledge to their administrators. It is high time that they think in favour of appointing hospital managers.

Education, learning and training thus make the ways for development of knowledge which keep you well informed regarding the day-to-day multidimensional developments taking place in the healthcare sector. If you adopt it as an ongoing process, your success in developing professional excellence besides value-engineering can't be obstructed.

Employee Development Programme (EDP)

We agree with this view that development of employees serving the hospitals assumes the same weightage as we find about the development of managers. In the hospitals or healthcare organisations, we find different types of employees in job who can make available to you the important feedback. Since you hold an important position in the hospital organisation and management, it is your prime responsibility to impart training facilities to your subordinates. To be more specific, when we find a drastic cut in the budget training and development programmes, it becomes your responsibility to take care of the employees' development programme.

In this context, you can organise a seminar or an in-service programme for employees. This would only not benefit the employees but would also increase your potentials of oral presentation vi-s-a-vis the public speaking skills. You are supposed to work as a trainer and therefore, you need to enrich your information bank. By imparting training facility to your staff, you will find a change in their potentials. The level of competence would be increased and a sense of cooperation and coordination would also be possible. It is in this context that we find significance of "bench strength." The term focuses our attention on the ability to have depth of talent across your entire department. We agree with this view that the bench strength is increased by having a diversity of talent and individual strengths. Undoubtedly enough, this can be increased by quality training.

You are supposed to establish creditability among your staff. If as a trainer you succeed in influencing your staff, it is quite natural that it would form a high opinion regarding your potentials. It is against this background that as a manager you need to assign due weightage to the training programme and to get yourself ready for the same so that the task of establishing credibility is made proactive. Demonstration of knowledge bears the efficacy of projecting a positive or even a negative image. If you have influenced them, they form a positive opinion regarding your professional excellence and conversely when you fail, they form a negative opinion.

By imparting training facilities to your staff, you get an opportunity to know about the specialities of an individual. You are found in a position to select the best among the available lot. Since you get an opportunity to interact, it is found easier to identify the specialities or the outstanding personalities. Relationships are found based on communication and trust. By training, you are in a position to communicate and receive. You come to know about the different categories of employees. You thus get information regarding the employees, their potentials, their weaknesses and these things help you in future.

The aforesaid facts make it clear that the development programmes for staff and employees would be beneficial to you as well as to them because this makes the ways for developing relationships. Since we talk about Employee Development Programme (EDP), it is quite natural that you also take care of their problems. The moment you start knowing about them informally and personally, the departmental relationships is made friendly where establishment of a strong organisational culture would not be found difficult. It is against this background that we make a strong advocacy in favour of EDP.

Individual Development Plan (IDP)

It is essential that being a manager, you also think about an Individual Development Plan which is considered to be a sound tool for establishing a group training programme. The IDP is found focusing on understanding the needs and requirements of an individual. It is quite natural that the potentials or qualities of all the employees working with you are not identical. You find some of them having high potentials whereas you also find a few of them potentially very weak. In Fig. 9.8, we find a sample of IDP.

Name : ________		IDP Date : ________
Position : ________		
Starting date : ________		
Supervisor's Manager's Name : ________		
Need	**Activity Time**	**Learning Value/Comments**
1. ADA Regulations	AHA Seminar	Competency
2. CQI Knowledge	In-services Programme	Can take lead in CQI Process
3. Time Management	University Course	Increased Efficiency
4. Budgeting	Participation in Process	Can back up Manager in Process
5. Patient Relations	Understudy Ongoing	Will assist on New Public Relations Project

Fig. 9.8. Sample of IDP Form

As it is clear in Fig. 9.8 that at the outset, you need to enter the name of an individual and the starting date, i.e., the date on which the IDP is started and the date of completion. You are required to put your signature or to mention your name as a manager or supervisor. Then write down the specific training needs identified for each individual, estimated time for training, learning value of the training programme and your comments. You need to prepare it annually.

You are supposed to ensure the rationale of the training programme for an individual. This focuses our attention on the need-analysis which clarifies the plus and minus points in an individual. Once you succeed in identifying the potentials or weaknesses of an individual, your task is then to conduct a basic inventory of the present skills of your employees in addition to the appraisal of performance for the last few years. If you feel essential, you can even discuss with your predecessor the potentials and weaknesses of each individual. But you are supposed to adopt it just as a source-material because if your predecessor has developed bias or prejudice to an individual knowing well that he/she is not potentially sound and does not like the adjective "weakness" therefore, it is right that you ask each employee about his/her aptitude that would provide you the right answer without displeasing them. Establish the goals of training and activities simultaneously. The estimated time of completion is considered to be an important aspect of IDP. The time range of one to two months would be ideal. You are also required to discuss with them the outcome of the training programme.

Value-orientation in Medical Profession

Education, training and development programmes for the personnel provide them an opportunity to be high performers, of course professionally. We can't negate that your professional excellence carries no meaning, if it is not to serve the interests of patients. If we turn our eyes on the performance or behaviour of hospital personnel, it is found that except a few, almost all of them contribute very abysmally to the process of value-engineering. We don't find any sense in becoming inhuman, indecent and unethical. Irrespective of the position you hold, the department you head, the expertise you possess, the process of value-engineering if not switched on in the right directions would hamper the accomplishment of organisational goals. You are not only supposed to cure the patients but you also bear the responsibility of making them convinced that you have just discharged your functional responsibilities and there is nothing like to feel obliged. In any case, we can't treat the medical profession as a business and albeit in business we find place for ethics and values. Either the employees work as a manager or a supervisor or a doctor or a nurse or a paramedical staff; he/she can't make a good-bye to the process of value-engineering because the medical profession is found standing on the same. It is against this background that we go through the problem of value inculcation while offering the facilities related to training and education.

Attitudes are substantially influenced by the brainwashing process. If all the sources motivate you to take part in the process of value-orientation, we find a basic change in your behavioural profile resulting into an attitudinal change.[8] If we find the process of value-generation taking its roots stronger and deeper even in the medical profession, it is due mainly to the fact that all the sources of inputs are closed. You don't get an opportunity in your family to learn from your parents because in a majority of the cases, they don't have courage to face you; you don't get an opportunity to learn from your teachers because they themselves have started making a good-bye to the process of value-orientation; you don't get an opportunity to learn from media because they have now been found promoting commercialisation for getting advertisements albeit at the cost of value-degeneration. Thus, the task of value-orientation is found difficult but being a hospital manager, you are supposed to be fully aware of the crisis management where your excellence is expected to be proactive even if the environment conditions are unfavourable. It is in this context that we focus on the problem of value-orientation while educating and training the different categories of hospital personnel.

We need to mention that Japanese media have been doing a good job by washing and storming the brains of their citizens and it is due mainly to the fact that roots of national excellence and ethics are found very deep specially in the Japanese society. The secondary and tertiary hospitals, the medical institutes and deemed universities, private institutes and even general schools and colleges need to redesign their syllabi in which ethics, values, morality, humanity, national excellence, social responsibility and so on are to be given due weightage. Before accreditation, the universities and institutes need to audit the multidimensional contributions of the students to be awarded degrees, certificates and diplomas. The policy decision makers bear the responsibility of activating the brain-washing process by redesigning the syllabi of almost all the courses. It is not only sufficient that your products are professionally sound. It is much more impact generating that your products are professionally excellent as well as well as personally committed.

Thus, the first thing that we need to do is a major change in our syllabi both for education and training. The syllabi for medical and paramedical staff, nurses and hospital managers need to be restructured in the face of emerging conditions. And in the same context, the accreditation process would also assign due weightage to the contributions of students to the process of value-orientation.

We find a number of cases to quote where the doctors are professionally sound but lack personal-touch-in-service, promote unethical practices and keep on moving the process of exploiting the patients and attendants. It is against this background that we need to link our compensation and motivation plans to the value-orientation process. The medical or paramedical staff, the nursing staff as well as the manager not evincing interests in the process or found promoting unethical or unfair practices are to be demotivated. On the other hand, they, if contribute substantially to the process of value-engineering, are to be motivated or rewarded suitably. Unless we think in this direction, the process of value-orientation would not be speeded up. It is in this context that we make much more advocacy in favour of linking the compensation and motivation plans for the hospital personnel to the value-orientation process.

The boardroom or the policy makers need to assign due weightage to this parameter while approving the budget for education and training because unless we motivate personnel for value-orientation; the process, the efforts are not to be result oriented. In addition, a hospital manager while making performance-audit is also required to assign an overriding priority to this dimension. Job promotion is an important tool in the hands of a hospital manager to motivate the hospital personnel for evincing their interests in value-orientation. If the patients and attendants have been commenting favourably on their contributions if the departmental heads have been remarking favourable regarding their participation in the value-orientation process, and they should be given promotion to the high position. Thus, while educating and training the hospital personnel, you need to make it clear that, the staff or employees not behaving properly and acting unethically would suffer a lot. In a true sense, your lessons should start with value-orientation and should be concluded with the same.

In US, we find the society more conscious. There are a number of healthcare organisations and associations, social organisations, non-governmental organisations, social activities, philanthropists taking part in the education and training programme for the hospital personnel. This in a true sense, helps personnel in perceiving the importance of value-orientation and we find an attitudinal change. To be more specific in the Indian society, we don't find multi-cornered cooperation because the society is found to be insensitive if social regulations start regulating the behaviour of hospital personnel.

In view of the above, it is right to mention that to activate the process of value-orientation, the education and training programmes for the hospital personnel are to be creative so that we succeed in inculcating values. So far as the professional excellence is concerned, we don't find it so much disappointing but the personal-touch-in-service has been found very much neglected and a hospital manager bears the responsibility of bringing the derailed systems on the rail.

Human Capital Formation and Productivity Acceleration

A hospital manager bears the responsibility of managing the personnel serving the hospitals or the healthcare organisations. They are supposed to increase the rate of staff productivity which makes it essential that the hospital personnel achieve the targeted level of efficiency. How to cultivate the available potentials or faculties so that the hospital personnel contribute substantially to the process of productivity acceleration is an important functional responsibility of a hospital manager. This makes it essential that the personnel are professionally sound and are well aware of the latest developments in the field of medical sciences. It is supposed that the education and training programmes focus on the recent developments in biomedical equipments and apparatus and the allied problems related to the management of equipment. We need a correlation between the evolving technologies and the personnel development programme. The experts related to the discipline are required to assign due weightage to recent developments so that we find personnel in a position to deliver goods to the hospitals. The medical and the paramedical staff need in-house training programme for the purpose because in a majority of the hospitals, we find the problem of abysmally low rate of technology-productivity. Of course, we find a pressure on the financial management of hospitals which have been facing the problem of financial crunch. On the one hand, we find shrinking avenues for generating revenues while on the other hand, we find mismanagement of even expensive technologies. This makes it essential that the world class trainers make available to the personnel an indepth knowledge regarding the maintenance, repairing, replacement and installation. Such a step would make the concerned personnel efficacious enough in increasing the rate of productivity of biomedical equipments and apparatus presently found to be a burden on hospitals or the healthcare organisations.

For the formation of human capital, it is pertinent that we make the personnel potentially sound.[9] Of late, the trainers can seek the cooperation of information superhighway for that very purpose. The increasing significance of Internet operations is to be conceptualised even in the education and training programme for the hospital personnel. The diagnostic measures as well as the treatment processes are now found completely changed but a majority of the hospital personnel are not aware of the recent developments. This makes it essential that we assign due weightage to the knowledge bank of personnel in general and with the help of Internet services or audio-visual exposure enrich the process of developing knowledge. The changes in the disease profile of vulnerable areas, the contracting effects of medicines, the increasing side-effects of antibiotics, the instrumentality of sophisticated information and communication technologies, are some of the key issues necessitating due care of the trainers. If we succeed in creating awareness, the potentials of hospital personnel would sizeably be increased.

Professionally sound personnel bear the efficacy of offering quality health care services, but failing professional commitments, we find personnel not sincere even to their defined functional responsibilities. This makes it essential that we motivate personnel and at the same time, also think about the demotivational measures for those personnel who have been found deliberate in degenerating the level of efficiency. It is against this background that we make a strong advocacy in favour of integrating professional commitments with personal commitments.

The trainers need to speed up the process of value-orientation because we find absence of work culture in almost all the hospitals and healthcare organisations. The value-engineering process if well directed and scientifically and professionally managed makes the ways for personal commitments. It is in this context that we make a strong advocacy in favour of ethics in hospitals. A structural change in syllabi is to be made possible and in addition, the personnel development programme is required to assign due weightage to value generation. Of late, we also find cases that doctors are professionally sound but since they lack personal commitments and we don't find personal-touch-in-service. This makes the ways for dissatisfaction to the patients at large. Keeping in view the absence of work culture, specially in the government hospitals, it is pertinent that the trainers make sincere and honest efforts to inculcate values in which ethics, humanity, personal-touch-in-service need due weightage.

A degeneration in the behavioural profile of personnel in general makes it essential that the trainers on their development agenda assign top priority to the behavioural dimension of personnel irrespective of the specialisation and discipline. We can't negate the instrumentality of behavioural scientists in the process of enriching the behavioural profile because failing it the personal commitments would not be possible. Professionally sound and personally committed personnel would help managers in accomplishing the organisational goals.

The trainers also need due emphasis on waste management because we find medical and paramedical staff throwing even the biomedical degradable waste here and there then what to talk about the biomedical non-degradable waste. The paramedical staff and the nurses need a special training programme related to the management of hospital waste. The harmful effects of waste mismanagement are to be transmitted to almost all categories of the hospital personnel. Infection management also draws attention of trainers because the sensitive or vulnerable points like OTs, wards, lavatories, urinals and dustbins prove to be a source for the multidimensional diseases. The trainers need to focus on infection management.

All of us agree with this view that aesthetic management is an important dimension of hospital management because this contracts avenues for the generation of diseases. The surroundings and premises of hospitals, the drains, sewage, etc. are to be given a new look. The sanitary inspector or supervisor, the hospital architects and planners need to be involved in the process so that the hospitals prove to be a centre for quick recovery. The forest department, the NSS team, the SCOUTS and the social organisations are to be involved in the process. At the same time, it is also pertinent that the trainers while educating the personnel focus on the effects of hygienic living conditions on the health of masses.

The aforesaid facts make it clear that we need concerted, sincere and honest efforts to develop the personnel. Our personnel if professionally-sound and personally-committed prove to be a capital or an asset to the hospitals and conversely, the personnel not having a fair mix of both the attributes prove to be a liability. If we educate and train the personnel in a right fashion, they prove to be capital contributing substantially to the process of acceleration of productivity.

Delegation of Responsibility

As a manager, it is imperative that you delegate as many responsibilities as possible while maintaining responsibility for the ultimate outcome of the project. You need to keep in your mind four basic delegation guidelines as presented in Fig. 9.9.

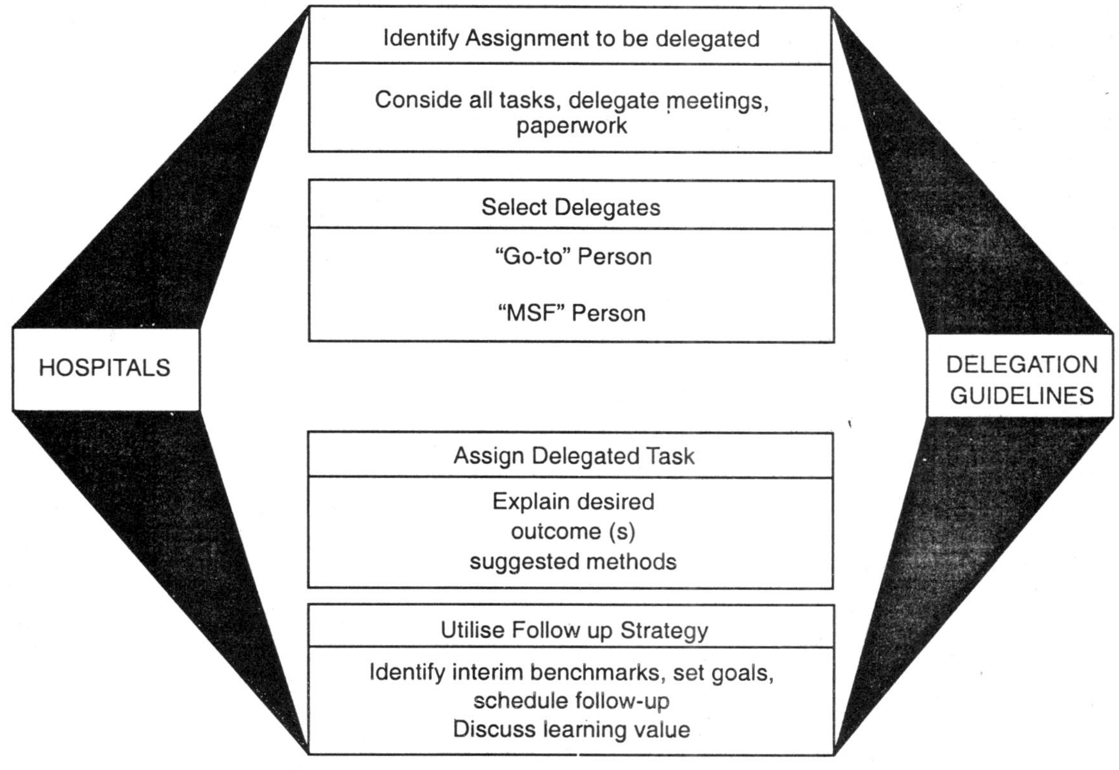

Fig. 9.9. Delegation Guidelines

The above mentioned figure focuses on the basic guidelines:

- Your first task is *to identify the delegatable assignments* and in this context, you need to consider all tasks that can be done by others in the same fashion. You are supposed to limit the list to things you dislike and consider delegating meetings, paperwork, audits and people related projects.
- Your second task *is to select a delegate* and in this context, you need to go to a person who has enough time and, who is highly competent. You need to consider time available for teaching task and the potentials of MSF persons.
- Your third task is to *assign the delegated task* and here you need to explain the desired outcome (s) and also to suggest the alternatives for accomplishment. You need to clarify, express confidence and to establish communicative follow up.
- Your fourth task is to utilise follow up strategy and here, you need to identify the interim benchmarks, set goals using time, numbers, percentage and cost containment. You are also required to schedule the follow up sessions and to discuss the learning value in depth.

In assigning the task, you need to identify the assignments that are not routine. To put it another way, you need not to limit your list of delegatable assignments to the things that bore you, things you don't like or things you would like to do but have never done and thus, have no frame of reference as to how to pursue the objective. You also need to review the learning value inherent in each delegated task and be sure to stress this to the employee when you assign the task. Meetings, paperwork, audit activities, investigation work and people-intensive activities are to be preferred to be delegated.

The motive of delegation is to increase the efficiency of your staff. As it is mentioned in Fig. 9.10, that there are two types of individuals to whom you would find it convenient to delegate. The first is the "go-to-go" individual who is the person who has done the task earlier and has achieved total competency but because he/she has achieved mastery of the task, the learning process could not be activated, and the second individual is the MSF (Maximum Stretch Factor) person who has no competency in the activity or task and can learn upto 100 per cent of the learning value of the task. And therefore, if you are not in haste, you need to prefer MSF person and he/she would learn and grow from the experience. This would also free the go-to-go person to complete another assignment that would teach a new competency such as assignment #2 as shown in Fig. 9. 10.

In assigning the delegated objective, you have three alternatives, viz., first, you are in a position to instruct the individual that how to do the task assigned to him/her which would guarantee a clear outcome but at the same time would limit creativity; second, you would ask the individual how he/she wants to do the task but without a frame of reference which he/she would not be in a position to answer; and the third option is, of course, the best in which you suggest to the individual how you have completed the task earlier, how others might have completed the task before and what the creative contributions mentioned in a paper of a journal suggests to complete the task. We find that in the process, a learner gets the frame of reference which makes the ways for creativity. Or as mentioned in Fig. 9.9, you can also use an appropriate follow-up strategy. In this context, you assign the objective using time, money, percentage and numbers.

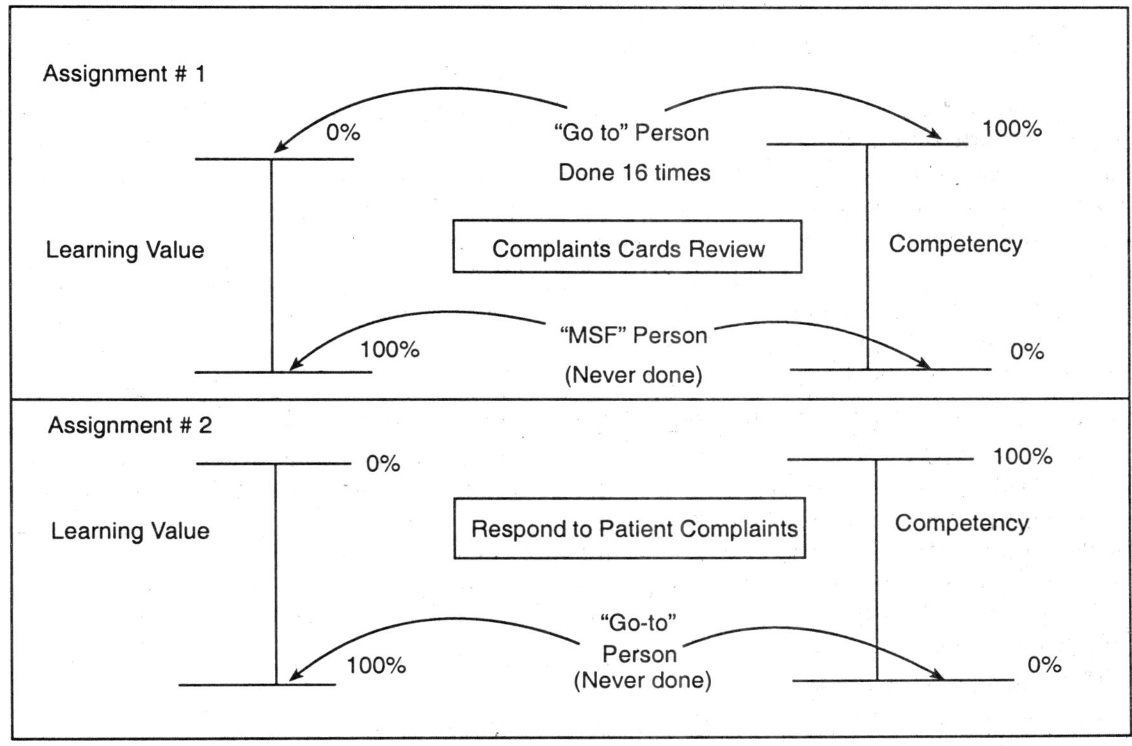

Fig. 9.10. Delegation Dynamics
Adapted from Lombardi, Healthcare, p. 323

After assigning the goals and delegating the task to the efficient employees, you are required to note the same in your calendar or in a set file for each employee or even in a notebook to ensure that you have informed the progress of employees. It is quite natural that when you find yourself a new person to manage the healthcare organisations, you find yourself in a true sense "delegatee and more often than the delegator or mentor." Since you need to learn something new each and everyday, the delegation would benefit you in many ways. It is quite natural that when you are new, an opportunity to learn something in the process of delegation would enrich your potentials.

Compensation and Motivation

It is not only sufficient that you select the right personnel; it is even not to help you substantially that you have made available to them quality educational aid and world class training facilities; it is important of all that you motivate them suitably so that they evince keen interest in delivering goods to an organisation where they work. The behavioural scientists as well as the personnel experts make a strong advocacy in favour of motivation. It is against this background that this constituent of the management of human resources occupies a place of outstanding significance.

You have been successful in getting the right and potentially sound people because the selection process followed by you were right. You have also been successful in developing their professional excellence since you have made available to them world class education and training facilities in addition to the enrichment of their behavioural profile. But unless you offer to them handsome incentives, your efforts for managing the human resources would not be fruitful. This makes it essential that being a hospital manager, you make sincere efforts to motivate them in a right fashion so that whatever they have gained in a learning process subserve the interests of patients and attendants. We find a number of devices to motivate people to help discharge the functional responsibilities as per the defined norms. You offer to them handsome wages and salaries; you offer to them a number of welfare facilities; you make available to them quality environment at the work and living places and you provide to them an opportunity to work in a friendly environment. If you blend all of them optimally, the people are motivated; not only motivated but albeit hypnotised. It is due mainly to the fact that the behavioural scientists as well as the industrial psychologists have been found making a strong advocacy in favour of a sound motivational plan for the human resources.

We can't negate the fact that hospitals and the healthcare organisations are required to work in a difficult condition. They are supposed to invest huge money for expensive inputs; they are also required to offer a sound scheme of motivation but they don't have a legitimate right of making profits. They are supposed to bear huge social costs. The state exchequer is not liberal to pay the grants. The corporate sector is found disinterested in promoting the health sector, specially as a corporate citizen. The avenues for mobilising the internal financial resources are regulated and the organisations and individuals are not found so much interested in offering to the hospitals and healthcare organisations charity and donations. However, the masses have high level of expectations from hospitals. Of course, it is a challenging task for a hospital manager more so, an acid test of his professional excellence to manage everything in a positive fashion.

We go through the problem of compensation and motivation and therefore, the following issues are to be discussed:

- Strategic decisions regarding the linking of financial incentives to the contributions of employees.
- Offering handsome wages and salaries to the efficients.
- Making available incentives for the involvement of family members.
- Enriching the environment at the workplace.
- Making the departmental relationship friendly.
- Establishing organisational culture.

Policy Decisions Regarding Incentives

At the outset, the boardrooms or the policy makers need to formulate a policy regarding the incentive plan. To be more specific, the financial incentives draw our attention on a priority basis. Of late, we find our wage and salary plans based on the number of days on monthly, weekly or even daily basis. In a majority of the hospitals, we find such type of provision. We also find hospitals or healthcare organisations where the financial incentives are based on contractual obligations. Thus, we find schemes promoting uniformity in the payment of financial incentives. It is against this background that we go through the policy imperatives necessitating a basic change. It is quite natural that the levels of efficiency of all the employees can't be uniform because we find some of them potentially very sound, some of them potentially sound and some of them potentially poor. The industrial psychologists feel that efficients should be rewarded suitably so that even inefficients attempt to evince keen interests in becoming efficients. The behavioural scientists opine that if we don't offer special incentives to the super performers, in the long run they would also be transformed to be potentially poor. These observations necessitate that the boardrooms or the policy makers deliberate upon the problem on a priority basis and make the ways for linking of the organisational incentive plans to the performance or contributions of employees. If in the government hospitals, we find performance degeneration, this is also due to the fact that they don't reward suitably to the high performers. Conversely, we find private leading hospitals offering more incentives to the super performers. Thus, the degenerating level of efficiency in the government hospitals makes it essential that the policy decision makers provide to the hospital managers a free hand in offering a package of benefits to the high or top performers.

The trade unions or staff associations need an attitudinal change. Of course, they have a legitimate right of protecting the interests of workers or employees but they also bear the responsibility of making it sure that the efficients are motivated suitably. If they start accepting the responsibility of generating the level of efficiency,[10] the copious avenues would be paved for establishing the organisational culture in which the level of work culture would be found to an acceptable level. It is really amazing that to be more specific in the Indian perspective we find unions and associations confining their attention only on the interests of employees and workers albeit at the cost of the existence of an organisation which in the long run aggravates the problem of financial crunch. It is in this context that we need to solicit the cooperation of trade unions and staff associations to contribute substantially to the process of efficiency-generation.[11] We need to close the ways for a vicious circle that make an organisation financially bankrupt.

In view of the above, it is right to mention that hospitals and healthcare organisations think over the policy imperatives, specially in the face of the decreasing level of efficiency and decelerating rate of overall productivity in a majority of the government hospitals. This would open new vistas for the development of hospitals because an increase in the performance level of employees would increase the productivity of almost all the inputs used in the process of generating and offering the world class healthcare services. It is high time that the policy decision makers think over the problem in the best interest of masses.

Compensation

We find compensation a comprehensive term which includes wages, salaries, allowances and benefits. Basically, we don't find difference in wages and salaries because wages are the remuneration paid to the skilled, semi-skilled and unskilled operative workforce whereas salary is the remuneration of those employees who provide mental labour to the employer, such as jobber, supervisor, office staff and all levels of executives. Generally, we find payment of salary on monthly basis whereas the wages are paid on daily or hourly basis. The process of compensation is a complex network of such process directed towards remunerating people for the services rendered and motivating them to attain a desired level of efficiency. Thus, we find compensation covering a number of incentives, such as wage and salary payments, the awarding of cost generating items, viz., allowance, leave facilities, housing, leave travel concession and essential non-cost generating offerings such as recognition, privileges and symbol of benefits. The primary compensation includes wages and salaries, the incentive compensation includes premium and bonus and the supplementary compensation includes DA, CCA, HRA, LTC, HTC or so. It is the prime responsibility of a hospital manager to synchronise all the three constituents of compensation, primary, incentive and supplementary in such a way that the employees are found motivated.

Motivation

We find motivation influencing the workers and employees considerably. Of course, the financial incentives play a commanding role in motivating the personnel in almost all the organisations but it is also right to mention that in addition to the financial incentives, a number of motivational schemes influence the employees and workers. We also talk about non-financial incentives, such as individual, group and institutional. In the individual non-financial incentives, we find status, promotion, responsibility, pleasant and interesting job, recognition of work and job security. In the group incentives, we find social importance, team spirit, competition and informal group. In the institutional category, we find human relations in industry, communication, workers' participation in management, morale building and discipline. Thus, motivation includes in its purview both financial as well as the different types of non-financial incentives.

We find motivation a managerial process to influence the instinct of employees in which the stimulation process is found very much active. The industrial psychologists feel that offering of financial incentives is not the only thing that a hospital manager is required to do for motivating the employees. In addition to the financial incentives, they also expect decent behaviour of superiors, quality environment at the work place, quality environment at the living places, recognition of their contributions to the smooth functioning of an organisation and so on. Thus, motivation has a big area. It is pertinent that a manager studies the changing expectations of employees as well as the fluctuating and shrinking potentials of an organisation and takes a decision relating to an optimal point where both the parties remain satisfied and the organisation prospers.

In view of the above, it is essential that the various components of motivation are managed in an effective way so that employees are found motivated.

Wage and Salary Administration-Wage Administration

The most important problem before a hospital manager is to manage salary and wages in an effective way so that the personnel are found motivated. The determination of wage rates, administration of wage policies and satisfying the employees to the wage rates are the important constituents of wage administration. In a true sense, the wage and salary administration is one of the major responsibilities of a hospital manager bearing the responsibility of managing the human resources. It is, of course, a line responsibility but existing complications have made it essential that we go through the problem of wage and salary administration with a new vision.

The question of wage determination is found important with the view points of socioeconomic transformation. It is a difficult task to take a decision that satisfies the trade unions. The increasing costs on hospital materials and other infrastructural facilities have been making the task of wage administration much more difficult to a hospital manager. This makes it essential that a hospital manager in consultation with the unions resolves the problem of offering a wage structure that is acceptable to both the parties. It is clear that wages focus our attention on the amount paid to labour for his/her services to the organisation. It is considered to be a source of creating utility.

We talk about a fair wage structure with the motto of improving the departmental relationships and making the workplace environment cohesive. Fair wages is that wages which the labour gets for his/her work which is very close to the minimum and living wages. Of course, we find the fair wages marginally higher to the living and minimum wages. In almost all the organisations, we find employment of a number of workers for diverse purposes. It is not a financially sound decision that for all purposes we prefer to employ regular employees. This draws our attention on the employment of workers. A number of workers, specially to use the tools and equipment, clean the surroundings and premises, plantation and gardening, throwing the garbage or the general medical waste are needed in the hospitals or healthcare organisations. A hospital manager is required to understand the requirements of different departments and to make available to them efficient workers.

Since we find the problem of making possible operational economy for increasing the rate of productivity, it is pertinent that a manager manages things in the face of the changing requirements of a particular department at a particular place. To be more specific, in the government hospitals where the problem of financial crunch is found at its peak, it is the prime responsibility of a hospital manager to prioritise the organisational requirements so that the process is made cost-effective. It is against this background that the problem of wage administration is discussed because in a majority of the cases the Trade Unions feel that workers are not getting fair wages and based on such realisation, we find enough scope for unfriendly and bitter relations and so on. To deal with the situation helpfully in satisfying both the parties is a challenging task which a hospital manager is supposed to perform tactfully, intelligently and professionally.

Salary Administration

In addition to the wage administration, we also find salary administration an important task for a hospital manager. We are well aware of the fact that basically, there is no difference between wage and salary. Payments made to manual labour are generally called as wages whereas payment made periodically, generally monthly, to those employees whose output can't be easily measured in units, such as clerical staff, supervisory staff or managerial personnel and paramedical staff is referred to as salaries. It is the responsibility of a hospital manager to make it sure that different categories of employees have been getting salaries as per the service conditions or in tune with their potentials.

Like administration of wages, we also find administration of salaries and in this context, it is pertinent that a manager is well aware of the emerging trends in inflation and the strategic decisions taken by other hospitals related to the payment of salaries and transmit the proposal for revision to the boardrooms. We find it judicious that the salary plan is linked to the pressure of inflation so that employees serving hospitals get it convenient to manage their family budgets. An important/decision making area in the very context is a time-to-time revision of the scale as and when the emerging trends in the economy necessitate the same. It is judicious that different categories of employees get different scales of pay as per their positions, credentials and experiences. The government as well as the private hospitals have been found adopting different scales. The main thing that we find in the salary administration is to make it attractive so that the world class professionals and other personnel prefer to join the hospitals or healthcare organisations. We agree with this view that the paramedical staff and nurses have till now been found neglected and therefore, efforts are to be made to make available to them hand, some salaries because they contribute considerably to the process of generation of quality services.

The salary administration thus, makes it essential that a hospital manager is fully aware of the financial limitations and keeping in view the fact the boardrooms think for a change in the pay-scale. Of course, we need to protect the interests of employees but at the same time, it is also pertinent that employees realise the difficulties of hospitals or healthcare organisations in a right perspective. Unless we find a sense of realisation prevailing on both sides of an organisation, the positive results can't be expected. To be more specific in the private hospitals, we find several complaints that they are not paid suitably. Both types of hospitals—government as well as private—need to assign due weightages to the salary plan of hospital personnel because they are a bit different from others.

The medical and paramedical staff, nursing staff and managerial staff serving hospitals or healthcare organisations need to be paid suitable incentives. It is the responsibility of a hospital manager that he/she makes it sure that the employees working with him/her are paid suitably. Not only salary but other financial incentives such as allowances of different types, bonus, special allowances are paid to them on time. The blending of different types of financial incentives in a right fashion is found significant to increase the level of efficiency of employees. It is judicious that we don't equate hospital personnel with other employees because the hospital personnel make a significant contribution to the process of social transformation even in a difficult condition.

Non-financial Incentives

Of course, we find financial incentives playing a significant role in motivating the hospital personnel but we can't devalue the instrumentality of non-financial incentives in transforming them into top performers. It is against this background that a hospital manager needs to blend the financial and non-financial incentives optimally. There are three categories in the non-financial incentives as presented in Fig. 9. 11.

Individual Incentives: In the individual incentives, we find focus on measures like:

1. *Status*: It is the ranking of positions, right and duties in the formal organisational future. We can't deny the impact of good status and high position on motivating the personnel.

2. *Promotion*: It is movement to a position in which responsibilities and prestige are found increased. It satisfies human beings serving an organisation in different ways, such as money, prestige and status. The avenues of promotion thus motivate the personnel.

3. *Responsibility and Challenge*: A number of people like a job of challenging nature. A manager needs to provide opportunities to the employees so that they prove their excellence by testifying their contributions.

4. *Pleasant and Interesting Job:* The pleasant and enjoyable job attract people because such type of job satisfies their natural instincts and generates interests in the work.

5. *Recognition of Work*: We also find a few of the employees acting and proving their excellence as top performers. If they get recognition, the motivation is found natural. A manager is supposed to recognise and appreciate the outstanding contributions of an individual.

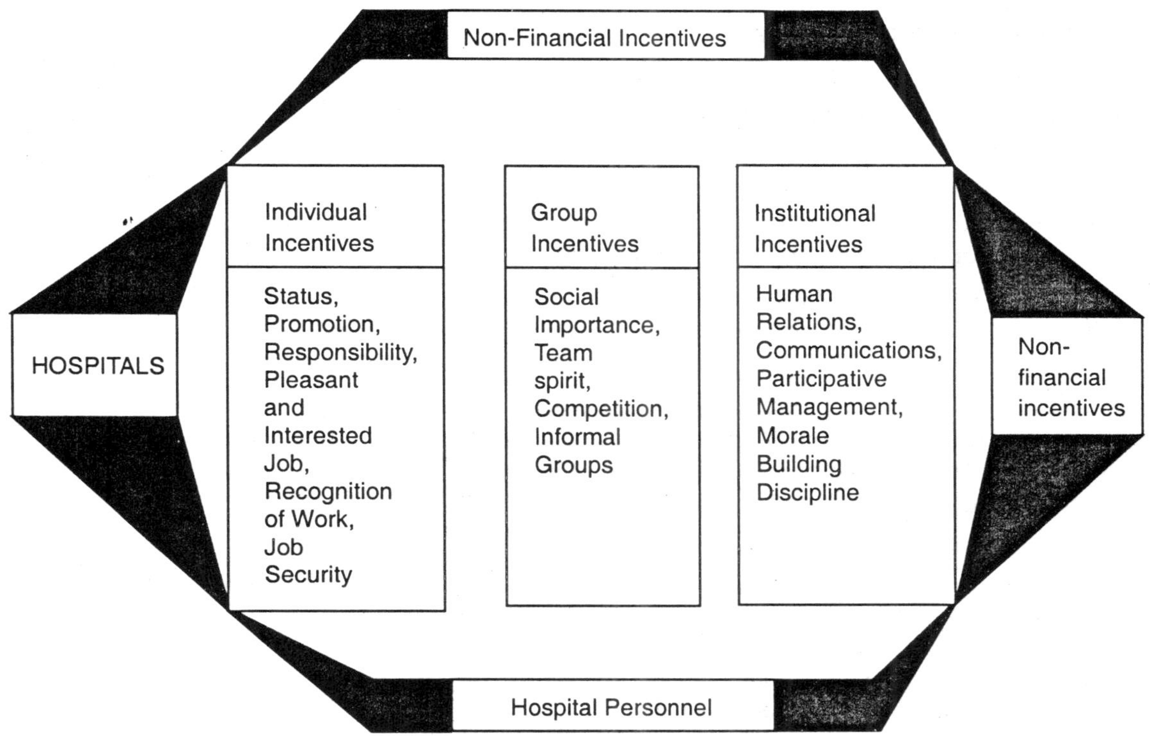

Fig. 9.11. Non-Financial Incentives

6. *Job Security:* We can't negate the instrumentality of job security in motivating the personnel because this motivates employees to demonstrate their worth and thus even the hidden potentials come out.

Group Incentives

1. *Social Importance of Work:* Employees, to be more specific in the hospitals and healthcare organisations work in a group and the recognition of the contributions of a group motivates employees of that group.

2. *Team Spirit:* To be more specific in the hospitals and healthcare organisations, a manager bears the responsibility of promoting and encouraging a team since we find the healthcare services considerably influenced by dedicated contributions and coordinated efforts of a team.

3. *Competition: A* sense of competition if generated in a right fashion among the employees serving an organisation proves to be motivational and subserves the interests of users as well as an organisation.

4. *Informal Groups:* Organisation of competition between different groups and individuals generate a sense of competition and motivate employees to establish an edge over their competitors. A manager is required to form informal groups so long as we don't find the process detrimental to the organisational efficiency and objectives.

Institutional Incentives

1. *Human Relations in Industry:* It is related to the development of a sense of belongingness in the employees to improve their efficiency. We find emphasis on physiological as well as psychological satisfaction by improving the quality of environment at the workplace.

2. *Participative Management:* If the employees get an opportunity to participate in the policy decision making processes, they are found motivated. In the Japanese management, we find the same process for improving the work culture.

3. *Morale Building:* We find morale as the attitudes of individual and groups towards work environment and towards voluntary cooperation to the full extent in the best interest of an organisation. High level of morale is found instrumental in accelerating the rate of productivity.

4. *Discipline:* We find discipline as obedience, application, energy behaviour and outward makes of respect shown by employees. It is a process of self control. It is the prime responsibility of a manager to maintain discipline by applying standards in a consistent, fair and flexible manner. This helps employees in enriching their behavioural profile.

The aforesaid non-financial incentives are found instrumental in motivating the personnel. Like other employees, even the employees serving hospitals and healthcare organisations also need to be motivated so that they evince their personal interests in generating efficiency. Of course, a hospital manager is required to assign due weightage to the non-financial incentives because in an age of materialism, it is difficult for us to think anything without financial incentives. The non-financial incentives help employees in getting suitable rewards, recognition, respect, friendly departmental-relationships, improved organisational climate and so on. In the hospitals or healthcare organisations where we find employees or the hospital personnel serving the patients, it is the prime responsibility of a hospital manager to make it sure that sincere efforts have been taken to improve the quality of non-financial incentives. Incentives to an individual or a group bear the efficacy of increasing the level of efficiency found essential for accelerating the rate of productivity.

Involving the Family Members

For getting personally-committed employees, it is essential that we motivate not only the employees but also their family members by offering to them different types of incentives directly or indirectly. The incentives made available to the children of employees for education and entertainment in a very natural way influence them and motivate them to think and act for the development of hospitals in which the employees are working. Like this, provision of a big playing ground, a think park, organisation of sports, painting competition or so influence the children of the employees. Besides, the availability of adequate infrastructural facilities at the living places, healthcare centre, women's club, etc. motivate the female members of the family. It is important to mention here that whatever the amenities and facilities the employers make available at the living places influence the members of the family. It is in this context that we find Japanese organisations assigning due weightage also to the quality of environment at the living places because if the interests of family members are found linked to the development of an organisation, the members in general develop a positive attitude towards the development of that organisation in which the head of a family is found working.

The hospitals and healthcare organisations need personally-committed employees so that they evince personal interests in offering the medicare or healthcare services. We talk about personal-touch-in-service which is found essential for good patient care. Unless the medical or paramedical staff or the nursing staff show personal-touch-in-service, the performance level would not be found satisfactory. Since we find users of the services or patients in a different condition, it becomes essential that the hospital personnel take personal care of the users so that they feel that they are getting special care and develop a positive attitude. This makes it essential that a hospital manager explores avenues for involving the personnel personally and it is in this context that we talk about special incentives to the family members of the hospital personnel.

In addition to the quality of environment at the living places, it is also impact generating that a hospital manager improves the quality of environment at the workplace so that the concerned employees don't develop monotony and fatigue and show personal interests in discharging their responsibilities. This draws our attention on the infrastructural facilities at the workplace. The power, water, sanitation, communications and other amenities, entertainment facilities where they relax are found essential to keep the employees fresh and active. Thus, a hospital manager is required to make it sure that quality of environment at the workplace generates comforts and conveniences to the employees working there.

In addition to the aforesaid aspects, it is also essential that we find friendly or conducive environment at the workplace. This draws our attention on the interdepartmental and intra-departmental relationships. If superiors start misbehaving with the subordinates and if subordinates start disobeying the superiors the environment at the workplace would not remain cohesive or conducive. Thus, for personal commitments, it is also significant that a hospital manager makes best of his/her efforts to improve the quality of environment at the work and living places so that not only the employees but even their family members develop a positive attitude towards the development of hospitals.

Performance Audit

You have gone through the problem of selection of hospital personnel; you have also made efforts to develop the potentials of hospital personnel by making available to them world class educational aid and the training facilities and more so, you are also offering to them suitable incentives. Now, it is essential that you get it confirmed that all your positive efforts based on world class professional excellence are contributing substantially to the process of increasing the level of efficiency. You have a target, you have a goal and in addition, you also have a mission. It is your professional responsibility to make it sure that goals, objectives and mission are fulfilled. It is against this background that we talk about performance audit or making an appraisal of the performance of different categories of employees serving the hospitals. It is quite natural that we commit mistakes and therefore, we don't find it surprising. It is really amazing that we commit mistakes but fail in realising and confessing the same. By doing such, we commit a blunder and damage the interests of not only the organisation where we work but also harm our own interests because our existence and prosperity are considerably influenced by the potentials of an organisation. Performance audit is a device to make an appraisal of the performance or the level of efficiency of different categories of employees serving an organisation. It is the last constituent of the management of human resources that makes the ways for the beginning of the first stage since we identify errors and find out the corrective measures which engineer a sound foundation for the human resources planning.

Like other organisations, the hospitals and healthcare organisations also need to audit the performance of their employees so that their grievances are taken care and at the same time, their positive or negative contributions are documented to practice the motivational or demotivational measures. There are a number of indicators helping a manager in making an appraisal of the performance of employees. A hospital manager is required to make use of all the indicators and to study the problem in depth because a mistake committed in the process may confuse him. In all the cases, we don't find a fall in the level of efficiency of employees only due to their negligence or mistakes. We also find cases where employees are found working satisfactorily but due to other shortcomings and weaknesses, the results are not so satisfactory. Particularly in the hospitals and healthcare services, we find a team work where a number of persons, equipment, apparatus, medicines and nursing care play an important role. This makes it essential that while making an appraisal of the performance of employees, we go through all the parameters and make a microscopic analysis of their contributions. Of late, we find computers used in almost all the hospitals and a hospital manager would find it convenient to audit the performance of employees and technologies so that the lapses, shortcomings, errors, sore spots are detected at an initial stage. We are well aware of the fact that the healthcare sector is full of risks and uncertainties wherein, addition to the contributions of personnel and technologies, we find almighty God playing a commanding role. The medical and paramedical staff are performing satisfactorily, the world class equipments, apparatus, medicines have been used in the process. However, the results may or may not be positive. This makes it essential that a hospital manager adopts more care and precaution while detecting the errors. With sensitive indicators or tools, a hospital manager may be successful in making a right appraisal.

Documentation

We find documentation the linchpin to successful performance evaluation. It is a process of taking notes and recording performance and performance levels. Managers and executives at almost all the levels of a hospital or a healthcare organisation rely on documentation based on a logbook.

Performance Documentation Logbook: We find logbook a simple spiral-bound notebook in which records, dates and events are noted. The logbook is not required to be used for finger printing but rather as a guide to chronicle individual and staff performance. The following are some of the examples of poor documentation.

Examples:

1. "Has a bad attitude."
2. "Didn't listen to what I said."
3. "Dresses like a clown."
4. "A racist snob."
5. "Never documents well on charts."
6. "Showed up late a couple of times."
7. "Even though I told him how to do it he didn't do it."
8. "Has a bad memory, poor attention span and lacks confidence."
9. "Disappears for long breaks."

Example 1: In this example, we don't find description of attitude. Its effect is not set forth. While going through or discussing attitude, consider adaptability, aggressiveness, perseverance and work ethic in addition to the effect. Besides, be sure that all the entries have been updated.

Example 2: It refers to an incomplete assigned task by an employee who did not follow a work direction. It is necessary for a manager to be more specific in terms of subject, time and process of directing.

Example 3: It relates to appearance. A manager should have researched the code policy of hospitals regarding dresses and should mention that how and in what conditions, the employee failed to comply.

Example 4: Here, a manager comes to a subjective conclusion that the employee in question didn't enjoy working with a particular ethnic group. The documentation must be clear-cut and should mention the effect on performance.

Example 5: Here, two words are used—first word "never" is non-specific and arguable whereas the second word "chart" is without a quantifying adjective. Essential information that the employee was required to use—their importance and the number of times the employee failed to document well on the specified charts are found essential information which should have been included while making entry.

Example 6: Here, two important time elements are unspecified, the first is the number of items and the second is related to duration. The lateness parameters must be specified and the next entry should indicate that the employee was counselled relative to the specific negative behaviour.

Example 7: It fails to provide direction and all of the characteristics like memory, confidence and attention span are the subjective, personal characteristics and we find little relevance to job conduct.

Example 8: This is the final example and the use of the word "disappear' is problematic.

The aforesaid entries make it clear that none of them were positive in nature or provided any positive direction and against this background, we find the entries in the logbook of no use.

Rules of Documentation

A hospital manager is required to follow the documentation rules as mentioned below :

- Don't forget to enter date.
- Use time, money, percentage and numbers or say the quantitative data as much as possible.
- Your language should be clear and simple.
- You are also required to use examples, episodes, cases, explanations or so to present a clear picture of the performance.
- You also need to use sound references.
- Don't forget to focus on both quality as well as quantity.
- Do not store information to use only at performance evaluation time but prefer to make feedback an ongoing process. You need to counsel employees.
- You are also required to document counselling sessions specially for your reference.

- Subjective based language should not be used.
- As and when the circumstances necessitate must enforce the disciplinary measures.
- Don't forget to document good examples of behaviour, sympathy, empathy, critical contributions of an individual or a group.

The aforesaid precautions would help you in having a sound documentation found essential for making an appraisal of the performance of employees. We have gone through the documentation of no use and you are not supposed to document in that way. Since observations are followed by documentation, it is essential that you document then and there.

An Ideal Appraisal Plan

You need to formulate a sound appraisal plan and in this context, you are required to go through the following factors:

- Your appraisal plan must secure full agreement of line management on the need and purposes.
- You should avoid to formulate a complicated plan.
- Appraisal plan must enlist the cooperation of supervisor not only in the drawing up the appraisal form but also regarding weightage to be assigned to each factor.
- Your appraisal plan must be explained indepth and more so in advance particularly in the interest of those who are likely to be affected.
- The supervisor requires training for that very purpose.
- Full line and staff cooperation and mutual checking of employee performance are found essential.
- Provisions are to be made for reviewing the observations.

An appraisal plan if found ideal or sound would simplify your task of performance audit that would be a base for further improvements.

Performance Indicators

Making an appraisal of the performance of employees is a difficult task. A hospital manager is required to audit the performance very minutely, specially with the help of authentic indicators so that possibilities of errors in getting the results are considerably minimised. Since the results are to influence your motivational and demotivational measures, it is pertinent that you don't take any decision in haste and make use of the performance indicators in a right fashion. The following sources are found credible:

1. *Your Own First Hand Knowledge:* We can't negate the fact that your own first hand information or knowledge helps the process substantially. Personal observation, conversation and written reports submitted by the employees would help you in getting the first hand knowledge. Since it is not subject to argument, we find this source very much effective. In this context, it is essential that whatever your hear from others are to be ascertained. This makes it essential that you use your logbook in a right way mentioning in detail everything.

2. *Compliance of Job Description:* While making an appraisal of the performance of your employees, the first task before you is to study the job description. This is an important source to

be reflective of the major duties of the job position. A "top 10" list is to be prepared for knowing what he/she does on a regular basis. All specific duties are to be covered on the job description and the same is to be used throughout the period of grading. The responsibilities are to be enumerated and specified for employees' job conduct. You and your employees need to maintain a copy of the job description that would be used as a reference in all discussions with the employees. The specific duties should be mentioned on the job description and the entire range of responsibilities are to be enumerated and specified for employee's job conduct.

3. *Attainment of Goal:* We are well aware of the concept of Management by Objectives (MBO) which refers to the goals agreed upon by the employees and a manager. The goals are to be made clear to the employees at the initial stage. If we find a system that does not formally identify the specific goals for completion, the hospital manager and the employees are required to design a list of goals above and beyond the job description. It provides to a manager an idea of what is to be expected from the employees. The actual performance of employees would be compared with the set goals. It makes the task of making an appraisal easier.

4. *Category of Working Numbers:* In the healthcare organisations and hospitals, we find any job significant to indicate the numbers reflecting the performance. The performance can be measured by percentages, time, money and members. As for example, a laboratory technician is required to complete X number of assays in a given time slot at a particular percentage of efficiency. As a manager, you are required to set objectives, document performance and educate the employees toward fully achieving the set parameters of performance.

5. *Peers as Input:* We find peer input an observation resource that yields data from managers in other departments of the hospitals. Besides, your fellow manager must be subjective in his/her evaluation of the individual's performance. This makes it essential that inputs must be viewed as a secondhand source.

6. *Organisational Input:* The secondhand source of performance appraisal is known as organisational input which refers to any communication you might receive from the organisation relative to the employees' performance. In this context, you are required to make entry in the logbook regarding the receipt of a letter citing the employee for a particular achievement and subsequently would incorporate into the performance evaluation. In addition, you may also receive letter of recognition from patients who were the employee's patient and felt the performance either positively or negatively outstanding. Besides, phone calls and other forms of communication would also let you know regarding the performance of the employees.

7. *Monthly Report: You* also use monthly report as a base for performance evaluation as a number of hospitals or healthcare organisations have been found suggesting their employees for presenting a written or oral report at monthly meetings. A good rule of thumb for you is to sit down with each employee on a monthly basis for at leasy 10 to 15 minutes to discuss the performance of the current month and to make it sure that in the next month, there would be additional progress in the performance.

8. *Critical Contributions:* We find some of the employees making some outstanding contributions even in an adverse condition. The critical contributions focus our attention on the outstanding contributions of employees. You are required to note, examine and review the performance of employees. The activities related to the outstanding or critical contributions may be above and below the call of the duty.

9. *Unit Performance:* We also find unit performance as a base for evaluating the performance of the employees. It refers to the contributions of an individual to overall departmental objectives. This also includes overall departmental relationships, the degree of technical expertise they provide to others and relations with peers in the department.

10. *Work Approach:* It is your duty to note anything that reflects the attitude of employees, people skills, managerial aptitude and team orientation. This focuses your attention on what the employee does and how he/she does it. Any performance examples are to be documented.

In view of the above, it is right to mention that you are required to use the aforesaid sources for making an appraisal of the performance of employees. You should try to get a comprehensive picture of the performance of employees to construct a programme review. The aforesaid facts also make it clear that performance appraisal is not only an equitable tool but a constructive and progressive one. You are supposed to trust your own instincts because you observe everything. You set the target and you get the actual results. It is essential that you use your appraisal measures on time so that the corrective measures are incorporated.

Since it is an ongoing process, you need to make it sure that the critical cases of negative nature are not repeated. At the same time, you also need to motivate the employees particularly for the critical contributions of positive nature. Result of performance evaluation provides you feedback regarding the top performers and even about the poor performers. If you delay the process of rewarding suitably the top performers, just tomorrow you find that even they are not sincere to their positive contributions. By doing such, you close doors for performance generation.

Critical Factors in Performance Audit

Your responsibility as an evaluator influences a number of factors and this makes it essential that while making an appraisal of the performance of hospital personnel, you show your professional excellence. We don't find anything wrong for the delay in the process of getting the results but we find the process of getting the wrong information and making the wrong decisions very much instrumental in tarnishing your image as a manager vis-a-vis the image of your hospitals in which you work. This makes it essential that you assign due weightage to the factors mentioned below.

1. *Appraisal process needs to be comprehensive:* Before coming to a conclusion, it is pertinent that you go through the entire breadth of the performance. This focuses our attention not only on the level of efficiency but in addition also the manner in which the employees perform the job role. An evaluation of organisational values and personality traits becomes significant in the process. If you fail to be comprehensive, of course you consider one factor but neglect another. In a true sense, you need to gravitate your attention on all the essential job elements.

2. *Eliciting stellar performance and encouraging professional growth::* While making an appraisal, it is significant that you take a full view of the job position that would provide you a comprehensive insight into the potentials of qualitative improvements within the scope of the job position. The critical incidents related to the job, job related training, development activities and other motivational data would be the sensitive bases for making an appraisal.

3. *Make it an ongoing process:* Performance audit is an everlasting process. From the first date of the commencement of work by an individual till his/her continual, you need to audit his/her

performance. The performance evaluation-cycle needs to provide a feedback on an ongoing basis and you are supposed to discuss and deliberate upon the problems as and when the circumstances necessitate so. We need continuity in the evaluation process because we find cases of performance degeneration cropping up even among the high performers. You need not make yourself sure that high performers of today would hold the same position for all the time. If you make it an ongoing process, the scope for degeneration would considerably be minimised.

4. *The evaluation process should be individualised:* You need to individualise the evaluation process. This necessitates due weightage to the individual traits or attributes. Nothing justifies the validity of making two identical evaluations on two different individuals in the same job position. This makes it essential that you eliminate the possibilities of identical evaluation. You are required to evaluate the attributes of employees individually and to look at his/her role within the job. Your actions promoting identical evaluation would project a negative attitude in the minds of employees that evaluation is nothing but just the completion of paper work, or discharging of the functional responsibilities and completion of the formalities.

5. *Make the evaluation process a motivational tool:* You make an evaluation of the performance of employees to know about their positive or negative contributions. If the employees contributing substantially are not motivated, the process of efficiency generation would hardly be cycled. This makes it significant that being a manager, you make it sure that the evaluation process is linked to their motivational plan and if the evaluation results are positive, they are to be motivated suitably.

6. *Prioritising performance evaluation and job description:* For promoting right evaluation, you need to prioritise performance evaluation and job description. The importance of functional responsibilities would be an important base in the very context. You are required to list job requirements in a "1-10" or "top-ten" fashion with 1 as the most important and 10 as the least important. Whatever technique you use for assigning weightage, a sense of priority is found essential.

7. *Performance evaluation needs to be situational in scope:* While making an appraisal, it is also pertinent that you take into consideration the situation in which an individual operates and performs. Of course, this is an acid test of your professional excellence which would provide to you the right results. In the work situation, if there are a number of constraints and difficulties and an individual is found performing excellently even in the unfavourable conditions, it is quite natural that he/she deserves to be a high performer. Thus, you are required to centralise your attention on the quality of environment at the workplace and the impact of the same on the job performance. This makes a strong advocacy in favour of analysis of a particular situation in which we find an individual working satisfactorily or inefficiently.

8. *Employee expectations of the job:* It is quite natural that expectations of all the employees from an organisation can't be identical in nature. We find a few expecting more and at the same time, we also find others expecting nothing. An ideal performance appraisal needs to provide employees an insight on what the organisation expects from them. Your perception regarding stellar performance should be made clear to the employees.

9. *No confusion in understanding the evaluation form:* It is your prime responsibility to make it sure that employees perceive the form supplied to them in a right perspective. The form obscured by "psychobabble" can't serve your purpose. Incomprehensible or misleading language should not be used in the form made available for evaluation. You are required to remember that a form

found vague promotes distrust and further eliminates opportunity to use the process as an educational tool.

10. *Performance evaluation should provide short-term direction:* It is also important that the performance evaluation provides a short-term direction. You are required to establish a strong set of objectives for the coming rating period. You are required to be proactive in establishing the job objectives for the next years. This helps the employees in having a clear picture of the expectations of the following year.

11. *Performance evaluation needs to he a tool for long-term evaluation:* In this context, it is also pertinent that the appraisal form that you supply or make available includes a section for a development plan. It is right that you ask employees to cite areas in which he/she can improve. We find a number of hospitals and the healthcare organisations providing lip service because it is not substantiated by a strong development plan which is considered to be a part and parcel of the performance appraisal form.

12. *Performance evaluation is required to be viable in scope:* While making an appraisal of the performance, it is also important that you make it a communication exercise in which all the parties participate and the listed goals are realistic and practical. By doing so, you communicate to the employees that goals are realistic, attainable and challenging.

13. *Financial consideration needs due weightage:* Being a manager, you need to assign due weightage to the financial limitations. Since you bear the responsibility of making the process cost-effective, it is essential that you establish a clear-cut difference between the potentials of different employees. If the rankings are like "above expectations", "meets expectations" and "below expectations", the financial consideration would play an important role. Of course, the employees bear the responsibility of performing satisfactorily but at the same time, they are also required to maintain economy.

14. *Performance evaluation should be legal in content:* It is your prime responsibility to make it sure that the contents of performance have legal validity. You are not supposed to show bias or prejudice. While making an audit, you are required to be fair, assigning due weightage to the performance of an individual and not thinking in terms of gender, race, ethnicity, regional or other considerations. Bonafide Occupational Qualifications (BFOQ) is found to be an important criterion. Before circulation, you need to discuss the same with the human resources department if you have some doubt regarding the legal validity of the form.

15. *Performance evaluation needs to be measurable:* In addition to the aforesaid facts, it is also important that the valuation process should use clear quantitative measures easily understandable to the employees. In using quantitative measures, you need to discuss with the employees how the measurement would be realistic and also try to collect their opinion regarding the realistic evaluation. This would increase the educational value of evaluation.

The aforesaid facts make it clear that making an appraisal of the performance of employees is a difficult as well as a challenging task which a hospital manager is required to perform efficiently. Since we talk about quality in totality, it is pertinent that you have world class hospital personnel. It is quite natural that before making an evaluation, you have perceived the right concept of quality people, specially in the changing conditions. The essence of performance evaluation is to know about the quality of employees serving the hospitals so that based on the findings or results, you activate the process of education and training in the changed perspective.

You also make an audit of the performance of employees to motivate the high performers and demotivate the poor performers. Your motivation plans or schemes need a close link with the results of performance evaluation. It is judicious that high performers are rewarded suitably whereas the poor performers are either given an opportunity to improve or to make a good-bye. Being a manager, it is your prime responsibility to make it sure that efficients are given an opportunity to be the top performers. It is against this background that we find performance audit considered to be an important dimension of the management of human resources.

To be more specific, and when we talk about hospitals or the healthcare organisations, it is significant that in addition to other aspects, we also think about humanity, human values, morality as important parameters because the hospital personnel need to conceptualise humanity and morality as important traits to be an important criterion for gauging the performance. Of course, you are supposed to assign due weightage to professional excellence of employees but it is not meant that these traits playing an incremental role in improving the overall productivity of hospitals and healthcare organisations are not given due importance. Modern principles of human resources management make it essential that employees serving an organisation are decent, fair, ethical and contribute substantially to the process of value-engineering.

Health Manpower Information System

In an age of information superhighway, we find significance of an independent information system for the development of hospital personnel. Of course, we find materials or inputs used in the process very much instrumental in activating the process of qualitative transformation but we can't deny the outstanding contributions of human resources because even in the robot culture, we need to solicit the cooperation of manpower. Of late, we have technologies for almost all the purposes. If we talk about developing an independent information system for human resources serving the hospitals, our prime focus is on a computer-driven manpower information system. It is against this background that we go through the problem of Health Manpower Information System.

The Health Manpower Planning, Production and Management Committee in 1987 recommended that the Education Commission for Health Sciences (ECHS) must be established as a central organisation on the lines of University Grants Commission for professional and paraprofessional education in health sciences inter *alla* to provide realistic projection for national manpower requirement and suitable mechanism to continuously review the projections based on felt needs. The Committee was of the view that for an effective support to the health manpower management, the information system is vital for managerial efficiency. The health manpower information should encompass all the components of the health manpower management. The Committee recommended development of National Health Manpower Information System as an important support to the health manpower development strategies. While recommending the establishment of Universities of Health Sciences, it was further emphasised that it is entirely likely that several new faculties will grow in the University of Health Sciences. It is expected that a faculty of health information system shall also be established in the Health Science Universities. In spite of these far reaching recommendations, the necessary action plans are yet to be concretised. Information Technology (IT) is now becoming one of the major components of the technological infrastructure for health management. All subsector dealings with the generation, transmission and utilisation of demographic and epidemilogical data such as Bioinformatics,

Biostatistics, Health Management Information System (HMIS) and Decision Supporting System (DSS) are now getting priority attention in health planning and management. With the nation-wide network, NICNET, under the Planning Commission giving health information support through its MEDLA1RS, Bio-Medical Informatics Programme and Tele-Medicine Programme, a viable nucleus has already been set up. 12 Policy initiatives are required to be taken by the policy makers to make it sure that a strong Health Manpower Information System is to serve the needs of the health sector of the country. We need qualitative improvements in the process so that the hospitals and healthcare organisations are benefited by having quality and value-based hospital personnel for the different purposes.

The development of University of Health Sciences would play an incremental role in making available to the hospitals and healthcare organisations world class personnel. The special focus of the UHS would be on initiating necessary steps to enhance computer literacy among medical students and expose them to emerging technologies and informatics and telematics which would be an important base for developing knowledge in the 21st century. We agree with this view that if in the health sector we find inadequacy of quality personnel, this is due mainly to the degenerating quality of universities and the institutes accepting the responsibility of developing quality people.

The development of information system for the manpower serving the health sector is found significant not only with the viewpoint of developing quality healthcare personnel but also with the motto of making their productive utilisation. The positive or negative contributions of the hospital personnel can be evaluated with the help of information technology and based on their contributions, the incentive plan can be made rational. The information technology would simplify the process of making an appraisal or performance audit that would help a healthcare manager in linking the incentive plan to the contributions of personnel. Thus, suitable incentives to the efficients would inspire even the inefficient personnel to be efficient. In an organisation, a number of negative developments take place and a manager finds it difficult to fix accountability. In this context, we find the information system playing a positive role. Of course, we need to document the positive or negative contributions of personnel and even this task is made easier if we have a technology-driven human resource information system. The information technology helps the process of development substantially and it is against this background that we favour development of an independent information system for managing the hospital personnel.

The multidimensional developments in the medical sciences are found based on intensive research undertaken by the dedicated academics and medical scientists. A number of researchers or the research scientists are found engaged in the process. With the joint efforts of people and technologies, we find the process of scientific inventions and innovations getting the right directions. We are aware of the fact that the task of intensifying research is made easier, if we have the support of information superhighway. Earlier the task was not only time taking but even complicated. With the development of a sound information system for the manpower, the hospitals or healthcare organisations may promote research which would benefit the healthcare sector and healthcare personnel in many ways. Of course, the development of an independent information for the human resources would involve huge finance and therefore, the big hospitals need to develop a network so that even small hospitals and healthcare centres get the advantages of information system. The availability of data and knowledge would benefit all the related streams. With more frequency in the development process, the hospital personnel may develop their awareness of the latest developments in the field of medical sciences. The information related to the new generation of information technology, new devices of diagnosis and treatment, new equipments, instruments, apparatus, new drugs and medicine would benefit both, doctors as well as the patients.

Of late, we find a changed scenario. The advancements in the field of information technology have paved avenues for telemedicine, telediagnosis and teleconferencing. The concept of e-Health has injected new life and strength to the healthcare services. The establishment of National Grid would benefit healthcare providers, trainers, beneficiaries and civil society in many ways. We cannot deny that increasing sophistication in the field of information technology has been helping Health Management Information System in different ways. In the Indian perspective where we find the healthcare services in the rural areas presenting a gloomy picture, telemedicine has been helping in bringing specialised healthcare services even to the remotest areas of the country. Tele-diagnosis, specially in the areas of cardiology, pathology, dermatology and radiology has been possible due to IT. The ISRO has been found much more instrumental in the entire process.

The e-Health is found emerging as a new dimension and the credibility for the same goes to the new generation of information and communication technology. We find today e-governance which has been simplifying the task of hospitals and healthcare centres in commanding and monitoring the services. The e-enabled services like disease surveillance, tele-consultations, health helpline, district hospital referral net and e-enabled mobile medical units have been found benefiting the masses. An optimal utilisation of inputs has been made possible duo to IT.

In the context of human resources management, we find education and training programmes for the development of different categories of health personnel gaining new experiences with e-health initiatives. Enriching the knowledge bank of healthcare personnel and making them potentially sound are due to multidimensional uses of e-Health. It is high time that we intensify the uses of electronic devices for developing quality healthcare personnel. It is the prime responsibility of tertiary hospitals to enrich the potentials of primary and secondary hospitals. Brushing up the knowledge of healthcare personnel has been possible due to latest electronics devices and in the coming years, we expect a number of innovative developments. The government policy makers need to make the devices much more popular.

Job Stress in Indian Hospitals

We find hospitals having a different service environment where medical and paramedical staff deal with emotions of life and death and feeling of pain and relief. They are supposed to be sympathetic and empathetic. They need professional touch as well as human orientation. At the workplace, they need a number of items in addition to the supporting infrastructural facilities. They have to remain alert because even minor lapses may result into irreparable losses. The medical and paramedical staff particularly on emergency duty witness a number of odds and however, they have to perform. Surprisingly, the hospital administration has not been found sincere to that moment and therefore, it is the prime responsibility of hospital managers to identify the situational barriers so that necessary preparations are made to remove the same. In a majority of the hospitals, we find psychosomatic complaints by the medical and paramedical staff specially while delivering emergency services. On the one hand, they have a different nature of complicated jobs while on the other hand, they are not made available the supporting infrastructural facilities. This makes the ways for a significant increase in the intensity of stress.

Because we find them all the time facing emergency cases, it is but natural what we find an increase in the psychosomatic complaints which crop up due to stress-friendly environment and intense involvement of staff in stressful work experiences. Mounting vehicular population, connectivity of highways to the entire nation and the speed at which the traffic flows are found to be the important reasons for a significant increase in the number of accident victims.

The emergency department deals with the reception and treatment of the patients, mostly the injured, as accident victims with the help of available supporting infrastructural facilities. However, we find attendants becoming a carrier for stress which is natural but must be regulated. Almost all the government hospitals have been found getting psychosomatic complaints from their emergency staff. In the private hospitals, we find a different scenario because they often deny admission to trauma cases. The medico-legal cases are found only in government hospitals where the medical and paramedical staff experience a different situation which is not witnessed by their counterparts working in the private hospitals. This focuses our attention on the coping mechanism so that the intensity of stress is minimized and the quality of services is improved. But before developing prescription, it is significant that our focus is on the reasons playing an important role in increasing the intensity of risk amongst the different categories of staff such as managers, doctors, nurses, technicians, ancillary staff and security/gatekeepers.[13]

Of course, it is not possible for us to change the service environment found in hospitals due to professional requirements but here, it is imperative that we balance the pressure of work because lack of leisure time, lack of time for subordinate needs, feelings of being occupied with work, lack of amenities and facilities at the workplace, obsession with work, lack of time for subordinates' needs, time pressure, etc. result into stress and make the ways for psychosomatic complaints. Though we find some of us not agreeing a correlation of psychosomatic problems with stress but we find this affecting it and ultimately causing not only a fall in the operational efficiency but even aggravating some of the major health problems in the working staff. Almost all the medical and paramedical staff face the problem of personal sacrifice for professional requirements and commitments but we do not take notice of their such sacrifices while offering to them the financial or non-financial incentives.

Though we find all the medical staff facing the problem of job stress but the stress among the ancillary staff is found of high magnitude. Since we find them extremely involved in their jobs, suffering from time pressure and overburdened with workloads, the intensity of stress is high. The ancillary staff is found involved in the diagnostic services, work as ward boys and Aayas whose work pressure is high due to an increased flow of patients in the government hospitals. They are supposed to remain alert and even highly alert specially when we find them working in the emergency department.

It is also found that freshers working in the emergency department have less stress in comparison with the persons already working for six months or more. The levels of stress are found equal among managers and doctors. The increasing pressure of work strengthens the realisation of medical and paramedical staff that they have been facing a never-ending problem. Here, we find the law of Parkinson applicable which focuses on the fact that work expands so as to fill the time available for its completion. The incessant job-stress experiences show deleterious effects and result into psychosomatic problems in the long run. The psychosomatic complaints come out in different forms such as trouble in breathing, feeling fidgety and poor appetite.

In view of the above mentioned facts, it is right to say that hospitals and healthcare organisations need to make an indepth study of the multidimensional problems related with the job stress. The hospital professional need to make a constant supervision, time-honoured help, and constant monitoring of the availability of staff and supporting infrastructural facilities. It is also pertinent that the working staff is made available all the required amenities and facilities at the workplace so that they relax as and when the situations permit. The nature of work is also an important factor because when we find increasing cases of medico-legal work found traumatic in nature, the intensity of stress is found high.

The hospital professionals in the very context need to assign due weightage to the service environment at the workplace. They require to make possible clear-cut protocols and procedures, providing scope for relaxing the working staff, much more frequency in rotation, availability of increased number of staff, less working hours, family counselling week and special leave packages. We cannot deny the instrumentality of financial and non-financial incentives in regulating the job-stress and therefore, it is to be made sure that medical and paramedical staff specially working in the emergency department get something more than their counterparts not facing the similar problems.

Retaining Quality People in Hospitals

Talent-nurture makes the ways for work culture. This is due to the fact that it paves avenues for organisational culture. If you create an environment in which people feel pleasure in performing, it is quite natural that all the doors for talent-volatility are sealed. Hence, the hospital professionals need to explore opportunities that how and in what way they can ensure a talent-nurturing environment. If quality doctors bid a good-bye to your hospitals, it is a direct loss to your organisation. We define talent as a capability applied to create value that is recognised and rewarded by primary stakeholders-owners, managers and customers. In an age of attrition and job hopping, the hospital managers need priority attention on managing quality people and their success-rate is found coiled in the essence of retaining quality people.

With the mounting competition, we find increased scope for talent volatility[14] because almost all the hospitals are found in search of quality people. The hospitals are known with the quality of doctors they have. The most burning problem before hospital professionals is to minimise the negative effects of attrition. This focuses on identifying the roots of attrition. The concept of attrition in modern world throws light on talent volatility. The hospital professional found bold enough to accept the talent volatility in a positive angle consider the following for attracting talent.

We cannot deny that attracting talent is one of the toughest challenges for any HR department in an organisation. In the health care organisations, the task is found much more challenging because the leading private hospitals offer to the talents lucrative incentives. The professionals need to go through the problems related to attracting talents, retaining them and making use of their names for creating a brand name. This necessitates identification of talents in hospitals. In the hospitals and healthcare organisations, the shortage of talent is considered to be the biggest obstacle to the development process. The quality doctors are developed by hospitals or hired or outsourced. From the very beginning, the leading hospitals should make professionalised efforts to develop quality medical and paramedical personnel.

The hospital professionals at the outset need to identify the quality medical staff whose services are found of world class. Attracting the talents require due focus on providing to the working quality staff a positive work culture to facilitate growth of talents. Talent incubation is a long term process which requires much more consistency. This focuses on providing to the people adequate research and training facilities so that they get an opportunity to enrich their excellence. In this context, we cannot underrate the behavioral dimension which is to touch the ego of people. An ambience which is to help the medical staff in particular while developing and performing becomes significant for attracting the talents.

Retaining talent is an important functional responsibility before hospital professionals and this draws our attention on some of the important dimensions. Lucrative incentives to the working medical and paramedical staff commensurate with their potentials needs priority attention. Proper reward and recognition are found essential for motivating them. In addition, the administration needs to consider the maximum amenities and facilities to be made available to them. Maximum promotional avenues would also motivate them for retaining in the same hospitals where they work. Adequate supporting infrastructural facilities to enable them to deliver in tune with their potentials cannot be underestimated. For the world class doctors, there should not be any age limit for superannuation. The policy makers and professionals need to make use of their potentials and to include them in their advisory board to tap their excellence. There should not be any discrimination on the basis of racial or gender considerations. Indeed, the available talents in an individual should be the guiding force. Providing to them the amenities and facilities for undertaking research and imparting the best training facilities to brush up their knowledge would also act as a motivational tool. In a true sense, the administration should make the incentives nationally and internationally competitive so that the quality medical and paramedical staff are lured.

We cannot deny the fact that the realities are something different, particularly in the government hospitals. What to talk of the general government hospitals when we find administration nurturing a negative attitude albeit in the world class hospitals like AIIMS. Of late, we find AIIMS and other government hospitals of same standard facing the problems of scarcity of quality doctors. And this is due mainly to the fact that even world class doctors are found demoralised. We make a strong advocacy in favour of motivational tools but conversely, we find there demotivational forces instrumental. This forces them for attrition and consequently, they have been found opting for private hospitals where they get maximum incentives and even due respect. Retention is found based on satisfaction. Unless and until we satisfy the working medical and paramedical personnel by offering to them lucrative incentives, it is not possible to retain them. Retaining talents is thus considered to be an important decision making area to enable hospitals to earn a brand name.

Discrimination is also found to be instrumental in promoting attrition. We also find cases specially in the government hospitals when based on political or other considerations, the talented doctors are demoralised. If the government hospitals want to create a brand name to contribute to the process of making India a healthcare destination, they have no option but to retain the quality medical and paramedical staff. Decent behaviour, lucrative financial incentives, sound service ambience and due weightage to their excellence are considered the guiding forces to transform their attitudes where they consider hospitals not only as an organisation where they work but indeed as an institution where they are nurtured. Particularly, when we find India emerging as a health destination, it is pertinent that hospitals in general and the government hospitals in particular retain and respect talents.

Developing Quality People for Healthcare Services

Ultimately, the quality people serve. The technology simply assists. During the yesteryears, a number of developments have taken place in the healthcare sector and the coming years would posit newer opportunities and challenges before medical and health education. We are required to educate, train and develop people found commensurate with our changing requires. We are making sincere efforts to correct the wrongs done in past. This focuses priority attention of hospitals on the problem of qualitative and quantitative gap in the development of people for the healthcare services. We find India potentially sound to become an important destination for healthcare services and for capitalising on the opportunities, it is significant that efforts are made to develop an effective information system. The concerned Ministries, Professional Councils, Technical Councils, UGC, Central and State Universities, Public Health Institutions and knowledgeable individuals from civil society are required to take part in the process of developing quality human resources for the healthcare sector.

NCMH (2005) has recommended additional funding for the establishment of new medical, nursing and other institutions, training of village level functionaries and in-service training of health personnel[15]. The resources required for developing human resources are to be shared by the Centre and States. The National Rural Health Mission would also be required to make significant contribution to the process. Additionally, the suitable partnership arrangements with the private sector and also through other available options are to be mobilised. It is high time that we consider healthcare sector as an infrastructure sector. In the face of increasing healthcare requirements and changing healthcare devices, a sum of Rs. 3,70,000/- crores would be required which cannot be mobilised only through the government sources and therefore, we need to motivate the private sector and to promote the PPP mode.

Ensuring availability of medical professionals in the rural areas on a permanent basis, posting of doctors with adequate monetary incentives and non-financial motivational schemes such as suitable accommodation, Class I status, preferential school admissions for children of doctors, transfer or posting of choice after a stipulated length of stay and training opportunities need priority attention of policy makers. The state governments in the very context are required to expand the pool of medical practitioners including a cadre of Licentiate Medical Practitioners on Indian Systems of Medicines and Homoeopathy (AYUSH). Increasing the age of superannuation to 65 years, retaining public health doctors on contract basis even after superannuation if they are interested in serving are some of measures which would act as a motivational tool to bridge the qualitative-cum-quantitative gap.

There are a number of areas where we find a stage of deficit or shortage of doctors such as public health, anaesthesia, psychiatry, geriatric care and oncology. In these areas, we need to motivate the private sector to participate in the venture. The efforts made by National Board of Examinations (NBE) are to be enhanced for overcoming the shortage of specialists and also to improve the quality of training. We need Councils to create a scientific data bank of health professionals. The establishment of new medical, nursing and dental colleges in the underserved areas of the country cannot be undermined. The NCMH (2005) made recommendations for reducing the existing inequality by establishing 60 Medical Colleges of deficit States like U.P.,

Rajasthan, M. P., Orissa, Chattisgarh and Bihar and 225 nursing colleges in underserved areas. We may think over the PPP mode for bridging the gap. In addition, the implementation of the recommendations of OSC for development of human resources for the healthcare sector, equipping medical graduates with the skills essential for providing broad-based community health care, stemming the high rate of attrition of academics teaching in professional colleges and private OPDs in the medical colleges are some of the measures to make available to the healthcare sector quality human resources.

Of late, we find a changed scenario. The adequate shortage of Medical Colleges and Nursing Schools has been found increasing the intensity of problem. The students interested in getting admission find it difficult to get a place. A number of government medical colleges are found in a depleted condition. They are found infrastructurally and managerially deficient. The private medical colleges and institutes have been charging exorbitant fee structure. The talents are thus demotivated to pursue medical education. This focuses our attention on increasing the number of medical colleges and institutes under the PPP mode. On the one hand, the state governments as well as the central government require to open new colleges in the underserved and backward areas while on the other hand, they also need to promote the private sector and the PPP mode.

It is amazing that even doctors have been facing the stage of unemployment. Even if they are employed, the financial and non-financial incentives are not found to be lucrative. They do not have an ambient condition for showing their excellence. A number of demotivational forces are found demoralizing and discouraging them. We find the government hospitals experiencing a number of problems concerned with the managerial deficiency. The politicians have been found managing and ruling the hospitals which create a condition where doctors are insulted, demoralised and even removed.

In view of the above, it is right to mention that developing quality people for the healthcare sector is a crying need of the hour which requires involvement of state governments, central government, private sector and public-partnership-mode. The supply position cannot be improved unless we find multi-cornered efforts to make an assault on the problem.

SUMMARY

You have gone through different dimensions of the management of hospital personnel. After going through the chapter, be sure that the following facts are well versed.

Perception of Human, Humane and Humanity: Since we go through the management of human resources, it is essential that we know about the perception of human, humane and humanity. The term human, refers to the process of developing essential qualities for the genus man. The term "humane" refers to the process of humanising which in due course makes possible humanity.

Leadership: In the field of healthcare, the term "leadership" focuses on the excellence of a hospital manager in managing hospitals efficiently.

Leadership Influences: There are a number of factors to influence leadership, such as family, media, friends, self-identity, peers, professional leaders, historical leaders and educators.

Universal Characteristics of Leadership: The universal characteristics are viable, a steady hand, smartness, emotion, a sense of humour, ability to confess and ability to listen.

La Guardia Model: The La Guardia Model of leadership focuses on energy, strength, intelligence, values, courage, spirit.

Categories of Personnel Serving Hospitals: Find different categories of employees serving hospitals, such as medical and paramedical personnel, nursing staff, managerial staff and general technicians.

Dimensions of Human Resources Management: The important dimensions of HRM are selected on, education, training and development, motivation and compensation and performance audit.

Managing the Preselection Process: The preselection processes are compiling a wish list, compiling an expectation list, reviewing the job description, reviewing recruitment tactics and reviewing resumes.

Managing the Selection Process: The management of selection process focuses our attention on getting right people on right time.

Managing Post-selection Process: The post-selection process starts with the employer's orientation and continues throughout the tenure.

Principles Governing Recruitment: The basic principles governing recruitment are centralised selection, work analysis, internal and external sources, required qualifications, clear recruitment policy and without a bias.

Education and Training: This dimension of the management of human resources focuses on the development of human resources in tune with the emerging conditions.

Benefits of Training: The benefits of training are to an organisation, to the employees, to a team, to the patients and to the formation of human capital.

Education and Development Programme: This includes management development, sources of learning.

Employee Development Programme: This is related to the education and training programme for the hospital personnel.

Management Development Programme; This is related to the development of executives.

Individual Development Programme: This is related to the development of an individual.

Value-orientation: This draws our attention of the process of value engineering.

Human Capital vs. Productivity: This establishes a correlation between the two.

Compensation and Motivation: In this dimension, we go through the problems like policy imperatives, perception of compensation and motivation, wage and salary administration, non-financial incentives.

Performance Audit: We go through documentation, performance indicators, and critical factors for performance evaluation.

Health Care Information System: The management of information focusing on information related to healthcare.

Job stress in Indian Hospitals: Medical and para-medical staff and managerial staff particularly serving the emergency department face the problem of psychosomatic due to job stress. The professionals need to improve the service environment.

Retaining Quality People in Hospitals: By improving service environment and providing lucrative financial and non-financial incentives, the quality people would be retained to enable hospitals to earn a brand name.

Developing Quality People for Hospitals: The professionals need to improve the quality of people in primary, secondary and tertiary streams by providing to them world class educational aid and training facilities.

KEY TERMS

Human	Industrial psychologists
Humane	Performance Audit
Human Capital	Linchpin
Information Superhighway	Logbook
National Rural Health Mission	Peers
RMPS	Rule of Thumb
ANMs	Performance Audit
Profanity	Psychobabble
Foibles	psychosomatic
Confession	Job-stress
Learning Curve	Attrition
Participative Learning	Retention
Compensation	Tele-conferencing
Motivation	Ancillary Staff
Incentives	Coping Mechanism
Personal-touch-in-service	Talent Incubation

REVIEW QUESTIONS

1. Define Humane, Human and Humanity. Focus on the development of human resources is in the healthcare services.
2. What do you mean by Leadership? Explain the factors influencing leadership in the context of hospital management.
3. Discuss the universal characteristics of leadership. Focus on the La Guardia Model of Leadership.
4. Explain the different main categories of personnel serving hospitals and throw light on their instrumentality in the healthcare services.
5. Discuss in brief the different dimensions of Human Resources Management with focus of healthcare sector.
6. What do you mean by selection? Explain the pre-selection process to be followed by a hospital manger in selecting quality people.
7. Throw light on the post-selection process for developing quality people in hospitals.
8. State and explain the different underlying principles governing recruitment of hospital personnel.
9. What do you mean by Training? Explain the importance of training for the development of quality hospital personnel.
10. Focus on the Management Development Programme for hospitals.
11. What do you mean by Compensation? Discuss the policy imperatives found instrumental in motivating the hospital personnel.
12. Explain the Wage and Salary Administration. Explain the role of financial incentives in motivating the hospital personnel.
13. What do you mean by Performance Audit? Do you find it helpful in increasing the level of efficiency? Justify you arguments.

14. What do you mean by non-financial incentives? Explain its different types to motivate the hospital personnel.
15. Explain the critical factors requiring priority attention while making an appraisal of the performance of hospital personnel.
16. Focus on the instrumentality of developing a techno-driven information system for improving the quality of hospital personnel.
17. Throw light on the professionalised efforts for retaining the quality people in the hospitals.
18. Explain the steps hospital professionals need to initiate to minimise the job-stress of hospital personnel working in the emergency department.
19. Focus on the policy making decisions, the government should initiate to minimise the shortage of quality people in the healthcare sector.

APPLICATION EXERCISES

1. As a hospital professional, you need enrich the potentials of employees working in different capacities. Throw light on the training programme helping you in the process.
2. A number of people are to be recruited in different areas for your hospitals. Comment on the techno-driven devices simplifying the process or recruiting quality hospital personnel.
3. You hospital has been facing the problem of attrition which would make an invision on your efforts for retaining quality people for establishing a brand name. Focus on the steps you find proactive for retaining quality people.
4. The emergency department of your hospital is found over-pressed which has been found increasing the psychosomatic complaints from different categories of staff. In the capacity of a hospital professional, focus on the measures you need to initiate for minimising job-stress.
5. Keeping in view the significant developments in the field of medical sciences, you need to initiate short and long-term training courses for your employees. Explain the structural changes you would prefer to develop the hospital people.
6. Your quality doctors have been leaving your hospital because lucrative incentives have been offered to them by other hospitals. Throw light on the measures you would like to suggest to motivate them.
7. In the capacity of a hospital professional, focus on the measures you would initiate to audit the performance of different categories of employees serving your hospital.
8. In addition to other incentives, the service ambience provided to medical and paramedical personnel also help in motivating and increasing their operational efficiency. Comment on this statement as a hospital manger.
9. While developing quality people for your hospital, what essential properties would you inculcate for improving the operational efficiency of paramedical staff ?
10. "The most important aspect while developing hospital personnel is value-engineering." In the light of this statement, explain the process of value-orientation for developing hospital personnel.
11. In the capacity of a hospital manger, establish a direct relation of human capital formation with the human resource development.

END NOTES

1. Jha S. M., *Perception of Human and Humane*, Bank Marketing , HPH, Mumbai, 2009
2. *Ibid*
3. Lombardi, D.N., *Healthcare*, p.72

4. *Ibid.*, pp. 78-80
5. *Ibid.*, pp. 80-82
6. *Ibid.*, pp. 232-37
7. *Ibid.*, p. 280
8. Jha S. M., *Social Marketing: Changes and Attitude Formation*, HPH, Mumbai, 2009
9. Jha S.M., *Decision Making Criteria for the Productive Human Resources*, Edited by B. L. Mathur, Human Resources Development, pp. 35-48.
10. Harish Kumar, *Trade Unions: Boosters of Barriers or Productivity*, Market Man, 1998, pp. 20-23.
11. Jha S. M., *Service Marketing*, HPH, Mumbai, 2009
12. Nabbi's Ninth Five Year Plan, Vol. I, pp. 472-73
13. Chandra Sekhar, *Stress and Psychosomatic Complaints Among Emergency Staff in Hospitals*; The Icfain Journal of Management Research, Vol. VII/7 July, 2008 pp. 7-16
14. Indrani Mutsuddi and Rini Mutsuddi, *Retaining Talents: The Key Knowledge to Organisation*; The Icfain Journal of Management and Research, Vol. VII/7 July, 2008 pp. 73-84
15. *Eleventh Five Year Plan*: Planning Commission, Government of India, New Delhi Vol. II pp. 57-115

Management of Finance in Hospitals

Shrinking avenues for generating revenues, contracting scope for charities and donations, a drastic cut in government grants, regulated pricing decisions specially in the government hospitals, a large-scale misuse of funds, increasing irregularities and frauds in managing finance and increasing financial burden on account of mounting social costs make a strong advocacy in favour of sound financial management.

CHAPTER OBJECTIVES

Introduction—Financial Management in Hospitals—Financial Planning—Financial Organisation—Budgeting—Exploring Avenues for Revenues in Hospitals—Managing the Financial Information—Break—even Analysis—Project Planning—Project Life Cycle—Feasibility Studies—Management of Books and Accounts—Computer—driven Accounting System—Formatting for Books and Accounts—Removing Financial Constraints for Health Care Services—Summary—Key Terms—Review Questions—Application Exercises—End Notes.

LEARNING OBJECTIVES

This chapter aims at studying the different dimensions of hospitals financing. The readers develop their awareness of the various dimensions of financial management with the motto of controlling the financial irregularities and making possible the best utilisation of funds. Wider avenues for the mobilisation of financial resources are to be tapped and all the doors for financial irregularities are to be sealed. The hospitals in general and the government hospitals in particular have been facing the problem of financial crunch. The financial directors, advisors and hospital managers need professionalised efforts to ensure productive utilisation of funds.

Introduction

Increasing use of new generation of expensive inputs, expanding requirement of supporting infrastructural facilities, mounting administration budget, increasing demand for attractive and comfortable buildings, growing temptation for environment-friendly surroundings and premises, mounting social responsibility and growing popularity of e-health are some of the key issues found very much instrumental in increasing the financial burden on the hospitals and healthcare organisations. On the other hand, shrinking avenues of generating revenues, contracting scope for charities and donations, a drastic cut in government grants, regulated pricing decisions specially in the government hospitals, a large scale misuse of finance, increasing irregularities and frauds are some of the alarming problems making the ways for financial crunch. Except a few of the leading private hospitals, we find almost all the hospitals and healthcare organisations facing financial insolvency.

A hospital manager bears the responsibility of managing finance in such a way that not only a stage of financial insolvency is removed but in addition, copious avenues are paved for expansion, modernization and development. If we need to promote the infusion of new generation of technology, equipment, instruments, apparatus for making available to the users world class services, we have no option but to assign an overriding priority to the management of finance. The managers in the very context need professional excellence of world class. The management of finance draws our attention on a number of accounting and auditing and other allied problems resulting into irregularities. It is really amazing that despite of the financial crunch, the intensity of mismanagement of finance in the government hospitals is found high. The increasing financial irregularities particularly in government hospitals and specially in purchasing hospital materials, managing stores and inventories have also been found aggravating the magnitude of problem. It is against this background that we make a strong advocacy in favour of professionalised management of finance.

The modern concept of hospital management is found considerably influenced by the holistic concept. The hospital and healthcare organisations bear the responsibility of offering quality medical services to the society. This is not to be possible unless they make use of quality inputs and assign number one priority to the quality of medical and paramedical staff. If it significant that a hospital manager explore avenues for mobilising finance. The different categories of paramedical staff, nursing and managerial personnel need to be paid lucrative financial and non-financial incentives. Unless they make us of both, the internal and external sources and regulate mismanagement of finance, the hospitals cannot be successful in bearing the social costs as a part of their corporate social responsibility. Of course, we find a number of e-devices to govern and regulate mismanagement of finance. For a sound financial management, it is significant that hospitals practise e-filing, e-accounting, e-governance which would simplify the process of making payments *vis-a-vis* receiving payments from different sources.

The modern hospitals bear the responsibility of providing quality medical services to the users. This is not possible unless they have quality inputs and the same would require huge financial allocation. The medical, paramedical, nursing and managerial staff is required to be paid lucrative incentives. This makes it essential that hospitals mobilise resources and keep on moving the process of channelising productive and investments so that their dependence on state exchequer is considerably minimised. This requires a new vision, a new strategy that helps in soliciting the cooperation of masses particularly for getting charities and donations both from individuals and institutions.

The management of finance in hospitals requires world class professional excellence because the hospitals and healthcare organisations make possible an optimal utilisation of the available financial resources. Of course, we find maintenance of books and accounts and routine control essential for managing finance but in addition, there are a number of facets to be practiced for a sound financial management. Financial allocation, cost analysis and control, establishment of revenue and cost centres and allocation of data, revenue and cost centrewise study of utilisation of resources, materials and stores management, budgetary control, review of actual and budgets, setting standards, management by exceptions, performance budgeting and management by objectives, review of project, and new schemes and investments therein, net work analysis, PERT, Internet services are some of the essential aspects requiring due care while managing finance. It is against this background that we find management of finance necessitating due care and world class excellence. Particularly in government hospitals where in a majority of the cases we find mismanagement of finance, the administration needs to take it on a priority basis.

In this context, we find three-dimensional problems, viz. Management of Accounts, Management of Financial Information and Management of Materials and Stores. Earlier we have gone through the management of materials and stores and therefore, we find focus on management of accounts and management of information. Though, we find emphasis on management of financial information even in the chapter Management of Information System here, we go through the problem specially with the viewpoint of managing the financial information in hospitals and healthcare organisations.

The management of accounts is considered to be an important dimension of financial management which includes in its purview books of accounts, periodical accounts, revenue and cost centres and cost collection. While going through the problem of management of financial information, we focus on budget and actual, analysis of variances for corrective action, utilisation of resources, cost analysis and information technology for managing financial information.

The aforesaid facts make it clear that management of finance includes in its purview a large number of problems and a financial director bearing the responsibility of managing finance or even a hospital manger bearing the responsibility of managing finance or even a hospital manager managing finance requires expertise in the related area. It is essential that we find an organisation with proper delegation of authority and responsibilities. The formulation of organisational structure for managing finance would depend on the size of the hospital or a group of hospitals. In almost all the hospitals or healthcare organisations, we need to hand over the responsibility of managing finance to the Financial Advisor who in consultation with the financial director would make the financial decisions. Since hospitals do not have a legitimate right of making profits, the financial advisor requires to manage various dimensions of financial management with a professional touch. In big hospitals, we find an independent position for the Financial Director. Even a hospital manager with specialization in finance can successfully manage financial problems in the hospitals and healthcare organisations.

The policy makers need due focus on various dimensions of financial management in hospitals so that the problem of financial crunch is removed. We cannot deny that today, the e-supported devices have been found successful in having a sound management of finance. Both the components such as mobilisation of financial resources and optimal allocation are found significant in the very context. Because we find hospitals and healthcare organisations distinct from others, it is imperative that managerial proficiency and professional excellence get due place. On the one hand, they have to pave avenues for modernisation, expansion and development while on the other hand, it is also pertinent that they strengthen their potentials of bearing the social costs. What to talk of the government hospitals when we find even the private hospitals initiating the process. It is high time that they accelerate the process and significantly contribute to the process of social transformation.

Financial Management in Hospital: the Perception

Financial management draws our attention on making financial decisions in the larger interests of an organisation vis-a-vis the stakeholders. Since we talk about the management of finance in hospitals, our prime focus is management of finance for the non-profit organisations in which avenues for revenues are found very limited. The management principles based on the holistic concept make it essential that hospitals generate surpluses so that they find themselves in a position to serve the society. This deprives a manager of using the term "profit" which complicates his/her functional responsibilities. It is against this background that we study the problem of financial management in hospitals in a bit different way. We are well aware of the fact that hospital is a non-profit organisation not having a legitimate right of making profits but at the same time, bearing the responsibility of serving and sub-serving the society.

Financial management involves making of three important decisions, viz., the decisions related to investment, the decisions related to generation and mobilisation and the decisions related to financial control. Since we find management of hospitals both under the public and private sectors, the managerial decisions are found a bit different in both the categories of hospitals. It is quite natural that when we talk about financial management, our focus would be on different constituents, like generation and mobilisation, allocation, accounting and auditing. The hospitals managed and controlled by the government receive grants from the government and in addition, they have a very limited internal sources for generating finance, such as paying wards, nominal fees charged from the patients, rental from the shopping complex, if they have or so. But the hospitals managed under the private sector generate finance from fees, charity and donations. This makes it clear that in both the categories of hospitals, we find limited avenues for generating revenues. However, they have a budget supposed to be formulated by the experts in the area of finance. For the government managed hospitals, the health department of the government is found responsible for making allocation and for the private hospitals. We find a governing body or the boardrooms responsible for formulating policies, making sanctions where a hospital manager supposed to be aware of the financial management or a financial adviser accepts the financial responsibilities and makes the managerial decisions in the area of finance.

The management of finance requires due emphasis on potential benefits in qualitative terms. The hospitals or the healthcare organisations need to make a number of decisions related to finance. They are required to invest for capital intensive machines, equipment and apparatus. The purchase of X-Ray machines, auto-analysers, surgical instruments, and other necessities of operation theatres such as operation table, trolleys, drums, autoclave machines, etc. and a number of equipments and apparatus for diagnosis and treatment and information management need huge amount for investment. We find them capital investment because it is used by hospitals for a long period. In addition, the hospitals also need sufficient working capital. They need drugs, linen, cotton, bedsheets, pillows, syringes, needles, etc. We call them short-term assets because we find them of day-to-day uses. In the management of working capital, a financial manager requires to consider average daily census, occupancy ratio, average length of stay of patients, number of different kinds of surgical operations, etc. This helps them in knowing the financial requirements for a particular period.

The aforesaid facts make it clear that the management of finance in hospitals is found a bit different from other profit making organisations. Since the product of hospitals are found of a sensitive nature, a financial adviser manager requires professional excellence to manage things efficiently.

Financial Planning

For managing anything effectively, the managerial natural impulse focuses our attention on planning. To move forward, we need a development plan but the formulation of a development plan carries no meaning unless we have a sound financial plan which paves avenues for the generation and mobilisation of resources besides making possible an optimal allocation and a result-oriented control and supervision. It is against this background that we, while going through the problem of financial management of hospitals centralise our attention on the financial planning.

Planning is considered to be the formulation of enterprise goals and objectives, the selection among alternative courses of action and the initiation of policies and programmes to achieve objectives.[1] Since we talk about hospital planning, the concept draws our attention on the formulation of the goals and objectives of hospitals or the healthcare organisations and the initiation of policies and programmes helping a manager in accomplishing the objectives of making available to the patients quality services. Thus, the financial planning is found to be a managerial device to explore avenues for the generation of financial resources, making possible an optimal allocation so that the multi faceted requirements of a hospital or healthcare organisations are given due weightage in the face of their impact on offering good patient care, following the accounting and auditing practices to ascertain that investments and expenses have been as per the required norms and budgetary provisions and regulating the irregularities by using different tools of control and supervision. Thus, on the one hand we find financial planning a managerial process to manage finance professionally while on the other hand, we also find it an administrative mechanism to check the irregularities and unfair practices.

Formulated both, for the short and long-terms, we find financial planning a device helping an organisation right from the first day of its inception to the last date of its existence. The short-term financial plan focuses our attention on the annual financial requirements of an organisation because we need working capital so as to attain and retain an optimal level of current assets. Conversely, we also go through the problem of long-term financial planning because an organisation needs different types of fixed assets of expensive and inexpensive nature which are found essential for delivering goods to the patients/users and it is not possible for a manager to make it possible with the very limited resources.

With the growing importance of expensive equipments, apparatus, machines, instruments, sophisticated information and communications technologies, a number of supporting infrastructural facilities for improving the quality of diagnosis and treatment, it is not possible for hospitals or the healthcare organisations to manage things in a right fashion unless they assign due weightage to the long-term plan which necessitates huge finance. A manager by formulating both the short and long-term plans comes to know about the short and long-term financial requirements of hospitals and exercises his/her professional excellence for making possible a time-honoured and cost-effective implementation so that the organisational goals are accomplished and the patients/users remain satisfied. It is in this context that the financial management of an organisation, be it profit-making or no-profit making, occupies a place of outstanding significance. And management without planning carries no meaning.

Financial Organisation

It is a sound organisation that simplifies the task of accomplishing the organisational goals. By formulating a sound organisational structure, an organisation succeeds in achieving mission and fulfilling its multidimensional objectives. This necessitates an idea about the financial organisation for hospitals or the healthcare organisations.[2] Gone are the days when hospitals worked with the support of a Medical Superintendent who was found all in one. Of late, we find specialisation making the ways for your desired, targeted growth and development. Yesterday, a medical superintendent looked after everything, e.g., medical services, financial accounting, general administration, purchases, stores and all the activities taking place under the umbrella of a hospital. Even till now, we find a number of government hospitals managed and controlled by a Medical Superintendent and all of us are well aware of the quality of performance of government hospitals. There is no doubt in it that a majority of the private hospitals have been found assigning due weightage to the conceptualisation of modern management principles and whatever the qualitative improvements that we find in the medical sciences have significantly

Governing Body

Medical Director

Financial Adviser	Medical Superintendent	G.M. Services	G.M. Pesonnel
Financial Management Budgeting Accouning Auditing Financial Information	Managing Finance in Government Hospitals Financial Information and Medical Service	Managing Services	Managing Hospital Personnel

Fig. 10.1. Financial Organisation

been contributed by management-orientation. The private hospitals, institutes, global health organisations and social organisations have made significant contributions to the process of development. We can't negate that in the medical or healthcare sector, we find a number of areas where specialisation assumes a place of outstanding significance. Purchase of expensive equipments, instruments machines, apparatus, information and communication technologies, increasing expectations of hospital personnel for financial and non-financial incentives, growing requirements for sophisticated peripheral services and mounting expectations of users/patients or attendants are some of the important problems requiring sound financial decisions which can only be made by a professional manager having world class excellence. An organisation framework is presented in Fig. 10.1.

In Fig. 10.1, we find a framework for organising finance for hospitals or healthcare organisations. At the top, we find the Governing Board and thereafter in the hierarchy, we find a financial director assisted by financial adviser, medical superintendent, general manager (services) and general manager (personnel). We find financial adviser responsible for all the aspects related to finance, such as formulation of a sound budget, analysis of cost management of books and accounts, auditing, management of financial information and a number of allied problems directly or indirectly affecting finance. Thus, with a big list of financial accountability, he/she bears the responsibility of managing finance for hospitals.

Budgeting

Budget is considered to be a comprehensive plan of operations expressed in monetary and quantitative terms. It is defined as a financial or a quantitative statement prepared and approved prior to a period of time of the policy to be pursued during that period for purposes of attaining a given objective. It is more than a forecast of income and expenditure. It reflects the policy being implemented. The formulation of an ideal budget is found essential to an optimal development of an organisation. It is the responsibility of a financial manager to formulate a budget that ensures proportionate and time-honoured development of an organisation for which it has been formulated.

Ideal Budget

While formulating a budget, there are certain essentials to be given due weightage.[3]

- Identification and clear understanding of the hospital financial and services goal become important before the formulation of a budget.
- Definite and accountable organisation with clearly defined responsibilities for each department of the hospitals or healthcare organisations.
- A system of accounting designed and maintained that would serve as a base for adequate reporting to provide a measure of performance and for holding the organisation (department) responsible.
- Represents a system of future accounts, stated in terms of organisation responsibility and with this end, there would be an active participation of hospital personnel in the preparation or formulation of the budget.
- Revealing the weaknesses and shortcomings.
- Providing a strong base for coordinated work.

- Lines of authority and responsibilities are established for execution of the tasks laid down.
- Decentralisation of authority and responsibility so as to place it as nearly as possible at the point of action.
- Planning for the future is facilitated.
- The Plant and Equipment Budget (Capital Budget) consists of investment in assets to be acquired during the period of budget.
- The estimates of operating revenues and expenses for the next budget year and for that formulating the operating budget.
- The formulation of cash budget for estimating the monetary requirements and the sources of funds for the budget period.

Formulation of a Budget

The formulation of an effective budget is found essential for the sound development of hospitals and the healthcare organisations. An effective budget can't be prepared on imagination and hence, we find different types of information essential which are to be collected from different departments. Our experiences as reflected in accounting and other records, modified or extended by future needs and requirements, knowledge of past performance, constructive examination of what has happened in past and accurate statistical information are found essential for the preparation of an effective budget.

Data of past performance are to be collected. Changes in the service mix are to be studied and the external factors affecting the hospitals, especially admissions and registration are to be identified. The adverse impact of policy decision is to be detected and the constraints in the process are to be observed. Because the budget would prove to be an effective tool for financial administration and control, it is necessary that actions necessary to reflect the anticipated effect of the above factors and to remedy the situation are to be planned. Measures are to be taken to ensure that the plan is being carried out and the objectives are to be accomplished.

At the very outset, it is significant that written instructions regarding procedures to be followed are to be issued which should be accompanied by illustrative forms and calculations are to be disseminated to all the personnel to be involved in the budget preparation. The different departments of hospitals then would formulate a budget for their department. Since we find salaries and wages accounting for at least 40 to 50 per cent of the total expenditure, it is pertinent that the budget is realistic or pragmatic. This focuses our attention on the compilation of a master list of the personnel in each department. Additional staff requirements, if necessary, are to be mentioned. Other expenses, such as food, drugs, supplies and expenses are to be projected on the basis of past year's expenses. Normally, we find an increase of 10 per cent in a particular head but keeping in view the inflationary pressure and other changes, it can be increased or adjusted. While estimating the expenses on operation of plant and maintenance including depreciation, and interest, some essentials are to be considered, such as any additional equipment like X-ray, laundry, sterliser etc., are anticipated and acquisition of additional vehicles is to be contemplated besides the anticipation of a major renovation. The effect of free care is also an important consideration requiring due attention. Generally, the cost of free care is covered in the charges levied. If an increase is found in the cost of free care, it is to be made clear.

Plant and Equipment Budget

To be more specific in the hospitals and healthcare organisations, the plant and equipment budget is found playing a dominating role. This dimension is related to the formulation of a capital budget. A well planned capital budget is found related to the different areas, such as addition to building and fixed equipment, addition to furniture and movable equipment and replacement of existing fixed asset. The managerial decisions related to capital budgeting are found based on needs of patients, necessity of expansion, cost-benefit analysis, effect of additional equipments on income and expenditure, replacement and most significantly, the availability of funds.

Because the hospitals in general have been found experiencing the problem of financial crunch, it is important that the capital budget prepared by the heads of different departments focus on priorities, such as

- Urgently Needed
- Essential
- Desirable
- Additional Service

We find a number of hospitals not making adequate provisions for depreciation and replacement. They are also found disinterested in creating a fund for reserve and depend on general funds. This necessitates creation of funds for the items mentioned in the capital budget. In this context, we find cash budget playing a significant role which is considered to be a forecast of cash receipts and payments and reflecting the way and means of hospitals. A financial manager requires to take care of the seasonal fluctuation in the process. Besides, grants and donations from different sources are to be encouraged. The cash outflow generally consisting of salaries, routine purchase of supplies, drugs, etc. require due care. The forecast is found essential for the capital purchase. If you have surplus, it is to be used for creating a safe margin.

Master Budget

The budgets formulated by the heads of different departments of hospitals are finally incorporated into a master budget. We find the Financial Adviser responsible for reviewing the same and finally presenting it to the Governing Body for approval. After approval, the concerned departmental heads are given the information explaining the amendments if any. Cash budget is formulated after the approval of the budget so that any changes if required to be made are incorporated. We also find preparation of cash budget along with other budgets.

We are well aware of the fact that formulation of an effective, realistic budget is found a challenging task because it is based on a number of information to be received from different sources and different departments of hospitals. A financial manager bears the responsibility of preparing a sound budget for hospitals so that we find an optimal allocation of funds for different heads on a priority basis. Since the hospitals in general are supposed to work with the motto of serving the patients, it is pertinent that while formulating budget, the heads related to the medicare or healthcare services are given due weightage. Of late, we find a well developed technology—driven management information system and we also think in favour of developing an independent financial information system and with its support, the collection of information can be made easier as well as authentic. To be more specific, the government hospitals find it difficult to solve the problem because the Department of Health of the state government is found controlling everything. It is against this background that we find a non-optimal budget for government hospitals where the allocation of fund on different heads is also found disproportionate to the changing needs and requirements. This makes it essential that the health department takes into consideration the fluctuating needs and requirements of the related command area and approves the budget accordingly.

For both categories of hospitals, government as well as the private, the formulation of an effective budget is found essential. A medical superintendent or a financial manager responsible for managing the finance requires to keep his eyes open. He/she is supposed to know the changing financial requirements of different departments and to allocate funds accordingly. It is also important that our budgets are essentially based on the existing potentials. There is no doubt that capital equipment budget needs to be assigned a top priority in both categories of hospitals but at the same time, the mismanagement of expensive equipments generally found in the government hospitals is also required to be regulated.

Exploring Avenues for Revenues in Hospitals

Quality inputs make available to you quality outputs. Quality inputs in a majority of the castes are found expensive. Quality hospital personnel have high expectations from you. They expect lucrative financial and non-financial incentives. The patients and attendants also have high expectations from you. They in addition to the quality healthcare services also expect innovative peripheral services from you. In the healthcare sector,-you need to project a positive image and this requires an optimal mix of all. Thus, the modern hospitals and healthcare organisations need to fulfil the expectations of all the segments which are found increasing even without a gap. You, of late, can do anything, if you have adequate finance and conversely, you can do nothing if you face the problem of finance. It is against this background that we go through the problem of exploring avenues for revenues in hospitals and the healthcare organisations. You need to explore both—the internal as well as the external sources. Your professional excellence can help hospitals in generating and mobilising the financial resources till now found either untapped or partially tapped.

Internal Sources

At the outset, you need to exhaust the internal sources which have not been used in an optimal fashion. Of course, we agree with this view that like other profit making organisations, the hospitals are not free to consider costs while setting fees but at the same time, it is also right to mention that our efforts in the very context have not been judicious. There are a number of sources from where we can get money, if our efforts are right and result-oriented.

1. Fee Structure: This is an important source for generating finance and the hospitals need to make an optimal use of the same. Both categories of hospitals—private and government—need a rational approach for setting fees for the different types of services. There is no doubt it that the private hospitals have been found making use of it as an important source but so far as the government hospitals are concerned, they need innovative policy decisions making ways for setting a rational fee structure. Till now, the government hospitals are not free to set fees in the face of increasing costs. They, in a majority of the cases, offer free of charge or subsidised or concessional services and thus, make the social costs very disproportionate to the potentials of hospitals. This results into the problem of financial crunch and creates a vicious circle in the management of finance. If hospitals managed by the government fail in initiating the process of qualitative or quantitative improvements, this is due mainly to the inadequacy of finance. The state exchequer finds it difficult to make available to the hospitals, the required grants. At this juncture, the government hospitals have no option but to think about the fee structure on a priority basis. Of course, we bear the responsibility of subserving the social costs but professionally sound managers have to make it sure that the burdens and potentials have a correlation. Earlier, we have talked about regulating the mismanagement of finance but this is not the only thing that we need to initiate and activate the process. Even the government hospitals need to charge fees, of course rational in character, affordable in effect and practical in behaviour. Pocket-friendly or user-friendly fee structure would help government hospitals in utilising the internal sources optimally in which in addition to the redressal of the grievances of poorest of the poor, the hospitals would also be in a position to pave avenues for multidimensional developments for qualitative and quantitative improvements.

2. Paying Wards: In the context of internal sources, the hospitals can generate revenues even from paying wards. In some of the hospitals, we find provision of paying wards but on a very limited basis. It is also right to mention that fee charged for the paying wards is right now very nominal and the beneficiaries in a majority of the cases belong to the affluent sections. This has been found making the ways for unfair practices, specially while allotting the same to the patients. This makes it essential that the hospitals initiate two-pronged measures, viz., firstly, the fee structure for the paying wards is linked to the income of patients and attendants and secondly, the hospitals construct more paying wards containing all the essential amenities and facilities. All of us are well aware of the fact that patients and attendants living in the private hospitals and clinics pay huge money and therefore, even if we increase the fee of the paying wards, the pressure on the users would be very nominal. The hospital planners and architects need to explore avenues for the same at the initial stage so that the hospitals generate revenues even from this source.

3. Shopping Complex: While generating revenues from the internal sources, it is also pertinent that hospitals think in favour of constructing a shopping complex. Since we find the patients and attendants not getting even the essential items at right prices in the general shopping centres, such a provision would not only increase the revenues of hospitals but would also protect the patients and attendants. It is quite natural that shops located within the walls of the hospitals would not exploit patients. Whatever the price they charge for the goods bought by the patients and attendants would also be spurious of quality and therefore, the possibilities of getting drugs would also be minimised.

4. Dispensary or Pharmacy: In the shopping complex of the hospitals, the dispensary or pharmacy would ensure supply of right medicines at the right prices. We also need to think in favour of pharmacy or dispensary managed by the hospitals mainly to regulate the unethical practices promoted outside the walls of the hospitals. In addition, the hospitals themselves would find it easier to check the harmful effects on patients due to spurious drugs besides making available the employment opportunities to the pharmacists. It is quite natural that the hospital-managed pharmacy would be in a position to supply cheap medicines to the patients and attendants because they would have the benefits of direct marketing.

5. Hospital-managed Transportation: The hospitals also need to make transportation provision for the patients, attendants and the visitors. In addition to the ambulance services, they need to offer general transportation services exclusively for the users of the services. We agree with this view that in a majority of the government hospitals, we don't find a provision of an ambulance then what to talk of general transportation services. We also find cases where the patients fail to reach to the hospitals on time since the transportation facilities, specially during odd time are not available. Thus, by developing a transportation network, in addition to innovating the peripheral services, the hospitals would also be successful in offering comforts and conveniences to the patients and attendants.

6. Pay-phones: In the shopping complex of the hospitals, the provision of pay-phone would help patients and attendants in many ways. Besides, the hospitals would also be successful in generating revenues from this head particularly as rent from the pay-phone provider. The fax and e-mail services would provide conveniences to the patients and attendants. Since they are located at the shopping complex of the hospitals, we find a source of generating revenues.

7. Advertisement Place: We agree with this view that hospitals are found located at a place where a number of persons from different parts of the country or even from abroad— if hospitals are of world class—come for treatment. In addition, the local population also attends hospitals. Thus, we find it a place where inflow of population is found very high. The hospitals are in a position to sell their eye-catching places to the advertising agencies for displaying advertisements. This would be a source for generating revenues which presently is not used. Though we find advertisements there they are unauthorised. It is against this background that we need to tap the source and to increase the revenues of hospitals. If we talk about a shopping complex, it requires huge investment but the use of place for advertisements is not to increase the financial liability and is indeed a big source of revenue.

8. Charity Shows: For generating revenues from the internal sources, the hospitals also need to organise charity shows and the amount received from the sell of tickets would be the revenues. To be more specific when we find it a tertiary hospital or even secondary hospital, there are a number of medical students who can organise programmes or events on a payment basis. Or, they can do it even with the support of local artists who in a natural way would not charge anything from them. The government hospitals need to promote such events for generating revenues.

9. Exhibition and Shows. In the context of generating revenues, the hospitals need to organise exhibition, shows, baby shows, flower shows and handicraft shows and shows promoting heritage which would help hospitals in collecting funds from the masses who are found interested in helping hospitals. In addition, this is also to increase the instrumentality of hospitals in contributing to the process of promoting mass-participation.

The aforesaid internal sources would help hospitals in generating revenues. The professional excellence of a manager is coiled in the essence of maximising their dependence on the external sources or to put it another way, to explore internal sources so that dependence on the external sources is considerably minimised. We agree with this view that right now, a majority of the government hospitals have been found depending on government grants. Not only this, they have been even found misusing the grants and aggravating the intensity of problem. If we talk about the government hospitals, it is almost all clear that what to talk of exploring avenues when they are found promoting unfair practices, irregularities, mismanagement of finance and so on. The existent financial crunch found in a majority of the government hospitals is a staunch testimony to this proposition that the hospital personnel in general and the financial authorities in particular have sizeably been responsible for the present stage of financial disaster. We talk more about a contraction or a drastic cut in grants but speak less about the mismanagement, theft, pilferages, financial irregularities and so on. Thus, it is high time that the health department of state governments, medical superintendents of government hospitals, financial advisers, etc. make sincere and honest efforts to explore avenues, specially or preferably the internal sources to improve the financial health of hospitals, which at present have been facing a critical condition. Of course, we need to tap the external sources but the internal sources are to be used on a priority basis.

External Sources

In addition to the internal sources, the hospitals also need to generate finance from the external sources. The following heads need due care of a manager:

1. Government Grants: *A* drastic cut in the government grants has been found aggravating the financial problems, especially in the government hospitals. Since in a welfare state, it is the prime responsibility of a government to make available quality healthcare services to the masses, it is pertinent that to be more specific, the government hospitals are given adequate grants. Though we make an advocacy in favour of charging fee even by the government, hospitals, however, it is essential that keeping in view the increasing financial pressure and the growing importance of sophisticated technologies, the process of allocating grants continues because the expensive inputs need huge money. If we make a strong advocacy in favour of sharing of social costs even by the private hospitals, it is judicious that they are also given nominal grants. Unless we make multicornered efforts for generating revenues, the intensity of the problem would not be minimised.

2. Charity and Donations: During the yester decades, we have witnessed several examples of charity and donations given by the individuals or institutions but now we find the process slowing down. Despite of the fact that we find provisions for a relief in the tax liabilities, the individuals or institutions have not been found evincing keen interest in offering donations and charity to the hospitals or the healthcare organisations. It is in this context that we need to promote charity and donations. The interested parties are to be encouraged for offering the maximum they can. Not only the private hospitals but even the government hospitals need charity and donations to improve the financial position.

3. Loans and Borrowings: The public sector commercial banks and other financial institutions need to promote hospitals and healthcare institutes by offering to them the credit facilities on the reasonable terms and conditions. To be more specific, for purchasing expensive equipments, instruments and machines, the credit facilities to be offered by the commercial banks or other financial institutions need due attention of government policy makers and the hospital professionals. The main thing in the process is the rate of interest charged by them. Of course, the hospitals and healthcare organisations deserve the maximum possible support from them.

4. Corporate Sector: The principles of social marketing make a strong advocacy in favour of cause related marketing to be promoted by the corporate sector as a corporate citizen. In this context, we find companies organising sponsored programmes, events, sports for the hospitals and healthcare organisations. This is an important source and the hospitals are required to use it. The amount collected from this source should be for both categories of hospitals—the government as well as the private. Of course, the private hospitals deserve a lion's share because they don't receive grants from the government. If the corporate sector switches on the process of generating funds for government and private hospitals, a stage of financial bankruptcy right now instrumental in degenerating the quality of services would also be removed.

5. Global Bodies and Social Organisations: There are a number of social welfare organisations at national and international levels found responsible for the development of backward states and vulnerable regions of the world. They need to extend the maximum possible financial support to hospitals.

The developing and less developed countries of the world have been found facing the problem of mass unawareness due mainly to the high rate of illiteracy, lack of nutritional awareness, high intensity of environment pollution, noise pollution, water-borne, food-borne diseases, communicable and vector-borne diseases and so on. This makes it essential that in addition to the financial help, the social organisations and global bodies also promote creative healthcare education.

6. Soliciting Cooperation of Large-sized Customers/users: The hospitals and healthcare organisations need to solicit the co-operation of large-sized indirect users who offer the benefits of reimbursement of medical bills to their employees. The leading undertakings or governmental organisations or even private corporations make such payments to the hospitals where their employees get specialised services. Since we find it an ongoing process, the concerned organisations may extend financial support on a lumpsum basis that would be adjustable. To be more specific while purchasing expensive equipments apparatus and such assistance would minimise their financial burden. It is in this context that we talk about the cooperation of large-sized organisations to the hospitals.

7. Soliciting Cooperation of Film Stars and Cricketers: Since we go through the problem of finance and all of us bear the responsibility of extending the best possible cooperation to hospitals and healthcare organisations, it is significant that cine artists and cricketers having a high mass image of making the audience crazy, come ahead, organise cultural shows and entertainment programmes and pay to the hospitals, the fund generated from the events. Thus, it is a problem of developing rapport with the persons having a high social or mass image.

The aforesaid facts make it clear that the hospitals and healthcare organisations also need to mobilise the external sources so that the adequacy of finance enables them to initiate and activate the process of qualitative-cum-quantitative transformation. A hospital manager supposed to be professionally sound requires to synchronise the internal and external sources in such a way that the patients/users get the desired levels of services. It is right to mention that with the increasing importance of sophisticated technologies, we find a basic change in the concept and perception of quality which is found increasing the level of expectations of patients and attendants. This makes it essential that hospital manager/financial adviser/medical superintendent makes the ways for innovative financial decisions to maintain the cash flow keeping in view the increasing financial requirements of hospitals.

Of late, a majority of the hospitals have been found facing the problem of financial crunch. What to talk of the government hospitals when even the private hospitals having world class excellence have been experiencing the problem of finance. In a true sense, we find it a situational compulsion that hospitals in general, assign a transcendental priority to increase the level of cash flow which is not possible unless they capitalise on all the available opportunities optimally. The internal as well as the external sources need to be used rationally. To be more specific, the government hospitals need to make it possible on a priority basis because they in a majority of the cases have been found financially bankrupt. It is hoped that they innovate the strategic financial decisions and pave avenues for the development of hospitals.

Generation with innovative efforts, control and supervision with sincerity are the devices to sensitise our efforts.

Managing the Financial Information

While going through the problem of management of information, we have also gone through the instrumentality of financial information in making the creative financial decisions. A hospital manager/financial adviser/ medical superintendent can't think of making the financial decisions innovative unless he/she is well supported by a technology-driven financial information system. Of late, we have a new generation of sophisticated information technology and we are well aware of its positive contributions to the process of making managerial decisions. It is in this context that we focus on the management of financial information for improving the financial health of hospitals and healthcare organisations. Organised and purposeful statistical data are found of real importance to the administration and management of a hospital for effective and time-honoured control.[4] It is due mainly to the fact that such statistics open new vistas of control. You act as a financial manager/adviser and this makes it essential that you consider data not only as historical documents but virtually as barometer; not only as mere results but as a crying need of the moment; not only as reflections but as something positive making the way for efficiency-generation.

You need to make quantitative as well as the qualitative analysis. The quantitative analysis would be helpful in the following ways:

- Establishing administrative control over financial activities.
- Providing a strong base for the preparation of operational budget.
- Rendering reports to the management, outside agencies, etc.
- Providing a base for the distribution of expenses while computing costs.
- Providing a base for the calculation of average income and cost per unit of the services offered.
- Providing basic data to plan for the future in a realistic fashion.

Reporting is an important dimension of management of information which is prepared daily, weekly, fortnightly and monthly. While preparing reports, the following aspects need due care:

- We find reports a statement of facts well supported by references.
- We find them a list of findings and conclusions based on observations.
- The reports also include recommendations or the corrective measures.

- The reports prepared are found-in-patients daily mid-night census report, clarifying average length of stay and the average daily census.
- This helps a manager in knowing the emerging trends in the patient stay and the occupancy ratio besides helping budgeting and planning the future financial policy.
- In the context of out-patients, the information related to visits daily by patients (old patients) for the second or third time, the information related to the number of new patients daily and patient visit by doctor is found important.
- The monthly reports indicate the trends of patient load, disciplinewise hospital days, deaths analysed into broad causes, in-patients by state, sex and age.
- Departmental operating and statistical reports for laboratory.
- X-ray and other specialised services, operating room, ECG, etc.
- Inventory reports of debtors, losses due to expiry of drugs, theft and pilferages, bad debts, etc.
- The monthly Income and Expenditure Statement of each department is compared with budget, unit costs services etc., are prepared and sent to the management.
- Taking support of information technology in the process of preparing report to be more specific, in the big hospitals where maintenance of statistical data is found complex. In this context, we find computers playing a big role in the maintenance of medical records, in billing to the patients and in compiling various statistical and accounting reports and transmitting the same to the management.
- The financial information related to the different areas would help researchers in undertaking research.

The main thing in the management of financial information is to make available to the management a clear picture of finance so that a manager finds it convenient to formulate the strategic decisions. You need to replace an expensive equipment or apparatus. This makes it essential that you come to know about the different sources, price structure of competitive organisations, terms and conditions of supplies, the acceptable mode of payment or so. You find the task much more difficult if everything is managed manually. At the same time, a technology-driven financial information system simplifies your task. Thus, the management of financial information is found significant to hospitals because this also helps them in knowing the qualitative values or effects of the financial decisions taken earlier. You invest, you spend and thus naturally you expect something positive for your investments. It is the responsibility of a financial adviser to make available to a manager the information related to effects of decisions so that any amendment, modification or change is made possible on time. It is against this background that we find management of financial information helping hospitals in knowing qualitative as well as the quantitative outcome of financial investments in hospitals.

We are well aware of the fact that financial reporting is an important dimension of the management of finance because this makes available to a manager the right directions, the positive or negative effects, the emerging trends in the occupancy ratio and the influx of patients and attendants and so on. Since the hospitals are not supposed to make profits, the performance rating is found based on the quantitative and qualitative results of financial decisions on improving the financial health of hospitals. The motive is to increase and maintain the cash flow so that the different departments of a hospital get the required finance for day-to-day requirements and in addition, the modernisation, expansion and development plans of hospitals are implemented on time. To be more specific, when we find government hospitals not assigning any significance to the maintenance and replacement of equipment, apparatus and instruments, the existing trend of financial insolvency would hardly be reversed unless the hospitals are financially sound. Reporting is found based on the management of financial information and to make the reports authentic, result-oriented and productive, we need to prepare a sound financial report.

Break-even Analysis

An important technique of financial analysis, the break-even analysis has gained outstanding significance in the modern financial management. The relationship between cost-volume-profit attracted the attention of financial experts while analysing the finance functions. It is right to mention that the technique of Cost-Volume-Profit Analysis is also called as break-even analysis.[5] In the process of making an analysis, we use the terms fixed and variable costs in a bit different way. Since we go through the problem of hospital financing, it is pertinent that we use the fixed costs and variable costs in relation to hospitals or healthcare organisations.

Fixed Costs: Fixed costs are considered to be the elements of cost which do not vary with the volume of production. It is based on the presumption that the installed production capacity is fixed and not to be changed. These costs are required to be incurred regardless of the level of output and sales. Depreciation, Property, Taxes, Interest, Insurance Premium, Rent, supervisory and management salaries are the typical examples of fixed costs. In the hospital management, we find use of equipments apparatus, machines and therefore, the depreciation cost is found important. It is the responsibility of a financial manager to know about the depreciation cost. If we find hospitals or healthcare organisations taking loans or borrowing from banks or financial institutions, they are supposed to pay interest. If we find hospitals running in the rented house, the rental cost becomes significant. In almost all the hospitals, we find payment of insurance premium specially to protect the property of hospitals from fire, theft and natural calamities. It is in this context that we find insurance premium significant. In hospitals, we find a number of employees working and they are paid salaries and therefore, we also talk about salaries. When we talk about the costs of the healthcare services in the computation process, we find fixed costs important.

Variable Costs: Variable costs are those which vary directly with the actual volume of production or sale. This makes it clear that the variable costs per unit of output is found constant and with a change in the output, we find a proportionate change in the total variable cost. In the eyes of a financial manager, the average variable cost is found constant but the economists feel that as output increases, the average variable cost at the outset comes down to a certain level and then starts increasing. Of course, we find more strength in the viewpoints of economists. Variable costs are also called direct costs, such as labour and raw materials.

An analysis of break-even point is found to be a popular control device. The break-even chart is a visual device to identify the relationship of sales and expenses in such a manner as to determine at what volume, revenues exactly cover costs or expenses. At lesser volume, we find loss and at a greater volume, we find profit. Because we talk about a no-profit making organisation, our prime focus in studying break-even analysis is to optimise the costs so that the cost-effectiveness is made possible. So far as the fixed costs are concerned, it is not possible to minimise the same but the variable costs can be minimised and an optimal stage would help hospitals and healthcare organisations in making possible cost economy. It is in this context that we find break-even analysis to be discussed while managing finance. The Cost-Volume-Profit Model (CVP) provides an important tool in the hands of a financial manager to analyse the relationship between revenues from sales and costs of production.

Semi-variable Cost: Some of the costs are purely fixed whereas some of the costs are purely variable. As for example, the rental of X-Ray machine is the fixed cost and the films used in the process is a variable cost.

Total Cast: We find total costs the aggregation or combination of all types of costs used in the process.

Break-even Analysis: We find break-even analysis a relationship between costs and revenue. In the Fig. 10.2, we find the break-even point which is considered to be the lowest point at which a firm can operate without loss. This is the point where the sales revenue received covers exactly the total costs incurred.[6] It is a point that occupies a place of outstanding significance specially for the public utility organisations working with the motto of serving the society. The hospitals or the healthcare organisations are supposed to serve the society and therefore, the BEP or break-even point would be important to them.

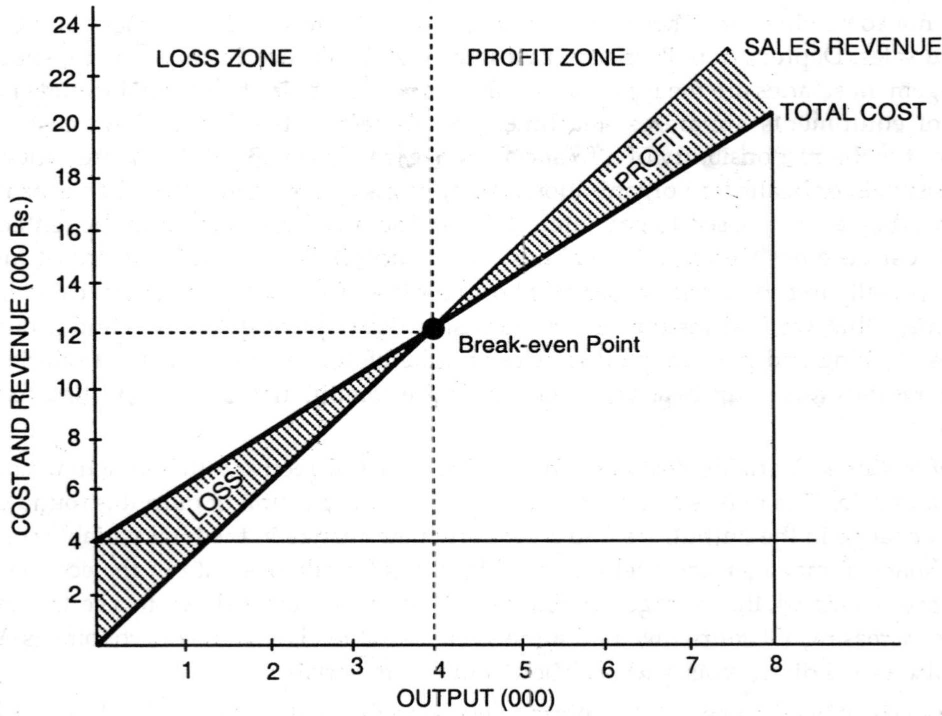

Fig. 10.2. Break-even Point

Of course, the hospitals are not supposed to make profits but at the same time, they are also not supposed to generate losses. To be more specific in the hospitals or healthcare organisations, we also find a provision that the patients or the users are offered free of charge or concessional services. It is quite natural that whatever the price or fees are charged from the patients are not even found cost-based in some of the special cases. This makes it essential that hospitals charge cost plus surplus from the affluent sections of the society so that losses on account of subsidised or free of charge services are adjusted. We don't find generation of profit a motive but even the generation of losses would also not be supported. With the help of break-even analysis, the hospitals come to know about the total costs of services offered and this helps them in adjusting the price structure. If we force hospitals or healthcare organisations to generate losses, the financial health would start deteriorating. Thus, a break-even analysis helps hospital managers in making the fee structure affordable. The process of adjustment helps hospitals in many ways.

In Fig. 10.2, the break-even point is the point at which the hospitals and healthcare organisations need to set their fee structure. It is neither supposed from them that they generate profits nor is expected from them that they would generate losses. Of course, the break-even point is not significant to the profit-making industries but specially for the no-profit making organisations, it is found to be the best strategic decision not only offering to the patients the quality healthcare services but in addition also paving copious avenues for the qualitative-cum-quantitative development of hospitals.

At the break-even volume, the total costs equal the total revenue. This is simply a geometric fact. The amount of loss or profit expected at any volume is the vertical distance between points on the total cost and revenue lines at that volume. The break-even volume is not the same as the standard volume used as a basis for determining overhead rates. The hospitals and healthcare organisations are supposed to subserve public interests and they need expensive inputs to improve the quality of their services. If in all the cases and for all the patients, they charge the fee structure at the break-even point, the task of implementing the schemes of modernisation, expansion, development would remain unfulfilled. This makes it essential that they charge a high fee structure from the affluent sections of the society found in a position to pay more but at the same time, charge less than the break-even point from the weaker sections of the society not in a position to afford even the cost based services. Whatever the losses they generate by offering free of charge and the concessional or subsidised services would be adjusted by charging more from the affluent sections and whatever the surpluses they get as revenues from the different sources would be used for development, modernisation and expansion.

The aforesaid facts make it clear that break-even point is the point at which the no-profit making organisations like hospitals and educational institutions safeguard their existence and whatever they generate above the point from charity, donations, grants, or other sources would enable them to march forward in the face of latest developments.

Project Planning

A project may be defined as any scheme, or a part of a scheme, for investing resources which can be analysed and evaluated or appraised as an independent unit. A project or a scheme can be subdivided into different parts for separate consideration and each of these parts would be a project if it can be analysed and evaluated as an independent unit. A project, is therefore, a work plan devised through scientific investigation and analysis to accomplish a set objective within a certain period. Thus, it is a course of action. It has its own objectives and it involves "one shot" or time-bound activities.

The experts have developed a self-contained and detailed technique for the formulation of project. Mathematical decision-making processes such as operation research makes it easier to evaluate systematically the alternative projects on the basis of their cost-benefit analysis. The boardrooms on the basis of a comparative analysis of the alternatives can study different alternatives and can pick up the best viable or feasible project. The process of project formulation is in a true sense a team work. To be more specific when we talk about the hospitals and healthcare organisations in a very natural way, our focus is on the instrumentality of hospital planners, architects and consultants who can show the right directions and the viable projects can be selected for implementation. The project manager bears the responsibility of planning, organising and controlling the activities involved in achieving the final objective.

Since we consider project as any item of investment which can be evaluated through cost-benefit analysis, the process of design consists of rejecting and accepting the alternatives. To maintain consistency in the process, we find administration of identical measures essential. The concerned technical authorities and the planners are to be influenced by the same rules and methods. This makes possible harmony in planning and evaluating the project. We agree with this view that maintaining harmony is found easier when we find organisations working with the motto of making profits but to be more specific in the hospitals and healthcare organisations, the task of maintaining harmony is found much more difficult because the organisations are supposed to work with the motto of subserving the social interests and more so are supposed to be very much instrumental in justifying their existence in the society by innovating the perception of quality.

Public Interests—A Criterion to Evaluate the Project

Here, we don't talk about the profit making organisations and therefore, our strategies would be a bit different. In the profit making organisations, we find profitability an important criterion for adoption and rejection of a project but here, we need an attitudinal change. We are supposed to assign an overriding priority to the social or public interests.

With the increasing importance of technologies in the healthcare services, we find a basic change in the nature and character of project to be found socially and environmentally friendly. In the Indian perspective, we find masses not in a position to afford the expensive healthcare services and this makes it essential that the hospital planners, architects, consultants, technical experts and management experts deliberate upon the social considerations and computation of social costs on a priority basis so that the services are also found pocket-friendly. Keeping in view the disease profile of a particular catchment area, we need a change in the nature and size of a healthcare project. The prime focus is to be on the intensity of public interest.

Of course in a developed society where the masses have high level of income can afford the expensive healthcare services but in the Indian context, the services are to be made affordable to the masses. When we find profit a criterion, the formulation of a project is found easier because in that case, the decisions are influenced by profitability. But when we find public/social interests as a criterion for project formulation, the task of hospital planners and architects becomes much more complicated.

The cost-benefit analysis happens to be an important criterion for approving or rejecting a project. It is right to mention here that to be more specific in the healthcare sector, we need to conceptualise the perception of benefit in a bit different way. To put it in another way, the social costs or the losses on account of increasing social burden due to free of charge or concessional services to the selected segments of the society would be the base for finalising the project. In this context, it is significant to mention that for the implementation of a project, the hospitals or healthcare organisations would need huge fund and later on for maintenance and replacement, they would need additional allocation. This makes it essential that the hospitals generate revenues from the project already implemented so that the process of development keeps on moving. It is against this background that the hospitals or the healthcare organisations are required to take the support of break-even analysis. They need to maintain the break-even point which would enable them to make provisions for the maintenance, development and expansion.

The feasibility is a term that gravitates the attention of hospital planners and architects. The perception of feasibility is required to be conceptualised by them in a bit different way. In the profit-making organisations, if we find a stage of loss or the goods or services not helping an organisation to make profits, they find the products (goods or services) unremunerative and don't prefer to continue the same because this is to make them financially sick. In the no-profit making organisations, we don't find profitability the term to be used for studying the feasibility because such a perception is to jeopardise the social orientation and mission. Hence, the hospitals and healthcare organisations in the very context are required to link feasibility/banefit with the public/social interests. A project is found to be feasible if the process of maintenance, replacement, development and expansion is not to be slowed down. They need to generate revenues till that point, specially from the affluent sections of the society. It is in this context that we find a discriminating pricing/fee strategy suitable for hospitals and healthcare organisations. We find focus on the same in the marketing of hospital services while going through the problem of price mix.

The aforesaid facts make it clear that project planning requires professional excellence. It is not only the excellence of a hospital planner or architect but even the world class professionalism of a manager or a financial adviser helping the planners and architects in formulating a project that is found socially affordable vis-a-vis and financially viable. The viability is not to be confused by making the ways for generating profits rather to the point which helps a manager in making the development an ongoing process. The multidimensional developments in the medical sciences make it essential that hospitals and healthcare organisations make possible frequency in initiating the process of qualitative improvements by innovating the perception of quality which sets international standards and enriches the potentials of hospitals to offer world class services and the process keeps on moving.

Project Life Cycle

The life cycle of a project helps a manager/planner/architect and a financial adviser in many ways. An idepth study of the project life cycle provides to them necessary information related to the elimination of a project in the face of multidimensional changes. It is against this background that we go through the project life cycle. A project normally passes through three distinct phases.

1. *The Pre-investment Stage:* This stage of a project covers setting of aims and objectives, forecasting of demand, selection of best means or strategies to fulfil objectives, evaluation of the nature and types of materials/inputs required for the project, projection of financial plan, cost-benefit analysis and finally, the pre-investment appraisal. In view of the results of the different studies, the idea may or may not be converted into a concrete investment proposal or scheme on

which the hospitals or healthcare organisations can base their investment decision. It is a stage that helps hospitals in identifying the benefits of the project for the segments or the catchment areas to be the beneficiaries. Of course, we find financial requirements an important consideration specially for the hospitals because like other organisations and other projects, it is not possible for the hospitals to generate revenues after the implementation and therefore, the promoters and financiers would find it difficult to extend to them the financial support.

2. *The Construction Phase;* The second stage of the project life cycle is the construction phase which is found based on the results of the first phase. After making the investment decision, it is pertinent that the hospital planners, designers, architects and consultants think about the phase of construction. This includes availability of land and buildings, plant and machinery, transport and communications, acquisition of materials and supplies, organising, marketing and managing personnel or so to develop a project which would be successful in achieving the set objectives.

3. *The Normalisation Phase:* The third and final phase of a project is to utilise the assets created in the second phase. Our focus is here on processing inputs for getting outputs. Since we talk about the healthcare services, it is pertinent that in the second phase, we are careful to the cost and time constraints. We find a time frame and a budgetary limit. It is much more impact generating that the construction phase has been completed within budgetary and time limits because this would help hospitals in making possible cost-effectiveness in the process. The gap between the construction and normalisation phase is to be minimised so that the projects switch on the process of offering the promised quality of services to the patients or the users.

A project related to the establishment of a special unit offering the world class services to the potential users is found assuming an outstanding significance in the healthcare sector. To be more specific in the Indian context, it is pertinent that hospitals and healthcare organisations, both the government as well as the private, assign due weightage to the projects found of mass use. This necessitates an indepth study of the specialities of a command or catchment area so that the nature and character of the disease profile is studied and the projects prove their instrumentality in achieving the set objectives or aims.

Feasibility Studies

We consider the project a dream unless it succeeds in taking a final shape as per the plan. The no-profit making organisations like hospitals are not supposed to expect profits from the said projects, rather the services aimed at are to be translated into actions. However, feasibility studies become important because they adopt different criteria for declaring a project feasible or viable. There are a number of areas to be taken up while undertaking feasibility studies. The technological requirements as per the hospital architects and consultants and technical feasibility related to the location, layout and economic feasibility studies dealing with the demand generated by the potential users of the services become significant in the very context. So far as the commercial feasibility studies are concerned, to be more specific, the healthcare organisations either government or private are not supposed to assign any weightage to the same. The feasibility studies help an organisation in getting an idea about the viability of the project. In almost all the profit-making organisations, we find commercial viability an important consideration while declaring a project viable but if we talk about hospitals, they need an attitudinal change and to keep due consideration the intensity of benefits to be made available to the users of the services. On the basis of feasibility studies, a feasibility report is prepared.

Feasibility Report

- At the outset, it is pertinent that we mention in the feasibility report, the demand position or the uses of the project for the potential users or patients. The relevance or rationale of the project for the concerned command area is the most significant aspect to be more specific in the healthcare services.
- While preparing feasibility report, the government policies related to the development and weightage to the healthcare sector is also to be mentioned.
- It is also significant that a feasibility report clarifies the regulatory support or constraint because while important technologies, if needed, the foreign exchange regulations are not to stand as a barrier.
- In addition, it is also important that while preparing a project feasibility report, we also mention the relevance of the project to the command area and focus on the worldwide developments in the process.
- The project in a very natural way would require a number of materials and the supporting infrastructural facilities and therefore, the availability of required materials would also be mentioned in the feasibility report.
- The availability of quality people or the human resources would also be mentioned in the feasibility report. If the new project is based on the new generation of technologies, the trained personnel would be required for this purpose.
- Factors favourable for location or providing the benefits to the maximum number of population would also be mentioned in the feasibility report.
- Cost of the project and sources of finance are also to be clarified in the feasibility report.
- This is found significant because in the hospitals or healthcare organisations, the financing of a project becomes difficult.
- The availability of land and buildings and the infrastructural facilities required for project implementation are also to be mentioned in the feasibility report.
- The cash-flow statement is also to be produced.
- The management of hospital waste related to the project is required to be clarified because hazardous biomedical waste would generate environmental problems.
- The future prospects of the existing project are also to be mentioned in the feasibility report because a project may gain its popularity in due course due to mass awareness that is not right now generated.
- The feasibility report requires to clarify the instrumentality of project in the context of public interests.

The aforesaid aspects need due attention while preparing the feasibility report. It is right to mention that based on the feasibility report, the top management of hospitals or the boardrooms would be required to make the policy decisions regarding the suitability of the project, its usefulness and implementation. A hospital planner and architect while preparing the feasibility report would also be required to clarify the names of interested parties or segments in the project to be implemented. May be that hospitals or the healthcare organisations have been seeking the cooperation of banks or financial institutions for financing. In this context, it is pertinent that in the feasibility report, we mention the name of that bank. May be that hospitals have generated internal funds for that very purpose and this is also to be made clear. The main thing in the process is to make it clear that from where the required finance would be made available. Since we go through the problem of healthcare services, it is also possible that a social organisation or a global organisation or a corporation or even an individual accepts the responsibility of financing. Sponsored projects don't create any problem because the financial constraint is not to obstruct the process of implementation.

We can't negate the fact that scheduling is found to be an important aspect for the time-honoured and cost-effective implementation of the project. The scheduling focuses our attention on an action plan or a time frame for the implementation of the project. A time-bound action plan helps to make the implementation process cost-effective. Not only this, but it is also to increase the real value of the project for the concerned or related segment. If we avoid scheduling, the process of implementation would be made much more complicated and the delayed implementation of the project can't be denied. This would also increase financial involvement because the rising inflationary pressure would increase the cost and the cost economy an important dimension of project implementation would not be made possible. It is against this background that we assign due weightage to scheduling and consider it an important dimension of the feasibility studies.

Management of Books and Accounts

Book-Keeping: It is a systematic and an orderly method of recording financial transactions and for this purpose, certain primary books of accounts are maintained. The objects of book-keeping are to ascertain the financial position of an undertaking as to the amounts owing to the creditors, the amounts owed by debtors, the amount and the nature of assets, such as cash, bank, debtors, investments, land, building and equipment, stores, etc., the amount and the nature of its liabilities, the amount of its gains or losses, the amount of its capital as represented by assets over liabilities. Recording of the dual effect of the transaction is known as double entry system and of one effect termed as a single entry. The transactions posted on the credit side or right side of the journal are sale of or decrease in asset value, increase in liabilities, increase in income and decrease in expenses. The transactions posted on the debit side of the journal or ledger are the purchase of or increase in asset value, decrease in liabilities, decrease in income and increase in expenses.

The hospitals managed and controlled by government follow the principles of single entry system and cash accounting while private hospitals follow the principles of double entry system and accrual accounting. It is important to mention that in the cash accounting system, the revenues are recognised only when cash is received. It is just an operating statement which is considered to be a summary of all receipts and payments and a balance sheet that is not true and that does not reflect the correct position. The accrual system of accounting recognises all revenues earned even though cash is not received and all expenses incurred during the time period even though payment is not made. With the motto of providing necessary qualities of completeness, accuracy and meaningfulness in accounting, the accrual basis is found significant.

We are well aware of the fact that in the government hospitals, the financial powers are delegated to different heads of department as well as to the administrative heads. The criteria for expenditure are proper vouching and propriety. In a government hospital, we find propriety playing an important role while incurring the expenditure.

Book-Keeping Cycle: The cycle of book-keeping begins with the recording of the transactions from the posting which is called journalising. After the completion of the journal, the informations mentioned in the journal are transferred to the ledger. The process of transfer is known as posting.

Books of Accounts and Registers: In respect of double entry system, the following primary books of accounts are maintained:

- Cash Book
- Journal (General and Special)
- Ledger (General and Subsidiary)

Cash Book: All cash receipts and cash payments are recorded chronologically in the cash book. The opening and closing balances are also recorded. The closing cash balance is tallied with the physical cash balance at the end of each day. There are two types of cash books maintained, viz., scroll cash book and main cash book. A scroll book is maintained by cashier who records all cash received and issues receipts and all cash payments against approved vouchers. The cheques received are also recorded. We also find a main cash book maintained by the finance section where on the basis of the same record, the cash receipts and payment vouchers are recorded and the closing cash balance is arrived at and tallied with the cash balance. In the main cash book, a column may be provided for recording the bank transactions. A reconciliation statement is prepared periodically between the bank balance as per the cash book and balance as per bank statement on the day of reconciliation. We call it in the accounting literature as Bank Reconciliation Statement.

In the hospitals, to provide conveniences to the patients, the cash may be collected at different points and this necessitates tightening of the safety and security measures. But there must be a main cash office to which the cash collected at various points is remitted. The provision for a Fidelity Guarantee Insurance is found essential for all who handle cash and besides, a Money in Till which is a compartment or drawer in a chest or Money in Transit Insurance for cash which remains in cash box or chest. Adequate safety and security measures are needed to minimise the possibilities of theft. It is essential to verify cash balance as per scroll book each and everyday. The cash collecting counters are required to be careful to the serial numbers of cash memos/receipts to be prepared in duplicate/triplicate.

Petty/Imprest Cash: *You* are required to avoid the petty payments from the main cash and for that petty cash is to be maintained separately. The petty cash vouchers are consolidated and accounted in the main cash book periodically and the total amount spent is reimbursed to petty cash. To be more specific in a large-sized hospital, the impress amounts may be given to the purchase officer or to a departmental head. The accounting process would be like petty cash.

Accounts Receivable

Generally, we don't find hospitals allowing credit to individuals but the selected organisations and institutions or the large-sized users of the services are allowed. It is the discretion of a medical superintendent or a hospital manager to allow or not to allow credit facilities or installment-payment facility. The patients are required to make payment of their bills before they are discharged from hospital and this minimises the need for maintaining the accounts receivable ledger of discharged patients and to expedite the process of recovery. The accounts are maintained for those patients who have just been admitted and are not supposed to leave the hospitals immediately. We find provision of collecting advances at the time of admission or registration. For the day-to-day requirements, we find issue of Charge Slips for X-ray, laboratory, operations, etc. The Billing section maintains and generally on weekly basis, the bills are sent to the concerned patients. This minimises the pressure on patients and at the same time, also makes available funds to the hospitals for the day-to-day expenses. Separate journals are maintained for in-patients and out-patients. Any items related to free care or subsidised services are posted in the general ledger. We find justifications for offering the concessional or subsidised or free of charge services to the poor sections of the society. In addition, the hospital staff is also offered free or subsidised services. All the concessions are approved by the medical superintendent or even by a hospital manager if we find a provision like this. It is right that all concessions are maintained in Patients Concessions Journals with a detailed address of patients. Periodically, a review of accounts receivable is essential.

Accounts Payable: Sundry Creditors or Accounts payable are related to the supplies bought on credit. In this context, we credit the sundry creditors and debit the supplies (goods) or services. When payment is made, the creditors account is debited and cash or bank is credited. It is right to mention that we find Accounts Department responsible for making payments against accepted supplies or services or against accounts approved by the competent authorities. At the time of payment, the necessary endorsement is found essential. Before making payments, the following aspects draw attention:

- It is to be ascertained that the price, terms, quality and quantity of supplies or services for which the payment is to be made is found in accordance with the purchase order. This makes it essential that a copy of the purchase order is made available in the Accounts Department.
- The certification by the stores is found essential to ascertain that the materials have been supplied. A copy of the note related to the supply of materials is also to be made available to the Accounts Department.
- It is also to be verified that the other charges mentioned in the bill are correct. The amount of sales tax charged is also to be verified.
- Besides, the computation is also to be checked.
- It is essential that all the payments against invoices or bills are made by Accounts Payee Cheque.
- All the purchases are to be entered in the Purchase Journal.

Pay Roll: We are well aware of the fact that in hospitals or healthcare organisations, the staff salaries are the largest single head of expense. This makes it essential that different items like pay-scales, increments, dearness and other allowances and necessary deductions like PF, Advance, House Rent, Income Tax, Premium of LIC, etc. are checked. Payment records are to be maintained in a right way. We also find Individual Learnings Record for knowing the total earnings of an individual and his/her accumulated earnings. If one person is found working in more than one department, his/her salary is to be allocated to each department, such as if a surgeon spends 50 per cent of his/her working hours in surgery, 25 per cent in wards and rest 25 per cent in OPD, then his/her salary would be allocated to the operating room, inpatient services (medical room) and OPD.

Capital and Revenue Expenditure

In this head, we talk about the expenditure incurred for the acquisition of assets for managing the services of hospitals, such as land and buildings, equipment and apparatus, instruments, furniture, etc. Besides, we also include the expenditure incurred for goods or services for managing the hospitals and the benefits of the same would not remain confined to a particular year but would be carried over from one accounting period to another, such as salaries, taxes, interest, consumable materials, repairs and maintenance or so. We call them Revenue Expenditure or Operating Expenditure. It is also to be clarified that such an expenditure related to a period is set-off against the income or earnings of the said period. We also find borderline cases where it becomes difficult to ascertain the expenditure as Capital or Revenue. In this context, if we find the benefits or uses of such an expenditure to continue even in the coming years, the expenditure is treated as Capital Expenditure.

We treat depreciation as a loss and therefore, we treat it as an expense. Of course, it is a nominal loss. It is essential to record the assets at cost because we use them for hospitals. In this respect, it is necessary that a charge for the utilisation of such services is debited to the operating expenses. The value of the fixed asset is reduced to the extent of depreciation charged. The net value is shown in the Balance Sheet. The cumulative depreciation is deducted from the original value of asset at the end of every year. The amount charged as depreciation is generally invested in a Sinking Fund which enables hospitals in making use of the same when the asset is completely depreciated. It is against this background that in a rising market, we find replacement cost more than the original price of the asset. We are well aware of the fact that a number of minor equipments are used such as basins, medical and surgical instruments, trays and baskets. Because we do not find them of permanent nature, we call them Minor Equipments. We also charge them at the time of incidence of expenditure taking place and keep only quantity inventory of the items. The inventory of the available equipment is taken and the cost of the same is credited at the end of the year. Alternatively, we also debit the cost to the Minor Equipment and treat the them as an asset. The inventory is taken at the end of the year. We also find in a few cases that the payment is made towards expenses like taxes and insurance covering a period beyond the accounting period. We treat them as Prepaid Expenses and classify them as an Asset.

Chart of Accounts: We find it the listing of account titles with numerical symbols used for the compilation of data concerning assets, liabilities, revenue and expenditure. The main purpose of chart accounting is to make available a planned segregation of business transactions. The process of numerical coding is found useful. The following plus points testify the same.

- For locating the accounts quickly, we find it significant.
- For identifying and remembering the account titles, it is impact generating.
- For classifying the transactions, it is convenient.
- For reducing the amount of time needed to identify and record the accounting data, it is effective.
- For facilitating the use of mechanical Book-keeping methods, it is useful.
- For helping management in planning and control, it is a guide.

Department Numbering: In the mechanised system of accounting, we find it of much use. It facilitates easy identification of income or expenditure to the department. The principles governing the classification are found relatively simple. Each department is given a number and any income or expenditure is not only assigned the numerical code but also identified with the department. In this context, a classified schedule of wards, departments and services which make up the complete organisation of the hospital is made at first. The classification is made keeping in view the units for the budgetary control, cost centres and the revenue centres. As for example, suppose, account 501 represents for salaries. If 110 is the Departmental code for X-ray, then the Account 501/110 would be identified with salaries related to the X-ray Department.

We find the Chart of Accounts and the Departmental Numbering helpful to be more specific when the accounting system is found mechanised.

Revenue Centres and Cost Centres

Revenue Centres are the beginning point in the system of hospital accounting. We find the centres significant because this makes the ways for the establishment of cost centres. The recording process makes it essential that the revenues are recorded in a fashion that makes possible identification with the concerned unit of hospital. We find the subdivision of revenue according to the type of patient, such as in-patient and out-patient. In hospitals, we find the revenue centres very numerous where the separation of daily-patient service, professional service and nursing service is found necessary. In the daily patient service, we, for example mention Paediatric, in the professional service-operating room or recovery room and in nursing service-laboratory or blood bank.

Cost Centres are established to parallel the revenue centres. This makes it clear that for each revenue centre, we find a cost centre. The number of cost centres is found very large. The centres follow the organisational lines and are found an important base for budget and planning. They also follow the operational lines specially to allocate costs to revenue centres for the determination of full cost of each service offered. We find the cost centre a centre of activity within the operations of the hospital. It is supposed to collect the cost separately. We find cost centres playing an incremental role in budgeting because it provides a logical activity for planning costs or for matching costs against plan especially for control and supervision purposes. We also find it established for pricing purposes providing a logical costing activity for allocation to revenue producing centres.

Financial Statements and Reports

The financial reports represent the end results. A number of methods and records for accounting have been discussed and we find all of them with the ultimate motto of preparing financial statements and reports which focus our attention on Income and Expenditure Statement and the Balance Sheet. We are well aware of the fact that we find both of them very much instrumental in making available to an organisation information related to financial performance of the hospital. We also agree with this view that the entire hospital accounting is aimed at providing information to the management for making right decisions.

Income and Expenditure Statement: The first step for preparing the Income and Expenditure Statement is to take out a trial balance of debit and credit from the general ledger accounts. The Income and Expenditure Statement reflects the results of the hospital operations for a particular period. The details are furnished in schedules. It is also essential to furnish the actuals of previous year as well as the budget for the said period. The financial indicators like In-patient Income and

Expenditure per patient day, out-patient income and expenditure per patient are given at the end of the Income and Expenditure Statement.

Balance Sheet: A Balance Sheet represents the financial position as of a specific date. We call it a statement of assets and liabilities and the assets, fixed or current are given on the right side and net worth is given on the left side. It reflects what the institution owes on that date. The figures are generally given against each classification of main account.

Budgetary Control

We find budgetary control as establishment of budgets relating to responsibilities of executives to the requirements of a policy and the continuous comparison of actuals with budgeted results to secure the objectives or to provide a basis for revision. For the efficient administration of finance, it is essential to have a close coordination of Income and Expenditure. It is considered to be a process of defining and establishing yardsticks with a view to recurring adherence to plan or revise it. Of course, we have gone through the problem of formulation of an ideal budget but this is not the only thing that we need for an effective financial administration. We find budgetary control fruitful if—

- A consistent and close watch over the budget is given due weightage;
- A continuous review of actuals with the budget is made frequent and deviation in the actual performance is analysed;
- Remedial action is taken for improving the operating performance as and when we find deviation;
- Efforts are taken to revise the budget if the changing conditions and circumstances necessitate so;
- Active participation of personnel responsible for the implementation of budget is essential.

Standard Costing

We find Standard Costing an estimated cost prepared in advance of production or supply, correlating a technical specification of materials and labour to the price and wage rates estimated for a selected period of time with the addition of an apportionment of overhead expenses estimated for the same period. It is the preparation of standard costs to clarify the financial results of a business particularly by the measurements of variations of actual costs from standard costs and the analysis of the causes of the variations for the purpose of maintaining maximum efficiency. The standard costing is aimed at controlling the cost, not only its ascertainment. We find control effective when standards of performance and actual costs are measured and compared and variances are tapped. Control with the help of Standard Costing is exercised on the principle of Management by Exception.

Standard cost may be computed on the basis of the study of material requirements and labour based on time and motion study. Standard cost may be fixed for some of the heads like laundry, canteen, pharmacy, maintenance, service department, etc. Budgetary control and Standard costing, no doubt, are the two distinct operations and therefore, each one can exist without other. However, if we blend the two optimally, the most effective instrument of cost control would be in your hand. Of course, we find some of us treating both the terminologies synonymous but undoubtedly enough, we find budget a broader term than standard cost. To put it another way, budget may apply to a department whereas standard cost applies to an operation. In hospitals, the standard costs are found fixed for laundry, kitchen, service departments, etc. Here, we need to be careful specially regarding specifications and standards. Since the hospitals or healthcare organisations need to make possible cost economy and quality in totality, we find both of them impact generating.

Cost Ascertainment and Cost Containment

Cost Ascertainment

Cost ascertainment is related to cost finding. In some of the hospitals, we find cost based on the size of deficit generated in the hospitals. They charge for their services in the face of deficit with the motto of bridging over the annual deficit. We find costing an important dimension related to pricing on which we find an indepth focus in the next chapter on marketing the hospital services. The costing system needs to provide for the ascertainment or finding of full cost of all departments producing revenue so that the cost of each service is computed. Full cost consists of direct cost of the department and the allocated costs of the General Service Departments. In this context, the first step is to identify the departmental expenses, such as salaries and wages, printing and stationery, travelling allowances but expenses like depreciation are to be distributed on a rational basis as mentioned below:

- The depreciation of building would be on the basis of floor area.
- The lighting charges would be ascertained on the basis of the floor area or wattage of the amps.
- The insurance charges would be on the basis of the value of insurable plant and equipment.
- The heating cost would be ascertained on the basis of the cubic feet.

After the ascertainment of direct costs, the next step is related to the allocation of accumulated costs of the service departments to the revenue earning departments. We find such allocation on the basis of the amount of services rendered to other departments. The expenses on house keeping would be on the basis of square footage, the laundry expenses could be on the basis of poundage of pieces, the dietary would be on the basis of number of meals, the nursing administration would be on the basis of salaries and wages of nurses and the general administration would be on the basis of number of staff or the total expenses. We call this method of distribution as step-down method. The direct costs are generally controlled by the departmental heads but the indirect costs allocated can't be controlled by the departmental heads. The cost data would help management in deciding on the rates to be charged for the services rendered.

The cost ascertainment in addition to a basis for fixing the fees also helps to identify the unfair practices in each department, such as the additional technicians may be hired for the laboratory because of the increase in the actual unit of the service. The cost system with a mix of budgetary control would be of outstanding significance to the management. The costs for each department and for each service can be budgeted and the actuals could be compared. It is right to mention that a study of variances would prove to be an effective tool in the hands of management for control and supervision.

Cost Containment

Cost Containment is a process of making possible cost economy by reducing costs or by controlling costs. To be more specific in the hospitals and healthcare services, we find cost containment significant to make the services affordable or pocket-friendly. It is quite natural that we find increase in the costs of materials and labour. There are a number of factors to influence hike or escalation. The increasing inflationary pressure is found very much instrumental in increasing the costs of materials used in the process.

We can't negate the fact that the costs if made optimal would make the services affordable. This requires professional excellence while exercising the following measures. You are not supposed to sacrifice quality but to regulate costs. You need not to perceive that higher quality costs more.

1. *Capital Controls, Utilisation Controls and Budget Controls:* You need more professional excellence in controlling costs because you have to contain costs without sacrificing quality. Eliminating unnecessary expenses, minimising the number of staff, increasing the rate of productivity of biomedical equipment and apparatus, making possible operational efficiency are some of the measures to be effective in minimising the costs. You need to minimise the investigations not needed, you need to minimise the expensive drugs/medicines not essential and these things would also help you in minimising the costs. One thing you need to remember that acceleration of productivity is linked to the optimisation of costs and if you succeed in the process, you, in a very natural way succeed in increasing the productivity of all the assets used in the process of diagnosing and treating the patients. How to increase the productivity of hospital employees is an important problem before a hospital manager. We find incentives, financial and non-financial, playing a commanding role in accelerating productivity because this is found effective in motivating the hospital employees. By making possible total motivation, viz., financial and non-financial incentives, improving the behavioural profile and departmental relationships, increasing the quality of physical environment at the workplace and improving the quality of environment at their living places make the ways for the development of quality-people, professionally-sound people and personally-committed people who open doors for optimal cost and high productivity. You are also required to assign due weightage to ethical dimensions of hospital personnel for controlling the overall costs of healthcare services.

2. *Cost Reduction by Optimising the Operational Expenses:* In this context, it is also important that you bring down the costs by substitution, value analysis, efficient purchase and sound material management, resource utilisation and use of reusables, elimination of wastage and pilferages. We can't negate that in a majority of the hospitals, the mismanagement of materials proves to be instrumental in increasing the costs. The misuse of materials, increasing cases of theft and pilferages can be checked if we have ethically sound hospital personnel. Optimising inventory is essential to reduce the operational expenses.

3. *Cost Containment by Other Measures:* In addition to the aforesaid measures, you also need to maintain economy in supplies and expenditure, standardisation, ABC analysis, inventory control, proper material management, proper contracts, good security and vigilance, proper scheduling and patient services, controlling the building costs, maintaining the equipment, planning of facilities are some of the measures to be effective in the process of maintaining cost economy.

4. *Promoting Sophisticated Technologies:* We agree with this view that the cost-effectiveness is a challenging task but at the same time, an essential condition, especially in the Indian perspective where masses need affordable services. It is in this context that we make a strong advocacy in favour of technology-driven diagnostic and treatment measures. Of course, the expensive equipment would make the process capital intensive but the potentials of hospitals would be increased and the duration of treatment would considerably be minimised. With the use of sophisticated biomedical equipment and apparatus, our requirements of hospital employees would come down. We can't make hospitals and healthcare organisations a labour-intensive industry.

Internal Audit

You need an automatic built-in-system to make it sure that everything in your hospital is OK. The financial decisions have shown positive effects and the cases of mismanagement and irregularities have been regulated. The diversion of funds has not been practiced and provisions like depreciation, repair and replacement have been as per the plan. It is in this context that we talk about a tool of financial management that helps you in many ways. We are well aware of the fact that internal audit is an in-built provision in an organisation for regulating financial irregularities and frauds.

The internal audit makes provision for checking of cash book and physical cash and other books of accounts, reviewing of bank reconciliation statement, checking of all payment vouchers, reviewing purchases and inventory, accounting of assets and safeguarding of assets against defalcation or other irregularities, ascertaining the reliability of statistical data, reviewing the performance of each centre, ensuring proper utilisation of the resources of hospitals and reviewing of the policies and procedures of hospitals related to finance.[7]

This makes it essential that a financial manager/adviser focuses his/her attention on the following:

1. *Cash Receipts and Payments:* In almost all the hospitals, we find transactions related to cash occupying a place of significance because it is a sensitive point where we find scope for misappropriation and frauds. The points where we find collection of cash need due attention and for this, we need to verify the bank reconciliation statement very carefully. The verification of cash at counters is also to be done minutely.

2. *Purchases and Stores:* We are well aware of the fact that of late, in modern hospitals, a number of expensive materials are used for diagnosis and treatment of patients. This makes the materials and purchase processes very much volatile. There are a number of avenues where financial irregularities can be promoted. We consider it a vulnerable point and need to divert our attention so that the irregularities are checked. The purchases of drugs, biomedical equipment and apparatus and expensive machines constitute not less than 40 per cent of the total budget. The purchasing processes, the payment methods, the inventories, the issues and the uses or misuses of hospital materials are some of the points where you need a rigid control. You are required to make a scrutiny of purchases in the face of quotations and specifications mentioned therein, stock on hand, outstanding orders or so. A periodical review of inventories is found important. You need to make it sure that proper documentation is made for the materials/items ordered and accepted and the rates.

3. *Free of Charge and Subsidised Services:* In almost all the hospitals and healthcare organisations, we find a provision and accordingly the poor or needy segment is offered free of charge and concessional or subsidised services. You need to make possible a continuous checking to ascertain that the free of charge or subsidized services are offered to the needy or deserving persons. Since we find misuse of this provision and it is related to finance which is to influence the financial health of hospitals, it is to be given due weightage especially while undertaking internal checking. The deprived sections need the concesssional or free of charge services on a priority basis and therefore, the provisions are not to be misused.

4. *Care on the Missing Charges:* We find possibilities of missing charges because it is possible that the nursing staff fails to make the required notations with respect to charges or forget to send the Charge Slips for investigations which may result into huge financial losses. This necessitates to evolve a system to make possible a control.

5. *Maintenance and Repair of Machinery and Equipment:* We also find scope for the misuse of biomedical equipments and apparatus in the hospitals. This makes it essential that a logbook is there and the data related to down-time are recorded. The equipments and machines are maintained, repaired as per the defined norms so that the rate of depreciation is minimised and the uses of equipments and machines are made rational. Since we find operation theatres making a large scale use of equipments and apparatus, you are required to make it sure that the misuse of the said assets of hospitals is regulated.

6. *Maintenance of Vehicles:* We also find it a vulnerable point in hospitals where the vehicles of hospitals and healthcare organisations have been found misused by the hospital staff. To be more specific in the government hospitals, we find it on a very large scale. This increases the maintenance and operation bill and to increase the financial pressure on the hospitals. It is in this context that we need to maintain a logbook for all the vehicles of hospitals. The private use of hospital vehicles is to be checked.

7. *Misuse of Infrastructure:* We can't negate the fact that by and large, in almost all the hospitals, the infrastructural facilities like, power, water, transportation, communications and other facilities are misused by the hospital staff. The increasing bill on infrastructure is to be checked and this requires a control.

8. *Boxes and Crates:* Of late, we find the boxes and crates supplied by the distributors or manufacturers of domestic use. Since the empty cartons, boxes and crates are found in a very large number, this requires auction selling of these items on a monthly interval. On the one hand, the problem related to the management of hospital waste would be minimised while on the other hand, you will also get some money that would increase revenue position of hospitals.

9. *Gift Items:* To be more specific, the private hospitals receive a number of gift items offered by charitable trusts or even individuals or corporations. So far as the purchases are concerned, we are found careful but in respect of gift items, we fail in taking the due care. This makes it essential that you are particular to the gift items and make it sure that proper inventories have been done for the same.

The aforesaid facts make it clear that being a financial manager or a financial adviser, you are supposed to check financial irregularities and cases of frauds and internal auditing or checking would considerably help you in regulating the unfair practices. Since we find hospitals facing the problem of financial crunch, it is pertinent that we assign due weightage to internal audit. You are not supposed to make an additional arrangement for the same because you have financial experts and auditors to take care of the internal financial irregularities. The hospitals in general and the government hospitals in particular need to promote internal audit for making an appraisal of the quality of financial management you have. The internal check would contract avenues for financial irregularities if the hospitals have a team of professionally and ethically sound people.

Computer-driven Accounting System

The process of technological sophistication influences almost all functional areas of an organisation. This is due mainly to the fact that technologies have proved their excellence in the transformation process by establishing an edge over the human resources who invented them. In a true sense, we now live in an age of robot culture in which the services of human resources are found outliving their significance. It is against this background that we find frequent inventions and innovations in improving the quality of information and communication technologies and our efforts have also been proactive in building a superhighway for information. The information technology has now moved to be knowledge technology because we now find information superhighway very much instrumental in enriching our knowledge bank. The increasing contributions of computers in almost all the areas and almost for all the purposes has paved avenues for managing even the accounting system with the help of computers. A number of businesses small or large have been found using computers for their accounting work. Increasing accessibility to computers has been found expanding the knowledge transformation process.

We appreciate the contributions of computers in terms of memory, accuracy and speed but at the same time, also feel that forms and records used in the manual systems are visible whereas the operations that go on inside a computer are invisible. The processes of practising computers for accounting purposes are found changing frequently. The data are entered into a computer by means of an input device. The data may be originally prepared in the form of a punched card or a paper tape and the computer may obtain them by reading an invoice or other source document with an optical scanning device or they may even come from cash registers or other machines which are wired so that they automatically transmit data to the computer. As soon as data are inputted, the computer translates them into a code which is found to be a combination of electrical states. After that, we find computer working with the coded data. The storage units or memory units hold data until the computer needs to work on them. The internal storage which is found inside the computer itself is arranged in such a way that the computer can locate a needed piece of data very rapidly but such type of storage is found expensive. It is in this context that we find users preferring external storage devices. These devices may be disks which resemble photograph records in appearance; reels of magnetic tape; or other devices on which data are coded. The external storage is found less expensive than the internal storage but the data retrieval from the external storage is found slower. It is right to make it clear that the processing unit consists of three types, viz., internal storage, a control unit and an arithmetic unit. The control unit instructs the computer to operate as per the programme. It instructs the computer to move data into an out of storage, to perform operations on these data and sends the results either back to storage or to the operating unit. The arithmetic unit performs the actual calculations. The output unit provides the results of the calculation. The arithmetic operations are in the form of addition, subtraction, multiplication and division whereas the results of calculation provided by the output unit may be in the form of hard copy, such as a printed report, or in the form of a cathode (negative terminal) ray tube display which is the same as the tube in the television set. The financial experts have now been found advocating much in favour of promoting computers in the field of accountancy. An accounting system operated manually performs exactly in the same fashion as we find by a computer-driven accounting system.

In the context of accounting, we find computers performing the following:

- Storing data.
- Retrieving data from its storage.
- Performing arithmetic operations on the data.
- Comparing two items of data for equality or inequality.
- Storing data or rearranging data.
- Preparing reports.

It is right to mention that even in a computer-driven accounting system, the rules for debit and credit are exactly the same as in a manual system. The storage unit in a computer-driven system serves the same purpose as the ledger in the manual system. The numbers of account found listed in the manual chart of accounts are called file numbers in a computer-driven system. It is also significant to mention that in the computer literature, each amount is called a file. Since we find the process of storage in the computer inexpensive and reusable and because locating and using data held in storage is also inexpensive, it is easier to have a large number of account classifications and cross classifications in a computer-driven system. The process of making summaries of various types from these files is also found easier in a computer-driven accounting system.

The input in a computer-driven system corresponds to the journal in a manual-driven system. The programme contains the information on the proper files to be debited and credited for nearly all types of transactions, the same function as performed by the special journals in a manual-driven accounting system. The computer makes adjusting entries if it is given the necessary information as input. The computer would make closing entries and would also prepare financial statements without human intervention, if it has been programmed to do so. It is also significant to mention that the computer performs these functions without the equivalent of a trial balance or a work sheet because its programme causes it to perform automatically and even without error but the same step in a manually-driven system is performed with the help of a work sheet. Since we find computers doing arithmetic very rapidly besides the sorting and rearranging the data, the amounts can be added up in individual files and in addition, the various cross classifications that the management needs. It may also calculate percentage and other useful statistics much more rapidly and accurately than is feasible in a manual-driven accounting system.

In view of the above, it right to mention the following facts:

- The computer operates much more rapidly. Of course at the initial stage, we find entering data relatively slow but once the data are translated into computer code, the operations are performed thereafter at the speed of electricity which is approximately the speed of light. It is authenticated by the fact that the large hospital or healthcare organisations can provide managers with a detailed report of the activities or the transactions of the preceding day in each store and for the whole company, just the following morning. This speaks of the speed that we find in a computer-driven accounting system.

- So far as the accuracy is concerned, we find computer essentially 100 per cent accurate. Unlike human beings, we don't expect from computers the arithmetical errors or even copying errors.
- It is important to mention that mistakes are committed by us, specially while writing the computer programmes or while preparing input data.
- So far as the costs are concerned, we find computers operating much less expensively. But the cost of programming of computers to perform a certain operation is much greater than the cost of educating and training a human to perform the same operation. Unless the scale of operation is high, the cost-effectiveness in the process is not possible.
- The computer and its equipment costs more than the journals and ledgers prepared in a manual-driven accounting system.
- In addition, we don't find computer using a sense of judgement. In a true sense, it does exactly what is told to do by its programmer or the computer is just to follow your command.

The aforesaid facts make it clear that a big hospital would find the process of using computers for accounting purposes cost-effective but so far as the small hospitals or healthcare organisations are concerned, they find the process expensive. The preparation of a programme is found time consuming vis-a-vis expensive in effect. It is against this background that we find establishment of *"Service Bureau"* engaged in operating computers and developing programme to be useful for different purposes to different types of organisations. Each of the clients share these costs by paying a fee for the work done. For example, we find drug stores sending to a service bureau sales invoices and remittances from customers and the service bureau does the accounts receivable work for each store, including the preparation of statement that customers need to support claimed income tax deductions or medicare payments for drugs purchased. In the same fashion, the records required for a company's pay-roll are fairly complicated. It is against this background that we find a very few organisations using the services of service bureau for preparing pay-roll.

In Fig. 10.3, we find Schematic of a computer.

On the basis of Figure 10.3, it is right to mention that data are entered into a computer by means of an input device. The data may be originally prepared in the form of a punched card or a paper tape. The computer obtains them by reading an invoice or other source document with an optical scanning device or from the cash registers or other machines which are wired. As soon as the data are inputted, the computer translates them into a code.[8] The increasing sophistication in the information technology has been making possible a number of changes. The use of a computer-driven accounting system is found cost effective but only to the big hospitals.

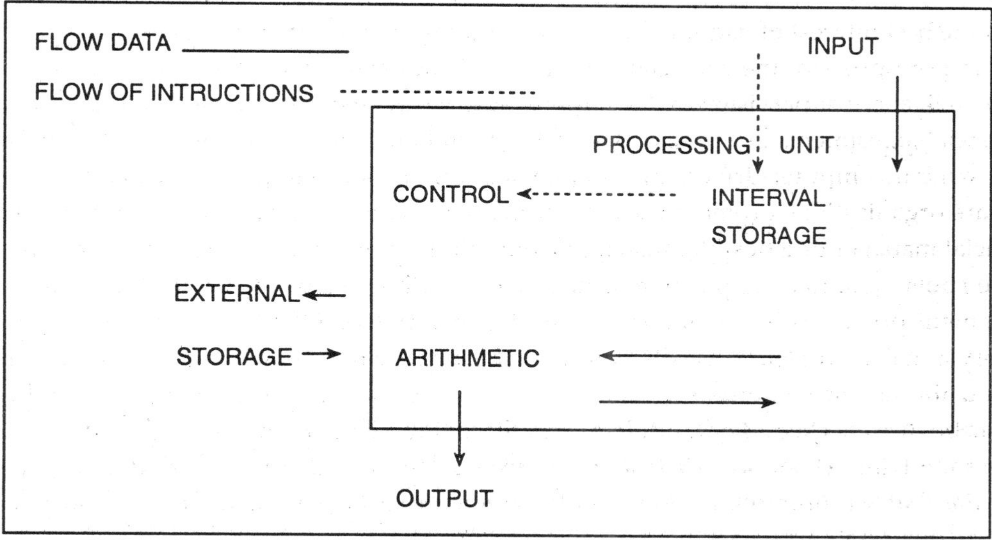

Fig. 10.3. A Schematic of a Computer

However, we need to promote the application of computers in the hospitals and healthcare organisations because this helps you in different ways. It is in this context that we advocate very strongly in favour of developing Health Management Information System and particularly the Health Management Financial Information System. Timely reporting and analysis of data from the system could also serve as an early warning of local outbreak of diseases so that appropriate interventions can be initiated. The Central Bureau of Health Intelligence is a nodal agency for the information system. Of late, we also find State Bureau of Health Intelligence being used by 13 states and union territories for sending district level information.[9] It is high time that the entire country is covered and all the data pertaining to Health and Family Welfare Programmes are collected, collated and reported from all the districts through the National Information Centre.

Way back in 1986, the Expert Committee on Health Manpower Planning, Production and Management (Bajaj Committee) recommended for an effective support to the health manpower management information system for managerial efficiency. Not only this, the management experts in general and the financial experts in particular felt the significance of information technology in managing finance efficiently. It was against this background that a number of large-sized organisations and even hospitals preferred computer-driven financial management in lieu of manual-driven financial management. It was realised that not only the presentation of accounts but the identification and detection of errors and frauds and financial irregularities would be much more effective specially with the help of information technology This also encouraged big hospitals to use computers for managing finance or the financial activities.

The aforesaid facts make it clear that computers play a very meaningful role in managing finance. To be more specific, the accounting practices and management of inventory are made more scientific and action-oriented if we use computers for that very purpose. Of late, we find even inexpensive computers which would be useful to the small hospitals. The main thing in the process is to perceive the usefulness of techniculture in a right fashion and to conceptualise the same in the best interest of users as well as the hospitals and healthcare organisations. If we keep on moving the process, the financial activities and the financial decisions would have a fresh look. We talk about supervision and control because we are required to know about the results of our financial investments in a project. The task is found much more difficult if it is manually done but the same if computer-driven, proves to be easier. This makes it essential that hospitals and healthcare organisations promote uses of information technology even for accounting purposes. A financial manager or a hospital manager would find it convenient to identify the errors, detect the sore spots, quantify the positive or negative contributions of personnel and finance in the development processes if we take the support of computers. Of late, we find management of inventory a major problem specially before the hospitals where a large number of materials are used and the use of computers would make the process action-oriented. Thus, the financial irregularities are checked, the fraudulent preferences are detected, the management of inventory is made sound, the accounting activities are made scientific and these positive contributions make it essential that we promote information technology and increase awareness of hospitals and healthcare organisations regarding the techniculture.

Working as a non-profit organisation, we find hospitals accepting the responsibility of making the society healthy and prosperous. It is in this context that we find productive use of funds occupying a place of outstanding significance, of course, in almost all the organisations but much more in the non-profit organisations. The emerging trends in information technology have been found influencing the accounting practices vis-a-vis the financial management. The modern developments have paved avenues for bechmarking, analysis of a competitive position, quality reporting and value-based management. Much more sophistication in information technology opens wider scope for making a microscopic analysis of the financial position. Hence, it is imperative that no only the tertiary hospitals but even the primary and secondary hospitals promote the use of new generation of computers which would help them in different ways.

e-accounting thus is becoming an integral part of managing hospital finance. The process has been gaining popularity and in the days to come, we expert wider application of computer-driven accounting in the hospitals and healthcare organisations. The increasing mismanagement of funds particularly in the government hospitals makes it essential that they promote computer-based operations which would help them in managing finance, materials and stores where we find possibilities for irregularities.

Formatting for Maintaining Books and Accounts in Hospitals

Maintaining books and accounts in hospitals is considered significant with the viewpoint of managing finance in a right way so that financial irregularities are controlled. During yester-decades, we have witnessed a number of changes in the accounting practices. The traditional methods of accounting have been found outliving their significance in the modern age. There is no doubt that information technology has firmly entrenched itself as a necessary tool for virtually every organization that is seriously working towards achieving the defined goals. Of late, we have also been found thinking in favour of digital tools which have been helping organisations in making decisions quickly. It is against this backdrop that we find even hospitals and healthcare organisations infusing new generation of technology for maintaining their books and accounts. The manual practices or techno-driven practices by and large follow the same format.

The following formats will provide to you an idea of the different areas where accounting practices for hospitals are to be followed. In different figures, we find different formats which have been shown from Figures 10.4 to Fig. 10.29.

10/4 Cash Memo
10/5 Cash Receipt
10/6 Cash Book
10/7 Bank Reconciliation Statement
10/8 Accounts Receivable Register (Patients)
10/9 In-patient Fee (Journal)
10/10 Out-patients Fee (Journal)
10/11 Statement of Collections and Concessions
10/12 Statements of Daily Collection (In-patient)
10/13 Statement of Daily Collection (Out-patient)
10/14 In-patient Bill
10/15 Purchase Register (Journal)
10/16 Pay Roll
10/17 Pay Roll (IEP)
10/18 Purchase Requisition
10/19 Purchase Order
10/20 Goods Received Note
10/21 Stores Requisition
10/22 Vehicles Logbook
10/23 Vehicles Maintenance Book
10/24 Income and Expenditure A/c
10/25 Budget (Salary)
10/26 Budget (Capital Expenditure)
10/27 Cash Budget
10/28 Proforma of Budget
10/29 Balance Sheet

Of course, you use a number of other format for maintaining books and accounts but the aforesaid format found of general use would help you in managing and supervising the workings of finance department which would minimise the possibilities of financial irregularities and fraudulent preferences at the very initial stage. There is no doubt in it that of late, we use computers even for managing and maintaining books and accounts but the aforesaid format would help you even in developing filing and programming to promote a computer-driven accounting system.

Name of the Hospital ____________

No. ____________ **Cash Memo**

Name ____________ Date ____________

Hospital No. ____________ Department ____________

Serial No.	Particulars	Rs.
1.		
2.		
3.		
4.		
5.		
6.		
7.		
Rs. Total		

Received Rs. ____________ Cashier Signature

CASH MEMO

You find cash memo an authentic paper prepared in duplicate/triplicate. It is to help you in collecting cash from the related party or parties. You are required to be careful of the serial number of the cash memo issued to the different collecting counters.

Fig. 10.4. Cash Memo

Name of the Hospital

Cash Receipt

Serial No. ____________ Date ____________

Received from ____________

Amount in words Rs. ____________

By Cash/Cheque/DD ____________

Credit Card

Towards ____________

Account No. ____________

Rs. ____________

Cashier Signature

CASH RECEIPT

The cash receipt is issued against the amount received at your counters by the cashier who is a competent authority to collect cash. The amount is received in cash/cheque/DD or of late, we also find use of credit cards for this purpose. It is required to be prepared in triplicate.

You are required to make it sure that Sl. No. is noted.

Fig. 10.5. Cash Receipt

Name of the Hospital ____________

Cash Book for the month of ____________

Receipts									Payments							
Date	R. No.	Particulars	L/F	Bank	Cash	IP	OP	Others	Date	Vr. No.	Particulars	L/F	Bank	Cash	S. Crs	Others

CASH BOOK

In the cash book, all cash receipts and payments are recorded chronologically. A scroll cash book is maintained by cashier whereas a main cash book is maintained by Finance Section. The opening and closing balance of the day are also recorded.

Fig. 10.6. Cash Book

Bank Reconciliation Statement for the month of —		Rs.	Rs.
Bank balance as per Cash Book, as on the last day of the month the last day of the month			
Add	Cheques issued but not debited by Bank.		
Add	Credit afforded by Bank but not accounted in Cash Book.		
	Deduct		
	Cheques received and accounted in Cash Book but not credited by Bank.		
	Debited raised by Bank but not accounted in Cash Book.		
	Balance as per Bank Statement/Pass Book, as on the last day of the month.		

Bank Reconciliation Statement

A reconciliation statement prepared periodically between the bank balance as per cash book and the balance as per bank Statement on the day of reconciliation is called the Bank Reconciliation statement. It helps in revealing frauds or wrongly posted amount. Any omissions or wrong entries can be detected. This helps you in many ways.

Fig. 10.7. Bank Reconciliation Statement

PATIENT'S ACCOUNTS RECEIVABLE REGISTER **NAME OF THE HOSPITAL**

Name of the Patient

Ward No. ______ Hospital No. ______

Bed No. ______

Admitted No. ______ Discharged on ______

Date	Room	Food	Medicare	Operation	Delivery	Anaes.	X-ray	Lab	Pharma	Other	Charges	Total	Payment	Deposit	Balance	
										Other Type	Charge Amt.		Rect. No.	Amt.	Dr.	Cr.
1	2	3	4	5	6	7	8	9	10	11	12	13	14	15	16	17

PATIENT'S ACCOUNTS RECEIVABLE REGISTER

As a general rule, the hospitals are not supposed to allow credit to individuals. However, the large-sized customers, such as organisations or institutions are offered credit facilities. In such a case, we find preparation of Accounts Receivable Register. The Medical Superintendent or a hospital manager exercises his/her discretion in this respect.

Fig. 10.8. Accounts Receivable Register (Patients)

IN-PATIENT'S FEES JOURNAL

Date	Bill No.	Room	Nsg. care	Operation room	Delivery room	X-ray	Lab	Pharma	Total	Adv.	Concession Paid	Cash Paid		Total
Totals														
Posted														

IN-PATIENT'S FEES JOURNAL

Separate journals for in-patients and out-patients are maintained. In the format, we find the in-patient's fees journal. Any free care or concessions are posted to General Ledger. All concessions should be approved by the Medical Superintendent or a Manager/Financial Manager. Concessions may occur when free service is authorised to poor patients or courtesy or professional discounts are given to the hospital personnel.

Fig. 10.9. In-Patient's Fees Journal

Out-patient's Fees Journal									
Medicine			X-ray			Surgery			
Date	Receipt	Amount No.	Date	Receipt	Amount No.	Date	Receipt	Amount No.	
Total									

OUT-PATIENT'S FEES JOURNAL

Like in-patient's fees journal, we find preparation of out-patient's fees journal. In the format, we find three columns, such as Medicine, X-ray and Surgery. It explains the amount against a particular head received on a particular date. The receipt number is required to be mentioned.

Signature

Fig. 10.10. Out-patient's Fees Journal

IP Billing Office Statement of Daily Collections and Concessions	
Date	No. of Bills
Hospital Days	
Total Amount:	Collection:
Refund Amount:	Due Amount:
	Advance:
	Drug Refund:
Analysis Concessions	
Unit	Amount Rs.
Med I/Med II/Med III/Med IV	
Surg I/II/III/IV	
OBG I/II	
Ortho I/II	
Urology I/II	
Paed I/II	
Paed Surgery	
Neurology/N-surgery	
Cardiology	
Skin	
CTU	
Oncology	
Psychiatry	
P T C D	
Dental	
Gastro-Enterology	
Others	
	Medical Records Officer In-charge IP Billing Officer

STATEMENT OF DAILY COLLECTIONS AND CONCESSIONS

It is a statement showing daily collections and concessions. There are a number of heads and the related head explains the collections and concessions given. An in-charge IP Billing Office is to issue the statement. We find this statement useful while justifying the concessions given to the persons/patients who deserved because it is directly to influence the hospital finance.

Fig. 10.11. Statement of Collections and Concessions

Statement Showing Daily Collection from IP Account Section

	Amount	
	Rs.	Rs.
Date:		
IP Collection:		
Bills Collection ______		
IP Advances ______		
Sundry Debtors ______		
Miscellaneous ______		
P.A.B.X. ______		
P.A.B.X. Debtors ______		
Central Office: ______		
Van Charges ______		
Bank Commission ______		
OP Collection: ______		
Registration ______		
Gastroscopy ______		
Physiotherapy ______		
Trauma-Centre ______		
Blood Bank ______		
X-ray Prof. Charges ______		
X-ray ______		
Onco. Spl. Consultant		
Burns Centre ______		
Laboratory ______		
Occupational Therapy ______		
OT Drugs ______		
Observation ______		
Miscellaneous Items		
1.		
2.		
3.		
4.		
Total		
Opening Balance		
Excess of Cash		
Less Remittance		
Less Refund		
Concessions		
S. Debtors		
O.P. Collection		
Closing Balance		

O.P. Credit
Registration
Physio
X-ray
Trauma
Burns ______
Total ______
Special Ward Collection

> **STATEMENTS SHOWING DAILY COLLECTION**
>
> This is a statement showing daily collection from IP Accounts Section. It contains IP and OP collection. IP collection on covers bills collection, PABX and central office van charges and ban commission. OP collection includes a number of charges. The miscellaneous items are in a separate head. It also includes OP credit and opening balance from which remittance, refund and concessions are deducted.

Accounts Assistant

Medical Records Officer
In-charge IP Building Officer

Fig. 10.12. Statement showing Daily Collection from IP Accounts Section

Statement of Daily Collection OP Accounts Section		Amount	Amount
Date	1. Registration		
	2. OEU Registration		
	3. Special Consultations:		
	Medical I/II/III/IV/V/VI		
	Surgery I/II/III/IV/V/VI		
	Ortho I/II		
	ENT I/II		
	Paediatrics I/II		
	OBG I/II		
	Eye		
	Psychiatry I/II		
	CTU		
	Skin		
	Neuro I/II		
	Plastic Surgery		
	Cardiology		
	Urology I/II		
	4. Services		
	Medicine		
	ENT		
	Ortho		
	Allergy Clinic		
	Clinical Lab		
	Surgery		
	Paed Surgery		
	Paediatrics		
	OBG		
	Treadmill Test		
	Dental		
	Dental (X-ray)		
	CTU		
	Skin		
	EMG/Neuro		
	ECG		
	Ultrasound		
	EEG		
	Echo		
	Yoga		
	Urology		
	Angiography		
	Laser Therapy		
	5. Professional Charges:		
	Eye-Cardio/Radiology/		
	GEC/Neurology		
	6. OEU Fund		
	7. IP Advance		
	8. Total		
	9. Add Opening Balance		
	10. Deduct Cash to Central Office/EGG/OPD		
	Closing Balance		
	Accountant OPD		

STATEMENT OF DAILY COLLECTION OF A/C

It is a statement of daily collection related to OP Accounts Section. The main heads are Registration. OEU Registration, Special Consultation Services, Professional Charges, OEU Fund, IP Advances.

The Opening Balance is added and cash remitted to Central Office, ECG and OPD are deducted. Finally, we find the closing balance.

Fig. 10.13. Statement of Daily Collection of Accounts Section

Name of the Hospital | In-patient Bill

Bill No. ------------------------------------ | Tel. --

Date --

Hospital No. ------------------------------ | Department ---

IP No. ------------------------------------ | Ward --

Name ------------------------------------- | Category ---

Address ---------------------------------- | Admission Date ------------------------------------

Discharge Date ------------------------------------

Discharge Time ------------------------------------

No. of Days ---

Charges for Hospitalisation	Amount Rs.
Admission Charges	--
Bed and Service Charges	--
Consultation Charges	--
Operation Charges	--
Investigation Charges	--

> **In-Patient Bill**
>
> It is a bill related to in-patients where we find details of charges, concessions and finally, the amount payable. It covers charges for hospitalisation.

-------------------------------- Total ---

Others --------------------------------

Less Advance Paid | Balance ----------------------------------

Less Concessions | Amount Payable ----------------------------------

Rs. ------------------------------------

Prepaid by | Checked by | Officer In-charge IP Building Section

Received with thanks

Rs. ------------------------------------ | Vide Receipt No. --

Cashier

Fig. 10.14. In-patient Bill

Name of the Hospital						Purchase Register/Journal									
Date	Sl. No.	S.Crs. Folio	Supplier's Name	Inv. No.	Total Amount	Gen. Stores	Linen Stores	Maintenance Repairs	X-ray	Pharmacy	Stationery	Oxygen	Misc.	Capital items	Remark
1	2	3	4	5	6	7	8	9	10	11	12	13	14	15	16

PURCHASE REGISTER JOURNAL

It is related to purchase register in which we find sixteen columns. The materials purchased by hospitals are entered in the purchase register. In the context of material management, the purchase register is found impact generating.

Fig. 10.15. Purchase Register/Journal

<table>
<tr><td colspan="5">Name of the Hospital</td><td colspan="4">Pay Roll</td><td colspan="5">Individual Earnings Card for the Year ......</td></tr>
<tr><td colspan="5">Name of the Employee ____________</td><td colspan="4">Employee Code ____________</td><td colspan="5">Designation ____________</td></tr>
<tr><td>For the month</td><td>1</td><td>2</td><td>3</td><td>4</td><td>5</td><td>6</td><td>7</td><td>8</td><td>9</td><td>10</td><td>11</td><td>12</td><td>Total for year</td></tr>
<tr><td>Basic Pay</td><td></td><td></td><td></td><td></td><td></td><td></td><td></td><td></td><td></td><td></td><td></td><td></td><td></td></tr>
<tr><td>D.A.</td><td></td><td></td><td></td><td></td><td></td><td></td><td></td><td></td><td></td><td></td><td></td><td></td><td></td></tr>
<tr><td>House Rent</td><td></td><td></td><td></td><td></td><td></td><td></td><td></td><td></td><td></td><td></td><td></td><td></td><td></td></tr>
<tr><td>Children Allowance</td><td></td><td></td><td></td><td></td><td></td><td></td><td></td><td></td><td></td><td></td><td></td><td></td><td></td></tr>
<tr><td>Others</td><td></td><td></td><td></td><td></td><td></td><td></td><td></td><td></td><td></td><td></td><td></td><td></td><td></td></tr>
<tr><td>Total Earnings</td><td></td><td></td><td></td><td></td><td></td><td></td><td></td><td></td><td></td><td></td><td></td><td></td><td></td></tr>
<tr><td>P.F.</td><td></td><td></td><td></td><td></td><td></td><td></td><td></td><td></td><td></td><td></td><td></td><td></td><td></td></tr>
<tr><td>Income Tax</td><td></td><td></td><td></td><td></td><td></td><td></td><td></td><td></td><td></td><td></td><td></td><td></td><td></td></tr>
<tr><td>Food</td><td></td><td></td><td></td><td></td><td></td><td></td><td colspan="5" rowspan="5">PAY ROLL IEC
The hospitals or healthcare organisations also prepare pay roll which includes the details of payment under different heads and the deductions and the total net amount payable. With the help of computers, you can also prepare pay roll. The name of employee and his/her code and position are to be mentioned at the top.</td><td></td><td></td></tr>
<tr><td>Electricity</td><td></td><td></td><td></td><td></td><td></td><td></td><td></td><td></td></tr>
<tr><td>Others</td><td></td><td></td><td></td><td></td><td></td><td></td><td></td><td></td></tr>
<tr><td>Total Deduction</td><td></td><td></td><td></td><td></td><td></td><td></td><td></td><td></td></tr>
<tr><td>Net Cash paid</td><td></td><td></td><td></td><td></td><td></td><td></td><td></td><td></td></tr>
</table>

Fig. 10.16. Pay Roll Individual Earning Card (Monthly)

Name of the Hospital ______	Pay Roll ______	Individual Earning Card ______
Name ______	Marital Status ______	Employee Code ______
Address ______	No. of Children ______	Department ______
______	Date of Joining ______	Grade ______
______	Date of Leaving ______	Designation ______

Year	Basic Pay	DA	House Rent	Children Allowance	Others	Total Earnings	P.F.	Income Tax	Food	Electricity	Others	Total Deductions	Net Paid

PAY ROLL-IEC

It is also a format showing the payroll which is found a bit different from the first one. The details of employees are found in the Pay Roll as mentioned at the top. It includes the details of payment in a year. The first one shows the payments in a month.

Fig. 10.17. Pay Roll IEC (Annual)

Purchase Requisition — Name of the Hospital

Identing Department:

P.R. No. ______________ Date ____________

Sl. No.	Item code	Item description	Present stock consumption	Average monthly	Quantity required	Unit cost	Total cost	Suggested vendor	Remarks

PURCHASE REQUISITION

It is requisition related to the purchase of hospital materials. It shows description of items for which requisition is made. It is issued by the Identing Department of a hospital. The requisition form clarifies the code for a particular item to be required. The name of vendor is also suggested which may or may not be accepted. The requisition is found based on the demand of the material department.

Identor — Approved by

Fig. 10.18. Purchase Requisition

No. ____________

Date ____________

To

M/s ______________________________ Ref: Your Tender No. Dated

Please supply the following stores on the following terms & conditions :

Sl. No.	Item Description	Quantity Ordered	Unit of Quantity	Rate per Unit	Total Value

Date of Delivery: ____________

Place of Delivery: ____________

Mode of Inspection: ____________

Terms of Payment: ____________

To be despatched by ____________ at

consignor's-carrier's/our risk

Freight at the rate of ____________

payable by us/or

Delivery free at the site indicated above.

Price Variation Clause, if any and other conditions ____________

Please acknowledge the receipt of this order. Signature

PURCHASE ORDER

It is related to purchase order. It clarifies the details regarding the materials for which order is placed. The description of item shows the details of items ordered. It includes quantity, unit and date.

FOR OFFICE USE

Acknowledgment received on ____________

First Reminder ____________ Second Reminder ____________ Third Reminder ____________

Date Delivered ____________ Date Inspected ____________ Brought on Charge ____________

Invoice No. and Date Voucher No. ...... Date ......

Fig. 10.19. Purchase Order

GOODS RECEIVED NOTE

NO. GRN

Supplier's Name ______________ Date ______________

P.O. No. ______________ Packing/Dly. Note Ref. ______________

Sl. No.	Description	Quantity Received	Quantity Accepted	Quantity Rejected	Remarks	Stocks available including this consignment

GOODS RECEIVED NOTE

It is a note for receiving goods. In the remarks column, reason for rejections, acceptance of excess supplied, etc. are to be noted. A copy of the purchase order is to be made available to inspector for making inspection. One copy of GRN to Accounts, one copy to Purchase file and one office copy are also made available. This notebook gives a detailed description of receiving or rejecting the goods.

Materials Inspected for quality specified in Purchase Order and accepted.
Signature Inspector

Quantity accepted and taken on Stores Charge Stores
Signature in-chage

Fig. 10.20. Goods Received Note

Stores Requisition No. ....

Identing Department Date

Sl. No.	Item Code	Item Description	Present Stock	Now Identified	Unit Price	Total Value	Remarks

STORE REQUISITION

It is a requisition related to stores issued by the Indenting Department. It mentions the details of item Code and Description. Present Stock, Unit Price and Total Value are also mentioned.

Fig. 10.21. Stores Requisition

Vehicles Log Book **Vehicle No.**

				Mileage			Time of Journey		Details of Overtime Allowance						Total
Date	Charges to	Place to	Purpose	From	To	No. of KM	From	To	Driver's Name	Duty From	Hrs. To	OT Hrs.	Allowances OT	Food	

VEHICLES LOG BOOK

This log book is to check the misuse of vehicles and fuels. It includes the details of journey and the total Kms in addition to the overtime. The name of driver and other details are also given.

Receipt Details			Credit Bill Details			Fuel		Details		Remarks
RT No. Date	Amt.	Remarks	Bill No.	Date	Amt.	Diesel	Petrol	Party's Name	Bill No. Date	

Fig. 10.22. Vehicle Log Book

Vehicles Maintenance Book Vehicle No. ...

Job No.	Defect Report No.	Repair Time		Mileage during Repair			Job Description	Materials	Description	Qty.	Labour			Total
		Date in	Date out	Km. in	Km. out	Total		Details Supplier's Name Bill No. Date			Amount A	Quantity	Amount B	Amount A + B

VEHICLE MAINTENANCE BOOK

This book is found related to the maintenance of vehicles. It includes details of repairs and the materials.

Contd....

Bill and Date	Materials sent to scrap and salvage Stores			
	Date	Description	Qty	Remarks

Fig. 10.23. Vehicles Maintenance Book

Name of the Hospital	Income and Expenditure Account		
Income and Expenditure	**Budget**	**Actual**	**Variance over Budget**
	Rs.	Rs.	Rs.
Income:			
In-patient			
Out-patient			
Others			
Total			
Expenditure			
Establishment			
Hospital Supplies			
Water & Electricity			
Printing & Stationery			
Repairs & Maintenance			
Postage			
Telephone			
Fee & Concessions			
Depreciation			
Others			
Total			
Surplus/Deficit			

INCOME & EXPENDITURE A/C

The Income and Expenditure A/c in a hospital is to show the details of income and expenditure. In a hospital, the sources of income are found very limited whereas they have a big list of different types of expenditure. The Income & Expenditure A/c shows surplus or deficit.

Fig. 10.24. Income & Expenditure A/c

SALARY BUDGET

Salary Budget for ________________ Department ________________

Name	Designation	Basic	DA	HRA	PF	Gross	Increment	Others	Total

SALARY BUDGET

The salary budget is to include the details of salary mentioning different heads of payment. It is meant for a financial year which generally is found from April to March. This helps a manager in knowing the payment under the head salary.

Fig. 10.25. Salary Budget

Particulars	Total Cost of project		Estimated Expenditure during the year
A. Buildings			
1. In respect of new works			
(a) Canteen Buildings:			
Civil			
Water Supply			
Electricity			
Other Services			
(b)			
(c)			
(d)			
(e)			
2. In respect of work in progress			
(a)			
(b)			
(c)			
(d)			
B. Machinery & Equipment, etc.			
1. New Items as per list			
2. Items ordered/to be ordered			

CAPITAL EXPENDITURE BUDGET

Capital Expenditure Budget focuses on budget related to the capital-intensive items, such as buildings, water, power, sanitation, machinery and equipment. In one column we find total cost of the project and in other column estimated expenditure during the year is shown.

Fig. 10.26. Capital Expenditure Budget

Cash Budget Year ______

Particulars	1 Jan.	2 Feb.	3 Mar.	4 Apr.	5 May	6 June	7 July	8 Aug.	9 Sep.	10 Oct.	11 Nov.	12 Dc.
Cash Balance												
Repairs:												
In-patients												
Out-patients												
Other Income												
Disbursements												
Salaries & Wages												
Supplies												
Other Exp.												
Capital Expenses												
Cash Balance (end of period)												
Less Cash Balance (Margin)												
Cash Surplus/Deficit												

CASH BUDGET

In the cash budget, we find details of receipts and disbursements.

Out of the total receipts and disbursements, the minimum cash balance is reduced. The balance is surplus/deficit.

It starts from beginning of the cash balance and finally, we find the cash balance for the end of the period.

Fig,. 10.27. Cash Budget

Budget Proforma

Income/Expenditure (Particulars)	Actuals of last year	Current Year		Budget Next Year	
		Budget	Actuals	Budget	Actuals
BUDGET PROFORMA It is a proforma related to budget for hospitals. We find details of Income and Expenditure. The actuals of last year and the budget and actuals of current year are shown in the budget.					

Fig. 10.28. Budget Proforma

Name of the Hospital			Balance sheet as at ....20...		
Liabilities and Net Worth			Assets		
Current Liabilities			Current Assets		
Accounts Payable Short-term Loans Due to other Funds Total Current Liabilities Total Long-term Liabilities Building and Equipment Funds Funds Others Net Worth Opening Balance			Cash in hand and Bank Security Deposit Investment Accounts Receivable Inventories Prepaid Expenses Due from other Funds Others Total Current Assets		
Gain/ Loss for the period Hospital Capital Total Net Worth Total			Fixed Assets Land and Building Machinery and Equipment Furniture and Vehicles Construction in Progress Total Fixed Assets Funds-Investments Total		

BALANCE SHEET

It is a statement of assets and liabilities. We find two sides of the Balance Sheet. In the left side, we show current liabilities and long-term liabilities. In the right side, we show the current assets and fixed assets.

Fig. 10.29. Balance Sheet

Removing Financial Constraints for Healthcare Services

The process of social transformation cannot gain a rapid momentum unless we find a minimum level of healthcare in the population. We cannot deny that since independence, India has built up a vast health infrastructure and health personnel at primary, secondary and tertiary centres and a number of medical and paramedical institutions have also been set up, Ayurveda, Yoga and Naturopathy, Unani, Siddha and Homeopathy (AYUSH) institutions have also been promoted but the qualitative and quantitative gap in the availability of hospitals and healthcare services has not been bridged. Of course, we find increasing pressure of demography expanding the gap and obstructing the process but even for that problem, the accountability rests on the shoulders of national policy makers not making sincere and honest efforts to resolve the problem. We consider health of a nation as wealth of a nation provided the masses are physically and mentally sound. And physical and mental soundness considerably rest on the hospital and healthcare services.

Poverty and ill health are found inter-related. The onset of a long and expensive illness can drive the non-poor into poverty. The problem of malnutrition is found closely associated with poverty and illiteracy. A number of diseases crop up due to unawareness such as food-prone, water-prone and communicable diseases which have a downward graph particularly in the states and countries where we find high level of literacy. Easily accessible, reliable and affordable quality healthcare services need due attention of policy makers. The rising costs of inputs have been found making it difficult to the hospitals and healthcare organisations to provide quality services. So far as the government hospitals are concerned, they are not free to generate financial resources from the internal sources. In addition, they do not get adequate grants from the government. On account of financial crunch, a majority of the government hospitals find it difficult to satisfy the users. Since a majority of the population depends on, government hospitals, it is pertinent that we remove their financial problems on a priority basis.

The two sources for mobilising financial resources are internal and external. The government hospitals get a very negligible portion of their income from fees charged for different services. They bear huge social costs and this is in tune with their defined objectives. We do no find them using consultancy services for improving their revenue position. Hence, they have no option but to depend on the grants from the government because even charities and donations as a source for mobilising resources are not used by them. Thus, the only source where we find focus is grants from the government which cannot be claimed to be adequate specially in the face of changing disease profile and the increasing demand position. It is in this context that the state governments as well as the central government need to assign due weightage to the problem of finance. Developing mass awareness will also require priority attention of state governments mainly with the help of hospital professionals and medical staff.

It is not only significant that we concentrate our attention only on the government hospitals and do not think about the development and well being of private hospitals found in good number and providing quality medicare services to almost all the segments. Keeping in view, the changing disease profile and increasing healthcare requirements, it is essential that central as well as the state governments motivate and promote private hospitals. Unless we consider healthcare sector as an infrastructure sector and offer to the interested persons, parties, agencies or organisations adequate incentives, the existing gap between the demand and supply of healthcare requirements would continue. By offering incentives, the private hospitals may be successful in bridging the gap and improving the quality. The avenues for charities and donations are required to be tapped by both the sectors. But this requires more incentives to the persons and organisations donating for the development of healthcare sector. Another alternative is development of PPP mode which would not only minimise the burden of state governments but would also be helpful in improving the service quality. Of course, the government would be required to monitor and regulate the behaviour of private hospitals with the motto of protecting the users because we find a number of cases where private hospitals do not honour the norms found essential for the healthcare sector.

We cannot deny the fact that quality of healthcare services in India has been found of world class. The fee structure has been globally competitive because in almost all the developed countries of the globe, the healthcare services are found very expensive. For improving the financial health of both the leading government and private hospitals, the government may provide more incentives to the tourism and hospitality sectors and with their cooperation may be successful in developing India as a healthcare destination. The development of medical or health tourism would be a positive step of innovative nature which would help hospitals in improving their financial health.

It is not only significant that we focus on mobilising financial resources but it is equally important that we regulate unfair and unlawful practices adopted by both the government as well as the private hospitals in different forms. If we make possible a productive use of our resources and contract scope for corrupt practices, the healthcare sector would be in a position to save their resources for important heads helping an acceleration in the process of qualitative-cum-quantitative transformation. It is right to mention that the national policy makers need to regulate the unfair practices. Regulating unproductive expenses would help in channelising and promoting productive expenses because the hospitals would be in a position to make the productive investments.

It is significant to mention that the existing level of government expenditure on health in India is about 1% which is unacceptably low. Hence, it is essential that sincere efforts are made to increase the total expenditure at the Centre and States to at least 2 % of the GDP by the end of Eleventh Five Year Plan. Innovative health financing mechanism is required to be introduced to improve the financial position of government hospitals. This throws light on the multifaceted measures such as increasing the government grants, incentives to the persons donating in the healthcare services and providing an opportunity to the hospitals to mobilise resources from fees charged for different types of services.

The health spending in India is around 4-5 % of the GDP. The results from the National Health Account (NHA) for the year 2001-02 showed that total health expenditure in the country was Rs. 105734 crore, accounting for 4.6 % of the GDP out of which public health expenditure constituted Rs. 21439 crore (0.94 %), private health expenditure constituted Rs. 81810 crore (3.58 %) and external support, Rs. 2485 crore (0.11 %).[10] The available statistics reveal that public health expenditure is required to be increased. On the other hand, professionals working for hospitals and health organisations also need to maximise the external support. The hospital professionals need to explore avenues for charities and donations. Studies also reveal that poor and other disadvantaged groups in both rural and urban areas spend a higher proportion of their income on healthcare than those who are better off. The burden on treatment is high on them while seeking inpatient care. Very often, they need to borrow money at very high interest to meet medicare. Hence, it is essential that the government policy makers make honest efforts so that the weaker sections of the society get the healthcare services either free of charge or at nominal fee which would help them in rationalising their household consumption needs. Meeting the cost of hospitalisation particularly for those who cannot afford is an urgent need of the hour.

The financial allocation for the health sector over the past decade indicates that the public expenditures on health, through the Central and State Governments, as a percentage of total government expenditure have declined from 3.12 % in 1992-93 to 2.99 % in 2003-04.[11] Healthcare is financed primarily by the State Governments and State allocations on health are usually affected by any fiscal stress they encounter. This sector has been plagued with instances of inefficiencies at several levels resulting in waste, duplication and non-optimal use of scarce resources. This has adversely affected the potentials of public healthcare services.

The above mentioned facts make it clear that during the Eleventh Fiver Year Plan, the Central Government will have to augment resources for health and the State Governments will be persuaded to assign at least 7-8 % of the State expenditure towards healthcare. In addition, it is also essential that state governments allocate more resources for drinking water, sanitation, nutrition, primary education, roads and connectivity.

The prime consideration before the Central as well as the State Governments is to make hospitals and healthcare organisations financially sound. We need to make our services of world class but this is not to be possible unless we find all the avenues for generating revenues and improving the financial position tapped in a right way. Our efforts for channelising e-Health services; our schemes for expanding the services in the remotest parts of the country; our proposals for strengthening the PPP mode make it essential that we solicit the cooperation of private sector because for meeting the healthcare requirements of present population we need almost Rs. 4,00,000 crore which cannot be provided only by the government. We need to mobilise 20% from the public sector and remaining 80% from the private sector either independently or through PPP mode. The States like Rajasthan, West Bengal, Uttarakhand, Gujarat, Arunachal Pradesh, Andhra Pradesh and Tamil Nadu have been found promoting PPP mode. It is significant that other states also activate the process and inject new life and strength to the healthcare services found almost sick.

Creation rests on satisfaction and satisfaction depends on the quality of our services provided to the users. And if we talk about quality, our focus must be on the quality of inputs used in processing the services. We are well aware of the fact that in the modern hospitals and healthcare organisations, the healthcare services sizably depend on the quality of technology. Retention can not be our motive specially in the context of healthcare services because the professional ethics make it essential that we make sincere and honest efforts to cure the patients and to sensitise the masses in such a fashion that they develop habits of healthy lifestyles. Nutritional deficiency, poor sanitation , insensitivity to food and water-prone diseases and communicable diseases are the roots of a number of diseases. The healthcare organisations need to make masses aware so that the healthcare spending is minimised. This would also be an indirect effort to improve the financial position of healthcare organisations.

Innovative low-cost technology also requires priority attention of hospital professionals. Additionally, the indigenous technology would also minimise the healthcare spending. The diagnosis and treatment of diseases based on low-cost indigenous technologies would considerably benefit the weaker sections of the society vis-a-vis the healthcare budget would also be minimised.

We find India in the midst of an epidemiological and demographic transition with increasing burden of chronic diseases, decline in mortality and fertility rates and ageing of the population. Non-Communicable diseases (NCDs) have increased the intensity of chronic disease burden on the healthcare system of India. If hospitals and healthcare organisations fail in sensitising the masses, the increasing healthcare spending would sizably affect the poor segments of the society. The doctor, paramedical and managerial staff need to play a distinct role. They have to be much more creative in their efforts healthy society is our target. On the one hand, we need to make hospitals potentiality sound and on the other hand, also bear the responsibility of making society aware.

Keeping in view the emerging problems, it is essential that we focus on innovative financial mechanisms helping the process as adopted by different States in the country such as Kerala, Uttar Pradesh, Jharkahnd, Haryana and Karnataka. In Kerala, we find constitution of risk pools around professionals of occupational groups, SHGs or micro credit groups, weavers, fishermen, farmers, agricultural labourers and other informal groups. Such a risk pool in Kozhikode covers 90% of the population under some form of network or the other. It is significant that other states also practice the same. The Vouchers Scheme for RCH services piloted in the Seven blocks of UP (Agra) for BPL population has been funded by State Innovations in Family Planning Services Agency. Such a Voucher Scheme may be useful even for other States. In Jharkhand, a Voucher Scheme was introduced to promote institutional delivery and routine immunization in 22 districts. The Vouchers are issued to BPL pregnant women at the time of registration of pregnancy. She has freedom to have the delivery at any government facility or at accredited private health providers. In Haryana, we find Vikalp considered to be an innovative approach to finance Urban Primary Healthcare for poor through a combination of PPPs and risk pooling using capitation fees for a package of primary healthcare services with the State Health Department and private providers. We cannot deny that the only alternative to improve the quality of healthcare services and to improve is the financial health of hospitals and healthcare organisations if promoting PPP mode which should be conceptualised even by other States. In Karnataka, Yeshasvini Co-operative Healthcare Scheme is a health insurance scheme targeted to benefit the poor. The scheme was initiated by Narayana Hridayalaya, a superspeciality heart hospital in Bangalore and by the Department of Co-operatives of the Government of Karnataka. All farmers who have been members of a cooperative society for at least a year are eligible to participate, regardless of their medical histories. The scheme provides coverage for all major surgeries.

Improving the quality of healthcare services is significant and the hospitals and healthcare organisations should not have any excuse that on account of financial sickness, they find themselves not in a position to provide even the basic medical aids. The government policy makers have to explore avenues that how and in what way they can make it possible. They need to enrich the government hospitals; they need to promote PPP mode; they need to offer incentives to individuals and institutions for providing charities and donations or any of the innovative financial mechanisms which cater to the changing healthcare requirements of society.

SUMMARY

You have gone through different dimensions of hospital financing. After going through the chapter, be sure that the following facts are well versed:

Financial Management in Hospitals—the Perception: The financial management of hospitals involves making of three important decisions, viz., investment, generation and control and supervision.

Financial Planning: Planning is considered to be the formulation of enterprise goals and objectives. The financial planning of hospitals focuses our attention on formulating a financial plan that paves avenues for the generation and mobilisation of financial resources.

Financial Organisation: The financial organisation is aimed at formulating a sound organisational structure for hospitals where quality personnel are available to manage hospital finance.

Budgeting: The formulation of a budget for hospitals draws our attention on the sources of revenues and expenditure in a hospital to enable a manager to make possible effective functioning of hospitals.

Exploring Avenues for Revenues in Hospitals: The problem of mobilisation of financial resources from the internal and external sources are discussed. In the internal sources, we find fee, paying wards, rent from the shopping complex, dispensary or pharmacy, transportation, pay-phone, advertisement places, charity shows and exhibition. In the external sources, we find government grants, charity and donations, loans and borrowings, corporate sector, global bodies and social organisations, co-operation of large-sized customers and film stars and cricketeers.

Managing the Financial Information: This draws our attention on the development of an independent financial system for managing information specially with the support of information technology.

Break-even Analysis: We are well aware of the fact that hospital is a no-profit making organisation and this deprives them of making profits and therefore, they are supposed to keep their costs at the break-even point where no-profit no-loss is the result.

Project Planning: The plan related to the beginning of a project keeping in view the requirements and potentials is called project planning which is found based on cost-benefit analysis. In hospitals, the term benefit focuses our attention on public interests and therefore, we find it an important criterion to approve a project.

Project Life Cycle: The life cycle of a project draws our attention on the pre-investment stage, construction phase and the normalisation phase.

Feasibility Studies: This is found to be a result-oriented study helping a manager in coming to the conclusion that the project should be taken up or should be stopped. A number of facts are taken into consideration while preparing the feasibility report.

Management of Books and Accounts: We go through practical problems in this context, such as book-keeping, books of accounts and registers, Accounts Receivable, Accounts Payable, Payroll, Capital and Revenue Expenditure, Revenue Control and Cost Centres, Income and Expenditure Statement, Budgetary Control, Standard Costing, Cost Ascertainment and Cost Containment, and finally, the Internal Audit.

Computer-driven Accounting System: This focuses our attention on the use of computers for accounting purposes.

Removing Financial Constraints for Healthcare Services: With the changing disease profile and existent insensitivity, it is pertinent that national policy makers bring a radical change in their policy decisions so that hospitals are found to be potentially sound. This focuses on tapping the possible avenues for the mobilisation of financial resources.

KEY TERMS

Computer-driven Accounting	Internet Audit
PERT	Storing Data
Holistic Concept	Retrieving Data
Financial Planning	Service Bureau
Capital Budgeting	Health Intelligence
Operating Revenue	Bank Reconciliation Statement
Fixed Cost	In-Patient Bill
Variable Cost	Pay Roll
Break-even Analysis	Cash Book
Cost-Volume Profit Model	Log Book
Feasibility Report	Financial Director
Book-keeping	Financial Advisor
Petty Cash	Accounting
Imprest Cash	Auditing
Budgetary Control	Equipment Budget
Standard Costing	Master Budget

REVIEW QUESTIONS

1. What do you mean by Hospital Financing? Focus on the different constituents of hospital financing.
2. Define Hospital Financing. Discuss the significance of a sound financial plan for a healthcare organisation.
3. Throw light on the financial organisation of a hospital. Explain the instrumentality of a sound financial manager in generating finance for hospitals.
4. What do you mean by Budgeting? Present the format of budget for hospitals.
5. Focus on the instrumentality of managing financial information in the healthcare organisations.
6. What do you mean by Break-even analysis? Do you find it relevant to the hospitals for pricing? Defend your answer.
7. Explain Project Planning. Discuss the different considerations to be given due weightage while preparing feasibility report of a project.
8. What do you mean by Project Life Cycle? Explain the various aspects to be studied while studying the project life cycle.
9. Explain the following in the context of hospitals:
   (*a*) Accounts Receivables
   (*b*) Accounts Payable
   (*c*) Pay Roll
10. Discuss the following:
    (*a*) Capital and Revenue Expenditure
    (*b*) Income and Expenditure Statement
    (*c*) Revenue Control and Cost Centre
11. What do you mean by Budgetary Control? Explain the measures to be taken for the same.

12. Write a brief note on Cost Ascertainment and Cost Containment with a reference to the hospital.
13. Discuss Internal Audit. Do you find it important to check the financial irregularities in the hospitals? Explain the process to be followed for the same.
14. Write short notes on the following:
    (*a*) Standard Costing
    (*b*) Computer-driven Accounting System.
15. Explain the instrumentality of information technology in maintaining hospital accounts.

APPLICATION EXERCISES

1. You have been working as a financial advisor in a hospital. Explain the precautions you need to manage hospital finance.
2. Design a financial plan for your hospital which is to help you in removing the problem of financial crunch.
3. Prepare an imaginary budget for your hospital.
4. You need to design a project for the expansion and development of your hospital. Focus on the considerations to guide you while preparing a feasibility report of a project.
5. As a hospital manager, focus on the steps you will take for budgetary control.
6. You need to check the financial irregularities in your hospital. Explain the process you will follow for the same.
7. In the capacity of a hospital manager, how you would promote the use of computers for managing and maintaining hospital accounts ?
8. In the capacity of a hospital manager, throw light on the role of a Financial Information System for managing finance.
9. Do you find a study of break-even point essential for making the pricing decisions for your hospital? Justify your opinion.
10. Do you find logbook as a guide to chronicle individual and staff performance? Defend your arguments as a hospital manger.
11. In the capacity of a financial manager serving a hospital, you need to promote the use of computers for maintaining books and accounts. Throw light on the steps you have to initiate for the infusion of new generation of information technology.

END NOTES

1. Weston and Brigham, *Essentials of Managerial Finance,* p. 9.
2. Krishna Swamy Rao H., *Financial Management and Cost Containment,* pp. 119-20.
3. *Ibid.,* pp. 141-142.
4. Goel, S.L. and Kumar R., *Hospital Administration and Management,* pp. 153-55.
5. Robbert C. Higgins, *Financial Management,* pp. 139-40.
6. *Ibid.*
7. H.R. Krishna Swamy Rao, *op. cit.,* p.152.
8. Anthony and Reace, *Management Accounting,* p. 106/
9. *Nabhi's Ninth Five Year Plan,* pp. 471-72.
10. *Eleventh Five Year Plan* : Planning Commission, Government of India, New Delhi, pp. 104-115.
11. *Ibid.,* pp. 104-105.

Marketing Hospital Services

Synchronisation of the different submixes of marketing requires world class professional excellence. By conceptualising social marketing principles, the healthcare and medicare organisations strike a balance between organisational and social considerations.

CHAPTER OBJECTIVES

Introduction—Hospital Marketing: the Perception—Rationale behind practising Marketing in Hospital Services—Segmentwise Users of Healthcare Services—Behavioural Profile of Users—Market Segmentation—Marketing Information Systems—Marketing Mix—Product—Mix Promotion Mix—Price Mix—Palace Mix—Process Mix—Physical Evidence and Attractions—People—Strategic Marketing—Summary—Key Terms—Review Questions—Application Exercises—End Notes.

LEARNING OBJECTIVES

This chapter aims at studying the different dimensions of hospital marketing. The hospital professionals develop their awareness of the different mixes of marketing helping them in improving the quality of healthcare services. Since we find users of services coming from different segments of society, it is pertinent that the hospital professionals have an indepth idea of the changing medicare requirements. The behavioural studies, study of information system, segmentation and marketing mix are the important areas where we find due focus.

Introduction

Of course, a number of factors are found instrumental in accelerating the pace of social engineering but of all the factors, the healthcare assumes a place of outstanding significance. "Health is above wealth", a proverb as effective as yesterday; is effective today and it will remain effective tomorrow and even a day after tomorrow. This is due mainly to the fact that a sound health is a prerequisite for a healthy and creative mind. To accelerate the pace of economic transformation, we appreciate the contributions of human resources and to improve the quality of human resources, we sizably appreciate the contributions of quality healthcare services. It is really amazing that even after decades and decades of attaining independence, we find Indian society considering healthcare management insignificant and this become very much instrumental in degenerating our productive efficacy. It is really unfortunate that the government policy makers, healthcare experts, hospital professionals and even the NGOs appear disinterested in bringing back the derailed healthcare systems on the rail. It is high time that we realise the gravity of the changing disease profile and make sincere and honest efforts to accelerate the pace of qualitative-cum-quantitative transformation.

We cannot deny that a majority of the hospitals and healthcare organisations are in a depleted condition. If the providers become insolvent and if the providers become managerially and professionally deficient, it becomes very much difficult to bridge the qualitative or quantitative gap. Decades and decades of neglécted care and treatment of the hospitals and healthcare organisations have virtually made them sick. The ultimate sufferers are the poor because affluent sections of society are found efficacious of availing the expensive services provided by the leading private hospitals. It is against this backdrop that the hospitals in general and government hospitals in particular, need to make themselves potentially sound.

Gone are the days when the classical physicians were found successful in diagnosing just with the clinical investigations. Of late, the services of modern hospitals are found considerably supported by the sophisticated equipments, instruments and new generation of information technology in addition to the world class professional excellence of the hospital personnel. A number of expensive technologies are used for diagnosing and treating the patients. Quality inputs generate quality outputs. Based on the principle, we find costs on different types of inputs rapidly increasing and making the healthcare services expensive making an invasion on the affordability of general masses. Hence, it is pertinent that we promote low-cost indigenous technologies go that even the weaker sections of society avail the quality healthcare services of government hospitals.

The concept of hospital marketing is found based on the perception that in lieu of offering poor quality of services to the users, it is judicious that we charge reasonably but offer world class services. Unless and until we find organisations potentially sound, it will be difficult for them to offer the best. Unless you are strong enough to resist the odds, it is difficult for you to protect your existence. And in the present materialistic age, unless you are financially sound, you find yourself weak. Based on the same principle, an organisation or an institution requires priority attention on improving its financial health because the process of enriching your strength is considerably influenced by your financial soundness. The management of marketing process would help hospital professionals in developing a sound marketing mix. We are aware of the fact that conceptualisation of modern marketing principles in the non-profit organisations paves wider avenues for an improvement in the quality of services to be instrumental in satisfying the users, protecting and promoting the social interests and engineering a sound foundation for the development and prosperity of an organisation. The holistic concept of management makes scope for the application of societal marketing principles particularly by the non-profit organisations like hospitals and educational institutions because this makes them stronger enough to bear the social costs. The hospital professionals play an important role in the formulation or blending process.

Synchronisation of the different submixes of marketing requires world class professional excellence so that the recent developments in the field of medical sciences are incorporated to serve and subserve social interests. The professionals are here supposed to make an indepth study of the changing needs and requirements of society in the face of changing disease profile so that quality healthcare services are made available. A techno-driven information system would make their tasks much more easier. Expectations never remain static. The multidimensional changes taking place in the marketing environment influence the levels of expectations and on the basis of behavioural studies, the hospital professional succeed in understanding and satisfying them. We live in an age of information technology and therefore, the development of a sound health information system is found to be a pre-requisite both, for the government and private hospitals.

The product mix for hospitals makes it essential that we make our services distinct to others by adding additional attractions and blending unique features. The core services, supportive services and peripheral services are required to be innovated in such a fashion that services are found of world class. It is not only significant that we improve the quality. It is equally important that we keep on moving the sensitisation process. The primary, secondary and tertiary hospitals and healthcare centres we find quality dimension not getting due place. Since we find healthcare sector on a boom, the hospitals need to focus on qualitative transformation. Capitalising on the opportunities in domestic as well as in the global markets cannot be possible unless the hospitals concentrate on the innovation process.

The hospitals and healthcare organisations also need to make use of creative promotional measures so that the users and potentials users develop their awareness of service quality. It is in this context that hospital professionals need to focus on advertising and other promotional measures with the prime motto of sensitising the masses. We need to advertise in a creative way; we need to publicice by developing a rapport with the media people and academics. We need personal selling so that users and potential users develop their awareness of the quality and affordability. We need to offer incentives to the people helping us in the sensitisation process and this drawsourattention on sales promotion. We can also make use of telemarketing for promoting and influencing the users. The word-of-mouth promotion would be active and positive when we find hospitals sincere to quality. Innovative services and creative promotional measures need due attention of hospital professionals.

The most important consideration particularly in the Indian context is pricing because we find a majority of our population having poor affordability. The low-cost indigenous technologies are to be given due weightage particularly in the government hospitals where we find a good number of weaker sections getting the medicare. The small hospitals even in the private sector should make use of low-cost indigenous technologies. At each and every stage, the hospital professionals are required to maintain cost effectiveness so that the healthcare services are found affordable.

The promised quality of services must be made available to the users on time and in a decent way. We find hospital and healthcare services considerably different to other services where even a minor delay may cause irreparable losses. This focuses our attention on the place mix.

In an age of new generation of information and communication technology, the processing of services requires priority attention of hospital professionals. It is to be made sure that apparatus, equipments and instruments are of quality and quality people are handling, operating and maintaining them in a right way. The possibilities of distortion or delay are to be regulated because time management occupies here a place of outstanding significance.

Being a sensitive sector, it is significant that hospital professionals are sincere to the physical evidence and attractions as a submix of marketing. The service ambience for hospitals must be productive and environment-friendly. The service environment where different categories of medical, paramedical and managerial staff feel pleasure in serving the environment where users and attendants gain new experiences while recovering and the ambience where new generation of technology, instruments, equipments become instrumental in performing need priority attention of hospital professionals in the development of service ambience. The most important aspect in the healthcare organisation is found concerned with cleanliness. The physical amenities and facilities, of late, have been found getting due attention in the healthcare sector. The medical and paramedical staff needs to be particular to the dresses or uniforms used by them. This simplifies the identification process both for the patients and attendants and the hospital staff. The paramedical and medical staff needs to keep their dresses and uniforms neat and clean with dismal possibility for infection.

Of course, we find all the submixes of marketing significant for improving the quality of services but out of all, the medical and paramedical staff are found much more significant because a team of doctors working and serving with professional touch, personal commitment, value-orientation and humanised behaviour considerably govern the service quality. Hence, the hospital professionals need to make it sure that healthcare organisations are made available quality people.

A fair synchronisation of all the submixes is found essential for satisfying the users and establishing a brand name. Healthcare sector is on a book and will continue to hold the position even in the days to come. The healthcare industry accounted for 5.2.% of India's GDP in 2002 and this figure is expected to rise to 7.5% of $47 billion by 2012. Now, we have the concept of state-of-art hospitals gaining popularity because India has been emerging as a healthcare destination. With the corporatisation of healthcare industry, we expect multidimensional sophistication in the transformation process which would help hospitals and healthcare organisations in attracting the users and potential users from different parts of the globe. To momentise the process or to increase the flow of foreign patients, the Indian hospitals need double-barreled efforts viz. first providing world class services and second, charging less fee for the services rendered. We cannot deny that healthcare services in India are of world class and the fees charged for the services are abnormally low. We have potentials and even opportunities are existent in the markets. We need to be professional to capitalise on the same. We have hospitals maintaining international standards such as AIIMS, Apollo Hospital, B.M. Birla Heart Research Centre, Tata Memorial Hospital, Apollo Cancer Hospital, Escorts Heart Hospital, Shankar Netralaya, Bangalore Heart Hospital and many others efficacious of offering world class services. It is high time that hospitals make use of the services of marketers and capitals on the opportunities.

HOSPITAL MARKETING—THE PERCEPTION

Before we go through other dimensions, it is essential that our focus in on the concept of hospital marketing. The changing cycle necessitates a change in the perception and if the conceptualisation process is delayed, our efforts and strategies get a lukewarm response. It is in this context that we need to perceive the concept in the changing environmental conditions.

By hospital marketing, we mean providing healthcare services to the different categories of users in such a fashion that they get quality services, at a reasonable fee structure, on right time and in a decent way.[1] The concept of Social Marketing principles focus on making available the services even to those segments of the users who are not in a position to afford.[2] It is in this context that we find marketing medicare or healthcare services a managerial process that helps a professional in formulating a sound marketing mix in tune with the fluctuating intensity of health problem. The social marketing also focuses on promoting the services in a creative way that informs, senses and motivates the users for managing a healthy living condition that minimises the possibilities of illness or ailments. The principles throw light on inculcating mass awareness so that the prospects or potential patients or users change their living conditions, food habits, preferences, life styles and the harmful effects of environmental pollution. Thus, contrary to other organisations, the healthcare organisations or hospitals are supposed to bring down the number of potential patients or users by injecting new life and strength to the preventive measures. If we improve the environmental condition; if we are aware of nutritional awareness; if we counter the food-borne, water-borne, noise-borne problems; if we regulate our living conditions as per the requirements, it is quite natural that the bed for the germination different types of diseases would be made barren.

A majority of us are found confused with the conceptual aspect of marketing. During the yester decades, the contours of development have undergone radical changes which has changed the perception of marketing. Marketing focused on profit generation; marketing concentrated on customer-satisfaction; marketing is now hammering on social-orientation.[3] This makes it clear that profit generation is not the only thing that we expect from the functional areas of marketing. Of course, the profit generation is an important condition but not an essential condition. We are well aware of the fact that the changing social problems engineer a sound foundation for a change in the concept and perception.

We can't negate that the management principles have speeded up the process of industrial transformation which have substantially helped multidimensional social developments but at the same time have also made the land more fertile for the germination and growth of a number of health problems. The perception that marketing is to be conceptualised only in the goods manufacturing sector obstructed the development of services-generating organisations in general and the healthcare and educational institutions in particular. To put it another way, the profit-making goods manufacturing organisations conceptualised principles of modern marketing but the services-generating profit-making organisations delayed the process. Later on, the profit-making service-generating organisations, viz., bank, insurance, transportation, communications, tourism, hotel and many others switched on the process but the no-profit making organisations like healthcare or hospitals, educational institutions, social organisations and political organisations are till now found in doldrums.

Of course, the no-profit making organisations of west have realised the instrumentality of marketing in increasing the efficacy of an organisation and have conceptualised marketing principles on a priority basis but the less developed countries and developing countries are yet to develop a strong sense of realisation. It is against this background that we find a major fall in the productive efficacy of no-profit making organisations in general and the healthcare organisations in particular. Once again, it is to remind that healthcare organisations and educational institutions don't have a legitimate right of making profits.

In a true sense, we find marketing an important functional area of modern management helping all the individuals or organisations and institutions in evincing interests in activating the process of qualitative-cum-quantitative transformation. Marketing is right now considered to be a managerial process and more so, a social process. This necessitates alignment of marketing albeit with the healthcare and educational services.

Since we find hospital marketing an aggregation or a compendium of two different areas, our focus is found on practicing the principles of modern marketing even in the no-profit making organisations. It is in this context that we go through the changing perception of marketing and its instrumentality in improving the productive efficacy of healthcare organisations or hospitals.

Because marketing is a managerial process, it throws light on the formulation of different sub-mixes of marketing. In the changing conditions, the marketing experts, specially for the hospitals and healthcare organisations find it proper to go through seven mixes, viz., Product Mix, Promotion Mix, Price/ Free Mix, Place Mix, People Mix, Physical Attractions and Processing. Thus, when we talk about hospital marketing, it is essential that we keep in our minds creative developments in all the seven areas. By the product mix, our focus is on the services generated by hospitals or healthcare organisations. A marketing professional is supposed to blend the different types of healthcare services optimally, e.g., the core services, supportive services, preventive services and the peripheral services. They bear the managerial responsibility of making quality upgradation an ongoing process. This helps them in practicing Product Uniqueness Proposition. Further, they also bear the responsibility of promoting the services in an innovative fashion so that the patients or the potential patients are informed and sensed in a right perspective. This draws our attention on the different constituents of promotion such as, advertising, publicity, sales promotion, personal selling, word-of-mouth promotion and telemarketing. By blending the different constituents, they are found successful in creating mass awareness. In addition, a marketing professional is also supposed to make the services affordable to the masses by making possible cost-effectiveness in the process. Besides, they are also supposed to locate the healthcare organisations or hospitals at a location point found accessible and safe. Further, they are also required to go through the problem of people management so that sympathy and empathy are found in the hospital personnel. The physical attractions make it essential that they sense the hospital personnel regarding the dresses/ uniform and personality development and the processing makes it essential that the hospital personnel with a decent behaviour bridges over the gap between the services ensured and services offered. Thus, a sound marketing mix is formulated. In the process of formulation, they also go through the marketing information system, behavioural studies, study of segmentation and so on.

In view of the above, it is right to say that hospital marketing is a managerial vis-a-vis a social process helping the process of social information in tune with the proverb, "Health is above wealth."

Rationale Behind Marketing Healthcare Services

Of late, the concept of managing hospitals professionally has gained prominence the world over. The management of a no-profit making organisations no doubt complicates that task of boardrooms and hospital manager in many ways. On the one hand, they need to offer world class healthcare services to the patients while on the other hand, they are not supposed to charge from them even a cost-based fee. The costs of inputs used in the process of offering the services are found increasing and for which they need to practice two-fold measures—first, exploring avenues for generating revenues and making the social costs proportionate or optimal to the potentials of the hospitals or healthcare organisations. For the successful marketing of services, it is pertinent that hospitals are professionally sound. This helps hospitals in many ways, such as an increase in the organisational potentials to bear the social costs, use of internationally accepted quality of inputs in the process of generating the healthcare services and availability of smooth ways for modernisation, expansion and time-honoured development. It is in this context that we make a strong advocacy in favour of practicing marketing principles in the hospitals or healthcare organisations.[4] The following facts testify the justification for such application.

1. To Keep users Satisfied: *We are* well aware of the fact that the main thing in the process of offering the quality services is to satisfy the users and to keep on moving the process even without a gap. Like other profit making organisations, the hospitals are also required to satisfy the customers and the principles of marketing help them substantially in the process. If the doctors and nurses are found soft, sympathetic, decent and show empathy, the users would remain satisfied. Of course, the quality of medical aid made available to them is found significant but we can't devalue the instrumentality of behavioural dimension in activating the process of satisfying the users. In the Indian perspective, the hospitals and healthcare organisations plan and act with this realisation that core services are the only thing they need to offer but this is not the only thing the users expect from you. By conceptualising marketing in a right fashion, we engineer a strong foundation for both, viz., you offer quality medical aid and you also show personal-touch-in-service. Thus, with the fulfilment of their expectations, we find the users satisfied if the hospital personnel in general assign due weightage to application.

2. Time-hononoured Services: To be more specific in the hospitals and healthcare organisations, we find time management more impact generating because this is to influence the success rate of your treatment-plan. With the passage of time, a number of developments have taken place in the medical sciences specially based on the contributions of new generation of biomedical equipments and apparatus. Sophisticated equipments and machines have virtually transformed the whole process of medicare management. The diagnostic and treatment devices are now found completely changed. We call them inputs which play a contributory role in the process of qualitative transformation. The hospitals in general find it difficult to install new generation of expensive bio-medical equipments due mainly to the financial constraint. If we talk about the government hospitals, the results are found very disappointing because they not only fail in replacing technology but also fail in maintaining and managing the new generation of sophisticated technologies. We can't expect quality services mix from the poor, substandard, traditional equipments and apparatus. This makes it clear that hospitals need to assign due weightage to the time honoured development plans to cater to the changing requirements and expectations of users.

The principles of hospital marketing focus on setting the fee structure in such a way that hospitals are in a position to improve the quality of inputs. Not only this, the principles of social marketing make it essential that different profit-making organisations help hospitals in countering the financial problem. Thus, we rationalise the fee structure and open new vistas for the generation and mobilisation of financial resources from different sources till now partially tapped or even untapped. All these developments help hospitals in enriching their services profile. It is also against this background that we find it judicious to practice the principles of modern marketing in the hospitals and healthcare organisations.

3. Inculcating Mass Awareness: The hospitals and healthcare organisations are required to play a creative role in creating mass awareness because specially in the Indian society, the low rate of literacy complicates the task. A majority of the population is not aware of the food-borne, water-borne, pollution-borne, vector-borne and communicable diseases. To be more specific, the population living in the rural areas is found innocent, illiterate and taking least interest in the healthcare devices. The principles of social marketing make it essential that hospitals and healthcare organisations accept the responsibility of making the healthcare education or communications more creative specially with the support of audiovisual exposure and creative advertisement and publicity measures. The hospitals are not only responsible to offer the curative services but they also need to assign an overriding priority to the preventive services which make it significant that they inform and sense the potential users or users regarding the impact of food, water and healthy living conditions on the disease profile. The hospitals with the support of professionally sound managers can be successful in inculcating mass awareness which would minimise the pressure on the hospitals because in the long run, there would a sharp fall in the number of patients coming to the hospitals. We are also aware of the fact that unlike other profit making organisations, the success rate of hospitals depends upon their contributions to bring down the number of potential users.

4. Identifying the Thrust Areas: Since we find the marketing principles assigning due weightage to the innovative measures in tune with the changing requirements, the identification of vulnerable areas is found possible. In the context of medical services, the viral diseases, communicable diseases, child care, women care and drug addiction are found important sources of influencing the disease profile. In the Indian perspective, it is pertinent that we have a special task force to make an assault on the sensitive problems. We need to activate child immunisation, vaccination for serious diseases, pre and post-maternity care to women, a crash programme for malaria, cholera, leprosy, typhoid or so. The marketing principles make it essential that we, in our service mix, assign an overriding priority to the thrust areas so that the possibilities of disease are minimised. The principles of societal marketing advocate in favour of a transcendental priority to this segment of the catchment area which would simplify the process of making the services effective. An indepth study of catchment area, a survey and research of the changing disease profile make it possible to know about the thrust areas and the vulnerable regions. This also supports application of marketing principles in the hospitals. It is right to mention that to make your disease control programme much more impact generating, you need to identify the thrust areas.

5. Identifying the Vulnerable Segment: With the viewpoint of healthcare services, we find some of the segments of vulnerable nature requiring special medical aid and care like the backward villages, urban slums, rural women and children population close to the industrial towns and cities or so. To make available the best possible medical aid to them, it is essential that we have detailed information regarding the nature and character of problem found identical or common. This draws our attention on the development of information network so that hospitals get the information and make available the required medical care. Earlier we have talked about the management information system and we also find marketing information system an essential part of the management of marketing activities in the healthcare organisations. The societal marketing principles advocate in favour of a transcendental priority to this segment of the population and the modern hospitals have been found assigning due weightage to the development of information technology.

6. Behavioural Dimension would be Given Due Weightage: We find justifications for conceptualising marketing in the healthcare services because the behavioural dimension is found to be an essential part of marketing management. To be more specific, in a majority of the government hospitals, we don't find behavioural dimension getting any place. In the syllabi for medical education, the behavioural dimension is found neglected. The application of marketing principle paves avenues for behavioural studies even in the healthcare sector. The hospital personnel are supposed to understand the changing behavioural profile of patients and attendants and in addition, they also bear the responsibility of becoming decent, polite, sweet, sympathetic or so.

7. Cost-effectiveness is Made Possible: Of late, we find almost all the organisations assigning due weightage to the cost economy which is found based on making the process of managing the services cost-effective so that the services are found pocket-friendly or affordable to the masses. The marketing principles explore avenues for bringing down the costs on generating and distributing the services to the end users. The management of hospital materials, stores, human resources and finance pave avenues for cost economy. It is in this context that we find almost all the hospitals making sincere and honest efforts to maintain cost-effectiveness. This makes it essential that a hospital manager makes the best possible efforts so that the right quality of hospital inputs, bought at a reasonable price structure succeed in generating the right quality of outputs. It is also due to the fact that we practice hospital marketing.

8. A Rational Fee Structure is Possible: With the application of marketing principles we find possibilities of making the fee structure rational. The principles of societal marketing make it clear that the benefits of scientific developments and advancements should also be harnessed by the weaker section of the society. This makes it essential that the hospitals or healthcare organisations prefer a fee strategy that is found acceptable to the masses. If we talk here about the pocket-friendly fee strategy, our focus is found on subserving the interests of weaker sections on a priority basis. Incomewise setting of fee structure would be a judicious approach to improve the financial health of hospitals. It is an important managerial problem requiring due attention of the hospital policy makers. Shrinking financial avenues make it essential that the hospital personnel make innovative efforts to generate and mobilise the financial resources.

9. Motivating Personnel: We agree with the view that our slogan of quality in totality can't be translated into the meaningful purposes unless the hospital personnel evince keen interest in offering world class services. We find services promotion an important dimension of motivation instrumental in influencing the different echelons of management. If we expect doctors showing empathy, personal-touch-in-service, decency in behaviour or so, this is substantially based on the motivational plans or schemes. The marketing principles also argue for a plan which is linked to efficiency. If a team of paramedical or even medical personnel launch a camp in the rural areas and more so, when we find epidemics, a hospital manager is required to launch a camp with all precautions as per the required norms.

In view of the above, it is right to mention that the process of application of marketing principles in the hospitals and healthcare organisation is found simplified, if the policy makers of government and private hospitals evince their personal interest. We consider hospital a social institution successful in accomplishing the organisational goals. This makes it essential that the hospital personnel are well aware of the organisational goals and make sincere efforts to fulfil them. It is not only the question of survival but more so, the problem of growth and prosperity. Because we find hospitals and healthcare organisations a social institution, it is important that we assign due weightage to public interests. Marketing principles help us in professionalising the services in tune with the defined goals and targets. Thus, the hospitals generate their own financial resources and this is due mainly to the application of marketing principles. The masses, specially in the Indian perspective are not in a position to afford the expensive services of private hospitals. Unless we allow the government hospitals to mobilise financial resources from the internal sources, the problem of financial crunch is not to be solved. Besides, the marketing principles help a manager in understanding the changing behavioural profile of patients and attendants. A study of behavioural profile is found an essential part of marketing. Satisfying the customers/users/ patients is the main thing in the management of marketing. The hospitals and healthcare organisations thus need to assign due weightage to the application of marketing principles. By conceptualising modern marketing and analysing the problem in the face of societal or social marketing, a hospital manager succeeds in solving a number of problems. It is against this background that we make a strong advocacy in favour of the application of marketing principles in the healthcare organisations. What to talk of the private hospitals, if we find marketing essential even for the government hospitals. By conceptualising marketing, we don't mean charging more or abnormal fees and earning profits. Our focus in a true sense is found on improving the quality of services, understanding the expectations of patients and attendants and thus, processing the services in such a fashion that makes the task of satisfying the users easier. We find some of the leading private hospitals practicing the same and hope that others would also promote the same. We do feel that even the government hospitals implement the same and for that, an attitudinal change in the policy makers is found essential.

Users of Healthcare Services—Segmentwise Classification

Since we go through the problem of marketing healthcare services, it is right that we know about the different types of users. It is quite natural that human beings belonging to different categories or segments act, expect and react in a different fashion. Because a marketing professional bears the responsibility of satisfying the users, it is pertinent that they come to know about the changing levels of expectations of different categories of users/patients using the services of hospitals or healthcare organisations.[5]

In Fig. 11.1, we find different types of users.

We are well aware of the fact that strategic decisions are substantially influenced by the quality of users availing the services. It is essential that the hospital personnel have an indepth study of different types of users. At the outset, we classify users into two parts, viz., individual and organisational or institutional. In the category of individual users, we find all of us availing the healthcare services directly without seeking institutional or organisational support. In the

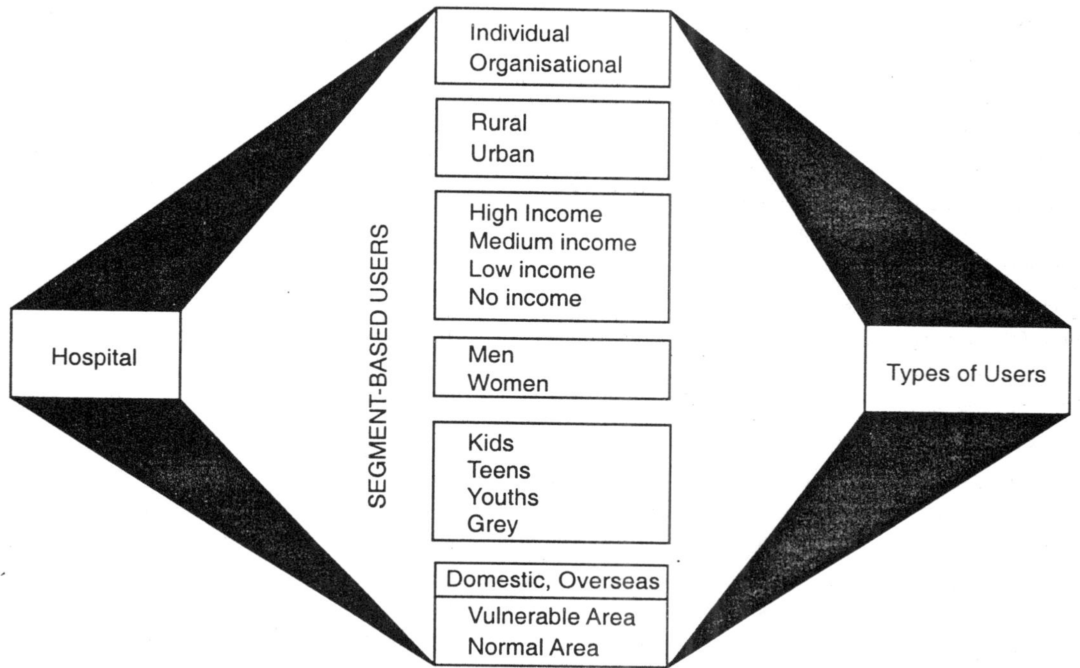

Fig. 11.1. Types of Users of Healthcare Services

category of institutional or organisational users, we find those industries or organisations or institutions making arrangements for the medicare or healthcare services of their employees. We find a link with a hospital or a healthcare institute and the employees avail the services and the medical bills are paid by the concerned organisation.

We also classify users on the basis of region such as the users living in villages and coming to hospitals for medicare and the users living in cities and towns and visiting hospitals for medicare. We find a difference in the expectations of both categories of the users. Like this, we also classify users on the basis of levels of income, viz., high income group, medium income group, low income group and no-income group. The behavioural profile of rich and poor can't be identical.

It is significant that we know about the users belonging to different income groups. The gender and age are also found to be important bases for making a classification of the users. The men and women act, react and expect in a different way. The hospital personnel are required to know about the levels of their expectations. Like this, the kids, teens, youths, grey have different levels of expectations.

With mounting qualitative transformation in the medicare services, there has been a significant increase in the number of overseas users. The emergence of a global market makes it essential that marketing professionals keep themselves aware of the changing levels of expectations so that the overseas users get an additional attraction and helps India in developing as a healthcare destination.

Since we go through the problem of medicare or healthcare, it is also pertinent that we know about the different categories of users living in vulnerable areas or in a healthy living condition. The users coming from rural areas or environmentally healthy areas have different problems.

This makes it essential that the hospital personnel also know about the vulnerable conditions and the normal conditions.

The hospital personnel are also found to be the users of services. The professional users have different levels of expectations. If you serve a hospital, it is quite natural that regarding the services of that hospital, you have a different perception of expectations.

Because the hospitals or healthcare organisations are supposed to subserve the interests of all, it is quite natural that they know about the concessional groups, such as students and downtrodden sections.

The classification of users is also found on the basis of nature and types of diseases. We find some of the users facing normal, minor problems and conversely, some others facing major health problems. It is natural that expectations and attitudes of all of them can't be uniform. The hospital personnel are supposed to know about them in detail so that they succeed in fulfilling or meeting their expectations.

In view of the above, it is right to mention that different categories of users use the services of hospitals or healthcare organisations and if we don't know about their behavioural profile, the task of fulfilling the same satisfying them would be much more difficult. It is in this context that we need to understand the different categories and types of users/patients availing the services of hospitals. Because we talk about the marketing management of hospitals or the healthcare organisations, it is significant that we assign due wightage to the users' satisfaction. Of course, a hospital manager bears the prime responsibility of making available to the patients, quality medicare or healthcare facilities but it doesn't mean that they don't go through the problem of satisfaction and dissatisfaction. The hospitals bear the responsibility of knowing about the significant changes in the disease profile of a particular catchment or command area. It is due mainly to the fact that problems of all the regions, all the personnel and all the patients are not identical. A study of the behavioural profile of different categories of users is found essential while studying the behavioural profile. At present, we have only gone through the problem of different types of users.

Of course in the eyes of hospital personnel, the needs and requirements of patients assume the place of outstanding significance but it is also right to mention that with the same quality of services, if you satisfy one segment, you dissatisfy another. Being a professional, it is your prime responsibility to inform, sense, influence, win and retain the users so that you are found successful in projecting a positive image. A study of the types of users of hospital services provides you important feedback to differentiate and generate unique service.

Behavioural Profile of Users of Healthcare Services

Though we have gone through the problem of behavioural management in an independent chapter, a brief study of their behaviour is found essential even in this chapter because here, we view the problem in the context of marketing. The providers are required to understand the behavioural profile of users which can't remain static.[6]

The doctors attending on a patient, the paramedical staff helping them in the process, the nursing staff simplifying their task and the managerial staff arranging everything for them need to understand the changing behavioural profile of patients and attendants. Of course, we find professional excellence of each of them playing a significant role in improving the quality of healthcare services but at the same time, it is also right to mention that their task of satisfying the patients and attendants would remain unfulfilled unless they have an indepth study of behavioural management. If we find two hospitals or healthcare organisations offering to the patients the same quality of medicare services but the personnel of one misbehaving and another promoting decency in behaviour, one generating tension, and another instrumental in diffusing the same; one looking serious and keeping mum, and another showing sympathy and empathy—the users in general would prefer the second one. The users without a choice or option may come to you but you need to create such a situation that they prefer to come to you even if they have a number of options or alternatives. It is against this background that a study of behavioural profile assumes a place of outstanding significance.

In the Indian perspective, we find a changed scenario. It is really amazing that even world class doctors offering quality healthcare services to the patients are found misbehaving with them. Of course, we find a very few of them specially coming from the new school having management orientation behaving decently with the patients and attendants. We don't find any sense in generating tension to the patients and attendants who have already been tensed by their own faults or by the decision of almighty God. In addition, the process of generating tension complicates the responsibility of hospital personnel because partially or substantially, all of us believe that our mental conditions have a close relation with the treatment received by us at different places and more so, when they are already tensed and work at a place found very sensitive to the multi-faceted odds. The decent behaviour of hospital personnel is to be impact-generating. It is in this context that we need to assign an overriding priority to the behavioural profile.

Attitudes, preferences, priorities and expectations are found to be the important constituents of behavioural profile. A number of factors are found influencing them generated at the places where we go or visit with a certain motive and high expectations. Of late, we find sophistication in the process of development of communications fantastically. The educated and conscious segment of the society come to know about the developments taking place in the different parts of the globe and if they experience or realise a gap, a strong base or foundation is engineered for negative developments in our mental conditions which shape the levels of expectations. If we live on a island having a complete communication gap, the expectations would remain static but in the society where we find significant developments in the field of transportation and communications and concerted efforts for building of a superhighway for information, the expectations move very fast.

It is against this background that we find the expectations of the users and potential users of the healthcare services increasing very fast. They come to know about the healthcare services made available to their counterparts in the leading modern hospitals, and expect the same standard and level where they become a customer. They on the one hand expect world class healthcare services while on the other hand, also expect decent behaviour in addition to the multi-dimensional amenities and facilities for their comfortable stay at the hospitals or healthcare centres. The leading private hospitals have perceived it in a right fashion and therefore, we find them managing hospitals in tune with the changing levels of expectations of patients and attendants but the government hospitals are yet to realise the same.

In view of the changing scenario, you bear the responsibility of innovating the core services, no doubt, but at the same time, you are also supposed to realise the instrumentality of peripheral services vis-a-vis the expectations of patients and attendants. This would inject new life and strength to the hospitals which, of late, have been found almost in a depleted condition. There is no doubt in it that the realisation of a hospital manager would not carry any meaning unless we find an attitudinal change in the policy makers. In a true sense, they are required to assign an overriding priority to the heath sector in the agenda of social engineering because all our programmes for the development of society turn into a fiasco if we don't succeed in offering to the masses at least the basic healthcare facilities.

Thus, an indepth study of the changing behavioural profile of users/patients is found essential and all of us need to perceive it in a right fashion. The doctors attending on the patients, the nursing staff serving the patients, the paramedical staff assisting the process and the managerial staff simplifying the functional responsibilities of all of them need an attitudinal change. To be more specific, we expect a lot from doctors in the very context because they are the leverspring of hospitals or healthcare organisations. May be that they have world class professional excellence; may be that they are sincere and honest but their professional excellence and sincerity and honesty need a positive approach and this makes it essential that they are also sympathetic to the patients and attendants and their behavioural profile change the realisation of the users and the attendants that doctors are indecent, inhuman and aggressive. It is really amazing that to be more specific in the Indian perspective, the doctors are yet to realise the instrumentality of decent behaviour, sympathy and empathy in the process of quick recovery of patients.

In view of the above, it is right to mention that the hospital personnel in general and the doctors in particular need an attitudinal change. We can't negate the fact that patients visit hospitals in a tensed situation and all of us need to make sincere efforts to diffuse it. The motive behind understanding the behavioural profile of patients and attendants is to change the functional behaviour of hospital personnel . On the one hand, they need world class professional excellence while on the other hand, they also need a personal-touch-inservice. This is not possible unless they assign due weightage to the behavioural profile. In addition, the concept of hospital marketing makes it essential that for motivating the patients and attendants, you need to sensitise the impulse of patients and the process would help you in increasing the number of patients which would increase the revenue position of your hospitals or healthcare organisations.

Market Segmentation

We find segmentation a process to divide and subdivide the markets into small categories so that the process of identification of the changing expectations of users is made easier. It is right to mention that the expectations of even two persons can't be identical. However, there are common properties, needs and requirements which prove to be an important base to divide them into the small categories. The rationale behind making segmentation is to understand the users' expectations. The management experts and to be more specific, the marketing experts feel that if we segment the market, the task of undertaking an indepth study of behavioural profile is found easier. Any change in the marketing mix without understanding the changing levels of expectations of potential users can't be proactive. It is against this background that we need to segment the market for the healthcare services offered by hospitals or healthcare organisations.[7]

In Fig. 11.1, we have classified users into different segments. This is a segmentwise study which would let you know the changing medical needs of the potential users. It is quite natural that when you come to know about their preferences and expectations, you innovate the process of formulating a sound marketing mix for them expecting a positive response. We go through the problem in the face of latest developments in the field of information and communication technologies which have been found to be an important reason for an increase in the levels of expectations of users. Of late, we find a number of developments taking place in the medical sciences which have been found making the ways for a basic change in the nature and form of diagnosis and treatment and at the same time, we also find a technology-driven healthcare system very much instrumental in shaping the levels of expectations. This makes it essential that the different types of mixes are innovated and the users are made available the desired level and standard of healthcare services. The task would be much more difficult if we don't assign due weightage to the studies related to market segmentation.

We find logic behind saying—"*Divide and Rule.*" It is considered to be a strategy helping you in modifying and developing the healthcare services. The level of awareness or consciousness is substantially influenced by education. We find educated persons acting, reacting and communicating with a sense. You come to know about their requirements and make efforts to fulfil them by making an adjustment in the marketing resources which develops a sound marketing mix expecting a positive response from the different segments. It is quite natural that the needs and requirements of high income group is found different to the medium income and low income groups. The affluents develop a high level of expectations and they are also in favour of fulfilling the same. But the low-income group people find the process complicated. Besides, we also find a variation on the basis of regional considerations. The prospects or the potential users living in the rural areas are found not aware of the developments taking place outside the world and therefore, they have limited expectations. The marketing experts feel that we find such variation also influenced by the nature and character of a particular command area. It is quite natural that some of the areas are found sensitive to disease because the people living in the areas have not increased their awareness, specially related to the healthcare requirements. Conversely, we find the urban population knowing everything related to the development in the medical sciences and therefore, they have high level expectations. Since they are in a position to afford even the expensive services, we don't find any change in their expectations.

The segmentation on the basis of age-group makes it clear that the medical of healthcare requirements of different age groups can't be identical. It is quite natural that kids and teens have different problems whereas the youths and gray also have different problems. If we make a microscopic study, it is found that kids living in the urban areas have different healthcare requirements to the kids living in the rural areas. Generally in the urban areas, we find mass awareness and therefore, we find child-care getting an important place in their family healthcare budget. But we don't find the same thing in the rural areas because the masses living in villages are found not so conscious to the healthy living conditions of their children. The requirements of gray-group would also be different to other groups because they have different health problems.

We find some of the areas more vulnerable and therefore, sensitive to the different types of diseases, such as heavily populated cities and towns and the industrialised cities and towns. They have different types of problems and therefore, we also find a change in their disease profile. On the other hand, the persons living in the hilly areas or eco-friendly areas have different types of health problems. Thus, we find intensity of population and pollution playing here an important role.

The healthcare organisations or hospitals have some of the organisational or institutional customers. In a true sense, they reimburse the medical bills of their employees who get medical aid in the hospitals. On the other hand, we also find individual users who are not financed or supported by anyone and therefore, we find a change in the levels of their expectations.

In Fig. 11.1, we find segmentwise classification of different types of users of the healthcare services. We assign due weightage to segmentation because like other services generating organisations, the healthcare organisations are also required to satisfy the users and for that, it is essential that they come to know about their expectations which depend upon their needs and requirements. If we find a hospital manager well aware of different segments of users living in the catchment or command areas, he/she may simplify the task of medical and paramedical personnel and to be more specific, the nursing staff who bear the responsibility of offering the services. In addition, our awareness regarding the disease profile or healthcare problems of a particular area would also simplify the task of managing the services in the face of changing requirements.

The aforesaid facts make it clear that market segmentation is an important dimension of marketing because it helps a decision maker and to be more specific, the hospital personnel in understanding the users' expectations which simplifies the task of innovating the services. The most important thing in the process is to satisfy the users which necessitates an indepth study of the users belonging to different segments. Since we talk about sympathy, empathy and decency in the behavioural profile of hospital personnel, it is pertinent that they are well aware of the population living in a particular segment and facing a particular problem. If the hospitals or healthcare organisations fail to study the same, the service profile would not be optimal to the changing requirements of different segments. It is against this background that a study of market segmentation is found impact generating even in the context of health care organisations. If you realise that satisfying the users is your important functional responsibility, the segmentation would help you significantly.

Marketing Information System

In an age of information superhighway, an organisation is required to consider the instrumentality of information system in making the marketing decisions creative which makes the ways for sensitivity and acceptability. We can't deny that even the healthcare organisations have been found facing the problem of competition and this necessitates an improvement in the quality of decision. The formulation of a sound marketing mix is found important to a hospital manager but the task is difficult because a number of changes have been found taking place everyday. The diagnostic as well as the treatment measures are found changing, the drugs and medicines are found changing, the equipment and apparatus are found changing and more so, the expectations of users have also been found changing. Not only this, on the other hand, we also find a change in the expectations of hospital personnel who expect more incentives in different forms. The environmental problems are found increasing, the water-borne, food-borne and pollution borne diseases have been found changing the nature and character of the disease profile. Thus, in the face of multidimensional changes, it is pertinent that a hospital manager and other hospital personnel keep themselves well informed so that the quality of services offered by them match to the changing requirements of the potential users. It is in this context that we go through the problem of marketing information system.

A technology-driven marketing information system is considered to be important to help a hospital manager and the hospital personnel in raising their awareness. We have talked about the management information system that studies the problems of all the functional areas of healthcare organisations in brief. Here, we make an indepth study of the marketing information system, specially with the viewpoint of making the marketing decisions. As and when we talk about a system, it is quite natural that we know about its different subsystems. We find marketing information system an aggregation or combination of different subsystems in which analytical marketing, marketing research, marketing intelligence and internal reporting are found to be important. The processing of data into information is the main thing in its functional area which helps a hospital manager in knowing about the nature and character of product or other mixes to cater to the changing healthcare needs of the society. Of late, we also talk about the Decision Supporting System (DSS) which helps a decision maker in selecting the best from the available alternatives. Of late, we find a basic change in the management of information because different types of technologies are also used in the process. Information and communication technologies have virtually changed the management of information. With more speed, accuracy and memory, we find technologies fantastically helping the process of managing the information. This makes it essential that hospitals and healthcare organisations take the support of marketing information system for improving the quality of their marketing decisions which would help them not only in satisfying the users but also in developing the potentials of providers to bear the social costs. It is against this background that we consider the importance of marketing information system in the hospitals or healthcare organisations.

We are well aware of the fact that there are different subsystems helping the process of managing the information and therefore, we need a brief idea of their instrumentality.

Internal Reporting: Internal Reporting System is to help the information system in identifying the levels of inventory, accounts receivables and accounts payables, spotting important opportunities, data related to the performance of the hospitals or healthcare organisations. The base of internal marketing information is the accounting system. We also call the data collected as the result data managed with the purpose of spotting opportunities.

Marketing Intelligence System: It is the second subsystem of the marketing information system which helps managers in getting information related to the current marketing environment besides identifying the emerging trends in the market. Census data, market news and reports, trade/health papers, health shows, medical books and journals, medical or health publications, publications of national and international health associations, publications of Medical Council, Health Reports prepared at national and international levels are the important sources of getting the information. In a true sense, the intelligence system acts as a mirror of marketing environment. It is also considered to be an organised feedback process of marketing communications. This subsystem supplies happening data which has a far-reaching impact on the making of sensitive marketing decisions. We find a number of publications of different institutions and organisations or hospitals and healthcare organisations which help hospitals in knowing about the latest developments in the medical sciences. Of late, we find information superhighway helping a lot in enriching the information bank. The processes of developing marketing intelligence system are undesired viewing, conditioned viewing, informal and formal research.

Marketing Research System: The marketing research system is also an important subsystem which offers special information on request when a manager is found encountering numerous problems necessitating unique information for countering the problems. The marketing research studies are found project-oriented. Generally, the information related to the behavioural profile and the changing levels of expectations of potential users/patients, advertising awareness, promotional efforts, emerging trends in competition and instrumentality or effectiveness of the publicity measures are collected through the marketing research.

Analytical Marketing Subsystem: This subsystem of the marketing information system is found useful for the collection of statistical procedures for extracting meaningful information from data. It is a computer based marketing decision support system which helps a manager in different ways.

The aforesaid subsystems of the marketing information system are used for getting meaningful or relevant information for making the decisions. We are well aware of the fact that a hospital manager bears the responsibility of collecting different types of information from the different sources and with the support of a marketing information system, he/she is required to make decisions which help hospitals or healthcare organisations in subserving the interests of patients. Of late, we find a number of changes in the medical sciences and we have the support of information in the health sector nationally or internationally. We talk about a technology-driven information system in which the information and communication technologies are required to play an incremental role. It is the responsibility of a hospital manager to develop and enrich the marketing information system so that the qualitative improvements are made possible. The instrumentality of marketing information system is coiled in the essense of making available to the manager relevant information.

In Fig. 11.2, we find different subsystems of the marketing information system.

The aforesaid facts make it clear that marketing information system is to help a healthcare manager in many ways. With the increasing intensity of competition, it is essential that a hospital or healthcare managers keeps himself/herself well informed so that whatever the new developments taking place in the medical sciences are incorporated in the marketing mix. The development of marketing resources depends upon the availability of information. If we have latest information, the educational and research activities in addition to the service profile can be innovated in the face of latest developments. With the development of the concept of hospital marketing, we find marketing information system occupying a place of importance.

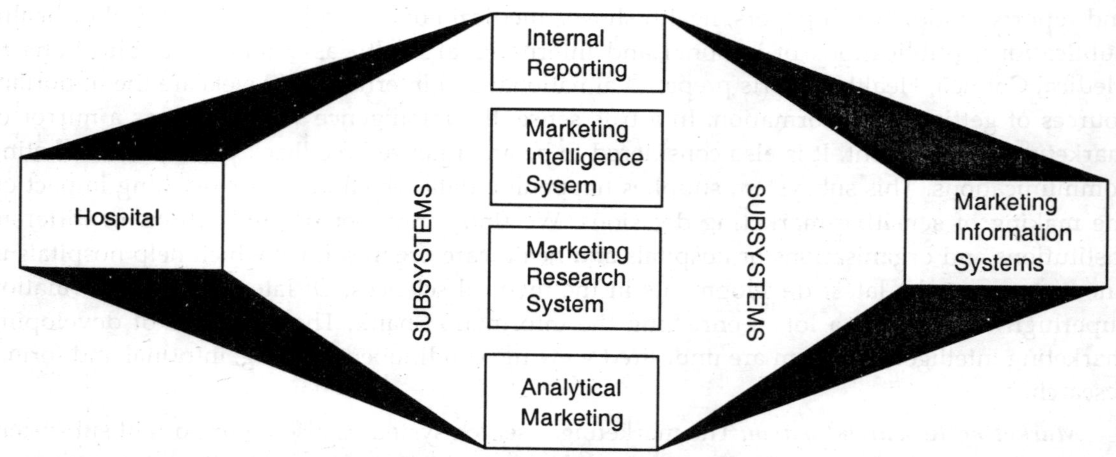

Fig. 11.2. Marketing Information System (Subsystems)

Of late, whatever the developments we find in the health sector or medical sciences can be used with the support of information superhighway or internet operations. This makes it essential that a hospital manager assigns due weightage to the organisation of marketing information system. The main purpose of healthcare organisation is to subserve the interests of masses by offering to them time honoured, economic/affordable and world class medicare services and this task would remain unfulfilled unless we take the support of a well organised and systematically developed marketing information system. There is no doubt in it that all the subsystems of the marketing information system would be useful to the healthcare organisations but the analytical reporting and intelligence system would be of outstanding significance because the financial informations would be received from the internal reporting and the external information would be received from the intelligence system.

In view of the above, it is right to say that like other organisations, the hospitals and healthcare organisations also need to develop an independent information system for marketing purposes because in view of the increasing costs of inputs, they have no option but to promote the concept of hospital marketing on the basis of the principles of social or societal marketing which on the one hand would make available to the masses affordable services and while on the other hand would also ensure the time honoured expansion and development of hospitals. If an organisation is found financially sound, its efficiency to bear the social costs is found at its peak. It is high time that we make hospitals and healthcare organisations financially sound which necessitates conceptualisation of hospital marketing even in the government hospitals.

Marketing Mix

We are well aware of the fact that under the product, we include both the categories —goods as well as the services. It is the prime responsibility of a marketer to make sincere efforts for merchandising customer benefit and services with the help of customer-oriented marketing decisions. It is the social responsibility of a marketer to make * sure that the organisations for which he/she has been working contributes significantly to the process of social transformation. The holistic concept of management and the defined principles of social marketing make it essential that organisations irrespective of the fact that they have or don't have a legitimate right of making profits bear an optimal burden of social costs. Of course, the healthcare organisations or hospitals don't have a legitimate right of making profits but it is not meant that they make the burdens of social costs so much non-optimal to their potentials that the process is to make the ways for their final departure. It is against this background that we make an advocacy in favour of marketing the healthcare services and propose to formulate the marketing mix which accomplish the organisational goals. We can't negate the fact that the formulation of a sound marketing mix for an organisation requires professional excellence.

The term "Marketing Mix" was first coined by Prof. Neil H. Borden of the Harvard Business School.[9] Both the term and concept have since been adopted the world over. At the initial stage of industrialisation, an organisation targeted the production facilities first and then adjusted all the other functional activities around it. A number of authorities realised that marketing is something that takes place after the manufacturing process is over. With the passage of time, the pace of industrialisation was sufficiently accelerated which paved the avenues or opened new vistas for the inclusion of a number of products in the profile. Thus, the stress could no longer be confined to manufacturing and gradually, we find development of service generating organisations. The conceptual framework of marketing mix has been designed by the different experts in different ways but perception by and large is found the same. Kotler, Keeley and Lazar, Davar and many others have gone through the conceptual aspect of the term but all of them agree that it is a fair blending of different sub-mixes which in the course of development may change the ingredients and the composition process. The ultimate goal of different submixes of marketing is to deliver standard goods or services to the customers/users. The product mix includes product line and quality, brand, packaging and services in course of processing or others. This draws our attention on the formulation of product or service mix. Like this, we go through promotion mix because it is not only sufficient that you contribute significantly to the production processes. Indeed it is much more impact generating that your prospects/potential customers come to know about your contributions so that they form a positive option about you and your product and make the buying decisions in your favour. There are a number of constituents to be included in the promotion mix, such as advertising, publicity, sales promotion, personal selling, word-of-mouth promotion and telemarketing. Both the categories of organisations—goods manufacturing or service generating need to charge for their product. If they discontinue the process sooner or later, today or tomorrow, they have no option but to make a final good-bye. This gravitates our attention on the price/fee mix which in true sense is a reward for your excellence of mixing the different ingredients.

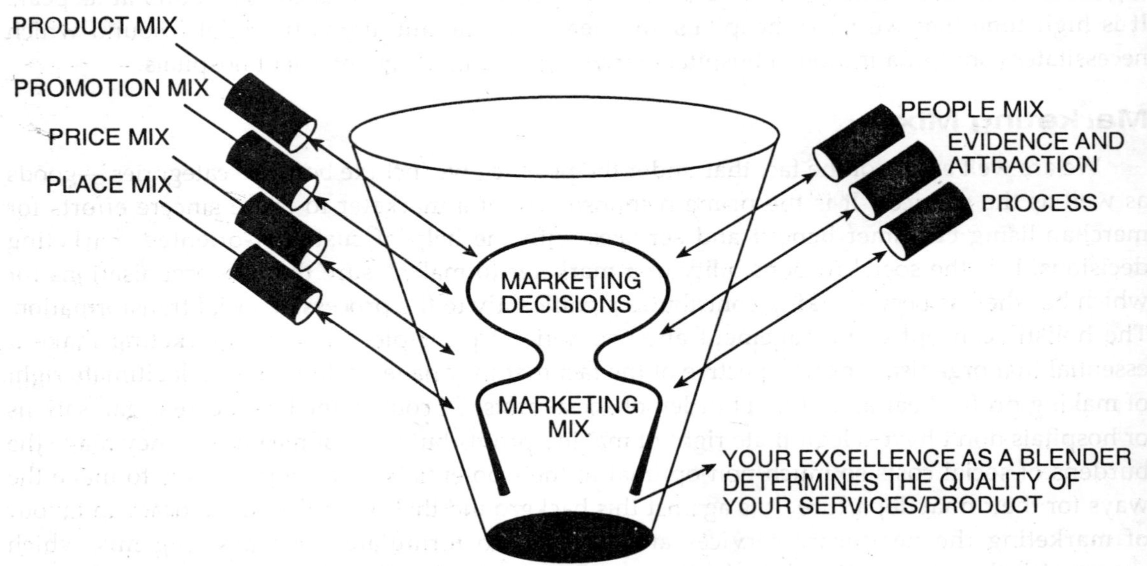

Fig. 11.3. Marketing Mix

You then bear the responsibility of delivering the goods or processing the services so that they reach to the ultimate or end users on right time and in a decent way. This focuses your attention on the place mix. Later on, the mounting intensity of competition necessitated inclusion of more mixes to change the fragrance of product and this included three more mixes in the marketing mix, viz., People, Physical Attractions and Processing. By the term "people" we focus on new people management which centralises our attention on development of quality people or human resources who are not only professionally sound but also personally committed. A degeneration in the process of value-orientation engineered a sound foundation for the development of the concept of New People Management.

The increasing domination of corporate sector in the process of socio-economic transformation paved avenues for the development of a new culture influenced by the corporate sector and this made it essential that your employees, human resources or working people project themselves in an attractive fashion so that the process of generating attraction is stimulated and it was against this background that physical attractions got a significant place in the marketing mix. It was also realised that goods/services are of quality but the people working there are not aware of the instrumentality of decency in making possible proficiency. This necessitated decent processing for making available the goods/services to the ultimate customers/users and we find inclusion of processing as a mix.

In Fig. 11.3, we find the marketing mix which focuses our attention on the fact that a marketer requires professional excellence for blending all the submixes like a cook who shows his/her excellence by mixing different ingredients or spices for preparing a delicious dish. It is quite natural that instrumentality of all the submixes in all the conditions and for all the purposes can't be uniform and therefore, based on your professional excellence you are supposed to identify the proportionate dose and the right time. If you have developed world class professional excellence, it is quite natural that you are well aware of the taste, preferences, expectations of customers/users of different categories living in different parts of the globe and therefore, you find yourself competent enough to market successfully not only in the national or domestic markets but even in the global markets. In this context, you need to remember that if we don't find a limit to quality of your goods/services, we even don't fix a boundary for the perfection or excellence or expertise you need to face the challenges and threats in the markets. Hence, you need to perceive that sky is the limit-quality (goods/services). Sky is the limit to perfection/excellence. If you develop your excellence with this notion, your task is fantastically simplified because the competitors find it difficult to accept your challenges and you succeed in excelling competition.

Formulation of Marketing Mix

The formulation of marketing mix requires professional excellence because we find it a process of blending the different submixes, the development of marketing resources or the tailoring of marketing resources in tune with the changing requirements. It is in this context that the managers to be more specific serving a no-profit making organisation require world class professional excellence. Whatever you offer today becomes outdated just tomorrow and the process of elimination and inclusion continues till an organisation is found existent. If you make possible more frequency in the process, the concept of Product Uniqueness gets an important place and this simplifies your functional responsibility of winning and retaining the customers/users as long as you keep on moving the process. Conversely, if the process is slowed down or stopped, the business is lost. Thus, the formulation of a sound marketing mix is an important managerial responsibility. Here, we go through the problem of healthcare organisations and therefore, a hospital manager requires world class professional excellence because based on his/her excellence he/she would be successful in accomplishing the mission, goals and objectives.

Product Mix

To be more specific in the service generating organisations, we find services mix occupying a place of outstanding significance because the high level of sensitivity and unfavourable conditions virtually prove to be an acid test of your expertise or professionalism. We are well aware of the fact that modern hospitals offer a number of services, such as core services, supportive services, peripheral services and the preventive services. In Fig. 11.4, we find the service mix/product mix of hospitals or healthcare organisations. It is an important functional responsibility of a healthcare manager to make it sure that whatever the services profile/product profile they develop bear the potentials of satisfying the users. How to make it possible is determined by the emerging trends in the medical sciences vis-a-vis the advancement in communications. Since we find formulation of a sound product mix a managerial process of mixing different types of services in the profile, it is quite natural that the process is substantially influenced by the scientific inventions and innovations. If we find researches getting due weightage in the healthcare sector, a basic change in the diagnostic and treatment process can't be denied. It is in this context that we find a technology-driven diagnostic and treatment processes gaining popularity the world over. For generating world class core services, you need the same quality of supportive services because unless the infrastructural facilities are of world class, it is meaningless to think about the generation of quality services. The mounting intensity of competition makes it essential that you establish an edge over the strategic decisions of your competitors and it is against this background that we find the peripheral services gravitating the attention of a manager the world over. We agree with this view that the core services help you in protecting your existence with peripheral sources simplifing your task of increasing the market share. Since by enriching the quality of peripheral services, you create product uniqueness, the users are gravitated. If the process keeps on moving, you even succeed in establishing leadership.

In Fig. 11.4, we find the service/product profile of healthcare organisations which is a combination of different types of services.

The services have been classified into four parts, viz., line services, supportive services, auxiliary services and the preventive services.

It is your professional excellence to gauge the changing healthcare requirements of a particular catchment area and to develop the mix accordingly so that the users experience uniqueness. Of course, it is important that you assign an overriding priority to the core and supportive services and due weightage to the auxiliary services but at the same, it is also pertinent that you promote the communication services, specially focusing on the creation of mass awareness related to the healthy living conditions. It is really surprising that a majority of the healthcare organisations don't assign any significance to the preventive services which has been aggravating the pressure on hospitals. To be more specific in the Indian perspective, it is of prime importance that creativity is made possible in the preventive services so that the masses come to know about the healthy living conditions and are found developing awareness regarding food-borne, water-borne, pollution-borne, vector-borne and communicable diseases. It is right to remind you that professional excellence of a hospital or healthcare manager is coiled in the essence of minimising the pressure on the hospitals which would not be possible unless we make the preventive measures creative.

Of late, we find modern healthcare organisations also innovating the peripheral services which focus our attention on a number of services making the stay and visit of patients and attendants comfortable and convenient. The seating arrangements, the potable water, the sanitation, the power, the transportation and communications, the entertainment facilities, the shopping complex, the restaurants and cafeteria to mention a few are playing a big role in

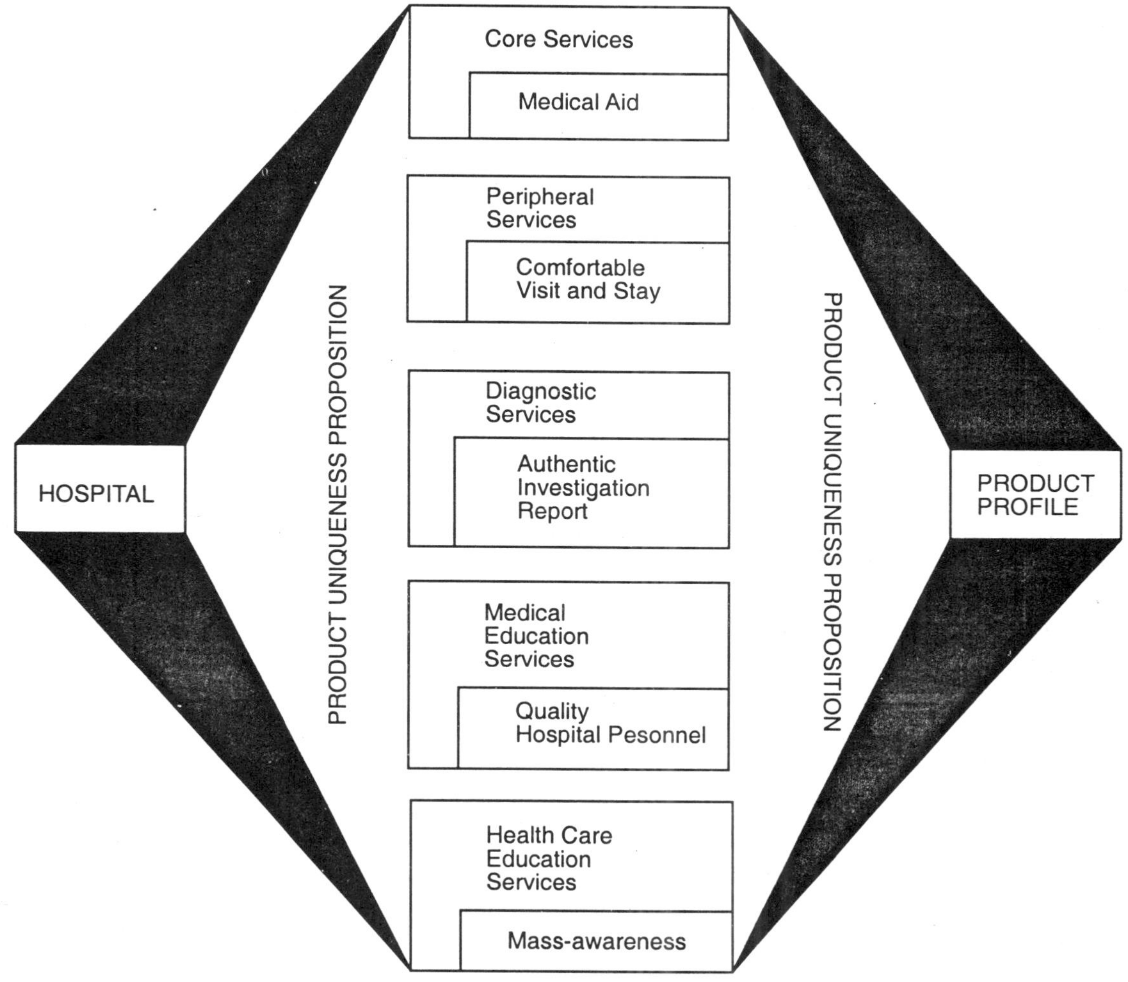

Fig. 11.4. Product Profile of Hospitals

making the stay of patients and attendants comfortable. Of course, you bear the responsibility of innovating the core services but at the same time, you also need to innovate the peripheral services because in the healthcare organisations, we find patients and attendants facing a number of problems very much instrumental in generating tension. It is your prime responsibility that you, by the innovative peripheral services of your organisation instrumentalise the process of diffusing tension.

The secondary, tertiary and other leading medical institutes not only generate different types of services but also produce different categories of personnel. We talk a lot about the quality of doctors, paramedical staff and the nursing staff but keep their development plans on the bottom of health manpower development programme. This has been found degenerating the quality of hospital personnel of almost all the categories. It is against this background that the hospitals or the healthcare organisations also need to take into consideration the quality educational aid to be made available to the medical students. The training institutes for nurses occupy a place of significance because they play an incremental role in improving the quality of services offered by you. The syllabi at all the levels and for all the hospitals offering educational aid and training facilities are to be updated in the face of emerging changes in the environmental conditions. In this context, it is also important to mention that we find educational institutions in general concentrating on developing the processional excellence of medical students. They don't feel that in addition to professional excellence, personal commitment is also to be given due weightage in the process of educating and training the medical students. It is due mainly to our neglected efforts and a negative attitude towards the development of ethics, human value and humanity that we find doctors becoming inhuman and indecent. Even the unfair practices promoted by the hospital personnel are the result of the irrational educational policy. It is against this background that we make a strong advocacy for promoting medical ethics, including it in the curriculum and making it sure that our products are not only professionally sound but even personally committed.

The formulation of product mix or development of product profile for hospitals and healthcare organisations thus makes it essential that you have blended the different dimensions optimally. Accreditation carries no meaning, professional excellence comes of no use, if the patients and attendants feel that doctors or other paramedical staff have been playing the role of a blood sucker. Thus, the formulation of a sound product profile is your functional responsibility and you are supposed to perform excellently. Like other organisations, you also bear the responsibility of satisfying the customers/users/patients and this makes it significant that your product profile is of world class. Of course, you need more frequency in the innovation process but with this feeling that services are made affordable because we find the masses poor.

Promotion Mix

It is not only significant that you perform well. It is much more impact generating that your customers/patients realise your constructive and positive contributions and this realisation would make the ways for promotion. You offer world class healthcare services to your patients; you are not only sympathetic to them but also show empathy, you not only offer time honoured services but your services are affordable too but unless these positive contributions of your organisation reach to the potential customers, your task of promoting the business is found much more complicated. It is against this background that an organisation requires to adopt creative promotional measures to inform and sense, motivate and influence the public at large because prospects of today are the customers of tomorrow. If you keep on moving the process of winning and retaining, your market share is found always moving upward. Like other organisations, the hospitals and healthcare organisations also need to promote and this makes it essential that they make sincere efforts and show professional excellence in synchronising the different constituents of promotion.

With the passage of time, a number of promotional measures have been included in the list which has raised the promotional budget of all the organisations promoting in a right fashion. But in the context of healthcare organisations, you bear the responsibility of increasing the effects and optimising the costs so that the services remain affordable to the masses. This complicates the functional responsibility of a healthcare manager. How to blend the different constituents of promotion so that the prospects are sensitised but the costs should remain proportionate is a challenging task which you need to perform efficiently and effectively. Unlike other organisations, the success rate of the promotional efforts of hospitals or healthcare organisations is considerably influenced by the fact that they have been successful in bringing down the number of prospects. You need to make it sure that your promotional measures have been so much effective that prospects have made their living conditions healthy and food containing nutritional values, potable water, eco-friendly environment, neat and clean sanitation, civic sense and aesthetic sense have fantastically helped them in improving their health and increasing their resistance power to counter the diseases. This makes it essential that your promotional measures are creative because creativity makes the ways for sensitivity which opens doors for acceptability.

There are a number of components of promotion, such as advertising, publicity, sales promotion, personal selling, word-of-mouth promotion and telemarketing. In Fig. 11.5, we present the different constituents of promotion.

Advertising: It is a paid form of persuasive communication. Like the goods manufacturing organisations, even the service generating organisations also need to advertise and like other profit-making service generating organisations, even the no-profit making organisations like hospitals and educational institutions also need to advertise. We find advertising a managerial process of informing and sensing the patients/prospects. In addition, we also find advertising a social process because the defined principles of social marketing make it essential. To be more specific, the healthcare organisations assign an overriding priority to social advertising, though others too bear the responsibility to contribute to the process of social transformation. Thus, the hospitals and the healthcare organisations need to assign due weightage to social advertising by making their slogans and campaigns more creative. May be that by doing such, they bring down the number of prospects.

While promoting, the healthcare organisations need to instrumentalise not only the personal promotion measures but also to intensify the non-personal. For making available the right quality of services to the right users at the right time, it is essential that we focus on personal promotion. In this context, we find hospital personnel in general playing a meaningful role. To be more specific, the front-line-personnel have been found playing a significant role in the very context. If nurses start neglecting the patients, if receptionists miscommunicate with patients and attendants, if doctors don't show humanity, the medical services even after the availability of world class personnel and sophisticated technologies fail in delivering goods to the society. Almost all of us are well aware of the most depressing contributions of personal promotion, specially in the healthcare sector. This makes it essential that we focus on advertising.

In an age of information and communication technology, we find innovative forms of advertisement. The hospitals also make use of banner advertisement. We also call it Internet advertising. Being a borderless and worldwide coverage, the hospital professionals can customize the ads for maximum viewership and thus, may reach to the target audience. We find banner advertising not only simple but even cost-effective. The users and potential users get detailed information online. It has a global exposure and corporate appearance. We find provision for the use of multimedia and therefore, it is used for exposure to a large audience. Thus, new generation of technology or hybrid technology has redefined advertising. The state-of-the-art hospitals need to make use of this form of advertising.

While advertising, it is pertinent that we assign due weightage to creativity since this bears the efficacy of making the messages and campaigns effective. By creativity, our emphasis is on adjusting the advertisement programmes, campaigns and slogans in tune with the receiving capacity of the prospects or in the face of changing conditions making the measures proactive.

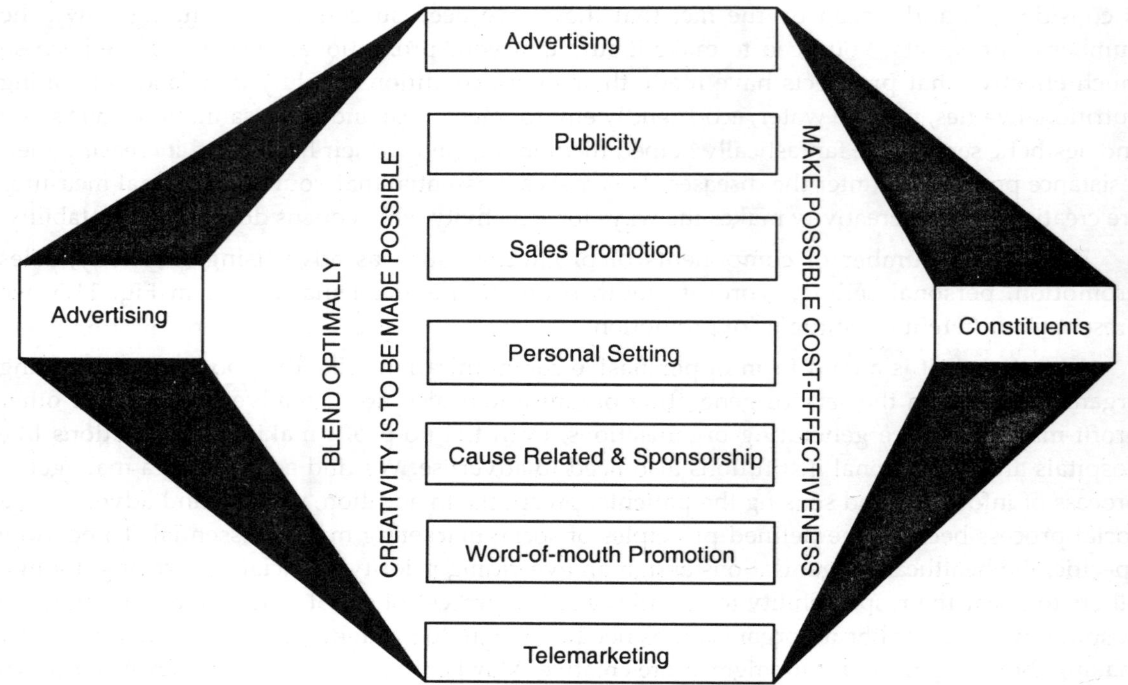

Fig. 11.5. Constituents of Promotion

While advertising, a hospital manager or a healthcare manager bears the responsibility of selecting the most effective media out of print media, broadcast media and the telecast media as per their requirements and budgetary limits. In the context of healthcare services, we need to take the support of print media and telecast media and to make a fair mix of the two. We need to prefer telecast media because it bears the potentials to sensitise even the insensitive rural and illiterate segments of the society. With the help of audio-visual exposure, the healthcare organisations and TV channels, private or government, can be successful in creating mass awareness. To be more specific in the context of healthcare education for the rural segment, we find telecast media much more effective in educating and informing, sensing and influencing the masses.

The health department, the hospitals, the healthcare organisations and the social organisations bear the responsibility of educating and sensing the masses. Almost all the profit making organisations are required to promote the healthcare education in a creative fashion so that the illiterate and poor segments of the society come to know about the sensitive problems instrumental in generating the health problems. The main theme of social advertising focuses on health sector on a priority basis. The municipal corporations and non-governmental social organisations are also required to evince keen interest in the process. Since we have a challenging task of sensing and influencing even the insensitive segments of the society, we find justifications for taking the support of professional advertising agencies who with the help of creative messages would boost up the process of sensitising the masses. Thus, the telecast media for the illiterate segment and print media for the literate segment would play a positive role in creating mass awareness.

We can't deny the fact that in the Indian perspective, we find even the literate and educated segment of the society, if not all of them, at least a majority of them, not assigning any weightage to the healthy living conditions. They develop a food habit inviting numerous health problems. In addition, the rural women have been found facing health problems on account of a number of children because they don't support the family welfare/planning measures. In a true sense, we find them generating two types of problems, viz., first due to more children, the health conditions of rural women are poor and on account of increasing population, the pressure on hospitals and healthcare organisations is found increasing very fast. This makes it essential that the concept of social advertising is given due place in the boardrooms and the corporate sector of the country accepts the responsibility of creating mass awareness.

Publicity: We find publicity an unpaid form of communication because an organisation is not supposed to pay anything while publicising whereas the advertising is a paid form. It is in this context that we need to assign an overriding priority to this constituent of the promotion mix. To be more specific, hospitals and healthcare organisations need to promote the same because they have been found facing the problem of financial crunch. While going through this constituent of the promotion mix, it is essential to make it clear that the healthcare organisations/ hospitals need to use it in two ways, first, by developing a rapport with the media people who would promote hospitals and second, by assigning due weightage to the public relations activities by developing a team of professionally sound Public Relations Officers.

So far as the first step is concerned, the hospitals/healthcare organisations are required to develop a rapport with the media personnel and even in this context, we find a public relations officer more effective because he/she is supposed to develop excellence of influencing and motivating the press correspondents for write ups and news items related to the positive contributions of their hospitals. If a tea party, get-together or lunch/dinner is organised for them, the process of sensitising the media would be sharpened. Of course, a public relations officer is required to have high communication excellence for the same so that the media personnel don't take it otherwise.

The sensitivity of public relations activities in the hospitals makes it essential that a hospital manager is well aware of the public requiring priority attention while publicising the services, viz., the patients and attendants, the government, the donors, the doctors, nurses, paramedical and managerial staff need to be influenced to activate the process. To enable hospitals to plan efforts to obtain a feedback on the present quality of services makes it essential that a hospital manager undertakes surveys with the support of professionally sound researchers and research scientists. They need to accept the responsibility of designing questionnaires and selecting the respondents and further collecting their opinions. If a hospital manager feels, the questionnaires can be designed by him/her keeping in view the emerging trends. The motive is to collect the opinions of selected respondents based on scientific sampling so that a hospital manager comes to know about the weaknesses and lapses and adopts the corrective measures. It is quite natural that while selecting respondents, a hospital manager would assign due weightage to all the concerned segments as detailed earlier. We agree with this view that communication with the stakeholders occupies a place of outstanding significance, specially in the healthcare sector because all of them, partially or substantially, are found influenced by the services of hospitals/healthcare organisations. After achieving your goal, it is essential that you come to know the reactions of the stakeholders so that you are in a position to change your strategic decisions, if the feedback necessitates so. It is against this background that in the context of injecting life to the publicity, we need to communicate with the stakeholders. It is essential that we find communications comprehensive, open and even repetitive if conditions warrant so. We don't find any risk in being redundant when you repeat the importance of the task and underscore the basic objective you have been trying to achieve with your positive efforts.

In view of the above, it is essential that you have an independent Public Relations Department. If we find it significant that hospitals/healthcare organisations offer world class healthcare services to the society and if we advocate that they should bear the social costs, it is also important that we publicise our positive contributions so that the public at large comes to know about the same. We are well aware of the face that a hospital manager gets an opportunity to develop contacts with almost all the segments of the society. May be that negative developments taking place in the hospitals and indecent behaviour of the hospital personnel are not coming to the knowledge of a hospital manager and therefore, the hospitals have been facing the image problem. This makes it essential that a hospital manager with the support of a professionally sound Public Relations Officer comes to know about the feelings of stakeholders regarding the services and takes appropriate measures to resolve the crisis. In a true sense, if you are interested in knowing about your positive or negative contributions, you need to develop rapport with the stakeholders. We don't find anything wrong, if mistakes are committed because it is quite natural that human beings working in an unfavourable condition fail to regulate themselves. We, of course, create blunder when we don't confess and repeat the mistakes again and again.

The aforesaid faces make it clear that hospitals/healthcare organisations need to strengthen the public relations activities by soliciting the cooperation of public relations department and the other health personnel working there. Of course, the projection of a positive image is found impact generating and even hospitals or healthcare organisations can't negate it. And the task of image projection is successfully done with the support of a Public Relations Officer who is supposed to be a high performer.

Dimensions of Public Relations

An important and internationally acclaimed authority on marketing, Kotler has thrown light on the different components of public relations as presented in Fig. 11.6.

Press Kits: Whenever you organise a get-together cable-talk press conference please distribute the kits to the press reporters containing writing materials which would influence them to write about your hospitals, of course in a positive fashion.

Speeches: Since you have sophisticated information and communication technologies at your working desk, please record them to make use of the same as and when the circumstances necessitate so.

Seminars: You are also required to organise seminars, workshops frequently and invite prospects, patients, attendants, industrial customers or large-sized customers, vocal persons, social activists, intellects and others to participate and deliberate upon the performance of hospitals.

Annual Reports: It is quite natural that you publish an annual report of your hospitals, specially in case of the private hospitals and prepare the reports mentioning the financial position of your hospitals.

Charitable Donations: In tune with the defined principles of social or societal marketing, you are also supposed to make significant contributions to the development and welfare of the

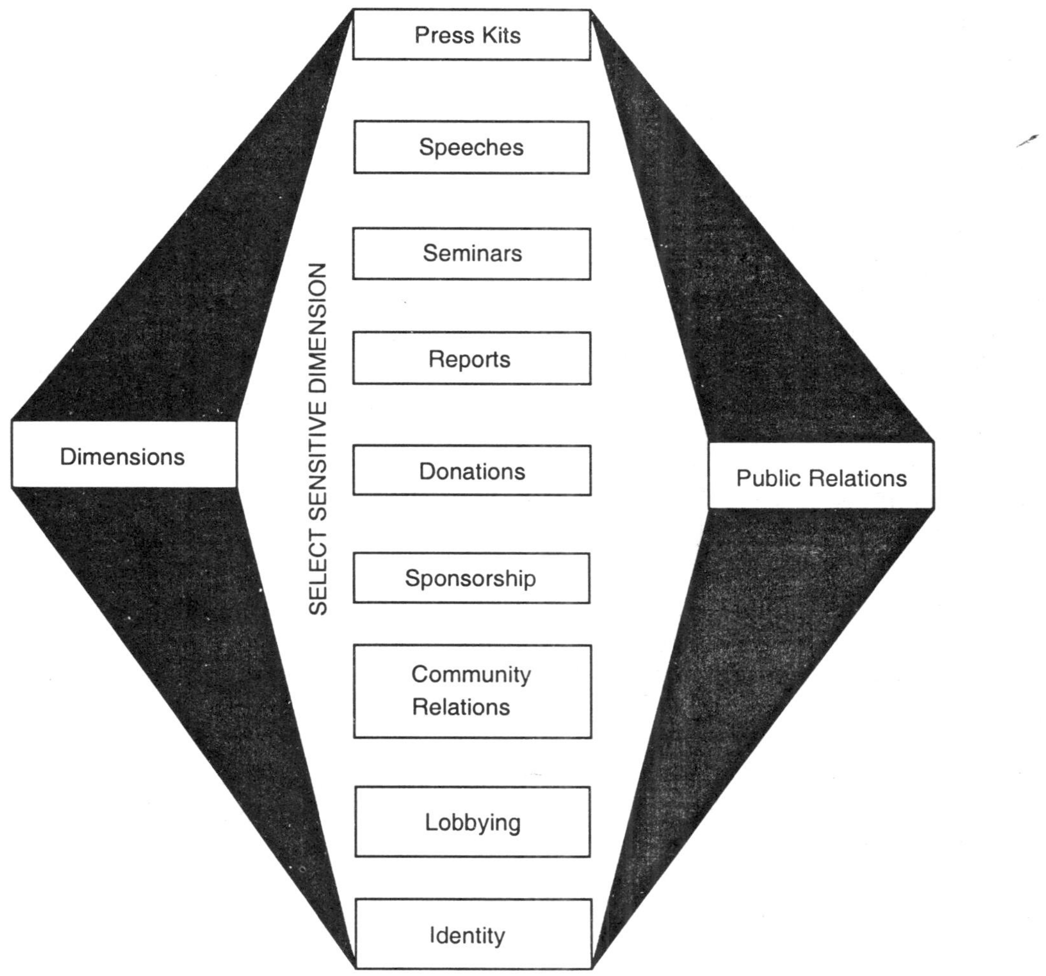

Fig. 11.6. Dimensions of Public Relations

society. While organising conferences, conventions and seminars, you may develop contact with industrial organisations making donations to your hospitals.

Sponsorships: To promote cause-related marketing, you are also required to develop rapport with the leading industrial organisations and business magnets evincing interests in the promotion of social welfare and interested in sponsoring events for making available to you financial support.

Community Relations: You are also required to develop community relations which would help you in projecting a positive image of your hospitals.

Lobbying: This focuses on lobbying the important personalities, VIPs and Social Reformists

Identity Media: You are required to take support of media helping you in the projection of a positive image.

Being a hospital manager, it is your responsibility to make use of all the components of public relations in the face of your requirements and situational requirements. This would help you not only in the projection a positive image but also in getting more business *vis-a-vis* the financial support.

Public Relations and Image Projection

If you fail to keep on moving your business, it is not difficult for you to regain, provided the innovative marketing practices are switched on. But if you fail to stop the process of tarnishing your image, your task is made much more complicated. It is against this background that almost all the organisations need to assign due weightage to the process of image projection. Like other service generating organisations, the hospitals/ healthcare organisations also need to project their image. To be more specific, when we find a majority of the government hospitals facing the problem of image, it is pertinent that a Public Relations Officer/hospital manager makes the best possible efforts to project a fair image. We can't negate the fact that distortion of the image of a hospital in general and the government hospitals in particular is due mainly to the degeneration found in the quality of healthcare services. The public relations activities, if promoted in a right fashion, would be successful in bringing their tarnished image on the rail. Thus, we find image projection an important need specially in today's situations when hospitals in general have been facing the image problem.

At the outset, it is essential that both the terminologies, viz., Image Projection and Image Building are clarified. A majority of us believe that image can't be built, but they are not hundred per cent correct in their observations. In a true sense, the term "image building" focuses on our positive efforts, deeds which change the perception of the receivers regarding the contributions of an individual or an institution. The purpose of image building is to project the right image based on facts and figures. The image building is a long-term result based on your positive contributions, dedicated efforts, deeds and value based services. To put it in another way, if we find hospitals/healthcare organisations offering world class services, subserving the interests of weaker or poorer sections, bearing social costs, we create a condition for image projection. This is one part of the process and therefore, the hospitals/healthcare organisations are required to make positive contributions and to make a case for image projection by activating the process of image building. If you are honest to the first process, it is quite natural that another part would be completed successfully and your responsibility of image projection would considerably be made easier.

The aforesaid facts make it clear that a Public Relations Officer/hospital manager while organising, strengthening and innovating the public relations activities needs to concentrate on both. They have to make it sure that their services are of world class and therefore, they have been making efforts to build a positive image. Now, the second task is to project your positive contributions specially with the help of sophisticated communication technologies so that you succeed in informing to the public at large about your positive efforts to improve the quality and to protect the interest of the publics. A hospital manager in the very context is required to go through the problems and if he/she feels it essential an efficient Public Relations Officer can be handed over the responsibility of image projection. It is right to mention that in the entire process of image projection, you need to solicit the cooperation of media personnel and that depends upon your professional excellence bearing the efficacy of influencing and motivating them in the right directions. Thus, the public relations activities can be helpful in projecting a positive image.

Factors Contributing to Image Building

Since your efforts for projection of a fair image are substantially influenced by your contributions to the process of image building, it is pertinent that you are well aware of the following factors:

1. *Behavioural Profile of the Hospital Personnel:* At the outset, you bear the responsibility of studying and understanding the behavioural profile of different categories of personnel. This necessitates an indepth study of their past records, reporting from the users' grievances cell or so. The hospital personnel in addition to the offering of quality services are also required to behave in a decent way. The cases of misbehaviour with the patients or attendants are to be collected and based on the same, a report is to be prepared. In this context, you need to assign due weightage to the behavioural profile of front-line-staff such as receptionists, cashier, paramedical staff and the centre for the collection of investigation reports, nursing staff or so. This would let you know about the behaviour profile of doctors attending on the patients. Unless the hospital personnel are decent in behaviour, it is difficult for you to project a positive image.

2. *Quality of Healthcare Services Offered:* We agree with this view that in the healthcare services, the quality of core services is found assuming a place of outstanding significance. This makes it essential that you make it sure that the different categories of hospital personnel are performing as per the defined norms. This focuses your attention on the offering of quality services to the patients. We also find cases that due to the negative attitude of front-line staff, the ensured quality of services is distorted and a gap is created between the quality of services promised and the quality of services offered. Hence, you are required to make it sure that your hospital has been offering quality services, assigning an overriding priority to the quality of core services and in addition, diverting due attention on the quality of peripheral services meant for the patients and attendants visiting the hospitals. Since we talk about quality in totality, it is pertinent that your professional excellence assigns due weightage to the blending of core and peripheral services optimally so that the services are made distinct. This helps you in creating product uniqueness simplifying your task of image building. Since we find a number of developments taking place everyday in the medical sciences, you need to make it sure that your services are in tune with the evolving technologies and in the face of the recent developments in the field of medical sciences.

3. *Performance of Hospital Personnel:* It is also significant for you to make sure that the hospital personnel in general are performing excellently. On the one hand, they are offering world class services based on their expertise while on the other hand, they are also showing personal-touch-in-service. They are found promoting ethical values, assigning due weightage to humanity and human values and thus, have been successful in proving their excellence as a top performer. If your personnel are found making sincere and honest efforts to show personal-commitments in addition to the professional excellence, your task of image building is found easier. It is against this background that the hospitals and healthcare organisations need to assign due weightage to the level of performance of their employees working in different capacities at different points in the different departments.

4. *Fulfilling the Expectations of Public at Large:* We find healthcare services considerably influenced by their contributions to the process of social transformation. If they offer concessional or subsidised services; if they offer free of charge services to the weaker sections of the society; if they evince keen interest in promoting social advertising, it is quite natural that the public at large would remain satisfied. Of late, we find the expectations of almost all categories of users of

the services increasing fast which are sizeably influenced by the sophistication in the process of development of communication technologies and the information superhighway. Being a healthcare manager, you need to identify the changing levels of expectations of prospects and to make it sure that a gap between the expectations and potentials of hospitals are bridged over. Of course, you are required to subserve social interests by offering quality services to almost all the segments without making any discrimination.

5. *You Contribute Substantially to Social Advertising:* For enriching your positive contributions, in addition to the aforesaid areas, you also need to make significant contributions to promote social advertising. In social marketing, we find social advertising getting an important place which is to promote advertisements directly or indirectly contributing to the process of creating mass awareness, such as nutritional awareness, regulating food habits, realising the importance of potable water and sanitation, inculcating civic sense, promoting family planning measures, awareness related to immunisation programme and vaccination, communicable diseases, irresponsible sexual behaviour and so on. We are well aware of the fact that hospitals/health care organisations also bear the responsibility of creating mass awareness and social advertising would help them in the process. The signpost, the slogans the wall paintings and related to healthcare would be successful in creating mass awareness.

The aforesaid facts are related to your positive contributions in promoting the healthcare services and therefore your deeds, contributions, mission make the way for image building. You, on the basis of your services are found in a position to project a positive image. Of course, the government hospitals have been facing the image problem and therefore, it is difficult for them to project a positive image. But we also find a few of the government hospitals and a majority of the private hospitals offering world class services and therefore, they would not find it difficult to project a fair image before the stakeholders or the public at large. Since you have sophisticated communication technologies, you find yourself in a position to project a positive image.

In a true sense, our deeds and misdeeds, positive and negative contributions, commercial and social considerations, decent and indecent behaviour, generation and diffusion of tension are the areas making the task of image building difficult or easier. If we find hospitals offering quality services to the patients, subserving the interests of weaker sections, innovating the peripheral services frequently and assigning due weightage to social advertising, it is not difficult for them to project a positive image because even if we fail in publicising, our satisfied group of users start acting like a hidden sales force and with the help of making word-of-mouth recommendations, they complete the task which remained incomplete even with the support of sophisticated promotional measures.

Projection of Image

Since you have made positive contributions and have achieved the mission by justifying your existence in the society, your rights of promoting the same can't be denied. By the projection of image, our emphasis is on adopting those measures which help us in bringing an attitudinal change in the stakeholders. Of course, hospitals subserving the social interests bearing the social costs need to project a fair image. The following measures would be helpful to you in activating the process of image projection.

1. *Organising and Participating the Exhibitions and Seminars:* It is essential that your public relations officers or your representatives or you yourself participate in the conferences, seminars,

workshops related to the health associations, medical councils and in addition also, organise seminars and workshops and inform the participants about the positive contributions of your hospitals. Since you have been making sincere efforts by subserving the social interests, the projection process would be proactive.

2. *Organising Patients Relations Programme:* Being a manager, you also bear the responsibility of organising Patients Relations Programme where your get-together and dialogues or face-to-face communications with the patients would help you in detailing out the positive contributions of your hospitals in addition to the feedback that you receive from them regarding the constraints and difficulties they feel. This would also help you in undertaking opinion survey.

3. *Get-together with the Opinion Leaders:* For projecting the image of your hospitals, it is also essential that you develop rapport with the opinion leaders, social activists and academicians, writing on the health problems found almost in all the catchment areas. The opinion leaders are those who have a say in the society and therefore, whatsoever they feel about your hospitals would help you in the projection process. The main thing you have to remember is to influence them and on the basis of your professional excellence, you can do it effectively.

4. *Contacting Philanthropists:* For the projection of a positive image, you also need to influence the philanthropists having love for mankind. To be more specific in the healthcare services, we find their feelings and comments more impact generating. Since we find the philanthropists all the time engaged in the social welfare activities, it is quite natural that masses trust on them.

5. *Contract with Local Population:* For the projection of a positive image, it is also significant that you develop contact with the important personalities in your command area. You explain to them the positive contributions of your hospitals and they recommend prospects as and when they get an opportunity.

6. *Due Weightage to Social Advertising:* Because you contribute significantly to the process of social transformation by changing the nature and character of your advertisement, it is natural that you get cooperation of stakeholders in general. You are required to promote social advertising by creating mass awareness and narrating the positive contributions of your hospitals. Advertisements related to child care, rural women, family welfare, sanitation, healthcare in general and nutritional awareness would help you in many ways.

7. *Rapport with Educational Institutions:* For the projection of a positive image, it is also essential that you develop rapport with local universities, institutes, colleges and schools to inform the masses regarding the positive contributions of your hospitals.

Sales Promotion: Since we talk about marketing the healthcare services, it is quite natural that we also talk about the sales promotion considered to be an important constituent of the promotion mix. In the hospitals/healthcare organisations by sales promotion, our focus is found on offering gifts or other incentives to both the parties, viz., providers and the users. We find hospital personnel playing the role of providers and the stakeholders are the users. Of course, the hospitals or the healthcare organisations need to use this component of promotion with a fresh look. If we make a strong advocacy in favour of professional and personal commitments, it is judicious that we also talk about the incentives to be offered to them for their positive contributions to the development of organisations and subserving of the interests of users. It is in this context that we talk about the sales promotion tools even in the hospitals and healthcare organisations. The promotion incentives to the hospital personnel for their outstanding contributions would induce others to contribute substantially to the process. The low echelon of hospital personnel needs due attention because they significantly contribute to the process of development.

In addition to the hospital personnel, we find justifications for promotional incentives even for the users specially belonging to the low income group or poor segment of the society. Because we talk about sales promotion, it is quite natural that limited incentives would remain effective just for the limited period when the pressure on hospitals or influx of patients in the hospitals is found low. Offering of small gifts and concessions during that period would help hospitals even in serving those segments who failed in availing the service based on fee or other considerations.

Personal Selling: We find personal selling an important constituent of the promotion mix where the instrumentality of an individual plays an incremental role in promoting the business. We are well aware of the difference that we find between the personal selling and salesmanship. By salesmanship, our focus is on the skill, excellence of sales personnel but in the context of personal selling, we find involvement or participation of not only the salespeople but even a hospital manager is supposed to be involved in the process.

In the context of personal selling, it is important that personal promoters communicate to the prospects or potential customers/patients/stakeholders in general regarding the outstanding services, salient features of hospitals or healthcare organisations which would, of course, be based on a comparative analysis of the contributions of other competitive hospitals. Essentially, you are not supposed to speak anything against your competitors but you have a right of making a comparative analysis of the features of your services. Since we go through the problem of hospitals, it is quite natural that our communications and deliberations are found based on specialities or the extraordinary facilities to the patients or attendants which are not made available by others. The frontline personnel of the hospitals, the receptionists, the nursing staff, the paramedical personnel and even the doctors and managers need to communicate effectively because we don't find anything wrong in communicating the right things.

In the context of personal selling, the managerial staff are supposed to play a contributory role because they are supposed to be excellent and creative in communicating and influencing the prospects or the potential patients. It is right to mention that a hospital manager needs to accept the responsibility of communicating with the industrial or organisational customers.

In the group of customers, they belong to the large sized customers not directly but using the services indirectly. They provide an opportunity to their employees to avail the services of hospitals and the medical bills are reimbursed to the hospitals or healthcare organisations. In this case, we find prospects for a big business and a hospital manager requires to motivate them so that they keep on moving the process of using their services. We find personal selling very much instrumental in the process of getting large sized customers, provided a hospital manager and his/her team evince interest in the process.

The aforesaid facts make it clear that personal selling may be effective if the front-line-staff, such as the receptionists, staff at the payment counters, nursing staff, paramedical staff and even the doctors and managerial staff assign due weightage to influence and motivate the patients and attendants. The personal selling is found based on personal relations in which the behavioural profile of employees play an effective role. It is against this background that we need to use this component of the promotion mix on a priority basis.

Word-of-mouth-Promotion: This component of the promotion mix is found based on the positive or negative contributions of hospital/healthcare organisations. If we find hospital personnel offering quality services, showing sympathy and empathy, decency in behaviour, charging reasonably, the word-of-mouth-communications act positively. Conversely, if we find hospitals offering substandard services, misbehaving with the patients and attendants, generating tension to them, it is quite natural that this tool of the promotion mix acts in the negative fashion. This makes it clear that the instrumentality of word-of-mouth promotion is considerably influenced by the quality of product profile of hospitals and in addition, the behavioural profile adds additional attractions and you succeed in winning the heart of patients and attendants who in exchange promote your services without charging anything from you.

The advertising may be ineffective, the publicity may be insensitive, the sales promotion may be unproductive and even the personal selling may or may not be proactive but even without an exception, we find word-of-mouth promotion to be effective—if you serve satisfactorily; it is in a positive fashion and if you serve half-heartedly, it is in a negative way. This makes it essential that a hospital manager makes best possible efforts to improve the quality of product profile because this provides him an opportunity to show the excellence of hospitals.

Word-of-mouth promotion is an exercise of communicating favourably and therefore, being a manager you are supposed to make use of this component of the promotion mix. We also call this mix of promotion as the instrumentality of hidden salesforce. The satisfied group of patients or attendants promote your business but you know nothing about them. To be more specific in the hospital/healthcare organisations, we find this component of promotion very much helpful to the promotion of business if the hospital personnel in general evince personal interests in offering quality services, showing decency in behaviour and making all possible efforts to fulfil the expectations of patients and attendants. But this component of the promotion mix also damages or harms your interest if you are not particular to the quality of product profile because no one would like to compromise with the quality. How to increase the number of word-of-mouth promoters is your important functional responsibility necessitating the cooperation of all the personnel engaged in generating and processing the services.

***Cause-related and Sponsorship Marketing*:** With the corporatisation of healthcare sector, we find significant developments in the filed of healthcare services. The concept of state-of art hospitals has added a new feather in the development and modernisation of hospitals where we find users not only getting the medicare services for quick recovery but in addition also, innovative devices with new features providing to the users an opportunity to gain new experiences. A number of leading private hospitals have been found developing in that fashion which has been attracting affluent sections from India or abroad. This focuses our attention on the increased societal role of hospitals particularly in the Indian perspective where general masses have been deprived of albeit the basic medicare facilities. It is in this context that we talk about this component of promotion in which an organisation is supposed to protect and promote social interest in different ways specially when we find an abnormal condition like natural calamities or war like problems or the problem of war refugee.

The cause-related and sponsorship marketing is a component of promotion in which hospitals and healthcare organisations generating surpluses are required to notice their participation by helping the victims of war or natural calamities. They get a platform to serve the society by organising a camp distributing relief materials or medicines and medicare facilities without charging anything from the users of services. Since we find them contributing to the process of social engineering, it is judicious that they make use of the platform for displaying their banners or advertising which is witnessed by a number of people. If we make efforts for image building, it is natural that we find ourselves in a position to project our positive image.

In the Indian perspective, we find a number of hospitals of world class such as AIIMS, Apollo Hospital, Tata Memorial Hospital, Apollo Cancer Hospital, Escorts Heart Hospital, Shankar Netralaya, Bangalore Heart Hospital and many others who have a well established brand name recognised nationally and globally. A number of high spending users visit hospitals making them financially sound and therefore, it is judicious that these hospitals significantly contribute to the process of social welfare. By making use of this component of promotion, they would be efficacious of promoting the quality of services for which they are well known.

The state-of-the art hospitals are to be popular even in the days to come. With the changing spending behaviour and increasing health consciousness, we find people preferring those hospitals and therefore, the cause-related and sponsorship marketing would provide to them an opportunity to promote the service quality. They can sponsor events and mobilize funds for protecting and promoting social interests where we find avenues for promoting the hospitals and attracting the niche customers. Thus, this component of promotion plays a dual role. On the one hand, the healthcare services are promoted while on the other hand, the interest of segments affected by abnormal conditions are also protected.

Telemarketing: Of late, we find telemarketing contributing substantially to the process of promoting and selling. In a true sense; we find scientific inventions and innovations paving new avenues for the development of information technology. Globally, the telemarketing blossomed in the later part of 1960s. With the introduction of inbound and outbound Wide Area Telephone Services (WATS), the avenues could be broadened for the use of telephonic services for the marketing of goods and services. Gradually, we find development of television and this could inject new life and strength to telemarketing. Automated-dialling and Recorded Message Players (ADRMPs) can dial numbers, play a voice-activated advertising message and take orders from the interested customers or users on an answering machine device or by forwarding the call to an operator. Thus, we find telephone an important instrument playing a commanding role in promoting the business. The sensitivity of telemarketing increased further with the advent of TV which is now found a growing medium for direct marketing both through network and cable channels. TV is used in two ways for marketing goods or services, first through direct response advertising and the second through home shopping channels where the entire TV programme or even the whole channel is dedicated to selling goods or services and we find instrumentality of telemarketing in the very context.

Like other goods manufacturing or service generating organisations, even hospitals/ healthcare organisations can use telemarketing for promoting or even for business purposes. The big or large sized hospitals can have a whole channel dedicated to the working of hospitals, the fees for different types of services, the accommodation available, the arrangements for attendants or so. The significant developments in the field of satellite communications have sharpened the instrumentality of telemarketing even in the Indian perspective. It is against this background that of late, we find e-commerce or e-business gaining popularity. The Health Department of State Governments or the Union Government can promote leading hospitals of the country to inform and sense the prospects in a right fashion. We also find big hospitals efficacious enough in taking the support of telemarketing. If the big hospitals desire, a network can be developed which would also benefit even the small hospitals.

In the context of telemarketing, we find telemarketers playing an important role. The hospitals/healthcare organisations telecasting their messages on the screen of TV are found benefited in two ways; first the patients or attendants come to know about the information, services, fee structure, amenities and facilities and second, the prospects can be persuaded in an effective way. They if sensed in the right directions and persuaded with creative dialogues of telemarketers can transform the potential customers into actual customers. We agree with this view that the instrumentality of telemarketing is substantially influenced by creativity. To be more specific in respect of healthcare services, we expect a lot from the telemarketers who are supposed to stimulate the impulse of the patients or attendants interested in using the services of hospitals. We can't deny the fact that the instrumentality of this new component of promotion substantially depends upon the quality of telephonic as well as the telecasting services. In the Indian context, the telemarketing may be useful to educate and influence the rural customers if we develop the network. It is the prime responsibility of a government that to ensure quality healthcare services, the government hospitals promote telemarketing because this would not only be related to the government hospitals but the leading hospitals would also be included. To promote the health services, the telemarketing is required to be encouraged in government as well as the private hospitals.

Strategic Areas in Promotion

Your task of informing, sensing, influencing, winning and retaining the customers/ patients need professional excellence of world class. Since the users of the services in a majority of the cases have been found educationally and financially sick, you need to promote creativity. You live in an age of technological sophistication where the pioneers are always promoted. By innovating the product profile, you have enriched the potentials of your hospitals to offer world class healthcare services. Now it is pertinent that you create mass awareness so that on the one hand, you succeed in attracting their attention while on the other hand, also minimise the possibilities of generating multidimensional diseases. This makes it essential that you promote with a sense. There are some of the thrust areas gravitating your priority attention and requiring due treatment. Being a professionally sound manager, you are supposed to formulate such a strategy that makes the promotional measures effective. The following strategic decisions would sharpen the instrumentality of promotion.

Inculcating Mass Awareness: It is well-known to you that the society for which you need to promote the healthdare services has been facing the problem of high level of illiteracy which has made the task of creating mass awareness much more difficult. We find a number of health problems due to ignorance or unawareness. We can't deny the fact that water-borne, food-borne and pollution-borne health problems can substantially be regulated if the masses develop awareness or consciousness. Contaminated water aggravates health problems and proves to be an important source for the water-borne disease. Like this, we find a number of diseases generated by the consumption of unhealthy food items. What to talk of the illiterate segment of the society when we find even the educated and literate segment not aware of the nutritional value for maintaining a sound health. Of course, we find eating/food habits playing an incremental role in the generation or regulation of diseases. With the passage of time and increasing impact of corporate culture on our food habits, we find a craze for fast food specially among the teens and youths. The latest in the area is "Fat Food" which has been found inviting nutritional deficiency and engineering a sound foundation for making your health conditions more sensitive to the different types of disease. Of course, we need variety in food since no single food provides us with all the nutrients that we need. Cereals like rice or wheat which form the staple food supply us only with a fraction of nutritional requirements. We need to supplement minor quantities of a number of vitamins and minerals to make our diet-chart balanced or proportionate. We need to remember, "larger our diet-sheet, the better our health will be." Carbohydrates, fats, water, minerals and vitamins are the different nutrients found in food stuff and we need to make them proportionate to our requirements. In Fig. 11.5, we find Energy Requirement Chart focusing on the Importance of food stuff in the maintenance of a sound health. It is your prime responsibility that while offering the preventive service, you make it sure that the promotional messages assign due weightage to the same. In the Indian perspective, we find most of us consuming good stuff providing to us more carbohydrates and fats than proteins. This makes it essential that we create mass awareness regarding the nutritional values. With the support of professionally sound advertising personnel, we can create mass awareness which would help us in many ways. In this context, it is significant to seek the cooperation of dieticians or nutritionists. In a true sense, we expect from doctors more positive efforts.

Category	*Age*	*Height*	*Weight*	*Energy Allow Kcal*	*Protein gm.*
Infants	0-5	60	6	650	13
	5-1	71	9	850	14
Children	1-3	90	13	1300	16
	4-6	112	20	1800	24
	7-10	132	28	2000	28
Males	11-14	157	46	2500	45
	15-18	176	66	3000	59
	19-24	177	72	2900	58
	25-50	176	79	2900	63
	51 +	173	77	2300	63
Females	11-14	157	46	2200	46
	15-18	163	55	2200	44
	19-24	164	58	2200	46
	25-50	163	63	2200	50
	51 +	160	65	1900	50

Fig. 11.7. Energy Requirements

Jha S.M., Services Marketing, p. 512/Millennium Edition 2000.

The most important thing in the process of promotion is to generate mass awareness and our promotional messages need creativity in the process so that we find masses well aware of the healthy living conditions. In addition to the food, water, sanitation and environmental pollution, our messages also need to focus on the population problem. To be more specific, the communicable diseases need a priority attention while creating mass awareness.

Instrumentalising Personal Promotion: While promoting, it is pertinent that we assign due weightage to the personal promotion measures. The personal promoters like doctors, paramedical staff, nursing staff and even the managerial staff bear the professional and situational responsibilities of activating the promotional measures. We need the constitution of a team of efficient, dedicated and committed hospital personnel related to almost all the echelons. If we find hospital personnel in general and the doctors in particular evincing interests in promotion, the effectiveness of our promotional measures would considerably be increased. The secondary, tertiary hospitals and even the big private hospitals and institutes are required to promote the healthcare services. The preventive services of hospitals/ healthcare institutions make it essential that the hospital personnel with the help of creative promotional messages and appeals make sincere and honest efforts to promote the services so that a pressure on hospitals is sizeably minimised. Your professional excellence would help the stimulation process and the prospects would come to know about the measures to maintain a sound health.

Technology-driven Promotion: In an age of information revolution, it is quite natural that we make use of the information and communication technologies for activating the promotional efforts. Of late, we find print and telecast media in an advanced form. The hospitals/healthcare organisations need to advertise/and publicise with the support of communications technologies. We find audio-visual exposure more effective in sensitising the prospects. To be more specific, the rural segment and specially the child and women segment need due care of a healthcare manager. We appreciate the positive contributions of modern print technology as a tool of promotion. The latest developments in the area are e-commerce and Internet services found more effective in the process of informing and sensing the masses. In addition, the concept of telemarketing would also help hospitals in promoting the services in a right fashion. The concept of cable-marketing would also instrumentalise the process. Thus, it is pertinent that the hospitals/healthcare organisations take the support of advanced and sophisticated technologies not only for medicare but even for creative promotion.

Innovations in Promotion: Unless the hospitals and healthcare organisations keep on moving the process of making the promotional efforts innovative, the results are not likely to be satisfactory. Your promotional efforts in a true sense are required to be a fair mix of curative and preventive measures taken by you. Of course, you need to innovate the product profile of your hospitals but at the same time, it is also impact generating that you make the processes of informing and sensing the patients/prospects creative. Creativity bears the efficacy of sensitising the prospects. Out of the available measures for promotion, such as advertising, publicity, sales promotion, personal selling, word-of-mouth promotion and telemarketing, you need to select the most effective constituents in tune with your changing requirements. It is quite natural that the promotional strategy varies in the face of changing segment vis-a-vis the disease profile. You are supposed to make your promotional budget optimal because the services are to be made affordable. Maintaining cost-effectiveness in the process of promoting the healthcare services is your prime responsibility and being a manager, you bear the responsibility of making it sure that a non-optimal budget is not to jeopardise your positive efforts. You need a fresh look, the innovative measures and creative efforts. How to increase the sensitivity of your promotional efforts is an important functional responsibility before you which is required to be performed satisfactorily.

An Overriding Priority to the Organisational Customers: While promoting, you also need to make *it* sure that the large-sized customers are sensitised in an effective way. We are well aware of the fact that some of the industries and institutions make provisions for treatment of their employees in a particular hospital. They pay the medical bills of their employees and this is found to be an important source for generating revenues for hospitals, specially under the private sector. Of course, you need to sensitise the rural masses but at the same time, you also bear the responsibility of paving avenues for revenues so that you enrich your hospitals of bearing the social costs on account of the facilities of free medical aid to the weaker segment of the society.

The aforesaid facts make it clear that being a manager, you need to make your strategic decisions result-oriented. Of late, it is possible because we have professionally sound advertising personnel in addition to the sophisticated communication technologies.

The ultimate task before a hospital manager is to make available an effective promotional strategy that informs and senses prospects efficiently and at the same time is also found successful in projecting a positive image of hospitals.

We can't deny that in hospitals/healthcare organisations, the word-of-mouth promotion or communication plays an outstanding role which is the result of a team-work, team-spirit and team-culture. The satisfied group of patients/users act like a hidden sales force. If we have made available to them quality healthcare services and they are found satisfied with the behaviour of the hospital personnel working there, it is very natural that they make it a matter of table-talk and communicate their experience to the friends, relatives and spouse who, if motivated prefer to use the services of that hospital as and when the circumstances necessitate so. This makes it clear that hospital or healthcare services depend on the instrumentality of a team. In Fig. 11.8, we find promotion programming for the healthcare services.

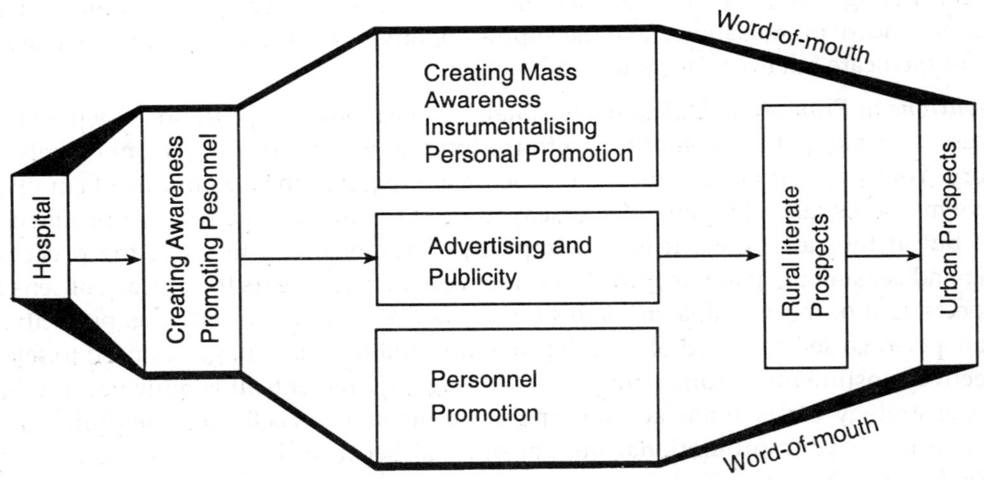

Fig. 11.8. Promotion Programming for Hospitals

The aforesaid facts make it clear that in the healthcare services, we find instrumentality of almost all the constituents of promotion but the word-of-mouth recommendations become much more impact generating which depend on the quality of services made available to the users. The advertisement budget, public relations activities, tools of sales promotion, instrumentality of personal promoters and services of telemarketers would hardly motivate the users if they feel that they are not made available quality healthcare services. It is against this background that while formulating a strategy for promotion, a healthcare manager is not required to formulate a non-optimal budget for promotion. In a true sense, the quality of services of hospitals or healthcare organisations proves to be a base and if you find the base weak, even if the promotional efforts are innovative and technologically-supported, the results or the sensitising processes are not to be effective. However, a hospital manager is required to think about promotion and to formulate a strategy for the same so that the prospects or patients come to know about the changing service and behavioural profile. Of course, the instrumentality of promotional measures in the context of educating and sensing the prospects or in the sphere of healthcare education for generating mass awareness is found occupying a place of outstanding significance and a hospital manager needs to show his/her professional excellence to sensitise the masses in the right directions.

Price Mix

In the Indian perspective, where a number of persons are found below the poverty line, the formulation of a price mix is found to be a challenging task. A hospital manager on the one hand bears the responsibility of making the healthcare services affordable while on the other hand, they are also supposed to open new vistas for the development of hospitals and healthcare organisations. Setting a balance between the two opposite considerations requires world class professional excellence. It is against this background that we go through the problem of formulating a sound price mix for the healthcare services. Quality services need expensive inputs and for which a hospital is required to be financially sound. Of late, we find costs of inputs used in the process increasing very fast. The Government hospitals in general have been found facing the problem of financial crunch because they are neither given a free hand while formulating a fee strategy nor are made available adequate financial grants from the government. They are supposed to improve the quality but to bring down the costs. Thus, a hospital manager requires professional excellence so that we find hospitals/healthcare organisations thriving significantly to cater to the increasing healthcare requirements of the society. It is in this context that we go through the problem of formulating a sound price mix.

The defined principles of social marketing make it essential that hospitals and healthcare organisations are given an opportunity to thrive so that they enrich their potentials of bearing the social costs on account of free of charge services to the poorest of the poor. It is against this background that modern hospitals need an innovative pricing strategy. The fee strategy for hospitals, private or public, should be income based. The quality of services would remain the same but the fee structure would be linked to the income-structure. For this purpose, we need to classify the society into four subheads, viz., high-income group, medium-income group, low-income group and no-income group. In Fig. 11.7, we find a pricing/fee strategy for modern hospitals which would help them in generating finance from the internal sources. For a social institution like hospital, it is pertinent that we promote discriminatory pricing strategy, or what the traffic will bear or a pocked-friendly strategy. In the Indian context, we find it judicious because a majority of our population finds it difficult to avail the expensive services of private hospitals. We don't find any sense behind regulating the pricing strategy of government hospitals more so when we are not in a position to provide to them the financial support they need to cater to the increasing healthcare requirements of the society.

In Fig. 11.9, the fee strategy for hospitals makes it clear that four strategic decisions would be effective for the four different segments. At the very outset, we go through the problem of no-income group because specially in the Indian setting, we find this segment often failing in harnessing the benefits of development in almost all the areas. They are not in a position to pay because whatever they earn are found inadequate to meet their family requirements of food and shelter. Hence, it is judicious that all of us who can afford partially or substantially contribute to the process by paying more than cost in proportionate to our incomes. The government hospitals as well as the private hospitals need a fresh look specially to subserve the interests of that segment. However, if we find a few of them even in that segment interested in contributing to the process of social transformation and we don't need to discourage them.

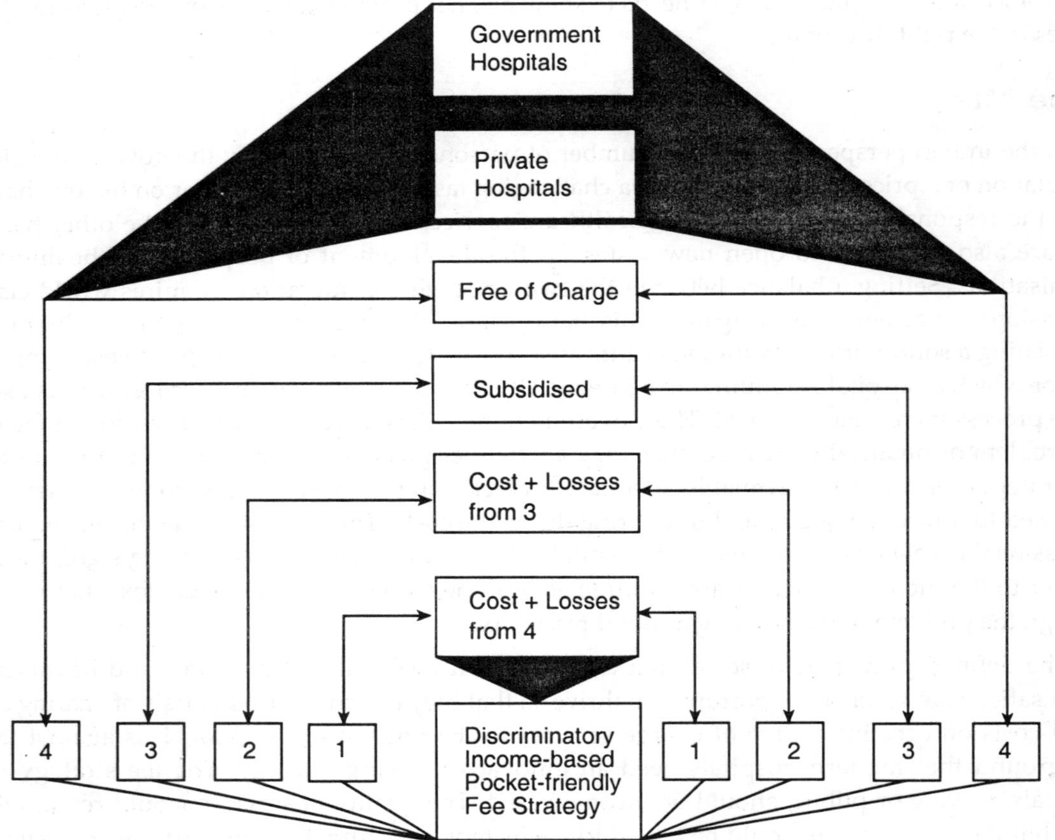

Fig. 11.9. Pricing/Fee Strategy for Hospitals

Jha. S.M., Services Marketing, Millennium Edition.

4 = No Income Group. He/she is not in a position to earn and therefore, the free of charge services would be made available to them.

3 = Low Income Group. He/she earns something and therefore, should pay a minor portion of his/her income to the hospitals as fee.

2 = Middle Income Group. He/she relatively earns more and therefore, the fee structure for them would be enough to make up the losses on account of the low income group.

1 = High Income Group. He/she earns more and therefore, the fee structure for them should be sufficient to make up the losses on account of no-income group.

This would be positive in two ways. First, there would a very nominal increase in the revenue of hospitals and the most important that a sense of participation would not demoralise them that they are living or surviving at the costs of others. Of course, there would not be any limit to the same and the psychological and situational factors would guide them.

The aforesaid facts make it clear that only from the internal sources, we find hospitals successful in making up the losses on account of concessional and subsidised services. So far as the development, expansion and modernisation programmes are concerned, the grants, charity, donations would be meant for that.

We find rationale behind adopting such strategy because even at the cost of all of us, the hospitals/healthcare organisations, private or government are required to be made available an opportunity to thrive and prosper so that qualitative as well as the quantitative developments are made possible to cater to the increasing healthcare requirements of society. We can't move forward with the strategy adopted earlier.

Place Mix

This submix of the marketing mix draws our attention on two important dimensions viz. channels for planning the services to the ultimate users and the location point for the hospitals considered as centre for generation and delivering the services.

Albert Einstein opines in favour of "the right patient, the right drug, the right route, the right time" for quality service delivery. When we talk about place mix, it is found concerned with the right route. We are aware that hospitals comprise many people-mobile assets such as beds, equipment and drugs and departments such as admissions, the emergency room, the operating room, the intensive care unit and the recovery room, associating with many documents at various points and stages in the total patient care process. It is quite natural that mistakes may be committed if we find a gap or delay in the transmission of information from one route to another. This makes it essential that health professionals assign due weightage to the application areas and routes.

With an acceleration in the process of technological sophistication, it is natural that we find its impact even in the placing of medicare services by the hospitals and healthcare organisations. On account of involvement of a number of people, technology, department and organisations, the new generation of IT has been found playing an incremental role in managing the supply chain. Of late, we find a major change in the supply chain management considerably influencing the operational efficiency of a particular route or channel. Radio Frequency Identification (RFID) has been successful in significantly enhancing supply chain processes and improving the customer services. RFID can be used to track certain medical devices when brought into patient's room for treatment purpose. It triggers a billing charge for use of the device automatically. This system can be used to track how employees go about their work such as moving equipment, caring for patients, etc. for streamlining the workflow. The active RFID tags have the ability to detect certain conditions such as movement, tamper or certain environmental conditions through the use of sensors incorporated into the tags.

The focal point is diversifying the use of new generation of sophisticated technology so that wastage of time and resources are minimised. The motive is minimising the gap or delay and maximizing the operational flow. We find leading hospitals adopting the strategy and getting the desired results. It is clear that when we talk about the healthcare services, the potential users are supposed to visit the centres or hospitals where the services are to be delivered. Right from diagnosis to treatment and recovery, we find different stages managed and controlled by different channels. The RFID technology has been found instrumental even in improving the functioning of monitoring devices, managing patient care and administrative devices such as identification of patients, routing and treatment, administration and inventory, laboratory examination, identification of departments and medical procedures. Hence, the healthcare professionals need to promote new generation of technology for getting the desired quality of services.

In the context of place mix, the health professionals bear the responsibility of making it sure that all the routes through which the services move are in perfect order and the different units or sections or departments contributing to the process have been following the tracks, maintaining the time schedule and monitoring everything involved in the process. Since we find services covering different states, it is pertinent that the concerned people behave in a decent way. This draws our attention on people in general and the front-line personnel in particular. Being a manager, you need to make it sure that service quality-gap due mainly to indecent behaviour of people is bridged. The service quality promised and the service-quality delivered may create a behavioural gap which may adversely affect the quality of services.

Additionally, the place mix also draws our attention on the location points for hospitals. Accessibility is an important consideration and therefore, it is to be made sure that the patients do not experience any difficulty while identifying and visiting the hospitals. If we find hospitals not having a convenient accessibility, lack of all weather proof roads and transportation facilities, the patients would experience difficulties which may result into irreparable losses. While locating hospitals, the hospital planners and professionals need to identify a place which is free from health hazards. The place identified must be peaceful and well connected with the transportation and communication services. In the changing scenario, we find safety also an important consideration and therefore, the health professionals need to consider the availability of fire brigade and administrative and protective services so that safety and security of hospital people, assets, patients and visitors or attendants are made sure. It we find hospitals close to big industries or population not having a sense, a number of problems would crop up which would affect the services quality vis-a-vis would make the service environment unsafe or insecure. Thus, trouble-free, peaceful well-connected and environment-friendly locations need due attention of healthcare professionals.

Processing

This submix of marketing focuses our attention on processing of healthcare services. In an age of technology, we find the concept of processing redefined. The new generation of sophisticated technology helps in increasing the operational flow. The involvement of people, instrumentality of technology and availability of service environment play an incremental role in processing the healthcare services. For right and time honoured processing, it is only not essential that medical, paramedical or other staff have been working properly but it is also impact generating that we find them behaving decently. They need to develop their awareness of sympathy and empathy. To be more specific, the frontline staff working as receptionists, nurses and even doctors need to know about behavioural dimensions. The healthcare services cross different windows, counters, departments and sections. Particularly, the people serving the government hospitals need to remember it because a large number of complaints have been found against the behavioural profile of hospital personnel.

This necessitates due weightage to the behavioural profile of personnel and a medical superintendent right now serving the government hospitals are required to educate and train them in the changing perspective. There are different points or stages where we need due attention, such as the cash counter, admission, registration, investigation reports and reception. It is pertinent that the patients or attendants at the sensitive counters are given due treatment so that the distortion in the process of offering the services is removed. A hospital manager/superintendent is required to bridge over the gap between the services-ensured and services-offered and this is not possible unless we find a full team of hospital personnel coordinating each other to make possible good patient care.

Thus, while going through the place mix, it is important that a hospital manager gravitates his/her attention on the windows and wards through which the services reach to the patients. He/she bears the responsibility of making it sure that different departments and the personnel working there are careful and in addition to the professional excellence, they also have the potential to understand the changing behavioural profile of patients and attendants. Right processing, time-honoured processing, decent processing are some of the small things showing significant impact on the level of efficiency of personnel vis-a-vis satisfaction to the users and attendants. It is against this background that we need a fresh look on the channelisation of services.

To be more specific, in the large-sized hospitals where we find local and outstation patients and attendants visiting the hospitals, it is essential that a hospital manager is particular to the influx of patients and the pressure on outdoor and emergency services are given due weightage. In specialised hospitals of excellence, we find arrival of patients from different parts of country or even from abroad and this makes it essential that the overcrowding problem is countered intelligently. Increasing pressure on hospitals of special category makes it clear that we find a gap in the demand and supply positions of the hospital because the available facilities in the hospitals are not to cater to the increasing demand position. It is in this context that a hospital manager while going through the problem of delivering the services to the ultimate users requires due support of a full team without which the processing would face the problem of degeneration both at the micro and macro levels.

We also find cases where the location point for a particular hospital assumes a place of significance. In addition to the comforts of patients and attendants, a hospital manager is also required to go through the constraints and difficulties before the hospital personnel specially while processing the services. There are a number of cases to prove that specially in the government hospitals, we find the problem of quality and therefore, a manager requires to ascertain that services are the most important thing in the management of hospitals. But even if you improve the quality and neglect the personnel, other constraints would influence the process. It is against this background that this mix of the marketing mix becomes instrumental in distorting while processing the services if a hospital manager is not to place right, efficient and decent personnel at the sensitive windows of the hospitals.

In view of the aforesaid facts, it is right to observe that place mix requires due care of a hospital manager. He/she requires right processing of services so that the patients are found satisfied. It is your professional excellence that would again determine the magnitude of your success.

Physical Evidence and Attractions

This additional submix of the marketing mix focuses our attention on physical amenities and facilities, surroundings and premises making possible qualitative improvements in the service environment and ensuring development of service culture where the hospital staff feels pleasure in performing and the patients and attendants gain new experiences while using the services. We find hospital and healthcare services distinct to others coiling much more sensitivity where albeit minor lapses result into irreparable losses. The environmental conditions where hospitals and healthcare organisations are located become a determining factor in improving the service quality. The modern hospital and healthcare services depend on a number of instruments, equipments, apparatus, machines, and more so, new generation of information and communication technology and even their intelligent and tactical display also become a part of service ambience. The interiors, exterior lighting, ventilation, sanitation, furnishing and allied services play an effective role in the development of service environment in hospitals. We cannot deny that cleanliness is considered to be the most significant dimension in the healthcare organisations where all our efforts turn into a fiasco if we find even a minor scope for infection. Further, the surrounding and premises if found environment-friendly may be helpful in improving the quality of healthcare services. The indoor, ornamental shadow plants, display of signposts, counters of receptionists, waiting lounges, parking places, lighting in the premises are also considered significant with the view point of making hospital a place for easy and quick recovery. Plantation and afforestation, safe and convenient accessibility, safety and security cannot be underestimated as a part of service environment.

Of late, we find hospitals and healthcare organisations witnessing qualitative transformation and credibility for such a new development is found due to corporatisation and techniculture. The increasing temptation and fascination for state-of-art hospitals make it clear that the healthcare sector has entered a new age and has been crossing a new phase where sophistication becomes an integral part of attraction and uniqueness. Thus, we have been defining and redefining the concept of service quality particularly in the context of state-of-the-art hospitals where modern amenities and facilities and innovative devices are given due weightage. For the different speciality medicare centres, we find the perception of state-of-art hospitals having a different list for service ambience and physical facilities. It is the responsibility of hospital professionals to keep into consideration their requirements and to make available the same. The state-of-the art for automated Pathology Department requires automated system for biochemistry, harmones, viral markers and drug-level assays, state-of-the art haematology analyzer for accurate enumeration of blood cells including differential counts, well-equipped histopathology units including facilities like frozen section, immunohistochemistry, tumor markers and cytopathology.

Ultramodern microbiology laboratory equipped with an automated blood culture monitoring system becomes essential for the state-of-the-art Pathology Department. The state-of-the-art cancer centres requires Solid Tumor Chemotherapy, HaematoOncology, Paediatric Oncology, Surgical Oncology, oral malignancies, Colo, Cervix, Head and neck., Rectum, Uterus, Thoracic and Endocrine surgery and Radiation Oncology. A number of technologies are required for this purpose such as linear accelerator, high energy radiation, precise/conformal radiation, Intensity Modulated Radiotherapy, etc. The focus is on the point that state-of-the-art facilities are found influenced by the speciality of a particular centre or hospital.

The hospital professionals need to ensure a service ambience where promised quality of services are made available to the users. They should make it sure that the users and attendants visiting hospitals or healthcare centres come to know the fact that the state-of-the-art hospitals are different to the general hospitals. In addition, they also need to make it sure that these technologies are managed, maintained and handled and operated by the right persons having expertise and experiences for the same. Right from the reception to the service delivery point, a number of aspects need due attention of professionals such as the signposts displayed at different sensitive points, the lighting and positioning and colour and intensity of light, the furnishing particularily in the lounges meant for visitors, the places for the relaxation of medical and paramedical staff, the ventilation, keeping in view the temperature and climatic condition, the sanitation services for patients and attendants, the instrumentality of information technology and the quality and generation of computers and computer professionals used for this purpose, etc.

Particularly in the healthcare organisations, the provisions for disinfection for sensitive places needs priority attention of hospital professionals. The surroundings and premises of hospitals also become significant because the healthy environmental conditions activate the process of quick recovery. If we find service lapses in the hospitals efficacious of developing a service ambience in which service environment is found of world class, thematical and paramedical staff may be successful in developing service culture. Hence, the hospital professionals bear the responsibility of developing and nurturing service culture for which they have to assign due weightage to ambient conditions which would help the hospital staff in performing and the patients and attendants in gaining new experiences.

The above mentioned facts make it clear that by managing service ambience, the hospital professionals may be successful in increasing the operational flow which would bring momentum in the service delivery process. If the technologies and hospital staff work in a right way, there will be a significant increase in the speed which would also make the process of diagnosis and treatment cost effective.

Physical Attractions

There is nothing more appealing than a man with a sense of wit and fun. There is nothing more paying than an aesthete. With the growing influence of corporate culture in the process of socio-economic emancipation, we find a basic change in the perception of personality development. Of late, the leading global organisations have been found assigning due weightage to physical attractions.[10] The subjective knowledge, no doubt, plays an important role in almost all the organisations but at the same time, the organisations also expect that their employees have a classic and an attractive look. A look that generates a positive image; a look that creates distinction; a look that magnifies optimism and a look that conveys elegance. In a true sense, we find look of employees narrating the image of the organisation in which they work. If you promote a poor, repulsive and pessimism-generating look, the public at large develops a negative attitude about your organisation. It is against this background that we find physical attractions occupying a place of significance in the marketing mix of modern organisations either producing goods or generating services; either working with the motto of generating profits or working to subserve social interests. We agree with this view that like other organisations, the healthcare organisations also need to assign due weightage to this submix of the marketing mix.

Since we go through the problem of hospitals or healthcare organisations, it is pertinent that we view the problem with a different vision. Of course, the dresses used by the hospital personnel narrate the culture of their hospital for which they work. The professional requirements, situational limitations, circumstantial compulsion, cultural barriers are some of the important considerations influencing the nature and types of dresses used by us. It is quite natural that technocrats, corporate executives, cine artists, singers, doctors or others are not supposed to have an identical look and therefore, the dresses used by them would have an apparent variation. The main thing in the process is to look smart and active and influencing the attitudes of users/customers/patients/attendants/prospects in a positive fashion. In a majority of the hospitals, we find uniform culture making a good-bye. Of course, we find a very few of the healthcare organisations considering it significant. This makes it essential that the policy makers, boardrooms, top-level managers and senior doctors assign an overriding priority to the uniform-culture.

Of late, we promote techniculture, develop human resources in the face of evolving technologies but devalue uniform culture. The Industrial Psychologists are of the opinion that we find a close relation between dresses used by us and participation expected from us. If we find Security, Police, Air Hostess, Hotel Personnel wearing the uniform/ dresses made available to them; a sense of participation is generated and he/she finds himself/herself on duty and in action. Like this, if we find doctors wearing uniform, nurses and other hospital personnel wearing the dresses made available to them by the hospitals, they start thinking about their profession. Not only this, it is also found significant with the viewpoint of changing the attitudes of patients, attendants or others. The behavioural profile of patients and attendants witness a change the moment they find doctors and nurses in the dresses made available to them. This makes it essential that hospitals or healthcare organisations irrespective of size, type, sex, age and sectoral variation promote uniform culture to activate work culture. The hospital personnel on duty need to assign an overriding priority to the same because a sense of responsibility would effectively be generated.

While promoting uniform culture, the main thing that you need to take care is that the dresses used by the personnel are neat and clean, well-pressed and infection-free. A hospital or a healthcare manager bears the responsibility of making it sure that specially the linen used at different places are not to generate the problem of infection. It is in this context that we find laundry management getting an important place in the management of hospital. It is quite natural that the uniform supplied to the different categories of people are not to generate inconveniences indeed to make the professional conditions proactive. Since you serve an organisation in which patients from diverse sections, groups, regions, cultural and family backgrounds come and stay for getting healthcare, it is pertinent that they form a positive opinion about your hospitals. It is not wrong to mention that in a majority of the hospitals, we find uniform culture making a good-bye and right now except nurses, we find a very few of them using uniform. Even if they use, we find them not well maintained. The laundry section of the hospital is found ill-maintained and deficiently managed and a medical superintendent finds it difficult to improve the working conditions. The patients coming to the hospitals form a negative attitude that the hospitals are financially insolvent and they have no funds to supply uniform and maintaining the same. In addition, the patients and attendants find it difficult to identify the hospital personnel. This makes it essential that particularly in the government hospitals, an attitudinal change is made possible. We can't deny the fact that private hospitals have been assigning due weightage to the uniform culture.

Since you serve an organisation promoting healthcare, educating and sensing masses; it is essential that different categories of employees working there don't provide to others an opportunity to make adverse comments regarding the different dimensions of physical attractions. Your dresses, physique, hair style, and facial expression throw significant impact on the behavioural profile of patients, attendants and visitors. This makes it essential that you are particular to the management of physical attractions and promote the same in the hospitals.

The aforesaid facts make it clear that a hospital manager needs to treat Physical Attractions as a submix of the marketing mix where attractions carry some meaning. Of course, your core services generate attractions; your peripheral services generate additional attractions but we find physical attractions linked to both. We talk about the high performer, a super performer and this makes it essential that all the dimensions are given a fresh look, a new vision, an innovative treatment so that the uniqueness proposition is found establishing distinction in almost all the areas. It is against this background that we feel the need of including this submix of the marketing mix even in the hospitals or healthcare organisations. Unless you generate additional attractions, unless you differentiate yourself, unless your make hospitals distinctive; the customers/patients would not be motivated. Of course, we find quality of healthcare services motivating them significantly but if you offer quality healthcare services and in addition, make make sincere efforts to generate additional attractions, the task of establishing an edge; the task of and increasing market share; the task of excelling competition and the task of establishing leadership would be fulfilled satisfactorily. These facts make it clear that physical attractions need to be incorporated in the marketing mix of hospitals.

People Mix

Of late, we find people mix occupying a place of special significance in almost all the organisations. In the healthcare services, we find people playing a commanding role. There is no doubt in it that despite of innovative biomedical equipment, apparatus, instruments, machines and robot, the techniculture becomes ineffective in establishing work culture if the people lack professionalism. It is against this background that we find developing the excellence of people an important task before the management of almost all the organisations. In the formulation of marketing mix, the instrumentality of people mix has gained significance because the top-level managers and the boardrooms based on their experiences have come to this conclusion that people serving an organisation need top priority on your development agenda. We need to educate, train and develop people in such a way that they are not only professionally sound but even personally committed because our professional excellence carries no meaning, if we lack personal care in services. This is substantiated by the fact that we find doctors having the world class excellence, technocrats extraordinarily efficient, administrators exceptionally proficient, teachers well qualified and experienced but the results almost all dismal, the level of efficiency coming down and the rate of productivity consistently decelerating due mainly to the fact that all of them lack personal commitment, ethics, values or so. This necessitates a fresh look, a new vision, an innovative strategy for the development of people. It is in this context that the concept of New People Management has gravitated priority attention of the management experts.

We can't negate the fact that it is the time-cycle that influences the nature and character of developments and an individual or an institution not evincing interest in conceptualising the same, suffers a lot. Change is a natural phenomenon. No one can stop the flow and albeit can turn the directions. Hence, it is wisdom that we keep our minds active, eyes open and do our best to foresee the developments to take place and innovate the strategic decisions accordingly. We have sophisticated world class technologies, supporting infrastructural facilities, comfort-based buildings but the lowest level of efficiency. Like other organisations, we find hospitals and healthcare organisations facing identical problems. If we divert our attention on the level of performance of government hospitals, except a very few, almost all of them present a disappointing result. The ultimate sufferers are the patients belonging to the poor segment because the private hospitals have been found subserving the interests of those who can afford. Of course, we appreciate the contributions of medical scientists who have made possible significant developments in the discipline but their mission would remain unfulfilled if we find poorest of the poor not harnessing the benefits of development in the world of medical sciences. We are well aware of the fact that hospitals or healthcare organisations don't have a legitimate right of making profits and therefore, the boardrooms or the policy makers are fantastically influenced by the social considerations. The government as well as the private hospitals need to serve the patients with the same motto. Both of them need to search an equilibrium point where time-honoured developments and interests of stakeholders are given due weightage.

The formulation of a sound people mix particularly for hospitals or healthcare organisations makes it essential that they have professionally sound, personally-committed and value-based people who not only play a commanding role in accomplishing the organisational objectives but contribute significantly to the fulfilment of organisational mission.

The most important task before a hospital manager is to develop a healthy and harmonious relationship with the employees to create a family and friendly feeling, a sense of belonging in the minds of employees, a feeling that employees and managers share the same fate. Thus, in the face of degenerating level of efficiency in the hospitals and healthcare organisations, it is pertinent that an organisation has people with special attributes who fulfil the organisational as well as the managerial mission.

Since we go through the problem of marketing the healthcare services, it is essential that we make sincere and honest efforts to make available to the hospitals quality people and for this, it is significant that a fair synchronisation of the individuals and organisational goals is made possible. This would help or inspire the hospital personnel to show personal-touch-in-service in addition to the professional excellence. We talk about world class excellence but it is not possible unless we find our incentive plans globally competitive. A self-motivated manager bears the efficacy of making it possible.

The hospitals or healthcare organisations have been facing numerous problems. They need to make possible good patient care. They need to bear a considerable amount of social costs. They need to achieve world class excellence. They need to assign an overriding priority to the satisfaction of patients and attendants. This makes it essential that a self-motivated manager accepts the responsibility of building friendly, harmonious, value-based and inter and intra-departmental relationships. By doing such, he/she succeeds in making the environment at the work place sound very much instrumental in generating the level of efficiency. It is in this context that we make a strong advocacy in favour of developing quality hospital personnel who play a dominating role in increasing the number of satisfied group of patients/users.

A hospital manager bears a challenging task of making the process of generating and processing the healthcare services cost-effective so that the services are found affordable even to the weaker sections of the society. Not only this, he/she also needs to make hospitals and healthcare organisations a centre of excellence found very much effective in promoting research and innovating the diagnostic and treatment measures to counter the multifaceted challenges before the healthcare sector. This makes it clear that in the changing social condition, it is pertinent that an innovative fee/pricing strategy is practised so that the hospitals or healthcare organisations find them in a position to enrich their potential to bear the social costs. Of course, he/she bears the responsibility of enriching the quality of biomedical equipment, apparatus, instruments, machines and infrastructual facilities but the important of all is the people that gravitate his/her attention on a priority basis. Unless we motivate people as per the international standards, it is difficult for us to achieve the world class excellence and unless we are globally competitive, our dream of becoming a leader would remain just a dream.

In view of the aforesaid facts, it is right to say that people mix of organisations in general and hospitals or healthcare organisations in particular need an overriding priority and in addition to a healthcare manager, the boardrooms or the policy makers also need an attitudinal change. It is in this context that we find management experts promoting the new perception of "Quality People" that requires a fair blending of professional excellence and personal commitments.

Strategic Marketing

The contours of development have undergone radical changes during the yester decades. We find transformation in almost all the areas. The scientific advancements have been opening new vistas for a structural change in the key areas of socio-economic transformation. If we turn our eyes on the healthcare sector, the multidimensional developments have been successful in defining and redefining healthcare services. There are a number of Indian hospitals maintaining international standards and establishing a strong brand name. The concept of state-of-the-art hospitals particularly initiated and activated by the corporate sector has injected new life and strength to the corporatisation process. Our healthcare services are of world class and affordable. The hospitals are well equipped, up-market and proficient and albeit may outshine any hospital in the West. What to talk of the private sector when we find some of the government hospitals having world class excellence.

Of course, we find the other side of the coin presenting a gloomy picture because a majority of the primary, secondary and tertiary sector hospitals have not been providing even the basic medical aids then what to talk of the speciality services. In 1946, the Health Survey and Development Committed headed by Shri Joseph Bhore recommended establishment of a well-structured and comprehensive health care with a sound primary healthcare infrastructure. We cannot deny that report of Bhore Committee provided a historical landmark in the development of public health system, however, the national policy makers have not been successful in offering even the basic healthcare facilities in the rural areas where a majority of the population live. The yawning gap between demand and supply of healthcare services draws priority attention of government policy makers on the depleted hospitals and healthcare organisations witnessing a stage of sickness.

At the time of attainment of independence, the national healthcare infrastructure was mainly urban based and clinically promoted. The hospitals and clinics provided curative care to patients who came to them. Outreach of rural healthcare services was found very limited. Gradually, we started development plans and a number of steps were taken to activate the process of qualitative-cum-quantitative transformation in the rural healthcare services. There is no doubt in it that today we have a vast network of government voluntary and private health infrastructure manned by a large number of world class medical, paramedical and managerial personnel. However, a qualitative or even quantitative gap is found existent. We need to bridge the gap which requires development of quality people by the different medical colleges and institutes and further, their time-to-time training for brushing up their knowledge by the hospital professionals. Thus, a persistent gap in manpower and infrastructural facilities if bridged over would make the healthcare sector sound enough to cater to the changing healthcare requirements of rural India vis-a-vis the weaker sections.

The hospital professionals while conceptualising marketing in the healthcare sector need to make it sure that hospitals and healthcare organisations have been successful in satisfying the users. Additionally, they have to ensure soundness of healthcare organisations in serving and subserving social interests so that the corporate players investing in the hospital or healthcare sector are successful in justifying their existence. It is also imperative that they assign due weightage to low cost indigenous technologies. Inadequacy of supporting infrastructural facilities, poor referral services, inadequacy of almost all categories of manpower, inadequacy of sophisticated biomedical equipment, apparatus, instruments, machines and technicians, lack of inter-sectoral coordination, increasing burden on account of communicable and non-communicable diseases are some of the constraints standing as a major barrier while developing the healthcare services.

Of course, we find State Governments investing huge fund for healthcare services but the level of efficiency of government hospitals is going down. On the one hand, the government hospitals complain abut the inadequacy of hospital personnel while on the other hand, we find their doctors all the time practising in the private clinics. The financial support by the government is found falling. The government hospitals do not have a freedom of generating revenues. The charities and donations are found decreasing and ultimately, we find them facing the problem of financial crunch. The potentials of hospitals are found decreasing whereas the demand for healthcare requirements are found increasing. The ultimate and the worst sufferers are the weaker sections of the society because the affluent sections make use of the world class services of private hospitals. It is against this background that the hospital professionals need to think in favour of strategic decisions which make the process of marketing the services innovative *vis-a-vis* proactive.

Present century breeds the next century. We have a long-term target of having a healthier 21st century and a short-term target of improving the quality of healthcare services. The modern hospitals bear the responsibility of protecting, sensing and serving the human resources considered to be the precious endowment. The formation of human capital is sizably influenced by the development of healthcare services. In modern India, the marketing of healthcare services is becoming difficult because a majority of us feel that it is the ultimate responsibility of government to promote the healthcare services. The hospitals for improving the quality of diagnostic, curative and other services need to implement a number of capital intensive projects in addition to the different supporting infrastructural facilities. At this juncture, we need to formulate an innovative strategy for the healthcare services.

Tailoring of marketing resources in the face of an action plan so that the marketing mixes provide to be proactive is known as strategic marketing. The hospital planners, architects, consultants, top-level doctors, professionals and the government policy makers need an attitudinal change. They need to identify the thrust areas and to develop marketing inputs accordingly.

General and Special Hospitals Need Quantitative Transformation: In view of the increasing healthcare requirements of society, it is essential that we bring a substantial increase in the number of both the categories of hospitals, viz., General and Special. In almost all the state capitals, a large-sized general hospital is to be started and in the selected towns and cities or even in the easily accessible suburbs and rural areas, a number of special hospitals either based on the character of disease or based on the organs of body are to be set up. These would be government supported hospitals where cost-based, free-of-charge, concessional or even surplus-generating fee structure would be charged. The hospitals would be well equipped with the sophisticated technologies and a team of committed and professionally sound medical and paramedical personnel. Modern management-orientation would be given top priority and different echelons of management would bear the responsibility of developing them as a centre of excellence in the discipline of medical science. In the rural sector, the primary health care centres would be restructured and the concept of referral hospital would be rejuvenated. There would be a close link between the primary healthcare centres and the referral hospitals and the cases if required necessary would be referred either to the general hospitals or to the special hospitals as the circumstances warrant. It is important to mention that these hospitals would be in addition to the existing strength of hospitals and therefore, we expect a big increase in the potentials of healthcare organisations to meet the increasing healthcare requirements of the society. A Special Health Care Fund would be created in which the State Government, Union Government and public at large would make financial contributions in the face of the levels of income. It is important to mention that the corporate sector would also make financial contributions as a corporate citizen in tune with the defined principles of social marketing.

The Existing Hospitals Need Qualitative Transformation: We agree with this view that by and large, almost all the government hospitals are found in a depleted condition. They have been facing the problem of financial crunch and more so, they have become financially bankrupt. It is quite natural that due to financial crunch, we find bankruptcy at almost all the levels. The traditional technologies and traditional management orientation have been found throwing them in the reverse gear. This makes it essential that a special task force is organised to overhaul them. The management-orientation, upgradation of biomedical equipment, apparatus, instruments, availability of uninterrupted supporting infrastructural facilities screening of the performance of almost all categories of medical and paramedical personnel and performance-based incentive plans need due attention of the policy makers. Since we go through the problem of government hospitals, it is natural that the Health Department of the state government evinces interest in the process of overhauling. So far as the financial requirements for that purpose are concerned, the

Union Government would be required to offer the matching grant. In addition, the global bodies taking part in the process are also to be approached. An important task before the government would be to make possible one hundred per cent fair use of the financial resources.

Private Hospitals to be Promoted: In this context, it is also pertinent that we promote the private hospitals. This draws our attention on the policy decisions to be given due weightage in the very context. Since we make a strong advocacy in favour of the bearing of social costs even by the private hospitals, it is pertinent that they are offered special incentives for the development of hospitals. It is significant that we promote the corporate sector for the opening of new hospitals in the vulnerable areas of the country. In a true sense, we need to practise a sense of coordination and cooperation between the government and private hospitals specially to counter the challenges on account of natural calamities or epidemics or immunisation and vaccination programmes. All of us agree with this view that in terms of infrastructual facilities and quality of apparatus and equipment, we find private hospitals in general establishing an edge over the government hospitals and this is mainly on account of their management orientation which they practise on a priority basis. Of course in terms of the quality of medical and paramedical personnel, we find government hospitals having an upper hand but this is not due to special incentives they get there but in a true sense due to the well established image of a few of the government hospitals and institutes. The government policy makers are required to go through the problems of private hospitals and to help them to counter the same. As and when they need to import biomedical equipment of world class which are not available in the domestic markets, they need multipronged facilities and the government should come forward to help them. If they need financial support, the public sector commercial banks and other financial institutions need to offer credit facilities on the reasonable terms and conditions. The supply of infrastructural facilities like power, water, communications are to be ensured. The law and order problems and the safety and security measures need due support of the government. The concept of small private clinics is to be given a shape so that they don't prove to be blood suckers. It is to be made sure that whatever the fee they charge is optimal to the quality of services they offer. In the beginning or at the initial stage, they need concessional services of infrastructural industries. Thus, we need to promote the private hospitals so that they develop and prosper and increase their potentials of bearing the social costs.

Government and Private Hospitals Need to Promote Social Advertising: Since we talk about management of hospitals on the basis of the defined principles of social marketing, it is pertinent that both of them evince keen interest in social advertising. By social advertising, our focus is on the advertisement promoting social interests, viz., advertisements related to family welfare, child care immunisation, noise pollution, water contamination, irresponsible sexual behaviour, food habits, drug addition, liquor consumption, use of tobacco or so. The messages related to the aforesaid problems would counter health problems. Since we find different categories of patients and attendants coming to the hospitals in a large number from different parts of the country or even from abroad, the advertisement slogans and messages would be required to be made effective.

If you expect from others, you also need to fulfil the exceptions of others. You expect that a corporate citizen should promote the healthcare sector by extending to you the financial support and in the same fashion, the society expects that you should also promote and subserve their interests by inculcating mass awareness. The slogans related to social advertising would be efficacious in fulfilling or meeting the expectations of public at large. Besides, the society would considerably be benefited because a number of social problems would successfully be countered if the messages of social advertising become effective in sensitising the mass.

Injecting Craze for Techniculture: Except a very few, we find almost all the hospitals, private or government, generating healthcare services with the help of traditional technologies. The latest developments in the medical sciences have been successful in innovating biomedical equipment, apparatus, instruments and in addition, the information technology has been found adding new dimensions by innovating the diagnostic and treatment process. The patients are benefited because of the authentic and quick diagnosis and the doctors are benefited by minimising the time gap between initiating investigations and coming to a final conclusion. It is against this background that we find justifications for injecting craze to promote techniculture which focuses our attention on aggravating the temptation for the new generation of medical technologies. Not only the government hospitals but even the private hospitals need to promote the same to meet the increasing levels of expectations of prospects at large. Since we make a strong advocacy in favour of quality in totality, it is the prime responsibility of a few of the leading hospitals of the country sensitive supposed to be leaders not only in the Indian context but even at global levels to inform and the new as well as the old hospitals to promote technologies and show their temptation to the techniculture.

Creativity in Health Care Awareness: We are well aware of the fact that a large number of diseases spreading like a wild fire in the present society are self-generated. Since we find a majority of the population illiterate and unconscious, they, due to wrong food habits, consumption of contaminated water, generation of noise and atmospheric pollution, drug addiction, non-optimal size of their family, early and late marriages, consumption of liquor, use of tobacco, irresponsible sexual behaviour, invite a number of health problems. It is in this context that we talk about healthcare awareness. Till now, a majority of the hospitals have not assigned due weightage to the preventive services. It is the responsibility of all categories of hospitals to accept this vital social responsibility of creating mass awareness so that the health problems are considerably minimised. Since we find you an expert knowing well about the instrumentality of creative messages and slogans in sensitising the impulse of masses, the slogans related to social advertising are required to be made creative. Of course, we find media instrumental in the process but the messages and campaigns promoted by the doctors and managing of hospitals would be found impact-generating. It is in this context that we need to sensitise the masses specially to the health problems and the healthcare measures.

Vaccination Culture to be Promoted: In view of the emerging health problems, it is also significant that hospitals in general promote vaccination culture. Vaccines are the most cost-effective agents for controlling the communicable diseases. In a true sense, a revolution is needed on the vaccinology front. The immunisation programme is to benefit the society in many ways.

A reduction in the infant mortality rate is the result of child immunisation. The Universal Immunisation Programme (UIP) has been aimed at a healthier 21st century. This can certainly be achieved if the government financing bodies and the core and paramedical personnel evince interests in the immunisation programme. An aggressive marketing strategy is needed to make the immunisation programme a grand success. We are witnessing the positive results of Pulse Polio Programme and expect that in the coming years, we also promote the Vaccination Programme for Hepatitis B. Tuberculosis is a major disease and in India about half a million people are dying of this disease every year. Of course, we have a vaccine like BCG in the immunisation programme but it is not found so effective against Pulmonary Tuberculosis. It is essential that we develop more effective medicines against tuberculosis. Cholera is still around and often appears as an epidemic. The old cholera vaccine is no longer used. Typhoid is another problem and we need to promote a vaccine for that. Since we are studying the managerial problem, it is right to focus on the managerial lapses that we find in the process. Of course, we are making efforts to promote immunisation programme but the vulnerable segments of the society the specially rural population have not been given due weightage. Thus, it is our prime responsibility to constitute a special task force to benefit the rural segment.

Yoga and Pranayam Need to be Promoted: Of late, even the medically developed countries of the west have realised the significance of *"Yoga"* and *"Pranayam"* in countering a number of health problems. The revived interest in Yoga is something which is welcome the world over. We find Yoga a beneficial system and an elegant way of regulating and exercising the mind, the brain, the respiration and other vital functions. Proper Yoga can give us a feeling of the well-being in the system which no drug can give. It is against this background that we make a strong advocacy in favour of Yoga. The hospitals of all categories bear the responsibility of creating interests of masses in Yoga. Since we find masses perceiving the suggestions of doctors and practising the same in a right fashion, the involvement or participation of doctors in generating interests among the masses would benefit the society in different ways. To be more specific, the poor rural society right now facing a number of hazardous health problems would substantially be benefited if they assign due weightage to Yoga in their health management programme.

Herbal Products to be Promoted: In view of the increasing health problem, it is essential that we promote herbal products and create mass awareness regarding the same and to promote the cultivation of plants having medicinal value. To be more specific in the Indian society, where masses find it difficult to buy the expensive medicines and in addition also find it difficult to make them apprised of the side-effects or optimal dose, it is essential that the hospitals and healthcare organisations bear the responsibility of promoting herb based medicines and cosmetics.

In view of the above, it is right to say that to cater to the increasing healthcare or medicare requirements of the society, the healthcare organisations need to activate qualitative-cum-quantitative measures. A gap between the demand and supply is to be bridged on a priority basis and this requires mass participation.

An Overriding Priority to the Quality Systems: Since we talk about quality in totality for marketing the healthcare services nationally and internationally, it is pertinent that we focus on developing quality systems found helpful in meeting the quality objectives. It also helps in satisfying the internal managerial needs of hospitals and healthcare organisations. It is found broader than the requirements of a particular patient who for satisfaction only evaluates the relevant part of the system, such as the curative services made available to him/ her. We find quality in totality a salient feature of an entity that depends on its ability to satisfy stated and implied needs. In this context, it is essential that hospitals or healthcare organisations know about the quality policy as formally expressed by the policy makers or the boardrooms.

For maintaining quality, we find quality management an important dimension in which all activities of the overall management function determining the quality policy are taken into consideration. For quality control, we find operational techniques and factors influencing or degenerating quality to be given due weightage. These things help in shaping quality assurance which proves to be an important constituent to evaluate the performance because a gap between the quality-assured and quality-offered is to dissatisfy the patients and attendants. Thus, it is significant that a healthcare manager for marketing the services in the future perceives the right meaning of quality because a mistake committed in the process would make all the marketing resources insensitive. All the activities influencing quality are to be managed in a right fashion.

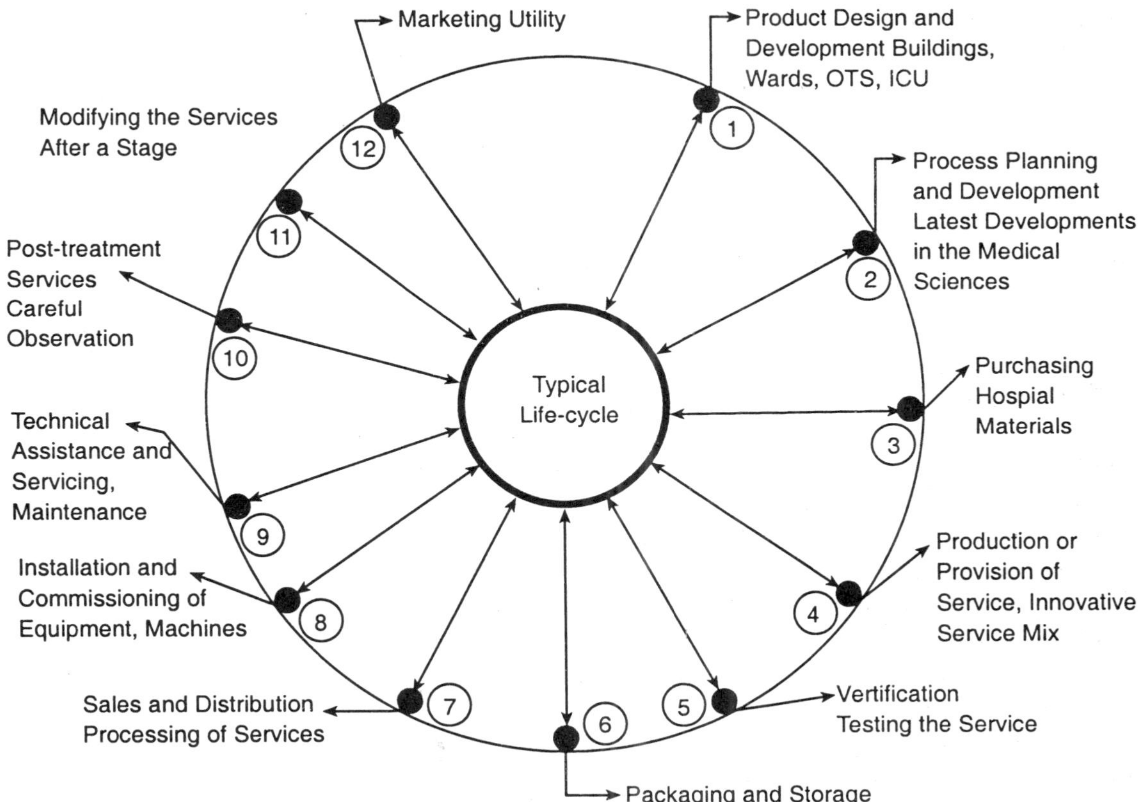

Fig. 11.10. Activities Influencing Quality
Adapted from: Quality Management Systems, UNCTAD/WTO/ISO, p. 13.

Behavioural Management to be Improved: In addition to the world class healthcare services, it is also essential that the hospital personnel improve their behavioural profile which not only minimises the gap between the services-assured and service-offered but also promotes, decency in processing. The hospital-personnel in general need to be sympathetic to the patients and attendants and in addition should also show empathy. This makes it essential that the behavioural profile of hospital personnel is given due weightage and for that a training and development programme is to be restructured. With the increasing level of expectations of users, the hospital personnel need to improve their behaviour.

Uniform Culture to be Promoted: To give a fresh look to the personality of hospital personnel, it is also pertinent that a hospital manager thinks of promoting the uniform culture. This makes it essential that all the personnel wear the uniform made available to them by the hospitals. It is also to be made sure that their dresses are neat and clean and infection-free. To be more specific, the linen supplied by the hospitals is to be washed, dried and pressed in a right way to counter the problem of infection. We find senior doctors not wearing dresses and therefore, whatever the dresses they wear should be neat and clean and well pressed. Your look is to generate a positive or negative image of hospitals and this makes it essential that you are very much careful to the uniform or dress culture to promote physical attraction.

Social Costs to be Made Optimal: To improve the financial health of hospitals, it is also essential that we make the social costs proportionate to the potentials of hospitals. The social cots are the losses on account of concessional or subsidised or free of charge services made available to the poor segment of the society. To be more specific, the government hospitals have been found facing problem on that account which has been making them financially insolvent. Of course, the poor sections need due care but it is not meant that in all the cases and for all the purposes, we promote free of charge or subsidised services. A basic change in the pricing policy is found imperative. On the other hand, the private hospitals need to promote the concessional or subsidised services because, they contribute non-optimally to the process of subserving the social or public interests.

Concept of Urbanisation to be promoted: Strategic marketing makes it essential that for the development of new hospitals, both in the private and public sector, the concept of urbanisation is to be promoted. This means opening and developing new hospitals in the rural areas or in the suburbs so that even the rural segment is benefited by the new developments in the field of medical sciences. If we develop big, specialised hospitals close to the villages or suburbs, the development of backward regions would also occur since the increasing number of patients and attendants coming to the hospitals for treatment are almost from all the segments. The multiplier effects would be found effective and a number of development centres would start functioning. But in this context, it is important that we locate hospitals at a place found round the year easily or smoothly accessible.

The aforesaid strategic decision would bring multidimensional improvements in the working of hospitals or healthcare organisations. The patients would get quality healthcare services, the hospital personnel would be motivated and the hospitals would thrive in the face of latest developments taking place in the medical sciences.

PPP Mode to be Promoted: A number of government hospitals have been found facing the problem of financial crunch. The grants received form the government are found inadequate to cater to the increasing medicare requirements of Indian society. This makes a strong advocacy in favour of PPP mode which focuses our attention on the public-private-partnership. It is significant to mention that during yesteryears, the Centre as well as the State Governments have initiated a wide variety of PPP arrangement to meet people's growing healthcare needs. Contract based operation is found to be the predominant model for PPP in India where some partnerships are on the basis of simple contracts such as laundry, diet, cleaning, etc. whereas other forms are found to be much more complex involving many stakeholders with their respective responsibilities. As for example, the Yeshaswini Health Insurance Scheme for farmers in Karnataka includes the State Department of Cooperatives, the Yeshaswini Trust with its almost 200 private hospitals, a corporate Third Part Administrator (TPA) and beneficiaries with the eligibility conditions.[12] It is also found that in most partnerships, the State Health Department is the principal partner with limited stakeholders consultation. We rarely find true partnerships which mean equality among partners, mutual commitment to goals, shared decision making and risk taking. Keeping in view the depleted conditions of government hospitals, it is pertinent that the government policy makers assign due weightage to equal partnership.

Medical Tourism to be Promoted

We find western countries making tremendous strides in the field of medicine. Of course, they have also been providing world class services to the users but the cost of treatment is so high that only affluent sections of the society can afford. Or, the people having full insurance can opt for treating some major diseases like cancer, cardiac problems and major surgeries like hip-joint, bypass, etc. Thus, the segments not having full insurance or not coming from the affluent sections have an option to get treatment in places or counties where cost is affordable and it is against this background that we find wider avenues for the development of medical or health tourism in India because qualitywise we offer world class healthcare services and at a competitive fee structure. In USA, we find about 48% of the population uninsured and another 25% under-insured and therefore, a major chunk of the population opts to get treatment in places where cost is affordable without compromising on the quality.[13] The African countries would not prefer to go to the USA for treatment. Hence, for a good number of population we find India as an option.

It is significant to mention that medical tourism is a totally different form of tourism. In this context, a person suffering from some illness goes to a place where we find the services having low cost. The healthcare services are of world class and affordable to the customers. The state-of-the art hospitals are found potentially sound to make the treatment process result-oriented. This also throws light on developing rapport with the media people.

State-of-the-art hospitals need to be promoted: We find India emerging as a healthcare destination. In a true sense, we find healthcare sector on a boom and the global financial crisis is not to affect it. Indeed, it is going to increase the demand position in the global markets where the healthcare services are becoming much more expensive. It is in this context that we make a strong advocacy in favour of state-of-the art hospitals where innovative technologies and world class amenities and facilities would attract domestic affluent users vis-a-vis the global customers where the healthcare services are very expensive. We find a number of hospitals having international standards and offering world class services at an abnormally competitive fee structure, or at third world cost. According to the Planning Commission Report (Times of India April 7, 2008), the hospitals established by private corporate players are of world class. They not only have the latest medical technologies but also services of Indian doctors and nurses with high degree of proficiency. The hospitals are completely equipped, up-market and proficient and can measure up or even outshine any hospital in the West."[14] It is against this background that during the yesteryears, we have witnessed the number of patients visiting India for medical treatment has been rising by 20%.

The overseas patients have been getting a comprehensive package in which we find special surgical rate packages, exclusive nursing attendants, excluding guest home facility, travel assistance such as ticket/taxi booking, information booklets of various places in India, arrangement of pick and drop service to the Airport/Station in luxury cars, sight seeing tours to various tourist spots, special laundry services, discounted accommodation at renowned hotels, exclusive onsite beauty treatments for ladies such as ayrvedic massages, facials, hair treatments, etc.

The state-of-the art hospitals would also get a domestic market generated by the affluent sections of the society. Such type of hospitals need due attention of the corporate sector, It is high time that coporatisation of healthcare services gains a rapid momentum. The National Accreditation Board for Hospitals and Healthcare providers should make it sure that these hospitals are providing world class services. In addition, it is also pertinent that these hospitals bear the social costs by offering services to the weaker sections of the society. If they provide even basic medical aids at their different camps located in the rural areas to the weaker sections of the society, they would justify their existence in the society.

The state-of-the art hospitals would play an effective role in promoting medical tourism showing multiplier effects and benefiting various sectors and segments of the society. Hence, the Union Government as well as the state governments need to promote state-of-the art hospitals for tapping the opportunities that we find in the healthcare sector.

Hospitals need a sound ambience: The healthcare services are considerably influenced by the ambient conditions provided to the hospitals for delivering the services to the patients. Particularly in the government hospitals, we find a different scenario where a majority of them lack a suitable service environment for processing and delivery of services. Poor lighting, furnishing, ventilation and sanitation services adversely affect the service quality. Lack of cleanliness and possibilities for infection at the sensitive points make hospitals a source for the development of diseases. The in availability and poor handling and maintenance of equipments, instruments and information and communication technology aggravate the magnitude of problem. The hospital personnel as well as the patients lack civic sense then what to talk of the aesthetic sense. The surroundings and premises are found ill maintained, safety and security, parking, transportation facilities, etc. remain neglected. Thus, the government hospitals in particular lack suitable service ambience where we can expect service environment vis-a-vis service culture. This necessitates development of servicescapes or service environment where the hospitals are efficacious of delivering quality services. The state-of-the-art hospitals assign due weightage to the ambient conditions which not only add additional attraction to the service environment but also help in minimising the duration of recovery. Civic and aesthetic sense significantly contribute to the process of qualitative transformation.

Thus, the above mentioned thrust areas need due focus in the changing scenario where healthcare services may be of world class and a majority of the hospitals and healthcare organisations may be successful in developing India as a healthcare destination. The following points are found important:

- Hospitals in general need qualitative-cum-quantitative transformation.
- Private Hospitals need to be promoted.
- Government as well as the private hospitals needs to focus on social advertising.
- Techniculture need priority attention. Low-cost indigenous technologies need due focus.
- Creativity in healthcare awareness is significant.
- Vaccination and immunisation culture need to be promoted.
- Yoga and Pranayam, Homoeopathic, Ayurvedic, Unani and Siddha (AYUSH) may serve the interest of general masses.
- Behavioural Management needs due attention.
- Uniform culture is to be promoted.

- PPP mode requires due focus.
- Medical Tourism is required to be promoted.
- State-of-the art hospitals need due attention.
- Hospitals need a sound service ambience where service culture can be nurtured.

SUMMARY

In this chapter, you have gone through the problem of marketing. The motive is to sensitise the readers to the instrumentality of marketing the healthcare services. After going through the chapter, be sure that the following facts are well versed.

Hospital Marketing—the Perception: The hospital marketing focuses our attention on the conceptualisation of modern marketing principle in the healthcare services with a holistic approach.

Rationale Behind Practising Marketing in Hospitals: We find justification for the application of marketing principles in the healthcare services because this would help keeping users satisfied, time honoured services would be made available to the patients, mass awareness would be created, thrust areas would be identified, vulnerable segments would be detected, behavioural dimension would be given due weightage, cost-effectiveness would be made possible, a rational fee structure can be introduced and hospital personnel can be motivated.

Segmentwise Users of Healthcare Services: We classify users of healthcare services on the basis of segment, viz., individual, organisational; rural-urban; high-income, medium-income, low-income and no-income; men and women; kids, teens, youths and gray; vulnerable and normal areas.

Behavioural Profile of Users: A hospital manager is required to know about the attitudes, life styles, preferences and level of expectations of the users.

Market Segmentation: It is a managerial process of dividing and sub-dividing the markets into small groups and segments so that the changing levels of expectations of the users are identified.

Marketing Information System: It is a system to manage marketing information, specially with the help of new generation of information technology. It is a process of transforming the marketing data into marketing information.

Marketing Mix: It is a managerial process of formulating the marketing mix which helps a manager in developing marketing resources in tune with the changing needs and requirements.

Product Mix: This focuses on core, supportive, peripheral and preventive services of the healthcare organisations. It is a process of blending the different types of healthcare services in the face of changing requirements.

Promotion Mix: This submix of the marketing mix focuses on the different constituents of promotion, e.g., advertising, publicity, sales promotion, personal selling, word-of-mouth promotion and telemarketing.

Price Mix: In this context, we go through the problem of setting fees by the hospitals and healthcare organisations.

Place Mix: This focuses our attention on location point for hospitals and the channels through which the services reach to the end users.

Process Mix: This submix of marketing mix throws light on the processing of services. The healthcare organisations for increasing the operational flow make use of different types of technologies. The sophisticated equipments, instruments, machines if rightly used by the experts improve the quality of healthcare services to be efficacious of satisfying the users.

Physical Evidence & Attractions: This submix focuses our attention on physical amenities and facilities helping hospital personnel in performing and users in gaining new experiences. This also includes in its purview the dresses and uniforms of hospital personnel.

People: In this submix, we go through the people responsible for marketing the healthcare services. The hospital professionals by making use of their excellence may be successful in satisfying the users. They need to be thematically sound, professionally excellent, personally-committed, value-based and having human touch in behaviour.

Strategic Marketing: The hospital professionals need to identify the thrust areas which may help them in capitalising on the opportunities available in domestic and global markets. The private as well as the government hospitals need to formulate a sound marketing strategy.

KEY TERMS

Indigenous Technology	Cause-related Marketing
Synchronisation	Telemarketing
GDP	Organisational Customers
State-of-the art hospitals	Service Ambience
Vector-borne diseases	Servicescapes
Communicable Diseases	Vaccination Culture
Market Segmentation	Immunization
Divine and Rule	Yoga
Marketing Information System	Pranayam
Internal Reporting	Social Costs
Analytical Marketing	Urbanisation
Marketing Research	Uniform Culture
Marketing Intelligence	Medical Tourism
Product Profile	PPP Mode
Core Services	Third World Cost
Peripheral Services	First World Services
Press Kite	AYUSH
Image Building	Service Culture

REVIEW QUESTIONS

1. What do you mean by Hospital Marketing? Focus on the rationale behind practising the principles of modern marketing by the hospitals.
2. What do you mean by Market Segmentation? Explain the segmentwise users of healthcare services.
3. Throw light on the behavioural profile of users of healthcare services.
4. What do you mean by Marketing Information System? Explain the different subsystems of MIS.
5. What do you mean by Marketing Mix? Explain in brief the different submixes of marketing mix in relation to healthcare organisations.
6. Focus on the product mix of hospitals. Explain the role of peripheral services in attracting the users.
7. Explain in brief the different components of promotion for persuading and transforming the healthcare users.

8. What do you mean by Public Reactions? Explain the role of public relations for promoting the healthcare services.
9. Explain the relevance of advertising for promoting the healthcare services.
10. Explain the role of additional submixes of marketing the healthcare services.
11. What do you mean by Personal Selling? Explain its relevance to the healthcare sector.
12. Explain the importance of servicescapes for healthcare organisations.
13. Pricing healthcare services in the Indian perspective requires cost-economy by promoting the use of low-cost indigenous technologies. Comment on this statement.
14. Focus on strategic marketing in the face of increasing demand of healthcare services in the domestic and global markets.

APPLICATION EXERCISES

1. In the capacity of a hospital professional, conceptualise societal marketing principles in your hospitals which may enable you to serve social interests.
2. "Image building makes the ways for image projects." In the light of this statement, explain the factors contributing to the process of image building and image projection.
3. As a professional, you need to be innovative. Focus on the measures to be initiated by you for making the healthcare services much more innovative.
4. The India healthcare sector is on a boom and is not to be affected by the global financial crises. Comment on this statement in the capacity of a hospital professional.
5. "You need to promote uniform culture to make the ways for work culture". Focus on this statement as a hospital professional.
6. In the capacity of a hospital professional, design service ambience simplifying your task of making the service environment eco-friendly.
7. The Indian healthcare sector provides First World services at the Third World Cost. Do you agree with this view? Defend your arguments as a hospital manager.
8. Innovative healthcare services and creative promotional measures need priority attention of hospital professionals in the Indian perspective. Comment on this statement as a hospital manager.
9. The State-of-the art hospitals have a big market. In the capacity of a hospital professional, throw light on the measures you need to initiate and activate for capitalising on the opportunities available in the global markets.
10. We are potentially sound for developing Medical Tourism. In the light of this statement, focus on the measures you will have to initiate for tapping the global markets.
11. Developing quality healthcare personnel is a prime consideration for the development of Indian healthcare sector. Comment on this statement in the capacity of a hospital manager.
12. The India healthcare sector provides First World services at Third World prices. Comment on this statement as a hospital manager and focus on the professionals requiring excellence for capitalising on the opportunities available in the global markets.

END NOTES

1. Jha, S. M. *Services Marketing*, HPH, Mumbai, 2009
2. Jha, S. M. *Social Marketing*, HPH, Mumbai, 2009, Chapter 1
3. Jha, S. M. *Services Marketing*, Old Edition, pp. 6-27

4. Jha, S. M. *Social Marketing*, HPH, Mumbai, 2009
5. Jha, S. M. *Services Marketing*, Chap. Hospital Marketing; 2009
6. Jha, S. M. *Services Marketing*, Chap. Hospital Marketing; 2009
7. Jha, S. M. *Services Marketing*, Chap. Hospital Marketing; 2009
8. *Ibid*
9. Jha, S. M. *Social Marketing*, Chap. Hospital Marketing; 2009
10. Jha, S. M. *The Hindustan Times*; Looks Make a Man April, 17, 2000.
11. Jha, S. M. *Employment News*; Strategic Issues in Medicare Services, 1998
12. *Eleventh Five Year Plan*: Planning Commission, Government of India, pp. 80-81
13. Subbaraman, K : *Pune as a Preferred Medical Tourist Destination in India for Foreigners*; Journal of IMS Group Vol. 5/2 July-Dec 2008, pp. 82-95
14. *Times of India*: April 7, 2008.

Management of Hospital Records

Records speak something with much more authenticity. They remind you to make an audit of your managerial decisions and keep on moving the process of defining and redefining quality. The modern hospitals need sound management of records.

CHAPTER OBJECTIVES

Introduction—Hospital Records: the a Perception Types of Records—Essentials of an Effective Record Management—Forms of Hospital Records—Sections of Medical Records-Dimensions of Records Management—Significance of record keeping—Key information for healthcare managers—Filing of Hospital Records—Arranging Files—Centralised and Decentralised Filing—Management of Hospital Records: Problems and Remedies—Modern Filing Devices—Recent Trends in Records Management—Summary—Key Terms—Review Questions—Application Exercises—End Notes.

LEARNING OBJECTIVES

This chapter aims at studying the different dimensions of management of records for hospitals and healthcare organisations. The readers develop their awareness of the relevance of records management to the process of innovating diagnostic and treatment devices. The records management also helps in promoting the research activities for getting innovative results. There have been multi-dimensional developments in the stores management where we find new generation of technology defining and redefining records management.

Introduction

Unless you are aware of your mistakes, you cannot remove them. Unless you know the intensity of effectiveness of your diagnostic and treatment plans, you cannot adopt them. You are supposed to manage the present; you are supposed to manage the future. You are required to file, you are required to document. You need to make use of your records and you also need to make them useful to the researchers and medical scientists. You need to sort out the records of no use and to destroy them which enables you to make place for the new. Testifying its instrumentality as a clinical, scientific, legal and managerial documents related to patient-care and other important matters, the management of hospital records has been found gravitating the attention of mangers, medical scientists and researchers to enable them to be creative and innovative. It is against this background that a hospital professional needs to assign due priority to the management of hospital records.

Records are the memory of internal and external transactions of an organisation and they speak something with much more authenticity. They remind you to go through the quality of your managerial decisions so that the process of defining and redefining quality keeps on moving. By the internal transactions, our focus is on the dealing in the external transactions, by persons in the organisations at all levels. And by external transactions, we know the contents of correspondence between the organisation and its clients such as suppliers, patients and attendants. We find records a written evidence, a true guide, a real friend to help in rough weather and more so, a true picture of our deeds and misdeeds, a mirror to witness the facts, identify the rights and wrongs done in past at all the levels by almost all the echelons of management. If you have to reward, you need records. Even if you have to punish, you need records. If you want to identify your errors, you need records. If you are interested in making your future fruitful, you need records. It is against this backdrop that we find management of records occupying a place of outstanding significance.

The management of records is found concerned with different types of problems. The record keeping, making use of the records, destroying the old records of no use, documentation of the vital and important records found useful for researchers and medical scientists are some of the important areas for the management of records. With the development of sophisticated information and communication technology, we find inclusion of new features in the management of records making the process scientific vis-à-vis easier. The management of records is found to be a programme involving the multidimensional functions such as creating, administering, retaining, submitting and destroying the records. Of late, we find managerial decisions as well as the diagnosis and treatment process considerably influenced by the case history and techno-driven management of records simplified the process.

This makes it essential that a hospital manager makes suitable arrangements for the management of records so that he/she makes use of them in the required conditions. Since we can also use records as a legal proof, it is found easier for us to protect and project the image of hospitals and the hospital personnel. Managing records with the motto of improving the quality of patient care is an important managerial responsibility. You are supposed to make the records useful. Once again, it is to be an acid test of your potentials and credentials as a manager of a non-profit organisations.

In the context of healthcare organisations, we find the record a clear, concise and accurate history of the life and illness which is written from the health and medical points of view. The statement of patients, observations of nurses and comments of doctors are mentioned in the medical records. The medical section of record consists or history sheet, physical examination sheet, provisional diagnosis, investigation reports, physicians order sheet, treatment record, anaesthesia and operation records, obstetric records, consultancy report, progress report, discharge summary and in case of death, the cause of death and autopsy report. There are different types of records such as vital records which are required to be protected and preserved for the long time; important records which are not of current use and transit record found useful only for a short period. A hospital manager is required to identify the nature and uses of records and to make provision for their safety and protection. Of late, we find e-filing which has made the process convenient and simple but at the same time expensive.

Since the problem is related to the effective management of hospital records, it essential that a hospital manager makes it sure that whatever the arrangements have been talked earlier are found helpful to the hospital personnel and researchers. The records are required to be comprehensive, planned, economic, time-honoured and classified in a right way. Because the records meet the diverse needs of almost all sections evincing interests in the healthcare problem, it is pertinent that a hospital manager makes the process of managing records scientific. The indexing or cataloguing should be innovative and simple so that the required records are identified and procured and made available to the concerned or needy persons. While managing we need to careful so that the records found irrelevant are identified and destroyed. It is significant to mention that techno-driven management of records requires priority attention of hospital professionals.

What to talk of the big hospitals when we find even small hospitals promoting e-filing with diverse motives. But in this context, it is imperative that hospital professionals are careful and side-by-side develop a manual system because the problem of virus and data insecurity may create numerous problems. Thus we find a techno-driven management of records gaining popularity and even in future, the trend will continue. However, we cannot bid a goodbye to the traditional system of filing because there are a number of cases to quote that techno-driven management of records, of course, a sophisticated device for managing records has created serious problems before the hospital manager.

The above mentioned facts draw our attention on the different constituents of records management, e.g. retaining, submitting and destroying. The process of record-keeping is found significant in the management of healthcare organisations which in addition to other aspects also draw our attention on the measures adopted for safety and protection of important records. It is quite natural that all the records are not found of identical character and therefore, a hospital manger is required to identify the vital records and important records helping doctors, researchers and the medical scientists in different ways. The control of insects and virus assumes a place of outstanding significance. In the context of submitting records, our focus is on making available the reports to the concerned people. The records are not only preserved but with the help of scientific and computer-based indexing, the identification process is found to be easier. It cannot be accepted that modern hospitals need to bid a good-bye to the manually-supported record-keeping because we also find cases when virus problem destroys the collected facts and figures. Hence, the vital records should have to-way devices for regulating the possibilities of data insecurity. With the help of computers, we find a basic change in the nature and requirements of records and it is in this context that we find record keeping an important process of regulating the misuse of records. It is also clear that all the records related to the different departments of secondary and tertiary hospitals cannot be effective for all the time. This makes it essential that a hospital manager assigns due weightage to the management of records so that we shape our present in the face of past and plan our future in the face of past and present.

HOSPITAL RECORDS: THE PERCEPTION

At the outset, it is essential that we go through the perception of hospital records. McGibony opines, "A chronicle of the pageantry of medical and scientific progress is found in the hospital records. There may be found in the running story, disconnected it is true of the drama, the comedy, the mystery, the miracles of medicines and hospital of 20th century." The viewpoints of McGibony make it clear that the records of a hospital present a true story of events in which the doctors, researchers, managers and medical scientists taking interest in the problems find everything they need. We find medical records, a clinical, scientific, administrative and legal document relating to patient-care which is to help them in different ways. In hospital records, we find sufficient date written in sequence of events to justify the diagnosis. The complicated cases may be diagnosed with the help of facts and figures found in the past records. The treatment and end results are found authentic. The management of hospital records is found based on the professional excellence of a hospital manager. Case history received form records simplified the task of doctors while diagnosing and treating. It is also emerging as a techno-driven process where computers play a dominating role in the management of records.

We find hospital records a clear, concise, written document specially from the health and medical point of view. It is in a true sense a story narrating the history of patients, observation made by nurses and paramedical staff, comments made by doctors and experts which in a written form is found to be a legal document. 'We find hospital records a clear picture of the problem of patients, the diagnosis and investigation reports, the medicines administered and their effects and side-effects, the results positive or negative, the books and accounts, letters, circulars, reports, contracts, minutes, vouchers. Thus, we find hospital records a statement, a story, an observation and more so, the details of patients and thus, a source of treatment for others or a back up material for undertaking and promoting research.

In view of the above, it is right to mention that hospital records cover a number of things coming from different sources and departments. We find the general section of a hospital providing administrative and personal data. The socio-economic record of the patients, such as the name of the patient, father's or husband's name, age, sex, income, religion, address of patients and address of nearest relatives. The administrative informations include the date of admission, the in-patient number, the name of the nursing unit and bed number. In addition to the general section, we find a nurse section where observations of trained nurses are recorded. Here, we find the details of treatment administered. This section prepares a graphic chart of temperature, pulse, respiration, blood pressure and observation, medicine administered, dose and duration of medicines, diet or so. Further, we also find a medical section covering the entire medical history of the patients, such as history sheet, physical examination sheet, provisional diagnosis, investigation reports, physicians order sheet, medical or surgical treatment prescribed, record of anaesthesia, record of operation, records of obstetric, consultancy report, progress report, final diagnosis, discharge summary and if death, causes of the death.

The aforesaid facts make it clear that for good patient care, we find hospital records an important source of information, specially with the viewpoint of diagnosing and treating the patients. Right from the first stage of admission to the last stage of discharge and further for adopting the line of treatment in identical cases or for undertaking research, we find hospital records making available to us an authentic back up material which in addition to the medical purposes may also be useful to the concerned persons for using the same as a legal document. These facts make it clear that a hospital manager requires to manage the hospital records in a scientific way so that the medical or paramedical staff, managerial or administrative staff, patients and attendants get and make use of the same conveniently as and when they need, as a source of information or as a legal document.

Types of Records

In hospitals or healthcare organisations, we find a large number of records for different purposes. It is quite natural that all records don't carry equal significance. We find some of the records to remain useful for all the time and this necessitates due management of records. In Fig. 12.1, we find different type of records.[2]

1. Vital Records: In the first category, we find vital records found of use without any time limit and therefore, a hospital manager is required to assign due weightage to the management of vital records. The records related to critical results, projection of wonderful results by the personnel, innovative efforts of doctors in treating the patients, cases of fraudulent preferences, etc. carry outstanding significance till the existence of hospitals. For references or for carrying on research, the records help substantially to the researchers, doctors, medical scientists and others evincing interests in promoting research. This makes it essential that a hospital manager makes it sure that the related records have been stored, documented or stored in the memory of computers.

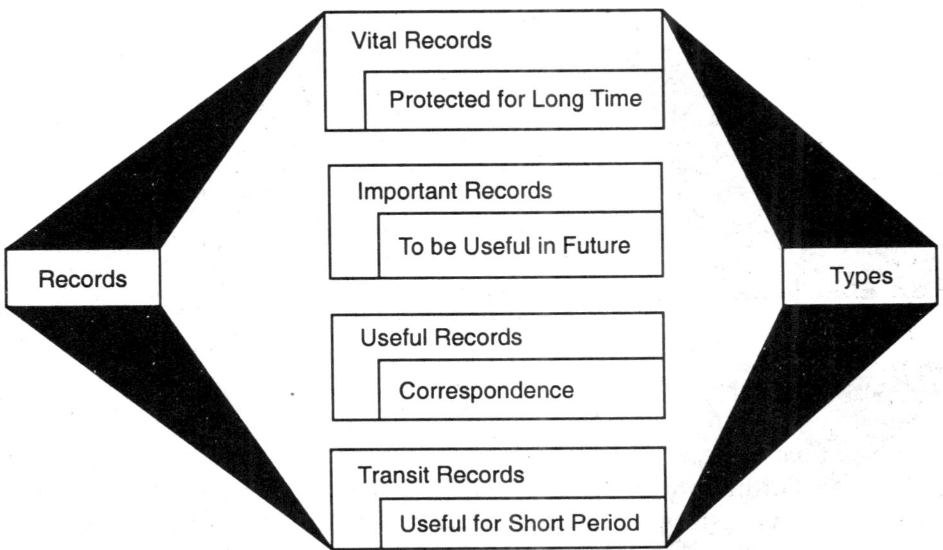

Fig. 12.1. Types of Records to be Made Keeping in View the Significance of Records.

2. Important Records: In this category, we find important records found significant or useful for future or for undertaking research. A hospital manager bears the responsibility of making available to the researchers the feedback or back up material for reference. If we find provision for computers, the information can be stored in the memory and if not, the documentation would be required.

3. Useful Records: In this category, we find useful records based on correspondences between the personnel of the hospitals and the clients which may include patients, attendants, suppliers of different types of materials or so. It is possible that even in this category, we find some of the correspondences useful and keeping in view the nature of urgency, a hospital manager is required to make suitable arrangements for their recording.

4. Transit Records: The records in this category are found of current or temporary use. This makes it essential that a hospital manager keeping in view the period or time limit make suitable arrangements for their documentation. It is also important that after the time limit, the records are destroyed. In the management of records, we find steps or decisions for destroying the records significant which should be taken after an indepth discussion with the heads of the related departments.

Essentials of an Effective Record Management

Being a hospital manager, you bear the responsibility of making it sure that the records related to different departments and healthcare services are managed in an effective way. For future reference, for legal proof, for developing rapport for rewarding or punishing, for promoting quality research and for not committing the mistakes, you have already committed, it is pertinent that you come to know about the essentials so that your records help you substantially in fulfilling the organisational objectives. It is against this background that we talk about the essentials of an effective record management. In Fig. 12.2, we find focus on different essentials.

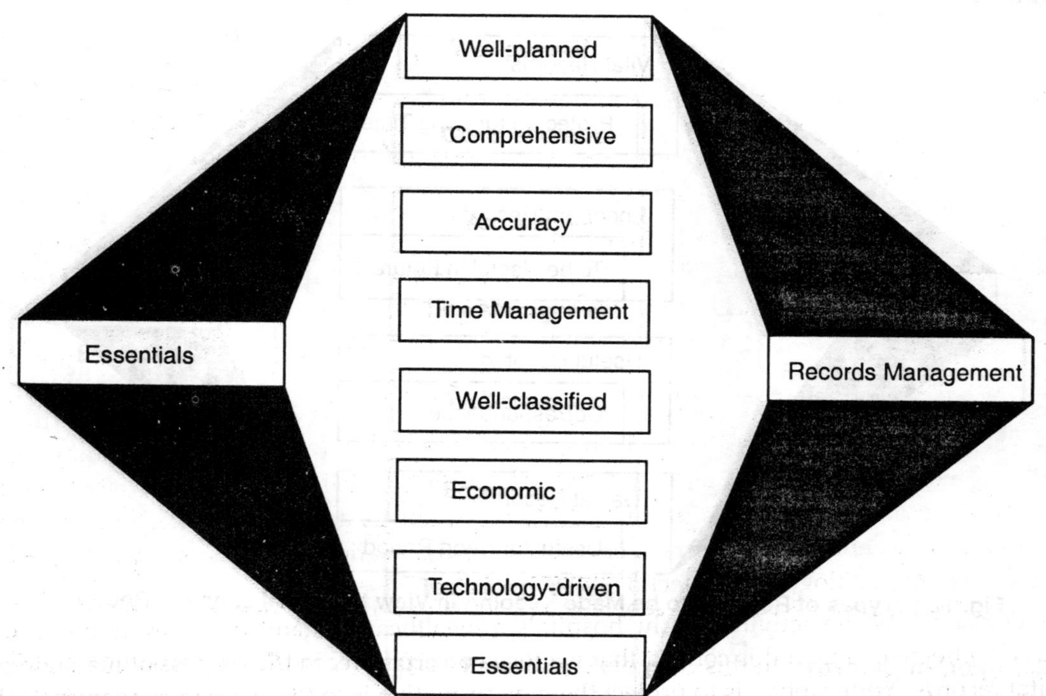

Fig. 12.2. Essentials of an Effective Record

1. *Well Planned:* This first consideration that we find significant in the very context is related to planning which focuses our attention on knowing about the records of different departments and making arrangements accordingly. If you are aware of the different types of records, it is easier for you to make necessary arrangements to protect, indeed and store them on the basis of their significance. You need special attention on some of the records because they are found vital and important not only at present but even in future whereas you also find records of temporary importance and you need to destroy them just after the fulfillment of your requirements. You need to screen the records at a regular interval, specially to weed out the information not of future use. The most important thing in planning for the management of hospital records is to minimise your requirements of space and this makes it essential that you know about the importance of records. Arrangements related to cataloguing or indexing and protection can't be made satisfactory unless you know everything in detail.

2. *Comprehensive:* Another quality is related to comprehensiveness which makes it essential that the management of records should speak everything in itself. When you retrieve old records for the formulation of a plan or for making policy recessions, the task of locating the required records should not be difficult. While managing records, you need to make suitable arrangements for their scientific indexing and if you have computers, you need to develop a file in the face of your requirements. Whatever the code, language you use or coin should easily be understandable. More simple and intelligent the coding and indexing, less time taking we find the processes of location and identification. It is in this context that you need to assign due weightage to the same.

3. *Accuracy:* In the context of records management, you need to make it sure that whatever the facts and figures, informations made available are accurate and authentic. Since the accuracy of records is to influence a number of policies and plans, almost all the decisions and processes vis-a-vis the credibility of your managerial excellence and professionalism, you are supposed to make it one hundred per cent sure that whatever the information the concerned persons or agencies get from the records department are authentic.

4. *Time Management:* Even in the context of records management, you need to assign due significance to time management. It is quite natural that different persons, departments, agencies and organisations come to the records department for collecting the information and if they find it a time-taking process, that would question your professional excellence. Scientific indexing or cataloguing simplifies the task of collection and the concerned individuals or agencies appreciate your managerial proficiency. This makes it essential that you are very much particular to the system of indexing you adopt for managing the records.

5. *Well-classified:* For making records management ideal, effective and purposeful, it is pertinent that you classify them in the face of their utility. Some of the records are found useful for all the time whereas some of the records are not useful today but are expected to be useful for tomorrow. You also find records useful for today but not for tomorrow. Since you face space constraint, it is essential that you on the basis of their classification make necessary arrangements for their indexing, cataloguing, protection or so.

6. *Economic: All* the activities in the hospitals or healthcare organisations are required to be made cost-effective. It is in this context that we focus on economy in the process of managing the hospital records. Your motive is to protect them, your motive is to locate them conveniently. It is not your motive that you spend or waste your time and money for managing the records of no

use. Of course, the vital and important records require due attention but records of no use need to be destroyed. It is essential that you have an indepth idea of their usefulness.

7. *Technology-driven:* In an age of information technology, the records management also need to be well supported by computers. This would minimise your functional responsibilities related to documentation because computers would make possible proper storing. The process of making the management of records technology-driven would also be cost-effective, if not in the short run, of course in the long-run. To be more specific, the task of collecting and recollecting the required documents and papers would be made easier if we take the support of computers.

The aforesaid qualities make the management of records effective not only with the viewpoint of locating or collecting the same but also with the motto of maintaining economy in the process. Being a manager, you have to make it possible and if the above-mentioned features are found in your records management, the task of researchers, medical scientists, doctors and others would fantastically be simplified. It is against this background that you need to manage records of your hospitals carefully. The excellence and expertise you show in the process help the healthcare management in different ways.

A majority or almost all of us believe that medical records are of vital importance clinically for immediate diagnosis and treatment and for use of future development and welfare plans. They play a positive role in making an appraisal of the services of hospitals, increasing the levels of efficiency and offering world class patient care. In the secondary and tertiary hospitals or in the medical teaching institutes, we find records helping faculty in educating and training the students and staff. The research activities are also promoted on the basis of medical records. Keeping in view the instrumentality of hospital records in almost all the areas, we find it essential that a hospital manager assigns due weightage to manage the hospital records in an effective way. This makes it essential that the hospital records must present a comprehensive picture of patients' illness with the physical findings and special reports such as X-ray and laboratory reports. It is pertinent that the reports are accurately written, properly filed and documented and made conveniently accessible. It is against this background that in a number of hospitals, we find provisions for an independent department for managing the hospital records.

An expert, K. Pennathur makes a strong advocacy in favour of sound management of records and feels that a hospital manager should make best of his/her efforts to make the management of hospital records scientific. Pennathur observes that the hospital records should serve specific needs and have specific objectives and purposes. Efforts should be made to minimise or optimise the scope and contents and be designed for expensive handling. It is also important that the hospital records are updated and are made available as and when the concerned persons agencies need or make a demand. The supervision activities can be made more result-oriented if the management of hospital records is found scientific. Thus, the line management based on records can be successful in identifying the weaknesses or lapses. The processes of record management should not be expensive and for that, the hospitals need to take the support of almost all the heads of the departments in addition to the record manager or a hospital manager.

The aforesaid facts make it clear that the management processes need to be made effective and of late, we need to do the same on a priority basis. The management information system substantially depends on the records department for enriching the information bank and if the system is made technology-based, the management of records can be made more effective. It is in this context that we find leading hospitals making efforts to take the support of computers for managing records. It is right to mention that the Department of Materials and stores supplies a number of documents to the records section and for developing contract with suppliers or for identifying the fraudulent activities, the old records can be more helpful. Of late, the process of documentation, if managed manually, is found cost-effective because we are supposed to invest a lot on the management of personnel and records. In addition, the accessibility to records is not found to be so smooth if the system is managed manually. It is against this background that we find computers used by a number of hospitals for managing the records. We can't negate the fact that manual documentation is expensive and even sensitive to unfair practices whereas we find computers making the process cost-effective and convenient. Of course at the initial stage, the process may be cost-ineffective but gradually we find a big fall in the management expenses. Keeping in view the similarities in the nature of management, it is significant that the library department of a hospital accepts the responsibility of managing the hospital records. Proper indexing and cataloguing would make the ways for the productive use of hospital records.

Form of Hospital Records

We find different sections and departments using a number of records for different purposes. It is significant that all the records after making classification and assigning weightage are documented by the records department or are stored in the memory of computers for future reference. The different forms[3] of hospital records are mentioned in Fig. 12.3.

Letters: A large number of letters are used by different departments for different purposes. The letters come from patients, attendants, clients, suppliers or others and it is the responsibility of a hospital manager to make it sure that all the important letters are placed at a right place. It is quite natural that all the letters don't carry equal importance and therefore, keeping in view their uses and significance at present or in future, a hospital manager/record manager bears the responsibility of ordering, indexing and cataloguing the important or vital letters.

Circulars and Reports: In hospitals, we also find circulation of orders of departmental heads, managers and government and it is essential that all the circulars are screened and important circulars are recorded for future reference. To be more specific, the circulars related to the service conditions of the hospital personnel or any change or revision therein are to be sorted out and vital or important circulars are to be recorded. Like this, the reports focus our attention on the investigation reports or the reports of any sub-committee or committee related to the workings of the hospital. In this connection, the annual reports of the health department of the government and private hospitals where annual reports are published are found significant.

Case Histories: We are well aware of the fact that in almost all the hospitals, the case histories of patients developing critical diseases and symptoms are recorded. This includes details of patients, such as his/her name, address, age, sex, disease, investigation reports, observation of reports, observation of doctors, drugs prescribed/operation suggested, routine, checking, precautions, diet sheet, effects and side-effects of medicines or so. Some of the cases are found of critical nature which are required to be recorded in a right way because doctors or researchers may find them significant, or of use in the future to diagnose and treat other patients. With the use of computers, we find the process of recording case histories becoming easier. Right from the admission or registration, the process of recording everything in the process starts which continues till the discharge of patients or till they are cured or even in future for future reference. We can't negate that some of the case histories become an important feedback or source materials for undertaking research. It is responsibility of a hospital manager to be aware of the important or critical case histories and to record them in a right order.

Contracts: In hospitals, to be more specific, the materials department is required to take a decision regarding the supplies. This makes it essential that for ensuring the supply of quality hospital material and biomedical equipment, a hospital manager comes to know about the name of the suppliers, specifications, actual supply position, conditions for installing and servicing so that we don't find any confusion. For renewing the contracts or for signing new contracts, or for changing or amending the provisions, the doctors, hospital managers, suppliers of biomedical equipment and apparatus need past reference and in this context, the scientific management of records would make their task easier. To be more specific, while supplying expensive biomedical equipment or other materials, a hospital manager needs to make it sure that the terms and conditions for supplying the related items have been fulfilled. The terms and conditions related to the maintenance or repairing of equipment need due attention in the very context.

Invoices: To be more specific, the material and stores department of hospitals for ensuring supply or for making payments for the supplies make use of invoices. Here, it essential that a hospital manager goes through the invoices and discusses the same with the material manager if circumstances necessitate so. This would ensure actual supplies and would also make it sure that the required quality of materials have been supplied on time.

Vouchers: We find vouchers an important document because whatever the payments we find for the supplies or other persons are to be substantiated through the vouchers. We find hospital materials and stores department playing a contributory role because a large number of vouchers are recorded by them when purchases are made.

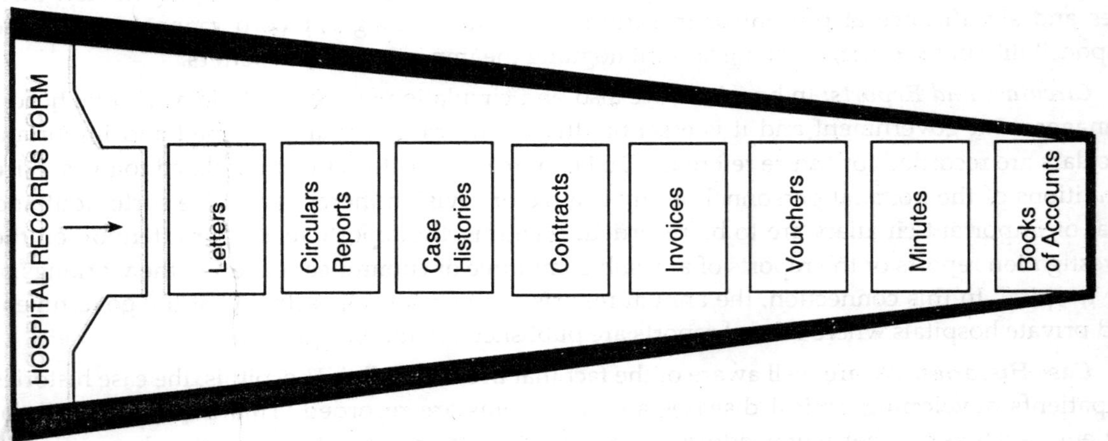

Fig. 12.3. Forms of Hospital Records

Minutes: We find different types of meetings and some of deliberations of the meeting may also be useful. It is the responsibility of a hospital manager to make suitable arrangements so that minutes are used as a legal document. This focuses on recording of the proceedings of a meeting.

Books and Accounts: This is related to the finance department, and therefore, while going through the books and accounts, it is also to make it sure that the details related to the health problems have been recorded and all the important papers are well protected. The vehicle log book and the vehicle fuel book need to be managed in a proper way. The pay roll is an important area and it is the prime responsibility of a hospital manager to make it sure that the expenses and revenue are taken into consideration. The Income and Expenditure Account, Accounts Receivables and Payables and Balance Sheet of the hospitals are some of the important documents found of use and the hospital manager/materials manager bears the responsibility of procuring, recording, protecting and making available the required information by the concerned or related person(s).

Sections of Medical Records

The medical record is found to be a complete history of the life of patients, nature of illness and all the problems related to the diagnosis and treatment.[4] It is in a true sense a true story of patients' illness which is explained by them and observed by the nursing staff and commented or remarked by the specialists and doctors. All the reports related to their illness are mentioned in the medical records. There are three important sections of medical record, viz., General Section, Nursing Section and Medical Section.

General Section: This section of the medical record consists of administrative and personal data. In this section, we find name of the patient, father's or husband's name, age, sex, religion, ethnicity, income, mailing address and the address of the nearest relative. In this section, we also find inclusion of administrative report which includes the date of admission, in-patient number, name of the nursing unit and bed number. Thus, in the general section of the medical record, we find mix of the two with the motto of collecting details regarding the patients.

Nursing Section: In the nursing section, we find observation of trained nurses and the details of treatment administered. It includes graphic chart prepared by the nurses consisting of temperature chart, pulse rate, blood pressure and other observations such as intake-output chart and administration of medicines. This section of the medical record is mainly related to the nurses who are supposed to take care of patients and to note the aforesaid details.

Medical Section: This section of the medical report includes statement on the studies, observations and conclusions and findings of the attending doctors or the intern (an immate of the boarding school) or the resident working under him. It includes a complete history of patients' medical profile. The important items to be included in the medical report are the following:

- A history sheet including the detailed medical history of patients.
- Physical examination sheet including the details of investigations and the reports and observations.
- Provisional diagnosis including the diagnosis of patients before experts come to a final conclusion.
- Order Sheet of Physicians including the instruction of doctors.
- Treatment—medical or surgical that determines the ways of treatment needed.
- Anaesthesist record which includes administration of anaesthesia or other devices and doses.
- Operation record includes the details of doctors / surgeons who have operated the patients and their observations.
- Obstetric record which is pertaining to midwifery.
- Consultancy report is related to the reports and observations of consultants.

- Progress report that clarifies the treatment schedule, administration of medicines and their effects or side effects on the related patients.
- Final diagnosis clarified or related to the observations based on the final investigation reports.
- Discharge summary is found related to the discharge of patients after recovery.
- Autopsy report which is related to death report.

Dimensions of Records Management

Management of hospital records is found significant not only with the viewpoint of making available to the different persons and agencies information pertaining to the working of hospitals but also with the motto of evaluating the performance of hospital personnel serving the different departments. If you manage hospital records scientifically and in a systematic fashion, your task of making possible qualitative-cum-quantitative improvements is considerably simplified. It is against this background that a hospital manager is required to be careful at the different stages of managing the hospital records. We agree with this view that with the development of information technology, a hospital manager finds it convenient to manage the hospital records. The different dimensions of managing the hospital records are presented in Fig. 12.4.

1. Creating the hospital records: This is the first constituent or dimension of records management which draws our attention on the development of filing system, indexing, cataloguing and record-keeping in view of the requirements of different departments for which the records are created. The creation focuses our attention on the system we adopt and quality we promote for the said purpose. It is well-known that almost all the departments of the hospital need to maintain records, such as the materials department, wards, engineering department, food and beverages or so. Of course, we use computers in place of records but it is also right to mention that development or creation of hospital records manually should also be promoted so that the faults developing at one side are identified on the other side. The mechanics determine the intensity of your success and you are not supposed to forget the same. It is also possible that the financial constraint is obstructing you to develop a technology-driven records management and therefore, instead of generating financial problems, you need to create manual filing system. The most important thing in the very context is your approach which would determine the magnitude of your success in managing the hospital records.

2. Administering the records: This is the second dimension of the management of hospital records which gravitates our attention on the implementation of the system of developing records that you have created. Irrespective of the fact that it is technology-driven or manual-driven, you need to make it sure that the system is functioning on your directions and instructions. The filing and programming are as per the changing needs and requirements of your hospitals. The records section and the personnel working there are efficient and maintaining records carefully. Of course, the sectional head would make a frequent inspection and supervision but you, as a manager also need to make a frequent inspection and time-to-time supervision to ascertain that records are administered in the right direction.

3. Retaining the hospital records: Since we find hospitals facing the problem of space constraint, it is right that you make a microscopic analysis of the facts that how and in what way the records are to be retained for future reference. While making classification of hospital records, you have come to know that some of the records are vital and important whereas some of the records are of temporary use. It is your professional excellence to foresee the future needs of records so that you are in a position to retain and document them in a right fashion. This dimension of the management or records makes it essential that at first stage, all the records are retained and only after making an indepth study of their needs in future, you make suitable arrangements for retaining and documenting them. You are not required to take a decision in haste because at the first stage, it becomes difficult to ascertain the usefulness of the same.

4. Submitting the records: This is the first stage before you take a decision to destroy the records. This dimension of the management of hospital records makes it essential that being a hospital manager, you come to know about the rationale behind documenting the same or storing the same in the memory of your computers. Protection is an important aspect to be given due weightage in the process because the files and programmes can be destroyed even by the insects and virus. We are well aware of the fact that the department of records or records section of your hospital or even in some of the cases, the library of the hospitals accept the responsibility of preserving the old records of hospitals and therefore, you bear the responsibility of making available to the records section all the facilities and devices they need to protect the same. In case of damage to the vital or important records, due mainly to the negligence of your staff, you need to fix accountability.

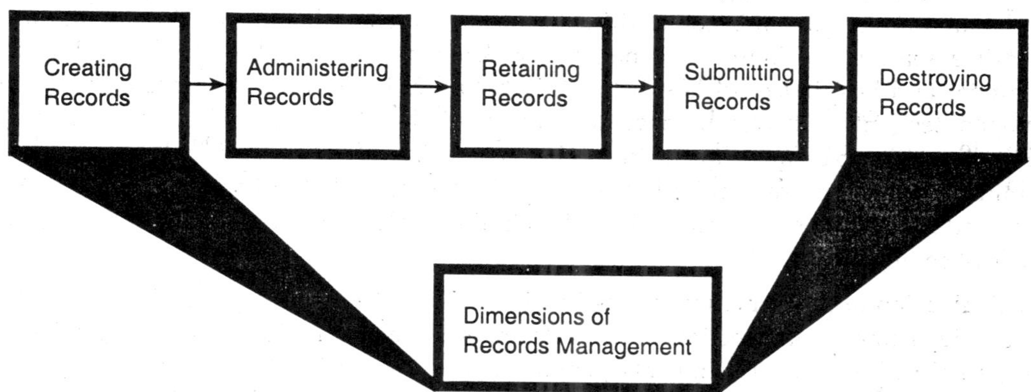

Fig. 12.4. Dimensions of Records Management

5. Destroying the hospital records: This dimension of records management is found occupying an outstanding place because once you take a decision, you are not in a position to make use of the same. This makes it essential that before taking a decision regarding the destroying of the records, you consult different heads of department and in consultation with them, take a final decision. In any case, you are not required to take a decision in haste. Of late, you have computers with high potentials of storing the same and therefore, only after a microscopic analysis of the problem, you need to instruct regarding the same. Since creation of records is an ongoing process, it is not essential that you preserve even the records of no use. The most important decision making area in the very context is to fix the time keeping in view of the urgency.

The aforesaid facts make it clear that different dimensions of records management are given due weightage because mistakes committed at one stage complicate the management process at the next stage. Of late, you have sophisticated devices and quality materials for managing the records and you need to make use of the same in tune with your potentials and requirements. You need not forget that old records act as a guide, friend and philosopher.

Significance of Record-Keeping

Of course, in almost all the organisations, we find record-keeping playing a significant role in improving the quality of managerial decisions but to be more specific in hospitals or healthcare organisations, we find their instrumentality even for improving the quality of healthcare services. Of late, the process has been made more scientific and albeit easier because we find computers playing an incremental role in managing the records. It is pertinent that you realise the instrumentality of record-keeping so that your managerial decisions assign due weightage to the management of hospital records. It is against this background that we go through the significance of record-keeping. It is also displayed in Fig. 12.5.

1. Quality decision-making: We agree with this view that sky is the limit to quality upgradation and sky is the limit even for achieving a stage of perfection. Of course, you have subjective knowledge and based on that you are in a position to manage hospitals in a right fashion. But at the same time, you also need to make it sure that your decisions establish an edge over the decision of the competing hospitals often challenging your excellence and expertise. The process of enriching knowledge is not to be slowed down because the moment you start realising that you are number one, it becomes difficult for you to retain the position for a long time. This makes it essential that being a manager, you keep on moving the process of knowledge-enrichment and hospital records substantially help you in the process. Since you have a well developed, technology-driven management information system, it is easier for you to make use of the information to be made available by the records. You are supposed to keep your eyes open and mind active. You are required to identify the lapses and shortcomings so that you make sincere and honest efforts to correct them. It is in this context that we talk about the significance of record-keeping.

2. Evaluation of performance is possible: Records in a true sense narrate the contributions of different departments and sections. The performance of an individual or a team can be gauged with the help of records. The mistakes committed in diagnosing and treating the patients, in purchasing the biomedical equipment, instruments, apparatus, machines or other materials in finalising the contract with the suppliers, in negotiating, in nursing, in operating or in almost all the areas can be identified if you go through the old records. Now the task is easier because you have a well-developed management information system and in addition, the computers are also available at your office desk. It is quite natural that the hospital personnel like the personnel of other sectors or organisations commit mistakes. But if they fail in realising and confessing their mistakes, they would commit a blunder which would result into irreparable losses. This makes it essential that being a manager, you go through the vital records and come to know the lapses in the different departments.

3. Making possible a comparative analysis: If you want to remain number one or at the top, it is pertinent that you not only know about yourself but also come to know about your competitors. It is in this context that we find hospital records helping you in making a comparative analysis of the performance of leading and internationally acclaimed hospitals and healthcare organisations.

The medical records would considerably help you in making a comparative analysis of the performance of your hospitals and the quality of healthcare services made available by you. In addition, you also need to collect records related to the complaints of patients and attendants. This would help you in studying the level of behavioural profile of your employees. The hospital records thus help you in different ways. The moment you come to know about the quality of different types of services made available by the competitive hospitals or healthcare organisations, you get an opportunity to correct the mistakes.

Fig. 12.5. Importance of Record-Keeping

4. Internal control is possible: The record-keeping if managed and monitored in a right fashion helps you in channelising the internal control. Since you have come to know the points, stages, reasons for the mistakes committed earlier, it is easier for you to be vigilant so that the employees don't repeat the same. "Prevention is better than cure." We agree with this proverb and the record-keeping helps you in adopting or channelising and sensitising the preventive measures. If you feel that based on records, the mistakes were committed while having a deal with the suppliers of materials, you try to remove the scope for the same. Like this, in almost all the areas and almost at all the stages, you can adopt preventive measures to exercise internal control.

5. Operational efficiency is increased: The hospital records substantially help you in increasing the level of efficiency of not only the personnel but also the equipment, instruments, plants and machines and instruments used in the process. If you succeed in increasing the level of efficiency of both the sources of efficiency-generation, it is quite natural that you succeed in making the process of diagnosis and treatment cost-effective which fantastically helps you in making the services affordable. Being a manager, you also bear the responsibility of making it sure that cost-effectiveness is made possible at almost all the stages. An optimal use of assets and human resources is found to be a prerequisite for accelerating the rate of productivity and you need to remember it. With the help of computers, you are in a position to maintain the efficiency, accuracy, speed and these things help you in the process of productivity-acceleration. In the management of hospitals or healthcare organisations, the most important responsibility before a healthcare manager is to make possible cost-effectiveness and this is not possible unless you increase the levels of efficiency of capital and human resources.

6. Statutory obligations to be fulfilled satisfactorily: We can't negate the fact that you need to meet the statutory obligations because failing it, you invite a number of problems. It is quite natural that like other organisations, you also face the problems like litigation, disputes or claims. To be more specific, the Consumer Protection Act has made it essential that you are vigilant so that cases of negligence are not to complicate your functional responsibility. If you maintain records, it is easier for you to substantiate or authenticate the arguments or testify the charges levelled by an individual or an organisation. The provisions of the Indian Companies Act, 1956 make it essential that you are maintaining books and accounts and keeping in view the statutory obligations. You have no option but to assign due weightage to records keeping. You find yourself more bold, you find your arguments more appealing and convincing, if the same substantiated or authenticated by records.

7. Strategic Management is found easier: With the help of records, it is easier for you to think about the strategic management which focuses your attention on the formulation of an action plan keeping in view the latest developments in the medical sciences vis-a-vis the emerging trends in the disease profile. It is in this context that we find record-keeping helping a manager while formulating an action plan. The moment an organisation is found satisfied with its achievements, we can't activate the process of qualitative or quantitative developments. It is quite natural that based on scientific invention and innovations, the process of technological sophistication keeps on moving. If you delay the process of adopting the same, you fail in establishing an edge over your competitors. To be more specific in the Indian perspective, we find a large number of problems engineering a sound foundation for the development of a new disease profile. The problems related to population, illiteracy and unawareness aggravate the magnitude of problems, specially in the Indian setting. The increasing problem of environmental and cultural pollution make the bed for the germination of diseases more fertile. The consumption of contaminated water, unhygienic food items, noise pollution, air pollution, irresponsible sexual behaviour have been found increasing the intensity of health problem. Thus, the hospitals and healthcare organisations need to open new vistas for qualitative and quantitative improvements so that a gap between the demand and supply is bridged. If the population is increasing fast, it is quite natural that the demand would increase and in absence of strategic management, it would be difficult for you to cater to the increasing healthcare requirements of the Indian society. With the help of record-keeping, it is easier for you to know about the changing healthcare requirement. For the information of a sound strategic plan, this happens to be essential because based on the future requirements, you can activate the process of development. It is against this background that being a hospital manager, it is essential for you to manage hospital records in a scientific way so that your action plan enables hospitals to keep on moving the process of development.

The aforesaid facts make it clear that we find record-keeping essential and being a manager, you are required to assign due weightage to the same. Of course, depending upon the financial limitations, you have to take a decision but it is also pertinent that you try your best to move with the emerging trends. The records keeping help you in many ways. You bear the responsibility of making the best use of hospital resources. You bear the responsibility of making it sure that services are made cost effective. You bear the responsibility of improving the quality. The record-keeping help you.

Key Information for Healthcare Managers

The hospital records make available to a hospital or healthcare manager different types of information which help them in making and innovating the managerial decision. We can't negate that medical records occupy a place of outstanding significance in the process of initiating and activating qualitative transformation in the healthcare services. For the day-to-day management of hospitals or healthcare organisations the hospital manager needs the following information:

1. *Death Rates of Patients:* For the sound management of healthcare organisations, it is pertinent that a hospital manager is well aware of the death rates. Here, our focus is on both types of the death rates, viz., Gross Deaths and Net Deaths. In the context of Gross Death, we find focus on all the deaths of admitted patients whereas the Net Deaths exclude the patients dying within 48 hours of their admission. In a true sense, we find net death rate an indicator of the working of a hospital. The calculation of net death rate is found on the basis of the following equation:

$$\frac{\text{Number of net deaths during a period of time}}{\text{Number of total discharges during the period of time}} \times 100 = \text{Death rate of patients}$$

Generally, we find in hospitals an average net death rate between 4-6 per cent. This makes it clear that on an average, we find 5 per cent net death rate as a normal phenomenon and a hospital manager is required to see that a stage of abnormal death rate exceeding 5 per cent is to be taken due care and the reasons for the same are identified. It is right to mention that there are a number of factors influencing the net death rate because in case of patients affected by epidemics, viral diseases and admitted at a critical stage, the death rate may be abnormal but the responsibilities are not on the doctors working there. Thus, before coming to any conclusion, a hospital manager needs to identify the reasons for an abnormal increase in the net death rate. If we don't find natural factors instrumental in the process of increasing the net death rate, a hospital manager is required to go through the fact that at what stage of the service areas, the failures in the healthcare systems could result into an increase in the net death rate. A hospital manager is required to keep a track of the performance of each and every unit department of the hospital by keeping a track of the net death rate. Thus, we find death rate an indicator helping a manager in improving the level of efficiency or in identifying the failures of personnel or technologies or the system as a whole.

2. *Average Length of Stay of Patients:* On the basis of hospital records, it is also possible for a manager to find out the average length of stay of patients in the hospitals. We agree with this view that in a majority of the hospitals, the date of admission is taken into consideration but the date of discharge is not given due weightage. In this context, it is important to mention that a hospital manager requires to know about the average length of stay which would be calculated on the basis of discharge analysis with the help of following equation:

$$\frac{\text{Total length of stay of discharged patients during a period of time}}{\text{Total discharges during that period of time}} \times 100 = \begin{array}{l}\text{Average length of stay}\\ \text{of patients of stay}\end{array}$$

The average length of stay of patients discharged during a particular period of time is worked out not only for the whole hospital but it is also calculated departmentwise or unit-wise.

This helps in locating or finding out the unnecessary length of stay which would be required to be discouraged. It is the responsibility of a hospital manager to bring down the unnecessary length of stay which would benefit the patients and hospitals in many ways. The vacancy due to discharge would be used for those patients who could not be admitted on account of accommodation constraints.

3. *Rate of Bed Turnover:* By the bed turnover rate, our focus is found on the number of patients who have been made available the services per bed per year. We calculate it on the basis of the following equation:

$$\frac{\text{Total Number of discharges during a year}}{\text{Total Number of authorised beds}} \times 100 = \text{Rate of Bed Turnover}$$

This rate is calculated with the support of average length of stay and the interval between discharge and successive admissions. We also call it in the medical literature T-interval. This helps a hospital manager in planning the optimal utilisation of hospital resources.

4. *Bed Occupancy Ratio:* The bed occupancy ratio focuses on the relationship between the availability of facilities and their utilisation. It is right to mention that an optimal bed occupancy is found between 85-90 per cent. If it is more than 90 per cent, it is clear that we find stress on a particular area of the hospital. It Is also right to mention that when we find the occupancy ratio 100 per cent or more than 100 per cent, the dilution in the facilities of a hospital can't be negated. Besides, it also focuses on the low level of efficiency. The bed occupancy ratio can be worked out for the whole hospital and also for each unit or stream of a hospital. The following equation would be used for calculation:

$$\frac{\text{Average Daily Census during a period of time}}{\text{Number of authorised beds}} \times 100 = \text{Bed Occupancy Rate}$$

The aforesaid information can be received from the medical records which would help a hospital manager in improving the quality of health care services. Hence, it is the responsibility of a hospital manager that he/she takes the support of medical records and attempts to get the aforesaid information on a priority basis. He/she bears the responsibility of minimising the average length of stay because this would make it clear that the quality of healthcare services is of world class. In addition, the waiting patients who could not be admitted or are waiting for vacancy would get an opportunity for admission. We can't negate the fact that in some of the hospitals, the patients are found deliberately overstaying due to personal reasons but it affects the level of efficiency of hospitals in an adverse way. This make it essential that a hospital manager on the basis of results received from the calculation takes a decision and tries to achieve the optimum level. We can't negate the fact that credibility of a hospital is substantially influenced by the emerging trends in the death rate but we can't come to a particular conclusion unless we know the nature of admission, stage of admission or so. Thus, on the basis of hospital records, the aforesaid information would help a hospital manager not only in improving the level of efficiency but also in identifying the high performing units, wards, team which would be an important base for rewarding or penalising, motivating or demotivating the healthcare personnel.

Filing of Hospital Records

The international standard calls for proper indexing and filing of records that can easily be retrieved. A simple means of indexing quality records is to maintain a register in the functional groups or departments concerned. The register should list the quality records in numerical order and these should be filed in sequence and kept in specified locations under the responsibility of designated persons.

Filing is found to be an important constituent of the management of records which is the process of classifying, arranging and storing records systematically. It is the systematic arrangement for keeping of business correspondences and records so that these may be found and delivered quickly as and when required for the future reference. It is the placing of documents in the acceptable containers according to some predetermined arrangements so that any of these when required may be located and made available to the concerned persons or agencies.

Arranging Files

There are a number of bases for arranging files and a manager is required to take a decision in the face of his/her requirements. The following bases are found used for arranging the files which are also shown in Fig. 12.6.

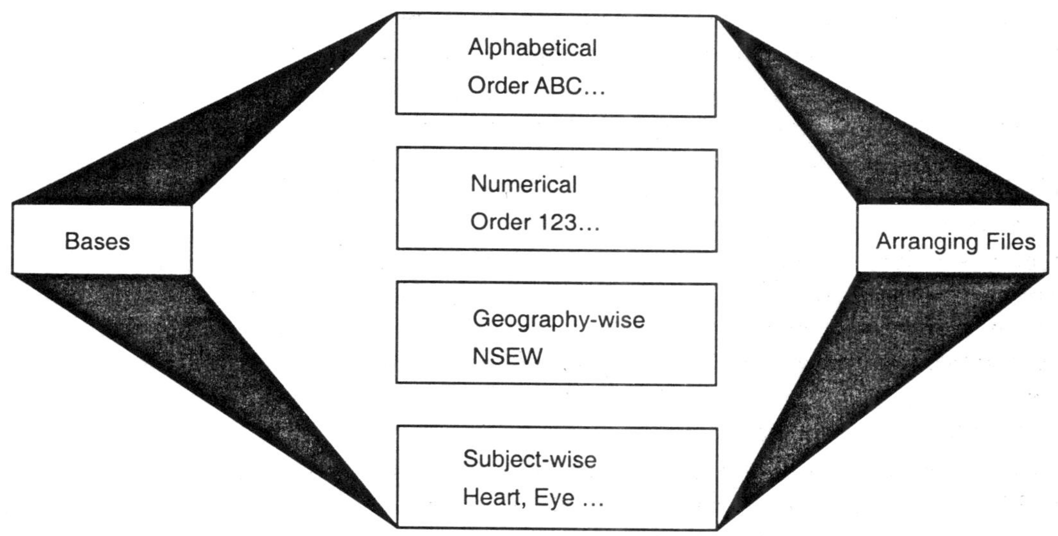

Fig. 12.6. Bases for Arranging Files

Alphabetical Order: By the alphabetical order, our focus is on the main subjects under the functions, such as establishment, common office services and budget which are listed under the functional group headings identified by capital letters, A, B, C or so.

Numerical Order: In this context, our emphasis is on arranging files in the numerical order. Each main subject or head under each of the functional group is assigned consecutive Arabic numericals beginning with 1 which may go up to 99. Like this, the sub-subjects or subheads under each main head are assigned consecutive Arabic numericals beginning with II which may also go up to 99.

The identifying subject numerals and sub-subjected numerals are separated by O. The group of numerals to the left of O refer to the main head while that to the right to its subhead, topic or aspect.

Files opened under the same subject are also given serial number 1, 2, 3, and are separated from the groups of numerals by an oblique. The year in which the file is shown separately from the file number by an oblique.

Centralised and Decentralised Filing

By the centralised filing system, our emphasis is on locating all the filing equipment and personnel in a single area of the office which should essentially be accessible to all departments by messengers, controlled by a centralised plan or index of the filing. The decentralised filing system focuses our attention on the system where each organisation makes its own arrangement for filing.[5]

The centralised filing system is found useful to an organisation because it ensures uniformity and standardisation of the filing equipment and procedure which can help in easy and quick location of records. It also eliminates the need of duplication and distribution to all concerned sections and encourages completeness of related documents. Besides, we find the system promoting economy of time for both the users as well as the personnel because we find the process centralised to send material to be filed. It is easier for the management to supervise and control effectively since one person or group alone is responsible which minimises oversights and loss of valuable records. The economy of filing equipment is also possible.

Thus, we find centralised filing system useful to an organisation and it is the responsibility of a manager to promote centralised filing system and to minimise scope for the decentralised filing system. The decentralisation is also to cause inconveniences and the users would find it difficult to fulfil their requirements. In the management of files, we find uniformity and standardisation playing a significant role but due to decentralisation, the task of ensuring uniformity and maintaining standards is found difficult. The possibilities of duplication may generate numerous problems and the users would find it difficult to locate unless they are well aware of the system adopted by an organisation. Of late, we find almost all the organisations facing the problem of space constraint and in the decentralised system of filing, we can't check the same. The records manager or a hospital manager finds it difficult to supervise and control the filing arrangements when the system is found decentralised.

In view of the above, it is right to adopt the centralised system of filing even by the hospitals and healthcare organisations. This would simplify the process, maintain economy and the users would find it accessible or convenient to locate if proper indexing and cataloguing are made possible.

Of late, we find technology-driven system of filing gaining popularity in almost all the leading hospitals of the world. With the development of information technology and its increasing uses even in hospitals, we now find a new perception of filing. The hospitals and healthcare organisations using computers for this purpose find it convenient to centralise the system which is not only economic but also requires the minimum possible space and makes the process of supervision and control proactive. The users with the help of indexing find it convenient to locate the file of their use very conveniently if they are aware of the computers. It is against this background the we find a majority of the well established hospitals or healthcare organisations preferring computers for the filing of records. To be more specific in the hospitals where diverse nature and character of records are used, it is pertinent that we promote the application of computers for making possible the management of records productive.

Management of Hospital Records: Problems and Remedies

The management of hospital records in the Indian context presents a very gloomy picture. Of course, the private hospitals have been found establishing an edge over the government hospitals even in respect of records management. In a majority of the government hospitals, we find a number of problems which require an immediate solution.

1. The use of outdated forms not in tune with the evolving technologies: Whatever the forms are used in the hospitals for records management are found outdated lacking a correlation with the evolving technologies. This makes it essential that the forms are revised and while revising, the instrumentality of information technology is given due weightage. The columns appearing obsolete in the forms are to be replaced with the new columns appearing obsolete in the face of use of computers, diagnostic and treatment devices so that the forms make available complete information.

2. Inadequacy of efficient personnel: It is also found that the records department has been facing the problem of inadequacy of efficient personnel, specially in tune with the changing system. It is strange and in a true sense amazing that the hospital authorities don't assign due weightage to the records department in improving the quality of personnel or technologies. The management of records requires completion of a number of processes and on account of inadequacy of efficient personnel, the records are not managed in a right fashion. The important documents/records are destroyed whereas records carrying no significance are dumped. Since we find records department an important source for making available to the different segments important information related to the workings of the hospitals, the mismanagement of records results into a degeneration in the quality of research. It is in this context that we find it important to recruit efficient personnel in the required number who are well educated and trained and are in a position to manage a technology-driven record department.

3. Ineffective handling and processing: It is also found that handling and processing of records are found time taking which complicates the task of a hospital manager or a doctor requiring old case histories or a researcher undertaking research. This makes it essential that a hospital manager takes up the issue on priority basis so that the processes are simplified and the collection process is made easier. We need to check the records frequently. A random checking is required to be promoted in which Accuracy Ratio and Activity Ratio are to given due importance.

The Accuracy Ratio is calculated with the help of following equation:

$$\frac{\text{Number of references not found}}{\text{Number of references found}} = \text{Accuracy Ratio}$$

The Activity Ratio is calculated with the help of following equation:

$$\frac{\text{Number of references found}}{\text{Number of documents filed}} = \text{Activity Ratio}$$

It is right to make it clear that if the accuracy ratio is half or one per cent, it is excellent. If it is three or more, it is poor. If the activity ratio is below 10 per cent, it magnifies abnormal or excess quantity of inactive material.

If it is in between 10-20 per cent, this requires improvement. When it is more than 20 per cent, it clarifies that the records are in bad shape. If we make evaluation based on both the ratios, we find possibilities of qualitative improvements in the management of records.

4. Determination of records retention period: The duration for the retention of records is an important aspect for managing records efficiently. Since the records of no use are to be destroyed and the records of vital use are to be retained, documented, stored in the memory of computers, it is pertinent that a hospital manager makes it sure that retention period has been given due importance. Though we don't find a hard and fast rule for retention of records, but this problem is required to be solved in consultation with the heads of departments or experts of the related area so that they take a decision regarding the retention keeping in view its uses for future reference. The vital records are to be kept for the long time and to be stored in the memory of computers or filed in a proper way. In this context, we need to turn our attention on the retention period as shown in Fig. 12.7. Of course, it is not essential that all the hospitals follow the same but this would provide to a majority of the hospital guidelines for the retention of records.

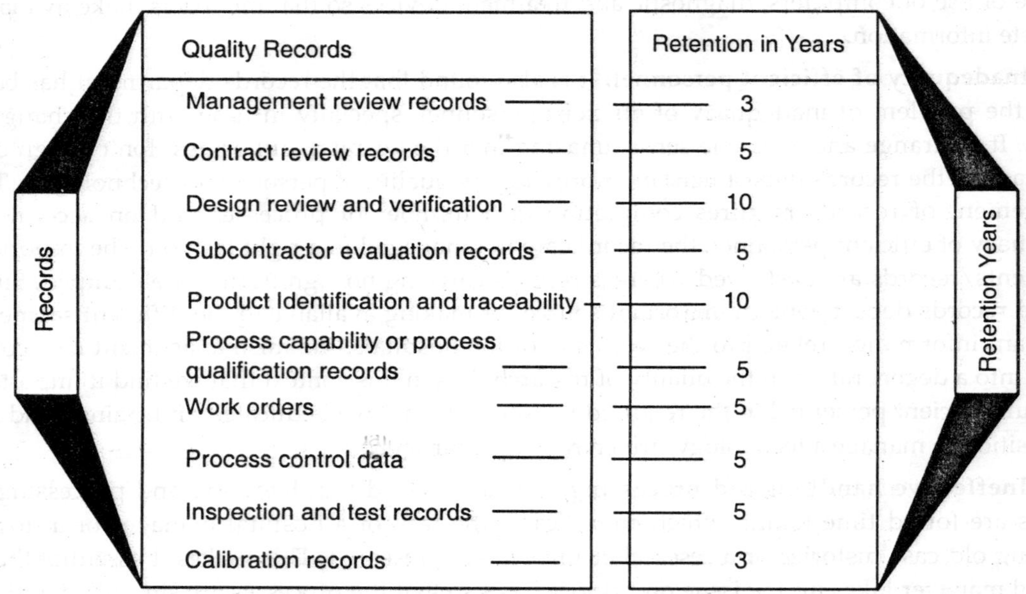

Pig. 11.7 Retention Period for Records

Adapted from: ISO 9000, Quality Management Systems, p. 163.

Before we talk about the transfer of records, it is pertinent that we go through the problem of dating of records found not important for the future reference. Since a decision is to be taken to destroy the records, it is essential that a hospital manager with the help and cooperation of experts comes to a final conclusion and destroys the records of no use and makes proper arrangements to file the records of vital use.

5. Lack of planning: It is also felt that in a majority of the hospitals, we find the problem of an effective plan for the management of hospital records. This draws our attention on the formulation of an ideal plan for the management of hospital records in the hospitals or healthcare organisations. It is pertinent that records are stored at a safe place where maximum protection to them is possible. The humidity, dampness, insects and virus generate and complicate the problems because even the vital records are destroyed due to mismanagement. In this context, it is proper to go through the suggestions of Secretariat Training School in its report on Work Study (III) as mentioned below.[7]

- It is significant that a table is provided for the important contexts of a file on cover which would facilitate of contents.
- The files and records should be kept separately which would make possible easy location.
- Papers covering informations are to be carried in a third folder separately from notes and correspondence.
- The vital elements of the records are to be compiled.
- A small alphabetical register of important files, cases, reports and other documents would make possible smooth location and disposal.

6. Improving the quality of medical records: It is felt that quality of medical records is not in tune with the improvements found in the whole system. This focuses our attention on the quality of hospital records in general and the medical records in particular. We can't negate the instrumentality of quality medical records in improving the quality of health care services. To be more specific, the case histories related to the critical cases, wonderful or excellent or innovative treatment results are required to be stored for the future reference. In case of investigation reports, we also find some of the reports carrying outstanding significance and it is the responsibility of a hospital manager that vital reports, cases and developments are given due weightage.

7. Information technology to be promoted: In the face of increasing pressure on almost all categories of the hospitals, it is pertinent that we promote computers even for managing the hospital records. Since we talk about the technology driven management information system, it is essential that we promote the use of computers having more capacity to store. It is quite natural that if we make a strong advocacy in favour of computers for managing the hospital records, our focus would also be on the quality of personnel responsible to operate, handle and maintain the same.

The aforesaid facts make it clear that management of records has been facing numerous problems and it is significant that we make possible qualitative improvements so that quality hospital records serve multidimensional interests of diverse sections requiring the same for constructive purposes. Your old mistakes make the ways for innovative efforts. The records let you know the mistakes you committed and the outstanding contributions you made. The records help researchers in getting the valuable information which may help them in innovating the medicare services. The records help a material manager in identifying the mistakes or lapses on the part of suppliers and a doctor in improving his/her credentials. We need to explore avenues for the sophisticated devices for managing records.

Modern Filing Devices

Like other organisations, the healthcare organisations also need to make use of the modern devices for filing which would help them in many ways. The motorized filing, reciprocating filing, Micro film filing and computer filing need due attention of hospital mangers.

Motorised Filing: During the yesteryears, we find emergence of new and modern office equipments to cater to the changing needs of an office. Motorised filing equipment has an eclectrically operated console in which the operator sitting at a desk presses the button and the relevant file is presented to the view. Usually, we find trays of reference cards suspended round a drum and on the depression of button, the drum revolves to bring the required tray. This system is found easier and the operator is not to face the fatigue problem. The operational flow is increased and in the filing system we find accommodation of hundreds of thousand of cards. But it is not possible for small organisations to install on account of huge investment.

Reciprocating Filing: This filing system is mechanically constructed in such a fashion that file tracks move along a route according to the requirements of clerical work flow. The operating clerk remains comfortable and the files move forward and backward in tune with the situational requirements. The working employees do not feel fatigue in the system and the possibilities for the wastage of time are minimised. The clerical staff is found in a position to increase the operational flow.

Microfilm Filing: It is a photographic process of retaining information given in the office documents and records.[8] At the outset, the record is photographed on a film at reduced size and after that the film is developed as a permanent record. The preparation of films is found with the help of original documents and then it is placed in the file cabinet which is specially built for microfilm. As and when the record is required, the operator locates the subject on the film, places the film on the projector-reader and then locates the references. The film can be enlarged to a large size. The system makes use of different types of format in the face of purpose, length or retention and frequency of retrieval. Roll Microfilm, Aperture Card, Microfiche and Jacketed Microfilm are formats used in the system.

In the roll microfilm, the documents are filmed on a roll on film normally found 16 mm or 35 mm which may be 100 feet long. In aperture card, we find a rectangular hole to which a single microfilm is affixed.

In Microfiche, a number of images are exposed onto a single sheet and the standard size is 5" x 6" containing 96 images.

In the jacketed microfilms, we find conversion of roll microfilm into a flat film or series of films are taken on a roll of film.

This system of filing saves considerable amount of storage space.

This device consists of a camera which may be 8 mm to 70 mm, reader for projecting image, photo printing attachments and special cabinets for storing film. Of course, it is expensive and therefore, cannot be afforded by small hospitals.

Computer Filing: In the modern world, we find computers emerging as an important device for filing. It has scope for storing large quantities of information which can be retrieved in graphical form and even in alphabetical and numeral characters. Whatsoever we store in the computer may be brought to screen within seconds and can be obtained in the form of a print out. It is significant to mention that use of computer as a means of filing and retrieving text is restricted because the original documents and records are required to be stored in a filing system for future reference vis-s-vis to meet the legal requirements. The computer system of filing proves to be expensive if all the information stored is copied in computers through a scanner to place it on record. It is due its expensive character that we find computer filing restricted to technical data and reference libraries.

In this context, it is essential to be aware of the filing equipment used, equipment of transporting the documents, rental value of space occupied by the files, the depreciation of filing equipment, the cost of accessories such as boxes, cards, folders forms and references cards, etc., lighting, heating, air conditioning, expenses for the room used for filing and cost of preservation of the documents in the files. The hospital professionals in the very context need to take into consideration the preservation of only indispensable documents.

The suitability of a particular system of filing depends on the nature and character of job of the concerned organisation for which we are managing records. In a true sense, there are five purposes of managing records such as keeping an orderly account of progress, facilitating preparation of statement of true condition, facilitating comparisons, detecting errors and waste and completing the legal formalities.

In healthcare organisations, the hospital professionals need to make it sure that records have been helping doctors, researchers and managers in undertaking research activities for initiating and activating the innovation process. The diagnosis and treatment processes considerably rest on the availability of records specially when the cases are found of critical nature. The hospital professionals while taking a decision regarding the management of records need to make it sure that the concerned persons, departments or organisations get the required records within the shortest possible duration. All the hospitals cannot adopt a particular method of managing records on account of variation in cost and requirements. It is upon the hospital professionals to identify the requirements and to adopt such a method of record management which is to help hospital professionals, doctors and researchers in undertaking the research activities for qualitative improvements in diagnosis and treatment processes.

Recent Trends in Records Management

During the yester years, we have witnessed a number of developments in the management of records as briefed below:

1. *Use of loose leaf and card systems:* Abandoning the bound book record and in this place, using the loose leaf or card record is the first requirement of an organisation.
2. *Avoiding useless copying:* Using one of the duplicating methods and avoiding copying of all kinds is another development that we find in the management of records. By classifying and filing much, useless copying is avoided.
3. *Questioning the necessity of each record:* The professionals investigate the necessity of each record and where the record is not being used and it is found to be irrelevant, it is discontinued.
4. *Coordinating the record-keeping:* Coordination of record-keeping is found essential with the motto of diversifying the uses of record keeping.
5. *Eliminating unnecessary motions:* It is significant to study the possibilities of reducing labour by minimising the amount of work necessary to produce the particular record.
6. *Exploring possibilities of using modern methods:* In the changing scenario, it is significant that a hospital manger explores possibilities for promoting the application of new generation of equipments with the motto of making the process of records

management much more economic. Since we find filing a form of record keeping, it is pertinent that even for filing, the hospital professionals explore possibilities of using new generation of equipments.

7. ***Promoting use of records for undertaking research activities:*** Since we find significant developments in the field of management of records and the medical scientists as well as the researchers need to promote and intensify research activities, it is imperative that hospital professionals focus on the records helping them in initiating and activating qualitative improvement in the healthcare services.

The above mentioned facts make it clear that due to significant developments in the field of technology, we find enough scope for diversifying the uses of technology for managing records and therefore, the hospitals and healthcare organisations need to explore avenues for innovating the methods of records management. We agree with the viewpoint of George Jemore Moscowitz that during the past two decades, man has managed to create more paper documents than he did during the 5000 years of recorded history preceding them., Hence, it is high time that the healthcare organisations focus on the significant developments in the field of records management and make use of them in tune with their requirements and affordability.

SUMMARY

In this chapter, you have gone through different aspects of records management. After going through the chapter, be sure that the following facts are well versed.

Hospital Records—the Perception: Hospital records are considered to be a cronicle of the pagentary of medical and scientific progress. We consider hospital records a true story of the events in which the doctors, researchers, managers and medical scientists keep valuable information.

Types of Records: There are different types of hospital records, viz., Vital Records, Important Records, Useful Records and Transit Records.

Essentials of an Effective Record Management: For an effective management of hospital records, the important essentials are planning, comprehensiveness, accuracy, timing, right classification, economy and technological support.

Form of Hospital Records: The different forms of hospital records are letters, circulars and reports, case histories, contracts, invoices, vouchers, minutes and books and accounts.

Sections of Medical Records: The different sections of medical records are General Section, Nursing Section and Medical Section.

Dimension of Record Management: The different dimensions while managing the hospital records are creation of hospital records, administration of records, retaining the records, submitting the records and destroying the records.

Significance of Record-keeping: We find record-keeping significant since based on effective hospital records, the quality of decisions can be improved, evaluation of performance is possible, a comparative analysis of the performance of government and private hospitals is possible, internal control is possible, operational efficiency is increased, statutory obligations are fulfilled and formulation of strategic management plan is found easier.

Key Information for Healthcare Managers: A hospital manager finds some of the information of outstanding nature which he/she gets from the records department, such as death rate of patients, average length of stay of patients, rate of bed turnover and bed occupancy ratio.

Filing of Hospital Records: Filing is found to be an important constituent of the management of hospital records which is the process of classifying, arranging and storing the records.

Arranging Files: The files are arranged in alphabetical order, numerical order, geographic subject-wise.

Centralised and Decentralised Filing: Centralised filing system helps a hospital manager in controlling the same efficiently whereas the decentralised filing complicates the process of management and control.

Management of Hospital Records: Problems and Remedies: In the management of record a hospital manager faces numerous problems such as frequent use of outdated forms, inadequacy of efficient personnel to manage the records, ineffective handling and processing, determination of retention period for the records, lack of planning, quality of medical records and non-optimal use of technology.

Modern Filing Devices: During yesteryears, we have found innovative devices for filing such as Motorised filing, Reciprocating filing, Microfilm filing and Computer filing. The hospitals need to explore opportunities for using new devices.

Recent Trends in Records Management: The emerging trends in records management focus on the use of loose leaf and card system, avoiding useless copying, questioning the necessity of each records, coordinating the record keeping, eliminating unnecessary motions, exploring possibilities of using modern methods and promoting use of records for undertaking research activities.

KEY TERMS

Vital Records	Creating Records
Important Records	Administering Records
Useful Records	Retaining Records
Transit Records	Submitting Records
Invoices	Destroying Records
Vouchers	Alphabetical Order
Minutes	Numerical Order
General Section	Centralised Filing
Nursing Section	Decentralised Filing
Medical Section	Motorised Filing
Circulars and Reports	Reciprocating Filing
Case History	Microfilm Filing
Accurate Ratio	Computer Filing

REVIEW QUESTIONS

1. What do you mean by Hospital Records? Explain the different types of hospital records.
2. Focus on the different essentials for an effective management of records in the healthcare organisations.
3. Discuss the different forms of hospital records.
4. Throw light on the different sections of medical records.
5. Explain the different dimensions of management of hospital records.
6. Focus on the instrumentality of hospital records in the development of healthcare organisations.
7. State and explain the key information a hospital manager needs while managing records.

8. What do you mean by Filing? Explain the centralised and decentralised filing in the management of hospital records.
9. Focus on the multifaceted problems in the management of hospital records and suggest remedies to counter the same.
10. Throw light on the instrumentality of innovative devices for managing the files of hospitals.
11. Explain the role of a hospital manager in the face of recent developments in the management of records in hospitals.

APPLICATION EXERCISES

1. In the capacity of a hospital manager, focus on the role of records management in diagnosing and treating the patents and promoting the research activities for innovating developments in the healthcare services.
2. You are a manager of a small hospital. Throw light on the management of records helping you in making the managerial decisions.
3. In the management of hospital records, we find medical records occupying a place of outstanding significance. In the light of this statement, focus on the different sections of hospital records.
4. For managing records, you need different types of information. In the capacity of a hospital professional, focus on the information you need for managing hospital records.
5. Do you find computer based management of records suitable for hospitals? Justify your opinion in the capacity of a hospital manger of a leading hospital.
6. A number of problems crop up while managing records. Name the problem and suggest the measures to be adopted for resolving the same.
7. During yesteryears, the techniculture has also influenced the process of records management in hospitals. As a hospital manager, throw light on the innovative techno-driven devices for managing files.

END NOTES

1. Gibony, *Principles of Hospital Administration*, New York, 1952
2. Goel S. L., *Records Management in Hospital*, p. 204
3. Ibid, p. 201
4. Dave N. V., *Hospital Management*, pp. 81-82
5. Goel S.L., *op. cit.*
6. ISO 9000, *Quality Management System*, p. 163
7. Report of the Secretariat Training School Work Study III
8. Littlefield & Rachel: *Office Administrative Management*
9. Leffingwell & Robinson: *Text book of Office Management*: Introduction to Administrative Office Management

Management of Control in Hospitals

Management control is usually perceived as a feedback system. Well-formulated policies and intelligently designed strategies need time-honoured, cost-effective and efficient monitoring. A microscopic audit of healthcare services in Indian perspective makes it clear that benefits of sophisticated developments have remained confined to the affluent sections. This focuses on increasing the public healthcare spending which is non-optimal to the changing disease profile.

CHAPTER OBJECTIVES

Introduction—Control: the Perception—Steps in the Control Process—Importance of Control Types of Control—Process—Precontrols in Healthcare Organisations—Effective Control—Features of Effective Control—Feed forward Control and Feedback Control Systems—Strategic Points in Managing Control—Problems in Establishing Effective Control Systems—Healthcare Services in India: A Microscopic Audit—Summary—Key Terms—Review Questions—Application Exercises—End Notes.

LEARNING OBJECTIVES

This chapter aims at studying the different dimensions of control. It is significant that hospital professionals make a microscopic analysis of plans, formulation and implementation processes, strategic decisions and targeted results. The readers develop their awareness of the process of control, strategic points in managing control and the ways for effective control. A microscopic evaluation of healthcare services makes it clear that public healthcare spending is required to be increased. We need to accelerate the pace of qualitative-cum-quantitative transformation to bridge the gap between demand and supply.

Introduction

Well-formulated policies and intelligently designed strategies need time-honoured, cost-effective and efficient monitoring during implementation and proper auditing after implementation. Your plans, policies and strategies, even if promoting innovations, carry no meaning unless you in succeed in translating them into meaningful sections. Being a hospital manager, you bear the responsibility of making possible quality in totality. This in a very natural way requires the cooperation of almost all the hospital personnel engaged in the process of generating, processing and delivering the services. It is not only important that you have recruited quality people; it is much more impact generating that you have assigned due weightage to their excellent contributions. It is not only important that you make available world class technology to the hospitals; it is much more significant that technologies have been significantly contributing to the process of productivity acceleration. It is not only significant that you have fixed or set a time-frame for implementation; it is much more pertinent that time management is given priority attention and time-honoured and cost-effective implementation of projects have been made possible. It is against this background that we find management of control and supervision occupying a place of outstanding significance for getting the desired results.

A hospital manager in addition to the formulation of an ideal and realistic plan, a national policy and an innovative strategy also bears the responsibility of making it sure that sincere and honest efforts are made to achieve the plan target. He/she is required to monitor the process of implementation and to identify the lapses, errors, shortcomings in the different departments where a large number of quality people and innovative technologies work together to generate world class healthcare services. He/she also needs to make it sure that the monitoring mechanism designed to implement the plans is working as per the set norms and directions and has been promoting and nurturing work culture. The hospital people are working efficiently and behaving decently. The bio-medical equipment, apparatus, instruments, plant and machines, new generation of information and communication technology have been installed, handled, maintained, repaired and replaced on time. The departmental relationship has been paving avenues for departmental harmony. The promised quality of healthcare services has been made available to the users on time and without any distortion. The services are not only of world class but affordable too. The hospital personnel have been taking due care of not only the patients but even attendants who feel duly treated. The hospitals are in a position to innovate the technology as and when the circumstances necessitate so because they are very sincere to the research and development activities. The new avenues have been explored and tapped for mobilising financial resources. He/ she also bears the responsibility of innovating the perception of quality in totality and making it sure that the services made available to the patients are of world class.

The aforesaid multidimensional functional responsibilities of a hospital manager makes it essential that the control function of management has been given an overriding priority. It is in this context that we go through different aspects of control. In the government hospitals, the control function has obviously been found neglected.

The management function of control is the measurement and correction of performance in order to make sure that organisational objectives and the plans formulated to attain them are accomplished. This makes it clear that we find a close relation between planning and controlling. Like other organisations, the healthcare organisations also need to exercise effective control and this requires deep involvement of almost all the echelons of management right from the President to Supervisor or from top to bottom involved in the process. Of course, we prove our professional excellence in formulating an ideal plan but the managerial responsibility remains incomplete unless we succeed in implementing the same. Managerial control is the same functional process of control that we find in physical, biological and social systems. Almost all the systems are found controlling themselves through the information feedback which help managers in knowing the deviations, distortion and degeneration in the service delivery process. It is in this context that we talk about the instrumentality of control in managing hospitals and healthcare organisations. Management control is usually perceived as a feedback system.

Presently, we find three modes of developing the healthcare services viz. public sector, where we find primary, secondary and tertiary hospitals functioning, private sector where we find even world class hospitals working on the basic of corporatisation and PPP mode where we find partnership between public and private sectors. We cannot deny that during yesteryears, there has been significant development in almost all the areas but the benefits of technological or other developments have not been optimally harnessed by rural regions and weaker sections of the society. On the one hand , we find a few of the leading private hospitals providing world class services to the affluent sections while on the other hand, we also find government hospitals in a good number where even basic medical aids are not available. Emerging qualitative and quantitative gap in the healthcare services make it essential that Union as well as the state governments and NGOs as well as the corporate sector promote sincere and honest efforts to improve the quality of healthcare to the population and is a critical constituent of the development process. The ultimate responsibility falls on the shoulders of government. Actually, we need a new vision based on faster, broad-based and inclusive growth.

We cannot deny that India is in the midst of an epidemiological and demographic transaction with increasing burden of chronic diseases, decline in mortality and fertility rates and ageing of the population. The communicable as well as the non-communicable diseases have been found increasing with a high pace. The disease profile is found becoming complicated and the governmental efforts are found shrinking.

The public health system has various drawbacks. The conceptualisation and planning of all programmes is centralised where strategic decisions lack sensitivity to regional problems. The approach towards disease control and prevention is fragmented resulting into a lack of vertical programmes for each and every disease. It is significant to mention that despite a steady increase in public healthcare infrastructure, utilisation of public health facilities by population for outpatient and inpatient care has not shown a positive trend. The NSSO (1986-2004) data clearly show a major decline in the utilisation of public health facilities. An audit of NRHM indicates that in order to improve the public health delivery, the situation needs to change on a fast track mode at the grassroots. Not only this, we find National Urban Health Mission lagging behind in ensuring need-based city specific urban healthcare system to meet the diverse health needs of the urban poor. The secondary as well as the tertiary healthcare services lack professionalised efforts. They face problem of infrastructural constraints and in addition, the inadequacy of quality people is also found at its peak. The medical as well as the paramedical staff lack work culture. In the government hospitals, we find the service ambience not instrumental in generating service fragrance which obstructs the process of nurturing service culture.

Of late, we find PPP mode essential for the development of healthcare services specially in the states where the government hospitals have not been successful to cater to the increasing healthcare requirements of general masses. In the Indian perspective, we find contracting as the predominant model for PPP. Lack of mutual commitment to goals, shared decision-making and risk-taking are rarely seen in the Indian context which need due attention of government policy makers while promoting PPP mode. The perception of true partnership will only be conceptualised when we find government positive to a corporate Third Party Administrator (TPA). When the State Health Department becomes the principal partner with limited stakeholders, we cannot expect equality among partners. The Yeshaswini Health Insurance Scheme" in Karnataka includes the State Department of Cooperative actually meant for farmers and involve many stakeholders and manage and maintain 200 private hospitals. We need to develop a generic framework for different categories of PPP at primary, secondary and tertiary levels of healthcare to improve cost-effectiveness, enhancing quality and expanding access through extensive stakeholders consultations. The state policy makers need to provide to them a number of incentives such as land at concessional rates, increasing floor areas ratio and ground coverage, tax holiday and loan at concessional rates so that private players significantly contribute to the development of healthcare service particularly in the backward areas of the country where the healthcare services need priority attention.

The corporatisation of healthcare sector has not been assigned due weightage and therefore, it is need of the hour that we are positive to the development of healthcare sector with the joint or independent support of big players.

It is also important to mention that in the Indian perspective, we find health system only a mix of the public and private sectors. The NGOs and Civil Society though found important have been found playing a very small role. Promoting research activities is an important task before the healthcare sector so that low cost indigenous technologies and AYUSH provide multi-dimensional services to the poor Indian society having poor affordability.

In view of the above, it is right to say that we need to audit the developments in the field of healthcare sector which requires a microscopic evaluation. With significant developments in the field of medical sciences, we find healthcare services becoming much more expensive. The weaker sections of the society cannot afford the expensive services of leading private hospitals. Hence, it is pertinent that particularly the government hospitals promote low cost indigenous technology which would increase the attractions of masses to the healthcare services of government hospitals. The doctors are found disinterested in going to the villages and therefore, it is imperative that the government policy makers link it with the medical education. The hospitals and healthcare organisations need to focus on informal education so that medical and paramedical personnel are not only thematically sound but are also concerned with civic sense, aesthetic sense, personal-commitment, value-orientation and human touch in behaviour. The healthcare organisations need to increase the retention rate of quality personnel and therefore, it is essential that we offer lucrative incentives blending both financial and non-financial. A hospital manager initiating the process of control requires to be sensitive while establishing standards, rating performance, correcting deviation plan from standard and to prefer a plan which simplified accomplishing the organisational goals vis-a-vis achieving the mission for justifying the existence of hospitals or healthcare organisations in the society. Making healthcare affordable is a crying need of the hour. We need to promote telemedicine, telediagnosis, teleconferencing so that specialised healthcare services reach even to the remotest parts of the country.

The most important task before healthcare organisations is to activate the sensitisation process so that masses develop their awareness of the water-prone, food-prone, communicable and non-communicable diseases. We need to make use of new generation of information and communication technology for promoting healthcare education, specially in the rural areas of the country.

CONTROL: THE PERCEPTION

At the outset, we go through the conceptual aspect of control. Control is found to be a managerial process of evaluating the performance of an organisation. It is measurement and control of performance in order to make sure that enterprise objectives and the plans desired to attain them are accomplished.[1] Further, Strong and Smith opine, "There are a number of controlling viewpoints regarding the best manner in which to manage an organisation. However, theorists as well as practitioners agree that good management requires effective control. A combination of well planned objectives, strong organisation, capable direction and motivation have little probability for success unless there exists an adequate system of control."[2]

To put it in another words, it is a managerial function that helps an organisation in accomplishing the organisational goals. We agree with this view that the function of control has evolved over time just as have the other basic functions of management. The traditional control through division of labour, specialisation of task and centralised authority structures. But we find a change in the traditional concept of control and of late, we find it a managerial process. The advent of the information revolution activated the process of change in the concept and perception of control and now, when we find an age of information superhighway exist. The control is found to be a device to improve the feedback system.

In view of the above, it is right to mention that control is vitally an important process through which managers assure that actual activities conform to planned activities. The process of control thus includes four basic steps, viz., establishment of standards and methods for measuring performance, the measurement of performance, the comparison of performance against the standards and taking the corrective action. It is quite natural that in the changing environment of an organisation, we find the process of control a bit difficult that complicates the managerial responsibility of making possible an effective control. Here, it is significant to mention that with the development of communication and information technology, the responsibility of controlling the activities of an organisation is found easier.

Out of all the management functions, we find control occupying a place of outstanding importance and it is pertinent that a manager managing an organisation having no legitimate right of making profits exercises the process of control in an effective way so that the process of control makes it possible to attain the organisational objectives. Time honoured and cost-effective implementation of plans become essential to make the healthcare services affordable and this function of management makes the way for the same. Control is thus proving its instrumentality as a feedback system similar to that which operates in the usual household thermostat.[3] The system places control in a more complex and realistic light. Of late, we view control not only as a matter of establishing standards, measuring performance and correcting deviations but more so, a process of programming the corrective action. Like other organisations, the hospitals or healthcare organisations also need to realise the instrumentality of this function of management and to process effective control.

Steps in the Control Process

We are well aware of the fact that management control is a systematic effort to set performance standards with planning objectives, to design information feedback systems, to compare actual performance with these predetermined standards, to determine whether there are any deviations and to measure their significance and to take any action required to assume that all corporate resources are being used in the most effective and efficient way possible in achieving corporate objectives.[4] This definition of management control clarifies the step as shown in Fig. 13.1.

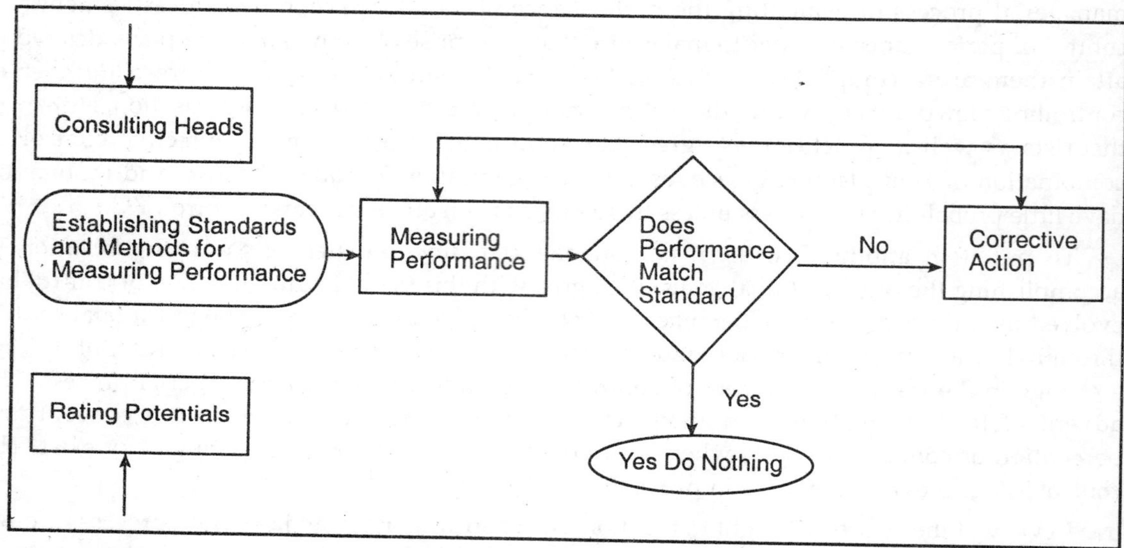

Fig. 13.1. Steps in the Control Process

1. *Establishing standard and methods for measuring performance:* In a true sense, we find control a measuring process in which we measure the performance in the face of established standards. This makes it essential that at the outset, we specify the standards in meaningful terms and this one essentially be accepted by the persons or people involved in the process. An organisation may set an objective to become the leader in the field. To be more specific, in the service generating industries, standards and measurements might include waiting time limits, the number of customers served per hour and the speed or quality of service. Since we go through the problem of hospitals or healthcare organisations, it is pertinent to make it clear that setting of standards would gravitate the attention of a manager on the waiting list for the patients to be admitted, the shrinking of queue in the OPD, the speed of serving the patients, the availability of investigation reports, the duration of recovery or so. A hospital manager by setting new paradigm may be a leader in the field but unless we find personnel agreeable and the technologies of world class, it is difficult for a manager to think in this direction. Thus, a hospital manager while setting standards needs to consult the different heads and besides, they also need to evaluate the potentials of technologies and consult their subordinates before setting standards.

2. *Measuring the performance:* This is the second stage in the context of management control and a hospital manager is required to measure the performance of the personnel and technologies in the face of standards set earlier. It is in this context that we need to consult the personnel and

evaluate our technological competence before setting the standards. To be more specific in the healthcare organisation, the process of performance evaluation should begin on new employees. Evaluation of current employees should start at first and only then other steps should be taken.

A manager while evaluating the performance of employees can take the support of a logbook as shown in Fig. 13.2.

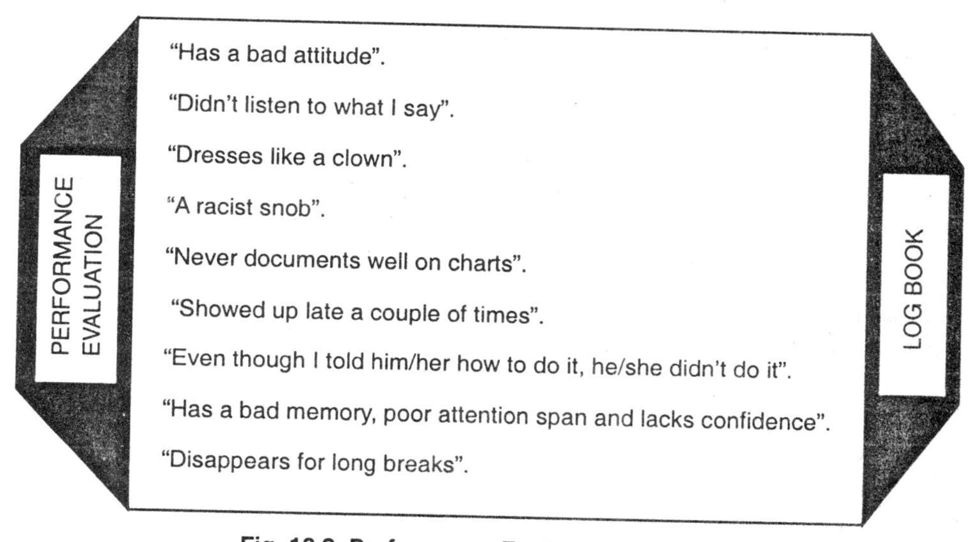

Fig. 13.2. Performance Evaluation Logbook

With the help of this logbook, it is easier for a hospital manager to evaluate the performance of employees. Here, it is important to mention that a hospital manager while evaluating the performance is also required to measure the performance of technologies used in the process of offering the diagnostic and treatment facilities to the patients.

3. *Matching of performance with the standards:* This is the third step in the evaluation process which makes it essential that on the basis of set standard, a hospital manager comes to know about the actual performance of employees. The comparison of measured results with the established targets or standards previously set is found easier. If performance matches the standards, a manager may assume that everything is under his/her control. Conversely, a manager would be required to identify the reasons for a gap that he/she finds between the set standards and the actual results.

4. *Taking corrective actions:* If a gap is existent between the set standards and actual results, a hospital manager is required to identify the reasons for the same. A degeneration in the level of efficiency, a gap in the set standards and actuals may be influenced by a number of factors. Without making an evaluation of the reasons, he/she is not supposed to come to a particular conclusion. The corrective action may include a change in one or more activities of the operations or working of healthcare organisations. At the outset, a hospital manager is required to divert his/her attention on the set standards. If it is found that the set standard was not optimal to the potentials, a hospital manager is required to change the same. Thus, inappropriate or non-optimal standards and inadequacy of sophisticated technologies and efficient personnel are some of the key areas where a manager is required to be careful.

A hospital manager, like the managers of other organisations, is required to carry out the process of control throughout the organisation. It should be kept in mind that financial control is not the only thing. In addition, we also need to control the quality of materials, quality of personnel engaged in the process, the use of technologies or so. Of late, we find use of technology even for controlling. Computers can integrate servicing points and can monitor the activities. Robots can be incorporated into line operations and various activities can be reviewed. Hidden camera may be used for knowing the instrumentality of personnel. Thus, a hospital manager can take support of different types of technologies for evaluating the performance. In the Indian perspective, it appears essential because the employees in general have been found making a goodbye to the work culture.

Importance of Control to Healthcare Organisations

The control mechanism is found essential, specially for a no-profit making organisation because at almost all stages of generation and distribution of services, a manager needs world class professional excellence to make the process cost-effective. The hospitals and educational institutions play a contributory role to the process of human capital formation and if they become insensitive to the problems of cost and quality, the public at large is considerably affected. It is against this background that we go through the importance of management of control of hospitals or healthcare organisations.

1. Organisational factors necessitate management control: In the business environment, we find multidimensional changes taking place everyday. Change has become a natural phenomenon because scientific inventions and innovations make possible new developments, make ways for new perception, new services, new regulations, new technologies or so. The competition is found increasing and the expectations of users are found mounting. If hospitals or healthcare organisations delay the process of incorporating the important changes, the potentials to serve the society start contracting. The professional excellence of a manager bears the efficacy of adjusting the significant developments so that the different stages of generating and processing the services are found making outstanding contributions to the process of development. An effective control thus becomes essential to counter the organisational problems. It is against this background that like other organisations, the hospitals or healthcare organisations also need to exercise control.

2. Cost-effectiveness necessitates control: The healthcare organisations need to make the whole process cost-effective. The management of hospital material is required to be made effective so that quality materials or inputs are used in the process. The management of human resources is required to be made productive because only quality hospital personnel would be instrumental in getting the quality outputs. The management of finance becomes essential to minimise the unproductive expenses. The management of marketing requires due weightage to generate revenues from the internal sources besides satisfying the users. The management of technologies becomes significant to generate the services of world class, All these functional areas of management need cost economy so that the services are made affordable. We agree with this view that in the management literature, we find control a word carrying outstanding significance because a manager finds it difficult to identify the errors unless and until, the control processes are effectively monitored. We need quality in totality and this in addition to other factors also requires cost economy. The organisations in general and the healthcare organisations in particular by improving the quality and maintaining economy, can set new paradigms and the public at large thus would considerably be benefitted. Control is a device to identify the errors, weaknesses, shortcomings, lapses and to find out appropriate solutions to counter the same. It is in this context that we find management control significant to the healthcare organisations because of late, we find a majority of the hospitals facing the problems of non-optimal costs.

3. Vanishing work culture requires management control: We agree with the view that in a majority of the government hospitals, we find lack of work culture which is the result of degenerating organisational climate. We can't expect work culture, if we find managerial deficiency. We can't expect work culture if we find environment at the work places unfriendly. Since the health care services are the result of a team work, the departmental harmony occupies a place of outstanding significance. With the management of control, it is possible to evaluate the performance of employees as well as the technologies used in the process. The work culture can be improved because the personnel contributing significantly to the process are to be motivated suitably. The improving organisational climate thus makes the ways for work culture.

4. Identification of mistakes: It is quite natural that people and technologies commit mistakes. With the management of control, it is easier to identify the errors and lapses at the very early stage. If the quality of healthcare services is found poor due to the poor quality of materials used in the process or it is due to the decreasing level of efficiency of hospital personnel or due to the mistakes committed by the paramedical and nursing staff, ultimately the quality is affected. With the help of control processes, a hospital manager finds it easier to identify the reasons and with the help of corrective measures, it becomes possible to resolve the same. The accountability can be fixed and the shortcomings can be removed.

5. Monitoring the progress is easier: We are well aware of the fact that a manager is also to delegate his/her task to the subordinates specially to speed up the process of generating and processing the services. With the management of control, a manager is found responsible to monitor the progress so that he/she is in a position to know the latest developments and to detect the lapses and the faults in the technologies used in the process. This makes him /her successful in achieving the set target within the stipulated time. Besides, we also find scope for removing the constraints obstructing the process. It is against this background that we find management of control helping a manager in monitoring the process. In a true sense, we find monitoring very much instrumental in making possible time honoured diagnosis and treatment which improves the quality of services.

The aforesaid facts make it essential that we make the control processes more effective so that healthcare organisations or hospitals succeed in improving the quality of services. A hospital manager with the help of different tools or variables evaluates the efficiency of personnel and machines or equipment and instruments and on the basis of results comes to a particular conclusion. Since we find control processes related to almost all the areas, sections, departments, technologies, materials, the task of fixing accountability would not be so much difficult. Of late, we also find use of computers for evaluating the performance of employees. In some of the organisations, we also find provision for a hidden camera for that very purpose. Robots are also used for evaluating the performance. These facts make it clear that a hospital manager needs to assign due weightage to this function of management which not only points out the lapses, identifies the shortcomings but also suggests the corrective measures. More scientific and technology-based control processes, more accurate, quick and dependable the healthcare services. Since we find management of control paving avenues for the formulation of a new plan based on the lapses and constraints found in the implementation processes of earlier plans, this function of management proves to be significant and effective. It is in this context that we find control processes occupying an outstanding place in the management of hospitals. In a true sense, based on the actual results/performance, a manager formulates a new plan and therefore, we find the least possible scope for a gap. The control thus appears to be the last and first function of management because without control, it is difficult to identify the lapses in the implementation of a particular plan.

Types of Control

To make the process of control effective, it is pertinent that we know about the different types of control methods which can be grouped into one of the four basic types, viz., Pre-action Control, Steering Control, Yes/No or Screening Control and Post-Action Control.[5] In Fig. 13.3, we find different types of control.

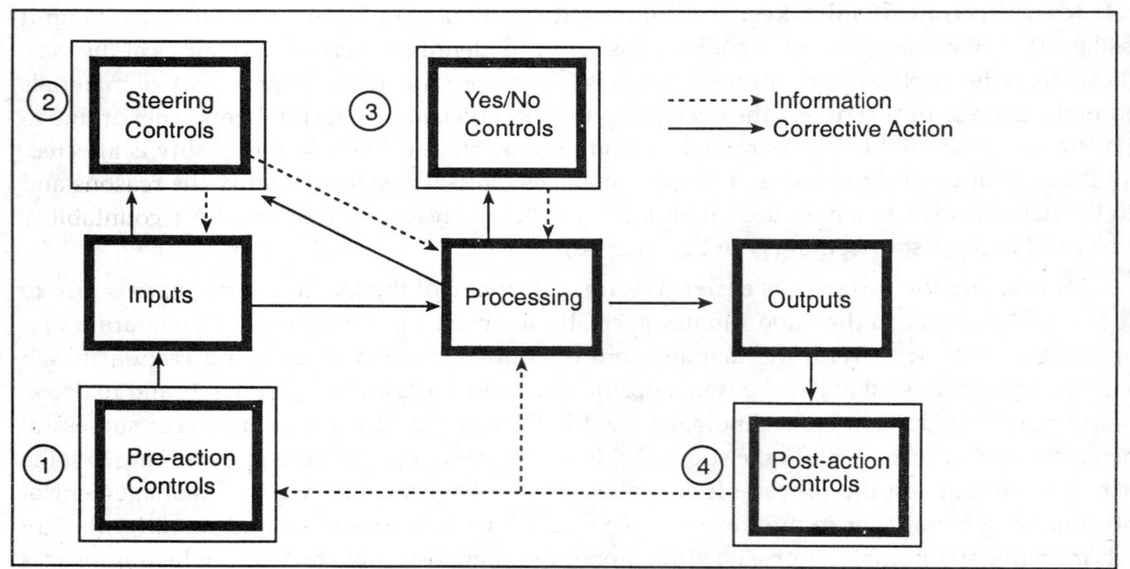

Fig. 13.3. Types of Control

(1) *Pre-action Control:* Precontrols or pre-action controls make it sure that in the healthcare organisations, the human, financial, material and marketing resources have been budgeted properly. It is quite natural that before we switch on the process, the necessary resources have been budgeted. The formulated budgets make it sure that the requisite resources would be available on time and in the types, quality, quantity and location needed. The budgets may call for hiring and training the new employees, the purchase of equipment, instruments, apparatus and materials and the designing and engineering works if needed. In a majority of the hospitals or healthcare organisations, if we find a problem while implementing the plans, this is due mainly to the resource constraints. The precontrol minimises the possibilities of resource constraints and makes possible time honoured and cost-effective implementation.

(2) *Steering Controls:* We also call Steering Control as Cybernetic or Fedforwarded Controls. This type of control is meant to detect deviation from some standard goals and also to permit the corrective measures.[6] It is essential to clarify the Steering Control which is a simple metaphor derived from the driving of an automobile in which the driver steers the car to prevent it from going off the roads or in the wrong direction. The success of steering control depends upon the fact that a manager has obtained timely and accurate information about changes in the environment or about progress towards the desired goal. It is significant to mention that if a hospital or a healthcare manager feels that there has been a degeneration in the quality of healthcare services, he/she could correct the same before losing too much business or reputation. Thus, we find steering control helping a manager in adopting the corrective measures much earlier than the adverse effects found tarnishing the image and credibility of the well established hospitals.

(3) *Yes/No or Screening Controls:* This is the third type of control which is also known as go/no go control method for screening procedures that must be followed or conditions that must be met before operations.

This method of control provides a screening process in which specific aspects of a procedure is required to be approved or specific conditions met before operations may continue. The screening control provides a means for taking the corrective action while a programme is still viable. An organisation is found using yes/no controls as double-check devices. To be more specific in the expensive projects or risk-bearing projects, we find such type of control effective. Since we find steering control rarely perfect, a number of organisations use screening control. We can't negate the fact that even in hospitals or healthcare organisations, we find screening control effective because we find some of the projects very expensive. Safety is found to be a key factor in the hospitals and healthcare organisations and in addition, we also find risk elements involved in the process of installing diagnostic and treatment methods. An extra margin of security is found essential in the very context and the screening control makes it possible.

(4) *Post-action Control:* This is the fourth type of control known as post-action control which measures the result of a completed activity. The post-action controls are also used as a basis for rewarding or encouraging service employees. In the hospitals or healthcare organisations, we find post-action control considerably effective because on the basis of evaluation results, a hospital manager comes to know about the positive or negative contributions of hospital personnel. Of course, we find some of the employees contributing fantastically whereas we also find other category of employees contributing very insignificantly to the process of generating and processing the healthcare services. It is not judicious that all categories of employees are offered the same incentives because by doing so, we discourage or demotivate the employees making outstanding contributions to the process of offering good patient care.

Thus, we have gone through different types of control and it is right to mention that all the four types of control methods complement each other. May be that we find hospitals or healthcare organisations selecting a particular method of control or combining all the tour while exercising effective control. It is right to mention that just as outfielders can't wait until a fly ball lands to see whether they should have been standing, the managers can't afford to wait until all the results are in before they begin to evaluate the performance. The steering controls help a manager in taking advantage of unexpected opportunities. Besides, this method of control also helps a manager in correcting the miscalculations. However, we don't find it essential that hospitals or healthcare organisations concentrate on a particular type or method of control. The motive behind control is to identify the errors and to adopt the corrective measures. It is quite natural that where human beings and technologies are working together, the mistakes are committed. Hence, a manager bears the responsibility of minimising the possibilities of errors and mistakes and therefore, pre-action control would help him/her in assessing the different types of resources required to generate and process the healthcare services. After this, a manager is required to motivate the employees contributing significantly and substantially to the process of development and for that, we find post-action control effective. This makes it clear that hospitals and healthcare organisations blend the pre-and post-action controls which would help them in improving the quality of healthcare services. They would come to know about the resource constraints and would also be aware of the gap generated by some of the employees or technologies used in the process.

Control Process

While exercising control, it is pertinent that a manager comes to know about the control process. William H. Newman has provided a discussion of the process for the establishment of a control system. In his opinion, there are five basic steps that can be practiced to all types of control activities in an organisation. The control process is presented in Fig. 13.4.

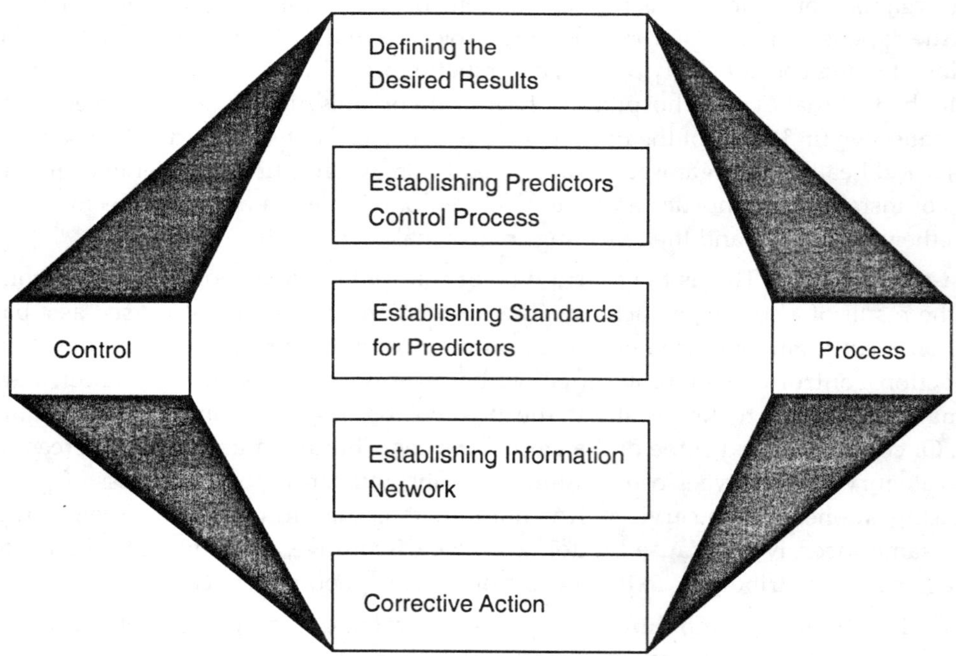

Fig. 13.4. Control Process

1. Defining the desired results: At the outset, it is significant that a manager defines the desired results which he/she desires to obtain. The desired results according to Newman should be linked to the responsible individual. It is quite natural that while defining the desired results, a manager would take into consideration the potentials of his/her organisation to achieve the same. The goals must be constructive such as a cut in the unproductive expenses by 10 per cent. It includes a yardstick by which he/she can measure the success or failure in achieving the objectives. If we link the desired results to an individual who is found responsible that would be related to a reduction in the time of diagnostic and treatment devices under the head of a particular individual. This step of the control makes it essential that a manager is well aware of the institutional/organisational/individual potentials and keeping in view the same, the goals are set.

2. Establishing predictors of results: This process of control focuses on finding out suitable or sensitive indicators or predictors for each of their goals. We find management experts devising several early-warning predictors helping managers in estimating whether the desired results would be achieved. Measurement of input, result of early step, symptoms, changes in assumed conditions are found significant in the very context. The measurements of inputs make it essential that a manager keeping in view the demand position in his/he command area makes it possible to measure the available inputs in the face of services to be offered. The results of early steps if found worse, the revaluation may be called for. The symptoms make it essential that circumstances are not sensitive to wrong and misleading interpretations which we find existent in a majority of the cases. The changes in assumed conditions make it clear that the original estimates are based on the assumption that normal conditions including expected changes would prevail. Any change made by the leading competitive hospitals would necessitate a change in the potentials of hospitals or healthcare organisations. As for example, if a sophisticated diagnostic biomedical equipment is installed by a leading hospital, it is essential that the goals set earlier are reviewed.

3. Establishing standards for predictors and results: The control process includes establishing standards or pars for predictors and final results which is considered to be its important part. It is essential to make it clear that a par has two basic aims, viz., to motivate and serve as a benchmark against which it is difficult to compare the actual performance. Obviously, we find the control system most effective when it succeeds in developing high performers. We find some people evincing interests in accepting the critical issues and therefore, their success in motivating a high or even tough standard may provide a great sense of accomplishment than meeting an easy or a smooth going responsibility. If we find a par impossible to meet, our motivational efforts can't be effective and therefore, we need to discourage them. It also clarifies that too difficult standards may degenerate performance. The experts are of the view that it is right to establish high performance generating attainable standards since this helps in encouraging employees to show wonders even if the actual goals are not attained. Peters and Waterman opine that the excellently managed organisations tend to accomplish a similar objective by setting goals found normally achievable.

4. Establishing the information and feedback network: Another control process is related to the establishment of information and feedwork network which is to establish the means for collecting information on the predictors and for comparing the predictors against their pars. Since we find the communication network working very effectively when the flows are not only upward but even downward to those who take corrective actions. We find communications control based on the management by exception principle. The management by exception principle suggests that the controlling managers should be informed about an operation's progress only if there is a significant deviation from the plan or standard.

5. Establishing information and taking corrective action: The final step in the control processes is the evaluation of information and taking the corrective actions, which is related to comparing predictors to pars; or deciding what action to take and then taking that action. In this process, the information about a deviation from a par must be evaluated because we find some of the deviations of purely temporary nature due to circumstantial or situational conditions which would not reflect the final result. In Fig. 13 5, we find the elements in a control cycle.

The aforesaid elements in the control process make it clear that it is better to set standards which can be achieved. Of course, a manager can set critical standards because some of the persons or employees are found showing special interests in achieving the critical objectives or showing wonders but all the employees can't make it possible and therefore, if we set the standards which can't be achieved, it is nothing but to promote degeneration of efficiency. In the healthcare organisations or hospitals, we find control process essential to set standards for before setting the standards, a hospital manager is required to make it sure that the healthcare organisations or hospitals have the potentials to achieve the same. Or, the hospital personnel are professionally-sound, personally-committed and in addition, getting the benefits of advanced or sophisticated biomedical equipment, instruments or so. We find some of the doctors accepting the responsibilities necessitating more excellence and covering more risks, but all the doctors don't prefer to promote the same.

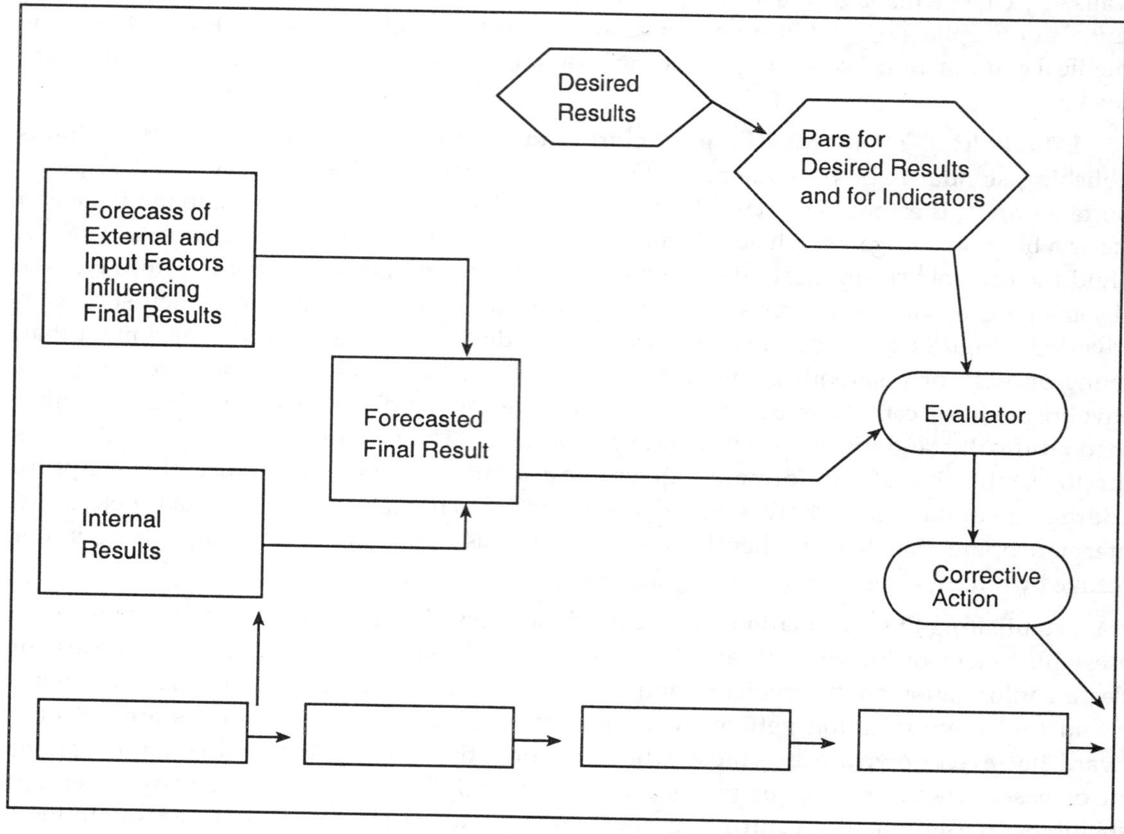

Fig. 13.5. Elements in a Control Cycle

It is right to mention that the alternative corrective actions are first required and then developed and evaluated.

In view of the above, it is right to mention that control process requires due weightage in almost all the organisations. We find relevance of the control process even in hospitals and healthcare organisations because there we find more critical responsibilities to be discharged in a very critical condition. We find some of the physicians, surgeons evincing interests in showing wonders but we can't generalise it for setting standards based on the same. We have gone through five basic steps that can be practiced even in hospitals. You, at the outset need to define the desired results. Being a hospital manager, you are well aware of the potentials of your hospitals and you are in a position to define the results that you expect. Here, it is important to mention that desired results are also to be linked to the responsible individual. Because we find some of the doctors having high potentials and if they are found successful in discharging the assigned difficult responsibilities successfully, the credit is to be given to his/her performance. Then in the second process we find establishing predictors of results and this focuses our attention on correcting deviations which necessitates some of the reliable indicators or predictors. The next process is establishing standards for the indicators and results and this gravitates our attention on making the predictors more rational with a pragmatic approach and a positive attitude. The fourth process is establishing the information and feedback network and this focuses on management by exception and fifth one is related to the establishment of information and taking the corrective action. Of late, we find information superhighway and a computer-driven information system helps you in getting the feedback which simplifies the decision-making process for corrective action.

Pre-controls in Healthcare Organisation

The hospitals or healthcare organisations need pre-action or pre-controls to make it sure that the formulated plans are not to face the financial or other constraints. Of late, we find capital intensive projects increasing the potentials of hospitals because the expensive biomedical equipment, instruments, apparatus, machines are used in the process and in addition, the developments, apparatus, machines are used in the process and further, the development of buildings or other infrastructural facilities require adequate financial support. It is quite natural that when we make use of sophisticated technologies in the process, the requirements for quality hospital personnel in tune with the evolving technologies can't be deferred. The hiring and training of personnel thus become essential. Besides, we find hospitals using a large number of materials for different purposes. Thus, to fulfil the increasing multifaceted requirements of hospitals or healthcare organisations, we find generation and mobiliation of funds from internal as well as the external sources gravitating the attention of a manager on a priority basis. The recent developments in the field of information and communications technologies also make it essential that healthcare organisations develop a technology-driven information system. The hospital planners, architects, consultants, managers and senior doctors bear the responsibility of budgeting, keeping in view the changing requirements of hospitals. It is against this background that we find pre-action control or pre-controls necessitating due attention of all of us so that the problem of resource constraints is not to obstruct the process of development.

Pre-controls or pre-action controls make it essential that in the healthcare organisations, the human, financial, material, marketing and information resources are budgeted properly. It is quite natural that before we switch on the process of development, the required resources to activate the process of development are optimally budgeted. The formulated budgets make it sure that the requisite resource would be available at the times and in the types, quality, quantity and location needed. The budgets may call for hiring and training the new employees, the purchase of sophisticated equipment, instruments, apparatus and different types of hospital materials and the designing and engineering works. In a majority of the government hospitals, we find the problem of resource constraints at the last moment of the plan execution that complicates and delays the process of implementation. It is in this context that we talk about precontrols to be instrumental in countering the problems.

In view of the changing healthcare requirements of society and the increasing inflationary pressure on the economy, we find it essential that the hospital managers and planners go through the problem in depth and find out an appropriate solution to make the implementation process time honoured and cost-effective. Since we find modern hospitals to be more capital intensive, it is pertinent that we go through the problem of finance on a priority basis. The pre-action controls make it essential that we budget all out requirements and generate financial resource accordingly. In a true sense, we find the problem directly related to the planning and budgeting. Thus, we need to focus on the budgeting for multifaceted requirements of hospitals. In Fig. 13.6, we find different types of resources needed for hospital and budgeting to avoid a crisis like situation at the last moment.

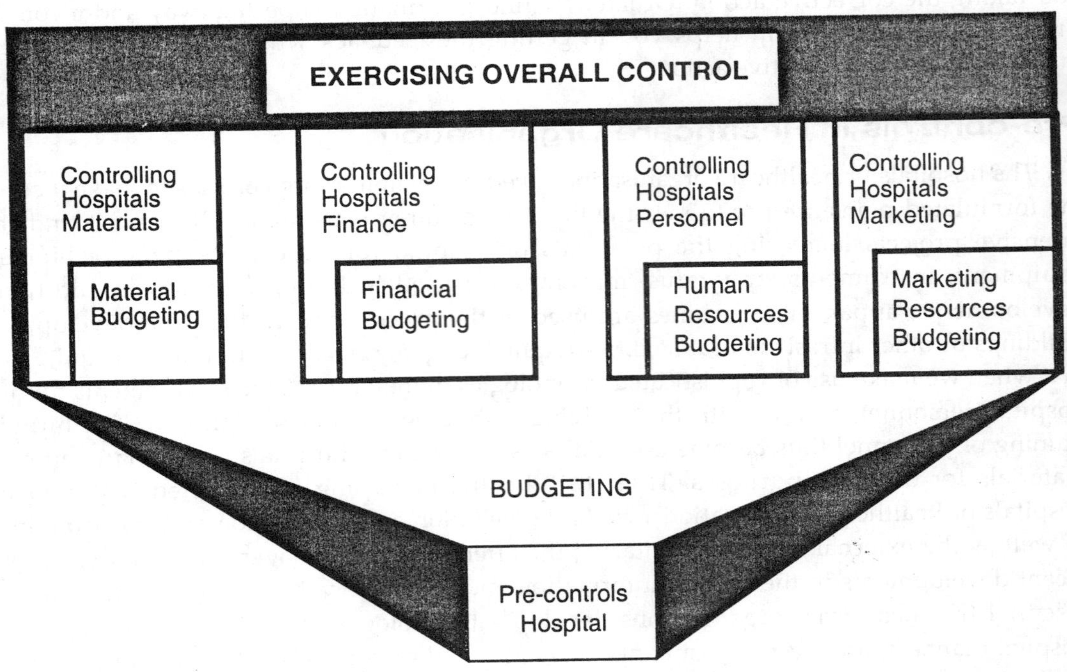

Fig. 13.6. Pre-controls of Healthcare Resources

At the outset, we turn our eyes on the financial budgeting to cater to the increasing financial requirements of hospitals. This diverts our attention on the generation of finance from internal as well as the external sources. The managers as well as the planners are required to estimate the financial requirements for the implementation of plans. Not only the private but even government hospitals also need to explore new avenues for generating the hospital revenues.

The hiring and training of hospital personnel of different categories can't be underestimated because ultimately, the hospital personnel, both medical and paramedical, are found responsible for generating the services with the help of different types of materials and the supporting infrastructural facilities. With the evolving technologies, the programmes for educating and training the personnel are to be innovated. We need to make it sure that the personnel are not only professionally-sound but also personally-committed. The behavioural profile, the ethical dimensions and the value-orientation are to be given due weightage in the process of developing the hospital personnel.

Besides, they also need to go through the problem of hospital materials and the supporting infrastructural facilities. We are well aware of the fact that in the hospitals and healthcare organisations, a large number of materials and infrastructural facilities are used. To be more specific for purchasing materials, they need to develop contact with the suppliers, installing biomedical equipment, plants and machines. The requirements of the supporting infrastructural facilities are to be assessed and made available.

They are also required to develop the marketing inputs so that the services are found in the face of increasing level of expectations of users. The processing of services is to bridge over the gap between the services-promised and services-offered. The hospital receptionists, nurses, paramedical staff and others need to satisfy the patients and attendants.

Effective Control

The main thing in the management of control is to make the process effective so that a manager is found efficacious in making an evaluation at the different stages of functioning of an organisation. The effective control focuses our attention on identifying the lapses, detecting the reasons, diagnosing the causes so that a manager is in a position to adopt the corrective measures. The word *"Control"* often has unpleasant connotations because it seems to threaten personal freedom and autonomy. The effective control focuses on finding out the right degree of control which if considered extreme or harmful would vary form one situation to another. On the other hand, the inadequate control would harm the organisation by wasting resources and by making it more difficult to attain the goals. In establishing control thus, the task for managers is to find out a balance between appropriate organisational control and individual freedom. With too much control, we find organisations generating unfriendly environment whereas with too little control, we find organisations becoming chaotic, inefficient and ineffective in achieving their goals. This makes it clear that effective control is an optimal point between too much and too little control and a manager is required to search the equilibrium point for controlling an organisation in an effective way. Because organisations, people, environment and technology keep changing, an effective control system requires continuing review and modification.[8] This makes it clear that effective control means controlling an organisation in the changing perspective so that the control processes are neither too much nor too little.

A hospital manager or a healthcare manager requires to exercise effective control and therefore, we find prime focus on controlling the workings of hospitals in the changing conditions. Since we find a change in technology, a change in regulations, a change in the expectations of patients and attendants, a change in the disease profile, a change in the profile of the hospital personnel and therefore, our control measures need to assign due weightage to all these elements and only then a manager can be successful in identifying the lapses or shortcomings. Effective control makes it essential that a manager is well aware of the quality of environment at the work places made available to the hospital personnel and in addition, the technological and infrastructural support are taken into consideration and based on the same, the variables are adopted. As for example, where we find sophisticated biomedical equipment available, computers helping a lot, personally committed and professionally sound hospital personnel, the parameters for measuring efficiency would be different because technologies increase the capacity to generate more services. The same parameter can't be effective in a manually driven hospital because there we find speed, accuracy and documentation or memory processes not so sound.

In view of the above, it is right to mention that a careful manager wants to have an adequate and effective system of controls to assist him/her in making sure that events control the plans. If a healthcare manager is found interested in making the control processes effective, he/she requires to be aware of the different essential features for the same. The most important thing that we need in the very context is the instrumentality of a manager in assessing the conditions in which the personnel have been working and the infrastructural facilities made available to them to accomplish the organisational goals.

Features of Effective Control

The following features are related to an effective control system and a manager is required to be aware of the same so that the control processes help him/her in improving the functional efficacy of an organisation.

1. Accuracy: The first feature is related to accuracy that makes it essential that whatever the information you collect from any source should be authentic. Inaccurate data from a control system would not only obstruct the process of removing or resolving the problems but would also make place for a number of complicated problems where the task of protecting the existence of an organisation would be found much more difficult.. This makes it essential that a manager makes it sure that the data collected by him/her is accurate.

2. Time-honoured Information: In this context, it is also pertinent that a manager is made available right information at the right time. The information must be collected, routed and evaluated quickly if you are really interested in resolving the same. If in the healthcare systems we find wrong practices continuing without a check, it is to generate irreparable losses. Hence, to be more specific in hospitals, the information regarding the problems are to collected on time.

3. Comprehensible: It is also significant that whatever the information you have been made available are understandable and be seen as an objective by the individuals who use it. The less subjective the control system, the great likelihood that individuals would react knowledgeably and efficiently to the information they receive. In order to avoid confusion and misunderstanding, we find it significant. A difficult control system is to aggravate the magnitude of problems.

4. Realistic: For an effective control system, it is also essential that whatever the information you collect are realistic and more so, economically realistic. This focuses our attention on minimising or optimising the costs on the collection of information. The cost of implementing a control system should not be more than the benefits that you expect from the same. In this connection, it is essential that you make it sure that the monitored activity would reach the desired goal.

5. Strategic Control Points: In any case, you are not supposed to allow deviations from the set standards and for that, you need to gravitate your attention on the sensitive points of deviations. The system should focus on the strategic points where the corrective actions can most effectively be applied.

6. Organisationally Realistic: In this context, we also find it essential that the control system is to be compatible with the organisational realities. You are required to concentrate on the point that your control measures are concerned with the generation of efficiency and for that, you are rewarding suitably the employees contributing significantly to the process of efficiency-generation. The standards set for must be realistic and the personnel working thereon must be clarified that if they achieve this much level of efficiency, this amount of rewards would be payable to them.

7. Coordination: For an effective control, it is also essential that the control informations are coordinated with the flow of work through the organisation because each step in the work system may affect the success or failure of the entire operation, and the control information must be made available to the personnel who need it.

8. Flexibility or Elasticity: In an effective control system, we need to have flexibility because of late, we find multidimensional changes in the business environmental conditions and to be more specific in the health sector, we find significant changes taking place very frequently. This makes it essential that controls have flexibility so that you get an opportunity to incorporate quickly and to overcome the adverse changes or to capitalise on the opportunities available.

9. Prescriptive: For an effective control, it is also essential that the systems indicate the deviation from the set standards and make available the appropriate solutions to resolve the same. The information should be in usable form.

10. Accepted by Members of the Organisation: In addition to the aforesaid features, for an effective control, it is also essential that whatever the control measures you adopt are accepted by all the members of your organisation. This makes it essential that controls must be related to meaningful and accepted goals reflecting the language and activities of the individuals to whom they pertain.

The aforesaid features for an effective control system make it clear that like other organisations, even the healthcare organisations need to control and this makes it essential that the healthcare managers are well aware of the aforesaid essential features for an effective control. Of course, we find a number of problems in activating the process of effective control but here, it is significant that whatever the measures you adopt or promote must be accepted by the members of the organisation. It is not only significant that you control, it is much more impact generating that whatever the measures you adopt are to help you in identifying or detecting the wrongs. Since you are going to accept it as an important base for rewarding or penalising the personnel and for replacing the equipment, you need to make it sure that whatever the information you have been made available are correct. Delay in coming to a particular conclusion is not wrong if you feel that by making haste, the blunders are to be committed. As a healthcare manager, you find a number of wrongs for which the hospital personnel are not responsible and therefore, you need to get it confirmed that if wrongs have been committed where are the roots.

You are well aware of the fact that working conditions of hospitals are found different to other organisations. The problems are of critical nature resulting into irreparable losses. You also need to realise that in the healthcare services, the results are found based on a team work and if you don't find a team culture to be nurtured in your hospitals in an effective way, whatever the qualitative developments you have made possible would not generate quality results to your expectations. Work culture, team culture, departmental harmony, friendly relations, cooperation and coordination are found playing a contributory role in the healthcare organisations and you can't negate it. You are not required to be too hard and you are also not required to be too liberal. The main thing in the process is to make the working conditions conducive and friendly. Of course, you need immediate solutions to the critical problems but you don't need to forget that critical problems make the ways for the generation of a large number of allied problems.

Feedforward Control and Feedback Control Systems

Of late, the management experts feel that control must be directed toward the future if it is to be effective. To be more specific in the healthcare services, we find multidimensional developments taking place each and everyday. Future-directed control is often disregarded in practice because we find a majority of managers depending upon accounting and statistical data for control purposes. Out of the better techniques of future-directed control in use today is network planning exemplified by PERT (Programme Evaluation and Review Technique) which enables managers to see that they would have problems in managing costs and time unless they resolve the problems right now. We find rationale behind practising feedforward control because this would also identify the important input variables. A model of the system would be developed which would take care to keep the model up-to-date or would be reviewed regularly to see whether the input variables identified. The data on input variables would be collected regularly and would be put into the system. The variations of actual data would regularly be assessed and action would be taken to solve the problems. In this connection, the managers need an adequate and effective system of controls to assist them in ascertaining that events conform to plans. This focuses on tailoring of plans and positions to the individual managers and their personalities to the needs for efficiency and effectiveness. The feedforward system monitors inputs into a process to ascertain whether inputs are as planned and if are not as per plans, the processes are changed to obtain the desired results.

We find a number of examples of feedforward control in human systems. An idea of feedforward in management control is also related to cash and inventory planning systems. One of the problems in all feedforward control systems is the necessity of watching for what engineers call disturbances. It is felt that feedback from the output of a system is not good enough for control. It is little more than a postmortem. We can't deny that a feedforward control system is really a kind of feedback system in which a manager measures the final system output.

In Fig. 13.7, we find a comparison of simple feedback and feedforward systems.

In an age of information technology, it is quite natural that sensitive organisations like hospitals assign due weightage to feedback and feedforward control systems to detect the errors and get the solutions. We are well aware of the tact that both the systems of control are found based on feedback and based on the same, the corrective measures are taken. The faults found at the initial stage can conveniently be removed. The biomedical equipment not working satisfactorily or other instruments, apparatus, machines not making available the correct findings

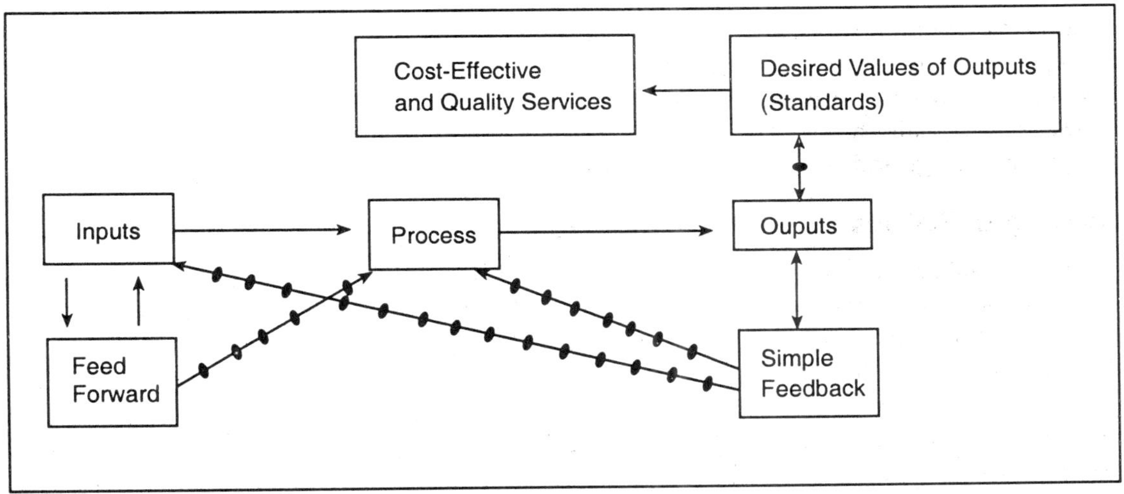

Fig. 13.7. Feed Forward and Feedback Systems

related to the diagnosis of diseases are required to be detected at the early stage. In addition, the infection is required to be controlled at the very initial stage and the managers need feedback to resolve the same. This makes it clear that transmission of necessary information related to the critical problems require an immediate solution and this is possible when we find feedforward and feedback systems working together. The most outstanding contribution of the feed control systems are related to the future oriented developments. A change in the disease profile of a particular catchment or command area and spreading of epidemics require immediate solutions because the problems can't be deferred. The feedback system of control would help healthcare managers in getting the necessary information besides the right solutions.

In the healthcare organisations, we find future-directed control assuming a place of significance because significant changes in the medical sciences are to be incorporated in the service profile of hospitals on a priority basis. The delay in the process of incorporation would obstruct the process of qualitative and quantitative improvements. The supply position would be made optimal and this would make it essential that a hospital manager with the support of a future-directed control succeeds in improving the same. The feedforward system helps a hospital manager in knowing about the emerging problems and therefore, he/she is found in a position to adopt the corrective measures on time. Taking action immediately is found significant in the management of healthcare services and the feedforward control system helps managers in the very context. For managing hospitals efficiently, we realise the instrumentality of management information system and the instrumentality of a technology-driven or a computer-based information system can't be underestimated in the very context. The feedforward system monitors inputs and on the basis of monitoring process, it is found easier to know about the availability of inputs in the face of their requirements. Not only this, a degeneration in the quality of supplied materials can also be detected which would help a hospital manager in checking the use of substandard materials. It is right to mention that the feedforward control systems can be effective even in controlling the human systems besides the cash and inventory planning.

The aforesaid facts make it clear that a hospital manager needs to make a fair mix of feedforward control and feedback control systems which would require due cooperation of management information system. It is significant to mention that in the healthcare organisations, the hospital manager is also required to depend upon the internal reporting and the complaints redressal cell would help managers in getting the feedback even from the patients and attendants. The main thing in the process is to know about the mistakes, errors, faults, wrongs at the very early stage and to find out the solutions without delaying the process.

Strategic Points in Managing Control

Since we talk about the healthcare organisations, it is pertinent that a hospital manager is well aware of the critical issues or strategic points determining the intensity of success of the healthcare organisations. The following issues are found important in the very context. Our focus in this respect would be on the standards and yardsticks for measuring the expected levels of performance. Of course in a simple operation, a manager might control through careful personal observation. However, in the healthcare operations, he/she requires to be more careful due mainly to the complexity of operations. A healthcare manager is required to choose points for special attention and to make it sure that whole operation is proceeding as planned. The points selected for control should be of critical nature. The principle of critical-point control advocates effective control and for this, special attention would be required on those factors critical to evaluate the performance of hospitals in the face of plans. It is against this background that we go through the critical or strategic points..

We can't negate the fact that ability to select critical points of control is an art that requires world class professional excellence and only professionally-sound healthcare managers can make it possible. In this context, there are certain questions and a manager is supposed to be aware of the answers. What will best reflect the goals of your hospital? What will best measure critical deviations? What will tell you who is responsible for any failure? What standards will cost the least? For what standards is information economically available? There are a number of variables to measure the performance, such as physical standards, cost standards, capital standards, revenue standards, programme standards, intangible standards and strategic plans. The type of healthcare organisation would determine the instrumentality of a particular variable. In the Indian context, the hospitals or healthcare organisations need to assign due weightage to the variables like cost and quality The healthcare services are to be made affordable and this requires an overriding priority to cost-effectiveness. Besides, the quality is also to be improved and this requires use of quality inputs in the process of generating and offering the services.

Physical Standards: The physical standards prove to be effective where we find use of labour, materials, services and the production of goods. In addition, the physical standards may also reflect quality such as hardness of bearings, closeness of tolerance, durability of a fabric or fastness of a colour.

Cost Standards: The cost standards are monetary measurements and are found common at the operating level. To be more specific, the healthcare organisations, specially in the Indian condition need to assign an overriding priority to this variable because the masses are not in a position to use the expensive healthcare or medicare services. The hospitals thus bearing the responsibility of minimising the costs need to go through the labour-hour cost and machine-hour costs. Since we find personnel and technologies playing a contributory role in the process of generating and offering the services, the costs are required to be made optimal.

Capital Standards: Monetary requirements to physical items is to determine the capital standards. We find its relation with the capital invested in the firm rather than with the operating costs and therefore, it is found related to the balance sheet not to the income statement. We are aware of the fact that the most widely used standard for new investment and overall control is (ROI) Return on Investment. The typical balance sheet clarifies other capital standards such as the ratios of current assets to the current liabilities, debt to net worth, fixed investment to the total investment, cash and receivables to payables and notes or bonds to stock and the size and turnover of investments. We can't negate the fact that even in healthcare organisations, we find investment of huge capital essential because the expensive equipment, instruments, machines, infrastructural facilities, construction of ICUs, OTs require huge capital without which the quality of healthcare services can't be improved. The monetary requirements for healthcare organisations are found increasing very fast. The capital intensive items determine the quality or standards of the healthcare services. Only world class doctors can't do anything unless they get the support of diagnostic and treatment devices found expensive in nature. This makes it clear that of late, even in the healthcare organisations, we find capital standards significant.

Revenue Standards: To be more specific in the healthcare organisations, we don't find revenue standards significant because the hospitals are not supposed to make profits. They don't have a legitimate right of making profits. However, it is significant that hospitals make their revenues proportionate to the increasing costs, otherwise, they would not be in a position to protect their existence then what to talk of offering the quality healthcare services. But we can't set revenue standards to measure or gauge the performance of hospitals.

Programme Standards: The programme standards are found related to the development of new products or offering new services and schemes. The healthcare organisations also need to introduce a new programme to improve the quality of different categories of personnel working, thereby imparting to them quality training facilities.

Intangible Standards: In business, we find a number of standards of intangible nature existent partially because adequate research into what constitutes the desired performance has not been done above the level of the accounting department. What do we find about the public relations department working in hospitals? Are supervisors loyal to the corporate objectives? Do we find the office staff alert ? What do the patients or attendants feel about the quality of healthcare services? Of course, we find these standards significant but it is difficult to quantify them due mainly to the intangibility that we find involved in their results and effects.

Goals Standards: Qualitative and quantitative goals are also used as standards for measuring the performance of an organisation. To be more specific, in the hospitals or healthcare organisations, we find both types of standards to be effective. On the one hand, the quantitative goals make it essential that the hospitals or healthcare organisations are in a position to offer services to a large number of population while on the other hand, they also need to improve the quality of healthcare services.

Problems in Establishing Effective Control Systems

Of course, we find effective control essential but it is difficult to establish the effective control systems, specially in the healthcare organisations where we find nature of services a bit difficult and complicated to others.

1. Items difficult to measure not getting due weightage: In the control process, we find organisations preferring the factors easily quantifiable and neglecting the factors generating difficulties in quantification. In the healthcare organisations, we find figures related to the turnover of hospital personnel getting attention but the quality of services offered by them is not carefully checked. The doctors offering world class services are hardly retained, motivated and rewarded. Thus, we find the control systems concentrating on small/minor matters even at the cost of important organisational goals. The quality of services offered by paramedical staff, nursing staff, hospital architects and consultants are not given due weightage because we find complications in the process of quantification.

2. Short-run factors getting overemphasised at the cost of long-run factors: The long run results are found more unpredictable than the short-run achievements. The designing of hospitals in general and to be more specific, the wards, OTs, ICUs are found important and effective in the long-run when we realise the conveniences or feel the difficulties. The goodwill on account of good patient care is found visible after the long-run and often, we undermine them while measuring the performance.

3. The Control System may not be adjusted to reflect shifts in the importance of various activities and goals over time: It is right to mention that no healthcare organisations can neglect things influencing quality, assured delivery or processing, offering of new diagnostic, curative, peripheral and preventive services and the control on the manufacturing or generation costs. To be more specific in hospital or healthcare organisations, we find them significant because a number of factors influence the quality; the gap is often generated by the health personnel, particularly between the quality of service assured and the quality of service offered. This makes it essential that while measuring the performance of hospitals or healthcare organisations, a manager makes it sure that whatever the changes or developments taking place in the environmental conditions due to a change in the social systems or disease profile or emergencies or natural calamities, are also used as variables or indices to measure the performance. It is quite natural that with a change in the environmental conditions, we find a shift in the organisational goals and the concerned organisations should have the potentials to achieve the same.

Effective control is found impact generating to improve the quality of services of hospitals or healthcare organisations but we find the variables not in tune with the changing social conditions. The private hospitals of course, offer quality services but expensive in nature and therefore, the masses find it difficult to avail the same. If we talk about the control system for hospitals or healthcare organisations, the variables like costs of services, gap between the quality of services assured and offered and the behavioural profile of medical and paramedical staff are found important but often neglected while rating the performance. We can't consider profitability as a criterion specially when we evaluate the performance of hospitals because they are considered as a no-profit-making organisation. Of course, the most important parameter for evaluating the performance of hospitals is the quality and economy or costs of services. The hospitals found successful in offering world class services at an affordable cost would be considered to be number one. Since they are supposed to make outstanding contributions to the process of social transformation, we can't undermine the same while evaluating their performance.

Health Care Services in India: A Microscopic Audit

Healthcare sector in India is emerging as a sunshine industry. The annual growth rate of 13%

testifies the multi dimensional developments in the healthcare industry. The increasing heat of globalisation has injected new life and strength to the healthcare organisations and we find a number of world class hospitals both in public and private sectors very much instrumental in defining and redefining service quality. A mix of Yoga, Meditation, Ayurveda, Allopathy, Homoeopathy, Aroma Therapy, Music Therapy and other systems of medicine are present and India offers a vast array of healthcare services which we find nationally and internationally competitive. The e-health initiatives have added new feathers in the development process. We cannot deny that contours of development have undergone radical changes during the yesteryears.

Modern hospitals offer multifaceted services to the patients but the services are not meant for the general masses because only a few of the affluent sections of society can afford. From village level to block level and from subdivision or taluk level to district level of the primary, secondary and tertiary hospitals working under the public sector, the results are very disappointing. In a true sense, the public health system meant for the general masses have been found witnessing multipronged constraints. We find centralised planning instead of decentralized planning, institutions based on population norms rather than habitations, fragmented disease specific approach rather than comprehensive healthcare, inflexible financing and limited scope for innovations, semi-used or dysfunctional health infrastructure, inadequate provision of human resources, no prescribed standards of quality, inability of the system to mobilize areas of safe water, sanitation, hygiene, and nutrition, inability to mobilize AYUSH and other locally available human resources are the constraints obstructing the development of public health system.

The National Rural Health Mission launched to address infirmities and problems across primary healthcare and to bring about improvements in the health system and health status of people living in the rural areas needs an overhauling on a fast track mode at the grassroots. The National Urban Health Mission to cater to the health needs of the urban poor particularly, the slum dwellers by making available to them essential healthcare services witnesses the problems like lack of high-caliber health professionals, appropriate technology through PPP mode and health insurance for the urban poor need priority attention. The District hospitals supposed to play a key role in providing health services to the poor need substantial improvement in supporting infrastructural facilities to perform their role in an effective fashion. We need to strengthen the Central Government hospitals and for that, the PPP mode may be preferred because the hospitals have been found witnessing the problem of financial crunch. The Government Medical Colleges and Hospitals are on the verge of derecognition because they fail to adhere to the infrastructure, equipment and staff norms as laid down by the MCI.

A majority of them do not make use of new generation of technology either for promoting the healthcare services or for innovating medical education.

It is significant to mention that to address the gap in health infrastructure and human resources, the National Rural Health Mission was launched on 12 April 2005[10] But we do not find NRHM showing the desired results. The NUHM is also found in the same boat. The Tenth Five Year Plan indicated the dismal picture of the health services infrastructure and emphasized the need to strengthen primary level care and referral services. A microscopic audit of the Plan not only throws light on the gap between the rhetoric and reality but also the framework within which the policies are formulated. The framework, design and approach within which the policy makers worked and low investment in health are the key reasons for the failures of NRHM and

NUHM. An attitudinal change appears to be a crying need of the hour to have the desired results from the programmes and policies we adopt for improving the healthcare services, both in qualitative and quantitative ways.

An analysis of drug policy indicates that despite efforts taken in this context, we find a number of complaints related to quality and price. We find increasing cases of spurious drugs and ineffectiveness of National Pharmaceutical Pricing Authority aggravating the magnitude of problem. The life saving drugs are not available at reasonable prices. In order to take up drug pricing, quality and clinical trials as recommended by the Mashelkar Committee (2003) and NCMH, (2005) a National Drug Authority (NDA) with an autonomous status was set up[11] but we do not find any change in the intensity of problem. This makes it clear that for improving the healthcare services, we need to make a multicornered attack. The drugs and medicines form a substantial portion of the out-of-pocket spending on health by households. The weaker sections are found to be the worst affected. This focuses on strengthening the drug regulatory system.

In view of the emerging problem, it is also right to mention that the Union as well as the State Governments have not made possible an optimal use of PPP mode. On the one hand, we find inadequacy of government grants while on the other hand, we also find less focus on PPP mode. We need to initiate and activate the efforts to promote PPP mode. Yeshaswini Health Insurance Scheme for farmers in Karnataka is an example which requires to be followed even by other states in the country. The States like Rajasthan, West Bengal, Uttarakhand, Karnataka, Gujarat, Arunachal Pradesh, Andhra Pradesh and Tamil Nadu have been found initiating the process of promoting PPP but they need to activate something more.

Though we find private sector moving forward in the right direction but the pace is required to be accelerated. Corporatisation of hospitals and healthcare organisations requires attitudinal transformation. The government as well as the private sector need to be positive to tap the potentials and capitalize on the opportunities. Since we find corporate sector potentially sound for activating the transformation process, it is pertinent that motivational plants are given priority attention.

This would increase flow of capital in the healthcare industry and would improve the supply position. It is significant to mention that about 80% of our healthcare requirements are met by the private sector and therefore, increased flow of capital in the development of healthcare organisations particularly by the corporate sector is to be an important policy decision. The big private planners like Escorts, Max Healthcare, Apollo Group, etc. have been successful in establishing a brand name and they have no option but to keep on moving the process of defining quality. It is against this background that we find due support and cooperation to the corporate hospitals considered as a need of the hour. The development of world class hospitals would make the ways for the development of medical tourism which would show multiplier effects on the economy.

Since we have not promoted low cost indigenous technologies, the healthcare services have become expensive adversely affecting the weaker sections of the society. Studies show that the poor and other disadvantaged groups both in the rural and urban areas spend a higher proportion of their income on healthcare than those who are better-off. The burden of treatment is high on them for which they have to borrow at very high interest to meet both medical and other household consumption needs. This makes a strong advocacy in favour of development of a mechanism having universal coverage of population for meeting the cost of hospitalization.

We find a majority of the government hospitals facing the problem of financial crunch which is primarily due to the inadequate financial support from the government. A sharp reduction in capital investment in public hospitals, low priority to preventive and promotive care and inefficiencies in allocations under national health programmes have made hospitals and healthcare organisations potentially deficient. On the one hand we find an increase in the cost of inputs required for quality healthcare services and on the other hand, we find the avenues for resource mobilisation shrinking. This makes it essential that government policy makers encourage charities and donations from individuals and organisations. Additionally, it is also essential that the PPP mode and corporate sector are prompted to channelise their investments in the healthcare services.

Almost all the government hospitals have been facing the problem of managerial deficiency. This makes their investments unproductive. A number of medical and biomedical equipments are mismanaged and non-optimally used. The materials and stores are found to be a source for unfair and unlawful practices. We also find them facing the problem of inadequacy of quality medical and paramedical personnel. They are not only thematically unsound but in addition, we also find them inefficient, dishonest, inhuman and aggressive in behavior. They lack a sense of personal commitment and assign due weightage to their personal interests. Actually, personal interest command the interest of users.

This automatically degenerates the quality of services offered by the healthcare organisations. We cannot negate that the healthcare services are found distinct to other services where personal and human touch, sympathy and empathy also contribute to the process of service quality. The medical college and institutes while educating and training people need to assign due weightage to the informal education.

Increasing healthcare spending of weaker sections of the society makes it essential that the government policy makers assign top priority to AYUSH. On the one hand, low cost indigenous technology and on the other hand, AYUSH would be very much instrumental in bringing down the healthcare costs. It is right to mention that we have not tapped the existent potentials of AYUSH and therefore, a change in the vision of AYUSH is considered significant. The thrust areas[13] need due attention of policy makers such as strengthening professional education, strategic research programmes, promotion of best clinical practices, technology upgradation in industry, setting internationally acceptable pharmacopoeial standards, conserving medical flora, fauna, metal and minerals, utilising human resources of AYUSH in the national health programmes with the ultimate aim of enhancing he outreach of AYUSH healthcare in an accessible, acceptable, affordable and qualitative manner would bring multifaceted improvements in the healthcare service quality. It is pertinent that we integrate AYUSH in NRHM which would considerably complement the conventional national health programmes vis-a-vis would enhance the quality and outreach of NRHM.

The research and development activities are considered as strong pillars of medical sciences which pave avenues for defining and redefining quality. In almost all the areas of health sector, we find government policy makers not to evince special interests which tell upon the costs and quality. It is in this context that we make a strong advocacy in favour/public as well as the private sector hospitals for promoting research. If we need innovative technologies for diagnosis and treatment; if we need to offer the world class services to the users; if we need to improve the quality of medicines and further to minimise their costs, we have no option but to keep on moving the process of undertaking research, inventing something innovative and producing and promoting something creative.

It is amazing that coverage of health insurance in India is abnormally limited. Current health insurance in government and private sector covers around 11% of the population.[14] The existing Employment Insurance Scheme, Central Government Health Scheme and Ex-servicemen Contributory Health Scheme provide services to industrial workers, government employees and ex-Armed Forces personnel along with their families. The Mediclaim covers mainly the upper-middle income Groups. The private health insurance schemes are found for urban-oriented and therefore, the most deserving weaker segments remain unprotected. The rural poor need a liberal attitude of government. It is judicious that the government policy makers assign due weightage to comprehensive health insurance on a risk pooling basis at least for the poor.

A microscopic audit of healthcare services in India makes it clear that the benefits of sophisticated development have been harnessed only by affluent sections of the society whereas the weaker sections are still continuing as a disadvantaged group. The public spending has not been found proportionate to the increasing requirements. Of course, we find a significant increase in the private spending where the service quality is, no doubt, of world class but not affordable to the masses. This necessitates a big jump in the public sector healthcare spending.

A majority of the hospitals lack a team of dedicated medical and paramedical personnel and resulting from which we do not find team spirit and team culture. The problem of managerial deficiency is found at its peak. This makes hospitals strategically deficient even if they are potentially sound. In the government hospitals, even expensive equipments are found becoming unproductive. The poor maintenance, handling in absence of skilled people deprive the general masses of getting the benefits of expensive technology. The healthcare organisations have not been found sincere to the development of low cost indigenous technology aggravating the problem of affordability. This makes it essential that medical colleges and institutes develop quality people found thematically sound, professionally excellent, value-based, personally committed and human-oriented.

The corporatisation of healthcare sector has been found gaining a rapid momentum but the leading private hospitals have not been sincere to their societal role. They have avenues for capitalising on the opportunities because we find niche markets both at domestic and global levels. The development of medical tourism would provide to them an opportunity to enrich their potentials which they can channelise for serving and subserving the interests of weaker sections of the society. Enriching their potentials for bearing social costs cannot be unjust.

In the Indian perspective, the primary hospitals and healthcare centres need to play a meaningful role. Since we find general masses very insensitive to the changing disease profile, it is pertinent that medical and paramedical personnel working there play in an outstanding role in the sensitisation process. If masses develop their awareness of food-prone, water-prone, communicable and non-communicable diseases, the intensity of health problem would considerably be minimised. Additionally, it is also essential that managerial people working there develop the awareness of masses to the vaccination and immunization culture and nutritional problems so that the increasing demand side shows a downward trend.

Healthcare problem requires multicornered support. Involvement of government, NGOs, private sector development of PPP mode and corporatisation of healthcare sector are the key measures to initiate and activate the process of qualitative-cum-quantitative improvements. Let's hope that the government policy makers accelerate the pace of attitudinal transformation.

SUMMARY

In this chapter, you have gone through different dimensions of control. After going through the chapter, be sure that the following facts are well versed.

Control—the Perception: The management control is a systematic effort to set performance standards with a planning objective.

Steps in the Control Process: The different steps in the control process are establishing standards and methods for measuring performance, matching of performance with the standards and taking corrective action.

Importance of Control: We find the management of control significant even to the healthcare organisations. The organisational factors necessitate management control, cost-effectiveness is made possible with the help of the control system, control can generate work culture, the mistakes can he identified with the support of control and the progress can also be monitored with the control system.

Types of Control: The different types of control are Pre-action Control, Steering Controls, No or Screening Control and Post-action Control.

Control Process: The control process is defining the desired results, establishing predictors or indicators, establishing standards for indicators, establishing information network and the corrective action.

Pre-controls in Healthcare Organisations: We find pre-controls significant to the healthcare organisations because with the help of resource budgeting, the precontrol measures can remove the problem of resource constraints. The control of hospital materials, finance, human resource and marketing are the areas for the budgeting of resources.

Effective Control: By effective control, our focus is on finding out the right degree of control.

Features of Effective Control: The features of effective control are accuracy, time-honoured availability of information, comphrensibleness, economically realistic, strategic control points, organisationally realistic, coordination, elasticity, prescriptive and acceptance of the members of the organisation.

Feedforward Control and Feedback Control Systems: The feedforward control and feedback control systems are found based on the information network. We also call it future-directed control which makes it essential that an organisation is well aware of the emerging problems and enriches the organisational potentials accordingly.

Strategic Points in Managing Control: The critical points in the management of control are related to the setting of standards, such as physical standards, cost standards, capital standards, revenue standards, programme standards, intangible standards and goals standards.

Problems in Establishing Effective Control Systems: A number of organisations commit mistakes while establishing effective control, such as the items found difficult to measure are not identified, short-run factors establishing an edge over the long-run factors and the control system is not in the face of latest developments.

Healthcare Services in India: A Microscopic Audit: It is essential for a hospital professional that he/she makes an audit of the working of hospitals or healthcare organisation so that the lapses, shortcomings or mistakes at different stages are identified and corrective measures are initiated. There are a number of processes for making the control process effective and it is upon a professional to make use of the same in tune with the changing requirements. The control processes need to be effective. Forward Control and backward control processes are adopted for getting the ideas regarding steps taken or to be taken.

KEY TERMS

AYUSH
Telemedicine
Telediagnosis
Teleconferencing
Indigenous Technology
Stakeholders
Health Insurance
Thermostat
OPD
Clown
Racist
Snob
Robot
Steering Control
Formation Network
Control Cycle
Pre-action Control
Overall Control
Strategic Control Points
Team Culture
Team Spirit
Feed Forward Control
Feedback Control
Log book
Cybernetic
Public Healthcare Spending

REVIEW QUESTIONS

1. What do you mean by Management Control? Focus on the control process.
2. Explain the importance of control to the development of hospital.
3. Discuss the different types of control. Do you find pre-action control important to the healthcare organisations? Present arguments in your favour.
4. What do you mean by Effective Control? Explain the features of an effective control.
5. Discuss the Feedforward and Feedback control in the context of healthcare organisations.
6. Focus on the sensitive standards with the viewpoint of healthcare organisations.
7. Throw light on the mistakes helping a hospital professional in identifying mistakes.
8. Make a microscopic audit of healthcare services in the Indian perspective.
9. Focus on the role of control in making the healthcare services cost effective.

APPLICATION EXERCISES

1. "The management of control is found significant to a healthcare organisation." Comment on this statement in the capacity of a hospital manager.
2. "We find pre-control significant to the healthcare organisation." In the light of this statement, throw light on the role of pre-controls in removing the problem of resources constraints.
3. Feedforward Control and Feedback Control systems help healthcare managers in identifying the problems at an early stage that simplifies the task of finding out an appropriate solution. Comment on this statement as a hospital professional.
4. "Setting of standards is an important managerial responsibility that requires professional excellence. "Comment on this statement and focus on the sensitive standards with the viewpoint of healthcare organisations.
5. "Hospital managers often commit mistakes in establishing effective control. "In the light of this statement, identify the mistakes making the control process ineffective.

6. "By making possible effectiveness in the control process, a healthcare manager is found successful not only in improving the quality of healthcare services but also in making the process cost-effective which makes the services affordable." Comment on this statement as a hospital manger.

END NOTES

1. Knonntz Weihrich, *Essentials of Management*, p. 293
2. Earl p. Strong and Robert D. smith, *Management Control Models*, New York, pp. 1-2
3. Robert J. Meckler, *The Management Control Process*, New Jersey, p.2
4. Ibid
5. William H. Newman, *Constructive Control*, New Jersey, pp. 6-9
6. Koontz and Bradspies, *Managing through Feedforward control, Business Horizon*, 4/3, pp. 25-26, 1972
7. William H. Newman, *op. cit.*
8. Stoner and Freeman, *Management*, pp. 572-73
9. Robert N. Anthony, *Management Control System*
10. *Eleventh Five Year Plan*: Planning Commission, Government of India, New Delhi, Vol. II, pp. 70-72
11. *Eleventh Five Year Plan*; Vol. II, pp. 57-115
12. Soni & Upadhyaya: India—*A Global Healthcare Brand; Journal or Marketing & Communication* Jan-April 2006, Vol. 1/3, pp. 6-76
13. *Eleventh Five Year Plan*; Vol. II, pp. 108-113
14. *Eleventh Five Year Plan*; Vol. II, pp. 82

Rural Healthcare Management

We often forget that development of urban economy rests on the transformation of rural society. In the Indian context, the rural-urban gap has been expanding with a high pace. Shrinking public healthcare spending and mounting insensitivity need priority attention of health professionals while improving the quality of rural health care and medicare services.

CHAPTER OBJECTIVES

LEARNING OBJECTIVES

This chapter aims at studying the different dimensions of rural healthcare management. The readers develop their awareness of the rural masses not getting proper healthcare and medicare facilities. Managing rural healthcare services is an important functional responsibility before health professionals. They need to know the different constituents for managing healthcare services in the Indian perspective. The thrust areas have been identified which would help in improving the quality of rural healthcare services.

Introduction

Our negative attitudes to the process of rural transformation generate a big gap between the rural and urban economies and the rural society fails in harnessing the benefits of sophisticated developments. We often forget that development of urban economy rests on the development of rural economy. In developing countries like ours, we find rural urban gap expanding with a high pace. The heat of globalization has been found aggravating the magnitude of problem. The inadequacy of infrastructural facilities, civic amenities, lack of education and awareness make the task of transforming the society much more complicated. It is against this background that villages in India have remained neglected and the process of transforming the rural areas into urban areas has virtually been slowed down. The rural population fails in getting even the basic healthcare facilities which makes it essential that national policy makers assign priority attention to the rural healthcare services.

In 1947, when we attained independence, the healthcare services were urban concerned and hospital based. With the development of Five Year Plans, we generated Primary Healthcare infrastructure making possible the emergence of Primary Health Centres and the Community Health Centres who were assigned the tasks of enriching the healthcare facilities but even till today, we find rural India not getting albeit the basic care and the primary healthcare. It is important to mention that the primary healthcare centres provide first level of services and contact between the providers and users. They are supposed to provide integrative, promotive, preventive, curative and rehabilitative services to the rural population close to their health and home. We cannot negate that since independence, India has built up a vast health infrastructure. Considerable achievements have been made over last decades in our efforts to improve health standards such as life expectancy, child mortality, infant mortality and maternal mortality. However, we find a big gap between rural and urban healthcare services. An unacceptably high proportion of population continues to suffer and die from the diseases emerging due to a change in the disease profile.

The national policy makers need to realise the strong link between poverty and ill health. The onset of a long and expensive illness can drive the non-poor into poverty. High healthcare costs can lead to exacerbation of poverty. This draws our attention on the shrinking public healthcare spending. During yesteryears, we have witnessed a significant increase in the cost of inputs for providing the healthcare services which has made possible a big jump in the price or fees charged for the services rendered. It is pertinent that we make the public healthcare accessible and affordable to the general masses.

Wrong location, poor access, lack of maintenance of equipment and instruments, inadequacy of quality medical and paramedical personnel, mismatch between the demand and supply position, lack of funds for drugs and the diagnostic measures, lack of First Referral Units for linkage of referral services are some of the critical problems making the rural healthcare services a big joke in the name of social transformation. The government policy makers, social scientists, non-government organisations and corporate sector need sincere and honest efforts the resolve the problems. The budgetary provisions and allocation to not carry any meaning if the operational mechanism is not well supported by the quality people.

In a true sense, we find the rural healthcare services very much neglected and it is in this context, that all the healthcare centres right from the village level to the block level need priority attention. The ASHA, AWW, VH & SC at village level and the subhealth centres at Gram

Panchayat level require due care. All the three levels of rural health care would suffice the healthcare demand.

In the context of rural healthcare services, we cannot undermine the Public Health Centres playing a commanding role. The functions of PHCs as explained by Department of Community Development are Medical care, Maternal and Child Health Services, School Health Services, Family Welfare, Control of communicable diseases, environmental, health education and involvement in the facilities for managing information.

The National Rural Health Mission (NRHM) launched to address infirmities and problems across primary health care and bring about improvement in the health system and health status of the rural population has failed in touching the desired target. The mission aims to provide universal access to equitable, affordable and quality healthcare accountable and responsive to the needs of the people and to achieve the goals set under the National Health Policy and the Millennium Development Goals (MDGs). This necessitates a sound management of primary health programmes. For promotive and preventive healthcare, a framework is required to be developed. The core and supplementary strategies need due attention in this regard. In the context of core strategies, we need an improvement in the capacity of PRIs to enable them to supervise and manage public health services. The ASHA, known as female health activities have to play a meaningful role for promoting healthcare at household level. Besides, the existing PHCs and CHCs are required to be strengthened. The National, State and District Health Missions for Public Health Management need technical support. The family welfare programmes need priority attention. The management of information also requires the due support. In the context of supplementary strategies, we find focus on regulation of private sector to ensure availability of quality services to citizens at a reasonable cost. Additionally, the PPP mode requires priority attention and medical care and medical ethics are to be an integral part of medical education. Social health insurance also needs due attention in this regard.

The plans, policies and strategies for the development of rural healthcare services do not carry any meaning if the society where we have to administer is found insensitive. We cannot deny that illiteracy is found to be a major problem aggravating insensitivity and therefore, our efforts must be proactive to promote healthcare education or to make the promotional measures much more creative to sense and sensitise the rural population. A majority of the rural population lacks awareness of food-prone, water-prone and communicable diseases. They are not aware of vaccination and immunization culture. They lack nutritional awareness. The disease profile is considerably influenced by these problems. Thus, the government policy makers not only bear the responsibility of developing the healthcare facilities in the rural areas but in addition, they also need to make it sure that healthcare professionals make use of their expertise for transforming the attitudes of rural population.

The healthcare centres and referral hospitals need to establish a direct link with secondary and tertiary hospitals. The professionals managing big hospitals in the towns and cities need to develop a direct contact with the rural heal centres in their command or catchments areas. Particularly, the government hospitals are required to accept the challenging task of channelising the rural healthcare services. The leading private hospitals also need to play a meaningful role by supporting the rural healthcare centres. The corporate hospitals need to accept their societal role and to promote the rural healthcare centres. If the government policy makers develop the supporting infrastructural facilities and offer to the corporate sector incentives, they may think in favour of locating big hospitals in the rural areas. This would not only provide to the rural population an opportunity to avail the quality healthcare services partially supported by the corporate hospitals but would also show multiplier effects and the rural economy would considerably be benefited.

Of course, a number of steps have been taken to improve the healthcare services in the rural areas but the results are found very disappointing. This focuses on managerial proficiency. We need to make possible a productive use of our resources. During yesteryears, we have witnessed sophistication and let's hope that sophistication that we have made possible in the field of healthcare technologies benefits the rural population.

RURAL HEALTHCARE SERVICES-THE GENESIS

It was way back in 1946 that the Bhore Committee recommended for setting up Primary Health Centre in India to serve as a focal point for providing comprehensive, curative and preventive healthcare services in the rural areas. Based on the recommendations of Bhore Committee, the rural healthcare services were redefined. The report recommended a primary health unit for a population of 20,000, a secondary unit for the population of 6,00,000 and a District Healthcare Organisation for a population of three million as a long-term development for the healthcare services in India. But as a short-term measure, the Committee recommended a Primary Unit for a population of 40,000, a secondary unit for a population of one and a half million and a district healthcare unit for a population of three million. To improve the operation of primary health centres, this Committee recommended a reduction in the population covered by them, expansion and strengthening of district hospitals and introduction of mobile teams of specialists to provide necessary supervisory and consultancy services in the periphery.

In pursuance of these recommendations, the Government of India appointed a committee on multipurpose workers under health and family planning programmes in October, 1972 which submitted its reports in September, 1973 recommending multipurpose workers for the delivery of health, family planning and nutrition services to the rural community, one PHC for every 50,000 population, each PHC to be divided into 16 subcentres and each having a population of 3,000 to 3,500 depending upon the topography and means of communication, each subcentre to have a team of one male and one female worker, one male and one female supervisor to supervise the work of four sub-centres, the doctors at PHC to divide the population on a geographical basis for their field visits, for effective integration of workers engaged in vertical programmes of health and family planning and the concept of integration to be expanded to the district and state levels.

The Government of India accepted the recommendations of the Committee except of PHC for every 50,000 population and one sub-centre for 3,000 to 3,500 population, instead of it was agreed to have a subcentre for 5,000 population.[3]

It is important to mention that India was one of the pioneers in health service planning with a focus on primary healthcare. We started the process way back in 1946 when the Health Survey and Development Committee under the Chairmanship of Sir Joseph Bhore recommended establishment of a well-structured and comprehensive health services with a sound primary healthcare infrastructure and we, of course, even till now are the backbenchers when even small countries starting the process of developing rural healthcare services, no doubt very late, but are found marching forward very fast to subserve the interests of rural masses. It is against this background that in the management of healthcare services in the Indian perspective, the rural healthcare management is required to be assigned an overriding priority. Not only on papers because we appear very intelligent in drafting the development programmes and designing the development schemes but all our intelligence and potentials start shrinking once we start the process; why? Not to be answered because all of us are well aware of the answer.

Management of Rural Healthcare Services

We can't negate that the healthcare services to be more specific in rural India are very much neglected. The rural masses have been found suffering and the government policy makers bear the responsibility of bringing the derailed healthcare systems back on the rail. This necessitates an attitudinal change, a new vision and an innovative strategy. Instead of making an anatomy of our

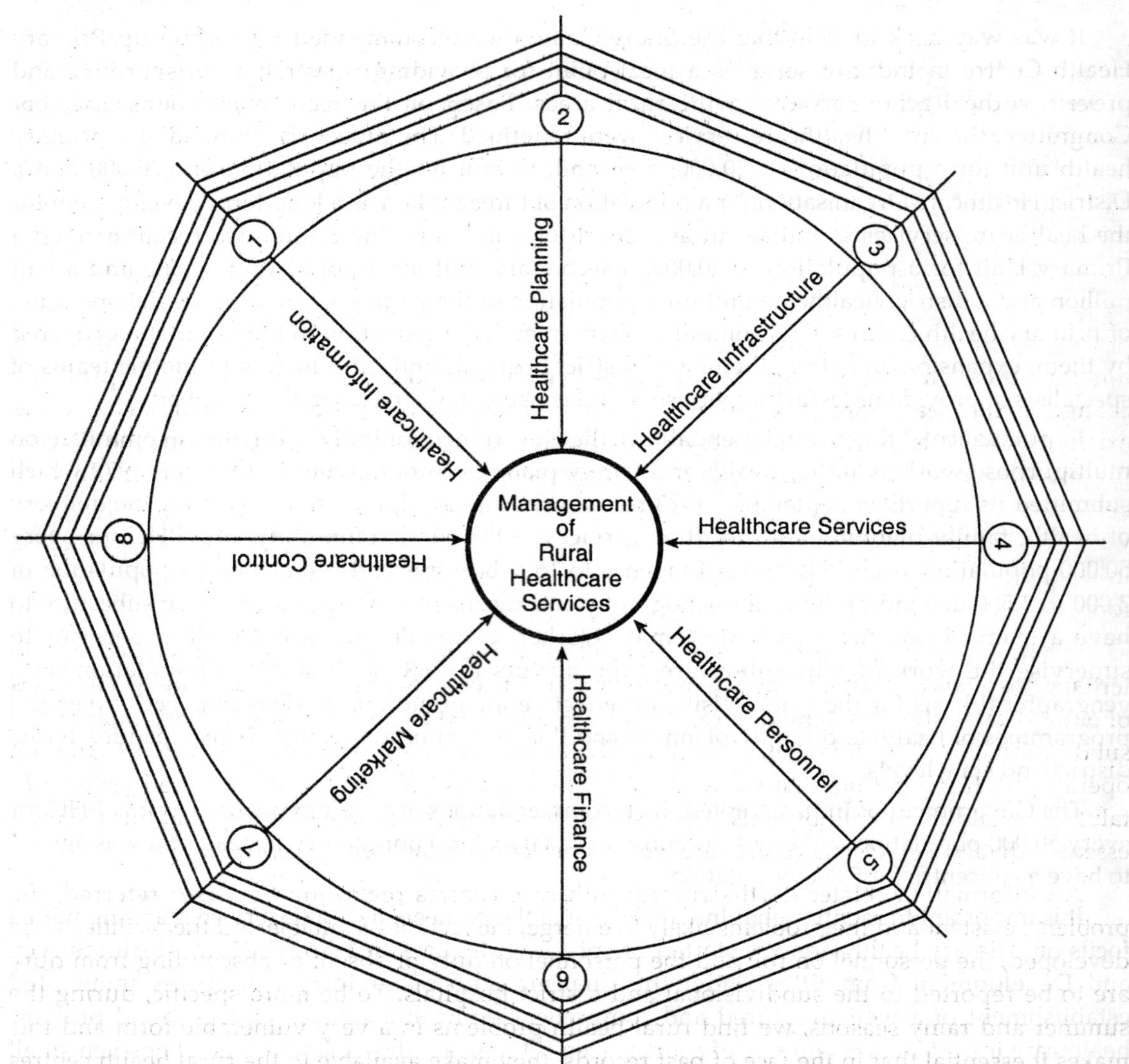

Fig. 14.1. Network of Rural Healthcare Services

wrongs and misdeeds, it is essential that we switch on the process from the very beginning. If we activate the process sincerely and honestly, the problems can considerably be resolved. It is against this background that we go through the problem of rural healthcare management in an innovative fashion. We agree with this view that during the yester decades, a number of developments have taken place in the medical sciences but a majority of the population has failed in harnessing the benefits of development. It is high time that the government policy makers take up the problem on a priority basis and develop a network as shown in Fig. 14.1. We start the process from the management of healthcare information for rural India because now we have communications network in a very sophisticated form. This would let us know the magnitude of requirements and the potentials can be developed on that basis. We don't find any sense in following the old paths when new avenues are likely to be more effective not only with the viewpoint of enriching the healthcare services but also with the motto of linking the healthcare services with the development programmes. This engineers a sound foundation in favour of developing large-sized hospitals in the rural areas so that the increasing influx of patients and attendants albeit from the urban areas open new vistas for the development of villages.

Rural Healthcare Information Management

In an age of information technology, we find it judicious that the benefits of technological sophistication are also made available to the rural population. The information superhighway can be more useful to the development of rural healthcare facilities. The secondary and tertiary healthcare organisations bear the responsibility of developing an information network that keeps updating the management regarding the çhanging nature and character of the disease profile, a change in the healthcare requirements of the population related to the catchment area, the existent potentials of rural healthcare centres, the requirements of financial and healthcare personnel keeping in view the seasonal fluctuations or so. Since we talk about the direct linkage between the rural health centres and secondary and tertiary hospitals, it is pertinent that they, with the support of sophisticated information and communication technologies collect information and make available to the planning department that bears the responsibility of formulating a plan.

Of late, we find a gap between the rural and urban healthcare facilities and the secondary and tertiary hospitals are not well aware of the emerging problems in the command areas. The cases of natural calamities, epidemics, viral and communicable diseases are not made available to the subdivisional or district hospitals on time. Of course, we find referral centres but virtually not operational. It is essential that we revive them and connect the same with the subdivisional or taluk hospitals or district hospitals. The cases are to be referred at an early stage and this makes it essential that all the referral centres are well connected with the feeding centres.

All information related to the rural health care centres regarding the cases referred, the problems existent and the problems likely to emerge, the facilities available and the facilities to be developed, the personnel on roll and the personnel on duty or absent or absconding from duty are to be reported to the subdivisional and district hospitals. To be more specific, during the summer and rainy seasons, we find rural health problems in a very vulnerable form and this makes it essential that in the face of past records, they make available to the rural health centres the preventive and curative devices. The Village Panchayats, the Public Health Centres, the schools for rural children need support of information and the policy makers here bear the responsibility of channelising the communication and information network.

We can't negate that by and large, almost all the rural health centres are in a depleted condition and therefore, minor treatments would hardly bring qualitative improvements in their potentials of generating the services. With the migration of rural population to the urban areas and to be more specific to the big industrial towns and cities for getting jobs we find wider avenues for the spread of communicable diseases due mainly to the irresponsible sexual behaviour. Of late, we find a number of villages in the grip of communicable diseases and due to communication gap, the reporting system is not found to be effective. The information network would enrich the reporting system and the vulnerable cases, communicable diseases would be referred for treatment at an early stage. The main purpose of developing information network in the rural areas is to help hospital planners and consultants so that they formulate a plan in the face of regional conditions. The would be switched on specially with the support of budgetary provisions which would estimate the multifaceted requirements of the rural health centres.

Rural Healthcare Planning

Based on information, the hospital planners need to formulate short and long-term plans for the development of rural healthcare facilities. We talk about formulation of a plan based on the demand and supply position. The rural health ventures managed and controlled by government have been found facing the problem of resource constraints. The government policy makers bear the responsibility of strengthening the centres and in addition, the corporate sector also needs to promote the rural healthcare or medicare measures to be more specific as a corporate citizen. We talk about planning for the development of rural healthcare services and this is not possible unless we find private sector to be involved in the process. In the face of emerging problems, the government as well as the private sector need to develop the healthcare facilities in the rural areas.

Till now, we find cities and towns getting priority attention while locating hospitals. But we need an attitudinal change so as to promote the development of hospitals or healthcare organisations in the rural areas or in the suburbs. If we find the opening of large sized specialized hospitals in the rural areas, the urban population would also be benefited because the location points for such hospitals would be easily accessible with the road or rail transportation services. A distance of 100 kms from the big towns and cities would not matter if we find all-weather proof roads and developed transportation facilities to and from the hospitals. With the opening of big hospitals, the development of villages would be channelised because new vistas would be opened for multidimensional developments. The accommodation facilities would open doors for the opening of hotels and apartments, shopping complexes, transportation services, communications services and so on. The availability of infrastructural facilities would make the villages potentially sound for showing the multiplier effects. The affluent sections or even the weaker sections living in the towns and cities would come for treatment which would change the economy of that region. The prices of even the agricultural produces would be increased which would benefit the poorer sections living in the villages. This makes it clear that hospitals or healthcare centres or organisations would be instrumental in transforming the economy of villages found till now backward.

While formulating a plan, it is also pertinent that the planners concentrate on the development of some of the centres, such as maternity centre, vaccination centre, immunisation centre, because we find high rate of mortality, specially in the rural areas mainly on that account. In villages where we don't find health centres, the healthcare personnel need to visit frequently and to refer the cases to the centres. Since we find the demand position increasing very fast mainly on account of the increasing rate of population, it is also important that family welfare centres are strengthened.

Of course, we find rural care centres facing the problem of financial constraint because the government is not to increase the financial support. This makes it essential that the charitable trusts and social organisations come forward and generate funds for the development of rural hospitals or healthcare centres. The requirements for healthcare personnel are also to be fulfilled and this makes it essential that the related doctors and nurses, paramedical staff live in the villages where they are posted. The villages in India need a plan based on the changing requirements.

Rural Healthcare Infrastructure

Of late, we find a sea change in the diagnostic and treatment devices. The increasing instrumentality of technology in the healthcare services makes it essential that the supporting infrastructural facilities are made available to the rural health centres or hospitals. The availability of power, water, communication, transportation facilities, diagnostic and treatment devices need due care. Whatever the qualitative improvements we find today in the healthcare services are considerably based on power and communication facilities. The hospital planners and the government policy makers need to expand the infrastructural support without an interruption.

At the time of independence, the healthcare services were mainly urban centred and hospital-based but now we find a change because the primary healthcare centres have been promoted. The current functional status of Primary Healthcare Infrastructure, Sub-centres, Primary Health Centres and the Community Health Centres make it essential that we enrich the infrastructural facilities. There is considerable backlog in terms of construction of buildings for subcentres and PHCs. Taking cognisance of the expanding disparities among the State in the availability of basic minimum services, the Conference of the Chief Ministers in July, 1996 recommended that Additional Central Assistance (ACA) may be provided by the states for correcting the existing gap in the provision of basic minimum services.[4] Of these, access to primary healthcare, safe drinking water and primary education were given higher priority with the mandate that universal access to these services would be achieved at the earliest possible but even till now, we don't find any concrete steps taken in the very context.

The channelisation of healthcare facilities in the rural areas makes it essential that the infrastructural facilities are made available to the rural hospitals and health centres on a priority basis. If we delay the process of enriching the infrastuctural facilities, the potentials of healthcare centres would hardly be tapped. We talk about sophisticated biomedical equipment. We also talk about the development of wards and the diagnostic centres. This makes it essential that infrastructural facilities in general and the power facilities in particular are given due weightage. Inappropriate location, poor access, lack of professional and nonprofessional healthcare staff, mismatch between the requirements and availability of health professionals, specially lack of funds for essential drugs and diagnosis and lack of First Referral Units (FRUs) for the linkage of referral services need an intensive care.

In view of the above, it is right to mention that rural healthcare services specially in the Indian perspective have been facing the problem of inadequacy of infrastructural facilities without which the healthcare services can't be of quality. It is against this background that we find the quality of healthcare services deteriorating rapidly. The hospital planners responsible for formulating an ideal plan, the consultants, the patients and attendants are required to be fully aware of the latest developments. Thus, the main thing in the process is to enrich the infrastructural facilities. This would enable quality technologies and personnel to be active in subserving the interest of the deprived of sections. There are a number of areas to be completed. The process would, course, be effective and we have no option but to enrich the infrastuctural facilities so that not only the government but even the private sector evinces interest in the process of generating and processing the rural healthcare services.

Healthcare Services

To promote healthcare facilities in the rural India, we find Public Health Centres playing a commanding role. The functions of PHCs according to the Department of Community Development are the following:

- Medical Care
- Maternal and Child Health Services
- School Health Services
- Family Welfare
- Control of Communicable diseases
- Environmental Sanitation
- Health Education and
- Collection of Vital Statistics.

The personnel to offer these services comprise a medical officer, a woman physician, a public health nurse, an health educator, a statistical clerk, a clerk-stenographer, a midwife,, a health inspector (Sanitation), a laboratory technician and several family planning field workers with a health assistant to assist the staff members.

Subcentres: We find subcentres an important rural primary healthcare infrastructure. The subcentres are being established on the basis of one subcentre for 5000 population in general and for every 3000 population in hilly, tribal and backward areas.

Primary Health Centres: We find Public Health Centres bearing the responsibility of offering healthcare services to the rural population on the basis of one PHC for every 30,000 population in the plains area and for every 20,000 population in the hilly, tribal and backward areas. However, there are marked disparities at the State and District levels. It is a matter of concern that many of the districts with poor health indices do not have adequate health infrastructure. There is a considerable backlog in terms of constitution of buildings for subcentres and Public Health Centres. Some states have been found adopting innovative measures including the mobilisation of local resources to clear the backlog. Involvement of the people's representatives, voluntary organisations and people themselves in these activities are to be promoted in the coming Five Year Plans.

While computing the requirements for the primary healthcare infrastructure for the increasing population, it is pertinent to increase the number of functionaries to cater to the needs of the population rather than increase in the number of centres. We find PHCs facing a number of problems and it is essential that we focus our attention on improving the functional potentials of centres. In a majority of the cases, we find locational problem because the centres are not easily accessible. They lack professional and para-professional staff and in addition, we also find the mismatch between the requirements and availability of health professionals, specially physicians at the Public Health Centres. Besides, lack of funds for essential drugs and diagnostic measures and lack of First Referral Units (FRUs) for linkage of referral services has been found aggravating the magnitude of problems. This makes it essential that we make possible qualitative improvements in the functional character of PHCs so that these centres substantially contribute to the process of developing the rural healthcare facilities.

Upgraded PHC: The establishment of rural hospitals with specialist facilities by upgrading the existing Public Health Centres would activate the process. The upgraded public health centres would have 30 beds. It is envisaged to cover a population of one lakh.

Community Health Centres are found not in a position to work as First Referral Units. In view of the serious implications of this lacuna in the establishment of a referral system as well as effective position of health MCH/FP care, there is an urgent need to rectify this. Improving the service conditions and providing a conducive environment is found essential so that specialists find themselves comfortable to work in the community health centres. We also find it essential that the community health centres need Public Health Specialists or anaesthetists to make possible emergency/routine surgery in the community health centres. The in-service candidates are to be trained in this speciality. It is pertinent to provide inter linkage between preventive, promotive and curative services in the CHCs. The health and family welfare programmes, disease surveillance and response mechanisms are required to be strengthened to improve the quality of services offered by the community health centres. We feel the need of specialists in public health to be posted in the community health centres and until they are posted, the existing specialists presently responsible for the curative services are required to be given Public Health orientation and training in Epidemiology and Health Management so that each one of them assumes the responsibility of looking after the Disease Control Programmes (DCP) in their respective areas of specialisation, e.g., Immunisation by paediatrician and FP by the obstetrician. This would be effective in improving the linkage between the PHCs and CHCs.

Tribal Healthcare

In the context of rural healthcare services, we find tribal areas getting a priority attention. The Scheduled Castes and Scheduled Tribes having the highest concentration in the North Eastern States and also in UTs of Lakshadweep and Dadra and Nagar Haveli and in the States of Madhya Pradesh, Orissa, Gujarat, Maharashtra and Bihar are found neglected where we find increased disease burden on account of poverty and undernutrition. The poor environmental sanitation, poor hygiene and lack of safe drinking water resulting into increased morbidity from water and vector-borne infections, lack of access to healthcare facilities, social barriers preventing utilisation of healthcare services and specific diseases found prone to genetic diseases are some of the critical problems necessitating a fresh look at the problems of tribal and hilly areas.

The healthcare planners and the policy makers need an innovative strategy to improve the quality of healthcare services to the tribal population. Ensuring availability of adequate infrastructure and personnel, Areas Specific RCH programme, 100% control plan funds of NMEP, effective implementation of the health and FW programmes and close monitoring, early detection of problems in implementation and midcourse correction need due weightage.

The main thing in the process is to study the changing problems and healthcare requirements and based on the findings to promote the healthcare devices so that the tribal population found till now neglected, get quality healthcare or medicare facilities. The problem in the tribal area is found of critical nature because the masses are illiterate and lack awareness. It is in this context that the preventive services are required to be made creative to sense the tribal population in the right direction.

Preventive Services

In the Indian rural society where the intensity of illiteracy is found at its peak, the social unconsciousness and unawareness make all our efforts insensitive. The masses don't assign any weightage to nutritional awareness, consumption of safe drinking water, pollution of noise and environmental conditions, irresponsible sexual behaviour, civic sense and waste management and this invites a number of health hazards. It is against this background that the most effective aspect for promoting rural healthcare services is to sensitise the society. The rural healthcare organisations/centres, in addition to the offering of curative services, also bear the responsibility of activating the preventive services so that the masses are found well aware of the living conditions increasing their resistance power to counter the health problems with a positive result. The preventive services focus our attention on the measures found instrumental in informing, educating and sensing the masses. If we turn our eyes on the disease profile of rural India, it is apparent that a majority of the diseases are found prone to food, water, sanitation, noise and environment pollution which would considerably be minimised if we find the hospitals, health centres, social organisations and media instrumental in increasing their awareness by making possible creativity in the advertisement and publicity measures.

The organisations, agencies and institutions bearing the responsibility of educating the society need to focus on the measures regulating their food habits, sanitation, civic sense, irresponsible sexual behaviour and so on. Of late, we find ourselves in a position to make the promotional measures more creative and it is high time that we realise their instrumentality and switch on the process. The sophisticated communication technologies, if used in a right fashion, the advertising professionals, if extend their best cooperation, the media, if come in action, the social organisations, if strengthen social regulations; we don't find any doubt in making the society healthier. Conversely, if we find all of them becoming insensitive, nothing can help them.

We find a number of provisions to offer to the rural population the healthcare devices. The rural healthcare centres are there, the media is there, the social organisations are there, the educational institutions are there but we find a big gap between the healthcare services assured and the health care services offered. It is this context that we need to strengthen the preventive measures. It is social participation; it is social regulation; it is multi-sector cooperation and coordination that would be effective in sensitising the rural society and we need to think in this direction.

Informing, educating and sensing the rural society would make an attack on the rural health problems. The diseases prone to food, water, sanitation, environmental pollution and unhealthy living conditions can be minimised to the extent that we even can't imagine. Of course, we need to enrich the healthcare measures but at the same time, our focus should also be on the preventive services benefiting the society fantastically but taxing the state exchequer very insignificantly.

The rural healthcare services thus need a fresh look, a new vision and an innovative strategy. In view of the increasing intensity of problem, we have no option but to activate multicornered measures. It is judicious that a majority of our population harnesses the benefits of developments taking place in the medical sciences.

Rural Healthcare Personnel

We agree with this view that in almost all centres of manufacturing goods or generating services, the human resources make a significant contribution and to be more specific, in the healthcare sector, we find them contributing very significantly. Of course, the technologies and infrastructural facilities influence their potentials but if they lack professional excellence and devalue personal commitments, even the world class technologies can't switch on the process of generating and processing quality healthcare services. It is against this background that we need due focus on the quality of healthcare personnel to be placed in villages. Since we go through the problem of rural healthcare services, it is pertinent that different categories of healthcare personnel placed at subcentres or health centres or at referral units are present on duty. We need due emphasis on this problem because we find a majority of the healthcare personnel though placed in villages attend the centres very casually. May be that they are professionally-sound but their professional excellence doesn't carry any meaning because they forget even the most essential condition that they are present.

Besides, it is also essential that the administration makes the working and living conditions for them conducive so that they get an opportunity to show their excellence. It is right to mention that by and large, almost all the health centres and referral units have been facing the problem of infrastructural facilities at the healthcare centres on a priority basis. The accommodation facilities for staff are also important and we need to develop the same so that the personnel don't have any excuse. The diagnostic and treatment management need due attention because in almost all the referral units, we don't find even small equipments and apparatus. What to talk of drugs and basis medical aids when we find the centres presenting a deserted look.

The doctors, paramedical staff, nursing staff or other personnel need due incentives to work in villages where a number of constraints are found. In a true sense, it is the prime responsibility of village panchayats to make it sure that the centres, subcentres and referral units are working as per the defined norms and conditions. The state exchequer is not in a position to make available to the hospitals or health centres even the basic healthcare facilities then what to talk of the advanced amenities and facilities. In view of the emerging problems, we have two options. First, let the centres and units suffer or second, make available to them at least the essential amenities and facilities to work. The masses are not in a position to afford the expensive medicare services of private hospitals and clinics. This makes it essential that the voluntary social organisations, corporate sector, public sector organisations, charitable trusts or others make efforts to make available to the centres and units the required infrastructural facilities and for which they need to generate funds locally.

The conditions at the workplace and the amenities and facilities at the living places play a significant role in motivating the employees. It is against this background that we make a strong advocacy in favour of mass-participation in the process because when rules, regulations, laws, acts, professional commitments become insensitive, the only option left in our hands is to activate social participation which bears the efficacy of synchronising professional and personal commitments. The healthcare personnel working or placed in the rural areas need to be monitored and controlled by the society and their incentive plans also need to be finalised by them because we need a solution in a system where all the subsystems are found collapsing.

Managing Finance for Rural Healthcare Services

We are well aware of the fact that state governments bear the responsibility of offering healthcare services to the society and against this background, we find the Health Department managed and controlled by the government. We find a budget and the different healthcare sectors, viz., primary, secondary and tertiary are financed by the government. In addition, we also find private sectors offering the healthcare services and charging fees for the services offered. Since we go through the problem of rural healthcare services where we find the contributions of private sector almost dismal, it is pertinent to think about the financial problem which has been found showing red, green and amber signals to all the sectors and units working either in the urban areas or in the rural areas. Nothing can happen unless we make available adequate finance. This in a natural way focuses our attention on the different constituents of financial management, specially for managing the rural healthcare services.

At the outset, we need to go through the problem of generation and mobilisation because the rural health centres and subcentres and the referral units operating in villages are found virtually non-existent. The healthcare personnel working there argue that they don't get any infrastructural support from the government and therefore, it is not possible for them to offer the healthcare services. On the other hand, we also find arguments from the government side that they provide everything but the personnel misuse and create artificial scarcity. Instead of justifying and countering arguments of both the sides, it is significant that we pave avenues for the generation of funds, specially to enrich the healthcare facilities in the rural areas where the masses have no option. All our developmental efforts become insensitive if we find the healthcare and educational services shrinking and degenerating.

At this juncture, we need to promote charity and donations and for that, the social reformists, cine artists and cricketers having a mass image are to be motivated. In almost all the villages, we find affluent sections and employees earning outside the villages and they should be approached and motivated to donate the best they can. If we find even poorest of the poor paying fees to the private hospitals much beyond their potentials, we don't find anything wrong in charging nominally from them as fees if they evince their interests in the process. The organisation of charity shows, cultural programmes, sports and dramas would also help the process of generation. To be more specific, the corporate sector needs to come ahead and to donate a very small percentage of their profits to the development of rural hospitals or health centres. We can't negate the fact that mass participation opens doors for mass control and supervision in which the employees don't get any option but to work and serve to the extent they can.

The aforesaid facts make it clear that the rural health centres and subcentres need mass support. We can't think of high level of efficiency, specially from the centres or units or hospitals facing multifaceted constraints. If we make available financial support, all the formalities and requirements would be completed and fulfilled because mass-generation regulates the process of misuse of funds, or mass-participation promotes productive utilisation. Thus, the financial management of rural healthcare centres needs a fresh look because we don't have any option. Instead of facing the problem of exploitation by the private clinics or hospitals, it is judicious, fair and ethical to charge reasonably from the users and to resolve their problems at the village levels because a majority of the problems are found not so much complicated if resolved at the very initial stage.

Marketing of Rural Healthcare Services

On the one hand, we find avenues for revenues shrinking while on the other hand, we find the responsibilities of healthcare centres mounting each and everyday. Of course, we find rural masses not in a position to pay for the healthcare services made available to them but the existent policy of offering free of charge services by the healthcare centres and subcentres would not only aggravate the magnitude of financial problem but would also degenerate the quality. It is against this background that we need to think about marketing of services which would make the ways for quantitative-cum-qualitative improvements, specially in the rural areas where the healthcare services present a very gloomy picture.

The marketing of rural healthcare services focuses our attention on a number of problems, viz., identifying the levels of expectations of users, information system, segmentation of market and tailoring of marketing inputs in the face of changing nature and character of health problems. The main focus in the process is found on making the healthcare services cost-effective found affordable even to the weaker sections of the society.[6] It is not essential that in all the cases and purposes, we need expensive drugs and medicines. It is not essential that for all the diseases, we need expensive diagnostic measures. We find avenues for making the healthcare processes cost-effective and to be more specific for rural India, this is likely to be an effective prescription. It is in this context that we find relevance of marketing not only for the big and large-sized hospitals working in the towns and cities but albeit for the small hospitals and health centres serving the rural society.

Of late, the marketing principles are considerably influenced by the holistic concept of management which makes it essential that even the private hospitals contribute significantly to the process of subserving the social interests. The government hospitals or health centres bear the responsibility of protecting the interests of public at large. In the process, we need formulation of a sound marketing mix. Of late, like the technocrats, even doctors need to have managerial excellence. The doctors leading the health centres, the secondary and tertiary hospitals assisting the health centres if assign due weightage to the principles of modern management, a large number of problems would smoothly be resolved.

While formulating the services mix, the doctors need to develop their knowledge about the specialities of the catchment or command area. This would let them know about the disease profile and the diagnostic and treatment plans to be formulated. In a majority of the villages, we find the problem of some special types of diseases prone to food, water, environmental pollution and irresponsible sexual behaviour. To be more specific related to women, we find diseases considerably linked to the large number of children and early marriage. The problem of under-nutrition due mainly to unawareness is found aggravating the magnituded of problem. The service mix of the catchment area would be based on the prevailing or emerging conditions. The poor sanitation services has also been found inviting a number of health problems. By formulating the service mix, the doctors or the healthcare personnel would concentrate on the services helping the population of a particular catchment area. In the face of emerging problems, the essential diagnostic and treatment measures would be developed. The doctors would prefer the drugs affordable to the masses.

Besides, the preventive services need an intensive care while formulating the service mix. The diseases found food-borne, water-borne, pollution-borne, sanitation-borne or so can be regulated, if we create mass awareness. The healthcare personnel in general and the doctors in particular need to educate the masses in a creative way.

In this context, the health centres and subcentres also need to make the promotional measures creative. The advertising professionals, the media, the educational institutions, the social reformists and voluntary social organisations are required to promote specially with the help of messages, slogans, campaigns bearing more creativity. A majority of the rural population faces health problems, specially on account of its own mistakes related to food, water and sanitation. This draws our attention on the formulation of a sound promotion mix, specially supported by the secondary and tertiary hospitals.

The rural health centres also need to think about the fee/pricing strategy. There is no doubt in it that a majority of the rural population is poor but at the same time, it is also right to mention that in a large number Indian villages, we find a few selected persons bearing the potentials of running a hospital then what to talk of soliciting their cooperation. The main thing is that the masses not in a position to pay are not required to pay but a few bearing the potentials of affording the expensive services, extend to the rural hospitals the maximum possible financial support which they can.

The rural hospitals and health centres are to be located at a point found smoothly accessible. We also find cases where particularly during the rainy seasons, the rural population finds it difficult to go to the health centre because we don't find all-weather proof roads. The healthcare personnel and the village panchayats need more care while selecting the location points for health centres. We expect the healthcare personnel to be honest and decent. To be more specific, the trained nurses and staff for maternity care need to have a decent behavioural profile so that women requiring the services are not found to be hesitant. In almost all the villages, where we find health centres, the services are not found to be hesitant. In almost all the villages, where we find health centres, the subsidised pharmacy is to be promoted, of course for the poorest of the poor.

The aforesaid measures would help smooth functioning of the health care centres. We need to make a goodbye to the assumptions that application of marketing principles would make the services expensive. Contrary to it, we find marketing principles to be practiced in the healthcare organisations or centres considerably influenced by the holistic concept of management in which we don't find a place for the commercial considerations. The hospitals or health centres practicing marketing would be found potentially sound and only sound persons or organisations can help others. If we find health centres or hospitals potentially weak, financially bankrupt and facing the problem of financial crunch, the ultimate sufferers would be the poor society because the affluent sections have a number of options.

Thus, the marketing principles, if practiced in a right fashion, would make hospitals and health centres sound enough to serve the masses. It is in this context that we make a strong advocacy in favour of marketing principles. Of late, we find private hospitals potentially-sound albeit in subserving the social interests and they can do more if the government hospitals and health centres make the environment competitive.

Rural Healthcare Management Control

We find control an important managerial responsibility very much instrumental in justifying the investments meant for channelising the healthcare services in the rural areas. Unless we control our investments, our results can't be made productive. It is against this background that we talk about testifying the rationale behind investments. We find subcentres, health centres and referral units and invest a lot on the personnel and other requirements. Since we talk about the services of healthcare organisations, the profitability is not to be adopted as a parameter to justify the investments. The important variable in the very context is healthcare services made available to the rural population. Another consideration is related to the levels of their satisfaction. If we find that the health centres or subcentres have been successful in offering the services to the extent of their potentials and the users or patients appear satisfied, the investments would be considered fruitful. Since the referral units bear the responsibility of referring the cases, it is to be evaluated on the basis of the cases they referred.

The control function of management focuses on evaluating the performance and based on the results identifying the positive and negative contributions of personnel and technologies used in the process. The personnel contributing significantly to the process are to be rewarded whereas the personnel making negative contributions are to be penalised. Since we don't find a well managed reporting system, the task of evaluating the performance is found much more complicated. To be more specific in the rural areas, the centres, subcentres and referral units have not been found performing satisfactorily. In a majority of the cases, we find healthcare personnel not on duty. So far as the healthcare materials are concerned in almost all the centres, the patients fail in getting even the facilities related to basic medical aid then what to talk of other diagnostic and treatment devices. The buildings meant for that purpose are found abandoned. The doctors prefer to live in the towns and cities. In a true sense, we don't find the rural healthcare services fruitful to the patients.

The aforesaid facts are a staunch testimony to this proposition that the rural healthcare services need to be managed and controlled by the professionals who would depend upon the reporting system made available by the village panchayats, social organisations and so on. This is based on the fact that the subdivisional and district hospitals have not been successful in managing and controlling the rural healthcare services. It is against this background that we find mass participation essential to manage and control the rural healthcare services because control by social regulations would force the healthcare personnel to be present at the workplaces meant for them. So far as the essential materials and inexpensive equipment and apparatus are concerned, the agencies and organisations bearing the responsibility of controlling the functional behaviour would make it sure that the patients have been getting the benefits. The direct reporting to the subdivisional or district hospitals would minimise the possibilities of misuse of funds.

It is really amazing that despite of a large number of health centres and subcentres, the rural population is forced to use the services of private clinics, quack and thus, are considerably exploited. This makes it essential that instead of increasing the number of health centres and sub-centres, we justify their relevance by channelising the services.

Thrust Areas in Rural Healthcare Management

Decades and decades of managing rural healthcare services make it clear that our policy planners, strategists and healthcare personnel need an attitudinal change. Of course, we have been channelising multidimensional investments for improving the quality of healthcare services of the rural population but even today, a majority of the population living in village fails in getting albeit the basic medicare services. The disease profile is becoming vulnerable and the public healthcare spending is found moving downward. Whatsoever the positive effects of techniculture and professional excellence that we find on the healthcare sector remain confined to the big towns and cities. We cannot deny the positive contributions of corporate sector to the healthcare services because we find a number of world class private hospitals very much instrumental in accelerating the pace of qualitative transformation but they have not been found sincere and honest to their societal role. The yawning gap between demand and supply position make makes it essential that we identify the thrust areas and develop a prescription to make an assault on the vulnerable problems. We cannot deny that launching of National Rural Health Mission on 12 April, 2005 (NRHM) was with the motto of improving the rural healthcare services at Village, Panchayat and Block levels and undoubtedly enough, we find some qualitative improvements but still they face numerous problems. It is against this background that we make a strong advocacy in favour of the following thrust areas:

Tribal Population Needs an Intensive Care: In the Indian perspective, we find high disease burden in tribals due to poverty and undernutrition, poor sanitation, non-availability of safe drinking water, genetic diseases, lack of awareness about healthy living conditions and access to healthcare and socio-economic barriers to the utilisation process. The SC and ST constitute about 17% and 1% respectively of the total population. The highest concentration is found in the North Eastern States and Union Territories of Lakshadweep and Dadara Nagar Haveli, M.P., Orissa, Gujarat, Maharashtra, Bihar, Jharkhand and Chhatisgarh.

The factors contributing to increased disease like G-6 PD deficiency infection (tawa) need due attention in the tribal areas.[7] The "Onges" in Andaman and Nicobar are a primitive tribe with very little access to education and healthcare. This makes it essential that the government policy makers formulate a differential area-specific strategy for each of the tribal areas to improve access and utilisation of health services.

Vulnerable diseases Need Concerted Efforts: In the rural areas of the country, we find a number of diseases instrumental in increasing the rate of morbidity. The vector-borne diseases such as Filariasis, Dengue, Japanese Encephalitis need to be controlled. We find Tuberculosis a major health problem in India. National Tuberculosis Programmes needs due attention. The National Leprosy Eradication Programme is also required to be strengthened.

The diseases like malaria and cholera increase the rate of morbidity in the rural areas. The sensitisation process is found essential to regulate the problem.

Sexually-transmitted diseases need due care: A large number of rural people go to big towns and cities for jobs and when they come back, we find them carrying AIDS due mainly to their irresponsible sexual behaviour. Increasing multi-partner sex and consequent increase in sexually-transmitted diseases and HIV infection in particular have been aggravating the intensity of problem and therefore, it is significant that health professionals keep on moving the sensitisation process so that mass awareness is developed.

Family Welfare Programme Needs due care: The birth rate is found high particularly in the illiterate rural segment which increases the intensity of demographic pressure and proves to be an important reason for the expansion of disease profile and draws our attention on the motivational and demotivational measures. We need to motivate the rural population for regulating the birth rate and in addition, we also need to demotivate those who become a party to the population problem. To be more specific, the rural women segment is found the worst sufferer which necessitates additional incentives to them and in addition, proper education for developing awareness. The creative promotional measures may be much more effective in sensitising the rural women.

Immunisation Programme to be Promoted: Vaccines are the most effective agents for controlling the communicable diseases. In a true sense, a revolution is needed on the vaccinology front. The immunisation programme is to benefit the society in many ways. The Universal Immunisation Programme (UIP) has been aimed at a healthier 21st century. Of course, we are doing well on the front of Polio, however, the results are not found to be very impressive. The rural masses lack awareness and perceive some confusions regarding the Polio Vaccine which requires due support of health professionals. In addition, we also need to promote vaccine for "Hepatitis B" which is found very dangerous. Typhoid is another problem and the medical scientists bear the responsibility of developing economic oral vaccine. If we succeed in promoting the vaccination and immunisation culture, this will minimise the problem of disease specially in the rural areas.

Creativity in Healthcare Promotion: We cannot deny that a number of diseases in the rural areas are food-prone, water-prone, pollution-prone and sanitation-borne which can be minimised to the desired level if healthcare professionals make use of creative promotional measures for sensitising them. The publicity measures may be much more effective and for that, we can solicit the cooperation of media people and academics. The social advertising measures initiated by the corporate sector my also be effective in developing mass awareness. The policy makers, the media, social organisations, global welfare organisations and the healthcare professionals need to play a meaningful role in initiating and activating the sensitisation process. The social evils such as liquor consumption, tobacco chewing, cigarette smoking, child marriage, poor sanitation, nutritional deficiency and high birth rate may be regulated with the help of social advertising.

Healthcare Insurance needs due attention: Particularly for protecting the poor, it is pertinent that we make provision for Healthcare Insurance. We cannot deny that the coverage of health insurance in government and private sectors cover around 11% of the population.[8] The existing Employees State Insurance Scheme, Central Government Health Scheme and Ex-Servicemen Contributory Health Scheme provide services to individual workers, government employees and ex-Armed Forced along with their families. Mediclaim covers mainly the upper-middle income groups. Private Health Insurances Schemes are mainly urban oriented and they have problems like unaffordable rate of premium, delay in settling claims, non-transparent procedures in deciding reimbursements, etc. This focuses on encouraging community risk-pooling. In this context, the local government would identify population at risk and would provide a revolving fund to be managed by a consortium of SHGs. This consortium would also encourage small savings by households and would pay needy households a cash support of Rs. 5,000 to Rs. 10,000 for hospitalization, catastrophic illness and death. The Community Based Health Insurance Schemes coupled with behavioural change campaigns and other interventions increase the quality of healthcare. Easy and low cost accessibility to healthcare protect the households from indebtedness arising from high medical expenditure forcing the weaker sections to borrow. We can implement these schemes in areas where institutional capacity is too weak to organise mandatory nationwide risk pooling. ACCORD, BAIF, karuna, Trust, Self Employed Women's Association (SEWA), DHAN Foundation and VHS are some of the examples. The motive is to protect and promote the interests of weaker sections of the society preferably living in the rural areas of the country.

Human Resources for Health need due weightage: Ensuring availability of medical professionals in rural areas on a permanent basis, posting of doctors with adequate monetary as well as non-monetary incentives such as suitable accommodation, class I Status, preferential school admissions for children of doctors living in remote areas, transfer or posting of choice after a stipulated length of stay and training opportunities need due attention of government policy makers. We cannot deny that doctors and paramedical staff do not prefer to go to the rural areas and therefore, unless we provide to them lucrative incentives, our all efforts for enriching the healthcare services in the rural areas would turn into a fiasco. In almost all the villages, we find shortage of all key cadre such as doctors, paramedical, ANMs, Nurses, Lab Technicians and OT Assistants.[9] This focuses our attention on improving the supply position by innovating motivational schemes.

Drug Accessibility and Affordability need due care: The rural masses need to be sensitized regarding the availability of drugs and medicines. Access to essential drugs and medicines form a substantial portion of the out-of-pocket spending on health by households. A system of guaranteeing essential drugs is considered an essential component of enriching primary healthcare services.[10] Timely supply of drugs of good quality involving procurement as well as logistics management is of critical importance in any health system.

Making Healthcare Services Affordable: The sophisticated developments in the field of medical sciences made ways for new generation of technology which increased the costs on diagnosing and treating the patients and made the services much more expensive. The rural poor required low cost technologies so that the services were found affordable to them. It is significant that we find technological solutions for making crucial equipments affordable such as anaesthesia machine, surgical equipment and lighting, sterilization equipment, defibrillator, ventilator, electrocardiogram (CG), blood pressure monitoring equipment, pulse oxymeter, etc. Our scientists and researchers need to develop indigenous technologies which would minimise the costs on healthcare services. The public health related technologies are to be used at all levels which may help preventing outbreaks of water borne diseases, maternal mortality related to unsafe deliveries and postpartum infections, anaemia, preventing acquisition of malaria and deaths due to childhood pneumonias, etc. Thus, inventions and innovations in the field of public health related technologies need to be promoted by the medical colleges and institutes so that the benefits of techniculture are harnessed even by the poor rural segment of the country. We need to publicise and practice the experiences of Jan Swasthya Sahyog (JSS) initiated by a group of dedicated young doctors from institutes like AIIMS, CMC, Vellore for making healthcare services available, affordable and accessible to the rural population[11]. We cannot deny that JSS technology has been successful in developing cheap, accurate and easy to use technology which can be used for prevention, diagnosis and treatment of diseases in remote tribal areas of different States. It has made the healthcare services much more economic because we find early detection of UTIs costing less then Rs. 2 per test, anaemia Rs. 1, diabetes Rs. 2, pregnancy Rs. 3. They have also developed low cost mosquito repellent creams, breath counters for detection of pneumonia among children, easy to read BP instruments to prevent preeclampsia and a simple water purification method whereby one can cycle for 15 minutes and get a bucket of potable water treated by UV light. Like this, a number of indigenous technologies may be invented which would protect and promote the larger interests of weaker sections of rural society.

e-Health needs priority attention: During the yesteryears, we have witnessed significant developments in the field of information and communication technology which has paved avenues for telemedicine, telediagnosis and teleconferencing for multi-dimensional uses. With the development of e-Health, it has been possible to set up a National Grid to be shared by healthcare providers, trainers, beneficiaries and civil society. Since we find the country having the advantage of a strong fibre backbone and indigenous satellite communication technology with trained human resources in this regard, it is easier for the government to make the e-Health devices much more popular. It is significant to mention that a number of pilot projects on e-Health have been set up by private concerns, corporate, NGOs, medical colleges and research institutions which may benefit the rural population in different ways.

Telemedicine may help to bring specialised healthcare to the remotest corners of the country. This may also provide the advantages of telediagnosis specially in the areas of cardiology, pathology, dermatology and radiology. Additionally, it may help in initiating qualitative improvements while innovating medical education. It is significant that even primary healthcare services make use of the benefits of e-Health. The disease surveillance, tele-consultations, health helpline, district hospitals referral net and e-enabled mobile medical units are possible with the help of e-Health. Additionally, the Geographical Information System, Resource Mapping of various health facilities, Laboratories, Training Centres and Health Manpower would also help in optimising the requirements. We cannot deny that the government policy makers need to promote e-Health particularly in the rural areas where the mobile telemedicine vans would benefit the rural and remote hospitals across the country through its geostationary satellites.

High concentration on AYUSH: We find AYUSH now emerging as an industry. Ayurveda, Yoga, Naturopathy, Unani, Siddha and Homoeopathy are the different constituents of AYUSH. In a country like India, where we find general masses not in a position to afford the increasing healthcare spending, it is pertinent that the government policy makers assign due weightage to AYUSH. The rural population would considerably be benefited with AYUSH if we find government strengthening professional education, promoting strategic research programmes and best clinical practices, initiating the process of technological sophistication, setting internationally accepted pharmacopoeic standards, conserving medical flora, fauna, metals, minerals with the ultimate aim of enhancing the outreach of AYUSH healthcare to be accessible, acceptable and affordable to the interested segments in general and the rural segment in particular. The focus must be on integrating AYUSH with the NRHM. We cannot deny that such integration would enhance quality and outreach of NRHM.

Other Key Areas: In addition to the above, the government policy makers need to make it sure that the geographically delineated rural areas are covered by all the three tier of primary healthcare institutions. In this context, it is also pertinent that we accord top priority to bridge the gap created in the CRH and FRU by restructuring and strengthening the existing block level PHCs, rural hospitals and subdivisional hospitals. All the FRUs need to ensure that specialised and trained medical and paramedical personnel are available in specialities like medicine, surgery, obstetrics, pediatrics and anaesthesia.

In the face of mounting intensity of rural health problem, it is significant that the corporate sector comes forward and accepts the responsibility of improving the quality of healthcare services. The poorest of the poor need priority attention. We need to strengthen our realisation that holistic concept of management would change the face and image of National Rural Healthcare. There is no doubt in it that the NRHM would open new avenues for the development of rural healthcare services. Healthcare management would help in achieving the mission in the larger interests of society, specially living in villages and getting the lowest share in the transformation process.

SUMMARY

In this chapter, you have gone through the problem of rural healthcare services. After going through the chapter, be sure that the following facts are well versed.

Rural Healthcare Services—the Genesis: After the attainment of independence in 1947 and to be more specific after the beginning of Five Year Plans, the contours of development underwent radical changes but the benefits of development could not be harnessed by the poor rural population. This necessitates an intensive care on rural healthcare services.

Management of Rural Healthcare Services: We need management orientation in developing and channelising the rural healthcare services. This gravitates our attention on different constituents, viz., Rural Healthcare Information, Rural Healthcare Planning, Rural Healthcare Infrastructure, Rural Healthcare Services, Rural Healthcare Personnel, Rural Healthcare Finance, Rural Healthcare Marketing and Rural Healthcare Control. By managing these constituents professionally, we expect qualitative-cum-quantitative improvements in the rural healthcare services which even till now have been found neglected.

Managing Information: We need a feedback, we need reporting and the information and communication technologies are to be used for this purpose.

Rural Healthcare Planning: We need to estimate the requirements and to develop the potentials helping us in fulfilling the healthcare requirements of the rural population.

Rural Healthcare Infrastructure: We need to enrich the infrastructural facilities by making available power, water, communication, transportation, buildings, biomedical equipment, educated and trained healthcare personnel.

Rural Healthcare Services: We need to assign due weightage to the curative, diagnostic and preventive services.

Rural Healthcare Personnel: The healthcare personnel are required to live in the villages or the catchment or command areas where they are posted. The inadequacy of personnel is required to be removed.

Rural Healthcare Marketing: We need to manage and market the rural healthcare services professionally. This would make possible cost-effectiveness and would let us know the changing requirements of a particular catchment area. We need to tailor the marketing input in the face of changing requirements.

Rural Healthcare Control: It is also pertinent that we develop a feedback system with the help of sophisticated information and communication technologies and make an appraisal of the performance of personnel and technologies used for the rural healthcare services.

Thrust Areas: In the thrust areas, we find focus on tribal health, vulnerable diseases, sexually transmitted diseases, family welfare measures, immunisation programme, cost-effective healthcare services and creativity in the healthcare promotion.

The mounting healthcare spending makes it essential that the government policy makers promote low cost indigenous technologies, AYUSH and make the rural healthcare services affordable to the poor people living in the rural areas. In an age of new generation of information and communication technology, the policy makers need to promote e-Health so that the services like telemedicine, teleconferencing, telediagnosis, etc. help the rural population in different ways. In addition, availability of quality and economic drugs, health insurance schemes and quality human resources cannot be undermined.

KEY TERMS

Public Healthcare Spending	Hepatitis B
Primary Healthcare	e-Health
Mortality	Jan Swasthya Sahog
AYUSSH	Postpartun
AHSA	Medicinal Flora
NRHM	Fauna
Rural healthcare information	Geographical Info System
First Referral Units	Resourse Mapping
Disease Control Programme	Environmental Sanitation
Immunisation	Primary Health Centres
Vaccination	Community Health Centres
Onges	Healthcare Spending
Universal Immunisation Programme	Indigenous Technology

REVIEW QUESTIONS

1. Explain the constituents helping the management of rural healthcare services in Indian perspective.
2. Discuss the instrumentality of curative and preventive measures for improving the quality of services in rural India.
3. Explain the importance of information system in managing the rural healthcare services.
4. Focus on the development of rural healthcare infrastructure for improving the quality of healthcare services in the rural India.
5. Explain the role of finance for managing healthcare services in village India.
6. Focus on the relevance of quality people for improving the quality of healthcare services in rural India.
7. Explain the relevance of marketing for improving the healthcare services in rural areas of the country.
8. Make an appraisal of healthcare services in rural India.
9. Focus on the thrust areas for enriching healthcare services in the rural areas of the country.

APPLICATION EXERCISES

1. "A majority of us feel that the rural healthcare services need managerial proficiency." Comment on this statement and throw light on the constituents you need to manage for making available to the rural masses quality healthcare services.

2. "While managing rural healthcare services, you, as a health professional need to assign due weightage to rural healthcare infrastructural facilities required for enriching the rural healthcare services in the Indian perspective.
3. As a health professional, throw light on the preventive measures you will adopt for sensitising the rural population found illiterate and unaware.
4. "The most critical factor in managing the rural healthcare services is finance. ":In the face of this statement, explain the measures to be adopted for mobilizing the financial resources particularly when the public healthcare spending is found decreasing.
5. "The location of large-sized speciality hospital in the rural areas would show multiplier effects. "Comment on this statement and in the capacity of a hospital professional, suggest the measures you would initiate to locate hospitals in the rural areas.
6. "Rural healthcare personnel need not only be thematically sound but in addition, personally-committed, value-based and human-oriented. "Comment on this statement in the capacity of a health professional.

END NOTES

1. *Nabhil's Ninth Five Year Plan*, Vol. I, pp.446-47
2. Goel, S.L. *Administration of Rural Hospitals;* Hospital Administration, Vol. III, p.11
3. *Nabhi's op.cit* p.451
4. *Ibid*
5. *India Depptt. of Community Development*, 1960, Primary Healthcare, Faridabad
6. Jha, S.M. *Social Marketing*, Himalaya Publishing House, Mumbai, 2009.
7. Nabhil's op. cit. p.455
8. *Eleventh Five Year Plan*; Planning Commission; Government of India, New Delhi, Vol. II, p. 82
9. *Eleventh Five Year Plan*: Vol. II, p. 96.
10. *Eleventh Five Year Plan*: Vol.II, p. 76
11. *Eleventh Five Year Plan*: Vol.II, p.86.

Strategic Management of Hospitals

Issues of strategic nature instrumental in improving the quality and minimising the costs gravitate priority attention of health professionals. Affordable and world class services make it essential that we are strategically and tactically sound. Providing First World Services at Third World Costs would help India an internationally acclaimed healthcare brand.

CHAPTER OBJECTIVES

Introduction—Strategy: the Perception—Strategic Management—Steps in the Formulation and Implementation of Strategy—Strategy Implementation—A Successessful Implementation Strategy—The Situation Analysis and TOWS Matrix—Strategic Issues in the Management of Hospitals—Summary—Key Terms—Review Questions—Application Exercises—End Notes

LEARNING OBJECTIVES

This chapter aims at studying the different dimensions of strategic management in the context of healthcare services. The readers develop their awareness of steps involved in the process of formulating and implementing strategy. Since we witness multidimensional changes in the disease profile, it is pertinent that health professionals design a strategy which is to meet the requirements of urban as well as the rural population. Bridging the qualitative and quantitative gaps in the healthcare requirements is the crying need of the hour.

Introduction

Affordable healthcare services is our objective. World class healthcare services is our target. Making the society absolutely disease-free is required to be our avowed mission.

It is our professional excellence that helps us in touching the target and accomplishing the objectives. It is our personal commitment that helps us in achieving the mission. And if we blend both of them in an optimal fashion, our managerial proficiency helps hospitals or healthcare organisations in establishing leadership and developing India as a global healthcare brand where professionals would be required to prove their excellence as a star or super performer. By developing world class professional excellence and managerial proficiency; by developing a temptation for showing personal-touch in service and ethical dimensions and more so, by developing a craze for humanised behaviour, we enrich our potentials and prove to be a star performer which helps us in showing some wonders.

The contours of development have undergone radical changes particularly during the yester-decades. On the one hand we have been successful in innovating quality healthcare services while one the other hand, we have also engineered a sound foundation for the development of a number of new diseases. On the one hand, we find corporate hospitals offering world class services while on the other hand, we also find a number of private hospitals cheating patients and exploiting them. We cannot negate that presently the benefits of development remain confined to the big cities and towns where world class hospitals offer quality services to the users. Five star hospitals cannot serve our purpose. Mounting insensitivity, changing disease profile, decreasing public healthcare spending and increasing personal health spending need priority attention of national health policy makers.

As and when we break the law of nature, our actions, sins and mistakes result into the development of a new disease. We are heavily punished and penalized for our mistakes and wrong decisions but don't prefer to obey the law of nature and unless and until the process of breaking the law of nature keeps on moving, the disease profile would continue to be much more complicated. We have polluted the environment; we have contaminated the water; we have frequently been taking pesticides-based food items; we do not regulate irresponsible sexual behaviour and we have also been advocating and legalising unnatural sex which is not prevalent albeit in the animal society. Unless we regulate our behaviour; unless we stop the process of disobeying the law of nature, the pace would continue to move forward without any break. Of course, we need to promote research so that innovative developments take place in the medical sciences but the most important thing in the process is to educate and sense the general masses in a creative fashion.

Of late, we find the Indian society facing a number of challenges. The mounting intensity of population, the harmful environmental influences of non-optimal developments, the decreasing respect for nature, the increasing temptation for animal culture if not regulated would make our tasks so much complicated that even medical scientists and world class doctors would find it difficult to resolve the same. It is against this background that we focus on the strategic management of hospitals and healthcare organisations.

The formulation of a sound strategy for hospitals is found important to improve the quality of healthcare services. We find hospital professionals bearing the responsibility of formulating and implementing the strategies. They are required to be aware of the changing requirements and expanding or contracting potentials so that a gap between the demand and supply is bridged. Strategic decisions are found at all the three levels viz. top-level or corporate-level strategy, middle-level or business-level strategy and operational or functional-level strategy. Because we find hospitals facing a number of challenges mainly on account of resource crunch, it is the responsibility of policy makers that to be more specific at the corporate-level, the strategic decisions pave new avenues for improving the financial health of hospitals. Particularly in the government hospitals, it is pertinent that the government policy makers bring a change in the policy decisions. The private hospitals in general and the corporate hospitals in particular also need an attitudinal change, specially while innovating the strategic decisions in the face of holistic concept of management so that not only the affluent sections of the society but even the weaker sections harness the benefits of qualitative improvements. In addition, the hospital managers need to bring a change in the business-level strategy so that the functional strategies are found to be proactive.

The formulation of strategy makes it essential that hospital professionals are aware of the emerging trends in the demand and supply. Since we find the intensity of demographic pressure increasing very fast, there would be a significant increase in the healthcare requirements of increasing population. It is in this context that hospital organisations would be required to improve the supply position by enriching their potentials. The boardrooms need to notice the problems because an increase in the potentials would require huge financial investment on different heads. Besides, the latest developments in the medical sciences have been found increasing the level of expectations of patients and attendants and this makes it essential that hospitals and healthcare organisations going ahead with the traditional technologies replace new generation of sophisticated technologies or develop low cost indigenous technology. Because the projects are to be capital intensive, the policy makers would be required to change the strategic decisions. To be more specific in the Indian perceptive, the hospitals and healthcare organisations need to make the services cost-effective so that the healthcare services are affordable. The hospital professionals having world class excellence can make it possible.

For the formulation of a sound strategy to ensure the development of hospitals, it is essential that a hospital manager undertakes situational analysis which would develop his or awareness of the actual potentials and the potentials required to deliver quality healthcare services. A change in the disease profile is found significant to quantify the strengths and weaknesses. The strategic decisions cannot be identical for the urban and rural masses. We find high rate of insensitivity in the rural community and therefore, the health professionals need to focus on preventive measures so that food-prone, water-prone, sanitation-prone, population-prone and noise prone diseases show a downward tend. The marketing dimension of healthcare services becomes significant in the very context.

The formulation of strategy, of course, is found significant but if we find the implementation process lacking professional excellence and the desired results cannot be achieved. The implementation process requires a team of dedicated medical, paramedical, technical and other required staff. Formulation of a team becomes important to generate team spirit and nurture team culture. The health professionals need to make sure that thematically-sound, personally committed, value-based and human-oriented people have been included in the team who are like minded and lack attitudinal variations. In the healthcare service, time element and behavioural dimension determine the targeted results.

We target a healthy 21st century. We need physically and mentally sound people. We require quality healthcare services both for the rural and urban masses on equal footing. The formulation and implementation of strategies would help hospital and healthcare organisations in many ways. Hence, the most important consideration that we find essential for fulfilling the target is the qualitative and quantitative transformation in the healthcare services. The primary, secondary and tertiary hospitals; the government as well as the private hospitals and albeit the corporate hospitals need to contribute to the process of improving the quality and minimising the cost. Accessibility and affordability need priority attention in the very context.

We cannot deny that India is developing as a healthcare destination and emerging as a global healthcare brand but establishment of small affluent islands around the vast sea of backwardness cannot serve our purpose. Synchronisation of modern and traditional systems, expensive and low cost indigenous technologies may improve the supply position. Creativity in promotional measures may bring contraction in the demand position. Thus, expansion and contraction are the two important facets necessitating due attention.

STRATEGY : THE PERCEPTION

A majority of us are not aware of the concept of strategy. It is a term coined from the military discipline. Strategy can be defined from the two different perspectives, vis. what an organisation intends to do and what an organisation eventually does. The firs perspective about strategy is the broad programme for defining and achieving and organisation's objective and implementing the mission.[1]

The second perspective about strategy is the pattern of the organisation's responses to the environment over time.[2]

Thus, we find strategy the broad programme for defining and achieving an organisation's objectives and further the mission of an organisation and in addition, the response of an organisation to its environment over time. Since we find change a natural phenomenon, a manager is required to go through the multidimensional changes taking place in the business environment. The objectives are considerably influenced by the emerging trends in the environmental conditions. Every organisation responsive to its nature and character has a strategy. It is quite natural that while going through the strategy, we keep in our minds both the perspectives. Prioritising and reprioritising the objectives become essential to survive and thrive.

The word, *"Strategy"* comes from the Greek *"Strategia"* which means the art and science of being a *"General."* The Greeks experienced the importance of Generalship in winning and losing the battles. Effective Generals needed to define the purpose of leading an army, winning, holding territory, protecting a city from invasion, wiping out the enemy and so forth. Each kind of objective required a different deployment of resources—different programmes. Gradually, the Greeks also realised that strategy is more than just fighting battles because effective Generals need to determine the right times of supply and to decide when to fight and when not to fight and manage the army's relationships with citizens, politicians and diplomats. Efficient generals not only need to plan but also to act well. Dating back to the Greeks, the concept of strategy thus could be integrated with planning and decision making.[3]

The aforesaid facts make it clear that the formulation of strategy is significant to an organisation and tailing it, we can't expect the plans to be effective, the objectives to be accomplished and the mission to be achieved. It is due mainly to the fact that we find strategy occupying a place of outstanding significance in almost all the organisations.

We also find strategy a "*game plan*"[4]. Here, our focus is on the fact that in a playground, all the players playing football have a target to move forward to the goal post. The players make efforts to touch the target and for that, the selected ways may be different depending upon the strategies of the opponents. The strategy in a true sense is thus found to be the way that we select for touching the target. Of course, the selection of a particular way is influenced by the professional excellence of a manager because even the opponents also follow a strategy. The main thing is to counter the challenges and to opt for offensive or defensive strategies keeping in view the choice or decision of the opponent.

The formulation of a strategy is thus found to be a difficult as well as a challenging task and like other organisations, the healthcare organisations also need to follow a strategy.

STRATEGIC MANAGEMENT—THE PERCEPTION

The term "strategic management" focuses our attention on managing an organisation with the help of an action plan which is found based on the changing organisational objectives redefined in the face of recent changes in the business environment. In this context, we find strategic decisions playing a significant role in planning and decision making and further implementation process for the strategic plan includes strategic control that helps a manager in accomplishing the organisational objectives within the limited time frame and budgetary limitations. A number of experts, no doubt, have gone through the problems of strategic management but Charles Hofer and Dan Schendel have surveyed the resulting literature in order to arrive at a composite definition and a strategic management approach.[5] They developed the following definitions which includes four components, viz.:

- The need to match products or markets with geographic territories or scope.
- Need to deploy a large quantity and variety of resources, both human and materials.
- Need to recognize and size competitive advantages.
- Need to convince a complex variety of functional divisions that departmental cooperation is better for overall organisational performance than isolated departmental activity.[6]

The aforesaid facts make it clear that overall designs of the organisation can be described only if objectives are included to policy and strategy as one of the key factors in management's operation of the organisational activities that we find in the process of strategic management. It is also right to make it clear that the implementation of strategy is found a strategic management process basically found to be an administrative task. It is significant that while formulating the strategy, we take into account the goals and strategy of an organisation. Finally, we find the strategic control which is a process of checking the implementation process in the face of the strategic plan already formulated. Once a strategy is to be implemented, its progress must be monitored.

In view of the above, it is right to mention that in the management of strategy, we find three important aspects, e.g., formulation of strategy, implementation and control of strategy and a manager, not particular to the different aspects, finds it difficult to accomplish the organisational goals. It is in this context that we find strategic decisions significant to the smooth functioning and desired development of an organisation.

Here, we talk about strategic management in the context of hospitals or healthcare organisations and this makes it essential that a healthcare manager is well aware of the multi-dimensional changes in the environmental conditions. The changing disease profile, diagnostic and treatment devices make it essential that our strategic decisions related to the management of hospitals redefine the objectives and reprioritise the requirements and potentials so that they are in a position to cater to the increasing healthcare requirements of the society. Since we find masses belonging to the poor segment, it is pertinent that the strategic decisions promote cost-effectiveness in the generation and processing of services. The process would make the healthcare services affordable. The innovative preventive services would sensitise the masses and they would be sensed in the right directions.

Levels of Strategic Management

We find three levels in the strategic management[7] such as corporate-level strategy, line or business-level strategy and operational strategy or functional-level strategy as presented in Fig. 15.1.

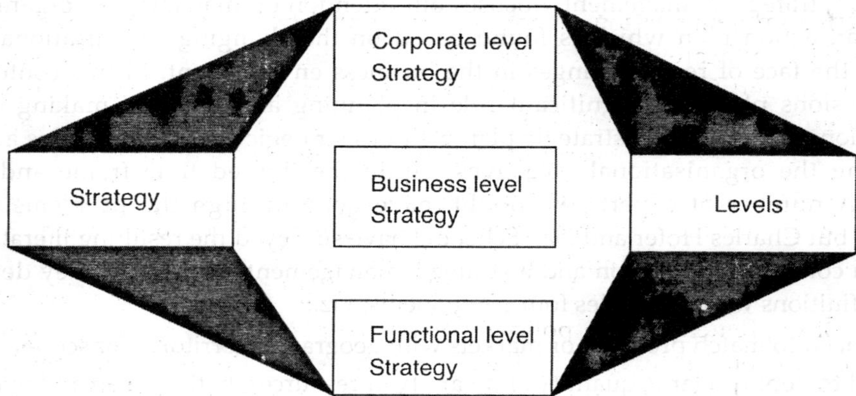

Fig. 15.1. Levels of Strategic Management

Corporate level Strategic Management: The corporate level strategy in a very natural way is formulated by the top-level management and therefore, we also call it top management-level strategy. We find strategic management vitally significant at the corporate or top-level management. It is right to mention that strategy at the top-level is found related to the sensitive problems such as different types of innovative services included or to be included in the service profile and the management of resources for them, specially the allocation of resources which makes it impact generating that the top management is fully convinced with the services to be eliminated, and services to be included. Of late, we find technologies very much instrumental in diagnosing and treating the patients and therefore, the rationale behind the use of innovative technologies for the generation or processing of services would also be taken into care. We are aware of the fact that top management-level strategy would take into consideration the financial health of the organisation and new avenues to be tapped because the hospitals and healthcare organisations now need expensive biomedical equipment, instruments, apparatus and machines to improve the quality of services. This makes it essential that the boardrooms are well aware of the latest developments taking place in the medical sciences vis-a-vis the changing disease profile of the command area and the potentials of hospital or healthcare organisations to counter the same.

Middle level Management Strategy: As and when we find a change in the strategic decisions taken by the top management, it is quite natural that we find their effects on the middle-level management. We also call it business-unit strategy. The strategic decisions in the very context and at this level are found concerned with managing the interests and operations of a particular business in a particular organisation. He/she while making the strategic decisions is required to know about the intensity of competition, the strategic decisions of the competitive healthcare organisations, the service mix to be offered, the segment or catchment area found in need of the services offered and managing all the functional areas, such as managing information, managing behavioural profile, managing healthcare personnel, managing marketing and so on. A strategic business unit groups together all business activities within a multi-business corporation that produces a particular type of product. We find hospital managers or healthcare managers managing the strategic decisions keeping in view a number of factors necessitating the innovation process.

He/she bears the responsibility of gauging the changing level of expectations of patients and attendants and managing the functional decisions accordingly. To make possible time honoured and cost-effective implementation of policies formulated by the top-level management, it is pertinent that the healthcare managers are not only professionally-sound but even personally-committed. Setting and framing of guidelines are done by the top-level management, whereas following the guidelines and implementing the same with the support and cooperation of supervisor or operative level management are expected from the middle level.

Functional-level or Operational-level Strategy: The task of implementing the policies falls on the shoulders of the healthcare managers but unless they act at the cooperation of functional-level, the task would remain much more difficult. The different categories of healthcare personnel, paramedical staff, other personnel instrumental in generating the services bear the responsibility of implementing the policies with the support and guidance of the healthcare managers. The functional level strategy creates the framework for the management functions, such as finance, research and development, management of healthcare personnel and marketing.

The aforesaid levels of strategic management make it clear that for the time-honoured and cost-effective accomplishment of organisational objectives, we need all the three level thinking and working together with the aim of achieving the mission. In the hospitals or healthcare organisations, we find a number of problems of diverse nature and character. Of late, we find the healthcare services of expensive nature and the masses are not in a position to afford the expensive diagnostic and treatment services. It is in this context that we find integration essential so that all of them devise ways to offer affordable curative services and innovative preventive services. We can't negate the fact that whatever the policy decisions we find at the government levels have not been successful in making the services cost-effective. There is no doubt in it that the private hospitals in a majority of the cases are found serious to the quality but the services become so expensive that the masses find it difficult to afford. This necessitates a basic change in the strategic decisions of top-level management at both the levels or in both the sectors.

The most important thing in the process is found related to the formulation of strategy and the changing healthcare requirements and the latest developments in the medical sciences make it essential that strategic decisions are given a fresh look. Unless we innovate the strategic decisions, the qualitative or quantitative improvements would hardly be possible. It is against this background that an indepth study of the different dimensions and steps is found impact-generating.

Steps in the Formulation and Implementation of Strategy

There are a number of steps involved in the process of formulating and implementing the strategy and a manager is required to be aware of the same as mentioned in Fig. 15.2.

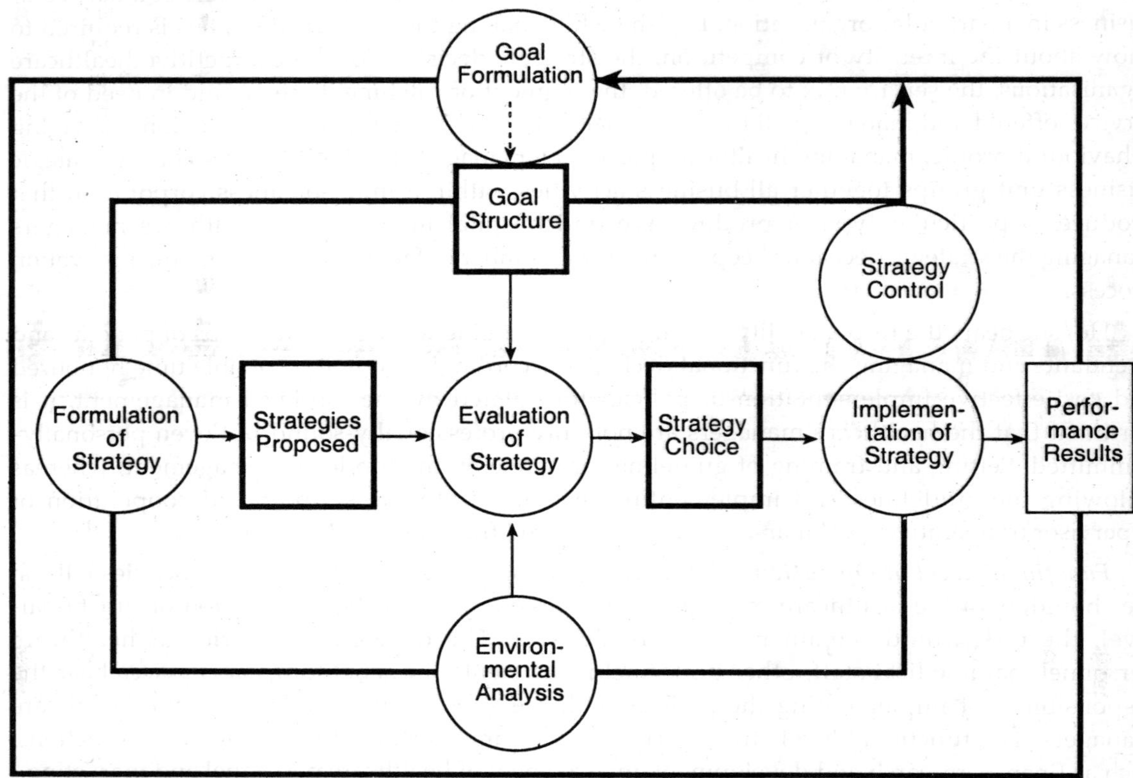

Fig. 15.2. Steps in the Formulation and Implementation of Strategy

First Step: The Formulation of Goal: The first step is the formulation of a goal and a healthcare top-level manager is required to set the goals of hospitals or healthcare organisations. It is right to mention that the middle-level management strategy is found instrumental in the process because the goals need to be formulated in the face of resources or potentials and this key responsibility is found on upper level managers. In any organisation, the setting of goal occupies a place of outstanding significance because if you don't know where you are going, then any road will take you there. The perception of strategy makes it essential that we start the process with some sense of which road we want to go down. The answer to this question goes by various means like *"mission", "objective", "goal", 'purpose."* It is right to mention that the formulation of goal includes reviewing and understanding the organisation's purpose, defining its mission and establishing the objectives that translate the mission into concrete terms. Thus, the key steps in the process of formulation of goal is defining the mission of the healthcare organisation. At the very outset, it is mentioned that hospitals or healthcare organisations need to work with the mission of making you highly resistive of the diseases. l he dream of quality, affordable and quick healthcare services can't be a speculation. Before deciding what their objectives are going to be, the hospital or healthcare managers must know the purpose and mission. This makes it essential to know that out of the available diagnostic, curative and preventive services which one to be eliminated and which one to be continued.

Second Step: Identification of Current Objectives and Strategy: After the setting of goals, the second step is related to the identification of current objectives and strategy. Once the mission of an organisation is defined and translated into the meaningful actions, we find managers ready for the next step which determines the basis for what must be done differently to achieve those objectives. In some of the cases, we find the newly defined mission and objectives quite similar to the mission and objectives on which the current strategy is based. We find a number of managers defining the current strategy by asking themselves some of the questions.

What is our service profile and what should it be?

Who are our patients/customers and who should they be?

Where are we heading?

What major competitive advantages do we enjoy?

In what areas of the services we excel competition?

Third Step: Analysis of Environment: This is the third step which focuses our attention on analysing the environment. It is the responsibility of a healthcare manager to make it sure that on the basis of the knowledge of the goals of hospitals and existing strategy which aspects of the environment would have the greatest influence on the potentials of the hospitals/healthcare organisations to achieve the objectives. It is right to mention that the purpose of making an indepth analysis of the environment is to identify the ways in which changes in an organisation's economic, social, technological, cultural, political, legal environment would directly influence the organisation and the ways competitors, suppliers, customers, government agencies and others can directly influence. We can't negate the fact that in the process of making an analysis of the environmental conditions, the measures helpful in making the environment eco-friendly are also to be taken into consideration. Out of the different factors, the effects of all the factors are not to be uniform. Some of the factors influence the process of change very significantly whereas we also find factors throwing minor effects. To be more specific, when we go through the problem of healthcare organisations, it is right to opine that environmental conditions, living conditions, social conditions and technological conditions play a very significant role and therefore, a healthcare manager is required to assign an overriding priority to these factors while making an analysis of environment.

If we find the society educated and literate, the management of healthy living conditions minimises the possibilities of diseases because we find them conscious and aware of the things showing positive or negative effects on their healthy living conditions. In the modern age, we also find economic factors influencing the process because the medical or healthcare services are now found expensive and the masses find it difficult to afford. The diagnostic, curative and preventive measures are now found in a changed form because we find new generation of technologies changing the basic concept. The society found conscious and organised manages everything in a right fashion and therefore, whatever the preventive measures are adopted are found effective in sensitising them. Conversely, the task of sensitising the illiterate, unconscious society is found much more difficult.

We find forecasting and management scientific methods effective for analysing the environment. It is right to mention that one key to successful environmental analysis is the detection of changes at an early stage or diagnosing and identifying the problems at the very beginning stage. To be more specific in the healthcare services, we find this aspect important because early and right diagnosis is to simplify the task of healthcare organisations and the doctors.

We find multidimensional changes in the environment resulting into environment pollution, noise-pollution, water-pollution throwing a positive impact on the formation of a hazardous disease profile. In addition, the large-scale use of pesticides in the processes of farming has been found making the food items very sensitive to disease. The deforestation has been found resulting into a change in cycle of nature. The increasing insensitivity among the masses has been found making the environmental conditions more volatile. It is essential that a healthcare manager keeps his/her eyes moving and manages the service mix in the face of changing disease profile.

Thus, an indepth study of the changing environmental conditions is found essential catering to the changing healthcare requirements of the society.

Fourth Step: Analysis of Resources: For the formulation of a sound strategy, it is also pertinent that a healthcare manager makes an analysis of the resources. We are well aware of the fact that in the medical sciences, we find a number of significant developments and the hospitals or healthcare organisations making use of the latest technologies have been found offering world class healthcare services. Unless you improve your quality, the task of excelling competition would remain unfulfilled. If you find it essential to emerge as a healthcare leader, you have no option but to make your organisation potentially sound. Like other organisations, you also need to take the help of SWOT or TWOS analysis to know about your potentials determining your strength. In addition, you are required to make an analysis of the potentials with you related to technologies and healthcare personnel. The management-orientation practiced by you, the innovative improvements delayed by you and so on. The question is not "What do we do well or poorly? But rather "What are we doing better or worse than anyone else? Of late, almost all the organisations take the benefit of competitive advantage which focuses our attention on the slogan "Differentiate or Perish." By offering something innovative which is not offered by others, you get an opportunity to motivate your patients which others don't practice. Thus, taking a competitive advantage paves avenues for excelling competition and you succeed in establishing an edge over your competitors. If all the hospitals or healthcare organisations in a particular command area offer the same quality of diagnostic, curative, preventive services, the task of taking a competitive advantage is found difficult. It is against this background that you need to keep your eyes open and to come to know about the latest developments taking place in the medical sciences, the services profile of leading hospitals or healthcare organisations and to innovate your marketing mix so that you differentiate your services, specially by innovating the peripheral services.

For making an analysis of healthcare resources of your hospital, there are certain considerations suggested by Hofer 8 and you are required to be aware of the following in the very context:

- You need to develop a profile of the key resources and expertise in the different streams like diagnostic, curative, preventive and peripheral.
- You are also required to focus on the quality of medical and paramedical staff available in your hospitals and the technological support taken by you in the process.

- You also need to determine the key success requirements with the viewpoint of excelling competition or taking a competitive advantage.
- You are required to compare the resource profile to the requirements for determining the major strengths on which an effective strategy can be based and in addition, also the major weaknesses required to be resolved.
- You need to compare the strengths and weaknesses of organisation with those of its major competitors to make it clear that what magnitude of strength would help your organisation in taking the competitive advantage.

Thus, an analysis of resources or potentials would help you in making a self-appraisal of the same which would help you in enriching the potentials in tune with the development efforts taken by competitive hospitals or healthcare organisations. Since you have a technology-driven management information system, the task is not found to be so much difficult.

Fifth Step: Identification of Strategic Opportunities and Threats: Here we go through the identification of opportunities and threats. Being a healthcare manager, it is your prime responsibility to study the opportunities and threats in the market. Here, your focus would be on the market potentials. Since you are marketing the healthcare services, you need to go through the fact that keeping in view the existent problems in the command area who are your prospect or potential customers. It is quite natural that while developing the healthcare services, you have taken into consideration the changing needs and requirements of the command area where your hospitals or healthcare organisations are located. Being a professional, you are supposed to be aware of the expertise required for tapping the opportunities optimally. Of course, we find a difference in the attitudes of professionals to be more specific when we find marketing of medicare services. This makes it essential that even if you find non-optimal supply the fee structure is not to be increased. You need to remember that with an optimal tapping of opportunities, you would also be successful in making the services cost-effective, This makes it essential that you increase awareness of prospects regarding the quality of services made available by you. The increasing influx of patients would make the services affordable.

Another problem in the very context which you need to study is the available threats, risks and challenges. It is quite natural that in the healthcare services, we find magnitude of risks of high intensity and this makes it essential that being a manager, you keep yourself well informed regarding the risk factors in the business environment and make professionalised efforts to counter the same successfully and effectively. The new or innovative services lack a sense of confidence among the potential customers and being a hospital manager, it is your responsibility to inform and sense the users in a right perspective.

Sixth Step: Determination of Strategic Change: After making an analysis of the business environment, you need to determine the extent of required change. An innovation in strategy is, of course, found to be significant but you also have to check an uncalled for change in the strategy. Any modification in the strategic decisions would not be made operational unless you find it pertinent to do the same. The performance-gap is found to be a significant indicator to rate the effectiveness of the strategic decisions. If you find a gap of negative nature, it is almost clear that your strategic decisions are getting a lukewarm response. Since you are a professional, it is important that you keep yourself aware of the performance-result and based on the same modify or mend the strategic decisions. The term performance-gap, is the difference that we find between the objectives and the actuals.

We find eases of performance-gap if the difficult objectives are chosen or it may be even from the failure of past performance to meet expectations due to the effective steps taken by the competitive hospitals or healthcare organisations. The natural calamities, epidemics and viral infections may also generate such a gap.

Seventh Step: Strategic Decision Making: It is the seventh step focusing our attention on the strategic decisions due to a performance gap generated by one or other factors. This gravitates our attention on the identification of alternative strategic decisions found to be effective to counter the challenges created by the circumstantial or situational factors. If only a minor change is found essential, the logical alternatives would be a few, as for example, a lag in new service or scheme introduction identified as a major cause of falling demand or shrinking demand, or a programme to improve the performance of the research and development department may also be the obvious choice. But if a major change is felt essential, it is essential to identify more alternatives. It is also pertinent that the alternative strategic decisions are evaluated. Richard 1' Rumelt " has focused his attention on four criteria for making an evaluation of the alternative strategic decisions as mentioned below:

- It is essential that strategy and its component parts have consistent goals, objectives and policies.
- It should have resources and efforts on the critical issues identified in the formulation of strategy.
- It should deal with subproblem efficacious of solution, given the organisation's resources and skills.
- The strategy should be capable of producing the intended results or promise of actually working.

After the evaluation of strategic alternatives, NVC find selection of strategic alternatives users best suited to the potentials of the healthcare organisations. It is right to mention that the successful strategic plans utilise the existing strengths of the organisation. New potentials can be acquired only through investment in the healthcare personnel and /or adoption of innovative sophisticated bio-medical equipment, instruments, apparatus.

Eighth Step: Strategy Implementation: This is the eighth step related to the implementation of strategy. After the formulation of strategy, the most significant aspect that we find in the process is the implementation of strategy. We are well aware of the fact that even innovative or creative strategy would not benefit an organisation unless it is implemented in a right fashion. The transformation of a formal strategic plan into the appropriate tactical plan is found essential. May be that your strategic plan makes a call for the introduction of a new line of services in five years. Now the human resources department would be required to develop a short-term hiring programme. The marketing department may be required to mate a short-term budget for that purpose and the research and development department may also set preliminary plans for the entire period of the new strategy. The production department may work out preliminary cost estimates and so on. Thus with the implementation of strategy, we find before a manager the last task of measurement and control of progress.

Nineth Step: Measurement and Control: The last stage control focuses our attention on exercising control. It is pertinent that a manager is well aware of the processes adopted or followed for implementation. It is his/her responsibility to make it sure that the strategy being implemented is as per plan as the intended results are achieved. This helps a manager in rating the contributions of human and technological resources used or involved in the process. It is not only significant that you plan to offer innovative services but also get it ascertained whatever the services/schemes are found in a final shape are in tune with your plan.

In Fig. 15.3, we present different steps or stages involved in the plan formulation and implementation. A healthcare or hospital manager bears the responsibility of making the services affordable without degenerating the quality and the task would be found much more easier if he/she makes it sure that the aforesaid steps are followed while formulating and implementing the strategies. It is pertinent to mention that monitoring is considered to be the best device to avoid the possibilities of errors and shortcomings. A healthcare manager can simplify his/her task by designing a sound monitoring mechanism.

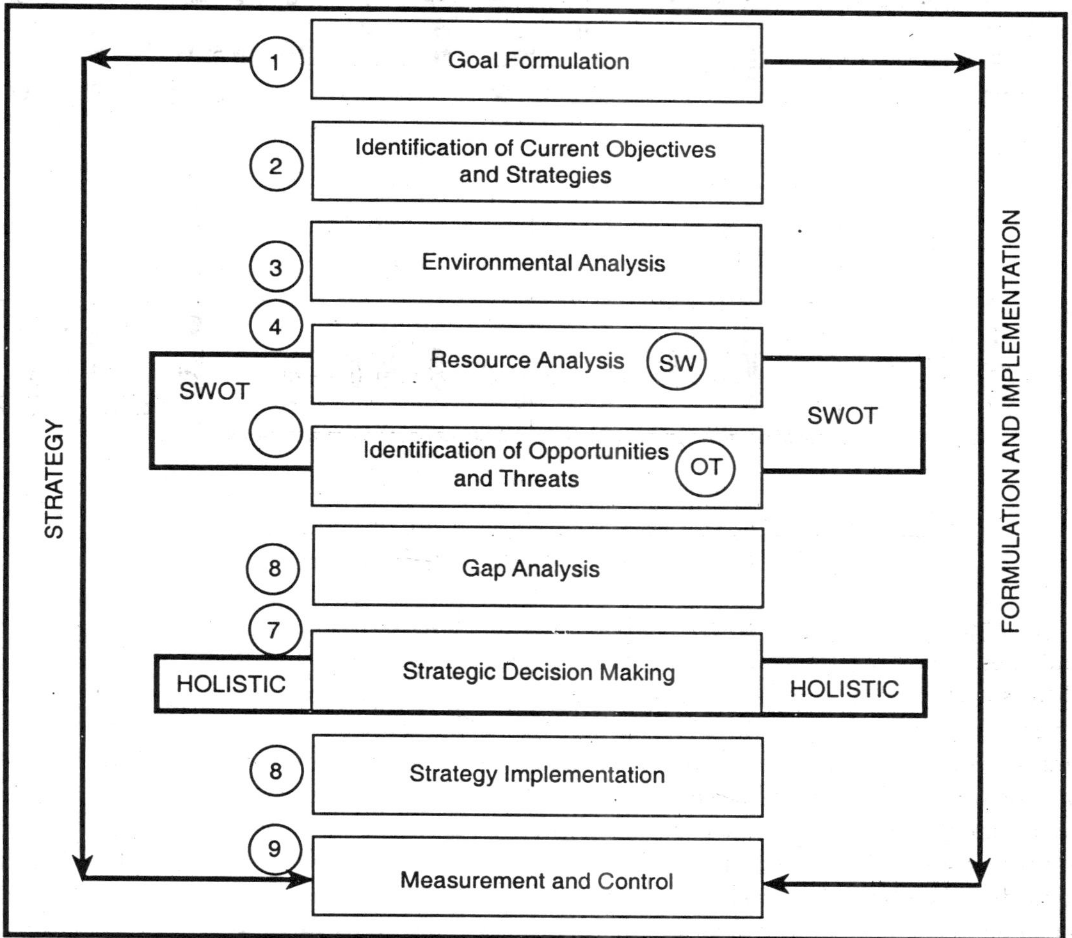

Fig. 15.3. Strategy Formulation and Implementation

Strategy Implementation

The formulation does not carry any meaning if you fail in implementing the strategy in an effective way. Hence, it is pertinent that your managerial excellence assigns due weightage to the effective formulation of strategy. Ideas are required to be put into action and only then your organisation is to be benefited. It is against this background that implementation of strategy occupies a place of significance. Lawrence Herbeniak and William Joyce have described four different approaches to strategy implementation.[10] The Fig. 15.4 clarifies implementation of strategy.

The successful strategy implementation depends on the structure of an organisation. The classic work of Alfred Chandlrt and his followers have gone through the problem. Before the implementation of strategy, it is essential that a strategy is operationalised, in which we find processing of strategies into specific actions and objectives that lower-level managers and employees can actually execute. It is pertinent that these objectives are capable of achieving the desired organisational goal. In addition, the strategy must be institutionalised or it must become a routine part of the day-to-day activities of an organisation, pervading its culture, systems and values.

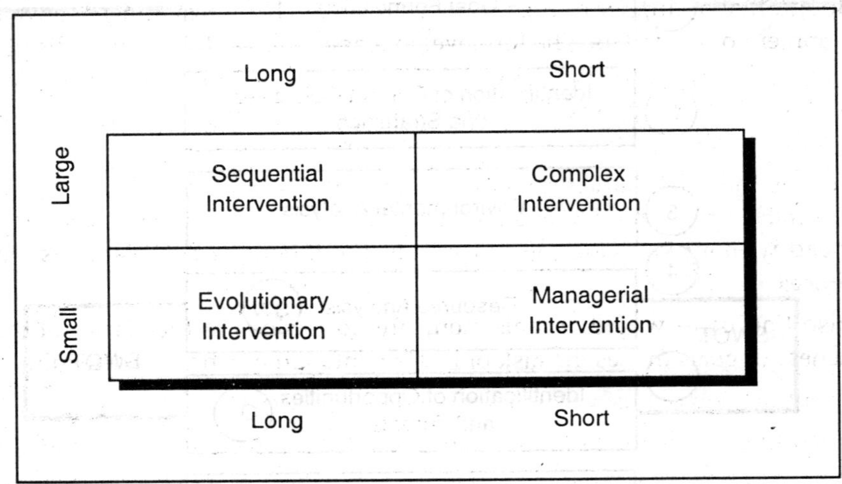

Fig. 15.4. Strategy Implementation Horizon

In Fig. 15.4, we find strategy implementation horizon focusing on long and short-term strategies. When time is available, a manager gets an opportunity to subdivide the problem and address each part in turn in a process called sequential intervention. A manager can carry out a series of changes. When the time is short, a manager is forced to make those changes simultaneously and this one according to a process called complex intervention. It requires a task force or some other mechanism to bring the interested parties together. A drastic change in the environmental conditions may commonly call for a complex intervention. As the environment grows more turbulent, we find intervention of complex nature. We can't negate that change can jeopardise the strategic decisions of an organisation if it is not anticipated. It is significant that managers recognise and preserve interrelationships among the different areas of an organisation even during the course of making changes. Thus, intervention in different forms is found existent.

Effective Implementation of Strategy

Being a healthcare manager, it is your prime responsibility to make it sure that strategies are formulated in the face of changing environmental conditions and the best possible efforts are taken to implement them in a right fashion. It is against this background that effective implementation of strategy assumes a place of outstanding significance because the expertise used in the process of formulation does not carry any sense if the process of implementation is delayed or is found cost-ineffective. It is pertinent that strategic planning to be effective must be accompanied by strategic thinking that also draws our attention on the designing of an appropriate organisational structure, an effective management information system, a scientific budgeting system to facilitate the accomplishment of objectives and in addition a reward system that supports and injects strength to the strategy. Before going through the problem of successful implementation of strategy, we find rationale for identifying the reasons entailed behind the failures of strategic planning.

Why Strategic Planning Fails?

A recent study[11] identifies the following reasons for the failures of strategic planning:

- It is found that a number of organisations have not been assigning due weightage to the development of managers. The top-level management has been found disinterested to the problem and they, of course, are particular to the professional soundness of middle-level managers but fail in perceiving the fact that professional-excellence without personal-commitments complicate the process of implementation.
- It is also found that a large number of organisations don't assign any significance to the management of information even in an age of information superhighway. If you plan to go ahead without knowing the constraints, the threats or risk elements would obstruct the process.
- We also find cases where organisations are not serious to the clarity of their goals and vagueness of goals makes the task of implementation much more difficult.
- The identification of business units is not done in a right way.
- We don't find reviewing of the strategic plans for the business units in an effective way.
- Often we find a gap between the strategic planning and control which complicates the implementation process.

We can't deny the fact that the goals and objectives to be meaningful are to be more than platitudes such as achieving excellence.[12] The overall strategic plan is required to be supplemented by specific action plans. This makes it essential that the line managers are well aware of the formulation of a strategic plan and the different functional departments such as the research and development, engineering, production, marketing, finance and human resources make sincere efforts to plan for the people required to carry out the plan. Of course, the integration process is found difficult and therefore a task-force is found essential so that the managers are found instrumental and successful in removing the functional barriers. Since we find plans the basis for control, it is essential that we make possible an integration of the strategic plan with the total managerial process.

Formulating a Successful Implementation Strategy

We can't deny the fact that formation and implementation are the two sides of the same coin carrying equal weightage. It is not only essential that a sound strategy is formulated in a right way. You may be successful in formulating a sound strategy but the implementation may not be effective if you neglect the processes to be followed. It is against this background that like other organisations, even the healthcare organisations need to assign an overriding priority to the implementation of strategy. There are certain steps[13] making the task of a healthcare manager easier and the process of implementation effective. It is in this context that we need to go through the different steps requiring due consideration. In Fig. 15.5, we find different steps helping you in making the implementation process effective.

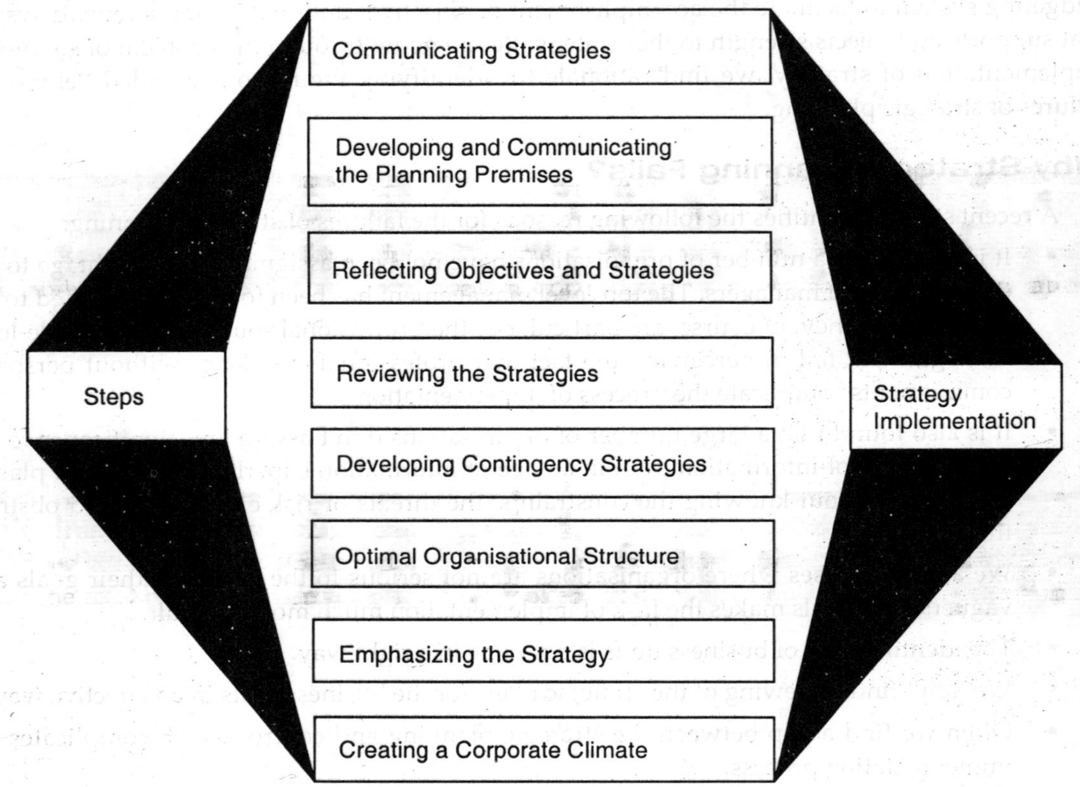

Fig. 15.5. Essentials for Effective Implementation of Strategy

1. *You need to communicate strategies to all the key decision makers:* Being a healthcare manager, you are well aware of the fact that healthcare services are based on a team-work and a team-culture. In the process, you find a number of experts involved and therefore, you can't isolate yourself. Nothing is found well communicated unless the receivers receive the same in the desired fashion. May be that you have perceived the strategies in a right fashion but unless other managers involved in the process also perceive in the same fashion, your task is likely to be much more complicated. This makes it essential that you communicate strategies in an effective way so that different managers to be involved in the process of implementation receive your messages without any barrier.

2. *You need to develop and communicate the planning premises:* Planning premises focus our attention on the critical or key issues related to the plans and the implementation processes. It is quite natural that because you have been involved in the process of plan formulation, you are also well aware of the critical points but your associates helping you in the implementation process

are also to be aware of the same. This makes it essential that you also communicate critical factors to the managers to be involved in the process. A clarification regarding the environmental conditions in which the plans are to be operated would make the process of implementation more effective.

3. *You need to ensure that your action plans reflect objectives and strategies:* Being a healthcare manager, it is also significant that you make it sure that your action plans clarify the key objectives and strategies because this helps you in soliciting the cooperation of the bottom-line of personnel. Vague hopes and useless intentions get an opportunity to grow if you fail in doing the same. This makes it essential that your action plans are tactical. The managers to be involved in the process are to be aware of the objectives and strategies and only then they can communicate the same to the line subordinates to seek their cooperation.

4. *You need to review the strategies regularly:* In this context, it is also important that you review the strategies frequently. To be more specific in the healthcare services, the process of reviewing is found much more impact generating because a number of uncontrollable variables complicate your task. This makes it essential that you link your strategies with the environmental conditions and as and when you find a change, the strategies are reviewed.

5. *You need to develop contingency strategies and programmes:* To make possible more effectiveness in the process of implementation of strategies, it is also important that you develop contingency strategies and programmes. We are aware of the fact that to be more specific in the healthcare sector, we find the environmental conditions more volatile aggravating the magnitude of contingencies. The uncertainties in the environmental conditions, the natural clamities, the epidemics, viral infections are some of the problems complicating the task of effective implementation. The contingency plans provide to you an opportunity, to make necessary preparation to counter the unexpected problems.

6. *You need to make the organisational structure optimal to the needs of planning:* In the process of effective implementation, it is also impact generating that you make efforts to formulate an organisational structure that is found optimal to the needs of strategic plans, The organisational structure with its system of delegations should be designed to help managers the accomplishment of goals. The end-result areas and key tasks are to be identified and assigned to a single position as far down the organisational structure as feasible.

7. *You need to emphasize the planning and implementation strategy:* For the successful implementation of strategy, it is pertinent that the managers continue to stress the nature and importance of strengthening and sensitising the process of increasing the awareness of their colleagues and the subordinates. Enriching the knowledge of your team is an important functional responsibility because we agree with this view that what you fail in delivering in the convention or conference halls, you make it possible in the day-to-day interactions and deliberations with the subordinates and the assisting teams.

8. *You need to create a corporate climate:* In addition to the aforesaid steps, it is also pertinent that you evince personal interests in creating a climate that helps you in activating the process of effective implementation. In a true sense, a successful healthcare manager needs to activate three-tier measures; first formulation of a sound strategy, second creation of a conducive environment for implementation and third monitoring the process of evaluation that all the members of the team are showing personal-touch-in service. Thus, the effective implementation would make the entire process cost-effective vis-a-vis time-honoured.

The Situation Analysis and TOWS Matrix

The healthcare services are influenced by a number of factors. We find some of the services influenced by artificial factors whereas some of the factors are also influenced by the natural factors. It is in this context that we find healthcare services a bit different from the services of other organisations. The hospitals or healthcare organisations face a number of problems on this account. They can't control natural calamities and even they can't foresee or apprehend. Of course, they are aware of the health problems generated due to our food and living habits. The food-prone, water-borne, pollution-borne diseases can be apprehended and preventive measures can also be taken to counter the same. But so far as the epidemics and viral infections are concerned or deaths or diseases on account of natural calamities or accidents are concerned, the task of forecasting becomes difficult which influences the supply position vis-a-vis the credibility of the hospitals or healthcare organisations in bridging the gap. It is against this background that the situational analysis is found impact generating to improve the quality of healthcare organisations. It is also important to mention that matrix developed by Heinz Weihrich[13] known as TOWS Matrix focuses on situational analysis an important factor not only to improve the quality of healthcare services but also to improve the potentials of hospitals or healthcare organisations to cater to the increasing and changing health care requirements of the society.

Of late, we find a number of matrixes developed by the experts for designing the strategic decisions but of all we find the matrix developed by Weirich assuming a place of outstanding significance to be more specific for the healthcare organisations. We are aware of the fact that in the context of formulation of strategy, the Boston Matrix developed by Boston Consultancy Group of USA also heralded new ideas but we find the TOWS matrix establishing an edge over the Boston Matrix. It is also significant to mention that the TOWS matrix has a wider scope which focuses on a conceptual framework for a systematic analysis that facilitates matching the external threat and opportunities with the internal weaknesses and strength of the organisation. It is a general practice that an organisation identifies its strength and weaknesses as well as the opportunities and threats in the external environment but we also find that while doing so, the task of combining the different factors is often left and this makes an advocacy in favour of distinct strategic choices. It is in this context that we find TOWS matrix instrumental. To clarify the Matrix:

T stands for THREATS

O stands for OPPORTUNITIES

W stands for WEAKNESSES

S stands for STRENGTHS

The TOWS Matrix thus starts with the Threats whereas the SWOT analysis starts with the Strengths. It is important to mention that according to the TOWS matrix, the Threats can't be devalued because unless you are aware of the risks factors disturbing you, the task of arranging the order of priorities would not be done in a required fashion. To be more specific for the healthcare organisations, we find Threats generated by a number of sources because not only the leading hospitals or health organisations generate Threats but even the natural factors and the mistakes committed by us also aggravate the magnitude of problems. This makes it clear that hospitals or healthcare organisations while formulating strategic decisions assign due weightage to the TOWS Matrix.

In Fig. 15.6, we find tour alternative strategies of the TOWS Matrix. The strategies are found based on the analysis of external environment (threats and opportunities) and the internal environment (weaknesses and strengths).

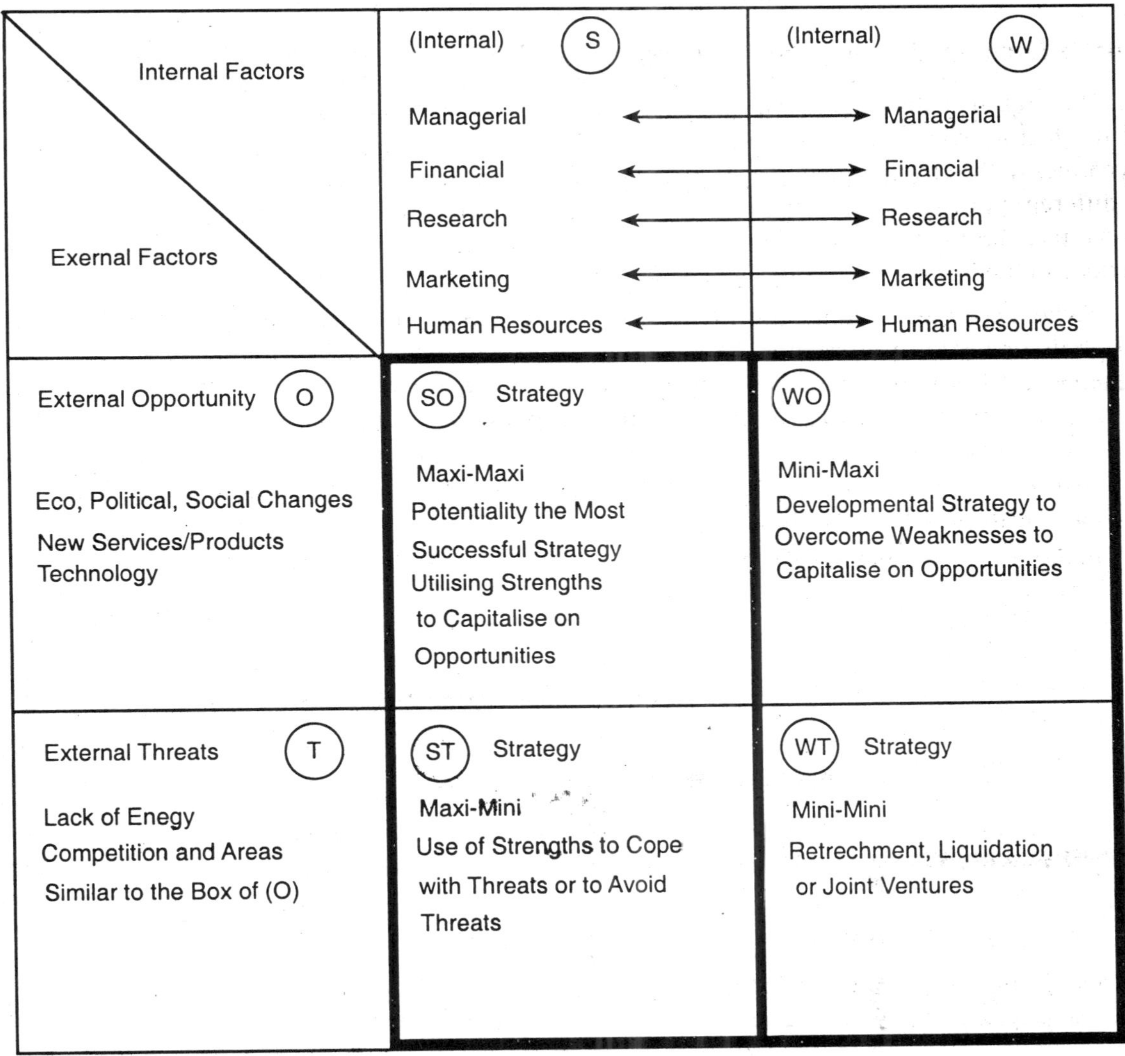

Fig. 15.6. TOWS Matrix

- The WT or mini-mini strategy found in the figure in the lower right-hand corner aims at minimising the magnitude of weaknesses and threats.
- The WO or mini-maxi strategy attempts at minimising the weaknesses and maximising the opportunities.
- The ST or maxi-mini strategy is based on the strengths of the organisation to deal with threats in the environment. The aim is to maximise the former and to minimise the latter. This helps an organisation in using its technological, financial, managerial and marketing

strengths to cope up with threats related to the offering of new or innovative services of world class.

- We find emergence of the most desirable situation when an organisation uses its strengths to take advantage of opportunities. (The SO or maxi-maxi strategy).

Time Dimension in the TOWS Matrix

We find the external and internal environment as the dynamics. It is quite natural that some of the factors change over time while others don't follow an analogous change. Due to the dynamics in the environment, the strategy designer is required to prepare several TOWS matrixes at different points in time as shown in Fig. 15.7. In this way, one may start with a TOWS analysis of the past, and may keep on moving the process even at present by focusing on different time periods in the future, such as T_1, T_2 or so (Fig. 15.7).

To be more specific in the healthcare services, we find significance of time management. The hospitals or healthcare organisations have been found developing a number of services and schemes but in the due course, we find possibilities of a change in the conditions which may counter the impact of diseases, may make the measures ineffective, insensitive or showing lukewarm responses. There are a number of instances to quote that when the innovative healthcare measure were introduced, the effects were of high magnitude but gradually the measures proved to be ineffective.

In Fig. 15.7, the dynamics of TOWS analysis focus on the time dimension.

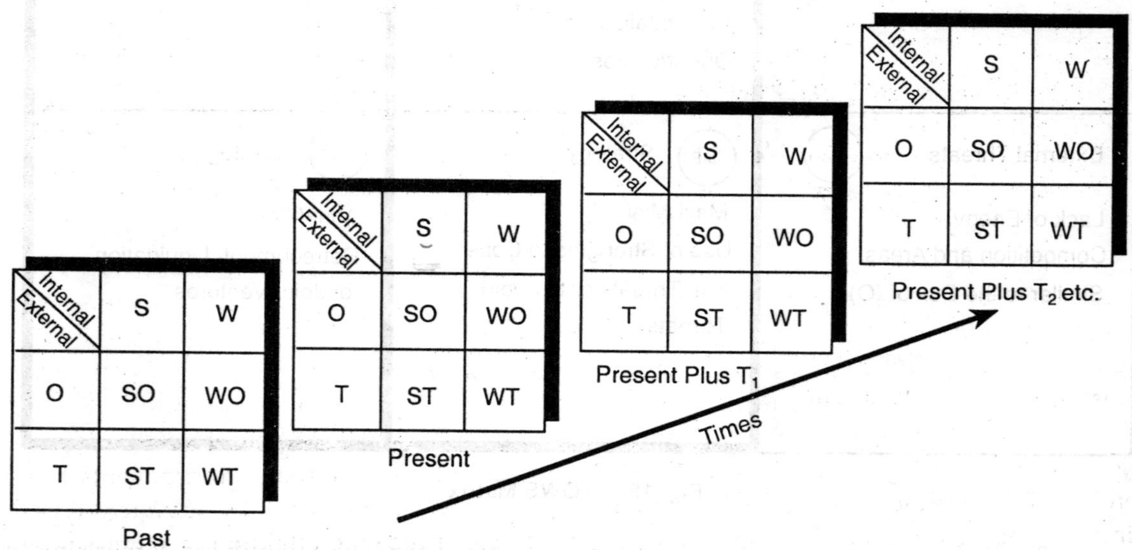

Fig. 15.7. Dynamics of TOWS Analysis

The past, present, present plus T1, present plus T2 etc. make it clear that the healthcare organisations need to study the multi-dimensional changes due to a change in the time-cycle.

The aforesaid facts make it clear that the TOWS Matrix developed by Weirich has a wider scope. Of late we find a number of matrixes showing the relationships of critical variables. We often talk about the Boston Consultancy Group Matrix but the TOWS Matrix has been developed very recently which is exclusively for the situational analysis. We can't negate the fact that the healthcare services are considerably influenced by the situational variation which necessitates a change in the strategies to be followed by the healthcare organisations. The natural and artificial factors substantially influence the nature of disease profile vis-a-vis the diagnostic and curative measures. It is significant that the hospitals and the healthcare organisations are aware of the emerging changes and while formulating or designing strategies incorporate the same optimally. It is not essential that the measures developed today would remain effective even tomorrow. The natural factors may aggravate or even minimise the intensity. We developed curative measures for Malaria. At the initial stage, the magnitude of effectiveness was so high that we considered it totally eradicated. Of late, we find it even in the most dangerous form and the curative measures are found not so much effective. Like this, there are a number of examples and cases to quote that healthcare problems change their nature and character and this makes it essential that the healthcare organisations and hospitals also keep their eyes open and the medical scientists keep on moving the process of inventing and innovating the diagnostic and curative measures so that even the critical problems are countered. This in a very natural way gravitates our attention on the situational analysis and the TOWS Matrix is found effective in the very context.

Strategic Issues in the Management of Hospitals

The hospitals or healthcare organisations bear the responsibility of offering world class services, affordable to the masses. A majority of the Indian population is not in a position to afford the expensive services offered by the private hospitals. Of course, we find a change in the nature and quality of inputs used for generating the healthcare services. However, with the support of professionally-sound and personally-committed healthcare personnel, the services can be made cost-effective. Hence, the main thing in the process is to make possible management-orientation with due focus on the holistic concept of management. The following issues are of strategic nature and gravitate an intensive care.

1. Making the healthcare services cost-effective: The healthcare managers to be more specific in the Indian perspective bear the responsibility of making the entire process cost-effective. This in a very natural way requires world class professional excellence while managing the different types of inputs in the process. On account of a basic change in the nature and character of diagnostic and curative devices, the inputs in general are found capital intensive. The sophisticated bio-medical equipment, instruments, apparatus, plants and machines, information and communication technologies are found used in the process of diagnosing and treating the patients. In addition, a number of peripheral services are also offered to the patients and attendants. The healthcare managers need to make possible an optimal use of the different types of inputs. The maintenance and operation of technologies need due attention to increase the potentials vis-a-vis to control the depreciation cost. The quality materials used in the process would be very much instrumental in improving the quality of services. The administration and establishment expenses are required to be made optimal to the changing requirements of hospitals. The misuse or non-optimal use of infrastructural facilities is to be regulated. The requirements for healthcare personnel are required to be minimised by promoting sophisticated technologies. We can't negate that these efforts would be helpful in minimising the costs or making the process cost-effective which would make the services affordable.

2. World class healthcare services: We are well aware of the fact that sky is the limit for quality-upgradation. With the increasing instrumentality of technologies in the process of generating the healthcare services, we find a new perception of quality getting due weightage in the boardrooms. We can't negate the fact that to be more specific in the Indian condition, the government hospitals, except a few, have failed in improving the quality. The masses have no option but to avail the poor quality of services because they can't afford the expensive services. A majority of the private hospitals have been found evincing interests in improving the quality. It is against this background that we find it essential that the hospitals or healthcare organisations in general make an organised effort to promote research because this would help them in innovating the services which would make place for a new perception of quality. We can't deny the fact that even quality services are to be cost-effective if the hospital or healthcare managers use world class professional excellence and the healthcare personnel in general are personally committed. By making the healthcare services of world class, the healthcare organisations would be efficacious in increasing the influx of high spending patients even from abroad which in the long run would make them financially sound.

3. Concept of Rurbanisation to be linked to the hospitals: The government policy makers, the boardrooms, the hospital planners, architects, consultants, doctors and managers need to realise the instrumentality of promoting large-sized and specialised hospitals preferably in the rural areas or suburbs so that the hospitals contribute substantially to the process of socioeconomic transformation. Till now, we have promoted healthcare organisations only in the big cities and towns which on the one hand have been increasing the influx of patients and attendants to the towns and cities already facing the problem of population congestion, while on the other hand have also been depriving the rural masses of not getting the benefits of latest developments in the medical sciences. This makes it essential that the policy planners promote big hospitals or the specialised hospitals in the rural areas so that they activate the process of urbanisation of villages by switching on the points of multiplier effects. It is quite natural that the rural hospitals would be accessible to all of us which would increase the influx of patients and attendants vis-a-vis would open new vistas for the development of regions in which the hospitals are located. We name it the process or rurbanisation or transforming the rural areas into the urban areas by promoting world class hospitals.

4. Immunisation culture to be promoted: Modern hospitals or healthcare organisations need to generate immunisation and vaccination culture that would help the poor rural masses in different ways. We can't deny the fact that till now, the vaccination culture has remained confined to the urban areas. There are a number of diseases spreading like wild fire and only vaccination can counter them effectively. The Hepatitis B, Typhoid, Cholera, Malaria, and many other diseases based on the pattern of Pulse Polio Programme are to be countered with the support of vaccination. This would help hospitals or healthcare organisations in minimising the influx of patients because the preventive measures, if activated in the right directions, close doors for a number of diseases.

5. Enriching the management information system: We find information technology gaining popularity the world over. It is found paving the avenues for the development of knowledge in almost all the areas. To be more specific with the development of information superhighway, we find new avenues for enriching the knowledge. The computers have made possible a fundamental change in the nature and character of improving the diagnostic and curative services of hospitals or healthcare organisations. The medical scientists, medical and paramedical personnel and the intellects are now in a position to get the required information related to the latest developments taking place in the globe. It is in this context that we find it essential to promote the use of information technology in the hospitals or healthcare organisations. It is quite natural that expansion of information technology would require a number of infrastructural facilities. Not only the large-sized hospitals but even the small-sized hospitals also need to increase their awareness regarding the significance of information technology to the development of healthcare services. This requires enormous cooperation of almost all the segments involved in the process. The government policy makers need to enrich the government hospitals on a priority basis because in a majority of the government hospitals, we find traditional practices making ways for managerial and other deficiencies. Thus, the information technology requires an intensive care.

6. Behavioural profile of healthcare personnel to be enriched: Of course, we find professional excellence significant to the development of quality healthcare services because only the world class medical and paramedical personnel can be successful in making possible qualitative-cum-quantitative transformation but at the same time, it is also impact generating that we improve the behavioural profile of almost all categories of the healthcare personnel. We can't negate that in a majority of the government hospitals, the doctors are professionally-sound but they lack decency and consequently fail in satisfying the patients and attendants. This makes it essential that the healthcare personnel have an indepth knowledge of behavioural management.

7. Developing personally-committed healthcare personnel: For improving the quality of healthcare services, it is not only important that we develop professionally-sound personnel but at the same time, it is also essential that we assign due weightage to personal commitments. The Industrial Psychologists are of the opinion that personal-touch-in-service is the most significant dimension to improve the quality of services. To be more specific in the healthcare services, the recovery period of patients in general can sizeably be minimised, if we find healthcare personnel showing personal-touch-in-service. The healthcare managers while developing personnel of different categories need to synchronise professional-commitments with personal-commitments. This would fantastically increase the levels of efficiency of hospitals. Not only this, the rate of productivity of almost all the assets used in the process would significantly be accelerated which would add strength to our efforts for making the services cost-effective.

8. Promoting herbs: Since we talk about cost-effectiveness and quality, it is pertinent that the healthcare organisations promote the use of herbs having medicinal value. The farming of herbs on a large-scale would not only make available cheap inputs to the pharmaceutical industry but would also improve the economy of villages. It is also testified that herbs as ingredients have dismal side-effects. We find a number of examples to quote that in the Indian perspective, the doctors or pharmaceutical industry promoting herbs have been successful in curing a number of diseases which required huge financial investments earlier. We have a long history and we need to inject new life, and strength to the process.

Recently, we find focus on AYUSH which would make the healthcare services rural-friendly. In this context, the national policy makers need due emphasis on standardisation of drugs and medicines. We need to make it an integral part of NRHM. The infrastructure and capacities of AYUSH research councils need to be upgraded to enable them to carry-out the state-of-the-art scientific work related drug standardisation and quality control, botanical standardisation, laying down of pharmacopeial standards and clinical trials.[14] Strengthening the regulatory mechanism with the motto of safety, control and increased efficacy of AYUSH drugs need priority attention.

9. Innovative IT and Communication Technology: To improve quality of healthcare services, it is pertinent that we promote the uses of new generation of information and communication technology. The devices like telediagnosis, telemedicine and teleconferencing have been instrumental in benefiting almost all the segments of society. The areas like cardiology, pathology, dermatology and radiology[15] and in addition, continuing healthcare or medical education have been innovated and the credibility for the same goes to the ISRO found very much instrumental in serving superspeciality hospitals with the help of mobile telemedicine vans. The geostationary satellites have been benefiting the remotest parts of the country. It is also significant that we take the support of sophisticated communication technology even for sensitising the general masses lacking awareness. The corporate hospitals need to play an incremental role in the sensitisation process with the support of media. This would increase their societal role. In addition, the educational institutions, government hospitals, media, NGOs, voluntary social organisations and even global organisations like UNICEF need to make the process of educating the rural masses much more proactive. The medical institutes and secondary and tertiary hospitals need to promote techno-driven services.

10. Professional-orientation: In the context of strategical decisions, the private as well as the government hospitals have to make possible professional excellence. The new generation of sophisticated technology cannot deliver expected quality of services unless at each and every stage, we find world class professionals. It is not only significant that we channelise our investments. It is equally important that we make our resources highly productive. This is not to be possible unless we have quality healthcare professionals.

11. Tactical issues cannot be undermined: Creativity makes the ways for sensitivity. This makes it essential that hospitals and healthcare organisations assign due weightage to creative promotional measures so that their positive contributions to the process of qualitative-cum-quantitative transformation simplify the projection of a positive image. The corporate hospitals need to come forward to accelerate the pace of sensitising the general masses vis-a-vis capitalising on the niche markets both at domestic and global levels.

We cannot negate that both i the developing and developed countries of the globe, we find tremendous opportunities with the creation of niche markets. During the yesteryears, we have been successful in developing India as an international brand in respect of medicare services and therefore we find even developed countries of the globe showing keen interests in using our services. The professionals need to make use of web pages so that potential users in any part of the globe get an indepth idea of our service quality. Our creative promotional measures would be very much instrumental in tapping the opportunities.

12. Synchronisation of Ancient and Modern Devices: We need to make use of the best either found in the ancient medical sciences or in the modern. The government as well as the private hospitals need to develop a mix of ancient and modern. Since we have a long history of practising medicare devices even 2000 years B.C. by Astreya, the experts need to promote those even today. It is in this context that we find AYUSH gaining popularity but the same should not remain confined only to the government hospitals rather than its best possible uses should also be made by leading private hospitals, specially in the larger interests of weaker sections of the society. The medical scientists and researchers need to focus on the diversified uses of AYUSH which during the yesteryears have outlived their significance.

Of course, we find a number of outstanding properties in the modern medical sciences. The diseases due to bacterial infections are now found effectively cured. The vaccination and immunisation devices have been successful in controlling a number of vulnerable diseases. The medical scientists need to intensify research activities so that a vaccine is developed to prevent AIDS. One of the recent developments in the field of modern medical sciences known as genetic engineering has paved wider avenues for making the treatment processes much more innovative and effective. R.D.N.A. technique is found revolutionising the modern medical sciences because a microscopic study is possible in the technique which may be helpful in regulating a number of vulnerable diseases. Another significant development in the modern medical sciences is the transplantation of human organs. Virtually, we find ultrasound and laser techniques now redefining quality of medicare services.

Blending the ancient and modern devices need priority attention, specially in the Indian condition where a majority of the people due mainly to poor affordability fail to get even the basic medicare services. Such a strategy needs due care of government as well as the private hospitals.

13. Developing World Class Service Ambiences: The medicare services considerably rest on the ambience provided by the hospitals. We cannot negate that specially the government hospitals are not sincere and professional while developing service environment which obstructus generating service culture. Curing patients depend on a number of factors and the surroundings, premises and physical facilities provided to the hospitals cannot be undermined. The location point for hospitals should be free from health hazards. The professionals need to consider the quality of environment where the people perform and patients stay. This makes it essential that professionals assign due weightage to plantation, cleanliness and disinfection processes.

The hospital is a place found distinct to others. It is place where we find providers working in different capacities generating tension, facing stress and realising constraints while performing. This draws our attention on furnishing, lighting, ventilation, sanitation, music, paintings, etc., which would provide to them an opportunity to perform and serve. The surroundings and premises must be efficacious of diffusing their tension. We cannot underestimate instrumentality of a sound ambience even for the patients coming to the hospitals for treatment. Thus, providers as well as the users would be benefited from the sound ambience. To be more specific the government hospitals where we find service ambience not getting due attention, it is required on a priority basis. They should learn something from the Five star hospitals and leading private hospitals who have been found spending huge money on the development of ambience.

The mismanagement of medical and biomedical wastes have been found obstructing the process of managing hospital ambience. Hence, it is pertinent that hospital professionals are sincere and professional while managing service ambience.

14. Satisfaction and Retention of Quality Hospital Personnel: Of course, we have witnessed a number of developments in the field of medical sciences and credibility for the same goes to the new generation of equipments and instruments; however we find our success story sizably influenced by the quality medical and paramedical personnel. We find AIIMS experiencing a number of problems because the quality doctors have been found opting for private hospitals.

The decreasing rate of retention has been adversely affecting service quality of AIIMS and making an invasion on the service culture/*vis-a-vis* its well established international image. When we fail in satisfying our personnel; they prefer to make a search for those hospitals where they are offered lucrative incentives, decent behaviour and world class ambience. Hence, the hospital professionals need to induce quality people by offering to them the required amenities and facilities which would increase the satisfaction level *vis-a-vis* would maximise the retention level.

Blending strategical and tactical issues by making use of world class professional excellence would make medicare services productive *vis-a-vis* cost effective. At each and every stage, the hospital professionals need holistic approach. Services need to be personalised and humanised. The government policymakers need to motivate private hospitals but in this context, it is also pertinent that private hospitals initiate the process of bearing social costs particularly while providing services to the weaker sections. They cannot undermine the supporting infrastructural facilities provided to them by the government and society for the development of services. The prime consideration in making hospitals socially and globally productive is liberal attitudes of government policymakers. Let hospital emerge as an international healthcare brand which would bring multiplier effects partially in the interest of society and partially in the interest of national economy. The acceleration process for socio-economic transformation thus would gain a rapid momentum.

SUMMARY

In this chapter, you have gone through different dimensions of strategy. After going through the chapter, be sure that the following facts are well versed.

Strategy —the perception: Strategy is a game plan that helps us in knowing the right ways for touching the target. It is the pattern of the organisation's response to the environment over time. It is the broad programme for defining and achieving an organisation's objective and implementing the mission.

Strategy Management—the Perception: The term strategic management focuses our attention on managing an organisation with the help of an action plan which is formulated in the face of changing internal and external environmental conditions.

Levels of Strategic Management: There are three levels of strategic management, viz., top-level-management strategy, middle-level management strategy and functional-level-management strategy.

Steps in the Formulation and Implementation of Strategy: In the strategic decisions, there are nine steps, e.g., formulation of goal, identification of current objective and strategy, analysis of environment, analysis of resources, identification of strategic opportunities and threats, determination of strategic change, strategic decision making, strategy implementation and measurement and control.

Strategy Implementation: For effective implementation of strategy, a manager is required to identify the reasons for the failures of strategic planning.

A Successful Implementation Strategy: There are different essentials for the successful implementation of strategy, viz., communicating the strategies to all the key decision makers, developing and communicating the planning premises, ensuring that the action plans reflect objective and strategies, reviewing the strategies regularly, developing contingency strategies, making the organisational structure optimal to the changing needs, emphasising the planning and implementation strategies and creating a corporate climate.

The Situation Analysis and TOWS Matrix: The situation analysis draws our attention on studying the internal and external environment that is found essential to identify the emerging trends. The TOWS matrix starts with Threats and ends with enriching the strengths. In the healthcare organisations, we find TOWS Matrix relevant.

Strategic Issues in the Management of Hospitals: There are some of the strategic issues in the healthcare services, *e.g.*, making the health services cost effective, making the services of world class, promoting hospitals in the rural areas, assigning due weightage to the immunisation programme, enriching the management information system, improving the behavioural profile of healthcare personnel, developing personally-committed and professionally-sound healthcare personnel, promoting herbs and innovating the healthcare education.

The significant developments in the field of AYUSH need to be linked with the NRHM so that rural masses of the country are considerably benefited. The new generation of IT and communication technology need due focus on telemedicine, telediagnosis and teleconferencing. The low cost indigenous technologies need priority attention of health professionals with the motto of making possible cost-effectiveness. At each and every stage, we need professional excellence so that quality healthcare services do not remain confined only to the affluent sections of the society. Quality Healthcare Services for all require a fair blending of strategical and tactical issues.

KEY TERMS

Star Performer	Gap Analysis
Five Star Hospitals	Sequential Intervention
Animal Culture	Complex Intervention
Strategeia	Evolutionary Intervention
Game Plan	Managerial Intervention
Mission	Corporate Climate
Corporate-level Strategy	Rurbanisation
Business-level Strategy	Immunisation
Functional-level Strategy	Herbs
Goal	Tactical Issues
Target	Demographic Pressure
TWOS Matrix	Team Culture
SWOT	Holistic

REVIEW QUESTIONS

1. What do you mean by Strategy? Focus on the levels of Strategic Management.
2. Explain Strategic Management. State and explain the steps in the formulation and implementation of strategy.
3. Focus on the effective implementation of strategy. Discuss the reasons for the failures of strategic planning.
4. Explain the different essentials for the successful implementation of strategy.
5. What do you mean by TOWS Matrix? Explain the relevance to TOWS matrix while innovating the strategic decisions.
6. What do you mean by Situation Analysis?
7. Focus on the strategic issues for managing the healthcare organisations in the changing scenario.

APPLICATION EXERCISES

1. You are working as a hospital manager and have been asked to formulate a strategy which is to help you in meeting the changing healthcare requirements. How and in what way, you will make use of your professional excellence in designing a strategy ?
2. In the capacity of a health professional, throw light on the steps in the formulation and implementation of strategy.
3. Your hospital has been witnessing failures of strategic planning. Focus on the reasons to be responsible for the same
4. Throw light on the essentials you will take care while implementing strategy for your hospital.
5. The strategic decisions of your hospitals are required to be innovated. Do you find TOWS Matrix to be helpful in the process? Justify you arguments.
6. Of late, we find significant changes in the disease profile. Focus on the strategic decisions which would help you in improving the quality of healthcare services both in the national and international perspectives.

END NOTES

1. Roger Evered, *So What is Strategy:* Long Range Planning, 16, No. 3, June 1983, pp. 57-72.
2. Dan E. Schendel and Charles W. Hofer (eds.), *Management—A New View of Business Policy and Planning,* 1979.
3. Daniel Gilbert, Edwin Haman, Jon Mauriel and Edward Freeman, *A Logic for Strategy,* 1988.
4. Jha S.M., *Strategic Issues in Medicare Services,* Employment News.
5. Dan E. Schendel and Charles W. Hofter, *op. cit.*
6. Mintzberg Henry, *Power In and Around Organizations,* Englewood Cliffs, S New Jersey.
7. Thompson A. Arthus and J. Strickland III also Paul Miesing and Joseph W, The Art and Science of Planning at the Business Unit Level; *Management Science,* pp. 773-81.
8. Dan E. Schendel and Charles W. Hofer. *op. cit.*
9. Richard P Rumelt, Evaluation of Strategy in Schendel and Hofer eds., *Strategic Management, A New Hew of Business Policy and Planning.*
10. Lawrence G. Hrebeniak and William F. Joyce, *Implementing Strategy,* Macmillan, 1984, pp. 19-22.
11. Koontz and Weihrich, *Essentials of Management,* p. 95.
12. *Ibid.*
13. *Ibid.*, pp. 100-102.
14. *Eleventh Five Year Plan*: Planning Commission, Government of India New Delhi, p-109, Vol. II
15. *Eleventh Five Year Plan*: p. 85

Bibliography

Alen Sheldon — Organizational Issues in Healthcare Management; Graduate School of Business Administration, Harvard University

Alexander Edythe L. — Nursing Administration in the Hospital Healthcare System; Mobsy St. Louis, 1972

Ammer S. — Purchasing and Material Management for Healthcare Institutions; North-eastern University, Lexington Books, DC Health and Company Massachusetts, London, 1975

Anand, KK — Hospital Management; Vikas Publication, ND 1996

Anderson C.L. — Health Principles and Practice; St. Louis, CV Mobsy, 1967

Anthony and Reece — Management Accounting; Irwin, 5th Edition, 1975

Argyris C. — Management and Organizational Development; McGraw-Hill, New York, 1971

Basil S. Geogropoulos — Sound Services in Healthcare Organization and Administration; WB Soundes Co., Philadelphia, London

Browne K. Freeling — The Doctor-Patient Relationship; E. and S. Living Stone Ltd. Burling Temple, London, 1967

The Give and Take in the Hospitals; G.P. Putnam's Sons Ltd.

C. Rao Subha — Pharmaceutical Marketing in India, Excel Books, 2006

Cuming Maurice W. — Hospital Staff Management; Heinemann, London, 1971

Davel Nalini V. — Hospital Management; Deep & Deep, New Delhi, 1999

Davies Julia — A Study of Hospital Management Training in its Organizational Context; Centre for Business Research in Association with Management Business School; University of Manchester, 1972

Divincart — Administration of Nursing Services; Little Brown & Co., Boston, 1972

Drucker P.F. — Management Revised and Abridged; Harper Collins, New York City, 1985

Durbin and Spring — Organization and Administration of Healthcare; Saint Louis, CV Mobsy, 1974

Edgar H. Schein — Organizational Psychology, PHI, 1983

Ferrar H.P. — The Health Services, Administration, Research and Management; London, Butter Worths, 1972

Goel S.L. & Kumar R. — Hospital Administration; Vol. I,II,III, Deep & Deep Publications, New Delhi

Healthcare Administration; Policy Making and Planning; ND, Sterling, 1981

Healthcare Administration: Ecology Principles and Modern Trends, New Delhi, Sterling 1981

Haywood S.C. — Managing the Healthcare Services, George Allen and Unwin Ltd., Raskin House, 1974,

ISO 9000 International Organization for Standardisation, Trade Support Services, Geneva

Jha, S.M. Social Marketing; HPH, Mumbai, 2009

Jha, S.M. Services Marketing; HPH, Mumbai, 2009

Jha, S.M. Marketing Non-profit Organizations; HPH Mumbai, 2004

Koontz & Weirisch Essentials of Management; McGraw-Hill International Edition

Lombardi Donald M. Handbook for the New Healthcare Manager. American Hospital Publishing Inc., 1988

Handbook of Personnel Selection and Performance Evaluation in the Healthcare; 1988

Progressive Healthcare Management Strategies, Chicago-American Hospitals Publishing, 1992

Stress and Healthcare Environment; Ann Arbor MI Health Administration Press, 1990

Luck G.M., Luckman J. B.W Smit., Stringert Patients, Hospitals and Operational Research; Tavistock Publications, London, 1971

Mac Eachern Malcalm T. Hospital Organization and Management; Physician's Record Co. Illinosis, 1962

Mc Gibony M.D., John R. Principles of Hospital Administration; GP Putnam's Sons, New York, 1969

M.Z. Bookman & K.R. Bookman Medical Tourism in Developing Countries, P. Macmillion, 2007

Mishra R.P. Medical Geography of India, NBT, New Delhi, 1970

Murdick, Ross, Cleggett Information Systems for Modern Management; PHI, 1995

Norman D. Bailey Hospital Personnel Administration, Physician's Record Co. Berwyn Illinots, 1966

Odiorne G.S. Strategic Management of Human Resources; San Francisco, Jossey-Bass, 1984

Owen Joseph Varlton and Modern Concepts of Hospital Administration; WB Saunders Co., Philadelphia

Raj Pruthi Medical Tourism in India; Arise Publisher & Distributor 2006

Ralph Rowbottom Hospital Organization; A Progress Report on the Burnel Health Services Organization, Project Heinemann, London

Robinson G.A. Hospital Administration; Buffer Worth, London, 1966

Runnels G. and Danielson N. Sterlization of Hospital Textiles; Hospital Topics, 1985

Samul Levey, N. Paul Loomba Healthcare Administration: A Managerial Perspective; Philadelphia; Toronto, 1973

Seal S.C. Health Administration in India; Dawn Books, Calcutta, 1975

Spencer J.A. Management in Hospitals; Faber and Faber, London, 1967

Stevens G.H. The Strategic Healthcare Management; San Francisco, Jossey-Bass, 1991

Stoner & Freeman Management; PHI, 1989

Syed Amin Tabish Hospital and Health Services Admn: Principles and Practices, Oxford Pub, ND 2001

Sykes G. Disinfection and Sterilization; E & F, London

William REO — Hospital Information; Lloyd-Lake, London, 1960

WHO Publications — Technical Report Series Public Health Papers, WHO Chronicle, Annual Report of the World Health Assembly and Executives Board
New Approaches to Health Education in Primary Healthcare, 1983
Hospital Planning and Administration, 1966
Hospital Administration, 1968
Alma-Ata, 1978
The Role of Healthcare Sector in Food and Nutrition, 1981
Information System for Health Services, 1981

Other Publications — Eleventh Five Year Plan Planning Commission, Government of India, New Delhi
Report of the Bhore Committee, Consumer Protection Act
Report of the Health Survey and Planning Committee
Ministry of Health, Government of India
August 1959/October, 1961
Annual Report of the Ministry of Health and Family Welfare, Government of India
Manorama Year Book, 2009
Manorama Year Book, 2010
Eleventh Five Year Plan, Planning Commission, Govt. of India, New Delhi
Journal of Academy of Hospital Administration, New Delhi
Vol. 11/2, 1999; Vol. 12/2, 2000; Vol. 15/1, 2003
Indian Journal of Medical Ethics; Vol. III/2—April-June, 2006
Indian Journal of Commerce; Vol. XXIII/3, 2005
Indian Management—Vol. 45/6, 2006
Abhigyan—Vol. XXIII/3, 2005
Indian Medical Tourism : Expro-2005
Business Standard, October 5/2005
The Hindu Magazine, 17 April, 2005
Express Healthcare Management; Feb. 16-28, 2005
Journal of Marketing & Communication—Vol. 1/3, 2006; Vol. 3/2, 2007
Journal of IPM Meerut—Vol. 7/2, 2006; Vol. 6/1, 2006
SCMS Journal of Indian Management— Vol. 3/I, 2006
Journal of IMS Group—Vol. 5/2, 2008
The Indian Journal of Management Research—Vol. VI/11, 2007
The Indian Journal of Management Research—Vol. VI/7, 2008
Health Data Management—Dec. 2004

www.health.gov.in
www.thehealthpages.com
www.expresspharmaonline.com
http://us.rediff.com/money/2003/dec/06 health.htm.ibef-17—March 2005
http://www.telegraphindia.com/141108/asp/business/story 3978459.asp

AF553090

Physiopathology of Clinical Disorders

NIPA® GENX ELECTRONIC RESOURCES & SOLUTIONS P. LTD.
New Delhi-110 034

About the Editor

Dr. Tanmoy Rana obtained his Bachelor of Veterinary Sciences and Animal Husbandry degree (B.V.Sc. & A.H.) and Masters (M.V.Sc) in Veterinary Medicine, Ethics & Jurisprudence from West Bengal University of Animal and Fishery Sciences, Kolkata, India. He secured his Doctor of Philosophy (Ph.D.) in Veterinary Science from the University of Calcutta, Kolkata, India. He works currently as an Assistant Professor of the Veterinary Clinical Complex at West Bengal University of Animal and Fishery Sciences, Kolkata, India. Previously he has also worked as a Veterinary Officer, Animal Resources Development Department, Government of West Bengal, India. He is actively engaged in teaching and clinical practices in veterinary medicine and research related to animal health, production, and disease monitoring regimes. His research interests involve arsenic toxicity, molecular diagnosis, molecular toxicology and medicine, oxidative stress, immunopathology, nanoparticles, Echinococcosis, and microbes. He has published several research articles in reputed international and national journals along with review articles in international journals. He is an editorial board member (especially BMC Veterinary Research, Associate Editor of Frontier in Veterinary Science), and a reviewer of international and national journals. He is a member of many international scientific societies and organizations importantly the West Bengal Veterinary Council (WBVC), The Indian Society for Veterinary Medicine (ISVM), the Association of Public Health Veterinarians, and The Indian Science Congress Association (ISCA). He is also an associate of the West Bengal Academy of Science & Technology, West Bengal, India. He is an editor and author of so many national and international books.

Physiopathology of Clinical Disorders

Tanmoy Rana, Ph.D., AFWAST, FVASc.
Assistant Professor
Veterinary Clinical Complex
(Veterinary Medicine, Ethics & Jurisprudence)
Department of Veterinary Clinical Complex
West Bengal University of Animal & Fishery Sciences
Kolkata-700037, West Bengal, India

NIPA® GENX ELECTRONIC RESOURCES & SOLUTIONS P. LTD.
New Delhi-110 034

NIPA® GENX ELECTRONIC RESOURCES & SOLUTIONS P. LTD.

101,103, Vikas Surya Plaza, CU Block
L.S.C. Market, Pitam Pura, New Delhi-110 034
Ph : +91-11-43860225, Mob.: +91 9717133558, 9540816132
E-mail: newindiapublishingagency@gmail.com
Website: www.nipaersources.com

Print ISBN: 978-93-58873-97-9
ebook ISBN: 978-93-58876-19-2

Composed and Designed by NIPA®.

Preface

Animal Physiology deals with the study of functioning of normal animal body systems. The basic subject is very interesting dealing with a powerful explanations about the physiology with macroscopic levels extending the continuation of the molecular. The basic subject is taught to the undergraduate as well as post graduate students of veterinary science at the beginning of the Veterinary Curriculum. So, the subject is of huge importance for the understating of normal as well as clinical physiology of various animals during clinical evaluation, diagnosis and treatment. There is a lacuna of MCQ book for the preparation of Clinical Animal Physiology in a well-structured manner. The MCQ book provides useful and updated information about the pathophysiology of Clinical Disorders, The students will not be bored in preparation of various competitive examination. I hope, the book will serve/ deliver its purpose fruitfully for the betterment of knowledge in this field. The book is sequentially organized covering various chapters of animal clinical physiology ranging at the graduate as well as post graduate levels. The book is also benefitted by the professionals. Enthusiasts, academicians, and job aspirants of various competitive examinations. The basic book is also useful for the students preparing for the various quiz competitions in their colleges and universities in academic curriculum. Lastly, the book helps the students to boost their confidence before ICAR (NET), ARS and SRF examination, State PSC, UPSC, and other competitive examinations. I always welcome constructive feedback and encouragement from my veterinarian colleagues all over the world.

Dr. Tanmoy Rana
Department of Veterinary Clinical Complex
West Bengal University of Animal & Fishery Sciences
Kolkata, India

Acknowledgement

I would like to convey my regards and sincere gratitude to Hon'ble Vice Chancellor, West Bengal University of Animal & Fishery Sciences, Kolkata, India for providing me an opportunity to edit the book. I am also extremely thankful to all contributors who contributed to the manuscript within the stipulated time in spite of their preoccupation with multiple tasks. I would also like to convey my sincere thanks to the departmental colleagues who provided me with extreme energy, and bits of knowledge for editing the book. I am also grateful to the all publisher who provided me a platform to publish such a nice book for the readership. . I also acknowledge and thank all veterinary practitioners, researchers, and academicians who directly or indirectly helped me to edit the book. Last, but not the least, I am indebted to my family who bear a lot for giving me the time for editing the book.

Dr. Tanmoy Rana
Department of Veterinary Clinical Complex
West Bengal University of Animal & Fishery Sciences
Kolkata, India

Contents

1

General Introduction of Physiology of Clinical Disorders

Aakanksha[1], Rajesh Kumar[1], Amrita Behera[2], Himalaya Bhardwaj[2], A.C. Saxena[3] and Tanmoy Rana[4]

[1]*Department of Veterinary Surgery and Radiology, Bihar Veterinary College Patna, Bihar*

[2] *Veterinary Biochemistry, Bihar Veterinary College, Patna, Bihar*

[3]*Division of Veterinary Surgery, IVRI, Uttar Pradesh*

[4]*Department of Veterinary Clinical Complex, West Bengal University of Animal and Fishery Sciences, Kolkata, West Bengal*

Introduction

Clinical physiology is the branch of medical science that focuses on understanding the functional processes within the body under both normal and disease conditions. It emphasizes how body systems respond to disease, injury, and therapeutic interventions, and, forms the foundation of many diagnostic and therapeutic practices in veterinary medicine.

Importance and scope of Clinical Physiology in Veterinary Medicine: Clinical physiology is indispensable and plays a pivotal role in veterinary medicine. The knowledge allows for early detection of diseases, select effective treatment plans, and improved outcomes for animal patients. It is used to monitor the effects of treatment interventions, adjusting medications or therapies based on the physiological responses observed in the patient. A solid understanding of cardiovascular physiology is essential to manage heart failure condition in dog, and, treating respiratory diseases in cats or gastrointestinal disorders in horses, relies on the knowledge of respiratory and digestive physiology. Beyond treatment, clinical physiology also plays a significant role in preventive medicine. Knowing the normal range of heart rates, blood pressure, and respiratory rates in different species allows veterinarians to quickly assess whether an animal is in distress or experiencing a pathological condition, and allow for timely intervention. It is also critical in managing the health of populations of animals, such as in livestock farming, where maintaining optimal physiological function is essential for productivity and welfare. The major systems in the body - including the cardiovascular, respiratory, digestive, nervous, endocrine, renal, musculoskeletal, reproductive, and immune systems, can be affected by a variety of diseases, and clinical physiology provides the framework for understanding these effects. It encompasses the study of physiological processes across a wide range of species, including companion animals, livestock, wildlife, and exotic animals.

Overview of Major Physiological Systems

***Cardiovascular System*:** The system includes the heart, blood vessels (arteries, veins, and capillaries), and blood, and is responsible for circulating blood throughout the body, delivering oxygen, nutrients and hormones to tissues, and removing waste products. Clinical physiology involves understanding how the heart pumps blood, how blood pressure is regulated, and how blood vessels maintain their integrity under various conditions. Conditions such as heart disease, hypertension, and shock are frequently encountered, and a deep understanding of cardiovascular physiology is necessary for their diagnosis and treatment. For instance, heart murmurs, arrhythmias, and congestive heart failure require precise knowledge of how the heart functions normally and how these conditions alter its function.

Respiratory System: The respiratory system includes the lungs, airways, and associated muscles and tissues that facilitate breathing, and, enables gas exchange, providing oxygen to the blood and removing carbon dioxide. Clinical physiology focuses on understanding the mechanics of breathing, gases exchange, and the regulation of breathing patterns. Respiratory diseases, such as pneumonia, asthma, and chronic obstructive pulmonary disease (COPD), are common in animals. In cases of respiratory distress, veterinarians must assess the efficiency of gas exchange and determine whether there is an obstruction in the airways or a problem with lung tissue itself.

Digestive System: The digestive system includes organs such as the mouth, esophagus, stomach, intestines, liver, and pancreas, and is responsible for breaking down food, absorbing nutrients, and eliminating waste. Clinical physiology involves understanding how these organs work together to process food, how nutrients are absorbed into the bloodstream, and how waste products are excreted. Disorders of the digestive system, such as colic in horses, pancreatitis in dogs, and gastrointestinal stasis in rabbits can be life-threatening if not managed correctly. Understanding the physiology of digestion, including the roles of digestive enzymes, gut motility, and the microbiome, is essential for diagnosing and treating these conditions.

Nervous System: The nervous system comprises the central nervous system (brain and spinal cord and the peripheral nervous system (nerves that extend throughout the body). It controls and coordinates body functions, from voluntary movements to involuntary processes such as heart rate and digestion. Clinical physiology includes studying how nerve impulses are generated and transmitted, how the brain processes information, and how the nervous system interacts with other systems in the body. Neurological diseases, such as epilepsy, neuropathy, and spinal cord injuries, require a deep understanding of nervous system physiology. Managing a seizure disorder in a dog involves knowledge of how electrical activity in the brain can become dysregulated and how medications can stabilize this activity.

Endocrine System: The endocrine system includes glands such as the thyroid, adrenal glands, pancreas, and pituitary gland, and regulates various physiological processes through the secretion of hormones. Clinical physiology focuses on how these glands function, how hormones are produced and regulated, and how hormonal imbalances can lead to disease. Endocrine disorders, such as diabetes, hyperthyroidism, and Cushing's disease require a thorough understanding of hormone physiology for effective treatment. Managing diabetes in a cat involves regulating blood glucose levels through insulin therapy, which requires an understanding of how insulin is normally produced and how it affects metabolism.

Renal System: The renal system includes the kidneys, ureters, bladder, and urethra, is responsible for filtering blood, regulating fluid balance, and maintaining electrolyte levels. Clinical physiology involves understanding how the kidneys filter waste products from the blood, how urine is produced and excreted, and how the kidneys help regulate blood pressure. Renal diseases, such as chronic kidney disease and urinary tract infections, are common in animals, particularly in older pets. Managing these conditions requires an understanding of how kidney function deteriorates over time and how this affects the animal's overall health. Treating chronic kidney disease in a dog involves managing blood pressure, fluid balance, and electrolyte levels to prevent further kidney damage.

Musculoskeletal System: The musculoskeletal system includes bones, muscles, tendons, ligaments, and joints, and provides structural support and enables movement. Clinical physiology focuses on how muscles contract, how bones grow and repair, and how joints function and withstand stress. Musculoskeletal disorders, such as arthritis, fractures, and muscle injuries often require surgical or therapeutic intervention. Understanding the physiology of bone healing, muscle repair, and joint function is essential for developing effective treatment plans. Treating arthritis in a horse involves managing inflammation and pain while promoting joint health through appropriate exercise and nutrition.

Reproductive System: The reproductive system involves organs such as the ovaries, testes, uterus, and mammary glands. Clinical physiology includes understanding the hormonal regulation of reproduction, ovulation and fertilization, and the development of fetus. Reproductive disorders, such as infertility, dystocia (difficult labor), and mastitis, require a deep understanding of reproductive physiology. Managing infertility in a mare involves understanding the hormonal cycles that regulate ovulation.

Immune System: The immune system includes components such as white blood cells, antibodies, and lymphoid organs like the spleen and lymph nodes, and protects the body from infections and diseases. Clinical physiology of the immune system involves understanding how the body detects and responds to pathogens, how immune cells are activated, and how immunity is regulated. Immune-mediated diseases, such as autoimmune disorders and allergies require an understanding of how the immune system can become dysregulated. Treating autoimmune hemolytic anemia in a dog involves suppressing the immune system to prevent it from attacking the animal's own red blood cells.

Comparative Physiology: It is he study of how different species' physiological systems function and adapt to their unique environments, lifestyles, and evolutionary histories, as different animal species vary widely in their physiological processes, which directly impacts their medical care. Comparative physiology examines the similarities and differences in physiological processes across species. Digestive system of a ruminant like a cow is vastly different from that of a monogastric animal like a dog. This difference affects how these animals digest food, absorb nutrients, and metabolize drugs. The cardiovascular system of a horse, which is adapted for high-speed running, differs from that of a sedentary animal like a cat.

Digestive System: Ruminants, such as cows and sheep, possess a complex stomach with four compartments (rumen, reticulum, omasum, and abomasum) designed to break down fibrous plant material through fermentation before it is digested. In contrast, monogastric animals like dogs and pigs have a single-chambered stomach, where digestion begins before food moves to the small intestine. Ruminants are prone to disorders such as bloat and acidosis, which require specific dietary management that differs significantly from the needs of monogastric animals.

Cardiovascular System: The cardiovascular system is adapted to different levels of physical activity. Horses have a highly efficient cardiovascular system with a large heart that can increase its output dramatically during intense exercise, supporting their ability to run at high speeds for extended periods. In contrast, animals like reptiles have a three-chambered heart that is less efficient at oxygenating blood, reflecting their lower metabolic rates and different environmental needs.

Respiratory System: Birds have a unique respiratory system that includes air sacs and a unidirectional flow of air through their lungs, allowing for more efficient gas exchange compared to mammals. This adaptation is critical for flight, as it ensures a constant supply of oxygen even during the intense physical demands of flying. In contrast, mammals have a bidirectional airflow system where air moves in and out of the lungs in the same path, which is less efficient but sufficient for their metabolic needs.

Nervous System: The nervous system also shows significant variation, particularly in sensory adaptations. Echolocation abilities of bats are a result of specialized neural mechanisms that process ultrasonic sound waves to create detailed images of their environment, allowing them to navigate and hunt in complete darkness. Highly developed olfactory system in dogs reflects their reliance on scent for communication and hunting, with a much larger portion of their brain dedicated to processing olfactory information.

Adaptations to Environment and Lifestyle: Animals have evolved physiological adaptations to survive and thrive in a wide range of environments, from the deep ocean to arid deserts.

Thermoregulation: Desert-dwelling animals like camels have evolved to withstand extreme heat by minimizing water loss through mechanisms such as highly efficient kidneys and the ability to tolerate significant fluctuations in body temperature. In contrast, animals like polar bears have developed thick layers of fat and fur to insulate against the cold, along with a circulatory system that conserves heat. Reptiles require precise temperature gradients for thermoregulation and specialized housing conditions in captivity.

Osmoregulation: Marine animals, such as fish, face the challenge of maintaining water and electrolyte balance in a saltwater environment. They have evolved specialized gills and kidneys that excrete excess salt while conserving water, allowing them to survive in high-salinity environments. Freshwater fish, on the other hand, must constantly excrete excess water while retaining salts to prevent their bodies from becoming too diluted.

Metabolic Adaptations: Animals adapted to environments with scarce food supplies, such as bears or desert rodents, have developed the ability to enter states of reduced metabolic activity, such as hibernation or torpor, to conserve energy during periods when food is unavailable.

Respiratory Adaptations: Aquatic mammals, such as whales and seals, have developed the ability to hold their breath for extended periods and efficiently use oxygen stored in their muscles and blood, allowing them to dive to great depths without suffering from decompression sickness. Their lungs are also adapted to collapse safely under pressure, reducing the risk of nitrogen absorption that could lead to the bends.

Reproductive Adaptations: Marsupials have short gestation periods followed by extended development outside the womb, while elephants have long gestation periods with fully developed offspring at birth. Understanding these reproductive adaptations is essential for managing breeding programs, pregnancy, and neonatal care in different species.

Implications for Veterinary Practice

Species-Specific Disease Management: Cats have a unique liver metabolism that makes them particularly sensitive to certain drugs, such as acetaminophen.

Nutritional Requirements: Ruminants require a diet high in fiber to support the fermentation processes in their stomachs, while obligate carnivores like cats require a diet rich in animal proteins and fats to meet their nutritional needs.

Anesthesia and Surgery: Rabbits are sensitive to stress and require careful monitoring during anesthesia, while reptiles have slower metabolism, which affect duration and recovery.

Reproductive Health: Timing and hormonal regulation of ovulation vary significantly between species, affecting success of artificial insemination or embryo transfer techniques.

Clinical Physiology in Diagnostics

Electrocardiogram (ECG): An electrocardiogram (ECG) measures the electrical activity of the heart. A prolonged QT interval can indicate electrolyte imbalances or the effects of certain medications, while the presence of abnormal P waves might suggest atrial enlargement or other structural heart changes.

Blood Pressure Measurement: Blood pressure is regulated by complex physiological mechanisms. Understanding these mechanisms is vital for interpreting blood pressure readings and determining the underlying causes of hypertension, whether it's due to renal disease, endocrine disorders, or primary hypertension.

Blood Gas Analysis: Blood gas analysis measures the levels of oxygen, carbon dioxide, and pH in the blood, providing critical information about respiratory function and acid-base balance. Hypoxemia (low blood oxygen levels) might indicate respiratory failure, while acidosis (low blood pH) can result from metabolic disturbances like ketoacidosis in diabetic animals or lactic acidosis due to shock.

Ultrasound and Imaging Techniques: An enlarged liver on ultrasound might indicate hepatic disease, while an echocardiogram showing abnormal heart valve movement could suggest valvular disease.

Endoscopy: It allows veterinarians to directly observe the mucosal surfaces, detect abnormalities like tumors or ulcers, and even take biopsies for further examination. Understanding the normal physiology helps in recognizing pathological changes.

Hemato-biochemistry: Elevated liver enzymes might indicate liver damage or disease, while a high white blood cell count could suggest infection or inflammation.

Urinalysis: Presence of protein in urine (proteinuria) might indicate kidney disease, while the detection of crystals could suggest urolithiasis (bladder stones).

Cytology and Histopathology: Cellular atypia can be seen in cancer, and, the infiltration of inflammatory cells in infections.

Molecular Diagnostics: PCR can detect specific pathogens like viruses or bacteria by amplifying their genetic material, while ELISA can measure the presence of antibodies or antigens in the blood, indicating an immune response.

Disease Pathophysiology and Management: Pathophysiology is the study of how disease processes affect the normal physiological functions of the body, which is essential for diagnosing diseases, predicting their progression, and developing effective treatment plans.

Cardiovascular Disease: Cardiovascular diseases are characterized by the inability of the heart to pump blood effectively. Understanding the pathophysiology of heart failure involves studying how changes in heart muscle contractility, valve function, and vascular resistance contribute to the clinical signs observed, such as exercise intolerance, coughing, and edema.

Respiratory Disorders: Asthma or chronic obstructive pulmonary disease (COPD), involve the narrowing of airways and difficulty in breathing. The pathophysiology often involves chronic inflammation, mucus production, and bronchoconstriction, which can allow appropriate therapies, such as bronchodilators and anti-inflammatory medications, to alleviate symptoms and improve the animal's quality of life.

Digestive Issues: Inflammatory bowel disease (IBD) or gastric ulcers, disrupt the normal processes of digestion and nutrient absorption. The pathophysiology involve immune-mediated inflammation, increased permeability of the intestinal lining, or the overproduction of gastric acid. Treatment strategies are designed to address these underlying issues, such as using immunosuppressants for IBD or proton pump inhibitors for ulcers.

Treatment Strategies Based on Physiological Understanding

Pharmacological Interventions: The use of beta-blockers in cardiovascular disease is to reduce the heart's workload by blocking the effects of adrenaline on the heart, thereby slowing the heart rate and reducing blood pressure. Similarly, insulin therapy in diabetic animals is to regulate blood glucose levels by facilitating glucose uptake into cells. Beta-lactam antibiotics, like penicillin, inhibit cell wall synthesis, making them effective against gram-positive bacteria. However, they are less effective against gram-negative bacteria, which have a different cell wall structure. Understanding the inflammatory process allows veterinarians to use anti-inflammatory drugs effectively while minimizing side effects, such as gastrointestinal irritation with NSAIDs or immunosuppression with corticosteroids. In cases of hypothyroidism, where there is insufficient production of thyroid hormones, veterinarians prescribe synthetic thyroid hormone (levothyroxine) to normalize metabolism. Similarly, in cases of adrenal insufficiency, corticosteroids may be used to replace the deficient hormones.

Surgical Considerations: For orthopedic surgery to repair fractures, veterinarians must understand the physiology of bone healing, including the role of osteoblasts and osteoclasts in bone remodeling. Spaying or neutering procedures require knowledge of reproductive physiology, including the hormonal regulation. Certain anesthetics may depress respiratory function, requiring careful monitoring and support during surgery. Understanding the series of physiological processes of wound healing, including inflammation, proliferation of new cells, and remodeling of the tissue, allows veterinarians to optimize wound healing by providing appropriate postoperative care, such as managing infection, controlling inflammation, and supporting tissue regeneration.

Rehabilitation and Physiotherapy: Rehabilitation in animals, such as physical therapy after surgery, is based on the principles of muscle and nervous system physiology. Hydrotherapy is often used in dogs with arthritis because it provides low-impact exercise that strengthens muscles while minimizing stress on joints. Controlled exercise, such as walking on a treadmill or swimming, can help strengthen muscles without putting excessive stress on joints or healing tissues. Physiotherapy techniques, like massage, cold and heat therapy, and acupuncture, influence the physiological processes involved in pain perception and inflammation, helping to reduce pain and improve the animal's quality of life. Positive reinforcement, gentle handling, and creating a stress-free environment can all contribute to the success of rehabilitation efforts

Objectives

1. What is the primary function of the alveoli in the lungs of animals?
   a) Filtering air b) Gas exchange
   c) Producing mucus d) Regulating blood pressure
2. Which part of the brain regulates the respiratory rate?
   a) Cerebellum b) Medulla oblongata
   c) Hippocampus d) Cerebrum
3. What condition is characterized by an excessive buildup of CO_2 in the bloodstream?
   a) Hypoxia b) Hypercapnia
   c) Hypocapnia d) Hyperoxia
4. What muscle primarily drives the process of inspiration in mammals?
   a) Intercostal muscles b) Diaphragm
   c) Abdominal muscles d) Pectoral muscles
5. Which respiratory structure is responsible for producing sound in animals?
   a) Trachea b) Larynx
   c) Bronchioles d) Pharynx
6. What is the normal tidal volume for a healthy adult dog?
   a) 5-10 mL/kg b) 10-15 mL/kg
   c) 15-20 mL/kg d) 20-25 mL/kg
7. Which respiratory disease is characterized by chronic inflammation and narrowing of the airways in animals?
   a) Asthma b) Pneumonia
   c) Bronchitis d) Emphysema
8. Which condition is commonly caused by a viral infection and leads to inflammation of the bronchi in dogs?
   a) Canine infectious respiratory disease b) Canine distemper
   c) Canine parvovirus d) Kennel cough
9. Which diagnostic tool is primarily used to visualize the structures of the respiratory tract in animals?
   a) X-ray b) Ultrasound
   c) MRI d) CT scan
10. In which condition does pulmonary edema commonly occur?
    a) Heart failure b) Kidney failure
    c) Liver failure d) Gastrointestinal disease

11. What is the primary clinical sign of chronic bronchitis in dogs?
    a) Coughing
    b) Vomiting
    c) Diarrhea
    d) Weight loss
12. What clinical sign is most indicative of a pleural effusion in animals?
    a) Dyspnea (difficulty breathing)
    b) Coughing
    c) Vomiting
    d) Lethargy
13. In horses, what condition is characterized by chronic airway obstruction and is commonly referred to as "heaves"?
    a) Pneumonia
    b) Recurrent airway obstruction (RAO)
    c) Exercise-induced pulmonary hemorrhage
    d) Pleuropneumonia
14. What is the term for decreased oxygen levels in the blood?
    a) Hypercapnia
    b) Hypoxemia
    c) Hypoxia
    d) Hyperoxia
15. What is the most common cause of respiratory acidosis in animals?
    a) Hyperventilation
    b) Airway obstruction
    c) Hypoventilation
    d) Metabolic acidosis
16. Which abnormal lung sound is typically associated with fluid accumulation in the lungs?
    a) Wheezing
    b) Crackles
    c) Stridor
    d) Pleural rub
17. What is the primary function of bronchodilators in respiratory therapy?
    a) Increase mucus production
    b) Decrease inflammation
    c) Relax bronchial smooth muscle
    d) Inhibit cough reflex
18. Which diagnostic test measures the concentration of gases in the blood?
    a) Complete blood count (CBC)
    b) Blood gas analysis
    c) Urinalysis
    d) Radiography
    d) Larynx
19. What is the primary purpose of using a pulse oximeter in animals?
    a) Measure blood pressure
    b) Measure heart rate
    c) Measure oxygen saturation
    d) Measure respiratory rate
20. What is the most common cause of epistaxis (nosebleeds) in horses?
    a) Sinus infection
    b) Exercise-induced pulmonary hemorrhage
    c) Nasal tumors
    d) Foreign bodies
21. What is the recommended treatment for a dog diagnosed with laryngeal paralysis?
    a) Antibiotics
    b) Surgical correction
    c) Antitussives
    d) Bronchodilators

22. Which respiratory condition in cattle is often associated with transport stress?
    a) Bovine respiratory disease complex b) Pulmonary edema
    c) Bovine tuberculosis d) Aspiration pneumonia
23. In birds, which structure allows for unidirectional airflow through the lungs?
    a) Air sacs b) Alveoli
    c) Bronchi d) Trachea
24. What is the main function of the cilia in the respiratory tract?
    a) Absorb oxygen b) Produce mucus
    c) Trap and remove particles d) Exchange gases
25. What is the primary effect of histamine release on the respiratory tract?
    a) Bronchodilation b) Bronchoconstriction
    c) Increased mucus clearance d) Decreased vascular permeability
26. What is the primary cause of cyanosis in animals?
    a) Hyperoxia b) Hypoxemia
    c) Hypercapnia d) Anemia
27. Which emergency condition is characterized by the accumulation of air in the pleural space?
    a) Pleural effusion b) Pneumothorax
    c) Hemothorax d) Chylothorax
28. What is the immediate treatment for upper airway obstruction in an animal?
    a) Bronchodilators b) Endotracheal intubation
    c) Chest compressions d) Intravenous fluids
29. Which respiratory condition is characterized by severe hypoxemia that does not improve with oxygen therapy?
    a) Asthma
    b) Chronic bronchitis
    c) Acute respiratory distress syndrome (ARDS)
    d) Pleural effusion
30. What is the best way to prevent kennel cough in dogs?
    a) Regular deworming b) Vaccination
    c) Flea control d) Dietary supplements
31. Which factor is a common trigger for feline asthma attacks?
    a) Dust b) Low humidity
    c) High altitude d) Low temperature
32. What is the primary focus of managing chronic respiratory diseases in pets?
    a) Reducing inflammation b) Increasing exercise
    c) Decreasing food intake d) Enhancing social interactions

33. A 6-year-old cat presents with chronic sneezing and nasal discharge. Which condition is most likely?
    a) Asthma
    b) Chronic rhinitis
    c) Pneumonia
    d) Pulmonary edema
34. A cow presents with open-mouth breathing and cyanosis. What is the first step in management?
    a) Administer antibiotics
    b) Provide oxygen supplementation
    c) Perform a thoracocentesis
    d) Start bronchodilator therapy
35. Which zoonotic disease is transmitted through the inhalation of contaminated dust or droplets from birds?
    a) Aspergillosis
    b) Avian influenza
    c) Psittacosis
    d) Histoplasmosis
36. What is the primary cause of respiratory infections in neonatal calves?
    a) Poor ventilation
    b) High humidity
    c) Contaminated water
    d) Inadequate colostrum intake
37. Which factor is a significant risk for developing equine influenza?
    a) Regular vaccination
    b) Contact with infected horses
    c) High altitude
    d) Dust-free environment
38. What is the primary route of transmission for Bordetella bronchiseptica in dogs?
    a) Direct contact
    b) Fecal-oral route
    c) Vector-borne transmission
    d) Aerosol transmission
39. Which preventive measure is recommended to reduce the risk of respiratory disease in poultry flocks?
    a) Regular deworming
    b) High-protein diet
    c) Biosecurity measures
    d) Vitamin supplements
40. What is the primary effect of pulmonary hypertension on the heart?
    a) Right ventricular hypertrophy
    b) Left ventricular hypertrophy
    c) Increased cardiac output
    d) Decreased heart rate
41. Which condition is characterized by an abnormal accumulation of lymphatic fluid in the pleural cavity?
    a) Pneumothorax
    b) Hemothorax
    c) Pleural effusion
    d) Chylothorax
42. Which respiratory disease in cattle is commonly referred to as “shipping fever”?
    a) Pneumonic pasteurellosis
    b) Tuberculosis
    c) Parainfluenza-3
    d) Contagious bovine pleuropneumonia
43. Which diagnostic tool is most useful for assessing pulmonary function in animals with chronic respiratory disease?
    a) Radiography
    b) Spirometry
    c) Blood gas analysis
    d) Computed tomography (CT) scan

44. What is the primary purpose of administering diuretics to an animal with pulmonary edema?
    a) Reduce inflammation
    b) Increase urine output
    c) Decrease fluid accumulation in the lungs
    d) Improve oxygenation

45. Which chamber of the heart receives oxygenated blood from the lungs?
    a) Right atrium
    b) Right ventricle
    c) Left atrium
    d) Left ventricle

46. What is the normal heart rate range for a healthy adult dog?
    a) 60-100 bpm
    b) 80-120 bpm
    c) 100-160 bpm
    d) 120-180 bpm

47. What is the function of the heart valves?
    a) To pump blood
    b) To oxygenate blood
    c) To prevent backflow of blood
    d) To store blood

48. Which part of the heart initiates the heartbeat?
    a) AV node
    b) SA node
    c) Bundle of His
    d) Purkinje fibers

49. What is the primary role of capillaries?
    a) To transport blood to the heart
    b) To exchange gases, nutrients, and wastes between blood and tissues
    c) To prevent blood clotting
    d) To store oxygen

50. Which of the following is a common sign of heart failure in animals?
    a) Increased appetite
    b) Exercise intolerance
    c) Hyperactivity
    d) Weight gain

51. Which disease is characterized by the thickening of the heart muscle in cats?
    a) Dilated cardiomyopathy
    b) Hypertrophic cardiomyopathy
    c) Restrictive cardiomyopathy
    d) Arrhythmogenic right ventricular cardiomyopathy

52. Which of the following diagnostic tools is commonly used to evaluate heart function in animals?
    a) Ultrasound
    b) MRI
    c) X-ray
    d) Electrocardiogram (ECG)

53. Which type of arrhythmia is most commonly seen in horses?
    a) Atrial fibrillation
    b) Ventricular tachycardia
    c) Bradycardia
    d) Premature ventricular contractions

54. Which congenital heart defect is characterized by a hole between the heart's chambers?
    a) Aortic stenosis
    b) Patent ductus arteriosus
    c) Ventricular septal defect
    d) Pulmonic stenosis

55. Which neurotransmitter is primarily involved in increasing heart rate?
    a) Acetylcholine
    b) Dopamine
    c) Norepinephrine
    d) Serotonin

56. What is the term for the volume of blood pumped by each ventricle in one minute?
    a) Stroke volume
    b) Cardiac output
    c) Heart rate
    d) Blood pressure

57. What is the Frank-Starling law of the heart?
    a) The relationship between heart rate and cardiac output
    b) The relationship between stroke volume and venous return
    c) The relationship between blood pressure and heart rate
    d) The relationship between oxygen consumption and cardiac output

58. Which electrolyte imbalance is most likely to cause cardiac arrhythmias?
    a) Hypokalemia
    b) Hypercalcemia
    c) Hypomagnesemia
    d) Hyponatremia

59. Which receptor type is primarily responsible for detecting changes in blood pressure?
    a) Chemoreceptors
    b) Photoreceptors
    c) Baroreceptors
    d) Mechanoreceptors

60. Which imaging technique uses sound waves to create a picture of the heart?
    a) X-ray
    b) MRI
    c) Echocardiography
    d) CT scan

61. Which blood test is commonly used to assess heart function?
    a) Complete blood count (CBC)
    b) Serum creatinine
    c) Blood urea nitrogen (BUN)
    d) Cardiac biomarkers

62. What is the primary purpose of performing a stress test on an animal?
    a) To evaluate the animal's response to exercise
    b) To measure resting heart rate
    c) To assess lung function
    d) To detect bone abnormalities

63. What does the P wave in an ECG represent?
    a) Ventricular depolarization
    b) Atrial depolarization
    c) Atrial repolarization
    d) Ventricular repolarization

64. What does the QRS complex in an ECG represent?
    a) Atrial depolarization
    b) Ventricular depolarization
    c) Ventricular repolarization
    d) Atrial repolarization

65. Which medication is often prescribed to reduce fluid buildup in heart failure?
    a) Diuretics
    b) Beta-blockers
    c) Calcium channel blockers
    d) ACE inhibitors

66. Which dietary modification is often recommended for animals with heart disease?
    a) High-sodium diet
    b) Low-fat diet
    c) Low-sodium diet
    d) High-carbohydrate diet

67. What is the mechanism of action of ACE inhibitors in the treatment of heart failure?
    a) Blocking the action of angiotensin II
    b) Increasing the heart rate
    c) Reducing blood glucose levels
    d) Promoting sodium retention

68. Which drug is commonly used to treat heartworm in dogs?
    a) Ivermectin
    b) Furosemide
    c) Digoxin
    d) Enalapril

69. Which genetic disorder is known to cause cardiac problems in Boxer dogs?
    a) Von Willebrand disease
    b) Degenerative myelopathy
    c) Arrhythmogenic right ventricular cardiomyopathy
    d) Progressive retinal atrophy

70. What is the purpose of a Holter monitor in cardiac evaluation?
    a) To measure blood pressure
    b) To assess heart function over 24-48 hours
    c) To evaluate lung function
    d) To detect bone abnormalities

71. What is the immediate treatment for an animal experiencing cardiac arrest?
    a) Administration of diuretics
    b) Cardiopulmonary resuscitation (CPR)
    c) Administration of antibiotics
    d) Application of a cold compress

72. What is a primary symptom of shock in animals?
    a) Hypertension
    b) Hyperactivity
    c) Hypotension
    d) Hyperthermia

73. Which type of shock is caused by severe blood loss?
    a) Cardiogenic shock
    b) Hypovolemic shock
    c) Anaphylactic shock
    d) Septic shock

74. Which emergency condition is characterized by the twisting of the stomach, often seen in large breed dogs?
    a) Gastric dilatation-volvulus (GDV)
    b) Intussusception
    c) Megacolon
    d) Gastric ulceration

75. Which dietary supplement is often recommended for improving cardiovascular health in animals?

a) Vitamin C
b) Omega-3 fatty acids
c) Iron
d) Calcium

76. A dog presents with coughing, difficulty breathing, and exercise intolerance. What is a likely diagnosis?

a) Liver disease
b) Heart failure
c) Kidney failure
d) Gastrointestinal disease

77. A cat with hypertrophic cardiomyopathy is at risk for which complication?

a) Liver failure
b) Kidney failure
c) Thromboembolism
d) Hyperthyroidism

78. A dog with a history of syncope (fainting) episodes is most likely to have which condition?

a) Hypothyroidism
b) Heart disease
c) Liver disease
d) Diabetes

79. A dog with heartworm disease is exhibiting signs of right-sided heart failure. What is a common symptom of this condition?

a) Coughing
b) Ascites (fluid accumulation in the abdomen)
c) Weight loss
d) Increased appetite

80. Which vitamin is essential for the synthesis of collagen in blood vessels?

a) Vitamin A
b) Vitamin B12
c) Vitamin C
d) Vitamin D

81. What is the primary cause of myocardial infarction in animals?

a) Hypoglycemia
b) Coronary artery blockage
c) Anemia
d) Hyperthyroidism

82. Which hormone regulates water balance by acting on the kidneys?

a) Insulin
b) Aldosterone
c) Antidiuretic hormone (ADH)
d) Glucagon

83. What is a common sign of kidney disease in animals?

a) Vomiting
b) Excessive thirst
c) Lethargy
d) All of the above

84. What is the primary function of the kidneys?

a) Production of red blood cells
b) Regulation of body temperature
c) Filtration of blood
d) Secretion of hormones

85. What is the primary nitrogenous waste product excreted by the kidneys?

a) Urea
b) Ammonia
c) Creatinine
d) Uric acid

86. Which part of the nephron is involved in the majority of nutrient reabsorption?
 a) Proximal convoluted tubule b) Distal convoluted tubule
 c) Loop of Henle d) Collecting duct
87. What is the functional unit of the kidney?
 a) Glomerulus b) Nephron loop
 c) Renal capsule d) Nephrons
88. Which diagnostic test is commonly used to evaluate kidney function and detect urinary tract disorders?
 a) Blood pressure measurement b) Urinalysis
 c) Ultrasound d) ECG
89. What does a high urine specific gravity indicate?
 a) Dilute urine b) Normal hydration
 c) Concentrated urine d) Liver dysfunction
90. Which combination of test results suggests kidney dysfunction?
 a) Elevated BUN and creatinine b) Low blood glucose
 c) High blood cholesterol d) Low blood urea nitrogen
91. Which condition is characterized by inflammation of the kidney pelvis and renal parenchyma?
 a) Nephritis b) Pyelonephritis
 c) Glomerulonephritis d) Nephrotic syndrome
92. What is the gradual loss of kidney function over time called?
 a) Chronic kidney disease (CKD) b) Acute kidney injury (AKI)
 c) Nephrotic syndrome d) Polycystic kidney disease
93. Which condition is associated with the formation of stones in the urinary tract?
 a) Nephritis b) Urolithiasis
 c) Pyelonephritis d) Glomerulonephritis
94. Which clinical finding is common in chronic kidney disease due to decreased erythropoietin production?
 a) Polycythemia b) Leukopenia
 c) Anemia d) Thrombocytosis
95. Which lab finding is typical in nephrotic syndrome?
 a) Hyperkalemia b) Hypernatremia
 c) Hyperphosphatemia d) Hypoalbuminemia
96. Which symptom is commonly seen in animals with renal failure?
 a) Anuria b) Polydipsia
 c) Diarrhea d) Polyphagia
97. Which clinical sign indicates an increased volume of urine output?
 a) Anuria b) Oliguria
 c) Polyuria d) Dysuria

98. Which symptoms are commonly associated with uremia?

a) Vomiting and diarrhea
b) Increased appetite
c) Hyperactivity
d) Weight gain

99. Which condition is often associated with nephrotic syndrome?

a) Polyuria
b) Polydipsia
c) Hematuria
d) Edema

100. Which electrolyte imbalance is commonly seen in chronic kidney disease?

a) Hypokalemia
b) Hypernatremia
a) Hyperphosphatemia
d) Hypocalcemia

101. What is a common diagnostic test for detecting bacterial infections in the urinary tract?

a) Blood culture
b) Imaging studies
c) Urine specific gravity
d) Urine culture

102. What are common causes of azotemia in animals?

a) Hyperthyroidism
b) Dehydration or kidney dysfunction
c) Anemia
d) Hyperlipidemia

103. What is a common treatment for acute kidney injury?

a) Antibiotics
b) Fluid therapy
c) Diuretics
d) Steroids

104. Which class of drugs is commonly used to manage proteinuria in animals with kidney disease?

a) Beta-blockers
b) ACE inhibitors
c) Calcium channel blockers
d) Diuretics

105. What is the purpose of erythropoietin therapy in animals with kidney disease?

a) To increase red blood cell production
b) To decrease proteinuria
c) To control blood pressure
d) To reduce urine output

106. Which medication is used to manage metabolic acidosis in chronic kidney disease?

a) Calcium supplements
b) Phosphate binders
a) Sodium bicarbonate
d) Diuretics

107. Which type of medication is commonly used to reduce fluid buildup in animals with kidney disease?

a) Diuretics
b) Antibiotics
c) ACE inhibitors
d) Beta-blockers

108. Which type of kidney stones are most commonly found in animals?

a) Uric acid
b) Struvite
a) Calcium oxalate
d) Cystine

109. Which process is responsible for the movement of substances from the nephron back into the blood?
a) Filtration b) Secretion
c) Reabsorption d) Excretion

110. Which hormone primarily acts on the distal convoluted tubule to regulate sodium and potassium balance?
a) ADH (antidiuretic hormone) b) Aldosterone
c) Insulin d) Glucagon

111. Which function is performed by the Loop of Henle in the nephron?
a) Filtration of blood b) Concentration of urine
c) Secretion of hormones d) Excretion of waste

112. What is a common electrolyte imbalance seen in animals with acute kidney injury?
a) Hypokalemia b) Hyperkalemia
c) Hypernatremia d) Hypocalcemia

113. What drives the filtration process in the glomerulus?
a) Oncotic pressure b) Osmotic pressure
c) Hydrostatic pressure d) Hydrostatic pressure

114. Which hormone increases water reabsorption in the collecting ducts of the nephron?
a) Aldosterone b) Cortisol
c) Antidiuretic hormone (ADH) d) Insulin

115. What is a common emergency procedure for relieving urinary obstruction?
a) Dialysis b) Nephrectomy
c) Urinary catheterization d) Cystoscopy

116. Which condition is characterized by dilation of the renal pelvis and calyces due to obstruction of urine flow?
a) Nephritis b) Hydronephrosis
c) Pyelonephritis d) Interstitial nephritis

117. What is a common cause of nephrotoxicity in animals?
a) Antibiotics b) Steroids
b) NSAID toxicity d) Antihistamines

118. What are the common symptoms of uremia in animals with kidney disease?
a) Vomiting b) Anorexia
c) Lethargy d) All of the above

119. Which treatment is commonly used for bacterial infections causing pyelonephritis?
a) Steroids b) Antibiotics
c) Diuretics d) ACE inhibitors

120. What is the primary function of antidiuretic hormone (ADH) in the kidneys?
a) Increase urine production b) Decrease urine production
c) Increase blood pressure d) Decrease blood pressure

121. Which test measures the ability of the kidneys to concentrate urine?
   a) Urine specific gravity
   b) Blood urea nitrogen (BUN)
   c) Serum creatinine
   d) Urinalysis
122. What is a common symptom of chronic kidney disease in animals?
   a) Polyuria and polydipsia
   b) Vomiting and diarrhea
   c) Weight gain
   d) Hyperactivity
123. Which enzyme is primarily responsible for the breakdown of proteins in the stomach?
   a) Amylase
   b) Lipase
   c) Pepsin
   d) Trypsin
124. Which condition is characterized by inflammation of the stomach lining in animals?
   a) Enteritis
   b) Gastritis
   c) Hepatitis
   d) Pancreatitis
125. What is the primary function of the gastrointestinal (GI) tract?
   a) Filtration of blood
   b) Oxygen transport
   c) Digestion and absorption of nutrients
   d) Hormone secretion
126. Where is bile produced?
   a) Stomach
   b) Pancreas
   c) Liver
   d) Gallbladder
127. What is the primary function of the pancreas in digestion?
   a) Secretion of digestive enzymes and bicarbonate
   b) Production of bile
   c) Absorption of nutrients
   d) Storage of glycogen
128. What is the function of villi in the small intestine?
   a) Secretion of digestive enzymes
   b) Increase surface area for nutrient absorption
   c) Movement of food
   d) Production of mucus
129. Which process moves food through the GI tract?
   a) Diffusion
   b) Filtration
   c) Peristalsis
   d) Osmosis
130. What is the function of hydrochloric acid in the stomach?
   a) Activate pepsinogen to pepsin
   b) Neutralize bile
   c) Absorb nutrients
   d) Lubricate food
131. Where is the hormone cholecystokinin (CCK) produced?
   a) Stomach
   b) Pancreas
   c) Small intestine
   d) Liver

132. What is a common clinical sign of gastroenteritis in animals?
a) Diarrhea b) Increased appetite
c) Weight gain d) Constipation

133. What is a primary symptom of gastric ulcers in animals?
a) Diarrhea b) Vomiting
c) Increased thirst d) Hyperactivity

134. What is the term for the backward flow of stomach contents into the esophagus?
a) Dysphagia b) Gastroparesis
c) Gastroesophageal reflux d) Gastric dilation

135. What is a common cause of pancreatitis in animals?
a) High carbohydrate diet b) High-fat diet
c) Low protein diet d) High fiber diet

136. What condition results from the twisting of the stomach in animals, especially in large breeds of dogs?
a) Hepatic lipidosis b) Gastric ulceration
c) Gastric dilation volvulus (GDV) d) Enteritis

137. What does a fecal examination commonly diagnose in animals?
a) Liver disease b) Kidney disease
c) Parasitic infections d) Heart disease

138. Which test is used to measure pancreatic enzyme levels in blood?
a) Liver function test b) Serum amylase and lipase
c) Blood urea nitrogen (BUN) d) Complete blood count (CBC)

139. What does the presence of occult blood in stool indicate?
a) Liver disease b) GI bleeding
c) Kidney disease d) Heart disease

140. Which blood test measures liver function in animals?
a) Serum ALT and AST b) Blood urea nitrogen (BUN)
c) Serum amylase d) Serum creatinine

141. Which test is used to detect pancreatic insufficiency in animals?
a) Serum trypsin-like immunoreactivity (TLI)
b) Serum ALT and AST
c) Blood urea nitrogen (BUN)
d) Serum creatinine

142. What is the primary treatment for gastric ulcers in animals?
a) Antibiotics b) Proton pump inhibitors (PPIs)
c) Antihistamines d) Antacids

143. Which dietary modification is often recommended for animals with inflammatory bowel disease (IBD)?
a) Hypoallergenic or novel protein diet b) High-fat diet
c) Low-protein diet d) High-carbohydrate diet

144. Which medication is commonly used to treat liver disease in animals?
   a) Ursodeoxycholic acid   b) Antihistamines
   c) Antiemetics   d) Antibiotics

145. What is a common cause of gastritis in animals?
   a) Dietary indiscretion   b) High protein diet
   c) Low fiber diet   d) Infection

146. What is the primary cause of colitis in animals?
   a) Liver disease
   b) Inflammatory bowel disease (IBD)
   c) Kidney disease
   d) Heart disease

147. What is the primary function of the enteric nervous system?
   a) Control of voluntary muscle movements
   b) Regulation of heart rate
   c) Regulation of GI motility and secretion
   d) Control of respiratory rate

148. Which cells in the stomach secrete hydrochloric acid?
   a) Chief cells   b) Parietal cells
   c) Mucous cells   d) G cells

149. What is the role of intrinsic factor in digestion?
   a) Breakdown of proteins   b) Absorption of vitamin B12
   c) Emulsification of fats   d) Digestion of carbohydrates

150. Which condition is characterized by the formation of fibrous scar tissue in the liver?
   a) Cirrhosis   b) Hepatitis
   c) Pancreatitis   d) Gastritis

151. What is the primary role of the hormone ghrelin?
   a) Inhibit appetite   b) Stimulate appetite
   c) Promote digestion   d) Regulate blood sugar

152. Which condition involves the outpouching of the intestinal wall?
   a) Gastritis   b) Diverticulosis
   c) Enteritis   d) Hepatitis

153. Which hormone increases the release of digestive enzymes from the pancreas?
   a) Cholecystokinin (CCK)   b) Gastrin
   c) Secretin   d) Ghrelin

154. What is a common clinical sign of liver disease in animals?
   a) Polyuria   b) Polydipsia
   c) Jaundice   d) Hyperactivity

155. Which symptom is commonly associated with exocrine pancreatic insufficiency (EPI) in animals?
   a) Steatorrhea (fatty stools)
   b) Vomiting
   c) Polyuria
   d) Polydipsia

156. Which condition is indicated by the presence of blood in the vomit?
   a) Hematuria
   b) Hematemesis
   c) Hemoptysis
   d) Hemarthrosis

157. What is a common symptom of intestinal obstruction in animals?
   a) Abdominal pain and vomiting
   b) Polyuria and polydipsia
   c) Weight gain
   d) Jaundice

158. Which clinical sign is commonly associated with gastric dilation volvulus (GDV) in dogs?
   a) Distended abdomen and unproductive retching
   b) Polyuria and polydipsia
   c) Weight gain
   d) Jaundice

159. What is the term for the presence of blood in the feces?
   a) Hematuria
   b) Hemoptysis
   c) Hematochezia
   d) Hematemesis

160. Which gland is known as the "master gland" of the endocrine system?
   a) Thyroid gland
   b) Pituitary gland
   c) Adrenal gland
   d) Pancreas

161. What hormone is produced by the pancreas to lower blood glucose levels?
   a) Glucagon
   b) Insulin
   c) Cortisol
   d) Epinephrine

162. Which hormone regulates calcium levels in the blood?
   a) Insulin
   b) Parathyroid hormone (PTH)
   c) Glucagon
   d) Aldosterone

163. Which part of the adrenal gland produces cortisol?
   a) Medulla
   b) Cortex
   c) Capsule
   d) Zona glomerulosa

164. Which hormone is responsible for the fight-or-flight response?
   a) Cortisol
   b) Epinephrine
   c) Insulin
   d) Glucagon

165. Which gland secretes melatonin?
   a) Pineal gland
   b) Thyroid gland
   c) Adrenal gland
   d) Pituitary gland

166. Which hormone stimulates the release of glucose from the liver?
   a) Insulin
   b) Glucagon
   c) Thyroxine (T4)
   d) Cortisol

167. Which hormone is primarily involved in the regulation of metabolic rate?
a) Insulin
b) Cortisol
c) Thyroxine (T4)
d) Aldosterone

168. Which hormone is secreted by the anterior pituitary and stimulates milk production?
a) Oxytocin
b) Prolactin
c) ADH
d) ACTH

169. Which hormone is released in response to low blood calcium levels?
a) Parathyroid hormone (PTH)
b) Calcitonin
c) Thyroxine (T4)
d) Insulin

170. Which hormone is responsible for the regulation of circadian rhythms?
a) Insulin
b) Melatonin
c) Cortisol
d) Thyroxine (T4)

171. Which condition is characterized by excessive thirst and urination due to lack of ADH?
a) Hypothyroidism
b) Diabetes insipidus
c) Addison's disease
d) Cushing's syndrome

172. Which clinical sign is often seen in animals with diabetes mellitus?
a) Vomiting
b) Polyuria and polydipsia
c) Hair loss
d) Seizures

173. Which endocrine disorder is characterized by the overproduction of cortisol?
a) Addison's disease
b) Cushing's syndrome
c) Hypothyroidism
d) Hyperparathyroidism

174. What is a common symptom of Addison's disease in animals?
a) Hyperactivity
b) Lethargy and weakness
c) Increased appetite
d) Weight gain

175. What is a common clinical sign of an adrenal tumor in animals?
a) Hair loss
b) Hypertension
c) Vomiting
d) Seizures

176. Which clinical sign is commonly associated with hyperadrenocorticism in animals?
a) Pot-bellied appearance
b) Weight loss
c) Lethargy
d) Vomiting

177. Which hormone is typically overproduced in Cushing's syndrome?
a) Insulin
b) Thyroxine (T4)
c) Cortisol
d) Parathyroid hormone (PTH)

178. What is the primary cause of secondary hyperparathyroidism?
a) Pituitary tumor
b) Adrenal tumor
c) Chronic renal failure
d) Pancreatic tumor

179. Which condition is caused by an adrenal tumor that secretes excessive catecholamines?
a) Addison's disease
b) Cushing's syndrome
c) Pheochromocytoma
d) Hypoparathyroidism

180. What is the primary pathophysiological feature of diabetes mellitus?
   a) Hyperglycemia due to insulin deficiency or resistance
   b) Hypoglycemia due to excess insulin
   c) Hypercalcemia due to excess PTH
   d) Hypocalcemia due to deficient PTH

181. What is a common diagnostic test for diabetes mellitus in animals?
   a) Blood glucose measurement
   b) Thyroid hormone levels
   c) Cortisol levels
   d) Parathyroid hormone levels

182. What is a common diagnostic test for Cushing's syndrome in animals?
   a) Blood glucose measurement
   b) Thyroid hormone levels
   c) ACTH stimulation test
   d) Serum calcium levels

183. Which diagnostic test is used to measure long-term glucose control in diabetic animals?
   a) Fructosamine test
   b) Serum thyroxine (T4) levels
   c) ACTH stimulation test
   d) Serum calcium levels

184. What is a common diagnostic test for hyperparathyroidism?
   a) Blood glucose measurement
   b) Serum calcium and PTH levels
   c) Serum thyroxine (T4) levels
   d) Serum cortisol levels

185. What is a common diagnostic test for diabetes insipidus?
   a) Water deprivation test
   b) Blood glucose measurement
   c) Serum cortisol levels
   d) Serum insulin levels

186. Which medication is commonly used to treat hypothyroidism in dogs?
   a) Levothyroxine
   b) Methimazole
   c) Prednisone
   d) Insulin

187. What is the primary treatment for hyperthyroidism in cats?
   a) Levothyroxine
   b) Methimazole
   c) Prednisone
   d) Insulin

188. What is the primary function of neurons in the nervous system?
   a) Structural support
   b) Transmission of electrical impulses
   c) Production of hormones
   d) Protection of organs

189. Which part of the nervous system controls voluntary movements?
   a) Autonomic nervous system
   b) Somatic nervous system
   c) Central nervous system
   d) Peripheral nervous system

190. Which neurotransmitter is primarily associated with the parasympathetic nervous system?
   a) Dopamine
   b) Serotonin
   c) Acetylcholine
   d) Norepinephrine

191. What is the main role of the cerebellum in the nervous system?
   a) Regulating emotions
   b) Coordinating voluntary movements and balance
   c) Processing sensory information
   d) Controlling autonomic functions

192. Which part of the brain is responsible for higher cognitive functions such as reasoning?
   a) Brainstem
   b) Cerebellum
   c) Cerebrum
   d) Hippocampus

193. What is the primary symptom of myasthenia gravis in animals?
   a) Seizures
   b) Muscle weakness
   c) Tremors
   d) Paralysis

194. Which disorder is caused by a deficiency in the neurotransmitter dopamine?
   a) Parkinson's disease
   b) Epilepsy
   c) Multiple sclerosis
   d) Alzheimer's disease

195. What is the primary cause of hydrocephalus in animals?
   a) Accumulation of cerebrospinal fluid (CSF) in the brain
   b) Inflammation of the meninges
   c) Degeneration of motor neurons
   d) Demyelination of nerve fibers

196. Which disorder is characterized by the demyelination of nerve fibers in the central nervous system?
   a) Parkinson's disease
   b) Multiple sclerosis (MS)
   c) Epilepsy
   d) Myasthenia gravis

197. Which condition results from the compression of the spinal cord?
   a) Epilepsy
   b) Intervertebral disc disease (IVDD)
   c) Meningitis
   d) ALS

198. What is the primary symptom of Wobbler syndrome in animals?
   a) Seizures
   b) Muscle atrophy
   c) Unsteady gait
   d) Cognitive decline

199. Which diagnostic tool is most commonly used to visualize the structure of the brain in animals?
   a) Electroencephalography (EEG)
   b) Magnetic resonance imaging (MRI)
   c) Electromyography (EMG)
   d) Ultrasound

200. Which test is used to measure the electrical activity of the brain?
   a) MRI
   b) Electroencephalography (EEG)
   c) Electromyography (EMG)
   d) CT scan
201. Which test can help diagnose conditions like myasthenia gravis by detecting abnormal muscle responses?
   a) MRI b) CT scan
   c) Electromyography (EMG) d) EEG
202. Which symptom is commonly associated with vestibular disease in animals?
   a) Seizures b) Muscle weakness
   c) Head tilt and loss of balance d) Paralysis
203. What is the primary clinical sign of Horner's syndrome in animals?
   a) Drooping eyelid and constricted pupil on one side of the face
   b) Unsteady gait
   c) Seizures
   d) Muscle atrophy
204. What is the primary clinical sign of intervertebral disc disease (IVDD) in animals?
   a) Seizures b) Head tilt
   c) Back pain and hind limb weakness d) Muscle tremors
205. Which condition presents with abnormal gait and difficulty walking?
   a) Seizures b) Ataxia
   c) Tremors d) Paralysis
206. Which disorder is characterized by the gradual loss of muscle function and control?
   a) Seizures b) Paralysis
   c) Tremors d) Ataxia
207. Which medication is commonly used to control seizures in animals?
   a) Antibiotics b) Phenobarbital
   c) Anti-inflammatory drugs d) Antivirals
208. Which treatment is used for reducing intracranial pressure in animals with head trauma?
   a) Antibiotics b) Mannitol
   c) Phenobarbital d) Anticholinesterase drugs
209. What is the main goal of physical therapy in animals with neurological disorders?
   a) To cure infections
   b) To manage seizures
   c) To improve mobility and muscle strength
   d) To reduce intracranial pressure

210. Which medication is used to manage chronic pain in animals with neuropathic pain?
a) Antibiotics
b) Gabapentin
c) Mannitol
d) Phenobarbital

211. Which condition is indicated by the presence of nystagmus (involuntary eye movement) in animals?
a) Vestibular disease
b) Seizures
c) Muscle weakness
d) Paralysis

212. What is the primary symptom of a radial nerve injury in animals?
a) Inability to extend the paw or bear weight on the limb
b) Seizures
c) Head tilt
d) Muscle atrophy

213. Which glial cell is responsible for forming the blood-brain barrier?
a) Microglia
b) Astrocytes
c) Oligodendrocytes
d) Schwann cells

214. What is the primary symptom of a lower motor neuron lesion?
a) Flaccid paralysis and muscle atrophy
b) Spastic paralysis
c) Hyperreflexia
d) Sensory loss

215. Which condition results from a deficiency in the neurotransmitter dopamine?
a) Parkinson's disease
b) Epilepsy
c) Multiple sclerosis
d) Alzheimer's disease

216. Which condition is indicated by a sudden onset of unilateral facial paralysis in animals?
a) Facial nerve paralysis
b) Seizures
c) Head tilt
d) Muscle atrophy

217. Which type of muscle is responsible for voluntary movements?
a) Smooth muscle
b) Cardiac muscle
c) Skeletal muscle
d) Involuntary muscle

218. What is the primary function of tendons?
a) Connect muscle to bone
b) Connect bone to bone
c) Protect organs
d) Produce synovial fluid

219. Which ion is essential for muscle contraction?
a) Sodium
b) Potassium
c) Calcium
d) Chloride

220. What is the basic contractile unit of a muscle called?
a) Myofibril
b) Sarcomere
c) Sarcolemma
d) Myofilament

221. Which disease is characterized by an abnormal immune response leading to joint inflammation?
   a) Osteoarthritis
   b) Rheumatoid arthritis
   c) Gout
   d) Tendinitis

222. Which of the following is a common clinical sign of hip dysplasia in dogs?
   a) Decreased appetite
   b) Lameness in the hind limbs
   c) Increased thirst
   d) Weight gain

223. Which muscle group is primarily involved in the extension of the elbow joint?
   a) Biceps brachii
   b) Triceps brachii
   c) Deltoid
   d) Latissimus dorsi

224. In which condition do animals typically exhibit a "bunny hopping" gait?
   a) Elbow dysplasia
   b) Hip dysplasia
   c) Intervertebral disc disease
   d) Cranial cruciate ligament rupture

225. Which vitamin is crucial for calcium absorption and bone health in animals?
   a) Vitamin A
   b) Vitamin C
   c) Vitamin D
   d) Vitamin K

226. What is the main structural protein found in bone?
   a) Actin
   b) Myosin
   c) Collagen
   d) Elastin

227. Which clinical disorder in horses is associated with inflammation of the laminae in the hoof?
   a) Tendinitis
   b) Laminitis
   c) Osteochondrosis
   d) Navicular disease

228. Which disorder is characterized by the breakdown of muscle tissue and the release of muscle fiber contents into the bloodstream?
   a) Rhabdomyolysis
   b) Muscular dystrophy
   c) Myasthenia gravis
   d) Polymyositis

229. What is the primary component of the extracellular matrix in cartilage?
   a) Elastin
   b) Collagen
   c) Chondroitin sulfate
   d) Hydroxyapatite

230. Which ligament is commonly injured in dogs, leading to stifle instability?
   a) Anterior cruciate ligament
   b) Medial collateral ligament
   c) Lateral collateral ligament
   d) Patellar ligament

231. Which type of muscle contraction occurs when the muscle length does not change despite tension?
   a) Isotonic contraction
   b) Isometric contraction
   c) Concentric contraction
   d) Eccentric contraction

232. Which vitamin deficiency is commonly associated with rickets in young animals?
   a) Vitamin A
   b) Vitamin B12
   c) Vitamin D
   d) Vitamin K

233. Which muscle group is primarily responsible for extending the hock joint in animals?
   a) Hamstrings
   b) Quadriceps
   c) Gastrocnemius
   d) Gluteals
234. Which bone disease is characterized by inadequate mineralization of the bone matrix?
   a) Osteoporosis
   b) Osteomalacia
   c) Paget's disease
   d) Osteopetrosis
235. Which structure serves as the site for hematopoiesis (blood cell formation) in bones?
   a) Periosteum
   b) Yellow marrow
   c) Red marrow
   d) Articular cartilage
236. What is the primary function of osteoblasts in bone tissue?
   a) Break down bone matrix
   b) Produce bone matrix
   c) Store minerals
   d) Resorb bone matrix
237. Which joint type allows for the greatest range of motion?
   a) Hinge joint
   b) Pivot joint
   c) Ball-and-socket joint
   d) Gliding joint
238. Which disorder is characterized by the excessive deposition of uric acid crystals in joints?
   a) Gout
   b) Osteoarthritis
   c) Rheumatoid arthritis
   d) Osteomalacia
239. Which condition is caused by a genetic mutation that affects collagen synthesis in bones, leading to brittle bones?
   a) Osteogenesis imperfecta
   b) Osteoporosis
   c) Osteomalacia
   d) Paget's disease
240. Which vitamin is essential for collagen synthesis in the body?
   a) Vitamin A
   b) Vitamin C
   c) Vitamin D
   d) Vitamin E
241. Which condition in animals is characterized by a lateral deviation of the spinal column?
   a) Lordosis
   b) Scoliosis
   c) Kyphosis
   d) Spondylosis
242. Which type of bone cell is primarily involved in bone remodeling by resorbing bone tissue?
   a) Osteoblasts
   b) Osteoclasts
   c) Osteocytes
   d) Chondrocytes
243. Which type of connective tissue forms the intervertebral discs in animals?
   a) Hyaline cartilage
   b) Elastic cartilage
   c) Fibrocartilage
   d) Articular cartilage

244. Which bone disease is characterized by the replacement of normal bone marrow with fibrous tissue?
   a) Osteopetrosis
   b) Osteoporosis
   c) Osteomyelitis
   d) Fibrous dysplasia

245. Which bone disorder is characterized by inflammation of the bone and marrow, usually due to bacterial infection?
   a) Osteomyelitis
   b) Osteoarthritis
   c) Osteosarcoma
   d) Osteopetrosis

246. Which type of immunity is present at birth and does not require prior exposure to an antigen?
   a) Adaptive immunity
   b) Innate immunity
   c) Passive immunity
   d) Acquired immunity

247. Which cells are primarily responsible for producing antibodies?
   a) T cells
   b) Macrophages
   c) B cells
   d) Neutrophils

248. Which organ is the primary site for the maturation of T cells?
   a) Bone marrow
   b) Spleen
   c) Thymus
   d) Lymph nodes

249. Which of the following is an example of passive immunity?
   a) Vaccination
   b) Antibody transfer from mother to offspring
   c) Infection recovery
   d) Immune memory

250. Which of the following cytokines is primarily responsible for inducing fever?
   a) Interleukin-1 (IL-1)
   b) Interleukin-2 (IL-2)
   c) Interferon-gamma (IFN-γ)
   d) Tumor necrosis factor-alpha (TNF-α)

251. Which immune cells are the first to arrive at the site of infection?
   a) Lymphocytes
   b) Neutrophils
   c) Eosinophils
   d) Basophils

252. Which type of hypersensitivity reaction is involved in allergic reactions?
   a) Type I
   b) Type II
   c) Type III
   d) Type IV

253. Which type of hypersensitivity reaction is responsible for autoimmune diseases such as systemic lupus erythematosus?
   a) Type I
   b) Type II
   c) Type III
   d) Type IV

254. Which of the following is the first antibody produced in response to an infection?
   a) IgA b) IgE
   c) IgG d) IgM

255. Which type of hypersensitivity reaction involves T cells and does not require antibodies?
   a) Type I b) Type II
   c) Type III d) Type IV

256. Which immunoglobulin is associated with allergic reactions and parasitic infections?
   a) IgA b) IgD
   c) IgE d) IgM

257. Which cells produce histamine in response to allergens?
   a) Eosinophils b) Neutrophils
   c) Mast cells d) B cells

258. Which type of hypersensitivity is characterized by the formation of immune complexes?
   a) Type I b) Type II
   c) Type III d) Type IV

259. Which immune cells are most involved in the response to parasitic infections?
   a) Neutrophils b) Macrophages
   c) Eosinophils d) Lymphocytes

260. Which of the following is a common immunologic disorder seen in young foals?
   a) Neonatal isoerythrolysis b) Autoimmune hemolytic anemia
   c) Rheumatoid arthritis d) Systemic lupus erythematosus

261. Which of the following is a common feature of autoimmune hemolytic anemia (AIHA)?
   a) Spherocytosis b) Lymphadenopathy
   c) Coughing d) Diarrhea

Answer Key

1	b	2	b	3	b	4	b	5	b	6	a	7	a
8	d	9	a	10	a	11	a	12	a	13	b	14	b
15	c	16	b	17	c	18	b	19	c	20	b	21	b
22	a	23	a	24	c	25	b	26	b	27	b	28	b
29	c	30	b	31	a	32	a	33	b	34	b	35	c
36	d	37	b	38	d	39	c	40	a	41	d	42	a
43	b	44	c	45	c	46	b	47	c	48	b	49	b
50	b	51	b	52	d	53	a	54	c	55	c	56	b
57	b	58	a	59	c	60	c	61	d	62	a	63	b
64	b	65	a	66	c	67	a	68	a	69	c	70	b

71	b	72	c	73	b	74	a	75	b	76	b	77	c
78	b	79	b	80	c	81	b	82	c	83	d	84	c
85	a	86	a	87	d	88	b	89	c	90	a	91	b
92	a	93	b	94	c	95	d	96	b	97	c	98	a
99	d	100	a	101	d	102	b	103	b	104	b	105	a
106	c	107	a	108	c	109	c	110	b	111	b	112	b
113	d	114	c	115	c	116	b	117	c	118	d	119	b
120	b	121	a	122	a	123	c	124	b	125	c	126	c
127	a	128	b	129	c	130	a	131	c	132	a	133	b
134	c	135	b	136	c	137	c	138	b	139	b	140	a
141	a	142	b	143	a	144	a	145	a	146	b	147	c
148	b	149	b	150	a	151	b	152	b	153	a	154	c
155	a	156	b	157	a	158	a	159	c	160	b	161	b
162	b	163	b	164	b	165	a	166	b	167	c	168	b
169	a	170	b	171	b	172	b	173	b	174	b	175	b
176	a	177	c	178	c	179	c	180	a	181	a	182	c
183	a	184	b	185	a	186	a	187	b	188	b	189	b
190	c	191	b	192	c	193	b	194	a	195	a	196	b
197	b	198	c	199	b	200	b	201	c	202	c	203	a
204	c	205	b	206	b	207	b	208	b	209	c	210	b
211	a	212	a	213	b	214	a	215	a	216	a	217	c
218	a	219	c	220	b	221	b	222	b	223	b	224	b
225	c	226	c	227	b	228	a	229	c	230	a	231	b
232	c	233	c	234	b	235	c	236	b	237	c	238	a
239	a	240	b	241	b	242	b	243	c	244	d	245	a
246	b	247	c	248	c	249	b	250	a	251	b	252	a
253	c	254	d	255	d	256	c	257	c	258	c	259	c
260	a	261	a										

2

Temperature Regulation and Maintenance

Lipika Sarma[1], Devojyoti Dutta[1], Mrinmoyee Sarma[2] and Monoshree Sarma[3]

[1]*Department of Veterinary Physiology, College of Veterinary Science, Assam Agricultural University, Khanapara, Guwahati-781022, Assam*

[2]*Department of Veterinary Public Health and Epidemiology, Institute of Veterinary Science and Animal Husbandry, Siksha O Anusandhan, Bhubaneswar, Odisha*

[3]*Department of Veterinary Pharmacology and Toxicology, Institute of Veterinary Science and Animal Husbandry, Siksha O Anusandhan, Bhubaneswar, Odisha*

Introduction

Temperature regulation is a critical physiological process that allows animals and birds to maintain homeostasis in varying environmental conditions. Thermoregulation involves a complex interplay of behavioral, physiological, and biochemical mechanisms that ensure the body temperature of these animals remains within a narrow, optimal range. This process is vital for maintaining metabolic functions, health, and productivity, particularly in agricultural settings where animals are often exposed to temperature extremes.In farm animals such as cattle, sheep, and pigs, thermoregulation is primarily managed through a combination of heat production, heat dissipation, and behavioral adaptations. Endothermic animals generate heat internally through metabolic processes, particularly in the muscles and liver. This heat is distributed throughout the body via the circulatory system. When ambient temperatures rise, farm animals activate various cooling mechanisms to prevent hyperthermia. These mechanisms include increased respiratory rates (panting), sweating (in species like cattle and horses), and vasodilation, where blood vessels near the skin surface expand to dissipate heat. Conversely, in cold environments, animals reduce heat loss by vasoconstriction, piloerection (raising of hair or fur), and seeking shelter or huddling together. Behavioral adaptations, such as seeking shade or water, also play a crucial role in temperature regulation.In poultry, thermoregulation is equally important but is managed differently due to their unique physiology. Birds lack sweat glands and have a higher metabolic rate compared to mammals, which means they rely more heavily on respiratory evaporative cooling and behavioral adaptations. Poultry regulate their body temperature by panting, which increases evaporative heat loss from the respiratory tract. Additionally, birds adjust their posture, such as spreading their wings or ruffling feathers, to enhance heat dissipation. During cold stress, poultry increase their metabolic rate, fluff their feathers to trap air for insulation, and reduce blood flow to peripheral areas to conserve heat. The thermal comfort zone, or thermoneutral zone, is narrower in poultry compared to larger mammals, making them more susceptible to temperature extremes.The ability of farm animals and poultry to regulate their body temperature is influenced by several factors, including age, breed, body condition, and acclimatization to the environment. Younger animals and certain breeds are more vulnerable to temperature stress due to their less developed thermoregulatory mechanisms or specific genetic traits. For instance, breeds with higher muscle mass or thicker coats may be more prone to heat stress, while those with lower body fat reserves may struggle in cold conditions. Acclimatization, or the gradual adaptation to a new thermal environment, plays a key role in enhancing the thermoregulatory capacity of these animals.

Environmental management is crucial for supporting the thermoregulatory needs of farm animals and poultry. Proper housing design, ventilation, and access to shade and water are essential strategies for mitigating temperature stress. In modern agricultural practices, technologies such as climate-controlled barns and precision livestock farming tools are increasingly used to monitor and manage environmental conditions, ensuring optimal temperatures for animal welfare and productivity.In conclusion, temperature regulation and maintenance in farm animals and poultry are vital for their survival, health, and productivity. Understanding the physiological and behavioral mechanisms involved in thermoregulation, along with the factors influencing these processes, is essential for effective animal management. As climate change continues to pose challenges to livestock farming, enhancing the thermoregulatory capacity of farm animals and poultry through improved breeding, nutrition, and environmental management practices will be increasingly important for sustaining agricultural productivity and animal welfare.

1. Hygrometer measures the;
   a) Wind velocity   b) Humidity
   c) Rainfall   d) Temperature
2. When a meteorological variable is averaged for a minimum of 30 years, it is referred to as;
   a) Macroclimate   b) Weather
   c) Microclimate   d) Climate
3. A seasonal year graph that shows how agricultural/climatic factors or human activity relate to each other is referred to as a
   a) Hythergraph   b) Ergograph
   c) Climograph   d) Climatogram
4. The term "microclimate" describes;
   a) The environment around the animal   d) Both a and b
   c) Climate in large space   a) Climate of the least space
5. A charted graph illustrating the correlations between temperature and precipitation is called
   a) Climograph   b) Ergograph
   c) Climatogram   d) Hythergraph

6. When it comes to regular chicken reproduction, the most significant environmental component is

a) Light
b) Humidity
c) Rainfall
b) Temperature

7. The term "bioclimatology" describes the relationship between:

a) Temperature, plant, animal and soil
b) Photoperiod, rainfall, animal and soil
c) Wind velocity, day length, animal and soil
d) Climate, plant, animal and soil

8. Evaporative Cooling: in summer includes

a) Sweating and:
b) Panting
c) none of the above
d) both of the above

9. When it comes to Zebu cows and milk production, the optimum temperature range is between;

a) 27-30°C
b) 30-35°C
c) 35-38°C
d) 20-25°C

10. The estimated decrease in milk production occurs with each degree (°c) increase in rectal temperature.

c) 1.2 kg
b) 1.0 kg
a) 0.5kg
d) 1.5 kg

11. Decrease in milk production is mainly due to

a) Extended daytime hours and moderate relative humidity
b) High temperature and high relative humidity
c) Low relative humidity and a high temperature
d) None of the above

12. In cases of extreme heat stress, increased heat generation and respiratory energy expenditure are referred to as:

a) Van't Hoff effect
b) Van't Hoff Arrhenius effect
c) Van Allen effect
d) Van't Hoff Arthur effect

13. The following raises erythropoietin levels:

d) Lower pH
b) Lower PO_2
c) Lower Hb
a) Lower PCO_2

14. Which organ uses the most oxygen per minute (in milliliters)?

a) Brain
b) Kidney
c) Liver
d) Skeletal muscle

15. Which bodily organ uses the most oxygen per minute (ml / 100 gm)?

a) Liver
b) Brain
c) Kidney
d) Skeletal muscle

16. Which bodily organ uses the least oxygen per minute (ml / 100 gm)?
    a) Skeletal muscle c) Liver
    d) Kidney b) Brain
17. Getting acquainted with high altitude causes all of the following except;
    a) Increase in the sensitivity of the carotid body
    b) Shift in the oxygen dissociation curve to left
    c) Increase in minute ventilation
    d) Increase in the sensitivity of central chemoreceptor
18. Estivators stop their activity during
    a) Rainy season b) Summer
    c) Winter d) None of the above
19. When compared to poikilotherms, homoeotherms produce more heat;
    a) 2-4 times b) 4-6 times
    c) 8-10 times d) 6-8 times
20. Animals whose body temperatures fluctuate in response to environmental temperature are referred to as;
    a) Temperature regulator b) Poikilotherm
    c) Homeotherm d) Warm-blooded
21. The thermoregulatory behavior known as gular flutter is present in;
    a) Mammals b) Birds
    c) Amphibians d) Reptiles
22. Sweat glands not found in;
    b) Rodents c) Birds
    a) Whales d) All of the above
23. What physiological reactions are utilized to detect an animal's stress level?
    a) Respiration rate b) Pulse rate
    c) Rectal temperature d) All of the above
24. Animals that can regulate their body temperature despite temperature fluctuations in their surroundings are referred to as;
    a) Homeotherm b) Cold-blooded
    c) Temperature conformer d) Poikilotherm
25. When animals are exposed to high ambient temperatures, their initial reaction is;
    a) Vasodilatation b) Vasoconstriction
    c) Non-shivering thermogenesis d) Decrease in heat production
26. THIindicates
    a) Thermal heat index b) Thermal humidity index
    c) Temperature humidity index d) Temperature humidity indicator
27. Panting not seen in;
    a) Horse b) Cat
    c) Poultry d) Dog

28. In higher mammals, the deep body temperature ranges between;
    a) 38 - 42 deg °C b) 39 - 45 deg °C
    c) 36 - 40 deg °C d) 40-50 deg °C
29. The summer heat load on animals can be reduced by;
    a) Increasing insulation b) Reducing body surface area
    c) Concentrate diet d) Decreasing heat production
30. What influences the rate of cutaneous evaporation is
    a) Air temperature b) Humidity
    c) Air movement d) All of the above
31. The effective method of regulating an animal's body temperature by;
    a) Conduction b) Sweating
    c) Panting d) Radiation
32. The main process by which heat loss occurs when the outside temperature is higher than the body's is;
    a) Convection b) Conduction
    c) Radiation d) Evaporation
33. Which area of a zebu cattle's body has the most capacity to produce sweat?
    a) Hump b) Rump
    c) Ventral d) All of the above
34. Shivering thermogenesis is linked to which hormone?
    a) Epinephrine b) Cortisol
    c) Nor-epinephrine d) Both a and c
35. Which hormone among those listed below is not necessary for cold-stimulated non-shivering thermogenesis?
    a) GH b) Cortisol
    c) Epinephrine d) None of the above
36. One of the following does not conserves heat:
    a) Vasodilatation b) Huddling
    c) Piloerection d) Vasoconstriction
37. Breeds and species that emerged in areas with temperate climates have;
    a) Medium body size b) Large body size
    c) Small body size d) None of the above.
38. Of the following, which range of temperatures represents the ambient temperature at which the least amount of heat exchange occurs between the environment and the animal?
    a) Zone of homeothermy b) Zone of thermal survival
    c) Zone of thermoneutrality d) None of the above
39. Reasonable heat loss implies the following procedure:
    a) Radiation b) Conduction
    c) Convection d) All of the above

40. Most heat resistant animal among the following?
    a) Sheep b) Goat
    c) Camel d) Cattle

41. When two heated items come into direct physical contact with one another, heat is dissipated in:
    a) Evaporation b) Conduction
    c) Radiation d) Convection

42. In the winter, a decrease in body temperature, heart rate, and respiration along with a cessation of coordinated locomotor activity are referred to as;
    a) Summer sleep b) Estivation
    c) Both a and b d) Hibernation

43. A trance-like state of sleep in the summer is referred to as;
    a) Hibernation b) Torpor
    c) Estivation d) Hibernation

44. Exertion-induced sweating is mediated by;
    a) Sympathetic adrenergic nerve fibre
    b) Parasympathetic cholinergic nerve fibre
    c) Sympathetic cholinergicnervefibre
    d) Adrenal cortex hormones

45. The animal's body's ability to transfer heat depends on;
    a) Length of coat b) Color of coat
    c) Thickness of coat d) All the above

46. An essential role for brown adipose tissue is thermoregulation during
    a) Cold stress b) No effect
    c) Heat stress d) None

47. Homeostasis was coined by?
    a) Walter Bradford Cannon b) Philip Bard
    c) Hans Selye d) Claude Bernard

48. Related to the Stefan-Bolzmann constant are
    a) Radiation b) Evaporation
    c) Convection d) Radiation

49. General Adaptation Syndrome (GAS) was given by;
    a) Walter Bradford Cannon b) Hans Selye
    c) Philip Bard d) Claude Bernard

50. An apparatus that tracks and measures both activity and rest is referred to as;
    a) Octameter b) Pedometer
    c) Actometer d) All of the above

51. The range of normal temperatures in which animals may thrive is
   a) 40 to +40°C b) -32 to +60°C
   c) -32 to +40°C d) -60 to +60°C

52. Heat regulation center is present in;
   a) Thalamus b) Hypothalamus
   c) Motor cortex d) None of the above

53. Thermoregulatory control centers regulating sweating, and panting are present in;
   a) Anterior hypothalamus b) Anterior pituitary
   c) Posterior hypothalamus d) Posterior pituitary

54. Which rule best describes how the protruding bodily organs are comparatively shorter in cooler than in warmer portions of the species' biological range?
   a) Wilson's Rule b) Bergman's rule
   c) Allen's rule d) Golger's Rule

55. The anterior portion of the hypothalamus reacts to afferent cutaneous and deep tissue sensors during thermoregulation by means of;
   a) Peripheral vasodilation b) Sweating
   c) Panting d) All of the above

56. Animals that have adapted well are characterized by anything but;
   a) High reproductive efficiency b) Longevity
   c) Loss of body weight d) High resistance to disease

57. Which rule best describes the situation where smaller breeds of a particular species happen to exist in warmer sections of the ecological zones and larger breeds are found in cooler regions?
   a) Allen's rule b) Golger's rule
   c) Bergmann's rule d) Wilson's rule

58. Which of the preceding rules connects climate and insulating cover?
   a) Golger's Rule b) Wilson's Rule
   c) Allen's rule d) Bergman's rule

59. Control centers for thermogenesis, which govern both shivering and non-shivering, are found in;
   a) Anterior pituitary b) Posterior hypothalamus
   c) Posterior pituitary d) None of the above

60. Which rule best describes the fact that breeds of birds and mammals that live in warm, humid climates have higher melanin pigmentation than breeds that live in colder, drier climates?
   a) Golger's Rule b) Bergman's rule
   c) Allen's rule d) Wilson's Rule

61. Acclimatization refers to
   a) Short term adjustments b) Long term adjustments
   c) None of the above d) Both a and b

62. Gradually fading sensitivity in response to a certain recurrent stimulation is referred to as:
    a) Learning b) Habituation
    c) Adaptation d) Conditioning
63. Quick changes in physiology and behavior are the hallmark of acute stress, which is commonly referred to as
    a) Cannon's Emergency syndrome b) General adaptations syndrome
    c) Fight or flight syndrome d) None of the above
64. An animal's expected total radiation exchange in a given habitat is calculated using
    a) Anemometer b) Dry and wet bulb thermometer
    c) Black Globe Thermometer d) Wind vane
65. Wind direction determined by?
    a) Wind vane b) Black Globe Thermometer
    c) Dry and wet bulb thermometer d) Anemometer
66. Speed of windis determined by?
    a) Dry and wet bulb thermometer b) Anemometer
    c) Wind vane d) Black Globe Thermometer
67. The areas with the biggest brown adipose tissue deposits include;
    a) Between muscles of neck and back
    b) Around thoracic and abdominal viscera
    c) In axillae and groin
    d) Around the kidney and adrenal gland
68. A graph illustrating the relationship between climate variables, human activity, and a cyclical year is called as.
    a) Ergograph b) Climograph
    c) Hythergraph d) Climatogram
69. The microclimate means;
    a) Climate in large space
    b) Climate in the immediate vicinity of animal
    c) Climate of a least space
    d) Both a and b
70. The term "bioclimatology" describes the relationship between;
    a) Temperature, plant, animal and soil
    b) Climate, plant, animal and soil
    c) Photoperiod, rainfall, animal and soil
    d) Wind velocity, day length, animal and soil
71. For every 100 meters above sea level, the air temperature drops by...;
    a) 0.65°C b) 0.65°C
    c) 6.5°C d) 6.5°C

72. A hygrometer measures the
   a) Temperature b) Humidity
   c) Wind velocity d) Rainfall
73. When physiological processes repeat itself more or less at constant intervals the phenomenon is known as;
   a) Circadian rhythm b) biological rhythm
   c) Diurnal rhythm d) All of the above
74. Which of the following rules describes the dependence of free running period on light intensity?
   a) Aschoff's rule b) Van't Hoff's rule
   c) Dalton's rule d) Kibler's rule
75. When a meteorological variable is averaged for a minimum of 30 years, it is referred to as;
   a) Weather b) Macroclimate
   c) Microclimate d) Climate
76. A charted graph illustrating the correlations between temperature and precipitation is called a
   a) Climatogram b) Hythergraph
   c) Ergograph d) Climograph
77. Short term day to day fluctuation of meteorological variable is called —
   a) Macroclimate b) Climate
   c) Microclimate d) Weather
78. General large-scale climatic conditions of the open atmosphere in large area are-
   a) Weather b) Microclimate
   c) Climate d) Macroclimate
79. Physiological Adaptations to high temperature
   a) Sweating and Panting b) Vasodilation
   c) Increased Respiratory Rate: d) All of the above
80. Transfer of heat from a warmer object to a cooler object by direct contact is term as-
   a) Convection b) Conduction
   c) Radiation d) Evaporation
81. The instrument composed of human hair used to measure humidity is called
   a) Hygrometer b) Dry bulb thermometer
   c) Thermometer d) Wet bulb thermometer
82. Physiological Adaptations to cold temperature are
   a) Vasoconstriction: b) Shivering
   c) Piloerection: d) All of the above
83. Biochemical changes during heat stress
   a) Depletion of liver enzyme b) Lower bodys mineral status
   c) Lower level of albumin, total protein d) All of the above

84. What is presented in an insensible heat loss mechanism?
    a) Radiation b) Convection
    c) Conduction d) Evaporation
85. The rhythm that will take more than a day but less than a year known as-----
    a) Chronobiology b) Ultradian rhythm
    c) Diurnal rhythm d) Infradian rhythm
86. Which of the following is more resistant to change in temperature
    a) Exotic animals b) Indeginous animals
    c) Crossbred animals d) None of the above
87. What is presented in a sensible heat loss mechanism?
    a) Convection b) Conduction
    c) Radiation d) All of the above
88. Which of the options that follow is frequently employed to aid animals in surviving in cold climates, enabling the organism to conserve energy that would otherwise be required to keep its body temperature high?
    a) Torpor b) Estivation
    c) Shivering d) Hibernation
89. A significant element that modifies the bird's body temperature and, eventually, its productivity is the
    a) Photoperiod b) Day period
    c) Gestation period d) Night period
90. Sweat glands absent in-
    a) Buffalo b) Sheep
    c) Poultry d) Dog
91. The range of temperatures known as ---- is the range over which changes in ambient temperature have no effect on metabolic heat production (HP).
    a) Huddling, Increased Activity b) Shivering, Piloerection
    c) Vasoconstriction d) All of the above
92. Milk yield of crossbred cows is unaffected within a temperature range of----
    a) 0-21°C b) 35-40°C
    c) 40-45°C d) 0-5°C
93. When birds experience cold exposure, they attempt to minimize their surface area and minimise heat loss. This is known as
    a) Sunning behavior b) Hunching
    c) Shivering d) Huddling behaviour
94. Rhythm taking place in less than a day is called as---
    a) Diurnal rhythm b) Chronobiology
    c) Ultradian rhythm d) Infradian rhythm

95. What is the temperature of the brain and core during flight?
   a) Increases
   b) Decreases
   c) Constant
   d) None of the above

96. Which of the tools listed below is used to measure the intensity of light?
   a) Sunset recorder
   b) Hygrometer
   c) Lux meter
   d) Evaporimeter

97. What temperature best represents the core temperature?
   a) Ear temperature
   b) Rectal temperature
   c) Skin temperature
   d) Ventral body temperature

98. Milk production decreases in
   a) Long day length and medium relative humidity
   b) High temperature and high relative humidity
   c) None of the above
   d) High temperature and low relative humidity

99. BMR encompasses all of the following, except:
   a) Fasting heat production
   b) Fasting anabolism
   c) Fasting catabolism
   d) Both a and b

100. Breathing too quickly results in respiratory
   a) No change in pH
   b) Alkalosis
   c) All of the above
   d) Acidosis

101. It takes the following to maintain constant alveolar ventilation under elevated physiological dead space:
   a) None
   b) Higher tidal volume
   c) Both a and b
   d) Higher respiratory frequency

102. The degree to which the body cools down before heat production starts is referred to as—
   a) Hypothermia
   b) Shivering
   c) Critical temperature
   d) Hibernation

103. The following causes the oxygen-hemoglobin dissociation curve to shift to the right:
   a) Increase in temperature
   b) Decrease in pH
   c) Increase in DPG
   d) All of the above

104. How farm animals balances high ambient temperature
   a) Seeking Shade: Reduced Activity:
   b) Increased Water Intake, Postural Change
   c) Sweating and Panting: Vasodilation:
   d) All of the above

105. Study of biological rhythm is called as-
   a) Chronobiology
   b) Cirannual cycles
   c) Ultradian rhythm
   d) Circadian rhythm

106. Which of the listed THI stress levels shows that there is severe stress

a) Up to 72 b) 72-78

c) 78-88 d) Above 88

107. Which of the listed THI stress levels shows that there is no stress?

a) Up to 72 b) 72-78

c) 78-88 d) Above 88

108. Nitric oxide synthetase action in heat stress animal is:

a) Vasodialtion b) Vasoconstriction

c) None of the above d) Shivering

109. Is a common thermometer that can be used to measure the dry air temperature, similar to a maximum thermometer.

a) Dry bulb thermometer b) Minimum thermometer

c) Maximum thermometer d) Wet bulb thermometer

110. When animals are exposed to high ambient temperatures, their initial reaction is:

a) Vasodilatation b) Non-shivering thermogenesis

c) Vasoconstriction d) Decrease in heat production

111. Goats typically have rectal temperatures of

a) 101.5ºF b) 102.3ºF

d) 102ºF c) 100ºF

112. Why indigenousbreeds are more resistant to harsh environmental temperature

a) Body coat colour b) Genetic makeup

c) Sweat gland d) All of the above

113. What kinds of sweat glands are there?

a) Apocrine b) Eccrine

c) Both a & b d) Exocrine

114. Which of the following is the function of HSP in heat stress?

a) Protect protein denaturation b) Protein proper structure

c) Maintain cellular integrity d) All of the above

115. Which of the following animals has the highest potential for thermoregulatory function-the removal of heat through sweating?

a) Horse b) Cattle

c) Sheep d) Dog

116. Which of the folowingrefers to a state of decreased physiological activity in an animal, usually characterized by a reduction in body temperature, metabolic rate, and energy consumption.?

a) Estivation b) Shivering

c) Torpor d) Hibernation

117. Which among the following animals has the best panting efficiency?

a) Sheep b) Horse

c) Cattle d) Dog

118. Which of the following is responsible for apoptosis during heat stress
a) Hsp b) Bax
c) Gpx d) Sod

119. A 24-hour period is used to describe a cyclical fluctuation in physiological, behavioural, or metabolic processes.
a) Ultradian rhythm b) Circadian rhythm
c) Cirannual cycles d) Chronobiology

120. Is a method by which animals generate heat.
a) Shivering b) Critical temperature
c) Hibernation d) Hypothermia

121. The process of sleeping in a safe burrow when hibernating is known as
b) Hibernation d) Hypothermia
c) Critical temperature a) Shivering

122. The maximum temperature for peak milk letdown of Zebu cows is between:
a) 35-38°C b) 30-35°C
c) 27-30°C d) 20-25°C

123. ----is a type of connective tissue that has a high mitochondrial density and colour due to cytochrome pigments.
a) Brown fat b) Yellow fat
c) Red fat d) White fat

124. Which of the following gives animals the highest possible heat load?
a) Metabolism c) Conduction
d) Convection b) Radiation

125. How The level of cortisol changes during chronic heat stress
a) Increses b) Decreses
c) No change d) None of the above

126. The following which of the this is more heat resistant
a) Tharparkar b) Red sindhi
c) Sahiwal d) HF

127. When a non-hibernating homeotherm's deep body temperature falls below normal, it's referred to as —
a) Hypothermia b) Hyperthermia
c) Homeostasis d) Thermostat

128. Which of the items listed below describes a moderate THI stress level?
a) Above 88 b) 72-78
c) 78-88 d) Up to 72

129. Changes that occur when an animal that is not acclimated to a fast drop in temperature include:
a) Tachycardia
b) Shift of blood from periphery to core

c) Increase in systolic blood pressure
d) Non-shivering thermogenesis

130. Which of the listed THI stress levels corresponds to mild stress?
a) Up to 72 b) 72-78
c) 78-88 d) Above 88

131. An apparatus that automatically determine humidity and temperature is---
a) Minimum thermometer b) Thermohygrograph
c) Thermograph d) Maximum thermometer

132. Is a standard thermometer that is used to measure the maximum temperature in a specific time period.
a) Thermohygrograph b) Minimum thermometer
c) Maximum thermometer d) Thermograph

133. The air's lowest temperature during a certain duration can be determined by:
a) Thermograph c) Maximum thermometer
b) Thermohygrograph d) Minimum thermometer

134. Muscular tremor occurs at a frequency of roughly ten times per second and is an involuntary function of the body.
a) Estivation b) Torpor
c) Hibernation d) Shivering

135. ----- Is a unique kind of thermometer, with a moist muslin cloth wrapped around the bulb.
a) Dry bulb thermometer b) Wet bulb thermometer
c) Minimum thermometer d) Maximum thermometer

136. The hours of brilliant sunshine during the day, from dawn to sunset, are recorded with this device.
a) Sunshine recorder b) Anemometer
c) Sunset recorder d) Wind vane

137. Molecular chaperon involved in protein structure maintenance in heat stress?
a) HSP b) SOD
c) IGF1 d) NOS

138. Which of the tools that follow is used to calculate the amount of rainfall that falls within a day, or 24 hours?
a) Sunshine recorder b) Sunset recorder
c) Rainguage d) Anemometer

139. ---Utilised to manually measure the total quantity of rainfall over a 24-hour period using a measuring cylinder and a collecting vessel.
a) Ordinary rainguage b) Rainguage
c) Automatic rainguage d) Sunset recorder

140. ....Utilised to automatically calculate the total amount of rainfall using a graph, not only for the entire day but also for brief intervals throughout a day.

a) Sunset recorder b) Automatic rainguage

c) Ordinary rainguage d) Rainguage

141. A wide, pan-like device that measures how quickly water evaporates from the top layer over the course of a day as a result of ambient heat is called—

a) Hygrometer b) Evaporimeter

c) Rainguage d) Sunset recorder

142. Most abundant hsp which protects cattle from heat stress

a) Hsp 90 b) Hsp160

c) Hsp 70 d) Hsp 60

143. The device that measures the atmospheric pressure is

a) Hygrometer b) Evaporimeter

c) Barometer d) Sunset recorder

144. Which of the following thermoanemometer measures both air temperature and speed of air movement?

a) Anemometer b) Kata Thermo anemometer

c) Dry bulb thermometer d) Maximum thermometer

145. During heat stress of cattle which of the following is immidiatly expresses

a) High rectal temperature b) High respiration rate

c) Swaeting d) All of the above

146. Which of the following hormone is responsible for thermoregulation in animal

a) Thyroid hormone b) Cortisol

c) Growth hormone d) Both a and b

147. Which of the following neutralize the free radical production in the body during heat stress

a) Sod b) Cat

c) Gpx d) All of the above

148. HSP are present in

a) Cytoplasm b) Nucleus

c) Mitochondria, ER d) All of the above

149. Function of black globe thermometer

a) Measure surface body temperature

b) Measure the combine effect of temperature, humidity solar radiation

c) Measure core body temperature

d) None of the above

150. Which of the following is the effect of heat stress on animal

a) Low reproduction b) Decrease feed intake

c) Increased mortality d) All of the above

Answer Key

1	b	2	d	3	d	4	a	5	a	6	a	7	d
8	d	9	b	10	b	11	b	12	a	13	b	14	c
15	b	16	a	17	b	18	b	19	b	20	d	21	b
22	d	23	d	24	c	25	a	26	c	27	a	28	c
29	d	30	d	31	b	32	d	33	a	34	d	35	a
36	a	37	a	38	b	39	d	40	c	41	b	42	d
43	c	44	c	45	d	46	a	47	a	48	a	49	b
50	c	51	d	52	b	53	a	54	c	55	c	56	d
57	c	58	b	59	b	60	a	61	b	62	b	63	b
64	c	65	a	66	b	67	d	68	a	69	d	70	b
71	a	72	b	73	a	74	a	75	d	76	b	77	d
78	d	79	d	80	c	81	a	82	d	83	d	84	d
85	d	86	b	87	d	88	a	89	a	90	c	91	d
92	a	93	b	94	c	95	a	96	c	97	b	98	b
99	c	100	b	101	c	102	c	103	d	104	d	105	a
106	d	107	c	108	a	109	a	110	a	111	b	112	d
113	c	114	d	115	a	116	c	117	d	118	b	119	b
120	a	121	b	122	b	123	a	124	a	125	b	126	c
127	a	128	b	129	b	130	b	131	b	132	c	133	d
134	d	135	b	136	a	137	a	138	c	139	a	140	b
141	b	142	c	143	c	144	b	145	b	146	d	147	d
148	d	149	b	150	d								

3

Enzymatic Regulation

K. Pallavi, S. Gurpreet, C. Amit, and N. Dawoud

College of Veterinary Science, Rampura Phul

Introduction

Enzymatic regulation refers to the mechanisms that control the activity of enzymes, ensuring that they function optimally and in accordance with the needs of the cell or organism. These mechanisms are crucial for maintaining homeostasis and regulating metabolic pathways. Here are the primary methods of enzymatic regulation:

1. **Allosteric Regulation:** Allosteric regulation involves the binding of regulatory molecules (allosteric effectors) at sites other than the active site (allosteric sites) on the enzyme. This binding can either enhance (activators) or inhibit (inhibitors) enzyme activity. Allosteric enzymes typically exhibit a sigmoidal (S-shaped) kinetics curve.
2. **Covalent Modification:** Covalent modification involves the addition or removal of specific chemical groups to an enzyme, altering its activity. The most common form is phosphorylation, where a phosphate group is added by kinases and removed by phosphatases. Other modifications include acetylation, methylation, and ubiquitination.
3. **Feedback Inhibition:** Feedback inhibition occurs when the end product of a metabolic pathway inhibits an enzyme involved earlier in the pathway. This prevents the overproduction of the end product and helps maintain balance within the cell.
4. **Proteolytic Activation:** Some enzymes are synthesized as inactive precursors (zymogens or proenzymes) that require proteolytic cleavage to become active. This mechanism is common in digestive enzymes and blood clotting factors.
5. **Enzyme Induction and Repression:** The synthesis of enzymes can be regulated at the genetic level. Induction increases the production of an enzyme in response to a substrate or other signal, while repression decreases enzyme synthesis. This regulation is often mediated by transcription factors and other regulatory proteins.
6. **Substrate Availability:** The availability of substrate can directly affect enzyme activity. High substrate concentrations can increase the rate of reaction up to a certain point (saturation), beyond which the enzyme operates at its maximum rate (Vmax).
7. **pH and Temperature:** Enzymes have optimal pH and temperature ranges within which they function most efficiently. Deviations from these optimal conditions can lead to decreased enzyme activity or denaturation.

8. **Compartmentalization:** Enzymes can be compartmentalized within specific organelles or regions of a cell, allowing for regulation based on the spatial and temporal needs of the cell.

Multiple Choice Questions

1. In Allosteric regulation, what type of curve is generally seen?
   a) Sigmoid b) Parabola
   c) Straight line d) None of the above
2. Which of the following acts as an allosteric activator of Phosphofructokinase enzyme?
   a) ATP b) Citrate
   c) Both of the above d) None of the above
3. NAG acts as an allosteric activator of which of the following enzymes?
   a) Lipase
   b) Hexokinase
   c) Carbamoyl phosphate synthetase I
   d) Carbamoyl phosphate synthetase II
4. Acetyl CoA-carboxylase is allosterically inhibited by which of the following given below?
   a) Acyl CoA b) Citrate
   c) Both of the above d) None of the above
5. AcetylCoA is the allosteric activator of which of the following enzymes?
   a) Hexokinase
   b) Carbamoyl phosphate synthetase I
   c) Carbamoyl phosphate synthetase II
   d) Pyruvate carboxylase
6. Which of the following statements given below is not a salient feature of allosteric regulation?
   a) It is partially reversible, when excess substrate is added
   b) Km is usually increased
   c) Vmax is incraesed
   d) All of the above
7. Most allosteric enzymes possess which type of the structure?
   a) Tertiary b) Secondary
   c) Quaternary d) None of the above
8. Cholesterol acts as allosteric inhibitor of which of the following enzymes?
   a) Hexokinase
   b) HMG CoA-reductase
   c) Carbamoyl phosphate synthetase I
   d) Carbamoyl phosphate synthetase II

9. Suicide Inhibition is kind of which type of inhibition of enzyme activity?
   a) Irreversible
   b) Reversible
   c) Both of the above
   d) None of the above
10. Lactate dehydrogenase, acting on pyruvate will form only L-lactate, but not the D variety is an example of which type of enzyme specificity?
   a) Stereospecificity
   b) Optical
   c) Bond specificity
   d) All of the above
11. Number of substrate molecules transformed per unit time by a single enzyme molecule or by a single catalytic site is termed as?
   a) Catalytic efficiency
   b) Turnover number
   c) Specific activity
   d) All of the above
12. Number of enzyme units present per milligram of protein (Vmax divided by the protein concentration) is termed as?
   a) Catalytic efficiency
   b) Turnover number
   c) Specific activity
   d) All of the above
13. Number of moles of substrate transformed per second per liter of sample is termed as?
   a) Catalytic efficiency
   b) Turnover number
   c) Specific activity
   d) Katal
14. Hexokinase can catalyse phosphorylation of glucose, galactose and mannose variety is an example of which type of enzyme specificity?
   a) Absolute
   b) Optical
   c) Bond specificity
   d) Group
15. Urea is the only substrate for urease is an example of which type of enzyme specificity?
   a) Absolute
   b) Optical
   c) Bond specificity
   d) Group
16. Methotrexate is a structural analogue of folic acid, and can inhibit folate reductase enzyme by which type of inhibition?
   a) Competitive
   b) Non-Competitive
   c) Both of the above
   d) None of the above
17. Dicoumarol can act as an anticoagulant by competitively inhibiting activity of which vitamin?
   a) Vitamin C
   b) Vitamin K
   c) Vitamin D
   d) Vitamin E
18. Inhibitors that have no structural resemblance to the substrate and an increase in the substrate concentration generally does not relieve the inhibition are known as?
   a) Competitive
   b) Non-Competitive/Irreversible
   c) Both of the above
   d) None of the above

19. Which of the following statements about Km value is incorrect?
    a) Km value is substrate concentration (expressed in moles/L) at half-maximal velocity
    b) It is the characteristic feature of a particular enzyme for a specific substrate
    c) It denotes that 100% of enzyme molecules are bound with substrate molecules at that particular substrate concentration
    d) Km denotes the affinity of enzyme for substrate
20. Which of the following enzymes doesnot contain Zinc?
    a) Carbonic anhydrase
    b) Carboxy peptidase
    c) Alcohol dehydrogenase
    d) Cytochrome oxidase
21. Penicillin antibiotic inhibits which of the following enzymes?
    a) Carbonic anhydrase
    b) Transpeptidase
    c) Carboxy peptidase
    d) Alcohol dehydrogenase
22. Inhibition of placental alkaline phosphatase (Regan iso-enzyme) by phenylalanine is an example of which type of inhibition?
    a) Competitive
    b) Uncompetitive/Non Competitive
    c) Both of the above
    d) None of the above
23. Zymogen activation by partial proteolysis and ADP ribosylation is an example of which type of enzyme modification?
    a) Covalent
    b) Ionic
    c) Electrostatic
    d) Hydrophobic
24. Certain enzymes of the pathway may be located in mitochondria whereas certain other enzymes of the same pathway are cytoplasmic is an example of following regulations given below?
    a) Feedback Inhibition
    b) Allosteric regulation
    c) Compartmentalization of enzymes
    d) None of the above
25. How many iso-enzymes of enzyme Lactate dehydrogenase (LDH) exist?
    a) 4
    b) 5
    c) 3
    d) 9
26. Actions of drugs, such as Sulphonamides, Methotrexate, Dicoumarol and Isoniazid are based on the principle of which type of inhibition?
    a) Competitive
    b) Uncompetitive/Non-Competitive
    c) Both of the above
    d) None of the above
27. Which of the following factors influences enzyme activity?
    a) Enzyme concentration and substrate concentration
    b) pH and temperature
    c) Presence of inhibitors
    d) All of the above

28. Hexokinase belongs to which category of enzymes?
    a) Oxidoreductases b) Transferases
    c) Hydrolases d) Ligase
29. Acetylcholine esterase belongs to which category of enzymes?
    a) Oxidoreductases b) Transferases
    c) Hydrolases d) Ligase
30. Which of the following statements about enzyme is incorrect?
    a) Enzymes doesn't require presence of a metal ion for their activity
    b) Area of an enzyme where the catalysis occurs is called the 'active site'
    c) Amino acid residues of the enzyme involved directly in the binding of the substrate are called 'catalytic residues'
    d) The activity of enzymes may be increased or decreased by covalent modification
31. Which of the following statements about enzyme is correct?
    a) The region of the enzyme where substrate binding and catalysis occurs is referred to as active site
    b) Although all parts are required for maintaining the exact three-dimensional structure of the enzyme, the reaction is taking place at the active site
    c) Generally active site is situated in a crevice or cleft of the enzyme molecule
    d) All of the above
32. Which of the following amino acids is not present at the catalytic site of Chymotrypsin enzyme?
    a) Histidine b) Aspartate
    c) Lysine d) Serine
33. When energy exchange is negligible, the reaction is easily reversible, the reaction is termed as?
    a) Isothermal b) Endothermic
    c) Exothermic d) All of the above
34. Which of the following statement given below is correct?
    a) At equilibrium, forward and backward reactions are equal
    b) Equilibrium is a dynamic state.
    c) Even though no net change in concentrations of substrate and product occurs, molecules are always interconverted
    d) All of the above
35. Effect of Temperature on the velocity of enzyme reaction is depicted by which shape of graph?
    a) Parabola b) Bell shape
    c) Straight Line d) None of the above
36. Usually enzymes have the optimum pH between?
    a) 2-3 b) 1-2
    c) 6-8 d) 12-14

37. In which type of enzyme inhibition, the structural analogue is converted to a more effective inhibitor with the help of the enzyme to be inhibited and new product irreversibly binds to the enzyme and inhibits further reactions?
    a) Suicide Inhibition
    b) Feedback inhibition
    c) Reversible Inhibition
    d) All of the above
38. Suicide inhibition is a type of which type of inhibition in which the inhibitor makes use of the natural reaction of the enzyme for inhibition?
    a) Reversible Inhibition
    b) Feedback inhibition
    c) Irreversible Inhibition
    d) All of the above
39. Which of the following enzymes are active in phosphorylated state?
    a) Acetyl-CoA carboxylase
    b) Glycogen synthase
    c) Pyruvate dehydrogenase
    d) Glycogen phosphorylase
40. Trypsin can hydrolyse peptide bonds formed by carboxyl groups of arginine or lysine residues in any protein is an example of which type of enzyme specificity?
    a) Absolute
    b) Optical
    c) Bond specificity
    d) Group
41. Drug 5-fluoro uracil is metabolized inside body into deoxy fluoro uridylic acid inhibits which enzyme, thereby acting as an anticancer drug?
    a) Acetyl-CoA carboxylase
    b) Glycogen synthase
    c) Pyruvate dehydrogenase
    d) Thymidylate synthase
42. Increasing the substrate concentration can overcome/abolish which type of enzyme inhibition?
    a) Competitive
    b) Non-Competitive
    c) Both of the above
    d) All of the above
43. Isonicotinic acid hydrazide, commonly used anti tuberculous drug works on the principle of which type of enzyme inhibition?
    a) Non-Competitive
    b) Competitive
    c) Both of the above
    d) All of the above
44. Malonate inhibits succinate dehydrogenase enzyme by which type of enzyme inhibition?
    a) Competitive
    b) Non-Competitive
    c) Both of the above
    d) All of the above
45. Which of the following amino acids is not present at the catalytic site of Carboxypeptidase enzyme?
    a) Histidine
    b) Arginine
    c) Tyrosine
    d) Lysine
46. Trypsin, Chymotrypsin, Clotting factors belong to which category of proteases?
    a) Serine protease
    b) Cysteine protease
    c) Aspartyl protease
    d) Carboxy protease

47. Aldolase belongs to which category of enzymes?
    a) Oxidoreductases b) Lyases
    c) Hydrolases d) Ligase
48. Enzymes link two substrates together, usually with the simultaneous hydrolysis of ATP are known as?
    a) Ligases b) Lyases
    c) Oxidoreductases d) Hydrolases
49. Protein part of the enzyme that is essential for the biological activity of the enzyme is termed as?
    a) Isoenzyme b) Coenzyme
    c) Isomer d) Holoenzyme
50. Increased activity of which fraction of lactate dehydrogenase enzyme in serum is an indicator of liver diseases?
    a) LDH1 b) LDH2
    c) LDH3 d) LDH5
51. Increased activity of which fraction of creatin kinase enzyme in serum is an indicator of myocardial infarction?
    a) CPK 1 b) CPK 2
    c) CPK 3 d) None of the above
52. Which of the following enzymes is deficient in patients suffering from congenital haemolytic anaemia?
    a) Glucose 6-phosphate dehydrogenase b) Urease
    c) Amylase d) Hexokinase
53. Which of the following enzymes levels are increased in the cancer of prostate gland?
    a) Glucose 6-phosphate dehydrogenase b) Urease
    c) Acid phosphatase d) Amylase
54. Which of the following enzymes levels are increased in the cases of acute pancreatitis?
    a) Glucose 6-phosphate dehydrogenase b) Amylase
    c) Urease d) Acid phosphatase
55. Enzymes which are immobilized by binding them to a solid, insoluble matrix which will not affect the enzyme stability or its catalytic activity are known as?
    a) Immobilized enzymes b) Inactive enzymes
    c) Zymogens d) All of the above
56. Which of the following enzymes prepared from *Streptococcus* is useful for clearing the blood clots?
    a) Glucose 6-phosphate dehydrogenase b) Amylase
    c) Urease d) Streptokinase

57. Which of the following cellular organelles contains enzymes Catalase; urate oxidase; D-amino acid oxidase; long chain fatty acid oxidation in higher levels?
    a) Nucleus b) Vacoule
    c) Peroxisomes d) Endoplasmic reticulum

58. For which of the following enzymes double reciprocal plots resemble that of non-competitive inhibition?
    a) K-class of allosteric enzymes b) V-class of allosteric enzymes
    c) Both of the above d) None of the above

59. The energy required by the reactants to undergo the reaction is known as?
    a) Activation energy b) Physical energy
    c) Chemical energy d) None of the above

60. Ribonuclease which cleaves phosphodiester bonds in a pyrimidine locus in RNA is a classic example of the role which type of enzyme catalysis?
    a) Substrate strain b) Covalent catalysis
    c) Proximity catalysis d) Acid Base catalysis

61. Lysozyme action is believed to be due to a combination of which two types of enzyme catalysis?
    a) Substrate strain and acid-base catalysis b) Proximity and acid-base catalysis
    c) Substrate strain and Proximity catalysis d) Substrate strain alone

62. Which of the following statement given below is incorrect?
    a) The catalyst (or the enzyme in the biological system) reduces the activation energy and this causes the reaction to proceed at a lower temperature
    b) Enzymes alter the equilibrium constants
    c) Enzymes only enhance the velocity of the reaction
    d) For any chemical reaction to occur, the reactants have to be in an activated state or transition state

63. Flavin mononucleotide (FMN) and Flavin adenine dinucleotide (FAD) coenzymes are derived from which of the following vitamins?
    a) Riboflavin b) Ascorbic acid
    c) Pyridoxine d) Biotin

64. Coenzyme A is derived from which of the following vitamins?
    a) Riboflavin b) Ascorbic acid
    c) Pantothenic acid d) Biotin

65. Which of the following coenzymes donates methyl group in biosynthetic reactions?
    a) SAM b) UTP
    c) CTP d) UDP

66. Which of the following coenzymes donates sulfate for the synthesis of mucopolysaccharides?
    a) SAM b) CTP
    c) UDP d) PAPS

67. Which of the following coenzymes is required in phospholipid synthesis as carrier of choline and ethanolamine?

a) UDP b) SAM

c) PAPS d) CDP

68. Which of the following coenzymes is carrier of monosaccharides (glucose, galactose), required for glycogen synthesis?

a) SAM b) UDP

c) PAPS d) CDP

69. The specificity of the enzyme is mostly dependent which of the following?

a) Apoenzyme b) Coenzyme

c) Both of the above d) None of the above

70. NAD and NADP coenzymes are derived from which of the following vitamins?

a) Riboflavin b) Ascorbic acid

c) Pyridoxine d) Niacin

71. Who proposed a more acceptable and realistic model for enzyme substrate complex formation and put forward that the active site is not rigid and pre-shaped?

a) Emil Fischer b) Koshland

c) Both of the above d) None of the above

72. Which of the following cellular organelles contains enzymes of fatty acid oxidation; amino acid oxidation; Krebs cycle; urea synthesis; electron transport chain and oxidative phosphorylation?

a) Mitochondria b) Nucleus

c) Peroxisome d) Lysosomes

73. Which of the following cellular organelles contains enzymes such as aminotransferases; peptidases; glycolysis; hexose monophosphate shunt; fatty acid synthesis; purine and pyrimidine catabolism?

a) Mitochondria b) Nucleus

c) Peroxisome d) Cytoplasm

74. Which of the following cellular organelles contains enzymes glucose 6-phosphatase; nucleotidase; glucosyl- and galactosyl-transferases?

a) Mitochondria b) Nucleus

c) Golgi body d) Cytoplasm

75. Which of the following statement given below is correct?

a) Constitutive enzymes levels are not controlled and remain fairly constant

b) Adaptive enzymes concentrations increase or decrease as per body needs and are well-regulated

c) Both of the above

d) None of the above

76. Half life of enzyme serum amylase is?

a) 3-5 hours b) 5-6 days

c) 5-6 minutes d) 18-60 hours

77. Half life of enzyme serum lactate dehydrogenase-1 is?
    a) 1-2 hours
    b) 8-12 hours
    c) 5-6 minutes
    d) 18-60 hours
78. Which enzyme is used in preparation of washing powders as industrial application?
    a) Amylase
    b) Urease
    c) Protease
    d) All of the above
79. Which enzyme is used in Polymerase chain reaction?
    a) Taq DNA polymerase
    b) Amylase
    c) Urease
    d) Protease
80. Which enzyme is used in gene transfer, DNA finger printing?
    a) Taq DNA polymerase
    b) Amylase
    c) Urease
    d) Restriction endonuclease

Answer Key

1	a	2	c	3	c	4	a	5	d	6	c	7	c
8	b	9	a	10	a	11	b	12	c	13	d	14	d
15	a	16	a	17	b	18	b	19	c	20	d	21	b
22	b	23	a	24	c	25	b	26	a	27	d	28	b
29	c	30	a	31	d	32	c	33	a	34	d	35	b
36	c	37	a	38	c	39	d	40	c	41	d	42	a
43	b	44	a	45	d	46	a	47	b	48	a	49	b
50	d	51	b	52	a	53	c	54	b	55	a	56	d
57	c	58	b	59	a	60	d	61	a	62	b	63	a
64	c	65	a	66	d	67	d	68	b	69	a	70	d
71	b	72	a	73	d	74	c	75	c	76	a	77	b
78	c	79	a	80	d								

4

Foodstuffs and Animal Nutrition

Neeti Lakhani and Gurslamat Singh

Department of Animal Nutrition, College of Veterinary Science, Rampura Phul Bathinda, GADVASU, Ludhiana, Punjab

Introduction

In the intricate tapestry of life, the relationship between foodstuffs and animal nutrition forms a fundamental thread, weaving its way through the intricate patterns of ecological balance, agricultural practices, and the sustenance of diverse life forms. The intersection of these two realms is not only pivotal for the flourishing of animals but also crucial for the well-being of ecosystems, human societies, and the planet at large. This intricate connection delves into the nuanced interplay between dietary components, physiological mechanisms, and the broader implications for the health of animals, both domestic and wild.

It is imperative to recognize that foodstuffs are not mere sustenance; they are the building blocks of life, the fuel for growth, and the source of energy that sustains the diverse array of creatures inhabiting our planet. From the microscopic organisms in the soil to the majestic mammals roaming vast landscapes, the quest for nourishment is a universal constant, intricately tied to the delicate balance of ecosystems.

At the heart of this relationship lies the fascinating science of animal nutrition—a field that scrutinizes the complex interactions between dietary elements and an organism's physiological functions. From the intricacies of nutrient absorption to the role of different foodstuffs in promoting health, animal nutrition serves as a compass guiding us through the intricate pathways of biology, agriculture, and environmental conservation.

The journey into understanding animal nutrition commences with a closer look at the varied foodstuffs that contribute to the dietary landscape. Foodstuffs, in this context, encompass a vast array of substances ranging from grains and forage to proteins and fats, each playing a distinctive role in the nutritional well-being of animals. The composition and quality of these foodstuffs are crucial determinants of an animal's growth, reproduction, and overall health. Unraveling the nutritional value of these components requires delving into the realms of biochemistry, physiology, and the intricate dance between macronutrients and micronutrients.

Macroscopic entities such as carbohydrates, proteins, and lipids stand as the pillars of animal nutrition. Carbohydrates, in the form of sugars, starches, and fibers, serve as the primary source of energy, fueling the metabolic processes that sustain life. Proteins, comprising amino acids, are the essential building blocks for growth, development, and the maintenance of bodily functions. Meanwhile, lipids, including fats and oils, play multifaceted roles, serving as energy reserves, structural components, and facilitators of nutrient absorption.

However, the nutritional tapestry extends beyond these macronutrients to embrace a symphony of micronutrients-vitamins and minerals that play indispensable roles in maintaining health and preventing deficiency-related disorders. The delicate balance of these elements, akin to a well-orchestrated melody, contributes to the overall harmony of an animal's physiology. Exploring the significance of vitamins and minerals unveils a captivating narrative of biological intricacies, where deficiencies or excesses can tip the scales from vitality to vulnerability.

In the realm of animal nutrition, the types and proportions of these nutrients are not uniform across species. The dietary requirements of a ruminant, such as a cow, vastly differ from those of a carnivorous predator like a cat. Understanding these variations is imperative for effective husbandry practices, whether in the context of livestock farming or the preservation of endangered species. As humans increasingly grapple with the responsibility of sustainable resource management, the nuances of animal nutrition assume a pivotal role in ensuring the well-being of domesticated animals and wildlife alike.

The story of foodstuffs and animal nutrition is intricately interwoven with the tapestry of agriculture-an art and science that humanity has cultivated for millennia. The domestication of animals, the cultivation of crops, and the symbiotic relationships between plants and animals have shaped the course of civilizations. Agriculture, in its essence, is not merely the act of growing food; it is a testament to the intricate dance between humans, animals, and the land they inhabit.

In the modern era, as agricultural practices have evolved to meet the burgeoning demands of a growing global population, the implications for animal nutrition have become increasingly complex. Intensive farming practices, while efficient in producing large quantities of food, pose challenges to the health and welfare of animals. Balancing the need for high yields with ethical considerations and environmental sustainability has become a tightrope walk, prompting the exploration of alternative approaches such as organic farming, agroecology, and precision agriculture.

The nexus between foodstuffs and animal nutrition extends beyond the realm of domesticated animals. Wild animals, navigating their ecosystems in pursuit of sustenance, face a delicate equilibrium that is easily disrupted by environmental changes, habitat loss, and human activities. Conservation biologists and ecologists delve into the nutritional requirements of wildlife to devise strategies that ensure the preservation of biodiversity.

As we traverse the landscapes of foodstuffs and animal nutrition, it becomes evident that this exploration is not confined to the realm of biology and agriculture alone. The choices we make, both as individuals and as societies, regarding food production, consumption, and waste, reverberate through the intricate web of life. The global challenges of malnutrition, food insecurity, and the ecological footprint of agriculture compel us to reevaluate our relationship with food and the systems that produce it.

1. DCP is a good source of

   a) Ca　　　　b) P

   c) Ca and P both　　　　d) None

2. Molasses is a rich source of

   a) Protein　　　　b) Cellulose

   c) Complex Carbohydrates　　　　d) Soluble Sugars

3. Prussicacid is anti-nutritional factor present in the
   a) Salseed meal b) Jowar white
   c) Tapioca meal d) GNC
4. ……………………… anti-nutritional factor is present in cotton seed meal
   a) Prussicacid b) Saponin
   c) Gossypol d) Ricin
5. Threonine is limiting amino acid in
   a) Wheat b) Sorghum
   c) Both d) None
6. Blood meal is rich in
   a) Lysine b) Isoleucine
   c) Both d) None
7. Corn gluten is rich in
   a) Tryptophan b) Isoleucine
   c) Both d) None
8. Sesame seed is rich in
   a) Lysine b) Methionine
   c) Both d) None
9. Soyabean is rich in
   a) Lysine b) Methionine
   c) Both d) None
10. Tapioca meal contains
   a) Prussic acid b) Tannin
   c) Trypsin inhibitor d) All
11. Energy rich concentrate feedstuffs contain
   a) < 20 % protein b) > 20 % protein
   c) > 35 % protein d) > 30 % protein
12. Protein rich concentrate feedstuffs contain
   a) < 20 % protein b) > 20 % protein
   c) < 15 % protein d) < 10 % protein
13. Byproduct of cereals left after harvesting
   a) Stower b) Fodder
   c) Hay d) Straw
14. Aerial parts with ears & husk are called
   a) Stower b) Fodder
   c) Hay d) Straw
15. Aerial parts without ears & husk are called
   a) Stower b) Fodder
   c) Hay d) Straw

16. Outer covering of beans & peas
    a) Hull
    b) Stower
    c) Husk
    d) Shells
17. Dry Outer covering of grains
    a) Hull
    b) Stower
    c) Husk
    d) Shells
18. Hard Outer covering of nuts
    a) Hull
    b) Stower
    c) Husk
    d) Shells
19. Moisture content in straw is ________
    a) 10%
    b) 20%
    c) 50%
    d) 75%
20. Moisture content in green grasses is ________
    a) 10%
    b) 20%
    c) 50%
    d) 75%
21. In general, stored feeds get moldy and spoiled when moisture level is above
    a) 5%
    b) 7%
    c) 9%
    d) 11%
22. Total carbohydrate in the feed areexpressed as
    a) Crude fiber
    b) NFE
    c) Both
    d) None of the above
23. Non-fiber carbohydrate of feed stuff can be calculated by
    a) NFC= 100-(%CP+ %NDF +%EE + % TA)
    b) NFC= 100-(%CP+ (%NDF-%NDICP) +%EE + % TA)
    c) Both
    D) None Of The Above
24. Rich source of essential fatty acid is
    a) Safflower oil
    b) Sunflower oil
    c) Groundnut oil
    d) Soyabean oil
25. Which of the following is true statement
    a) Straws are bulky roughages
    b) Brans are bulky concentrates
    c) Less bulky ness reduce milk yield
    d) All of the above
26. To improve the urea utilization N:S ratio should be
    a) 5:1
    b) 10:1
    c) 15:1
    d) 50:1
27. Urea toxicity result from
    a) Rumen 80mg/100 ml
    b) Blood 1 mg /100 ml
    c) Both
    d) None of the above

28. Lipid absorption in avian is done by
    a) Small intestine b) Lymphatic system
    c) Portal vein d) All
29. Lipid content of average ruminant diet is_____ on DMB
    a) 2% b) 3-5%
    c) 10% d) 10%
30. Legume seed are rich in the
    a) Calcium b) Phosphorus
    c) Chlorine d) Fluorine
31. Cereal grains are rich in the
    a) Calcium b) Phosphorus
    c) Chlorine d) Fluorine
32. Goitrogens are present in
    a) Peanuts b) Brassica family
    c) Soybeans d) All
33. Mottling occurs when fluorine in water is above
    a) 1ppm b) 2-5ppm
    c) 1.5ppm d) All
34. Sulphur containing vitamins are
    a) Thiamin b) Biotin
    c) Niacin d) A & B both
35. Which of the following is source of carotenoids
    a) Maize b) carrots
    c) Egg yolk d) All
36. Very rich source of Vitamin D is
    a) Cod-liver Oil b) Milk
    c) Cereals d) Butter
37. Plant containing lipoxygenase which readily destroy the carotene & xanthophylls
    a) Soybean b) Carrots
    c) Maize d) All
38. α-tocopherol is destroyed in alfa-alfa meal and maize due to
    a) Storage b) Dehydration
    c) High temperature d) All of the above
39. Oligosaccharides are example of
    a) Probiotics b) Prebiotics
    c) Nutraceutical d) Ionophores
40. DCP content of productive type of roughages is
    a) > 5% b) 3-5%
    c) <3% d) None of the above

41. DCP content of maintenance type of roughages is
    a) > 5% b) 3-5%
    c) <3% d) None of the above
42. DCP content of Non-maintenance type of roughages is
    a) > 5% b) 3-5%
    c) <3% d) None of the above
43. Forages contain_____ CF and _____ cell wall
    a) < 18% &< 35% b) >18% &>35 %
    c) <18% &>35% d) >18% &<35 %
44. Concentrate contain_____ CF and _____ cell wall
    a) < 18% &< 35% b) >18% &>35 %
    c) <18% &>35% d) >18% &<35 %
45. Moisture level of hay should be less than
    a) 15% b) 18%
    c) 20% d) 25%
46. Hull, husk and shell contain higher amount of
    a) Protein b) Fiber
    c) Fats d) Minerals
47. % of fat present in oil cakes obtained from hydraulic pressure method
    a) 1% b) 3%
    c) 6% d) 8%
48. % of fat present in oil cakes obtained from expeller pressure method
    a) 1% b) 3%
    c) 6% d) 8%
49. % of fat present in oil cakes obtained from solvent extraction method
    a) 1% b) 3%
    c) 6% d) 8%
50. Stage b/w initiation of bloom and stage in which $1/10^{th}$ of the plants are in bloom
    a) Early bloom b) Mid bloom
    c) Full bloom d) Milk stage
51. Stage in which 1/10 to 2/3 of the plants are in bloom
    a) Early bloom b) Mid bloom
    c) Full bloom d) Milk stage
52. Stage in which 2/3 or more of the plants are in bloom
    a) Early bloom b) Mid bloom
    c) Full bloom d) Milk stage
53. Stage in which seeds well formed, soft and immature
    a) Early bloom b) Mid bloom
    c) Full bloom d) Milk stage

54. Increase in the heat production following consumption of food when animal is in thermo neutral environment is known as

a) Heat increment | b) Digestible energy
c) Metabolic energy | d) Heat of fermentation

55. Total digestible nutrients (TDN) can be calculated as

a) TDN = (DCP X X2.25) +DCF+DNFE+DEE
b) TDN = DCP+(DCF X 2.25)+DNFE+DEE
c) TDN = DCP+DCF+DNFE+(DEE X2.25)
d) TDN = DCP+DCF+DNFE+DEE

56. Ideal nutritive ratio for horse and cattle

a) 1:9 | b) 1:6
c) Narrow ratio | d) Medium ratio

57. Ideal nutritive ratio for fattening of flock

a) 1:9 | b) Wide ratio
c) Narrow ratio | d) Medium ratio

58. Nutritive ratio for young stock

a) Wide ratio | b) 1:6
c) Narrow ratio | d) Medium ratio

59. Respiratory quotient value for glucose is

a) 1.4 | b) 1
c) 0.6 | d) 0.8

60. Respiratory quotient value for protein is

a) 1.4 | b) 1
c) 0.6 | d) 0.8

61. Respiratory quotient value for fats is

a) 1.4 | b) 1
c) 0.6 | d) 0.8

62. Respiratory quotient value for rapidly fattening animal is

a) 1.4 | b) 1
c) 0.6 | d) 0.8

63. Impact grinding of feed is done by

a) Roller mill | b) Hammer mill
c) Both A & B | d) All of the above

64. Before mixing molasses is pre heated to reduce its viscosity

a) 95-100°F | b) 140-210°F
c) 80-85°F | d) 215-220°F

65. What is the temperature of dry heat in popping/puffing of grains

a) 150-200°C | b) 100-150°C
c) 370-425°C | d) 200-300°C

66. What is the temperature of flames for roasting of grains
   a) 100ºC b) 148.9ºC
   c) 200ºC d) 189.9ºC

67. Time and temperature required for stem rolling at atmospheric pressure
   a) 8-20 min, 100ºC b) 1-2 min ,121-148.9ºC
   c) 8-20min, 300ºF d) 1-2 min, 212 ºF

68. Time and temperature required for stem rolling at 60 psi pressure
   a) 8-20 min, 100ºC b) 1-2 min ,121-148.9ºC
   c) 8-20min, 300ºF d) 1-2 min, 212ºF

69. Rapid expansion of grain due to Sudden decrease of pressure from 250 psi to atmosphericpressure
   a) Pressure cooking b) Popping
   c) Puffing d) Exploding

70. Soaking of paddy removes
   a) Ca b) Gossypol
   c) Oxalates d) Protein

71. Which one of the following is density of cubed hay
   a) 7 lb/cft b) 25-32 lb/cft
   c) 40lb/cft d) All of the above

72. Upper permissible dose of aflatoxins in poultry and duck feed
   a) 15ppb b) 20ppb
   c) 25ppb d) 30ppb

73. Promising method for the commercial treatment of mycotoxins to destroy aflatoxin
   a) Ammonia treatment b) CaCl treatment
   c) Salt water d) Sodium bicarbonate

74. The process of conservation of green fodder is known as
   a) Tillage b) Soilage
   c) Ensilage d) All

75. What Is the percentage Loss of carotene during the process artificial drying of forage
   a) 0-5 % b) 5-15%
   c) 15-20% d) >20%

76. What is the ratio of fodder and legumes for silage preparation
   a) 1:1 b) 2:1
   c) 3:1 d) 4:1

77. Stage of harvesting of crop for silage
   a) Early bloom b) Mid bloom
   c) Full bloom d) Milk stage

78. Why Activity of proteases stop after 5-7 day of silage making
a) CO_2 level rise
b) O_2 level decrease
c) Ph drop below 6
d) None of the above

79. During ensiling Clostridia convert lysine in to ____________
a) Putrescine
b) Tyramine
c) Cadaverine
d) Tryptamine

80. Buffering properties of herbage is attributed to the ____________
a) Anions
b) Cations
c) Chlorophyll
d) Carotene

81. Yellowish green color of silage is due to presence of
a) Chlorophyll
b) Phaeophytin
c) VFA
d) Organic acids

82. Chlorophyll converted into phaeophytin due to the action of ____________
a) Organic acid
b) H_2SO_4
c) HCl
d) All of the above

83. Which vitamin decompose during silage preparation
a) A
b) B
c) C
d) D

84. Method used for evaluation of silage quality
a) TDN estimation
b) DCP
c) Fleig Index
d) All of the above

85. What is the maximum moisture level of the hay
a) 5-6%
b) 6-8%
c) 10-14%
d) >15%

86. Best time for cutting crop for hay making is
a) 1/3-1/2 in blossom
b) Early boom
c) Milk stage
d) All

87. Which vitamin decompose during hay preparation
a) A
b) B
c) C
d) D

88. Loss of carotene during hay making
a) 20%
b) 50%
c) 90%
d) 99.99%

89. Butyric acid will predominate in silage making if fodder is rich in
a) Carbohydrate
b) Protein
c) Crude fat
d) None of the above

90. Young chicken on raw soyabean diet develop presence of
a) Trypsin inhibitor
b) Gossypol
c) Tannins
d) Oxalic acid

91. Protease inhibitor which only inhibit chymotrypsin only
    a) Kunitz b) Bowman-brick
    c) Both A & B d) None of the above
92. Protease inhibitor which only inhibit trypsin
    a) Kunitz b) Bowman-brick
    c) Both A & B d) None of the above
93. Name of the haemagglutinins present in the castor bean
    a) Kunitz b) Bowman-brick
    c) Ricin d) Saponin
94. Which antinutritional factor present in Lucerne cause bloat
    a) Dhurrin b) Saponin
    c) Amygdalin d) Linamarin
95. What is the name of cyanogenetic glycoside present in the immature jowar
    a) Dhurrin b) Saponin
    c) Amygdalin d) Linamarin
96. Most susceptible animal for the cyanogen's/glycosides
    a) Horse b) Goat
    c) Pig d) Cattle
97. Glucosinolates are antinutritional factors present in the which plants
    a) Cabbage b) Turnip
    c) Mustard green d) All of the above
98. Glucosinolates are antinutritional factors present in crucifera family depress the synthesis of which hormone
    a) T_3 b) T_4
    c) D d) Both A & B
99. Most susceptible animal for the gossypol
    a) Horse b) Goat
    c) Pig d) Cattle
100. Most resistant animal for the gossypol
    a) Horse b) Goat
    c) Pig d) Cattle
101. Change in the colour of yolk due to gossypol
    a) Red spot b) Olive green colour
    c) Brown colour d) None of the above
102. Anti-nutritional factor present in the cotton seed cake
    a) Dhurrin b) Saponin
    c) Gossypol d) Linamarin

103. What is the optimum level of inclusion of poultry droppings in concentrate mixture

a) 25% b) 20%
c) 15% d) None of the above

104. What is the maximum level of inclusion of mahua cake in concentrate mixture

a) 25% b) 20%
c) 15% d) None of the above

105. What is the maximum level of inclusion of Guar cake in concentrate mixture

a) 25% b) 20%
c) 15% d) None of the above

106. Name of the deleterious factor present in the Neem seed cake

a) Gossypol b) Karanjine
c) Nimbin d) Mowrin

107. Name of the deleterious factor present in the cottonseed cake

a) Gossypol b) Karanjine
c) Nimbin d) Mowrin

108. Name of the deleterious factor present in the Karanj cake

a) Gossypol b) Karanjine
c) Nimbin d) Mowrin

109. Name of the deleterious factor present in the Mahua seed cake

a) Gossypol b) Karanjine
c) Nimbin d) Mowrin

110. HCN is deleterious factor present in the

a) Cassava b) Rubber seed meal
c) Both d) None of the above

111. What is the Seed rate of Maize

a) 10 kg/ha b) 25 kg/ha
c) 30kg/ha d) 40kg/ha

112. What is the Seed rate of Sorghum

a) 10 kg/ha b) 25 kg/ha
c) 30kg/ha d) 40kg/ha

113. What is the Seed rate of berseem

a) 10 kg/ha b) 25 kg/ha
c) 30kg/ha d) 40kg/ha

114. What is the Seed rate of lucerne

a) 10 kg/ha b) 20 kg/ha
c) 30kg/ha d) 50kg/ha

115. What is the cause of low availability of Zinc then caesin in Soyabean meal
   a) Prussic acid   b) Phytic acid
   c) Biotin   d) Avidin

116. Phytate present in the feed reduce the availability of
   a) Zinc   b) Calcium
   c) Phosphorus   d) All of the above

117. Oxalates present in the feed reduce the availability of
   a) Zinc   b) Calcium
   c) Phosphorus   d) All of the above

118. Which compound can reduce the level of biotin in feed
   a) Avidin   b) Streptavidin
   c) Starvidin   d) All of the above

119. Gossypol present in the feed stuff increase the requirement of which element
   a) Iron   b) Zinc
   c) Phosphorus   d) Copper

120. Which among the following is examples of nutrient interrelationship
   a) Choline and methionine   b) Ca , Mn & Cu
   c) B_{12}& methionine   d) All of the above

121. Which among the following is examples of nutrient interrelationship
   a) Fe & P   b) Mo, Cu & S
   c) Na & K   d) All of the above

122. Which among the following is Indigenous grasses
   a) Hariali grass   b) Doob grass
   c) Gaddi grass   d) All of the above

123. Which among the following is perennial cultivated grasses
   a) Napier grass   b) Guinea Grass
   c) Para grass   d) All of the above

124. Energy produced by fat is .... Times more than carbohydrate
   a) 2.50   b) 6.25
   c) 2.25   d) 6.35

125. Energy produced by fat is_________________
   a) 9Kcal   b) 2Kcal
   c) 4Kcal   d) 5kcal

126. Energy produced by protein is_________________
   a) 9Kcal   b) 2Kcal
   c) 4Kcal   d) 5kcal

127. Energy produced by carbohydrate is_________________
   a) 9Kcal   b) 2Kcal
   c) 4Kcal   d) 5kcal

128. Balanced diet includes
   a) Proteinsand vitamins
   b) Carbohydrates, fats and proteins
   c) Carbohydrates, fats, proteins and vitamins
   d) Carbohydrates, fats, proteins, minerals, vitamins and water

129. To get sufficient carbohydrates one should take .
   a) Meat b) Rice
   c) Carrots d) Ground nuts

130. The most important food element for growth and repair of tissue is
   a) Glucose b) Proteins
   c) Vitamins d) Calcium

131.

132. Feed additives that are used for the prevention and treatment of diseases are ____________
   a) Antibiotics b) Supplements
   c) Anthelmintics d) Growth regulators

133. Best source of phosphorus in polultry diet
   a) Fishmeal b) Meat meal
   c) Wheat bran d) Salt

133. Kellner's starch equivalent values are values for:
   a) Body fat production b) Net calories retained
   c) None d) All

134. Which is the most effective essential fatty acids:
   a) Oleic b) Linoleic
   c) Linolenic d) Arachidonic

135. Dietary essential vitamin on straw roughage based complete diet is:
   a) Vitamin B b) Cyanocobalamin
   c) Vitamin A d) None

136. Most of the magnesium is present in:
   a) Blood b) Blood plasma
   c) Muscles d) Bones

137. The association of lignin with hemicellulose and cellulose in a feed markedly reduces the digestibility of:
   a) Lignin b) Hemicellulose
   c) Cellulose d) Pectin

138. Calcium and phosphorus are examples of what type of nutrients
   a) Vitamin b) Mineral
   c) Protein d) None

139. The most refined measure of food energy in poultry is

a) ME b) GE

c) DE d) NE

140. Which of the following is needed for maturation of RBC in poultry

a) Biotin b) Pantothenic

c) B6 d) folic acid

141. The chief source of calcium in poultry diet is

a) Bone meal b) Calcium phosphate

c) Oyster shell d) None

142. Protein content of egg is

a) 12% b) 10%

c) 15% d) 6%

143. Find the antifungal feed additive

a) Propionic acid b) Sodium propionate

c) Nystatin d) All of the above

144. Soyabean meal is an example of

a) Roughage b) Cereal grain

c) Cereal byproduct d) Oil seed cake

145. Alfa Alfa is an example of:

a) Roughage b) Cereal grain

c) Cereal byproduct d) Oil seed cake

146. FOS is an example of

a) Prebiotic b) Probiotic

c) Synbiotic d) None

147. Stiff lamb disease caused due to deficiency of

a) Vit E b) Se

c) Both d) None

148. Major components of food which are necessary for our body are called:

a) Minerals b) Vitamins

c) Nutrients d) None

149. Scandinavian feed unit system evaluates food in terms of the production they promote in the animal and is in relation to the values of a common food:

a) Maize b) Barley

c) Oats d) None

150. For fat production in body, highest ATP is formed by:

a) Acetic acid b) Propionate

c) Protein d) Glucose

Answer Key

1	c	2	d	3	c	4	c	5	c	6	a	7	b
8	b	9	a	10	a	11	a	12	b	13	d	14	b
15	c	16	a	17	c	18	d	19	a	20	d	21	d
22	c	23	b	24	b	25	d	26	b	27	c	28	c
29	b	30	a	31	b	32	d	33	b	34	d	35	d
36	a	37	a	38	d	39	b	40	a	41	b	42	c
43	b	44	a	45	a	46	b	47	d	48	c	49	a
50	a	51	b	52	c	53	d	54	a	55	c	56	a
57	d	58	c	59	b	60	d	61	c	62	a	63	b
64	a	65	c	66	b	67	a	68	b	69	d	70	c
71	b	72	b	73	a	74	c	75	b	76	c	77	d
78	c	79	c	80	a	81	b	82	a	83	c	84	c
85	c	86	c	87	a	88	c	89	b	90	a	91	b
92	c	93	c	94	b	95	a	96	d	97	d	98	d
99	c	100	d	101	b	102	c	103	c	104	b	105	c
106	c	107	a	108	b	109	d	110	c	111	d	112	d
113	b	114	d	115	b	116	a	117	b	118	d	119	a
120	d	121	d	122	d	123	d	124	c	125	a	126	c
127	c	128	d	129	b	130	b	131	a	132	c	133	a
134	b	135	c	136	c	137	c	138	b	139	a	140	d
141	c	142	a	143	d	144	d	145	a	146	a	147	c
148	c	149	b	150	d								

5

Important Physiological Disorders/ Dysfunctions

Mohsinkhn M. Pathan

Department of Veterinary Physiology & Biochemistry, College of Veterinary Science & Animal Husbandry, Kamdhenu University, Anand, Gujarat

Introduction

Physiological disorders or dysfunctions in domestic animals are prevalent and can significantly impact the health and well-being of these animals. Understanding the fundamentals of these disorders is essential for veterinarians, animal scientists, and anyone involved in the care and management of animals. This chapter covers a diverse range of physiological disorders, including cardiovascular, respiratory, gastrointestinal, renal, endocrine, musculoskeletal, neurological, dermatological, reproductive, and ocular disorders. These conditions can manifest differently across species and breeds. This MCQ chapter serves as an introduction to the basics of physiological disorders in domestic animals and aims to test your knowledge on this important subject.

1. What is a physiological disorder in domestic animals?
   a) A genetic condition that affects an animal's appearance
   b) A disease caused by parasites
   c) An abnormality in the normal functioning of the body
   d) An injury or trauma to the animal
2. Which of the following is not a physiological disorder in domestic animals?
   a) Respiratory infection b) Lameness
   c) Diabetes d) Coat colour variation
3. What is a common physiological disorder in dairy cattle?
   a) Bovine Respiratory Disease (BRD) b) Mastitis
   c) Equine Influenza d) Avian Salmonellosis
4. Which of the following physiological disorders primarily affects a horse's digestive system?
   a) Bloat b) Foot rot
   c) Pneumonia d) Tapeworm infestation

5. Which domestic animal is particularly susceptible to heat stress as a physiological disorder?
   a) Dogs b) Cats
   c) Sheep d) Poultry
6. What physiological disorder is caused by a deficiency of iron in the diet of piglets?
   a) Rickets b) Anemia
   c) Botulism d) Foot-and-mouth disease
7. Which of the following is a physiological disorder related to the nervous system in horses?
   a) Founder b) Tetanus
   c) Ringworm d) Hoof abscess
8. In poultry farming, what physiological disorder can occur due to the overconsumption of calcium?
   a) Coccidiosis b) Marek's disease
   c) Hypocalcemia d) Eggshell quality issues
9. What is a common cause of physiological disorders in domestic animals?
   a) Genetic mutations b) Environmental factors
   c) Viral infections d) Lack of exercise
10. Which of the following can be a cause of respiratory physiological disorders in animals?
    a) Improper grooming b) Nutritional deficiencies
    c) Fungal infections d) Social interaction
11. What is the primary cause of lameness in horses and cattle?
    a) Sunburn b) Bacterial infections
    c) Parasitic infestations d) Dental problems
12. Which of the following factors can lead to heat stress in domestic animals?
    a) Adequate ventilation b) Moderate temperatures
    c) High humidity d) Proper hydration
13. What is a common cause of reproductive physiological disorders in livestock?
    a) Adequate nutrition b) Hormonal balance
    c) Inbreeding d) Vaccination
14. What is a major cause of metabolic disorders in dairy cattle?
    a) Balanced diet b) Regular exercise
    c) High milk production d) Low environmental temperature
15. Which of the following is a primary cause of gastrointestinal physiological disorders in animals?
    a) Proper sanitation b) Contaminated feed and water
    c) Adequate socialization d) Regular vaccination

16. What can lead to skin and coat disorders in pets like dogs and cats?
    a) Proper grooming and hygiene b) Frequent bathing
    c) Lack of interaction with other animals d) Indoor housing
17. Which of the following is a common gastrointestinal disorder in horses that can lead to colic?
    a) Bloat b) Equine influenza
    c) Gastric ulcers d) Tetanus
18. What gastrointestinal disorder is caused by the accumulation of gas in the stomach of ruminant animals like cattle and sheep?
    a) Colic b) Bloat
    c) Gastric ulcers d) Enteritis
19. Which of the following parasites can cause severe gastrointestinal disorders in dogs and cats?
    a) Ticks b) Fleas
    c) Roundworms d) Ear mites
20. What is the primary cause of enteritis in domestic animals?
    a) Viral infections b) Dietary allergies
    c) Lack of exercise d) High humidity
21. Which gastrointestinal disorder is characterized by inflammation of the stomach lining and is common in cats?
    a) Colic b) Bloat
    c) Gastric ulcers d) Feline gastritis
22. What condition is often the result of foreign objects, like swallowed toys or bones, causing a blockage in a dog's digestive system?
    a) Gastroenteritis b) Colitis
    c) Gastric dilatation-volvulus (GDV) d) Intussusception
23. Which domestic animal is particularly prone to coccidiosis, a gastrointestinal disorder caused by protozoan parasites?
    a) Horses b) Cattle
    c) Poultry d) Dogs
24. What gastrointestinal disorder is associated with the overconsumption of rich, high-starch feed in horses and can lead to colic and laminitis?
    a) Gastroenteritis b) Grain overload
    c) Bloat d) Enteritis
25. What respiratory disorder in horses is often characterized by a harsh, dry cough, nasal discharge, and fever?
    a) Influenza b) Colic
    c) Tetanus d) Botulism

26. Which of the following is a common respiratory disorder in dogs caused by inflammation of the airways?
   a) Pneumonia b) Bronchitis
   c) Arthritis d) Gingivitis
27. What respiratory disorder is commonly associated with sniffling, sneezing, and nasal discharge in cats?
   a) Asthma b) Bronchitis
   c) Rhinotracheitis d) Glaucoma
28. In poultry farming, which respiratory disorder is highly contagious and can cause respiratory distress, coughing, and sinusitis in birds?
   a) Marek's disease
   b) Feline immunodeficiency virus (FIV)
   c) Newcastle disease
   d) Avian influenza
29. What is a common respiratory disorder in cattle that results in labored breathing and a characteristic "bellowing" sound?
   a) Colic
   b) Pneumonia
   c) Respiratory distress syndrome
   d) Bovine respiratory disease (BRD)
30. Which of the following is a fungal respiratory disorder affecting the respiratory system of horses?
   a) Equine herpesvirus (EHV) b) Equine infectious anemia (EIA)
   c) Strangles d) Aspergillosis
31. What respiratory disorder primarily affects the upper airways of dogs and is characterized by a "goose-honk" cough?
   a) Pneumonia b) Kennel cough
   c) Feline leukemia d) Feline calicivirus
32. What respiratory disorder in pigs can result in coughing, fever, and pneumonia, and is often caused by Mycoplasma hyopneumoniae?
   a) Porcine respiratory and reproductive syndrome (PRRS)
   b) Swine flu
   c) Atrophic rhinitis d) African swine fever
33. Which reproductive disorder in cattle is characterized by inflammation of the uterus and can result in infertility or pregnancy loss?
   a) Bovine respiratory disease (BRD) b) Bloat
   c) Metritis d) Strangles
34. What is a common reproductive disorder in female dogs, leading to an abnormal swelling and inflammation of the uterus?
   a) Pyometra b) Cystitis
   c) Ovarian cysts d) Testicular torsion

35. Which reproductive disorder can lead to prolonged gestation and difficulty during parturition in mares?
    a) Cryptorchidism
    b) Equine herpesvirus (EHV)
    c) Dystocia
    d) Feline immunodeficiency virus (FIV)
36. What reproductive disorder in cats is characterized by excessive or inappropriate mating behavior, often leading to persistent vocalization and restlessness?
    a) Cryptorchidism
    b) Pseudopregnancy
    c) Rhinotracheitis
    d) Feline leukemia
37. In poultry farming, what is a common reproductive disorder in hens that results in the laying of soft-shelled or shell-less eggs?
    a) Coccidiosis
    b) Marek's disease
    c) Egg drop syndrome (EDS)
    d) Avian influenza
38. Which reproductive disorder in swine can lead to sows crushing their piglets due to poor maternal behavior?
    a) Porcine reproductive and respiratory syndrome (PRRS)
    b) Mastitis
    c) Agalactia
    d) Foot-and-mouth disease
39. What is a common reproductive disorder in male horses, where one or both testes fail to descend into the scrotum?
    a) Cryptorchidism
    b) Orchitis
    c) Ovarian cysts
    d) Testicular torsion
40. In dogs, which reproductive disorder can occur when the uterine horns become twisted, leading to a blockage in the reproductive tract?
    a) Pyometr
    b) Cystitis
    c) Ovarian cysts
    d) Testicular torsion
41. Which musculoskeletal disorder in horses is characterized by inflammation of the joints, resulting in lameness and swelling?
    a) Colic
    b) Tetanus
    c) Arthritis
    d) Botulism
42. What is a common musculoskeletal disorder in dogs, especially in large breeds, that affects the hip joints?
    a) Osteosarcoma
    b) Hip dysplasia
    c) Lyme disease
    d) Glaucoma
43. Which musculoskeletal disorder in cattle is often related to overgrowth of hooves and can lead to lameness?
    a) Founder
    b) Bloat
    c) Foot rot
    d) Enteritis

44. What musculoskeletal disorder is common in cats and is characterized by inflammation of the joints, resulting in pain and decreased mobility?
    a) Osteosarcoma b) Hip dysplasia
    c) Osteoarthritis d) Feline calicivirus
45. In poultry farming, what is a musculoskeletal disorder that affects the legs and wings of birds, leading to lameness and deformities?
    a) Marek's disease b) Feline leukemia
    c) Newcastle disease d) Avian influenza
46. Which musculoskeletal disorder in pigs is characterized by lameness, joint swelling, and reluctance to move, often caused by bacterial infections?
    a) Porcine reproductive and respiratory syndrome
    b) Swine flu
    c) Arthritis
    d) African swine fever
47. What is a common musculoskeletal disorder in cattle that leads to inflammation and swelling in the hooves, often due to environmental factors and nutrition?
    a) Founder b) Bloat
    c) Foot rot d) Mastitis
48. In dogs, which musculoskeletal disorder is characterized by inflammation of the spine, resulting in pain, stiffness, and mobility issues?
    a) Osteosarcoma
    b) Spondylosis
    c) Lyme disease
    d) Feline immunodeficiency virus (FIV)
49. What is a common dermatological disorder in dogs characterized by itchy and inflamed skin often related to allergies?
    a) Flea infestation b) Ringworm
    c) Atopic dermatitis d) Feline leukemia
50. Which dermatological disorder in horses results in hair loss, often in circular patterns, and is caused by a fungal infection?
    a) Rain rot b) Sweet itch
    c) Scratches d) Laminitis
51. What is a highly contagious dermatological disorder in cats caused by parasitic mites, leading to intense itching and hair loss?
    a) Ringworm b) Sarcoptic mange
    c) Demodectic mange d) Coccidiosis
52. In poultry farming, what dermatological disorder is caused by feather-pecking behaviors in chickens, leading to feather loss and skin damage?
    a) Avian influenza b) Feather mites
    c) Cannibalism d) Egg drop syndrome (EDS)

53. Which dermatological disorder in cattle is associated with a skin infection caused by the bacterium Dermatophilus congolensis?
   a) Bovine respiratory disease (BRD) b) Foot rot
   c) Dermatophilosis d) Enteritis
54. What is a common dermatological disorder in rabbits, resulting in hair loss and flaky skin due to fungal infections?
   a) Psittacosis b) Fur mites
   c) Rabbit syphilis d) Ringworm
55. Which dermatological disorder in dogs is characterized by the thickening and darkening of the skin in the axillary and groin areas?
   a) Atopic dermatitis b) Acral lick dermatitis
   c) Lipoma d) Lyme disease
56. In swine, what dermatological disorder results in raised skin lesions and is caused by the Sarcoptes scabiei mite?
   a) Mange b) Swine flu
   c) Erysipelas d) African swine fever
57. Which endocrine disorder in dogs is characterized by an overproduction of cortisol, resulting in symptoms such as increased thirst, urination, and abdominal distension?
   a) Hypothyroidism b) Cushing's disease
   c) Hyperthyroidism d) Diabetes mellitus
58. In horses, which endocrine disorder is associated with insulin resistance and can lead to laminitis and obesity?
   a) Equine metabolic syndrome (EMS) b) Hyperadrenocorticism
   c) Hyperthyroidism d) Diabetes insipidus
59. What is a common endocrine disorder in cats characterized by an overactive thyroid gland, resulting in weight loss, increased appetite, and restlessness?
   a) Hypothyroidism b) Hyperadrenocorticism
   c) Hyperthyroidism d) Diabetes insipidus
60. Which endocrine disorder in cattle is related to the deficiency of iodine and results in an enlarged thyroid gland?
   a) Bovine spongiform encephalopathy (BSE)
   b) Foot-and-mouth disease
   c) Actinobacillosis
   d) Goiter
61. In poultry farming, what is a common endocrine disorder in hens, characterized by a reduction in egg production and ovarian dysfunction?
   a) Marek's disease b) Egg drop syndrome (EDS)
   c) Newcastle disease d) Avian influenza

62. What endocrine disorder in pigs is related to the deficiency of thyroid hormones, resulting in poor growth and decreased feed efficiency?
    a) Porcine reproductive and respiratory syndrome
    b) Swine flu
    c) Osteochondrosis
    d) Goiter
63. In dogs, which endocrine disorder is characterized by an underactive thyroid gland, leading to weight gain, lethargy, and skin issues?
    a) Hyperadrenocorticism
    b) Hyperthyroidism
    c) Hypothyroidism
    d) Diabetes mellitus
64. What endocrine disorder in horses can result in excessive drinking and urination, muscle wasting, and excessive sweating, often due to a deficiency of antidiuretic hormone?
    a) Equine metabolic syndrome (EMS)
    b) Diabetes insipidus
    c) Equine influenza
    d) Botulism
65. What neurological disorder in dogs is characterized by seizures, often with no identifiable underlying cause?
    a) Vestibular disease
    b) Hydrocephalus
    c) Epilepsy
    d) Rabies
66. In horses, which neurological disorder is caused by the protozoan parasite Sarcocystis neurona and can lead to muscle atrophy and incoordination?
    a) Equine protozoal myeloencephalitis (EPM)
    b) West Nile virus
    c) Tetanus
    d) Equine herpesvirus (EHV)
67. What is a common neurological disorder in cats that results in the loss of coordination, often due to inflammation of the central nervous system?
    a) Vestibular disease
    b) Toxoplasmosis
    c) Feline immunodeficiency virus (FIV)
    d) Feline infectious peritonitis (FIP)
68. In cattle, which neurological disorder is caused by the consumption of certain plants and can result in symptoms such as tremors, staggering, and paralysis?
    a) Bovine respiratory disease (BRD)
    b) Bovinespongiform encephalopathy
    c) Actinobacillosis
    d) Plant poisoning (locoweed toxicity)
69. What neurological disorder in birds, especially parrots, is characterized by feather-plucking behavior and self-mutilation?
    a) Avian influenza
    b) Psittacosis
    c) Preening disorder
    d) Proventricular dilatation disease

70. Which neurological disorder in pigs is associated with tremors and nervousness, often due to nutritional imbalances, especially with calcium and phosphorus?
    a) Swine flu b) Pseudorabies
    c) Atrophic rhinitis d) Staggers

71. In dogs, which neurological disorder is characterized by the inflammation of the vestibular nerve and can result in head tilting and loss of balance?
    a) Hydrocephalus b) Vestibular disease
    c) Epilepsy d) Distemper

72. What is a severe and fatal neurological disorder in horses caused by the equine herpesvirus, resulting in incoordination and difficulty walking?
    a) Equine protozoal myeloencephalitis (EPM)
    b) West Nile virus
    c) Tetanus
    d) Equine herpes myeloencephalopathy

73. What cardiovascular disorder in dogs is characterized by abnormal heart sounds, such as murmurs, and can result from congenital defects or acquired diseases?
    a) Congestive heart failure (CHF) b) Hypertension
    c) Cardiomyopathy d) Mitral valve disease

74. In horses, which cardiovascular disorder is associated with irregular heart rhythms and can result in poor exercise performance?
    a) Aortic stenosis b) Hypertension
    c) Arrhythmia d) Tetanus

75. What is a common cardiovascular disorder in cats, especially in older cats, characterized by thickening of the heart muscle?
    a) Congestive heart failure (CHF) b) Aortic stenosis
    c) Hypertrophic cardiomyopathy d) Lyme disease

76. Which cardiovascular disorder in cattle is related to a bacterial infection and can result in inflammation of the heart lining?
    a) Foot rot
    b) Bovine spongiform encephalopathy
    c) Endocarditis
    d) Botulism

77. In poultry farming, what is a cardiovascular disorder that affects the heart and blood vessels of chickens, often caused by certain toxins in feed?
    a) Marek's disease b) Ascites
    c) Coccidiosis d) Avian influenza

78. Which cardiovascular disorder in pigs is characterized by high blood pressure and can lead to heart and kidney damage, often associated with obesity?
    a) Swine flu b) Hypertrophic cardiomyopathy
    c) Hypertension d) African swine fever

79. In dogs, which cardiovascular disorder is a genetic condition in some small breeds, leading to a narrowing of the aortic valve?
 a) Dilated cardiomyopathy b) Aortic stenosis
 c) Arrhythmia d) Myocarditis

80. What cardiovascular disorder in horses is caused by a protozoal parasite and can result in inflammation of the blood vessels in the brain and spinal cord?
 a) Aortic stenosis
 b) Hypertension
 c) Equine protozoal myeloencephalitis (EPM)
 d) Tetanus

81. What is a common urinary tract disorder in cats, characterized by the formation of mineral crystals or stones in the urinary tract?
 a) Diabetes mellitus b) Cystitis
 c) Urolithiasis d) Feline leukemia

82. Which urinary tract disorder in dogs results in the inability to control urination and is often caused by weakened or damaged sphincter muscles?
 a) Cystitis b) Diabetes mellitus
 c) Incontinence d) Pyometra

83. What urinary tract disorder in horses is related to the accumulation of sand or grit in the bladder and can lead to colic and urinary obstruction?
 a) Equine herpesvirus (EHV) b) Sand colic
 c) Urolithiasis d) Tetanus

84. In poultry farming, what urinary tract disorder in hens is characterized by the deposition of urate crystals in the kidneys, causing kidney dysfunction?
 a) Ascites b) Nephritis
 c) Gout d) Avian influenza

85. Which urinary tract disorder in cattle is caused by a bacterial infection and can result in inflammation of the bladder and urinary tract?
 a) Bovine respiratory disease (BR d) b) Cystitis
 c) Urolithiasis d) Pyometra

86. What is a common urinary tract disorder in rabbits, especially in males, resulting in the accumulation of mineral deposits in the bladder?
 a) Cystitis b) Urolithiasis
 c) Ascites d) Encephalitozoonosis

87. In pigs, which urinary tract disorder is related to the inability to excrete excess nitrogen from the body and can lead to kidney damage?
 a) Swine flu b) Hypertrophic cardiomyopathy
 c) Urolithiasis d) Water belly (urinary ascites)

88. What urinary tract disorder in dogs is characterized by the inflammation of the bladder and can result in frequent urination and discomfort?

a) Diabetes mellitus b) Cystitis

c) Incontinence d) Pyometra

89. What is a common immune system disorder in dogs, characterized by an abnormal immune response to environmental allergens, leading to itching and skin problems?

a) Diabetes mellitus b) Atopic dermatitis

c) Hypothyroidism d) Leishmaniasis

90. Which immune system disorder in cats is a viral disease that can lead to immunosuppression, weight loss, and an increased risk of other infections?

a) Feline leukemia b) Hypertrophic cardiomyopathy

c) Feline immunodeficiency virus (FIV) d) Feline infectious peritonitis (FIP)

91. What is a common immune system disorder in horses, characterized by an abnormal immune response to proteins in forage, resulting in hives, itching, and swelling?

a) Equine infectious anemia (EIA)

b) Sweet itch

c) Equine protozoal myeloencephalitis (EPM)

d) Equine influenza

92. In poultry farming, which immune system disorder in chickens is caused by a parasitic protozoan, leading to decreased immunity and increased susceptibility to other diseases?

a) Marek's disease b) Egg drop syndrome (EDS)

c) Coccidiosis d) Avian influenza

93. Which immune system disorder in cattle is characterized by an abnormal immune response to certain proteins in the diet, resulting in inflammation of the intestinal lining?

a) Bovine respiratory disease (BR d) b) Foot rot

c) Johne's disease d) Allergic gastroenteritis

94. What immune system disorder in rabbits is characterized by the presence of white lumps or abscesses on the skin, often caused by bacterial infections?

a) Psittacosis b) Dermatophilosis

c) Rabbit syphilis d) Encephalitozoonosis

95. In swine, which immune system disorder is associated with bacterial infections and can result in swollen joints and lameness?

a) Swine flu

b) Erysipelas

c) Porcine reproductive and respiratory syndrome

d) Strep throat

96. What immune system disorder in dogs is characterized by inflammation of the immune system's blood vessels, leading to symptoms such as fever and joint pain?

a) Lupus b) Rheumatoid arthritis

c) Panosteitis d) Leptospirosis

97. What is a common metabolic disorder in dogs characterized by an inability to regulate blood sugar levels, leading to excessive thirst and urination?

a) Osteosarcoma b) Hyperthyroidism

c) Diabetes mellitus d) Feline leukemia

98. In cattle, what metabolic disorder results from a deficiency of calcium, often occurring around calving, and can lead to muscle tremors and weakness?

a) Bovine respiratory disease (BRD) b) Hypocalcemia (milk fever)

c) Ketosis d) Botulism

99. Which metabolic disorder in cats is related to the overproduction of thyroid hormones, resulting in weight loss, increased appetite, and restlessness?

a) Hypothyroidism b) Hyperthyroidism

c) Cushing's disease d) Lyme disease

100. What is a common metabolic disorder in horses, often associated with obesity, and characterized by insulin resistance and laminitis?

a) Laminitis

b) Equine metabolic syndrome (EMS)

c) Equine protozoal myeloencephalitis (EPM)

d) Tetanus

101. In poultry farming, what is a metabolic disorder in laying hens caused by a deficiency of calcium and can result in brittle bones and eggshell quality issues?

a) Ascites b) Rickets

c) Egg drop syndrome (EDS) d) Avian influenza

102. Which metabolic disorder in pigs is associated with a deficiency of thiamine (Vitamin B1), leading to neurological symptoms and uncoordinated movements?

a) Swine flu b) Polioencephalomalacia

c) Osteochondrosis d) African swine fever

103. What metabolic disorder in dogs is characterized by an excess of cortisol production by the adrenal glands, leading to symptoms such as increased thirst, urination, and abdominal distension?

a) Cushing's disease b) Hypocalcemia

c) Acromegaly d) Leptospirosis

104. In dairy cattle, which metabolic disorder occurs when the energy demands of lactation exceed energy intake, often leading to weight loss and ketone production?

a) Milk fever

b) Bovine respiratory disease (BRD)

c) Ketosis

d) Foot rot

Answer Key

1	c	2	d	3	b	4	d	5	d	6	b	7	b
8	d	9	b	10	c	11	b	12	c	13	c	14	c
15	b	16	a	17	c	18	b	19	c	20	a	21	d
22	c	23	c	24	b	25	a	26	b	27	c	28	c
29	d	30	d	31	b	32	c	33	c	34	a	35	c
36	b	37	c	38	c	39	a	40	c	41	c	42	b
43	c	44	c	45	a	46	c	47	a	48	b	49	c
50	a	51	b	52	c	53	c	54	d	55	b	56	a
57	b	58	a	59	c	60	d	61	d	62	b	63	c
64	b	65	c	66	a	67	a	68	d	69	c	70	d
71	b	72	d	73	d	74	c	75	c	76	c	77	b
78	c	79	b	80	c	81	c	82	c	83	b	84	c
85	b	86	b	87	d	88	b	89	b	90	c	91	b
92	c	93	d	94	b	95	b	96	b	97	a	98	b
99	b	100	b	101	b	102	b	103	a	104	c		

6

Metabolism

Abhishek Kumar Singh[1] and Abhay Kumar Singh[2]

[1]*FVAS, IAg Sc, Banaras Hindu University, Varanasi, Uttar Pradesh*

[2]*Department of Livestock Production Management, BASU, Patna, Bihar*

Introduction

Metabolism encompasses a series of cellular reactions essential for sustaining life in living organisms. These reactions are part of interconnected pathways within cells, ultimately providing the necessary energy for cellular functions. The importance and evolutionary benefits of these pathways are evident as they are conserved across animals, plants, fungi, and bacteria. In eukaryotes, metabolic pathways operate within the cytosol and mitochondria, with glucose and fatty acids being the primary sources of cellular energy in animals. Metabolism is organized into distinct pathways to optimize energy capture or minimize energy expenditure. It can be divided into two main processes: anabolism, which involves the synthesis of complex macromolecules, and catabolism, which involves their degradation.

Carbohydrates are the major source of energy in the animal's diet. Absorbed glucose could be utilized by the animal for several functions. The first priority is the formation of glycogen in the liver, which is stored in muscle and hepatic tissue. However, the body stores very little as glycogen (a starch-like compound), and glycogen could be rapidly hydrolyzed back to glucose through a process called glycogenolysis. This helps in maintaining blood glucose at a narrow range in normal healthy animals. The second priority is oxidation to form energy (a major function) and is described in the next sections. Since glycogen storage is limited, excess glucose is converted to fat and is stored in adipose tissue. This is accomplished by the breakdown of glucose to pyruvate through a process called glycolysis, which is then available for fat synthesis. The catabolism of glucose occurs in two metabolic pathways: glycolysis and the tricarboxylic acid (TCA; also called citric acid or Kreb's) cycle.

Glycolysis: Enzymes for glycolysis are located in the cytosol of the cell, and glycolysis occurs in this part of the cell. Glycolysis is the breakdown of 6 C glucose into two 3 C end product pyruvates in aerobic metabolism and lactic acid in anaerobic metabolism. It is a catabolic pathway involving oxidation and yields ATP and NADH (reduced NAD) energy. Glycolysis is the pathway by which other sugars (e.g., fructose, galactose) are catabolized by converting them to intermediates of glycolysis. Fructose can be converted to fructose-6-phosphate by hexokinase. Galactose can enter glycolysis by being converted to galactose-1-phosphate followed by conversion (ultimately) to glucose-1-phosphate and subsequently to glucose-6-phosphate (G6P), which is a glycolysis intermediate.

Energy Production Process through Glycolysis: Glycolysis has two phases: an energy investment phase requiring the input of ATP (preparatory phase) and an energy realization phase (pay off) where ATP is made. Cells that utilize glucose have an enzyme called hexokinases, which use ATP to phosphorylate the glucose (attaches a phosphorus group) and changes it into G6P. At this point, the cellular "machinery" can begin to process the glucose. Briefly, in the first reaction of glycolysis, hexokinase catalyzes the transfer of phosphate to glucose from ATP, forming glucose-6-phosphate. Thus this step uses ATP, which provides the energy necessary for the reaction to proceed. Glucose-6-phosphate is converted to fructose-6-phosphate and subsequently to fructose-1,6-biphosphate, which is cleaved to dihydroxy acetone phosphate (DHAP) and glyceraldehyde-3-phosphate (G3P). During this process, an additional ATP is required to phosphorylate the intermediate fructose-6-phosphate. Therefore, the "preparation" of glucose results in two molecules of ATP being used for every glucose molecule processed. During the payoff phase, G3P is further processed to produce pyruvate. During this phase, one NADH and two ATP are produced during the intermediate steps. The DHAP produced can be simply converted into G3P and processed in a similar manner as the first G3P. Therefore, one glucose molecule will result in the production of two NADH, four ATP, and two pyruvate molecules.

Glycolysis (Aerobic)

Input: = 1 glucose molecule

Requires = − 2 ATP (Activation)

Produces

+ 2 pyruvate molecules + 4 ATP + 2 NADH (= 6 ATP)

Total = 6 + 4 =10 ATP

Net gain =10 − 2 = 8 ATP

Fates of Pyruvate

- Lactic acid production
- Acetyl CoA production

Anaerobic metabolism of glucose produces two ATP per glucose molecule. Pyruvate dehydrogenase links glycolysis with the TCA cycle by converting pyruvate into acetyl CoA. TCA cycle, citric acid cycle, or Kreb's cycle (named after Hans Krebs who discovered the pathway in 1937) includes a series of enzyme-catalyzed chemical reactions that occur in the matrix of the mitochondria. Several B vitamin–containing enzymes function as coenzymes in the pathway (e.g., thiamine, riboflavin, niacin). The TCA cycle is the key part of aerobic respiration in cells. The TCA cycle also serves as a source of precursors for storage forms of fuels (lipids) and building blocks, such as amino acids, in the animal body. One mole of glucose produces 24 ATP through the TCA cycle.

Protein Metabolism

- The liver is the major site of amino acid metabolism.
- Nonessential amino acids are synthesized through the process of transamination.
- Degradation of amino acid involves two processes (deamination and transamination).
- Deamination is the removal of amino groups from the C skeleton and the release of ammonia.

- Toxic ammonia is disposed through the urea cycle for detoxification of NH3 into urea (mammals) or uric acid (birds).
- Two important functions of the urea cycle are detoxification of ammonia (liver) and provisioning of arginine (kidney) to form urea and ornithine.
- Two nonprotein amino acids (ornithine and citrulline) are involved in the urea cycle.
- The C skeleton then can be used for energy, glucose, other amino acids, or ketone body synthesis.
- All amino acids except leucine and lysine are glucogenic.
- Four amino acids are both ketogenic and glucogenic (e.g., tyrosine, tryptophan, isoleucine, phenylalanine).
- Protein synthesis requires transcription and translation. The DNA template is transcribed into messenger RNA (mRNA), which in turn, serves as a template (translation) for protein synthesis.
- Transfer RNA (tRN a) carries the individual amino acid to the ribosomes and links together to form a polypeptide chain. Twenty individual amino acids are required at the same time to complete this task.
- There are constant turnovers of proteins in the body, and there is a loss of proteins in the body as well, mainly in feces.
- Protein need depends on age, physiological status, and quality of the protein supplied in the diet.

The ammonia liberated from amino acid degradation is toxic to the central nervous and needs to be excreted or detoxified. Most mammals detoxify ammonia and excrete it as urea in the urine, while birds excrete it as uric acid (a white substance in the excreta). The detoxification of ammonia to form urea is brought about by the urea cycle through two tissues, Liver and Kidney. Poultry cannot synthesize carbamoyl phosphate and hence they cannot make urea. Instead, glutamic acid, glycine, and methionine are used for uric acid synthesis. Hence poultry need high levels of methionine, arginine, and glycine in their diet for optimum production.

Protein turnover is a dynamic process involving continuous and simultaneous protein synthesis and protein degradation. The net rate of protein gain or loss is governed by the balance of synthesis and degenerative processes. Constant turnovers of proteins in the body and the loss of proteins, mainly in feces, are the basis for protein requirement. Even when an animal is not growing, it still has a protein requirement. The amount of protein needed in the diet depends on age, physiological (e.g., pregnancy, lactation) and pathological status, and quality of the protein supplied.

Lipid Metabolism

- Chylomicrons enter the liver and are packaged into very-low-density lipoproteins (VLDL).
- VLDL delivers triacylglycerols (TAGs) from the liver to extrahepatic tissues. Once they unload the TAGs at the target tissues, their density increases and thus the LDL and HDL increase as well.

- LDL carries most of the cholesterol to tissues. Once they unload the cholesterol at the target tissues, their density increases, and thus HDL increases as well.
- HDL offloads all the remaining cholesterol and triglycerides to liver and is marked for excretion.

Lipid Storage

- For TAGs to enter the cells, lipoprotein lipase is required to hydrolyze them into fatty acids and glycerol again. The formation of TAGs requires a glycerol backbone, which can only come from glycolysis. Consequently, glucose is the key signal for fat storage.

Lipid Mobilization

- Mobilized lipids are used for energy production. Mobilization of fat out of adipose tissue requires another lipase. Hormone-sensitive lipase hydrolyzes TAGs and releases fatty acids and glycerol into blood circulation and provides other tissues with the substrate for energy.

β-Oxidation of Fatty Acids (Energy Production)

Activation of fatty acid is done by acetyl CoA synthase to yield fatty acyl CoA is ATP dependent, needs two ATP Transportation into the mitochondria (carnitine needed)

Degradation of two carbon fragments (β-oxidation) provides one NADH and one FADH per each acetyl CoA.

Ketogenesis occurs under negative energy balance conditions in the liver.

- Excessive acetyl CoA accumulated from β-oxidation cannot be used in the TCA cycle; low incoming glucose due to starvation force the liver to make ketone bodies that can serve as an alternate energy source. However, continued synthesis leads to an accumulation of ketone bodies in the blood.

Fatty Acid Synthesis

- The location is cytosol.
- The starting material is acetyl CoA.
- The key enzymes are acetyl CoA carboxylase and fatty acid synthase complex.
- Starting with acetyl CoA (mainly from carbohydrates), two carbon units are added from the carboxyl to the methyl end.
- The cycle continues through the addition of malonyl CoA (building block for synthesis) and loss of CO2 up to 16 C.
- Further elongation and desaturation take place to form long-chain fatty acids. However, mammals cannot insert double bonds beyond Δ-9 position.
- Two fatty acids, linoleic and α-linolenic, are essential and should be included in the diet.

1. Which enzyme initiates carbohydrate digestion in the mouth?

   a) Pepsin b) Amylase

   c) Lipase d) Maltase

2. The primary site of carbohydrate digestion in non-ruminant animals is:
   a) Stomach b) Small intestine
   c) Large intestine d) Mouth
3. What is the main form of carbohydrate storage in animals?
   a) Starch b) Glycogen
   c) Cellulose d) Glucose
4. Which pathway is responsible for converting glucose to pyruvate?
   a) Glycolysis b) Gluconeogenesis
   c) Pentose phosphate pathway d) TCA cycle
5. What is the end product of glycolysis under anaerobic conditions in muscle cells?
   a) Pyruvate b) Lactate
   c) Acetyl-CoA d) Ethanol
6. Which enzyme converts pyruvate to acetyl-CoA?
   a) Pyruvate carboxylase b) Pyruvate dehydrogenase
   c) Pyruvate kinase d) Pyruvate decarboxylase
7. Where does the citric acid cycle occur in the cell?
   a) Cytoplasm b) Nucleus
   c) Mitochondria d) Endoplasmic reticulum
8. What is the main regulatory step of glycolysis?
   a) Hexokinase reaction b) Phosphofructokinase reaction
   c) Pyruvate kinase reaction d) Glucose-6-phosphatase reaction
9. Which molecule is the primary electron acceptor in the oxidative phase of the pentose phosphate pathway?
   a) NADH b) NADPH
   c) FADH2 d) ATP
10. In ruminants, volatile fatty acids (VFAs) are the primary end products of:
    a) Protein digestion b) Carbohydrate fermentation
    c) Fat digestion d) Nucleic acid metabolism
11. Which VFA is the major glucose precursor in ruminants?
    a) Acetate b) Butyrate
    c) Propionate d) Lactate
12. Gluconeogenesis primarily occurs in which organ?
    a) Liver b) Muscle
    c) Brain d) Adipose tissue
13. Which hormone increases glycogen synthesis in the liver?
    a) Glucagon b) Insulin
    c) Epinephrine d) Cortisol

14. What is the key regulatory enzyme in gluconeogenesis?
    a) Glucose-6-phosphatase b) Phosphofructokinase
    c) Pyruvate carboxylase d) Fructose-1,6-bisphosphatase
15. Which process converts lactate back to glucose in the liver?
    a) Glycolysis b) Gluconeogenesis
    c) Glycogenesis d) Pentose phosphate pathway
16. Which hormone promotes glycogen breakdown in the liver?
    a) Insulin b) Glucagon
    c) Somatostatin d) Aldosterone
17. The Cori cycle is primarily involved in the inter-conversion of:
    a) Glucose and glycogen b) Glucose and lactate
    c) Glucose and pyruvate d) Glycogen and starch
18. Which enzyme catalyzes the hydrolysis of sucrose into glucose and fructose?
    a) Sucrase b) Lactase
    c) Maltase d) Amylase
19. During prolonged fasting, which of the following becomes a major source of blood glucose?
    a) Glycogenolysis b) Gluconeogenesis
    c) Ketogenesis d) Lipolysis
20. Which molecule is a common intermediate in the metabolism of carbohydrates, fats, and proteins?
    a) Glucose b) Pyruvate
    c) Acetyl-CoA d) Oxaloacetate
21. In the absence of oxygen, pyruvate is converted into:
    a) Acetyl-CoA b) Lactate
    c) Oxaloacetate d) Ethanol
22. What is the primary role of the enzyme glycogen phosphorylase?
    a) Glycogen synthesis b) Glycogen breakdown
    c) Glucose phosphorylation d) Glucose dephosphorylation
23. Which enzyme is responsible for the conversion of fructose-6-phosphate to fructose-1,6-bisphosphate in glycolysis?
    a) Hexokinase b) Phosphofructokinase
    c) Aldolase d) Triose phosphate isomerase
24. Which carbohydrate is a major energy source for ruminants?
    a) Starch b) Cellulose
    c) Glycogen d) Lactose
25. In which cellular location does the pentose phosphate pathway occur?
    a) Mitochondria b) Cytoplasm
    c) Nucleus d) Endoplasmic reticulum

26. Which enzyme is responsible for the hydrolysis of lactose into glucose and galactose?
   a) Sucrase b) Lactase
   c) Maltase d) Amylase
27. Which intermediate of the citric acid cycle is also a substrate for gluconeogenesis?
   a) Citrate b) α-Ketoglutarate
   c) Succinyl-CoA d) Oxaloacetate
28. Which process describes the formation of glucose from non-carbohydrate precursors?
   a) Glycolysis b) Gluconeogenesis
   c) Glycogenesis d) Glycogenolysis
29. Which compound is not an end product of glycolysis?
   a) ATP b) NADH
   c) Pyruvate d) Acetyl-CoA
30. Which hormone stimulates the uptake of glucose into muscle and adipose tissue?
   a) Glucagon b) Insulin
   c) Epinephrine d) Cortisol
31. What is the major metabolic fate of glucose-6-phosphate in the liver during the fed state?
   a) Glycogen synthesis b) Glycogen breakdown
   c) Ketone body synthesis d) Gluconeogenesis
32. Which metabolic pathway generates NADPH and ribose-5-phosphate?
   a) Glycolysis b) Citric acid cycle
   c) Pentose phosphate pathway d) Urea cycle
33. In ruminants, which VFA is primarily converted to ketone bodies in the liver?
   a) Acetate b) Butyrate
   c) Propionate d) Lactate
34. Which enzyme is the key regulator of the glycogenolysis pathway?
   a) Glycogen synthase b) Glycogen phosphorylase
   c) Glucose-6-phosphatase d) Phosphoglucomutase
35. During intense exercise, the muscle converts pyruvate to:
   a) Acetyl-CoA b) Oxaloacetate
   c) Lactate d) Ethanol
36. Which enzyme catalyzes the first committed step in glycolysis?
   a) Hexokinase b) Phosphofructokinase
   c) Aldolase d) Pyruvate kinase
37. In the liver, which process is activated during fasting to maintain blood glucose levels?
   a) Glycogenesis b) Glycolysis
   c) Gluconeogenesis d) Lipogenesis

38. Which carbohydrate cannot be digested by most monogastric animals?
    a) Starch b) Glycogen
    c) Cellulose d) Sucrose

39. What is the primary function of the citric acid cycle?
    a) ATP production b) Glucose synthesis
    c) NADPH production d) Fatty acid synthesis

40. Which pathway is crucial for generating reducing power in the form of NADPH?
    a) Glycolysis b) Citric acid cycle
    c) Pentose phosphate pathway d) Urea cycle

41. Which intermediate is formed by the action of aldolase during glycolysis?
    a) Fructose-1,6-bisphosphate b) Glyceraldehyde-3-phosphate
    c) Dihydroxyacetone phosphate d) Both b and c

42. What is the main storage form of carbohydrates in plants?
    a) Starch b) Cellulose
    c) Glycogen d) Fructose

43. Which pathway allows for the production of glucose from amino acids?
    a) Glycolysis b) Gluconeogenesis
    c) Pentose phosphate pathway d) Beta-oxidation

44. The conversion of glucose-6-phosphate to ribulose-5-phosphate occurs in which pathway?
    a) Glycolysis b) Citric acid cycle
    c) Pentose phosphate pathway d) Glycogenesis

45. What is the primary role of the enzyme hexokinase in carbohydrate metabolism?
    a) Phosphorylation of glucose b) Dephosphorylation of glucose
    c) Isomerization of glucose d) Oxidation of glucose

46. Which process describes the synthesis of glycogen from glucose?
    a) Glycolysis b) Gluconeogenesis
    c) Glycogenesis d) Glycogenolysis

47. In the citric acid cycle, acetyl-CoA combines with which molecule to form citrate?
    a) Oxaloacetate b) Pyruvate
    c) Succinate d) α-Ketoglutarate

48. Which enzyme catalyzes the conversion of glucose-1-phosphate to glucose-6-phosphate?
    a) Hexokinase b) Phosphoglucomutase
    c) Glucose-6-phosphatase d) Glucokinase

49. Which carbohydrate polymer serves as a structural component in the cell walls of plants?
    a) Starch b) Cellulose
    c) Glycogen d) Chitin

50. Acetyl CoA enters the TCA cycle and condenses with this 4 C compound to form citrate _____.
   a) Malate b) Oxaloacetate
   c) Fumarate d) Pyruvate-

51. Which enzyme initiates protein digestion in the stomach?
   a) Pepsin b) Trypsin
   c) Chymotrypsin d) Carboxypeptidase

52. The main site of amino acid absorption in non-ruminant animals is:
   a) Stomach b) Small intestine
   c) Large intestine d) Mouth

53. Which process describes the removal of an amino group from an amino acid?
   a) Transamination b) Deamination
   c) Amination d) Peptide bond formation

54. The urea cycle primarily occurs in which organ?
   a) Kidney b) Liver
   c) Muscle d) Pancreas

55. Which amino acid is a major carrier of ammonia in the blood?
   a) Alanine b) Glutamine
   c) Serine d) Tyrosine

56. Which enzyme converts arginine to urea in the urea cycle?
   a) Arginase b) Carbamoyl phosphate synthetase
   c) Ornithine transcarbamylase d) Argininosuccinate lyase

57. Where does the initial step of protein digestion occur in ruminants?
   a) Rumen b) Omasum
   c) Abomasum d) Small intestine

58. Which amino acid is considered essential in the diet of monogastric animals?
   a) Glycine b) Proline
   c) Lysine d) Glutamate

59. Which amino acid is the primary precursor for the synthesis of nitric oxide?
   a) Arginine b) Lysine
   c) Histidine d) Tryptophan

60. The carbon skeletons of amino acids can be used for which metabolic pathways?
   a) Gluconeogenesis b) Ketogenesis
   c) Both a and b d) None of the above

61. Which amino acid is involved in the synthesis of the neurotransmitter serotonin?
   a) Tyrosine b) Tryptophan
   c) Phenylalanine d) Methionine

62. Which enzyme catalyzes the conversion of glutamate to α-ketoglutarate?
    a) Glutamate dehydrogenase
    b) Glutamine synthetase
    c) Glutaminase
    d) Transaminase
63. Which of the following is an essential amino acid for cats?
    a) Glycine
    b) Taurine
    c) Alanine
    d) Aspartate
64. Which amino acid is the main precursor for the synthesis of epinephrine?
    a) Tryptophan
    b) Tyrosine
    c) Methionine
    d) Lysine
65. Which enzyme is responsible for the initial step of protein digestion in the stomach?
    a) Pepsinogen
    b) Trypsinogen
    c) Chymotrypsinogen
    d) Carboxypeptidase
66. Which process converts.amino acids to glucose in the liver?
    a) Transamination
    b) Deamination
    c) Gluconeogenesis
    d) Ketogenesis
67. Which of the following amino acids is glucogenic?
    a) Leucine
    b) Lysine
    c) Isoleucine
    d) Alanine
68. What is the primary nitrogenous waste product excreted by birds?
    a) Urea
    b) Ammonia
    c) Uric acid
    d) Creatinine
69. Which amino acid is involved in the synthesis of both creatine and glutathione?
    a) Glycine
    b) Cysteine
    c) Methionine
    d) Serine
70. Which enzyme is deficient in phenylketonuria (PKU)?
    a) Tyrosine hydroxylase
    b) Phenylalanine hydroxylase
    c) Tryptophan hydroxylase
    d) Homogentisate oxidase
71. Which amino acid serves as a precursor for melanin synthesis?
    a) Tryptophan
    b) Tyrosine
    c) Methionine
    d) Lysine
72. The conversion of ammonia to urea takes place in the:
    a) Kidneys
    b) Liver
    c) Muscle
    d) Intestine
73. Which amino acid is essential for the synthesis of collagen?
    a) Serine
    b) Cysteine
    c) Proline
    d) Glycine

74. Which metabolic disorder is characterized by the accumulation of branched-chain amino acids?
 a) Alkaptonuria b) Maple syrup urine disease
 c) Homocystinuria d) Phenylketonuria

75. Which amino acid can be synthesized from pyruvate?
 a) Alanine b) Leucine
 c) Lysine d) Valine

76. Which enzyme catalyzes the conversion of ornithine to citrulline in the urea cycle?
 a) Arginase b) Carbamoyl phosphate synthetase
 c) Ornithine transcarbamylase d) Argininosuccinate synthetase

77. Which amino acid is primarily metabolized in muscle tissue?
 a) Alanine b) Leucine
 c) Glutamate d) Glycine

78. Which amino acid is a precursor for the synthesis of heme?
 a) Glycine b) Tyrosine
 c) Tryptophan d) Phenylalanine

79. Which amino acid is the precursor for the neurotransmitter GABA?
 a) Glutamate b) Aspartate
 c) Glycine d) Serine

80. Which enzyme is responsible for synthesis of carbamoyl phosphate in urea cycle?
 a) Arginase
 b) Carbamoyl phosphate synthetase I
 c) Ornithine transcarbamylase
 d) Argininosuccinate synthetase

81. Which amino acid is a precursor for the synthesis of histamine?
 a) Histidine b) Tyrosine
 c) Tryptophan d) Serine

82. Which amino acid is most commonly found in the blood as a transport form of nitrogen?
 a) Alanine b) Glutamine
 c) Glycine d) Aspartate

83. Which amino acid is involved in the synthesis of purines and pyrimidines?
 a) Glutamine b) Serine
 c) Cysteine d) Tyrosine

84. Which process converts amino acids to fatty acids in the liver?
 a) Transamination b) Lipogenesis
 c) Deamination d) Gluconeogenesis

85. Which amino acid is crucial for the detoxification of ammonia in the brain?
   a) Alanine b) Glutamate
   c) Glutamine d) Aspartate
86. Which amino acid is a precursor for the synthesis of creatine?
   a) Lysine b) Arginine
   c) Methionine d) Histidine
87. Which amino acid is essential for the synthesis of thyroid hormones?
   a) Tyrosine b) Tryptophan
   c) Methionine d) Phenylalanine
88. Which process involves the transfer of an amino group from one amino acid to a keto acid?
   a) Deamination b) Transamination
   c) Decarboxylation d) Hydrolysis
89. Which amino acid is a key component of the antioxidant glutathione?
   a) Glutamine b) Glycine
   c) Cysteine d) Methionine
90. Which amino acid is used in the treatment of liver diseases due to its role in ammonia detoxification?
   a) Glutamine b) Arginine
   c) Ornithine d) Aspartate
91. Which amino acid is synthesized from phenylalanine?
   a) Tyrosine b) Tryptophan
   c) Leucine d) Lysine
92. Which enzyme catalyzes the conversion of homocysteine to methionine?
   a) Methionine synthase b) Cystathionine β-synthase
   c) Homogentisate oxidase d) Tyrosine hydroxylase
93. Which amino acid is important for the synthesis of polyamines such as spermidine and spermine?
   a) Ornithine b) Lysine
   c) Arginine d) Histidine
94. Which enzyme catalyzes the conversion of cysteine to taurine?
   a) Cysteine dioxygenase b) Cystathionine γ-lyase
   c) Glutamate dehydrogenase d) Methionine synthase
95. Which amino acid can be directly deaminated to produce pyruvate?
   a) Alanine b) Glutamate
   c) Glycine d) Serine
96. Which amino acid is involved in the synthesis of carnitine?
   a) Lysine b) Methionine
   c) Arginine d) Both a and b

97. Which amino acid is the precursor for the synthesis of the pigment melanin?
    a) Tryptophan b) Tyrosine
    c) Methionine d) Histidine
98. Which enzyme catalyzes the conversion of glycine to serine?
    a) Serine hydroxymethyltransferase b) Glycine decarboxylase
    c) Alanine transaminase d) Aspartate aminotransferase
99. Which amino acid is essential for the synthesis of the hormone epinephrine?
    a) Tryptophan b) Tyrosine
    c) Methionine d) Lysine
100. Which amino acid plays a significant role in the formation of bile salts?
    a) Glycine b) Taurine
    c) Cysteine d) Methionine
101. Which enzyme is primarily responsible for the hydrolysis of triglycerides in adipose tissue?
    a) Lipoprotein lipase b) Hormone-sensitive lipase
    c) Pancreatic lipase d) Phospholipase A2
102. In which cellular organelle does β-oxidation of fatty acids occur?
    a) Cytosol b) Mitochondria
    c) Endoplasmic reticulum d) Golgi apparatus
103. Which molecule is the primary carrier of fatty acids in the blood?
    a) Albumin b) Hemoglobin
    c) Myoglobin d) Transferrin
104. Which enzyme catalyzes the first step of fatty acid β-oxidation?
    a) Acetyl-CoA carboxylase b) Carnitine acyltransferase I
    c) Fatty acyl-CoA synthetase d) Acyl-CoA dehydrogenase
105. The synthesis of fatty acids occurs primarily in which part of the cell?
    a) Mitochondria b) Cytosol
    c) Nucleus d) Golgi apparatus
106. Which cofactor is essential for the activity of acetyl-CoA carboxylase in fatty acid synthesis?
    a) NAD+ b) FAD
    c) Biotin d) Coenzyme A
107. Which of the following fatty acids is considered essential in the diet of mammals?
    a) Oleic acid b) Palmitic acid
    c) Linoleic acid d) Stearic acid
108. Which lipoprotein is primarily responsible for the transport of dietary lipids from the intestines to other tissues?
    a) HDL b) LDL
    c) VLDL d) Chylomicrons

109. Which enzyme is responsible for the conversion of acetyl-CoA to malonyl-CoA in fatty acid synthesis?
   a) Fatty acid synthase
   b) Carnitine acyltransferase I
   c) Acetyl-CoA carboxylase
   d) HMG-CoA reductase

110. Which apolipoprotein is a key activator of lipoprotein lipase?
   a) ApoA-I
   b) ApoB-100
   c) ApoC-II
   d) ApoE

111. What is the primary function of bile salts in lipid metabolism?
   a) Hydrolysis of triglycerides
   b) Emulsification of fats
   c) Transport of lipids in the blood
   d) Synthesis of cholesterol

112. Which enzyme catalyzes the rate-limiting step in cholesterol biosynthesis?
   a) HMG-CoA synthase
   b) HMG-CoA reductase
   c) Squalene epoxidase
   d) Mevalonate kinase

113. Which fatty acid is the precursor for the synthesis of prostaglandins?
   a) Arachidonic acid
   b) Palmitic acid
   c) Stearic acid
   d) Oleic acid

114. Which metabolic process involves the conversion of acetyl-CoA into ketone bodies?
   a) Glycolysis
   b) Lipogenesis
   c) Ketogenesis
   d) Gluconeogenesis

115. Which enzyme is responsible for the esterification of free cholesterol in cells?
   a) Cholesterol ester transfer protein (CETP)
   b) Acyl-CoA:cholesterol acyltransferase (ACAT)
   c) Lecithin-cholesterol acyltransferase (LCAT)
   d) Lipoprotein lipase

116. Which fatty acid is commonly used as an energy source by the heart muscle?
   a) Oleic acid
   b) Stearic acid
   c) Palmitic acid
   d) Linoleic acid

117. Which hormone promotes the storage of fats in adipose tissue?
   a) Glucagon
   b) Epinephrine
   c) Insulin
   d) Cortisol

118. In fatty acid synthesis, which molecule is the direct donor of two-carbon units?
   a) Acetyl-CoA
   b) Malonyl-CoA
   c) Citrate
   d) Pyruvate

119. Which process describes the formation of lipid droplets within cells?
   a) Lipolysis
   b) Lipogenesis
   c) Adipogenesis
   d) Lipidation

120. Which enzyme is inhibited by malonyl-CoA, thereby preventing the transport of fatty acids into mitochondria for β-oxidation?

a) Acetyl-CoA carboxylase
b) Carnitine acyltransferase I
c) Hormone-sensitive lipase
d) Fatty acid synthase

121. Which fatty acid cannot be synthesized de novo by mammals and must be obtained from the diet?

a) Palmitic acid
b) Stearic acid
c) Linolenic acid
d) Oleic acid

122. Which enzyme is responsible for the hydrolysis of triglycerides in the intestine?

a) Pancreatic lipase
b) Hormone-sensitive lipase
c) Lipoprotein lipase
d) Phospholipase A2

123. Which molecule is a key regulator of acetyl-CoA carboxylase activity?

a) AMP-activated protein kinase (AMPK)
b) Protein kinase A (PKA)
c) Glycogen synthase kinase-3 (GSK-3)
d) Calmodulin-dependent protein kinase

124. Which lipoprotein particle is known for its role in reverse cholesterol transport?

a) LDL
b) VLDL
c) HDL
d) Chylomicrons

125. Which enzyme converts diacylglycerol to triacylglycerol in adipocytes?

a) Hormone-sensitive lipase
b) Diacylglycerol acyltransferase (DGAT)
c) Lipoprotein lipase
d) Monoacylglycerol lipase

126. Which ketone body is the primary source of energy for the brain during prolonged fasting?

a) Acetoacetate
b) β-Hydroxybutyrate
c) Acetone
d) Citrate

127. Which fatty acid oxidation pathway occurs in peroxisomes?

a) β-Oxidation
b) α-Oxidation
c) ω-Oxidation
d) None of the above

128. Which enzyme catalyzes the rate-limiting step in bile acid synthesis from cholesterol?

a) Cholesterol 7α-hydroxylase
b) HMG-CoA reductase
c) Acetyl-CoA carboxylase
d) Squalene epoxidase

129. Which fatty acid is a major component of sphingolipids?

a) Palmitic acid
b) Stearic acid
c) Arachidonic acid
d) Ceramide

130. Which molecule is the immediate precursor of eicosanoids?
   a) Cholesterol b) Palmitic acid
   c) Arachidonic acid d) Linoleic acid

131. Which condition is characterized by an inability to degrade very long-chain fatty acids?
   a) Gaucher's disease b) Tay-Sachs disease
   c) Adrenoleukodystrophy d) Niemann-Pick disease

132. Which enzyme deficiency leads to the accumulation of phytanic acid?
   a) Acyl-CoA dehydrogenase b) Phytanoyl-CoA hydroxylase
   c) Hormone-sensitive lipase d) Lipoprotein lipase

133. Which enzyme is responsible for the conversion of citrate to acetyl-CoA in the cytosol?
   a) Citrate synthase b) Citrate lyase
   c) Citrate dehydrogenase d) Citrate permease

134. Which enzyme catalyzes the final step in the synthesis of triglycerides?
   a) Acetyl-CoA carboxylase b) Fatty acid synthase
   c) Diacylglycerol acyltransferase (DGAT) d) Monoacylglycerol lipase

135. Which class of lipids are primarily involved in the structure of cell membranes?
   a) Triglycerides b) Phospholipids
   c) Steroids d) Glycolipids

136. Which fatty acid is known for its anti-inflammatory properties?
   a) Linoleic acid b) Arachidonic acid
   c) Eicosapentaenoic acid (EPA) d) Palmitic acid

137. Which lipoprotein is primarily responsible for the transport of cholesterol to peripheral tissues?
   a) HDL b) LDL
   c) VLDL d) Chylomicrons

138. Which enzyme catalyzes the initial step in the β-oxidation of fatty acids?
   a) Acyl-CoA synthetase b) Acyl-CoA dehydrogenase
   c) Enoyl-CoA hydratase d) β-Ketothiolase

139. Which pathway involves the conversion of fatty acids into glucose?
   a) β-Oxidation
   b) Lipogenesis
   c) Gluconeogenesis
   d) There is no pathway for this conversion

140. Which lipid is a major component of the myelin sheath in nerve cells?
   a) Triglyceride b) Cholesterol
   c) Sphingomyelin d) Phosphatidylcholine

141. Which condition is associated with the buildup of cholesterol in lysosomes?
a) Gaucher's disease
b) Niemann-Pick disease type C
c) Tay-Sachs disease
d) Fabry disease

142. Which process describes the formation of ketone bodies from acetyl-CoA?
a) Lipogenesis
b) Ketogenesis
c) Glycogenesis
d) Gluconeogenesis

143. Which enzyme is inhibited by statins to reduce cholesterol synthesis?
a) HMG-CoA synthase
b) HMG-CoA reductase
c) Squalene epoxidase
d) Mevalonate kinase

144. Which molecule is a precursor for the synthesis of steroid hormones?
a) Palmitic acid
b) Cholesterol
c) Arachidonic acid
d) Linoleic acid

145. Which enzyme converts glycerol to glycerol-3-phosphate in the liver?
a) Glycerol kinase
b) Glycerol-3-phosphate dehydrogenase
c) Glyceraldehyde-3-phosphate dehydrogenase
d) Aldolase

146. Which lipid acts as a second messenger in cell signaling pathways?
a) Triglyceride
b) Cholesterol
c) Diacylglycerol
d) Phosphatidylcholine

147. Which enzyme is responsible for the conversion of phosphatidic acid to diacylglycerol?
a) Phospholipase C
b) Diacylglycerol kinase
c) Phosphatidate phosphatase
d) Lipoprotein lipase

148. Which fatty acid oxidation process produces hydrogen peroxide as a byproduct?
a) β-Oxidation
b) α-Oxidation
c) ω-Oxidation
d) Peroxisomal β-oxidation

149. Which enzyme catalyzes the conversion of acetyl-CoA to malonyl-CoA?
a) Acetyl-CoA carboxylase
b) Fatty acid synthase
c) Citrate lyase
d) HMG-CoA reductase

150. Which lipid is essential for the formation of lipid rafts in cell membranes?
a) Triglyceride
b) Cholesterol
c) Sphingomyelin
d) Phosphatidylcholine

Answer Key

1	b	2	b	3	b	4	a	5	b	6	b	7	c
8	b	9	b	10	b	11	c	12	a	13	b	14	d
15	b	16	b	17	b	18	a	19	b	20	c	21	b
22	b	23	b	24	b	25	b	26	b	27	d	28	b
29	d	30	b	31	a	32	c	33	b	34	b	35	c
36	b	37	c	38	c	39	a	40	c	41	d	42	a
43	b	44	c	45	a	46	c	47	a	48	b	49	b
50	b	51	a	52	b	53	b	54	b	55	b	56	a
57	a	58	c	59	a	60	c	61	b	62	a	63	b
64	b	65	a	66	c	67	d	68	c	69	a	70	b
71	b	72	b	73	d	74	b	75	a	76	c	77	b
78	a	79	a	80	b	81	a	82	b	83	a	84	b
85	c	86	b	87	a	88	b	89	c	90	a	91	a
92	a	93	c	94	a	95	a	96	d	97	b	98	a
99	b	100	b	101	b	102	b	103	a	104	d	105	b
106	c	107	c	108	d	109	c	110	c	111	b	112	b
113	a	114	c	115	b	116	c	117	c	118	b	119	c
120	b	121	c	122	a	123	a	124	c	125	b	126	b
127	b	128	a	129	d	130	c	131	c	132	b	133	b
134	c	135	b	136	c	137	b	138	b	139	d	140	c
141	b	142	b	143	b	144	b	145	a	146	c	147	c
148	d	149	a	150	b								

7

Physiology of Ageing

Afreed Muhammed N.V.[1], Mohamed Hasif G.[2] and Monalisha Debbarma[3]

[1]*Department of Veterinary Physiology, Indian Veterinary Research Institute Bangalore, Karnataka*

[2]*Department of Veterinary Physiology, Siksha O Anusandhan University, Odisha*

[3]*Department of Veterinary Anatomy and Histology, Siksha O Anusandhan University Odisha*

Introduction

Ageing, a multifaceted and intricate process, is characterized by a series of transformations that occur at various levels of biological hierarchy, ultimately culminating in death. This phenomenon, marked by its complexity, involves numerous factors that interact simultaneously and operate across different levels of functional organization. The diversity of ageing phenotypes among individuals of the same species and the disparities in longevity among different species underscore the significant roles of both genetic and environmental influences in shaping the lifespan.At its core, ageing is an ontogenic journey—a process of growing old that encompasses all physiological, genetic, and molecular changes occurring from fertilization to death. The biology of ageing pertains to the progressive accumulation of random molecular defects within tissues and cells, leading to age-related functional impairments in tissues and organs. This relentless, deleterious, and intrinsic phenomenon was famously described by Medawar in 1952 as an "unsolved problem in biology." Despite the enduring mystery of the ageing process, research has advanced significantly since Medawar's time, expanding our understanding of this intricate biological conundrum.

Goldberger *et al.* (2002) define senescence as the progressive deterioration of bodily functions over time, noting that normal human ageing is associated with a loss of complexity in various physiological processes and anatomical structures. Although ageing and senescence are often used interchangeably, they encompass distinct concepts. Senescence refers to a post-maturational process that leads to diminished homeostasis and increased vulnerability to death, while ageing encompasses any time-related process that begins at conception and continues until death. The mechanisms driving ageing are partially intrinsic, influenced by genetic and epigenetic factors, and partially extrinsic, shaped by environmental factors such as nutrition, radiation, temperature, and stress. Genetic factors account for approximately 25% of the variance in human lifespan, with the remainder determined by nutritional and environmental influences.

Theories of Ageing

To better understand the ageing process and develop strategies to enhance lifespan, various theories have been proposed, classified based on the targeted level of the ageing mechanism: evolutionary theories, systemic theories, and molecular and cellular theories.

Evolutionary Theories

Evolutionary theories propose that ageing results from a decline in the force of natural selection. Since evolution primarily aims to maximize reproductive fitness, longevity is selected only if it benefits reproductive success. Consequently, lifespan is shaped by selective pressures and exhibits significant plasticity within and among species.

Disposable Soma Theory

This theory posits that the somatic organism is maintained only for reproductive success and is subsequently deemed disposable due to limited resources. It suggests that bodily resources are invested in reproductive success, with somatic maintenance and longevity determined by the balance or imbalance in resources allocated for reproduction. While this theory explains the specific length of time we live, it does not pinpoint a specific cause for ageing.

Mutation Accumulation Theory

Proposed by Peter Medawar, this theory suggests that detrimental late-acting mutations accumulate in the population, ultimately leading to pathology and senescence. Medawar considered ageing a non-adaptive trait, asserting that functions providing no reproductive advantage are unsupported by selective pressure and lost in future generations. For instance, deleterious mutations expressed early in life reduce reproductive chances, exemplified by conditions like Progeria, where individuals exhibit premature ageing signs and shorter lifespans, making it less likely for them to pass on mutant genes.

Antagonistic Pleiotropy Theory

This theory proposes that certain genes selected for their beneficial effects early in life may have unselected deleterious effects in old age, contributing to senescence. For example, mutations causing overproduction of sex hormones in youth may enhance reproductive success but lead to conditions like prostate cancer in older age.

Systemic Theories

Systemic theories relate the ageing process to the decline of organ systems essential for controlling and maintaining other systems within the organism.

Neuroendocrine Theory

This theory suggests that ageing results from changes in neural and endocrine functions crucial for coordinating communication and responsiveness of all body systems with the external environment. A key component is the hypothalamus-pituitary axis (HPA), with a failing HPA linked to decreased stress survival in old age. However, organisms with ageing phenotypes similar to higher vertebrates lack complex neuroendocrine systems, implying that neuroendocrine changes may be secondary manifestations of fundamental age-related cellular changes.

Immunologic Theory

Proposed by Walford in 1969, this theory posits that normal ageing is related to a faulty immune process. Observations supporting this theory include the decline in immune system functionality with age, evidenced by decreased T cell response to mitogens and reduced resistance to infections, and the increase in autoimmunity phenomena.

Molecular and Cellular Theories

These theories delve into the mechanisms of the ageing process at cellular and subcellular levels.

Error Catastrophic Theory

Proposed by Leslie Orgel in 1963, this theory, also known as "Orgel's hypothesis," suggests that errors in molecular copying processes (transcription or translation) result in flawed protein synthesis. Damaged proteins accumulate with age, leading to cellular dysfunction and further damage accumulation, culminating in senescence. However, experiments feeding animals abnormal amino acids failed to shorten lifespan, leading to the hypothesis's rejection.

Free Radical Theory

In 1956, Denham Harman proposed that free radicals produced during aerobic respiration cause cumulative oxidative damage, resulting in ageing and death. Free radicals target lipids, nucleic acids, and proteins, leading to lipid autoxidation, protein and nucleic acid cross-linking, altered cell membrane properties, and peptide fragmentation. Despite supporting evidence from invertebrate studies, contrasting results from other experiments and the ineffectiveness of antioxidant supplementation in decelerating ageing have challenged this theory.

Ageing Changes in Organs, Tissues, and Cells

As ageing progresses, all vital organs experience functional decline, affecting the body's cells, tissues, and organs. Cells, the fundamental building blocks of tissues, undergo various changes with age, becoming larger and less capable of division and multiplication. These changes include increased pigmentation and fatty substance accumulation within cells, loss of cellular function, or abnormal functioning. Waste products build up in tissues, with fatty brown pigments like lipofuscin and other fatty substances collecting in many tissues. Connective tissue becomes stiffer, making organs, blood vessels, and airways more rigid. Cell membranes change, hindering oxygen and nutrient acquisition and waste removal. Tissue mass decreases, leading to atrophy, while some tissues become lumpy or more rigid. Consequently, ageing organs slowly lose function, although this loss is often unnoticed due to the organs' reserve ability to function beyond usual needs.

In conclusion ageing is an inherent physiological process in all mammals, accelerated by various factors, with stress significantly promoting the ageing process. Despite the detrimental effects of stress and ageing on well-being, humans have evolved a lifestyle with low annual mortality, allowing more resources for maintenance and less for reproduction. In contrast, species in high-risk environments invest more heavily in reproduction, allocating fewer resources to maintenance. This adaptive radiation of mammals across different ecological niches has resulted in a wide range of longevities. While ageing is no longer an unsolved problem at the organismal level, the detailed molecular and cellular changes underlying the ageing phenotype remain largely unknown. The principal mechanisms of deterioration are related to the generation of reactive oxygen species (ROS) and protein glycosylation, both influenced by environmental factors.

MCQ

1. What is the primary function of telomeres?
   a) Coding for proteins b) Protecting chromosome ends
   c) Facilitating cell division d) Repairing DNA damage
2. What happens to telomeres as cells divide?
   a) They lengthen b) They remain the same length
   c) They shorten d) They disappear
3. Which enzyme helps maintain telomere length in certain cells?
   a) DNA polymerase b) Telomerase
   c) RNA polymerase d) Ligase
4. Cellular senescence is characterized by which of the following?
   a) Uncontrolled cell division b) Permanent cell cycle arrest
   c) Increased apoptosis d) Decreased protein synthesis
5. Which type of DNA damage is most commonly associated with aging?
   a) Double-strand breaks b) Base pair mismatches
   c) Single-strand breaks d) Cross-linking
6. What is the role of the p53 protein in cellular aging?
   a) Promotes DNA repair b) Inhibits apoptosis
   c) Regulates the cell cycle d) Stimulates telomerase activity
7. What is the main consequence of oxidative stress on cells?
   a) Increased protein synthesis b) Enhanced cellular division
   c) DNA, protein, and lipid damage d) Improved mitochondrial function
8. Mitochondrial dysfunction in aging is primarily due to:
   a) Increased ATP production
   b) Decreased oxidative phosphorylation
   c) Enhanced mitochondrial biogenesis
   d) Improved calcium homeostasis
9. Which pathway is primarily involved in the removal of damaged proteins?
   a) Ubiquitin-proteasome system b) Glycolysis
   c) Krebs cycle d) Gluconeogenesis
10. Epigenetic changes in aging commonly involve:
    a) DNA methylation b) RNA editing
    c) Protein folding d) Telomere elongation
11. What is the main function of sirtuins in cellular aging?
    a) Promoting telomere shortening b) Enhancing DNA repair
    c) Inhibiting cellular senescence d) Increasing oxidative stress

12. Caloric restriction has been shown to:
    a) Decrease lifespan
    b) Increase telomere length
    c) Enhance autophagy
    d) Inhibit mitochondrial function
13. What is autophagy?
    a) Programmed cell death
    b) Cellular energy production
    c) Degradation of damaged cellular components
    d) DNA replication
14. Which of the following is a marker of cellular senescence?
    a) Increased ATP levels
    b) Enhanced telomerase activity
    c) Senescence-associated β-galactosidase (SA-β-gal)
    d) Decreased oxidative stress
15. Which molecule is often referred to as the "guardian of the genome"?
    a) Telomerase
    b) p53
    c) Sirtuin
    d) Ubiquitin
16. DNA damage response (DDR) mechanisms include:
    a) Telomere elongation
    b) Cell cycle arrest
    c) Increased protein synthesis
    d) Enhanced glycolysis
17. Aging cells often exhibit an increase in which of the following?
    a) DNA repair efficiency
    b) Mitochondrial biogenesis
    c) Reactive oxygen species (ROS)
    d) Telomere length
18. Which process is involved in the maintenance of genomic stability?
    a) Protein aggregation
    b) Telomere shortening
    c) DNA repair mechanisms
    d) Mitochondrial dysfunction
19. The accumulation of which molecule is associated with cellular aging?
    a) ATP
    b) NAD+
    c) Reactive oxygen species (ROS)
    d) Glucose
20. Which cellular process declines with age, contributing to the accumulation of damaged proteins?
    a) Proteasome activity
    b) Glycolysis
    c) Lipid synthesis
    d) Protein translation
21. What is the role of reactive oxygen species (ROS) in aging?
    a) Promote cell division
    b) Enhance DNA replication
    c) Cause oxidative damage to cells
    d) Improve mitochondrial function
22. Which of the following is a major consequence of mitochondrial dysfunction in aging?
    a) Increased ATP production
    b) Decreased oxidative stress
    c) Reduced energy production
    d) Enhanced protein synthesis

23. What is the effect of advanced glycation end-products (AGEs) on proteins?
    a) They enhance protein function
    b) They cause protein misfolding and cross-linking
    c) They promote protein synthesis
    d) They protect proteins from degradation
24. Which molecular change is associated with increased insulin resistance in aging?
    a) Enhanced insulin receptor sensitivity
    b) Decreased production of insulin
    c) Impaired insulin signaling pathways
    d) Increased glucose uptake by cells
25. What is the primary function of heat shock proteins (HSPs) in aging cells?
    a) Promote protein degradation
    b) Facilitate protein folding and repair
    c) Increase mitochondrial biogenesis
    d) Enhance oxidative stress
26. Which process is responsible for the removal of damaged mitochondria in aging cells?
    a) Autophagy
    b) Glycolysis
    c) Apoptosis
    d) Proteasome activity
27. What happens to the NAD+/NADH ratio in aging cells?
    a) It remains constant
    b) It decreases
    c) It increases
    d) It becomes irrelevant
28. Which molecular change is associated with reduced proteostasis in aging?
    a) Increased protein synthesis
    b) Enhanced protein degradation
    c) Accumulation of misfolded proteins
    d) Improved protein folding mechanisms
29. What is the impact of decreased sirtuin activity on aging?
    a) Enhanced mitochondrial function
    b) Improved DNA repair
    c) Increased oxidative stress and cellular damage
    d) Reduced insulin resistance
30. What role does the ubiquitin-proteasome system play in aging?
    a) Synthesizes new proteins
    b) Degrades damaged or misfolded proteins
    c) Enhances telomere length
    d) Promotes cell division
31. What is one of the consequences of epigenetic changes in aging cells?
    a) Increased genetic diversity
    b) Altered gene expression patterns
    c) Enhanced cellular proliferation
    d) Reduced DNA methylation

32. Which molecule accumulates as a result of oxidative damage in aging cells?
    a) ATP
    b) Glucose
    c) Lipofuscin
    d) Collagen
33. Which molecular change contributes to the chronic inflammation seen in aging?
    a) Decreased production of pro-inflammatory cytokines
    b) Enhanced anti-inflammatory responses
    c) Increased secretion of pro-inflammatory cytokines
    d) Reduced immune cell activation
34. What is the impact of decreased mitochondrial biogenesis in aging cells?
    a) Improved energy production
    b) Increased oxidative stress
    c) Enhanced ATP synthesis
    d) Reduced ROS production
35. Which of the following is a characteristic of senescence-associated secretory phenotype (SASP)?
    a) Secretion of pro-inflammatory cytokines and proteases
    b) Enhanced telomerase activity
    c) Increased cell proliferation
    d) Reduced oxidative stress
36. What happens to the levels of autophagy in aging cells?
    a) They remain constant
    b) They increase
    c) They decrease
    d) They become irrelevant
37. Which of the following is a common feature of aging in the extracellular matrix?
    a) Increased collagen synthesis
    b) Accumulation of cross-linked proteins
    c) Enhanced tissue elasticity
    d) Improved tissue regeneration
38. What is the effect of decreased AMP-activated protein kinase (AMPK) activity in aging?
    a) Enhanced energy production
    b) Reduced oxidative stress
    c) Impaired cellular energy homeostasis
    d) Increased mitochondrial biogenesis
39. Which of the following contributes to the decline in protein homeostasis with aging?
    a) Accumulation of damaged proteins
    b) Enhanced proteasome activity
    c) Increased autophagy
    d) Improved chaperone function
40. What role does DNA methylation play in the aging process?
    a) Enhances gene expression
    b) Silences genes and contributes to aging
    c) Increases genetic mutations
    d) Promotes telomere elongation

41. Which cardiovascular change is commonly observed with aging?
    a) Increased heart rate
    b) Decreased blood pressure
    c) Arterial stiffness
    d) Reduced blood viscosity
42. What is a common age-related change in the musculoskeletal system?
    a) Increased muscle mass
    b) Decreased bone density
    c) Enhanced joint flexibility
    d) Improved muscle strength
43. Which of the following conditions is often associated with aging of the nervous system?
    a) Alzheimer's disease
    b) Increased neurogenesis
    c) Enhanced cognitive function
    d) Reduced synaptic plasticity
44. How does aging affect the endocrine system?
    a) Increased hormone production
    b) Enhanced insulin sensitivity
    c) Decline in sex hormone levels
    d) Elevated thyroid function
45. What is a common change in the immune system with aging?
    a) Increased production of white blood cells
    b) Enhanced immune response
    c) Immunosenescence
    d) Improved antibody production
46. Which of the following is a typical age-related change in the respiratory system?
    a) Increased lung elasticity
    b) Reduced alveolar surface area
    c) Enhanced oxygen exchange
    d) Improved lung capacity
47. What is sarcopenia?
    a) Bone weakening
    b) Loss of muscle mass and strength
    c) Increased bone density
    d) Enhanced muscle function
48. How does aging typically affect the renal system?
    a) Increased glomerular filtration rate (GFR)
    b) Decreased kidney size and function
    c) Enhanced ability to concentrate urine
    d) Improved waste elimination
49. Which gastrointestinal change is commonly seen in aging?
    a) Increased gastric acid production
    b) Enhanced nutrient absorption
    c) Slower gastrointestinal motility
    d) Improved digestive enzyme activity
50. What is a common change in the skin with aging?
    a) Thinning of the epidermis
    b) Enhanced skin elasticity
    c) Increased collagen production
    d) Reduced susceptibility to UV damage

51. Which sensory change is often observed with aging?
    a) Improved vision
    b) Enhanced hearing
    c) Presbyopia (difficulty focusing on close objects)
    d) Increased taste sensitivity
52. How does aging affect the cardiovascular system's ability to respond to stress?
    a) Enhanced heart rate variability
    b) Increased cardiac output
    c) Reduced responsiveness to stress
    d) Improved vascular compliance
53. What is osteoarthritis?
    a) Inflammation of the muscles
    b) Degenerative joint disease
    c) Autoimmune bone disorder
    d) Increased bone density
54. Which of the following changes in the nervous system is commonly associated with aging?
    a) Increased synaptic density
    b) Decreased brain volume
    c) Enhanced cognitive flexibility
    d) Increased neuroplasticity
55. What is a typical age-related change in the gastrointestinal system?
    a) Increased saliva production
    b) Enhanced gastric motility
    c) Reduced production of digestive enzymes
    d) Improved nutrient absorption
56. How does aging typically affect the reproductive system?
    a) Increased fertility
    b) Decreased levels of sex hormones
    c) Enhanced reproductive function
    d) Improved libido
57. Which age-related change is commonly observed in the cardiovascular system?
    a) Increased elasticity of blood vessels
    b) Decreased incidence of hypertension
    c) Thickening of the heart walls
    d) Improved blood flow
58. What is a common change in the endocrine system with aging?
    a) Decline in adrenal hormone levels
    b) Enhanced thyroid function
    c) Increased growth hormone production
    d) Improved glucose metabolism
59. How does aging affect the sensory system?
    a) Improved sense of smell
    b) Enhanced tactile sensitivity
    c) Decline in auditory and visual acuity
    d) Increased taste sensation
60. What is a common change in the respiratory system with aging?
    a) Increased lung compliance
    b) Reduced lung elasticity
    c) Decreased residual volume
    d) Enhanced oxygen diffusion capacity

61. What is the primary effect of aging on basal metabolic rate (BMR)?
    a) It increases
    b) It remains the same
    c) It decreases
    d) It fluctuates
62. How does aging typically affect mitochondrial function?
    a) Mitochondrial function improves
    b) Mitochondrial function remains unchanged
    c) Mitochondrial function declines
    d) Mitochondrial function fluctuates
63. What is sarcopenia?
    a) Increased muscle mass
    b) Decreased muscle mass and strength
    c) Enhanced muscle function
    d) Reduced bone density
64. Which of the following hormones typically decreases with age, affecting metabolic regulation?
    a) Insulin
    b) Growth hormone
    c) Cortisol
    d) Epinephrine
65. What is the impact of aging on insulin sensitivity?
    a) It increases
    b) It remains unchanged
    c) It decreases
    d) It fluctuates
66. How does aging affect lipid metabolism?
    a) Decreases fat accumulation
    b) Enhances lipid clearance
    c) Increases fat accumulation
    d) Reduces fat oxidation
67. What role does adiponectin play in aging?
    a) Promotes inflammation
    b) Increases insulin sensitivity
    c) Reduces glucose uptake
    d) Enhances lipid storage
68. Which metabolic pathway is often impaired in aging cells, leading to reduced ATP production?
    a) Glycolysis
    b) Oxidative phosphorylation
    c) Lipogenesis
    d) Gluconeogenesis
69. How does aging typically affect appetite and food intake regulation?
    a) Appetite decreases
    b) Appetite remains unchanged
    c) Appetite increases
    d) Food intake regulation improves
70. What is the effect of caloric restriction on lifespan and metabolic health in aging?
    a) Extends lifespan and improves metabolic health
    b) No effect on lifespan
    c) Reduces lifespan
    d) Increases metabolic disorders

71. How does aging affect the body's ability to utilize glucose?
    a) Glucose utilization improves
    b) Glucose utilization remains unchanged
    c) Glucose utilization declines
    d) Glucose utilization fluctuates
72. Which hormone's decline with age is linked to reduced thermogenesis?
    a) Insulin
    b) Thyroid hormone
    c) Cortisol
    d) Epinephrine
73. What is a common metabolic change in aging related to body composition?
    a) Increased muscle mass
    b) Increased fat mass
    c) Decreased fat mass
    d) Decreased water retention
74. How does aging affect protein metabolism?
    a) Reduces protein synthesis
    b) Decreases protein degradation
    c) Increases protein synthesis
    d) Enhances amino acid utilization
75. What is the effect of aging on energy expenditure during physical activity?
    a) Energy expenditure increases
    b) Energy expenditure remains unchanged
    c) Energy expenditure decreases
    d) Energy expenditure fluctuates
76. Which of the following is a consequence of reduced mitochondrial biogenesis in aging?
    a) Increased ATP production
    b) Decreased oxidative stress
    c) Reduced cellular energy capacity
    d) Enhanced mitochondrial function
77. How does aging affect the regulation of hunger and satiety hormones?
    a) Increases ghrelin levels
    b) Reduces ghrelin production.
    c) Enhances leptin sensitivity
    d) Decreases leptin sensitivity
78. What is the impact of aging on basal metabolic rate (BMR)?
    a) Decreases BMR
    b) Increases BMR
    c) BMR remains constant
    d) BMR fluctuates significantly
79. Which age-related change affects the body's ability to maintain glucose homeostasis?
    a) Increased insulin production
    b) Reduced insulin sensitivity
    c) Enhanced pancreatic function
    d) Improved glucose uptake
80. How does aging impact the production of reactive oxygen species (ROS) and oxidative damage?
    a) Decreases ROS production
    b) Increases ROS production and oxidative damage
    c) No effect on ROS production
    d) Reduces oxidative damage

81. What is a common cardiovascular change associated with aging?
    a) Decreased arterial stiffness
    b) Increased arterial stiffness
    c) Reduced heart rate
    d) Enhanced heart contractility
82. Which of the following is a systemic effect of aging on the immune system?
    a) Immunosenescence
    b) Increased immune response
    c) Enhanced production of antibodies
    d) Decreased inflammation
83. How does aging typically affect the endocrine system?
    a) Increased hormone production
    b) Enhanced thyroid function
    c) Decline in hormone levels such as growth hormone and sex hormones
    d) Improved glucose metabolism
84. What is a common musculoskeletal change in aging?
    a) Increased bone density
    b) Enhanced muscle strength
    c) Decreased bone density and muscle mass
    d) Improved joint flexibility
85. Which sensory system change is often observed with aging?
    a) Improved hearing
    b) Enhanced vision
    c) Decline in auditory and visual acuity
    d) Increased taste sensitivity
86. How does aging affect the respiratory system?
    a) Increased lung elasticity
    b) Reduced lung capacity and alveolar surface area
    c) Enhanced oxygen exchange
    d) Improved respiratory muscle strength
87. What is a systemic effect of aging on the gastrointestinal system?
    a) Increased gastric motility
    b) Reduced production of digestive enzymes
    c) Enhanced nutrient absorption
    d) Improved bowel regularity
88. Which change in the renal system is commonly associated with aging?
    a) Increased glomerular filtration rate (GFR)
    b) Enhanced kidney function
    c) Improved waste elimination
    d) Decreased kidney size and function
89. How does aging affect the skin?
    a) Increased collagen production
    b) Enhanced skin elasticity
    c) Thinning of the epidermis and reduced elasticity
    d) Reduced susceptibility to UV damage

90. What is a common systemic effect of aging on metabolic function?
    a) Decreased insulin sensitivity and metabolic rate
    b) Enhanced energy expenditure
    c) Increased basal metabolic rate (BMR)
    d) Improved lipid metabolism
91. How does aging affect the cardiovascular system's ability to respond to physical stress?
    a) Increased responsiveness to stress
    b) Enhanced cardiac output
    c) Reduced responsiveness to stress
    d) Improved vascular compliance
92. Which cognitive change is commonly observed with aging?
    a) Increased cognitive flexibility
    b) Decline in memory and cognitive processing speed
    c) Enhanced memory retention
    d) Improved problem-solving abilities
93. What is a systemic effect of aging on the musculoskeletal system?
    a) Increased muscle mass and strength
    b) Enhanced bone density
    c) Loss of muscle mass (sarcopenia) and bone density (osteopenia/osteoporosis)
    d) Improved joint health
94. How does aging affect thermoregulation?
    a) Improved ability to regulate body temperature
    b) Enhanced heat dissipation
    c) Reduced ability to regulate body temperature
    d) Increased sweat production
95. What systemic effect does aging have on the nervous system?
    a) Increased neuroplasticity
    b) Reduced brain volume and slower neural processing
    c) Enhanced synaptic density
    d) Improved neurotransmitter production
96. Which age-related change affects cardiovascular health?
    a) Thickening of the heart walls and arterial stiffness
    b) Decreased incidence of hypertension
    c) Increased blood vessel elasticity
    d) Improved cardiac output
97. How does aging affect immune function?
    a) Enhanced production of immune cells
    b) Decreased immune response and increased susceptibility to infections
    c) Improved response to infections
    d) Increased inflammation resolution

98. What systemic effect does aging have on hormone regulation?
   a) Increased production of sex hormones
   b) Enhanced adrenal function
   c) Decline in sex hormone levels and growth hormone production
   d) Improved thyroid function
99. How does aging typically affect the gastrointestinal tract?
   a) Increased saliva production
   b) Enhanced gastric motility
   c) Improved nutrient absorption
   d) Reduced motility and digestive enzyme production
100. What is a systemic effect of aging on sensory perception?
   a) Improved sense of smell
   b) Enhanced tactile sensitivity
   c) Increased sensitivity to pain
   d) Decline in sensory perception such as vision, hearing, and taste
101. What is a common age-related change in the extracellular matrix (ECM)?
   a) Increased collagen synthesis
   b) Decreased collagen cross-linking
   c) Accumulation of advanced glycation end-products (AGEs)
   d) Enhanced elasticity of ECM components
102. How does aging affect collagen in connective tissues?
   a) Increases collagen turnover
   b) Reduces collagen cross-linking
   c) Enhances collagen flexibility
   d) Leads to collagen fragmentation and stiffness
103. Which component of the ECM is primarily responsible for providing tensile strength to connective tissues?
   a) Elastin b) Proteoglycans
   c) Collagen d) Fibronectin
104. What is the effect of aging on elastin fibers in the ECM?
   a) Increased elastin synthesis
   b) Enhanced elasticity of elastin fibers
   c) Fragmentation and loss of elasticity
   d) Improved structural integrity of elastin fibers
105. How does the aging process affect the proteoglycan content of the ECM?
   a) Enhances proteoglycan degradation
   b) Reduces proteoglycan synthesis and water retention
   c) Increases proteoglycan production
   d) Maintains proteoglycan levels constant

106. What is a characteristic change in the ECM of aged skin?
   a) Increased hydration
   b) Enhanced elasticity
   c) Thinning and loss of structural proteins
   d) Improved barrier function

107. Which enzyme is involved in the degradation of ECM components and is often elevated in aged tissues?
   a) Collagenase
   b) Elastase
   c) Hyaluronidase
   d) Matrix metalloproteinases (MMPs)

108. How does aging affect the mechanical properties of connective tissue?
   a) Increases flexibility
   b) Enhances tensile strength
   c) Reduces elasticity and increases stiffness
   d) Improves resilience

109. What role do advanced glycation end-products (AGEs) play in aging connective tissues?
   a) Promote collagen cross-linking and stiffness
   b) Increase tissue elasticity
   c) Improve ECM repair
   d) Enhance proteoglycan synthesis

110. Which age-related change occurs in the basement membrane of tissues?
   a) Thinning of the basement membrane
   b) Increased permeability
   c) Thickening and reduced permeability
   d) Enhanced filtration function

111. How does aging impact the fibroblasts responsible for maintaining ECM integrity?
   a) Increases fibroblast proliferation
   b) Enhances fibroblast function
   c) Reduces fibroblast activity and ECM production
   d) Maintains fibroblast function unchanged

112. What is the effect of aging on the turnover rate of ECM components?
   a) Increases turnover rate
   b) Reduces turnover rate
   c) Maintains turnover rate constant
   d) Enhances ECM remodeling

113. How does the accumulation of AGEs in the ECM affect connective tissues?
   a) Improves tissue flexibility
   b) Reduces tissue stiffness
   c) Increases tissue stiffness and reduces elasticity
   d) Enhances collagen synthesis

114. Which age-related change occurs in the connective tissue of joints?
   a) Degradation of cartilage and loss of joint function
   b) Enhanced cartilage regeneration
   c) Increased synovial fluid production
   d) Improved joint flexibility

115. What is a common change in the connective tissue of blood vessels with aging?
   a) Increased elasticity
   b) Decreased collagen content
   c) Stiffening and loss of elasticity
   d) Enhanced smooth muscle cell function

116. How does aging affect wound healing in connective tissues?
   a) Slows down wound healing and reduces regenerative capacity
   b) Enhances inflammatory response
   c) Speeds up wound healing
   d) Improves collagen deposition

117. Which structural protein in the ECM is most affected by glycation during aging?
   a) Fibronectin b) Laminin
   c) Collagen d) Elastin

118. How does aging impact the interstitial matrix of tissues?
   a) Increases matrix hydration
   b) Leads to matrix stiffening and decreased cell adhesion
   c) Reduces matrix degradation
   d) Enhances nutrient diffusion

119. What effect does aging have on the connective tissue of the lungs?
   a) Increases lung elasticity b) Enhances alveolar function
   c) Reduces lung compliance and elasticity d) Improves respiratory efficiency

120. Which glycoprotein in the ECM is involved in cell adhesion and is affected by aging?
   a) Collagen b) Elastin
   c) Fibronectin d) Hyaluronan

121. What is the term used to describe the end of a woman's reproductive years?
   a) Menarche b) Menopause
   c) Andropause d) Puberty

122. Which hormone primarily declines during menopause?
   a) Testosterone b) Progesterone
   c) Estrogen d) Luteinizing hormone (LH)

123. What is a common symptom associated with menopause?
   a) Increased fertility b) Hot flashes
   c) Enhanced libido d) Weight loss

124. How does reproductive aging typically affect male fertility?
   a) Sperm count and motility remain unchanged
   b) Sperm count and motility increase
   c) Sperm count and motility decrease
   d) Testosterone levels increase

125. What is andropause?
   a) The onset of puberty in males
   b) The male equivalent of menopause
   c) The decline in testosterone levels in aging men
   d) The peak reproductive age for men

126. Which hormone's levels are typically measured to confirm menopause?
   a) Follicle-stimulating hormone (FSH) b) Testosterone
   c) Insulin d) Cortisol

127. How does aging affect ovarian reserve in women?
   a) Ovarian reserve increases with age b) Ovarian reserve remains constant
   c) Ovarian reserve decreases with age d) Ovarian reserve is not affected by age

128. What is a common effect of reproductive aging on the menstrual cycle in women?
   a) Menstrual cycles become more regular
   b) Menstrual cycles become irregular and eventually cease
   c) Menstrual cycles become shorter
   d) Menstrual cycles increase in frequency

129. Which of the following is a potential consequence of decreased estrogen levels in postmenopausal women?
   a) Improved bone density b) Increased risk of osteoporosis
   c) Enhanced cardiovascular health d) Reduced risk of breast cancer

130. How does reproductive aging affect sexual function in men?
   a) Decreased libido and erectile function
   b) Increased libido and sexual function
   c) Sexual function remains unchanged
   d) Improved sperm quality

131. What is a common change in visual acuity with aging?
   a) Improved night vision
   b) Decreased visual acuity, especially for near vision
   c) Increased visual acuity
   d) Enhanced color discrimination

132. Which condition is commonly associated with aging and involves clouding of the lens?
   a) Glaucoma b) Macular degeneration
   c) Cataract d) Diabetic retinopathy

133. How does aging typically affect the auditory system?
   a) Improved hearing sensitivity
   b) Increased ability to distinguish high-frequency sounds
   c) Decreased ability to hear high-frequency sounds
   d) Enhanced sound localization

134. Which of the following is a common cause of age-related hearing loss?
    a) Increased production of cerumen
    b) Degeneration of hair cells in the cochlea
    c) Improved auditory nerve function
    d) Enhanced auditory cortex processing
135. How does aging affect taste perception?
    a) Increased sensitivity to all taste qualities
    b) Decreased sensitivity to bitter and sweet tastes
    c) Enhanced taste discrimination
    d) Improved ability to detect umami flavors
136. What is a common change in olfactory function with aging?
    a) Improved sense of smell
    b) Enhanced olfactory discrimination
    c) Reduced ability to detect and identify odors
    d) Increased sensitivity to strong odors
137. Which part of the sensory system is typically affected by presbyopia?
    a) The inner ear
    b) The retina
    c) The lens of the eye
    d) The olfactory bulb
138. How does aging affect proprioception?
    a) Increases proprioceptive accuracy
    b) Reduces proprioceptive sensitivity and balance
    c) Enhances spatial awareness
    d) Improves joint position sense
139. What is a common effect of aging on the somatosensory system?
    a) Increased sensitivity to touch
    b) Decreased ability to sense vibration and pressure
    c) Enhanced tactile discrimination
    d) Improved pain threshold
140. Which factor contributes to the decline in sensory function with aging?
    a) Increased number of sensory receptors
    b) Decreased neural processing speed
    c) Improved sensory integration
    d) Enhanced receptor regeneration
141. How does regenerative capacity generally change with aging?
    a) It remains unchanged   b) It increases significantly
    c) It decreases significantly   d) It improves in all tissues

142. Which type of cell is known for its limited regenerative capacity in aging tissues?
   a) Neurons
   b) Epithelial cells
   c) Muscle cells
   d) Blood cells

143. What is a common effect of aging on skin regeneration?
   a) Increased rate of wound healing
   b) Enhanced collagen synthesis
   c) Improved epidermal regeneration
   d) Decreased rate of wound healing and slower regeneration

144. How does aging impact the regenerative capacity of the liver?
   a) Liver regeneration is unaffected by aging
   b) Liver regeneration becomes faster
   c) Liver regenerative capacity decreases but remains functional
   d) Liver regeneration becomes more robust with age

145. What is a significant factor contributing to reduced regenerative capacity in aging tissues?
   a) Accumulation of cellular damage and senescence
   b) Enhanced cellular repair mechanisms
   c) Increased stem cell activity
   d) Improved tissue repair efficiency

146. Which of the following tissues typically shows the greatest decline in regenerative capacity with age?
   a) Bone tissue
   b) Blood tissue
   c) Cartilage tissue
   d) Epithelial tissue

147. What effect does aging have on stem cells in various tissues?
   a) Increased stem cell proliferation
   b) Enhanced stem cell differentiation
   c) Decreased stem cell number and function
   d) Improved stem cell regenerative potential

148. How does aging affect the regenerative ability of muscle tissue?
   a) Muscle regeneration is enhanced with age
   b) Muscle regenerative capacity decreases, leading to slower repair
   c) Muscle tissue regenerates more efficiently in older individuals
   d) Muscle regeneration remains unaffected by aging

149. What is a typical change in the regenerative capacity of the central nervous system (CNS) with aging?
   a) Increased neuronal regeneration
   b) Enhanced repair of neural damage
   c) Reduced ability to regenerate neurons and repair neural damage
   d) Improved synaptic plasticity

150. Which process is often impaired in aging tissues and affects their regenerative capacity?

a) Cellular apoptosis
b) Cellular senescence
c) Enhanced tissue growth
d) Improved cellular turnover

Answer Key

1	b	2	c	3	b	4	b	5	a	6	c	7	c
8	b	9	a	10	a	11	b	12	c	13	c	14	c
15	b	16	b	17	c	18	c	19	c	20	a	21	c
22	c	23	b	24	c	25	a	26	a	27	b	28	c
29	c	30	b	31	b	32	c	33	c	34	b	35	a
36		37	b	38	c	39	a	40	b	41	c	42	b
43	a	44	c	45	c	46	b	47	b	48	b	49	c
50	a	51	c	52	c	53	b	54	b	55	c	56	b
57	c	58	a	59	c	60	b	61	c	62	b	63	b
64	c	65	c	66	b	67	b	68	c	69	a	70	a
71	b	72	c	73	b	74	a	75	c	76	b	77	d
78	a	79	b	80	b	81	a	82	c	83	c	84	c
85	b	86	b	87	c	88	d	89	c	90	a	91	c
92	b	93	c	94	d	95	c	96	a	97	b	98	c
99	d	100	d	101	c	102	d	103	c	104	b	105	a
106	c	107	d	108	c	109	a	110	c	111	b	112	c
113	c	114	a	115	c	116	a	117	c	118	b	119	c
120	b	121	c	122	b	123	c	124	c	125	a	126	c
127	b	128	b	129	c	130	a	131	b	132	c	133	b
134	b	135	c	136	c	137	b	138	b	139	b	140	c
141	a	142	c	143	d	144	c	145	a	146	c	147	b
148	c	149	b	150	c								

8

Physiology of Membranes

Tanumoy Samui[1], Smruti Smita Mohapatra[2], Femi Francis[3]
Mukesh Kumar Bharti[4], Manish Kumar[4], and
Thulasiraman Parkunan[1]

[1]*Department of Veterinary Physiology, Faculty of Veterinary and Animal Sciences West Bengal University of Animal and Fishery Sciences, Belagachia, Kolkata West Bengal*

[2]*Regional IYRP Support Group of South Asia, Jammu, Jammu & Kashmir UT*

[3]*Department of Vocational Higher Secondary Education, Kerala*

[4]*Department of Veterinary Physiology and Biochemistry, Faculty of Veterinary and Animal Sciences, Institute of Agricultural Sciences, Rajiv Gandhi South Campus, Barkachha, Banaras Hindu University, Uttar Pradesh*

Introduction

Intracellular transport of molecules plays a crucial role in maintaining cellular function and organization. The genetic and biochemical processes that regulate membrane trafficking, such as membrane bending, budding, fusion, and fission, ensure the efficient movement of molecules within cells. Despite substantial advances in understanding the molecular aspects of these processes, the broader, or "supramolecular," regulation of membrane trafficking, which coordinates the overall balance and response to environmental changes, remains less explored. This involves the transport and exchange of membranes and proteins between organelles in a highly organized manner, critical for maintaining cellular homeostasis.

Membrane Trafficking Pathways

Membrane trafficking consists of well-defined pathways connecting cellular compartments like the endoplasmic reticulum (ER), the Golgi apparatus, and the plasma membrane (PM). Proteins and lipids are transferred from the ER to the Golgi and then directed either to the PM or other intracellular destinations. These pathways must be tightly regulated to maintain cellular balance, as any disruptions in membrane flow can lead to cellular dysfunction. In addition to routine cellular maintenance, these pathways must adapt to signals from the environment, ensuring that cells respond appropriately to external stimuli.

Signaling Pathways in Membrane Trafficking

Signaling molecules, including G proteins, kinases, and phospholipases, play a fundamental role in the regulation of membrane trafficking. One such example is the **cAMP-PKA**

(protein kinase

A. **Pathway**, a well-studied signaling cascade that affects various trafficking steps. PKA, composed of regulatory and catalytic subunits, becomes activated when the second messenger cAMP binds to the regulatory subunits, freeing the catalytic subunits to perform their function. This pathway regulates several steps in intracellular transport, including retrograde transport from endosomes to the Golgi and ER, and trafficking from the ER to the Golgi.

The **cAMP-PKA pathway** also influences the trafficking between the Golgi and the plasma membrane, allowing the cell to adjust membrane flow and protein delivery in response to environmental changes. For example, PKA is known to localize to the Golgi apparatus, where it modulates the movement of vesicles between compartments, playing a key role in maintaining cellular homeostasis and adaptation.

Role of Membrane Proteins and Lipid Interactions

Membrane proteins are critical to cellular processes, embedded within the lipid bilayers that form cellular membranes. These proteins can be classified into two groups: integral proteins that span the membrane and peripheral proteins that associate with the membrane surface. Their interaction with lipids helps maintain the bilayer's integrity and function. For instance, transmembrane proteins can influence the organization of lipids, affecting the membrane's fluidity and thickness, which in turn influences cellular transport and signaling processes.

Lipids, meanwhile, are highly dynamic and perform various roles beyond forming the membrane's structural backbone. They participate in signaling and protein localization processes, where lipid-protein interactions are crucial for maintaining membrane integrity. G proteins, essential for signal transduction, often associate with specific lipid regions, such as hexagonal (HII)-prone areas, demonstrating the importance of lipid environments in regulating protein activity.

Complexity of Membrane Lipids

The lipid composition of cellular membranes is remarkably diverse, including glycerol-based lipids, cholesterol, and ceramide-based sphingolipids. Phospholipids are the most abundant membrane lipids, forming bilayers that serve as the basis of biological membranes. These lipid bilayers are dynamic, allowing for processes such as vesicle formation, protein sorting, and signal transduction to occur efficiently.

Membrane lipids are not uniformly distributed; specific lipid compositions form microdomains known as lipid rafts. These rafts, enriched with specific lipids and proteins, serve as signaling platforms, assisting in processes like endocytosis and vesicle trafficking. The non-covalent interactions between lipids and proteins help ensure that membranes remain flexible yet robust, capable of adjusting to various physiological demands.

Lipids in Cellular Communication

Lipids also play a vital role in cellular communication by guiding signaling proteins to specific membrane regions where they can interact with other molecules. Membrane lipids regulate the localization and function of peripheral proteins, which control various processes such as signal transduction and intracellular transport. For example, G proteins interact with specific lipids, ensuring their proper localization and enabling efficient signaling.

These lipid-protein interactions are central to many signaling pathways, such as those involving Ras, a family of small GTPases involved in cell growth and differentiation. Ras proteins are known to localize to specific membrane regions, including the Golgi and plasma membrane, where they influence signaling pathways important for cell survival and growth.

Membrane Transport Mechanisms

Membrane transport occurs via two primary mechanisms: active and passive transport. **Active transport** requires energy, usually in the form of ATP, to move molecules against their concentration gradient. This process is vital for maintaining cellular functions such as nutrient uptake and waste removal. On the other hand, **passive transport** does not require energy and occurs through diffusion or osmosis, where molecules move down their concentration gradient.

Passive transport can be further divided into simple diffusion, facilitated diffusion, and osmosis. In **simple diffusion**, molecules move directly across the membrane, while **facilitated diffusion** involves the use of transport proteins to aid molecule passage. **Osmosis**, a specific type of passive transport, moves water across semipermeable membranes to equalize solute concentrations.

Key Pathways: cAMP-PKA and DAG-PKC

The **cAMP-PKA pathway** is pivotal in regulating various steps of membrane trafficking. It accelerates transport from the ER to the Golgi, stimulates intra-Golgi transport, and influences exocytosis from the trans-Golgi network to the plasma membrane. PKA also regulates retrograde transport from endosomes to the Golgi and the Golgi to the ER. This is achieved through specific targets, such as the **KDEL receptor (KDELr)**, which retrieves ER-resident chaperones that have escaped during transport. Another significant pathway is the **DAG-PKC (diacylglycerol-protein kinase c) pathway**, where PKC regulates various cellular processes, including apoptosis and membrane transport. PKC localizes to the Golgi apparatus, where it facilitates vesicle formation and trafficking. Certain PKC isoforms also play roles in apoptosis, such as the ceramide-induced translocation of PKC to the Golgi, which can trigger programmed cell death.

G Proteins and Ras Signaling

Heterotrimeric G proteins have pivotal roles in signal transduction at the plasma membrane and influence intracellular transport. G protein subunits, such as Gαi3, localize to the Golgi complex, where they regulate ER-to-Golgi transport. Other subunits, like Gαz, are involved in maintaining the Golgi's structural integrity, demonstrating the widespread influence of G proteins in cellular transport and signaling.

Ras proteins, a family of small GTPases, are also involved in membrane trafficking and signaling. These proteins modulate pathways associated with cell growth and differentiation, with Ras localized to both the Golgi and plasma membranes. Their activity is crucial for controlling intracellular transport processes that influence cell survival and proliferation.

Conclusion

Intracellular membrane trafficking is a highly coordinated process involving a complex network of signaling pathways, protein-lipid interactions, and membrane structures. The regulation of this system ensures that cells maintain balance, adapt to environmental changes, and respond to external signals. Key signaling molecules, such as PKA, PKC, and G proteins, play essential roles in coordinating these processes, emphasizing the importance of understanding membrane dynamics in cellular physiology.

Multiple Choice Questions Quiz

1. What is the cell membrane composed of?
   a) Phospholipid bilayer with many organic compounds
   b) Long amino acid chains
   c) Phospholipid bilayer only
   d) Cytosol
2. Who was/were the first to propose that cell membranes are phospholipid bilayers?
   a) H. Davson and J. Danielli b) C. Overton
   c) S. Singer and G. Nicolson d) E. Gorter and F. Grendel
3. The sodium-potassium ATPase (sodium pump) is ___________.
   a) A symporter b) An uniporter
   c) An antiporter d) Secondary active transporter
4. Cell membrane is ______________.
   a) Composed of protein molecules.
   b) Impermeable to fat-soluble substances.
   c) Permits glucose transport at a greater rate in the presence of insulin in some tissues.
   d) Unchanged throughout the life.
5. The substance that contributes maximally to the osmolality inside the cell is ______.
   a) Protein b) Phosphate
   c) Urea d) Potassium
6. The resting membrane potential of a cell __________.
   a) Is dependent on the permeability of the cell membrane to K+ being greater than Na+.
   b) Falls to zero if Na+/K+ ATPase in the membrane is inhibited.
   c) Is equal to the equilibrium potential for K+.
   d) Is equal to the equilibrium potential of Na+.
7. The term '*Milieu interior*' was coined by ________.
   a) Laplace b) Claud Bernard
   c) Carl Lansteiner d) Charles Boyle
8. Which of the following is an example of a co-transport system?
   a) Na+ glucose transport b) Na+-K+ pump
   c) Ca++ pump d) Na+- H+ pump
9. What is the polar head of a phospholipid composed of?
   a) Glycerol b) Fatty acids
   c) Proteins d) Vesicles

10. Which ways do the nonpolar tails face in the phospholipid bilayer?
    a) Towards the exterior
    b) Towards the interior
    c) The directions are scattered
    d) No tails exist in the phospholipid bilayer.
11. What is the cytoplasm made of?
    a) Microfibers
    b) Cytosol
    c) Carbon dioxide and iron
    d) Plasma membrane
12. Where are peripheral proteins attached?
    a) The surface of the cell membrane
    b) The rough endoplasmic reticulum
    c) The Golgi apparatus
    d) The interior of the cell membrane
13. Integral/ transmembrane proteins include what structure?
    a) Pumps
    b) Cell membrane
    c) Protein channels and carrier proteins
    d) Vesicles
14. What organic compound is often attached to integral proteins?
    a) Carbohydrates
    b) Proteins
    c) Lipids
    d) RNA
15. Carbohydrates are often attached to integral proteins in a process known as ________.
    a) Glycosylation
    b) Carboxylation
    c) Decarboxylation
    d) None of the above
16. What determines the concentration gradient?
    a) How fast a molecule crosses the membrane
    b) How fast the cell will fill up
    c) How fast the cell can move
    d) How fast the flagellum will be able to grab onto an object
17. If the concentrations are vastly different, the molecules will move ____________. If the concentrations are similar the molecules will move ____________.
    a) Slowly/quickly
    b) Quickly/slowly
    c) Quickly/at the same speed
    d) At the same speed/slowly
18. Which of the following are the types of passive transport?
    a) Exocytosis, endocytosis, pumps
    b) Exocytosis, endocytosis, osmosis
    c) Simple diffusion, Facilitated diffusion, Osmosis
    d) Pumps, Simple diffusion, Facilitated diffusion
19. When does simple diffusion occur?
    a) When a particle moves from a higher concentration to a lower concentration randomly
    b) When a particle moves from a lower concentration to a higher concentration

c) When a particle stays the same concentration

d) When a particle starts to eat away at the cell membrane

20. When does active transport occur?

a) When energy is needed to feed the cell

b) When no energy is needed to help substances move

c) When energy is needed to move a substance across the cell membrane

d) When small bits of energy are needed to make the cell move more quickly

21. Which of the following is characterized by carrier-mediated transport down a chemical concentration gradient?

a) Active transport
b) Facilitated diffusion
c) Diffusion
d) Osmosis

22. Deficiency of ___________ glycoprotein complex causes different forms of inherited muscular dystrophies and renders muscle much more susceptible to injury with eccentric stretch.

a) Dystrophin
b) Relaxin
c) Renin
d) Elastin

23. Dystrophin is part of the __________ superfamily of cytoskeletal proteins which lend elasticity to the muscle plasma membrane, as well as provide the structural cornerstone of the muscle costamere.

a) Spectrin
b) Relaxin
c) Glycoprotein
d) Elastin

24. The ____________ is a focal adhesion-like complex assembled at regular intervals along the sarcomere, providing a stabilizing connection between the cytoskeletal apparatus via the intermediate filament network, through the plasma membrane, and out to the extracellular matrix.

a) Elastomere
b) Costamere
c) C-protein
d) None of the above

25. ____________ is persistently elevated in patients with muscular dystrophy.

a) Creatine kinase
b) Phosphate kinase
c) Aldosterone
d) Cortisol

26. X-linked inherited disorder ______________ is the most common form of muscular dystrophy in boys.

a) Duchenne's muscular dystrophy
b) Acromegaly
c) Gigantism
d) None of the above

27. In 1999, a new gene ___________ was identified as the cause of a form of inherited muscular dystrophy.

a) Dysferlin
b) Dystrophin
c) Relaxin
d) Elastin

28. The dimensions of serum albumin are ________.
    a) 8nM X 8nM X 3 nM
    b) 3nM X 8nM X 3 nM
    c) 2nM X 8nM X 3 nM
    d) 8nM X 3nM X 8 nM

29. The process of __________ of membrane lipids and proteins renders muscle fibers more susceptible to injury with subsequent challenges in muscular dystrophy.
    a) Oxidation
    b) Decarboxylation
    c) Glycosylation
    d) Hydrolysis

30. _____________ is particularly sensitive to ischemia.
    a) Kidney
    b) Heart
    c) Liver
    d) Brain

31. Programmed cell death is _______________.
    a) Necrosis
    b) Apoptosis
    c) Cytosis
    d) Autophagy

32. ___________ proteins are central players in the evolution of the eukaryotic endomembrane system.
    a) SNARE
    b) Syntaxin
    c) SNAP
    d) VAMP

33. _____________ belongs to an ancient family of vesicle fusion proteins.
    a) Dysferlin
    b) Calpain
    c) Dystrophin
    d) Calcitonin

34. The skeletal muscle plasma membrane is called ___________.
    a) Sarcolemma
    b) Sarcomere
    c) Nuclear membrane
    d) None of these

35. _____________ is a late-onset form of muscular dystrophy, manifesting in older teenagers or adults, and is characterized by the absence or marked reduction of dysferlin protein in the skeletal muscle of affected patients.
    a) Dysferlinopathy
    b) Sarcopathy
    c) Musculopathy
    d) Neuropathy

36. ___________ are an ancient family of thiol-proteases, present in protozoa, plantae, and eukaryota kingdoms.
    a) Calpains
    b) Dysferlin
    c) Elastin
    d) Relaxin

37. ____________ is an abundantly expressed natural and specific inhibitor of calpain-1 and-2.
    a) Calplastatin
    b) Fibroblatin
    c) Myostatin
    d) Dystrophin

38. 'Calpain overactivity' due to aberrant calcium handling is often associated with pathologies of membrane injury in _______________.
    a) Alzheimer's disease
    b) Multiple sclerosis
    c) Cataract formation
    d) All of these

39. A polymorphism within intron 3 of ________ has been implicated as a susceptibility factor for type 2 diabetes.
    a) Calpain -1
    b) Calpain - 2
    c) Calpain -10
    d) Calpain - 3a
40. There are14 genes encoding large catalytic calpain subunits in ________.
    a) Feline
    b) Canine
    c) Avian
    d) Homo sapiens
41. The role of calpains in neurite sealing was confirmed by _______.
    a) Godell
    b) Xie and Barrett
    c) Morpholino
    d) Karl Landsteiner
42. _______________ is an ancient family of calcium-sensitive phospholipid-binding proteins.
    a) Annexin
    b) Calpain
    c) Dysferlin
    d) Dystrophin
43. The term annexin is derived from *annexare* (Latin) and *annexer* (French) meaning ________.
    a) To join
    b) To connect
    c) To attach
    d) All of these
44. __________ is widely used as a marker of apoptosis.
    a) Annexin A1
    b) Annexin A11
    c) Annexin A5
    d) Annexin A2
45. _______________ was first identified as part of an immunoproteomic study to derive monoclonal antibodies against skeletal muscle triad proteins.
    a) Mitsigumin-53
    b) Annexin A
    c) CAPNS1
    d) Caveolin-3
46. Mucolipin-1/TRPML-1 is one of three members of the vertebrate mucolipin-sub family of the ________ channels.
    a) TRP cation
    b) Calcium
    c) Potassium
    d) Sodium
47. The devastating neurodegenerative disorder Mucolipidosis type IV is caused due to the mutation of ____________ gene.
    a) MCOLN-1
    b) ALG-2
    c) ESCRT
    d) MG53
48. ____________ is one of the most highly conserved eukaryotic proteins, showing 85% identity between human, yeast, and plant actin isoforms.
    a) Actin
    b) Tubulin
    c) Myosin
    d) Cytosine
49. Colchicine, a microtubule destabilizing agent, is used to cure ______________.
    a) Mediterranean fever
    b) Gout
    c) Arthritis
    d) All of the above

50. The 1972 fluid mosaic model of _____________ is a commonly used representation of the cell membrane structure and dynamics.

a) Singer and Nicolson
b) Davson and Danielli
c) Overton
d) Gorter and Grendel

51. The first atomic model of a membrane water channel, isolated from human red blood cells is __________.

a) Aquaporin 1
b) Aquaporin 3
c) Aquaporin 4
d) Aquaporin 6

52. Transmembrane proteins are also known as ____________.

a) Intact proteins
b) Integral membrane proteins
c) Both 'a' and 'b'
d) Neither 'a' nor 'b'

53. ___________ is known as the cell's degradation centre.

a) Mitochondria
b) Lysosome
c) Endoplasmic reticulum
d) Golgi apparatus

54. Integral membrane proteins comprise _______% of the human proteome.

a) 25
b) 35
c) 45
d) 55

55. __________________ is used predominantly to determine molecular masses of ions with high accuracy.

a) Mass spectrometry
b) Molecular spectrometry
c) Atomic spectrometry
d) None of the above

56. Which of the following is used for the direct analysis of liquid protein samples?

a) 252-californium desorption
b) Matrix-assisted laser desorption ionization (MALDI)
c) Electrospray ionization (ESI)
d) All of the above

57. For the study of proteins in the gas phase, mass spectrometry can be integrated with which of the following chemical labelling processes to obtain information about the solution structure?

a) Hydrogen/deuterium exchange
b) Hydroxyl radical footprinting
c) Chemical cross-linking
d) All of the above

58. Mutations disrupting _______________ function cause the lysosomal storage disease mucolipidosis type IV.

a) TRPML 1
b) TRPML 2
c) TRPML 3
d) All the above

59. An MS analysis of the intact ATPase from ___________ revealed the presence of six phosphatidylethanolamine (PE) molecules.

a) *Thermus thermophilus*
b) *Enterococcus hirae*
c) *Mycobacterium spp.*
d) *Staphylococcus aureus*

60. What is the type of phase in which lipids form spherical droplets with their polar head groups on the surface and their hydrophobic tails creating an oily core?
   a) Lamellar b) Micellar
   c) Inverted Hexagonal d) Inverted cubic
61. Ten-cardiolipin central lipid plug is observed in the rotor ring of ________.
   a) *Enterococcus hirae* b) *Thermus thermophilus*
   c) *Enterococcus hirae* d) *Mycobacterium spp.*
62. What is the thickness of the lysosomal glycoprotein coat?
   a) 8 nm b) 9 nm
   c) 10 nm d) 15 nm
63. Juvenile neuronal ceroid lipofuscinosis is caused by the mutation of which lysosomal membrane protein?
   a) CLN7 b) CLN3
   c) CLC7 d) Cystinocin
64. Danon disease, a disorder characterized by serious skeletal and cardiac myopathy, is caused by the mutation of which lysosomal membrane protein?
   a) LAMP-2 b) LIMP-2
   c) LMBRD1 d) NPC1
65. The concept of intrinsic (spontaneous) curvature in membranes was introduced by ________.
   a) Seymour Jonathan Singer b) W. Helfrisch
   c) Garth L. Nicolson d) Evert Gorter
66. Salla disease is caused by the mutation of which lysosomal membrane protein?
   a) Sialin b) Cytokinin
   c) Cystinocin d) None of the above
67. Who proposed in 1838 that the basic unit of all life on our planet is the cell?
   a) Schleiden and Schwann b) Meyer and Overton
   c) Davson and Danielli d) Palade and Sjörstrand
68. ________________ is the ability to maintain within acceptable limits, a constant cellular composition to permit normal cellular metabolism.
   a) Entropy b) Homeostasis
   c) Acclimation d) Acclimatization
69. Which organelle is responsible for decomposing the hydrogen peroxide produced by cells?
   a) Microbodies b) Peroxisomes
   c) Both A and B d) None of the above
70. Ganglioside is an example of ___________.
   a) Glycerophospholipid b) Sphingophospholipid
   c) Glyceroglycolipid d) Sphingoglycolipid

71. ___________ are formed when fatty acids attach to the amino groups of sphingoid bases.

a) Cardiolipins b) Ceramides

c) Ergosterol d) Phytosterol

72. Which are the membrane carriers exclusively expressed in kidney proximal tubule cells?

a) OCT2 b) GLUT9

c) SGLT2 d) All the above

73. Who measured the electric capacitance of red blood cells to estimate the thickness of their cell membrane in 1925?

a) Hugo Fricke b) Theodor Schwann

c) Debey Hückel d) Moritz Traube

74. Who built the double helix model of DNA structure?

a) Watson and Crick

b) Rosalind Franklin and Raymond Gosling

c) Davson and Danielli

d) Debey and Hückel

75. The process where proteins move phospholipids between the leaflets of a membrane bilayer is known as _______________.

a) Scrambling b) Osmosis

c) Antiport d) Transversion

76. Which of the following statements are true?

a) Lipid bilayers provide a basic matrix and continuity for biomembranes

b) Membrane components attempt to maximize compatible molecular interactions to approach the lowest free energy state

c) Biomembranes are not automatous structures

d) All of the above

77. What are the functions of TRP channels?

a) They act as cation channels b) They help in nociception

c) They help in thermal sensitivity d) All of the above

78. Cell drinking is ____________.

a) Exocytosis b) Endocytosis

c) Pinocytosis d) Phagocytosis

79. The type of intercellular junction found in animal cells is ________.

a) Plasmodesmata b) Desmosomes

c) Middle lamella d) All the above

80. Which of the following theories explains that plasma membrane is selectively permeable?

a) Unit membrane Theory b) Cascade Theory

c) Sandwich Theory d) Fluid Mosaic Theory

81. In the plasma membrane, the best method to study the properties of integral membrane proteins is ____________________.
   a) Atomic force microscopY
   b) Freeze-fracture analysis and electron microscopy
   c) Cryo-sectioning and electron microscopy
   d) All of the above

82. Which of the following proteins are expressed during heat shock?
   a) HSP 60 b) HSP 70
   c) Both of them d) None of the above

83. The first active transport of lipids across the plasma membrane, i.e., requiring ATP, was reported by ____________________.
   a) Watson and Crick b) Bishop and Bell
   c) Seigneuret and Devaux d) Nicolson and Sanger

84. A prime example of the "apoptotic mimicry" is infection by __________.
   a) HIV-1 virus *b) Vaccinia* virus
   c) Both of them d) None of the above

85. Membrane protein integrase (MPIase) is a glycolipid found in the inner membrane of __________.
   a) *E. coli* *b) Staphylococcus aureus*
   c) Lyssa virus *d) Adeno* virus

86. Monogalactosyldiacylglycerol (MGDG) and digalactosyldiacylglycerol (DGDG) are the main components of the ______, which are the sites of photosynthesis in cyanobacteria and plants.
   a) Thylakoid membrane b) Nuclear membrane
   c) Cytoplasmic membrane d) None of the above

87. Merozoite surface antigen is the structural anchor in ________________ parasite.
   a) Trypanosoma brucei b) Plasmodium falciparum
   c) Leishmania major d) Toxoplasma gondii

88. Which organ synthesizes GPI-PLD (GPLD1) serum protein in mammals?
   a) Liver b) Blood
   c) Kidney d) None of the above

89. Which of the following biomolecules is 'water-hating'?
   a) Lipid b) Fat
   c) Both of them d) None of the above

90. Menisci of the stifle joint is formed by ____________ cartilage.
   a) Fibrocartilage b) Elastic cartilage
   c) Hyaline cartilage d) None of the above

91. Mutations in membrane protein spectrin cause which of the following hereditary diseases?
   a) Alzheimer's disease
   b) Parkinson's disease
   c) Dementia
   d) Hemolytic anaemia
92. Which of the following diseases is Glycophorin involved in?
   a) Viral fever
   b) Common cold
   c) Asthma
   d) Malaria
93. The membrane responsible for regulating the myoplasmic Ca++ concentration during sustained contractions in smooth muscle is ________________.
   a) Sarcoplasmic reticulum
   b) Caveoli
   c) Sarcolemma
   d) Transverse tubule
94. The resting potential of most cells is most dependent on the transmembrane concentration gradient of ____________.
   a) Sodium
   b) Potassium
   c) Chloride
   d) Calcium
95. The resting potential of the membrane depends upon the electrochemical gradient for potassium ions because
   a) Cells contain largely potassium
   b) The permeability to sodium ions is small except during action potentials
   c) The permeability of the resting membrane to potassium is higher than for other ions
   d) Of the activity of the sodium/potassium ATPase.
96. An organism with a cell wall would have the most difficulty doing which process?
   a) Diffusion
   b) Osmosis
   c) Active transport
   d) Phagocytosis
97. WBCs engulf bacteria through what process?
   a) Exocytosis
   b) Phagocytosis
   c) Pinocytosis
   d) Osmosis
98. For a protein to be an integral membrane protein, it would have to be which of the following?
   a) Hydrophilic
   b) Hydrophobic
   c) Amphipathic
   d) None of the above
99. What kinds of molecules pass through a cell membrane most easily?
   a) Large and hydrophobic
   b) Small and hydrophobic
   c) Large polar
   d) Ionic
100. Which of the following is a characteristic feature of a carrier protein in a plasma membrane?
   a) It is a peripheral membrane protein
   b) It exhibits a specificity for a particular type of molecule.
   c) It requires the expenditure of cellular energy to function.
   d) It works against diffusion.

Conflict of Interest: None declared

Answer Key

1	a	2	d	3	c	4	c	5	c	6	a	7	b
8	a	9	a	10	b	11	b	12	a	13	c	14	a
15	a	16	a	17	b	18	c	19	a	20	c	21	b
22	a	23	a	24	b	25	a	26	a	27	a	28	a
29	a	30	d	31	d	32	a	33	a	34	a	35	a
36	a	37	a	38	d	39	c	40	d	41	a	42	a
43	d	44	c	45	a	46	a	47	a	48	a	49	d
50	a	51	a	52	c	53	b	54	a	55	a	56	d
57	d	58	a	59	a	60	b	61	a	62	a	63	b
64	a	65	b	66	a	67	a	68	b	69	c	70	d
71	b	72	d	73	a	74	a	75	a	76	a	77	a
78	c	79	b	80	d	81	b	82	c	83	c	84	c
85	a	86	a	87	b	88	a	89	c	90	a	91	d
92	d	93	c	94	b	95	c	96	d	97	b	98	c
99	b	100	b										

9

Physiology of Growth

B. Divya Sri[1], and Dangeti VVN Durga Prasad[2]

[1]Department of Veterinary Physiology & Biochemistry, School of Veterinary & Animal Sciences, Centurion University of Technology & Management, Paralakhemundi

[2]Section of Veterinary Anatomy, ICAR -IVRI Izatnagar, Bareilly, Uttar Pradesh

Introduction

Cell Cycle: Growth at the cellular level involves the cell cycle, which includes phases of growth (G1), DNA replication (S), and cell division (M). During these phases, cells prepare for and execute division to increase cell numbers.

Mitosis and Meiosis: Mitosis results in two identical daughter cells, crucial for tissue growth and repair. Meiosis, on the other hand, is essential for producing gametes (sperm and eggs) and ensures genetic diversity.

Hormonal Regulation

Growth Hormone (GH): Secreted by the pituitary gland, GH stimulates liver cells to produce insulin-like growth factor 1 (IGF-1), which promotes cell growth and division throughout the body.

Thyroid Hormones: Thyroxine (T4) and triiodothyronine (T3) from the thyroid gland regulate metabolic rate and are vital for normal growth and development, particularly in the nervous system.

Sex Hormones: Estrogens and androgens influence the growth of secondary sexual characteristics and contribute to the final stages of skeletal growth during puberty.

Nutritional Factors

Proteins: Amino acids from dietary proteins are necessary for the synthesis of new proteins and enzymes, which are crucial for cell growth and repair.

Vitamins: Vitamins such as A, C, and D are essential for various growth processes. For instance, vitamin D is vital for bone growth and calcium absorption.

Minerals: Calcium and phosphorus are key for bone development, while zinc and iron are important for cellular functions and overall growth.

Genetic Factors

Genetic Blueprint: Growth patterns and potential are largely determined by genetic factors. Genes influence growth rates, final height, and the development of various body structures.

Growth Disorders: Genetic mutations or abnormalities can lead to growth disorders such as dwarfism or gigantism, illustrating the role of genetics in growth regulation.

Environmental Factors

Socioeconomic Conditions: Access to adequate nutrition, healthcare, and a supportive environment influences growth. Poor socioeconomic conditions can limit growth potential.

Health and Diseases: Chronic illnesses, malnutrition, and infections can impair growth by affecting nutrient absorption, metabolism, or overall health.

Stress and Psychological Factors: Stress and emotional well-being can also impact growth, particularly in children. Stress may affect hormonal balance and overall health.

Interaction of Factors

Growth Phases: Growth occurs in different phases, such as infancy, childhood, adolescence, and adulthood. Each phase has distinct physiological changes and requirements.

Adaptive Responses: Organisms adapt to varying environmental conditions, which can impact growth patterns. For example, humans may experience growth spurts in response to nutritional changes.

In summary, growth is a multifaceted process influenced by a combination of cellular mechanisms, hormonal signals, genetic instructions, nutritional inputs, and environmental conditions. Understanding these elements provides insights into normal development and helps identify and address growth-related disorders.

MCQs

1. What is growth primarily defined as?
   a) Increase in height
   b) Directive coordination of diverse processes
   c) Production of energy
   d) Decrease in cell size
2. Which of the following is NOT involved in growth from a single cell to an adult?
   a) Cell multiplication b) Cell hypertrophy
   c) Inclusion of exogenous substances d) Decrease in cell number
3. What is an example of cell hypertrophy?
   a) Cleavage of an embryo b) Increase in numbers of RBCs
   c) Increase in size of neurons d) Growth of ectodermal cells
4. What are the two main types of growth?
   a) Zygotic and embryonic growth b) Cellular and tissue growth
   c) Prenatal and postnatal growth d) Somatic and germinal growth
5. What is the primary nature of prenatal growth?
   a) Degenerative b) Developmental
   c) Static d) Regressive
6. Which process is involved in the specialization of cells during prenatal growth?
   a) Cleavage b) Differentiation
   c) Organogenesis d) Histogenesis

7. Which cells in the blastocyst stage form the fetal membranes?
   a) ICM cells
   b) Trophoblast cells
   c) Mesodermal cells
   d) Endodermal cells
8. The ectoderm differentiates into which of the following?
   a) Circulatory system
   b) Liver
   c) Nervous system
   d) Digestive system
9. What does organogenesis involve?
   a) Increase in cell size
   b) Development of bodily organs
   c) Formation of zygote
   d) Breakdown of tissues
10. Which of the following is an example of histogenesis?
    a) Formation of fetal membranes
    b) Development of contractile elements in muscle cells
    c) Increase in fetal size
    d) Formation of the blastocyst
11. What is meant by "developmental horizons"?
    a) The process of cell multiplication
    b) Time periods of organ development
    c) The stages of cleavage
    d) The differentiation of cells
12. What is a common method used to measure fetal length?
    a) Blood tests
    b) X-ray or ultrasound
    c) Physical examination
    d) Genetic testing
13. What is C-R length in fetal measurement?
    a) Length from head to feet
    b) Length from mouth to tail
    c) Length from skull to rump
    d) Length of the vertebral column
14. What does CVR length measure in a fetus?
    a) Crown-rump length
    b) Vertebral column length
    c) Total fetal length
    d) Length from mouth to tail
15. What does VR length represent?
    a) Length from skull to rump
    b) Curved crown-rump length
    c) Length of vertebral column
    d) Length from mouth to point of tail
16. What does BCVRT length measure in a fetus?
    a) Length from highest point on the skull to rump
    b) Curved crown-rump length
    c) Total length from mouth to point of tail
    d) Length of vertebral column

17. Which measurement is considered a good indicator of fetal development or age?
    a) Fetal weight
    b) Fetal length
    c) Blood pressure
    d) Heart rate
18. Why is fetal weight not commonly used to determine fetal age?
    a) It's not accurate
    b) It can't be easily measured in utero
    c) It varies too much between individuals
    d) It is not related to fetal age
19. What does VRT length in a fetus refer to?
    a) Length of the vertebral column and tail
    b) Length from mouth to tail
    c) Curved crown-rump length
    d) Length from highest point on the skull to rump
20. Which of the following best describes prenatal growth?
    a) Degenerative processes
    b) Growth after birth
    c) Development from a zygote into an organism
    d) Increase in size of existing cells
21. Which of the following factors is NOT listed as influencing prenatal growth?
    a) Fetal hormones
    b) Environmental pollution
    c) Maternal nutrition during pregnancy
    d) Heredity
22. What is the role of fetal hormones in prenatal growth?
    a) They are always crucial for fetal development
    b) They are only produced after birth
    c) They are important if the target systems can respond
    d) They do not affect fetal development
23. Which hormone is important for the development of precocial young?
    a) Thyroid hormone
    b) Androgens
    c) Growth hormone (STH)
    d) Estrogen
24. In which animals are the young born immature with closed eyes, called altricial young?
    a) Cows and goats
    b) Dogs and laboratory animals
    c) Horses and sheep
    d) Birds and reptiles
25. What is the significance of the thyroid hormone produced by the fetal thyroid gland?
    a) It is essential for parturition
    b) It is crucial for fetal metabolism
    c) It is needed for morphogenesis and nervous system development
    d) It influences the descent of testes

26. What is the role of androgens produced by fetal testes?
    a) Development of the left oviduct
    b) Differentiation of the nervous system
    c) Descent of testes into the scrotum
    d) Increase in fetal growth rate
27. Which factor primarily determines fetal size?
    a) Maternal nutrition
    b) Genetic makeup
    c) Placental size
    d) Ambient temperature
28. How does the size and age of the dam affect fetal growth?
    a) Larger and older dams generally have smaller fetuses
    b) Fetal growth is inversely related to maternal size
    c) Fetal growth is directly related to maternal size
    d) Age of the dam has no effect on fetal size
29. Why are mules generally larger than hinnys?
    a) Mules have a different genetic makeup
    b) Mules are carried in mares, while hinnys are carried in jennies
    c) Hinnys receive less maternal nutrition
    d) Hinnys are affected by lower ambient temperatures
30. What effect does maternal undernutrition during pregnancy have on the fetus?
    a) It increases the birth weight
    b) It reduces the growth rate and birth weight
    c) It has no effect on fetal growth
    d) It accelerates fetal development
31. In sheep, proper nutrition during which period of pregnancy is especially important?
    a) First third
    b) Second third
    c) Last third
    d) Entire pregnancy
32. What is the relationship between litter size and birth weight in monotocous animals?
    a) Twinning increases birth weight
    b) Twinning decreases birth weight
    c) Litter size has no effect on birth weight
    d) Birth weight is highest with single births
33. Why might increased litter size decrease birth weight?
    a) Due to decreased maternal age
    b) Because of the direct effect of the number of fetuses
    c) Due to increased placental size
    d) Due to better maternal nutrition
34. How does the sex of the fetus influence prenatal growth?
    a) Female fetuses generally grow faster
    b) Male fetuses generally grow slower
    c) Male fetuses generally grow faster and have higher birth weights
    d) Sex has no influence on fetal growth

35. What is the relationship between placental size and fetal growth?
   a) Smaller placenta results in increased fetal growth
   b) Fetal growth is directly proportional to placental size
   c) Placental size has no effect on fetal growth
   d) Larger placentas decrease fetal growth
36. What effect do high ambient temperatures during gestation have on fetal growth?
   a) They increase fetal growth
   b) They reduce fetal growth
   c) They have no effect on fetal growth
   d) They only affect the growth of male fetuses
37. What is the result of decreased environmental temperatures during gestation?
   a) Increased fetal growth
   b) Decreased fetal growth
   c) No change in fetal growth
   d) Increased birth weight
38. Which of the following factors is related to the development of genitalia in the fetus?
   a) Fetal pituitary hormones
   b) Thyroid hormone
   c) Fetal gonadal hormones
   d) Placental hormones
39. Which hormone is involved in the development of the left oviduct in birds?
   a) Androgens
   b) Estrogens
   c) STH
   d) Progesterone
40. How does the genetic makeup of the fetus influence its prenatal growth?
   a) It has no influence
   b) It only affects postnatal growth
   c) It primarily determines fetal size
   d) It affects the mother's nutritional needs
41. What is isometric growth?
   a) When an organ does not grow
   b) When an organ grows faster than the body
   c) When an organ grows at the same rate as the body
   d) When an organ grows slower than the body
42. Allometric growth implies that an organ grows at a different rate than the general body growth. Which of the following is an example of allometric growth?
   a) The liver growing at the same rate as the body
   b) The CNS reaching its maximum size before other organs
   c) All organs growing at the same rate
   d) No organs growing
43. During prenatal development, which system reaches its maximum size first?
   a) Muscles
   b) Circulatory system
   c) CNS (Central Nervous System)
   d) Adipose tissue

44. Which bodily regions grow first during postnatal life?
 a) Legs and head b) Pelvis and thorax
 c) Loins d) Adipose tissue

45. According to Schloss (1911), postnatal growth is defined as:
 a) Increase in body fat
 b) Increase in body mass at definite time intervals
 c) Irreversible time change in body dimensions
 d) Growth determined by external factors only

46. Which definition of growth takes both size and weight into consideration and excludes fluctuation due to non-availability of feed, gestation, lactation, or disease?
 a) Schloss's definition b) Brody's definition
 c) Allometric growth definition d) Isometric growth definition

47. Which of the following statements is TRUE regarding fattening and growth?
 a) Fattening is entirely separate from growth
 b) Fat represents only a reserve food source
 c) Fat serves other purposes besides being a food reserve and is part of growth
 d) Fattening is not considered a part of growth

48. Which of the following is the most commonly used measure of postnatal growth?
 a) Increase in height b) Increase in length
 c) Weight gain over a period of time d) Increase in diameter

49. What does the average growth rate represent?
 a) Weight gain per unit of height
 b) Absolute weight gain per unit of time
 c) Relative weight gain in a given time
 d) Instantaneous weight gain

50. Which growth rate measure is more useful when the time span is short?
 a) Relative growth rate b) Average growth rate
 c) Cumulative growth rate d) Instantaneous growth rate

51. Relative growth rate is expressed as:
 a) Absolute weight gain per unit of time
 b) Weight gain in relation to initial weight over a given time
 c) Average weight gain over a lifetime
 d) Instantaneous weight gain

52. Which equation is associated with relative growth rate expressed as a percentage?
 a) Minot's equation b) Brody's equation
 c) Schloss's equation d) Isometric growth equation

53. Which growth rate measure considers the instantaneous weight gain and the weight of the animal at the time of gain?
 a) Relative growth rate b) Cumulative growth rate
 c) Instantaneous growth rate d) Average growth rate

54. Which measure of growth includes increase in size, such as length, height, and diameter?
    a) Average growth rate
    b) Instantaneous growth rate
    c) Cumulative growth rate
    d) Measurement of postnatal growth
55. Why are rapid growth rates desirable in breeding stock, dairy animals, and meat animals?
    a) To attain mature weights quickly
    b) Because final weight is more important than growth rate
    c) Because few animals are allowed to reach mature weights
    d) To increase fat reserves
56. Why is maximum growth not desirable at all ages?
    a) Because it affects the quality of meat
    b) Due to changes in body composition at different ages
    c) Because it leads to early maturity
    d) Because it reduces lifespan
57. What kind of growth predominates before puberty?
    a) Growth of fatty tissue
    b) Growth of bones and muscles
    c) Growth of adipose tissue
    d) Growth of internal organs
58. Why might it be desirable to accelerate growth at certain periods and retard it at others?
    a) To ensure even fat distribution
    b) To maximize final weight
    c) To optimize body composition based on developmental needs
    d) To increase overall size
59. What shape does the growth curve take when plotting body weight against age?
    a) Linear
    b) Exponential
    c) Sigmoid
    d) Bell-shaped
60. In humans, puberty is attained when the body weight reaches what percentage of adult weight?
    a) 30%
    b) 50%
    c) 60%
    d) 75%
61. The increasing slope of the growth curve is known as which phase?
    a) Growth retarding phase
    b) Self-accelerating phase
    c) Point of inflection
    d) Negative growth phase
62. The point on the growth curve where growth rate is maximum is called?
    a) Pubertal point
    b) Point of stagnation
    c) Point of inflection
    d) Maturity point
63. What happens during the negative growth phase?
    a) Growth continues indefinitely
    b) Growth accelerates
    c) Tissues start degenerating
    d) Growth remains constant

64. Which of the following indicates the time of maximum velocity of growth rate?
    a) Point of inflection
    b) Self-retarding phase
    c) Self-accelerating phase
    d) Maturity point
65. Which phase of growth is characterized by cell hyperplasia and hypertrophy?
    a) Negative growth phase
    b) Self-retarding phase
    c) Growth stagnation phase
    d) Self-accelerating phase
66. Which of the following is NOT a factor affecting postnatal growth?
    a) Nutrition
    b) Litter size
    c) Atmospheric pressure
    d) Hormones
67. What is the primary factor in controlling the economics of meat and milk production?
    a) Environmental factors
    b) Plane of nutrition
    c) Breed of the animal
    d) Hormonal balance
68. Which group of pigs had the lowest cost of production per pound of meat in the study?
    a) High – High
    b) High – Low
    c) Low – High
    d) Low – Low
69. What is the effect of a low plane of nutrition during the accelerating phase of growth?
    a) It enhances growth
    b) It induces greater retardation
    c) It has no effect
    d) It only affects fat growth
70. Which vitamin group is especially important for normal growth?
    a) Vitamin K
    b) Vitamin D
    c) Vitamin B-complex
    d) Vitamin E
71. Which feed additive improves growth rate by reducing unnecessary physical activity?
    a) Antibiotics
    b) Tranquilizers
    c) Hormones
    d) Anthelmintics
72. Which group of hormones is known to be generalized protein anabolic agents?
    a) Androgens
    b) Estrogens
    c) Thyroid hormones
    d) Adrenal corticoids
73. Which animal product has a significant growth-promoting ability in young animals?
    a) Eggs
    b) Milk
    c) Meat
    d) Wool
74. In which type of animals does the nervous system control growth by regulating the release of hormones?
    a) Mammals
    b) Birds
    c) Reptiles
    d) Amphibians
75. Which environmental factor directly influences the growth rate in animals?
    a) Altitude
    b) Wind speed
    c) Climate
    d) Soil type

76. What is the effect of estrogens on skeletal growth?

a) Increase bone growth
b) Delay ossification
c) Decrease skeletal growth
d) No effect

Answer Key

1	b	2	d	3	c	4	c	5	b	6	b	7	b
8	c	9	b	10	b	11	b	12	b	13	c	14	a
15	c	16	c	17	b	18	b	19	a	20	c	21	b
22	c	23	c	24	b	25	c	26	c	27	b	28	c
29	b	30	b	31	c	32	b	33	b	34	c	35	b
36	b	37	b	38	c	39	b	40	c	41	c	42	b
43	c	44	c	45	b	46	b	47	c	48	c	49	b
50	b	51	b	52	a	53	c	54	d	55	c	56	b
57	b	58	c	59	c	60	c	61	b	62	c	63	c
64	a	65	d	66	c	67	b	68	b	69	b	70	c
71	b	72	a	73	b	74	a	75	c	76	c		

10

Physiology of Genetic Code and Protein Synthesis

A. Rajendra Prasad

Department of Animal Genetics and Breeding, College of Veterinary Science Mamnoor, Warangal, PVNRTGVU, Telangana

Introduction

The genetic code and protein synthesis are fundamental processes that underlie the expression of genetic information within all living organisms. These processes are integral to understanding how DNA, the hereditary material, dictates the production of proteins, which are essential molecules that carry out various functions in the body, from structural support to catalyzing biochemical reactions.

Genetic Code

The genetic code consists of rules that guide the translation of information stored in DNA or RNA sequences into proteins within living cells. It is nearly universal across all organisms, underscoring the shared evolutionary origins of life. The genetic code is composed of codons, which are sequences of three nucleotides in mRNA (messenger RNA) that correspond to specific amino acids or stop signals during protein synthesis.

Each of the 20 amino acids used in protein synthesis is encoded by one or more codons. For instance, the codon AUG not only codes for the amino acid methionine but also serves as the start signal for translation, marking the beginning of a protein-coding sequence. The redundancy of the genetic code, where multiple codons can specify the same amino acid, provides a protective mechanism against mutations, as some changes in the nucleotide sequence do not alter the resulting protein.

Protein Synthesis

Protein synthesis is the process by which cells construct proteins based on the instructions encoded in mRNA. This process takes place in two primary stages: transcription and translation.

Transcription: Transcription is the first step of gene expression, where a particular segment of DNA is copied into RNA by the enzyme RNA polymerase. During transcription, one of the two DNA strands serves as a template for the formation of a complementary RNA strand, This newly synthesized RNA strand, known as pre-mRNA, undergoes further processing, including splicing, capping, and addition of a poly-A tail, to become mature mRNA, which is then exported from the nucleus to the cytoplasm in eukaryotic cells. In contrast, in prokaryotes, both transcription and translation occur within the cytoplasm.

Translation: Upon entering the cytoplasm, the mature mRNA is prepared for translation, during which proteins are synthesized by ribosomes. Ribosomes, which are made up of ribosomal RNA (rRNA) and proteins, read the mRNA sequence in groups of three nucleotides at a time. Each three-nucleotide codon on the mRNA matches with a complementary anticodon on a tRNA (transfer RNA) molecule. Each tRNA molecule carries a specific amino acid that matches its anticodon to the corresponding codon on the mRNA.

As the ribosome progresses along the mRNA, it enables the attachment of tRNA molecules and the sequential incorporation of their respective amino acids into the elongating polypeptide chain. This chain elongates as each new amino acid is added, forming a protein. Translation proceeds until the ribosome encounters a stop codon (such as UAA, UAG, or UGA), which signals the end of protein synthesis. The newly synthesized protein then undergoes folding and possible post-translational modifications before becoming fully functional.

Significance and Regulation

The processes of transcription and translation are tightly regulated to ensure that proteins are synthesized in the right amounts, at the right times, and in the right places. Regulation can occur at multiple levels, including transcriptional control, RNA processing, mRNA stability, and the efficiency of translation.

Mutations or errors in any step of these processes can lead to diseases, including various genetic disorders and cancers. Understanding the physiology of the genetic code and protein synthesis is crucial not only for basic biology but also for medical and biotechnological applications, such as gene therapy, the production of recombinant proteins, and the development of new treatments for genetic diseases.

In summary, the genetic code and protein synthesis are central to the flow of genetic information from DNA to functional proteins. These processes ensure that the instructions encoded in the genome are accurately translated into the diverse array of proteins that sustain life.

Multiple Choice Questions

1. The sequence of three nucleotides that codes for a specific amino acid is called a
   a) Gene b) Chromosome
   c) Codon d) Anticodon
2. In the genetic code, how many codons specify the termination of protein synthesis?
   a) 1 b) 2
   c) 3 d) 4
3. Which of the following is a start codon?
   a) UGA b) AUG
   c) AGU d) GUA
4. The function of mRNA in protein synthesis is to
   a) Carrying genetic information from DNA to the ribosome
   b) Transporting amino acids to the ribosome

c) Catalyzing peptide bond formation
d) Modifying proteins after synthesis

5. The enzyme responsible for synthesizing mRNA from a DNA template is
a) DNA polymerase b) RNA polymerase
c) Reverse transcriptase d) Helicase

6. What is the first step of transcription?
a) Binding of RNA polymerase to the promoter
b) Splicing of introns from mRNA
c) Attachment of ribosome to mRNA
d) 5' capping & 3'polyadenylation

7. During transcription, which of the following is synthesized?
a) DNA b) Protein
c) Polysaccharides d) RNA

8. The molecule brings amino acids to the ribosome during translation is
a) mRNA b) rRNA
c) tRNA d) miRNA

9. The role of the ribosomes in protein synthesis is
a) Synthesizing RNA b) Synthesizing Proteins
c) Replicating DNA d) Modifying proteins

10. In which part of the cell does translation occur?
a) Nucleus b) Mitochondria
c) Cytoplasm d) Endoplasmic reticulum

11. To which site on the ribosome does the initiator tRNA bind first?
a) A site b) P site
c) E site d) T site

12. The function of rRNA in the ribosome is
a) Coding for proteins
b) Catalyzing the formation of peptide bonds
c) Transporting amino acids
d) Inhibiting translation

13. Which of the following sequences would be recognized by a tRNA with an anticodon sequence of UAC?
a) AUG b) UGA
c) GAC d) CUA

14. The type of bond formed between amino acids during protein synthesis is
a) Hydrogen bond b) Ionic bond
c) Phosphodiester bond d) Peptide bond

15. The component is necessary for the initiation of transcription is the
    a) Start codon b) Enhancer
    c) Terminator signal d) Promoter
16. Which of the following processes occurs immediately after translation?
    a) Protein degradation b) Post-translational modification
    c) RNA replication d) mRNA splicing
17. The enzyme is responsible for adding amino acids to tRNA is
    a) RNA polymerase b) RNA topoisomerase
    c) Aminoacyl-tRNA synthetase d) Ribosomal transferase
18. Which type of RNA is involved in both the structure and function of the ribosome?
    a) mRNA b) tRNA
    c) rRNA d) miRNA
19. The sequence of nucleotides in mRNA is translated into a sequence of
    a) Carbohydrates b) Amino acids
    c) Lipids d) Nucleotides
20. What does a stop codon do?
    a) Stops transcription b) Stops protein modification
    c) Stops replication d) Stops translation
21. In eukaryotes, where is the mRNA processed before it is translated?
    a) Nucleus b) Ribosome
    c) Golgi apparatus d) Cytoplasm
22. The commonly added modification to the 5' end of eukaryotic mRNA is
    a) Acetylated thymine cap b) Methylated guanine cap
    c) Phosphorylated cytosine cap d) Polyadenylation cap
23. Which of the following modifications is commonly added to the 3' end of eukaryotic mRNA?
    a) Methyl group b) Acetyl group
    c) Poly-A tail d) Cap structure
24. The molecule serves as a template during translation is
    a) DNA b) mRNA
    c) tRNA d) rRNA
25. During translation, what ensures that the correct amino acid is added to the growing polypeptide chain?
    a) DNA sequence b) mRNA sequence
    c) mRNA anticodon d) tRNA anticodon
26. The post-translational modification involves the addition of carbohydrate groups to proteins is
    a) Phosphorylation b) Glycosylation
    c) Methylation d) Acetylation

27. The scientist credited with the discovery of the structure of tRNA is
    a) Francis Crick
    b) Robert W. Holley
    c) Rosalind Franklin
    d) James Watson
28. The role of a signal peptide in protein synthesis is
    a) To direct the protein to its proper location
    b) To bind to the ribosome
    c) To elongate the mRNA strand
    d) To initiate transcription
29. Which of the following is a characteristic of eukaryotic transcription but not prokaryotic transcription?
    a) Occurs in the cytoplasm
    b) Requires a promoter region
    c) Involves splicing of introns
    d) Utilizes ribosomes
30. The two subunits of eukaryotic ribosomes are
    a) 60S & 40S
    b) 50S & 30S
    c) 60S & 50S
    d) 50S & 40S
31. The Shine-Dalgarno sequence is important for the initiation of translation in
    a) Eukaryotes
    b) Prokaryotes
    c) Viruses
    d) Fungi
32. The process responsible for the conversion of genetic information in mRNA into a sequence of amino acids is called as
    a) Replication
    b) Transcription
    c) Translation
    d) Transduction
33. The role of polyadenylation in mRNA processing is
    a) To initiate translation
    b) To add a 5' cap
    c) To splice out introns
    d) To protect mRNA from degradation
34. A common site for post-translational modification is
    a) Nucleus
    b) Golgi apparatus
    c) Ribosome
    d) Cytosol
35. During translation elongation, new amino acids are added to the growing polypeptide chain at which site on the ribosome?
    a) E site
    b) P site
    c) A site
    d) T site
36. The process of alternative splicing allows for
    a) One gene to produce multiple proteins
    b) The removal of the 5' cap from mRNA
    c) Efficient transcription
    d) Protein degradation

37. The molecule directly involved in recognizing the stop codon during translation is
    a) tRNA
    b) mRNA
    c) Release factor
    d) rRNA
38. What is the function of the TATA box in eukaryotic promoters?
    a) It terminates transcription
    b) It binds RNA polymerase II
    c) It codes for a start codon
    d) It stabilizes mRNA
39. During translation initiation, the initiation complex is formed by
    a) RNA polymerase, mRNA, and tRNA
    b) DNA, RNA polymerase, and ribosome
    c) tRNA, rRNA, and mRNA
    d) mRNA, ribosome, and tRNA
40. The correct folding of a protein into its functional shape is aided by
    a) Ribosomes
    b) DNA polymerase
    c) Chaperone proteins
    d) mRNA
41. The function of elongation factors during translation is to
    a) Terminate protein synthesis
    b) Assist with mRNA splicing
    c) Facilitate the movement of the ribosome along mRNAD
    d) Bind amino acids to tRNA
42. The Kozak sequence is important for
    a) Transcription initiation
    b) mRNA capping
    c) Polyadenylation
    d) Translation initiation in eukaryotes
43. The proteasome is involved in
    a) Protein degradation
    b) Protein synthesis
    c) RNA transcription
    d) RNA splicing
44. In bacteria, the molecule that recognizes the promoter and initiates transcription is the
    a) RNA polymerase I
    b) Sigma factor
    c) Rho factor
    d) Transcription factor
45. Which of the following processes occurs at the ribosome?
    a) DNA replication
    b) mRNA capping
    c) Protein synthesis
    d) RNA splicing
46. Which of the following is NOT a post-translational modification?
    a) Splicing
    b) Ubiquitination
    c) Glycosylation
    d) Phosphorylation

47. During translation, the ribosome moves along the mRNA in which direction?
   a) 3' to 5' b) 5' to 3'
   c) Random direction d) Both directions

48. The function of RNA polymerase II in eukaryotic cells is
   a) Transcription of mRNA genes b) Transcription of rRNA genes
   c) Transcription of tRNA genes d) Transcription of snRNA genes

49. The molecule is known as the "molecular adapter" in protein synthesis is
   a) mRNA b) tRNA
   c) rRNA d) shRNA

50. What is the function of the ribosomal E site?
   a) Entry of tRNA b) Exit of the empty tRNA
   c) Exit of the growing polypeptide chain d) Entrance of the mRNA

51. The genetic code is said to be "degenerate" because
   a) One codon can specify multiple amino acids
   b) Each codon specifies a unique amino acid
   c) Codons have no role in protein synthesis
   d) One amino acid can be specified by multiple codons

52. Which factor is involved in the termination of transcription in prokaryotes?
   a) Rho factor b) Sigma factor
   c) Release factor d) Initiation factor

53. Which of the following is true about the genetic code?
   a) It is universal for all organisms b) It is non-overlapping
   c) Degeneracy d) All of the above

54. In the context of protein synthesis, the "wobble" refer to the
   a) Flexible pairing between the third base of a codon and anticodon
   b) Movement of ribosomes along mRNA
   c) Modification of tRNA
   d) Termination of translation

55. During eukaryotic transcription, role of the carboxy-terminal domain (CTD) of RNA polymerase II is to
   a) Facilitates the termination of transcription
   b) Assists in mRNA splicing and capping
   c) Enhances translation efficiency
   d) Represses gene expression

56. Which eukaryotic RNA polymerase transcribes majority of rRNA?
   a) RNA polymerase I b) RNA polymerase II
   c) RNA polymerase III d) RNA polymerase IV

57. Which of the following scientist(s) received the Nobel prize for 'Deciphering the genetic code'?
    a) Marshall Nirenberg
    b) Har Gobind Khorana
    c) Robert W. Holley
    d) All of the above

58. In eukaryotes, the complex binds to the 5' cap of mRNA to initiate translation is
    a) RNA polymerase
    b) Small ribosomal subunit
    c) Large ribosomal subunit
    d) Spliceosome

59. The bond holds amino acids together in a protein is
    a) Hydrogen bond
    b) Disulfide bond
    c) phosphodiester bonds
    d) Peptide bond

60. Which of the following statements about the genetic code is false?
    a) It is redundant
    b) It is universal
    c) It overlaps
    d) It is read in triplets

61. In eukaryotic cells, transcription and translation are
    a) Spatially and temporally separated
    b) Occurring in the same location
    c) Occurring simultaneously
    d) Not related processes

62. The molecule acts as the primary template for translation is
    a) DNA
    b) mRNA
    c) rRNA
    d) tRNA

63. In prokaryotic cells, the function of the -35 and -10 promoter regions is
    a) To terminate transcription
    b) To initiate translation
    c) To bind RNA polymerase and initiate transcription
    d) To terminate translation

64. In Eukaryotes, tRNA is synthesized by
    a) RNA Polymerase I
    b) RNA Polymerase II
    c) RNA Polymerase III
    d) RNA Polymerase IV

65. Role of EF-Tu play in prokaryotic translation is
    a) It translocates the ribosome along mRNA
    b) It facilitates the binding of aminoacyl-tRNA to the ribosome
    c) It catalyzes peptide bond formation
    d) It terminates translation

66. During transcription, RNA is synthesized in which direction?
    a) 5' to 3'
    b) 3' to 5'
    c) 5' to 5'
    d) 3' to 3'

67. The most abundant RNA is the cell is
    a) mRNA
    b) tRNA
    c) miRNA
    d) rRNA

68. The primary function of the ribosomal large subunit is
   a) Binding to mRNA
   b) Catalyzing peptide bond formation
   c) Binding to tRNA
   d) Splicing RNA

69. Which of the following is a function of small nuclear ribonucleoproteins (snRNPs)?
   a) Protein synthesis
   b) DNA replication
   c) Splicing pre-mRNA
   d) Degradation of mRNA

70. The ribosome is composed of
   a) DNA and proteins
   b) RNA and lipids
   c) DNA and RNA
   d) RNA and proteins

71. The template DNA for transcription runs in which direction?
   a) 5' to 5'
   b) 3' to 5'
   c) 5' to 3'
   d) 3' to 5'

72. The wobble hypothesis explains
   a) The degeneracy of the genetic code
   b) The initiation of translation
   c) The formation of peptide bonds
   d) The termination of transcription

73. The fundamental theory of central dogma was developed by
   a) Har Gobind Khorana
   b) Francis Crick
   c) James Watson
   d) Nirenberg

74. The 5'-cap structure on eukaryotic mRNA is added
   a) During transcription
   b) After transcription
   c) Before transcription
   d) During translation

75. The enzyme responsible for catalyzing the formation of peptide bonds during protein synthesis is
   a) DNA topoisomerase
   b) RNA topoisomerase
   c) Ligase
   d) Peptidyl transferase

76. The process that allows a single gene to code for multiple proteins is
   a) DNA replication
   b) mRNA capping
   c) Alternative splicing
   d) Protein degradation

77. The role of 3' untranslated region (UTR) of mRNA is
   a) It codes for the amino acid sequence of the protein
   b) It helps in mRNA stability and translation regulation
   c) It is involved in transcription initiation
   d) It binds to the promoter

78. In eukaryotic cells, which process occurs in the nucleolus
   a) mRNA splicing
   b) rRNA synthesis & ribosome assembly
   c) Protein folding
   d) DNA replication

79. Pribnow box is seen in the promoter of
    a) Prokaryotes
    b) Eukaryotes
    c) Viruses
    d) Both Prokaryotes & eukaryotes
80. In prokaryotic cells, the transcription and translation occurs in
    a) Nucleus
    b) Mitochondria
    c) Cytoplasm
    d) Endoplasmic reticulum
81. In the DNA, promoter is located at the ____________ of the coding sequence.
    a) Upstream
    b) Downstream
    c) Both upstream & downstream
    d) Middle
82. Function of the ribosome's A site during translation is
    a) To accommodate incoming aminoacyl-tRNA
    b) To hold the growing polypeptide chain
    c) To exit the ribosome
    d) To initiate translation
83. Which of the following is a type of post-translational modification that affects protein function?
    a) Polyadenylation
    b) RNA splicing
    c) Phosphorylation
    d) mRNA capping
84. How do silent mutations affect protein function?
    a) They change the amino acid sequence
    b) They introduce a premature stop codon
    c) They do not alter the amino acid sequence
    d) They alter the DNA sequence
85. In prokaryotic cells, the structure that acts as the ribosomal binding site on mRNA is
    a) Shine-Dalgarno sequence
    b) TATA box
    c) Kozak sequence
    d) Poly-A tail
86. Scientist known for discovering the enzyme RNA polymerase is
    a) Roger Kornberg
    b) Arthur Kornberg
    c) Francois Jacob
    d) Severo Ochoa
87. The role of aminoacyl-tRNA synthetase is to
    a) Catalyze peptide bond formation
    b) Charge tRNA with its corresponding amino acid
    c) Facilitate ribosome movement
    d) Add a 5' cap to mRNA
88. The amino acid coded by AUG codon is
    a) Tryptophan
    b) Threonine
    c) Serine
    d) Methionine

89. Total number of codons in the genetic code is
   a) 64 b) 61
   c) 84 d) 20

90. In eukaryotic cells, the primary role of the nucleolus is
   a) DNA replication
   b) RNA synthesis and ribosome assembly
   c) Protein modification
   d) mRNA splicing

91. The function of the eukaryotic transcription factor TFIID is
   a) It terminates transcription
   b) It initiates translation
   c) It binds to the promoter region to start transcription
   d) It adds the 5' cap to mRNA

92. The two subunits of prokaryotic ribosomes are
   a) 50S & 20S b) 40S & 30S
   c) 40S & 20S d) 50S & 30S

93. 5S rRNA is synthesized by
   a) RNA polymerase I b) RNA polymerase II
   c) RNA polymerase III d) RNA polymerase IV

94. The role of the P site in the ribosome during translation is
   a) It holds the growing polypeptide chain
   b) It exits the ribosome
   c) It accommodates the incoming aminoacyl-tRNA
   d) It binds the mRNA

95. During translation, what happens at the E site of the ribosome?
   a) New tRNA molecules enter b) Peptide bonds are formed
   c) Empty tRNA molecules exit d) mRNA is translated

96. The organelle in which protein folding primarily occurs is
   a) Nucleus b) Endoplasmic reticulum
   c) Golgi apparatus d) Mitochondria

97. The scientists discovered the ribosomes and showed its crucial role in protein synthesis is
   a) Frederick Sanger b) Albert Claude
   c) George Beadle d) Barbara McClintock

98. At which end of the tRNA molecule does the amino acid attach?
   a) 3' end b) 5' end
   c) Anticodon loop d) D-loop

99. Total number of the standard amino acids used in protein synthesis are
   a) 03 b) 61
   c) 64 d) 20

100. What is unique about the first methionine used in translation in prokaryotes
   a) Modified with phosphate group   b) Modified with a formyl group
   c) Modified with nitrate group   d) Modified with a glycine

Answer Key

1	c	2	c	3	b	4	a	5	b	6	a	7	d
8	d	9	b	10	c	11	b	12	b	13	a	14	d
15	d	16	b	17	c	18	c	19	b	20	d	21	a
22	b	23	c	24	b	25	d	26	b	27	b	28	a
29	c	30	a	31	b	32	c	33	d	34	b	35	c
36	a	37	c	38	b	39	d	40	c	41	c	42	d
43	a	44	b	45	c	46	a	47	b	48	a	49	b
50	b	51	d	52	a	53	d	54	a	55	b	56	a
57	d	58	b	59	d	60	c	61	a	62	b	63	c
64	c	65	b	66	a	67	d	68	b	69	c	70	d
71	d	72	d	73	a	74	a	75	d	76	c	77	b
78	b	79	a	80	c	81	a	82	a	83	c	84	c
85	a	86	d	87	b	88	d	89	a	90	b	91	c
92	d	93	c	94	a	95	c	96	b	97	b	98	a
99	d	100	b										

11

Clinical Physiology of Neurological Disorders

Mamta Mishra and Manish Arya

Department of Veterinary Surgery and Radiology, College of Veterinary and Animal Sciences, Kishanganj, Bihar Animal Sciences University, Bihar

Introduction

The nervous system in animals is a complex group of highly specialized cells capable of collecting and transmitting information in response to external stimuli via receptors and highly specialized sensory organs. It aids in the regulation of muscle coordination, the release of hormones, neurotransmitters, and other chemical mediators, all of which facilitate numerous bodily activities.

The nervous system is divided into two systems: the central nervous system (CNS), which includes the brain and spinal cord, and the peripheral nervous system. Within these systems, there is another autonomic nervous system (ANS), which is distinguished by higher centers of the hypothalamus, midbrain, pons, and medulla, as well as tracts and nuclei in the spinal cord. The ANS is further divided into sympathetic and parasympathetic systems, which help maintain homeostasis and activate emergency mechanisms in response to external stimuli. The brain is normally covered by three meninges: piameter, arachnoid, and durameter. These meninges create three spaces: the subarachnoid space (between pia mater and arachnoid), the subdural space (between arachnoid and dura mater), and the epidural space (between dura mater and the ligamentum flavum in the spinal canal). The subarachnoid space includes cerebrospinal fluid, which is isolated from cerebral blood by the morphological and enzymatic activity of cells with tight junctions that regulate intercellular diffusion and solute exchange inside the cells. These cells form a barrier known as the "blood-brain barrier".

The blood-brain barrier works as a selective permeable membrane, allowing only certain chemicals and medications to pass through while excreting essential components from the central nervous system via energy-dependent efflux pumps like p-glycoprotein. These proteins are encoded by genes such as ABCB1, and mutations in them can result in severe effects such as Ivermectin poisoning in the Colie breed of dogs. Similarly, it aids in the relative isolation of the neurological system from the immune system by establishing an immune-suppressive parenchymal milieu. However, various infections, trauma, and developmental defects can result in underdevelopment or damage to different cerebellar structures. As a result, depending on the portion implicated, it might cause changed behavioral changes in animals such as muscle incoordination, depression, and paralysis. These clinical symptoms may be excitatory.

Cerebrospinal fluid (CSF) is a fluid found in the brain that is created by the choroid plexus, arteries, and arterioles in the piameter and arachanoid spaces. Any change in CSF composition may indicate an infection or underlying pathology in the neurological system. CSF is typically collected from the cisterna magna/atlanto-occipital and lumbosacral regions (in dogs, L4-L5/L5-L6, and in cats, L6-L7). It also regulates intracranial pressure, maintains electrolyte and acid-base homeostasis, acts as an intracerebral transport channel for neurotransmitters and hormones, and excretes metabolic products. The lumbosacral area is commonly preferred for CSF collection since it does not require general anaesthesia. The collection location is the midway of the lumbosacral space, which is identified as the midline depression between the last palpable dorsal lumbar spine (L6 in cattle, goats, and horses; L6 or L7 in sheep and pigs).

A correct neuroanatomical diagnosis is critical since it aids in the location of lesions in the nervous system and, as a result, the development of an appropriate treatment plan. Neuroanatomical diagnosis is usually followed by a thorough physical examination of all body systems, as other systemic illnesses, such as hepatic encephalopathy in animals, can damage the nervous system and cause seizures. It also aids in the differential diagnosis of disorders that can confuse doctors due to similar clinical signs, such as an animal with cranial cruciate ligament rupture resulting in pelvic limb abnormalities. Physical examinations often comprise an assessment of the animal's mental state and behavior, its position at rest when walking and standing, the presence or absence of aberrant involuntary movements, various nerve reflexes such as cutaneous, palpebral, and sensory evaluation.

Radiography, ultrasound, and magnetic resonance imaging are all diagnostic imaging modalities that can be used.

Multiple Choice Questions

1. Collection of neuronal bodies in PNS and other surrounding structures is
   a) Glial cells b) Corpora neurona
   c) Both a and b d) Schwann cells
2. Axons differ from dendrites in
   a) Narrow and non- tapering ends b) have little endoplasmic reticulum
   c) Impulse conduction away from body d) All of the above
3. Cerebrospinal fluid is present in CNS in
   a) Between pia mater and arachnoid
   b) Between arachnoid and dura mater
   c) Between dura mater and the ligamentum flavum in the spinal canal
   d) Schwann cells
4. Radial nerve originates from
   a) First lumbar and seventh thoracic vertebrae
   b) Supraspinatus and infraspinatus process
   c) Eight cervical vertebrae and first thoracic vertebrae
   d) Radius and ulna

5. Cognitive or mental status of animal is called as
   a) Reflex b) Sign
   c) Sensorium d) All of the above
6. Cranial Nerve originating from dorsal aspect of brain is
   a) Trigeminal b) Trochlear
   c) Oculomotor d) Optic
7. Central nervous system is generally originated from
   a) Endoderm b) Mesoderm
   c) Ectoderm d) All of the above
8. Nerve plexus present in intestine is
   a) Mesenteric reflex b) Pampiniform plexus
   c) Auerbach's plexus d) None of the above
9. Recurrent laryngeal nerve supplies all laryngeal muscles except
   a) Thyroarytenoideus b) Cricoartyenoideus
   c) Cricothyroideus d) Arytenidous transverse
10. Cranial nerve with smallest size
   a) Trigeminal b) Vestibulocochlear
   c) Optic d) All of the above
11. Largest nerve in body
   a) Ischiatic nerve b) Trigeminal
   c) Vagus d) Optic
12. Site of collection of CSF is
   a) Cisterna pontis b) Cisterna lumber
   c) Cisterna cervical d) Cisterna magna
13. Largest sensory nucleus of brain is
   a) Hypothalamus b) Thalamus
   c) Substansia niagra d) Corpus callosum
14. Nerve supply to tongue is given by
   a) Buccinator b) Trigeminal
   c) Glossopharyngeal d) Hypoglossal
15. CSF is formed mainly by
   a) Choroid plexus
   b) Arteries and capillaries in piameter and arachanoid
   c) Both of the above
   d) None of the above
16. Eye movement in animals is controlled by
   a) IX, X and XII b) III, IV and VIII
   c) III, IV and VI d) None of the above

17. Eye preservation reflex in animals is controlled by
    a) Trigeminal nerve b) Facial nerve
    c) Sciatic nerve d) Glossopharyngeal nerve
18. Flexor spinal response in animals is observed by
    a) Sciatic nerve b) Facial nerve
    c) Trigeminal nerve d) Glossopharyngeal nerve
19. Macroglial cells in brain are
    a) Schwann cells b) Astrocytes
    c) Oligodendrocytes d) Both b and c
20. Brain and spinal cord are covered by protective covering is called
    a) White matter b) Grey matter
    c) Meninges d) Myelin sheath
21. Complex mesh of intertwined arteries and capillary beds around pituitary gland is called as
    a) Pampiniform plexus b) Aurebach plexus
    c) Rete mirabile d) Neurolemma
22. Gag reflex in animals is controlled by
    a) Cranial nerve X b) Cranial nerve IX
    c) Cranial nerve III d) Both a and b
23. Withdrawl pelvic reflex in animals is generally controlled by
    a) L6–S1 b) L6–S2
    c) C6–T2 d) S1-S3
24. Patellar reflex in animals is present in
    a) L6–S2 b) C7–T2
    c) S1–S3 d) L4–L6
25. Which cranial nerve is responsible for inward rotation of eyeball
    a) VII b) IV
    c) III d) I
26. Schirmer tear test is done for evaluation for sympathetic activity of
    a) Cranial nerve VII b) Cranial nerve VIII
    c) Cranial nerve X d) Cranial nerve XII
27. Area of skin corresponding to specific nerve root and spinal cord segment is called
    a) Dermatome b) Desmetocele
    c) Skin graft d) Epidermis
28. Maintenance of equillbrium and regulation of muscle tone is maintained by
    a) Cerebral hemisphere b) Cerebellum
    c) Spinal cord d) Medulla oblongata

29. Peripheral nervous system consists of
    a) 12pair of cranial nerves and 36 pair of spinal nerves
    b) 36 pair of cranial nerves and 12 pair of spinal nerves
    c) 28 pair of cranial nerves and 30 pair of spinal nerves
    d) 25 pair of cranial nerves and 46 pair of spinal nerves
30. Consciousness in animal is maintained by
    a) Ascending reticular system b) Thalamic reticular system
    c) Hyposubthalamic reticular system d) All of the above
31. Visceral motor activity in brain is maintained by
    a) Ascending reticular system b) Thalamic reticular system
    c) Hyposubthalamic reticular system d) Limbic system
32. Vision in animals is controlled by
    a) Cranial nerve III b) Cranial nerve IV
    c) Cranial nerve II d) Cranial nerve I
33. Blinking in animals is controlled by
    a) Cranial nerve II b) Cranial nerve III
    c) Cranial nerve I d) Cranial nerve VII
34. Constriction of the pupil is mediated by
    a) Cranial nerve II b) Cranial nerve III
    c) Cranial nerve I d) Cranial nerve VII
35. Afferent pathway for generation of pupillary light reflex in animals originates from
    a) Lateral geniculate nuclei b) Choroid plexus
    c) Rete mirabile d) Auerbach's plexus
36. Physiological nystagmus is controlled by
    a) Optic nerve b) Trigeminal nerve
    c) Vestibulocochlear nerve d) Vagus nerve
37. Corneal reflex is controlled by
    a) Cranial nerve VIII b) Cranial nerve VI
    c) Cranial nerve IX d) Cranial nerve VII
38. Brachial plexus originates receive nerve from
    a) T1–T3 b) T4-L1
    c) C6–T1 d) C4-C5
39. Extraocular muscles in eye are supplied by cranial nerves:
    a) III b) IV
    c) VI d) All of the above
40. Which of the following help in maintaining position of the eyes, trunk and limbs in reference to the position of the head
    a) Vestibular system b) Limbic system
    c) Ascending reticular system d) Descending reticular system

41. Cranial nerve IX, X and XI originates from
    a) Rete mirabile
    b) Nucleus ambigus
    c) Geniculate
    d) None of the above
42. Withdrawal reflex in thoracic limb of dogs is controlled by (c)
    a) L6-S1
    b) T12-L3
    c) C6-T2
    d) C5-T1
43. Withdrawal reflex in pelvic limb of dogs is controlled by (a)
    a) L6-S1
    b) T12-L3
    c) C6-T2
    d) C5-T1
44. Triceps reflex is mediated by radial nerve involving (d)
    a) C5-T1
    b) T12-L3
    c) C1-C2
    d) C7-T2
45. Biceps reflex is mediated by which nerve involving C6-C8 segments
    a) Musculocutaneous nerve
    b) Radial nerve
    c) Vagus nerve
    d) Trigeminal nerve
46. Area of skin involving single nerve is called
    a) Supracutaneous nerve
    b) Subcutaneous area
    c) Cutaneous area
    d) Neuromuscular
47. Gag reflex in animals is controlled by
    a) Glossopharyngeal
    b) Vagus
    c) Hypoglossal nerves
    d) All of the above
48. Cutaneous area innervated by single nerve is called
    a) Overlapping zone
    b) Autonomouis zone
    c) Both a and b
    d) None of the above
49. Lateral aspect of digit V is innervated by
    a) Median nerve
    b) Ulnar nerve
    c) Radial nerve
    d) Saphenous nerve
50. Caudal surface of brachium is innervated by
    a) Median nerve
    b) Ulnar nerve
    c) Radial nerve
    d) Musculocutaneus nerve
51. Palmer surface of the paw is innervated by
    a) Median nerve
    b) Ulnar nerve
    c) Musculocutaneus nerve
    d) Both a and b
52. Medial aspect of pelvic limb is innervated by
    a) Saphenous nerve
    b) Median nerve
    c) Musculocutaneus nerve
    d) Ulnar nerve
53. Area of skin innervated by afferent fibers from a single spinal or cranial nerve is called
    a) Cutaneous
    b) Autonomous zone
    c) Overlapping zone
    d) Dermatome

54. Small vertical projection on the thoracic vertebrae which can be used as landmark on thoracolumbar radiographs is

a) Anticlinal vertebrae
b) Floating vertebrae
c) Transverse process
d) Vertical spine

55. Fibrocartilaginous tissue surrounding center of disc material with concentric lamellae of collagenous fibers running at an angle of 100-120° between adjacent vertebrae is called

a) Nucleus pulpous
b) Annulus fibrosus
c) Intervertebral disc
d) None of the above

56. Which of the following is related with unconscious perception?

a) Spinothalamic tract
b) Spinocerebellar tract
c) Rubrospinal tract
d) Vestibulospinal tract

57. Which of the following is related with increase in extensor tone on the ipsilateral side and flexor tone on the contralateral side

a) Spinothalamic tract
b) Spinocerebellar tract
c) Rubrospinal tract
d) Vestibulospinal tract

58. Area of brain responsible for induction of vomiting i.e. Chemoreceptor trigger zone is located in

a) Corpus callosum
b) Fourth ventricle
c) Pons
d) Thalamus

59. Sheets of connective tissue separating cerebellum and cerebral hemispheres is

a) Falx cerebri
b) Corpus callosum
c) Durameter
d) Tentorium cerebelli

60. Connective tissue sheet separating two cerebral hemispheres are

a) Falx cerebri
b) Corpus callosum
c) Durameter
d) Tentorium cerebelli

61. Myelin sheath is secreted by

a) Schwann cells
b) Dendrites
c) Oligodendrocytes
d) Axon hillock

62. Which of the following cells are able to detect chemical changes in brain and ensuring matching blood flow to neuronal activity

a) Dendrites
b) Astrocytes
c) Schwann cells
d) Oligodendrocytes

63. Normal range of intracranial pressure in brain of dogs and cats

a) 8 to 15 mm Hg
b) 15 to 20 mm Hg
c) 20 to 30mm Hg
d) 30-35mm Hg

64. CNS is protected from immune system by

a) Astrocytes
b) Dendrites
c) Blood-brain barrier
d) Meninges

65. Evaluation of muscle coordination is done by
   a) Wheelbarrow test b) Flexor reflex
   c) Patellar reflex d) Sway reaction
66. Flexing of limb on firm implement with caudolateral aspect of distal limb is called
   a) Crossed extensor reflex b) Babinski reflex
   c) Wheelbarrow test d) Patellar reflex
67. Production of CSF is done under the influence of
   a) Glutathione peroxidase b) Lipase
   c) Carbonic anhydrase d) None of the above
68. Control centers for autonomic nervous system is located in
   a) Spinal cord b) Hypothalamus
   c) Brainstem d) All of the above
69. Which of the following will increase contractility of heart?
   a) Sympathetic system b) Parasympathetic system
   c) Autonomic nervous system d) Peripheral nervous system
70. Most potent cerebral vasoconstrictor is
   a) Acetylcholine b) Prostacyclin
   c) Thromboxane-A_2 d) None of the above
71. Production of 'supranormal blood flow 'above normal metabolic requirement in brain occur in
   a) Luxury perfusion syndrome b) Intracerebral- steal syndrome
   c) Robin Hood syndrome d) None of the above
72. Decrease in cerebral vascular resistance of non-ischemic brain region causing blood shunting away area of from vasomotor paralysis is observed in
   a) Luxury perfusion syndrome b) Intracerebral- steal syndrome
   c) Robin Hood syndrome d) None of the above
73. Increase in cerebral vascular resistance in normal cerebral region causing shunting of blood towards area of vasomotor paralysis is observed in
   a) Luxury perfusion syndrome b) Intracerebral- steal syndrome
   c) Robin Hood syndrome d) None of the above
74. Which of the following techniques can cause marked increase in spinal blood flow
   a) Hypoxia b) Hypercapnia
   c) Hyperoxygenation d) Both a and b
75. Anesthetic agents cause sedation in animals by acting at
   a) β-1 GABA receptors b) β-2 GABA receptors
   c) β-3 GABA receptors d) β-4 GABA receptors
76. Anesthetic agents cause hypnosis in animals by acting at
   a) β-1 GABA receptors b) β-2 GABA receptors
   c) β-3 GABA receptors d) β-4 GABA receptors

77. General anaesthesia produces immobility in animals by acting at
    a) Brain b) Spinal cord
    c) Pons d) Medulla
78. Which of the following substrate is most inhibitory neurotransmitter in brain
    a) GABA b) Glutamate
    c) Acetylcholine d) None of the above
79. Which of the following molecules is responsible for recruitment of neutrophils in central nervous system
    a) Acetylcholine b) Prostacyclin
    c) Thromboxane-A2 d) Integrins
80. Appearance of alpha waves in EEG represent
    a) Sedation b) Ataxia
    c) Cerebral hypoxia d) Consciousness
81. Disturbing sensory and emotional experience due to actual or potential tissue damage is called as
    a) Ataxia b) Pain
    c) Reflex d) Nociception
82. The neuronal process of converting sensory information to motor information in response to noxious stimuli is known as
    a) Neurotmesis b) Plasticity
    c) Axon potential d) Nociception
83. Exaggrated response of nervous system to noxious stimuli is called
    a) Hyperalgesia b) Allodynia
    c) Hyperesthesia d) Reflex
84. Low intensity pain response to normally innocuous stimulus is called
    a) Hyperalgesia b) Allodynia
    c) Hyperesthesia d) Reflex
85. Increase in concentration of carbon dioxide will result in
    a) Increase in cerebral vascular resistance b) Decrease in cerebral blood flow
    c) Increase in cerebral blood flow d) Both a and b
86. Which of the following adrenoreceptors mediate vasoconstriction
    a) Beta-1 b) Beta-2
    c) Alpha-2 d) Alpha-1
87. Normal angle between atlas and axis should be
    a) More than 162 degrees b) Less than 162 degrees
    c) Equal to 162 degrees d) None of the above
88. Onion peel like structure present around axon is
    a) Schwann cells b) Nodes of Ranvier
    c) Epineurium d) Perinurium

89. Connective tissue present around entire nerve is called (a)
    a) Epineurium b) Perineurium
    c) Myelin sheath d) Neurolemma

90. Bands responsible for transmission of stresses and strain generated during movement of verterbrae is present in
    a) Nucleus palposus b) Annulus fibrosus
    c) Vertebral body d) None of the above

91. Which of the following ligament provide greater resistance to dorsal herniation of nuclear material than in other areas of the spinal column
    a) Dorsal longitudinal ligament b) Interspinous ligament
    c) Ventral longitudinal ligament d) None of the above

92. Which structure is used as landmark for counting correct intervertebral disc
    a) Last rib b) T11
    c) C5 d) C7

93. Paralysis of all the limbs in animal is
    a) Monoparesis b) Paresis
    c) Tetraparesis d) Hemiparesis

94. Onset of paralysis with retention of consciousness in animal is known as
    a) Cataplexy b) Tremor
    c) Ataxia d) Circling

95. Decreased sense of smell is known as
    a) Hyposomia b) Hypersomia
    c) Parasomia d) Anoxia

96. Cerebellar ataxia is type of
    a) Excitatory dysfunction b) Inhibitory dysfunction
    c) Both a and b d) None of the above

97. Irritation phenomena occur due to
    a) Anemic Hypoxia b) Experimental decerebration
    c) Tumours, infectious agents and poison d) Both a and c

98. Animal exhibiting acting in biazzare way and unaware of its surrounding is called
    a) Ataxia b) Incoordination
    c) Mania d) Circling

99. Animal exhibiting violent activity with unaware of its surroundings is called (b)
    a) Mania b) Frenzy
    c) Epilepsy d) Aggression

100. Sudden onset of unconsciousness in animal is called d)
    a) Coma b) Shock
    c) Narcolepsy d) Syncope

101. Continuous repetitive twitching movement of skeletal muscle is called
   a) Tremor   b) Tic
   c) Tetanus   d) Convulsions
102. Sustained spasm of the neck and limb muscles causing dorsal and caudal extension of the head and neck with rigid extension of the limbs
   a) Myoclonus   b) Opisothotonus
   c) Clonic   d) Tetanus
103. Spasmodic twitching movements in animal at longer interval due to traumatic injury to spinal cord injury is called
   a) Tics   b) Tetanus
   c) Convulsions   d) None of the above
104. Intermittent tetanic contraction of skeletal muscles causing rigidity of whole body followed by relaxation
   a) Myoclonus   b) Opisthotonus
   c) Tetanus   d) None of the above
105. Convulsions in hypomagensimic tetany occur due to
   a) Intracranial origin   b) Extracranial origin
   c) Both a and b   d) None of the above
106. Increased range of excess movement of limbs with overreaching of limbs is called
   a) Hypermetria   b) Hypometria
   c) Dysmetria   d) None of the above
107. Goose stepping is exhibited as common sign in
   a) Hypermetria   b) Hypometria
   c) Dysmetria   d) Opisthotonus
108. Head tilting accompanied by tight circle in animals is characteristic of
   a) Cerebellar lesion   b) Vestibular lesion
   c) Spinal cord lesion   d) Cerebral lesion
109. Unconscious proprioceptive defect causing incoordination in muscle while walking
   a) Narcolepsy   b) Ataxia
   c) Convulsions   d) None of the above
110. Severe compressive injury of thoracolumbar spinal cord resulting in extensive rigidity of forelimbs and hindlimb paralysis in dogs occur in
   a) Schiff–Sherrington syndrome   b) Tremorgenic mycotoxicoses
   c) Both a and b   d) None of the above
111. Functional blindness is seen in
   a) Acetonemia   b) Keratoconjuctivitis
   c) Poliencephalomyelopathy   d) All of the above

112. Mania in animals occur due to lesion in
   a) Cerebral brainstem reticular system   b) Brainstem of cerebral cortex
   c) Cerebellum   d) Cerebrum-limbic system
113. Coma in animals generally occur due to lesion in
   a) Cerebral-visual cortex   b) Vestibular apparatus
   c) Cerebral-brainstem reticular system   d) Cerebellum
114. Lesion in vestibular nucleus is seen in
   a) Brain abscess   b) Listeriosis
   c) Both a and b   d) None of the above
115. Central blindness in animals is observed in
   a) Poliencephalomalacia and lead poisoning
   b) Lesion in cerebral cortex
   c) Both a and b
   d) None of the above
116. BAER test in animal is used to diagnose lesion of
   a) Facial nerve   b) Vestibuloconchlear nerve
   c) Hypoglossal nerve   d) Spinal accessory nerve
117. Hypermetria without paresis is seen in
   a) Spinocerebellar   b) Cerebellar
   c) Both a and b   d) None of the above
118. Dysmetria in animals is observed due to lesion in
   a) Cerebellar   b) Spinocerebellar
   c) Thoracolumbar   d) All of the above
119. Localized unilateral sweating of the neck and cranial shoulder is seen in
   a) Pseudorabies   b) Bovine viral diarrohea
   c) Rabies   d) Horner syndrome
120. Clasp-knife release is seen in
   a) Tetanus   b) Black Quarter
   c) Spastic Parasis   d) Rabies
121. Lead-pipe rigidity is seen in
   a) Tetanus   b) Black Quarter
   c) Spastic Parasis   d) Rabies
122. Laryngeal auditory reflex is accessed in horses by
   a) Electromyogram   b) BAER
   c) Slap test   d) None of the above
123. Increase in protein content of CSF is recorded in
   a) Froin syndrome   b) Schiff–Sherrington syndrome
   c) Both of the above   d) None of the above

124. Queckenstedt's test is done in animals
  a) For evaluation of CSF protein
  b) For evaluation of electrical conductivity
  c) For evaluation of CSF pressure
  d) Both a and b

125. Protein content in CSF is estimated by
  a) Pandy test b) BAER test
  c) Both of the above d) Queckenstedt's

126. Accidental intracarotid injection of promazine in horses can cause
  a) Interstitial edema b) Vasogenic edema
  c) Cytotoxic edema d) All of the above

127. Interstitial edema in animals occurs in
  a) Hydrocephalus b) Poliencephalomalacia
  c) Brain abscess d) Meningitis

128. Type of respiration observed in meningitis
  a) Biot's breathing b) Cheyne–Stokes breathing
  c) Both of the above d) None of the above

129. Yellowish tinge to CSF is called
  a) Xanthochromia b) Cyanochromia
  c) Acetchromia d) None of the above

130. Primary demyelination of CNS is observed in
  a) Bacterial diseases b) Viral diseases
  c) Fungal diseases d) Protozoan diseases

131. Which of the following is example of demyelinating encephalitis
  a) Toxoplasmosis b) Listeriosis
  c) Visna d) None of the above

132. Thromboembolic meningitis in calves is caused by
  a) *P. multocida* b) *H. somni*
  c) *S. typhimurium* d) *E.coli*

133. Which of the following is both inflammatory and demyelinating in nature
  a) Visna b) Visceral larva migrans
  c) Leukoencephalomyleitis d) Listeriosis

134. Unusual irritation phenomenon is exhibited by
  a) Rabies b) Pseudorabies
  c) Scrapie d) Both a and b

135. Inflammation of the spinal cord is
  a) Myelitis b) Encephalitis
  c) Meningitis d) Encephalomyelitis

136. Premature degeneration of neurons due to an inborn metabolic error of development in neurons is called

a) Neurotrophy b) Neurotmesis
c) Abiotrophy d) Encephalomalacia

137. Cerebral herniation, Wallerian type of degeneration of optic nerves and elevated CSF pressure is observed in

a) Hypovitaminosis A b) Copper deficiency
c) Salt toxicity d) Toxoplasmosis

138. Cerebrocortical necrosis in animals may occur due to

a) Toxoplasmosis b) Hypovitaminosis A
c) Salt toxicity d) Thiamine deficiency

139. Irregular swellings in degenerative neurons indicating ability to maintain normal shape is called as

a) Kleiods b) Myeloma
c) Spheroids d) None of the above

140. Chewing gum fits in cattle is observed in

a) Toxoplasmosis b) Plumbism
c) Zn deficiency d) Selenium toxicity

141. Encephalopathy in plumbism occur due to

a) Hypervitaminosis b) Copper toxicity
c) Hypomagnesemia tetany d) Lead toxicity

142. Perivascular cuffing is observed in

a) Brain b) Liver
c) Testes d) Spleen

143. Intravenous Intralipid emulsion containing 20% soyabean oil has been used in treatment of

a) Copper toxicity b) Aminoglycosides toxicity
c) Macrolytic lactones toxicity d) Phenothiazine toxicity

144. Bilateral laryngeal hemiplegia in horses occur due to

a) Macrolytic lactone poisoning b) Organophosphate poisoning
c) Copper toxicity d) Antihelminth toxicity

145. Negri bodies in brain is found in

a) Pseudorabies b) Enterotoxemia
c) Rabies d) Meningoencephalitis

146. Fluorescein antibody test is generally done in

a) Rabies b) Visna
c) Listeriosis d) Pseudorabies

147. Vacuolation of grey matter neuropil and nibbling scratch is observed in

a) Visna
b) Bovine spongiform encephalopathy

c) Scrapie
d) Western equine encephalomyelitis

148. Gid or Coenurosis in goats is caused by
a) Oesophagostomum spp. *b) T. multiceps*
c) T. saginata *d) C. perfringenes*

149. Thiamine deficiency in horses is caused by ingestion of
a) Bracken fern b) Horsetail
c) Carrot grass d) Both a and b

150. Micro abscess in brain is generally reported in
a) Listeriosis b) Gid
c) Rabies d) Louping-ill

151. Vestibular disease in animals occur due to injury of cranial nerve
a) VII b) VII
c) X d) V

152. Tongue paralysis in animals is due to injury of cranial nerve
a) VIII b) XII
c) V d) VII

153. Masseter atrophy, weakness and hypalgesia of the nostrils and skin of the face is caused due to injury of
a) VII b) XII
c) I d) V.

154. Lateral curvature of spine is
a) Scoliosis b) Lordosis
c) Kyphosis d) Torticolisis

155. Ventral curvature of the spine is
a) Kyphosis b) Torticollis
c) Scoliosis d) Lordosis

156. Undulating vermiform movement of overlying skin due to contraction of small muscle fibers is called as
a) Opisthotonus b) Myoclonus
c) Myokymia d) Myotonia

157. Which of the following drugs is contraindicated in increased cranial pressure
a) Xylazine b) Ketamine
c) Propofol d) Diazepam

158. Minimum volume of CSF required for analysis is
a) 0.6ml b) 0.5ml
c) 5ml d) 3ml

159. Site for collection of CSF from lumbar site in cats is
    a) L6–L7 b) L4–L5
    c) L1-L2 d) L3-L4
160. Mysthenia gravis in humans is diagnosed by
    a) Electroencephalogram b) Single fibre electromyography
    c) Electromyography d) MRI
161. Screening test for identification of complete deafness in Dalmatians
    a) BAER b) EEG
    c) ECG d) BAEP
162. Failure of segmentation in the developing vertebrae is called
    a) Hemivertebrae b) Transitional vertebrae
    c) Block vertebrae d) Vertebral hypoplasia
163. Failure of formation of part of the vertebra T7–T9 in animals is called
    a) Hemivertebrae b) oTransitional vertebrae
    c) Block vertebrae d) Vertebral hypoplasia
164. Failure of fusion of neural tube and overlying tissue in Manx cats
    a) Discospondylitis b) Spondylosis
    c) Spina bifida d) None of the above
165. Mineralization of soft tissue of C1-C2 vertebrae in animals
    a) Calcinosis circumscripta b) Multiple cartilaginous exostoses
    c) Tumoral calcinosis d) Both a and c
166. Myelography in animals is done by injecting contrast medium
    a) Iohexol b) Mannitol
    c) Air d) Barium sulphate
167. USG in nervous system can be used to diagnose
    a) Hydrocephalus
    b) Cerebellar herniation associated with Chiari-like malformations
    c) Both a and b
    d) Encephalitis
168. Focal seizures involving progressive movement of facial, neck, shoulder or limb is called
    a) Jacksonian seizures b) Grand mal
    c) Petite mal d) Generalized
169. Most common used benzodiazapines in veterinary medicine for treatment of seizures is
    a) Phenobarbitone b) Thiopentol
    c) Diazepam d) Xylazine
170. Antileptic drug used for treatment of neuropathic pain in dogs
    a) Gabapentin b) Diazepam
    c) Midazolam d) Phenobarbitone

171. Sulphamate-substituted mono -saccharide with ability of preventing the spread of seizures via potentiating GABA activity in the brain is

a) Felbamate
b) Topiramate
c) Levetiracetam
d) Zonisamide

172. Structural analogue of GABA which inhibits depolarization of calcium influx and thus preventing seizures is

a) Zonisamide
b) Lamotrigine
c) Levetiracetam
d) Pregabalin

173. Antileptic drug which is not used in dogs due to its conversion into cardiotoxic metabolite is

a) Rufinamide
b) Lamotrigine
c) Potassium bromide
d) Lacosamide

174. Benzodiazepine not undergoing hepatic metabolism in cats is

a) Diazepam
b) Midazolam
c) Clorazepate
d) Clonazepam

175. Drug which binds to the presynaptic vesicular protein, SV2A, causing decrease in glutamate neurotransmitter release is

a) Levetriacetam
b) Clonazepam
c) Zonisamide
d) Phenobarbitone

176. The mental process of 'knowing', which includes perception, recognition, judgement and sensation is called

a) Awareness
b) Cognition
c) Delirium
d) Alert

177. Alteration in mental activity of animals due to illusions, hallucinations, cerebral excitement, physical restlessness and incoherence is called

a) Awareness
b) Cognition
c) Delirium
d) Alert

178. The observable response of an animal to a given situation is called (

a) Reflex
b) Behaviour
c) Spasm
d) None of the above

179. Animal with decerebrate rigidity may have lesion in

a) Spinal cord
b) Cerebellum
c) Medulla oblongata
d) Cerebral hemispheres

180. Animal having increased intracranial pressure show

a) Biot's respiration
b) Cheyne-strokes respiration
c) Apneustic respiration
d) Shallow respiration

181. Herniation of cerebral hemisphere into falx cerebri as result of unilateral hemispheric lesion is called

a) Transtentorial herniation
b) Falcine herniation
c) Both a and b
d) None of the above

182. Abnormal dilatation of the ventricular system within the cranium generally occur due to
   a) Hydrocephalus   b) Pyocephalus
   c) Hydrometra   d) None of the above
183. Setting sun sign (bilateral strabismus) is characteristic of
   a) Encephalitis   b) Meningitis
   c) Hydrocephalus   d) Myelitis
184. Most common type of tumours in brain
   a) Meningiomas   b) Gliomas
   c) Ependymomas   d) Choroid plexus tumours
185. Drug for treatment of aggressive gliomas is
   a) Hydroxyurea   b) Carmustine
   c) Lomustine   d) Temozolomide
186. Which of the following breed is susceptible for Ivermectin poisoning
   a) Coolie   b) Labrador
   c) German Shephard   d) Pugs
187. Which of the following test determine integrity of facial nerve and cortical awareness
   a) Pupillary light reflex   b) Dazzle reflex
   c) Jone's test   d) Menace response
188. Acute blindness in animals suffering from sudden retinal degeneration can be confirmed by evaluating
   a) Chromatic PLR   b) High intensity PLR
   c) Dazzle reflex   d) None of the above
189. Which reflex can be taken into account for evaluation of ophthalmic nerve
   a) Withdrawl and patellar reflex   b) Cutaneous and patellar reflex
   c) Palpebral and corneal reflex   d) None of the above
190. Reduced tear production can indicate insult to which cranial nerve
   a) Vagus   b) Facial
   c) Trigminal   d) Vestibuloconchlear
191. Horner syndrome occur due to disturbance in
   a) Sympathatic function   b) Parasympathetic function
   c) Sensory function   d) Motor function
192. Which of the following technique can be used for evaluation of both rod and cone photoreceptors
   a) Electroretinography   b) Visual evoked potential
   c) Direct opthalamoscopy   d) Slit-lamp
193. Which of the following techniques record signals from occipital cortex in response to light
   a) Electroretinography   b) Visual evoked potential
   c) Direct opthalamoscopy   d) Slit-lamp

194. Neurogenic keratitis in animals may be due to insult to

a) Vagus
b) Facial
c) Trigminal
d) Vestibuloconchlear

195. Inflammation of nerve tissue is called

a) Neuritis
b) Encephalitis
c) Dendritis
d) None of the above

196. Bilateral ventrolateral strabismus is seen in

a) Retinal degenration
b) Descemotocele
c) Hydrocephalus
d) Horner syndrome

197. Brief oscillations of pupil size is known as

a) Twitch
b) Hippus
c) Spasm
d) Pitch

198. Bilateral pupillary dilation showing no response to light with presence of third eyelid prolapse in presence of normal light is feature of

a) Static anisocoria
b) Pupilotonia
c) Dysautonomia
d) Hemi-dilated pupil

199. External ophthalmoplegia in eye occur due to which cranial nerve

a) III, IV and VI
b) IV, V, and II
c) IV, V and VII
d) V, VI and VIII

200. Congenital bilateral divergent strabismus is known as

a) Enotropia
b) Exotropia
c) Endotropia
d) Occulotropia

201. Loss of sensation in cornea may occur due to lesion in

a) Trigeminal nerve
b) Facial nerve
c) Vestibulo-conchlear nerve
d) None of the above

202. Ptosis in dogs may occur due to

a) Lesion in cranial nerve III
b) Loss of sympathetic supply to head
c) Both a and b
d) None of the above

203. Out of the following which is parasympathomimetic

a) Mannitol
b) Pilocarpine
c) Atropine
d) Tropicamide

204. Involuntary rhythmic oscillations of eyeball is called

a) Strabismus
b) Blepharospasm
c) Blinking
d) Nystagamus

205. Rotation of head around C1 vertebrae causing movement of one ear above the other is

a) Called head tilting
b) Indicative of vestibular deficit
c) Both a and b are true
d) Both a and b are false

206. Involuntary eye movement involving no fast or slow component can be classified as
   a) Pendulus nystagamus
   b) Jerk nystagamus
   c) Resting nystagamus
   d) Positional nystagamus
207. Involuntary rhythmic oscillation of Eye movement observed during resting period is called as
   a) Pendulus nystagamus
   b) Jerk nystagamus
   c) Resting nystagamus
   d) Positional nystagamus
208. Slow rotation of eyeball in one direction and movement in another direction is called
   a) Pendulus nystagamus
   b) Jerk nystagamus
   c) Resting nystagamus
   d) Positional nystagamus
209. Rotation of head into unusual position can elicit
   a) Pendulus nystagamus
   b) Jerk nystagamus
   c) Resting nystagamus
   d) Positional nystagamus
210. Which of the following technique can be used to evaluate otitis media and interna in animals
   a) Radiography
   b) Ultrasonography
   c) MRI and CT
   d) All of the above
211. Which of the following metabolic disease can cause association with peripheral vestibular disease and leading to positional strabismus
   a) Osteoporosis
   b) Hypothyroidism
   c) Diabetes mellitus
   d) All of the above
212. Which of the following disease can be seen in association with vestibular disease
   a) Facial nerve paralysis
   b) Neurogenic KCS
   c) Horner's syndrome
   d) All of the above
213. Which of the following is complication of Ventral bulla osteotomy
   a) KCS
   b) Otitis media
   c) Horner's syndrome
   d) Otitis media
214. Which of the following can cause compression of the brainstem and cerebellum, and result in signs of central vestibular disease
   a) Channelopathies
   b) Chiari like formation
   c) Haw syndrome
   d) Kleinfelter syndrome
215. Most common predilection site for supracollicular or quadrigeminal cysts in brachycephalic breeds is
   a) Hippocampus
   b) Geniculate nucleus
   c) Cerebellum
   d) Quadrigeminal cistern
216. Inflammation of brain and other surrounding structures is
   a) Myelitis
   b) Meningoencephalitis
   c) Neuritis
   d) Neuromyelitis

217. Dropped jaw in animals occur due to injury of

a) Cranial nerve V b) Cranial nerve IV

c) Cranial nerve VII d) Cranial nerve VIII

218. Wide grimacing mouth and narrowing of palpebral fissure is seen in

a) Botulism b) Tetanus

c) Haemorrhagic septicemia d) None of the above

219. Dysphonia in animals can occur due to lesion in

a) Cranial nerve IV b) Cranial nerve VI

c) Cranial nerve X d) Cranial nerve I

220. Megaoesophagus in animals may occur due to

a) Mysthenia gravis b) Polymyositis

c) Botulism d) All of the above

221. Difficulty or distortion in performing voluntary movements is called)

a) Rigidity b) Tremor

c) Dyskinesia d) Myokymia

222. Continuous involuntary muscle twitching that gives the appearance of worm-like rippling of the muscles

a) Rigidity b) Tremor

c) Dyskinesia d) Myokymia

223. Involuntary contractions or twisting of groups of muscle fibers is called

a) Fasciculation b) Tremor

c) Dyskinesia d) Myokymia

224. Involuntary and forcibly paroxysmal, prolonged and severe contraction of muscles that do not relax is called

a) Spasm b) Cramp

c) Tetany d) Cramp

225. Abnormal muscle tone in animals causing muscle stiffness and persistent contraction due to underlying spontaneous repetitive firing of motor unit potentials is called

a) Myokymia b) Neuromyotonia

c) Axonmetasis d) Eclampsia

226. Intention tremors are most common associated with

a) Cerebellar disease b) Cerebral hemisphere

c) Pons d) Medulla

227. Deviation of neck and head towards one side due to mid and rostral brainstem and cerebral lesions is called

a) Myoclonus b) Opisthotonus

c) Pleurothotonus d) None of the above

228. Inability to support weight or a deficiency in the ability to generate gait is called

a) Paresis b) Plegia

c) Paralysis d) Ataxia

229. Inability to support both pelvic limbs is called
   a) Complete paresis b) Paraparesis
   c) Hemiparesis d) Orthoplegia
230. Absence of generating gait in thoracic and pelvic limbs on one side of the body is called
   a) Complete paresis b) Paraparesis
   c) Hemiparesis d) Orthoplegia
231. Most common type of paresis observed in thoracolumbar herniation
   a) Lower motor neuron paresis b) Upper motor neuron paresis
   c) Peripheral motor neuron paresis d) None of the above
232. Disruption of ascending general proprioceptive tracts resulting in hindered spatial location of muscle tone of limb, trunk and neck cause
   a) General proprioceptive ataxia b) Vestibular ataxia
   c) Cerebellar ataxia d) None of the above
233. Floating type appearance of thoracic limbs is observed in
   a) Vestibular ataxia b) General proprioceptive ataxia
   c) Cerebellar ataxia d) None of the above
234. General proprioceptive ataxia is characterized by
   a) Hypermetria b) Incoordination
   c) Upper motor neuron paresis d) All of the above
235. Dysmetria in animals is characterized by
   a) Cerebellar ataxia b) General proprioceptive ataxia
   c) Vestibular ataxia d) None of the above
236. Acupoint used for treatment of seizures in dogs is located on
   a) Near anal region b) At base of ear
   c) Near thoracolumbar region d) Interdigital space
237. Angle of head tilting while cisternal myelography for easy flow of contrast medium in cisternal myelography is
   a) 10-15 degree b) 20-25 degree
   c) 10-12 degree d) 11-14 degree
238. Instruments for rapid removal of dorsal lamina in dorsal laminectomy is
   a) Gelpi retractors b) Lempert rongeurs
   c) Distractors d) Kerrison rongeur
239. Anti-epileptic properties of acupuncture contribute in hippocamus by
   a) Increasing glycine, taurine and GABA
   b) Decreasing somatostatin, aspartate and glutamine
   c) Both of the above
   d) Increasing somatostatin, aspartate and glutamine

240. Which of the following is referred to as internal winds in traditional Chinese veterinary medicine
 a) Ataxia
 b) Seizure
 c) Coma
 d) Poisoning

241. Application of electric stimulus to alleviate pain by application of needles at specific points is
 a) Diathermy
 b) BAER
 c) Electroacupuncture
 d) None of the above

242. Principle of Electropuncture pain control involves
 a) Stimulation of peripheral sensory afferent nerves
 b) Reducing concentration of substance P
 c) Inhibition of encephalinergic internuncial neurons
 d) All of the above

243. Presence of increased tone preventing forced flexion of the limb by the examiner until it suddenly gives way to complete flexion without resistance is
 a) Clasp-knife reflex
 b) Wheelbarrowing reflex
 c) Limb withdrawl reflex
 d) Crossed extensor reflex

244. Lesion in upper motor neurons results in
 a) Myotonia
 b) Hypertonia
 c) Hypotonia
 d) Atonia

245. Medial strabismus generally occurs due to dysfunction of
 a) Olfactory nerve
 b) Facial nerve
 c) Trigeminal nerve
 d) Abducens nerve

246. Angle of tip of microdissectors for retrieval of disc material in ventral slot procedure
 a) 45°
 b) 90°
 c) 50°
 d) 65°

247. Which of the following techniques can be used to produce active muscle contraction
 a) Electroacupuncture
 b) Neuromuscular electrical stimulation
 c) Ultrasonic diathermy
 d) Low level laser therapy

248. Which of the following techniques has been used in dogs and cats for accelerating wound healing and decreasing pain associated with osteoarthritis
 a) Electroacupuncture
 b) Neuromuscular electrical stimulation
 c) Ultrasonic diathermy
 d) Low level laser therapy

249. Which of the following technique is contraindicated in cancer and infection
 a) Interferential electrical stimulation
 b) Neuromuscular electrical stimulation

c) Ultrasonic diathermy
d) Low level laser therapy

250. Technique of massaging over stroking or gliding over the muscles with the hands is called
a) Effleurage b) Petrissage
c) Friction d) None of the above

251. Technique of kneading action or pressure and release along the entire length of muscle groups is
a) Effleurage b) Petrissage
c) Friction d) None of the above

252. Condition of loss of sympathetic innervation in eye causing enophthalmos, ptosis, elevation of the nictitating membrane, and miosis is called
a) Horner syndrome
b) Optic neuritis
c) Optic disc atrophy
d) Sudden acquired retinal degeneration

253. Testing of medial aspect of nasal mucosa by gently touching it with pen tip or closed hemostats
a) Vestibuloconchlear nerve b) Abducens nerve
c) Trigeminal nerve d) Oculomotor nerve

254. Dysphagia in animals occur due to lesion in
a) Cranial nerve IX and X b) Cranial nerve IV and V
c) Cranial nerve III and IV d) Cranial nerve VI and VII

255. Identification of hyperesthetic region in animals can be done by
a) Wheelbarrowing test b) Cutaneous trunci test
c) Patellar reflex test d) Tibial thrust test

256. Anisocoria in animals occur due to
a) Cranial nerve III b) Cranial nerve II
c) Cranial nerve I d) Cranial nerve VII

257. "Two-engine" gait in animals can be observed due to lesion in
a) Cranial cervical segment b) Thoracolumbar segment
c) Lumbosacral segment d) Cervicothoracic segment

258. Spinal shock in animals is observed due to lesion in
a) C1-C3 b) T3-L3
c) L3-L5 d) T1-T2

259. Clinical signs such as anisocoria, decreased tear secretion and salivation, bradycardia may be seen in
a) Myopathic syndrome b) Motor neuropathic syndrome
c) Sensory neuron myopathy d) Autonomic dysfunction

260. Generalised muscle weakness, exercise intolerance, localized or general muscle atrophy/ hypertrophy with "percussion dimple contracture", megaoesophagus, ventroflexion of head and neck can be seen in
   a) Myopathic syndrome   b) Motor neuropathic syndrome
   c) Sensory neuron myopathy   d) Autonomic dysfunction

261. Paralysis of innervated structures, neurogenic muscle atrophy, reduced/absent reflexes, muscle tone and fasciculations can be seen in
   a) Myopathic syndrome   b) Motor neuropathic syndrome
   c) Sensory neuron myopathy   d) Autonomic dysfunction

262. Decreased pain response (hypalgesia), sensation (hypesthesia), proprioceptive deficits, abnormal sensation/sensitivity (paresthesia) of the face, trunk, or limbs, self-mutilation etc) can be seen in
   a) Myopathic syndrome   b) Motor neuropathic syndrome
   c) Sensory neuron myopathy   d) Autonomic dysfunction

263. Electromyogram signals observed during denervating diseases or myopathies is called
   a) Fibs   b) End plate spikes
   c) Miniature end-plate potentials   d) Insertional activity

264. "Dive bomber" potentials in electromyogram are referred to as
   a) Fibs   b) Miniature end-plate potentials
   c) Myotonic potentials   d) Insertional activity

265. Recording of orthodromic propagation of action potentials along a nerve causing release of acetylcholine at the neuromuscular junction, and myofiber depolarization is called
   a) Fibs   b) M-waves
   c) F-wave   d) Miniature end-plate potentials

266. Values providing information about sensory input to spinal cord as result of depolarization of interneurons in the cervicothoracic and lumbosacral intumescences is called
   a) Cord drum potentials   b) F-wave
   c) Miniature end-plate potentials   d) Fibs

267. Electrical sensation running down the back and into the limbs upon neck flexion is called
   a) F-waves   b) Lhermitte's sign
   c) Myotonic potentials   d) Miniature end-plate potentials

268. Technique for identifying myasthenia gravis and botulism in animals is
   a) Repetitive nerve stimulation   b) BAER
   c) Electromyography   d) MRI

269. During single-fiber electromyography, elicitation of stimulus from latency to consecutive muscle fibers, fluctuations observed are called as
   a) F-waves   b) Myotonic potentials
   c) Jitter   d) Fibs

270. Radiographic examination of spinal cord and other surrounding structures by administration of injection of contrast medium into the subarachnoid space is called
   a) Myelography b) Encephalogram
   c) Encephalomyelogram d) None of the above

271. Which of the following MRI technique can be used for evaluating CSF movement, cranial nerve and inner ear
   a) Diffusion-weighted imaging
   b) Multiecho Gradient Echo—Echoplanar Imaging
   c) Diffusion tensor imaging
   d) Balanced Steady-state Free Precession

272. Most common type of cerebral oedema observed in animals
   a) Cytotoxic b) Vasogenic
   c) Interstitial d) Toxic

273. Ischemic type of cerebral edema can be detected on
   a) Diffusion tensor imaging
   b) Multiecho Gradient Echo—Echoplanar Imaging
   c) Diffusion-weighted imaging
   d) Balanced Steady-state Free Precession

274. Administration of contrast medium into central canal is done to diagnose
   a) Channelopathies b) Syringomelia
   c) Ceroid lipofuscinosis d) Globoid cell leukodystrophy

275. Which of the following statement is true?
   a) Brain is acute dividing tissue
   b) There is no side effect of radiotherapy on nervous system
   c) Radiation dose for neural tumours mass should be given in smaller fractions
   d) Radiation dose for brain tumours should be given in single dose

276. Drugs causing inhibition of P-glycoprotein in brain are
   a) Ketoconazole b) Dopamine
   c) Diltiazem d) Both a and c

277. Which of the following drugs can potentiate the ivermectin toxicity in brain
   a) Ketoconazole b) Dopamine
   c) Enrofloxacin d) Digoxin

278. Treatment of CNS protozoan infection in horses is done by
   a) Pencillins b) Cephalosporins
   c) Pyrimethamine + sulfadiazine d) Cefpodoxime proxetil

279. Which of the following drugs can lead to ataxia in animals
   a) Metronidazole b) Enrofloxacin
   c) Sulphonamides d) Ceftiofur

280. Which of the following anti-fungal drug is administered through intrathecal route

a) Itraconazole b) Amphotericin-B
c) 5-flucytosine d) Fluconazole

281. Which of the following anti-fungal drug can lead to neurotoxicity in cats?

a) Enilconazole b) Posaconazole
c) Voriconazole d) Itraconazole

282. Which of the following drug is commonly used for cryptococcal meningitis orally?

a) Fluconazole b) Itraconazole
c) Voriconazole d) Amphotericin-B

283. Which of the following drug has been used for treatment of myasthenia gravis?

a) Mycophenolate b) Ciclosporin
c) Leflunomide d) Azathioprine

284. Which of the following drugs can be used in patients refractory to other immunosuppressive agents?

a) Leflunomide b) Ciclosporin
c) Azathioprine d) Lemoustin

285. The drug used for treatment of granulomatous meningoencephalomyelitis in dogs

a) Leflunomide b) Ciclosporin
c) Azathioprine d) Lemoustin

286. Treatment of meningoencephalitis of unknown origin in dogs by compound obtained from sponge

a) Leflunomide b) Ciclosporin
c) Cytarabine d) Azathioprine

287. Which of the following antimetabolite anti-cancer drug used for CNS tumours

a) Cyclophosphamide b) Methotrexate
c) Vincristine d) Cis-platin

288. Which of the following drugs has been used for treatment of methotrexate

a) Leukovorin b) Hydroxycarbamide
c) Cytarabine d) Yohimbine

289. Which of the following drugs can be used to treat *Pseudomonas aeuroginosa*?

a) Ceftazidime b) Chloramphenicol
c) Meroprenem d) Clindamycin

290. Which of the following drugs can lead to CNS toxicity in coolie

a) Ivermectin b) Loperamide
c) Diazepam d) Both a and b

291. Removal of part of bony cadaver or space occupying lesion to relieve pressure due to compression of neural tissue is called

a) Decompression b) Fenestration
c) Mass resection d) Spinal stabilization

292. Creation of an opening in the intervertebral disc by removal of a section of the annulus fibrosus to allow the removal of nucleus pulposus
   a) Decompression b) Fenestration
   c) Mass resection d) Spinal stabilization
293. Slot-like opening created ventrally through the intervertebral disc and cranial and caudal vertebrae endplates in the cervical region is called
   a) Ventral slot procedure b) Hemilaminectomy
   c) Foramenotomy d) Deep dorsal laminectomy
294. Best surgical approach for resection of peripheral nerve and spinal cord tumours is
   a) Lateral laminectomy b) Dorsal laminectomy
   c) Ventral slot procedure d) Hemilaminectomy
295. Lesions in disc spaces adjacent to fused disc space after placement of implants i.e. Domino lesions is commonly found in
   a) Chondrodystrophic breeds b) Dobermann
   c) Brachycephalic breeds d) None of the above
296. Subsequent decrease in in proteoglycan content, with consequent dehydration and accumulation of mineral in nucleus of intervertebral disc causing loss of capacity of withstanding pressure is noticed in
   a) Hansen I b) Hansen II
   c) Hansen III d) None of the above
297. Replacement of dehydrated nucleus with fibrinoid tissue causing increase in content of annulus fibrous leading to compression of spinal cord is called
   a) Hansen I b) Hansen II
   c) Hansen III d) None of the above
298. Which of the following drugs can lead to decrease in CSF?
   a) Ketamine b) Mannitol
   c) Fentanyl d) Halothane
299. Which of the following drugs can be used safely in patients with increased CSF?
   a) Enflurane and Corticosteroids b) Furosamide and Ketamine
   c) Isoflurane and fentanyl d) Halothane and mannitol
300. Which of the following technique is better for visualization of the ventral and lateral aspects of spinal cord
   a) Lateral laminectomy b) Dorsal laminectomy
   c) Ventral slot procedure d) Hemilaminectomy
301. Out of the following techniques, which is generally used for exploratory and prolapse disc mass?
   a) Lateral laminectomy
   b) Hemilaminectomy
   c) Ventral slot procedure
   d) Thoracolumbar lateral corpectomy

302. Which of the following technique is used for treatment of lateralized thoracolumbar chronic (type II) disc disease in dogs without manipulation of spinal cord
   a) Lateral laminectomy
   b) Hemilaminectomy
   c) Ventral slot procedure
   d) Thoracolumbar lateral corpectomy

303. Which of the following technique can be used for direct visualization of cauda equina at L7–S1?
   a) Lateral laminectomy
   b) Ventral slot procedure
   c) Dorsal laminectomy
   d) Foramenotomy

304. Which of the following technique can be used for relieving entrapment of L7 nerve root leading to lumbosacral stenosis?
   a) Lateral laminectomy
   b) Foramenotomy
   c) Dorsal laminectomy
   d) Both b and c

305. Which of the following technique can be used for access to olfactory and frontal lobe
   a) Suboccipital craniotomy
   b) Transfrontal craniotomy
   c) Rostrotentorial craniotomy
   d) Caudal fossa craniectomy

306. Lesion involving olfactory and rostro lateral portions of the frontal lobes is done by
   a) Bilateral transfrontal craniotomy
   b) Caudal fossa craniectomy
   c) Rostrotentorial craniotomy
   d) Suboccipital craniotomy

307. Which of the following technique can be used for direct visualization of cerebellomedullary angle, tentorial region and lateral aspect of the cerebellum
   a) Bilateral transfrontal craniotomy
   b) Caudal fossa craniectomy
   c) Bilateral rostrotentorial craniotomy
   d) Suboccipital craniotomy

308. Which of the following technique can be used for lowering of intracranial pressure
   a) Suboccipital craniotomy
   b) Bilateral rostrotentorial craniotomy
   c) Caudal fossa craniectomy
   d) Bilateral transfrontal craniotomy

309. Treatment of syringomyelia in caudal brainstem can be done by
   a) Suboccipital craniotomy
   b) Bilateral rostrotentorial craniotomy
   c) Caudal fossa craniectomy
   d) Bilateral transfrontal craniotomy

310. Which of the following anesthetics can provide neuroprotection in cerebral hypoxia
   a) Ketamine
   b) Propofol
   c) Thiopentone
   d) Xylazine

311. Diffuse axonopathy in German Shephard dogs due to necrosis in lateral and ventral funiculi of the thoracolumbar spinal cord segments (T3-L3) leading to secondary demyelination and astrogliosis and subsequently upper motor neuron paresis and proprioceptive ataxia in the pelvic limb is observed in
   a) Meningomyelitis
   b) Degenerative Myelopathy
   c) Chronic intervertebral disc disease
   d) Infectious meningoencephalomyelitis

312. Degenerative myopathy in Welsh Corgi dogs occur due to mutation in
   a) Superoxide dismutase
   b) Glutathione peroxidase
   c) Carbonic anhydrase
   d) Cytochrome oxidase

313. Sporadic disorder characterized by episodes of profound cervical hyperesthesia, depression and ataxia in animals causing menace deficit, anisocoria, increased erythrocyte sedimentation rate and elevated alpha-2 globulin fraction in animals is observed in
   a) Steroid-responsive meningitis-arteritis
   b) Degenerative Myelopathy
   c) Chronic intervertebral disc disease
   d) Infectious meningoencephalomyelitis

314. Which of the following molecules mediates steroid responsive meningitis arteritis in dogs
   a) CD11
   b) Matrix metalloproteinase
   c) Both of the above
   d) None of the above

315. Angiocentric, nonsuppurative, mixed lymphoid inflammatory process predominantly affecting predominantly the white matter of the brain and spinal cord is observed in
   a) Steroid-responsive meningitis-arteritis
   b) Granulomatous Meningoencephalomyelitis
   c) Chronic intervertebral disc disease
   d) Degenerative Myelopathy

316. During induction and maintenance of anesthesia, electroencephalogram frequency will reveal which type of pattern
   a) Low-voltage, fast-wave pattern
   b) High-voltage, slow-wave pattern
   c) Low-voltage, slow-wave pattern
   d) High- voltage, fast-wave pattern

317. Decrease in beta activity and a concomitant increase in both α and δ activity of electroencephalogram pattern will indicate
   a) Increase in Anaesthetic depth
   b) Decrease in Anaesthetic depth
   c) First increase and then decrease in Anaesthetic depth
   d) First decrease and then decrease in Anaesthetic depth

318. Which of the following is used to measure depth of hypnosis during administration of general anaesthesia

a) Index of consciousness
b) Cerebral state index
c) Narcotrend index
d) Bispectral index

319. The phenomenon of rapid increase in intracranial pressure causing arterial hypertension, slow heart rate, irregular respiration and subsequently brain herniation with compression, unconsciousness and subsequent death is called

a) Stewart-Hamilton phenomenon
b) Starling phenomenon
c) Cushing phenomenon
d) Hering-Breuer phenomenon

320. Which of the following drugs is avoided in anaesthesia of patients having seizures

a) Ketamine
b) Propofol
c) Benzodiazepines
d) Opoids

321. Ischemic necrosis of spinal cord as a result of acute insult due to neuronal anoxia is observed in

a) Menigioencephalitis
b) Meningomalacia
c) Myelitis
d) Intervertebral disc disease

322. Bilateral facial weakness, decreased palpebral reflexes, marked pelvic limb lameness, cervical ventroflexion and megaoesophagus in dogs and cats may be seen in

a) Menigioencephalitis
b) Cerebral hypoxia
c) Myasthenia gravis
d) Meningomalacia

323. Cerebellitis in older dogs may occur due to

a) Trauma
b) Canine distemper
c) Rabies
d) Toxoplasmosis with neosporosis

324. Bacterial or fungal infection of intervertebral disc causing inflammatory changes leading to paralysis, febrile, anorexia in dogs is

a) Discospondylitis
b) Spondylosis
c) Osteomyelitis
d) Meningoencephalitis

325. Surgical diversion of Cerebrospinal fluid from intracranial to extracranial site is done for management of

a) Cerebral oedema
b) Hydrocephalus
c) Meningitis
d) None of the above

326. Placement of ventriculoperitoneal shunt for management of hydrocephalus is done in

a) Lateral ventricle
b) Corpus callosum
c) Lumbosacral region
d) Cisterna magna

327. Spinal nerve root disease of segments C6-T2 result in

a) Monoparesis
b) Hemiplegia
c) Paraplegia
d) Paresis

328. Reduced stride length of thoracic limb followed by increased stride length of pelvic limbs resulting in "two-engine gait "occur due to lesion in

a) C1-C5 b) C1-C3

c) C5-T11 d) C6-T2

329. Loss of deep pain perception in dogs may occur due to damage of

a) Motor neurons of phrenic nerve b) C5-C7 spinal segments

c) Both a and b d) None of the above

330. "Root-signature" position in animals may occur due to lesion in

a) C1-C5 b) C1-C3

c) C5-T11 d) C6-T2

331. Process of reconstruction of denervated nerve by using nerve graft or reconstruction of nerve is called

a) Neurotization b) Neurorrhaphy

c) Neurectomy d) None of the above

332. Which of the following drugs cause marked increase in intracranial pressure

a) Ketamine b) Desflurane

c) Halothane d) All of the above

333. Type of injury caused by intervertebral disc disease is

a) Contusion b) Ischaemia

c) Compression d) Both a and c

334. Removal of extruded disc material by removing caudal aspect of cranial vertebral body without removal of large portion of annulus fibrosus is observed in

a) Slanted Ventral Slot Procedure b) Dorsal laminectomy

c) Ventral slot d) Hemilaminectomy

335. Disease of cervical spine commonly seen in large breeds of dog due to stenosed vertebral canal, torsion of caudal vertebral spine and large volume disc is commonly observed in

a) Spondylosis b) Wobbler syndrome

c) Intervertebral disc disease d) Discospondylitis

336. Stressed myelography is normally employed for diagnosis of

a) Spondylosis b) Discospondylitis

c) Wobbler syndrome d) Intervertebral disc disease

337. Effective procedure for treatment of restoring perfusion in dogs is

a) Durotomy b) Neurectomy

c) Ventricular shunt placement d) None of the above

338. Inverted cone technique is generally used for treatment of

a) Intervertebral disc disease b) Spondylosis

c) Wobbler syndrome d) None of the above

339. Modified Glasgow comma scale is used for scoring of
   a) Brain injury b) Spinal cord injury
   c) Orthopaedic injuries d) None of the above

340. Technique of removal of dorsal spinous process, laminae, articular processes, and approximately half of the pedicles of a vertebra to gain access to the spinal canal is known as
   a) Funkquist A b) Funkquist B
   c) Ventral slot d) None of the above

341. Technique of removal of dorsal spinous process and laminae by keeping articular processes intact is known as
   a) Funkquist A b) Funkquist B
   c) Ventral slot d) None of the above

342. Failure of vertebral segment during development is known as
   a) Block Vertebra b) Hemivertebra
   c) Butterfly Vertebra d) Spina bifida

343. Incompletely formed vertebrae during development is known as
   a) Block Vertebra b) Hemivertebra
   c) Butterfly Vertebra d) Spina bifida

344. Sagittal cleft with in vertebral body giving appearance like butterfly on radiograph
   a) Block Vertebra b) Hemivertebra
   c) Butterfly Vertebra d) Spina bifida

345. Failure of lamina of vertebrae to fuse dorsally is known as
   a) Block Vertebra b) Hemivertebra
   c) Butterfly Vertebra d) Spina bifida

346. Herniation of meninges and spinal cord through bony defect
   a) Meningocele b) Meningomyelocele
   c) Cerebrocele d) None of the above

347. Incomplete separation of neuroectoderm from ectodermal tissue due to entrapment of viable ectodermal in central nervous system is known as (
   a) Cholesteatoma b) Osteochondromatosis
   c) Pseudocysts d) None of the above

348. Condition of vertebral column causing mineralization of soft tissue
   a) Pseudocysts b) Tumor calcinosis
   c) Calcium circumscripta d) Both b and c

349. Degenerative, non-inflammatory condition of vertebral cartilage in dogs causing formation of osteophytes is known as
   a) Pseudocysts b) Spondylosis deformans
   c) Discospondylitis d) Cauda equina syndrome

350. Neurological condition characterized by myokymia, persistent muscle contraction, cramp or impaired muscle relaxation in animals is known as
   a) Ataxia b) Dyskinesia
   c) Neuromyotonia d) None of the above

351. Back press test is done for diagnosis of which condition
   a) Cauda equina b) Intervertebral disc disease
   c) Wobbler syndrome d) Calcinosis circumscripta

Answer Key

1	a	2	d	3	c	4	a	5	c	6	b	7	c
8	c	9	c	10	b	11	a	12	d	13	b	14	d
15	c	16	c	17	b	18	a	19	d	20	c	21	c
22	d	23	b	24	d	25	b	26	a	27	a	28	b
29	a	30	a	31	d	32	c	33	d	34	b	35	a
36	c	37	b	38	c	39	d	40	a	41	b	42	c
43	a	44	d	45	a	46	c	47	d	48	b	49	b
50	d	51	d	52	a	53	d	54	a	55	b	56	b
57	d	58	b	59	d	60	a	61	c	62	b	63	a
64	c	65	a	66	b	67	c	68	d	69	a	70	c
71	a	72	b	73	c	74	d	75	b	76	c	77	b
78	a	79	d	80	d	81	b	82	d	83	a	84	b
85	d	86	c	87	a	88	a	89	a	90	b	91	a
92	a	93	c	94	a	95	a	96	b	97	d	98	c
99	b	100	d	101	a	102	b	103	a	104	a	105	a
106	a	107	c	108	d	109	b	110	a	111	a	112	d
113	c	114	c	115	c	116	b	117	c	118	a	119	d
120	c	121	a	122	c	123	a	124	c	125	a	126	b
127	a	128	b	129	a	130	b	131	c	132	b	133	c
134	d	135	a	136	c	137	a	138	d	139	c	140	b
141	d	142	a	143	c	144	c	145	c	146	a	147	c
148	b	149	d	150	a	151	a	152	b	153	d	154	a
155	d	156	c	157	b	158	b	159	a	160	b	161	d
162	c	163	a	164	c	165	d	166	a	167	c	168	a
169	c	170	a	171	b	172	d	173	b	174	d	175	a
176	b	177	c	178	b	179	d	180	a	181	b	182	a
183	c	184	a	185	d	186	a	187	d	188	a	189	c
190	c	191	a	192	a	193	b	194	c	195	a	196	c
197	b	198	c	199	a	200	b	201	a	202	c	203	b
204	d	205	c	206	a	207	c	208	b	209	d	210	d

211	b	212	d	213	c	214	b	215	d	216	a	217	a
218	b	219	c	220	d	221	c	222	d	223	b	224	d
225	b	226	a	227	c	228	a	229	b	230	c	231	b
232	a	233	b	234	d	235	a	236	b	237	a	238	d
239	c	240	b	241	c	242	d	243	a	244	b	245	d
246	b	247	b	248	d	249	a	250	a	251	b	252	a
253	c	254	a	255	b	256	a	257	d	258	b	259	d
260	a	261	b	262	c	263	a	264	c	265	b	266	a
267	b	268	a	269	c	270	a	271	b	272	b	273	c
274	b	275	c	276	d	277	a	278	c	279	a	280	b
281	c	282	a	283	d	284	a	285	d	286	c	287	b
288	a	289	a	290	d	291	a	292	b	293	a	294	a
295	b	296	a	297	b	298	b	299	c	300	d	301	b
302	d	303	c	304	d	305	b	306	a	307	c	308	b
309	a	310	c	311	b	312	a	313	a	314	c	315	b
316	b	317	a	318	b	319	c	320	d	321	b	322	c
323	d	324	a	325	b	326	a	327	a	328	d	329	c
330	d	331	a	332	d	333	d	334	a	335	b	336	c
337	a	338	c	339	a	340	a	341	b	342	a	343	b
344	c	345	d	346	b	347	a	348	d	349	b	350	b
351	a												

12

Clinical Physiology of Cardiovascular Disorders

Bhavanam Sudhakara Reddy, Sirigireddy Sivajothi Kambala Swetha and Dadireddy Narmada Raghavi

*College of Veterinary Science - Proddatur, Sri Venkateswara Veterinary University Andhra Pradesh**

Introduction

Heart failure can develop as a complication of almost all congenital and acquired cardiac diseases in dogs and cats. Cardiac disease is a significant global health concern, impacting both humans and domestic animals, particularly dogs. In the animal kingdom, the cardiovascular system consists of essential components, including the heart, veins, arteries, and capillary beds. Its proper function depends on complex mechanisms, such as the atrioventricular valves (mitral and tricuspid) and the semilunar valves (aortic and pulmonic), which ensure that blood flows in only one direction through the heart. The activity of the cardiovascular system, including heart contraction rates and strengths, as well as blood vessel diameter adjustments, is regulated by the autonomic nervous system (both sympathetic and parasympathetic branches) and various hormones.

The strength of ventricular contractions is influenced by several factors, primarily end-diastolic volume (preload) and myocardial contractility (inotropy). Preload is the amount of blood in the ventricles just before they contract, while contractility refers to the ability of the heart muscle fibers to contract. Preload is determined by the difference between the end-diastolic pressure in the ventricle and the pressure in the pleural space, adjusted for the stiffness of the ventricular myocardium. This pressure is influenced by the ratio of blood volume to the heart muscle's compliance. Low-pressure volume receptors in the heart and large veins primarily regulate preload. When these receptors detect increased blood volume or vein distension, they trigger responses such as increased urine production and vein dilation, which help reduce blood volume and lower venous pressures. Increased end-diastolic volume (preload) stretches the ventricular wall, enhancing contraction strength through the Frank-Starling mechanism, or Starling's law of the heart. This stretching activates receptors in the atria and ventricles, leading to the release of natriuretic peptides like brain natriuretic peptide (BNP) from the ventricles and atrial natriuretic peptide (ANP) from the atria) These peptides promote natriuresis, relax smooth muscle, and counteract vasopressin and angiotensin II. In dogs, levels of BNP and NT-proBNP are directly related to cardiac stretch. Myocardial contractility depends on the availability of ATP and calcium, which facilitate myosin-actin interactions. ATP production is partly regulated by norepinephrine binding to myocardial beta1-adrenergic receptors. In heart failure, there is often a decrease in myocardial beta1-receptors, impacting contractility. Conditions that increase afterload (e.g., pulmonary valve stenosis, subaortic stenosis, systemic or pulmonary hypertension) or preload (e.g., mitral valve insufficiency, left-to-right shunting defects, dilated cardiomyopathy) can elevate myocardial tension. When stenotic lesions are absent, afterload is influenced by arterial stiffness and arteriolar constriction. Vascular smooth muscle tone, which affects afterload, is modulated by various substances: constrictors such as adrenergic agonists, angiotensin II, vasopressin, and endothelin, and relaxants like norepinephrine, atriopeptin, bradykinin, adenosine, and nitric oxide. Increased afterload is common in heart failure and often requires therapeutic measures to reduce it. Most of the resistance to blood flow, or vascular resistance, comes from arteriolar constriction, with additional resistance from the stiffness of large arteries closest to the ventricles, known as impedance. Impedance includes external factors that oppose left ventricular ejection and is closely related to afterload. During systole, the ventricles eject blood into the proximal great arteries, which expand to accommodate the volume. During diastole, these arteries recoil to help maintain continuous blood flow through the arterioles into the capillaries. The aortic and pulmonic valves prevent the backflow of blood into the ventricles. Systemic vascular resistance is the resistance encountered as blood moves through the peripheral circulation and is calculated as the difference between mean arterial pressure and central venous pressure, divided by cardiac output. Right atrial pressure can substitute for central venous pressure in this calculation. Similarly, pulmonary vascular resistance is determined by the difference between mean pulmonary artery pressure and pulmonary arterial wedge pressure, divided by cardiac output, with left atrial pressure used instead of pulmonary arterial wedge pressure if needed. Increased pulmonary vascular resistance can occur with conditions like pulmonary vascular obstruction or pulmonary hypertension.

A key feature of heart failure is the elevated resistance of arterial, arteriolar, and venous smooth muscle due to increased levels of angiotensin II, vasopressin, and endothelin. Since heart failure often impairs the left ventricle's ability to expel a normal stroke volume, reducing vascular resistance through arterial vasodilation becomes a crucial therapeutic goal. In heart failure and cardiomyopathy, improper calcium handling can lead to arrhythmias and contribute to decreased contractile force and impaired relaxation, affecting both systolic and diastolic functions. Cardiac output is essential for delivering oxygenated blood to organs through the systemic (left ventricular) or pulmonary (right ventricular) arteries, which is vital for maintaining proper organ function. Normal cardiac output ranges from 100–200 mL/kg/min in dogs and approximately 120 mL/kg/min in cats.

Abnormalities in the cardiovascular system can arise from several mechanisms: 1. Valvular Disease: The heart valves may not close or open properly. 2. Myocardial Disease: The heart muscle may pump inefficiently or fail to relax adequately. 3. Arrhythmia: The heart may beat too slowly, too quickly, or irregularly. 4. Vascular Disease: The systemic blood vessels may impede blood flow excessively. 5. Cardiac Shunts: Abnormal connections between the heart's left and right sides or between the systemic and pulmonary circulations. 6. Volume Imbalance: Too little or too much blood relative to the vessels' capacity. 7. Parasitic Infections: Such as heartworm disease affecting the cardiovascular system.

Cardiac diseases in animals are classified as either congenital defects or acquired conditions. Notable examples include: 1. Degenerative Mitral Valve Disease: Leading to mitral regurgitation, especially common in dogs. 2. Hypertrophic Cardiomyopathy (HCM): Frequently seen in cats. 3. Dilated Cardiomyopathy (DCM): Affects dogs.

Congestive heart failure (CHF) occurs when the left side of the heart cannot pump enough blood to meet the body's needs, no matter what activity level is required. This condition is marked by symptoms resulting from both insufficient blood flow and fluid buildup in various organs. As the heart's ability to pump blood weakens, it becomes increasingly difficult to supply adequate blood to the kidneys and muscles, even during light physical activities that cause only small increases in energy demands. When the heart fails, the body tries to compensate through various systems, including the heart itself, the kidneys, the central nervous system, and the peripheral blood vessels. These systems respond to heart failure with neurohumoral and endocrine signals. While these responses are meant to compensate for the reduced cardiac function, they can sometimes worsen the condition by increasing the heart's workload and creating a harmful cycle of neuroendocrine activation. As renal function declines, the renin-angiotensin-aldosterone system (RAAS) is activated, which further deteriorates heart function. Elevated levels of certain hormones, such as norepinephrine, RAAS components, endothelins, and arginine vasopressin, lead to increased blood vessel constriction, which exacerbates heart failure. High levels of catecholamines, for example, not only increase the heart's oxygen demand but also can trigger arrhythmias and are linked to worse outcomes in patients with CHF. The actions of neuroendocrine systems in heart failure are counterbalanced by vasodilators, diuretics, and natriuretic factors, such as natriuretic peptides and nitric oxide (NO). Elevated levels of atrial natriuretic peptide (ANP) are observed in various cardiac disorders, even in asymptomatic dogs. It is believed that increased ANP activity may help counteract the effects of the renin-angiotensin-aldosterone system (RAAS) in these cases. Symptomatic dogs treated with angiotensin-converting enzyme (ACE) inhibitors, along with standard therapy, show reduced mortality rates, highlighting that changes in the neuroendocrine profile not only reflect the severity of heart failure but can also exacerbate it. Currently, measuring these hormones helps in studying heart disease pathophysiology and, to some extent, assessing treatment success, as seen with aldosterone. However, natriuretic peptides, such as B-type natriuretic peptide (BNP) and atrial natriuretic peptide (ANP), are becoming increasingly valuable as diagnostic tools for heart disease and indicators of heart failure severity.

Write correct alphabet of the answer in the given bracket

1. Nical sign of inadequate blood supply to the tissues in dogs
   - a) Peripheral vasoconstriction
   - b) Exercise intolerance
   - c) Syncope
   - d) All the above
2. Clinical sign associated with raised filling pressure
   - a) Cough
   - b) Dyspnea
   - c) Ascites
   - d) All the above
3. Principle sign of left sided heart failure is
   - a) Pulmonary edema
   - b) Generalized edema
   - c) Limb edem
   - d) All the above
4. Increased left atrial pressure results in
   - a) Pulmonary venous congestion
   - b) Pulmonary edema
   - c) Both a & b
   - d) None of the above

5. Signs in right side heart failure
   a) Ascites b) Pleural effusions
   c) Distended jugular vein d) All the above
6. Signs in chronic congestive failure
   a) Cachexia b) Fluid build up
   c) Shortness of breath d) All the above
7. Cardiac cachexia due to
   a) Poor tissue perfusion b) Cellular hypoxia
   c) Malabsorption d) All the above
8. Specific mucous membrane changes in dogs with CHF
   a) Pallor b) Cyanosis
   c) Prolonged CRT d) All the above
9. Positive hepatojugular reflex indicative of
   a) Increase right side atrial pressure b) Increase left side atrial pressure
   c) Increase left side atrial pressure d) Increase left ventricular pressure
10. Left side location of apex beat palpation in dogs
   a) 5th ICS b) 4th ICS
   c) 6th ICS d) 7^{h} ICS
11. Precordial thrill because of
   a) Effusions b) Murmurs
   c) Both a & b d) None of the above
12. S1 heart sound associated with
   a) Closure of AV valves
   b) Closures of semilunar valves
   c) Rapid ventricular filling in early diastole
   d) Blood flowing rapidly in to ventricles
13. S4 heart sound associated with
   a) Rapid ventricular filling in early diastole
   b) Closures of semilunar valves
   c) Blood flowing rapidly in to ventricles
   d) Closure of AV valves
14. S3 heart sound associated with
   a) Rapid ventricular filling in early diastole
   b) Blood flowing rapidly in to ventricles
   c) Closure of AV valves
   d) Closures of semilunar valves
15. S2 heart sound associated with
   a) Closure of AV valves
   b) Blood flowing rapidly in to ventricles

c) Closures of semilunar valves
d) Rapid ventricular filling in early diastole

16. Gallop sounds noticed in dogs are
a) S1, S2 b) S3, S4
c) Both a & b d) None of the above

17. Fusion of S3, S4 noticed in
a) Dogs b) Cats
c) Both a &b d) None of the above

18. Cardiac murmurs noticed in
a) Alteration in blood flow b) Tachycardia
c) Bradycardia d) None

19. Location of pulmonic valve to hear normal heart sounds in dogs
a) Left 2nd -4th ICS b) Left 4th ICS
c) Left 5th ICS d) Right 3-5th ICS

20. Location of aortic valve to hear normal heart sounds in dogs
a) Left 5th ICS b) Right 3-5th ICS
c) Left 4th ICS d) Left 2nd -4th ICS

21. Location of mitral valve to hear normal heart sounds in dogs
a) Left 4th ICS b) Left 2nd -4th IC
c) Right 3-5th ICS d) Left 5th ICS

22. Location of tricuspid valve to hear normal heart sounds in dogs
a) Right 3-5th ICS b) Left 4th ICS
c) Left 5th ICS d) Left 2nd -4th ICS

23. Which type of murmurs commonly seen in dogs
a) Diastolic b) Systolic
c) Both a &b d) None of the above

24. Grade 2 murmur can be assessed by
a) Soft murmur
b) Murmur intensity equal to heart sounds
c) Murmur intensity louder than heart sounds
d) Louder murmur with precordial thrill

25. Grade 4 murmur can be assessed by
a) Louder murmur with precordial thrill
b) Murmur intensity louder than heart sounds
c) Murmur intensity equal to heart sounds
d) Very loud murmur heard away from heart

26. Grade 3 murmur can be assessed by
a) Murmur intensity louder than heart sounds
b) Louder murmur with precordial thrill

c) Very loud murmur heard away from heart
d) Murmur intensity equal to heart sounds

27. Grade 5 murmur can be assessed by
a) Very loud murmur heard away from heart
b) Murmur intensity equal to heart sounds
c) Murmur intensity louder than heart sounds
d) Louder murmur with precordial thrill

28. Grade 6 murmur can be assessed by
a) Louder murmur with precordial thrill
b) Murmur intensity louder than heart sounds
c) Very loud murmur heard away from heart
d) Murmur intensity equal to heart sounds

29. Most objective measurement of heart size in dogs
a) VHS b) Radiography
c) Electrocardiography d) All the above

30. VHS normal level in dogs
a) 6 to 8 b) 8 to 10.5
c) 11 to 12 d) 11-14

31. Teratology of Fallot leads to
a) Right side cardiomyopathy b) Left side cardiomyopathy
c) Both a & b d) None of the above

32. Cor pulmonale leads to
a) Left side cardiomyopathy b) Right side cardiomyopathy
c) CHF d) All the above

33. Heartworm disease leads to
a) Right sided cardiomyopathy b) Left sided cardiomyopathy
c) Both a & b d) None of the above

34. Etiology of left side cardiomyopathy is
a) Valvular disease b) DCM
c) HCM d) All the above

35. Enlargement of caudal vena cava noticed in
a) Pericarditis b) Right sided heart failure
c) Left sided heart failure d) Both b and c

36. PDA more commonly noticed in
a) Males b) Females
c) No sex discrimination d) Both a & b

37. Continuous machinery murmur noticed in
a) Teratology of Fallot b) Hydropericardium
c) PDA d) All the above

38. Pulmonic stenosis leads to
   a) Left ventricular hypertrophy   b) Right ventricular hypertrophy
   c) Left atrium hypertrophy   d) Right atrium hypertrophy
39. Aortic stenosis leads to
   a) Concentric Left ventricular hypertrophy
   b) Concentric Right ventricular hypertrophy
   c) Both a & b
   d) None of the above
40. Cardiac abnormalities in cats
   a) Hypertrophic cardiomyopathy   b) Restrictive cardiomyopathy
   c) Dilated cardiomyopathy   d) All the above
41. Signs in cats with hypertrophic cardiomyopathy
   a) Paresis   b) Dyspnea
   c) Tachycardia   d) All the above
42. Round heart disease is seen in which season
   a) Winter   b) Summer
   c) Rainy   d) All the above
43. Clinical examination of cat with hypertrophic cardiomyopathy
   a) Pulmonary crackles   b) Gallop sounds
   c) SORT systolic murmurs   d) All of the above
44. Hypertrophic cardiomyopathy in cats characterized by
   a) Increase left ventricular wall   b) Increase ventricular septum
   c) Left ventricular outflow obstruction   d) All the above
45. Hypertrophic cardiomyopathy in cats characterized by
   a) Concentric hypertrophy   b) Dilated chambers
   c) Regurgitation   d) Fatty degeneration
46. DV projection reveals hypertrophic cardiomyopathy in cats as
   a) Round shape   b) Triangle shape
   c) Valentine shape   d) None of the above
47. Hypertrophic cardiomyopathy in cats characterized by
   a) Increase in FS   b) Decrease in FS
   c) Normal FS   d) None of the above
48. Calcium channel blockers used to treat arrythmias are
   a) Digoxin   b) Diltiazem
   c) Sotalol   d) Propranolol
49. Beta – adrenergic blockers used to treat arrhythmias
   a) Diltiazem   b) Digoxin
   c) Sotalol   d) Propranolol

50. Feline dilated cardiomyopathy is due to
    a) Taurine deficiency b) Cobalt deficiency
    c) Pericarditis d) Endocarditis
51. Cats with DCM characterized by
    a) No ascites b) Taurine deficiency
    c) Both a & b d) None of the above
52. Peritoneopericardial diaphragmatic hernia (PPDH)
    a) Congenital b) Acquired
    c) Idiopathic d) None
53. Benign pericardial cyst leads to
    a) Teratology of Fallot b) Cardiac tamponade
    c) Aortic stenosis d) None of the above
54. Pericardial effusions caused by
    a) Coccidiosis b) Aspergillosis
    c) Foreign body penetration d) All the above
55. Most common cause of pericardial effusion in dogs
    a) Lymphoma b) Hemangiosarcoma
    c) Fibrosarcoma d) All the above
56. Cardiac tamponade results in
    a) Decrease cardiac output
    b) Elevation of ventricular diastolic pressure
    c) Pulsus paradoxus
    d) All the above
57. Pericardial effusion cannot cause----- in dogs
    a) Increase in sympathetic tone b) Activation of RAAS system
    c) Increased filling pressure d) Activation of ANP
58. Radiographic appearance of pericardial effusion in dogs
    a) Enlarged and global cardiac silhouette b) Tracheal elevation
    c) Widening caudal vena cava d) All the above
59. Low voltage QRS complex indicative of
    a) RAE b) Pericardial effusion
    c) LAE d) All the above
60. Swinging motion of heart within the fluid is noticed in
    a) Endocarditis b) Ascites
    c) Pericardial effusions d) DCM
61. Inversion of right atrial free wall indicative of
    a) Decrease intrapericardial pressure b) Increase intrapericardial pressure
    c) Both a & b d) None of the above

62. Recurrent tamponade leads to
   a) Constrictive pericarditis b) Destructive pericarditis
   c) Endocarditis d) Valvular disease
63. Treatment option for idiopathic pericardial effusions
   a) Diuretics b) Glucocorticoids
   c) Both a & b d) Pericardiectomy
64. Causes for muffled heart sounds
   a) Pleural effusions b) Thoracic mass
   c) Diaphragmatic hernia d) All the above
65. Causes of low voltage QRS complex
   a) Pleural effusions b) Obesity
   c) Hypothyroidism d) All the above
66. Causes of prominent enlargement at cardiac silhouette on radiography
   a) DCM b) Tricuspid dysplasia
   c) Pericarditis d) All the above
67. Effusive constrictive pericarditis is
   a) Idiopathic b) Metallic FB
   c) Actinomycosis d) All the above
68. Effusive constrictive pericarditis leads to
   a) Signs at right sided CHF b) Signs at left sided CHF
   c) Exercise intolerance d) None
69. Infective stage of *D.immitis* in dogs
   a) L1 b) L2
   c) L3 d) L5
70. Most pathogenic stage of *D.immitis* is
   a) L1 b) L2
   c) L3 d) L5
71. *D.immitis* can cause---in dogs
   a) Cor pulmonale b) Pericarditis
   c) Endocarditis d) All the above
72. Cor pulmonale is consequences of the
   a) Activity pattern of dog b) Number of worm burden
   c) Both a& b d) None of the above
73. Pulmonary hypertension due to *D.immitis*
   a) Embolization b) Obstruction
   c) Both a& b d) None of the above
74. Reverse D shape heart on the ventro dorsal view indicative of
   a) Right heart hypertrophy b) Left heart hypertrophy
   c) Pericarditis d) All the above

75. Nutritional deficiency which are responsible for canine cardiomyopathy
    a) Carnitine b) Taurine
    c) Both a& b d) Vit-D
76. Secondary cardiomyopathy results from
    a) Volume overload b) Valvular diseases
    c) Left to right shunt d) All the above
77. Most commonly DCM leads to
    a) Systolic dysfunction b) Diastolic dysfunction
    c) Normal function d) None of the above
78. Most commonly HCM leads to
    a) Systolic dysfunction b) Normal function
    c) Diastolic dysfunction d) None of the above
79. Which are the cause of the atherosclerosis
    a) High blood cholesterol b) High lipid content
    c) Ageing process d) All of the above
80. Arrhythmogenic right ventricular cardiomyopathy seen in
    a) Boxer b) Beagle
    c) Pug d) Bull dogs
81. Fibrofatty replacement of cardiomyocytes of ventricles leads to
    a) VD b) DCM
    c) HCM d) ARVC
82. DCM noted more commonly in
    a) Spitz b) Doberman
    c) Boxers d) Dalmatian
83. Cardiomyopathy affecting
    a) Decreased SV b) Activation of RAAS
    c) Increased sympathetic tone d) All the above
84. Increased diastolic pressure on left side results in
    a) Pulmonary edema b) Ascites
    c) Pleural effusions d) All the above
85. Increased diastolic pressure on right side results in
    a) Pulmonary edema b) Ascites
    c) Pleural effusions d) All the above
86. Mechanical dysfunction of heart is known as
    a) Heart failure b) Heart attack
    c) Cardiac arrest d) None of the above
87. Electrical dysfunction of heart
    a) Coughing b) Syncope
    c) Exercise intolerance d) Both a & b

88. Signs in low cardiac output
    a) Exercise intolerance b) Weakness
    c) Cold extremities d) All the above
89. Signs in end stage disease
    a) Hypotension b) Shock
    c) Multiple organ dysfunction d) All the above
90. Valvular regurgitation more commonly seen in
    a) Toy breeds b) Giant breeds
    c) Deep chested breeds d) None of the above
91. Hallmark findings of DCM
    a) Reduced systolic function b) Ventricular enlargement
    c) Both a& b d) None of the above
92. Identification of echo cardiogenic evidence of DCM in asymptomatic dogs is
    a) Occult DCM b) Symptomatic DCM
    c) Asymptomatic DCM d) All the above
93. Treatment of heart failure
    a) Diuretics b) ACE inhibitors
    c) Steroids d) Both a& b
94. Choice of diuretics for refractory heart failure
    a) Thiazide b) Furosemide
    c) Mannitol d) All the above
95. Nutritional supplement required for management of heart failure
    a) Taurine b) Carnitine
    c) Co enzyme Q d) All the above
96. Vasodilation achieved by
    a) Nitroglycerine b) Hydralazine
    c) Sodium nitroprusside d) All the above
97. Inotropic agents are
    a) Digoxin b) Dobutamine
    c) Pimobendan d) All the above
98. Diseases causing concentric hypertrophy
    a) Hyperthyroidism b) Aortic stenosis
    c) Hypertension d) All the above
99. Diastolic dysfunction determined by
    a) X ray b) Tissue doppler imaging
    c) B -mode d) Color flow
100. Diastolic dysfunction noticed by
    a) Delayed relaxation pattern at mitral inflow velocity
    b) Restrictive pattern at mitral inflow velocity

c) Both a & b
d) None of the above

101. Parasitic aneurysm is mainly caused by
 a) *Dioctophyma renale* b) *Strongylus vulgaris*
 c) *Dictyocalus* d) *Ascarid*

102. Parasitic aneurysm in anterior mesenteric artery leads to
 a) Bloat b) Acid indigestion
 c) Colic d) Acute kidney failure

103. Inflammation of the veins is known as
 a) Salpingitis b) Mastitis
 c) Phlebitis d) Atherosclerosis

104. Patent ductus arteriosus is common in
 a) Dogs b) Cat
 c) Cattle d) Horses

105. Atrial septal defect could be failure of closure of the
 a) Foramen ovale b) Ductus arteriosus
 c) Interventricular foramen d) None

106. Atrial septal defect is common in
 a) Cat b) Dog
 c) Cattle d) Horse

107. Which of the conditions are produced by atrial septal defect
 a) Cardiac failure b) Pulmonary hypertension
 c) Cyanosis d) All the above

108. Tetralogy of Fallot" is reported as an inherited disease in
 a) Cat b) Cattle
 c) Dog d) Horse

109. _____is narrowing of the passage or orifice, and is usually formed by fusion of the Causes
 a) Stenosis b) Transposition
 c) CHF d) None of the above

110. Subaortic stenosis is most commonly seen in
 a) Pigs b) Dogs
 c) Cats d) Both a& b

111. Mitral dysplasia is common in
 a) Cats b) Dogs
 c) Cattle d) Both a & b

112. Endocardial fibroelastosis is common in
 a) Dogs b) Cats
 c) Cattle d) Horses

113. Mulberry heart disease is associated with ________deficiency
  a) Vit-E b) Vit-C
  c) Vit-A d) Vit-D

114. ________is the inability of the heart to maintain adequate circulation
  a) Cardiac tamponade b) Cardiac arrest
  c) Cardiac failure d) CHF

115. In acute cardiac failure, which chamber is commonly affected
  a) Right atrium b) Right ventricle
  c) Left atrium d) Left ventricle

116. Liver shows nut –mug appearance in which sided heart failure
  a) Left sided b) Right sided
  c) Both a & b d) None of the above

117. Portocaval shunt results in nervous system syndrome known as _____
  a) Epilepsy b) Hepatic encephalopathy
  c) Canine distemper d) Meningitis

118. Animals with phlebitis complicated by thrombosis hare the risk of
  a) Septic embolism b) Endocarditis
  c) Pulmonary abscess d) All the above

119. Dilation of lymph vessels is known as
  a) Lymphedema b) Lymphadenitis
  c) Lymphangiectasis d) None

120. Secondary cardiomyopathies is caused by
  a) Systemic hypertension b) Endocrine disorders
  c) Hereditary d) All the above

121. _____ is the occlusion of arteries by lodgment of foreign material, such as broken fragment of thrombi
  a) Thrombosis b) Embolism
  c) Atresia d) Aneurysm

122. Embolism is caused by ______ in to the pulmonary circulation
  a) *Dioctophyma renale* b) *Dirofilaria immitis*
  c) *Fasciola hepatic* d) Fasciolopsis

123. Embolism is cause by *Dirofilaria immitis* in pulmonary circulation in ______
  a) Cattle b) Horse
  c) Dog d) Cat

124. Bred and butter appearance of heart is known as
  a) Rouhgy heart b) Shaggy heart
  c) Cor pulmonale d) Cor bovinum

125. Pericarditis is seen in this condition
   a) Pasteurellosis
   b) Contagious bovine pleuropneumonia
   c) black quarter
   d) All the above

126. Which breed is susceptible to idiopathic myocarditis
   a) Labrador
   b) Boxer
   c) Germen shepherd
   d) Pug

127. Which breed is prone to stenosis of bundle of his
   a) Pugs
   b) Boxer
   c) Germen Shepherd
   d) Labrador

128. Which breeds are more prone to patent ductus arteriosus
   a) Pugs
   b) Boxer
   c) Poodles
   d) Labrador

129. Gas within pericardium due to bacterial infection will emit tympanic sound on percussion. This condition is termed as
   a) Pneumo-pericardium
   b) Hydropericardium
   c) Hemopericardium
   d) None

130. Atrial standstill is also termed as
   a) Silent atrium
   b) Silent ventricle
   c) Atrial flutter
   d) All the above

131. Which is a rapid and pre fibrillatory stage of ventricular tachycardia
   a) Ventricular flutter
   b) Ventricular fibrillation
   c) Both a & b
   d) None

132. Which is the force acting to strength the ventricular fibers at the end of diastole and to determine the maximal resting length of the sarcomeres
   a) After load
   b) Pre load
   c) A and B
   d) None

133. What is the change in the hearts ability to do work when the preload, after load and heart rate are kept constant
   a) Contractility
   b) Diastole
   c) Relaxation
   d) No change

134. Which is the index for the after load?
   a) Systole
   b) Diastole
   c) End-systolic wall stress
   d) End- diastolic wall stress

135. Increase in the preload leads to
   a) Decrease in contractibility
   b) Increase in contractibility
   c) No change
   d) May increase / decrease

136. Which is the biochemical leakage markers of cardiac disease?
   a) Epinephrine
   b) Renin
   c) C-reactive protein
   d) Cardiac troponin I

137. The presence of a pre cordial thrill defines the most intense _______
   a) Cardiomegaly
   b) Cardiac murmur
   c) A and B
   d) None
138. Which of the possibilities does not suggest, when an ECG indicating a right ward shift in the mean electrical axis
   a) Pulmonic stenosis
   b) Tricuspid valve dysplasia
   c) Tetralogy of Fallot
   d) Sub aortic stenosis
139. Which of the possibility suggest, when an ECG indicating a left word /left sided shift
   a) Mitral dysplasia
   b) Pulmonic stenosis
   c) Tetralogy of Fallot
   d) Tricuspid valve dysplasia
140. Which is typical for patent ductus arteriosus
   a) Dilation of the heart
   b) Dilation of the proximal ascending aorta
   c) Dilation of the Pulmonary aorta
   d) Constriction of the Pulmonary aorta
141. Increased 'R' wave and widened 'P' waves indicate
   a) Left ventricular & Left atrial enlargement respectively
   b) Right ventricular & right atrial enlargement respectively
   c) Left ventricular & Right atrial enlargement respectively
   d) Both a & b
142. Animals with reversed PDA commonly associated with
   a) Irreversible obstructive pulmonary valvular disease
   b) Reversible obstructive pulmonary valvular disease
   c) A and B
   d) None
143. When abnormal cardiac function leads to the accumulation and retention of sodium and water, resulting in
   a) Cardiac arrest
   b) Congestive heart failure
   c) Cardiac arrhythmia
   d) Vegetative endocarditis
144. Volume overload affects _______ ventricle, resulting in _____ sided heart failure
   a) Right,Right
   b) Right, Left
   c) Left, Left
   d) Left, Right
145. Jugular venous distension & pulses are common findings in cause of _______
   a) Mitral dysplasia
   b) Tricuspid dysplasia
   c) CHF
   d) All the above
146. Which is a life threatening disorder caused by microorganisms colonizing the cardiac endocardium
   a) Infective endocarditis
   b) Valvular disease
   c) DCM
   d) HCM

147. Persistent bacteremia is a prerequisite for the development of
   a) Dilated valvular disease
   b) Mitral valve regurgitation
   c) HCM
   d) Infective endocarditis
148. Functions of Pericardium
   a) Prevent over dilation of heart
   b) Prevent heart from infections
   c) Forming adhesions to surrounding tissue
   d) All the above
149. Highly sensitive cardiac troponin in dogs
   a) Cardiac troponin I
   b) Cardiac troponin T
   c) A and B
   d) None
150. Which is the gold standard for evaluating peripheral vascular disease due to its ability to characterize normal and abnormal vascular anatomy
   a) Angiography
   b) Electrocardiography
   c) Echocardiography
   d) Both b & c

Answer Key

1	d	2	d	3	a	4	c	5	d	6	d	7	d
8	d	9	a	10	a	11	b	12	a	13	c	14	a
15	c	16	b	17	b	18	a	19	a	20	c	21	d
22	a	23	b	24	a	25	b	26	d	27	d	28	c
29	a	30	b	31	a	32	b	33	a	34	d	35	b
36	b	37	c	38	b	39	a	40	d	41	d	42	b
43	d	44	d	45	a	46	c	47	a	48	b	49	d
50	a	51	c	52	a	53	b	54	d	55	b	56	d
57	d	58	d	59	b	60	c	61	b	62	a	63	d
64	d	65	d	66	d	67	d	68	a	69	c	70	d
71	a	72	a	73	c	74	a	75	c	76	d	77	a
78	c	79	d	80	a	81	d	82	b	83	d	84	a
85	c	86	a	87	b	88	d	89	d	90	a	91	c
92	a	93	d	94	a	95	d	96	d	97	d	98	d
99	b	100	c	101	b	102	c	103	c	104	a	105	a
106	b	107	d	108	c	109	a	110	d	111	d	112	b
113	a	114	c	115	b	116	b	117	b	118	d	119	c
120	d	121	b	122	b	123	c	124	b	125	d	126	b
127	a	128	c	129	a	130	a	131	a	132	b	133	a
134	c	135	b	136	d	137	b	138	d	139	a	140	b
141	a	142	a	143	b	144	a	145	b	146	a	147	d
148	d	149	a	150	a								

13

Clinical Physiology of Digestive Disorders of Monogastric Animals

Abhishek Kalundia

Cornerstone Pet Clinic Hyderabad-89

Introduction

The digestive system is essential for the survival and overall health of all animals, and its proper function is crucial for the digestion, absorption, and metabolism of nutrients. In monogastric animals-those with a single-chambered stomach, such as dogs, cats, pigs, and horses-the digestive process is both complex and finely tuned to meet their specific nutritional needs. Understanding the clinical physiology of digestive disorders in monogastric animals is vital for veterinary professionals, animal caretakers, and researchers, as it enables them to recognize, diagnose, and treat various gastrointestinal conditions that may impact these species. This introduction provides an overview of the fundamental aspects of digestive physiology in monogastric animals, outlines common digestive disorders, and highlights the importance of this knowledge in clinical practice.

The digestive tract of monogastric animals consists of several organs that work together to break down food, absorb nutrients, and expel waste. The primary components include the mouth, esophagus, stomach, small intestine, large intestine, and associated glands such as the salivary glands, liver, and pancreas.

The digestive process begins in the mouth, where food is mechanically broken down by chewing and mixed with saliva, which contains enzymes like amylase to initiate the breakdown of carbohydrates. The bolus of food is then transported through the esophagus to the stomach via coordinated muscular contractions known as peristalsis.

In the stomach, food is mixed with gastric secretions, including hydrochloric acid (HCl) and digestive enzymes like pepsin, which help break down proteins. The stomach's acidic environment also plays a critical role in killing pathogens and aiding the digestion of certain nutrients, such as vitamin B12. The stomach of monogastric animals differs from that of ruminants, as it does not possess multiple compartments for fermentation but rather relies on enzymatic digestion.

The chyme (partially digested food) passes into the small intestine, where most digestion and nutrient absorption occur. The small intestine is composed of three segments-the duodenum, jejunum, and ileum-each with specialized functions. Enzymes secreted by the pancreas and bile from the liver facilitate the digestion of carbohydrates, proteins, and fats. The intestinal lining, with its villi and microvilli, maximizes the surface area for nutrient absorption.

The large intestine, including the cecum, colon, and rectum, is primarily responsible for water absorption, electrolyte balance, and the formation and expulsion of feces. Although limited, some fermentation of undigested fibers occurs in the large intestine, particularly in species like horses, where the cecum plays a significant role in fiber digestion.

Digestive disorders in monogastric animals can result from a variety of factors, including dietary imbalances, infections, genetic predispositions, and environmental influences. These disorders can manifest in different ways, from mild gastrointestinal upset to life-threatening conditions. Understanding the clinical physiology of these disorders is crucial for effective diagnosis and treatment.

GERD is characterized by the backward flow of stomach acid into the esophagus, leading to inflammation, pain, and discomfort. In monogastric animals, GERD can be caused by factors such as obesity, certain medications, or anatomical abnormalities like hiatal hernias. Clinical signs include regurgitation, salivation, and esophagitis. Management may involve dietary changes, medications that reduce stomach acidity, and in severe cases, surgical intervention.

Gastric ulcers are a common digestive disorder in monogastric animals, particularly in horses and pigs. They result from an imbalance between protective factors (such as mucus and bicarbonate) and aggressive factors (like gastric acid and pepsin). Ulcers can cause pain, anorexia, weight loss, and, in severe cases, perforation. Risk factors include stress, nonsteroidal anti-inflammatory drugs (NSAIDs), and high-grain diets. Treatment typically involves acid suppression, mucosal protectants, and dietary modifications.

Pancreatitis, or inflammation of the pancreas, is particularly prevalent in dogs and can occur acutely or chronically. It often results from dietary indiscretion (such as high-fat meals), obesity, or other underlying conditions like hyperlipidemia. Clinical signs include vomiting, abdominal pain, lethargy, and anorexia. Diagnosis relies on clinical signs, blood tests, and imaging studies, while treatment focuses on supportive care, pain management, and dietary modifications.

Inflammatory Bowel Diseases, IBD encompasses a group of chronic gastrointestinal disorders characterized by inflammation of the intestinal lining. It can affect both the small and large intestines and is relatively common in dogs and cats. The exact cause of IBD is unknown, but it is believed to result from an abnormal immune response to intestinal microbes or food antigens. Clinical signs include chronic diarrhea, vomiting, weight loss, and lethargy. Diagnosis typically involves ruling out other conditions, and treatment may include dietary management, immunosuppressive drugs, and probiotics.

Colic is a broad term used to describe abdominal pain in horses, and it is one of the most common and potentially serious digestive disorders in this species. Causes of colic can range from simple gas accumulation and impaction to more severe conditions like intestinal torsion or strangulation. Clinical signs include restlessness, rolling, pawing, and sweating. Early diagnosis and prompt veterinary intervention are critical for successful management, which may involve medical treatment, fluid therapy, or surgery.

6.*Exocrine Pancreatic Insufficiency EPI is a condition where the pancreas fails to produce sufficient digestive enzymes, leading to malabsorption and nutrient deficiencies. It is particularly common in certain dog breeds, such as German Shepherds. Symptoms include weight loss, diarrhea, steatorrhea (fatty stools), and increased appetite. Diagnosis involves measuring serum trypsin-like immunoreactivity (TLI) levels, and treatment typically involves enzyme supplementation and dietary management.

The liver plays a vital role in digestion by producing bile, which aids in fat emulsification and absorption. Liver diseases, such as hepatitis, hepatic lipidosis, and cirrhosis, can impair these functions and cause digestive disturbances. In monogastric animals, liver diseases may manifest with signs such as jaundice, vomiting, diarrhea, and ascites. Management depends on the underlying cause and may include dietary changes, medications, and supportive care.

Understanding the clinical physiology of digestive disorders in monogastric animals is essential for several reasons:

Knowledge of the normal physiology of the digestive system allows veterinarians to identify abnormalities and diagnose disorders accurately. For instance, understanding the clinical signs of pancreatitis in dogs or colic in horses enables prompt recognition and appropriate intervention, potentially saving lives.

Effective management of digestive disorders requires a thorough understanding of their underlying pathophysiology. For example, knowing that gastric ulcers in horses are often related to excessive gastric acid secretion and inadequate protective factors informs the use of acid-suppressing drugs and dietary modifications.

Knowledge of digestive physiology and common disorders also aids in the development of preventive strategies. For example, understanding the role of diet in the development of conditions like GERD, pancreatitis, or colic can help in formulating feeding practices that minimize the risk of these disorders.

Gastrointestinal disorders can significantly impact the welfare and quality of life of animals. Understanding their clinical physiology enables early detection and appropriate management, improving the overall health and longevity of monogastric animals.

The clinical physiology of digestive disorders in monogastric animals is a complex and multifaceted field that encompasses numerous conditions affecting the gastrointestinal tract and associated organs. By understanding the normal physiological processes and the pathophysiology of common digestive disorders, veterinary professionals can provide better care, ensure accurate diagnoses, and implement effective treatments, ultimately enhancing the health and well-being of monogastric animals.

This introduction provides a comprehensive overview of the clinical physiology of digestive disorders in monogastric animals, suitable for setting the context for a multiple-choice questionnaire.

1. Example of monogastric animals

   Mark only one oval.

   a) Pigs b) Humans

   c) Cats d) All the above

   Other:

2. Digestion begins in the

   Mark only one oval.

   a) Mouth b) Buccal cavity

   c) Stomach d) Intestines

   Other:

3. Enzyme Present In Saliva

Mark only one oval.

a) Amylase b) Lipase

c) Protease d) All the above

Other:

4. Amylase helps in digestion of

Mark only one oval.

a) Carbohydrates b) Proteins

c) Fats d) All the above

Other:

5. Protease helps in digestion of

Mark only one oval.

a) Carbohydrates b) Proteins

c) Fats d) All the above

Other:

6. Lipase helps in digestion of

Mark only one oval.

a) Carbohydrates b) Proteins

c) Fats d) All the above

Other:

7. 1St Peristaltic Contractions Start In

Mark only one oval.

a) Oesophagus b) Stomach

c) Intestine d) Mouth

Other:

8. J shaped organ that stores and partially digestes food is

Mark only one oval.

a) Oesophagus b) Stomach

c) Intestine d) Mouth

Other:

9. Hcl and presinogen are secreted by

Mark only one oval.

a) Oesophagus b) Stomach

c) Intestine d) Mouth

Other:

10. 10. Chyme is formed in

Mark only one oval.

a) Oesophagus b) Stomach

c) Intestine d) Mouth

Other:

11. Most of the digestion and absorption occurs in
Mark only one oval.
a) Oesophagus
b) Stomach
c) Intestine
d) Mouth
Other:

12. Chayme is received by
a) Duodenum
b) Jejunum
c) Ileum
d) All the above
Other:

13. Nutrient absorbtion portion of SI
Mark only one oval.
a) Duodenum
b) Jejunum
c) Ileum
d) Both 2 and 3
Other:

14. Primary function of LI
Mark only one oval.
a) To absorb water and electrolyte To
b) Store feces
c) Both
d) None
Other:

15. End of digestiove tract
Mark only one oval.
a) Rectum
b) Colon
c) Anus
d) All The Above
Other:

16. Pepsinogen to pepsin is activated in
Mark only one oval.
a) LI
b) Stomach
c) SI
d) All The Above
Other:

17. Pepsis helps in digestion of
Mark only one oval.
a) Proteins
b) Carbohydrates
c) Fats
d) All The Above
Other:

18. Final stage of degestion
Mark only one oval.
a) Absorption of water in LI
b) Defecatiuon
c) None
d) Both 1 and 2
Other:

19. Surface Area of Absorption is Ibncreased By

Mark only one oval.

a) Villi b) Microvilli

c) None d) Both 1 and 2

Other:

20. Villi and micriovilli are present in

Mark only one oval.

a) S b) I

c) L d) I

Other:

21. Carbohydrates are converted into

a) Glucose b) Amino acids

c) None d) Fatty acids

Other:

22. Proteins are converted into

Mark only one oval.

a) Glucose b) Amino acids

c) None d) Fatty acids

Other:

23. Fats are converted into

Mark only one oval.

a) Glucose b) Fatty acids

c) Glycerol d) Both 2 and 3

Other:

24. Proteins are essential for

Mark only one oval.

a) Synthesis of enzymes b) Hormones

c) Repairing of tissue d) All the above

Other:

25. Process of taking food into mouth is called

Mark only one oval.

a) Ingestion b) Mastication

c) Digestion d) All the above

Other:

26. Process of breaking down complex food into simpler substances and absorbing is call

Mark only one oval.

a) Ingestion b) Mastication

c) Digestion d) All the above

Other:

27. Functions of saliva

Mark only one oval.

a) Swallowing Secretion

b) Of enzyme

c) Breaking of carbohydrate to simple sugars

d) All the above

Other:

28. Bile produced by the liver is stored in

Mark only one oval.

a) Stomach

b) GB

c) LI

d) All the above

Other:

29. Gut microbiota helps in sysnthesis of which vitamins

Mark only one oval.

a) Vit

b) K

c) Vit B

d) Both 1 and 2 None

Other:

30. Function of gut microibiota

Mark only one oval.

a) Synthesis of vitamins

b) To mailtain gut health

c) Regulate immune funtion

d) All The above

Other:

31. Procedure That Allows Veterinarians To Examine Digestive Tract Inserting An Instrument Is Called

Mark only one oval.

Endoscopy

Laparoscopy

Both 1 and 2

None

Other:

32. Esophagoduodenoscopy examines

Mark only one oval.

a) Stomach

b) Oesophagus

c) Portion of SI

d) All The Above

Other:

33. Colonoscopy examin

Mark only one oval.

a) Colon

b) Rectum

c) Caecum

d) Both 1 and 2

Other:

34. Capsule endoscopy is used for
Mark only one oval.
a) Location of bleeding
b) To take images of SI
c) None
d) Both 1 and 2
Other:

35. Enlargement of esopahus is called
Mark only one oval.
a) Megaoesophagus
b) Oesophageal ecstasia
c) Esophageal dilatation
d) All the above
Other:

36. Causes of megaoesophagus
a) Congenital
b) Neuromuscular disorder
c) Obstruction
d) All the above
Other:

37. Inflammation of esophagus
Mark only one oval.
a) Oesophagitis
b) Gastritis
c) Enteritis
d) All the above
Other:

38. Causes of esophagitis
Mark only one oval.
a) Foreign bodies
b) Gastroesophageal
c) ReZux Infections
c) All the above
Other:

39. Narrowing of esophagus
Mark only one oval.
a) Oesophagitis
b) Oesophageal stricture
c) Barrets oesophagus
d) All the above
Other:

40. Precancerous condiiton of esophagus
Mark only one oval.
a) Oesophagitis
b) Oesophageal stricture
c) Barrets oesophagus
d) All the above
Other:

41. Causes of oseophageal stricture
Mark only one oval.
a) Chronic Oesophagitis
b) Megaoesophagus
c) Barrets oesophagus
c) All the above
Other:

42. Causes of gastric ulcers

Mark only one oval.

a) Stress
b) Nsaid
c) Infections
d) All the above

Other:

43. Delayed emptying of stomach cointents into duodenum is called

Mark only one oval.

a) Gastritis
b) Enteritis
c) Gastroparesis
d) All the above

Other:

44. Causes of gastroparesis

Mark only one oval.

a) DM
b) Neurological disorders
c) Both 1 and 2
d) Mone of the above

Other:

45. Bacteria present in the stomach

Mark only one oval.

a) E Coli
b) Staphylococcus
c) Helicobacter pylori
d) None of the above

Other:

46. Causes Of Intestinal Malabsorption Syndrome Is

Mark only one oval.

a) EPI
b) Pancreatitis
c) Lymphamgiectasia
d) All of the above

Other:

47. Intestinal malabsorbtion causes

Mark only one oval.

a) B1 de\ciency
b) B2 de\ciency
c) Vit K de\ciency
d) Cobalamin de\ciency

Other:

48. Beneficial Bacteria That Helps in Restoring Gut Health

Mark only one oval.

a) Probiotics
b) Prebiotics
c) Both 1 and 2
d) None of the above

Other:

49. Inflammation of Gall bladder is called

Mark only one oval.

a) Cholangitis
b) Cholecystitis
c) Hepatitis
d) Both 1 and 2

Other:

50. Inflammation of bile duct is called

Mark only one oval.

a) Cholangitis
b) Cholecystitis
c) Hepatitis
d) Both 1 and 2

Other:

This content is neither created nor endorsed by Google.

Answer Key

1	d	2	a	3	a	4	a	5	b	6	c	7	a
8	b	9	b	10	b	11	b	12	a	13	c	14	c
15	c	16	b	17	a	18	b	19	d	20		21	a
22	b	23	d	24	d	25	a	26	c	27	d	28	b
29	d	30	d	31	a	32	d	33	d	34	d	35	d
36	d	37	a	38	c	39	b	40		41		42	d
43	c	44	c	45	c	46	d	47	d	48	a	49	b
50	a												

14

Clinical Physiology of Digestive Disorders of Ruminants

Bhavanam Sudhakara Reddy, Sirigireddy Sivajothi, Gude Harini and Singareddy Sreeya

College of Veterinary Science - Proddatur, Sri Venkateswara Veterinary University, Andhra Pradesh

Introduction

In cattle, the digestive system consists of four primary compartments: the rumen, reticulum, omasum, and abomasum, followed by the small and large intestines. The rumen plays a crucial role as a fermentation chamber, maintaining anaerobic conditions and ensuring thorough mixing, as well as regulating temperature and pH levels. Food, which is frequently re-chewed, enters the rumen through the esophagus, where fermentation occurs. The byproducts of fermentation are either absorbed within the rumen or moved on for further digestion and absorption in other parts of the digestive system.

Simple indigestion in ruminants is a temporary disruption in gastrointestinal function, usually caused by a sudden change in the quality or quantity of their diet. Consuming large amounts of indigestible feed can impair rumen function for 24 to 48 hours after ingestion, as the accumulation of this feed can physically disrupt ruminal activity. Additionally, the breakdown of proteins in the rumen can produce toxic substances such as amides and amines, including histamine. This condition can lead to a significant drop in milk production due to a marked reduction in the production of volatile fatty acids in a hypotonic reticulorumen. Ruminal impaction is a condition seen in ruminants like cows, sheep, and goats, where the rumen's contents become compacted, obstructing their movement through the digestive tract. This condition can arise from various causes, including the ingestion of plastic waste, grazing habits, mineral deficiencies, negative energy balance, urbanization, inadequate water intake, low-fiber or high-grain diets, changes in feed or grazing patterns, and stress. The accumulation of foreign material can block fermentation, interfere with the mixing of rumen contents, and disrupt the rumen's microflora, leading to indigestion. Acute ruminal acidosis is often caused by the sudden intake of large amounts of carbohydrate-rich feed, particularly grains. Subacute ruminal acidosis (SARA) occurs in dairy cattle and is characterized by disrupted ruminal fermentation. It typically results from feeding large amounts of concentrates with insufficient fiber, a practice often used to boost milk production during early lactation. This imbalance in diet can disturb rumen pH and microbial populations, leading to various metabolic and digestive problems. Chronic ruminal acidosis can lead to complications such as rumenitis, which is inflammation of the rumen, and laminitis, a painful condition affecting the hooves. Alkaline indigestion, also known as ruminal alkalosis, occurs when the pH of ruminal fluid rises above 7.5. This condition can be triggered by factors such as the sudden intake of protein-rich feed, urea supplementation, abrupt dietary changes, consumption of contaminated water, and prolonged feeding of straw. Soybean meal, which is commonly fed to dairy cows and growing cattle due to its high energy and nitrogen content, can also contribute to alkalosis. In the rumen, excess ammonia production can occur when microbes are unable to utilize all of the available ammonia efficiently. Ruminal tympany, also known as bloat, occurs when the rumen and reticulum become excessively distended due to the retention of fermentation gases. This condition can present in two forms: as a persistent foam mixed with rumen contents (frothy bloat) or as free gas separated from the ingesta (free-gas bloat). Normally, gas bubbles produced in the rumen coalesce, rise to the top, and are expelled through eructation. A common sign of ruminal tympany is left-sided distension, visible from the rear or side of the animal. This distension typically affects the left upper and lower quadrants, and tympanic resonance can be detected over the left paralumbar fossa. Gaseous pings associated with ruminal tympany are usually higher-pitched in cases of frothy bloat compared to free-gas bloat. Vagus indigestion is a syndrome marked by a range of clinical symptoms thought to result from damage or inflammatory changes to branches of the vagus nerve as it travels through the thoracic cavity, the perireticular area, or the pyloric region. Although the ventral vagus nerve is more commonly affected, there are cases where no lesions are found on the vagus nerve or its branches.

Diseases of the abomasum are common in adult dairy cattle, and consist of five important entities: Left displaced abomasum, Right displaced abomasum, Abomasal volvulus, Abomasal impaction, Abomasal ulcers.

In large ruminants, two common types of intestinal obstruction are mechanical and functional. Mechanical obstructions can be either luminal or extraluminal in origin. Luminal obstructions include conditions such as hemorrhagic jejunitis, trichobezoars, phytobezoars, cecocolic volvulus, impacted ingesta, and congenital issues like atresia coli, recti, and ani. Extraluminal obstructions occur due to factors such as strangulation, intussusception, volvulus, or the compression of the intestines by an expanding abdominal mass, such as fat necrosis or lymphosarcoma. Unlike mechanical obstructions, functional obstruction, also known as paralytic ileus, results from the cessation of peristaltic movement in the intestines. The exact cause of functional stenosis is not well understood but is linked to management or dietary factors, parasite infections, phytobezoars, enteritis, peritonitis, or electrolyte imbalances. Paralytic ileus is characterized by reduced intestinal motility or atony without any gross abnormalities and is more common than mechanical obstruction, particularly in pregnant or recently parturient cows. Cecal dilatation in cattle may initially present without symptoms but can progress to cecal volvulus, which may require surgical intervention. Cecal distention or volvulus typically produces a ping in the right paralumbar fossa and caudal quadrant, sometimes extending cranially and ventrally depending on the severity of the distention. When viewed from the side, cecal distention is often noticeable in the paralumbar fossa, while from the rear, significant distention of the right paralumbar fossa is evident. Splashing sounds within the distended cecum can be detected by performing succussion. Diarrhea is the most consistent clinical sign of infectious enteritis, but determining the specific cause based on clinical examination alone is challenging. In ruminants, infectious enteritis can be caused by bacterial, viral, or parasitic pathogens. Laboratory diagnostic tests are required to accurately identify the cause, which often has herd-wide implications.

Write correct alphabet of the answer in the given bracket

1. Rumen collapse is a physiological sign of
   a) Prolonged lameness b) Prolonged anorexia
   c) Acidosis d) Hyper anxiety
2. Vomiting noticed in calves with
   a) White muscle disease b) Pharyngeal muscular dystrophy
   c) Otitis media/interna d) All
3. Vomiting while passing stomach tube cattle is indicative of
   a) Pharyngeal disease b) Reticular disease
   c) TRP d) All
4. Peak occurrence of LDA seen in
   a) 6 weeks after lactation b) 6 months after lactation
   c) 6 months after lactation d) All
5. Displacement of abdomen by
   a) Excessive production of VFA b) Hypocalcaemia
   c) Periparturient metritis d) All
6. Signs of displacement of abomasum in cattle
   a) Sprung rib cage present on the side of displacement
   b) Ping sound under rib cage
   c) Off feed and down on milk
   d) All
7. Signs of cattle with abomasal perforation
   a) Fever b) Pneumoperitoneum
   c) Ping sounds d) All
8. Pathophysiological changes noticed in cattle with abomasal displacement
   a) Hypochloremia b) Hypokalemia
   c) Metabolic alkalosis d) All
9. Consequence to prolonged or severe metabolic alkalosis with displaced abomasum
   a) Paradoxic aciduria b) Acidosis
   c) Anuria d) All
10. Treatment of abomasal atony
    a) Rumenotorics b) Oral laxatives
    c) Antacids d) All
11. Suitable physiotherapy in cattle with LDA
    a) Rolling method b) Swimming
    c) Standing d) All

12. Hypokalemia associated with LDA managed by
    a) Oral potassium chloride b) Potassium sulphate
    c) Potassium carbonate d) All
13. Right side ping sound produced by
    a) RDA b) Ceacal dilatation
    c) Distension of colon d) All
14. Abomasal ulcers caused by
    a) Acidic diets b) Stone
    c) Silage feed d) All
15. Most commonly separated period of abomasal ulcers
    a) 4 to 6 weeks of lactation b) 14 to 16 weeks of lactation
    c) 4 to 6 months of lactation d) All
16. Perforating abomasal ulcers leads to
    a) Peritonitis b) Metritis
    c) Rumenitis d) Reticulitis
17. Causes for abomasal ulcers in cattle
    a) Lymphosarcoma of abomasum b) Prolonged NSAIDS usage
    c) Theileriosis d) All
18. Signs in cows with abomasal ulcers
    a) Reluctant to move
    b) Audible grunt with each respiration
    c) Peripheral parts become cold
    d) All
19. Diagnostic test for abomasal ulcers in cattle
    a) Serum protein b) Faecal occult blood
    c) Radiography d) All
20. Sweetish order of digested blood at the perineal region
    a) Abomasal ulcers b) Abomasal displacement
    c) Rumenitis d) Enteritis
21. Abomasitis in calves due to
    a) Clostridium b) Salmonella
    c) Sarcinia d) All
22. Severe colic in cattle due to
    a) Torsion at root of the mesentry b) Volvulus
    c) Torsion d) All
23. Signs of colic in cattle
    a) Kicking at abdomen b) Lordosis
    c) Reluctant to stand d) All

24. Cattle with intussusception may show colic sings only during
    a) 12 to 24 hours of obstruction
    b) 24 to 48 hours of obstruction
    c) 12 to 96 hours of obstruction
    d) 12 to 196 hours of obstruction
25. Rasp berry color dung is indicative of
    a) Rumenitis
    b) Omasal impaction
    c) Intussusception
    d) Enteritis
26. Important diagnostic tool for diagnosis of intussusception
    a) Radiography
    b) Ultrasonography
    c) Endoscopy
    d) All
27. Most common cause of small intestine obstruction in calves
    a) Hemorrhagic bowel syndrome
    b) Enteritis
    c) Colitis
    d) Rumenitis
28. Commonly associated toxins with hemorrhagic bowel syndrome
    a) *Clostridium perfringens* A with beta toxin
    b) *Clostridium perfringens* B with beta toxin
    c) *Clostridium perfringens* A with alpha toxin
    d) *Clostridium perfringens* B with alpha toxin
29. Colic noticed in condition
    a) Pyelonephritis
    b) Renal calculi
    c) Intestinal obstruction
    d) All
30. Colic noticed in cattle with
    a) Caecal dilatation
    b) Uterine torsion
    c) Hematoma of mesentery
    d) All
31. Post operative ileus management by administration of metoclopramide dose
    a) 0.1 to 0.25 mg per kg
    b) 1 to 2.5 mg per kg
    c) 10-20 mg per kg
    d) 100 to 250 mg per kg
32. Dose of erythromycin as prokinetic agent in cattle
    a) 0.08 mg per kg
    b) 0.8 mg per kg
    c) 8mg per kg
    d) 80 mg per kg
33. Drugs which will interfere with motility of intestines
    a) Atropine
    b) Methoscopolamine
    c) A and B
    d) Procaine penicillin
34. Ceacal dilatation
    a) Ceacum distends with gas and fluid
    b) Apex begins to rise in the abomasum
    c) Rotation of caecum
    d) All

35. Highly fermentable moist condition leads to
    a) Intestinal obstruction
    b) Intussusception
    c) Ceacal dilatation
    d) All
36. How to differentiate colon and cecal dilatation
    a) Radiography
    b) Ultrasonography
    c) Endoscopy
    d) Physical examination
37. Rectal laceration is due to
    a) Ignorant roughness while rectal examination
    b) Poorly restrained animals
    c) Natural service
    d) All
38. Signs in rectal lacerations
    a) Fresh blood on the sleeve after rectal examination
    b) Tenesmus
    c) Enteritis
    d) A and B
39. Rectal laceration leads to
    a) Septic peritonitis
    b) Arched stance
    c) Increased heart rate
    d) All
40. Diet restriction in cattle with rectal laceration
    a) High fiber
    b) Low fiber
    c) Laxatives
    d) High protein
41. Etiology for pneumo rectum
    a) Dystocia
    b) Tenesmus
    c) Enteritis
    d) Rumenitis
42. Cows with vicious cycle of sucking air by rectum and straining leads to
    a) Enteritis
    b) Pneumo rectum
    c) Mastitis
    d) Ceacal dilatation
43. Developed ping sounds in pneumo rectum
    a) Right para lumbar fossa
    b) Left para lumbar foss
    c) Both
    d) None
44. Short-term epidural analgesia attained for management of rectal prolapse
    a) Xylazine
    b) Lidocaine
    c) Morphine
    d) A&B
45. Conditions for pneumo peritoneum
    a) Exploratory laparotomy
    b) Rupture of abdominal organs
    c) Abomasal perforations
    d) All

46. Evacuation of air from pneumo peritoneum by puncture at
    a) Left paralumbar fossa b) Right paralumbar fossa
    c) Both d) None
47. Etiology of rectal prolapse in cattle
    a) Coccidiosis b) Colitis
    c) Dysuria d) All
48. Etiology for rectal prolapse in cattle
    a) Spinal lymphoma b) Spinal abscess
    c) Dystocia d) All
49. Most common complication of tail amputation in sheep
    a) Rectal prolapse b) Enteritis
    c) Colitis d) Recumbency
50. Dietary modification recurred for cattle with rectal prolapse
    a) Legume diet b) Mineral oil
    c) Magnesium hydroxide d) All
51. Most common gastro intestinal site affected by simple indigestion
    a) Rumen b) Small intestine
    c) A and B d) None
52. Indigestion most common in which stage
    a) Few weeks after parturition b) 3rd month after parturition
    c) Last trimester of pregnancy d) Early pregnancy
53. Diagnosis of ruminal indigestion diagnosed by
    a) History b) Signs
    c) Ultrasonography d) All
54. Clinical signs in ruminal dysfunction
    a) Rumen stasis
    b) Increased ruminal contractions
    c) Decreased strength of rumen contractions
    d) All
55. Signs in cattle with small intestinal indigestion associated with colic
    a) Tachycardia b) Tachypnea
    c) Both d) Bradycardia
56. Signs of colic due to small intestinal indigestion
    a) Kicking at belly b) Getting up and down frequently
    c) Treading with hindfeet d) All
57. Pathophysiology of cattle with small intestinal indigestion
    a) Increased fluid b) Increased gas
    c) Severe tension on the mesentry d) All

58. Sequelae to the rumen indigestion in cattle
    a) Laminitis b) Sole ulcers
    c) Toe abscess d) All
59. Signs associated with recovery after small intestinal stasis
    a) Diarrhea b) Bloat
    c) GDV d) Rumenitis
60. Serum biochemical abnormality associated with simple indigestion in cattle
    a) Hypocalcemia b) Hypochloremia
    c) Hyponatremia d) All
61. Serum biochemical abnormality associated with small intestinal indigestion
    a) Hypocalcemia b) Hypochloremia
    c) Hyponatremia d) A and B
62. Treatment goals with simple indigestion in cattle
    a) Re establish gastrointestinal motility
    b) Establish normal rumen microflora
    c) A and B
    d) None
63. Excessive alkalizing agents administration leads to
    a) Reduction in calcium levels b) Metabolic alkalosis
    c) Hyper magnesia d) All
64. Commonly used alkalizing products
    a) Magnesium sulphate b) Magnesium oxide
    c) Magnesium hydroxide d) All
65. Cattle with acidosis have
    a) Dehydration b) Splashy rumen
    c) Tachycardia d) All
66. Biochemical changes noticed in cattle with acidosis
    a) Azotemia b) Hypocalcemia
    c) Lactic acid increase d) All
67. Rumen lactic acidosis caused by ingestion of
    a) Finely grounded corn b) Small grain silage
    c) Improper mixing of TMR d) All
68. Isomer of lactic acid present in the acidosis
    a) D form b) L form
    c) A and B d) None
69. Organisms present during acidosis
    a) *S.aureus* b) *S.intermedius*
    c) *S.bovis* d) None

70. Ruminal fluid pH in acidosis
    a) 6 to 7   b) 7 to 8
    c) 4 to 5   d) 2 to 3
71. Systemic acidosis increases in
    a) D form lactic acid   b) L form lactic acid
    c) A and B   d) None
72. Rumen acidosis can cause
    a) PEM   b) Laminitis
    c) Production loss   d) All
73. Treatment option for acidosis
    a) Hypertonic solution   b) RL
    c) Sodium bicarbonate solution   d) All
74. Pathological changes in cattle with acidosis
    a) Chemical Rumenitis   b) Bacterial Rumenitis
    c) Mycotic Rumenitis   d) All
75. Bacterial Rumenitis is caused by
    a) *Fusobacterium*   b) *Staphylococci*
    c) *Streptococci*   d) All
76. Sequelae of ruminal acidosis in cattle
    a) Embolic infection at brain   b) Pneumonia
    c) Hepatic abscess   d) All
77. Most common type of acidosis in cattle
    a) Acute   b) Sub acute
    c) Chronic   d) Per acute
78. Sub acute ruminal acidosis can cause
    a) Caudal venacava thrombosis syndrome   b) Saw dust liver
    c) Laminitis   d) All
79. Acute free gas bloat occurs due to
    a) Hypocalcemia   b) Ileus
    c) Esophageal obstruction   d) All
80. Damage to vagal nerve roots with pharyngeal injurious leads to
    a) Rumenitis   b) Frothy bloat
    c) Free gas bloat   d) all
81. Ingestion of large quantity of succulent green forage leads to
    a) Rumenitis   b) Frothy bloat
    c) Free gas bloat   d) All
82. Frothy bloat can origin from due to
    a) Fiber   b) Chloroplast
    c) Nitrogen   d) All

83. Free gas bloat occurs in cattle
    a) Over ingestion of grains b) Tetanus
    c) Listeriosis d) All
84. Presence of fluid and gas bloat seen in calves with
    a) Rumenitis b) Bloat
    c) Acidosis d) All
85. Free gas bloat can be treated with
    a) Polaxalene b) Vegetable oil
    c) Emergency rumenotomy d) All
86. Trocarisation in cattle leads to
    a) Peritonitis b) Fever
    c) Rumenitis d) A&B
87. Chronic cause of bloat in calves
    a) Thymic lymphosarcoma b) Dilated esophagus
    c) Enlarged mediastinal lymph nodes d) All
88. Neoplasms responsible for development of bloat in cattle
    a) Fibropapillomas of the distal esophagus
    b) Lymphosarcoma
    c) Actinobacillus lesions at distal esophageal region
    d) All
89. Signs of pericarditis in cattle
    a) Ventral edema b) Brisket edema
    c) Intermandibular edema d) All
90. Vagus indigestion due to vagus nerve
    a) Inflammation b) Injury
    c) Destruction d) All
91. Heart rate in vagus indigestion
    a) Tachycardia b) Bradycardia
    c) Asystole d) All
92. Notifiable Bradycardia in cattle due to
    a) Reflex retrograde irritation at the vagus nerve
    b) Hypermotility of rumen
    c) Pericarditis
    d) All
93. Roman motility in cattle with vagal indigestion
    a) Hyper motility b) Hypo motility
    c) Atony d) All

94. L- shaped rumen sewn in cattle with
    a) Acid indigestion
    b) Alkaline indigestion
    c) Vagal indigestion
    d) All
95. Vomiting and normal regurgitation occurs due to
    a) Oral Pharyngeal neuromuscular function
    b) Cranial nerve deficits
    c) A&B
    d) None
96. Etiology for vagal indigestion in cattle
    a) Esophageal laceration
    b) Chemical phelgma
    c) Inflammation of cervical region
    d) All
97. Etiology for vagal indigestion in cattle
    a) Reticular abscess
    b) Liver abscess
    c) RDA
    d) All
98. Negative prognostic signs include
    a) Poor appetite
    b) Scanty dung
    c) Recurrent bloat
    d) All
99. Rumen void syndrome due to
    a) Septic metritis
    b) Septic mastitis
    c) Pneumonia
    d) All
100. Differential diagnosis of development of ping sound on left abdomen
    a) Rumen collapse
    b) LDA
    c) Pneumoperitoneum
    d) All
101. The main toxic amines produced may include in which is known to cause ruminal atony
    a) Ammonia
    b) Histamine
    c) Serotonin
    d) Dopamine
102. Which is a potent alkalizing agent used in ruminants as an antacid and mild laxative
    a) Magnesium oxide
    b) Sodium bicarbonate
    c) Calcium lactate
    d) Sodium lactate
103. Sudden ingestion of huge quantity of readily fermentable carbohydrate rich feed leads to
    a) Acidosis
    b) Alkalosis
    c) Vagus indigestion
    d) Peritonitis
104. Sub acute ruminal acidosis occurs in dairy cattle fed with .....% fiber.
    a) Less than 20%
    b) Less than 40%
    c) Less than 60%
    d) Less than 80%
105. Choice of medication for alkaline indigestion in a cow is
    a) Acetic acid
    b) Sulfuric acid
    c) Sodium bicarbonate
    d) MgO

106. Drug that can break down starch in the rumen
    a) Acetic acid b) Sulfuric acid
    c) Chloral hydrate d) MgO
107. Major clinical findings in malabsorption is
    a) Indigestion b) Constipation
    c) Diarrhea d) Vomitous
108. Ruminal fluid with milky grey colour is an indication of
    a) Vagal indigestion b) Alkaline indigestion
    c) Acid indigestion d) All the above
109. Papple shape abdomen seen in
    a) Vagal indigestion b) Alkaline indigestion
    c) Acid indigestion d) LDA
110. Slab shaped abdomen seen in
    a) Vagal indigestion b) Alkaline indigestion
    c) Acid indigestion d) LDA
111. Liptak test is used for detection of
    a) Vagal indigestion b) Alkaline indigestion
    c) Acid indigestion d) LDA
112. Ruminal hypermotility noticed in
    a) Vagal indigestion b) Alkaline indigestion
    c) Acid indigestion d) LDA
113. Ping sound noticed while simulations auscultation and percussion in
    a) Vagal indigestion b) Alkaline indigestion
    c) Acid indigestion d) LDA
114. Fresh blood and mucus in faeces indicate .... bowl infection
    a) Small bowl b) Large bowl
    c) Acid indigestion d) LDA
115. Increased frequency of defecation indicative of
    a) Small bowl b) Large bowl
    c) Acid indigestion d) LDA
116. Williams method of auscultation is used to diagnose the .... In cattle
    a) TRP b) Large bowl
    c) Acid indigestion d) LDA
117. L shape rumen in cattle is observed during rectal examination
    a) TRP b) RDA
    c) Vagus indigestion d) LDA
118. SARA can cause in ruminants
    a) Low milk fat b) Ruminal parakeratosis
    c) Laminitis d) All

119. Presence of fresh blood and mucus streaks in the dung indicative of
   a) Colitis
   b) Alkaline indigestion
   c) Acid indigestion
   d) Enteritis
120. Abducted elbows, careful gait are associated with
   a) TRP
   b) Pericarditis
   c) Pleurisy
   d) All
121. Mediastinal lymphnode enlargement in cattle can results in
   a) Constipation
   b) Frothy bloat
   c) Enteritis
   d) Free gas bloat
122. Mediastinal lymph node enlargement in cattle can results in
   a) Constipation
   b) Frothy bloat
   c) Enteritis
   d) Free gas bloat
123. Synthetic surfactant used for leguminous bloat
   a) Polaxalene
   b) Mineral oil
   c) Vegetable oil
   d) All
124. Which type of bloat left paralumbar fossa will be elevated
   a) Free gas
   b) Leguminous bloat
   c) A and B
   d) None
125. Diagnostic method for abomasal ulcers in cattle
   a) Abomasal fluid analysis
   b) Rumen fluid examination
   c) Ultrasonography
   d) Radiography
126. What is the best treatment for displaced abomasum
   a) Dietary modifications
   b) Fluid therapy
   c) Surgical intervention
   d) All
127. Which condition characterized by development of fibrous tissue in the abomasum
   a) Abomasal lymphoma
   b) Abomasal ulcers
   c) Abomasal displacement
   d) All
128. Primary cause of chronic bloat in ruminants
   a) High fiber diet
   b) Consumption of high protein feed
   c) Low water intake
   d) Excessive consumption of legumes
129. Clinical signs indicative of Johns diseases
   a) Chronic diarrhea
   b) Sudden death
   c) ARDS
   d) Rapid weight gain
130. Diagnostic method approach for detecting the hardware disease in ruminants
   a) Rumenocentesis
   b) Ultrasonography
   c) Endoscopy
   d) Radiography

131. Method to detect the fluid accumulation in the rumen
    a) Ultrasonography b) Endoscopy
    c) Blood test d) Radiography
132. Clinical signs in cattle with bloat
    a) Distension of left paralumbar fossa
    b) Distension of right paralumbar fossa
    c) Excessive urination
    d) All
133. Common cause of ruminal impaction in ruminants
    a) Excessive water intake
    b) High fiber diet
    c) Inadequate fiber intake
    d) Over consumption of concentrates
134. Signs of sub acute ruminal acidosis in ruminants
    a) Weight gain b) Hyperactivity
    c) Increased appetite d) Decreased milk production
135. What is the common preventive measure for reducing the incidence of ruminal impaction
    a) Providing adequate roughage b) Increase water intake
    c) Administrating probiotics d) Reducing concentrate intake
136. What is the common treatment for ruminal acidosis
    a) Sodium bicarbonate b) High protein feed
    c) Antibiotics d) Increase fiber intake
137. What is the common cause of sudden death in ruminants associated with the digestive system
    a) Lactic acidosis b) Bloat
    c) Rumen stasis d) Peritonitis
138. Consumption of high level of silage in ruminants leads to
    a) Abomasal ulcers b) Bloat
    c) Enteritis d) Ruminitis
139. Treatment for ruminal impaction in cattle
    a) High fiber diet b) Low fiber diet
    c) Surgery d) Antibiotics
140. What is the primary cause of abomasal displacement in ruminants
    a) High fiber diet b) Low protein diet
    c) Post partum uterine contractions d) Excessive water intake
141. Which condition leads to inadequate rumen contractions lead to bloat
    a) Abomasal displacement b) Ketosis
    c) Rumen stasis d) Rumen acidosis

142. Clinical signs is commonly associated with a chronic form of ruminal acidosis
   a) Increased milk production   b) Diarrhea and laminitis
   c) Decreased production   d) Bloat
143. Which type of bloat is due to the physical obstruction of esophagus or rumen
   a) Frothy bloat   b) Free gas bloat
   c) Frothy bloat   d) Rumen impaction
144. Which digestive disorders in ruminants is typically treated with rumenotomy
   a) Bloat   b) Rumen impaction
   c) Grass tetany   d) Abomasal impaction
145. Which diagnostic tool is most commonly used to assess rumen health
   a) Rumenocentesis   b) Ultrasonography
   c) Radiography   d) Endoscopy
146. Etiology for abomasal ulcers in ruminants
   a) Excessive fiber intake   b) High protein diet
   c) Stress   d) None of the above
147. Condition characterized by the back flow of abomasal contents into the rumen
   a) Abomasal displacement   b) Ruminal tympany
   c) Enteritis   d) Rumen impaction
148. The condition where the omasum twists around its axis is known as
   a) Omasitis   b) Omasal torsion
   c) Abomasitis   d) Rumenitis
149. Characteristic symptom of peritonitis
   a) Diarrhea   b) Abdominal distension
   c) Salivation   d) Increased urination
150. Dietary modifications for required for a cattle with rectal prolapse
   a) Legum diet   b) Mineral oil
   c) Magnesium hydroxide   d) All

Answer Key

1	b	2	d	3	d	4	a	5	d	6	d	7	d
8	d	9	d	10	d	11	a	12	d	13	d	14	d
15	a	16	a	17	d	18	d	19	b	20	a	21	d
22	b	23	d	24	a	25	c	26	b	27	a	28	a
29	d	30	d	31	a	32	c	33	c	34	d	35	c
36	d	37	d	38	d	39	d	40	c	41	a	42	b
43	a	44	d	45	d	46	b	47	d	48	d	49	a
50	d	51	c	52	a	53	d	54	d	55	c	56	d
57	d	58	d	59	a	60	a	61	d	62	c	63	d

64	d	65	d	66	d	67	d	68	a	69	c	70	c
71	c	72	d	73	d	74	d	75	a	76	d	77	b
78	d	79	d	80	c	81	c	82	b	83	d	84	a
85	d	86	d	87	d	88	d	89	d	90	d	91	b
92	a	93	d	94	c	95	c	96	d	97	d	98	d
99	d	100	d	101	b	102	a	103	a	104	a	105	a
106	c	107	c	108	c	109	a	110	d	111	d	112	a
113	d	114	b	115	a	116	a	117	c	118	d	119	a
120	d	121	d	122	d	123	a	124	a	125	a	126	c
127	a	128	d	129	a	130	d	131	a	132	a	133	d
134	d	135	a	136	a	137	b	138	d	139	a	140	c
141	c	142	b	143	b	144	b	145	a	146	c	147	a
148	b	149	b	150	d								

15

Clinical Physiology of Endocrinal Disorders

Richa Arora[1] and Arpit Tyagi[2]

[1]*Department of Veterinary Biochemistry, College of Veterinary and Animal Sciences, Kishanganj, Bihar Animal Sciences University, Patna, Bihar*

[2]*Chilkahar, Ballia, Department of Animal Husbandary, Government of Uttar Pradesh*

Introduction

The endocrine system comprises a network of glands responsible for producing and releasing hormones that regulate essential bodily functions, particularly the conversion of calories into energy for cellular and organ function. Endocrinology, a medical branch, focuses on these disorders, which often present complexities involving a combination of hypersecretion and hyposecretion due to intricate feedback mechanisms within the endocrine system. Glands within this system release distinct hormones into the bloodstream, where they travel to various cells, playing a pivotal role in coordinating and controlling numerous physiological processes. The coordination of normal physiological processes involves the interplay between the endocrine and nervous systems. Neurons with neurosecretory functions in the supraoptic and paraventricular nuclei of the hypothalamus generate peptides and amines.

Endocrine disorders refer to a broad range of conditions that affect the endocrine system, a complex network of glands responsible for producing and regulating hormones in the body. Hormones play a crucial role in controlling various bodily functions, including growth and development, metabolism, electrolyte balance, and reproductive processes. When the endocrine system fails to function properly, it can lead to a wide range of disorders that can significantly impact an individual's quality of life.

The endocrine system comprises several glands located throughout the body, each producing specific hormones that regulate various physiological processes. The main endocrine glands include:

1. **Pituitary gland:** Often referred to as the "master gland," the pituitary gland regulates the function of other endocrine glands and produces hormones that control growth and development.
2. **Thyroid gland:** Located in the neck, the thyroid gland produces hormones that regulate metabolism, energy production, and growth.
3. **Adrenal glands:** Situated on top of the kidneys, the adrenal glands produce hormones that control electrolyte balance, blood pressure, and stress response.

4. **Pancreas:** While primarily an exocrine gland, the pancreas also contains endocrine cells that produce hormones regulating blood sugar levels, such as insulin and glucagon.
5. **Ovaries (in females):** Produce hormones that regulate the monthly cycle, pregnancy, and lactation.
6. **Testes (in males):** Produce hormones that regulate sperm production, fertility, and male characteristics.

Endocrine disorders can arise from various factors, including

1. **Glandular dysfunction:** Hypofunction (underactive) or hyperfunction (overactive) of endocrine glands.
2. **Hormonal imbalances:** Excess or deficiency of specific hormones.
3. **Tumors or cysts:** Benign or malignant growths on endocrine glands.
4. **Genetic disorders:** Inherited conditions affecting endocrine gland function or hormone regulation.
5. **Infections or inflammation:** Damage to endocrine glands due to infection or inflammation.
6. **Certain medications or treatments:** Iatrogenic causes, such as steroid-induced Cushing's syndrome.

Common endocrine disorders include

1. **Diabetes mellitus (types 1 and 2):** A metabolic disorder characterized by high blood sugar levels.
2. **Hypothyroidism (underactive thyroid):** Insufficient thyroid hormone production.
3. **Hyperthyroidism (overactive thyroid):** Excess thyroid hormone production.
4. **Cushing's syndrome:** Excess cortisol production, often due to pituitary or adrenal gland dysfunction.
5. **Addison's disease:** Adrenal insufficiency, leading to inadequate cortisol and aldosterone production.
6. **Polycystic ovary syndrome (PCOS):** A hormonal disorder affecting ovulation and fertility in females.
7. **Growth hormone deficiency or excess:** Impaired growth and development due to insufficient or excessive growth hormone production.
8. **Thyroid nodules or cancer:** Abnormal growths on the thyroid gland.
9. **Adrenal tumors or hyperplasia:** Benign or malignant growths on the adrenal glands.
10. **Parathyroid disorders:** Hyperparathyroidism (excess parathyroid hormone) or hypoparathyroidism (insufficient parathyroid hormone).

Endocrine disorders can manifest in various ways, depending on the specific condition and affected gland. Common symptoms include:

- Weight changes (gain or loss)
- Fatigue or weakness
- Mood changes (anxiety, depression, irritability)

- Sleep disturbances
- Changes in appetite or thirst
- Skin issues (acne, dry skin, thinning skin)
- Hair loss or changes
- Reproductive issues (infertility, irregular periods)
- Muscle weakness or cramps
- Bone density changes (osteoporosis)

Early diagnosis and treatment are crucial to manage endocrine disorders effectively and prevent long-term complications.

Laboratory Tests for diagnosis of Endocrine disorders

- **Blood Tests:** Measure hormone levels (e.g., thyroid hormones, insulin, cortisol, growth hormone). Common tests include:
  - **Thyroid Function Tests:** TSH, Free T4, Free T3
  - **Glucose Tolerance Test:** For diabetes diagnosis
  - **Hemoglobin A1c:** For long-term glucose control in diabetes
  - **ACTH Stimulation Test:** For adrenal insufficiency
  - **LH, FSH, Estrogen, Testosterone:** For reproductive hormone evaluation
- **Urine Tests:** Measure hormones and their metabolites.
  - **24-hour urine collection:** For cortisol in Cushing's syndrome.
- **Dynamic Endocrine Testing:** Tests that involve stimulating or suppressing hormone production to diagnose certain conditions (e.g., dexamethasone suppression test for Cushing's syndrome).

Imaging Studies for diagnosis of Endocrine disorders

- **Ultrasound:** Commonly used for thyroid gland evaluation.
- **CT Scan or MRI:** Used for detailed imaging of adrenal glands, pituitary gland, and other endocrine organs.
- **Nuclear Medicine Scans:** (e.g., radioactive iodine uptake for thyroid disorders).

Specialized Tests for diagnosis of Endocrine disorders

- **Biopsy:** In cases where there's a suspicion of cancer (e.g., thyroid nodules).
- **Genetic Testing:** For inherited endocrine disorders like Multiple Endocrine Neoplasia (MEN) syndromes.

Common Endocrine disorders diagnosis

1. **Diabetes Mellitus:**
   - **Symptoms:** Frequent urination, excessive thirst, unexplained weight loss, fatigue.
   - **Tests:** Fasting blood glucose, Hemoglobin A1c, Oral glucose tolerance test.
2. **Thyroid Disorders (Hypothyroidism, Hyperthyroidism):**
   - **Symptoms:** Weight changes, temperature sensitivity, fatigue, changes in heart rate.
   - **Tests:** TSH, Free T4, Free T3, Thyroid antibodies.

3. **Adrenal Disorders (Addison's Disease, Cushing's Syndrome):**
   - **Symptoms:** Fatigue, muscle weakness, weight loss, high blood pressure, skin changes.
   - **Tests:** Serum cortisol, ACTH levels, 24-hour urine free cortisol, ACTH stimulation test.
4. **Pituitary Disorders (e.g., Acromegaly, Prolactinoma):**
   - **Symptoms:** Vision changes, headaches, growth abnormalities, menstrual irregularities.
   - **Tests:** IGF-1 levels, Prolactin levels, MRI of the pituitary gland.
5. **Parathyroid Disorders:**
   - **Symptoms:** Bone pain, kidney stones, fatigue, depression.
   - **Tests:** Serum calcium, PTH levels, 24-hour urine calcium.

Accurate diagnosis is crucial for effective treatment.Treatment options vary depending on the specific condition and may include:

- Hormone replacement therapy (HRT)
- Medications to regulate hormone production or balance
- Surgery to remove tumors or affected glands
- Lifestyle modifications (diet, exercise, stress management)
- Monitoring and management of related conditions (e.g., hypertension, dyslipidemia)

In conclusion, endocrine disorders encompass a broad range of conditions affecting the endocrine system, leading to hormonal imbalances and various physiological consequences. Understanding the causes, symptoms, and treatment options for these disorders is essential to provide effective management and improve quality of life for individuals affected.

Multiple Choice Questions

1. The endocrine system and the _____ system are both intimately involved in maintaining homeostasis.

   a) Cardiovascular b) Digestive
   c) Nervous d) Respiratory

2. Chemical signals that affect the behavior of other glands and tissues are _____.

   a) Enzymes b) Hormones
   c) Carbohydrates d) Metabolites

3. Which of the following is NOT a function of hormones?

   a) Maintain homeostasis b) Influence metabolism
   c) Innfluence growth and development d) Breaking down nutrients

4. What are the two categories based on chemical makeup in which hormones are classified?

   a) Glands and cortex b) Protein and carbohydrates
   c) Peptides and steroids d) Endocrine and ectocrine

5. Hormone communicate by binding to a receptor and further activates _____.

   a) Second messenger b) Third messenger
   c) First messenger d) All of the above

6. What is the hormone produced by adipose tissue which signal satiety?
   a) Glucagon b) Insulin
   c) Melatonin d) Leptin
7. Which of the following hormones does NOT aid in regulating fuel metabolism?
   a) Insulin b) Aldosterone
   c) Glucagon d) None of the above
8. Which of the following is true of female sex hormones?
   a) Progesterone is responsible for female secondary sex characteristics.
   b) Estrogen is necessary for maturation of the ovum.
   c) Estrogen does not aid in breast development.
   d) Progesterone helps the uterus to grow.
9. Which of the following is NOT true of glucagon?
   a) Produced by the pancreas b) Increases blood glucose levels
   c) Decrease blood glucose levels d) None of the above
10. Which of the following is the endocrine gland present within the brain?
    a) Adrenal gland b) Pancreas
    c) Pituitary gland d) Parathyroid gland
11. Which of the following is the endocrine gland present at top of kidney?
    a) Adrenal gland b) Hypothalamus
    c) Pancreas d) Thyroid gland
12. Which of the following hormone (s) are produced by hypothalamus?
    a) Oxytocin b) Antidiuretic hormone
    c) Releasing and Inhibitory hormones d) All of the above
13. The target organs of ADH are the:
    a) Adrenal cortex and liver b) Kidney and blood vessels
    c) Liver and kidney d) Pituitary and thyroid gland
14. ADH will stimulate _____ water reabsorption by the kidneys and ______ of the blood vessels; thus _____ blood pressure.
    a) Decrease: constriction: increase b) Decrease: dilation: decrease
    c) Increase: constriction: increase d) Increase: dilation: decrease
15. Identify the hormone that stimulates uterine contraction and the release of milk during lactation.
    a) ADH b) Glucagon
    c) Prolactin d) Leptin
16. Exemplify hormones secreted by the anterior pituitary.
    a) Anti-diuretic hormone and oxytocin b) ACTH and insulin
    c) Growth hormone and LH d) Thyroxine and Cortiosol
17. Identify a gland that is controlled by an anterior pituitary hormone.
    a) Pancreas b) Parathyroid
    c) Adrenal Medulla d) Ovary

18. Which of the following is NOT true of growth hormone?
    a) Stimulates rate of amino acid entrance into the cell
    b) Stimulates protein synthesis in bones, cartilage, and muscles
    c) Promotes glucose metabolism
    d) Promotes fat metabolism
19. What gland requires iodine in order to produce its hormones?
    a) Adrenal cortex b) Pancreas
    c) Parathyroid glands d) Thyroid gland
20. Identify a hormone that increases metabolic rate.
    a) Thyroid hormone b) Calcitonin
    c) Aldosterone d) Parathyroid hormone
33. Identify the gland that secretes cortisol and aldosterone.
    a) Thyroid b) Parathyroid
    c) Pancreas d) Adrenal
34. Which of the following is NOT related to adrenal medulla structure and function?
    a) Inner portion of adrenal gland.
    b) Controlled by the nervous system.
    c) Regulates level of glucose and minerals in blood.
    d) Produces epinephrine and norepinephrine.
35. Identify functions of calcium within the body.
    a) Clotting b) Hardens bone
    c) Nerve and muscle contraction d) All of the above
36. The main mineralocorticoid produced by the adrenal cortex is _____.
    a) Cortisol. b) Glucagon
    c) Epinephrine d) Aldosterone
37. Which of the following is NOT true of aldosterone?
    a) Targets kidney tubules to absorb sodium and water and to excrete potassium.
    b) It is a mineralocorticoid.
    c) Causes a decrease in urine volume.
    d) It causes a decrease in blood pressure.
38. Atrial natriuretic hormone (ANH) is produced by cells of the ___.
    a) Kidney tubules. b) Right atrium of the heart.
    c) Adrenal cortex. d) Pancreas.
39. The antagonistic hormone to insulin is __________.
    a) Glucagon b) Leptin
    c) Prolactin d) Melatonin
40. When blood glucose levels are low, the _____ will increase the secretion of _____.
    a) Adrenal cortex: aldosterone b) Pancreas; glucagon
    c) Pancreas: insulin d) Posterior pituitary: ADH

41. The most common second messengers for peptide hormones are ______ and ______.
    a) Peptide hormones and calcium
    b) Calcium and glucose
    c) CAMP and calcium
    d) CAMP and sodium.
42. The inability to produce ADH causes ______.
    a) Diabetes mellitus.
    b) Uterine contractions.
    c) Diabetes insipidus.
    d) Decreased urine volume.
43. Adrenocorticotropic hormone (ACTH) stimulates the ___ to produce and release its hormones.
    a) Anterior pituitary
    b) Adrenal medulla
    c) Adrenal cortex
    d) Kidneys
44. Underproduction of growth hormone during the growing years produces ______.
    a) Myxedema
    b) Gigantism
    c) Pituitary dwarfism
    d) Acromegaly
45. Identify the gland that secretes cortisol and aldosterone.
    a) Thyroid
    b) Parathyroid
    c) Pancreas
    d) Adrenal
46. Which of the following is not true about glucagon?
    a) Produced by the pancreas
    b) Increases blood glucose levels
    c) Promotes the use of fat and protein instead of glucose
    d) Stimulates the liver to store glucose as glycogen
47. Identify a characteristic of type I diabetes (IDDM).
    a) Development has a correlation with obesity.
    b) Most common form of diabetes.
    c) Body cells do not respond to insulin.
    d) Treatment usually involves insulin injections.
48. Identify a common function of atrial natriuretic hormone (ANH), aldosterone and antidiuretic hormone.Which of the following hormones does NOT help regulate blood pressure and volume?
    a) Atrial natriuretic factor
    b) Aldosterone
    c) Oxytocin
    d) Antidiuretic hormone
49. Which of the following is NOT an action of insulin?
    a) Stimulates cellular absorption of glucose.
    b) Stimulates cellular usage of glucose for energy.
    c) Stimulates the breakdown of glycogen.
    d) Lowers blood glucose levels.
50. Growth hormone is secreted by which gland?
    a) Hypothalamus
    b) Pituitary gland
    c) Adrenal gland
    d) Thyroid gland

39. Which of the following form of hypothyroidism is treated by antithyroid drugs and surgery?

    a) Addison disease b) Grave's disease
    c) Gigantism d) Acromegaly

40. Which term is used to describe the bulging or protruding eyes that characterize hyperthyroidism?

    a) Exopthalmos b) Goiter
    c) Acromegaly d) Grave's disease

41. Which of the following is the disease occurring by taking high doses of steroids for long period of time?

    a) Diabetes mellitus b) Diabetes insipidus
    c) Cretinism d) Cushing's syndrome

42. Which of the following disease condition is characterized by insufficient production of hormones by the adrenal glands.

    a) Addison's disease b) Cushing Syndrome
    c) Grave's disease d) Cretinism

43. The disease condition caused by hypersecretion of somatotropic hormones is.................

    a) Myxedema b) Dwarfism
    c) Gigantism d) Acromegaly

44. If left untreated, which of the following condition progresses to ketoacidosis?

    a) Diabetes insipidus b) Diabetes mellitus
    c) Acromegaly d) Grave's disease

45. Which of the following endocrine condition occurs when there is an overproduction of the prolactin hormone that promotes lactation?

    a) Cushing syndrome b) Diabetes insipidus
    c) Addison's disease d) Hyperprolactemia

46. Which of the following are signs of hypothyroidism?

    a) Weight loss and hyperglycemia b) Fatigue and cold intolerance
    c) Tachycardia and diarrhea d) Polydipsia and polyphagia

47. Which of the following endocrine condition occurs when the kidney is compromised in its ability to concentrate urine?

    a) Addison disease b) Cushing syndrome
    c) Diabetes mellitus d) Diabetes insipidus

48. Fatigue, headache, blurry vision and dry itchy skin are signs and symptoms of:

    a) Hyperglycemia b) Hypoglycemia
    c) Both of the above d) None of the above

49. Which type of diabetes mellitus is where the beta cells produce insufficient insulin?

    a) Gestational b) Type I
    c) Type II d) None of the above

50. Which of the following terms means "increased appetite?"
    a) Glycosuria b) Polyphagia
    c) Polydipsia d) Polyphagia
51. Which of the following is not the sign of Hypothyroidism?
    a) Diarrhoea b) Lethargy
    c) Anorexia d) Weight gain
52. Which of the following hormone is responsible for the "Fight-or-Flight" response?
    a) Thyoxine and Melatonin b) Insulin and Glucagon
    c) Epinephrine and Norepinephrine d) Oestrogen and progesterone
53. Among the following which hormone is not secreated by hypothalamus?
    a) PRH b) FSH
    c) CRH d) TRH
54. Which of the following is not an endocrine gland?
    a) Adrenal b) Thyroid
    c) Lacrimal d) Pituitary
55. Where are islets of langerhans found?
    a) Anterior Pituitary b) Cortex
    c) Spleen d) Endocrine pancreas
56. Diabetes Mellitus is a hormonal condition in which
    a) Ketone bodies increases in urine b) Ketone bodies decreases in urine
    c) Urine becomes more dilute d) None of the above
57. What does Somatostatin do?
    a) Inhibit release of Insulin and glucagon
    b) Stimulate release of insulin and glucagon
    c) Stimulate glucagon release while inhibit insulin release
    d) Inhibit glucagon release while stimulate insulin release
58. In Which of the Following Pairs, the Hormone of Endocrine Glands and Its Primary Action Is Incorrect or Mismatched?
    a) Calcitonin - Lower blood calcium levels
    b) Parathyroid - Raises blood calcium levels
    c) Somatostatin - Inhibits release of glucagon
    d) Melatonin - Regulates the rate of cellular metabolism
59. Which of the Following Endocrine Glands Contributes to Setting the Body's Biological Clock?
    a) Pituitary gland b) Pineal gland
    c) Thymus gland d) Adrenal gland
60. Which of these is a male sex hormone?
    a) Aldosterone b) Androgens
    c) Pheromones d) Insulin

61. Which of the Following Hormones Regulate Blood Sodium and Potassium Levels in the Body?
    a) Cortisol
    b) Glycogens
    c) Aldosteone
    d) Pheromones
62. Following statements about type I diabetes are true, except:
    a) Shows classic symptoms of insulin deficiency such as polydipsia, polyphagia, polyuria
    b) Obesity is usually present
    c) Absolute deficiency of insulin caused by destroyed β cells
    d) Both a) and c)
63. Which of these is true of the endocrine system?
    a) secretes hormones that are transported to target cells by blood.
    b) causes changes in metabolic activities.
    c) effects are prolonged.
    d) All of above are true.
64. The endocrine gland responsible for the body's circadian rhythm is the:
    a) Thymus gland
    b) Pineal gland
    c) Parathyroid gland
    d) Pituitary gland
65. An ACTH stimulation test is commonly used to diagnose:
    a) Grave's disease
    b) Cystic fibrosis
    c) Hashimoto's disease
    d) Adrenal insufficiency and Addison's disease
66. The most common benign tumor of the pituitary gland is
    a) Glioma
    b) Prolactinoma
    c) Carcinoid tumor
    d) Islet cell tumor
67. What is the treatment of hyperparathyroidism?
    a) Synthetic thyroid hormone
    b) Desiccated thyroid hormone
    c) Surgical removal of glands
    d) Calcium and phosphates
68. Short stature and undeveloped ovaries suggest which of the following disorder:
    a) Polycystic ovarian syndrome
    b) Prolactemia
    c) Grave's disease
    d) Turner's syndrome
69. Adrenaline and non adrenaline are hormones and act as ________.
    a) Neurotransmitters
    b) Energy storing substance
    c) Food storage material
    d) Energy producing agentsAcromegaly

70. Which of the following is not the effect of Addison's disease?
    a) Muscle weakness
    b) Lethargy
    c) Hyperglycemia
    d) All of the above
71. The principle sex hormone in female is
    a) Testosterone
    b) Estrogen
    c) Androgens
    d) Dihydrotestosterone
72. Which of the following is NOT a primary gonadal hormone?
    a) Estrogen
    b) Insulin
    c) Progesterone
    d) Testosterone
73. What is the primary function of estrogen in females?
    a) Development of female secondary sexual characteristics
    b) Maintenance of pregnancy
    c) Regulation of cholesterol levels
    d) Regulation of blood sugar levels
74. Which hormone is crucial for preparing the uterine lining for pregnancy and its maintenance?
    a) Adrenaline
    b) Estrogen
    c) Progesterone
    d) Testosterone
75. In males, where are the primary gonads located?
    a) Ovaries
    b) Fallopian tubes
    c) Testes
    d) Uterus
76. The complex system of interactions involving the hypothalamus, pituitary gland, and gonads is known as:
    a) Hypothalamic-Pituitary-Gonadal axis
    b) Hypothalamic-Pituitary-Thyroid axis
    c) Hypothalamic-Pituitary-Adrenal axis
    d) Hypothalamic-Pituitary-Pancreas axis
77. Which hormone is produced by the ovaries and is responsible for the release of an egg during ovulation?
    a) Estrogen
    b) Follicle-stimulating hormone (FSH)
    c) Luteinizing hormone (LH)
    d) Progesterone
78. Choose the correct answer, Polycystic Ovary Syndrome (PCOS) is characterized by:
    a) Decreased levels of luteinizing hormone (LH)
    b) Excessive production of prolactin
    c) Elevated levels of androgens
    d) Elevated levels of estrogen

79. Which of the following statement is FALSE regarding oxytocin?
    a) Suckling is the major stimulus for oxytocin secretion.
    b) Dilation of the cervix increases oxytocin.
    c) Oxytocin causes contraction of the uterus.
    d) None of the above.

80. All the following statements are correct regarding the hyperprolactinemia(prolactin excess) EXCEPT:
    a) It results from hypothalamic destruction or prolactin-secreting tumors.
    b) It causes galactorrhea and decreased libido.
    c) It causes failure to ovulate and amenorrhea by inhibiting GnRH.
    d) Increased Domaine secretion.

81. Proopopmelanocorticotropin (POMC) is a precursor for the following peptides, EXCEPT:
    a) Adrenocorticotropic hormone (ACTH)
    b) Thyroid Stimulating hormone (TSH)
    c) Beta-lipotropin
    d) Beta-endorphin

82. Which of the following factors increases prolactin secretion?
    a) Dopamine
    b) Bromocriptine
    c) Somatostatin
    d) Thyrotrophin-releasing hormone

83. Which of the following increases the secretion of growth hormone?
    a) Insulin-like growth factor-1
    b) Somatostatin
    c) Hypoglycemia
    d) Exogenous GH administration

84. Glomerular area of adrenal cortex is responsible for ________.
    a) Water and electrolyte balance
    b) Steroid hormone secretion
    c) Blood pressure
    d) Carbohydrate metabolism

85. What is the name of the cells producing the hormone in adrenal medulla?
    a) F cells
    b) Chief cells
    c) Principal cells
    d) Chromaffin cells

86. Adrenal gland consists of ________.
    a) ACTH and BCTH
    b) Inner and outer layer of kidney
    c) Inner medulla and outer cortex
    d) Lower adrenal and upper adrenal

87. The adrenal ____________ secretes small amount of both sex hormones.
    a) Medull
    b) Cortex
    c) Accessory gland
    d) Cells

88. ADH acts on ________.
    a) Loop of Henle
    b) Collecting ducts of testes
    c) Collecting tubules of kidneys
    d) PCT

Answer Key

1	c	2	b	3	d	4	c	5	a	6	d	7	b
8	d	9	c	10	c	11	a	12	c	13	b	14	d
15	c	16	a	17	d	18	a	19	d	20	a	21	c
22	d	23	a	24	a	25	c	26	b	27	d	28	c
29	a	30	b	31	d	32	b	33	d	34	d	35	d
36	d	37	d	38	b	39	a	40	b	41	c	42	c
43	c	44	c	45	d	46	d	47	d	48	c	49	c
50	b	51	b	52	a	53	d	54	a	55	c	56	b
57	d	58	b	59	d	60	a	61	b	62	b	63	a
64	c	65	b	66	c	67	d	68	a	69	d	70	c
71	b	72	b	73	c	74	d	75	d	76	b	77	d
78	b	79	c	80	d	81	a	82	c	83	b	84	b
85	a	86	c	87	c	88	a	89	c	90	a	91	b
92	d	93	b	94	d	95	c	96	a	97	d	98	b
99	b	100	c										

16

Clinical Physiology of Eye and Ear

Aakanksha[1], Chaithra S.N.[2], Rajesh Kumar[1] and A.C. Saxena[2]

[1]*Department of Veterinary Surgery and Radiology, Bihar Veterinary College, BASU Patna, Bihar*

[2]*Division of Surgery, Indian Veterinary Research Institute, Izatnagar, Uttar Pradesh*

Introduction

Eye

Visual perception, eyesight, sight, or vision is the ability to interpret the surrounding environment using light in the visible spectrum reflected by the objects in the environment. The eyes are the sensory organs that are extension of the brain; they receive visual information from the environment and transmit them to the visual sensory area of the brain for interpretation.

The pineal and para-pineal glands are photoreceptive in non-mammalian vertebrates. Birds have photoactive cerebrospinal fluid (CSF)-contacting neurons within the paraventricular organ that respond to light in the absence of input from the eyes or neurotransmitters.

Accessory Structure of the Eye

Eyelids - (Palpebrae) The free margins of the eyelids form the palpebral fissure. The edges where the upper and lower eyelids meet are called the lateral and medial canthus. The palpebral margins are lined by eyelashes. The eyelids are supported internally by sheets of connective tissue that form the tarsal plate.

Glands associated with the eyelids

Glands of Zeis - These are sebaceous glands associated with the eyelashes.

Tarsal glands - (Meibomian glands) - These glands line the inner margin of the lid and produce a lipid-rich product that prevents the lids from sticking together.

Lacrimal caruncle - This is a mound of tissue in the medial canthus that produces thick secretions.

Conjunctiva It is the epithelium that lines the inner surface of the eyelids and continues onto the outer surface of the eye.

Palpebral conjunctiva lines the inner surface of the eyelid.

Bulbar conjunctiva lines the anterior surface of the eye.

Lacrimal Apparatus It produces, distributes and removes tears. Tears reduce friction, remove debris, prevent bacterial infection and provide nutrients and oxygen for the conjunctiva. Lacrimal glands are located near the lateral canthus of the eye. Tears flow over the cornea and are drained into the nose by the nasolacrimal duct.

Nictitating membrane or the third eyelid is found in the medial canthus and it aids in protection of the eye and its glands also produce tears. Tear is also produced by the harderian glands, which is one of the lacrimal glands found in many bird and mammals except in carnivores.

Structure of eye The eye is a ball-shaped organ placed in the orbital fossa and has two cavities:

Posterior cavity: It is behind the lens and contains vitreous humor which is a hydrogel that contains hyaluronic acid and collagen fibers. It supplies nutrition to the retina.

Anterior cavity: It is in the front of the lens and is filled with a clear liquid called aqueous humor. It is further subdivided into anterior and posterior chambers by the iris.

Anterior chamber: The space between the cornea and the lens.

Posterior chamber: It lies between the iris and the suspensory ligament.

Eyeball tunics: The wall of the eye has three concentric layers called tunics.

Outer layer (fibrous tunic): The eyeball is enveloped by a tough outer protective fibrous sheet of connective tissue called sclera; anteriorly modified into the transparent cornea.

Middle vascular layer (uvea): It has three regions namely

Choroid: In nocturnal animals this layer contains a reflecting pigment called tapetum lucidum which causes "eye shine" in the night.

Ciliary body: It supports iris and lens. It secretes fluid called aqueous humor

Iris: It is a diaphragm of varying size and is a pigmented structure containing dilator and constrictor smooth muscle which controls diameter of its central opening called pupil.

Inner Layer (neural tunic) / Retina: Innermost layer of the eye which is light sensitive. Its main functions are photoreception and impulse transmission. It is a part of the central nervous system (CNS) and is actually brain tissue. The retina is interrupted at a point called *optic disk*, where the axons of the retina's ganglion cell layer leave the retina to the brain. The optic disk gives rise to the optic nerve (2nd cranial nerve). Arteries and veins enter the eye at the optic disk and provide nutrition to the retina. There are no photoreceptors present in the retina where the optic nerve leaves the eye, and this region is called *blind spot*. The *fovea* is an area located at the back of the retina, dorso-lateral to the optic disc, where the light rays are not distorted. In man and primates, cones are concentrated at fovea which provides sharp visual image. In domestic animals fovea is absent, but a homologous area is present referred to as *area centralis or macula or visual streak.*

The retina consists of two layers

Outer Pigmented layer / Retinal Pigmented Epithelium (RPE)

Inner Neural layer: It consists of three layers of cells that include the photoreceptors, bipolar cells and ganglion cells from outer to inside. The neural layer extends anteriorly to the boundary called the *ora serrata*.

- **Photoreceptors: Rods** are more sensitive to light and are responsible for night (scotopic) vision but **cones** are less sensitive to light and function in bright light and provide color discrimination and greater detail. They are responsible for day (photopic) vision. Rods have globular proteins called visual pigment rhodopsin or visual purple. Each molecule consists of a protein called opsin and a vitamin

A derivative called retinal (retinene). In cones, the pigment is called photopsin (iodopsin). Retina of domestic animals contains mostly rods while retina of birds contains mostly cones.

- **Bipolar cells:** They are the first order neurons of the visual pathway and transmit signals from the photoreceptors to the ganglion cells, cells directly or indirectly (via amacrine cells). The transmission of visual information through the bipolar cells is modulated by horizontal cells found in this layer. Horizontal cells are the laterally interconnecting neurons that connect different photoreceptors.
- **Ganglion cells:** They are the largest neurons of the retina, arranged in a single layer close to the vitreous body. They are second –order neurons of visual pathway. The transmission at this layer is modulated by amacrine cells. Amacrine cells are inhibitory neurons in the retina.

Lens (aquula): The lens is a transparent, biconvex structure in the eye that, along with the cornea, helps to refract light to be focused on the retina. The lens, by changing shape, functions to change the focal distance of the eye so that it can focus on objects at various distances. This adjustment of the lens is known as *accommodation*. It is suspended behind pupil by a ring of fibers called suspensory ligaments which are attached to ciliary body. Ciliary muscle contraction increases the convexity of the lens and focuses near objects on the retina. When lens becomes opaque it is called cataract. The lens itself lacks nerves, blood vessels, or connective tissue.

Glaucoma: It is increase in the intra-occular pressure. The ciliary process produce aqueous humor and it flows into the anterior chamber through the pupil. It is absorbed into the venous system at right angle between the cornea and the iris. If the absorption is obstructed, intraocular pressure increases which is called glaucoma.

Color Perception: Different animals have different kinds of color vision. Some have very poor color vision and others have very good color vision. In fact some birds and bees have super color vision and see colors that humans don't see. Dogs, cats, swine, mice, rats and rabbits have very poor color vision. In fact, they see mostly greys and some blues and yellows. Monkeys, ground squirrels, birds, insects, and many fish can see a fairly good range of color. Cattle, sheep and goat are red-green colour blind. Domestic animals have dichromatic color vision.

Night blindness (nictalopia) occurs with severe vitamin A deficiency.

Light adaptation: This occurs when we move from the dark into bright light. Rods and cones are both stimulated and large amounts of the photopigment are broken down instantaneously, producing a flood of signals resulting in the glare.

Dark adaptation is reverse of light adaptation; occurs when going from a well light to a dark area.

Visual acuity (VA) refers to the clarity and sharpness of vision. Cone cells provide better acuity than rod cells. The highest visual acuity is provided by area centralis where the cone cells concentration is more.

Accommodation of eye is the ability of the eye lens to adjust its focal length by changing its curvature for focusing the image to the retina for both near and distant vision.

In horse, the retina is placed at different distances from cornea because of the ramp shaped retina. The ciliary muscles are weak and are unable to alter the curvature of the lens to change the focal length. The animal simply raises or lowers its head or eye to allow the image to fall on the retina. In domestic animals – the predatory animals as dogs and cats can increase the power of their lenses more than horses and ruminants (ie, accommodative power is more in dogs and cats). Birds are good accommodators and each eye in birds can accommodate independently of the other. In birds, ability to accommodate reduces with age (as human).

Presbyopia is the condition of the eye characterized by gradual loss of power of accommodation, which is associated with loss of emmetropia (ability to focus parallel rays of light on retina).

Refraction errors of eye Ametropia: If the eye lens is unable to adjust its focusing capacity to focus image on the retina. It is of three types:

Myopia / short or near vision: Abnormal increase in the anterior posterior diameter of the eyeball or the excessive refraction of the eye lens causes focusing of the image just before the retina.

Hypermetropia (long or far sight): It is a common defect in wild animals, shortening of the anterior posterior diameter of the eyeball or less refraction of the eye lens, thus image fall behind the retina.

Astigmatism: The difference in the radius of curvature of the cornea causes the light to focus not to a common point on the retina, which results in both myotropic and hypermetropic visions.

Electroretinogram (ERG) is recording of the electrical activity generated by neural and non-neuronal cells in the retina in response to a light stimulus. It is composed principally of A, B and C waves.

Electroocculogram: It is a record of potential difference between the front and back of the eye ball.

Tonometry is the procedure to determine the intraocular pressure (IOP), the fluid pressure inside the eye. The normal range is 10-21 mmHg

Ophthalmoscopy, also called funduscopy, is a test that allows to see inside the fundus of the eye and other structures using an ophthalmoscope (or funduscope).

Ear

The Auditory System is designed to detect and analyse sound in the environment. Much of animal communication relies on this system. Sounds are travelling vibrations through air or liquid characterized by alternating regions of increased pressure caused by compression of molecules and region of decreased pressure caused by rarefaction of molecules. The auditory system perceives the frequency of sounds as pitch (unit is hertz) and their amplitude as loudness (unit is decibel). The neural perception of sound is called hearing.

Structure of ear The ear consists of three parts; external ear (outer ear), middle ear and inner ear. External ear: The external ear is made up of pinna and external auditory meatus. Pinna guides sound waves down the ear canal and acts as a resonating structure. In birds, external ear lacks a flap or pinna and is hidden by specialized feathers known as auricular feathers. The auditory canal conducts the sound waves into the middle ear. In dogs, the ear canal is long and and bent (L shaped) and often traps wax or provides an ideal habitat for mites, yeast and bacteria.

Tympanic membrane or ear drum is a separation between the outer and the middle ear.

Middle ear: It is air filled cavity, separated from the external ear by the tympanic membrane and from the inner ear by vestibular window (oval window) and cochlear window (round window). containing ossicles and Eustachian tube. The ear ossicles are bony structures namely malleus (hammer), incus (anvil), and stapes (stirrup). They conduct the vibrations toward the inner ear. In birds only one bone called columella is present.

Eustachian tube (auditory tube): It is a collapsible tube that connects middle ear with the pharynx. It opens periodically to equalize middle ear pressure with external atmospheric pressure and to clear fluid from middle ear. In horse, it has a ventral diverticulum called guttural pouch.

Inner Ear (Labyrinth): It is made up of bony labyrinth, within it is located the membranous labyrinth. The membranous labyrinth is surrounded by fluid called perilymph. Membranous labyrinth consists of cochlea (acoustic part) and vestibular organ (non-acoustic part).

Cochlea : Cochlea looks like a coiled up snail shell. It consists of three parallel, fluid filled canals that are coiled around a central bony axis called modiolus. Modiolus contain ganglion cells of auditory portion of cranial nerve VIII called spiral ganglion.

The cochlea of the bird differs considerably from that of the mammal. It is short and nearly straight, rather than coiled.

Scala vestibuli (vestibular duct) are the fluid filled tubes. It is the uppermost canal that starts at the oval window and ends at the tip (apex) of the cochlea. It is separated from scala media by Reissner's membrane (vestibular membrane).

Scala tympani (tympanic duct): It is the lowermost canal that starts at the round window and terminates at the apex of cochlea and is separated from the scala media by the basilar membrane.

Scala media (cochlear duct): It is the fluid filled canal present between the scala vestibuli and scala tympani. Scala vestibuli and scala tympani are connected with each other at the apex of cochlea at a region called helicotrema.

Both the scala vestibuli and scala tympani are filled with a fluid called perilymph, while scala media is filled with endolymph.

Organ of corti (spiral organ): The sensory organ of the auditory system is the organ of corti. It converts vibrations into nerve impulses. The organ of corti consists of sensory cells, supporting cells and tectorial membrane.

The sensory cells or hair cells are thin, stiff sensory hairs (microvilli or stereocilia) protruding into the endolymph. The hair cells in the row nearest the axis of the cochlea are called inner hair cells, while the hair cells in the remaining 3-5 rows are called outer hair cells. The inner hair cells detect sound while the outer hair cells amplify sound waves (cochlear tuning).

Surrounding the hair cells is a highly organized system of supporting cells and directly above is a gelatinous membrane called the tectorial membrane which is secreted by the supporting cells.

Mechanism of hearing Sound waves enter the ear, vibrate the tympanic membrane causing the middle ear ossicles to vibrate. The stapes is in contact with the oval window causing the vibration to be transmitted to the fluid of the the scala vestibuli. The moving fluid can either transfer the movement laterally to the other 2 tubes, the scala media and scala tympani or travel to the end of the scala vestibuli and, through an opening called the helicotrema into the scala tympani. These travelling waves in turn cause vibrations in the basilar membrane, which causes tectorial membrane to slide back and forth over inner and outer hair cells of the organ of Corti. Bending of stereocilia in the direction of tallest stereocilia cause pulling of tip link and causes depolarization. The bending of stereocilia away from the tallest stereocilium causes hyperpolarization of hair cells.

Auditory pathway The nerve impulse from the cochlear nerve to carried to the vestibulocochlear nerve. The vestibulococlear nerve terminates in cochlear nucleus of medulla. The axons from the cochlear nucleus terminates into inferior colliculus of mid brain. From here the axons will project into the median geniculate body of thalamus and from there to the primary and secondary auditory cortex of temporal lobe of cerebral cortex. Primary auditory cortex functions to study features of sound (frequency, loudness and pattern). The secondary auditory cortex process the information further for recognition of sound.

Auditory agnosia: Inability to hear

Vestibular system Sensory information about motion, equilibrium, and spatial orientation is provided by the vestibular apparatus, which in each ear includes the anterior utricle, posterior saccule, and three semicircular canals. The otolith organs (utricle and saccule) detect gravity (information in a vertical orientation) and linear movement. The semicircular canals detect rotational movement.

Otolith organs (gravireceptor): They have a 2 by 3 mm patch called macula composed of hair cells and supporting cells. Each hair cell of a macula has 40-70 stereocilia and one true cilium called a kinocilium. The tips of these cilia are embedded in an otolithic membrane (gelatinous membrane). This membrane is weighted down with protein- calcium carbonate granules called otoliths. These otoliths add to the weight and inertia of the membrane and enhance the sense of gravity and motion.

Vestibulo-ocular reflex (VOR) is a reflex eye movement that stabilizes images on the retina during head movement by producing an eye movement in the direction opposite to head movement, thus preserving the image on the center of the visual field. It is by means of vestibular projections from the semicircular ducts.

MCQs

1. Which of the following structures is responsible for the production of aqueous humor in the eye?
   a) Cornea b) Lens
   c) Ciliary body d) Retina
2. The cornea receives its nourishment primarily from:
   a) Blood vessels b) Aqueous humor
   c) Tear film d) Both B and C
3. Which part of the eye contains the highest concentration of photoreceptors?
   a) Optic nerve b) Cornea
   c) Retina d) Lens
4. The condition characterized by increased intraocular pressure is known as:
   a) Cataracts b) Glaucoma
   c) Uveitis d) Retinitis

5. The tapetum lucidum is found in the:
   a) Cornea
   b) Lens
   c) Retina
   d) Choroid
6. Rod cells in the retina are primarily responsible for:
   a) Color vision
   b) Daylight vision
   c) Night vision
   d) Peripheral vision
7. What is the primary function of the lens in the eye?
   a) Protection of internal structures
   b) Regulation of light entry
   c) Focus light on the retina
   d) Production of aqueous humor
8. Which of the following structures drains aqueous humor from the eye?
   a) Ciliary body
   b) Canal of Schlemm
   c) Optic nerve
   d) Vitreous body
9. The macula is part of the:
   a) Cornea
   b) Lens
   c) Retina
   d) Iris
10. Which vitamin is crucial for maintaining healthy vision?
    a) Vitamin A
    b) Vitamin B12
    c) Vitamin C
    d) Vitamin D
11. The conjunctiva is a membrane that covers the:
    a) Lens
    b) Cornea
    c) Eyelid
    d) Sclera
12. Which structure is responsible for the sharpest vision in the eye?
    a) Cornea
    b) Lens
    c) Fovea centralis
    d) Optic disc
13. Which of the following is NOT a layer of the cornea?
    a) Epithelium
    b) Endothelium
    c) Bowman's layer
    d) Sclera
14. Which cranial nerve is primarily responsible for the movement of the eyeball?
    a) Optic nerve
    b) Oculomotor nerve
    c) Trigeminal nerve
    d) Facial nerve
15. What is the name of the reflex that protects the eye by closing the eyelid?
    a) Pupillary reflex
    b) Blink reflex
    c) Accommodation reflex
    d) Light reflex
16. The anterior chamber of the eye is located between the:
    a) Cornea and lens
    b) Iris and lens
    c) Cornea and iris
    d) Lens and retina
17. Which condition is characterized by clouding of the lens?
    a) Glaucoma
    b) Cataracts
    c) Retinitis
    d) Conjunctivitis

18. The photoreceptors responsible for color vision are:
    a) Rods b) Cones
    c) Bipolar cells d) Ganglion cell
19. Which part of the eye adjusts its shape to help focus light?
    a) Cornea b) Sclera
    c) Lens d) Retina
20. The optic nerve transmits visual information from the retina to the:
    a) Cornea b) Lens
    c) Brain d) Iris
21. The vitreous body is located:
    a) In the anterior chamber b) In the posterior chamber
    c) Between the lens and the retina d) Between the cornea and the iris
22. The dark adaptation process in the eye involves:
    a) Decrease in pupil size b) Increase in rod activity
    c) Increase in cone activity d) Decrease in retinal sensitivity
23. Which layer of the retina contains photoreceptors?
    a) Inner nuclear layer b) Outer plexiform layer
    c) Ganglion cell layer d) Outer nuclear layer
24. The main purpose of the tear film is to:
    a) Protect and lubricate the eye b) Refract light
    c) Support the lens d) Absorb excess light
25. Which structure helps maintain the shape of the eye?
    a) Cornea b) Aqueous humor
    c) Sclera d) Retina
26. Which part of the eye contains the highest concentration of blood vessels?
    a) Cornea b) Lens
    c) Choroid d) Retina
27. The light-sensitive pigment in rod cells is:
    a) Rhodopsin b) Melanin
    c) Hemoglobin d) Chlorophyll
28. Which of the following structures is avascular?
    a) Cornea b) Retina
    c) Sclera d) Iris
29. The condition where the eye's lens loses its ability to focus, often due to aging, is known as:
    a) Myopia b) Hyperopia
    c) Presbyopia d) Astigmatism
30. Which part of the eye contains the densest population of cones?
    a) Peripheral retina b) Macula
    c) Optic disc d) Sclera

31. Which of the following layers is the outermost layer of the eye?
    a) Retina b) Choroid
    c) Sclera d) Lens
32. The optic disc is also known as the:
    a) Macula b) Blind spot
    c) Fovea d) Iris
33. Which gland is responsible for producing tears?
    a) Sebaceous gland b) Lacrimal gland
    c) Sweat gland d) Meibomian gland
34. The process by which the eye adjusts to focus on near or far objects is called:
    a) Refraction b) Accommodation
    c) Convergence d) Divergence
35. What is the name of the colored part of the eye that regulates the amount of light entering the eye?
    a) Cornea b) Iris
    c) Lens d) Retina
36. The refractive power of the cornea is measured in:
    a) Diopters b) Millimeters
    c) Centimeters d) Degrees
37. The part of the retina responsible for the highest visual acuity is the:
    a) Optic disc b) Macula
    c) Periphery d) Vitreous body
38. Which structure controls the size of the pupil?
    a) Lens b) Ciliary body
    c) Iris d) Cornea
39. Which of the following is responsible for draining tears from the eye into the nasal cavity?
    a) Lacrimal gland b) Nasolacrimal duct
    c) Meibomian gland d) Scleral venous sinus
40. Which cells in the retina are primarily responsible for detecting light intensity?
    a) Ganglion cells b) Bipolar cells
    c) Rod cells d) Cone cells
41. The term "emmetropia" refers to:
    a) Nearsightedness b) Farsightedness
    c) Normal vision d) Astigmatism
42. Which of the following is NOT a component of the uveal tract?
    a) Iris b) Ciliary body
    c) Choroid d) Retina

43. Which condition involves inflammation of the uveal tract?
    a) Uveitis
    b) Conjunctivitis
    c) Keratitis
    d) Blepharitis
44. The lens is held in place by the:
    a) Optic nerve
    b) Ciliary muscles
    c) Zonular fibers
    d) Cornea
45. The refractive index of the lens is higher than that of the:
    a) Cornea
    b) Aqueous humor
    c) Vitreous humor
    d) Sclera
46. Which of the following is a function of the choroid?
    a) Light refraction
    b) Protection of the eye
    c) Nourishment of the retina
    d) Light absorption
47. Which structure in the eye is avascular and transparent?
    a) Retina
    b) Cornea
    c) Sclera
    d) Choroid
48. Which layer of the eye provides most of the blood supply to the outer retina?
    a) Sclera
    b) Choroid
    c) Retina
    d) Cornea
49. Which part of the eye is responsible for changing the shape of the lens?
    a) Iris
    b) Ciliary body
    c) Cornea
    d) Retina
50. Which of the following is NOT a function of the aqueous humor?
    a) Providing nutrients
    b) Maintaining intraocular pressure
    c) Light refraction
    d) Draining waste products
51. The fovea centralis is part of the:
    a) Cornea
    b) Lens
    c) Retina
    d) Sclera
52. Which of the following is a common cause of blindness in older dogs?
    a) Glaucoma
    b) Conjunctivitis
    c) Cataracts
    d) Retinal detachment
53. The sensory cells that respond to dim light are:
    a) Rods
    b) Cones
    c) Bipolar cells
    d) Ganglion cells
54. What is the function of the pigment epithelium in the retina?
    a) Light absorption
    b) Light refraction
    c) Color vision
    d) Blood supply
55. The clear, jelly-like substance that fills the space between the lens and the retina is the:
    a) Aqueous humor
    b) Vitreous humor
    c) Lacrimal fluid
    d) Plasma

56. The first step in the process of vision involves the:
    a) Optic nerve
    b) Retinal ganglion cells
    c) Photoreceptor cells
    d) Lens

57. The optic nerve exits the eye at the:
    a) Fovea
    b) Macula
    c) Optic disc
    d) Ciliary body

58. What is the main function of the sclera?
    a) Light refraction
    b) Protection
    c) Nourishment of the retina
    d) Tear production

59. Which layer of the cornea is the thickest?
    a) Epithelium
    b) Stroma
    c) Descemet's membrane
    d) Endothelium

60. The clear, outermost layer of the eye is the:
    a) Sclera
    b) Cornea
    c) Retina
    d) Iris

61. What is the function of the Meibomian glands?
    a) Tear production
    b) Oil secretion
    c) Aqueous humor production
    d) Light absorption

62. Which structure is responsible for the "red-eye" effect in photographs?
    a) Retina
    b) Choroid
    c) Iris
    d) Cornea

63. The part of the eye that provides most of the eye's refractive power is the:
    a) Lens
    b) Cornea
    c) Aqueous humor
    d) Vitreous humor

64. Which structure is responsible for the pupillary light reflex in the eye?
    a) Lens
    b) Retina
    c) Iris
    d) Cornea

65. The part of the eye that changes in diameter to adjust the amount of light entering the eye is the:
    a) Lens
    b) Cornea
    c) Pupil
    d) Retina

66. Which layer of the eye is continuous with the dura mater of the brain?
    a) Retina
    b) Choroid
    c) Sclera
    d) Cornea

67. The clear, watery fluid in the anterior chamber of the eye is called:
    a) Vitreous humor
    b) Aqueous humor
    c) Lacrimal fluid
    d) Plasma

68. The eye condition characterized by inflammation of the conjunctiva is known as:
    a) Uveitis
    b) Conjunctivitis
    c) Keratitis
    d) Blepharitis

69. Which part of the eye helps to maintain intraocular pressure?
    a) Cornea b) Aqueous humor
    c) Lens d) Retina
70. Which cells in the retina are responsible for transmitting visual information to the brain?
    a) Rod cells b) Cone cells
    c) Bipolar cells d) Ganglion cells
71. The process by which the eye adapts to low-light conditions is called:
    a) Light adaptation b) Dark adaptation
    c) Accommodation d) Refraction
72. Which of the following is NOT a layer of the retina?
    a) Ganglion cell layer b) Inner nuclear layer
    c) Outer nuclear layer d) Descemet's membrane
73 Which of the following structures is NOT involved in the refraction of light in the eye?
    a) Cornea b) Lens
    c) Sclera d) Aqueous humor
74. Which of the following conditions is caused by an irregular curvature of the cornea or lens?
    a) Myopia b) Hyperopia
    c) Astigmatism d) Presbyopia
75. Which part of the eye contains no photoreceptor cells?
    a) Macula b) Optic disc
    c) Fovea d) Peripheral retina
76. Which of the following conditions is caused by inflammation of the cornea?
    a) Uveitis b) Conjunctivitis
    c) Keratitis d) Blepharitis
77. The process by which the eyes adjust to different light intensities is called:
    a) Adaptation b) Accommodation
    c) Refraction d) Divergence
78. The main protein found in the lens is:
    a) Hemoglobin b) Collagen
    c) Keratin d) Crystallin
79. Which part of the eye is most sensitive to light?
    a) Iris b) Cornea
    c) Retina d) Sclera
80. The anterior and posterior chambers of the eye are filled with:
    a) Vitreous humor b) Aqueous humor
    c) Blood d) Lymph

81. The condition where the cornea has an irregular shape, causing distorted vision, is called:
   a) Myopia
   b) Hyperopia
   c) Astigmatism
   d) Presbyopia

82. The vitreous body is composed mainly of:
   a) Aqueous humor
   b) Blood
   c) Collagen and water
   d) Adipose tissue

83. The central visual field is processed in which part of the retina?
   a) Peripheral retina
   b) Fovea
   c) Optic disc
   d) Macula

84. Which enzyme is involved in the phototransduction pathway in rod cells?
   a) ATPase
   b) Phosphodiesterase
   c) Kinase
   d) Lipase

85. The reflex that allows both eyes to move in the same direction is known as:
   a) Convergence reflex
   b) Divergence reflex
   c) Consensual light reflex
   d) Yoked reflex

86. Which condition is caused by the detachment of the retina from the underlying tissue?
   a) Cataract
   b) Glaucoma
   c) Retinal detachment
   d) Macular degeneration

87. The term for nearsightedness is:
   a) Hyperopia
   b) Presbyopia
   c) Myopia
   d) Astigmatism

88. Which muscle is responsible for changing the shape of the lens during accommodation?
   a) Rectus muscle
   b) Oblique muscle
   c) Ciliary muscle
   d) Sphincter muscle

89. Which vitamin deficiency can lead to night blindness?
   a) Vitamin A
   b) Vitamin B12
   c) Vitamin C
   d) Vitamin D

90. Which of the following is NOT a part of the fibrous tunic of the eye?
   a) Cornea
   b) Sclera
   c) Choroid
   d) All of the above

91. Which condition is characterized by the degeneration of the macula, leading to central vision loss?
   a) Glaucoma
   b) Cataracts
   c) Macular degeneration
   d) Uveitis

92. Which part of the eye is responsible for absorbing excess light and preventing it from scattering within the eye?
   a) Cornea
   b) Lens
   c) Retina
   d) Choroid

93. The process by which the eye's lens becomes less flexible with age is known as:
    a) Myopia b) Hyperopia
    c) Presbyopia d) Astigmatism
94. Which of the following layers is NOT part of the retina?
    a) Ganglion cell layer b) Inner plexiform layer
    c) Outer nuclear layer d) Zonular layer
95. The term for farsightedness is:
    a) Myopia b) Hyperopia
    c) Presbyopia d) Astigmatism
96. Which of the following is NOT a function of the aqueous humor?
    a) Providing nutrients to the lens and cornea
    b) Maintaining intraocular pressure
    c) Refracting light
    d) Draining excess fluid from the eye
97. What is the primary function of the tapetum lucidum in ruminants?
    a) Refract light b) Absorb light
    c) Enhance night vision d) Provide nutrients to the retina
98. The most common cause of conjunctivitis in ruminants is:
    a) Viral infection b) Bacterial infection
    c) Trauma d) Allergies
99. Which bacterium is a common cause of keratoconjunctivitis (pink eye) in cattle?
    a) Escherichia coli b) Moraxella bovis
    c) Streptococcus agalactiae d) Clostridium tetani
100. What is the role of the nictitating membrane in ruminants?
    a) Refract light b) Protect the eye
    c) Focus light d) Absorb nutrients
101. What is the most common site of ocular neoplasia in cattle?
    a) Cornea b) Retina
    c) Eyelid d) Nictitating membrane
102. The menace response in ruminants is used to assess the function of which cranial nerve?
    a) Optic nerve (CN II) b) Oculomotor nerve (CN III)
    c) Trigeminal nerve (CN V) d) Facial nerve (CN VII)
103. The primary cause of corneal ulcers in ruminants is:
    a) Trauma b) Bacterial infection
    c) Fungal infection d) Nutritional deficiency
104. Which diagnostic test is commonly used to detect corneal ulcers in ruminants?
    a) Schirmer tear test b) Fluorescein staining
    c) Tonometry d) Slit-lamp examination

105. The primary cause of infectious bovine keratoconjunctivitis is:
   a) Viral infection
   b) Fungal infection
   c) Bacterial infection
   d) Parasitic infection

106. The condition of having unequal pupil sizes is termed:
   a) Mydriasis
   b) Miosis
   c) Anisocoria
   d) Strabismus

107. Which vitamin deficiency is associated with the condition known as 'xerophthalmia' in ruminants?
   a) Vitamin A
   b) Vitamin B1
   c) Vitamin C
   d) Vitamin D

108. Which diagnostic test measures the intraocular pressure in ruminants?
   a) Fluorescein staining
   b) Schirmer tear test
   c) Tonometry
   d) Slit-lamp examination

109. Which condition is characterized by inflammation of the retina in ruminants?
   a) Keratitis
   b) Uveitis
   c) Retinitis
   d) Conjunctivitis

110. The tear film in ruminants is composed of three layers: lipid, aqueous, and:
   a) Mucous
   b) Protein
   c) Carbohydrate
   d) Electrolyte

111. Which reflex involves the constriction of the pupil in response to light?
   a) Accommodation reflex
   b) Pupillary light reflex
   c) Corneal reflex
   d) Blink reflex

112. The most common diagnostic test to assess tear production is:
   a) Schirmer tear test
   b) Fluorescein staining
   c) Tonometry
   d) Slit-lamp examination

113. The condition where the eye's lens is dislocated is called:
   a) Cataract
   b) Glaucoma
   c) Lens luxation
   d) Conjunctivitis

114. Which condition is often referred to as "pink eye" in small animals?
   a) Uveitis
   b) Keratitis
   c) Conjunctivitis
   d) Retinitis

115. The normal range of intraocular pressure (IOP) in small animals is typically between:
   a) 5-15 mmHg
   b) 10-20 mmHg
   c) 15-25 mmHg
   d) 20-30 mmHg

116. Which condition involves the inflammation of the uveal tract, including the iris, ciliary body, and choroid?
   a) Uveitis
   b) Retinitis
   c) Keratitis
   d) Conjunctivitis

117. Which of the following conditions is characterized by a dry eye or reduced tear production?
 a) Keratoconjunctivitis sicca b) Glaucoma
 c) Cataract d) Conjunctivitis

118. The condition where the eyelids are inverted is called:
 a) Entropion b) Ectropion
 c) Blepharitis d) Chalazion

119. Which structure in the eye reflects light to improve vision in low-light conditions in some small animals?
 a) Retina b) Tapetum lucidum
 c) Sclera d) Cornea

120. Which structure in the eye has the highest refractive power?
 a) Cornea b) Lens
 c) Retina d) Iris

121. Which of the following is a common sign of ocular trauma in small animals?
 a) Excessive tearing b) Squinting
 c) Redness d) All of the above

122. Which of the following conditions is characterized by a loss of vision due to damage to the optic nerve?
 a) Glaucoma b) Cataract
 c) Retinal detachment d) Optic neuritis

123. The external ear consists of the:
 a) Tympanic membrane and ossicles
 b) Pinna and external auditory canal
 c) Cochlea and vestibule
 d) Semicircular canals and auditory nerve

124. Which part of the ear is primarily responsible for equilibrium and balance?
 a) Cochlea b) Tympanic membrane
 c) Semicircular canals d) Ossicles

125. The ossicles are located in the:
 a) External ear b) Middle ear
 c) Inner ear d) Cochlea

126. Which structure transmits sound vibrations to the oval window?
 a) Tympanic membrane b) Cochlea
 c) Stapes d) Semicircular canals

127. The cochlea is a part of the:
 a) External ear b) Middle ear
 c) Inner ear d) Tympanic membrane

128. What is the function of the Eustachian tube?
   a) To amplify sound
   b) To balance pressure between the middle ear and the atmosphere
   c) To transmit sound to the inner ear
   d) To detect head movement
129. The organ of Corti is located within the:
   a) Cochlea b) Vestibule
   c) Semicircular canals d) Eustachian tube
130. Which type of cells in the ear are responsible for detecting sound?
   a) Hair cells b) Rod cells
   c) Cone cells d) Ganglion cells
131. The tympanic membrane separates the:
   a) External ear from the middle ear
   b) Middle ear from the inner ear
   c) Cochlea from the vestibule
   d) Semicircular canals from the cochlea
132. Which structure in the ear helps to detect rotational movement?
   a) Cochlea b) Utricle
   c) Saccule d) Semicircular canals
133. What is the role of the auditory nerve?
   a) To amplify sound
   b) To transmit sound from the outer ear to the middle ear
   c) To carry auditory information to the brain
   d) To balance ear pressure
134. The vestibule is involved in the sensation of:
   a) Sound b) Linear acceleration
   c) Rotational acceleration d) Both B and C
135 Which structure connects the middle ear to the pharynx?
   a) Cochlea b) Eustachian tube
   c) Semicircular canals d) Auditory canal
136. Which ossicle is attached to the tympanic membrane?
   a) Malleus b) Incus
   c) Stapes d) Cochlea
137. Which structure transmits vibrations from the stapes to the fluid-filled inner ear?
   a) Tympanic membrane b) Oval window
   c) Round window d) Semicircular canals
138. The utricle and saccule are parts of the:
   a) Cochlea b) Vestibular system
   c) Middle ear d) Auditory canal

139. What fluid fills the membranous labyrinth of the inner ear?
   a) Endolymph b) Perilymph
   c) Cerebrospinal fluid d) Synovial fluid
140. Which part of the ear is responsible for converting sound waves into neural signals?
   a) External ear b) Middle ear
   c) Inner ear d) Eustachian tube
141. The round window is located in the:
   a) Middle ear b) Inner ear
   c) External ear d) Tympanic membrane
142. Which structure in the ear contains the hair cells that detect sound vibrations?
   a) Cochlea b) Semicircular canals
   c) Vestibule d) Eustachian tube
143. Which of the following is a function of the middle ear?
   a) Balance b) Amplification of sound
   c) Sound transduction d) Equalization of pressure
144. What structure in the ear is primarily responsible for detecting linear acceleration?
   a) Cochlea b) Semicircular canals
   c) Utricle d) Stapes
145. The auditory cortex, where sound is processed, is located in the:
   a) Frontal lobe b) Temporal lobe
   c) Parietal lobe d) Occipital lobe
146. Which of the following is NOT a part of the ossicles?
   a) Malleus b) Incus
   c) Stapes d) Cochlea
147. What is the primary function of the cochlea?
   a) Balance b) Hearing
   c) Regulating ear pressure d) Protecting the ear from infection
148. The semicircular canals are primarily involved in detecting what type of movement?
   a) Linear acceleration b) Sound waves
   c) Rotational movement d) Air pressure changes
149. What type of fluid fills the cochlea?
   a) Endolymph b) Perilymph
   c) Plasma d) Interstitial fluid
150. The hair cells in the cochlea are responsible for converting sound vibrations into:
   a) Electrical signals b) Mechanical movements
   c) Chemical signals d) Light signals
151. Which cranial nerve is involved in transmitting auditory information to the brain?
   a) Facial nerve (VII) b) Glossopharyngeal nerve (IX)
   c) Vagus nerve (X) d) Vestibulocochlear nerve (VIII)

152. The main function of the pinna is to:
a) Transmit sound to the brain
b) Protect the middle ear
c) Collect and funnel sound waves
d) Balance air pressure

153. Otitis externa refers to inflammation of which part of the ear?
a) Inner ear
b) Middle ear
c) External ear canal
d) Tympanic membrane

154. Which organism is commonly associated with otitis externa in dogs?
a) Streptococcus
b) Malassezia pachydermatis
c) Escherichia coli
d) Clostridium

155. A common sign of otitis media in small animals is:
a) Head tilt
b) Itching
c) Excessive earwax
d) Loss of balance

156. What is the most likely cause of aural hematoma in dogs?
a) Infection
b) Trauma from scratching or shaking
c) Allergies
d) Foreign body

157 Which diagnostic tool is most commonly used to examine the ear canal and tympanic membrane?
a) Ultrasound
b) MRI
c) Otoscope
d) CT scan

158. Vestibular disease in small animals often presents with:
a) Paralysis
b) Vomiting
c) Diarrhea
d) Nystagmus

159. Which type of ear infection can lead to deafness if untreated?
a) Otitis externa
b) Otitis media
c) Otitis interna
d) All of the above

160. A BAER test is used to evaluate:
a) Hearing function
b) Balance
c) Middle ear pressure
d) Ear infections

161. What is the role of cerumen in the ear canal?
a) Transmit sound
b) Balance pressure
c) Protect and lubricate the ear
d) Facilitate equilibrium

162. In cases of suspected ear mite infestation, which diagnostic method is most appropriate?
a) Radiograph
b) Cytology
c) Skin scraping
d) Blood test

163. Which condition is characterized by excessive ear wax production?
a) Otosclerosis
b) Ceruminous otitis
c) Aural polyps
d) Vestibular disease

164. Which structure in the ear contains the otoliths?
   a) Cochlea
   b) Semicircular canals
   c) Utricle and saccule
   d) Tympanic membrane
165. The main function of the round window is to:
   a) Balance air pressure in the ear
   b) Transmit sound vibrations
   c) Allow movement of fluid within the cochlea
   d) Protect the inner ear structures
166. What condition is characterized by the abnormal formation of bone in the middle ear?
   a) Otosclerosis
   b) Osteoarthritis
   c) Osteomyelitis
   d) Osteochondritis
167. Which type of sensory receptors are found in the semicircular canals?
   a) Photoreceptors
   b) Mechanoreceptors
   c) Chemoreceptors
   d) Thermoreceptors
168. The fluid in the semicircular canals that helps with balance is called:
   a) Plasma
   b) Endolymph
   c) Perilymph
   d) Cerebrospinal fluid
169. Which part of the ear is responsible for converting mechanical vibrations into neural signals?
   a) Tympanic membrane
   b) Ossicles
   c) Cochlea
   d) Eustachian tube
170. The basilar membrane plays a crucial role in which auditory process?
   a) Sound wave collection
   b) Sound wave amplification
   c) Sound frequency differentiation
   d) Balance maintenance
171. What is the function of the otolith organs in the vestibular system?
   a) Detect rotational movement
   b) Detect linear acceleration and gravity
   c) Transmit sound to the brain
   d) Equalize ear pressure
172. For ear cleaning, which solution is recommended to avoid ear irritation?
   a) Alcohol
   b) Hydrogen peroxide
   c) Saline solution
   d) Soap and water
173. What is the preferred method for diagnosing otitis interna?
   a) Physical examination
   b) CT scan or MRI
   c) Otoscopic examination
   d) Blood test
174. Vestibular disease in older dogs is often idiopathic, meaning:
   a) It is caused by an infection
   b) It has no known cause
   c) It is hereditary
   d) It is due to trauma

175. Which type of ear infection is most likely to cause facial nerve paralysis?
   a) Otitis externa b) Otitis media
   c) Otitis interna d) None of the above

Answer Key

1	c	2	d	3	c	4	b	5	d	6	c	7	c
8	b	9	c	10	a	11	d	12	c	13	d	14	b
15	b	16	c	17	b	18	b	19	c	20	c	21	c
22	b	23	d	24	a	25	c	26	c	27	a	28	a
29	c	30	b	31	c	32	b	33	b	34	b	35	b
36	a	37	b	38	c	39	b	40	c	41	c	42	d
43	a	44	c	45	b	46	c	47	b	48	b	49	b
50	c	51	c	52	c	53	a	54	a	55	b	56	c
57	c	58	b	59	b	60	b	61	b	62	b	63	b
64	c	65	c	66	c	67	b	68	b	69	b	70	d
71	b	72	d	73	c	74	c	75	b	76	c	77	a
78	d	79	c	80	b	81	c	82	c	83	b	84	b
85	d	86	c	87	c	88	c	89	a	90	c	91	c
92	d	93	c	94	d	95	b	96	c	97	c	98	b
99	b	100	b	101	c	102	a	103	a	104	b	105	c
106	c	107	a	108	c	109	c	110	a	111	b	112	a
113	c	114	c	115	b	116	a	117	a	118	a	119	b
120	a	121	d	122	d	123	b	124	c	125	b	126	c
127	c	128	b	129	a	130	a	131	a	132	d	133	c
134	d	135	b	136	a	137	b	138	b	139	a	140	c
141	b	142	a	143	b	144	c	145	b	146	d	147	b
148	c	149	b	150	a	151	d	152	c	153	c	154	b
155	d	156	b	157	c	158	d	159	d	160	a	161	c
162	b	163	b	164	c	165	c	166	a	167	b	168	b
169	c	170	c	171	b	172	c	173	b	174	b	175	c

17

Clinical Physiology of Female Reproductive System

Thulasiraman Sarath[1], Sakthivel Manokaran[2], Annadurai Thangamani[2], Ramasamy Rajkumar[1] and Abdul Reshma[2]

[1]Veterinary Clinical Complex, [2]Department of Veterinary Gynaecology and Obstetrics Veterinary College and Research Institute, Salem, Tamil Nadu Veterinary and Animal Sciences University (TANUVAS), Tamil Nadu

Introduction

Normal reproduction in the female depends on hormones, which specific chemical substances produced by specialized glands are called endocrine glands. These secretions pass into the blood and lymph fluids and are transported to various parts of the body, where they exert several specific effects. Reproductive hormones may originate in the hypothalamus, pituitary, gonads, uterus, or placenta. Hypothalamic hormones are produced in the hypothalamus, a portion of the brain that is the neural control center for reproductive hormones. The role of hypothalamic hormones is to regulate the release of other hormones from the pituitary gland, and many hypothalamic hormones are therefore called releasing hormones. The primary releasing hormone of reproduction is gonadotropin-releasing hormone (GnRH). GnRH controls the release of follicle-stimulating hormone (FSH) and luteinizing hormone (LH) from the pituitary gland, located at the base of the brain. These pituitary hormones regulate the production of estrogen and progesterone from the ovary. FSH stimulates the follicle's growth, development, and function, while LH causes the follicle to rupture and the corpus luteum to develop. The female hormone estrogen is produced by the Graafian follicle on the ovary. Another hormone originating from the ovary is progesterone, which is produced by the corpus luteum. Each has an important role in the female reproductive process.

A relatively new discovery in reproductive physiology is that follicular growth is not continuous in the bovine, but occurs in waves (2 to 4 waves per cycle). Each wave begins when the dominant follicle in the previous wave gains maximal size, at which time numerous small follicles begin a period of rapid growth. From this group of follicles, one follicle is allowed to grow to a much larger size than the others. This large follicle is called the dominant follicle, because it has the ability to regulate and restrict the growth of the smaller follicles. A few days after reaching maximum size, the dominant follicle begins to degenerate and die.

Infertility is one of the primary factors for cattle reproduction in the present scenario. Reproduction-related immuno-infertility mainly involves immunization against the antigens related to reproductive hormones (LHRH, GnRH, Gonadal steroids, PGF2α and oxytocin), spermatozoa, seminal plasma and ovum. Anovulation, delayed ovulation, sperm immobilization, failure of fertilization, prolonged uterine involution, extended calving interval, prolonged post-partum estrus and reduced conception rate could be a result of immuno-infertility that occur due to the blockage of receptor site by antibodies formed against hormones, sperm and ovum. The mean interval to the first observed post-partum oestrus was 14 days in milked cows. Pregnancy corpora lutea were quite degenerate by Day 7 postpartum. At Day 14 post-partum, they were approximately 9mm in diameter and remained at this size, at least to Day 30. There was an increase in follicular size following parturition. At Day 7, the mean diameter of the largest follicle was 9 mm; at Day 14, it was 11 mm; at Day 30, the largest follicle averaged 13 mm. Neither the presence of suckling calves, nor anaemia delayed uterine involution. Caruncular tissue sloughed and was expelled from the uterus between Day 7 and Day 14 post-partum.

The success of dairy cattle husbandry depends on ensuring proper and optimal reproductive rhythm of individual female in the herd. Impairment in the normal reproductive function results in infertility and sterility leading to economic losses due to decrease in milk production, the number of calves produced and increase in culling rate. It is estimated that around 18 - 40% cattle are culled due to infertility or sterility in India. Ovulation in the cow normally occurs 25 to 35 hours after the onset of behavioural oestrus and 18 to 26 hours after the ovulatory LH peak. During estrus and after the end of estrus, several follicles undergo development but usually one, or occasionally two, ovulate; the other follicles regress and become atretic. A number of defects associated with ovulation viz. delayed ovulation, anovulation and cystic ovarian degeneration can occur. The consequences for fertility of an ovulatory defect two-fold; either the oocyte is not liberated and hence cannot be fertilized, or it is liberated too late so that the spermatozoa are now incapable of fertilization, or else the oocyte has aged and is not capable of normal development.

Ovulatory defects occur due to endocrine deficiency or imbalance, failure of the development of hormone receptors at the target tissue or mechanical factors. If the quantity of luteinizing hormone (LH) released is insufficient, or its timing is incorrect, then ovulation is delayed or fails to occur. In few cases, because of extensive lesions involving adhesions of the ovarian bursa to the surface of the ovary, the physical process of ovulation is prevented.

Estrus synchronization is the tool to bring a group of female animals to come into estrus during a short, predetermined interval by manipulating their reproductive process without altering their fertility.

Cattle naturally exhibit sexual receptivity once in every 18-21 days. This period of sexual receptivity is called estrus period/heat and the 18-21 day cycle is called as oestrus cycle. Nowadays, different technologies are invented to control the oestrus cycle for our advantage. Oestrus synchronization is one such technology. Synchronization of estrus means making estrus period of different animals in the same time by using different hormones. Prostaglandins are used in cyclic cattle by destroying the corpus luteum in the ovary which secretes the hormone called progesterone during luteal phase. Cysts are non-ovulating liquid-filled structures with a diameter of over 2.5 cm which persist on the ovary for over 10 days simultaneously with absence of the CL. Injection of GnRH causes higher LH secretion from the pituitary gland, which leads to luteinization of cystic follicles or promotes other follicles to ovulate.

Reproductive problems are seldom accompanied by alarming signs of disease. Furthermore, there often is a time interval between when a failure occurs and when it becomes apparent. A systematic procedure for reproduction specialists to conduct a herd infertility examination is outlined and discussed hereunder. The procedure should involve evaluation of breeding history, feeding and management practices and examination of health records, herd, and laboratory results to make an objective diagnosis.

1. Metabolic cues that affect the onset of puberty
   a) Leptin b) Blood glucose
   c) Free fatty acid d) All of the above
2. First estrus at onset of puberty may be
   a) Sub estrus b) Anovulatory estrus
   c) Silent estrus d) All of the above
3. Gonadostat theory related to
   a) Ovulation b) Parturition
   c) Sexual behaviour d) Fertilization
4. Ferguson reflex related to
   a) Ovulation b) Parturition
   c) Sexual behaviour d) Fertilization
5. Flehmens reflex related to
   a) Ovulation b) Parturition
   c) Sexual behaviour d) Fertilization
6. Presence of blood over the tail or perineal region of cow after estrus indicative of
   a) Proestrual bleeding b) Metestrual bleeding
   c) Diestrual bleeding d) Anestrual bleeding
7. Metestrus bleeding also known as
   a) Post estrual bleeding b) Proestrual bleeding
   c) Diestrual bleeding d) Menstrual bleeding
8. Heat signs observed during pregnancy known as
   a) Silent heat b) Gestational heat
   c) Post conception heat d) Both B & C
9. Life span of CL in cow and buffaloes
   a) 16 days b) 18 days
   c) 20 days d) 22 days
10. Window period for CL is
    a) 5-15 days of cycle b) 10-20 days of cycle
    c) 6-16 days of cycle d) 8-18 days of cycle
11. Maximum concentration of progesterone hormone detected in
    a) Early-luteal phase b) Late-luteal phase
    c) Mid-luteal phase d) Early-follicular phase

12. Blood supply to the ovary increased during
    a) Proestrus
    b) Estrus
    c) Metestrus
    d) Diestrus & Anestrous
13. The principle hormone that regulates the estrous cycle length in cow and buffaloes is
    a) Estrogen
    b) Prostaglandins
    c) Progesterone
    d) Inhibin
14. Female will remain in constant follicular phase until copulation occur in
    a) Rabbit & cat
    b) Camel & ferret
    c) Mink & llama
    d) All of the above
15. Seasonal breeder like mare, transition of non-breeding season into breeding season by
    a) Decrease in melatonin
    b) Increase in melatonin
    c) No alteration in melatonin
    d) None of the above
16. Hormone which regulates the breeding in seasonal breeder is
    a) Estrogen
    b) Prostaglandins
    c) Progesterone
    d) Melatonin
17. Short day breeders
    a) Cow and buffalo
    b) Sheep and goat
    c) Mare and Cat
    d) Mare and mink
18. Long day breeders
    a) Cow and buffalo
    b) Sheep and goat
    c) Mare and sow
    d) Mare, mink and cat
19. Follicular phase and luteal phase equal duration in
    a) Cow
    b) Bitch
    c) Women
    d) Mare
20. Prolonged follicular and luteal phase characteristics features of which animal
    a) Cow
    b) Bitch
    c) Women
    d) Mare
21. Inter estrus interval in bitch
    a) 1-2 months
    b) 2-4 months
    c) 4-6 months
    d) 6-8 months
22. Breed of Dog having single estrous cycle per year
    a) Labrador
    b) Basenji
    c) Chippipari
    d) Rajapalayam
23. Average duration of estrus and proestrus about
    a) 9 days
    b) 9 month
    c) 21 days
    d) 2 months

24. Pheromone which present in vaginal mucus during estrus for communication is
    a) Melatonin b) Methylhydroxy benzoate
    c) 5 alpha androstenodione d) Hydroxy progesterone
25. Hormone which is responsible for pseudopregnancy in canine
    a) Estrogen b) Prostaglandins
    c) Progesterone d) Prolactin
26. Pseudopregnancy in bitches can be treated by
    a) Cabergoline b) Bromocriptine
    c) Metergoline d) All of the above
27. Sterile mating in cat lead to
    a) Pyometra b) Pregnancy
    c) Pseudopregnancy d) All of the above
28. Camel administered with seminal plasma from male that will induce
    a) Parturition b) Ovulation
    c) Estrus d) Puberty
29. Regarding ovulation camel is a)
    a) Induced ovulator b) Spontaneous ovulator
    c) Modified induced ovulator d) None of the above
30. Species which ovulation occur in metestrus
    a) Bovine b) Caprine
    c) Ovine d) Equine
31. Riding test/back pressure test for detection of estrus in
    a) Cow and buffalo b) Sheep and goat
    c) Sow and cat d) Mare and mink
32. Normal inward curvature of lumbar and cervical region of spine is called as
    a) Scoliosis b) Kyphosis
    c) Campylorrachis d) Lordosis
33. Luteotrophic hormones in cow and buffalo
    a) LH b) Estrogen
    c) Prolactin d) Progesterone
34. Luteotrophic hormones in sow
    a) LH b) Estrogen
    c) Prolactin d) Progesterone
35. Luteotrophic hormones in bitch and ewe
    a) LH b) Estrogen
    c) Prolactin d) Progesterone
36. Fern pattern of cervical mucus is associated with high content of
    a) Calcium b) Potassium
    c) Chloride d) Magnesium

37. Who said that CL is a gland
    a) Corius b) Malphigi
    c) Ion Wilmot d) Morrow
38. The enzyme involved in melatonin synthesis
    a) Acid phosphatase
    b) Methyl hydroxylase
    c) 17-alpha hydroxylase
    d) Hydroxy-indol-O-methyl transferase (HIOMT)
39. A male fetus born co-twin with a female fetus is called as
    a) Wilgil b) Freemartin
    c) Male pseudohermaphoridism d) Female pseudohermaphoridism
40. Vascular anastomosis in freemartin occurs at
    a) 35-39 days of pregnancy b) 45-49 days of pregnancy
    c) 55-59 days of pregnancy d) 65-69 days of pregnancy
41. Theory that explains the freemartin
    a) Hormonal theory b) Cellular theory
    c) Gonadostat theory d) Both A & B
42. Under developed ovary and genitalia, tuft of vulval hair characteristics features of
    a) Wilgil b) Freemartin
    c) Male pseudohermaphoridism d) Female pseudohermaphoridism
43. Most accurate method of identifying freemartin condition in cattle
    a) External appearance b) Karyotyping
    c) Sex chromosome analysis d) Both B & C
44. Ovaries and oviduct are normal, but other genital portions are abnormal in which condition
    a) Wilgil b) Freemartin
    c) White heifer disease d) Pseudohermaphoridism
45. Fish hook vulva and prominent phallus seen in which condition
    a) Wilgil b) Freemartin
    c) White heifer disease d) Pseudohermaphoridism
46. Animal phenotypically resembles female but having testicles often called as
    a) Wilgil b) Freemartin
    c) Male pseudohermaphoridism d) Female pseudohermaphoridism
47. Animal phenotypically resembles male but having ovaries often called as
    a) Wilgil b) Freemartin
    c) Male pseudohermaphoridism d) Female pseudohermaphoridism
48. Segmental aplasia of mullerian duct related to
    a) pseudohermaphoridism b) Freemartin
    c) White heifer disease d) Virgin heifer disease

49. Most common non-pathological ovarian cyst in cow
    a) Follicular cyst b) Luteal cyst
    c) Cystic corpora lutea d) Nabothian cyst
50. Mature CL also known as
    a) Yellow body b) White body
    c) Bloody body d) Black body
51. Corpus albicans also known as
    a) Yellow body b) White body
    c) Bloody body d) Black body
52. Corpus haemorrhagicum also known as
    a) Yellow body b) White body
    c) Bloody body d) Black body
53. Corpus nigricans also known as
    a) Yellow body b) White body
    c) Bloody body d) Black body
54. High protein diet and High milk yield animal predisposed for
    a) BOD b) COD
    c) RBC d) SOD
55. More common cause for COD is
    a) Hormonal cause b) Nutritional cause
    c) Physical cause d) None of the above
56. Hormone which is cause for cystic endometrial hyperplasia-pyometra complex in canine
    a) Estrogen b) Relaxin
    c) Prolactin d) Progesterone
57. Cattle Breed predisposed for COD condition is
    a) HF b) Cross breed HF
    c) Jersey d) Cross breed Jersey
58. Sterility hump is characteristics feature of
    a) Follicular cyst b) Luteal cyst
    c) Mineral deficiency d) Vitamin deficiency
59. Treatment for follicular cyst
    a) Gynarich b) Hucog
    c) Cyclix d) Both A & B
60. Treatment for luteal cyst
    a) Gynarich b) Hucog
    c) Cyclix d) Both A & B
61. A frequent prolonged sign of estrus and short interval between successive estrus is observed in follicular cyst condition this often called as
    a) Estrumania b) Sterility hump
    c) Nymphomania d) All of the above

62. The predominant immunoglobulin present in the follicular fluid
    a) IgA b) IgG
    c) IgD d) IgM
63. The predominant immunoglobulin present in the vagina.
    a) IgA b) IgG
    c) IgD d) IgM
64. The follicle said to be dominant follicle when it reaches diameter of
    a) 5mm b) 6mm
    c) 9mm d) 8mm
65. Growth of follicle up to the stage of antrum formation is
    a) Gonadotropin independent b) Gonadotropin dependent
    c) Steroid independent d) Steroid dependent
66. Hormone which controls the Oocyte mitosis and antrum formation in graafian follicle
    a) FSH b) LH
    c) Estrogen d) Progesterone
67. The maximum duration of completion of each follicular wave in domestic cow is about
    a) 5-6 days b) 8-10 days
    c) 12-14 days d) 14-15 days
68. Post pubertal cow and buffaloes have primordial follicle in ovarian reserve is about
    a) 15,000-20,000 lakh b) 20,000-3 lakh
    c) 20,000-25,000 lakh d) 50,000-1 lakh
69. Following up the same follicle at different interval is often known as
    a) Ovulation b) Persistence dominance
    c) Follicular dynamics d) Estrus cycle
70. The innermost layer of follicle contains cells they often known as
    a) Granulosa cell b) Thecal cell
    c) Luteal cell d) Follicular cell
71. The circulating hormone which required to initiation of next follicular wave is
    a) LH b) Estrogen
    c) Progesterone d) FSH
72. Hormone which is have negative feedback effect on FSH hormone
    a) Inhibin b) Activin
    c) Melatonin d) Both A & C
73. Follicular dynamics process includes
    a) Recruitment b) Selection
    c) Dominance & Atresia d) All the above

74. Hormonal profiles during recruitment-choose the correct one
    a) High FSH, Low LH, No Inhibin
    b) Low FSH, Moderate LH, Low Inhibin
    c) Low FSH, High LH, High Inhibin
    d) None of the above
75. Hormonal profiles during selection-choose the correct one
    a) High FSH, Low LH, No Inhibin
    b) Low FSH, Moderate LH, Low Inhibin
    c) Low FSH, High LH, High Inhibin
    d) None of the above
76. Hormonal profiles during dominance-choose the correct one
    a) High FSH, Low LH, No Inhibin
    b) Low FSH, Moderate LH, Low Inhibin
    c) Low FSH, High LH, High Inhibin
    d) None of the above
77. Species in which maximum number of follicular wave reported
    a) Bovine b) Ovine
    c) Caprine d) Equine
78. Maximum number of follicular wave in cow
    a) Two b) Four
    c) Five d) Three
79. Maximum fertility observed during ovulation from (follicular wave)
    a) Second b) Fourth
    c) Fifth d) Third
80. Buffaloes maximum number of follicular wave
    a) Two b) Four
    c) Five d) Three
81. Species in which most probably ovulation occur in first follicular wave
    a) Bovine b) Ovine
    c) Caprine d) Equine
82. Number follicle selected during estrus
    a) 10-25 b) 25-30
    c) 30-35 d) 40-50
83. All species Oogenesis completed before birth itself, except
    a) Bovine b) Porcine
    c) Canine d) Ovine
84. Size of the Oocyte in primordial follicle
    a) 10-20 micron b) 60-80 micron
    c) 20-40 micron d) 120-180 micron

85. Size of the mature Oocyte
   a) 100-120 micron b) 160-180 micron
   c) 120-140 micron d) 120-180 micron
86. Largest cells in the body
   a) Sperm b) Oocyte
   c) Hepatocytes d) Renal Cells
87. Vitamin which is required for gametogenesis
   a) Vitamin D b) Thiamin
   c) Vitamin A d) Vitamin B12
88. Primary Oocyte remain arrested in which stage
   a) Diplotene stage of Meiosis I b) Diplotene stage of Meiosis II
   c) Diplotene stage of Mitosis I d) Diplotene stage of Mitosis II
89. First meiotic division of Oocyte completed before ovulation in all species, except
   a) Canine b) Porcine
   c) Equine d) Both A & C
90. First meiotic division of Oocyte completed after ovulation
   a) Canine b) Porcine
   c) Equine d) Both A & C
91. Process of follicular growth and degeneration known as
   a) Recruitment b) Selection
   c) Dominance & Atresia d) Follicular dynamics
92. Animal which is resistant to luteolytic effect of PGF_2 alph a)
   a) Cow b) Doe
   c) Mare d) Bitch
93. Animal which is sensitive to luteolytic effect of PGF_2 alph a)
   a) Queen b) Sow
   c) Mare d) Bitch
94. All Species regulation of CL regression depend on uterine PGF_2 alpha, except
   a) Cow b) Human
   c) Mare d) Doe
95. Species in which regulation of CL regression depend on ovarian PGF_2 alph
   a) Bovine b) Human
   c) Equine d) Caprine
96. The lowest progesterone found in milk on ------ days after estrus
   a) 12 b) 22
   c) 30 d) None of the above
97. Embryo division without growth is known as
   a) Zygote b) Nidation
   c) Cleavage d) Morula

98. The pH of cervical mucus
   a) 2.5-3.5
   b) 4.3-5.5
   c) 6.2-7.5
   d) 7.5-8.5
99. The estrogen used along with PRID is
   a) Estradiol benzoate
   b) Estradiol valerate
   c) Stilbesterol
   d) None of the above
100. Blood flow to ovary is higher during
   a) Proestrus
   b) Estrus
   c) Metestrus
   d) Diestrus

Answer Key

1	d	2	d	3	a	4	b	5	c	6	b	7	a
8	d	9	a	10	c	11	c	12	b	13	c	14	d
15	a	16	d	17	b	18	d	19	c	20	b	21	c
22	b	23	a	24	b	25	d	26	d	27	c	28	b
29	b	30	a	31	c	32	d	33	a	34	b	35	c
36	c	37	b	38	d	39	b	40	a	41	d	42	b
43	d	44	c	45	d	46	c	47	d	48	c	49	c
50	a	51	b	52	c	53	d	54	b	55	a	56	d
57	a	58	a	59	d	60	c	61	c	62	b	63	a
64	c	65	b	66	a	67	b	68	d	69	c	70	a
71	d	72	a	73	d	74	a	75	b	76	c	77	c
78	d	79	d	80	a	81	d	82	a	83	c	84	c
85	d	86	b	87	c	88	a	89	d	90	d	91	d
92	d	93	c	94	b	95	b	96	b	97	c	98	c
99	b	100	d										

18

Clinical Physiology of Haematological Disorders

Bhavanam Sudhakara Reddy, Sirigireddy Sivajothi Malaka Malavika Reddy and Kambala Swetha

College of Veterinary Science - Proddatur, Sri Venkateswara Veterinary University, Andhra Pradesh

Bleeding disorders can be either congenital, present from birth, or acquired, developing later in life. Defects in blood clotting proteins typically result in delayed bleeding and deep tissue bruising, whereas platelet defects often lead to superficial bruises, nosebleeds, black stools, and prolonged bleeding at injection sites or during surgery. Blood clotting tests can identify animals with defective clotting proteins, but they are not very sensitive.

Congenital Clotting Protein Disorders

Congenital clotting protein disorders are present from birth, and severe deficiencies or defects in these proteins typically manifest early in life. Such severe defects can be fatal, with affected animals often being stillborn or dying shortly after birth. Additionally, a lack of clotting proteins or vitamin K in a newborn can exacerbate clotting issues. If the level of a specific clotting protein is only 5 to 10% of normal, the newborn might survive but is likely to show signs of illness before reaching 6 months of age.

Hypofibrinogenemia, characterized by an abnormal shortage of fibrinogen in the blood and severe bleeding, has been observed in Saint Bernards. Dysfibrinogenemia, which involves abnormally functioning fibrinogen, has been reported in an inbred family of Russian Wolfhounds. Affected dogs experience mild bleeding problems, such as nosebleeds, but may suffer life-threatening bleeding from injuries or surgeries. The best treatment for this condition is intravenous transfusion with fresh or fresh-frozen plasma.

Factor II (prothrombin) disorders are rare. Prothrombin is a key protein in blood clotting. In Boxer dogs, prothrombin is present in normal amounts but does not function properly. Affected puppies may experience nosebleeds and bleeding gums, which tend to improve with age. In adult dogs, easy bruising and inflamed skin are common. Treatment involves transfusions of whole blood or plasma.

Factor VII deficiency has been reported in several breeds, including Beagles, English Bulldogs, Alaskan Malamutes, Miniature Schnauzers, Boxers, and mixed-breed dogs. This condition can lead to prolonged bleeding after giving birth and is often diagnosed incidentally during clotting tests.

Hemophilia A (Factor VIII deficiency) is the most common inherited bleeding disorder in dogs. Typically, females carry the gene without showing symptoms, while males do exhibit signs. Affected puppies may experience prolonged bleeding from the umbilical cord at birth, bleeding gums during teething, and excessive bleeding after surgery. Treatment involves repeated transfusions of whole blood or plasma until bleeding is controlled.

Hemophilia B (Factor IX deficiency) is less common than Hemophilia A and has been reported in several purebred and mixed-breed dogs. Females are usually carriers and often do not show symptoms. Affected animals may experience bleeding similar to Hemophilia A.

Acquired Clotting Protein Disorders

Most clotting proteins are produced in the liver, so liver disease can result in decreased levels of these proteins, particularly Factors VII, IX, X, and XI, as well as proteins involved in breaking up clots. Severe liver disease may also lead to disseminated intravascular coagulation (DIC). Additionally, fibrinogen, which is made in the liver and converts to fibrin in response to tissue damage, and von Willebrand's factor, which is produced outside the liver and helps platelets adhere to blood vessel walls and to each other, can be elevated in liver disease.

Disseminated intravascular coagulation (DIC) is a condition where small blood clots form throughout the bloodstream, obstructing small blood vessels and depleting the platelets and clotting factors necessary for controlling bleeding. Maintaining normal circulation with intravenous fluids is crucial. Prompt treatment of the underlying cause is essential, and anti-clotting medications may be required. DIC is a severe and often fatal disorder, but early diagnosis can improve survival chances. However, early detection is challenging and typically requires specialized testing.

Platelet Disorders

Platelet disorders can involve having too few platelets or having platelets that do not function properly. These disorders can be either congenital or acquired later in life. Thrombocytosis, which is an excessive number of platelets, may result from a physiological response or a disease process. In rare cases, it may be associated with blood cancer.

Congenital Thrombocytopenia: Gray Collies can develop a condition known as cyclic hematopoiesis, which involves 12-day cycles during which all types of blood cells, including platelets, decrease. This disorder can lead to mild to severe platelet shortages and an increased risk of excessive bleeding. Cyclic hematopoiesis is a severe and often fatal condition; most affected dogs die from infections before reaching 6 months of age.

Acquired Thrombocytopenia: Acquired thrombocytopenias are common in dogs. Many causes have been identified, most involving the immune system destroying platelets. Rickettsial diseases, caused by organisms in the genera *Ehrlichia* and *Anaplasma*, cause mild to severe loss of platelets in dogs. Infection may include short- and longterm changes in the number of platelets and other blood cells. Ticks are the usual carriers of the infection. Infected dogs may show no signs or may have nosebleeds, bleeding into the bowels, bleeding of the gums, and prolonged bleeding after vaccination or surgery. Thrombocytopenia due to immune system dysfunction occurs when the immune system makes antibodies that destroy platelets or platelet-producing cells in the bone marrow. Signs include tiny, purplish red spots on the gums or skin (called petechiae), bruising, bleeding into the bowels resulting in black stools, or nosebleeds. Thrombocytopenia caused by vaccination has been reported in dogs that have been vaccinated repeatedly with certain types of vaccines (modified live adenovirus or paramyxovirus vaccines). The platelet loss occurs 3 to 10 days after repeat vaccination, usually lasts for only a short time, and may be so mild that it is not noticed unless it happens at the same time as another clotting disorder. Thrombocytopenia caused by drugs has been reported in dogs. Some drugs and classes of drugs (including estrogen and some antibiotics) suppress the production of platelets in the bone marrow. Other drugs (including aspirin, acetaminophen, penicillin, and others) destroy platelets circulating in the bloodstream. Thrombocytopenia caused by cancer can occur in dogs. Certain types of cancers can trigger a condition called disseminated intravascular coagulation, which destroys many platelets.

Anemia is a common condition in dogs and cats and can be classified into two main types: regenerative and nonregenerative. Regenerative anemia: occurs when the bone marrow is functioning properly and responds to the loss or destruction of erythrocytes (red blood cells). This type of anemia is typically caused by external blood loss, such as from injury, surgery, or bleeding disorders, or by internal destruction of red blood cells (hemolytic anemia). Erythrocyte morphology is crucial for diagnosing regenerative anemia.

Nonregenerative anemia: It arises when the bone marrow does not produce enough red blood cells, despite its normal function. This form is more challenging to diagnose and can result from various conditions, including inflammation, renal or liver disease, endocrine disorders, and neoplasia. Severe cases may be due to aplastic pancytopenia, myelodysplasia, leukemia, pure red cell aplasia, or certain infections. Blood loss anemia: It is a type of regenerative anemia that occurs due to significant blood loss from injury, surgery, or bleeding disorders. Internal bleeding caused by conditions such as cancer, ulcers, or parasites can also lead to this form of anemia. Although the bone marrow attempts to increase red blood cell production, it may not be able to meet the demand.

Hemolytic anemia: involves the destruction of red blood cells within the body. This type of anemia can result from immune-mediated hemolytic anemia (IMHA) or autoimmune hemolytic anemia (AIHA), or from non-immune mediated causes such as hereditary diseases, parasites, toxins, or low phosphorus levels. Immune-Mediated Hemolytic Anemia (IMHA): It is an autoimmune disorder where the body attacks its own red blood cells, leading to anemia and potentially requiring blood transfusions. IMHA can cause serious complications, such as blood clots in the brain or lungs. There are two forms: Primary AIHA: occurs when the immune system inappropriately targets red blood cells, accounting for about three-quarters of IMHA cases. Secondary AIHA: It happens when red blood cells are altered by underlying diseases or toxins, causing the immune system to attack them. Triggers for secondary AIHA include cancer, Ehrlichiosis, Leptospirosis, parasites, drug reactions, snakebites, chemicals, toxins, or bee stings. Aplastic or nonregenerative anemia: It results from inadequate production of red blood cells and can be caused by toxin exposure, bone marrow disease, kidney disease, certain medications, chemotherapy, or parvovirus.

Leukocytes, or white blood cells, include neutrophils, lymphocytes, monocytes, eosinophils, and basophils. These cells differ in their production sites, circulation durations, and responses to factors that regulate their movement within the intricate network of blood vessels throughout the body. Normal white blood cell counts vary by species. Leukocytosis refers to an increase in the total number of circulating white blood cells, while leukopenia indicates a decrease. Changes in the numbers of specific types of white blood cells can help diagnose various disorders. Neutrophilia: It is characterized by an elevated number of neutrophils in the bloodstream, typically due to inflammation. Severe inflammation can lead to toxic changes in neutrophils. Neutropenia: It is a decrease in neutrophils, which may result from adherence to damaged blood vessel walls, destruction of neutrophils, or reduced production in the bone marrow. Neutropenia can occur during severe bacterial infections and as a side effect of certain drugs, potentially leading to pancytopenia (a reduction in red and white blood cells and platelets). Eosinophilia: It is an increase in eosinophils, which are involved in allergic reactions and parasite control. Elevated eosinophil levels can be triggered by substances like histamine and specific antibodies, and can occur with parasitic infections (e.g., heartworms or fleas) or inflammation of the intestines, kidneys, lungs, or skin. Eosinopenia: It is a decrease in eosinophils, commonly due to stress or corticosteroid treatment. Basophils: Basophils are rare in domestic animals and produce histamine, playing a role in allergic reactions and combating parasites. Basophilia: It is an increase in basophils, is uncommon but can be observed in some dogs with heartworm disease. Lymphocytosis: It involves an increase in lymphocytes and can be caused by certain hormones, immune system stimulation from infections, chronic diseases like arthritis, or leukemia (a cancer of the immune system). Lymphopenia: It is a decrease in lymphocytes, often due to corticosteroid use, decreased lymphocyte production, certain viral infections, or hereditary diseases. Monocytosis: It is an increase in monocytes and is usually associated with long-term inflammation. Leukemia: It is a malignant cancer characterized by an increase in abnormal white blood cells in the bloodstream. Lymphoma: It is a related cancer that originates in lymph nodes or other lymphoid tissues. When there is an elevated white blood cell count, leukemia should be considered as a potential cause.

Write correct alphabet of the answer in the given bracket

1. Which of the following occurs in absence of erythropoietin?
   a) Hypoxia b) Decreased RBC production
   c) Increased RBC production d) Both A and B
2. What is the main cause of megaloblastic anemia?
   a) Iron deficiency b) Vitamin B12 or folate deficiency
   c) Chronic blood loss d) Bone marrow failure
3. Clinical signs in anemi a)
   a) Lethargy b) Dyspnea
   c) Heart murmurs d) All the above
4. Epinephrine, norepinephrine and prostaglandins
   a) Stimulate erythropoietin production
   b) Blocks erythropoietin production
   c) Both a&b
   d) None of the above
5. Principle hormone that stimulate RBC production
   a) ACTH b) Thyroxin
   c) Erythropoietin d) All of the above

6. Conditions which can cause artificial elevation of haemoglobin
   a) Lipemia b) Excessive Heinz bodies
   c) A and B d) Hemolysis
7. What is needed for maturation of erythrocytes?
   a) Vitamin B12 b) Cobalt
   c) Both a & c d) None
8. Which condition is characterized by an abnormal increase in red blood cell mass?
   a) Anemia b) Leukemia
   c) Polycythemia vera d) Thrombocytopenia
9. What is the primary defect in hereditary spherocytosis?
   a) Hemoglobinopathy b) Membrane protein defect
   c) Enzyme deficiency d) Abnormal iron metabolism
10. The cellular stroma that remains after hemolysis is called
    a) Shadow b) Ghost corpuscles
    c) Both a & b d) None
11. What is the characteristic cell found in Hodgkin's lymphoma?
    a) Reed-Sternberg cell b) Plasma cell
    c) Auer rod d) Smudge cell
12. Which coagulation factor is deficient in hemophilia B?
    a) Factor VIII b) Factor IX
    c) Factor XI d) Factor XIII
13. What is the hallmark of aplastic anemia?
    a) Increased WBC
    b) Pancytopenia
    c) Elevated hemoglobin
    d) Hyper segmented neutrophils
14. Which is the respiratory pigment of erythrocytes?
    a) Hemoglobin b) Deltaglobin
    c) Chlorophyll d) None
15. Which of the following is a characteristic finding in multiple myeloma?
    a) Philadelphia chromosome b) Bence Jones protein inurine
    c) Rouleaux formation d) Smudge cells
16. Which test is used to diagnose glucose 6 phosphate dehydrogenase deficiency?
    a) Coombs test b) G6PD enzyme assay
    c) Hemoglobin electrophoresis d) Osmotic fragility test
17. Which is the derivative of hemoglobin formed by oxidation of ferrous ion of hemoglobin to the ferric state?
    a) Methemoglobin b) Carboxy haemoglobin
    c) Both a and b d) None

18. Which is the true oxide of haemoglobin?
    a) Oxy hemoglobin b) Methemoglobin
    c) Both a and b d) None
19. Significant pathophysiology in anemia.
    a) Bradycardia b) Arrhythmia
    c) Insufficient delivery of oxygen to vital organs
    d) Insufficient delivery of nutrition to vital organs
20. Most pathological changes due to anemia
    a) Hepatomegaly b) Splenomegaly
    c) Cardiomegaly d) All
21. Which vitamin deficiency leads to a decrease in prothrombin and other clotting factors, resulting in bleeding tendencies?
    a) Vitamin A b) Vitamin C
    c) Vitamin D d) Vitamin K
22. Which of the following is a common cause of microcytic hypochromic anaemia
    a) Vitamin B12 deficiency b) Folate deficiency
    c) Iron deficiency d) Bone marrow failure
23. Bone marrow aplasia results in
    a) Complete cessation of erythropoiesis b) Aplastic anaemi
    c) Megaloblastic anaemia d) Both a and b
24. Deficiency of cyanocobalamine and folic acid causes
    a) Complete cessation of erythropoiesis b) Aplastic anaemi
    c) Megaloblastic anaemia d) Both a and b
25. Defective absorption due to malfunction of gastric mucosa causes
    a) pernicious anemia b) Hemolytic anemia
    c) Both a&b d) None
26. Examples of hereditary acquired hemolytic anemia
    a) sickle cell anemia b) Erythroblastosis fetalis
    c) Both a&b d) None
27. Which of the following is a typical future of chronic lymphocytic leukaemia (CLL)
    a) High blast count in peripheral blood **b)** Presence of smudge cells
    c) Increased reticulocyte count d) Reed-Sternberg cells
28. Which of the following is not a feature of disseminated intravascular coagulation?
    a) Prolonged prothrombin time b) Decreased fibrinogen level
    c) Thrombocytopenia d) Increased levels of factor VIII
29. What is the primary treatment of pernicious anaemia
    a) Oral iron supplements b) Intravenous iron therapy
    c) Vitamin B12 injections d) Folic acid supplements

30. Which laboratory finding is indicative of hemolytic anaemia
    a) Decreased lactate dehydrogenase
    b) Decreased reticulocyte count
    c) Increased haptoglobin level
    d) Increased unconjugated bilirubin level
31. Eosinophils take
    a) Acid dye b) Basic dye
    c) Neutral dye d) None
32. Basophils take
    a) Acid dye b) Basic dye
    c) Neutral dye d) None
33. What is the most common cause of iron deficiency anemia worldwide
    a) Chronic disease b) Dietary deficiency
    c) Blood loss d) Genetic mutation
34. Which of the following cells are responsible for producing antibodies
    a) T cells b) Macrophages
    c) Neutrophils d) B cells
35. Which of the following is a common symptom of acute leukaemia.
    a) Increased appetite b) Enlarged spleen
    c) Decreased white blood cell count d) Joint pain
36. Which test is most commonly used to diagnose anemia
    a) Blood glucose level b) Complete blood count
    c) Liver function test d) Kidney function test
37. Thrombocytopenia refers to a deficiency of which blood component
    a) RBC b) WBC
    c) Plasma d) Platelets
38 What is the main function of haemoglobin in red blood cells
    a) Immune response b) Oxygen transport
    c) Blood clotting d) pH regulation
39. Which condition is characterized by an over production of red blood cells
    a) Anemia b) Polycythemia vera
    c) Leukopenia d) Thrombocytosis
40. An antiviral compound produced by lymphocytes
    a) Interferon b) Complement
    c) Both a and b d) None
41. Which cells are concerned with humoral immunity
    a) B cells b) T cells
    c) Both a and b d) None
42. Ideal level of PCV in dogs for blood transfusion
    a) 10% b) 20%
    c) 30% d) 40%

43. Which of the following organ is important in formation of bile pigments and iron storage
    a) Thymus
    b) Spleen
    c) Both a and b
    d) None
44. Which of the following is a term used to indicate increase in the number of immature neutrophils?
    a) Shift to left
    b) Shift to right
    c) Both a and b
    d) None
45. Which of the following is the chief pigment the imparts color to the plasm
    a) Bilirubin
    b) Biliverdin
    c) Both a and b
    d) None
46. Which of the following plasma protein is not synthesized in liver?
    a) Albumins
    b) Globulins
    c) Fibrinogen
    d) Prothrombin
47. Best donar dog
    a) Negative for DEA 1
    b) Positive for DEA 1
    c) Positive for DEA 2
    d) All
48. Which of the following is most abundant immunoglobulin present in blood?
    a) IgA
    b) IgE
    c) IgG
    d) IgM
49. Substance which promote coagulation are called
    a) Procoagulants
    b) Clotting factors
    c) Anticoagulants
    d) None
50. Prevention of blood loss when blood vessels are damaged is called
    a) Hemostasis
    b) Hematinic
    c) both a and b
    d) None
51. Chronic renal failure leads to
    a) Reduced clotting factor
    b) Reduced survival time
    c) Blood loss
    d) All
52. Classification of anemia done by assessing
    a) MCHC
    b) MCV
    c) MHC
    d) All the above
53. In Hypoadrenocortism
    a) Regenerative anemia
    b) Non regenerative anemi
    c) Aplastic anemia
    d) All the above
54. In Hypothyroidism
    a) Decreased erythropoiesis
    b) Increased erythropoiesis
    c) No relation
    d) Both A & B

55. In Hyperestrogenism
a) Aplastic anemia b) Regenerative anemia
c) Non regenerative anemia d) None

56. Drugs induced aplastic anemia
a) Trimethoprim b) Griseofulvin
c) Quinidine d) All the above

57. Exogenous estrogen produces
a) Thrombocytopenia b) Normocytic anemi a
c) Non regenerative anemia d) all

58. In cats, chloramphenicol administration leads to
a) Reversible bone marrow suppression
b) Irreversible bone marrow suppression
c) Both a & b
d) None

59. In cats, Griseofulvin administration
a) Non-regenerative Pancytopenia b) Regenerative Pancytopenia
c) Both a & b d) None

60. Drugs induced folate deficiency due to administration of
a) Phenobarbital b) Methotrexate
c) Sulfasalazine d) All

61. Folate deficiency leads to
a) Anemia b) Neutropenia
c) Thrombocytopenia d) All

62. Lead poisoning leads to
a) Mild anemia b) Abnormal erythropoiesis
c) Increased RBC fragility d) All

63. Demarcation of basophilic striplings indicative of
a) Lead poisoning b) Folate deficiency
c) Cyanide poisoning d) All

64. Replacement of normal hemopoietic tissue in bone marrow
a) Myelopthesis b) Polycythemia
c) Anemia d) None

65. Relative or absolute increase in red cell mass
a) Polycythemia b) Anemia
c) Both a and b d) None

66. Etiology for erythrocytosis due to hypoxi a)
a) High altitude b) Chronic pulmonary disease
c) Right to left shunt d) All

67. Tumors which produce erythropoietin
    a)Renal lymphoma   b) Renal carcinoma
    c) Renal fibrosarcoma   d) All
68. Physiological neutrophilia is due to release of
    a) Epinephrine   b) Nor epinephrine
    c) Both a and b   d) None
69. Etiology for physiological neutrophili a)
    a) Stress   b) Fear
    c) Parturition   d) All
70. Administration of glucocorticoids leads to
    a) Anemia   b) Allergy
    c) Neutrophilia   d) All
71. Presence of a greater number of immature neutrophils
    a) Right shift   b) Left shift
    c) Both   d) Anemia
72. Neoplasms that produce cytokines
    a) G-CSF   b) GM-CSF
    c) Both   d) None
73. Eosinophilia is due to
    a) Parasitism   b) Parturition
    c) Stress   d) All
74. T-cells dependent eosinophils associated with
    a) FL-S   b) GM-CSF
    c) Both   d) None
75. Immune mediated reactions cause
    a) Neutrophilia   b) Eosinophilia
    c) Basophilia   d) All
76. Mast cell degeneration leads to eosinophils leads to
    a) Release of igE   b) Release of igM
    c) Release of igA   d) None
77. Hyper eosinophilic syndrome in cats due to
    a) Idiopathic   b) Eosinophilic leukemia
    c) Both a and b   d) None
78. In cats mastocytosis leads to
    a) Neutrophilia   b) Basophilia
    c) Eosinophilia   d) All
79. Major cross matching
    a) Donar cells and Patient serum   b) Patient cells and Donar serum
    c) Both   d) Tridot method

80. Cats with intestinal mastocytoma leads to
   a) Neutrophilia   b) Basophilia
   c) Eosinophilia   d) All
81. Cytokines responsible for basophilia
   a) SCF   b) IL-3
   c) IL-5   d) All
82. Lymphocytosis is caused by
   a) Ehrlichia   b) Rickettsia
   c) Fungi   d) All
83. Minor cross matching
   a) Donar cells and Patient serum   b) Patient cells and Donar serum
   c) Both   d) Tridot method
84. What is the initial (30 min) blood transfusion rate
   a) 0.25 ml/kg   b) 0.5 ml/kg
   c) 5 ml/kg   d) 25 ml/kg
85. Inflammatory left shift is noticed in
   a) Pyometra   b) Pneumonia
   c) IMHA   d) All
86. Inflammatory right shift is noticed in
   a) Hypo adrenocorticism   b) Glucocorticoid administration
   c) Both a and b   d) None
87. Feline chediak-Higashi syndrome noticed in
   a) Blue smoke Persian cats with yellow colour
   b) Blue smoke Persian cats with blue colour
   c) Both a and b
   d) None
88. Lysosomal storage diseases in dogs and cats expressed as
   a) Seizures   b) Ataxia
   c) Bone deformities   d) All
89. Most common systemic fungal infection in cats
   a) Ringworm   b) Histoplasmosis
   c) Both a and b   d) None
90. Von wille-brands disease
   a) Inherited   b) Acquired
   c) Accidental   d) None
91. Clotting profiles
   a) Fibrinogen   b) PT
   c) APTP   d) All

92. After exercise elevation of platelet count indicative of
   a) Epinephrine b) Nor epinephrine
   c) Both d) None
93. Rickettsial organisms responsible for thrombocytopenia
   a) E.canis b) E.ewingii
   c) E.eceeci d) All
94. Thrombocytopenia leads to which haemorrhages
   a) Petechial b) Ecchymosis
   c) Both d) None
95. Assessment of improvement while blood transfusion done by
   a) TLC b) Haemoglobin
   c) PCV d) RBC
96. Immune mediated caused by which hypersensitive reaction
   a) Type II b) Type I
   c) Type III d) Type IV
97. Disseminated intravascular coagulation leads to
   a) Increased consumption of platelets
   b) Increased consumption of clotting factors
   c) Both
   d) None
98. Endotoxemia from
   a) Gram negative bacteria leads to endothelial damage
   b) Platelet activation
   c) Both a and b
   d) None
99. Reduced thrombopoiesis in dogs due to
   a) CDV b) CPV
   c) Ehrlichia d) All
100. Reduced thrombopoiesis in cats due to
   a) FELV b) FPV
   c) FIP d) All
101. Drugs which can cause thrombocytopeni a)
   a) Cisplatin b) Cyclophosphamide
   c) Doxorubicin d) All
102. Changes in the size of red blood cells
   a) Poikilocytosis b) Anisocytosis
   c) Polychromasia d) All
103. Changes in the shape of red blood cells
   a) Poikilocytosis b) Anisocytosis
   c) Polychromasia d) All

104. Myeloid leukaemia in
   a) FELV
   b) FPV
   c) FIP
   d) All
105. What are the blood types in dogs
   a) DEA1.1 , 2.2
   b) DEA3,4
   c) DEA5,7
   d) all
106. Ideal blood donor in dogs
   a) DEA1.2 negative
   b) DEA1.1negative
   c) a&b
   d) DEA 1.1 positive
107. Most common blood type in cats
   a) Type A
   b) TypeB
   c) Type C
   d) Type D
108. Incompatibility between the blood groups expected by
   a) roileaux formation
   b) red cell formation
   c) a&b
   d) none
109. Ideal feline donor
   a) >3kg body weight
   b) pcb>35%
   c) age 1to 7 yrs
   d) all
110. Changes in the color of red blood cells
   a) Poikilocytosis
   b) Anisocytosis
   c) Polychromasia
   d) Both a & b
111. Ideal blood to drawn from a donor
   a) 50 ml per kg
   b) 5 ml per kg
   c) 150 ml per kg
   d) 30 ml per kg
112. Common transfusion reactions
   a) hemolysis
   b) Dysnea
   c) opisthotonus
   d) all
113. Dacrocyte
   a) tear shaped RBC
   b) pear shaped RBC
   c) round RBC
   d) all
114. Signs in IMHA
   a) Icterus
   b) Fever
   c) Necrosis of tail
   d) All of the above
115. IMHA characterized by
   a) Increased plasma fibrinogen
   b) Increased MCV
   c) Reduced MCHC
   d) All the above
116. Definitive test for IMHA
   a) Coombs test
   b) HIA
   c) Blood smear
   c) VNT

117. Coombs test detect the
   a) Antibody attached to red blood cells
   b) Antibody attached to white blood cells
   c) Antibody attached to Platelets
   d) All

118. Treatment of IMHA involves
   a) Glucocorticoids b) Azathioprine
   c) Cyclosporin d) All of the above

119. Assessment of IMHA done by demonstration of red blood cells
   a) Rouleaux formation in a wet mount of blood
   b) Tight red cell clusters after addition of saline
   c) Aggregations of erythrocytes
   d) All of the above

120. Etiology for formation of Heinz bodies in dogs
   a) Onion toxicity b) Acetaminophen toxicity
   c) DL-Methionine d) All of the above

121. Common cause of Heinz bodies formation in cats
   a) Diabetic ketoacidosis b) Hyperthyroidism
   c) Lymphoma d) All of the above

122. Dirofilariasis in dogs can cause
   a) Postcaval syndrome b) Mechanical damage to RB
   c) Hemolysis d) All of the above

123. In dogs, zinc toxicity can cause
   a) Intravascular hemolysis b) Extravascular hemolysis
   c) A and B d) None

124. Treatment option for zinc toxicity in dogs
   a) Calcium EDTA b) PAM
   c) Both a & b d) Atropine sulphate

125. Presence of 20-30 % of reticulocytes in circulation indication of
   a) Pyruvate kinase deficiency b) Zinc toxicity
   c) DIC d) None

126. Bone marrow failure to produce RBC
   a) Hemolysis anemia b) Aplastic anemia
   c) Hemorrhagic anemia d) All of the above

127. Thin erythrocytes are
   a) Hypochromia b) Leptocytes
   c) Hyperchromic d) Both a& b

128. Pappenheimer bodies
    a) Hypochromia b) Leptocytes
    c) Hyperchromic d) Focal basophilic stippling
129. Hepatozoon app gametocyte affect the
    a) Neutrophils b) Monocytes
    c) Lymphocytes d) A & B
130. Canine distemper virus affects the
    a) Neutrophils b) Monocytes
    c) Lymphocytes d) A & B
131. Histoplasma capsulatum affects the
    a) Neutrophils b) Monocytes
    c) Lymphocytes d) Eosinophils
132. Proliferation mitotic pool in bone marrow composed of
    a) Myeloblast b) Progranulocytes
    c) Myelocytes d) All
133. Cytokines released during anemi a)
    a) TNF b) Interferon
    c) IL-1 d) All
134. Storage maturation pool in bone marrow composed of
    a) Metamyelocytes b) Band neutrophils
    c) Segmented neutrophils d) All
135. Immune mediated diseases causes of Neutrophilia
    a) Polyserosidis b) Polymyocytis
    c) Rheumatoid arthritis d) All
136. Which toxicity responsible for neutrophilia in dogs
    a) Blue green algae toxicity b) Botulism
    c) Endotoxemia and uremia d) All
137. In cats ,which is the cause of pancytopeni a)
    a) Feline pan Leukopenia b) Feline leukemia virus
    c) Feline immunodeficiency virus d) All
138. Obliteration of Marrow spaces by increased fibrous connective tissue
    a) Myelofibrosis b) Myelodysplasia
    c) Both d) None
139. Abnormal cellular morphology with or without blast cells
    a) Myelofibrosis b) Myelodysplasia
    c) A & B d) None
140. Precence of blast cells in circulation
    a) Myeloproliferative disease b) Myelofibrosis
    c) Myelodysplasia d) All

141. bone marrow hypoplasia reversed by
   a) Lithium carbonate
   b) Calcium carbonate
   c) Lithium chloride
   d) All
142. Granulocytic ehrlichiosis leads to
   a) Polyarthritis
   b) Normocytic normochromic anemia
   c) Thrombocytopenia
   d) All the above
143. Monocytic ehrlichiosis in dogs leads to
   a) Hypercellular bone marrow
   b) Increased M:E ratio
   c) Anemia
   d) All the above
144. Canine cyclic hematopoisis treated by
   a) G-CSF
   b) GM-CSF
   c) Botha&b
   d) None
145. Lymphopenia in dogs due to
   a) Chylothorax
   b) lymphangiectesis
   c) Hyperadrenocortisis
   d) All
146. Immature cells of leukocytosis
   a) Band cells
   b) Metamyelocytes
   c) Myelocytes
   d) All
147. Stress leukogram is
   a) Mature Neutrophilia
   b) Lymphopenia
   c) Eosinopenia
   d) All
148. Feline leukemia virus leads to
   a) Hemolytic anemia
   b) Non regenerative anemia
   c) Red cell hypoplasia
   d) All of the above
149. Non regenerative anemia
   a) Decreased PCV
   b) Lack of polychromasia
   c) Lack of reticulocyte s
   d) All
150. Pure redcell aplasia
   a) Low PCV
   b) Normal leukocyte count
   c) Normal platelet count
   d) All
   e) Round RBC

Answer Key

1	d	2	b	3	d	4	a	5	c	6	c	7	c
8	c	9	b	10	c	11	a	12	b	13	b	14	a
15	b	16	b	17	a	18	b	19	c	20	b	21	d
22	c	23	d	24	c	25	b	26	c	27	b	28	d
29	c	30	d	31	a	32	b	33	c	34	d	35	b
36	b	37	d	38	b	39	b	40	a	41	a	42	b
43	b	44	a	45	a	46	b	47	a	48	c	49	a
50	a	51	d	52	d	53	b	54	a	55	a	56	d
57	d	58	c	59	a	60	d	61	d	62	d	63	a
64	a	65	a	66	d	67	d	68	a	69	d	70	c
71	b	72	c	73	a	74	c	75	b	76	a	77	c
78	b	79	a	80	b	81	d	82	d	83	b	84	a
85	d	86	c	87	a	88	d	89	b	90	a	91	d
92	a	93	d	94	c	95	a	96	a	97	c	98	a
99	d	100	d	101	d	102	b	103	a	104	a	105	d
106	c	107	a	108	c	109	d	110	c	111	a	112	d
113	a	114	d	115	d	116	a	117	a	118	d	119	d
120	d	121	d	122	d	123	a	124	a	125	a	126	b
127	b	128	d	129	d	130	c	131	c	132	d	133	d
134	d	135	d	136	d	137	d	138	a	139	b	140	a
141	a	142	d	143	d	144	a	145	d	146	d	147	d
148	d	149	d	150	d								

19

Clinical Physiology of Haemo-lymphatic Disorders

***Avinash Palli*[1] *and D.V.V.N. Durga Prasad*[2]**

[1]*Department of Veterinary Physiology and Biochemistry, School of Veterinary and Animal Sciences, Centurion University of Technology and Management, Paralakhemundi, Gajapati, Odisha*

[2]*Section of Veterinary Anatomy, ICAR-IVRI, Izatnagar, Bareilly, Uttar Pradesh*

Introduction

The haematological system, essential for sustaining life and comprising blood and its components, is fundamental to human and animal physiology. Blood is a unique connective tissue that performs several critical functions, including transporting oxygen, nutrients, and hormones to cells and removing metabolic wastes. It also plays a pivotal role in immune response, haemostasis, and the regulation of body temperature and pH. This section provides an in-depth overview of the clinical physiology of the haematological system, covering the composition of blood, haematopoiesis, haemostasis, and common haematological disorders. Blood is composed of two main elements: plasma and blood cells. Plasma, the liquid component, constitutes approximately 55% of blood volume and consists predominantly of water, electrolytes, proteins, waste products, and dissolved gases. Plasma is the medium for transporting nutrients, gases, hormones, and waste products throughout the body. It contains important proteins such as albumin, which maintains osmotic pressure; globulins, which are involved in immune responses; and fibrinogen, which is crucial for blood clotting. The blood cells include erythrocytes (red blood cells), leukocytes (white blood cells), and platelets. Erythrocytes are the most abundant cells in the blood, with the primary function of transporting oxygen from the lungs to tissues and carbon dioxide from tissues back to the lungs. This is facilitated by haemoglobin, an iron-containing protein within erythrocytes that binds to oxygen. The lifespan of an erythrocyte is approximately 120 days, after which it is phagocytosed by macrophages, which are a type of myeloid phagocytic cells in the spleen and liver. Leukocytes are integral to the immune system, protecting the body against infections and foreign pathogens. They are categorized into granulocytes (neutrophils, eosinophils, and basophils) and agranulocytes (lymphocytes and monocytes). Each type of leukocyte has a specific function: neutrophils are the first responders to infection, eosinophils are involved in allergic reactions and parasitic infections, basophils release histamine during inflammatory responses, lymphocytes are central to adaptive immunity, and monocytes differentiate into macrophages and dendritic cells that engulf and digest pathogens. Platelets, or thrombocytes, are small, anucleate cells that originate from megakaryocytes in the bone marrow. They play a critical role in haemostasis by forming a temporary plug at the site of blood vessel injury. Upon activation, platelets release granules that promote further platelet aggregation and initiate the coagulation cascade, leading to the formation of a stable fibrin clot.

Haematopoiesis is the process by which blood cells are produced in the bone marrow. It begins with multipotent haematopoietic stem cells (HSCs), which have the potential to differentiate into all types of blood cells. The process of haematopoiesis is tightly regulated by a complex interplay of cytokines, growth factors, and hormones.

Erythropoiesis is the production of erythrocytes, regulated primarily by erythropoietin (EPO), a glycoprotein hormone produced by the kidneys in response to hypoxia.

Erythropoiesis involves the differentiation of HSCs into proerythroblasts, which undergo several stages of maturation, including the extrusion of the nucleus, to become reticulocytes. Reticulocytes are released into the bloodstream, where they mature into fully functional erythrocytes.

Leukopoiesis refers to the production of leukocytes. This process is driven by various cytokines and colony-stimulating factors, such as granulocyte colony-stimulating factor (G-CSF) and interleukins, which promote the differentiation of HSCs into specific leukocyte lineages. Granulopoiesis, the production of granulocytes, involves the differentiation of myeloid progenitors into neutrophils, eosinophils, and basophils. Lymphopoiesis, the production of lymphocytes, occurs in primary lymphoid organs, such as the bone marrow and thymus, where lymphoid progenitors differentiate into B cells, T cells, and natural killer cells. Thrombopoiesis is the production of platelets, regulated by thrombopoietin (TPO), a hormone primarily synthesized by the liver. During thrombopoiesis, HSCs differentiate into megakaryocytes, large polyploid cells that fragment into thousands of platelets. These platelets are then released into the circulation, where they remain ready to respond to vascular injury. Haemostasis is the physiological process that prevents blood loss following vascular injury. It involves a series of regulated steps that ensure the rapid formation of a clot at the site of injury while maintaining blood flow elsewhere in the circulatory system. The haemostatic process is divided into three major phases: vascular spasm, platelet plug formation, and coagulation.

Vascular spasm is the immediate response to blood vessel injury, characterized by vasoconstriction, which reduces blood flow to the affected area. This response is mediated by the release of endothelin from damaged endothelial cells and the reflex contraction of smooth muscle cells in the vessel wall.

Platelet plug formation is the second phase of haemostasis. Platelets adhere to exposed collagen fibers at the site of injury, becoming activated and releasing adenosine diphosphate (ADP), thromboxane A2, and other mediators that amplify the platelet response. This results in the recruitment and aggregation of additional platelets, forming a temporary plug that seals the injury site. Coagulation is the final phase of haemostasis, involving the formation of a stable fibrin clot. The coagulation cascade, involving a complex series of enzymatic reactions, is initiated through either the intrinsic or extrinsic pathway, both of which converge on the activation of thrombin. Thrombin catalyses the conversion of soluble fibrinogen into insoluble fibrin strands, which interlace with the platelet plug to form a stable clot. The coagulation process is tightly regulated by anticoagulant mechanisms that prevent excessive clot formation and ensure that clots are confined to the site of injury.

Disorders of the Haematological System

The clinical physiology of the haematological system is fundamental to understanding a wide range of haematological disorders. These disorders can arise from abnormalities in the production, function, or regulation of blood cells and plasma proteins.

Anaemias are characterized by a reduction in the number of erythrocytes or the amount of haemoglobin, resulting in the decreased oxygen-carrying capacity of the blood.
Anaemia can be caused by various factors, including iron deficiency, vitamin B12 or folate deficiency, chronic disease, and bone marrow failure. Clinical symptoms of anaemia include fatigue, pallor, shortness of breath, and tachycardia.

Leukemias are malignancies of the haematopoietic system, characterized by the uncontrolled proliferation of abnormal leukocytes. Leukemias are classified based on the type of leukocyte involved and the clinical course of the disease, which may be acute or chronic. The abnormal leukocytes in leukemia crowd out normal haematopoietic cells in the bone marrow, leading to symptoms such as anaemia, increased susceptibility to infections, and bleeding disorders.

Thrombocytopenias are conditions characterized by a low platelet count, which can result in an increased risk of bleeding. Thrombocytopenia may be caused by decreased platelet production in the bone marrow, increased destruction of platelets in the circulation, or sequestration of platelets in the spleen. Clinical management of thrombocytopenia depends on the underlying cause and may involve platelet transfusions, immunosuppressive therapy, or splenectomy.

Haemophilia, sickle cell disease, thalassemia, polycythemia vera, and myelodysplastic syndromes are among the significant blood disorders in humans, while babesiosis, feline infectious anaemia, canine ehrlichiosis, haemorrhagic disease in deer, and bovine leukemia virus infection are notable blood-borne diseases affecting domestic and wild animals.

The lymphatic system serves as a crucial auxiliary to the circulatory system, maintaining fluid balance by collecting excess interstitial fluid and returning it to the bloodstream. It acts as a diligent courier, transporting dietary fats from the small intestine to various tissues via lymphatic vessels, ensuring a direct and efficient supply of nutrients for cellular processes. The lymphatic system plays a pivotal role in immune defense, with lymphoid organs like the thymus, spleen, and lymph nodes housing specialized cells (lymphocytes) that orchestrate immune responses against pathogens.

Lymphocytes undergo maturation and activation within lymphoid tissues, patrolling the body through lymphatic vessels and congregating in lymph nodes to mount immune responses against antigens. The lymphatic system's involvement in cancer metastasis highlights its dual nature, serving as both a defender against disease and a conduit for its spread. Understanding the anatomy and function of the lymphatic system is essential for developing effective strategies to combat diseases such as cancer and to promote overall health and well-being in animals. The Lymphatic System: A Vital Component of Immunity. The lymphatic system is an essential part of the immune system in vertebrates. It complements the circulatory system and plays a crucial role in maintaining fluid balance, defense against infections, and nutrient transport.

Questions

1. What is the primary function of red blood cells in animals?
   a) Fighting infections b) Transporting oxygen
   c) Producing hormones d) Breaking down fats
2. Which blood cell type is primarily responsible for clot formation?
   a) Red blood cells b) White blood cells
   c) Platelets d) Plasma cells
3. Where is the majority of blood produced in adult animals?
   a) Liver b) Spleen
   c) Bone marrow d) Kidneys
4. What is the term for the liquid component of blood?
   a) Serum b) Plasma
   c) Haemoglobin d) Lymph
5. Which of the following is NOT a function of blood?
   a) Nutrient transport b) Waste removal
   c) Hormone production d) Immune response
6. Which hormone regulates red blood cell production?
   a) Insulin b) Erythropoietin
   c) Thyroxine d) Cortisol
7. The process of blood cell formation is called:
   a) Hemopoiesis b) Hemolysis
   c) Hemostasis d) Hematocrit
8. What is the average lifespan of a red blood cell in most animals?
   a) 10 days b) 30 days
   c) 60 days d) 120 days
9. Blood protein essential for clotting?
   a) Albumin b) Fibrinogen
   c) Haemoglobin d) Myoglobin
10. Which organ is primarily responsible for the removal of old or damaged red blood cells?
    a) Kidney b) Liver
    c) Spleen d) Heart
11. In veterinary haematology, which condition is characterized by an abnormal increase in the number of red blood cells?
    a) Anaemia b) Leukaemia
    c) Polycythaemi d) Thrombocytopenia
12. Which species-specific variation must be considered when analyzing hematology results?
    a) Platelet count b) Haemoglobin structure
    c) Hematocrit value d) Differential count of White blood cell

13. The diagnostic test which measures the percentage of red blood cells in a blood sample?
    a) Complete Blood Count (CBC)
    b) Hematocrit
    c) Blood smear
    d) Coagulation profile
14. What is the primary difference between plasma and serum?
    a) Serum lacks clotting factors
    b) Plasma lacks water
    c) Serum contains red blood cells
    d) Plasma contains antibodies
15. Which condition in veterinary medicine is diagnosed with a Coombs test?
    a) Immune-mediated haemolytic anaemia
    b) Leukopenia
    c) Thrombocytopenia
    d) Hemophilia
16. Which component of blood is primarily responsible for transporting oxygen?
    a) Platelets
    b) Red blood cells
    c) White blood cells
    d) Plasma
17. What is the main function of white blood cells?
    a) Clotting
    b) Oxygen transport
    c) Immune response
    d) Nutrient distribution
18. What percentage of blood is made up of plasma?
    a) 10%
    b) 25%
    c) 55%
    d) 75%
19. Which component of blood carries hormones to different parts of the body?
    a) Red blood cells
    b) White blood cells
    c) Plasma
    d) Platelets
20. Which type of white blood cell is most abundant in healthy animals?
    a) Eosinophils
    b) Basophils
    c) Neutrophils
    d) Lymphocytes
21. What is the primary function of albumin in the blood?
    a) Clotting
    b) Oxygen transport
    c) Maintaining osmotic pressure
    d) Immune response
22. Which cell type is responsible for antibody production?
    a) Erythrocytes
    b) T-cells
    c) B-cells
    d) Platelets
23. How do red blood cells in mammals differ from those in birds?
    a) Mammalian red blood cells are nucleated
    b) Bird red blood cells are larger
    c) Mammalian red blood cells lack a nucleus
    d) Bird red blood cells lack haemoglobin
24. Which blood parameter indicates the oxygen-carrying capacity of the blood?
    a) Hematocrit
    b) Haemoglobin concentration
    c) White blood cell count
    d) Platelet count

25. Which organ synthesizes the majority of plasma proteins?
    a) Heart b) Liver
    c) Spleen d) Kidney
26. In veterinary hematology, what is the significance of the mean corpuscular volume (MCV)?
    a) It measures the average size of white blood cells
    b) It indicates the oxygen saturation in the blood
    c) It determines the average volume of red blood cells
    d) It assesses the clotting ability of platelets
27. What does a high reticulocyte count indicate in an animal's blood test?
    a) Bone marrow failure b) Active red blood cell production
    c) Low platelet count d) Chronic infection
28. Which type of leukocyte is primarily involved in the response to parasitic infections?
    a) Neutrophils b) Lymphocytes
    c) Eosinophils d) Monocytes
29. Which protein in red blood cells binds to and transports oxygen?
    a) Albumin b) Globulin
    c) Haemoglobin d) Fibrinogen
30. Which diagnostic test is used to measure the various components of blood, such as red and white blood cells, haemoglobin, and hematocrit?
    a) Complete Blood Count (CBC) b) Blood Chemistry Panel
    c) Urinalysis d) Coagulation Test
31. Which cell type is the precursor to all blood cells?
    a) Myeloid cells b) Lymphoid cells
    c) Hematopoietic stem cells d) Erythrocytes
32. Which blood cells are primarily responsible for immune responses?
    a) Erythrocytes b) Leukocytes
    c) Thrombocytes d) Platelets
33. Organ which produces erythropoietin?
    a) Heart b) Liver
    c) Kidney d) Bone marrow
34. Immature red blood cells found in the bloodstream can be called as?
    a) Megakaryocytes b) Reticulocytes
    c) Erythroblasts d) Myeloblasts
35. Which white blood cell type is involved in allergic reactions and parasitic infections?
    a) Neutrophils b) Basophils
    c) Eosinophils d) Monocytes
36. In hemopoiesis, what role do megakaryocytes play?
    a) They produce red blood cells b) They produce platelets
    c) They produce white blood cells d) They produce plasma

37. The type of lymphocyte matures in the thymus?
    a) B cells
    b) T cells
    c) NK cells
    d) Dendritic cells
38. Which growth factor is crucial for the differentiation of myeloid progenitor cells?
    a) Granulocyte-macrophage colony-stimulating factor (GM-CSF)
    b) Interleukin-2 (IL-2)
    c) Thrombopoietin
    d) Erythropoietin
39. What is the primary site of hemopoiesis in the fetus?
    a) Liver
    b) Bone marrow
    c) Spleen
    d) Kidney
40. Which disorder is characterized by the overproduction of immature white blood cells?
    a) Leukaemi
    b) Anaemia
    c) Thrombocytopeni
    d) Polycythaemia
41. Which term describes the percentage of blood volume occupied by red blood cells?
    a) Hematocrit
    b) Haemoglobin
    c) Reticulocyte count
    d) Platelet count
42. Which interleukin is primarily involved in the stimulation of B-cell growth and differentiation?
    a) IL-1
    b) IL-4
    c) IL-6
    d) IL-10
43. What is the primary concern when transfusing blood between animals?
    a) Matching blood types
    b) Matching body weight
    c) Matching fur color
    d) Matching diet
44. Which blood component is most commonly transfused to treat anaemia?
    a) Plasma
    b) Platelets
    c) Red blood cells
    d) White blood cells
45. What is the main purpose of a crossmatch test before a blood transfusion?
    a) To check for parasites
    b) To determine blood type
    c) To test for compatibility
    d) To measure haemoglobin
46. An adverse reaction to a blood transfusion can be called as?
    a) Anaphylaxis
    b) Haemolytic reaction
    c) Hemostasis
    d) Immunodeficiency
47. In which species is blood type B more common?
    a) Dogs
    b) Cats
    c) Horses
    d) Cows

48. What is the primary reason for performing a blood type test in animals before surgery?
    a) To diagnose diseases
    b) To determine anesthesia dosage
    c) To prepare for potential transfusions
    d) To check liver function
49. Which component of the blood is typically used in the treatment of clotting disorders?
    a) Red blood cells
    b) Platelets
    c) Plasma
    d) White blood cells
50. Which condition is a common indication for a plasma transfusion in veterinary patients?
    a) Anaemia
    b) Hypoproteinaemia
    c) Leukopenia
    d) Thrombocytopenia
51. Which genetic factor determines blood type in animals?
    a) Chromosomes
    b) Alleles
    c) Mitochondria
    d) Enzymes
52. What is the primary immunoglobulin involved in blood transfusion reactions?
    a) IgA
    b) IgD
    c) IgE
    d) IgG
53. Which anticoagulant is commonly used in blood transfusion bags?
    a) Heparin
    b) Warfarin
    c) Citrate
    d) Aspirin
54. Which blood type system is commonly used in dogs?
    a) ABO
    b) DEA (Dog Erythrocyte Antigen)
    c) Rh factor
    d) MNS system
55. In which situation is an emergency blood transfusion performed without prior blood typing?
    a) Chronic anaemia
    b) Elective surgery
    c) Severe trauma
    d) Routine check-up
56. What is the first step in the haemostatic process following an injury?
    a) Fibrinolysis
    b) Platelet aggregation
    c) Vasoconstriction
    d) Coagulation
57. Which protein is converted to fibrin during coagulation?
    a) Prothrombin
    b) Fibrinogen
    c) Thrombin
    d) Plasminogen
58. What is the role of thrombin in the coagulation cascade?
    a) Converts fibrinogen to fibrin
    b) Activates platelets
    c) Breaks down fibrin
    d) Inhibits factor X
59. Which vitamin is essential for the synthesis of clotting factors?
    a) Vitamin A
    b) Vitamin B12
    c) Vitamin C
    d) Vitamin K

60. Which pathway is initiated by tissue factor in the coagulation cascade?
    a) Intrinsic pathway
    b) Extrinsic pathway
    c) Common pathway
    d) Alternative pathway

61. Which test is used to evaluate the extrinsic pathway of coagulation?
    a) Activated partial thromboplastin time (aPTT)
    b) Prothrombin time (PT)
    c) Thrombin time (TT)
    d) Bleeding time

62. What is the primary function of plasmin in hemostasis?
    a) Fibrin formation
    b) Fibrinolysis
    c) Platelet activation
    d) Vasoconstriction

63. Which anticoagulant is commonly used to prevent clotting in blood samples?
    a) Heparin
    b) Warfarin
    c) Aspirin
    d) Vitamin K

64. Which factor deficiency is associated with Hemophilia A?
    a) Factor V
    b) Factor VII
    c) Factor VIII
    d) Factor IX

65. Which color-coded blood collection vial is typically used for glucose testing?
    a) Red top (no additive)
    b) Blue top (sodium citrate)
    c) Green top (heparin)
    d) Gray top (potassium oxalate/sodium fluoride)

66. Which laboratory test measures the functionality of the intrinsic and common coagulation pathways?
    a) Prothrombin time (PT)
    b) Activated partial thromboplastin time (aPTT)
    c) Thrombin time (TT)
    d) Bleeding time

67. Which inherited coagulation disorder is most commonly seen in dogs?
    a) Von Willebrand disease
    b) Hemophilia A
    c) Hemophilia B
    d) Factor XII deficiency

68. Which condition is characterized by the widespread activation of coagulation and subsequent bleeding?
    a) Hemophilia
    b) Disseminated intravascular coagulation (DIC)
    c) Thrombocytopenia
    d) Von Willebrand disease

69. The type of anaemia which is caused by a deficiency of vitamin B12 or folic acid?
    a) Aplastic anaemia
    b) Haemolytic anaemia
    c) Megaloblastic anaemia
    d) Sickle cell anaemia
70. Which condition is characterized by the destruction of red blood cells within blood vessels?
    a) Intrinsic hemolysis
    b) Extrinsic hemolysis
    c) Intravascular hemolysis
    d) Extravascular hemolysis
71. Which diagnostic test is most useful in differentiating between regenerative and non-regenerative anaemia?
    a) Hematocrit
    b) Reticulocyte count
    c) Blood smear
    d) Coombs test
72. What is the most common cause of iron deficiency anaemia in young animals?
    a) Chronic infection
    b) Blood loss
    c) Dietary deficiency
    d) Bone marrow failure
73. Which breed of dog is particularly prone to hereditary spherocytosis?
    a) German Shepherd
    b) Golden Retriever
    c) Cocker Spaniel
    d) Dachshund
74. Which enzyme deficiency is commonly associated with haemolytic anaemia in dogs?
    a) Glucose-6-phosphate dehydrogenase
    b) Pyruvate kinase
    c) Lactate dehydrogenase
    d) Hexokinase
75. Which autoimmune condition results in the destruction of red blood cells?
    a) Immune-mediated haemolytic anaemia (IMHA)
    b) Thalassemia
    c) Polycythemia vera
    d) Sickle cell anaemia
76. Which hormone is often elevated in response to chronic anaemia?
    a) Insulin
    b) Erythropoietin
    c) Cortisol
    d) Thyroxine
77. Which test is used to diagnose iron deficiency anaemia in animals?
    a) Serum ferritin
    b) Haemoglobin electrophoresis
    c) Bone marrow biopsy
    d) Reticulocyte count
78 Which red blood cell morphology is commonly seen in cases of regenerative anaemia?
    a) Spherocytes
    b) Schistocytes
    c) Target cells
    d) Polychromatophilic cells
79. Which type of leukocyte is primarily involved in the body's response to bacterial infections?
    a) Eosinophils
    b) Basophils
    c) Neutrophils
    d) Lymphocytes

80. Which disorder is characterized by an abnormally high white blood cell count?
a) Leukopenia
b) Leukocytosis
c) Thrombocytopenia
d) Erythrocytosis

81. Which type of white blood cell is most commonly associated with allergic reactions?
a) Neutrophils
b) Basophils
c) Lymphocytes
d) Monocytes

82. What is the primary function of macrophages in the immune system?
a) Produce antibodies
b) Engulf and digest pathogens
c) Produce histamine
d) Transport oxygen

83. Which leukocyte disorder is characterized by a decrease in neutrophil count?
a) Lymphocytosis
b) Eosinophilia
c) Neutropenia
d) Monocytosis

84 Which inherited disorder results in recurrent infections due to a defect in neutrophil function?
a) Chronic granulomatous disease
b) Severe combined immunodeficiency
c) Chediak-Higashi syndrome
d) Hyper-IgM syndrome

85. Which leukocyte abnormality is commonly seen in animals with chronic stress?
a) Eosinophilia
b) Lymphopenia
c) Basophilia
d) Monocytopenia

86. What is the hallmark finding in a blood smear of an animal with leukaemia?
a) Presence of blast cells
b) Increased platelets
c) Fragmented red blood cells
d) Increased basophils

87. Which leukocyte disorder is characterized by the clonal proliferation of plasma cells?
a) Lymphoma
b) Multiple myeloma
c) Myelodysplastic syndrome
d) Polycythemia vera

88. Which white blood cell count is typically elevated in parasitic infections?
a) Neutrophil count
b) Eosinophil count
c) Basophil count
d) Lymphocyte count

89. Which technique is used to evaluate bone marrow cellularity and architecture in veterinary patients?
a) Complete Blood Count (CBC)
b) Bone marrow aspiration
c) Flow cytometry
d) Blood smear

90. What does an elevated erythrocyte sedimentation rate (ESR) indicate?
a) Increased red blood cell production
b) Inflammation or infection
c) Enhanced coagulation
d) Decreased platelet count

91. The molecular technique which is used for the diagnosis of specific genetic mutations in haematological disorders?
    a) Polymerase Chain Reaction (PCR)
    b) Western Blotting
    c) Enzyme-Linked Immunosorbent Assay (ELISA)
    d) Immunofluorescence

92. What is the primary use of flow cytometry in Veterinary Haematology?
    a) To count red blood cells
    b) To identify cell surface markers
    c) To measure haemoglobin levels
    d) To assess platelet function

93. Which staining technique is commonly used to identify reticulocytes in blood smears?
    a) Wright's stain
    b) Giemsa stain
    c) New methylene blue stain
    d) Hematoxylin and eosin stain

94. In a dog presenting with severe thrombocytopenia, which diagnostic test is most appropriate to determine the underlying cause?
    a) Blood smear evaluation
    b) Bone marrow biopsy
    c) Coagulation profile
    d) Reticulocyte count

95. What is the most likely diagnosis for a cat with elevated neutrophils, toxic granulation, and Dohle bodies in a blood smear?
    a) Chronic lymphocytic leukaemia
    b) Acute inflammation or infection
    c) Iron deficiency anaemia
    d) Immune-mediated haemolytic anaemia

96. Which diagnostic finding is characteristic of immune-mediated haemolytic anaemia (IMHA) in dogs?
    a) Schistocytes
    b) Spherocytes
    c) Howell-Jolly bodies
    d) Target cells

97. In a case of suspected von Willebrand disease, which specific diagnostic test should be performed?
    a) Prothrombin time (PT)
    b) von Willebrand factor antigen assay
    c) Activated partial thromboplastin time (aPTT)
    d) D-dimer test

98. Which laboratory test can help differentiate between regenerative and non-regenerative anaemia in a horse?
    a) Serum iron levels
    b) Bone marrow biopsy
    c) Erythropoietin levels
    d) Reticulocyte count

99. Which advanced imaging technique is used for detailed evaluation of hematologic organs such as the spleen and bone marrow in veterinary patients?
    a) Ultrasound
    b) MRI (Magnetic Resonance Imaging)
    c) CT (Computed Tomography) scan
    d) X-ray

100. Which novel therapeutic approach involves the use of genetically engineered cells to treat hematologic cancers in veterinary medicine?
    a) Chemotherapy
    b) Immunotherapy
    c) Gene therapy
    d) Bone marrow transplant

101. Which technology is being increasingly used for rapid and comprehensive analysis of blood cell populations in veterinary diagnostics?
    a) Flow cytometry
    b) Next-generation sequencing
    c) Mass spectrometry
    d) Electron microscopy

102. Which biomarker is being studied for its potential to provide early diagnosis of sepsis in veterinary patients?
    a) C-reactive protein (CRP)
    b) Procalcitonin
    c) Lactate
    d) Tumor necrosis factor (TNF)

103. The cell-based therapy which is gaining attention in veterinary medicine for the treatment of immune-mediated hematologic disorders?
    a) Stem cell therapy
    b) Platelet transfusion
    c) Erythropoietin administration
    d) Leukocyte transfusion

104. Which inherited disorder is characterized by a defect in the production of the alpha or beta chains of haemoglobin in animals?
    a) Thalassemia
    b) Sickle cell disease
    c) Hemophilia
    d) von Willebrand disease

105. Which blood disorder is marked by the presence of Heinz bodies in erythrocytes on a blood smear?
    a) Iron deficiency anaemia
    b) G6PD deficiency
    c) Pyruvate kinase deficiency
    d) Haemolytic anaemia

106. What is the primary pathophysiological mechanism in disseminated intravascular coagulation (DIC)?
    a) Excessive platelet production
    b) Uncontrolled activation of the coagulation cascade
    c) Immune-mediated destruction of red blood cells
    d) Increased erythropoiesis

107. Which condition is characterized by excessive production of immunoglobulin by a single clone of plasma cells?
    a) Polycythaemia
    b) Multiple myeloma
    c) Lymphoma
    d) Leukemia

108. Which hematologic condition involves the destruction of red blood cells due to antibodies against one's own erythrocytes?
   a) Autoimmune haemolytic anaemia b) Aplastic anaemia
   c) Hemophilia d) Thrombocytopenia
109. Which rare congenital disorder in dogs is characterized by the presence of large granules in leukocytes due to a mutation in the LYST gene?
   a) Pelger-Huet anomaly b) Chediak-Higashi syndrome
   c) Hyper-IgM syndrome d) Canine cyclic neutropenia
110. Which advanced laboratory technique is used for detecting minimal residual disease in hematologic malignancies?
   a) Karyotyping b) Immunohistochemistry
   c) Quantitative PCR d) Southern blotting
111. Which blood disorder is identified by the presence of Bence Jones proteins in the urine?
   a) Hemophilia b) Multiple myeloma
   c) Iron deficiency anaemia d) Sickle cell anaemia
112. Which genetic technique can be used to correct mutations causing haemophilia in animals?
   a) CRISPR-Cas9 b) RNA interference
   c) Gene knockdown d) Protein therapy
113. Which condition is marked by pancytopenia and hypocellular bone marrow in veterinary patients?
   a) Thalassemia b) Aplastic anaemia
   c) Hemophilia d) Leukaemia
114. Which coagulation factor deficiency is most common in Hemophilia B?
   a) Factor V b) Factor VIII
   c) Factor IX d) Factor XI
115. Which laboratory technique uses antibodies to detect specific antigens in blood samples?
   a) Flow cytometry b) ELISA
   c) PCR (Polymerase Chain Reaction) d) Western blotting
116. Which growth factor is crucial for the differentiation of myeloid progenitor cells?
   a) Granulocyte-macrophage colony-stimulating factor (GM-CSF)
   b) Interleukin-2 (IL-2)
   c) Thrombopoietin
   d) Erythropoietin
117. Which cytokine is critical for the differentiation of lymphoid progenitor cells into T cells in the thymus?
   a) Interleukin-2 (IL-2) b) Interleukin-4 (IL-4)
   c) Interleukin-7 (IL-7) d) Interleukin-10 (IL-10)

118. Which transcription factor is essential for the differentiation of hematopoietic stem cells into erythrocytes?
   a) GATA-1 b) PU.1
   c) NF-κB d) STAT3

119. What is the primary role of colony-stimulating factors (CSFs) in haematopoiesis?
   a) Induce apoptosis of defective blood cells
   b) Stimulate the proliferation and differentiation of blood cell precursors
   c) Inhibit erythropoiesis
   d) Decrease platelet production

120. Which cell type is responsible for the production of antibodies in the adaptive immune response?
   a) T cells b) B cells
   c) Macrophages d) Neutrophils

121. Which condition results from a mutation in the GATA2 gene affecting hematopoietic stem cells?
   a) Diamond-Blackfan anaemia
   b) Severe combined immunodeficiency (SCID)
   c) Myelodysplastic syndrome
   d) Chronic granulomatous disease

122. Which blood group antigen is most immunogenic in dogs, leading to severe transfusion reactions if mismatched?
   a) DEA 1.1 b) DEA 1.2
   c) DEA 3 d) DEA 4

123. Which complication is a risk when using stored blood products for transfusion in veterinary patients?
   a) Bacterial contamination
   b) Citrate toxicity
   c) Transfusion-associated circulatory overload (TACO)
   d) All of the above

124. In cats, which blood type can result in neonatal isoerythrolysis if kittens are born to a mismatched type B queen?
   a) Type b) Type B
   c) Type AB d) Type O

125. Which blood transfusion reaction is characterized by haemoglobinuria and acute kidney injury?
   a) Febrile non-haemolytic transfusion reaction
   b) Acute haemolytic transfusion reaction
   c) Transfusion-related acute lung injury (TRALI)
   d) Allergic transfusion reaction

126. What is the primary cause of non-infectious transfusion-related acute lung injury (TRALI) in veterinary medicine?
  a) Donor antibodies against recipient leukocytes
  b) Bacterial contamination of blood products
  c) Iron overload
  d) Volume overload

127. Which clotting factor is deficient in Hemophilia C, a rare bleeding disorder in animals?
  a) Factor VIII b) Factor IX
  c) Factor XI d) Factor XIII

128. Which diagnostic test is used to assess platelet function and the integrity of primary hemostasis in veterinary patients?
  a) Prothrombin time (PT)
  b) Bleeding time
  c) Activated partial thromboplastin time (aPTT)
  d) Thrombin time (TT)

129. What is the role of von Willebrand factor in the coagulation process?
  a) Activates thrombin
  b) Cross-links fibrin
  c) Inhibits fibrinolysis
  d) Mediates platelet adhesion to damaged endothelium

130. Which genetic mutation is associated with Factor V Leiden thrombophilia in animals?
  a) G1691A mutation in the F5 gene b) C282Y mutation in the HFE gene
  c) JAK2 V617F mutation d) Prothrombin G20210A mutation

131. Which laboratory finding is most indicative of disseminated intravascular coagulation (DIC) in a veterinary patient?
  a) Elevated D-dimer levels b) Increased hematocrit
  c) Low white blood cell count d) Normal fibrinogen levels

132. Which form of anaemia is associated with a defect in the spectrin protein in red blood cells, leading to spherocytosis?
  a) Iron deficiency anaemia b) Haemolytic anaemia
  c) Hereditary spherocytosis d) Megaloblastic anaemia

133. Which laboratory test is used to differentiate between anaemia of chronic disease and iron deficiency anaemia in animals?
  a) Serum ferritin b) Haemoglobin electrophoresis
  c) Bone marrow biopsy d) Reticulocyte count

134. Which condition is characterized by ineffective erythropoiesis and ringed sideroblasts in the bone marrow?
  a) Aplastic anaemia b) Megaloblastic anaemia
  c) Sideroblastic anaemia d) Haemolytic anaemia

135. Which genetic mutation is associated with pyruvate kinase deficiency in dogs, leading to haemolytic anaemia?

a) PFKM gene mutation
b) PKLR gene mutation
c) G6PD gene mutation
d) HFE gene mutation

136. Which clinical sign is most commonly associated with vitamin B12 deficiency in animals?

a) Hyperpigmentation of the skin
b) Neurological deficits
c) Joint swelling
d) Hypercalcemia

137. Which leukocyte disorder is characterized by a clonal proliferation of lymphocytes and is often associated with a retroviral infection in cats?

a) Chronic lymphocytic leukemia (CLL)
b) Feline leukemia virus (FeLV)-associated lymphoma
c) Canine cyclic neutropenia
d) Feline infectious peritonitis (FIP)

138. Which enzyme deficiency results in chronic granulomatous disease, affecting neutrophil function in dogs?

a) Myeloperoxidase deficiency
b) NADPH oxidase deficiency
c) Superoxide dismutase deficiency
d) Glutathione peroxidase deficiency

139. Which leukocyte abnormality is often seen in animals with Ehrlichiosis?

a) Lymphocytosis
b) Monocytosis
c) Neutropenia
d) Eosinophilia

140. Which inherited disorder is characterized by defective neutrophil chemotaxis and recurrent infections in Irish Setters?

a) Canine cyclic neutropenia (Gray Collie syndrome)
b) Pelger-Huet anomaly
c) Leukocyte adhesion deficiency
d) Chediak-Higashi syndrome

141. Which hematologic disorder in dogs is associated with a mutation in the c-kit gene, leading to mast cell proliferation?

a) Multiple myeloma
b) Mast cell tumour
c) Acute myeloid leukemia
d) Chronic lymphocytic leukemia

142. Which anticoagulant is commonly used in blood transfusion bags?

a) Heparin
b) Warfarin
c) Citrate
d) Aspirin

143. In which situation is an emergency blood transfusion performed without prior blood typing?

a) Chronic anaemia
b) Elective surgery
c) Severe trauma
d) Routine check-up

144. Which enzyme deficiency is commonly associated with haemolytic anaemia in dogs?

a) Glucose-6-phosphate dehydrogenase b) Pyruvate kinase
c) Lactate dehydrogenase d) Hexokinase

145. Which hormone is often elevated in response to chronic anaemia?

a) Insulin b) Cortisol
c) Thyroxine d) Erythropoietin

146. Which red blood cell morphology is commonly seen in cases of regenerative anaemia?

a) Spherocytes b) Schistocytes
c) Target cells d) Polychromatophilic cells

147. Which inherited disorder results in recurrent infections due to a defect in neutrophil function?

a) Chronic granulomatous disease
b) Severe combined immunodeficiency
c) Chediak-Higashi syndrome
d) Hyper-IgM syndrome

148. What is the hallmark finding in a blood smear of an animal with leukaemia?

a) Presence of blast cells b) Increased platelets
c) Fragmented red blood cells d) Increased basophils

149. Which white blood cell count is typically elevated in parasitic infections?

a) Neutrophil count b) Lymphocyte count
c) Basophil count d) Eosinophil count

150. Match the Following:

Column A		Column B	
I	Erythropoiesis	a)	Protein in red blood cells that carries oxygen
II	Haemoglobin	b)	Condition characterized by a low platelet count
III	Neutrophil	c)	Process of red blood cell formation
IV	Thrombocytopenia	d)	A white blood cell type involved in the immune response
V	Lymphocyte	E	A type of white blood cell primarily involved in fighting bacterial infections

a) I-C, II-A, III-E, IV-B, V-D b) I-A, II-B, III-C, IV-D, V-E
c) I-D, II-B, III-E, IV-A, V-C d) I-E, II-D, III-C, IV-B, V-A

151. Match the Following Questions

	Column A		Column B
I	Polycythemia	A	Increased number of red blood cells
II	Anaemia	B	Reduced red blood cell count or haemoglobin levels
III	Leukemia	C	White blood cell cancer originating in the bone marrow
IV	Immune-mediated haemolytic anaemia (IMHA)	D	Excessive breakdown of red blood cells due to autoimmune response
V	Von Willebrand Disease	E	Genetic disorder affecting platelet function

a) I-C, II-A, III-E, IV-B, V-D
b) I-A, II-B, III-C, IV-D, V-E
c) I-D, II-B, III-E, IV-A, V-C
d) I-E, II-D, III-C, IV-B, V-A

152. What is the primary function of the lymphatic system?
a) To transport hormones
b) B) To regulate temperature
c) To maintain fluid balance and protect against pathogens
d) To produce red blood cells

153. Which of the following is a primary lymphoid organ?
a) Spleen
b) Lymph node
c) Thymus
d) Tonsil

154. Lymphatic capillaries are known for:
a) High-pressure fluid transport
b) Presence of red blood cells
c) Being impermeable to proteins
d) Absorbing interstitial fluid

155. The lymphatic system plays a role in:
a) Digestion of fats
b) Oxygen transport
c) Blood clotting
d) Hormone secretion

156. Which cells are responsible for the immune functions of the lymphatic system?
a) Erythrocytes
b) Platelets
c) Lymphocytes
d) Neutrophils

157. The structure of a lymph node is organized into which of the following regions?
a) Cortex and medulla
b) Hilum and cortex
c) Medulla and hilum
d) Capsule and sinus

158. Which of the following cells are not typically found in a lymph node?
a) Macrophages
b) B-lymphocytes
c) Neurons
d) T-lymphocytes

159. High endothelial venules (HEVs) are unique to which type of lymphoid organ?
a) Primary lymphoid organs
b) Secondary lymphoid organs
c) Both primary and secondary lymphoid organs
d) Neither primary nor secondary lymphoid organs

160. What is the main function of the spleen in the lymphatic system?
   a) To produce lymphocytes
   b) To filter blood and remove old red blood cells
   c) To produce hormones
   d) To regulate body temperature

161. Lymphatic vessels are most similar to which type of blood vessel?
   a) Arteries   b) Arterioles
   c) Capillaries   d) Veins

162. Which of the following is a characteristic feature of lymphatic capillaries?
   a) They have a continuous basement membrane
   b) They are impermeable to macromolecules
   c) They have valves to prevent backflow
   d) They contain red blood cells

163. The thymus is responsible for the maturation of:
   a) B-cells   b) T-cells
   c) Macrophages   d) Dendritic cells

164. Mucosa-associated lymphoid tissue (MALT) includes all of the following except:
   a) Peyer's patches   b) Tonsils
   c) Spleen   d) Appendix

165. Which of the following is not a function of the lymphatic system?
   a) Maintaining fluid balance   b) Transporting dietary lipids
   c) Conducting nerve impulses   d) Defending against pathogens

166. The lymphatic system interacts with the circulatory system by:
   a) Delivering oxygen to tissues
   b) Removing waste products from the bloodstream
   c) Transporting hormones
   d) Returning interstitial fluid to the bloodstream

167. Which of the following is not a component of the lymphatic system?
   a) Lymph   b) Lymph nodes
   c) Heart   d) Lymphatic vessels

168. The inner region of a lymph node is called the:
   a) Cortex   b) Medulla
   c) Hilum   d) Capsule

169. Lymphatic tissues that are not encapsulated are referred to as:
   a) Nodular lymphatic tissue   b) Diffuse lymphatic tissue
   c) Organized lymphatic tissue   d) Disorganized lymphatic tissue

170. The germinal centers found in lymph nodes are mainly associated with:
   a) T-cell activation   b) B-cell proliferation
   c) Macrophage aggregation   d) Neutrophil storage

171. Which of the following best describes the lymphatic capillaries?
   a) They have a thick muscular wall
   b) They are closed at one end
   c) They contain valves similar to veins
   d) They are larger than blood capillaries

172. The thymus is most active during:
   a) Infancy
   b) Adolescence
   c) Adulthood
   d) Old age

173. Which of the following is true about the spleen?
   a) It is the largest lymph node
   b) It is a primary lymphoid organ
   c) It filters lymph
   d) It filters blood

174. The lymphatic system is involved in the absorption of which substance from the digestive tract?
   a) Glucose
   b) Amino acids
   c) Fatty acids and glycerol
   d) Nucleic acids

175. Hassall's corpuscles are unique to which lymphoid organ?
   a) Lymph node
   b) Spleen
   c) Thymus
   d) Bone marrow

176. The lymphatic system's role in lipid absorption occurs primarily in the:
   a) Liver
   b) Small intestine
   c) Stomach
   d) Pancreas

177. Lymph nodes are encapsulated structures that:
   a) Produce red blood cells
   b) Filter lymph
   c) Store plateletsd
   d) Secrete digestive enzymes

178. The outermost layer of a lymph node is called the:
   a) Cortex
   b) Medulla
   c) Hilum
   d) Capsule

179. Which of the following is not a function of the spleen?
   a) Blood filtration
   b) Immune surveillance
   c) Hormone production
   d) Removal of aged erythrocytes

180. The thymus differs from other lymphoid organs because it:
   a) Does not filter lymph
   b) Is not involved in immunity
   c) Lacks afferent lymphatic vessels
   d) Contains Hassall's corpuscles

181. Which of the following best describes lymph?
   a) A type of white blood cell
   b) A plasma-derived fluid that lacks proteins
   c) A plasma-derived fluid that contains proteins
   d) A red blood cell-containing fluid

Answer Key

1	b	2	c	3	c	4	b	5	c	6	b	7	a
8	d	9	b	10	c	11	c	12	d	13	b	14	a
15	a	16	b	17	c	18	c	19	c	20	c	21	c
22	c	23	c	24	b	25	b	26	c	27	b	28	c
29	c	30	a	31	c	32	b	33	c	34	b	35	c
36	b	37	b	38	a	39	a	40	a	41	a	42	b
43	a	44	c	45	c	46	b	47	b	48	c	49	c
50	b	51	b	52	d	53	c	54	b	55	c	56	c
57	b	58	a	59	d	60	b	61	b	62	b	63	a
64	c	65	d	66	b	67	a	68	b	69	c	70	c
71	b	72	c	73	c	74	b	75	a	76	b	77	a
78	d	79	c	80	b	81	b	82	b	83	c	84	a
85	b	86	a	87	b	88	b	89	b	90	b	91	a
92	b	93	c	94	b	95	b	96	b	97	b	98	d
99	b	100	c	101	a	102	b	103	a	104	a	105	d
106	b	107	b	108	a	109	b	110	c	111	b	112	a
113	b	114	c	115	b	116	a	117	c	118	a	119	b
120	b	121	c	122	a	123	d	124	a	125	b	126	a
127	c	128	b	129	d	130	a	131	a	132	c	133	a
134	c	135	b	136	b	137	b	138	b	139	c	140	c
141	b	142	c	143	c	144	b	145	d	146	d	147	a
148	a	149	d	150	a	151	b	152	c	153	c	154	d
155	a	156	c	157	a	158	c	159	b	160	b	161	d
162	c	163	b	164	c	165	c	166	d	167	c	168	b
169	b	170	b	171	c	172	a	173	d	174	c	175	c
176	b	177	b	178	d	179	c	180	c	181	c		

20

Clinical Physiology of Male Reproduction Disorders

Abhay Kumar Yadav, Abhinav Gupta, Rajesh Kumar and Sushant Srivastav

Department of Veterinary Gynaecology and Obstetrics, College of Veterinary Science & Animal Husbandry, Acharya Narendra Deva University of Agriculture & Technology, Ayodhya, Uttar Pradesh

Introduction

The testicle is a unique and important reproductive organ that serves two main purposes. The primary purpose is the development of mature spermatozoa that are able to fertilise the egg.The production of hormones, which plays a role in ensuring that mature spermatozoa are delivered to mature eggs where fertilisation may take place, must be considered a supplemental function to the development of germ cells. The induction of behavioristic reactions—also referred to as sex drive or mating instincts—and the provision of a means of transportation for spermatozoa, as well as the regulation of ejaculate—either its release into the aquatic medium surrounding the egg in the case of lower vertebrates or its introduction into female passages through an organ of intromission—are the two concrete necessities involved. The animal loses its ability to reproduce as long as either the production of germ cells or the propensity to mate is impaired, even though the two processes undoubtedly work in tandem to achieve the end result.

1. What are the two principal functions of the testicle?
   a) Formation of mature spermatozoa and secretion of hormones
   b) Production of testosterone and estradiol
   c) Regulation of the hypothalamic-pituitary-gonadal axis
   d) Secretion of inhibin B and Mullerian inhibiting substance (MIS)
2. What is the primary function of the epididymis?
   a) Sperm transport and maturation
   b) Sperm storage and fertilization
   c) Regulation of testosterone levels
   d) Production of seminal fluid
3. What is the main function of the hypothalamic-pituitary-gonadal axis?
   a) Regulation of sperm production
   b) Production of testosterone and estradiol

c) Promotion and maintenance of sexual development and function
d) Regulation of the menstrual cycle

4. What is the role of inhibin B and Mullerian inhibiting substance (MIS) in the male reproductive system?
a) Regulation of sperm production
b) Regulation of testosterone levels
c) Inhibition of sperm maturation
d) Promotion of sexual development

5. What is the primary source of testosterone in the male body?
a) Leydig cells in the testes
b) Sertoli cells in the testes
c) Adipose tissue
d) Hypothalamus

6. What is the function of 5-alpha-reductase in the male reproductive system?
a) Conversion of testosterone to dihydrotestosterone
b) Conversion of testosterone to estradiol
c) Regulation of sperm production
d) Promotion of sexual development

7. What is the function of aromatase in the male reproductive system?
a) Conversion of testosterone to dihydrotestosterone
b) Conversion of testosterone to estradiol
c) Regulation of sperm production
d) Promotion of sexual development

8. What is the role of follicle-stimulating hormone (FSH) in the male reproductive system?
a) Regulation of sperm production
b) Regulation of testosterone levels
c) Promotion of sexual development
d) Inhibition of sperm maturation

9. What is the role of luteinizing hormone (LH) in the male reproductive system?
a) Regulation of sperm production
b) Regulation of testosterone levels
c) Promotion of sexual development
d) Inhibition of sperm maturation

10. What is the primary function of the scrotum in the male reproductive system?
a) Production of testosterone
b) Storage of sperm
c) Regulation of temperature for sperm production
d) Protection of the testes

11. What is the function of the epididymis in terms of spermatozoa?
a) Storage of spermatozoa
b) Maturation of spermatozoa
c) Transport of spermatozoa
d) Fertilization of egg cells

12. What is the role of Sertoli cells in the male reproductive system?
a) Production of testosterone
b) Production of spermatozoa

c) Regulation of sperm maturation

d) Secretion of inhibin B and Mullerian inhibiting substance (MIS)

13. What is the function of gonadotropin-releasing hormone (GnRH) in the male reproductive system?

a) Regulation of sperm production

b) Regulation of testosterone levels

c) Promotion of sexual development

d) Regulation of the hypothalamic-pituitary-gonadal axis

14. What is the effect of seasonal breeding on spermatozoa production?

a) Continuous production of spermatozoa

b) Production of spermatozoa only during breeding season

c) Increased production of spermatozoa during breeding season

d) Decreased production of spermatozoa during breeding season

15. What is the role of light in regulating spermatozoa production in some species?

a) Stimulation of pituitary activity

b) Inhibition of pituitary activity

c) Direct stimulation of spermatozoa production

d) Direct inhibition of spermatozoa production

16. What is the effect of dietary phenomena such as severe inanition or lack of vitamin B on spermatozoa production?

a) Increased production of spermatozoa

b) Decreased production of spermatozoa

c) No effect on spermatozoa production

d) Variable effect on spermatozoa production

17. What is the effect of androgens on spermatozoa production?

a) Stimulation of spermatozoa production

b) Inhibition of spermatozoa production

c) No effect on spermatozoa production

d) Variable effect on spermatozoa production

18. What is the role of pituitary materials in regulating spermatozoa production?

a) Stimulation of spermatozoa production

b) Inhibition of spermatozoa production

c) No effect on spermatozoa production

d) Variable effect on spermatozoa production

19. What is the effect of cryptorchism on spermatozoa production?

a) Increased production of spermatozoa

b) Decreased production of spermatozoa

c) No effect on spermatozoa production

d) Variable effect on spermatozoa production

20. What is the primary cause of decreased spermatozoa production in cryptorchism?
    a) Higher temperature of the abdomen
    b) Lower temperature of the scrotum
    c) Hormonal imbalance
    d) Genetic defect
21. What is seminal vesiculitis?
    a) Inflammation of the seminal vesicles
    b) Infection of the epididymis
    c) Inflammation of the testes
    d) Infection of the prostate gland
22. What is brucellosis?
    a) Bacterial disease affecting the reproductive organs of male
    b) Viral disease affecting the reproductive organs of female
    c) Fungal infection of the skin
    d) Parasitic infection of the gut
23. What is leptospirosis?
    a) Bacterial disease affecting the reproductive organs of male
    b) Viral disease affecting the reproductive organs of female
    c) Fungal infection of the skin
    d) Parasitic infection of the gut
24. What are enteroviruses?
    a) Bacterial contaminants of semen
    b) Viral contaminants of semen
    c) Fungal contaminants of semen
    d) Parasitic contaminants of semen
25. What is the mode of transmission of enteroviruses?
    a) Through oral exposure to contaminated feces
    b) Through airborne transmission
    c) Through skin contact
    d) Through sexual transmission
26. What is the effect of enteroviruses on spermatozoa production?
    a) Increased production of spermatozoa
    b) Decreased production of spermatozoa
    c) No effect on spermatozoa production
    d) Variable effect on spermatozoa production
27. What is the function of the testes in the male reproductive system?
    a) Production of seminal fluid
    b) Storage of spermatozoa
    c) Regulation of testosterone levels
    d) Formation of mature spermatozoa

28. What is the role of the epididymis in the male reproductive system?
    a) Production of seminal fluid
    b) Storage of spermatozoa
    c) Regulation of testosterone levels
    d) Maturation of spermatozoa
29. What is the function of the prostate gland in the male reproductive system?
    a) Production of seminal fluid
    b) Storage of spermatozoa
    c) Regulation of testosterone levels
    d) Maturation of spermatozoa
30. What is the role of the vas deferens in the male reproductive system?
    a) Production of seminal fluid
    b) Storage of spermatozoa
    c) Regulation of testosterone levels
    d) Transport of spermatozoa
31. What is the function of the seminal vesicles in the male reproductive system?
    a) Production of seminal fluid
    b) Storage of spermatozoa
    c) Regulation of testosterone levels
    d) Maturation of spermatozoa
32. What is the role of the scrotum in the male reproductive system?
    a) Production of seminal fluid
    b) Storage of spermatozoa
    c) Regulation of testosterone levels
    d) Regulation of temperature for sperm production
33. What is the function of the penis in the male reproductive system?
    a) Production of seminal fluid
    b) Storage of spermatozoa
    c) Regulation of testosterone levels
    d) Intromission of spermatozoa into the female reproductive tract
34. What is the role of gonadotropin-releasing hormone (GnRH) in the male reproductive system?
    a) Regulation of sperm production
    b) Regulation of testosterone levels
    c) Promotion of sexual development
    d) Regulation of the hypothalamic-pituitary-gonadal axis
35. What is the function of testosterone in the male reproductive system?
    a) Regulation of sperm production
    b) Regulation of testosterone levels
    c) Maintenance of male secondary sex characteristics
    d) All of the above
36. What will happen when levels of estradiol increase in males ?
    a) weak bones
    b) development of breasts
    c) loss of libido or infertileity
    d) all of the above
37. Leydig cells are found in
    a) Interstitial cell of testis
    b) Epididymis
    c) Vasdefrens
    d) None of above

38. Sertoli cells are found in
    a) Periphery of seminiferous tubules
    b) Interstitial cell of testis
    c) Lumen of vas effentia
    d) none of the above
39. blood-testis barrier is found by
    a) Ledig cells
    b) Sertoli cells
    c) Myoid cells
    d) Germ cells
40. Androgen Binding Protein is formed by
    a) Myoid cells
    b) Germ cells
    c) Ledig cells
    d) Sertoli cells
41. Germ cells are found in
    a) Inside seminiferous tubules
    b) Outside seminiferous tubules
    c) Inside and outside both
    d) None of the above
42. Disorders of the male reproductive system includes
    a) Loss of libido
    b) failure to ejaculate
    c) infertility
    d) All of the above
43. Germs cells produced in rat at the age of
    a) About 20-30 days
    b) About 35-40 days
    c) About 45-50 days
    d) After 80 days
44. In the guinea pig spermatozoa are found in the testis by
    a) 30th-40th days
    b) 100-110 days
    c) 50th-70th days
    d) 20th-30th days
45. The ability of sperm to fertilize ova is acquired in
    a) Vas deferens
    b) Ampullae
    c) Rete testis
    d) Epididymis
46. Sperm stored in which part of epididymis
    a) Head
    b) Body
    c) Tail
    d) All
47. The process of separation of head of spermetids is referred as
    a) Spermiation
    b) Spermiogenesis
    c) Spermatogenesis
    d) Capasitation
48. Which part of epididymis involves in active absorption of seminal fluid
    a) Head
    b) Body
    c) Tail
    d) Only head and body
49. What changes occure in the process of maturation of sperm
    a) changes occur in the sperm DNA-protein complex
    b) changes occure in plasma membrane
    c) changes occure in axonemal complex
    d) All of the above

50. During the maturation of spermatozoa the cytoplasmic droplets migrate
   a) From proximal to distal position on the sperm midpiece
   b) From distal to proximal position on the sperm midpiece
   c) From head to midpiece
   d) From midpiece to tail region
51. terminal portions of the ductus deferens is called as
   a) Epididymis b) Ampullae
   c) Urethra d) Rete testis
52. Ampullae is most prominent in whice species
   a) DOG b) Cat
   c) Horse d) Bull
53. Ampullae is absent in which species
   a) Dog and cat b) Pig and horse
   c) Bull d) Ram and buck
54. The ductus deferens open (via the ampullae) into
   a) Cranial portion of the pelvic urethra
   b) Caudal portion of the pelvic urethra
   c) Cranial portion of the penie urethra
   d) Caudal portion of the penile urethra
55. Largest portion of the semen ejaculate is contributed by
   a) Cowper's gland b) Sminal veicles
   c) Prostate gland d) Ampullae
56. Which accessory sex gland is lobulate
   a) Prostate gland b) Ampullae
   c) Cowper's gland d) Sminal veicles
57. Whice accessory sex gland semen produce odour in semen
   a) Sminal veicles b) Ampullae
   c) Prostate gland d) Prostate gland
58. Testicular temperature in bulls for effective production of fertile spermatozoa
   a) 2 to 6° C b) 1 to 3° C
   b) 7 to 8° C d) 6 to 7° C
59. Pampiniform plexus is a cpmplex network of
   a) Testicular artries b) Testicular vein
   c) Lymphatic vessels d) Vas deferens
60. Which statement is true about thermoregulation of testis
   a) Scrotal skin lack subcutaneous fat
   b) Scrotal skin is richly supplied by sweat gland .
   c) Pampiniform plexus takes part in thermoregulation of testis
   d) All

61. Cryptorchidsm is most coomonly seen in
    a) Bull b) Stallion
    c) Boar d) Buck
62. Testicular hypoplasia is caused by
    a) Single recessive autosomal gene b) Single dominant autosomal gene
    c) Sex linked recessive gene d) None
63. Inflammation of testis called as
    a) Posthitis b) Balanitis
    c) Orchitis d) Seminal vesiculitis
64. Seminal vesiculitis is commonly observed in
    a) Bull and boar b) Bull,ram and boar
    c) Bull, stallion amd boar d) None
65. Which of the following diseases causing infertility in bull
    a) Brucellosis b) Laptospirosis
    c) Campylobacteriosis d) All
66. Medusa cells are chiefly found in
    a) Testicular degeneration b) Testicular hypoplasia
    c) Both d) None
67. Yellow colour of semen is due
    a) Riboflavin b) Xanthophylls
    c) Caratenoid d) None
68. Prostate secretion of which spercies is high in zinc
    a) Bovine b) Equine
    c) Canine d) Caprine
69. Development and function of accessory sex gland in male is dependent on
    a) GnrH b) LH
    c) FSH d) Testosterone
70. Testosterone is converted to dihydrotestosterone by an enzyme known as
    a) Aromatase b) 17 alpha hydroxylage
    c) 5- alpha reductase d) 5- ketoreductase
71. Hypothalamic releasing hormones reach adenohypophysis through
    a) Nerve tract b) Hypophysialportal system
    c) Hypophyseal vein d) All
72. Which of the following is all called as nurse cell of testis
    a) Germ cells b) Leydig cells
    c) Sertoli cells d) None
73. Sertoli cells of testis secrete
    a) Inhibin b) ABP
    c) AMH d) All

74. Function of pampiniform plexus is to
   a) Regulate testicular temperature
   b) Decrease arterial pulse
   c) Maintain increase testosterone level in testis
   d) All

75. Which of the following is most sensitive to heat
   a) Sertoli cells b) leydig cells
   c) Both a and d) Germ cells

76. The cells which are most sensitive to irradiation is
   a) spermatogonia b) Leydig cells
   c) Sertoli cells d) Spermatocyte

77. Sperm gain motility in
   a) Caput epididymis b) Corpus epididymis
   c) Cauda epididymis d) All

78. Migration of cytoplasmic droplets occurs in
   a) Caput epididymis b) Corpus epididymis
   c) Cauda epididymis d) None

79. Which of the following gland act as reservoir of sperm
   a) Bulbourethral gland b) Prostate gland
   c) Ampulla d) None

80. Fructose & citric acid in semen is secreted by
   a) Seminal vesicle b) bulbourethral gland
   c) Prostate gland d) Epididymis

81. Riboflavin and ascorbic acid in semen is secreted from
   a) Seminal vesicle b) cowper's gland
   c) Prostate gland d) Epididymis

82. Fate of unejaculated epermatozoa is
   a) Resorbtion in epididymis b) Phagocytosis
   c) Voided in urine d) All

83. Size and functions of accessory glands are mainly regulated by
   a) Gonadotrophins b) Seminal Plasma protein
   c) Androgen d) None

84. Muscle present in spermatic cord which controls thermoregulation of testis is
   a) Tunica dotos c) Both a and b
   b) Cremaster muscle d) Retractor penis muscle

85. Testes move into and out of body cavity throughout their life through a patent inguinal canal in
   a) Rat b) Rabbit
   c) Elephant d) Both a and b

86. Which of the following constitute impotentia generandi
   a) Penile deviatio
   b Penile frenulum
   c) Testicular Hypoplasia
   d Penile neoplasia
87. Testis is pulled into scrotum during testicular descent by
   a) Gubernaculum
   c) Pampiniform plexus
   b) Scrotal ligament
   d) Spermatic cord
88. A thick white capsule of connective tissue immediately surrounding testes is
   a) Tunica dartos
   b) Tunica vaginalis
   c) Tunica albuginea
   d) None
89. Principal functions of testicle that make it specific-
   a) Spermatozoa production
   b) Hormone production
   c) Both
   d) None
90. Primary sex organ of male is-
   a) Testes
   b) Penis
   c) Scrotum
   d) Prostate
91. The cutaneous pouch in which testicles are located-
   a) Tunica dartos
   b) Scrotum
   c) Tunica vaginalis
   d) none
92. The major male androgen is-
   a) Progesterone
   b) Estrogen
   c) LH
   d) Testosterone
93. The male androgen is produced from-
   a) Leydig cells
   b) Sertolicells
   c) Myoid
   d) Germ cells
94. Testosterone can be converted into estradiol by-
   a) Aromatase
   b) Cytochrome P450
   c) 5-alpha-reductase
   d) All
95. Mullerian inhibiting substance (MIS) hormone is secreted by-
   a) Leydig cells
   b) Sertoli cells
   c) Myoid cells
   c) Germ cells
96. LH and FSH are released from-
   a) Posterior pituitary
   b) Anterior pituitary
   c) Hypothalmus
   d) Testes
97. Secretion of LH and FSH is regulated by-
   a) GnRH
   b) Estrogen
   c) Progesterone
   d) Testeosterone
98. Testosterone can be converted to estradiol via aromatase from-
   a) Reticular tissue
   b) Epithelial tissue
   c) Adipose tissue
   d) Lymph tissue

99. Estradiol/estrogen can play a role in-
   a) bone resorption b) epiphyseal closure
   c) gynecomastia d) All

100. Functional cells of the male reproductive system primarily consist of-
   a) Leydig cel b) Sertoli cell
   c) Both d) None

Answer Key

1	a	2	a	3	c	4	a	5	a	6	a	7	b
8	a	9	b	10	c	11	b	12	d	13	d	14	b
15	a	16	b	17	b	18	a	19	b	20	a	21	a
22	a	23	a	24	b	25	a	26	b	27	d	28	d
29	a	30	d	31	a	32	d	33	d	34	d	35	d
36	d	37	a	38	a	39	b	40	d	41	a	42	d
43	b	44	c	45	d	46	c	47	a	48	a	49	d
50	a	51	b	52	c	53	a	54	a	55	b	56	d
57	c	58	a	59	b	60	d	61	b	62	a	63	c
64	c	65	d	66	b	67	a	68	c	69	d	70	c
71	b	72	c	73	d	74	d	75	d	76	d	77	b
78	b	79	c	80	a	81	a	82	d	83	c	84	b
85	d	86	c	87	a	88	c	89	c	90	a	91	b
92	d	93	a	94	a	95	b	96	b	97	a	98	c
99	d	100	c	101		102		103		104		105	

21

Clinical Physiology of Respiratory Disorders

Bhavanam Sudhakara Reddy, Sirigireddy Sivajothi Kambala Swetha and Appana Satya Rajeswari

College of Veterinary Science - Proddatur, Sri Venkateswara Veterinary University Andhra Pradesh

Introduction

Respiratory diseases are a common clinical issue in dogs, particularly in those housed in environments like pet shops, shelters, breeding and boarding kennels. Puppies and senior dogs are at a higher risk of developing respiratory infections compared to adult dogs. The respiratory system is one of the body's four major systems, comprising the upper airways (pharynx, larynx, and trachea and the lower airways (bronchi, bronchioles, and alveoli). The pharynx, which serves as a common passageway for both the respiratory and gastrointestinal systems, explains the relatively high incidence of aspiration pneumonia. The luminal diameter of the pharynx is the widest, followed by the larynx and trachea. The ratio of tracheal diameter to thoracic inlet height (TD:TI) remains relatively constant, regardless of the animal's size or respiratory phase. The respiratory tract is typically protected from harmful pathogens by physical, chemical, and immunologic barriers, including mucus, mucociliary clearance, innate antimicrobial factors, alveolar macrophages, and the pulmonary immune response. The entire respiratory tree is lined with ciliated epithelial cells, except for the bronchioles, which are lined by non-ciliated granular secretory cells known as club cells. The respiratory system's primary function is achieved through four major processes: pulmonary ventilation; diffusion of oxygen and carbon dioxide between the alveoli and the blood; transport of these gases in the blood and body fluids to and from the body's tissue cells; and regulation of ventilation and other respiratory factors. The pulmonary alveoli, the main sites for gas exchange between air and blood, are highly vulnerable to injury if the body's defense mechanisms are compromised, underscoring the importance of prompt emergency treatment for respiratory diseases.

Clinical signs of chronic respiratory diseases in dogs include dyspnea, costal or abdominal breathing, coughing, nasal discharge and congestion, lung edema and consolidation, lethargy, and weight loss. Typically, dogs exhibit a thoracic or costal breathing pattern, but abdominal breathing may become more prominent during painful thoracic conditions, such as pleuritis. Coughing is a crucial physiological response that helps clear harmful substances like foreign bodies, mucus, or debris from the airways, maintaining the respiratory tract's health. Coughing is triggered by stimulating cough receptors located in the larynx, trachea, or bronchi, whereas irritation in the smaller bronchi, bronchioles, and alveoli usually does not elicit a cough. In these lower parts of the respiratory tract, the luminal flow is insufficient to generate the shear forces needed to clear mucus and debris or produce a cough. Overall, respiratory signs in dogs can be varied and sometimes vague, ranging from a mild, non-productive cough to severe pneumonia with systemic changes.

Diseases affecting the nasal cavity and paranasal sinuses in dogs typically present with symptoms such as nasal discharge, sneezing, facial deformities, stertor, lethargy, loss of appetite, weight loss, and, in rare cases, central nervous system signs. Brachycephalic breeds are particularly prone to upper respiratory tract disorders due to anatomical features like stenotic nares, enlarged tonsils, elongated soft palate, everted laryngeal saccules, narrowed rima glottidis, laryngeal collapse, and tracheal hypoplasia.

Rhinitis is primarily an inflammatory condition, chronic nasal disease in dogs can also result from fungal infections, neoplasia, retained foreign bodies, or oral diseases. Common diagnoses in canine nasal conditions include inflammatory and neoplastic diseases. The most common intranasal tumors in dogs include squamous cell carcinoma, adenocarcinoma, and undifferentiated carcinoma. Infectious rhinitis in dogs can result from bacterial, viral, or fungal infections, although primary bacterial rhinitis is quite rare. Canine viral rhinitis is most commonly caused by the canine distemper virus and less frequently by adenovirus, reovirus, herpesvirus, and influenza virus. Fungal causes of canine rhinitis include Aspergillus and Penicillium species, with canine nasal aspergillosis being particularly common. Dolichocephalic and mesocephalic breeds are more susceptible to these fungal infections, while brachycephalic breeds are rarely affected. Allergic rhinitis in dogs is associated with hypersensitivity to airborne antigens present in the nasal cavity and sinuses. Clinical signs of allergic rhinitis include sneezing, nasal congestion, and serous or mucopurulent nasal discharge, which may be seasonal, continuous, or intermittent, and can manifest in acute or chronic forms. Parasitic rhinitis is rare in dogs, with common nasal parasites including mites (*Pneumonyssoides caninum*) and nematodes (*Capillaria boehmi*).

Coughing in dogs can often be differentiated by body weight, with respiratory diseases typically seen in dogs that are normal or obese, and cardiac diseases more common in dogs that are thin or experiencing weight loss. The two most prevalent chronic tracheobronchial conditions in dogs are tracheobronchial collapse and chronic bronchitis.

Tracheal collapse is characterized by the progressive, dorsoventral flattening of the tracheal lumen. This condition is most commonly observed in middle-aged, small-breed dogs, though it can also occur in large breeds. The severity of clinical signs correlates with the extent of the collapse and can range from mild airway irritation and paroxysmal "goose-honking" coughing to respiratory distress and dyspnea. Factors such as obesity, exposure to pollutants, environmental allergens, and kennel cough have been associated with the progression of this disease.

Chronic bronchitis in dogs is a chronic inflammatory pulmonary condition characterized primarily by a persistent cough, which can also lead to exercise intolerance and respiratory distress. A hallmark of chronic bronchitis is expiratory wheezing. In dogs with this condition, airway narrowing occurs due to thickening of the airway walls and excessive mucus production and accumulation, resulting in increased airway resistance.

Infectious tracheobronchitis is commonly known as kennel cough, is an acute, contagious respiratory disease in dogs that affects the larynx, trachea, bronchi, and sometimes the lower respiratory tract. Various pathogens have been identified as potential causes of this condition. The primary agents responsible for kennel cough include *Bordetella bronchiseptica,* canine parainfluenza virus (PI), and canine adenovirus type-2 (CAV-2). Other pathogens that can contribute to kennel cough include bacteria such as *Pasteurella multocida, Streptococcus zooepidemicus,* and *Mycoplasma cynos,* as well as viruses like canine herpesvirus, canine influenza virus, and canine respiratory coronavirus.

Bacterial pneumonia is one of the most common clinical diagnoses in dogs with acute or chronic respiratory diseases. It is characterized by the colonization of the airways or pulmonary parenchyma by bacteria, leading to exudation and lung consolidation. Common causes of bacterial pneumonia include the aspiration of gastrointestinal contents, reduced ciliary function, and infections with opportunistic pathogens due to immunosuppression. Aspiration pneumonia, a serious and potentially life-threatening inflammatory lung condition, occurs as a result of esophageal disease, prolonged anesthesia, seizures, persistent vomiting, and laryngeal dysfunction. This condition can cause pathological lung damage, leading to ventilation-perfusion mismatch and hypoxemia.

Infectious or community-acquired pneumonias in dogs often occur following viral colonization and infection of the upper respiratory tract by pathogens such as canine respiratory coronavirus, pneumovirus, herpesvirus, and parainfluenza virus. These infections are more common in dogs living in overcrowded, stressful environments. While these diseases are typically acute and self-limiting, they can compromise the host's immune defenses, making the dog more susceptible to bacterial respiratory infections.

Bronchiectasis is a permanent and debilitating condition that results from chronic or severe airway injury, leading to progressive and irreversible airway dilation. The highest prevalence of bronchiectasis has been recorded in Cocker Spaniels, Miniature Poodles, and older dogs of various breeds.

Lung lobe torsion (LLT) is a condition where a lung lobe rotates along its long axis, causing the bronchovascular pedicle at the hilus to twist. In dogs, the right middle lobe is most commonly affected due to its long, narrow shape and loose attachment to the mediastinum, thoracic wall, and adjacent lobes. LLT can be classified as idiopathic or secondary to factors such as tumors, trauma, pleural effusions, or prior thoracic surgery.

Eosinophilic bronchopneumopathy (EBP) is a condition marked by eosinophilic infiltration of the lungs and bronchial mucosa, previously known as pulmonary infiltrates with eosinophilia (PIE). This disorder predominantly affects Siberian Huskies and Alaskan Malamutes. Although the precise cause of EBP remains unknown, it is believed to be related to hypersensitivity to airborne allergens.

Write correct alphabet of the answer in the given bracket

1. Viral rhinitis in dogs is due to
   a) Canine distemper b) Parvo virus
   c) Infectious canine hepatitis d) All the above
2. Bacterial rhinitis in dogs due to
   a) Bordetella b) Mycoplasm
   c) Both a & b d) None of the above
3. Viral rhinitis in cats due to
   a) Feline herpes virus b) Feline calci virus
   c) Both a & b d) None of the above

4. Presence of mucous production and mucopurulent nasal discharges noticed in
   a) Bacterial rhinitis b) Viral rhinitis
   c) Fungal rhinitis d) All the above
5. Sneezing leads to nasal bleeding in cats due to damage of …
   a) Nasal mucosa b) Turbinate
   c) Nasal planum d) Nasal bone
6. Rhinitis in dogs required
   a) Cleaning of nares b) Nasal decompensation
   c) Nutritional support d) All the above
7. Chronic rhinitis leads to
   a) Hyperplasia b) Hypertrophy
   c) Mucous secretion d) All the above
8. Best view to examine the nasal cavity while radiography
   a) Dorsoventral b) Intraoral projection
   c) Lateral d) Both a &b
9. Mottled appearance at nasal cavity in radiography is indicative of
   a) Hyperplastic rhinitis b) Hypoplastic rhinitis
   c) Acute rhinitis d) All the above
10. Biopsy sample required for hyperplastic rhinitis in dogs
   a) Snares b) Turbinate
   c) Lungs d) All the above
11. Dental diseases which are predispose to rhinitis in dogs
   a) Periapical abscess b) Oronasal fistul
   c) Cleft palate d) All the above
12. Ciliary dyskinesia
   a) Leads to respiratory problems
   b) Congenital
   c) Impairs the ability to move fluids, mucous effectively
   d) All the above
13. Irish wolfhound rhinitis diagnosed by
   a) Immunological testing b) Radiography
   c) Hematological values d) None of the above
14. Nasopharyngeal polyps associated conditions
   a) Vestibular disease b) Horner's disease
   c) Polyps d) All the above
15. Destructive rhinitis due to
   a) Bacterial b) Fungal
   c) Viral d) None of the above

16. Most common cause of fungal rhinitis in dogs
    a) Aspergillosis b) Cryptococcus
    c) Candidiasis d) All the above
17. Most common cause of fungal rhinitis in cats
    a) Aspergillosis b) Cryptococcus
    c) Candidiasis d) All the above
18. Fungal rhinitis mainly noticed in dog breeds of
    a) Brachycephalic b) Dolichocephalic
    c) Mesocephalic d) All the above
19. Depigmentation and ulceration at the rhinarium noticed in which rhinitis
    a) Bacterial b) Fungal
    c) Viral d) Parasitic
20. Localized antifungal agent for fungal rhinitis
    a) Ketoconazole b) Itraconazole
    c) Enilconazole d) Fluconazole
21. Most common tumor of nasal cavity in dogs is
    a) Adenocarcinoma b) Lymphoma
    c) Osteosarcoma d) Fibroma
22. Most common tumor of nasal cavity in cats is
    a) Adenocarcinoma b) Lymphoma
    c) Osteosarcoma d) Fibroma
23. Dogs with heavy bouts of epistaxis following violent sneezing is
    a) Intranasal neoplasia b) Rhinitis
    b) Pneumonia d) None of the above
24. Extent of tumor in dogs assessed by
    a) CT scan b) X - ray
    c) Ultrasonography d) Endoscopy
25. Honking cough noticed due to
    a) Pneumonia b) Tracheal collapse
    c) Reverse sneezing d) None of the above
26. Most common cause of coughing in dogs
    a) Infectious trachea bronchitis b) Canine distemper
    c) Cryptococcus d) None of the above
27. Parasite which cause respiratory distress in dogs
    a) *Trichuris* b) *Toxocara*
    c) *Pneumocystis carinii* d) None of the above
28. Signs in dogs with bronchopneumonia
    a) Tachypnea b) Dyspnea
    c) Cyanosis d) All the above

29. In bronchopneumonia thoracic auscultation reveals crackles
    a) Exudates in lungs b) Bronchoconstriction
    c) Pleuritis. d) Consolidation
30. On auscultation which lung sound are noticed in bronchoconstriction
    a) Crackles b) Wheezes
    c) Pleural friction rub d) No respiratory sound
31. On auscultation which lung sound are noticed in pleuritis
    a) Crackles b) Wheezes
    c) Pleural friction rub d) No respiratory sound
32. On auscultation which lung sound are noticed in lung consolidation
    a) Crackles b) Wheezes
    c) Pleural friction rub d) No respiratory sound
33. Fluid therapy in dogs with bronchopneumonia
    a) To maintain the mucociliary function b) Clearance of secretion
    c) Both a & b d) None of the above
34. Nebulization in dogs with bronchopneumonia
    a) To maintain the mucociliary function
    b) Clearance of secretion
    c) Maintain adequate hydration and secretion
    d) All the above
35. Bronchodilators used to treat in dogs with which condition
    a) Bronchospasm b) Pleural effusions
    c) Pneumothorax d) Both b and c
36. Non resolving pneumonia can be treated with
    a) Lifelong medical management b) Lobectomy
    c) Both a &b d) None of the above
37. Rupture of bronchial and alveolar walls leads to
    a) Emphysema b) Pneumonia
    c) Consolidation d) All the above
38. Presence of chronic cough usually dry , unproductive due to
    a) Pneumonia b) Effusions
    c) Bronchitis d) Consolidation
39. Cough is elicited by tracheal palpation in
    a) Bronchitis b) Tracheal collapse
    c) Rhinitis d) All the above
40. Coughing at night or early hours in the morning due to
    a) Rhinitis b) Bronchitis
    c) Tracheal stenosis d) None of the above

41. In radiography peri bronchial infiltration is visualized as
    a) Bronchial pattern of lungs b) Alveolar pattern of lungs
    c) Both a &b d) None of the above
42. In radiography patchy alveolar infiltration is visualized as
    a) Bronchial pattern of lungs b) Interstitial pattern of lungs
    c) Both a &b d) None of the above
43. In radiography peri bronchial infiltration is noticed as
    a) Doughnuts b) Tramline
    c) Both a &b d) None of the above
44. Condition in which bronchoscopy reveals loss of parallelism at bronchial walls
    a) Bronchoconstriction b) Bronchiectasis
    c) Bronchitis d) All the above
45. Feline asthma is due to
    a) Bronchoconstriction b) Hypertrophy
    c) Increased mucus production d) All the above
46. Feline asthma is due to
    a) Smoke b) Feathers
    c) Aerosol sprays d) All the above
47. Commonly used bronchodilators in dogs
    a) Theophylline b) Terbutaline
    c) Both a &b d) Azithromycin
48. Hilar lymphadenopathy is commonly noticed in
    a) PIE b) Bronchitis
    c) Pneumonia d) Tracheitis
49. Pulmonary infiltration with eosinophilia is shown in
    a) Eosinophilic granuloma b) Pneumonia
    c) Parasitic rhinitis d) All the above
50. Circulatory basophilia is significance in
    a) PIE b) Eosinophilicgranuloma
    c) Pleuritis d) None of the above
51. During bronchoscopy , yellowish green mucopurulent discharges noticed in
    a) Eosinophilic granuloma b) PIE
    c) Parasitic rhinitis d) All the above
52. Choice of medication for PIE in dogs
    a) Prednisolone b) Bronchodilators
    c) Antibiotics d) None of the above
53. Irreversible dilatation at the bronchi is seen in
    a) Lung consolidation b) Pleuritis
    c) Bronchiectasis d) None of the above

54. Dogs with ciliary dyskinesis are more prone to
    a) Bronchiectasis
    b) Lung consolidation
    c) Effusions
    d) All the above
55. Etiology for bronchiectasis
    a) Chronic bronchitis
    b) Airway obstruction
    c) Smoke inhalation
    d) All of the above
56. *Oslerus osleri* mode of transmission is
    a) Milk
    b) Water
    b) Direct contact
    d) Droplets
57. Presence of larvae at tracheal wash indicative of
    a) *Taenia solium*
    b) *Taenia saginata*
    c) *Oslerus osleri*
    d) All of the above
58. Drugs to treat *Oslerus osleri* in dogs
    a) Fenbendazole
    b) Praziquantel
    c) Piperazine
    d) None of the above
59. Worm present in the pulmonary artery and right ventricle
    a) Angiostrongylus vasorum
    b) Oslerus osleri
    c) *Taenia saginata*
    d) Trichuris
60. Inhaled tracheal foreign bodies leads to
    a) Cough
    b) Bronchitis
    c) Pneumonia
    d) Both a & b
61. Prominent feature in inhaled tracheal foreign bodies is
    a) Pneumonia
    b) Halitosis
    c) Rhinitis
    d) None of the above
62. Pulmonary granuloma formation noticed due to
    a) Nocardiosis
    b) Tuberculosis
    c) Fungal infection
    d) All the above
63. Tracheal collapse frequently seen in
    a) Giant breeds
    b) Toy breeds
    c) Brachycephalic
    d) All the above
64. Etiology of tracheal collapse in dogs
    a) Obesity
    b) Recent endotracheal tube intubation
    c) Obstructive airway disease
    d) All the above
65. Pathophysiology in tracheal collapse
    a) Reductant dorsal tracheal membrane prolapse
    b) Reductant ventral tracheal membrane prolapse
    c) Both
    d) None of the above

66. Chronic, persistent paroxysmal cough noticed in
    a) Bronchitis b) Pneumonia
    c) Tracheal collapse d) None of the above
67. Views of radiography for diagnosing tracheal collapse
    a) Inspiratory radiograph b) Expiratory radiograph
    c) Skyline projection d) All the above
68. Most significant radiographic changes in tracheal collapse
    a) Narrowing of thoracic trachea b) Narrowing of cervical trachea
    c) Both d) None of the above
69. Dynamic tracheal collapse not demonstrated by
    a) Ultrasonography b) Fluoroscopy
    c) Serum analysis d) Both a & b
70. Confirmation and extent of tracheal collapse done by
    a) Bronchoscopy b) Tracheoscopy
    c) Endoscopy d) None of the above
71. Antitussives used to treat tracheal irritation
    a) Diphenoxylate hydrochloride b) Hydrocodone
    c) Codeine phosphate d) All the above
72. Difficulty in breathing is called as
    a) Tachypnea b) Distress
    c) Dyspnea d) All the above
73. Increased respiratory rate is known as
    a) Distress b) Tachypnea
    c) Dyspnea d) None of the above
74. Increased depth of respiration known as
    a) Hyperpnea b) Tachypnea
    c) Dyspnea d) All the above
75. Unusual position to ventilate
    a) Hyperpnea b) Orthopnea
    c) Hypopnea d) Apnea
76. Dogs with abducted elbow, reluctant to lie down
    a) Meningitis b) Pleuraleffusions
    c) Hepatitis d) Cardiac Block
77. Accumulation of abnormal quantity of fluid in pleural space is known as
    a) Pleural effusions b) Pericardial effusions
    c) Ascites d) All the above
78. Pleural effusions in dogs and cats are
    a) Unilateral b) Bilateral
    c) Focal d) None of the above

79. Signs in pleural effusion
    a) Reduced lung sound ventrally   b) Orthopnea
    c) Muffled heart sounds   d) All the above
80. Which view of radiographic positioning is not recommended in dogs with pleural effusions
    a) Dorsal   b) Ventral
    c) Lateral   d) All the above
81. Unilateral pleural fluid is indicative of
    a) Pyothorax   b) Chylothorax
    c) Reactive effusions   d) All the above
82. Radiographic appearance of pleural effusions
    a) Retraction of lung lobes from thorax wall
    b) Scalloped appearance ventrally
    c) Interlobar pleural fissures
    d) All the above
83. Emergency procedure to relieve pain from pleural effusions
    a) Abdominocentesis   b) Thoracocentesis
    c) Analgesics   d) All the above
84. Anatomical location of simple thoracocentesis in dogs is
    a) 7-9 th ICS   b) 4-6 th ICS
    c) 9-11 th ICS   d) 2-5 th ICS
85. In cats pyothorax associated with
    a) FIV   b) FIP
    c) Both a &b   d) None of the above
86. Pyothorax most commonly noticed in
    a) Gun dog breeds   b) Miniature
    c) Brachycephalic   d) All the above
87. Pyothorax ended with
    a) Anaphylactic shock   b) Hypovolemic shock
    c) Septic shock   d) Both a & b
88. Anaerobic bacteria which will cause pyothorax
    a) Bacteroides   b) Nocardia
    c) Staphylococcus   d) Both a &c
89. Aerobic organisms which will cause pyothorax
    a) Nocardia   b) Bacteroides
    c) Pseudomonas   d) Both b &c
90. In pyothorax characteristic fetid odor noticed in dogs affected with
    a) Bacteroides   b) Staphylococcus
    c) Nocardia   d) None of the above

91. Best solution of tracheal lavage is
   a) Normal saline b) Ringer's solution
   c) Distilled water d) All the above
92. Complications of thoracotomy
   a) Pneumothorax b) Pulmonary edema
   c) Bradycardia d) All the above
93. Penetrating wounds produce
   a) Effusions b) Pneumonia
   c) Pneumothorax d) Both a& b
94. Air enter in to the pleural cavity but it cannot leave by the same point of entry during expiration
   a) Tension pneumothorax b) Lung consolidation
   c) Bronchiectasis d) None of the above
95. Increased air filled apace in pleural cavity and collapse of lung lobe
   a) Bronchoconstriction b) Tracheal collapse
   c) Pulmonary neoplasia d) Pneumothorax
96. Increased resonance sound over the thorax while thoracic percussion
   a) Effusions b) Pneumothorax
   c) Pulmonary edema d) Both a &c
97. Elevated cardiac silhouette from sternum in the lateral recumbency projection indicative of
   a) Pneumothorax b) Pulmonary edema
   c) Infection d) All the above
98. Chylothorax is due to
   a) Neoplasia b) Right side heart failure
   c) Trauma d) All the above
99. Chylothorax more commonly presented in
   a) Deep chested breeds b) Brachycephalic breeds
   c) Toy breeds d) All the above
100. Complication of pleural effusion with lung lobe torsion
   a) Pneumothorax b) Pyothorax
   c) Chylothorax d) None of the above
101. Chylothorax confirmed by
   a) High proteins b) High triglycerides
   c) Low proteins d) Low triglycerides
102. Staining used to detect chylothorax
   a) H&E stain b) Gram stain
   c) Sudan III d) Field stain

103. Concentration of triglycerides is more in pleural space than serum is indicative of
    a) Pyothorax b) Chylothorax
    c) Pneumothorax d) Hemothorax
104. Nutritional modification for a dog with chylothorax
    a) High carbohydrate b) Low fat diet
    c) Both a &b d) None of the above
105. Best medium chain triglycerides for a dog with chylothorax
    a) Coconut oil b) Olive oil
    c) Fatty acids d) None of the above
106. Non anticoagulant coumarin for treating chylothorax
    a) Warfarin b) Vitamin k
    c) Rutin d) None of the above
107. Surgical options for chylothorax are
    a) Ligation of thoracic duct b) Pleuroperitoneal shunts
    c) Pleurodesis d) All the above
108. Tests to differentiate chyle and pseudo chyle
    a Sudan III b) Triglycerides
    c) Both a &b d) None of the above
109. Cytology in chylothorax
    a) Lymphocytes& Fat globules b) Neutrophils & Fat globules
    c) Neutrophils & Basophils d) Lymphocytes & Basophils
110. Ascultation of thorax in dogs with diaphragmatic hernia reveals
    a) Muffled heart sounds b) Borborygmi
    c) Absent lung sounds d) All the above
111. Most common cause of diaphragmatic hernia in dogs
    a) Heart failure b) Effusions
    c) Trauma d) None of the above
112. Radiographic appearance of diaphragmatic hernia
    a) Presence of diaphragmatic line b) Loss of diaphragmatic line
    c) Loss of serosal details d) None of the above
113. Accumulation of excessive fluid in the lungs
    a) Pneumonia b) Effusions
    c) Pulmonary edema d) All the above
114. Cardiogenic cause of pulmonary edema is
    a) Left side heart failure b) Right side heart failure
    c) Both a & b d) Pulmonic stenosis
115. Non cardiogenic cause of pulmonary edema is
    a) Anaphylaxis b) Hypoproteinemia
    c) Fluid overload d) All the above

116. Blood tinged, frothy edema fluid from mouth and nostrils
   a) Pleural effusions
   b) Pulmonary edema
   c) Both a & b
   d) none of the above
117. Pulmonary edema due to acute cardiogenic origin
   a) Edema of wide spread & patchy distribution
   b) Edema at perihilar region
   c) Both a & b
   d) None of the above
118. Pulmonary edema due to chronic in origin
   a) Edema of wide spread & patchy distribution
   b) Edema at perihilar region
   c) Both a & b
   d) None of the above
119. Pulmonary edema due to noncardiogenic origin
   a) Edema at perihilar region
   b) Edema of wide spread & patchy distribution
   c) Edema at caudal dorsal lung lobe
   d) All the above
120. Pulmonary edema treatment
   a) Oxygen
   b) Diuretics
   c) Glucocorticoids
   d) All the above
121. Destruction of alveolar septa and convalescence of the alveoli in to large cavernous space
   a) Pulmonary emphysema
   b) Pulmonary edema
   c) Lung consolidation
   d) None of the above
122. Signs in pulmonary emphysema are
   a) Progressive expiratory dyspnea
   b) Inspiratory crackles
   c) Wheezes
   d) All the above
123. Complication of chronic bronchitis and bronchiectasis
   a) Pulmonary edema
   b) Pulmonary emphysema
   c) Pleural effusions
   d) None of the above
124. Radiographic appearance in pulmonary emphysema
   a) Flattering diaphragm
   b) Increased radiolucency of lungs
   c) Pruned pulmonary blood vessels
   d) All the above
125. Treatment for congenital lobar emphysema
   a) Lobectomy
   b) Antibiotics
   c) Diuretics
   d) None of the above

126. Treatment for pulmonary emphysema
   a) Bronchodilators
   b) Glucocorticoids
   c) Both a & b
   d) None of the above
127. Coumarin toxicity leads to
   a) Cardiac failure
   b) Pulmonary hypertension
   c) Pulmonary hemorrhages
   d) None of the above
128. Dyspnea, tachypnea, coughing and hemoptysis noticed in
   a) Pulmonary hemorrhages
   b) Pulmonary edema
   c) Pneumonia
   d) All the above
129. Obstruction of pulmonary artery with thrombi called as
   a) Pulmonary stenosis
   b) Pulmonary thromboembolism
   c) Pulmonary contusion
   d) None of the above
130. Etiology for pulmonary thromboembolism
   a) Fractured ribs
   b) Penetrating wounds
   c) Infection
   d) Both a& b
131. Etiology for pulmonary thromboembolism
   a) Autoimmune hemolytic anemia
   b) Neoplasia
   c) Both a & b
   d) None of the above
132. Common components causing pulmonary thromboembolism
   a) Fat
   b) Air
   c) Emboli
   d) All the above
133. Platelet degranulation leads to vasoconstriction and bronchoconstriction leads to
   a) Autoimmune hemolytic anemia
   b) Pulmonary thromboembolism
   c) Pulmonary stenosis
   d) All the above
134. Treatment for pulmonary thromboembolism is
   a) Diuretics
   b) Glucocorticoids
   c) Heparin
   d) Bronchodilators
135. Paraquat poisoning leads to
   a) Alveolitis
   b) Fibrosis
   c) Renal tubular damage
   d) All the above
136. Dyspnea, coughing, regurgitation noticed in
   a) Mediastinal disease
   b) Pneumothorax
   c) Pleural effusions
   d) All the above
137. Fungal diseases which will produce the signs of respiratory, digestive, and liver infection is
   a) Cryptococcus
   b) Mycoplasma
   c) Histoplasmosis
   d) None of the above
138. Esophageal perforation in dogs leads to
   a) Pneumothorax
   b) Tracheitis
   c) Bronchitis
   d) None of the above

139. Pneumothorax leads to
   a) Progressive loss of intrapleural negative pressure
   b) Non progressive loss of intrapleural negative pressure
   c) Progressive loss of intrapleural positive pressure
   d) Non progressive loss of intrapleural positive pressure

140. Complications of bullous emphysema leads to
   a) Bronchitis
   b) Bronchoconstriction
   c) Pneumothorax
   d) None of the above

141. Tension pneumothorax leads to
   a) Accumulation of intrapleural air without hemodynamic compromise
   b) Accumulation of intrapleural air with hemodynamic compromise
   c) No accumulation of intrapleural air with hemodynamic compromise
   d) No accumulation of intrapleural air without hemodynamic compromise

142. Pneumothorax leads to
   a) Reduction of ventilatory capacity
   b) Reduction of cardiac output
   c) Both a &b
   d) None of the above

143. Spontaneous pneumothorax related to
   a) Trauma
   b) Non traumatic
   c) Bullous emphysematous
   d) Both b &c

144. Brachycephalic airway syndrome affects dog breeds with
   a) Shortened skull
   b) Widened skull
   c) Deep chested
   d) None of the above

145. Brachycephalic airway syndrome seen in dogs with anatomical features of
   a) Stenotic nares
   b) Elongated soft palate
   c) Hypoplastic trachea
   d) All the above

146. Which dog breeds are commonly affected by brachycephalic airway syndrome
   a) Bull dogs
   b) Grey hounds
   c) Beagles
   d) German shepherds

147. Acute respiratory distress syndrome means
   a) Shock lung
   b) Fluid build up in small air sacs
   c) Life threatening
   d) All the above

148. Aspiration pneumonia
   a) Improper administration of medicines
   b) Animals that breathe in vomit
   c) Megaesophagus
   d) All the above

149. Flail chest means
   a) Fracture of multiple ribs
   b) Instability and asynchronous movement of the chest wall during respiration
   c) Trauma
   d) All the above

150. Animals with pneumonia benefit from
   a) Warm and dry environment
   b) Warm and humid environment
   c) Both a & b
   d) None of the above

Answer Key

1	a	2	c	3	c	4	a	5	b	6	d	7	d
8	d	9	a	10	b	11	d	12	d	13	a	14	d
15	b	16	a	17	b	18	b	19	b	20	c	21	a
22	b	23	a	24	a	25	b	26	a	27	c	28	d
29	a	30	b	31	c	32	d	33	c	34	c	35	a
36	b	37	a	38	c	39	a	40	b	41	a	42	b
43	c	44	b	45	d	46	d	47	c	48	a	49	a
50	a	51	b	52	a	53	c	54	a	55	d	56	a
57	c	58	a	59	a	60	d	61	b	62	d	63	b
64	d	65	a	66	c	67	d	68	a	69	c	70	b
71	d	72	c	73	b	74	a	75	b	76	b	77	a
78	b	79	d	80	a	81	d	82	d	83	b	84	a
85	c	86	a	87	c	88	a	89	a	90	a	91	b
92	d	93	c	94	a	95	d	96	b	97	a	98	d
99	a	100	c	101	b	102	c	103	b	104	c	105	a
106	c	107	d	108	c	109	a	110	d	111	c	112	b
113	c	114	a	115	d	116	b	117	a	118	b	119	c
120	d	121	a	122	d	123	b	124	d	125	a	126	c
127	c	128	a	129	b	130	d	131	c	132	d	133	b
134	c	135	d	136	a	137	c	138	a	139	b	140	c
141	b	142	c	143	d	144	a	145	d	146	a	147	d
148	d	149	d	150	a								

22

Clinical Physiology of Skin Disorders

Anil Kumar Singh

Department of Veterinary Physiology and Biochemistry, College of Veterinary Science & Animal Husbandry, Nanaji Deshmukh Veterinary Science University Rewa, Madhya Pradesh

Introduction

The skin, also known as the integumentary system, is the largest organ of the human body and protects animals from external factors. It consists of different tissues (epidermis, dermis, hypodermis, glands, hair and nails) and plays an important role in maintaining homeostasis, especially in regulating body temperature, protecting the body from damage and sensing the outside world.

The skin consists of three main layers: epidermis, dermis and subcutaneous tissue; each has its own specific function. The epidermis is the outermost layer of keratinocytes that produce keratin as a protective layer. The dermis, beneath the epidermis, is rich in collagen and elastin, which give the skin strength and elasticity. The subcutaneous tissue beneath the dermis consists of fatty tissue and acts as an insulator for the body. Dermal fibroblasts are the primary cells that synthesize and maintain the skin's extracellular matrix, contributing to its structural integrity and function. The integumentary system also plays an important role in regulating temperature, providing sensation, synthesizing biochemicals, absorbing nutrients, and protecting the body from various types of damage. In general, the integumentary system plays an important role in the body's overall health and function by regulating body temperature, providing a sense of well-being, producing important biochemicals, absorbing nutrients, and protecting the body from external factors.

The clinical physiology of the skin varies depending on factors such as location, age, gender, medications, and health status. Disruption of skin balance can lead to various skin diseases. Some skin diseases in animals include acne, atopic dermatitis, cellulite, psoriasis, folliculitis, burns, and cancer.

Unlike humans, who often develop acne in their youth, animals tend to develop acne in middle age. Acne in animals is caused by dirt, oil, and debris clogging the skin follicles. There are two types of acne in dogs and cats: non-inflammatory acne and inflammatory acne. Short-haired breeds such as Dobermans, Bulldogs, Great Danes, and Boxers are prone to acne. Treatment for acne in dogs includes cleaning the affected area, oral medications, and topical treatments such as lotions and shampoos.

Atopic dermatitis, also known as eczema, is a type of skin disease caused by a combination of genetic and environmental factors. It is characterized by itching and pain caused by an allergy to certain proteins. Treatment for atopic dermatitis in animals includes reducing itching and inflammation, may require combination therapy, antibiotics, and long-term interventions.

Cellulitis is an inflammation of the tissue under the skin, usually caused by bacteria entering through a cut or wound. Cellulitis treatment usually includes antibiotics and antifungals to control infection and reduce inflammation.

Psoriasis is a rare disease in animals, but dogs can develop symptoms similar to psoriasis. Psoriasis is characterized by red bumps with silvery scales. Psoriasis and folliculitis may require specific treatment to control symptoms and resolve the problem.

Folliculitis is a dermatological condition characterized by itchiness in a pet's fur. It involves the inflammation of one or more hair follicles and generally refers to the inflammation of the pilosebaceous unit. Clinically, it manifests as papules and pustules centered around the hair follicles. Various factors can lead to folliculitis, including bacteria, fungi, viruses, or parasites, with Staphylococcus aureus being the most prevalent cause. To prevent folliculitis, it is essential to manage the underlying issues, such as allergies to fleas.

Burns can be caused by heat, cold, electricity, chemicals, or electrical damage to the skin or other tissues. Improper use of flames, hot liquids, or heating devices can cause immediate cell death. Burns can lead to serious consequences, including dehydration, sepsis, and death. The severity of the burn depends on the depth of the skin and its location. First-degree burns affect only the surface of the skin, causing redness and pain. Second-degree burns penetrate through the layers, causing blisters and possibly scars. Third-degree burns cover all layers of the skin and may not hurt at first. Fourth-degree burns are the most severe and extend into muscles, tendons, or bones. Burns should be treated promptly to prevent complications and speed healing. Treatment for burns includes wound management, surgery, and medications to promote healing and prevent infection. A healthy diet rich in protein, minerals, and vitamins is essential for healing. Adhering to proper wound management is key to minimizing complications and aiding the healing process.

Animal tumors are abnormal changes that can occur in the skin or subcutaneous tissue due to exposure to various carcinogens in the environment, hormonal imbalances, and genetic factors. The most common types of breast cancer are squamous cell carcinoma, malignant melanoma, and mast cell carcinoma. Squamous cell carcinoma often affects areas exposed to the sun and can appear as red, scaly patches or bumps. Basal cell carcinoma begins in the deepest part of the skin and is usually caused by exposure to ultraviolet light. Melanoma is a dangerous skin cancer that can be mild or severe and can occur on the head and legs of older dogs. Mast cell cancer affects the immune system and can occur anywhere in the body; boxers, pugs, Rhodesian Ridgebacks and Boston terriers are more likely to develop the cancer. Mast cell cancer can be diagnosed using a fine needle and surgery is recommended for large tumors, radiotherapy and chemotherapy may be selected. Cancer treatment may include surgery, chemotherapy, or other interventions, depending on the type and severity of cancer. Surgical resection is the best treatment for low-grade tumors; if the resection is not clean, additional surgery or radiation therapy may be required.

In general, keeping your pet's skin healthy is essential to their health. Understanding the structure and function of the skin can help veterinarians and pet owners recognize early signs of disease and provide appropriate treatment. By addressing skin issues quickly and effectively, your pet's overall health can be improved, thus improving their quality of life.

Multiple Choice Questions

1. What layer of the skin protects against bacteria, chemical damage, and mechanical injury?
   a) Epidermis b) Dermis
   c) Hypodermis d) Sebum layer
   e) Subcutaneous layer
2. Which fibrous protein contributes to skin's strength and water resistance?
   a) Keratohyalin b) Eleidin
   c) Collagen d) Keratin
   e) Elastin
3. Melanocytes are located in which layer of the epidermis?
   a) Stratum basale b) Stratum corneum
   c) Stratum granulosum d) Stratum lucidum
   e) Stratum spinosum
4. Body odor is produced by bacteria metabolizing the secretions of which glands?
   a) Apocrine sweat b) Ceruminous
   c) Eccrine sweat d) Merocrine sweat
   e) Sebaceous
5. How does the body react to an increase in temperature?
   a) Blood flow to the skin decreases b) Blood flow to the skin increases
   c) Melanocyte activity increases d) Sweat gland activity decreases
   e) Vasoconstriction occurs
6. Which macrophages are found in the epidermis?
   a) Basal cells b) Langerhans cells
   c) Melanocytes d) Merkel cells
   e) Squamous cells
7. Which glands release oils into hair follicles?
   a) Apocrine sweat b) Ceruminous
   c) Mammary d) Merocrine sweat
   e) Sebaceous
8. In which layer of the skin, cells actively divide through mitosis?
   a) Stratum basale b) Stratum corneum
   c) Stratum granulosum d) Stratum lucidum
   e) Stratum spoinosum

9. What is the response of the arrector pili muscles?
   a) Hair fall
   b) Itching
   c) Piloerection
   d) Skin color change
   e) Sweating
10. In the epidermis, which cells are most abundant?
   a) Adipocytes
   b) Keratinocytes
   c) Langerhans cells
   d) Melanocytes
   e) Merkel Cells
11. Which of the following helps to maintain healthy skin?
   a) Colour
   b) Elasticity
   c) Pigmentation
   d) Vibrancy
   e) All of the above
12. The medical branch of science that deals with the study of skin, its functions, diseases, & treatment is:
   a) Anatomy
   b) Dermatology
   c) Etiology
   d) Pathology
   e) Physiology
13. What are the typical effects on the skin when there is a reduction in the oxygen levels in the bloodstream?
   a) Cyanosis
   b) Flushing
   c) Jaundice
   d) Paleness
   e) None of the above
14. Which layer of the skin is devoid of blood vessels?
   a) Corium
   c) Cutis
   b) Dermis
   d) Epidermis
   e) Hypodermis
15. What is an alternative term for the stratum germinativum?
   a) Stratum basale
   b) Stratum corneum
   c) Stratum granulosum
   d) Stratum lucidum
   e) Stratum spinosum
16. The specific layer of the epidermis responsible for the shedding of keratinocytes, which are continuously replenished, is known as the?
   a) Stratum corneum
   b) Stratum granlosum
   c) Stratum lucidum
   d) Stratum mucosum
   e) Stratum spinosum
17. What characteristic of the stratum corneum functions as a protective barrier for the underlying body?
   a) Continuously desquamation
   b) Made of apoptotic cells
   c) Rich in keratin
   d) Semi-permeable
   e) All of the above

18. Which epidermal layer listed below is absent in thin skin?
    a) Stratum Basale b) Stratum Corneum
    c) Stratum Granulosum d) Stratum Lucidum
    e) Stratum Spinosum
19. Which cells are responsible for determining the colour of our skin?
    a) Goblet cells b) Keratinocytes
    c) Langerhans cells d) Markel cells
    e) Melanocytes
20. Which of the following does not represent a function of the skin?
    a) Calcium synthesis b) Excretion
    c) Protective function d) Thermoregulation
    e) All of the above
21. Animals with atopic dermatitis may also exhibit:
    a) Acne b) Allergies
    c) Cellulitis d) All of the above
    e) None of the above
22. Factors that may exacerbate atopic dermatitis include which of the following?
    a) Dry conditions b) Hot or cold temperature
    c) Stress d) All of the above
    e) None of the above
23. Which group of animals is more likely to develop atopic dermatitis?
    a) Adult animals b) Growing animals
    c) Old animals d) Young animal
    e) None of the above
24. Atopic dermatitis is frequently referred to as:
    a) Acne b) Eczema
    c) Pimples d) Psoriasis
    e) None of the above
25. What are the symptoms of an atopic reaction?
    a) Blisters b) Itchy and inflamed skin
    c) Pimples d) Patches
    e) Whiteheads
26. Animals with atopic dermatitis may develop following symptoms:
    a) Thick, leathery skin b) Raised bumps on the skin
    c) Red, scaling skin d) All of the above
    e) None of the above
27. Which component of the skin's structure is accountable for its sensitivity to light touch?
    a) Dermal papillae b) Hair plexus
    c) Meissner's corpuscle d) Pacinian corpuscle

28. Animals with atopic dermatitis have skin that is more vulnerable to:
    a) Herpes simplex
    b) Skin infections
    c) Warts
    d) All of the above
    e) None of the above
29. Which of the following is a key initial feature of atopic dermatitis?
    a) Dry, lichenified lesions
    b) Erythroderma
    c) Pruritus
    d) White dermographism
    e) All of the above
30. What factors assist in distinguishing atopic dermatitis from other skin conditions?
    a) Appears only on the face
    b) Appears only on the hands
    c) Appears on the extensor surfaces
    d) Appears on the flexural surfaces
    e) All of the above
31. What role do Meissner corpuscles serve in the papillary region?
    a) Pain sensations
    b) Touch sensations
    c) Sensation of coolness
    d) Sensation of warmth
    e) All of the above
32. Animals that possess albinism demonstrate a lack of tyrosinase within which layer of the epidermis?
    a) Stratum basale
    b) Stratumgranulosum
    c) Stratum lucidum
    d) Stratum spinosum
    e) All of the above
33. What structures of skin are composed of connective tissue, blood vessels, and nerves?
    a) Papillary dermis
    b) Papillary and reticular dermis
    c) Epidermis, papillary and reticular dermis
    d) Reticular dermis
    e) None of the above
34. What is the primary role of Pacinian corpuscles located in the hypodermis?
    a) Itching sensation
    b) Coloration
    c) Sensation of coolness
    d) Sensation of warmth
    e) Tickling sensations
35. Which of the following is the feature of reticular region?
    a) Epidermal ridges
    b) Hair follicles
    c) Sebaceous glands
    d) All of the above
    e) None of the above
36. What is periorbital cellulitis?
    a) Preseptal cellulitis
    b) Conjunctivitis
    c) Keratitis
    d) Orbital abscess

e) Orbital cellulitis

37. What is another term for periorbital cellulitis?
a) Anterior uveitis
b) Preseptal cellulitis
c) Postseptal cellulitis
d) Septal cellulitis
e) None of the above

38. What are the common causes of periorbital cellulitis?
a) Bacteria
b) Fungi
c) Parasites
d) Viruses
e) None of the above

39. Which of the following cells are associated with the sensory function of skin?
a) Keratinocytes
b) Langerhans cells
c) Melanocytes
d) Merkel cells
e) All of the above

40. When assessing a patient with symptoms indicative of cellulitis, the diagnosis is established through:
a) Blood culture
b) History
c) Physician examination
d) Wound culture
e) None of the above

41. What is the most prevalent pathogen responsible for causing cellulitis among the options listed?
a) Escherichia coli
b) Proteus mirabilis
c) Pseudomonas aeruginosa
d) Streptococcus pyogenes
e) All of the above

42. What is the most common form of psoriasis, accounting for about 80-90% of cases?
a) Plaque
b) Pustular
c) Guttate
d) Inverse
e) None of the above

43. Which areas of the body are commonly impacted by psoriasis?
a) Abdomen
b) Elbows
c) Knees
d) Scalp
e) All of the above

44. To which category of diseases does psoriasis belong?
a) Autoimmune disease
b) Genetic disease
c) Infectious disease
d) Neoplasm
e) Both a and b

45. What factors can exacerbate psoriasis?
a) Beta blocker medicines
b) Dry climate
c) Stress
d) All of the above
e) None of the above

46. In psoriasis, what is a notable change in the behavior of skin cells?
    a) Keratitis develop
    b) Skin cells die before becoming mature
    c) Skin cells pile up before becoming mature
    d) All of the above
    e) None of the above
47. What health issue may also arise in conjunction with psoriasis?
    a) Arthritis b) Conjunctivitis
    c) Gingivitis d) Hives
    e) All of the above
48. What is the treatment of psoriasis?
    a) Immunotherapy b) Phototherapy
    c) Topical medicines d) All of the above
    e) None of the above
49. What is the impact of psoriasis that affects multiple systems in animals?
    a) Inflammation b) Itching
    c) Scaling and flaking d) Thickening of the skin
    e) All of the above
50. In psoriasis, which of these suggestions can help to relieve the itching?
    a) Use the calamine lotion b) Use the cool compresses
    c) Use the moisturizers d) All of the above
    e) None of the above
51. Which of these skin problems is an inherited autoimmune disorder?
    a) Epidermis b) Melanoma
    c) Psoriasis d) Scabies
    e) All of the above
52. Which body parts are mostly affected in the folliculitis?
    a) Axillae b) Face
    c) Inguinal area d) Scalp
    e) All of the above
53. What are the potential causes of folliculitis, a skin infection that impacts one or more hair follicles?
    a) Exposure to a poorly chlorinated hot tub b) Showering in a stall
    c) Using a rusty razor blade d) Using dirty towels
    e) None of the above
54. Which of the following home remedies could potentially lead to the resolution of a skin abscess?
    a) Applying antibiotic ointment b) Applying warm compresses
    c) Covering it with a bandage d) Leaving it open to dry out
    e) All of the above

55. Identify which of the following does not represent a recognized risk factor for the development of folliculitis?
 a) Living in crowded conditions
 b) Having a chronic skin condition
 c) Having a family member with folliculitis
 d) Poor hygiene
 e) All of the above

56. What is the definition of the term erythema, which is commonly linked to inflammation, injury, or infection?
 a) Damaged skin
 b) Infection
 c) Itching
 d) Poor perfusion
 e) Redness

57. Which assertion accurately describes necrotising fasciitis?
 a) It is usually bilateral
 b) Mortality correlates to time to surgical intervention
 c) Patients are systemically well
 d) Slowly spreading infection
 e) Treatment should be with oral antibiotics

58. What does not result from erythroderma, commonly referred to as exfoliative dermatitis?
 a) Cancer
 b) Cardiac failure
 c) Fluid loss
 d) Heat loss
 e) Thromboembolism

59. Which receptors in the skin are responsible for maintaining a continuous response throughout the duration of a tactile stimulus?
 a) Pacinian corpuscle
 b) Meissner's corpuscle
 c) Merkel's disk
 d) Hair follicle afferent
 e) All of the above

60. Which skin infection is attributed to the poxvirus genus?
 a) Cellulitis
 b) Impetigo
 c) Molluscum contagiosum
 d) Verruca
 e) All of the above

61. What is the primary cause of burns?
 a) Chemicals
 b) Electricity
 c) Friction
 d) Heat
 e) All of the above

62. Which of the following classifications pertains to a type of burn?
 a) First-degree burn
 b) Second-degree burn
 c) Third-degree burn
 d) All of the above
 e) None of the above

63. What are the defining characteristics of a first-degree burn?
    a) Blistering and charring
    b) Redness and swelling
    c) Open sores and exposed bone
    d) Numbness and loss of sensation
    e) None of the above
64. What type of burn penetrates all layers of the skin and reaches the underlying tissues?
    a) First-degree burn
    b) Second-degree burn
    c) Third-degree burn
    d) Fourth-degree burn
    e) All of the above
65. Which of the following represents a symptom associated with a burn?
    a) Numbness
    b) Redness
    c) Tingling
    d) All of the above
    e) None of the above
66. What category of burn necessitates prompt medical intervention?
    a) First-degree burn
    b) Second-degree burn
    c) Third-degree burn
    d) Fourth-degree burn
    e) All of the above
67. What is the objective of applying a dressing to a burn wound?
    a) To apply pressure
    b) To prevent infection
    c) To promote healing
    d) To reduce pain
    e) None of the above
68. What is the main mechanism through which heat is lost in burns, accounting for 80-90% of the overall heat loss?
    a) Conduction
    b) Convection
    c) Evaporation
    d) Radiation
    e) None of the above
69. Which type of burn is defined by injury to both the dermal and epidermal layers, and carries the possibility of resulting in scarring?
    a) First-degree burn
    b) Second-degree burn
    c) Third-degree burn
    d) Fourth-degree burn
    e) None of the above
70. What is the term used to describe the syndrome that presents with hypovolemia, acidosis, and hypothermia in patients with severe burns?
    a) Burn shock
    b) Hypovolemic shock
    c) Sepsis
    d) Tissue hypoxia
    e) None of the above
71. What is the main objective of managing burn wounds during the initial 24 to 48 hours following the injury?
    a) Control of infection
    b) Debridement and grafting
    c) Fluid resuscitation and stabilization
    d) Wound closure
    e) None of the above

72. What burn complication arises from the release of inflammatory mediators, resulting in heightened vascular permeability and edema?
    a) Infection
    b) Hypertension
    c) Sepsis
    d) Systemic inflammatory response syndrome
    e) All of the above
73. The burn injury is classified as having affected areas that are white and resemble leather, with the absence of blisters and bleeding, and minimal pain experienced.
    a) Full thickness
    b) Partial-thickness deep
    c) Partial-thickness superficia
    d) Superficial
    e) None of the above
74. What classification is appropriate for this injury characterized by a red burned area, the presence of blisters, and significant pain?
    a) Full thickness
    b) Partial-thickness deep
    c) Partial-thickness superficial
    d) Superficial
    e) None of the above
75. Which vitamin deficiency is most likely to result from a full-thickness burn injury?
    a) Vitamin A
    b) Vitamin B
    c) Vitamin C
    d) Vitamin D
    e) Vitamin E
76. Which burn-related complication listed below is most successfully treated with hyperbaric oxygen therapy?
    a) Gas gangrene
    b) Hypovolemic shock
    c) Sepsis
    d) Wound infection
    e) All of the above
77. What is the main objective of fluid resuscitation during the initial 24 hours following a significant burn injury?
    a) To correct acidosis
    b) To prevent organ failure
    c) To reduce the sepsis
    d) To restore blood pressure
    e) None of the above
78. What is the main reason for performing an escharotomy in patients with burns?
    a) To improve motion
    b) To promote wound healing
    c) To reduce infection
    d) To relieve circumferential eschar constriction
    e) All of the above
79. Which of the medications listed below is frequently prescribed for the management of anxiety and insomnia associated with burns?
    a) Antidepressants
    b) Antipsychotics
    c) Benzodiazepines
    d) Sedatives
    e) All of the above

80. What is the primary indication for skin grafting in patients with critical burn injuries?
   a) To cover large areas of denuded skin
   b) To improve range of motion
   c) To promote wound healing
   d) To reduce the risk of infection
   e) All of the above

81. Which of the following broad-spectrum topical antimicrobial is commonly used in the management of burn injuries?
   a) Bacitracin ointment
   b) Mafenide acetate
   c) Povidone-iodine
   d) Silver sulfadiazine
   e) All of the above

82. Which of the following burn wound dressings is recognized for its capacity to maintain a moist environment, alleviate pain, and improve the healing process?
   a) Bioengineered skin dressings
   b) Foam dressings
   c) Hydrocolloid dressings
   d) Non-adherent dressings
   e) None of the above

83. What is the main objective of managing pain in patients with burns?
   a) To improve quality of life
   b) To improve range of motion
   c) To promote wound healing
   d) To reduce the risk of infection
   e) All of the above

84. What is the characteristic of benign tumours?
   a) Do not metastasize
   b) Grow slowly
   c) Remain localized
   d) Well-defined border
   e) All of the above

85. What is the primary characteristic of malignant tumours?
   a) Benign growth
   b) Localized invasion
   c) Metastasis to distant sites
   d) Regeneration of normal tissue
   e) All of the above

86. Which of the following tumour types is most frequently linked to genetic mutations?
   a) Carcinoma
   b) Leukemia
   c) Lymphoma
   d) Sarcoma
   e) None of the above

87. What is the objective of tumour staging?
   a) To determine the type of tumour
   b) To diagnose the tumour
   c) To monitor treatment response
   d) To predict the prognosis
   e) All of the above

88. What is the predominant type of tumour observed in young animals?
   a) Leukemia
   b) Lymphoma
   c) Brain tumor
   d) Bone tumor
   e) All of the above

89. Which type of tumour is most frequently linked to exposure to radiation?
a) Carcinoma
b) Leukemia
c) Sarcoma
d) Thyroid cancer
e) None of the above

90. What is the primary therapeutic approach for malignant tumours?
a) Chemotherapy
b) Radiation therapy
c) Surgery
d) Combination therapy
e) None of the above

91. What is a frequently encountered complication associated with tumour treatment?
a) Infection
b) Hair loss
c) Nausea and vomiting
d) All of the above
e) None of the above

92. What is the most prevalent form of tumour found in dogs?
a) Hemangiosarcoma
b) Lymphoma
c) Mast cell tumour
d) Osteosarcoma
e) All of the above

93. Which type of tumour is frequently observed in older cats?
a) Hyperthyroidism
b) Lymphoma
c) Melanoma
d) Osteosarcoma
e) All of the above

94. What is the most reliable prognostic indicator for melanoma?
a) Dermal spread
b) Diameter
c) Epidermal spread
d) Mitosis
e) Rate of growth

95. What is the most reliable diagnostic finding of melanoma?
a) Cytoplasmic pigmentation
b) Forming nests or clusters
c) Prominent nucleus
d) To be seen in the dermis
e) None of the above

96. Based on their origin, what is the primary classification of tumours?
a) Benign *vs.* Malignant
b) Carcinoma *vs.* Sarcoma
c) Epithelial *vs.* Connective Tissue
d) Neoplasia *vs.* Hyperplasia
e) None of the above

97. Which of the tumour types listed below arises from epithelial cells?
a) Carcinoma
b) Leukemia
c) Lymphoma
d) Sarcoma
e) All of the above

98. What is the classification of tumours that arises from connective tissue cells?
a) Carcinoma
b) Leukemia
c) Lymphoma
d) Sarcoma
e) All of the above

99. What type of tumour affects the skin of cats, causing ulcers, bleeding, and other skin lesions?

a) Basal cell carcinoma
b) Kaposi's sarcoma
c) Melanoma
d) Squamous cell carcinoma
e) None of the above

100. How koilocytosis is different from other epithelial cells?

a) Intracellular keratin inclusions
b) Neutrophil aggression in epidermis
c) Separated epidermal cells
d) SPV inclusions
e) All of the above

Answer Key

1	a	2	d	3	a	4	a	5	b	6	b	7	e
8	a	9	c	10	b	11	e	12	b	13	a	14	d
15	a	16	a	17	e	18	d	19	e	20	a	21	b
22	b	23	d	24	b	25	b	26	d	27	c	28	d
29	c	30	d	31	b	32	a	33	b	34	e	35	d
36	a	37	b	38	a	39	d	40	c	41	d	42	a
43	e	44	e	45	d	46	c	47	a	48	d	49	e
50	d	51	c	52	e	53	a	54	b	55	c	56	e
57	b	58	a	59	c	60	c	61	d	62	d	63	b
64	c	65	d	66	c	67	b	68	c	69	b	70	a
71	c	72	d	73	a	74	c	75	d	76	a	77	b
78	d	79	c	80	a	81	d	82	c	83	a	84	e
85	c	86	a	87	d	88	a	89	b	90	d	91	d
92	c	93	b	94	a	95	b	96	c	97	a	98	d
99	d	100	c										

23

Clinical Physiology of Urinary Disorders

Pubaleem Deka[1], Ritu Gupta[1] and Gunajit Das[2]

[1]Department of Veterinary Medicine, Institute of Veterinary Science and Animal Husbandry, Siksha 'O' Anusandhan, Deemed to be University, Bhubaneswar, Odisha

[2]Assam Agricultural University- Zonal Livestock Research Station, Mandira, Assam

Introduction

The renal system is primarily responsible for the filtration of waste products from blood plasma through urine production. The kidneys, along with the ureters, bladder, and urethra, are part of the urinary system responsible for removing waste products from blood and eliminating them in urine. They filter around 120 ml of blood plasma per minute and perform homeostatic roles such as regulating blood volume and pressure, pH and electrolyte composition, stimulating erythropoiesis, and supporting vitamin D biosynthesis. Nephrons, with around 1-1.3 million per adult kidney, are primarily cortical, with 80-85% of them located in the renal cortex. The remaining 15-20% are called juxtamedullary nephrons. The kidneys remove nitrogenous compounds like urea, uric acid, and creatinine, as well as metabolic waste products, toxins, excess hormones, water, and electrolytes. Urine formation involves three main stages: glomerular filtration, tubular reabsorption, and secretion. The kidneys produce renal filtrate, which contains blood components that can be filtered out, and the body recovers 99% of the water and electrolytes from the filtrate. The renal corpuscle, comprising the Bowman's capsule and glomerular capillaries, is responsible for filtration of blood plasma and producing renal filtrate. Its structural elements allow for efficient filtration, with glomerular capillaries having a 100-fold greater permeability to water, small ions, and solutes. The glomerular capillaries also have increased pressure due to the smaller diameter of the efferent arteriole. The filtration membrane consists of endothelium, basement membrane, and podocytes. The proximal convoluted tubule in the kidneys plays a crucial role in reabsorption of water and electrolytes, including sodium, chloride, potassium, calcium, and bicarbonate. It reabsorbs approximately 80% of filtered bicarbonate, with further reabsorption from the loop of Henle and distal convoluted tubule. This reabsorption regulates the body's acid-base balance, contributing to the acidic nature of urine. The proximal convoluted tubule is the only region able to reabsorb glucose. The loop of Henle is a crucial region in the kidney, responsible for concentrating urine and facilitating water and electrolyte reabsorption. It regulates fluid volume, blood pressure, and acid-base balance through bicarbonate reabsorption. The loop consists of two main regions: the descending limb and the ascending limb. The descending limb, initially thick, drops into the renal medulla and returns to the renal cortex. The distal convoluted tubule plays a crucial role in electrolyte and water reabsorption, as well as blood-pressure regulation. The juxtaglomerular apparatus, a complex structure formed by macula densa, JG cells, and extraglomerular mesangial cells, is central to this function, ensuring effective blood-pressure regulation through local and wider means. Filtrate is fine-tuned in collecting ducts before being channeled to renal pelvis, regulating electrolytes, acid-base balance, extracellular volume, water balance, and blood pressure. The collecting ducts, through specialized membrane transport and hormonal control, are crucial for the body's reabsorption of sodium and chloride, promoting water reabsorption, and reabsorbing approximately 9% of the filtrate's water content. The functions of renal system include-

Blood volume and pressure regulation

Renin, produced, stored, and secreted by JG cells, is a crucial enzyme in regulating blood pressure, with kidneys playing a crucial role in this process, acting as a rate-limiting step. The RAAS is a crucial system that regulates blood pressure, extracellular volume, and blood-sodium levels through hormonal and enzymatic interactions between the kidneys, liver, lungs, and heart. Its secretion is triggered by hypotension and hyponatraemia, causing the breakdown of angiotensinogen into angiotensin I, a relatively inactive peptide hormone. Angiotensin-converting enzyme is produced in the lungs, converting angiotensin I to angiotensin II. This process increases blood volume and pressure, leading to the release of aldosterone, antidiuretic hormone, hypothalamus, vasoconstriction, and hypertrophy. Atrial natriuretic peptide and brain natriuretic peptide are hormones that maintain blood-sodium concentration and blood pressure. They are produced by cardiomyocytes of the heart's atria and secreted by increased blood pressure, detected through myocardial stretching. These peptides work primarily on the nephrons to increase sodium excretion, resulting in a decrease in blood volume and pressure. In contrast, the RAAS' effects are directly influenced by the production of atrial and brain natriuretic peptides.

Red blood cell regulation

Erythropoiesis, the process of producing red blood cells, is regulated by the glycoprotein hormone, EPO. During fetal development, liver hepatocytes are the primary source of EPO, but demand is met by renal cortex cells from birth. Interstitial peritubular fibroblasts produce EPO in response to hypoxia, which is typically caused by blood loss, anemia, tissue damage, or high altitude. Renin-producing cells can undergo metaplastic transformation to produce EPO. Once released into circulation, EPO binds to EPO receptors on erythroid progenitor cells, promoting cell survival and proliferation. EPO receptors are also expressed by cells of other tissues, including the heart, nervous, and muscular systems.

Platelet regulation

Platelets, essential for blood clotting, are produced in the bone marrow through thrombopoiesis from megakaryocyte precursor cells. The hormone thrombopoietin, produced by liver cells and kidneys' proximal convoluted tubules, regulates this process. It binds to thrombopoietin-receptors on cell surfaces, triggering biochemical signaling cascades that change cell proliferation, survival, and differentiation into platelets. This process is primarily regulated by liver cells and kidney cells.

Activation of vitamin D and maintenance of bone density

The kidneys play a crucial role in vitamin D activation, producing vitamin D3 through sunlight and dietary intake, a precursor to the more active form, calcitriol. Vitamin D is converted to calcitriol by the liver and kidney, which is transported via the blood. Its main effects include promoting calcium reabsorption in the intestines, suppressing parathyroid hormone production, and maintaining calcium content in the nephrons, ultimately contributing to bone-density maintenance and overall calcium homeostasis.

MCQs

1. The renal system allows excretion of-
   a) Toxins b) Metabolic waste products
   c) Excess ions d) All
2. The main functions of kidney-
   a) Regulates plasma osmolarity b) Acid-base balance
   c) Both d) None
3. Kidney produces___________ which stimulates the production of red blood cells
   a) Renin b) Rennin
   c) Erythropoietin d) Cytokinin
4. Kidney produces ________ for blood pressure regulation and carries out the conversion of _____ to its active form
   a) Renin, Vitamin A b) Renin, Vitamin D
   c) Rennin, Vitamin D d) Rennin, Vitamin A
5. The major waste products removed in urine are
   a) NPN componds b) Urea and Uric acid
   c) Creatinine d) All
6. The process of urine formation has the following stage-
   a) Glomerular filtration b) Tubular reabsorption
   c) Secretion d) All
7. In __________ renal filtrate is produced, containing components of the blood that can be filtered out
   a) Glomerular filtration b) Tubular reabsorption
   c) Secretion d) All
8. During tubular reabsorption, the body recovers ______ of the water and electrolytes from the renal filtrate
   a) 99% b) 80%
   c) 70% d) 50%
9. Secretion – waste products such as urea, uric acid and metabolites are removed in urine through
   a) Distal convoluted tubule b) Collecting duct
   c) Both d) None

10. The proximal convoluted tubule is the only region of the nephron able to permit the reabsorption of ______

a) Glucose b) Bicarbonate

c) Water d) None

11. The ascending limb is also responsible for the reabsorption of _____ and ____ by the body

a) Calcium, magnesium b) Calcium, bicarbonate

c) Phosphorus, magnesium d) Water, calcium

12. Which of the following is not a component of the JG apparatus

a) Macula densa b) Jg cells

c) Extraglomerular mesangial cells d) Loop of henle

13. Which of the following enzyme is pivotal to electrolyte and blood-pressure regulation through activation of the renin-angio tensin-aldosterone system (RAAS)

a) Renin b) Rennin

c) Erythropoietin d) None

14. Which of the following component is involved in the production of renin and erythropoietin (EPO), serving to stimulate the production of red blood cells

a) Macula densa b) Jg cells

c) Extraglomerular mesangial cells d) Loop of henle

15. In the collecting ducts, approximately 9% of the filtrate's water content can be reabsorbed, under the control of_____ hormone, a crucial aspect of blood-pressure regulation

a) Renin b) Parathyroid

c) Antidiuretic d) Calcitriol

16. Which of the following hormones maintain blood-sodium concentration and blood pressure, in direct contrast with the effects of the RAAS?

a) Atrial natriuretic peptide b) brain natriuretic peptide

c) Both d) None

17. Natriuretic peptides are produced principally by-

a) Kidney b) Liver

c) Heart d) Spleen

18. Thrombopoietin, a glycoprotein hormone produced by

a) Liver b) Kidney

c) Both d) Heart

19. Which of the following hormones is responsible for activation of vitamin D and maintenance of bone density?

a) Cholecalciferol b) Thrombopoietin

c) Calcitrol d) Parathyroid hormone

20. Antidiuretic hormone – a peptide hormone also known as vasopressin is released from?
    a) Posterior pituitary gland
    b) Anterior pituitary gland
    c) Parathyroid gland
    d) Adrenal gland
21. Urea is synthesized in the _____ via the ornithine cycle from ammonia derived from amino acid catabolism
    a) Adrenal gland
    b) Liver
    c) Kidney
    d) None
22. Renal excretion of urea occurs by
    a) Glomerular filtration
    b) Passive reabsorption
    c) Both
    d) None
23. Which of the following clinical conditions characterized by increased catabolism also can increase BUN concentrations?
    a) Starvation
    b) Infection
    c) Fever
    d) All
24. BUN concentrations can be decreased by
    a) severe hepatic insufficiency,
    b) portosystemic shunting
    c) Starvation
    d) Both a and b
25. Normal BUN concentrations in dog-
    a) 8 to 25 mg/dL
    b) 5 to 15 mg/dL
    c) 15 to 25 mg/dL
    d) 20 to 45 mg/dL
26. Nonenzymatic breakdown product of phosphocreatine in muscle is?
    a) Urea
    b) Creatinine
    c) Protein
    d) Kinase
27. In chronic progressive renal disease, the urinary concentrating ability is impaired after ______ of the nephron population has become nonfunctional.
    a) Two-third
    b) One-third
    c) Half
    d) One-fourth
28. Normal urine is yellow because of the presence of _______ pigment
    a) Bilirubin
    b) Biliverdin
    c) Urochrome
    d) None
29. Urine for urinalysis may be collected by
    a) Voiding (midstream sample),
    b) Catheterization,
    c) Cystocentesis
    d) All
30. Most preferred method of collection of urine for urinalysis is?
    a) Voiding (midstream sample),
    b) Catheterization,
    c) Cystocentesis
    d) All
31. Which substance is derived from the breakdown of heme by the reticuloendothelial system?
    a) Biliverdin
    b) Bilirubin
    c) Ketone
    d) Creatinine

32. Bilirubin is transported to the liver, where it is conjugated with _______ and excreted in the bile.
    a) Diazonium salt b) Glucuronide
    c) Magnesium salt d) Sodium
33. In dogs with _______ disease, bilirubin may be detected in the urine before its serum concentration is increased.
    a) Lung b) Liver
    c) Kidney d) Pancreatic
34. The main causes of bilirubinuria are
    a) Hemolysis b) Liver disease
    c) Extra-hepatic biliary obstruction, d) All
35. Which test is specific for pyuria in canine urine samples?
    a) Leukocyte Esterase test b) Nitroprusside test
    c) Benzidine test d) Benedict's test
36. The presence of________ in the urine is evidence of severe muscle damage
    a) Creatinine b) Myoglobin
    c) Urea d) Protein
37. The condition where leukocytes are found in urine indicating inflammatory exudation in the renal pelvis or bladder is-
    a) Proteinuria b) Pyuria
    c) Anuria d) Oliguria
38. An abnormally frequent passage of urine istermed as
    a) Anuria b) Oliguria
    c) Dysuria d) Pollakiuria
39. Renal blood flow (RBF), glomerular filtration rate (GFR) is brought about by vasoconstriction initiated by reflexes through the vasomotor centre in
    a) The medulla and pons
    b) Anterior pituitary
    c) Frontal lobe
    d) Middle lobe
40. The glomerulus has a high pressure of ____mm Hg and peritubular capillaries have a low pressure of___ mm Hg which helps in rapid fluid filtration.
    a) 50, 20 b) 60, 13
    c) 60, 10 d) 70, 13
41. Which cells are involved in feed back mechanism that assist regulation of renal blood flow and glomerular filtrate rate?
    a) Vasa recta b) Juxta glomerular cells
    c) Macula densa d) Lacis cells

42. If Glomerular Hydrostatic Pressure = 60 mm Hg, Colloidal Osmotic Pressure in glomerulus = 32 mm Hg and capsular pressure (Bowman's capsule Hydrostatic Pressure) = 18 mm Hg. Then, the Filtration pressure will be?
    a) 20 mm Hg. b) 10 mm Hg.
    c) 15 mm Hg. d) 28 mm Hg.
43. Transport of fluid from the Bowman's capsule to the renal pelvis is accomplished by a difference in the ?
    a) Hydrostatic pressure. b) Osmotic pressure
    c) Capsular pressure d) None
44. Which process involves transport of water and solutes from the tubular fluid to the peritubular capillaries.
    a) Tubular reabsorption b) Glomerular filtration
    c) Tubular secretion d) None
45. The colloidal osmotic pressure in the Bowman's capsule is negligible due to very low ________ content?
    a) Protein b) Calcium
    c) Sodium d) None
46. The finger like projections which form slit pores through which glomerular filtrate filters lining the outer surface of the glomerulue are termed as
    a) Villi b) Podocytes
    c) Pseudopodia d) Cilia
47. The __________ is composed of a meshwork of collagen and proteoglycan fibrillae which can filter large amount of water and small solutes.
    a) Basement membrane b) Bowman's capsule
    c) Glomerulus d) Glomerular capillary membrane
48. Uremia or azotemia, is the elevated level of waste products in the blood, particularly nitrogen-containing compounds like urea and creatinine
    a) Azotemia b) Azoturia
    c) Creatinuria d) None
49. Clearance rate of different substances are determined by analyzing the concentration of substance simultaneously in plasma and urine and measuring the rate of urine formation is termed as
    a) Renal clearance b) Plasma clearance
    c) Creatinine clearance d) All
50. The substance used to measure GFR which must be freely filtered at the glomerulus and should not be reabsorbed or secreted by the tubular epithelium after it enters the nephron is
    a) Insulin b) Inulin
    c) Fructose c) Creatinine
51. Animals which excrete uric acid are known as:
    a) Uricotelic b) Ureotelic
    c) Guanotelism d) Ammonotelism

52. The first metabolic cycle discovered i.e; urea cycle that produces urea ($(NH_2)_2CO$) from ammonia (NH_3) in many animals is also known as:
    a) Arginine cycle
    b) Ornithine cycle
    c) Krebs cyle
    d) TCA cycle

53. Reduction in daily output of urine is known as _________ & complete absence of urine is known as __________.
    a) Oliguria & anuria
    b) Dysuria & stranguria
    c) Anuria & Stranguria
    d) Polyuria & oliguria

54. An increased no. of postures for urination, usually accompanied by decreased volume of urine is known as:
    a) Ployuria
    b) Pollakiuria
    c) Oliguria
    d) Postration

55. Abdominal pain and painful urination is called as _________ & difficult and slow urination is called as ___________.
    a) Oliguria & anuria
    b) Dysuria & stranguria
    c) Anuria & Stranguria
    d) Polyuria & oliguria

56. Aciduria is always accompanied by urine excretion of
    a) Sodium
    b) Phosphorus
    c) Bi-carboantes
    d) Calcium

57. A small amount of ketonuria is normally present in dairy cows in _______ lactation.
    a) Late
    b) Mid
    c) Early
    d) All of the above.

58. A clinically useful index of proximal tubular injury is by determining which of the following enzyme activity in urine
    a) Gamma glutamyl transferase (GGT)
    b) Creatine kinase
    c) Alkaline phosphatise
    d) Lactate dehydrogenase

59. __________ is a common PM findings in horses suffering from chronic renal failure.
    a) Chronic interstitial fibrosis
    b) Nephrosis
    c) Hydronephrosis
    d) None of the above

60. _____________ is an occasional sequelae to patent urachus but omphalitis & urachal abscess may also develop as complication.
    a) Nephritis
    b) Cystitis
    c) Cholecystitis
    d) Urolithiasis

61. Ingestion of plants with high oxalic acid content is associated with formation of ________ calculi in sheep.
    a) Oxalates
    b) Calcium carbonates
    c) Silica
    d) Ammonium chloride

62. Common calculi in cattle, sheep and goats eating a high grain diet is
    a) Struvite
    b) Ammonium chloride
    c) Calcium carbonates
    d) Oxalates

63. Normal specific gravity of urine of most species of animals is
    a) 1.020- 1.030 b) 1.008- 1.012
    c) 1.015-1.035 d) None of the above
64. In enzootic hematuria of cattle, hemorrhage originates from tumour of
    a) Urinary bladder b) Liver
    c) Kidney d) Bone marrow
65. Presence of blood in urine is known as
    a) Hematemesis b) Hematuria
    c) Hamoptysis d) Apoplexy
66. Which of the follwowing act as a chemoreceptor function
    a) PCT b) DCT
    c) Loop of Henle d) Macula densa
67. Specific gravity of urine is highest in
    a) Cattle b) Horse
    c) Dog d) Pig
68. Which of the responsible for decrease glmerular filtration rate
    a) Endothelin b) Angiotensin II
    c) Nor epinephrin d) All of the above
69. Macrophage of kidney is
    a) Kuffer cell b) Microglia
    c) Astrocyte d) Mesengial cell
70. Which of the following responsible for decrease glomerular filtration rate (GFR)
    a) Nor epinephrine b) Angiotensin
    c) Endothelin d) All of the above
71. Which of the following is a part of Juxta glomerular system of kidney
    a) Extra glomerular mesengial cells b) Macula densa
    c) Juxta glomerular cell d) All of the above
72. Bowman's capsule hydrostatic pressure is
    a) 10 mm Hg b) 18 mm Hg
    c) 80 mm Hg d) 60 mm Hg
73. Countercurrent mechanism of the nephron is formed by
    a) PCT b) DCT
    c) Vasa recta d) Loop of henle
74. Obligatory water re-ansorption occurs in
    a) PCT b) DCT
    c) Loop of henle d) Collecting duct
75. Normal filtration fraction at glomerulus of kidney is
    a) 5% of renal plasma flow b) 20% of renal plasma flow
    c) 30% of renal plasma flow d) 40% of renal plasma flow

76. Micturation centre is located at
    a) Pons b) Medulla
    c) Kidney d) Hypothalamus

77. Normal glomerular filtration rate(GFR)
    a) 100 ml/min b) 200 ml/min
    c) 150 ml/min d) 125 ml/min

78. Agranular cells of juxtaglomerular apparatus are known as
    a) Lasic cells b) Polkissen cells
    c) Goormaghtigh cells d) All of the above

79. Juxtaglomerular apparatus cell are known as
    a) Juxtaglomerular cell b) Extraglomerular mesengial cells
    c) Macula densa cell d) All of the above

80. Which of the following produced by Juxta glomerular cell
    a) Renin b) Rennin
    c) Both of the above d) None of the above

81. Significant function of juxta glomerular apparatus
    a) Glomerular hemodynamic regulation b) Renin release control
    c) Both of above d) None of above

82. Horse urine normally cloudy due to
    a) Calcium carbonate b) Mucus
    c) Both of above d) None of above

83. Hyposthenuria refers to
    a) Production of concentrated urine
    b) Production of small amount of urine
    c) Production of diluted urine
    d) All of the above

84. In renal azotemia urine specific gravity range in cattle and dogs
    a) 1.025-1.030 b) 1.008-1.029
    c) 1.035-1.040 d) None of above

85. Renal azotemia is typically associated with
    a) 75% reduction of renal function b) 50% reduction of renal function
    c) 25% reduction of renal function d) 15% reduction of renal function

86. What is renal threshold of glucose in dogs
    a) 80 mg/dl b) 140mg/dl
    c) 180mg/dl d) 240mg/dl

87. Which of the following crystal form in acidic urine
    a) Amorphous phosphate b) Calcium carbonate
    c) Magnesium ammonium phosphate d) Calcium oxalate

88. Which of the following crystal form in alkaline urine
    a) Calcium carbonate
    b) Ammonium urate
    c) Uric acid
    d) Calcium oxalate
89. Magnesium ammonium phosphate crystalluria common in
    a) Dog
    b) Cat
    c) Cattle
    d) All of above
90. Magnesium ammonium phosphate (struvite) crystal shaped
    a) Needle like
    b) Coffin lid-shape
    c) Octahedrons
    d) None of above
91. What are iatrogenic cause of crystalluria
    a) Sulfa drug
    b) Allopurinol
    c) Both of above
    d) None of the above
92. Most common cause of acute renal failure
    a) Ethylene glycol intoxication
    b) Nephrotoxic therapeutic agent
    c) Ischemic injury
    d) All of the above
93. Apical surface of thick ascending loop contains
    a) Na^- -Cl^+ co-transporter
    b) Na^+- K^+-2CL co-transporter
    c) Na^+ - K^+ atpase
    d) Na-HCO_3^- co-transporter
94. Most common indicator of acute kidney failure
    a) Increase BUN
    b) Decrease GFR
    c) Azotemia
    d) All of the above
95. Albuminuria occurs in condition of
    a) Tubular nephrosis
    b) Glomerulonephritis
    c) Renal infarction
    d) All of the above
96. Urine sample after collection should be evaluate within half hour. If time is exceeding, how should the sample be stored until analysis?
    a) Frozen upto48 hour
    b) Addition of acidifier agent
    c) Refrigerated for 24 hour
    d) Dark cabinet for 24 hour
97. Amorphous urate in urine sediment is common urolithiasis in
    a) Dalmatians
    b) English bulldogs
    c) Both of above
    d) None of above
98. Renal tubular cast form due to the accumulation of proteinaceous matrix presence in urine sediment called
    a) Crystalluria
    b) Cylinduria
    c) Ketonuria
    d) None of the above
99. Toxic nephrosis occur due to
    a) Arsenic
    b) Cadmium
    c) Gentamicin
    d) All of above

100. Renal ischemic injury associated with
a) Hypovolemia
b) Hypotension
c) Both of above
d) None of the above

Answer Key

1	d	2	c	3	c	4	a	5	d	6	d	7	a
8	a	9	c	10	a	11	a	12	d	13	a	14	c
15	c	16	c	17	c	18	c	19	c	20	a	21	b
22	a	23	d	24	d	25	a	26	b	27	a	28	c
29	d	30	c	31	b	32	b	33	b	34	d	35	a
36	b	37	b	38	d	39	a	40	b	41	b	42	b
43	a	44	a	45	a	46	b	47	a	48	a	49	b
50	b	51	a	52	b	53	a	54	b	55	b	56	d
57	c	58	a	59	a	60	b	61	b	62	a	63	c
64	a	65	b	66	c	67	b	68	d	69	d	70	d
71	d	72	b	73	c	74	a	75	b	76	a	77	a
78	d	79	d	80	a	81	c	82	c	83	c	84	b
85	a	86	c	87	d	88	a	89	a	90	b	91	c
92	d	93	b	94	d	95	d	96	c	97	c	98	b
99	d	100	c										

24

Experimental Physiology

T. Sathyabama*[2], G. Rameshkumar[2], Femi Francis[3], Thulasiraman Parkunan[4], Mukesh Kumar Bharti[4] and Manish Kumar[4]

[1]*Professor and Head, Dept. of Veterinary Physiology & Biochemistry, Veterinary College and Research Institute, Udumalpet, Tamil Nadu Veterinary and Animal Sciences University (TANUVAS), Tamil Nadu*

[2]*Assistant Professor, Dept. of Veterinary Physiology & Biochemistry, Veterinary College and Research Institute, Udumalpet, Tamil Nadu Veterinary and Animal Sciences University (TANUVAS), Tamil Nadu*

[3]*Vocational Teacher, Department of Vocational Higher Secondary Education, Kerala*

[4]*Assistant Professor, Department of Veterinary Physiology and Biochemistry, Faculty of Veterinary and Animal*

Sciences, Institute of Agricultural Sciences, Rajiv Gandhi South Campus, Barkachha, Banaras Hindu University, Uttar Pradesh

Introduction

Experimental physiology is a fundamental aspect of medical, veterinary and biological sciences that seeks to understand how living systems function through controlled experiments. It plays a crucial role in exploring the mechanisms behind normal and abnormal physiological processes. With roots in ancient medicine, experimental physiology was notably advanced by Claude Bernard in the 19th century, who introduced key concepts like homeostasis and experimental methods that are still in use today. The interdisciplinary nature of this field connects it with disciplines such as biochemistry, pharmacology, and bioengineering, promoting a more comprehensive understanding of biological processes.

Investigating Physiological Processes

Experimental physiology aims to explore how organisms function at the cellular, molecular, organ, and systemic levels. This field investigates both normal physiology and the mechanisms behind diseases, offering insights into how organs and systems interact. Laboratory-based experiments are central to this learning process, allowing students and researchers to apply theoretical knowledge to practical scenarios. By observing how tissues, organs, and entire systems respond to stimuli, experimental physiology enables the exploration of the relationship between structure and function in biological organisms. The practical experience gained in the lab is critical for medical and veterinary education, as theoretical knowledge alone is insufficient. In fields like physics and chemistry, materials can often be stored for future use. However, in biology, especially physiology, fresh live tissue is often needed for fundamental experiments. For example, muscle and nerve tissues require careful handling and immediate use after isolation to study their responses to electrical stimuli. In **in vivo** experiments, live organisms are studied in their natural context, while **in vitro** studies use isolated cells, tissues, or organs to understand their behavior in a controlled environment.

Techniques in Experimental Physiology

Various advanced techniques are used in experimental physiology to explore complex biological systems. One major method is **electrophysiology**, which records electrical activity in cells or tissues to study nerve and muscle function. This approach is invaluable in understanding how electrical signals regulate the body's communication networks, including the nervous and muscular systems.

In cardiovascular research, experimental physiology contributes significantly to understanding blood flow, hemodynamics, and cardiac function. These studies help address conditions such as hypertension, heart disease, and other cardiovascular disorders. **Imaging techniques**, *such as MRI, CT scans, and fluorescence microscopy, are also essential in visualizing physiological processes, providing detailed views of organs and tissues in living organisms.*

Genetic and molecular research is another area where experimental physiology is essential. Techniques like **PCR (Polymerase Chain Reaction)**, gene editing, and protein assays allow scientists to study how genes and proteins influence physiological functions. These techniques provide a deeper understanding of how diseases disrupt normal biological processes and pave the way for new treatments.

Contributions to Medicine and Research

The findings from experimental physiology have broad applications in medicine, helping to develop new treatments and improve understanding of diseases. For example, researchers use this field to study the pathophysiology of conditions such as cancer, diabetes, and cardiovascular disorders. By identifying how these diseases affect normal physiological processes, experimental physiology helps discover new therapeutic targets.

One of the field's major contributions is in **pharmaceutical development**. Before new drugs are released to the public, they must undergo rigorous testing to ensure efficacy and safety. Experimental physiology plays a crucial role in this process, offering insights into how drugs interact with the body, their mechanisms of action, and potential side effects.

Moreover, experimental physiology supports **personalized medicine**, which tailors treatments to individual patients based on their genetic makeup and physiological responses. This approach minimizes adverse effects and improves treatment outcomes by considering the specific needs and characteristics of each patient.

Rehabilitation and Athletic Performance

Insights from experimental physiology also enhance rehabilitation strategies. For patients recovering from injuries or surgeries, understanding how tissues and organs heal is essential for creating effective rehabilitation programs. By analyzing how the body recovers, therapists can develop targeted interventions that accelerate healing and optimize recovery.

Furthermore, experimental physiology aids in optimizing **athletic performance** and preventing injuries. Researchers study how exercise impacts physiological systems, such as cardiovascular fitness, muscle function, and metabolism, to develop training protocols that enhance performance and reduce injury risk. This knowledge is valuable for athletes looking to improve their physical abilities and recover from strenuous activity.

Current Research and Ethical Considerations

Current areas of research in experimental physiology include the influence of the **gut microbiome** on health, the effects of stress and aging, and the development of personalized medicine. These research avenues aim to deepen our understanding of how external factors, such as diet, environment, and lifestyle, impact physiological processes.

Ethical considerations are vital in experimental physiology, particularly when conducting animal experiments or human trials. Researchers must follow strict ethical guidelines to ensure humane treatment of animals and secure informed consent from human participants. Ethical review boards assess the risk and benefit of these experiments to protect the welfare of all involved.

Conclusion

Experimental physiology serves as a bridge between theoretical knowledge and practical application, making it a key component of medical and biological education. Its interdisciplinary approach integrates various fields to provide a more in-depth understanding of complex biological systems. By exploring physiological processes, developing new medical treatments, and contributing to personalized medicine, experimental physiology plays an essential role in advancing healthcare and scientific knowledge. Researchers and students gain hands-on experience that informs their understanding of how biological systems function, ultimately improving human health and well-being.

Multiple Choice Question

1. The time lapse exists between the point of application of stimulus and beginning of contraction is

   a) Gap phase b) Latent phase

   c) Log phase d) Lapse phase

2. The time duration of latent/lag phase is

   a) 0.01 sec b) 0.1 sec

   c) 0.001 sec d) 0.2 sec

3. Adjustment of distance between the primary and secondary coil in Dubois' Raymond Induction coil alters / converts the intensity of

   a) galvanic current b) AC to DC

   c) DC to AC d) Faraday's current

4. Preparation of experimental animal involves the following except

   a) tissues from anaesthetized

   b) tissues from live anaesthetized

   c) tissues from recently morbid

   d) Tissues from dead animal

5. Pithing is the process destroys

a) Brain only
b) Both brain and Spinal cord
c) Spinal cord alone
d) Brain stem

6. The Frog's Ringer's solution is
a) 0.89% NaCl
b) 1.0% NaCl
c) 0.65% NaCl
d) 0.1% NaCl

7. In amphibians the pace maker of the Heart is
a) Sinus Venous
b) SA node
c) Venus Sinous
d) AV node

8. The resting membrane potential is the voltage difference
a) across the cell membrane when cell is at rest
b) exists during contraction of cell
c) between negative and positive potential in the cell
d) between Na+ and K+ ionic flow of cell

9. In the isolated heart lung preparation, Starling's law proves
a) inherent rhythmicity of heart
b) inherent rhythmicity and conductivity of heart independent of nerves.
c) Homeometric regulation of Cardiac Output
d) Heterometric regulation of Stroke Volume

10. The mammalian ringer's solution differ from that of Amphibian's with the presence of
a) Na ion
b) Glucose
c) K ion
d) Calcium

11. The addition of Na+ and K+ ions in the ringer's solution is to maintain
a) Systolic function of heart
b) Diastolic function of heart
c) pH stability
d) membrane stability of cell

12. The effect of Acetyl choline in heart muscle is
a) Negative Chronotrophic
b) Negative Ionotrophic
c) Both a and b
d) Postive Chronotrophic and Ionotrophic

13. The effect of adrenaline in heart muscle is
a) Negative Chronotrophic
b) Postive Chronotrophic and Ionotrophic
c) Positive excitotrophic
d) Negative Ionotrophic

14. The receptor of sympathetic division of ANS present in heart muscle is
a) alpha 1
b) alpha 2
c) beta 1
d) beta 2

15. The nerve inhibitory to heart is

a) Vagus nerve b) Vasovagal nerve
c) Carotid nerve d) Coronary nerve

16. The reason for vagal escape is due to
a) Strong continuous bursts of action potential
b) Slight inhibition of heart due to electrical stimuli
c) Stoppage of action potential for few milliseconds
d) Shifting of pace maker to other ectopic sites (ectopic foci)

17. Cutting of both the Vagus nerve to heart causes
a) Heart rate accelerates b) Heart attact
c) Vagal escape d) BP increases

18. Which part of vagus nerve is more inhibitory to heart
a) Right branch b) Left branch
c) Both Right and Left branch d) Collateral branch

19. The 'heart as a pump' dependent on
a) Extrinsic control b) Intrinsic control
c) Both a and b d) Humoral control

20. Deinnervation of sympathetic division of ANS to heart
a) No effect b) Increases CO
c) Increases Heart Rate d) Decreases Heart Rate

21. In isolated muscle-nerve preparation, pick out the correct option below
a) All or None law is followed at motor unit level
b) All or None Law not at all followed
c) All or None Law is followed by individual motor nerve fibre
d) All or None Law is not followed by motor nerve fibre

22. The stimulus applied in muscle twitch is
a) Threshold Stimuli b) Supra Threshold Stimuli
c) Sub Threshold Stimuli d) Maximum Threshold Stimuli

23. Application of supra maximal stimuli causes the force of contraction to (be)
a) Maximum b) Increase
c) Decrease d) Constant

24. The stimuli required to lift of a pen is
a) Sub threshold b) Threshold
c) Supra threshold d) Supra Maximal

25. The heart muscle is never be tetanized because of
a) Longer refractory period b) Slow Ca^{2+} channels
c) Slow Na^{2+} channels d) Synctium

26. Successive continuous application of stimuli to a contracting muscle leads to
a) Tetanus b) Fatigue
c) Summation d) Refractoriness

27. The Stimuli (Strength) applied to modify the Heart Rate is

a) Supramaximal
b) Threshold Stimuli
c) Threshold
d) Sub Threshold Stimuli

28. The changes occurred during cold Ringer's solution(5°C) is
a) Decreased Heart Rate
b) Increase frequency of contraction (Cold rigors)
c) Decreased amplification of contraction in ventricle
d) All of the above

29. Pick out the change(s) occurring with Hot Ringer's Solution(32°C)
a) Increased Heart Rate
b) Decreased Frequency of contraction
c) Increased amplification of contraction
d) All the above

30. The changes in Heart Rate upon changes in Ringer's Solution temperature is due to
a) Increased enzymatic reaction
b) Increased metabolic activity
c) Increased ionic flow in muscle
d) All of the above

31. Pick out the correct sequence of heart activity modifiers
a) CaCl2 – Decrease Heart Rate
b) K+ - Increase Heart Rate
c) Pilocarpine – Decrease Heart Rate
d) Adrenaline – Decrease Heart Rate

32. The following chemicals increase the Heart Rate except
a) Adrenaline
b) NaCl
c) $CaCl_2$
d) KCl

33. When stimulus of same strength is applied at short interval the contraction will be increased due to
a) Tetanus
b) Beneficial effect
c) Summation
d) Treppe

34. The beneficial effect of increased height of contraction is due to
a) Decreased Viscosity in muscle
b) Increased Ca2+ level
c) mild Increase in temperature
d) All of the above

35. When sub minimal stimuli is repeatedly applied, the outcome of response is
a) Summation
b) Super position
c) Stair case phenomenon
d) Tetanus

36. The effect of atrophine in heart is
a) Blocking of Ach
b) Unblocking of Ach
c) Increased rate
d) Decreased contraction

37. The following are Ach Blockers except

a) Pilocarpin b) Atrophine
c) Neostigmine d) Digitalis

38. The Epinephrine solution mimics the effect of
a) Sympathetic ANS b) Parasympathetic ANS
c) CNS d) PNS

39. The effect of excess K^+ on heart (hyperkalemia) causes all except
a) decreased resting membrane potential
b) decreased force of contraction
c) Ventricular fibrillation
d) increased conduction rate

40. The arrhythmia produced in heart is due to the presence of
a) K^+ ion b) Na^+ ion
c) $Ca2^+$ ion d) Cl^- ion

41. The nurotransmitter in sympathetic division is
a) Adrenalin b) Atrophine
c) Acetyl choline d) Aspirin

42. The following are the changes occurred during HOT ringer's solution on simple muscle twitch except
a) Decreased contraction period b) Decreased Latent period
c) Decreased height of contraction d) Decreased Relaxation period

43. The following are the changes occurred during COLD ringer's solution on simple muscle twitch except
a) Increased contraction period b) Increased Latent period
c) Increased height of contraction d) Increased Relaxation period

44. The muscle and nerve involved generally for experiments related to skeletal muscle is
a) Gastrocnemius and sciatic nerve
b) Semi tendinous and sciatic nerve
c) Semi membranous and sciatic nerve
d) Achillis tendon

45. Skeletal muscle cannot be contracted automatically because they are
a) Involuntary b) Voluntary
c) Excitatory d) Inbititory

46. The following are true regarding muscle twitch except
a) It is the mechanical activity produced by initiation of electrical activity
b) It is the electrical activity produced by initiation of mechanical activity
c) A minimum current is applied for longer time to produce response
d) Can be applied with threshold stimuli

47. The beneficial effect observed in stair case phenomenon is not due to

a) Increase in Ca^{2+} in cytosol
b) Increase in temperature of muscle
c) Increased viscosity of muscle
d) Decreased resistance of muscle movement

48. Fatigue is not characterized by
a) Lack of energy source
b) Exhaustion of NT
c) Increased latent period
d) Decreased accumulation of lactic acid

49. The recovery time in isolated muscle-nerve preparation is long due to
a) Increased synaptic delay
b) Increased muscle inertia
c) delay in neurotransmitter release
d) Excitation-Contraction delay

50. The decrease in the mechanical efficiency of muscle contraction on sustained repetition stimulation is
a) Fatigue
b) Clonus
c) Tonus
d) Tetanus

51. When fatigue sets in the muscle, the muscle remain in the state of partial contraction called
a) Fatigue
b) contraction reminder
c) contracture
d) Tone

52. The following are the immediate sources of energy for muscle contraction
a) ATP
b) Creatine Phosphate
c) Glucose
d) Creatinine

53. The site of fatigue in intact animal is
a) Synapse in CNS
b) NMJ
c) End plate
d) Antigravid muscle

54. The following are the effects of cold calcium exposure on muscle contraction
a) Increased latent period
b) Increased contraction period
c) Increased force of contraction
d) Increased relaxation period

55. Any external agent elicit a visible response is
a) Stimuli
b) Reflex
c) Shock
d) Impulse

56. Which is not the characteristic of tonic muscle fibres
a) Smaller fibres
b) more number of sarcosomes
c) Increased Ca^{2+} release from SR
d) Fast in action

57. Which is not the characteristic of phasic muscle fibres

a) Smaller fibres
b) more number of sarcosomes
c) Increased Ca^{2+} release from SR
d) Fast in action

58. Greater amount of work is directly proportional to heat is explained by
a) Fenn effect
b) Starling's effect
c) Von Hoff's Rule
d) Dales effect

59. The force of contraction is directly proportional to
a) Initial length of muscle fibre
b) Number of motor units recruited
c) Stimuli applied initially
d) Amount of ATP stored

60. The work done by the muscle is calculated from
a) Height of curve obtained
b) Distance of load from joint
c) Length of curve obtained
d) All the above

61. Raising the head is an example for
a) 1st order lever
b) 2nd order lever
c) 3rd order lever
d) 4th order lever

62. Most of the human body works as
a) 1st order lever
b) 2nd order lever
c) 3rd order lever
d) 4th order lever

63. Standing on tip of toe is an example for
a) 1st order lever
b) 2nd order lever
c) 3rd order lever
d) 4th order lever

64. An electrical device used in experimental physiology is
a) Physiograph
b) ECG
c) ERG
d) EEG

65. The phenomenon not undergone in intact animal is
a) Contracture
b) Tone
c) Contraction
d) Excitation

66. The ability of a tissue to respond to external stimuli is
a) Excitability
b) Irritability
c) conductivity
d) Rhythmicity

67. When a second stimuli does not elicit a response, then the muscle be in the state of
a) Absolute refractory period
b) Resting period
c) Relative refractory period
d) accomadation period

68. When a stronger second stimuli elicit a response, then the muscle be in the state of
a) Absolute refractory period
b) Resting period
c) Relative refractory period
d) accomadation period

69. In smooth muscle, occurrence of short action potential is due to

a) Summation b) Clonus
c) Superposition d) Tonus

70. The muscle fatigue is due to the accumulation of
a) Carbon-dioxide b) Lactic acid
c) Hydrogen ions d) Lactose

71. Duration of one muscle twitch is
a) 0.1 sec b) 0.01 sec
c) 1.0 sec d) 0.001 sec

72. Father of experimental physiology is
a) Claudius Galenus b) Claude Bernaud
c) Von Haller d) Galileo Galilei

73. Fonnder of experimental physiology is
a) Claudius Galenus b) Claude Bernaud
c) Von Haller d) Galileo Galilei

74. For genesis of tetanus, sciatic nerve is stimulated at
a) Supramaximal b) Threshold Stimuli
c) Threshold d) Sub Threshold Stimuli

75. Choosing frog as an experimental hosts the benefit of
a) superior survivability of preparation than warm blooded tissues
b) easy to handle and disposal of wastes
c) invitro ability without oxygenation and temperature control
d) All of the above

76. The instrument records movements in a moving surface is
a) Ergograph b) Myograph
c) Kymograph d) Electrograph

77. Cold rigor is due to the development of all of the following except
a) Coagulation of muscle proteins b) failure to delink of myosin head
c) Cold shock d) Inhibition of calcium pump

78. The rigidity developed in the muscle after death is
a) Rigor b) Contracture
c) Contraction d) rigor mortis

79. Increasing the number of contracting motor units results in
a) Spatial Summation b) Temporal summation
c) Superposition d) Tonus

80. Increasing the rapidity of contracting motor units results in
a) Spatial Summation b) Temporal summation
c) Superposition d) Tonus

81. In cardiac muscle, All or none law is applicable to

a) Single motor unit b) individual muscle fibre
c) whole muscle d) Motor neuron

82. In intact animal the muscle contractions are
a) Single muscle twitches
b) Summated twitches
c) Fused muscle twitches
d) Fused smooth muscle twitches

83. In the locomotor system the site which is (are) easily fatigued
a) CNS b) Muscular system
c) NMJ d) All of the above

84. Which muscle, along with the sciatic nerve, is commonly used for experiments related to skeletal muscle
a) Biceps brachii b.Gastrocnemius muscle
c) Quadriceps muscle d.Lateral corticospinal tract

85. Which nerve is often used in conjunction with the hypoglossus muscle for experimental purposes
a) Hypoglassal nerve b) Sciatic nerve
c) Facial nerve d) Trigeminal

86. At what frequency of repetitive stimuli does muscle contraction typically become tetanic
a) 10-20 Hz b) 30-50 Hz
c) 100-200 Hz d) 1-5 Hz

87. The brief contraction of a muscle in response to a single stimulus is termed as
a) Tetany b) Twitch
c) Tonic contraction d) Phasic contraction

88. Which muscle fiber type is more resistant to fatigue
a) Fast-twitch b) Type IIA
c) Slow-twitch d) Type IIB

89. Which electromyogram (EMG) signal affect fatigue
a) Increased amplitude b) Increased motor units
c) Increased intensity d) Increased frequency

90. The heat generated during muscle contraction is
a) Potential energy b) Mechanical energy
c) Electrical energy d) Kinetic energy

91. The refractory period is easily demonstrated in isolated muscle preparation is by
a) Heating the nerve b) Time lapse between stimulus
c) Cooling the nerve d) Blocking the nerve

92. To measure the velocity of conduction, stimulate the nerve near

a) Spinal cord b) Tendon insertion
c) Belly of the muscle d.

93. The state of weight applied after the muscle begins to contract is
a) Load b) Afterload
c) Excess load d) Lifting load

94. The state of weight applied before the muscle begins to contract is
a) Preload b) Afterload
c) Excess load d) Lifting load

95. The preparation used for demonstration of drug action
a) Biceps brachii-femoral nerve b) Hioglosses-Hypoglassal nerve
c) Gastrocnemius- sciatic nerve d) Satorious-Sciatic nerve

96. The change occurs during muscle contraction
a) Electro chemical b) Physio chemical
c) Ionic changes d) Osmotic changes

97. The stimulus used to elicit fatigue
a) Sub threshold b) Threshold
c) Maximal threshold d) Supra Maximal

98. The stimulus applied for action of drug on muscle
a) Sub threshold b) Threshold
c) Maximal threshold d) Supra Maximal

99. The muscle nerve preparation for experiments generally involve the following except
a) Gluteus -thigh b) Hioglosses-lower jaw
c) Gastrocnemius- leg d) Satorious-thigh

100. The abnormal electrical response of an insured muscle is not due to
a) Loss of rhythmicity b) Loss of nutrients
c) Loss of conductivity d) Loss of excitability

Answer Key

1	b	2	a	3	c	4	d	5	b	6	c	7	a
8	a	9	b	10	b	11	d	12	c	13	b	14	c
15	a	16	d	17	a	18	a	19	c	20	a	21	c
22	a	23	d	24	a	25	a	26	b	27	a	28	d
29	d	30	d	31	c	32	d	33	b	34	d	35	a
36	a	37	d	38	a	39	d	40	a	41	a	42	c
43	c	44	a	45	b	46	b	47	c	48	d	49	a
50	a	51	c	52	a	53	a	54	c	55	a	56	c
57	d	58	a	59	a	60	d	61	a	62	c	63	b

64	a	65	a	66	a	67	a	68	c	69	a	70	b
71	a	72	a	73	b	74	a	75	d	76	c	77	a
78	d	79	a	80	b	81	c	82	d	83	d	84	b
85	a	86	b	87	b	88	c	89	d	90	a	91	c
92	a	93	b	94	a	95	b	96	a	97	c	98	d
99	a	100	a